WESTERN CIVILIZATION

A Social and Cultural History

SECOND EDITION

Volume 1: Prehistory–1750

MARGARET L. KING

Brooklyn College and the Graduate Center
City University of New York

Prentice Hall Inc., Upper Saddle River, NJ. 07458

Published 2003 by Prentice Hall Inc.
A Division of Pearson Education
Upper Saddle River, New Jersey 07458

A CIP catalog record for this book is available from the Library of Congress.
ISBN 0-13-045005-7

10 9 8 7 6 5 4 3 2 1

This book was designed and produced by
LAURENCE KING PUBLISHING LTD.,
London, www.laurenceking.co.uk

Senior Managing Editor: Richard Mason
Senior Editor: Samantha Gray
Commissioning Editors: Damian Thompson, Melanie Hill
Design: Ian Hunt Design
Cover Design: Design Deluxe
Picture Research: Peter Kent
Maps: Andrea Fairbrass and Ailsa Heritage
Printed in China

Cover: Red-figure cup, detail (Staatliche Museen, Berlin).
Photo: B.P.K., Berlin
Giovanni Boccaccio, *A Woman Copying a Manuscript*
(Bibliothèque Nationale, Paris)

Contents

CHAPTER 3

The Greek Polis

The New Politics of Ancient Greece

(1000–300 B.C.E.)

CHAPTER 4

The School of Hellas

Poetry, Ideas, and the Arts in Ancient Greece

(800–300 B.C.E.)

PART TWO

The Origins of the West

From Roman Dominion to the New Peoples of Europe

(300 B.C.E–1300 C.E.)

CHAPTER 5

Our Sea

The Mediterranean World in the Hellenistic and Early Roman Eras

(300–27 B.C.E.)

CHAPTER 6

PAX ROMANA

Society, State, and Culture in Imperial Rome

(27 B.C.E.–500 C.E.)

CHAPTER 7

PAGANS, JEWS, AND CHRISTIANS

Religions of the Mediterranean World

(500 B.C.E.–500 C.E.)

CHAPTER 8
AFTER ANTIQUITY
New Peoples of Europe and Other Peoples of the World
(300–1300 C.E.)

PART THREE
THE WEST TAKES FORM
Medieval Society, Politics, Economy, and Culture
(500–1500)

CHAPTER 9
WORKERS, WARRIORS, AND KINGS
Politics and Society in the Middle Ages
(800–1500)

CHAPTER 10

THE SPIRITUAL SWORD

Religion and Culture in the Middle Ages

(500–1500)

CHAPTER 11

IN THE NAME OF PROFIT

Cities, Merchants, and Trade in the Middle Ages

(1000–1500)

PART FOUR

THE WEST EXPANDS

The Self, the State, the World

(1200–1750)

CHAPTER 12

CITY LIFE

Public and Private Life in the Late Medieval Cities

(1200–1500)

CHAPTER 15

Absolute Power

War and Politics in Early Modern Europe

1500–1750)

CHAPTER 16

Europe Reaches Out

Global Voyages and Cultural Encounters

(1500–1750)

Witnesses

TIMELINES

Society, Politics, and Economy	Religion and Ideas	Europe and the Americas
Rulers, Nations, Warfare, and Revolution	Civilization, Art, and Science	Africa, the Middle East, Asia, and Oceania
	Beyond the West	

MAPS

WINDOWS ON

PREFACE

On September 11, 2001—a day that the citizens of the United States of America will not easily forget—four planes, hijacked by four squads of suicidal terrorists, were piloted deliberately toward four monuments that symbolized the achievements and strivings of our society. Three hit their targets; one crashed before it could do so, probably because of the prompt and courageous intervention of some of the doomed passengers. Nearly 4,000 people died in the four incidents, including hundreds of citizens of foreign nations resident in this country.

As these horrific events were pondered, while grief subsided and understanding dawned, the concept of "Western civilization" was mentioned rather more than it usually is in our bold and boisterous national discourse. Somehow, it was felt by many, these attacks had to be attacks on the fundamental structures of Western society: not just objections to American foreign policy, or resentment of American success, but a more basic blow to the values that sustain the democratic societies of the Western world. It is possible that some good will proceed from the great evil of September 11, and that one of the consequences of that day's events may be a renewed interest in the development of the West. The second edition of this book therefore begins with some very basic questions: where, and what, is the West?

WHERE IS THE WEST?

When I teach the introductory history course at Brooklyn College of the City University of New York, I start each semester by asking my students "Where is the West?" I send an unfortunate victim to the map of the world mounted on the back wall of the room. A finger roams around the continents of the globe. The class suggests many possibilities: western Europe? The western hemisphere? The wild west? The search goes on all semester—a search of special complexity for the many students who, speaking tens of languages, professing all the world's major religions, and hailing from all its inhabited continents, have no association by birth with Western civilization. To begin, I tell my students about Greenwich, England, where the Prime Meridian begins.

Visitors gathered outside the gates of the old Royal Observatory in Greenwich, England, may read a sign announcing that they now stand "at the center of time and space." From that spot an imaginary line circles the earth from pole to pole, slicing the globe in half. The two halves are the Eastern and the Western hemispheres. The line is the Prime Meridian, the first and last of the infinite series of lines of longitude by which any location on the globe, East or West, can be accurately denoted by its precise variation in hours, minutes, and seconds from Greenwich time.

The packs of schoolchildren who come to Greenwich are often photographed grinning as they stand astride the Prime Meridian—each with one foot in the East and one in the West. Yet both feet are in England, in Europe, and in the zone of Western Civilization. Part of England and most of Europe (and all of Australia and New Zealand) lie in the Eastern hemisphere. Yet they belong to the West. A good fraction of Africa lies in the Western hemisphere. Yet it does not belong to the West. The people of the nations of Latin America lie in the western hemisphere, accept an official language which is European, and adhere for the most part to the Roman Catholic Church—is their civilization "Western?" Or does a struggling economy, or a large population of peoples of mixed indigenous and African heritage, mark them as non-Western?

What is the West? It isn't the "west" of the old movies, where for a brief moment cowboys prowled the frontier, and the native peoples of North America resisted the incursions of Europeans arriving from the East. It isn't the "west" of the Cold War era (1945–1991; see Chapter 30) when eastern and western zones of Europe adhered to different ideologies, and the boundary between their mental and political battles was designated by an Iron Curtain in part mythical, in part real. It is not only the zone of western, Catholic Christianity (which includes Poland, a nation solidly in "eastern" Europe), but embraces also the nations whose majorities embrace eastern, Orthodox Christianity: Greece, Serbia, perhaps even Russia. The West is not defined by any number of terms which contain, in their designations, the word "west": the Western hemisphere, the North American West, or Western Europe. What is the West? It is not, in fact, a place.

Neither is the West a specific people, or race, or set of nations. Although all of the nations of Europe are Western, so too are other nations far away—the nations of the Americas, Australasia, and the Asian zones of Russia—that were settled by Europeans who bore with them, along with their tools and skills, the elements of their civilization. In these scattered zones of Western civilization, and in the European homeland now as well, as migrations of peoples have altered its original population, people of greatly different origins—Asian, African—have adopted aspects of Western civilization. Just as anybody may learn French, or become a Methodist, anyone who so chooses may adopt and transmit the civilization of the West. Although at times in the Western past, theorists argued that civilization was linked to what

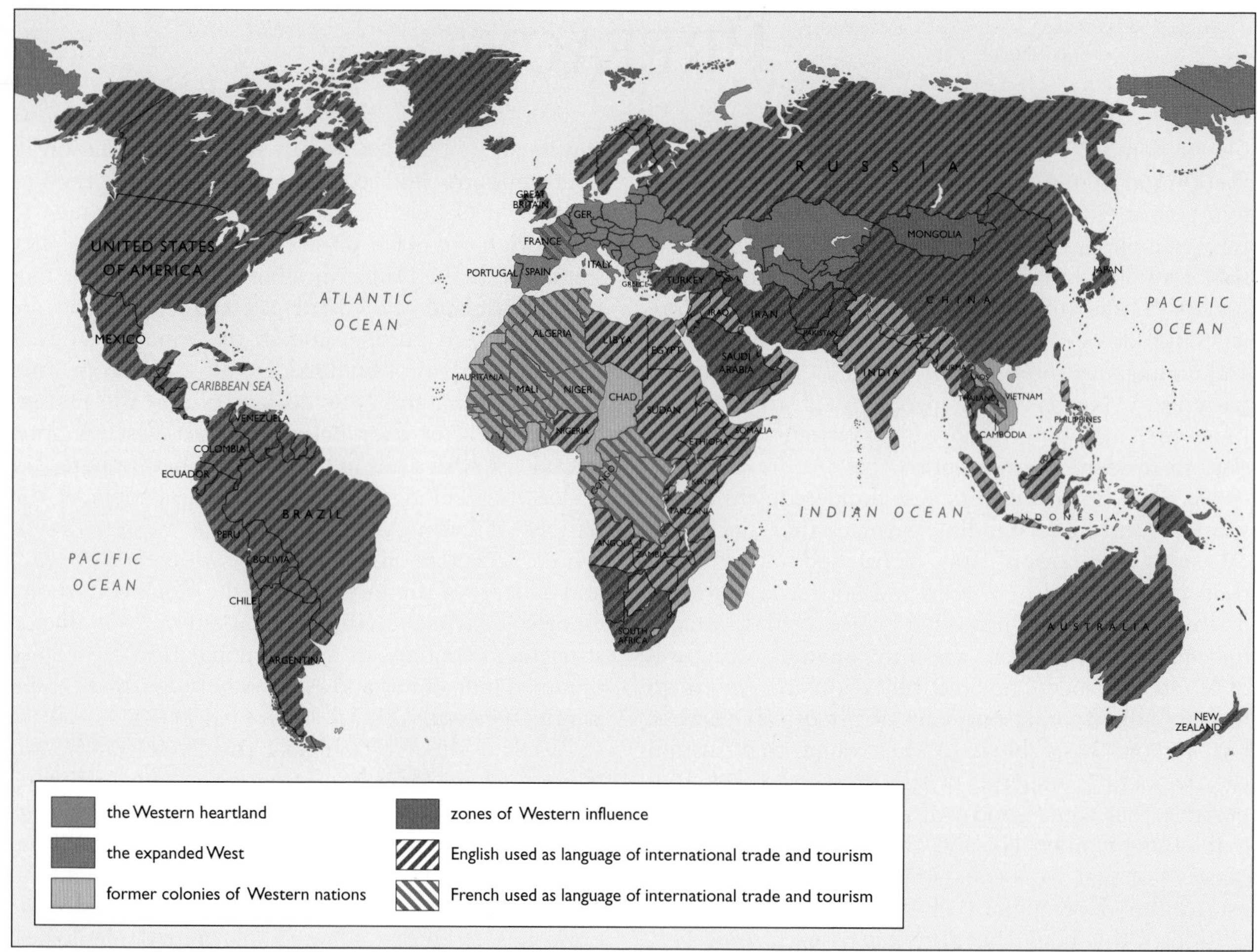

Where is the West: *Shown here is one way of thinking about the West geographically. Its heartland is Europe, where the cultural, social, and political traditions of the West developed their modern form after about 1000 C.E. "The expanded West" includes regions of European settlement, where Western civilization was transplanted from Europe after 1500 but where it has since developed in modified form because of contacts with other peoples. "Former colonies of Western nations" include those regions where Western civilization was imposed upon other nations, nations now largely liberated from colonial rule but still retaining some features of that civilization. Finally, areas designated as "zones of Western influence" have been largely free of any period of direct domination by Western nations, but have to a greater or lesser extent adopted selected Western political and economic institutions.*

was then, erroneously, called "race," the events of the last century have at long last obliterated those notions. Among the millions destroyed in the maelstrom of genocidal war were those considered to be by race outside the bounds of Western civilization; but their language and values were solidly Western, and their appeals for justice recapitulate the patterns of Western thought.

WHAT, THEN, IS THE WEST?

The West is a body of ideas, values, customs, and beliefs. These were forged over a period of centuries on the continent of Europe, which lay to the west of the then more advanced civilizations of the East. They triumphed during the centuries of European expansion: from approximately 1000 to 1900 of the Common Era, when Western values followed Western merchants, travelers, armies, and governors into every other corner of the inhabited globe. They are what the West means, and they are truly the meaning of the West.

Here are a few of the many concepts that have made the West and that constitute its core meaning:

- The principle of human dignity: that all human beings are equal in worth (if not in talents, beauty, or size), that they possess rights which cannot be taken away, and that to the greatest possible degree they are free.
- The ideal of justice: that no person should be unfairly privileged above another.
- The value of democracy: that the power to shape the future of a community belongs to its people as a whole and not to arbitrarily selected leaders.
- The method of rationalism, which assumes that all phenomena (even those pertaining to God, essence, or spirit) may be subject to the critical scrutiny of the human mind.

- The inclination to progress, to work toward goals to be achieved in the future.
- The habit of self-examination, which encourages human beings to examine themselves seriously and often to test whether they have fulfilled their promise and their responsibilities.

These, among others, are the habits and values that together characterize Western civilization, and which have caused it to develop in the directions it has—the very habits and values that have provoked the enemies to strike cruelly and violently against the innocent citizens of New York City and Washington DC on September 11, 2001.

THE WEST AND THE REST OF THE WORLD

We learn more about the Western world when we also examine the rest of the world. Some features of Western civilization are not unique to the West. They appear also in the cultural systems of other people around the globe, although not all of them appear in the same way in any other civilization. In many cases, particularly in the era of its origins, the West borrowed customs and ideas from the civilizations of Asia and Africa. More recently, a fully developed Western culture has lent, shared, or imposed its values on those civilizations and the newer ones of the Western hemisphere (see map, facing page).

This book will frequently pause in its narration of Western development to consider key aspects of non-Western civilizations, in the past and now. The ancient civilizations of the Mediterranean region, which confer upon the later West its first patterns of urbanization and political rule, its religious traditions and its alphabet, are, of course, considered. But so, too, are the ancient and medieval civilizations of China, India, Africa, and the Americas (Chapters 1, 2, 8, and 16). In the modern era, this book considers at length not only the process by which Western nations came to control much of the globe in the nineteenth century (Chapter 24), but also how colonized regions freed themselves from that domination in the twentieth (Chapter 29). To isolate the West from other regions which have helped shape it, and upon which it has impacted, makes no sense—especially in an age which is now no longer dominated by the West but is truly **global**.

A global perspective transcends any claims for the superiority of one civilization to another. The civilization of the West is the focus of this book not because it is better (arguable) or because it is ours (it is not "ours" to many Americans by virtue of birth), but because it embodies principles of permanent value that will survive as long as there are those who learn them, reflect on them, and teach them to future generations, in the West and elsewhere in the world.

It is hoped that this *Second Edition* of *Western Civilization: A Social and Cultural History* will help introduce students of the post 9/11/2001 world to the civilization that we all, whatever our origins or ethnicity, now share, and which can only be more treasured than it had been before. Please see the Walkthrough section of these preliminary pages for a detailed description of what is new in the second edition.

CHANGES TO THE SECOND EDITION

Drawing on the comments of the many reviewers of the original edition of *Western Civilization: A Social and Cultural History*, a number of changes and enhancements appear in this new edition.

The narrative has been changed at several points. Chapter 1 has been updated. In the modern era, the Epilogue: The Future of The West has been entirely rewritten. Chapter 20, which in the original edition had dealt with European politics from the Old Regime through the creation of the German and Italian states, has been split into two full-length chapters. The revised Chapter 20 deals with the French Revolution and Napoleon, while a new Chapter 23 carries the political narrative forward from the Congress of Vienna through the proclamation of the German empire and the Parisian Commune. Other chapters have been updated to reflect current scholarship or modified to improve the flow of the narrative.

Many elements have been updated or replaced. The *Witnesses* boxes, which contain, normally, two or more texts which "speak" to each other on an issue pertaining to the adjacent narrative, have all been equipped with brief introductions which focus on the issue under discussion, to aid the student in the critical reading of the selected passages. As well, 24 new *Witnesses* boxes or new *Witnesses* texts have been supplied, and some of the texts appearing in the original edition dropped.

In the same way, many of the illustrations in the original edition have been replaced, approximately 50 in color and 50 in black and white, and two new *Windows On* boxes have been created—most conspicuously a two-page spread on the impact of the French Revolution on both men's and women's costume. Moreover, each *Windows On* box now includes a *Windows On the Web* activity, which uses the Internet to continue the investigation presented in the text. In addition, new maps have been created for the Chinese world up to 800 C.E., German confessionalization in the sixteenth and seventeenth centuries, poverty in London, 1898–99, the fall of South Vietnam, 1975, and African political systems, 1996. There are also five new *How Many?* boxes, eight new *Must Reads*, and eight new *Who's Who* as well. Descriptions for these features can be found in the *Walkthrough* section that follows.

These changes to the narrative and features and updates throughout should make this *Second Edition of Western Civilization: A Social and Cultural History* more accessible to students than the original edition, and more appealing to faculty as well.

ACKNOWLEDGEMENTS

The single name of the author appearing on the title page disguises the reality that I have had many guides and helpers in the creation of this book. I am grateful to the staff at Laurence King Ltd. (Damian Thompson, Samantha Gray, Ian Hunt, Richard Mason, Nell Webb, Melanie White, Lee Greenfield, Judy Rasmussen, and especially Laurence King) who have had confidence in the project, assisted it in every way, and alternately soothed and bullied its restive author.

At Prentice Hall I would also like to thank Yolanda deRooy, President of the Humanties and Social Sciences Division, Charlyce Jones-Owen, Editorial Director for the Humanities and Social Sciences, and especially Charles Cavaliere, Senior Acquisitions Editor, who has been a fund of good ideas for revitalizing the second edition.

My colleagues in the History Department at Brooklyn College, especially Leonard Gordon, have contributed ideas and criticisms for which I am immensely grateful; as has former colleague Michael Mendle, now in the History Department at the University of Alabama (Tuscaloosa), former student and associate Michael Sappol, now at the National Library of Medicine (Bethesda, Maryland); and Brooklyn staffer Brian Bonhomme, now at the University of Arkansas, a young scholar whose insight and imagination contributed greatly to all the chapters of the second volume.

My severest critics and most valiant sustainers have been my sons and my husband—David, Jeremy, and Robert Kessler. They have waited patiently for the day when the stacks of books on the floor of my study return to their home on library shelves, and normalcy to our household.

Margaret L. King
Brooklyn College and the Graduate Center
City University of New York
December, 2001

The author and publisher would like to thank the many scholars and teachers whose thoughtful and often detailed comments helped to shape this book.

First Edition

John F. Battick, University of Maine
Wood Bouldin, Villanova University
Blaine T. Browne, Broward Community College
Amy Burnett, University of Nebraska-Lincoln
Jack Cargill, Rutgers University
Anna Clark, University of North Carolina at Charlotte
Cyndia Susan Clegg, Pepperdine University
Jessica A. Coope, University of Nebraska Lincoln
Gerald Danzer, University of Illinois at Chicago
Steven Fanning, University of Illinois at Chicago
Allan Fletcher, Boise State University
Neal Galpern, University of Pittsburgh
Richard Gerberding, University of Alabama
Gay Gullickson, University of Maryland
Jeff Horn, Stetson University
Patrick Kelly, Adelphi University
Mavis Mate, University of Oregon
John Mauer, Tri-County Technical College
Eleanor McCluskey, Broward Community College
Marion S. Miller, University of Illinois at Chicago
Joseph R. Mitchell, Howard Community College
Jim Murray, University of Cincinnati
Jasonne Grabher O'Brien, University of Kansas
William Percy, University of Massachusetts, Boston
John Powell, Penn State University at Erie
Thomas Preisser, Sinclair Community College
Carole A. Putko, San Diego State University
Timothy A. Ross, Arkansas State University
Roger Schlesinger, Washington State University
Hugo B. Schwyzer, Pasadena City College
James Smither, Grand Valley State University
Francis Stackenwalt, East Central University
Emily Sohmer Tai, Queensborough Community College
Robert W. Thurston, Miami University
Michael Weiss, Linn-Benton Community College
Norman J. Wilson, Methodist College
Michael Zirinsky, Boise State University.

Second Edition

Linda Bregstein, Mercer Community College (vol 1)
Tim Crain, University of Wisconsin-Milwaukee (comb)
Meaghan N. Duff, Western Kentucky University (vol 1)
Charles W. Hope, Tarrant County Junior College (comb)
Herbert Luft, Pepperdine University (comb)
Michael G. Paul, Boston College (vol 2)
William Benton Whisenhunt, College of DuPage (comb)
Steven Jay White, University of Kentucky Lexington Community College (comb)

THE MEANING OF THE WEST,
EXAMINED IN A LIVELY NEW EDITION OF

WESTERN CIVILIZATION

A Social and Cultural History

AVAILABLE IN THE FOLLOWING FORMATS:

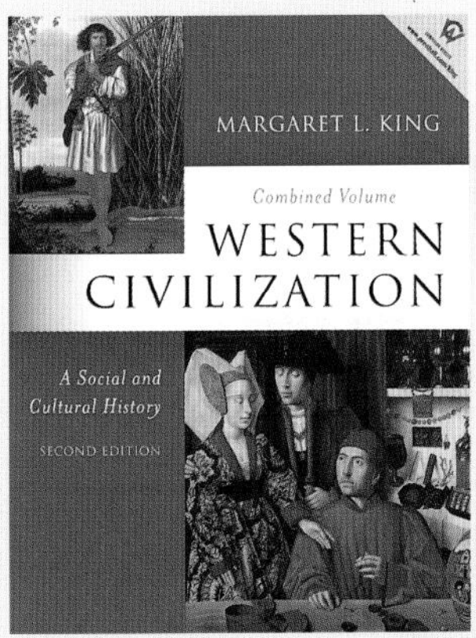

Combined Edition
Chapters 1–30, casebound

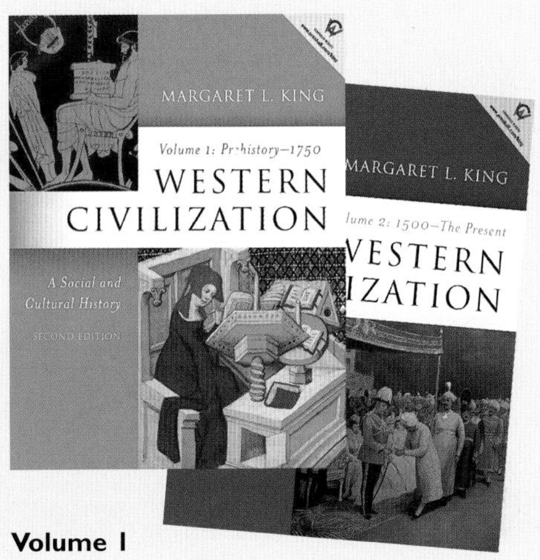

Volume 1
Prehistory to 1750
Chapters 1–16, paper
Volume 2
1500 to the Present,
Chapters 15–30, paper

Volume A: To 1500,
Chapters 1–12, paper
Volume B: 1200–1871,
Chapters 12–20, paper
Volume C: Since 1750,
Chapters 20–30, paper

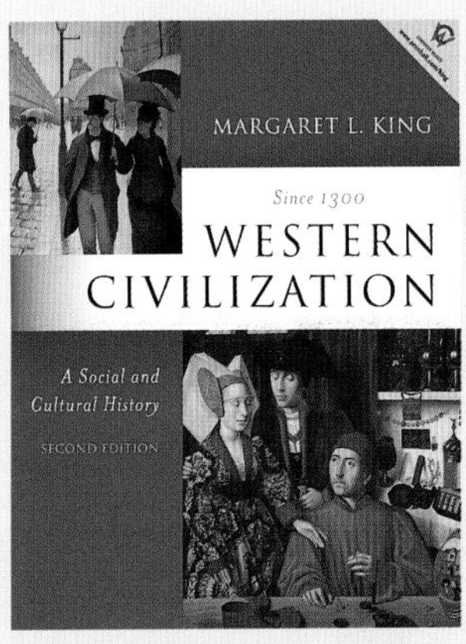

Since 1300
Chapters 11–30, casebound

WHY IS WESTERN CIVILIZATION, SECOND EDITION, ORGANIZED THEMATICALLY?

Because this book gives special attention to the history of culture and society, its organization is topical. Some chapters focus on politics, others on society, others on religion or ideas. Often two or three chapters in succession will deal with the same historical period, but from different topical vantage points. The chapters on the Middle Ages, for instance, examine the whole of that thousand-year period, stressing first politics and society (Chapter 9), then religion and ideas (Chapter 10), then commerce and urbanization (Chapter 11). A topical division has the virtue that students are introduced systematically to the variety of ways that historians study the past.

The consequence of a focus on social and cultural themes is a deemphasis of the political narrative. That shift of priorities parallels the tendency of historical scholarship since 1960, which has elevated the richness of multiple themes, and highlighted the many voices of past reality. Accordingly, attention is paid to the experience of workers, the poor, and marginalized groups (modifying the traditional emphasis on rulers and elites), to the changing roles of women and children, to the structure and growth of cities, to war as an expression of social values, to religious experience and behavior (as well as doctrine and organization), to popular and high culture, to the settings of intellectual discourse and the role of the powerful in shaping culture.

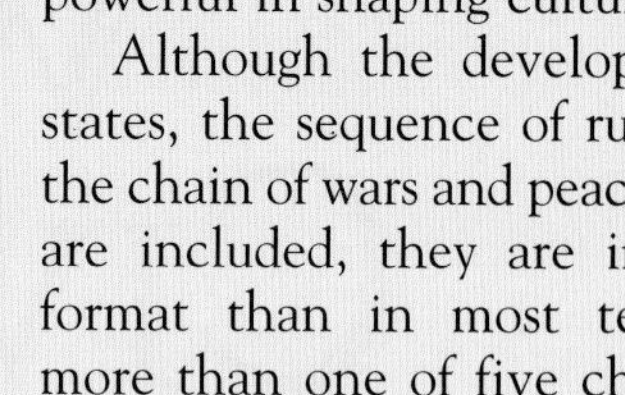

Although the development of states, the sequence of rulers, and the chain of wars and peace treaties are included, they are in briefer format than in most texts. No more than one of five chapters is devoted primarily to political discussion (Chapters 2, 15, 20, 23, 26, 29); only six others contain large sections dedicated to political narrative (Chapters 3, 5, 6, 9, 19, 28). Nearly two-thirds of the whole centers on social and cultural themes. Some chapters are particularly dedicated to language, religion, and ideas (Chapters 1, 4, 6, 7, 10, 13, 14, 17, 25, 27); others to social or economic problems, including world trade, migrations, urbanization, social structures, technology, development, and the environment (Chapters 3, 9, 11, 12, 16, 18, 21, 22, 30).

A topical organization means that students must read, and teachers must teach, different chapters in different ways. But in all cases, that reading and teaching is supported by maps, graphical, visual, and documentary materials that bring the material to life, and aid the student in gaining a rich and up-to-date vision of the past, and in developing an appreciation of Western civilization that is based not only on the recitation of its triumphs of war and state, but also on the impressive foundations of its social and cultural heritage.

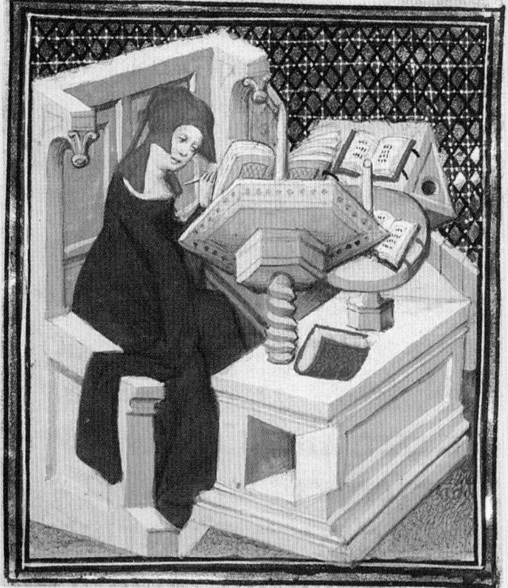

***Giovanni Boccaccio,* A Woman Copying a Manuscript, fifteenth century**

***Hans Holbein,* The Ambassadors, 1533**

Etruscan sarcophagus (coffin) from Veii, c. 520 B.C.E.

FEATURES OF THE SECOND EDITION

PART THREE

THE WEST TAKES FORM

Medieval Society, Politics, Economy, and Culture (500–1500)

Peasants and nobles created the society of the European Middle Ages. As Roman institutions crumbled and waves of invaders destroyed communities, medieval peasants devised new patterns of agricultural work and life, generally on the manors, or large estates, of noble landholders. The nobles, as an elite group of military men, warded off invaders and struggled among themselves for power.

Amid the bounds of mainly local authority, the first European kingdoms emerged, and kings employed violence and persuasion to assert their authority over nobles. The Crusades sent knightly armies east to the Levant (Palestine and Syria, on the eastern Mediterranean shores), while knights who stayed home at court developed the rituals of chivalry. In the late medieval centuries, which were gripped by famine and plague, peasant rebellions against landholders were frequent.

Providing cohesion to the disparate communities of Europe was the Catholic Church, centered in Rome under the pope, whose authority was at its height around 1300 after a process of reform, centralization, and resistance to the encroachments of secular rulers. A powerful Church summoned Christians to respect celibacy, the priestly administration of the sacraments, and the examples of saints and martyrs; and it disciplined those who strayed from orthodoxy. Providing access to libraries and schools, the Church trained most of Europe's intellectuals, who elaborated a rational system of theology and laid the foundations for modern philosophical, political, legal, and scientific thought.

As monarchical and ecclesiastical institutions crystallized, a new social group and setting emerged: merchants and towns. By 1300, towns stretching from the Mediterranean to the North Sea coasts housed artisans, merchants, bankers, and entrepreneurs. By 1500, their commercial ventures, extending to Africa, the Middle East, and Asia, made Europe rich and ready to expand.

9 Workers, Warriors, and Kings
Politics and Society in the Middle Ages, 800–1500

10 The Spiritual Sword
Religion and Culture in the Middle Ages, 500–1500

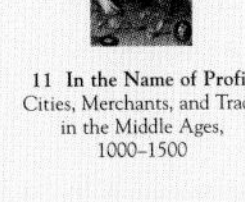

11 In the Name of Profit
Cities, Merchants, and Trade in the Middle Ages, 1000–1500

227

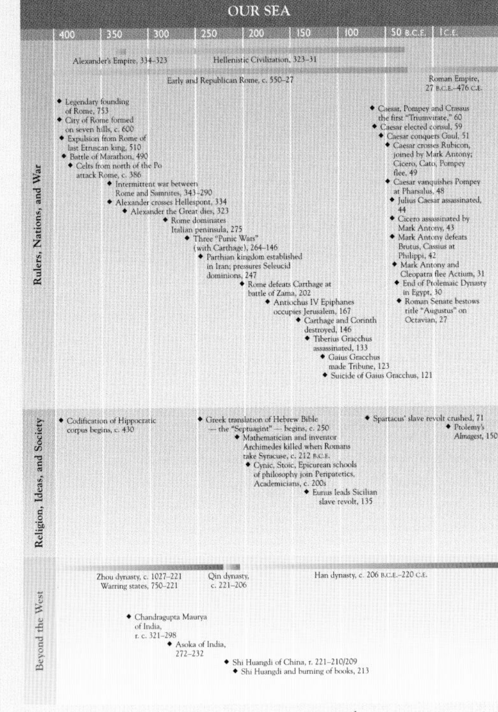

110

Part Opener

Western Civilization is divided into seven parts that group the chapters into a cohesive, thematic framework. Part-opening essays set the stage for discussions that follow.

Chapter Opener Timeline

Organized thematically, and arranged into color-coded sections, chapter-opening timelines show the chronology of major events and developments.

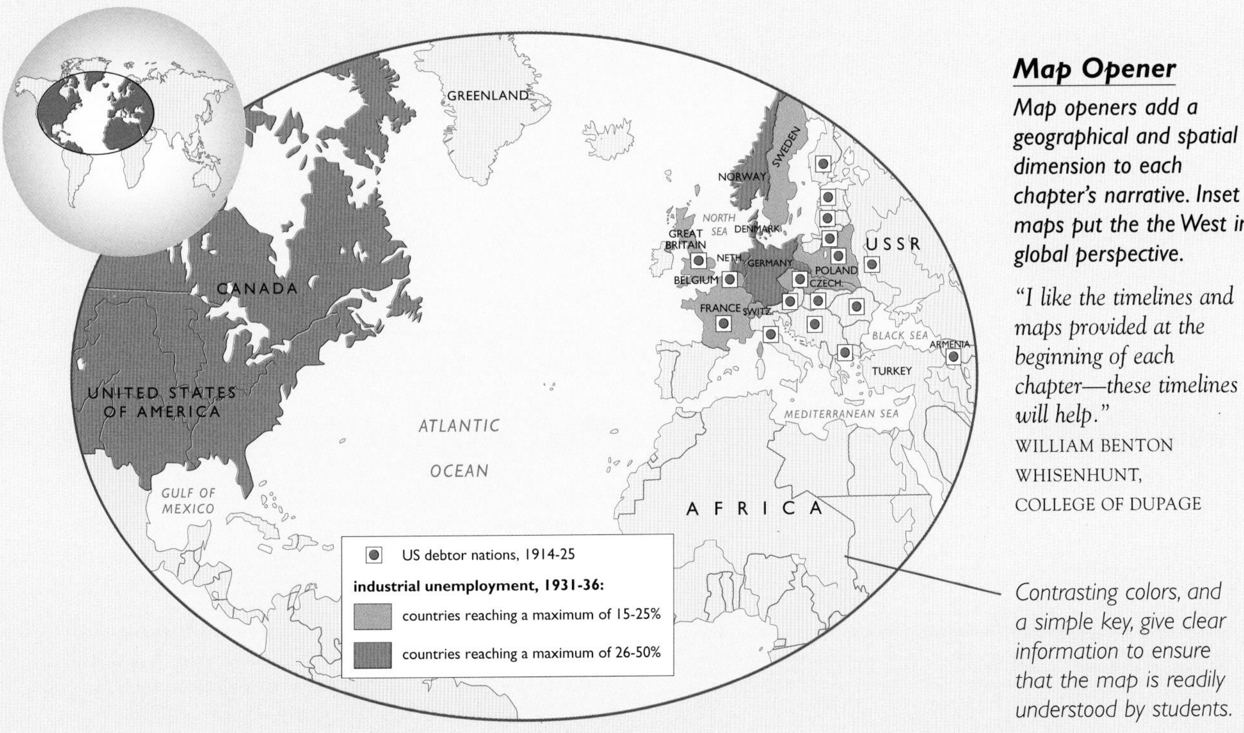

Map Opener

Map openers add a geographical and spatial dimension to each chapter's narrative. Inset maps put the the West in global perspective.

"I like the timelines and maps provided at the beginning of each chapter—these timelines will help."

WILLIAM BENTON WHISENHUNT,
COLLEGE OF DUPAGE

Contrasting colors, and a simple key, give clear information to ensure that the map is readily understood by students.

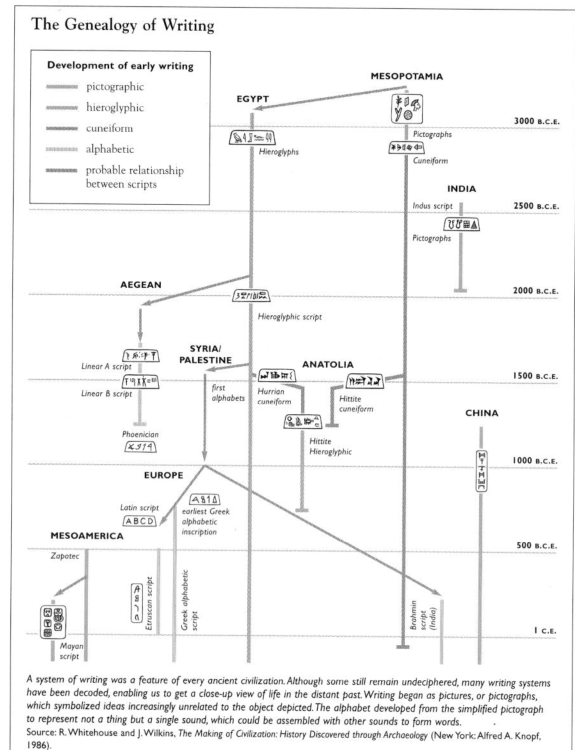

A system of writing was a feature of every ancient civilization. Although some still remain undeciphered, many writing systems have been decoded, enabling us to get a close-up view of life in the distant past. Writing began as pictures, or pictographs, which symbolized ideas increasingly unrelated to the object depicted. The alphabet developed from the simplified pictograph to represent not a thing but a single sound, which could be assembled with other sounds to form words.
Source: R. Whitehouse and J. Wilkins, *The Making of Civilization: History Discovered through Archaeology* (New York: Alfred A. Knopf, 1986).

Patterns of European Economic Development: 1850–1873

	1850	1869	1873
Britain			
Railroad	6,621	15,145	16,082
Coal	37,500	97,066	112,604
Steam power	1,290	4,040	
Pig iron	2,249	5,446	6,566
Raw cotton	266.8	425.8	565.1
Germany			
Railroad	3,639	10,834	14,842
Coal	5,100	26,774	36,392
Steam power	260	2,480	
Pig iron	212	1,413	2,241
Raw cotton	17.1	64.1	117.8
France			
Railroad	1,869	10,518	11,500
Coal	7,225	21,432	24,702
Steam power	370	1,850	
Pig iron	406	1,381	1,382
Raw cotton	59.3	93.7	55.4
Belgium			
Railroad	531	1,800	2,335
Coal	3,481	7,822	10,219
Steam power	70	350	
Pig iron	145	535	607
Raw cotton	10.0	16.3	18.0

By five measures of economic development—total railroad mileage (statute miles), coal production (1000 metric tons), steam power capacity (1000 horsepower), pig iron output (1000 metric tons), and raw cotton consumption (1000 metric tons)—Britain outpaced her three leading European rivals from 1850 to 1873. The gap narrowed, however, especially between Germany and Britain. Note Germany's sevenfold increase in coal production, compared to Britain's threefold increase, and Germany's sevenfold increase in cotton consumption, compared to Britain's, which slightly more than doubled.
Source: Based on D. Landes, The Unbound Prometheus (Cambridge: Cambridge University Press, 1969), p. 194.

Illustrated Information

Numerous tables, charts, and graphs display information visually. Complex processes and data are presented in an easy-to-read format that facilitates student learning.

Captions give a concise overview of visually presented information.

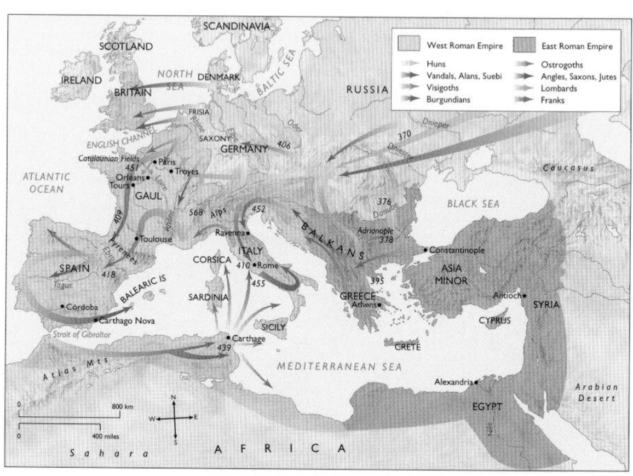

Map 8.1 Migrants, Raiders, and Conquerors, 100–800 C.E.: *Beginning in the first century C.E., nomadic peoples of the central Asian steppes began to expand both west and east, disrupting civilization in both the Mediterranean region and in China. China resisted determinedly, and had attained some stability by around 600. In the west, the movement of Asian peoples triggered the dispersion first of Germanic, and then of Slavic peoples, which was to cut western Europe off from the Mediterranean and the Eastern Roman Empire centered at Constantinople, and to result in the failure of Roman rule in the west. (Compare map 6.3, p. 179, showing the region when Rome, governed from its single capital, held unquestioned dominion over the region; and map 8.2, p. 235, showing the position of successor kingdoms to western Rome.)*

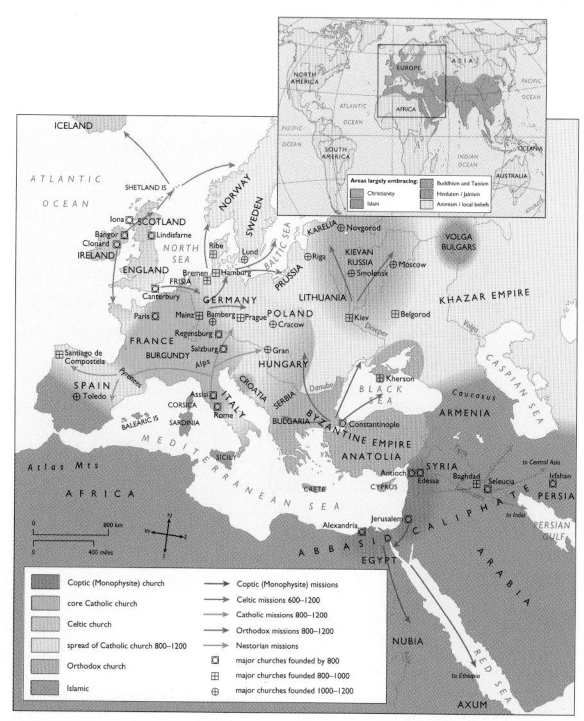

Map 10.1 Christianity and other World Religions, to 1500: *Over many centuries, Christianity spread from Constantinople and Rome; from Celtic Ireland, Anglo-Saxon England, and the eastern Frankish kingdom; from Moscow and Novgorod. As Christianity expanded from its Mediterranean homeland to touch the remotest boundaries of Europe, it took its place as a major actor among the matured religious systems of the world.*

Maps

In each chapter, a range of colorful maps (many featuring topography) help students to place events in their geographical context. Throughout the book, they chart the political, social, and economic changes that have taken place globally during the course of Western civilization.

"The colors of the maps and pictures should hold students' attention. With the emphasis of this book being social and cultural, this may be the type of book we are looking for."
CHARLES HOPE, TARRANT COUNTY JUNIOR COLLEGE

High Quality Art Reproductions

A stunning gallery of art focuses on the diverse experiences of people throughout Western history.

"I think the text is accessible, and the images are the best I have EVER seen in a textbook."
LINDA BREGSTEIN, MERCER COUNTY COMMUNITY COLLEGE

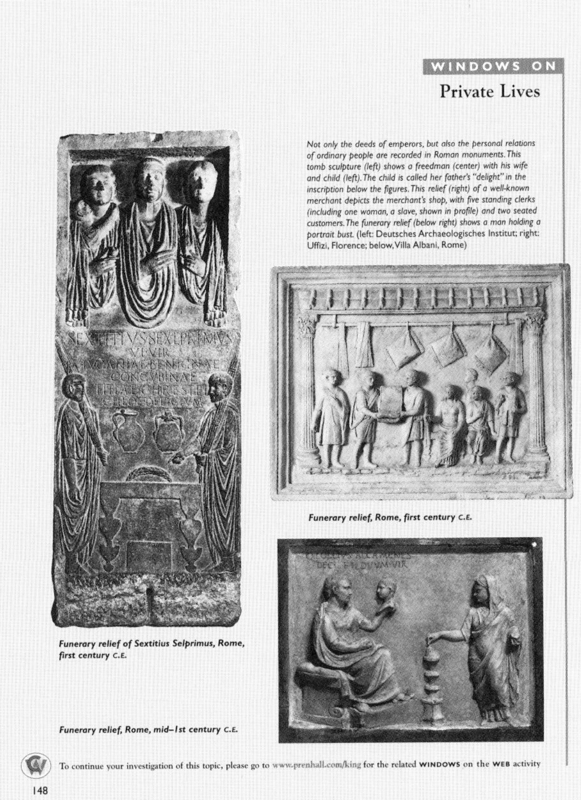

WINDOWS ON

Private Lives

Not only the deeds of emperors, but also the personal relations of ordinary people are recorded in Roman monuments. This tomb sculpture (left) shows a freedman (center) with his wife and child (left). The child is called her father's "delight" in the inscription below the figures. This relief (right) of a well-known merchant depicts the merchant's shop, with five standing clerks (including one woman, a slave, shown in profile) and two seated customers. The funerary relief (below right) shows a man holding a portrait bust. (left: Deutsches Archaeologisches Institut; right: Uffizi, Florence; below, Villa Albani, Rome)

Funerary relief of Sextitius Selprimus, Rome, first century C.E.

Funerary relief, Rome, first century C.E.

Funerary relief, Rome, mid–1st century C.E.

To continue your investigation of this topic, please go to www.prenhall.com/king for the related WINDOWS on the WEB activity

148

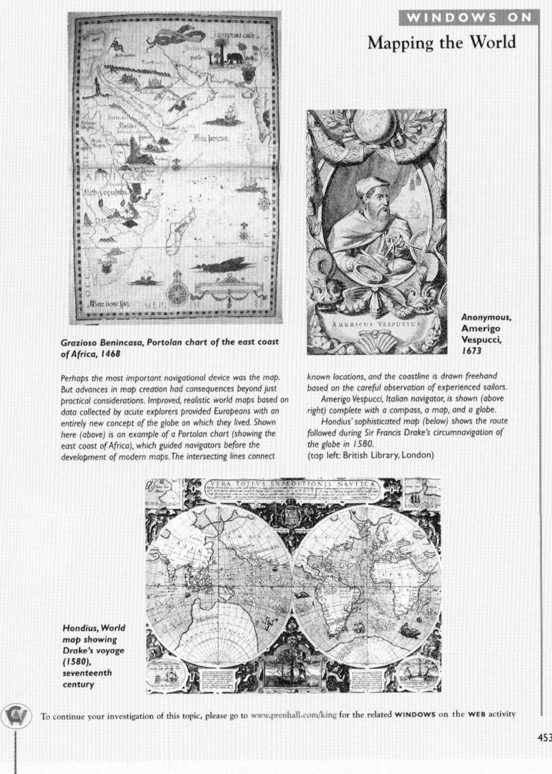

WINDOWS ON

Mapping the World

Grazioso Benincasa, Portolan chart of the east coast of Africa, 1468

Anonymous, Amerigo Vespucci, 1673

Perhaps the most important navigational device was the map. But advances in map creation had consequences beyond just practical considerations. Improved, realistic world maps based on data collected by acute explorers provided Europeans with an entirely new concept of the globe on which they lived. Shown here (above) is an example of a Portolan chart (showing the east coast of Africa), which guided navigators before the development of modern maps. The intersecting lines connect known locations, and the coastline is drawn freehand based on the careful observation of experienced sailors.

Amerigo Vespucci, Italian navigator, is shown (above right) complete with a compass, a map, and a globe.

Hondius' sophisticated map (below) shows the route followed during Sir Francis Drake's circumnavigation of the globe in 1580.
(top left: British Library, London)

Hondius, World map showing Drake's voyage (1580), seventeenth century

To continue your investigation of this topic, please go to www.prenhall.com/king for the related WINDOWS on the WEB activity

453

'Windows On' *boxes*

Windows On *boxes illuminate subjects of high interest by gathering together a range of provocative visual sources.*

"The text covers a vast amount of material and is extremely well written–college students will like the King text."
TIM CRAIN, UNIVERSITY OF WISCONSIN, MILWAUKEE

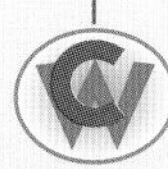

'Windows on the Web' activities extend the scope of the Windows On feature by combining documents, images, and Web-based material to explore concepts and problems in more depth. Each Windows on the Web activity can be found at **www.prenhall.com/king**

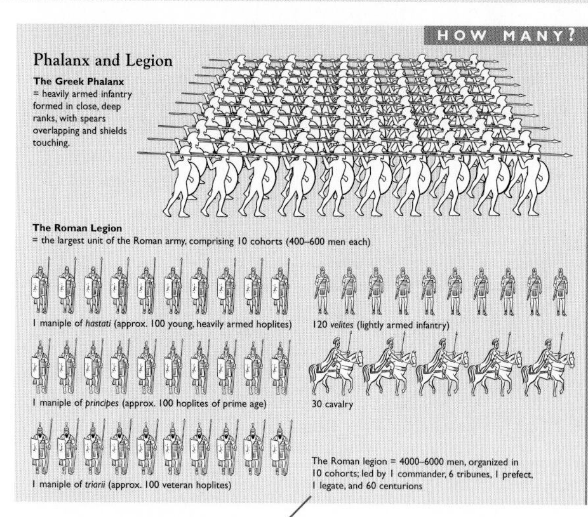

'How Many' *boxes*

Unique to Western Civilization, How Many? *boxes present useful data clearly and visually.*

WITNESSES

Women Protest against Husbands and Predators

In the sixteenth century, women's voices were finally heard—after centuries of near silence. Their works were composed mostly in the vernacular, which unlike Latin did not require an advanced education. The printing press made possible the publication of many copies, circulated widely, as in the case of Moderata Fonte's The Worth of Women represented in the first excerpt here. Women artists, too, became more conspicuous, as in the case of Artemisia Gentileschi, represented in the second excerpt. Both women protest against the actions of men: the first, broadly and theoretically, condemning them for "usurping" women's rights; the second, concretely and particularly, testifying in a trial against a man who raped her.

A Venetian woman lambasts the tyranny of men (1592): If men usurp our rights, should we not complain and declare that they have wronged us? Or if we are their inferiors in status, but not in worth, this is an abuse that has been introduced into the world and that men have then, over time, gradually translated into law and custom; and it has become so entrenched that they claim … that the status they have gained through their bullying is theirs by right. … And we would suffer it. … if they did not insist on exerting such absolute control over us and in such an arrogant manner, treating us like slaves who cannot take a step without asking their permission or say a word without their jumping down our throats. … As fathers, as brothers, as sons or husbands or lovers or whatever other relationship they have to us, they all abuse us, humiliate us, and do all they can to harm and annihilate us.
(Moderata Fonte (Modesta da Pozzo), *The Worth of Women, Wherein is Clearly Revealed their Nobility and their Superiority to Men*, 1592; ed. and trs. V. Cox, 1997)

Artemisia Gentileschi, painter, testifies at the trial of her rapist (1612): Agostino put his head on my breast … and said: "Let's walk together a while, because I hate sitting down." … After we had walked around two or three times, each time going by the bedroom door, when we were in front of the bedroom door, he pushed me in and locked the door. He then threw me onto the edge of the bed, pushing me with a hand on my breast. … Lifting my clothes, which he had a great deal of trouble doing, he placed a hand with a handkerchief at my throat and on my mouth to keep me from screaming. … I felt a strong burning and it hurt very much, but because he held my mouth I couldn't cry out. However, I tried to scream as best I could.

I scratched his face and pulled his hair and … I even removed a piece of flesh. … And after he had done his business he got off me. When I saw myself free, I went to the table drawer and took a knife and moved toward Agostino saying: "I'd like to kill you with this knife because you have dishonored me."
(From M. D. Garrard, *Artemisia Gentileschi*, 1989)

'Witnesses' *boxes*

Bringing to life the events narrated in the text, authentic voices from the past provide personal accounts of social and political change. Brief headnotes introduce the documents and place them in comparative perspective.

"The Witnesses *boxes are an excellent idea. I am pleased that primary sources are so numerous and varied."*
MEAGHAN DUFF, WESTERN KENTUCKY UNIVERSITY

MUST READS

Books and Pamphlets from the French Revolution

Emmanuel Sieyès	*What Is the Third Estate?* (1789)
Edmund Burke	*Reflections on the Revolution in France* (1790)
Olympe de Gouges	*Declaration of the Rights of Woman and the Citizen* (1791)
Tom Paine	*Rights of Man* (1791)
Mary Wollstonecraft	*A Vindication of the Rights of Woman* (1792)

MUST READS

Key Books by Key Leaders

Vladimir Ilyich Lenin	*What Is To Be Done?* (1902)
Adolf Hitler	*Mein Kampf (My Struggle)* (1925)
Winston Churchill	*The Speeches of Winston Churchill* (1941–1945)

'Must Reads' *boxes*

Must Reads *boxes list books of exceptional importance to the meaning of the West—books students may wish to read.*

WHO'S WHO

Fading Empires in Africa

Patrice Lumumba (1925–1961), first premier of the state of Zaire (formerly the Congo) upon Belgian withdrawal in 1960, but assassinated by rivals in 1961.

Joseph (Sese Seko) Mobutu (1930–1997), seized power in Zaire after Lumumba's death, and held it for 32 years, with US support.

Kwame Nkrumah (1909–1972), pan-Africanist prime minister of Ghana upon its independence in 1957, and president in 1960; ousted by a military coup in 1967.

Robert Mugabe (1924–), Marxist leader of Rhodesian revolutionary party which ousted prime minister Ian Smith; became head of nation re-named Zimbabwe.

Desmond Tutu (1931–), South African Anglican archbishop who aroused world outrage against the segregationist apartheid policy of the white Afrikaner government of South Africa; winner of the 1984 Nobel Prize.

Nelson Mandela (1918–), leader of African National Congress imprisoned in 1964 and released in 1990; in 1994, won election to the presidency of South Africa.

Muammar el-Qaddafi (1942–), seized power in Libya in 1969 after toppling the pro-Western monarchy, nationalizing foreign petroleum assets, and, during the Cold War, accepting Soviet aid and arms.

'Who's Who' *boxes*

Important figures are identified and listed in Who's Who *boxes, and their principal contributions noted.*

Stone, Bronze, and Word, 2 million–500 B.C.E. **29**

REVIEW QUESTIONS

1. Describe the evolution of the human species. Why were the advances in the New Stone Age so important? What role did women play in Neolithic society?

2. Where did the first civilizations arise? What functions did cities serve in these cultures? Why did iron implements largely replace bronze ones? Why were trade and cultural links significant?

3. Describe the social hierarchy of early civilizations. How did women's status influence these societies? How did the status of women differ in Egypt and Mesopotamia?

4. Why was the invention of writing in early civilization so important? Why did writing evolve from the first pictograms to the alphabet? What is the difference between writing and language?

5. How did the custom of sacrifice develop? Why were Akhenaten's religious innovations such a break with Egyptian religion?

6. By what process did the Israelites become monotheists? Why was the Israelite concept of a righteous God so radical in the ancient world? What role did ethics play in the development of early Confucianism and Buddhism?

SUGGESTED RESOURCES

Before History

Cavalli-Sforza, Luigi Luca, *Genes, Peoples, and Languages*, trans. Mark Seielstad (New York: Farrar, Straus & Giroux; North Point Press, 2000). Linking complex genetic and linguistic evidence, Cavalli-Sforza proposes to map the history of the migrations of all the world's peoples.

Fagan, Brian M., *The Journey from Eden: The Peopling of Our World* (London: Thames & Hudson, 1990). A critical overview of theories of human origin, arguing on the basis of recent historical, paleoanthropological, and genetic research that fully modern humans evolved in Africa and from there colonized the rest of the world.

Leakey, Richard and Roger Lewin, *Origins Reconsidered: In Search of What Makes Us Human* (New York: Doubleday, 1992). Reflections by a renowned paleoanthropologist on his own discoveries of early hominid life in East Africa. Leakey incorporates ideas from philosophy, anthropology, molecular biology, and linguistics to investigate not only how we evolved anatomically but how we acquired the qualities that make us human: consciousness, creativity, and culture.

McElvaine, Robert S., *Eve's Seed: Biology, the Sexes, and the Course of History* (New York: McGraw Hill, 2000). Fills in the history between the culmination of human evolution and the estabilishment of civilization, a period when women's role was dominant before envious men overturned power relations.

Civilization and the City

Diamond, Jared, *Guns, Germs and Steel: The Fates of Human Societies* (New York: W.W. Norton, 1997). A brilliant exploration of the geographical and material conditions that permitted Eurasian civilizations to advance and gain dominance.

Hodder, Ian, *The Domestication of Europe: Structure and Contingency in Neolithic Societies* (Cambridge, MA: Basil Blackwell, 1990). A bold if controversial attempt to reconstruct human societies in the Near East and Europe at the end of the Ice Age.

Kramer, Samuel Noah, *The Sumerians: The History, Culture and Character* (Chicago: University of Chicago Press, 1971). A classic history of Sumer, 4500–1750 B.C.E., with selected translations of Sumerian texts. Details Sumerian achievements in government, education and literature, philosophy, law, agriculture, and medicine.

Lerner, Gerda, *The Creation of Patriarchy I: Women and History* (New York/Oxford: Oxford University Press, 1986). A pioneering feminist study of the origin of Western women's subordination, linking it to the rise of property-conscious agricultural societies in Mesopotamia, Israel, and Greece.

Nissen, Hans J., *The Early History of the Ancient Near East, 9000–2000 B.C.* (Chicago: University of Chicago Press, 1988). A balanced political and cultural history of Mesopotamia, based on archaeological sources and analysis of material culture.

The Indus Valley civilization:
http://www.historyofindia.com/indus.html
http://www.harappa.com/har/har0.html

Writing, Language, and Consciousness

Frankfort, H. and H. A., John A. Wilson, Thorkild Jacobsen, *Before Philosophy: The Intellectual Adventure of Ancient Man* (Baltimore: Penguin, 1949). A challenging description of ancient Egyptian and Mesopotamian mythopoetic interpretations of phenomena, in contrast to the philosophical outlook of later Hellenic culture.

Martin, Henri Jean (trans. Lydia G. Cochrane), *The History and Power of Writing* (Chicago: University of Chicago Press, 1995). A comprehensive study by a preeminent scholar of the book. Examines the technologies, forms, and structures of writing throughout history.

The Analects of Confucius:
http://classics.mit.edu/Confucius/analects.html

Evolving Religions

Bergmann, Martin S., *In the Shadow of Moloch: The Sacrifice of Children and its Impact on Western Religions* (New York: Columbia University Press, 1993). An eye-opening account of the ritual convention of child sacrifice and its shaping of ancient cultures.

Cross, Frank Moore, *Canaanite Myth and Hebrew Epic: Essays in the History of the Religion of Israel* (Cambridge, MA.: Harvard University Press, 1973; reprint 1997). Traces continuities between early Israelite religion and its underlying Canaanite culture. Explores re-emergence of Canaanite mythic material in the apocalypticism of early Christianity and the Dead Sea Scrolls.

Leeming, David A. & Jake Page, *Goddess: The Myths of the Female Divine* (Oxford: Oxford University Press, 1994). A biography of the "goddess," the compelling, commanding, threatening female divinity revered by human populations from the Ice Age to modern times, showing how ancient themes endure in modern religion and psychology.

Bible tools—text and history: http://bible.crosswalk.com

End of chapter matter

Review Questions *stimulate critical thought and understanding.* Suggested Resources *direct students to further study by recommending books and websites.*

Conclusion

THE EARLIEST CIVILIZATIONS AND THE MEANING OF THE WEST

Much of what distinguishes human life today was first attained by the ancient people of the first civilizations. The ability to control nature, to manage food production, to build cities, to conduct trade, to develop technology, to understand science and mathematics, to create works of literature, to establish systems of law, and to ask thoughtful questions about the cosmos and our place in it—all of these were bequeathed to later generations by the first civilizations, and to the "West" specifically by the ancient civilizations of the Middle East. These civilizations offer lessons as well about the organization of the state and the fragility of power. The next chapter will consider this other dimension of life in antiquity.

'Conclusion' *boxes*

Conclusion *boxes look at how the events discussed in each chapter influenced the course of Western civilization, and provide insights into their consequences.*

SUPPLEMENTS FOR

WESTERN CIVILIZATION

Second Edition

PRINT SUPPLEMENTS

The Instructor's Manual with Test Item File combines teaching resources with testing material. The Instructor's manual includes chapter outlines, overviews, key concepts, discussion questions, and audiovisual resources. The Test Item File offers a menu of multiple choice, true-false, essay, and map questions for each chapter. A collection of blank maps can be photocopied and used for map testing or other class exercises.

The Study Guide (Volumes I and II) provides, for each chapter, a brief overview, a list of chapter objectives, study exercises, and multiple-choice, short-answer, and essay questions. In addition, each chapter includes a number of specific map questions and exercises.

The Documents Set (Volumes I and II) is a collection of additional primary and secondary source documents that underscore the themes outlined in the text. Organized by chapter, this set for each of the two volumes includes review questions for each document.

A Transparency Pack provides instructors with full-color transparency acetates of all maps, charts, and graphs in the text for use in the classroom.

Understanding and Answering Essay Questions suggests helpful analytical tools for understanding different types of essay questions, and provides precise guidelines for preparing well-crafted essay answers. This brief guide is available free to students when packaged with *Western Civilization: A Social and Cultural History*.

Reading Critically About History This brief guide prepares students with helpful strategies for reading a history textbook. Available free when packed with *Western Civilization, Second Edition*.

History on the Internet is a brief guide to the internet that provides students with clear strategies for navigating the Internet and World Wide Web. Exercises within and at the ends of the chapters allow students to practice searching for the myriad resources available to the student of history. Free to students when packaged with *Western Civilization: A Social and Cultural History*.

ELECTRONIC SUPPLEMENTS

The Companion Website™
www.prenhall.com/king
The Companion Website™ works in tandem with the text to help students use the World Wide Web to enrich their understanding of Western civilization. Built around the primary subtopics of each chapter, it includes study questions, web links, and document questions. Features new to the Second Edition include interactive map exercises, "Windows on the Web" activities and, for instructors, maps and graphics from the text available for downloading in Power Point presentations.

Instructor's Resources CD-ROM An ideal tool for classroom presentations, this CD-ROM contains all of the maps and charts from the text, PowerPoint lectures that match the sequence of topics in the text, and lecture outlines, chapter summaries, and test items.

Course Management Systems As the leader in course-management solutions for teachers and students of history, Prentice Hall provides a variety of online tools. Contact your local Prentice Hall representative for a demonstration or visit. **www.prenhall.com/demo**

Prentice Hall Custom Test, a commercial-quality, computerized, test management program is available for Windows and Macintosh environments. This allows instructors to select items from the Test Item File in the Instructor's Manual and design their own exams.

PART ONE

BEFORE THE WEST

The Inhabited World from the First Civilizations to Alexander the Great (d. 323 B.C.E.)

The Western world has not always existed; in fact, it is rather new. Many things needed to happen before there was a "West." It was necessary for the human species to evolve from earlier primates; to learn to grow food and live in villages; and to develop the first civilizations. Those civilizations formed about five to six thousand years ago far away from Europe (the heartland of the "West") in Asia and Africa. They are recognized by certain features: a high level of organization; a political system, or state, ruled by kings or priests; technical achievements such as the crafting of bronze metal implements or the use of the wheel; the ability to write, and so to record knowledge and remember the past. Even when living in simpler communities, people had demonstrated advanced skills and a creative imagination; but the capacity of peoples in the earliest civilizations to invent tools, organize systems, store information, and express feeling, beliefs, and ideas immeasurably expanded the possibilities of life for human beings everywhere in the world.

Several other civilizations emerged through contact with these earliest civilizations (while at least two, in China and the Americas, developed independently). One was that of the Israelites, whose worship of a single just God distinguished them from many of their neighbors. Another was that of the Greeks, although its characteristic forms developed some centuries later. From their mythological traditions, the Greeks developed philosophy, science, and drama, while modern concepts of the state and people's rights derive from the unique model of the Greek city. The beliefs of the Israelites and ideas of the Greeks would count among the cultural foundations of the West.

In the fourth century B.C.E., Alexander the Great of Macedonia conquered the cities of Greece, and the empires of Persia and Egypt. Under his successors Greek civilization became established throughout the ancient Mediterranean world.

STONE, BRONZE, AND WORD

2.5m | 100,000 | 10,000 | 5000 | 3500 | 3000 | 2500 | 2000 | 1500 | 1000 | 500 B.C.E.*

Prehistory and Evolution

Last Ice Age, c. 1.6m–10,000

Upper Paleolithic, c. 100,000–10,000

Mesolithic, c. 10,000–8000

Neolithic, c. 8000–2000

Cereal cultivation and domestication of animals, after 10,000

- ◆ Stone tools evolve, c. 2.5 m
- ◆ *Homo habilis*, c. 2 m
- ◆ *Homo erectus*, c. 1.8 m–500,000
- ◆ *Homo sapiens*, c. 500,000
- ◆ Neanderthal Man, c. 200,000–35,000
- ◆ Anatomically modern *homo sapiens*, c. 50,000–30,000

Civilization

Bronze Age, c. 6000–1000

Iron Age, from c. 1200

- ◆ Pottery, weaving, c. 9000
- ◆ Jericho, c. 9000
- ◆ Çatal Hüyük, c. 8000
- ◆ Woven flax, wool, c. 7000
- ◆ Ground and fermented grain, c. 7000
- ◆ Mesopotamian civilization, c. 3500; Egyptian, c. 3100
- ◆ Wheel, plow, draft animals, sail, after 3500
- ◆ Indus Valley civilization, c. 2500–after 2000
- ◆ Domestication of horses in Mesopotamia/Egypt, c. 2500
- ◆ Chinese civilization, c. 2200
- ◆ Iron metallurgy, 1200 B.C.E
- ◆ Silk weaving, after 1300
- ◆ New World civilization, c. 1200

Monuments and Artifacts

- ◆ Royal graves of Ur, c. 2600
- ◆ Egyptian pyramids, Old Kingdom, after 2600
- ◆ Ziggurat of Ur, 2100
- ◆ Mycenaean shaft graves, after 1600
- ◆ *Tholos* tombs, after 1500
- ◆ Deir el-Bahri, by 1479
- ◆ Egyptian temple of Medinet Habu (Ramses III), 1174
- ◆ Temple of Solomon, c. 960
- ◆ Palaces of Sargon II, c. 720
- ◆ Ashurbanipal of Assyria's monuments, c. 650

Religion and Ideas

- ◆ Cuneiform, from 3300
- ◆ Hieroglyphic, from 3200
- ◆ Egyptian, Sumerian decimal, sexagesimal systems, after 3000
- ◆ Egyptian solar calendar, after 3000
- ◆ *Gilgamesh*, after 2675
- ◆ Egyptian *Books of Wisdom*, from 2650
- ◆ Indian pictograms, c. 2500
- ◆ Ptah-hotep's *Instructions* to son, c. 2400
- ◆ Hammurabi's *Code*, c. 1790
- ◆ *Book of the Dead*, from 1575
- ◆ Egyptian clinical studies, brain surgery, after 1550
- ◆ Alphabet, after 1500
- ◆ Hittite *Chronicle*, after 1500
- ◆ Indian *Vedas*, from 1500
- ◆ Chinese pictograms, c. 1500
- ◆ *Ramayana*, *Mahabharata*, after 1000
- ◆ *Psalms* of David, c. 970
- ◆ *Upanishads*, from 800
- ◆ *Iliad*, c. 750; *Odyssey*, c. 725
- ◆ Hebrew Bible, c. 500

*Before Common Era

Note: timelines illustrate only major periods, movements, and events covered in the chapter or part.

CHAPTER

1 Stone, Bronze, and Word

Prehistory and Early Civilizations

2 MILLION–500 B.C.E.

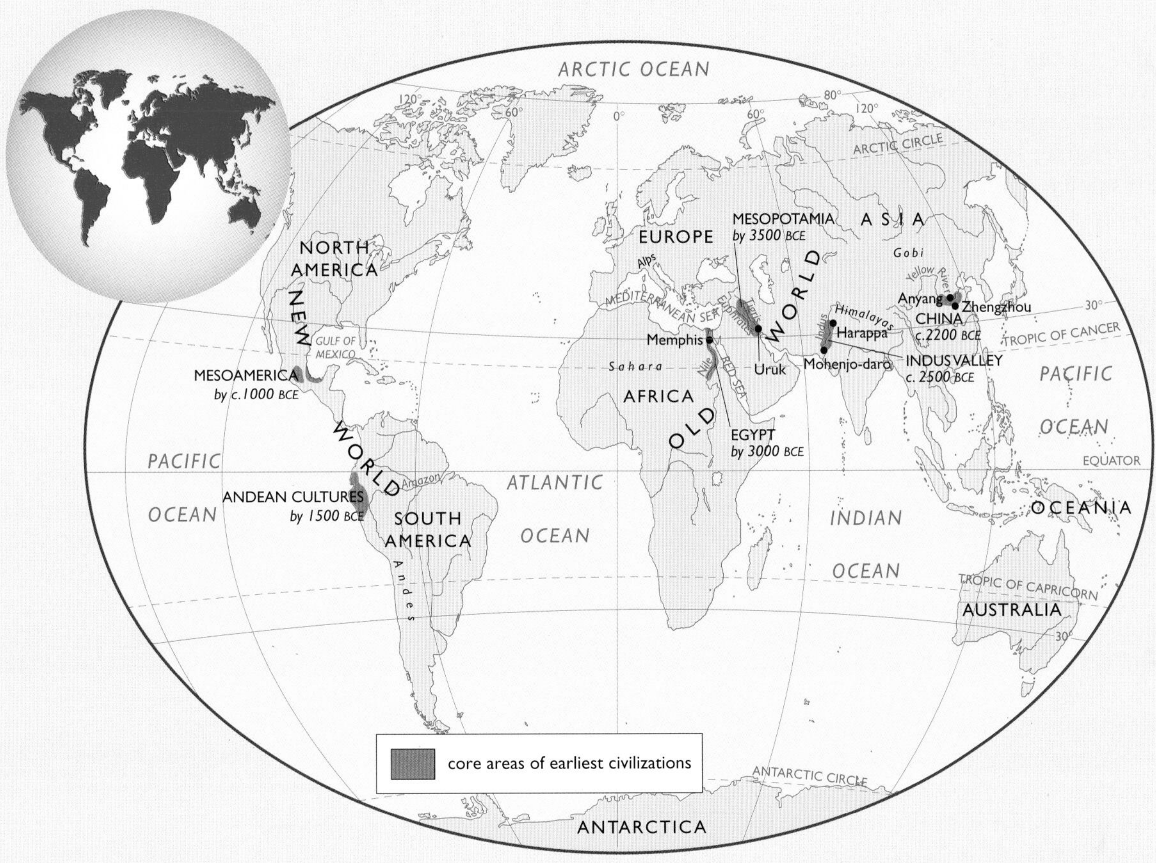

KEY TOPICS

- **Before History:** The human species evolves, settles down in villages, and learns to plant crops, weave textiles, make pots, and build fortifications.
- **Civilization and the City:** Civilizations arise at five different points on the globe—Mesopotamia, Egypt, India, China, and the Americas.
- **Writing, Language, and Consciousness:** People invent writing to manage their wealth, memorialize their kings, record their thoughts, and explain the cosmos.
- **Sacrifice, Myth, and Conscience:** People sacrifice to the gods, and ultimately come to worship one God.

The Unbinding of Isaac *An old man, Abraham, led his cherished son Isaac to a hilltop, obedient to the God who had ordered him long ago to leave the land of his birth. He drew a knife and laid wood for the fire, in preparation for the unimaginable deed he had been commanded to do. The deity demanded a sacrifice, Abraham's son must die. Satisfied by Abraham's steadfastness, and before the slaughter could take place, God sent a messenger to tell Abraham that he should set the child free. Abraham seized a ram caught in a nearby thicket, sacrificed the animal, and released his child.*

Written down nearly 3000 years ago, this story originated even earlier, not long after the appearance of the first human **civilization**. It is recorded in the Bible (Genesis 22:1–13), known also as the Hebrew Bible, the Old Testament, Scripture ("what is written"), or the Word, the fundamental book of the Western world. The story of Abraham and Isaac marks a key moment in the civilizing process. The value of human life, the strength of human love, the power of the will are all recognized in that moment when Isaac was rescued from the sacrificial knife. The unbinding of Isaac is preconditioned by the spiritual, or psychological, unbinding of Abraham. Freed from the fear of the unknown that drove his contemporaries to placate the gods, Abraham may trust, love, reflect, and choose between good and evil.

By the time the story of Abraham and Isaac was recorded, at least some members of the human **species** had completed one phase of a long journey, and entered the era of civilization: they had settled in villages and cities, used metal tools and weapons, learned to write and, equipped with words, to reason about the human condition. That journey extended over the vast expanse of time that had passed since the first appearance on earth of the human species about 500,000 years before. It is the subject of this chapter.

BEFORE HISTORY

The universe began some 15 billion years ago. The planet Earth took form as long as 4.5 billion years ago. The first living cells developed nearly 4 billion years ago. About halfway into the last billion years the first animals walked on land—dinosaurs and early mammals. About 65 million years ago, the mammals flourished, evolving in many ways. Some 55 million years ago, the first primates appeared, the group of mammals to which humans belong. Between 5 and 6 million years ago evolved the first human-like primate (or **hominid**). This critical development occurred in Africa in the Old World, the land mass made up of the three continents of Africa, Asia, and Europe.

The Arrival of the Human Being

The increased size of fossil skulls tells us that between 1 and 2 million years ago, these African hominids developed significantly larger brains. This distinction identified a new being, recognizably human and thus called by the genus name *Homo*—Latin for "man" or "human." The first species of human was called ***Homo habilis*** or "skilled man," which referred to the ability to make tools from stone. The second, ***Homo erectus***, was so called because scientists at first believed that this was the first primate to walk on two legs, with a fully upright posture. It is now known that earlier hominids had also walked in this way.

Homo sapiens, or "wise man," probably evolved from *Homo erectus*. Until recently it was believed that *Homo sapiens* developed independently in several parts of the world, from populations of *Homo erectus* that had migrated from Africa. Today it is generally believed that *Homo sapiens* originated only in Africa, as many as 2 million years ago, or as few as 200,000 years ago. Many authorities put the date at about 500,000 years ago (see *How Many?*).

Homo sapiens had a body and brain like ours. His hands were equipped with a prehensile thumb more dexterous than that of his primate ancestors, which could grasp and manipulate tools to do work. His brain could link words with ideas to create language. He could chip rock into a hatchet to kill his prey, or wield two sticks to start a fire in which to roast his victim. She could gather fruits and grains found growing wild to share with her mate and her children, whom she kept close by her longer than mothers in the animal kingdom.

The evolution of early forms of *Homo* and their migration to the Middle East, Asia, and Europe

HOW MANY?

From Then to Now

Approximate years B.C.E. (Before Common Era)

15,000,000,000	birth of the universe
4–5,000,000,000	formation of the earth
500,000,000	first land animals
55,000,000	first primates
6–5,000,000	first hominids
2,000,000	*Homo habilis*
1,800,000	*Homo erectus*
last 500,000	*Homo sapiens*
last 50,000–30,000	anatomically modern *Homo sapiens*

occurred during the Stone Age, so named after the material—pebbles and stones—from which humans made the tools used to hunt and dig and defend themselves. The Stone Age, which extends from about 2.5 million to 5000 years ago, is further divided into "old," "middle," and "new" periods. Using Greek terms, scientists refer to these respectively as Paleolithic, Mesolithic, and Neolithic. The **Paleolithic** was by far the longest, reaching to within 10,000 years of our own time.

Toward the end of the Paleolithic period, "Neanderthal man" appeared, probably a distinct species of *Homo* rather than a sub species of *Homo sapiens*. They were named after the Neander Valley in western Germany where their skeletal remains were first found. Neanderthalers lived scattered throughout Europe and southwest Asia, from perhaps 200,000 to 35,000 years ago. They made their homes in caves, hunted in packs, and appeased the spirits of nature—so the evidence suggests—with ceremonies that have left traces in the heaps of skulls and bones of the bears they revered. They gathered around fires, wore clothing, and buried their dead with tools and ornaments to accompany them to the afterworld. Their behavior implies a belief in a form of afterlife. Beginning with the Neanderthals, human beings have known that they are born to die, and that awareness shaped their culture. The rite of burial marks the appearance of religion within the human population.

Undisputably a form of *Homo sapiens* were the Cro-Magnon humans, so called after the site in southern France where their remains were first discovered. When they evolved at least 30,000 years ago, similar anatomically modern humans had already emerged in Africa and Asia. But European Cro-Magnons were extraordinarily creative. They used tools more refined than those of the Neanderthalers. They sewed clothes from animal skins, using needles of bone. They crafted statuettes of plump women with exaggerated breasts and bellies, who may have represented the source of life and new birth. Cro-Magnon artists adorned their cave walls with paintings of beasts whom the hunters had vanquished, or wished to vanquish. Some of the finest of these cave paintings can be seen at Lascaux, in France, illustrated on p. 6 and Altamira, in Spain. They bear witness to the emerging creative power of the human mind.

With Cro-Magnon humans, and their counterparts around the world, the evolution of humankind, as it exists today, was nearly complete. The human species that dominates the earth today is technically called *Homo sapiens sapiens*, indicating a supreme level of intelligence; some scientists prefer the term "anatomically modern *Homo sapiens*." Nevertheless, modern humans have learned to apply that brainpower in ever more sophisticated ways. Intelligence is essential to human nature, creating the capacity for **culture** or learned behavior, including social customs, religion, language, and the arts. Their capacity for culture distinguishes human beings from their close relatives, the apes—even more so than a dexterous thumb or an erect posture.

As humans evolved, so did the conditions in which they lived. Between about 1.6 million and 10,000 years ago, the Arctic ice cap repeatedly expanded over the land masses of the northern hemisphere. During this period, called the Pleistocene era, glaciers flowed into the valleys of the temperate zones of Asia, Europe, and North America. These ice ages made life hard for humans and animals alike, and they often migrated in search of warmer climes. The spread of glaciers also resulted in low sea levels, as ice deposits on the land surface stole water from the rivers and oceans. Coastal areas extended farther into the sea than they do today, and land outcroppings or bridges that have since disappeared under the sea made possible the human colonization of Australia and the Western Hemisphere—every continent except Antarctica.

Settling Down

The final recession of the ice cap, around 10,000 years ago, was a turning point in the evolution of human culture. As the climate warmed, human beings entered a new phase of their development—the **Neolithic**, or New Stone Age. During this era, they made important discoveries which radically changed their way of living and laid the foundations for the development of civilization. These achievements of the Neolithic age, made gradually over millennia, cumulatively amount to the most dramatic change in the way human beings lived until the modern era.

Foremost among the discoveries of the Neolithic period are farming and animal husbandry. In early human communities men hunted for food and the women gathered it: picking fruits from trees and bushes, gleaning grain from fields sown with seeds borne by animals or wind, digging edible roots from the earth. For almost all of human history, food was found in grassland or forest, growing wild or running free. Only recently have foodstuffs been deliberately cultivated. In the 5000 years after the end of the last Ice Age (about 10,000 years ago), human beings learned to control the plant and animal resources upon which their survival depended. That process is called "domestication."

It was probably a woman who first observed that a kernel she had neglected to pick and that happened to fall on soft, damp soil, soon germinated and formed a new plant. Countless people may have observed that process before one of them thought to break up the earth with a tool—probably only a stick—and sow it with grain. When she did so, agriculture began. It was a discovery of monumental importance for the human species. Now human beings—driven, perhaps,

Bull Worship: *The religious rituals of early peoples are not completely understood. We do know that tens of thousands of years ago and all over the globe, they revered figures representing fertility—male and female, human and animal, such as these powerful bulls painted on a cave wall in southern France by a Neolithic hunter about 100 centuries before civilization began.* (Lascaux, France, 16,000–10,000 B.C.E.)

by the overpopulation of their homeland into areas less productive—could cultivate the land, produce their own food, settle in one place, form stable communities, and increase in population. These were the preconditions of further achievements.

Agriculture was first enduringly established in the highlands of the Middle East after 8000 B.C.E. Fields of wheat, millet, oats, and, especially, barley fed the growing population of that region. The cultivation of these and a variety of other crops extended gradually into Asia Minor, southeast Europe, northern Africa, and Asia.

Three to four thousand years later, inhabitants of northern China and the Indus Valley and of The Americas, independently discovered how to sow and harvest. They grew wheat, millet, and rice in Asia, maize (corn) and potatoes in the Americas. From these centers, agricultural technology spread around the globe and eventually to nearly all its inhabitants—all but the fraction of about 1 percent who still live in hunting-and-gathering communities.

Neolithic farmers prepared their grains—ancestors of the kinds consumed today—to make a palatable food by boiling, soaking, pounding, and grinding them, as is known from the grinding stones discovered in several sites. They stewed the grains in water to form a porridge, molded them into a loaf or a cake for baking, and brewed them to make a fermented sludge, the precursor of modern beer. For thousands of years in all the civilizations of the globe, such foodstuffs were the basis, or staple, of the human diet.

Perhaps even before the first grain crops were cultivated, some animals had been trained and bred to suit the needs of human masters. Donkeys and horses learned to accept a bit, and dogs to follow the hunt. Early attempts to domesticate other animals, such as stags, antelopes, and lions, failed; and many centuries passed before the camel was tamed. But other animals—cows, goats, sheep, pigs, and fowl—soon proved their usefulness. Herding animals for later slaughter was an alternative to hunting. Beasts intended for future consumption grazed in open pastures or ate plant foods grown for their fodder. Sheep and cows, goats and pigs provided early livestock farmers, or pastoralists, with clothing and milk as well as meat. Eventually, humans learned to use strong animals, such as oxen, water buffalo, and horses, to haul loads and help them with their work.

Caring for crops and animals entailed a new way of life for the first farmers. They settled down in one place. They built shelters close to the fields, using the reeds and clay or timber and stones of the land about them. They clustered into communities larger than the groups of thirty or so persons whose tasks had been simply to hunt and gather. The new villagers numbered in the hundreds, even the thousands.

Traces of Neolithic villages exist in the Middle East at Jericho (9000 B.C.E., Jordan River valley), Jarmo (7000 B.C.E., modern Iraq), and Çatal Hüyük in Asia Minor (8000 B.C.E, modern Turkey). These may have been the first villages. By 8000 B.C.E. in Jericho, closely packed, round, mud-brick houses covered 4 acres (1.6 ha.) and housed a population of around 2000. For defense against invasion by wild beasts or other humans, the residents erected walls; these measured nearly 10 feet (3 m.) thick and 12 feet (3.6 m.)

Mother Goddesses

Hittite and Minoan art: *The numerous prehistoric figurines of female figures promising fertility (see also p. 3) reappeared in more sophisticated form thousands of years later. Shown here are two figures from the Bronze Age: a Hittite bronze statuette of a mother with child (left) and a decorated earthenware (faience) figure depicting a Minoan snake goddess, or attendant, from Knossos, c. 1600* B.C.E. *(below).* (below: Archaeological Museum, Herakleion, Crete)

Mother and child** (left),* ***Horoztepe, c. 2100–2000 B.C.E.

Minoan snake goddess, Knossos, c. 1600 B.C.E.

The Diet of Early Civilizations

Middle East	barley, wheat, rye, lentils
China	rice, millet, soy beans
Africa	yam, millet, rice, sorghum
Americas	cocoa, maize (corn), tomatoes

high, and were guarded from a watchtower. In the seventh millennium—that is, in the thousand-year period from 7000 to 6000 B.C.E.—the smaller village of Jarmo, perched on a hillside in the Zagros Mountains, boasted a watchtower rising to a height of 40 feet (12 m.), built of stone and set in stone walls.

Çatal Hüyük sprawled over 32 acres (13 ha.) and had a population of between 5000 and 7000 by the sixth millennium B.C.E. Here archaeologists have unearthed evidence of woven cloth, intricate stone weaponry, and technically advanced pottery. The crafters of these goods lived in a complex of connected homes, each accessed via a ladder through a window or roof opening. Within, religious worship seems to have been organized around a building (forty shrines on nine building levels) apparently designed for that purpose. The inhabitants adorned their temple with the heads of bulls and triple images of a fertility goddess in her youth, prime, and old age.

Artisans and Specialists

Of the human inhabitants of the globe, a small fraction were now farmers, herders, and villagers, better fed, housed, and protected than their hunting and gathering forebears. Soon these communities began to develop technical skills which enabled them to make their lives more comfortable and secure. The most competent or powerful assumed positions of leadership and undertook the task of placating the gods.

To store the products of their harvests, early farmers devised baskets and pots made of the same materials, reeds and clay, that they used to build their huts. The development of pottery skills—a major advance, as pots could be used to store grain and liquids—took place some 8000 years ago in the Old World zones of advanced human culture, from North Africa to Japan. In the Americas this innovation came independently and later—at around 2000 B.C.E.

Potters then learned to shape their products on a turning wheel—an object used for this purpose even before it was used as a means of transport. They learned to select the best clay and to make the clay vessels harder and more durable by heating them at a certain temperature for the right length of time. They took the time to decorate the clay before firing, producing useful vessels that were also works of art. When villages disappeared,

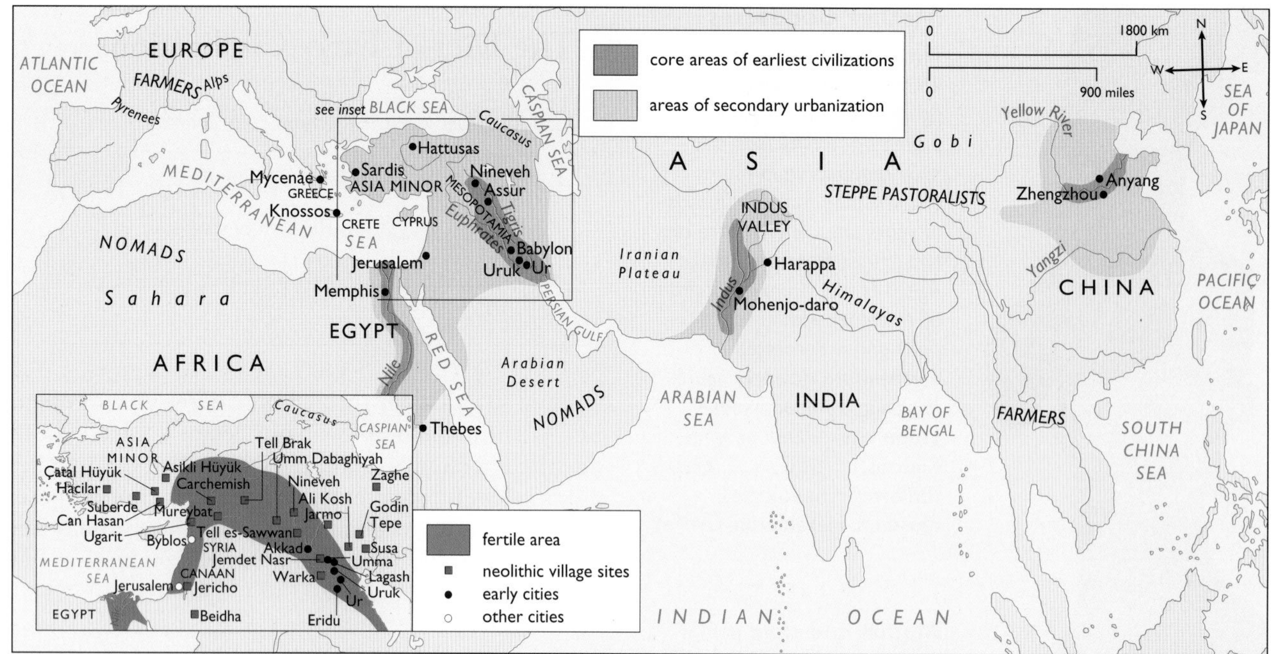

Map 1.1 Agriculture and Urbanization: From the Neolithic Era to the Era of the First Civilizations: *After the icecap began to recede about 10,000 years ago, farming began in some human communities, spreading from these eventually to every part of the globe. Where the crops were most abundant, some people were freed from farm labor for other tasks. Here advanced civilizations began at five different points and times: Mesopotamia, Egypt, India, China, and The Americas.*

fragments of the pots were buried in the soil underneath ash and dust and stone. Archaeologists today read in these deposits a record of the inhabitants' ways of life.

Other workers learned to process plant or animal fibers to form linen, cotton, wool, and (in China) silk, spinning the fibers into thread, then weaving them into cloth. Both of these textile-manufacturing tasks were nearly always performed by women. Spinning was accomplished by first wrapping a raw fiber around a simple stick, the distaff, then drawing a strand from the distaff and winding it onto a turning, weighted stick, the spindle. The thread could then be woven into cloth. A simple loom allowed the first weavers to craft both plain fabrics and more intricately patterned textiles. Villagers could put aside the animal skins that had warmed their ancestors and clothe themselves in light and flexible fabric.

Spinning, weaving, and sewing were women's work. In those early pre-agricultural communities where distinctions of sex roles were already established, women contributed as gatherers to feeding the family. As in traditional societies today, they may have provided 60 to 80 percent of the food supply. Women's role changed upon crossing the threshold to an agricultural society. Now men took on the jobs of farming—the hard work of herding and plowing (for the ox-drawn plow soon replaced the woman's hoe). Women took responsibility for the household and its numerous tasks: textile production, food preparation, water carrying, and the bearing and rearing of children.

This simple division of labor into farming and domestic work was gradually replaced by a more complex one, as some people became specialists in particular tasks. Among them were potters and tool-makers. While other villagers farmed and herded, the labor of these experts was freed for the highly skilled work that they alone could perform. Other specialists also emerged: managers who coordinated village labor; warriors, expert in fighting; priests who proclaimed the will of the gods.

Neolithic peoples feared and revered forces of nature with an attitude we call "worship." Those terrifying forces included the shifting winds and recurrent sun, flood and fire, lightning and thunder, the sheer heights of trees and mountains, the mysterious depths of caves, the new life of the springtime, and the inexplicable phenomenon of human birth from the body of a woman—all these were recognized as the work of a god. Gods had their own concerns. But human beings could summon their attention with gifts, with **icons**, with charms, with chants.

In this regard Neolithic people differed little from their Paleolithic ancestors, whose caves and graves yield evidence of artifacts used to claim the attention of the gods. Some ancient peoples revered the bull as an emblem of potency and painted or sculpted images of the beast. Others worshiped a goddess whose good will furthered both human and plant fertility. Archaeological sites worldwide have yielded a harvest of little statues of goddesses or magical figures, endowed with ample breasts, hips, and abdomens and sometimes shown in the act of suckling or giving birth (two examples are shown on p. 7). The bodies of these "Venuses" (so called later after the Roman goddess of love) symbolize the power of women to bring forth life and, by extension, the power of nature to provide all things bountifully.

To possess such images and to please the spirits they represented was the core of early religion. Some men and women took on the role of communicating the will of the gods and arranging for its fulfillment. These were the priests and priestesses, shamans or medicine men, prophets and prophetesses who mediated between the divine and the human. Since their services were thought to be necessary if the fields were to bear fruit and if new generations of human beings were to be born, priests and priestesses held special status in Neolithic societies. They remained important in the civilizations that soon emerged.

CIVILIZATION AND THE CITY

About 6000 years ago, some complex Neolithic societies crossed the threshold between pre-history and history and formed the first civilizations. These societies consisted of concentrated populations, a complex social organization, and advanced technical skills. Their peoples joined together to drain or irrigate the soil, to sow and harvest and serve the gods, as directed by their priests. They lived in walled cities, ruled by kings and defended by armies. They built temples, tombs, and palaces for gods and rulers, and lived in families that resembled ours. Their more efficient farming yielded a surplus of food, so that some workers were freed to pursue other tasks. They began to forge metals—first bronze, then iron—into weapons and tools, and they learned to write. Now they could use language to keep records of their possessions and lists of their kings; and soon, to convey their visions, fears, and longings, to speculate about the cosmos, and to develop moral thought.

The First Civilizations

As the chart on p. 10 shows, civilizations developed at different times at five points on the globe: in four river valleys of the Old World and on the coasts of the New World. The earliest of these arose in the river valleys of the Middle East—an area reaching from the Nile to the Tigris and Euphrates rivers and called the Fertile Crescent: the first in Mesopotamia (modern Iraq), around 3500 B.C.E.; the second in Egypt, around 3000 B.C.E. Another civilization arose around 2500 B.C.E. in the valley of the Indus River, in south Asia (in modern Pakistan), and around 2200 B.C.E. a further Asian civilization developed in the valley of the Yellow River (Huang He) (in modern China). In c. 1200 B.C.E. the first **Amerindian** civilizations developed along the Pacific coast of South America and in Mexico (see Chapter 8).

From the nuclei of the first four Old World civilizations developed all the subsequent civilizations of Afro-Eurasia and their offspring in the New World, Australia, and Oceania. The first New World civilizations were succeeded by later and more splendid Amerindian empires.

But what about the West? Paradoxically, the civilization we call "Western" did not begin in the West: not in Europe, where its culture was refined, nor in the Western Hemisphere whose Amerindian civilizations Westerners would later destroy (see Chapter 16). "Western" civilization, rather, derives from the civilizations of ancient Asia (Mesopotamia) and Africa (Egypt). During the first three millennia of the history of civilization, Europe lagged far behind these areas in development.

In the valleys formed by the Tigris and Euphrates (the region called Mesopotamia) and Nile rivers, the soil was potentially very fertile. Crops would grow abundantly in the hot climate, but only if they had the right amount of water. In both regions, the crucial task of water management required coordinated labor.

In Egypt, where rainfall was practically unknown, the Nile River made a fertile valley of what would otherwise be a parched and sterile desert. The Nile flooded its banks every summer and receded every fall. This inundation created a green strip on both banks about 15 miles (24 km.) wide. Here plant and animal life flourished, ripe for human exploitation. The deposit of alluvial soil formed an ideal bed for the cultivation of grains, which Egypt produced in quantities so great that its surplus regularly fed other peoples of the ancient world.

To take full advantage of the Nile waters, the Egyptians developed a system of storage pools. When the land was flooded, peasants rowed around to these pools, shutting the vents to trap some of the water. After the river had receded, the plowing and sowing took place, as shown on p. 12, under the direction of supervisors; keeping the growing crops watered entailed carrying water from the pools to the fields. Although much hard labor was involved, the reliability of the annual flood enabled the Egyptians to farm efficiently and productively. Writing in the fifth century B.C.E. the Greek historian Herodotus described the good fortune of the Egyptians (somewhat oversimplifying the case): "They obtain the fruits of the field with less trouble than any other people in the world … the husbandman waits till the river has of its own accord spread itself over the fields and withdrawn again to its bed, and he sows his plot of ground … after which he has only to await the harvest." Benefitting from this bountiful harvest, the Egyptian population tripled between 3000 and 1250 B.C.E.

Mesopotamian peasants faced a tougher task. Unlike the Nile, the Tigris and Euphrates rivers flooded unpredictably, furiously, and dangerously. When they were calm, it was necessary to carry water

The First Civilizations

Civilization	Time	Continent/Region	Waterway	Features
Mesopotamia	after 3500 B.C.E.	Asia	Tigris and Euphrates Rivers	ziggurat, Hammurabi's *Code*
Egypt	after 3100 B.C.E.	Africa	Nile River	pyramid, *Book of the Dead*
Indus	after 2500 B.C.E.	Asia	Indus River	citadels and bathhouses, mother goddess
China	after 2200 B.C.E.	Asia	Yellow River	bronze ritual vessels, Confucius
Olmec	after 1200 B.C.E.	Mesoamerica		temples, giant head monuments

or channel it from the river to the fields. Laborers constructed dams to hold back the flood-waters and canals to channel them. Managers and foremen organized the workforce for the diverse jobs of sowing and harvesting, building, and irrigation.

The Earliest Cities

True cities developed in all the early civilizations. They housed large populations, with distinct groups of rulers and workers. They were surrounded by walls which encompassed palace or temple complexes as well as the homes of ordinary families. In these cities artisans pursued their crafts. They learned to forge bronze and, later, to cast iron to make tools and weapons. This was the first major technological innovation since a human being first used a stone to kill a beast or ward off an enemy.

By the early third millennium B.C.E., the Sumerians, the founders of the first civilization in southern Mesopotamia, dominated the southern zone of the Tigris-Euphrates Valley from a dozen walled city-states. The walls of the city of Uruk, which by 2700 B.C.E. had a population of about 50,000 people, had a circumference of over 5 miles (8 km.), and its inner ramparts were more than 12 feet (3.6 m.) thick. The city of Ur was enclosed by thick walls, with a circumference of more than a mile (1.6 km.). Ur had some 25,000 residents, and the population of its surrounding area may have been 200,000. Among smaller cities, Lagash may have numbered 19,000, and Umma 16,000 residents. Although small by modern standards, these cities are comparable in size to many medieval European towns.

Within the walls of a Mesopotamian city were jumbled tenements amid unpaved pathways, a few avenues, and public squares. The ordinary artisan lived in a one-story building of mud-brick consisting of a few rooms opening onto a communal courtyard. The rich man's house, whose blank brick walls (built thick to ward off heat) were both plastered and whitewashed, had two stories and a dozen rooms opening onto an interior courtyard. It had a kitchen, shrines, and reception areas, with walls and floors covered by rugs or mats. The family's dead were often buried below the house, though sometimes in cemeteries outside the city walls.

When civilization first emerged in Egypt, it did so in a form quite different from that in Mesopotamia. As elsewhere in the Fertile Crescent, walled cities were established as centers of trade. By 3100 B.C.E., Egypt's kings, or pharaohs, had destroyed these cities and created a centralized state. After that time, Egyptians lived in villages governed directly by the pharaoh. The pharaohs' administrative centers at Thebes and Memphis were a form of capital city, and they were inhabited by a huge staff of bureaucrats and temple priests.

Sometime after 2500 B.C.E., a third Old World civilization began to arise along the Indus River valley in the Indian subcontinent. Although its origins were independent, it was in contact with Middle Eastern civilizations by both land and sea routes. As in Mesopotamia, cities were centrally important features of the Indus civilization. Its two principal cities were Mohenjo-daro, in the lower Indus Valley, and Harappa, almost 400 miles (644 km.) to the northeast. Their populations extended to 30–40,000, and included merchants, artisans, and farmers. Dominated by a citadel complex enclosing temples and other public buildings, these unwalled cities were peaceful centers of agriculture. Below the high citadels, the lower cities were built neatly on a grid pattern formed by streets as much as 30 feet (9 m.) wide. The streets had gutters; cleanliness and an efficient water supply were clearly important to these people. Their houses contained plumbing systems to carry water and waste from or to external cisterns, drains, and sewers. Mohenjo-daro also had a public bathhouse. Despite a glorious start, the Indus civilization vanished completely after 2000 B.C.E.. This civilization that so respected water may have been weakened by flood and drought before falling prey to the armies of invading **Aryans** (see Chapter 2).

HOW MANY?

Populations

Global populations	about 4,000,000 10,000 B.C.E.
	about 6,000,000,000 in 2000 C.E.
City populations	about 2000 in Jericho, 8000 B.C.E.
	about 50,000 in Uruk, after 3000 B.C.E.
	about 1,000,000 in Rome, first century C.E.

By the time the civilization of the Indus Valley disappeared, a fourth Old World civilization had emerged along the Yellow River (Huang He) in eastern China. The region soon came under the domination of city-states headed by well-armed warlords. Together these Yellow River cities constituted an urban zone which nurtured industries and entrepreneurs.

By about 1550 B.C.E., the city of Anyang was established as the capital of the first known **dynasty** of Chinese rulers, the Shang (see Chapter 2). An earlier Shang capital, dating from about 1700 B.C.E., lies buried underneath modern Zhengzhou. Unlike Anyang, which had no wall, this was a walled rectangle with a perimeter of about 4 miles (7 km.). In size it compares with the larger cities of Mesopotamia, but like the Egyptian capitals, it was a center of administration not commerce. Merchants and food-producers lived outside the walls, with the houses, workshops, and tombs of the workers. Within the walls dwelt the privileged **elite** of kings, officials, and priests who directed the business of civilization.

Tools and Trade

Urban life was one of the hallmarks of civilization. So also was the manufacture of metals. The technological breakthrough was achieved with bronze, the first alloy that could be used to make effective tools and weapons. Neolithic workers had extracted copper from its ore from at least the eighth millennium B.C.E., but this soft metal had limited uses. About the time the first cities were forming in the Middle East, metalworkers discovered the secret of casting bronze, an alloy of copper and other elements, usually tin. Now miners in remote regions unearthed ores which merchants shipped to the cities. There artisans extracted copper from its ore and fused it with tin to produce bronze. From bronze could be crafted the sharp-edged implements that have lent their name to the whole era: the **Bronze Age**.

Bronze was too expensive to replace stone for agricultural use. It was a luxury metal, used to create the implements of war and ritual required by the two dominant social groups, nobles and priests. Nevertheless, its manufacture and distribution fueled the commerce of the ancient world, and in its working—riveting, soldering, hammering, and decoration—people's artistic vision was expressed.

Between the societies of the Middle East and the Indus River valley there was frequent contact, allowing the spread of bronze manufacture from one civilization to another. But the Chinese, remote from this contact, probably discovered the technique on their own. Cast bronze vessels were a central feature of Shang civilization—striking for their intricate design (unmatched elsewhere in antiquity), and great beauty. Far away in the New World Amerindian civilizations bronze metallurgy also developed independently, but much later (around 1100 C.E.)

Iron, a stronger metal than bronze, came into use only after 1200 B.C.E., long after the beginning of the Bronze Age. To forge useful iron implements, it was necessary not merely to extract the metal from the ore, but also to develop techniques to harden it. Artisans working in the Hittite Empire (see Chapter 2) in Asia Minor learned to combine the raw metal with a small percentage of carbon, a process called carburizing. This process, together with high and sustained heat, yielded tough iron implements, both cheaper and more durable than those of bronze.

Once the forging of iron was perfected, iron tools spread throughout the Middle East (although not to the exclusion of bronze weapons), used not only by elite warriors but also by common laborers. The iron plowshare opened a new era in agriculture, while iron spears made warfare more lethal. Iron manufacture was developed much later in China and Africa. It was never developed by Amerindians, who used stone.

As they developed advanced metallurgical techniques, Bronze and Iron Age peoples also extended the trade networks begun by their Neolithic ancestors, who had traded natural and manufactured goods sometimes over very great distances. Merchants now procured the raw materials needed by artisans and distributed their manufactured goods. The invention of the sail, soon after 3500 B.C.E., aided the expansion of trade. Using as roadways the same rivers that watered the fields, merchants organized the transport of stone and metal, of pots and tools, of grain and weapons between cities.

To transport merchandise to markets isolated from waterways, Bronze Age merchants utilized the wheel (see p. 12), which was invented around the same time as the sail. Wheeled carts replaced heavy sledges, whose load had overtaxed draft animals. After 2000 B.C.E., when camels were at last domesticated in the Middle East, merchants led caravans across the deserts and plateaus to distribute goods from the

The Ancient Toolbox

Wheel and cart: *The stone tools used by prehistoric humans for hunting and defense developed into machines and skills for farming, transportation, and manufacture in the first civilizations. Of great importance was the wheel, shown in a Sumerian stone relief, c. 3000* B.C.E. (British Museum)

Book of the Dead *(below): An Egyptian papyrus (detail, c. 1000* B.C.E.*) depicts the plow. Both wheel and plow were invented after 3500* B.C.E.. (Egyptian Museum, Cairo)

Arabian Peninsula and the Indian subcontinent. Pack animals carried goods overland between China and India and across the belly of Eurasia.

By river, ocean, road, and desert, Old World merchants transported grain and wine and oil, the produce of the farms, decorative pottery, ores and finished implements, and ornaments made of metal and gems. They traded silk from China, cotton cloth from India, and linen and **papyrus** (see above) from Egypt—the latter produced from the reeds that grew wild in the Nile. The system of trade routes established in antiquity endured until the opening of the Atlantic and Pacific trade routes in the sixteenth century by Europeans (see Chapter 16).

The Social Hierarchy

Even Neolithic villages had chiefs and priests, artisans and workers, warriors and weavers. In the cities of the first civilizations, the differentiation of the population according to skill and rank became more pronounced. A **hierarchy** developed, a vertically arranged sequence of social groups. The process by which social groups became defined and arranged in hierarchical patterns is called **stratification**.

At the top of the social hierarchy were those who ruled: priests and priestesses, nobles and kings. The members of this privileged elite lived in palaces, or administered temple buildings and land. On their death, some were buried in spectacular tombs built by great armies of ordinary men to perpetuate their status in the next world. At the bottom of the social hierarchy were slaves, who owned nothing. In between these two levels were merchants and artisans, laborers and scribes, wives, widows, and children.

The imprint of social division is seen in the collections of laws that survive from various Mesopotamian cities. The most famous of these is the code of the Babylonian king Hammurabi (c. 1792–1750 B.C.E.), based on Sumerian legal traditions (see *Witnesses*, p. 13, and *Windows On*, p. 22). These codes define crime and punishment according to the social position of the perpetrator and the victim. A poor man assaulting a rich man might pay with his life, whereas a rich man could assault a poor man and be subject only to a fine. A rich man who stole another man's animals would be fined three times more heavily than a poor thief—and both would be put to death if unable to pay their fines.

Lower than the poor man in the social hierarchy was the slave. The first slaves were the products of war, survivors made captive after one city or kingdom defeated another. Initially, women and children predominated among slave captives; men usually were slaughtered. Other slaves were taken from among the poor of the native population. For example, debtors might sell themselves, or, more often, their wives, or their children, who were sold into slavery to pay their debts. That practice further blurred the line dividing the condition of women or children from that of slaves or prostitutes, for which conditions women and children were likely recruits.

Two types of slaves could be found in ancient societies—those who served private families, and those used by temples and palaces as agricultural workers, stewards, or prostitutes. Most household slaves performed domestic tasks, but some acquired training in marketable skills and worked at a profit, which filled the pockets of their owners. Domestic slaves often bought their own freedom. The slavery practiced in these first civilizations—although intrinsically cruel, as all slavery is—was arguably much milder than that later found in Rome or in the Americas.

Nobles and kings derived their authority from their status as warriors. Priests and priestesses derived theirs from their power (as they claimed) to communicate with the gods. Performing sacred tasks, some of which predated the advent of civilization, they informed mortals of the immortals' demands, and appeased those deities with rites and human or animal sacrifices. A goddess might be represented by a priestess. Just as priests were often of the same rank or blood as kings and nobles, so priestesses were often women drawn from the highest class and in some cases from royalty.

WITNESSES

Breaking the Law

The creation of law is one of the great achievements of civilized societies. Below are extracts from two famous ancient law codes. The first comes from the laws codified under Hammurabi, the Babylonian king, based on even older Sumerian legal traditions. These laws are characterized (as were many ancient law codes) by attention to the status of the victim or perpetrator as well as to the nature of the crime: if the victim is of low, or the perpetrator of high rank, the penalty is generally less. The laws of the Hebrews, which deal with the plain matters of everyday life—including food conventions and relations with servants—are framed by higher moral and religious laws, still considered sacred by millions of Jews and Christians today. The faithful believe that they were conveyed directly by God to Moses, who led them from slavery to freedom.

Hammurabi's laws vary with the social condition of the criminal and his victim (c. 1790 B.C.E.):

Personal injuries, class by class:

196 If a nobleman has destroyed the eye of a member of the aristocracy, they shall destroy his eye.

198 If he has destroyed the eye of a commoner ..., he shall pay one mina of silver.

199 If he has destroyed the eye of a nobleman's slave ..., he shall pay one-half [the slave's] value.

229 If a builder constructed a house for a nobleman but did not make his work strong, with the result that the house which he built collapsed and so has caused the death of the owner of the house, that builder shall be put to death.

230 If it has caused the death of a son of the owner of the house, they shall put the son of that builder to death.

231 If it has caused the death of a slave of the owner of the house, he shall give slave for slave to the owner of the house.

Fathers and sons:

188 If a member of the artisan class took a son as a foster child and has taught him his handicraft he may never be reclaimed.

189 If he has not taught him his handicraft, that foster child may return to his father's house.

195 If a son has struck his father, they shall cut off his hand.

On noble marriages:

128 If a nobleman acquired a wife, but did not draw up the contracts for her, that woman is no wife.

129 If the wife of a nobleman has been caught while lying with another man, they shall bind them and throw them into the water ...

142 If a woman so hated her husband that she has declared, "You may not have me," ... that woman, without incurring any blame at all, may take her dowry and go off to her father's house.

(From "Code of Hammurabi," *Ancient Near Eastern Texts relating to the Old Testament*, 2e, ed. J. B. Pritchard, 1955)

Yahweh's commandments are for all:

You shall have no other gods before me.
You shall not make for yourself a graven image, or any likeness of anything that is in
heaven above, or that is in the earth beneath, or that is in the water under the
earth; you shall not bow down to them or serve them ...
You shall not kill.
You shall not commit adultery.
You shall not steal.

(Exodus 20: 3–4, 13–15)

As they presided over the temples that housed their gods, priests and priestesses oversaw the warehousing of their society's wealth. Ancient peoples struggled hard to satisfy their gods. However hard the peasant labored, however well the artisan wrought, however fearlessly the merchant ventured forth to trade in distant lands, they were mere servants of the will of the gods. These workers bore to the temples a fat share of the produce of the earth, or the bounty of trade and manufacture, all commandeered by the priests for use of the deity—or by the priests themselves, who lived on this largesse. Their offerings were received in the temple precinct, a self-sufficient inner city. The god owned slaves and received taxes; leased such equipment as plows, wagons, and boats to the workers; stored wealth in the temple warehouse; and managed flocks of cattle or sheep. In Sumer especially, all of society was organized around the management of the gods' property.

The great religious importance of temples to ancient society was matched by the originality of their architectural design and the heroic feat of their construction. Beginning about 2900 B.C.E. and continuing until the sixth century B.C.E., the civilizations of Mesopotamia built distinctive structures called ziggurats for their gods. Artificial hills made of mudbrick, with sides ascending stepwise from foot to summit, these structures were elaborate bases for the temple at the peak. The temple was the "house of the god," lifted so high it seemed to sit in heaven, while the stepped hill suggested a staircase leading to the upper world of the gods. The ziggurat at Ur constructed by the king Ur-Nammu around 2100 B.C.E., shown on p. 15, rose to a height of about 80 feet (24 m.). Built in Babylon around 600 B.C.E., the ziggurat of Etemenanki rose 300 feet (92 m.), its commanding presence visible above the surrounding plain. This structure may have been the model for the biblical "Tower of Babel" (Genesis 11:1–9).

In their different way, the pyramids of Egypt expressed that society's concept of the divine. The pyramid was not a temple, but the tomb of the pharaoh, the god-king himself, who would return after his death to the heavens from which he had come. His resurrection ensured the continued processes of life and creation: the river's flood, the sun's warmth, the crops' growth, the social order. Unlike the ziggurat, the pyramid had smooth sides and was built of stone. Broad at the surface of the earth, it soared confidently toward the sphere of heaven, from which royal power derived. The precise geometry of its form succinctly expressed the Egyptian idea of the relations of earth and sky, of right and justice.

Most of the great pyramids were built for Egypt's earliest pharaohs, those who reigned between about 2700 and 2200 B.C.E. Later pharaohs were buried in less spectacular tombs, choosing instead to have themselves immortalized by vast temple complexes. Erected in the name of the sun-god Amon-Ra (or Re), the temple of Karnak (c. 1320–1237 B.C.E.) was designed so that on two mornings a year the sun's rays penetrated deep inside the temple to illuminate the statues that at all other times stood unseen in interior darkness. The royal temple at Medinet Habu (built to honor the conquering pharaoh Ramses III, c. 1198–1155 B.C.E.) required a staff of governors and

Tombs and Temples

Pyramids of Menkure, Khafre, and Khufu: *Ancient civilizations recruited immense labor forces to build monuments suitable for the worship of their gods or the welfare of their rulers. On this page and the following are two examples from the third millennium B.C.E. Below is a photograph of the Giza group of pyramids for Menkure, Khafre, and Khufu (or Cheops), with the latter, dating from c.2570–2530 B.C.E. in the foreground.*

Ziggurat of Ur-Nammu: *To the left is the Sumerian ziggurat built by Ur-Nammu, king of Ur around 2112* B.C.E.*, in a photograph taken during the monument's excavation. Although contemporary, Khufu's pyramid and Ur-Nammu's ziggurat were built for different purposes: the first to house the body of a divine ruler intended for immortality, the second to support a temple for the worship of a god.*

officials, housed with scribes within the temple precincts. Temple bureaucrats managed acres of land and herds of cattle, fleets, and workshops, fifty-six Egyptian towns and nine foreign cities.

The temple built in Jerusalem by King Solomon of the Israelites was small, compared to the gigantic temples of Egypt, for example. According to the biblical account (in 1 Kings chapter 6; see *Witnesses*, p. 16), it was 60 cubits long, 20 broad, and 30 high (or 88 by 29 by 44 feet [27 × 8.8 × 13 m.], using 17½ inches [44 cm.] as the approximate length of that ancient unit). However, it was made of the richest materials. Built of stone, it was paneled inside with precious cedar, overlaid with gold, and embellished with sculpture. King Solomon's building fulfilled the pledge of his father David to build a house for the Ark of the Covenant, the wooden chest that housed the Law, which forms the basis of Judaism.

Besides building temples, pyramids, and ziggurats to honor the gods and provide for their own afterlife, ancient rulers built splendid residences for themselves. The palace of King Sargon II of Assyria (in northern Mesopotamia) contained 209 rooms. The 71-room palace at the late Assyrian capital of Nineveh housed the superb library of King Ashurbanipal (r. c. 688–627 B.C.E.). Adorned with relief sculptures of lion hunts and other fierce subjects, it proclaimed the king's prowess in war, as well as his role as a patron of arts and literature.

Fathers, Women, and Children

Just as ancient society was arranged in hierarchical patterns, so also was the family, the basic unit of society. Prehistoric peoples had grouped themselves in **clans**, which worshiped a common ancestor. Clan organization persisted into the era of civilization. But increasingly, as agricultural communities found that the control of property was the key to survival, nuclear family units became more important and the wider network of kin less so. In the early cities, people lived in a family: a small group of closely related persons dominated by one man, father and husband. His subjects were his wife and children.

Among the ancient civilizations, Egypt offered women and children the fairest treatment. Egyptian relief sculptures, wall paintings, and papyrus illustrations often depict families—mother, father, child—united in perfect harmony and even equality. Women had the same legal rights as men and the same claim on the afterlife. They could enjoy high social status, although they could hold no public position. The high valuation of women in Egypt was matched by the high valuation of children, implied by the amulets children were given to wear to protect them from danger. Children of both sexes were nurtured, and almost all children were raised.

Outside Egypt, women's condition was less satisfactory. Women were excluded from public life—a pattern that endured, with few exceptions, in east and west, Old World and New, until recent times. Marriage and motherhood constituted a woman's life, yet she (and her husband) had little say in selecting a mate. Fathers, or parents acting together, arranged the marriages of their daughters and sons. Contracts, often required for a valid marriage, specified exchanges of property: given by the bride's family to a desirable groom, by the groom's to a valuable bride. Marriage was an economic arrangement that answered the aspirations of families—for status, for offspring, for allies. It was not designed to suit the inclinations of the individuals whose lives it affected.

Once married, a woman was subject to her husband's authority, as she had previously been to her father's. She could not act independently in society, although in some communities she could hold property. In some societies husbands could flog or mutilate even high-status wives they believed to be disobedient. In exchange for obedience, a woman received protection, a critical factor in determining her status. In Assyrian society, a married woman was always veiled: only those without male protection went unveiled. The veil declared women's relationships to men—their husbands, their fathers, and their brothers—and

WITNESSES

Skyscrapers of the Past

Among the earliest monuments created by human beings are the temples of the gods and the tombs or palaces of kings. In these three passages are described the building of three famous structures: an Egyptian pyramid, a royal tomb for a divine monarch; the first temple of the Israelites in Jerusalem, by King Solomon; the splendid renovation of the palace in Nineveh of the Assyrian King Ashurbanipal.

The Greek historian Herodotus describes an Egyptian pyramid (c. 450 B.C.E.): [Cheops] closed the temples, and forbade the Egyptians to offer sacrifice, compelling them instead to labour, one and all, in his service. Some were required to drag blocks of stone down to the Nile from the quarries ...; others received the blocks after they had been conveyed in boats across the river ... One hundred thousand men laboured constantly, and were relieved every three months by a fresh lot. It took ten years' oppression of the people to make the causeway for the conveyance of the stones ... The pyramid itself was twenty years in building. It is a square, 800 feet each way, and the height the same, built entirely of polished stone, fitted together with the utmost care.
(Herodotus, *Persian Wars*; ed. G. Rawlinson, 1924)

Solomon's temple (Jerusalem) according to the Hebrew Bible: So Solomon built the house [of the Lord], and finished it. He lined the walls of the house on the inside with boards of cedar; from the floor of the house to the rafters of the ceiling, he covered them on the inside with wood; and he covered the floor of the house with boards of cypress. He built twenty cubits of the rear of the house with boards of cedar from the floor to the rafters, and he built this within as an inner sanctuary, as the most holy place ... The inner sanctuary he prepared in the innermost part of the house to set there the ark of the Lord ... and he overlaid it with pure gold.
(1 Kings 6:14–16, 19–20)

Ashurbanipal rebuilds his Assyrian private apartments at Nineveh (c. 650 B.C.E.): At that time, ... the private apartment of the palace in Nineveh,the noble city, beloved of Ninlil, which Sennacherib, king of Assyria, the father of the father, my begetter, had built for his royal abode, ... its walls had given way. I, Ashurbanipal ... tore down its ruined portions ... In a favorable month, on an auspicious day, I laid its foundations upon that terrace and built its brickwork ..., I put down its floor, I laid its mud walls ... The kings of Arabia, who had violated the oaths sworn to me, whom I had taken alive in the midst of battle with my own hands, I made to carry the basket and headpad, and to do taskwork, for the building of those apartments. Molding its bricks, performing labor upon it, they passed their days to the accompaniment of music. Amidst gladness and rejoicing I completed it from its foundation to its top ... [and] filled it with splendid furnishings.
(From D. D. Luckenbill, *Ancient Records of Assyria and Babylon*, 1968)

thereby their social value. Unveiled women were considered outcast and available for exploitation.

Just as they had little choice in entering a marriage, women had little choice in its dissolution. In Mesopotamia and the Near East, a man could divorce his wife summarily and return her in disgrace to her father's house. The ancient Israelites considered such a woman irreparably defiled. In Babylon, a high-status woman could divorce her husband for sufficient cause, but she too returned with her bridal property to her father's house. In China, a wife who was not obedient to her husband's family was sent home, disgraced.

Once admitted to her husband's family, a woman was considered to belong to that family. If her husband died she was expected, in many societies, neither to leave nor to remarry. If she were allowed to remarry it was to a near male relative of her deceased husband. By that strategy, the family alliance originally secured by the marriage would be continued. These restrictions were all the more pressing if the woman, while married, had borne a child. Rarely did a woman take away with her the child of her dead husband. In India and China, sanctions against remarriage were especially severe. In some cases (a custom practiced especially among the elites), an Indian widow surrendered herself to be burned on her husband's funeral pyre in the infamous (to Westerners) custom of *sati* (or *suttee*), an expression of woman's absolute loyalty to man.

Harsh as were the restrictions that encircled wife or widow, her status was higher than that of an unmarried woman not under male protection: a prostitute, a slave, or simply a woman without property. The rape or assault of a married woman was judged a more serious offense than the same crime directed against a slave woman or prostitute. If an assault caused a woman to miscarry, the punishment was heavier if the victim was of high status. In Babylon, the fine for such an assault on the daughter of a noble was double that for an assault on the daughter of a merchant. Physical crimes against women were understood to be actually crimes against men, whose female property was thus damaged.

According to Babylonian law, if a man and a woman were caught in adultery, both could be killed. A woman who was accused of adultery could prove her innocence by jumping into the river and managing not to drown. A man's situation was different. Adultery was construed as a man having sex with another man's *wife*, not simply with another woman. The penalty for this was death. If, however, a man's lover was neither another man's legitimate wife nor his virgin daughter—in other words, his property—he could freely have sex with her.

Marriage customs in ancient societies often allowed polygamy and concubinage. In the Middle East, men could have more than one legal wife—the custom of polygamy. Or they could have one wife and one or more concubines. The latter were usually slaves but lived as though married to a householder. Examples of these arrangements abound in the Hebrew Bible. Abraham's wife Sarah urged upon him the concubine Hagar, a slave woman, to be the mother of Abraham's son Ishmael before she gave birth to Isaac. Jacob, Abraham's grandson, had two wives, the sisters Leah and Rachel, and also fathered children by the female slaves given to each by their father.

In Babylonian law, the status of concubines relative to the first, free-born wife varied with their fertility. Once a concubine had borne a child to the husband, she could not be sold by the first wife. The children of such concubines were raised as free-born members of the family, whereas a child born to a slave but fathered by a man outside the family unit was marked as a slave. Concubinage thus offered slave women a chance for higher status.

The ability of women to bear children gave them what status they possessed in ancient societies. But not all children were welcomed. Fathers might sell their children into slavery, or "expose" (that is, abandon) unwanted infants. By contrast, if a woman aborted her own child, she might be executed. Abandoned infants often died. Those who survived might be claimed from the crossroads or dumps where they had been left. The lucky ones would be raised by other families as servants or dependents, the less fortunate (male and female) by managers of brothels as prostitutes.

Infanticide, although rare in Egypt, was especially common in eastern Asia and India. In these areas, evidence of disproportionately high numbers of men attests to the widespread infanticide of females. Girls caused great expense because of the dowries they were expected to provide. (The dowry was a sum of money by which the bride's natal family discharged its obligations to support a daughter.) Also, they could not carry on the family line. To preserve the honor and property of their families, they were often abandoned.

By contrast, property-owning families greatly valued their healthy male children. In the cities of the Middle East, upper-class fathers educated their sons for high-level occupations, while merchants and artisans placed theirs out as apprentices. Family farms and family businesses were jointly operated by men and their sons, who expected to inherit family wealth. But

WITNESSES

All in the Family

Were human relations the same or different 3,000 years ago? These brief statements—an Egyptian woman's love for her husband, a Jewish man's expectations of a wife, and an Egyptian father's advice to his son—sound familiar to us, despite the great dissimilarities between the societies in which these speakers lived and our own.

An Egyptian in love:

My god, my husband, I come to you.
It is pleasant to go into the pool and
I rejoice that you wish me
To plunge in and bathe before you.
I let you see my beauty
In a tunic of fine royal linen
When it is wet
I go into the water with you
And emerge with a red fish for you
Pulsating in my hands.
I lay it on my breast.
O my man, my brother,
Come and see me!

(From B. Watterson, *Women in Ancient Egypt*, 1991)

A good Hebrew wife:

A good wife who can find?
She is far more precious than jewels.
The heart of her husband trusts in her,
and he will have no lack of gain ...
She seeks wool and flax,
and works with willing hands ...
Strength and dignity are her clothing,
and she laughs at the time to come.
She opens her mouth with wisdom,
and the teaching of kindness is on her tongue.

(Proverbs 31:10–11, 13, 25–26)

An Egyptian father advises his son to become a scribe: I have considered violent manual labor—give your heart to letters ... I have seen the blacksmith, directing his foundrymen, but I have seen the metal-worker at his toil before a blazing furnace ... And every carpenter who works or chisels, has he any more rest than the plowman? ... The weaver sitting in a closed-up hut has a lot that is worse than that of a woman. His thighs are drawn up close to his breast, and he cannot breathe fully ... Verily there is no occupation than which better cannot be found except the calling of the scribe which is the best of all ... One day spent in the chamber of instruction is better for you than eternity outside it; the works thereof endure like the mountains ...

(From J. B. Bernal, *Science in History*, 1969; modernized)

boys also faced some of the same restrictions faced by women. They were completely under their father's control. The penalty was severe for a son's crime against his father.

WRITING, LANGUAGE, AND CONSCIOUSNESS

Slaves, children, women, and the poor participated scarcely at all in the greatest cultural achievement of antiquity: the invention of writing. Its development is shown on p. 19. Art in verbal form could and did exist without writing, in poetry and song and story repeated orally and transmitted over many generations. But writing allows words to be preserved, reviewed, and analyzed. Writing furthered the development of critical thought, the "storage" of thought in texts inscribed on durable surfaces, and the communication of those thoughts to later generations. From this point onward, people speak to us directly, in words, rather than their tangible remains—however eloquent these may be. Hence the period before the invention of writing, in a given society, is called "prehistoric." With the written word, history became possible.

Words and Pictures

Human beings learned to write so as to keep lists: lists of the measures of grain stored in the gods' treasury, records of fees owed to the god by the citizens, inventories of tools and ornaments, records of planetary motion or the rise and fall of river waters threatening flood or drought. The first surviving written documents (from Sumer, around 3300 B.C.E.) record the sale of cattle and sheep, milk and grain. Of the tens of thousands of inscribed tablets found in that region, more than 90 percent deal with commercial transactions.

To make lists, it was necessary to learn to write. Priests, the guardians of temple wealth, were the first list makers and the first scribes. To transmit the complex art of writing to others, the priests formed schools for scribes. Bureaucrats and entrepreneurs sent their sons to these schools, the first in human history, so that they might master the new and crucial skill. Sumerian schools enrolled children of the city elites (governors, temple administrators, tax officials, scribes, and accountants) for instruction in writing. Their textbooks, mathematical tables, and dictionaries, some of which have survived, provide evidence of the process of teaching and learning 4000 years ago. In Egypt, the pharaoh's huge bureaucracy offered an appealing career to ambitious young people and learning to write was the prerequisite.

The first writing was based on **pictographs**. A pictograph is a simplified picture of an object: an ox, a house, a serpent. By 3000 B.C.E., thousands of such pictographs were in use in Mesopotamia and in Egypt. Mesopotamian scribes recorded pictographs by pressing the point of a wedge-shaped (**cuneiform**) stylus in a wet clay tablet, which was then left to harden and form a durable document. Thousands of these tablets have been unearthed.

Egyptian scribes painted pictograms called **hieroglyphs** (Greek: "sacred carving") on walls, carved them in stone, or wrote them on papyrus. Papyrus, a valued commodity of ancient trade, was manufactured from woven strips of fibers found in the pithy stem of the papyrus plant which grew along the Nile. Papyrus panels laid end to end and pasted together produced a roll, the standard book of antiquity. From Mesopotamian cuneiform and Egyptian hieroglyph derive all the writing systems of the ancient Mediterranean world and their modern descendants.

Other systems of writing developed independently outside the Middle East, in Asia and the Americas. By about 2500 B.C.E., the Indus Valley civilization had created a pictographic language, which died with the civilization that produced it. By 1500 B.C.E., the Chinese had developed a pictographic system with about 2000 characters. Later rulers standardized and preserved the precious legacy. Though modified, this Chinese system of writing has never since gone out of use. Amerindian civilizations also independently developed writing (see Chapters 8, 16).

Once invented, writing spread from people to people as neighboring communities on the fringes of the first civilizations eagerly borrowed this practical art. Mesopotamian kingdoms all adapted cuneiform to communicate the words of their own languages. It was used for Sumerian as well as for the **Semitic** languages Akkadian, Ugaritic, and Aramaic. (Semitic was a family of languages from Africa and Southwest Asia, which also featured Amharic, Arabic, and Hebrew). Egyptian scribes learned Akkadian, and Ugaritic texts were known to scribes of the Aegean region. Words, techniques, and symbols passed easily from group to group across the sites of Old World civilizations.

Mastery of ancient pictographs required powerful memory and great patience. Scribes were tempted to simplify the original elaborate pictures by reducing their detail and altering their forms in the direction of a flowing script. Egyptian scribes developed two levels of simplified hieroglyphic writing: the **hieratic** (or "priestly") and **demotic** (or "popular"). Meanwhile, Mesopotamian scribes developed new scripts in which the graphic image represented the initial sound associated with an object: a **phonogram**. At first, these figures represented syllables; later, the sounds of individual consonants.

As the pictograph yielded to the phonogram, so the phonogram ultimately led to the alphabet. Soon after 1500 B.C.E., the priestly scribes of the city of Ugarit (in present-day Ras Shamra) in northern Syria (whose population spoke a mixture of Semitic as well as Indo-European languages) assigned single

The Genealogy of Writing

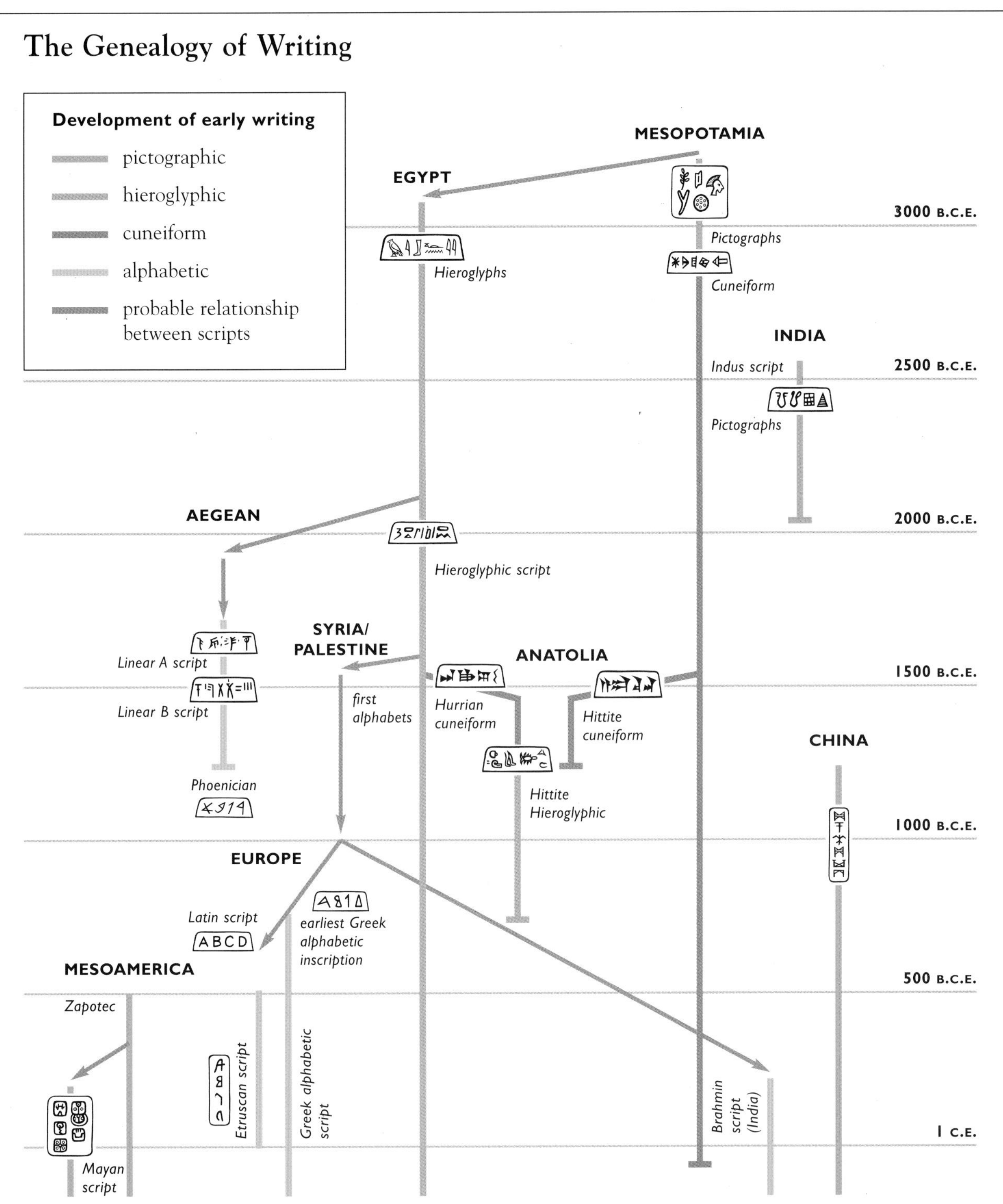

A system of writing was a feature of every ancient civilization. Although some still remain undeciphered, many writing systems have been decoded, enabling us to get a close-up view of life in the distant past. Writing began as pictures, or pictographs, which symbolized ideas increasingly unrelated to the object depicted. The alphabet developed from the simplified pictograph to represent not a thing but a single sound, which could be assembled with other sounds to form words.

Source: R. Whitehouse and J. Wilkins, *The Making of Civilization: History Discovered through Archaeology* (New York: Alfred A. Knopf, 1986).

consonantal sounds to thirty cuneiform signs. This set of figures and sounds was the first true alphabet. In an alphabet, each figure denotes not an object, nor an idea, nor a syllable, but an individual sound. A few figures can be combined flexibly in any number of patterns to represent the sounds of any words in the language—and in other languages, too. Easy to learn, an alphabet facilitated commerce with other peoples. It threatened the status of the scribes, however, whose rare and specialized skills were no longer needed.

At about the same time, the scribes of neighboring Phoenicia created a modified set of twenty-two signs based on Egyptian hieroglyphs. Abandoning the wedge-shaped stylus, they could write the figures of their alphabet with pen and ink on papyrus. This material had first been introduced to the Phoenician harbor city of Byblos and from there exported to Greece. The Greeks called papyrus *byblos*, after this port, and the word yielded in their language the word for "book" (*biblion*) and in ours the word for "the book," the Bible. The Phoenician alphabetic script, modified, also passed to the Greeks (who added symbols for vowel sounds), to the Romans and Etruscans, to the Persians and speakers of Aramaic and Hebrew, and to modern Hindi, Arabic, and European languages.

Languages and Peoples

Writing is a tool. It can be used, and was used in antiquity, to record a variety of languages. Languages are much more. They are an expression of the life, beliefs, and history of a community. People who share the same language are united in a way that is different from kinship by blood or common loyalty to a ruler or constitution but, in its own way, just as strong.

The skill of writing, once attained, has never been lost to the human species. But individual human communities that once were literate have subsequently lost the ability to write. Similarly, a language may "die," in the sense that no one speaks it anymore, although scholars may study it. Sumerian, Egyptian, Hittite, Phoenician, and ancient Greek are all "dead" languages; Latin has all but died, apart from some use in medicine, law, and Christian music. But many modern languages are derived from ancient ones.

The different languages spoken by the people of ancient civilizations fall into several distinct groups, or families. The oldest languages spoken by civilized persons were Sumerian and Egyptian. The former, unrelated to any modern language, disappeared completely when its speakers were absorbed by other groups. Ancient Egyptian stemmed from the "Hamitic" family of north African languages (so called after Ham, one of the three sons of Noah in the Hebrew Bible).

Closely related to the Hamitic are the "Semitic" languages (so called after Shem, Ham's older brother). These prevailed in the Fertile Crescent after the Sumerian period. The ancient peoples of the Middle East known as Akkadians and Amorites, Canaanites and Assyrians, Israelites and Aramaeans all spoke Semitic languages. The common language of Mesopotamia in the second millennium B.C.E. was Akkadian. In the first millennium, it was Aramaic. These languages were used for communication between different groups, even by peoples who retained their own language among themselves.

Most languages spoken in the West today (in Europe and the lands of European settlement) are distinct in origin from the Hamitic and Semitic languages of ancient Egypt and Mesopotamia. They mostly descend from those spoken by nomadic tribes who originated in the steppes of Eurasia between the Black and Caspian seas. These are called **Indo-European** languages, grouped as a family because they share many elements of basic vocabulary. Derived from them are classical Greek and Latin and their descendants, and the Celtic, Germanic, and Slavic languages of the European peoples who settled from the Alps to the Arctic. Other members of the Indo-European family are Persian, spoken by settlers on the Iranian plateau, and many Indian languages (classical Sanskrit, modern Hindi, and Urdu).

The grouping of peoples by language traditions is distinct from racial or ethnic classification. The human species has traditionally been divided into **races**—although many geneticists now question the validity of that classification, finding that the genes shared by visibly different peoples are vastly more numerous than the genes that cause them to have a distinctive appearance. The Caucasoid, Mongoloid, and Negroid races (which some specialists would divide into many sub groups) are no longer understood as biologically distinct species, but as groups of people who share certain physical traits that are transmitted genetically. They include features such as skin color, shape of head, and blood type.

Races (in this sense) emerged late in the process of human evolution but well before the first civilizations. Racial divisions do not coincide with language or culture or degree of technical achievement. Caucasoid peoples may speak Indo-European or Semitic (or other) languages, for example; and not all speakers of Semitic tongues are Caucasoid. And although some speakers of ancient Indo-European tongues called themselves Aryans, there is no Aryan race—a notion created by nineteenth-century race theorists and adopted with catastrophic consequences by the dictator Adolf Hitler (see Chapter 28).

How linguists learned to read the languages of antiquity is an intriguing detective story. In 1821, Jean-François Champollion (1790–1832), completing work begun by Thomas Young (1773–1829), deciphered the hieroglyphs carved on the Rosetta Stone, the prize brought back from Egypt by a French army under Napoleon. The partly eroded stone displayed a document dated to 196 B.C.E. written in three scripts: hieroglyphs, Egyptian demotic, and Greek. Because the Greek was familiar to European scholars, it was the key to interpreting the Egyptian, and so reading other Egyptian texts. In a similar way, the British soldier Henry Rawlinson (1810–1895) deciphered carvings on a rock face in Behistun in present-day Iran. Comparing the texts inscribed in three languages (Old Perisian, Elamite, and Babylonian), he succeeded, by 1850, in making the Persian and Babylonian texts legible to modern scholars. (The

Elamite text was finally deciphered by scholars early in the twentieth century.) Another ancient script, the Linear B of the ancient Mycenaeans—who lived in Greece and its neighboring islands in the second millennium B.C.E.—was decoded only recently. In the 1950s, the British linguist Michael Ventris (1922–1956) studied the clay tablets accidentally burned in the devastation of Mycenaean cities around 1200 B.C.E. After lengthy analysis of the script, Ventris discovered that the language recorded was an early form of Greek. His work finally unlocked the history of the warrior civilization whose exploits and values are recorded in the *Iliad* by Homer (see Chapter 4). Another ancient script from this region, Linear A, is still undeciphered.

Words and Ideas

Written language was first used to make lists; soon, ancient scribes employed their skills to publish royal decrees and codes of law which, like the kings themselves, were considered divine. They inscribed these laws on tablets and stone.

The first law codes from ancient Sumer are lost, or survive only in fragments. But extant still is the Babylonian law code, assembled by Hammurabi around 1790 B.C.E., inscribed on tablets called **stelae**, and displayed in several cities for all to consult. The code of Hammurabi is the most extensive surviving set of laws created until the compilation of Roman law ordered by the emperor Justinian at the end of the ancient era (see Chapter 8).

Hammurabi's pronouncements aimed to replace tribal systems of blood vengeance with a system of compensations. For each offense a punishment, corporal or monetary, is specified. As was often the case in ancient societies, these punishments were proportional to social status and gender. The code does not deal only with crime. Of its 282 regulations, about one-third deal with land tenure and commercial transactions, and one-quarter with the family.

Hammurabi claimed that he received these laws from the god Shamash, who is depicted with the king on the stone slab, or **stele**, on which the laws were inscribed (see *Windows On*, p. 22). Later, other Middle Eastern civilizations produced laws. These included the Assyrians, whose law codes also survive, and the Israelites, whose laws, recorded in the Hebrew Bible, are fundamental to modern Judaism.

There is no comparable document of legal thought from the civilization of Egypt. There the pharaoh himself was the law. He embodied the principal of *Ma'at*, or cosmic justice. No legal system was required where the pharaoh's living word took its place.

Ancient civilizations also laid the foundations of science. Priests and scribes observed planetary motions, measured the passage of time and the surface of the earth, and studied and healed disease. Babylonian mathematicians devised the multiplication table and certain theorems of geometry. They could calculate squares of numbers and square roots, exponents and percentages, and, in their **sexagesimal** system (based on the sacred number 60) of reckoning quantities, they divided the year into twelve months, the circle into 360 degrees, and the hour into 60 minutes, all divisions that are still in use. From observations of the moon, Babylonian scientists developed a calendar based on the lunar cycle of 28 days.

In Egypt, the annual flooding of the Nile encouraged observers to devise a solar calendar of 365 days, the basis of our own. The faceless plain created each year by the receding river encouraged the development of another skill, that of surveying. Medicine and surgery developed from Egyptian religion as tools in the struggle against ever-present demons. Descriptions of surgical operations (of which forty-eight survive) reveal that Egyptian practitioners performed abortions and explored the cavity of the skull.

The human venture of writing could have stopped with lists, laws, and numbers; indeed for nearly 1000 years it did. But in the first millennium B.C.E. some scribes discovered in writing the tool for a deeper exploration of the meaning of their lives. They began to write down the **myths** and legends of their people, producing the first documents of literature and, in due course, of history. Epics and chronicles of the experience of the Aryans (India) and Akkadians, the Israelites and the Hittites were inscribed on clay tablets and papyrus rolls. The first libraries numbered among their treasures works from earlier civilizations.

In the ruined library of the Assyrian king Ashurbanipal at Nineveh was found one of the key surviving texts of the Babylonian epic *Gilgamesh*, the first major surviving work of world literature, recorded on 12 tablets in 3000 lines of cuneiform (see *Witnesses*, p. 23). Son of the goddess Ninsun and himself called "two-thirds god, one-third man," the legendary hero Gilgamesh was probably based on an actual King Gilgamesh of Uruk, in Sumer, who reigned around 2675 B.C.E. and is credited with establishing its powerful walls. According to the story, Gilgamesh journeys abroad in search of adventure, accompanied by his friend Enkidu. When Enkidu dies, Gilgamesh struggles with his great sorrow and greater fear of death. Setting out again, this time on a quest for immortality, he returns home, sobered by his new-found understanding of the grim limits of the human condition, to perform his duty as sovereign.

Much of ancient literature was religious. Hymns and prayers, incantations and charms meant to sway the will of a thousand deities fill many clay tablets and sheets of papyrus. The Egyptian *Book of the Dead* is only one collection of a genre known as "wisdom literature," of which there are also samples in the Hebrew Bible. This literature consists of meditations on the conditions of human life and its destiny. The

WINDOWS ON

Laws as Hard as Stone

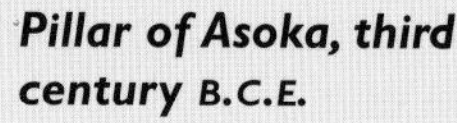

***Pillar of Asoka, third century* B.C.E.**

***Stele of Hammurabi, c. 1790–1750* B.C.E.**

In the Hebrew Bible Moses is recorded as receiving the Law, or Ten Commandments, inscribed by God himself on stone tablets. Similarly, ancient legislators, sometimes portrayed as recipients of divine favor, had their laws inscribed on the most durable materials available: stone and bronze. Shown here (left) are the basalt stele containing Hammurabi's Code, representing the king receiving the laws from the god Shamash; a limestone pillar inscribed with the Laws of Asoka (far left); and a stone with a law code inscription from Crete (below).
(left: Louvre, Paris)

***Law code inscription** (below)**, Dreros, Crete, c. 600* B.C.E.**

To continue your investigation of this topic, please go to www.prenhall.com/king for the related **WINDOWS** on the **WEB** activity

Bible contains many other genres of literature: poetry and history, law and prophecy.

The **brahman** priests who were the guardians of the sacred texts of Indian civilization transmitted orally (they were committed to writing only in the first millennium C.E.) the four sacred *Vedas* and the commentaries upon these known as the *Upanishads*. Two epics of that era—the *Ramayana* and the *Mahabharata*—retell the experience of legendary princes and warriors and are laced with mystical theology and stories of the gods. The *Mahabharata*, a vast anthology, incorporates the *Bhagavad-Gita* ("Song of God"), in itself a classic of Indian religious thought.

Thus the invention of writing enabled ancient civilizations to record the achievements of heroes and observations of scholars, to announce ethical and legal standards for successful community life, and to express their highest aspirations.

SACRIFICE, MYTH, AND CONSCIENCE

Ancient peoples inherited the custom of sacrifice from prehistoric times. The gods required sustenance, and were fed on the altars with the scarce foodstuffs offered up by worshipers hoping to avert their fury. In time, worshipers created myths, stories about the gods that helped explain the workings of the cosmos. By the last millennium before the Common Era, some communities of the Middle East and Asia developed new understandings of the divine. They believed that what was required of them was not only the sacrifice of beast or wealth, but obedience or faith, and good behavior. That understanding is expressed in the biblical account of Abraham, who was permitted to sacrifice a ram and spare his son Isaac. Abraham's faith alone satisfied his God.

WITNESSES

He Who Saw Everything

King Gilgamesh of Uruk, in Sumer, who reigned more than 3,000 years ago, is also the subject of the first major epic in world literature. Its themes, first expressed in the language and rhythms of a culture now lost, are the themes endlessly explored by the human imagination: the quest for glory, the poignancy of friendship and love, the purpose of life, and the meaning of death.

Gilgamesh will strive for glory (after 2675 B.C.E.):

"If I fall, I shall have made my name;
'Gilgamesh,' they will say, 'against fierce Huwawa
Has fallen!' And long after,
My descendants born in my house
Shall honour my name ...
I will ready my hand,
I will fell the cedar trees.
I will make my name a name that endures!"
(*Epic of Gilgamesh*, 28, Tablet III; trs. R. Temple, 1991)

Gilgamesh grieves for his friend Enkidu and commissions a statue (after 2675 B.C.E.):

"O Enkidu, my younger friend,
How you hunted the wild ass in the hills,
Chased the panther on the steppe!
We,
We two,
Have conquered all, climbed all ...
What is this sleep that has now come over you?
You have gone dark and cannot hear me!"
But Enkidu does not raise his head.
Gilgamesh felt for his heartbeat
But there was none.
Then he drew a veil across Enkidu's face
As if he were a bride.
He roared like a lioness
Who has had her cubs taken from her.
Backwards and forwards he went before his friend,
And tore his hair, ...
He tore off his beautiful clothes,
Flung them down
As though they were filth ...
Then Gilgamesh proclaimed unto the land:
"Come smith, come workman,
Come fashioner of copper,
Come worker in gold,
Come inscriber in metal!
Shape you the image of my friend!
My friend whose stature is beyond compare;
May his breast be lapis lazuli,
May his body be of gold ..."
(*Epic of Gilgamesh*, 80–81, Tablet VIII)

Gilgamesh contemplates the end for which he, too, is born (after 2675 B.C.E.):

"Fearing death, I roam over the steppe.
The fate of my friend
Lies heavy upon me,
On distant ways I roam the steppe.
The fate of Enkidu, my friend,
Lies heavy upon me.
How can I be silent?
How be still?
My friend whom I loved has turned to clay!
And I,
Shall I too, like him,
Lie down,
Never to rise—
Never again—
For ever and ever?"
(*Epic of Gilgamesh*, 108, Tablet X)

MUST READS

Books of the Ancient World

Gilgamesh	(after 2675 B.C.E.)
Ptah-hotep	*Instructions to his Son* (c. 2400 B.C.E.)
Hammurabi	*Code of Law* (c. 1790 B.C.E.)
Upanishads	(from 800 B.C.E.)
Hebrew Bible	(first codified from older materials, c. 500 B.C.E.)

Gods of Earth and Sky

The same storm gods and flood gods, round and full-breasted earth mothers, fierce and fertile bulls worshiped by Neolithic peoples were worshiped still by the peoples of the first civilizations. These gods looked like human beings or animals or both; many of the Egyptian gods had human bodies and animal heads. The gods resided in splendid and costly temples, on mountain tops, or in trees, streams, or oceans. They were immortal and numberless.

Ancient peoples shared and exchanged their gods and goddesses, just as they did their writing and metallurgical techniques. The whole ancient world teemed with a multiplicity of deities. The gods of a friendly neighbor or conquered foe were adopted or fused with native gods in a process called **syncretism**.

In Mesopotamia, the Sumerians revered Enlil and Anu, gods of storms and the atmosphere, and Enki, the god of wisdom and water. They worshiped fertility goddesses such as the earth mother Ninhursag, and the goddess of love and war, Ishtar, and the ubiquitous bull, whom the heroes Gilgamesh and Enkidu fought and vanquished. The Babylonians and Assyrians worshiped the sun gods Shamash and Assur (or Ashur). Assur was also associated with storms and with war.

Some of the most important Egyptian gods and goddesses personified the sun and moon and the river Nile. The gods Ra and Aten represented the sun in different aspects, rising or setting. Amon was the chief god of Thebes. Through his association with Ra, as Amon-Ra he became a sun god and the official king of the gods. At one moment, in the reign of Akhenaten, he had to fight for supremacy with Aten, god of the solar disk. Hathor was the Egyptian goddess of love, joy, and music, and was represented variously as a lovely woman and as a great golden cow, crowned with a solar disk. Osiris, god of justice, and his consort Isis, goddess of the moon and of fertility, were related to the worship of the pharaoh.

The Semitic Canaanites, who dwelt on the eastern Mediterranean shore (see Chapter 2) worshiped fertility gods with orgiastic rites, which attracted many of their Israelite neighbors but outraged the prophets. Like the Sumerians, they worshiped Ishtar, whom they called Astarte. Their chief deity, El, one of many gods bearing this name, was represented as a bull. Late into antiquity, the fifth century C.E., adherents still worshiped these deities by washing their bodies in the blood of slaughtered bulls, or having sexual union with temple prostitutes. From Palestine, these rites spread to the Hittites and the Assyrians, to the Phoenicians and their far-flung colonies, and finally to Greece and Rome.

The Indo-European Hittites, rulers of Asia Minor during the second millennium B.C.E. (see Chapter 3), proclaimed themselves the "people of a thousand gods." Among these were deities of the sky and the earth: a weather god (the "king of heaven"), a sun goddess, her son, god of the harvest, and the Canaanite Baal. The people of Crete, the Minoans, appear to have had no temples, although shrines have been found in some of their palaces. They also worshiped divine spirits on mountain tops, in caves, and in sacred groves. They celebrated a mother goddess and fertile bull with dancing and games in which young men and bare-breasted women participated, some of whom may have been sacrificial victims. The Mycenaean Greeks also worshiped fertility goddesses, and a sky god known later as Zeus, chief of all the Greek gods.

To the east, on the Indian subcontinent, during the formative years of Hinduism, people worshiped gods of thunder and lightning, fire and dawn, as well as the fertility goddesses inherited from the lost Indus civilization and from the indigenous peoples of the Ganges region. In China, ancestor worship was the most important form of religious observance. Nature gods and demons abounded, but they were later disdained by the philosophies that edged out traditional religion in that vast empire. In addition to worship of their ancestors, many Chinese revered semi-historical figures: the Three Sovereigns, the Five Emperors, founders of their well-managed kingdom.

Appeasing the Gods

Ancient peoples attempted to appease the gods and goddesses, and thereby bring order to their world, by offering sacrifices. The spirits of forest and desert, the gods of sun and moon, required grain, wine, or meat. If neglected, they would strike out furiously at their human subjects, whose very reason for existence was to satisfy the needs of divine beings. To the altars of their temples people brought their offerings. Here priests scattered grain and spilled wine, slew rams and goats to feed the greedy powers of the other world with the smell of roasted meat. The Persians sacrificed the horses central to the culture of their nomadic ancestors, and the Chinese developed complicated rituals of sacrifice in which a bronze-cast vessel of distinctive shape was used for each ritual substance. In some cultures, elaborate rules of cleanliness and order evolved, a kind of sacrificial behavior undertaken in honor of the deity. Among the Israelites and Hindus, for example, only certain foods might be eaten, in certain vessels and with certain companions.

Some gods demanded more than a sheep or a pigeon or spilled wine. They required a human sacrifice: a young man or woman, or a child. Both the Hebrew Bible and Greek mythology record traces of these sacrifices: Abraham was prepared to offer up his son Isaac at God's command, and King Agamemnon permitted his daughter Iphigenia to be slaughtered on the altar of an angry Greek god. In Shang China and in Canaan during the formative years of Israel and Judah, human beings were sacrificed to the gods. In the royal tombs of Sumerian Ur and the Shang city of Anyang were found, scattered around the body of the king, the remains of courtiers, slaves, and animals sacrificed in tribute to the dead monarch. In the Phoenician city of Carthage, crowds of children were surrendered by their parents for sacrifice into the hands of the officiating priests.

Explaining the Cosmos

Besides making sacrifices to the gods, ancient peoples created myths about them, in an attempt to make sense of the universe, to find order in the cosmos. In their sacred books (notably the *Enuma Elish*, c. 2000 B.C.E.), the Sumerians depicted the process of creation. According to this myth, the gods emerged from chaos and proceeded to create order, fighting battles over mysterious forces of darkness, monsters of chaos and death. Victorious, they arranged the universe neatly, with a heaven and an earth, in a form their worshipers understood as a box. The god's task was to keep the universe in order, in a perpetual repetition of the the creation of the cosmos.

The Sumerians' creation myth was transmitted to later peoples of the Middle East. These included the Israelites, who wove parts of the Sumerian creation legend into their own Bible. Another Sumerian tale, that of a universal flood that extinguished all human life except for a few individuals, also reappears in the biblical story of Noah and the Ark. That legend is first encountered in the epic *Gilgamesh* described above. In *Gilgamesh*, too, the hero's friend Enkidu is fashioned by the gods from clay, as the biblical Yahweh creates Adam.

The Sumerians also developed, from their ancient fertility beliefs, rituals celebrating resurrection and rebirth. In April, the month of resurgent growth, they celebrated their main festival: a ritual marriage of king and priestess, followed by the king's apparent death, representing the marriage and death of the god Dumuzi. His consort Inanna searches the bleak underworld for him, and he achieves a glorious resurrection. The goal of this festival was to ensure the fecundity of the earth. Elsewhere the same ritual was performed with a different cast of characters such as the Babylonian Shamash and the Canaanite Tammuz. Later echoes of this myth would be found in the Greek story of Persephone (see Chapter 4), and in the Christian narrative of the death and resurrection of Jesus of Nazareth (see Chapter 7).

Egyptian religion centered on the belief in immortality, related to notions of rebirth and resurrection. The soil's abundance encouraged that belief, and the dry desert conditions permitted the preservation of bodies. It was thought that the pharaoh, associated with the god Horus (son of Osiris, god of death, rebirth, and justice), was resurrected after death and rose as Horus to be united with Osiris. At first, immortality was seen as being the special destiny of the pharaoh. Eventually it was understood to be available to all faithful and just servants of the divine will.

In the second millennium B.C.E. the pharaoh Amenhotep IV (c. 1379–c. 1362 B.C.E.) abandoned the **polytheism** of his people and took a step toward **monotheism**. He changed his name to Akhenaten (meaning "he who serves Aten" or "the glory" or "the delight of Aten") to signal his intent to worship one God above all: the god of the setting sun, represented by a winged solar disk. His hymn of praise is quoted in *Witnesses*, p. 26.

Akhenaten practiced the reformed rites of his deity at a new capital he built called Akhetaten (meaning "horizon of Aten"), today's Tell el-Amarna. There he was joined in a life of worship by his children and his queen Nefertiti, who was renowned for her beauty. He or his priests composed moving hymns to their deity, including a hymn of praise to Aten as creator of the world. As a work of ancient religious literature, it deserves to be placed alongside the creation accounts of the Sumerians and the Hebrews.

Good and Evil

In a few ancient religious communities, the force of the divine was fundamentally reconceived. Not merely a master (or mistress) who demanded sacrifice, or a participant in cosmic dramas of creation and resurrection, the deity was identified with a single force for goodness, truth, and justice.

To arrive at that notion, it was necessary to conceive of one, not many deities—the conception of monotheism. Akhenaten was not really a monotheist. For him, Aten was not the only god, but *his* God, who showed special favor to him and his family. The more conservative priests continued to worship Amon-Ra, and Akhenaten's successors quickly reinstated conventional forms of Egyptian religion. It would take another thousand years for true monotheism to develop. It arose among the Israelites, who struggled for centuries to define themselves as worshipers of

WITNESSES

Forms of Worship

The gods ruled the first human civilizations, and they were fearsome beings. As these civilizations matured, however, so did people's understandings of the cosmos, and the relationship between divine power, the true, and the good. The four passages here give voice to four different understandings of divinity. In the first, an Egyptian pharaoh speaks of his relationship with the sun god Aten, identified as the one or principal all-powerful deity. In the second, a Mesopotamian goddess is portrayed as the powerful and universal force of nature. In the third, the Hebrew god is revealed as not merely powerful, but intimately in contact with the worshiping psalmist. In the fourth, the Four Noble Truths of Buddhism are explained, which define a way of life that touches the infinite.

Pharaoh Akhenaten adores his Creator, the Sun (c. 1362 B.C.E.):

Thou appearest beautifully on the horizon of heaven,
Thou living Aten, the beginning of life!
When thou art risen on the eastern horizon,
Thou has filled every land with thy beauty ...
When thou settest in the western horizon,
The land is in darkness, in the manner of death ...
Darkness is a shroud, and the earth is in stillness,
For he who made them rests in his horizon ...
The world came into being by thy hand,
According as thou hast made them.
When thou hast risen they live,
When thou settest they die.
Thou art lifetime thy own self,
For one lives only through thee.

(From J. B. Pritchard ed., *Ancient Near Eastern Texts relating to the Old Testament*, 2e, 1955)

The Mesopotamian goddess Inanna sings her own praises: I am Nature, the universal Mother, mistress of all the elements, primordial child of time, sovereign of all things spiritual, queen of the dead, queen also of the immortals, the single manifestation of all gods and goddesses that are ... Though I am worshiped in many aspects, known by countless names, and propitiated with all manner of different rites, yet the whole round earth venerates me ... and the Egyptians who excel in ancient learning and worship me with ceremonies proper to my godhead, call me by my true name, namely, Queen Isis.

(*ibid.*, 3e, 1969, supplement)

Psalm 63: 1–8:

1 O God, you are my God, I seek you, my soul thirsts for
you; my flesh faints for you, as in a dry and weary land
where there is no water. 2 So I have looked upon you in
the sanctuary, beholding your power and glory. 3 Because
your steadfast love is better than life, my lips will praise
you. 4 So I will bless you as long as I live; I will lift up
my hands and call on your name. 5 My soul is satisfied as
with a rich feast, and my mouth praises you with joyful
lips 6 when I think of you on my bed, and meditate on
you in the watches of the night; 7 for you have been my
help, and in the shadow of your wings I sing for joy.
8 My soul clings to you; your right hand upholds me.

Buddhism's Four Noble Truths (c. 500 B.C.E.): This is the Noble Truth of Sorrow. Birth is sorrow, age is sorrow, disease is sorrow, death is sorrow, contact with the unpleasant is sorrow, separation from the pleasant is sorrow, every wish unfulfilled is sorrow—in short all the five components of individuality are sorrow.

And this is the Noble Truth of the Arising of Sorrow. [It arises from] thirst, which leads to rebirth, which brings delight and passion, and seeks pleasure now here, now there—the thirst for sensual pleasure, the thirst for continued life, the thirst for power.

And this is the Noble Truth of the Stopping of Sorrow. It is the complete stopping of that thirst, so that no passion remains, leaving it, being emancipated from it, being released from it, giving no place to it.

And this is the Noble Truth of the Way which Leads to the Stopping of Sorrow. It is the Noble Eightfold Path—Right Views, Right Resolve, Right Speech, Right Conduct, Right Livelihood, Right Effort, Right Recollection, and Right Meditation.

(From A. L. Basham, *The Wonder that Was India*, 1954)

Yahweh distinct from the cultists who surrounded them in Canaan (see Chapter 2).

According to the Bible, the Israelites' journey to monotheism did not follow a straight line. In imitation of the neighboring Canaanites, some of Abraham's descendants worshiped images of their deity Baal, and they may have celebrated the feasts of indigenous fertility goddesses with ritual prostitution and even human sacrifice. Some, as was charged, may have brutalized the poor and homeless and wallowed in luxury. They were accused of all these crimes by the **prophets**, the Israelites' spiritual leaders, who may have demanded meticulous obedience to religious law. Micah and Hosea and Amos, Isaiah and Jeremiah and others warned their people, in a stream of eloquence, that Israel's neglect of God's will would lead to its destruction.

In the end, the Israelites suffered the fate of which the prophets had warned—devastation and exile (see Chapter 2). Those deported to Babylon in 586 B.C.E. continued to live in exile for nearly fifty years, clinging to their memories of nationhood. With no temple

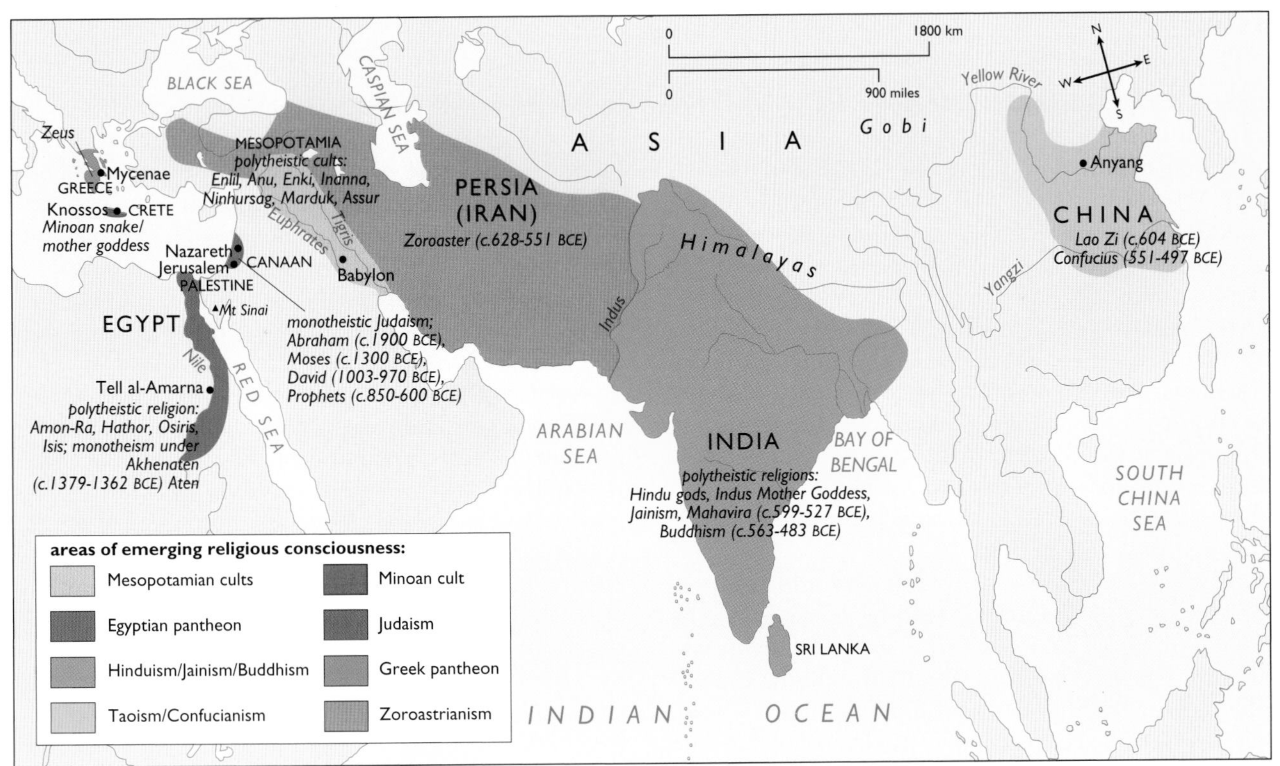

Map 1.2 Old and New Religions: *The peoples of prehistory and the first civilizations were animists or polytheists, revering the spirits of nature or deities understood to control natural forces. From late in the second millennium B.C.E., critics and innovators began to forge from these ancient polytheisms religious outlooks that were spiritually more inward and psychologically more demanding.*

or homeland, their leaders came to believe that an omnipotent God had no need of temples or kingdoms but demanded only righteous obedience. At some point thereafter, the mature Jewish faith emerged. It was a true ethical monotheism, the first such religion in the history of humankind.

The bedraggled remnant of the Israelites who returned from Babylonian exile to the Persian province of Judah in 538 B.C.E. had forged a new relationship with their Lord. Jews, as they were now called (after Judah), continued to make sacrifices of beasts and birds. But now it was, rather, strict observance of the Law that defined a Jew. According to Jewish tradition, the Law referred to a body of laws, which Yahweh himself had conveyed to Moses, leader of the Hebrew-speaking tribes who fled Egypt for the land of Canaan. Yahweh inscribed the commandments on stone tablets on the summit of Mount Sinai in the Arabian desert. The Law consisted of a body of dietary and domestic regulations. It also included principles of the highest ethical nature, intoned with the sonorous "thou shalt" or "thou shalt not" of the commandments. A righteous God was worshiped by righteous action. The nation that first proclaimed this notion had a revolutionary impact on future generations. It had defined ethical behavior as the central purpose of human life.

Independently, in China, in India, and in Iran, other sages sought in the divine realm a revelation of truth or justice or enlightenment. For the Chinese, the universe was simply the expression of the forces of nature (heaven, sun, earth, grain). No mystery, no sin, no apocalypse, could even be imagined in a system where the central challenge was to conform to the harmony already prevailing in the world. To achieve that harmony, one followed "the Way" or *Tao*. Taoism is the religion, or philosophy, that underlies most other patterns of Chinese thought.

The sage Lao Zi (born c. 604 B.C.E.) taught his followers how to reach the enlightenment of the Tao through a moral regimen promoting quiet and unassertive behavior. Two generations later, the master-teacher Kong Fuzi (551–479 B.C.E.; anglicized as "Confucius") would offer another path to enlightened, ethical behavior, specifically in the context of government. Confucius formed his views in an age of political stress, when there was great longing for the imagined good government of past regimes. His principles, which avoided the worship of gods or the pursuit of metaphysics, constituted a system of ethics for the ruling class. Public officials, he taught, must demonstrate high skill, loyalty, honesty, and selflessness. Since virtue existed independent of status, such rulers could come from any rank of society. This notion, common in modern democratic societies, was original with Confucius.

In India, two noblemen, both contemporaries of Confucius, taught followers the means of reaching higher knowledge and tranquillity. These are the two sages Nataputta Vardhamana (traditionally 599–527 B.C.E.), known as the "hero" or Mahavira, founder of Jainism, and Siddhartha Gautama (c. 563–c. 483 B.C.E.), known as the Buddha, originator of Buddhism.

Both Mahavira and the Buddha were concerned with freeing the soul from the endless cycle of rebirth and its burdens of anxiety and suffering, a belief central to Indian religions. These concerns were not fundamentally different from the Brahmanic beliefs (later Hinduism) that had jelled during the fifteen hundred years since the Aryan conquest (see Chapter 2). But both of these religious leaders opposed the **caste** system—the hereditary division into classes—linked with Hinduism, and both saw the possibility for the "release" or salvation of the individual soul regardless of caste or class. Jainism valued extreme asceticism as the means of extinguishing desire and attaining peace. Buddhism favored a "middle way" between an unregulated life of pleasure-seeking and bleak asceticism. The Four Noble Truths of Buddhism are cited in *Witnesses* on p. 26.

The Buddha preached that human fulfillment was attained not by the ardent seeking of goals but by extinguishing all desire. Its true goal, he taught, was **nirvana**, that condition in which all suffering is abolished, along with all personal cravings and qualities. Nirvana could be reached only by following the Eightfold Path of right behavior: in understanding, aspiration, speech, livelihood, ethics, action, thought, and contemplation. Buddha's message succeeded abroad, in east and southeast Asia, spread by missionaries over many centuries. In India, it lost its appeal and became reabsorbed into Hinduism.

The Persian religious reformer Zoroaster (or Zarathustra; c. 628–c. 551 B.C.E.), who was active a century before either Buddha or Confucius, also preached a religion based on righteous conduct. Crusading at first against the corrupt priests known as Magi, who performed the rites of Persian polytheism, he acknowledged only one God, Ahura Mazda ("Wise Lord"), proclaiming him the supreme deity of truth and light. This deity, resembling in some ways both the Egyptian Aten and the Jewish Yahweh, is opposed by a counter-force of evil and darkness, called Angra Mainyu. Throughout past, present, and future, for nine millennia in all, the two struggle. In the end, that struggle will result in victory for the good.

In the universe as conceived by Zoroaster, each individual would face a judgment after death; the righteous would go to heaven, the wicked to hell. This was a new idea in antiquity, where the immortality of the gods was assumed but the stubborn mortality of human beings was known as a certainty. Zoroastrianism appealed to many peoples throughout the Middle East, and at home it enjoyed the support of the Persian emperors. It lingered to enrich Jewish, Christian, and Islamic thought with its hatred of evil and its hope for the triumph of the good.

Judaism and Taoism and the messages of Confucius and Buddha and Zoroaster challenged the polytheistic religions of early civilization. They also made many people less willing to sacrifice wealth and blood to the appetites of gods and goddesses who cared little for humankind. This was the change represented by the event with which this chapter opened: the unbinding of Isaac, freed from the fate of sacrifice but committed to service of the divine will.

The advent of ethically-based monotheistic religions did, however, have at least one seriously negative effect. Because the new deity, the new righteousness, the new heaven were thoroughly masculine, women had even less status than under polytheism. Goddesses—and the priestesses ministering to them—disappeared.

Polytheism continued to flourish in many later civilizations, notably those of Greece and Rome—and in our own time in India, in the Hindu religion. And the Mother Goddess has survived in many guises, all over the world. The Egyptian goddess Isis (see Chapter 7), whose cult flourished in late Roman times, inspired many of the images associated with the Virgin Mary, mother of Jesus. The reverence accorded her by Christians (especially in the Roman Catholic and Orthodox churches) testifies to the enduring strength of the maternal principle in religion.

At the beginning of human civilization, the gods of prehistoric times were securely established as guardians of the known. By the end of the first millennium before the Common Era, among some peoples, these manifold gods had become one God, or one Principle or Source, identified with all the good toward which the human spirit would strive.

Conclusion

THE EARLIEST CIVILIZATIONS AND THE MEANING OF THE WEST

Much of what distinguishes human life today was first attained by the ancient people of the first civilizations. The ability to control nature, to manage food production, to build cities, to conduct trade, to develop technology, to understand science and mathematics, to create works of literature, to establish systems of law, and to ask thoughtful questions about the cosmos and our place in it—all of these were bequeathed to later generations by the first civilizations, and to the "West" specifically by the ancient civilizations of the Middle East. These civilizations offer lessons as well about the organization of the state and the fragility of power. The next chapter will consider this other dimension of life in antiquity.

REVIEW QUESTIONS

1. Describe the evolution of the human species. Why were the advances in the New Stone Age important? What role did women play in Neolithic society?

2. Where did the first civilizations arise? What functions did cities serve in these cultures? Why did iron implements largely replace bronze ones? Why were trade and cultural links significant?

3. Describe the social hierarchy of early civilizations. How did women's status influence these societies? How did the status of women differ in Egypt and Mesopotamia?

4. Why was the invention of writing in early civilization so important? Why did writing evolve from the first pictograms to the alphabet? What is the difference between writing and language?

5. How did the custom of sacrifice develop? Why were Akhenaten's religious innovations such a break with Egyptian religion?

6. By what process did the Israelites become monotheists? Why was the Israelite concept of a righteous God so radical in the ancient world? What role did ethics play in the development of early Confucianism and Buddhism?

SUGGESTED RESOURCES

Before History

Cavalli-Sforza, Luigi Luca, *Genes, Peoples, and Languages*, trans. Mark Seielstad (New York: Farrar, Straus & Giroux; North Point Press, 2000). Linking complex genetic and linguistic evidence, Cavalli-Sforza proposes to map the history of the migrations of all the world's peoples.

Fagan, Brian M., *The Journey from Eden: The Peopling of Our World* (London: Thames & Hudson, 1990). A critical overview of theories of human origin, arguing on the basis of recent historical, paleoanthropological, and genetic research that fully modern humans evolved in Africa and from there colonized the rest of the world.

Leakey, Richard and Roger Lewin, *Origins Reconsidered: In Search of What Makes Us Human* (New York: Doubleday, 1992). Reflections by a renowned paleoanthropologist on his own discoveries of early hominid life in East Africa. Leakey incorporates ideas from philosophy, anthropology, molecular biology, and linguistics to investigate not only how we evolved anatomically but how we acquired the qualities that make us human: consciousness, creativity, and culture.

McElvaine, Robert S., *Eve's Seed: Biology, the Sexes, and the Course of History* (New York: McGraw Hill, 2000). Fills in the history between the culmination of human evolution and the estabilishment of civilization, a period when women's role was dominant before envious men overturned power relations.

Civilization and the City

Diamond, Jared, *Guns, Germs and Steel: The Fates of Human Societies* (New York: W.W. Norton, 1997). A brilliant exploration of the geographical and material conditions that permitted Eurasian civilizations to advance and gain dominance.

Hodder, Ian, *The Domestication of Europe: Structure and Contingency in Neolithic Societies* (Cambridge, MA: Basil Blackwell, 1990). A bold if controversial attempt to reconstruct human societies in the Near East and Europe at the end of the Ice Age.

Kramer, Samuel Noah, *The Sumerians: The History, Culture and Character* (Chicago: University of Chicago Press, 1971). A classic history of Sumer, 4500–1750 B.C.E., with selected translations of Sumerian texts. Details Sumerian achievements in government, education and literature, philosophy, law, agriculture, and medicine.

Lerner, Gerda, *The Creation of Patriarchy I: Women and History* (New York/Oxford: Oxford University Press, 1986). A pioneering feminist study of the origin of Western women's subordination, linking it to the rise of property-conscious agricultural societies in Mesopotamia, Israel, and Greece.

Nissen, Hans J., *The Early History of the Ancient Near East, 9000–2000* B.C. (Chicago: University of Chicago Press, 1988). A balanced political and cultural history of Mesopotamia, based on archaeological sources and analysis of material culture.

The Indus Valley civilization:
http://www.historyofindia.com/indus.html
http://www.harappa.com/har/har0.html

Writing, Language, and Consciousness

Frankfort, H. and H. A., John A. Wilson, Thorkild Jacobsen, *Before Philosophy: The Intellectual Adventure of Ancient Man* (Baltimore: Penguin, 1949). A challenging description of ancient Egyptian and Mesopotamian mythopoetic interpretations of phenomena, in contrast to the philosophical outlook of later Hellenic culture.

Martin, Henri Jean (trans. Lydia G. Cochrane), *The History and Power of Writing* (Chicago: University of Chicago Press, 1995). A comprehensive study by a preeminent scholar of the book. Examines the technologies, forms, and structures of writing throughout history.

The *Analects* of Confucius:
http://classics.mit.edu/Confucius/analects.html

Evolving Religions

Bergmann, Martin S., *In the Shadow of Moloch: The Sacrifice of Children and its Impact on Western Religions* (New York: Columbia University Press, 1993). An eye-opening account of the ritual convention of child sacrifice and its shaping of ancient cultures.

Cross, Frank Moore, *Canaanite Myth and Hebrew Epic: Essays in the History of the Religion of Israel* (Cambridge, MA.: Harvard University Press, 1973; reprint 1997). Traces continuities between early Israelite religion and its underlying Canaanite culture. Explores re-emergence of Canaanite mythic material in the apocalypticism of early Christianity and the Dead Sea Scrolls.

Leeming, David A. & Jake Page, *Goddess: The Myths of the Female Divine* (Oxford: Oxford University Press, 1994). A biography of the "goddess," the compelling, commanding, threatening female divinity revered by human populations from the Ice Age to modern times, showing how ancient themes endure in modern religion and psychology.

Bible tools—text and history: http://bible.crosswalk.com

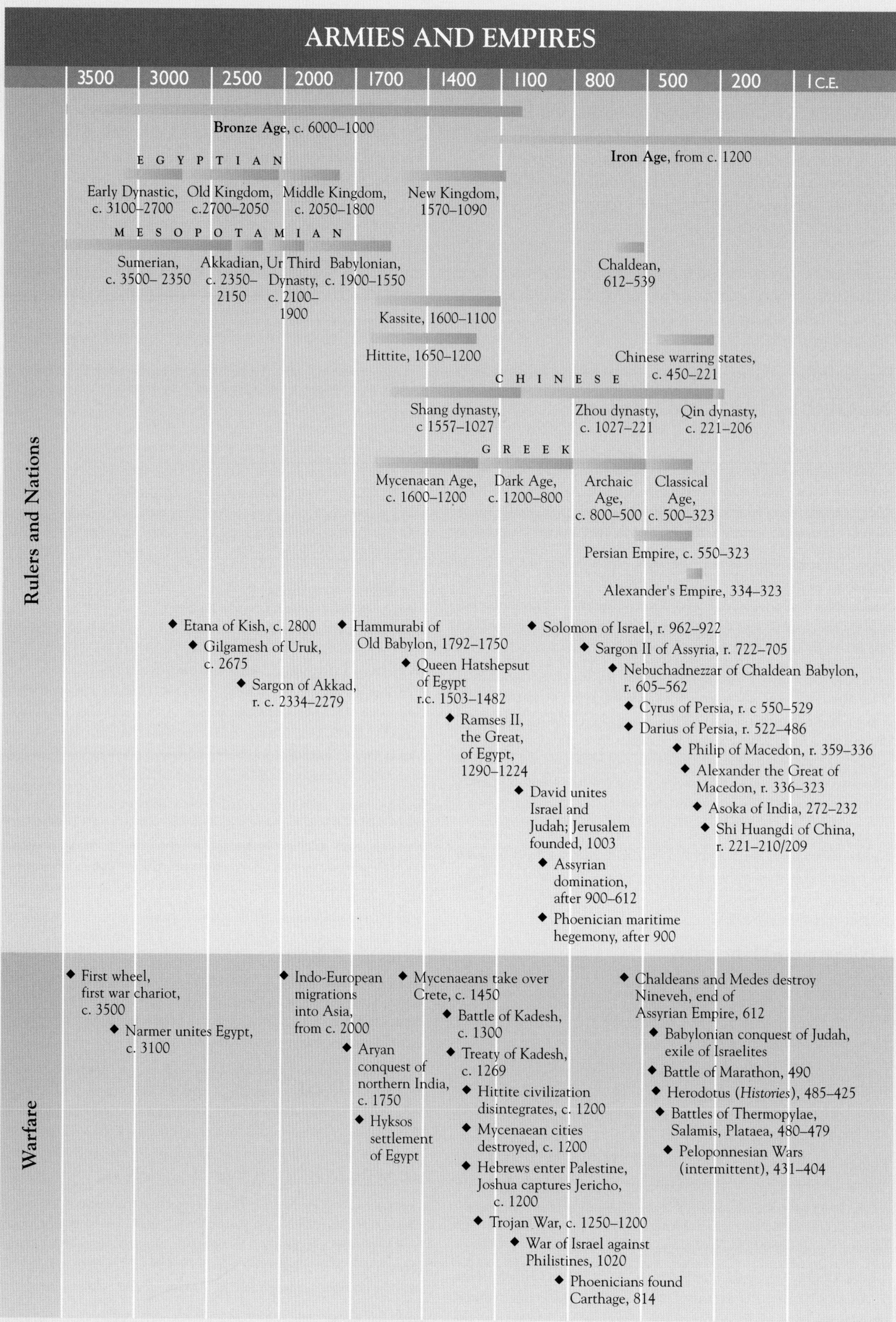
ARMIES AND EMPIRES
3500
3000
2500
2000
1700
1400
1100
800
500
200
I C.E.
Rulers and Nations
Bronze Age, c. 6000–1000
Iron Age, from c. 1200
EGYPTIAN
Early Dynastic, c. 3100–2700
Old Kingdom, c.2700–2050
Middle Kingdom, c. 2050–1800
New Kingdom, 1570–1090
MESOPOTAMIAN
Sumerian, c. 3500– 2350
Akkadian, c. 2350–2150
Ur Third Dynasty, c. 2100–1900
Babylonian, c. 1900–1550
Chaldean, 612–539
Kassite, 1600–1100
Hittite, 1650–1200
Chinese warring states, c. 450–221
CHINESE
Shang dynasty, c 1557–1027
Zhou dynasty, c. 1027–221
Qin dynasty, c. 221–206
GREEK
Mycenaean Age, c. 1600–1200
Dark Age, c. 1200–800
Archaic Age, c. 800–500
Classical Age, c. 500–323
Persian Empire, c. 550–323
Alexander's Empire, 334–323
◆ Etana of Kish, c. 2800
◆ Gilgamesh of Uruk, c. 2675
◆ Sargon of Akkad, r. c. 2334–2279
◆ Hammurabi of Old Babylon, 1792–1750
◆ Queen Hatshepsut of Egypt r.c. 1503–1482
◆ Ramses II, the Great, of Egypt, 1290–1224
◆ David unites Israel and Judah; Jerusalem founded, 1003
◆ Assyrian domination, after 900–612
◆ Phoenician maritime hegemony, after 900
◆ Solomon of Israel, r. 962–922
◆ Sargon II of Assyria, r. 722–705
◆ Nebuchadnezzar of Chaldean Babylon, r. 605–562
◆ Cyrus of Persia, r. c 550–529
◆ Darius of Persia, r. 522–486
◆ Philip of Macedon, r. 359–336
◆ Alexander the Great of Macedon, r. 336–323
◆ Asoka of India, 272–232
◆ Shi Huangdi of China, r. 221–210/209
Warfare
◆ First wheel, first war chariot, c. 3500
◆ Narmer unites Egypt, c. 3100
◆ Indo-European migrations into Asia, from c. 2000
◆ Aryan conquest of northern India, c. 1750
◆ Hyksos settlement of Egypt
◆ Mycenaeans take over Crete, c. 1450
◆ Battle of Kadesh, c. 1300
◆ Treaty of Kadesh, c. 1269
◆ Hittite civilization disintegrates, c. 1200
◆ Mycenaean cities destroyed, c. 1200
◆ Hebrews enter Palestine, Joshua captures Jericho, c. 1200
◆ Trojan War, c. 1250–1200
◆ War of Israel against Philistines, 1020
◆ Phoenicians found Carthage, 814
◆ Chaldeans and Medes destroy Nineveh, end of Assyrian Empire, 612
◆ Babylonian conquest of Judah, exile of Israelites
◆ Battle of Marathon, 490
◆ Herodotus (Histories), 485–425
◆ Battles of Thermopylae, Salamis, Plataea, 480–479
◆ Peloponnesian Wars (intermittent), 431–404

CHAPTER

2 ARMIES AND EMPIRES

Politics and Power in the Bronze and Iron Ages

3500–300 B.C.E.

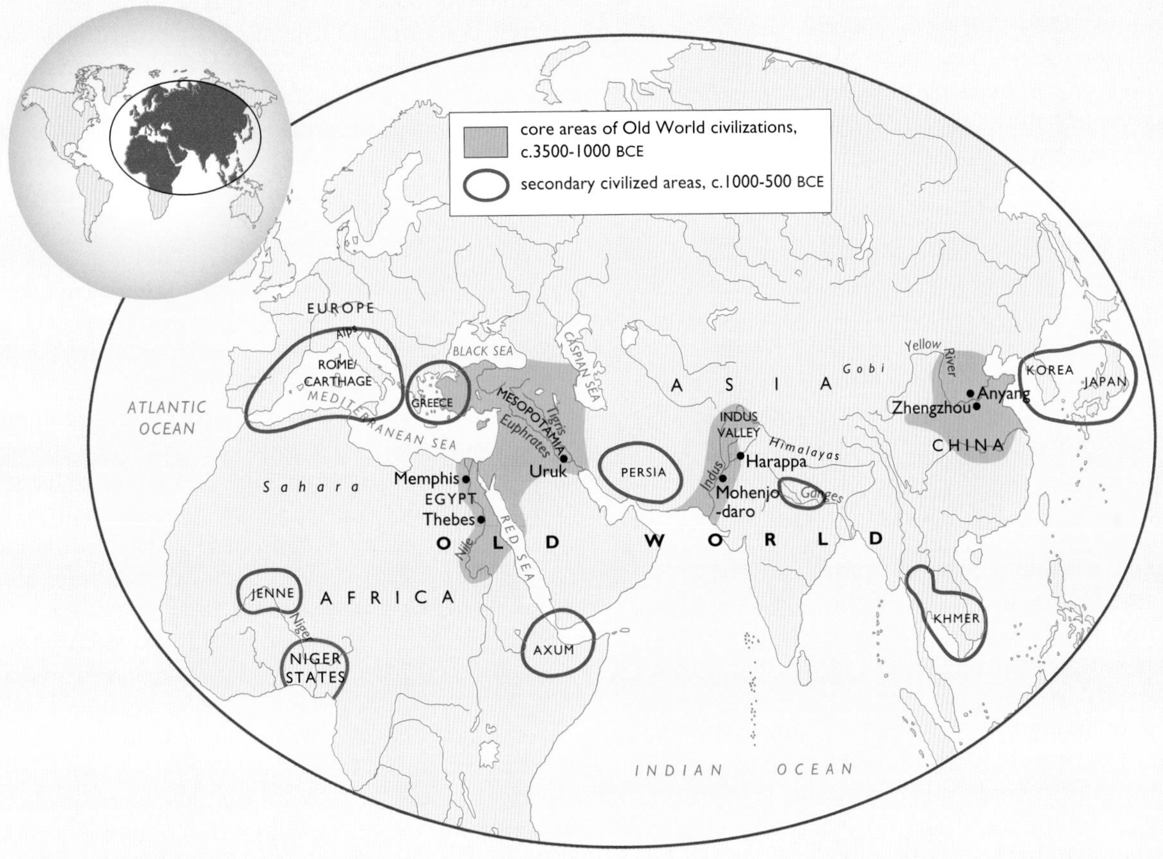

KEY TOPICS

- **Power and Civilization:** Kings wage war to enlarge their kingdoms, win glory, and establish dynasties that last for decades or centuries.
- **Bronze Age Kingdoms: Egypt, Mesopotamia:** Akkadians, Amorites supplant Sumerians in Mesopotamia; Egypt's pharaohs struggle for power.
- **Bronze Age Kingdoms: the Aegean, the Near East:** Newly formed Mycenaean and Hittite civilizations compete with older states until the region suffers calamities c. 1200 B.C.E.
- **Iron Age Empires of the Middle East:** Assyria and Babylon are overcome by the Persians, who subdue the entire Middle East.
- **Bronze and Iron Age Kingdoms: East and South Asia:** The Chinese Shang dynasty is followed by the Zhou and the Qin; Aryans invade India.
- **The Birth of the West:** Aegean peoples (later called Greeks) defeat the Persians, the first time a Western civilization gains supremacy.

A Notable Refusal *During the reign of King Xerxes of Persia (r. 486–465 B.C.E.), two citizens of the ancient Greek city of Sparta journeyed to the Persian court on an official mission. It was the custom for visitors to prostrate themselves before the King of Kings, as Xerxes called himself. Ordered to do so, the Spartans refused "and said they would never do any such thing, even were their heads thrust down to the ground; for it was not their custom to worship men ..." The Spartans' refusal to abase themselves before a king announces a theme that would recur often in the history of the Western world.*

Long before these Spartans faced the Persian monarch, who could have ordered their execution with a nod of his head, the power of kings, who reigned in nearly all the civilized regions of the globe, had grown vigorous and irresistible. Their taste for war wrought devastation and enslaved multitudes. Their need for weapons to fight these wars spurred innovation and trade. Their zeal for glory inspired great tombs and monuments, which also testify to the genius of the artists who made them. Their quest for domination led to the creation of larger and larger empires. The struggles that resulted from this accumulation of power in the hands of kings forcefully shaped the course of civilization.

POWER AND CIVILIZATION

Kings appeared almost as soon as civilization began. They reigned in most nations of the world for some 5000 years, until, early in the twentieth century, world war started to close the chapter on most kings. Until then, the history of world politics is largely the history of **monarchy**, or "the rule of one." Ancient monarchs were mostly male, and nearly divine. They were gods, they claimed, or became gods, or took the place of gods (see *Witnesses*, p. 33). Although religion buttressed monarchy, kings still imposed their will by force. They forged empires and held power by accumulating weapons and waging war. Some of these important rulers are listed in *Who's Who* on pp. 34, 37, 48, 49, and 50.

Kings, Queens, and Priests

Monarchy developed partly from the religious beliefs of early civilizations. People believed that they were governed by the gods, represented by their priests. Such societies are called **theocracies**. Gradually the rule of priests gave way to that of a single person, although the priests remained a privileged group. This individual cast himself as a representative of the gods, or the son of a god, or even a god himself. The Egyptian pharaoh was believed to rise from death in the form of the god Horus, son of the divine judge Osiris, and to reign with him eternally. This divine afterlife is expressed in the pyramid, a monument whose clear, converging lines bridge earth and heaven. The superhuman status of King Sargon of Akkad (r. c. 2334–2279 B.C.E.) is indicated by his having been miraculously rescued in infancy from a basket set adrift on the Euphrates River (like the biblical story of Moses). Hammurabi (c. 1792–1750) was depicted receiving directly from the Supreme God, Shamash, the code of laws he published (see *Windows On*, p. 22). Assyrian kings were priests of the warrior god Assur, and Hittite kings, called "Sun" while alive, were hailed as gods upon their death. Chinese monarchs claimed to rule by the mandate of heaven.

Rarely did a woman rule in her own right from the outset. The biblical judge and perhaps mythical prophetess Deborah (Judges: 4–5), and the legendary Amazon queens (see Chapter 3) were thought to have done so. Most monarchs were male. Where the legitimate male ruler had died or was still a child, his widow or mother might rule in his stead. Hatshepsut of Egypt (r. c. 1503–1482 B.C.E.), Summuramat of Assyria (ninth century B.C.E.) (the legendary Semiramis), and Artemisia (fifth century B.C.E.) of Halicarnassus (a city in Asia Minor) were **surrogate**, or substitute, rulers of this kind.

Apart from their claims to divinity, kings acquired power through their military skills. Violence threatened early societies. Even before human communities grew from village to city, people preyed upon each other. Paleolithic remains show that the stone weapons used to bring down bear and bull were also used to smash human skulls and limbs: evidence of homicide, at least, if not of battle. Skeletons from Neolithic times, in mass graves and marked by multiple injuries, testify to the invention of organized war.

Even the oldest towns archaeologists have explored had thick walls and tall watchtowers (see Chapter 1). These structures guarded town dwellers from attack not only from wild beasts roaming outside the walls, but from other humans like themselves. Especially fit and skilled men were chosen to hold the battlements and direct the defense, or to lead and pursue an assault. Some of these war chiefs became kings. Their fellow warriors became the nobility, professionals equipped with the finest weapons.

Weapons and Warriors

The earliest weapons were only the sticks and stones that early humans found readily at hand, but during the Neolithic age and the first civilizations weapons became increasingly sophisticated and effective. With the mace (stone head, wooden handle) Neolithic warriors could smash their enemies, and with a carved stone dagger stab them. With a sling

WITNESSES

The Idea of the King

The kings who ruled ancient civilizations claimed extraordinary powers; the whole later history of politics can be seen, in part, as the story of the moderation of, or restraint on, the kingly power possessed by ancient monarchs. The first passage is from an edict of the reforming Buddhist king of India, Asoka, who sets forth a different ideal: that of the monarch's responsibility for the welfare of his people. The second and third passages testify to the high claims of the monarchs of Egypt and Persia. The fourth contains a warning against the power of kings by the Hebrew judge Samuel, who would anoint David and Saul as kings of Israel.

King Asoka issues an edict about the duty of the ruler for the welfare of his people (c. 250 B.C.E.): In the past, state business was not transacted nor were reports delivered to the king at all hours. But now I have given this order, that at any time, whether I am eating, in the women's quarters, the bed chamber, the chariot, ... the park or wherever, reporters are to be posted with instructions to report to me the affairs of the people so that I might attend to these affairs wherever I am. And ... when urgent business presses itself ..., if disagreement or debate arises in the Council, then it must be reported to me immediately. ... Truly, I consider the welfare of all to be my duty, and the root of this is exertion and the prompt despatch of business. There is no better work than promoting the welfare of all the people and whatever efforts I am making is to repay the debt I owe to all beings to assure their happiness in this life, and attain heaven in the next. Therefore this ... edict has been written to last long and that my sons, grandsons and great-grandsons might act in conformity with it for the welfare of the world.
(From The Edicts of King Asoka, trans. Ven. S. Dhammika, 1993)

Obey the divine pharaoh:
He is Re [the sun], by whose beams one sees,
He is the one who illumines the Two Lands [of Egypt] more than the sun disc.
He is one who makes the land greener than [does] a high Nile,
For he has filled the Two Lands with strength and life ...
He whom the king has loved will be a revered one,
But there is no tomb for a rebel against his majesty,
And his corpse is cast into the water.
(From J. B. Pritchard ed., *Ancient Near Eastern Texts relating to the Old Testament*, 2e, 1955)

Darius, king of Persia, says who he is (c. 500 B.C.E.): A great god is Ahuramazda, who created this earth, who created yonder sky, who created man, who created happiness for man, who made Darius king, one king of many, one lord of many. I am Darius the Great King, King of Kings, King of countries containing all kinds of men, King in this great earth far and wide, son of Hystaspes, an Achaemenian, a Persian, son of a Persian, an Aryan, having Aryan lineage ... Ahuramazda, when he saw this earth in commotion, thereafter bestowed it upon me, made me king; I am king ... This which has been done, all that by the will of Ahuramazda I did.
(From R. G. Kent, *Old Persian: Grammar, Texts, Lexicon*, 2e, 1953)

Advised by Yahweh, Samuel warns the Israelites about kings: So Samuel reported all the words of the Lord to the people who were asking him for a king. He said, "These will be the ways of the king who will reign over you: he will take your sons and appoint them to his chariots and to be his horsemen, and to run before his chariots; and he will appoint for himself commanders of thousands and commanders of fifties, and some to plow his ground and to reap his harvest, and to make his implements of war and the equipment of his chariots. He will take your daughters to be perfumers and cooks and bakers ... He will take one-tenth of your flocks, and you shall be his slaves. And in that day you will cry out because of your king, whom you have chosen for yourselves; but the Lord will not answer you in that day."
(1 Samuel 8:10–18)

of wood and leather they could hurl a small stone, or with a wooden bow they could launch a wooden arrow tipped in stone.

These primitive weapons remained effective even into later ages when metal began to be used. According to the Bible, the Israelite youth David opposed the Philistine hero Goliath with sling and stone. "Am I a dog," Goliath sneered, "that you come to me with sticks?" But David's simple weapon prevailed over the Philistine's bronze sword (I Samuel 17:41–50). Centuries later, the Roman army, the most formidable military force of the ancient world, still massed slingers, whose missiles were of stone, and bowmen in its rear lines.

But metal was better. The sharp edge of a bronze weapon allowed a warrior to penetrate (rather than smash) the body of his enemy. The stone dagger would break if it met resistance, but the long bronze sword ripped through flesh. The bronze-bladed axe could do much more damage than the mace. Wheeled chariots staffed with spearmen were deadlier than a line of bowmen, even those equipped with bronze arrowheads. Iron weapons mimicked those of bronze, but were cheaper and stronger. Hence iron made possible the multiplication of weapons and of wars.

Weapons were not only useful, they were also a form of wealth, whose possession conferred status. Military equipment was elaborate and expensive.

Besides weapons, it included pieces of armor: shin-plates (greaves) and chestplate, shield and helmet, each piece invested with the glamour of rarity and power. These objects were buried with monarchs as tokens of their rank. The artisan or peasant possessed little bronze, as it was rarely used to make the implements of their daily life. Although it gave its name to the whole age, it was in fact the attribute only of the rich who ruled.

Like their kings, the upper-class warriors of the first civilizations came to the field armed in bronze—one form of wealth. For their prowess, they were rewarded with land or treasure. For millennia, the social order of noble warriors would rank higher than that of any laborer—merchant, farmer, or artisan.

Waging War

Then, as now, these warriors dealt in mass destruction. They devastated cities, the centers of civilization, and ravaged whole populations, who faced the alternatives of death or **slavery**. The colossal walls around a city could not offer total protection. The population could be surrounded and starved and those sturdy walls breached—by surrender, by storming, or by treachery. Then the unleashed invading army would run through the streets to loot and burn. Many accounts of ancient battles depict the storm and sack of cities (see *Witnesses*, p. 36). According to the Bible, Jericho was seized (its walls felled by the sound of trumpets) by the Israelites under Joshua, who "put everyone to the sword, men and women, young and old, and also cattle, sheep, and asses" (Joshua 6:21). Ur, in Sumer, was devastated by Sargon of Akkad in c. 2000 B.C.E., and Troy, according to legend, was sacked and ravaged by the Greeks, its men killed and its women enslaved (see Chapter 4).

The captors of a city might kill or deport the vanquished king, along with his brothers and sons, advisors and noble retinue, and other prominent persons, such as the temple priests and the skilled artisans. Sometimes the entire population was killed, or exiled to another city, to vanish as a people. Some of the lost kingdoms and lost peoples of the ancient world, such as the Indus Valley civilization, may have disappeared in this way. Alternatively, the male inhabitants of the conquered city might be slain, but the captive women and children would have been brought home to labor as servants, concubines, and prostitutes (see Chapter 1)—history's first slaves.

From the outset of civilization, war and peace were seen as the poles of human experience. An oblong box from ancient Sumer, known as the "Royal Standard of Ur," is decorated in mosaic with scenes of war on one side, those of peace on the other. In the same way, war and peace are the alternate modes of life depicted on the shield made by the god Hephaistos for the warrior Achilles, as recounted in the *Iliad* (18:478–613), the eighth-century epic poem attributed to Homer (see Chapter 4).

Kings and nobles, armies bristling with bronze weapons, the consolidation of states, the destruction of cities and even whole populations—all these were well-established in early antiquity. Over three millennia, a ceaseless cycle of warfare caused the appearance and disappearance of human communities as monarchs built or acquired their kingdoms, their dynasties, and empires.

BRONZE AGE KINGDOMS IN EGYPT AND MESOPOTAMIA

From the birth of the Bronze Age until about 1200 B.C.E., rulers of single cities expanded their authority over surrounding lands, creating kingdoms for themselves (see Map 2.1). The first to do so were the pharaohs of Egypt, who created a unified kingdom that would endure for nearly 3000 years. Meanwhile the war chiefs of the Sumerian cities extended their rule over neighboring communities, to be engulfed in turn by kings based in Akkad and Babylon. These Bronze Age kingdoms were the earliest to form in the history of humankind. They were pioneers in the concentration of power, the extension of rule, and the control of subject populations. Directly or indirectly, their model has influenced most of the world's subsequent political systems.

Egypt and its Pharaohs

The pharaohs came to power by absorbing the small communities of the region. Before civilization began, people of the Nile River valley clustered in towns headed by local chiefs. These clusters were scattered throughout the region, extending deep into the upper Nile zone of present-day Sudan, known in antiquity as Nubia. Some chiefs were sovereign over a single town, some over several. In time, these separate communities were absorbed into two kingdoms: those of Upper Egypt to the south, and Lower Egypt to the

WHO'S WHO

In Egypt

Narmer (r. c. 3100 B.C.E.) (traditionally called Menes) King who unites Egypt.

Hatshepsut (r. c. 1503–1482 B.C.E.) Pharaoh of Egypt, one of the few ancient queens to hold sovereign power.

Ramses II the Great (1290–1224 B.C.E.) Pharaoh of Egypt, who extends Egyptian power into Palestine and contends with the Hittites at Kadesh.

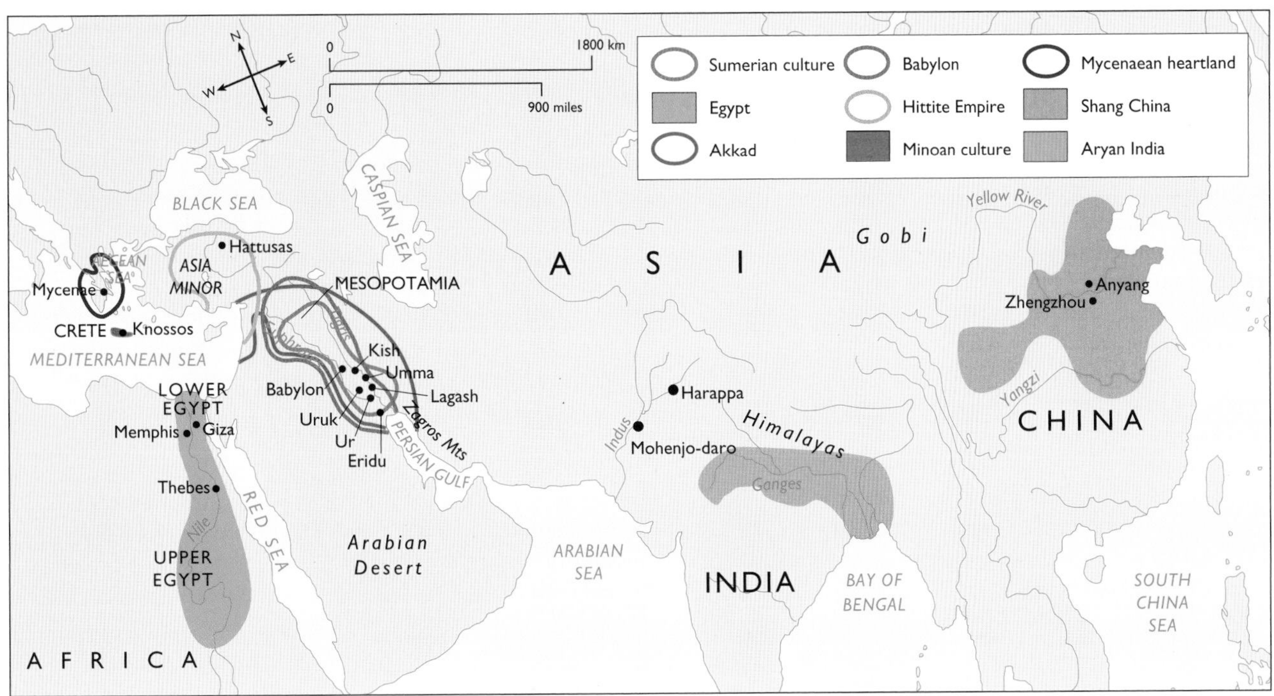

Map 2.1 Bronze Age Empires of the Old World, 3500–1200 B.C.E.: *In the zones of the first civilizations, rulers and dynasties contended with each other, and the form, core, and extent of their domains shifted constantly.*

north. The identity of the rulers of these two adjoining kingdoms remains unknown.

By 3100 B.C.E., these kingdoms were united under a single ruler, King Narmer (traditionally called Menes). Where there had been many kings, then two, there was now one. Narmer's achievement was announced and celebrated with complex imagery as shown on the Palette of Narmer on p. 37. He was depicted as wearing two crowns: the peaked White Crown and flatter Red Crown, of Upper and Lower Egypt respectively. The symbol of Narmer's clan, the falcon, was associated with the god Horus, a divine association strengthening his claim to sovereignty.

Narmer established the capital of his kingdom at Memphis in Lower Egypt, not far from the site, at Giza, where later pharaohs would raise the greatest of the pyramids. Under his successors, of the First and Second dynasties, Egypt grew in size, prosperity, and technical expertise, including the arts of building and writing. By about 2700 B.C.E. the main features of Egyptian civilization were established.

The pharaohs of the following five centuries—a period known as the Old Kingdom—enjoyed absolute power (see *Witnesses*, p. 33). Even during the political changes of later periods, Egyptian life and culture remained remarkably stable. The annual flooding of the Nile was a constant factor that regulated economic life, and the pharaoh in every dynasty personified the principle of cosmic constancy and justice expressed by the word *Ma'at*.

The pharaohs of the Middle Kingdom (who ruled from about 2050 to nearly 1800 B.C.E.) pursued a mainly defensive military strategy. Already protected by the desert to the west and the Red Sea to the east, they needed a minimal force to guard the frontier.

When Egypt was settled around 1700 B.C.E. by a nomadic people called the Hyksos, the newcomers met little resistance. Taking possession of Egypt, these "Kings of foreign lands" ruled from Avaris, in the eastern delta, for about 150 years. Then, beginning in about 1570 B.C.E., a new line of pharaohs gained power, launching the New Kingdom (1570–1090 B.C.E.). They expelled the Hyksos and pursued a strategy of expansion which continued to the brink of the **Iron Age**. After a confrontation with the Hittites in the 1200s, Egypt ceased to expand. Later, successive conquests by the Persians, Macedonians, Romans, Arabs, and Turks would put Egypt under foreign domination for the better part of 2000 years.

Mesopotamian Kingdoms

The first pharaohs of Egypt created a large, centralized state. The earliest kings of lower Mesopotamia, in contrast, ruled cities: one, two, or perhaps as many as ten. But although they had relatively modest powers over a small area, these kings were revered for their achievements and allegedly divine attributes.

Among the earliest written documents we possess are "king lists" from Sumer, the first political power of ancient Mesopotamia. The first ruler noted in these chronicles was Etana (c. 2800 B.C.E.) of the city of Kish, described as "he who stabilized all the lands" and as having later "ascended to heaven."

Sumer did not have dynasties, in the modern sense of the word (unless a family could establish a

WITNESSES

To War in Sumer, Canaan, and Assyria

Ancient war was total war. The conquering army razed the walls of the enemy city, looted and raped, slaughtered combatants and innocents, and enslaved whole populations. Some scenes of these conflicts are given here: the destruction of Sumerian Ur, the Israelite conquest of Jericho, and, in three separate boastful reports, the devastation wrought by Assyrian kings.

A poet laments the destruction of the city of Ur (c. 2000 B.C.E.):

Its walls were breached; the people groan.
In its lofty gates, where they were wont to promenade, dead bodies were lying about;
In its boulevards, where the feasts were celebrated, scattered they lay ...
Ur—its weak and its strong perished through hunger;
Mothers and fathers who did not leave their houses, were overcome by fire;
The young lying on their mothers' laps, like fish were carried off by the waters. ...

(From J. B. Pritchard ed., *Ancient Near Eastern Texts relating to the Old Testament*, 2e, 1955)

Joshua and the Israelites take the city of Jericho with a shout: On the seventh day they rose early, at dawn, and marched around the city in the same manner seven times. ... And at the seventh time, when the priests had blown the trumpets, Joshua said to the people, "Shout! For the Lord has given you the city. The city and all that is in it shall be devoted to the Lord for destruction. ... " So the people shouted, and the trumpets were blown. As soon as the people heard the sound of the trumpets, they raised a great shout, and the wall fell down flat; so the people charged straight ahead into the city and captured it. Then they devoted to destruction by the edge of the sword all in the city, both men and women, young and old, oxen, sheep and donkeys.

(Joshua 6:15–17, 20–21)

Tiglathpileser I reports his conquests (c. 1100 B.C.E.): Assur and the great gods, who have made my kingdom great, and who have bestowed might and power as a ... gift, commanded that I should extend the boundary of their land, and they intrusted to my hand their mighty weapons, the storm of battle. Lands, mountains, cities, and princes, the enemies of Arrus, I have brought under my sway, and have subdued their territories. With sixty kings ... I fought, and established (my) victorious might over them. I was without an equal in battle, or a rival in the fight. I enlarged the frontier of my land, and all of their lands I brought under my sway.

(From D. D. Luckenbill ed., *Ancient Records of Assyria and Babylonia 1*, 1968)

Assurnasirpal puts down a revolt (c. 870 B.C.E.): While I was staying in the land of Kutmuki, they brought me the word: "The city of Suru of Bit-Halupe has revolted, they have slain Hamatai, their governor, and Ahiababa, the son of nobody, whom they have brought from Bit-Adini, they have set up as king over them." ... to the city of Bit-Halupe I drew near, and the terror of the splendor of Assur, my lord, overwhelmed them. The chief men and the elders of the city, to save their lives, came forth into my presence and embraced my feet, saying: 'If it is thy pleasure, slay! If it is thy pleasure, let live! That which thy heart desireth, do!" Ahiababa, the son of a nobody, whom they had brought from Bit-Adini, I took captive. In the valor of my heart and with the fury of my weapons I stormed the city. All the rebels they seized and delivered them up ... Azi-ilu I set over them as my own governor. I built a pillar over against his city gate, and I flayed all the chief men who had revolted, and I covered the pillar with their skins; some I walled up within the pillar, some I impaled upon the pillar on stakes, and others I bound to stakes round about the pillar; many within the border of my own land I flayed, and I spread their skins upon the walls; and I cut off the limbs of the officers, of the royal officers who had rebelled. Ahiababa I took to Nineveh, I flayed him, I spread his skin upon the wall of Nineveh.

(From A. Ferrill, *Origins of War: From the Stone Age to Alexander the Great*, 1985)

Sennacherib triumphs over Hezekiah (c. 688 B.C.E.): As to Hezekiah, the Jew, who did not submit to my yoke, I laid siege to 46 of his strong cities, walled forts; and to the countless small villages in their vicinity, and conquered them by means of well-stamped ramps and battering-rams brought near to the walls combined with the attack by foot soldiers, using mines, breeches as well as sapper work. I drove out 200,150 people, young and old, male and female, horses, mules, donkeys, camels, big and small cattle beyond counting ... Himself I made a prisoner in Jerusalem, his royal residence, like a bird in a cage. ... Hezekiah himself, whom the terror-inspiring splendour of my lordship had overwhelmed ... did send me, later, to Nineveh, my lordly city, together with 30 talents of gold, 800 talents of silver, precious stones, antimony, large cuts of red stone, couches, inlaid with ivory ... daughters, concubines, male and female musicians.

(From H. V. F. Winstone, *Uncovering the Ancient World*, 1986)

WHO'S WHO

In Mesopotamia

Etana of Kish (r. c 2800 B.C.E.) first Sumerian ruler to form a kingdom beyond his own city.

Gilgamesh of Uruk (c. 2675 B.C.E.) Sumerian king whose deeds are recorded in history's oldest epic, *Gilgamesh*.

Sargon of Akkad (r. c. 2334–2279 B.C.E.) conquers Sumerian cities and builds the first empire.

Hammurabi of Babylon (r. 1792–1750 B.C.E.) Amorite king, famed for his *Code of Laws* (c. 1790 B.C.E.).

dynasty), but a "kingship," which passed from one city to another. After Kish's heyday, the kingship passed to the city of Uruk, which nurtured some renowned kings. Among them was Dumuzi, identified with a god who dies and is resurrected. Better known, however, was Dumuzi's successor, Gilgamesh. As immortalized in legend, the hero Gilgamesh symbolized the tragedy of human existence. The historical Gilgamesh ruled Uruk at about the time the kings of Ur also gained prominence, in about 2675 B.C.E. There would follow the kings of Lagash and Umma and Eridu, each of whom was a divinely appointed ruler of a different Sumerian city.

Another king of Uruk, Lugalzaggesi ("lugal" meant "king"), was captured after twenty years of military triumph and brought in chains to the city of Nippur as the booty of King Sargon the Great. By 2331 B.C.E., Sargon had conquered and unified many of the cities of the Tigris-Euphrates Valley and beyond, from the Syrian tip of the Fertile Crescent down to the Persian Gulf. He thereby achieved for the region a consolidation comparable to Narmer's earlier unification of Egypt.

An imaginative administrator and clever fashioner of his own image, Sargon built a new capital c. 2300 B.C.E., called Akkad, which had a population of about 5400. Here, he presided over a huge court of nobles and officials. Akkad gave its name to Akkadian, the civilization founded by Sargon, and also to the Semitic language spoken by its people. For 1000 years Akkadian was the universal tongue of the Middle East.

The Akkadian conquerors imposed their language on the vanquished Sumerians. Yet, in a pattern that would often be repeated, the Akkadians were themselves "conquered." They adopted many of the innovations of Sumerian life, and so perpetuated the civilization of their victims. The wheel and the sailing boat, myth and poetry, ceramic and metallurgical techniques, agricultural methods and reckoning of

***Victory in Egypt** (Palette of Narmer, front and back):* *Narmer, king of Upper Egypt, became the first pharaoh and began the political history of Egyptian civilization by conquering the lands of his rival, the king of Lower Egypt (c. 3100 B.C.E.). On the front of the slate palette commemorating the victory from Hierakonpolis (left), Narmer seizes his enemy by the hair and raises his mace to strike. Below his feet are represented two of his defeated foes.* (Egyptian Museum, Cairo)

weights and measures developed by the civilization of Sumer, and above all its system of writing were used by the Akkadians as well. Cuneiform writing, which had recorded the Sumerian language (now dead), passed into the service of a Semitic language which even today has many relatives.

Like all other kingdoms, Sargon's eventually fell—in the reign of his descendant Naramsin, around 2250 B.C.E. Now, wrote a contemporary, Akkad's "canalboat towpaths grew nothing but weeds," the chariot roads were overgrown, and "no human being walks because of the wild goats, vermin, snakes, and mountain scorpions." The Sumerian cities briefly revived around 2100 B.C.E. under the leadership of the Third Dynasty of Ur. Then, early in the second millennium B.C.E., control of the region was seized by Babylon, capital of a Semitic people called the Amorites. The Amorites migrated from Syria to the Mesopotamian valley around 1900 B.C.E. and established themselves not far from Akkad. Among their kings was the renowned Hammurabi, codifier of the laws (see Chapter 1).

After 1600 B.C.E., other rulers displaced the descendants of Hammurabi in the Mesopotamian heartland. Dynasty yielded to dynasty over 1500 years, leaving behind destroyed cities, lost peoples, and memories of great deeds. Meanwhile, new and energetic kingdoms were forming farther west, in Asia Minor and around the Mediterranean.

BRONZE AGE KINGDOMS IN THE AEGEAN AND THE NEAR EAST

While the power of Mesopotamian and Egyptian monarchs was at its zenith, peoples speaking Indo-European languages spread into many parts of Europe and Asia. Their strong kingdoms would challenge those of the senior civilizations, while they easily overcame their lesser rivals. Of these new kingdoms, the Mycenaean and Hittite were the first to flourish.

The Arrival of the Indo-Europeans

By 2000 B.C.E., the long migrations of Indo-European speakers from their barren homelands north of the Black and Caspian seas ended, and they settled in new and more hospitable regions closer to the centers of civilization (see Chapter 1 and Map 2.2). They had pushed west and northwest into Europe as far as Iceland; south and east into India; south into Iran; and south and west into the Balkans, Greece, and Asia Minor. They brought with them new gods and goddesses, swift horses, and a militarist tradition.

Indo-European peoples brought to their new homes a religion centered on the worship of a preeminent sky god, the wielder of lightning and thunder. This deity appears among the Aryan settlers of India with the name Dyaus Pitar, among the Greeks as Zeus, among the Romans as Jupiter (note the similarity in the sounds of the names).

Indo-European tribesmen were master horsemen. Hitching a light cart to their racing mounts, they created the chariot of ancient warfare. Unlike the noble warriors of Mesopotamia or Egypt, they followed chiefs into battle who owed no allegiance to an all-powerful king. When the united tribes needed a leader, the chiefs together chose one of their number, who ruled with only a limited mandate and no expectation of hereditary succession.

The culture of the newcomers—their language, use of horses, and patterns of authority—impressed itself on the peoples among whom they settled. At the same time, the natives' culture supplied elements that

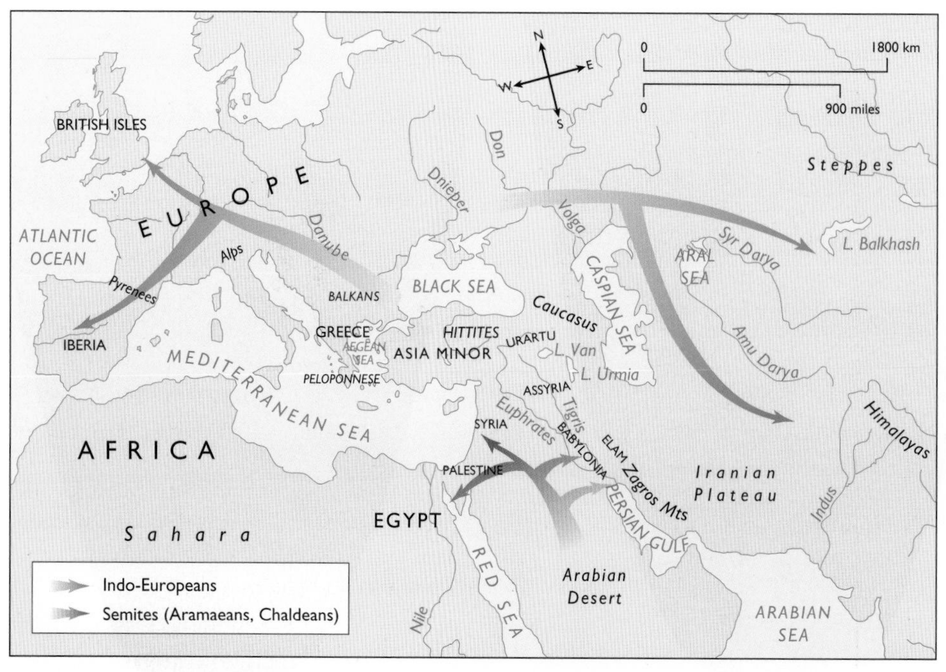

Map 2.2 Semitic and Indo-European Speakers, 3000–2000 B.C.E.: *Although the pioneers of civilization, the Sumerians, spoke a language now extinct, most of the founders of the Middle-Eastern kingdoms spoke either a Semitic (or related Hamitic) or an Indo-European language. During the third and second millennia B.C.E., speakers of both language groups were on the move.*

the invaders' lacked. The word "ocean," absent from the vocabulary of a people whose entire past was on the land-locked **steppes**, was borrowed from the Mediterranean people they conquered. The word *thalassa*, meaning "sea," was absorbed into early Greek from the non-Indo-European language of the indigenous Aegean people.

Civilizations of the Aegean and Asia Minor

Two Indo-European kingdoms grew to dominate the region around the Aegean Sea. One, the Mycenaean, occupied part of the Greek mainland and its islands; the other, the Hittite, controlled the area of Asia Minor. Both were characterized by strong monarchies and an aggressive program of expansion.

The Indo-Europeans who migrated south through the Balkans and settled in mainland Greece were the ancestors of the Greeks. Intermingling with native populations, whom they easily subdued, they created a new civilization, discovered only in the last hundred years or so. It is called Mycenaean, after **Mycenae**, the name given by archaeologists to one of the chief cities excavated and one which may possibly be the kingdom of Mycenae in Homer's *Iliad*. Other Mycenaean sites have been located at Thebes (not to be confused with the Egyptian city of that name) and at Tiryns, Pylos, Corinth, and Athens.

Mycenaean civilization revered horses and cherished weapons. The treasuries of kings were packed with the implements of war, crafted in bronze—helmets, shields, swords, knives, the parts of chariots. The same objects were found in the tombs of Mycenaean kings, as was the mask depicted on p. 40. These took two forms: shaft graves under the earth (c. 1600 B.C.E.) and after about 1500 B.C.E. "beehive" or **tholos** tombs, huge earthwork mounds constructed on the surface. More than eighty of these monuments have been uncovered, the largest reaching to a height of over 43 feet (13 m.).

The military focus of Mycenaean civilization is visible in the fortified palaces of its kings. Mycenaean monarchs ruled self-sufficient but loosely allied city-states. The king's residence was a complex arranged around the central hall where the business of state was managed. Here the king and his consort sat enthroned before a sacred hearth, symbolic of the hearth of the whole city. Other rooms and storehouses radiating around the central hall housed an army of bureaucrats, who administered the king's land, treasure, and trading ventures.

Beyond the royal precinct was the city itself, populated mainly by artisans, and enclosed by massive stone walls pierced by an imposing gate, as shown in *Windows On* on pp. 44–5. Outside the walls were the lands worked by peasants but owned by the priests and the kings' warrior companions.

The primary source of wealth for the kings and their companions was the booty taken by raiding other communities in the Aegean region. Profits came also from trade. Mycenaeans participated in the commercial networks of the eastern Mediterranean in the second millennium B.C.E. Their sailing ships reached Crete and Asia Minor, Egypt, and the eastern shore of the Mediterranean. Their excellent pottery, decorated with their favorite themes of men in battle, circulated all over the region. An example is shown in *Windows On* on p. 61.

The roaming Mycenaeans absorbed many important lessons from neighboring peoples. Above all, they were influenced by the Minoan civilization, the first to develop in Europe, which was established around 2200 B.C.E. on the island of Crete, south of the Greek mainland. Cretan kings lived in expansive palace complexes that extended up to three acres (1.2 ha.) and had two or three stories. Palace walls were painted with **frescoes** and these rooms were supplied with bathrooms, running water, and sewage systems. Within the royal precincts were organized the region's food supply and manufactures, the inventories carefully documented on clay tablets. Or so it is presumed: the tablets cannot be read, as the language spoken on Crete has not been deciphered.

Crete had no true cities, no walls, and no fortifications—unique in these respects among the civilizations of the ancient Middle East. Its commercial relations with the Syrian cities and the ports of Egypt suggest strong cultural links with those regions. Around 1450 B.C.E., Mycenaean Greeks conquered Crete and inherited its cultural traditions. For the next two centuries, the lands west of the Aegean were under the power of the Mycenaean kings, until these also perished.

Across the Aegean Sea, the Indo-European people called the Hittites established their own kingdom in the mountainous interior of Asia Minor (modern Turkey). This was the first civilization not located on a river or the ocean coast. By 1500 B.C.E., the Hittites had established their capital at Hattusas (modern Bogazköy). In that inhospitable setting, possessing only thin soil, the Hittites nevertheless organized themselves as a rich and powerful nation. They seem to have been the first people to smelt iron successfully (although their warriors continued to use armor and weapons made of bronze).

Innovators in iron technology, the Hittites showed themselves willing to learn skills from their neighbors. They were the first major Indo-European people to absorb, to a substantial degree, Mesopotamian culture: writing, religion, political organization, and more. The Hittites were earnest recorders of commercial and administrative data, as the 10,000 or so of their surviving cuneiform tablets attest. In the political arena, their conception that a "covenant," like a contract, defined the relations between ruler and

The Tombs of Rulers

The "mask of Agamemnon": *When we die, we leave our wealth behind, but ancient kings tried to take it with them. Buried in the tholos tombs of the Mycenaean kings are all the glittering bronze helmets, spears and daggers, chariot wheels, and armor that those warriors were likely to require in the afterlife. The so-called "mask of Agamemnon" from Mycenae, c. 1500 B.C.E., which was excavated from a grave circle shaft, records the features of one such king.* (National Archaeological Museum, Athens)

ruled may underlie the conception found in the Hebrew Bible of a "covenant" between God and his "chosen people."

Like other Indo-European peoples, the warlike Hittites were, by tradition, expert horsemen and chariot drivers. From their ancestors they had also inherited the tribal custom of electing their kings. These rulers were selected by a council of nobles and, unlike other Middle Eastern monarchs, could not claim divinity or divine favor. No ruler could hold secure power, nor establish a dynasty and an enduring regime. Around 1520 B.C.E., this practice was modified. King Telipinus seized the throne, then compelled the Hittite chiefs to recognize a unified and hereditary dynasty. Under a king who could command their allegiance, the Hittites posed the first challenge to the dominance of Mesopotamia and Egypt.

Within two centuries of Telipinus's coup, Hittite power had grown to rival that of Egypt. King Suppiluliumas (r. c. 1380–1346) was even invited by the young widow of the pharaoh Tutankhamen to send one of his sons to be her husband. Although the marriage never materialized, and the Hittites thus failed to secure a profitable alliance, they pursued power more forcefully, expanding into the neighboring regions of northern Mesopotamia and Syria. Suppiluliumas himself went into battle with an army of about 30,000, which included infantry and chariots (equipped with heavy three-man crews whose task was to charge through enemy lines). He was protected by a bodyguard of seasoned troops.

Under later rulers, Hittite forces reached far enough south and east to harry the rulers of Babylon. To the south and west, the Hittites struggled with Egypt for dominance in the Near Eastern region known as Canaan.

Near Eastern Rivalries and the End of the Bronze Age

Sandwiched between the Hittites, the Mesopotamian kingdoms, and Egypt, small communities of Semitic peoples flourished in Canaan. In the second millennium Canaan was culturally rich and commercially vigorous, but militarily weak. Into this power vacuum the Hittites pushed from the north, the Egyptians from the south.

In the southern part of Canaan, an area later known as Palestine, the Canaanites farmed and herded sheep and clustered in walled cities such as Jericho and Jerusalem. Their religion and culture, including cuneiform writing, were similar to those of neighboring Mesopotamia.

Farther north lay the cities of Syria and Phoenicia (akin to modern Lebanon), which were the commercial crossroads of the ancient Middle East. Through Damascus and Ugarit, Sidon, Byblos, and Tyre streamed the wealth of Egypt and Mesopotamia. Because of the crucial location and cosmopolitan culture of these cities, innovations made here in spoken and written language had an impact on the whole region of the Middle East. In Syria, scribes developed the alphabetic script now used in modified form by many modern languages. The same scribes recorded oral myths and legends of the Canaanite peoples which were circulating through the region.

Following their expulsion of the Hyksos, in about 1570 B.C.E., the Egyptians had pursued an aggressive policy of foreign conquest. In warfare they adopted the horse-drawn chariot introduced by the Hyksos (who had themselves perhaps copied it from the Hittites). Formidably armed, they pushed northeast into Canaan and beyond.

***Chinese warriors:** In northern China the emperor Shi Huangdi was buried with 7000 lifesize terracotta statues of the soldiers, servants, horses, and chariots he wished to protect him in the afterlife, 210 B.C.E..*

One of these New Kingdom pharaohs, Hatshepsut, is the first known of the queens who ruled effectively as surrogates for male relatives. Daughter and wife of deceased pharaohs, Hatshepsut began her reign (c. 1503) by acting as regent for her minor stepson and nephew Thutmose III. When he reached adulthood, she usurped his rule. Her claim to full power is expressed by the honorary beard with which she is depicted in painting and sculpture. She arranged for the celebration of her achievement with a mortuary temple at Deir el-Bahri, one of the great architectural sites on the Nile in Upper Egypt. The reliefs carved on the walls, including those celebrating her divine birth (she considered herself the daughter, through her human mother, of the god Amen) were defaced by order of her successor, Thutmose III.

Hatshepsut herself launched no wars of conquest, but Thutmose III (r. 1479–1447 B.C.E.) engaged in many. With these conquests he created a new imperial role for Egypt. He penetrated western Asia seventeen times, reaching the Euphrates River. Once content to use military force only to police their frontier, Egypt was now, like other kingdoms of the ancient world, organized as a military state.

For the next century and a half after Thutmose's death in 1447 B.C.E., the Egyptians and the Hittites struggled for supremacy in Palestine. The pharaoh Ramses II (r. 1290–1224) finally faced the Hittites at Kadesh in about 1300 B.C.E., a battle that left neither party a victor. The lines of battle are shown on the chart on p. 52. He settled with his Hittite opponents in 1269 B.C.E. in a written treaty of peace—the first known to historians—which survives today in both Hittite and Egyptian versions (see *Witnesses*, p. 42).

This agreement, which established separate spheres of influence in Syria and Palestine, achieved not so much peace as limits to the exploitation of the powerless by competing powers. It is important as a model of the kind of agreement that can be made between different sovereign states. Also, its expressions of peace and material commitment evoke other covenants that were found in ancient civilization, such as that in the Hebrew Bible between Yahweh and the children of Israel.

As the rivalry of the Egyptians and the Hittites drew to a close, the civilizations of the Aegean were on the brink of disaster. Under Mycenaean domination after 1450 B.C.E., Minoan civilization dwindled and disappeared. Not long thereafter, during the years 1250 to 1100 B.C.E., the Mycenaean cities of the mainland, already weakened by social and political stresses, succumbed to invasions, or revolutions, or both. The result was devastation; the Mycenaean centers were literally incinerated. It was the heat of the fire at Pylos around 1200 B.C.E. that accomplished the baking—and thus the preservation—of clay tablets inscribed with royal accounts. After this disaster, the population of Mycenaean cities and even the number of inhabited sites dropped sharply—the population of Pylos fell to 10 percent of what it had been, while the number of Mycenaean sites in the area of Laconia dropped from thirty to seven, in Boeotia from twenty-seven to three. Of 320 sites inhabited in the 1300s, only 40 were known two centuries later. Of the major cities, Athens alone survived, weak and depopulated. The Mycenaean civilization to which it had once belonged vanished utterly.

Shortly before the Mycenaean cities crumbled, they may have joined forces around 1250 B.C.E. to raid Troy. Troy was a city on the Aegean cost of Asia Minor, not far from the Hellespont (the strait separating Greece from Asia Minor and the gateway to Black Sea ports). Six cities stood successively on the same point of land, each abandoned or destroyed in turn before there developed the rather poor one that was the target of the Mycenaean raid. The siege and capture of Troy by the Mycenaeans lingered in folk memory during the period of the "Dark Ages" which followed the collapse of the civilization of the Mycenaean kings. The story reappeared in the epic

WITNESSES

The Quiet Voice of Peace

Amid the warfare endemic in the ancient world, some indications of a desire for peace do appear. In the first of the passages here, a historic treaty is arranged between the Egyptians and the Hittites, the 3000-year-old archetype of subsequent peace treaties in human history. In the second, the Greek poet Homer, who lived some 500 years later, sketches an ideal picture of a world at peace, which is engraved, ironically, on the shield of the hero Achilles, fighter par excellence.

The Egyptians and the Hittites make peace (c. 1269 B.C.E.): Behold, Hattusils, the Great Prince of Hatti, has set himself in a regulation with User-maat-Re Setep-en-Re, the great ruler of Egypt, beginning from this day, to cause that good peace and brotherhood occur between us forever, while he is in brotherhood with me and he is at peace with me, and I am in brotherhood with him and I am at peace with him forever. ... The land of Egypt, with the land of Hatti, shall be at peace and in brotherhood like unto us forever. Hostilities shall not occur between them forever.
(J. B. Pritchard ed., *Ancient Near Eastern Texts relating to the Old Testament*, 2e, 1955)

A vision of peace on the shield of Achilles (c. 750 B.C.E.):

On it [Hephaistos] wrought in all their beauty two cities of mortal
men. And there were marriages in one, and festivals.
They were leading the brides along the city from their maiden chambers
under the flaring of torches, and the loud bride song was arising.
The young men followed the circles of the dance, and among them
the flutes and lyres kept up their clamour as in the meantime
the women standing each at the door of her court admired them. ...
But around the other city were lying two forces of armed men
shining in their war gear.

(Homer, *Iliad*, 18:490–496, 508–509; ed. R. Lattimore, 1951)

poem believed to have been composed by a blind man named Homer around 750 B.C.E. (see Chapter 4). This is the *Iliad*, a sacred book to the ancient Greeks and a classic of Western civilization.

The years around 1200 B.C.E. brought upheaval to other kingdoms of the late Bronze Age. Piratic "Sea Peoples" raided Egypt and threatened the eastern Mediterranean coast. Among these were the Philistines, speakers of an Indo-European language, who had migrated from their Aegean homes to settle on the coast of Canaan. Other invaders, the Indo-European Phrygians, attacked the Hittites, whose civilization, like that of the Mycenaeans, vanished. Both civilizations were forgotten until rediscovered by twentieth-century archaeologists.

The great Bronze Age empires were now dead or in eclipse. In the Iron Age that followed, new nations would contend for power in the Middle East. Iron Age empires are shown on Map 2.3.

IRON AGE EMPIRES OF THE MIDDLE EAST

In the centuries of turmoil following 1200 B.C.E., the small nations along the eastern Mediterranean held the stage in the Middle East. Pioneers of culture and commerce, they seized a brief moment of glory before the iron-wielding giants of late antiquity—Assyria, Babylonia, and Persia—overpowered them. By the middle of the sixth century B.C.E., the Indo-European Persians had created an empire that united and dominated most of the region, including the whole of Egypt and Mesopotamia, where the first civilizations began.

Philistines, Israelites, and Phoenicians

Sometime after 1200 B.C.E., two different peoples, the Philistines and Israelites, arrived in Canaan. The Philistines were expert fighters, well equipped with iron tools and weapons. The Israelites were endowed with a religious and ethical tradition that constituted the world's first major monotheism. Farther north a diverse people joined together as the Phoenicians to develop a different kind of empire—an empire of commerce—facilitated by their navigational, industrial, and communications skills.

Philistines and Israelites The Philistines arrived by sea and established a dominion along the coastal plain, an area that, from the eleventh century B.C.E. onward, was called Palestine. The Hebrew-speaking peoples who would be known first as Israelites and later as Jews arrived from the Sinai Desert. According to the Book of Exodus (chapters 1–15), these were led by Joshua, lieutenant of Moses (who had died during the forty-year migration from his native Egypt). Moses not only had led his people out of Egypt, but also had bestowed upon them, carved in stone, the law code decreed by their one God.

The Israelites, who believed that they were descended from Abraham (whom their tradition depicted as an immigrant to Canaan around 1900 B.C.E.), thought of Canaan as their homeland despite generations of slavery in Egypt. In around 1200 B.C.E. they finally returned to Canaan.

Convinced that they were obeying God's will, the Hebrew-speaking migrants founded the nation of Israel. Joshua's dramatic capture of Jericho (see Chapter 1 and *Witnesses*, p. 36) was allegedly accomplished by faith and the sound of trumpets. In reality, detachments of armed men were required to carve out a domain in a land already thickly settled with inhabitants. Organized after the death of Joshua as a loose confederation of twelve tribes under military leaders called "judges," the Israelites labored persistently to erode the significant power of the Canaanites who dwelled between the Jordan River and the Mediterranean shore.

At the same time, Israelite armies contended with the Philistines who also aimed to relieve the Canaanites of their villages and cities. Disciplined and aggressive, heavily armed with weapons of iron and bronze, the Philistines were extremely formidable opponents of the nomadic Israelites. Despite the Philistines' superior strength, they were subdued in the tenth century by King David of the Israelites. The Philistines' power waned from then on. In the end they retained sovereignty over only five city-states: Gaza, Ashkelon, Ashdod, Gath, and Ekron.

King David was the successor to the first king, Saul. Saul himself had been anointed by the priest Samuel around 1020 B.C.E. although Samuel had warned the Israelites against kings (see *Witnesses*, p. 33) when the inadequacy of the rule of the "judges" became apparent. King David (r. c. 1003–962 B.C.E.)

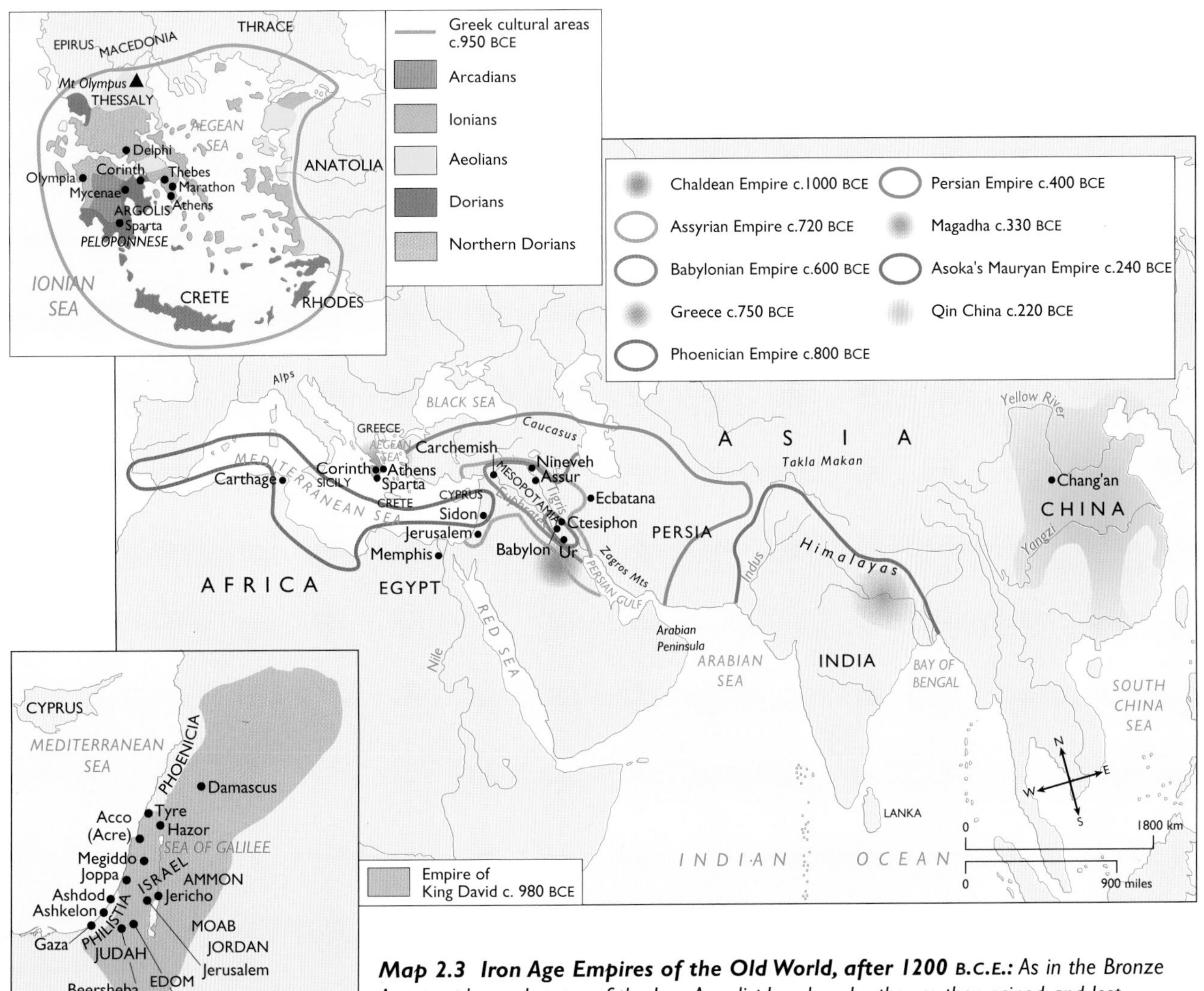

Map 2.3 Iron Age Empires of the Old World, after 1200 B.C.E.: *As in the Bronze Age, peoples and states of the Iron Age displaced each other as they gained and lost territory and supremacy.*

Tools of War

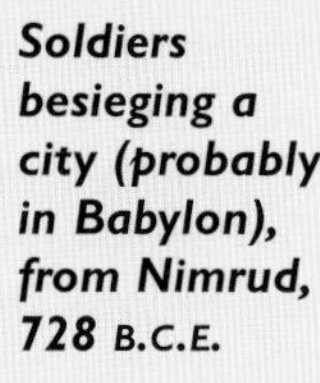

Hand axe, Gray's Inn, London, c. 250,000 B.C.E.

Soldiers besieging a city (probably in Babylon), from Nimrud, 728 B.C.E.

Our human ancestors engaged in violence even before they learned to form or sew clothing, as we see from the stone hand-held axe (top left), a weapon which is a quarter of a million years old. More sophisticated is the ornate carving on the bronze dagger blade, from a shaft grave at Mycenae. As soldiers besiege a city (above) one soldier holds a body shield in front of himself and two others in an early example of teamwork. The relief (below) shows horses and chariot being used in warfare. (Top left: British Museum, London: top right: British Museum, London; center: National Archaeological Museum, Athens; below: British Museum, London)

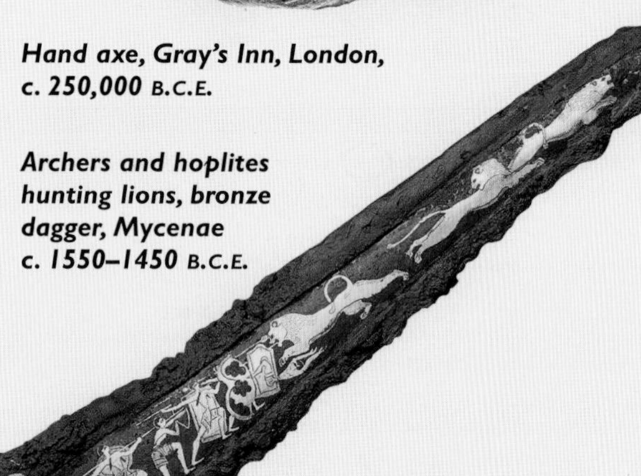

Archers and hoplites hunting lions, bronze dagger, Mycenae c. 1550–1450 B.C.E.

King Ashurnasirpal in chariot, from Nimrud, c. 865 B.C.E.

Assyrian army attacking the city Upa, believed to be the city of Medes 728 B.C.E.

Fortified camp, Nimrud, 870–860 B.C.E.

By the first millennium B.C.E., the notoriously aggressive Assyrians had developed powerful engines of war. The relief (top left) features a line of archers on the right, soldiers scaling the enemy's fortifications with siege ladders, and a wheeled assault chariot assigned with the task of breaching the city's gate. Not long afterwards, the Greeks developed the phalanx, a line of citizen soldiers who charged into battle as though they were a single machine of war, held together by discipline and high morale.

In the relief (center left) a schematic view of a circular fortified camp shows food being prepared and a priest in a flat hat examining entrails of sacrifice. To the right horses are being groomed while, to the far right, a guard stands watch. Depicted on a vase (below left) is a rank of Mycenaean foot-soldiers, with helmets, shields, and spears. Defense was as important as offense. The massive stone Lion Gate to the citadel of Mycenae (below right) assertively expressed the military determination of its masters.

(top: British Museum, London; center: British Museum, London; below left: National Archaeoligical Museum, Athens)

Greek vase, from Mycenae, c. 1300 B.C.E.

Lion Gate, Mycenae, 1500–1300 B.C.E.

To continue your investigation of this topic, please go to www.prenhall.com/king for the related **WINDOWS** on the **WEB** activity

unified the Israelites into a nation. He captured the city of Jerusalem from its Canaanite inhabitants and established it as his capital. Here he hoped to build a temple to Yahweh that would house the Ark of the Covenant, the shrine containing the two stone tablets inscribed with the Ten Commandments.

David's objectives were realized by his son and successor, Solomon (r. 962–922 B.C.E.). Surrounded by soldiers and advisers, a bureaucracy and a harem, Solomon reigned in splendor. He built the temple and fortified and adorned the capital, including some magnificent royal palaces. This extravagance (at odds with his legendary wisdom) was resented by his heavily-taxed subjects, and on his death the kingdom split into two parts. The northern state comprised ten of the twelve original tribes and was known as the kingdom of Israel. The southern state, centered on the temple at Jerusalem and comprising the other two tribes, was known as the kingdom of Judah.

The people of Judah would later become known as Jews, and their religion as Judaism. By the time of Solomon, many of the formative experiences of the Jewish people had already occurred (see Chapter 1). But their ethical, monotheistic faith had yet to reach maturity. It would do so during the period of exile that followed the defeat of both Israel and Judah by, respectively, Assyria and Babylon.

While the kingdoms of Israel and Judah were still taking shape in Palestine, the communities to the north crystallized. These were peopled by Semitic natives, Philistine and Canaanite refugees from the south, and Aramaean immigrants from desert regions to the east. The latter established strongholds throughout the region (in modern-day Syria), including the important commercial center of Damascus. Their language, Aramaic, replaced Akkadian as the common language of the Middle East, and would become the official language of the Persian empire. This language maintained its primacy into the period of Greek domination.

The Phoenicians The Phoenicians, another Canaanite people, were established in the narrow zone west of Syria between the Lebanon mountains and the Mediterranean coast (modern Lebanon). Along that coast stood their principal cities: Tyre, Byblos, and Sidon. The Phoenicians continued to practice the religious rites of Canaan, which included child and animal sacrifice and temple prostitution. At the same time, they possessed the most advanced culture of the whole region. The best-skilled sailors of antiquity (their navigation guided by sightings of the North Star), the Phoenicians not only traded with the coastal cities of the eastern Mediterranean but also colonized its western shores. They founded Carthage on the north coast of Africa (modern Tunis) in 814 B.C.E., and reached as far west as Spain and the mouth of the Atlantic.

Wherever they traveled, the Phoenicians purveyed a reddish-purple dye extracted from a marine snail of the genuses *Murex* or *Purpura* (from which the name "purple" is derived). So costly was Tyrian purple that the color became associated with power. Cherished by royalty and nobility, who alone could afford it, the dye colored the robes of kings and, later—in the form of a modest stripe—the white togas of Roman senators. The Phoenicians also exported cedar from the forests of Lebanon and transported luxury goods from remoter parts of Asia. They spread abroad the alphabetic script their ancestors had devised, and supplied ancient empires with mercenary warriors. Yet these enterprising, literate, and wealthy Phoenicians were no match for the later empires that successively dominated the Mediterranean and the Middle East from the seventh century B.C.E.

Assyria, Babylon, and Persia

The Iron Age dawned in about 1200 B.C.E. when the iron-smelting technology developed by the Hittites began to spread rapidly through the Middle East. Iron was now available to make swords and spears and knives for a whole army. So equipped, an opportunistic king could rule not only a kingdom but an empire.

The Assyrians The kings of Assyria were the first to exploit iron for this purpose. Located at the northern bend of the Fertile Crescent, the cities of Assur and Nineveh successively served as capitals for Assyrian kings. The Semitic people they ruled had been established there since the third millennium B.C.E. and had absorbed the main features of Mesopotamian culture. From the thirteenth to the tenth centuries, they had been harassed by the Hurrians of Mittani (a people probably originating in Armenia before their expansion into Anatolia and Mesopotamia), and challenged by the Aramaean tribes of the northern Euphrates and Syria. Now, beginning in about 900 B.C.E., they began to expand into neighboring kingdoms. The Hittites were gone. There was room for a new, aggressive contender in this maelstrom of nations.

The Assyrians were equipped with an experienced army, unprecedented weapon strength, and relentless ferocity. For the Assyrians, war was a profession and a commitment, as the name of their first capital indicated: for Assur was the Assyrian god of war and chief god in their pantheon. Their art, too, glorified war. Their cult of strength is expressed by the bulls and lions, crouching, leaping, and dying, some bearded and half-human, carved in relief or monumentalized in statues in their palace complexes. These savage creatures and their human companions told the stories of Assyrian conquest.

The ferocity expressed in those images was not lost on the peoples unlucky enough to fall to the Assyrian advance. Assyrian kings went to war each year, and viciously subdued the conquered. King Assurnasirpal II (r. c. 884–859 B.C.E.) excelled in the ruthless tactics that won Assyria infamy (see *Witnesses*, p. 36). In the wake of victory, he ordered the mass deportation of whole populations. These captives were brought back to Assyria as slave laborers and set to work building the walls, towers, and palaces on which was brazenly proclaimed in sculpted relief the relentless power of their masters.

Each monarch surrounded himself with a personal bodyguard or security force—the troops, as these kings often described them, "who in a place hostile or friendly never leave my feet." In addition to these, the monarch commanded a standing army of faithful Assyrians, and a "grand army," numbering some 100,000 to 200,000—certainly the largest assembled to that date—which included auxiliaries drawn from conquered provinces.

At the head of this force marched standard-bearers and priests. At the rear followed engineers, specialists in Assyrian technology, with equipment for bridge- and road-building, portable ramps, and battering rams. In between were ranks of heavy and light infantry, spearmen, archers, and slingers. Here, too, were chariot and cavalry units, for the Assyrians brought the management of horses in warfare to a new level of efficiency. The later armies of the Persians, of the Macedonians, and of the Romans profited from Assyrian innovations in tactical military organization.

To this vast human and material force, the Assyrians added psychological weapons: they deliberately broadcast far and wide warnings of their brutal tactics. Such warnings of rape and mayhem and massacre often sufficed to deter a defeated enemy from harassing the conqueror with guerrilla counterattacks. Better still was to release a few wounded prisoners of high rank to describe to their compatriots the might of the conqueror: "Their leaders, men who understood battle and who had fled before my weapons," crowed Sargon II (r. 722–705 B.C.E.), "drew near to them covered with the venom of death, and recounted to them the glory of Assur, ... so that they became like dead men."

In the eighth century B.C.E., the Assyrian king Tiglathpileser III (r. 745–727 B.C.E.) seized the Aramaean kingdom centered at Damascus, in north Syria, and pushed into Arabia. A successful conqueror, he was also an efficient manager. He built roads, started a postal service, and trimmed provincial government. His successors Shalmaneser V (r. 727–722 B.C.E.) and Sargon II destroyed the northern kingdom of Israel and deported its people. The tens of thousands of captives said to have been marched back to Assyria to slave on construction projects subsequently lost their national identity. These were the "Ten Lost Tribes" of the ancient Israelites. The Assyrians recolonized Israel's former territory (now known as Samaria) with foreigners, and these intermingled with the resident population to form the "Samaritan" culture (despised in the time of Jesus for its lukewarm or lapsed Judaism).

Sargon's son Sennacherib (r. 705–681 B.C.E.), having relocated the Assyrian capital to Nineveh, crushed the Phoenicians, north of Samaria, and captured forty of the fortified cities of the kingdom of Judah, whose king, Hezekiah (r. 787–699 B.C.E.), was stranded in Jerusalem. By the end of the seventh century B.C.E., the Assyrians controlled all the lands arching upward from Egypt, through Palestine and Asia Minor, and down to the Persian Gulf.

Although known for power and cruelty, Assyria made some important cultural contributions to the ancient world. Its huge cities were filled with vital, awe-inspiring sculpture commissioned by Assyrian kings. From Nineveh, their later capital, Assyria's conquest-hungry rulers managed state affairs with competence and even benevolence. Their skills built the first true empire, encompassing not only related peoples and kingdoms but a **polyglot** assortment of unrelated states. The Assyrians encouraged the general use of the Aramaic language throughout their domain (in preference to their native Akkadian), and through this medium, the accumulated culture of the whole of Mesopotamia was disseminated.

Among the cultural achievements of the Assyrians, none exceeds those of King Ashurbanipal (r. 668–631 B.C.E.), who died only nineteen years before the extinction of the Assyrian Empire. This grandson of the conqueror Sennacherib created at Nineveh a major research library. It contained about 22,000 clay tablets, consisting mainly of literature useful for magicians and priests. But it also included, on twelve tablets, the Akkadian version of the epic of *Gilgamesh* which is our main source of this work. Editions of other works of literature were standardized by the critical skills of Assyrian scribes, who also recorded the deeds of their kings. Ashurbanipal ordered his agents to gather works of which there were not yet any copies known in their homeland: "If you hear of any tablet or ritualistic text that is suitable for the palace," he instructed them, "seek it out, secure it, and send it here." His empire fell, but many of the works from his library survive.

The Babylonians Assyria aroused the envy of its neighbors. In 612 B.C.E., the two independent nations of the Chaldeans, centered at Babylon, and the Medes, centered at Ecbatana, united to defeat the oppressor. The allied forces captured and obliterated Nineveh, visiting upon it the same savage destruction that the Assyrians had so often inflicted on the cities of their foes.

As fruits of victory, the Chaldeans assumed the domination of the Fertile Crescent, while the Medes consolidated their power on the Iranian plateau, to

WHO'S WHO

Hittites, Israelites, and Assyrians

Suppiluliumas (c.1380–1346 B.C.E) the Hittites' greatest king expands their boundaries.

David (1003–962 B.C.E) unites the Hebrew-speaking kingdoms of Israel and Judah, and founds city of Jerusalem.

Solomon (962–922 B.C.E.) David's son; erects the first temple at Jerusalem.

King Assurnasirpal (r. 884–859 B.C.E.) launches military terror tactics; begins process of Assyrian expansion.

King Ashurbanipal (r. 668–631 B.C.E) last Assyrian king; palace-builder and creator of one of the first great libraries.

the north. Among the other main contenders for power in the Middle East were a fading Egypt and the new state of the Lydians, in Asia Minor. Babylonian armies wrested Syria and Palestine from the pharaoh, whom they defeated at Carchemish (in modern Turkey) in 605 B.C.E., and asserted their authority in that corridor.

In 597 B.C.E., the Babylonians suppressed a revolt in Judah, deporting the king, his family, and 8000 leaders. When the remnant of the nation rebelled a second time, the Babylonians spared no one. In 586 B.C.E., they seized Jerusalem and blinded King Zedekiah and his sons so that they could cause no more trouble. The nation of the Jews (excepting the poorest, who were left behind) was marched to captivity in Babylon, where for forty-seven years two generations of priests and scholars would reflect on the meaning of their history and their exile.

Babylon at this brief moment of its supremacy—between the fall of Nineveh in 612 B.C.E. and its conquest by the Persians in 539 B.C.E.—was a cosmopolitan city, filled with boulevards and lovely parks. Bold public buildings formed a palace complex and temple precinct, on whose glazed brick walls strode fantastic beasts. According to legend, King Nebuchadnezzar II (or Nebuchadrezzar; r. 605–562 B.C.E.) built in his palace for his consort Amytis, a Median princess, the Hanging Gardens, constructed on stone arches above ground and watered by the Euphrates through a sophisticated engineering system. Babylon was both a center of luxury and the cultural capital of the Middle East. Here philosophers observed the heavens and created astronomy, which later they would teach to the Greeks.

The study of astronomy caught the imagination of King Nabonidus (r. 556–539 B.C.E.), who was one of Nebuchadnezzar's successors. Nabonidus was an ardent adherent of a moon cult. As a scholar, like Ashurbanipal of Assyria, and as a mystic, like Akhenaten of Egypt, he promoted his heretical cult over the objections of the priests of the traditional and heretofore unchallenged god Marduk. These priests took advantage of the King's unpopularity—in a time when Babylon was afflicted by famine and illness—to lead an uprising against him. He was forced into exile, leaving his son Belshazzar as regent.

The Persians In 539 B.C.E., the priests conspired to open the gates of Babylon to the Persian army waiting outside the walls. The Persians seized Babylon and its empire and established their sway over the whole Middle East. These events are the subject of the Book of Daniel, in which the Jewish scholar Daniel decodes for Belshazzar the fatal "writing on the wall" which tells of the impending fall of his kingdom.

The craft of empire building that the Hittites had learned from Mesopotamia, that Egypt learned from the Hyksos and the Hittites, that Assyria learned from its warrior neighbors, the Medes learned from Assyria, and the Persians borrowed from the Medes. During the last generations of Assyrian kings, the Medes, with their subjects and dependents, including, ironically, the Persians, had been building a desert state to the east of Assyria. By 625 B.C.E., they had become an independent kingdom under their king Cyaxerxes (r. 625–585 B.C.E.). In 612 B.C.E., they joined the Chaldeans in the sack of Nineveh. Before their forces were able to venture farther westward, the Persian subject king Cyrus II, called the Great (r. c. 550–529 B.C.E.), ousted the Median king in a swift ***coup d'état***. He then set about expanding his domain. Within the next twenty years the Persians created an empire reaching from the Mediterranean to the Indus River.

As the Assyrians excelled at war, the Persians excelled at domination, thanks largely to their policy of toleration. The kings who ruled from 550 to 486 B.C.E.—Cyrus, Cambyses, Darius—all permitted their subjects to practice their native customs and religions. This policy won the support of the conquered, or at least made the condition of servitude more endurable. Tolerance of the ethnic and cultural distinctiveness of each people was a new value in the political world of antiquity—a principle that would endure, if often violated, into our own time.

Cyrus conquered Lydia in about 546 B.C.E., and Babylonia, Palestine, and Syria in 539–538 B.C.E. He liberated the Jews from their "Babylonian Captivity," as this exile became known, and allowed them to return to their homeland (now re-organized as the Persian province of Judaea) to reestablish their temple and their reinvigorated faith. Cambyses (r. 529–522 B.C.E.) conquered Egypt in 525 B.C.E., terminating the independence of that most enduring of kingdoms. Darius (r. 522–486 B.C.E.) pushed into Europe north of the Black Sea and across the Aegean, into the Balkans.

WHO'S WHO

Persians and Chaldeans (Babylon)

Nebuchadnezzer (r. 605–562 B.C.E.) conqueror of Judah; deports the Jewish people wholesale to his splendid city of Babylon, capital of the short-lived Chaldean Empire.

Cyrus (r. 550–529 B.C.E.) seizes leadership from the Medes for the Persian people and conquers much of the Middle East, including Babylon.

Darius (r. 522–486 B.C.E.) launches Persian attempt to conquer Greece.

King Darius set a new standard in the efficient governing of an empire. He directly controlled only his ceremonial capital, Persepolis (in modern Iran). From his administrative capital at Susa, Darius governed his vast empire through officials called **satraps**, each of whom had charge of a province. The satraps collected the tribute due the King of Kings (as the Persian rulers styled themselves) and kept the peace, closely watched by the military commanders of local garrisons and financial officers that Darius also appointed in each province.

The tireless Darius read the reports submitted in writing by all three sets of officials and cross-checked to make sure that they were all in agreement. In addition, he appointed traveling inspectors to supervise all of the provincial officials. To enable this network of officials and bureaucrats to function, he had an immense highway system constructed. The Royal Road (which the Romans would later imitate; see Chapter 6) stretched across the empire from Susa to Sardis (in modern Turkey), spanning a vast 1000 miles (1600 km.).

The Persian conquest of the ancient Middle East was decisive. The Persians had forged into a political and cultural unity the proliferating kingdoms of an earlier era, the culmination of a struggle for empire that had engaged the Middle East from the creation of the first civilizations. That political and cultural unity persisted even as—in the centuries that followed—Persian rule succumbed to Greek and Parthian, Sassanid and Roman, Arab and Turkish leadership.

BRONZE AND IRON AGE KINGDOMS IN EAST AND SOUTH ASIA

While Egyptians, Hittites, Assyrians, Persians, and others were competing for power in the Middle East, advanced civilizations coalesced in east and south Asia (see Map 2.1). Around 1557 B.C.E., the Shang rulers of China established a kingdom on the Yellow River (Huang He). Later dynasties refined the principles and mechanisms of Chinese rule, which were, by the end of the Han dynasty (220 C.E.) the most advanced in the world. In India, Aryan conquerors invading around 1750 B.C.E. created a civilization that briefly achieved political unification.

Heaven's Mandate in China

Over nearly 2000 years, Chinese monarchs labored to create a strong, centralized kingdom. It was the divine will, they believed, that such political unity be achieved, and they ruled by the command or "mandate" of heaven.

Around 1557 B.C.E. in east Asia, the Shang kings conquered and unified the cities of the Yellow River (Huang He) valley, establishing themselves as rulers of this region. Central to their government was a dynastic cult, managed by priests, which involved the worship of the royal ancestors upon whose favor the welfare of the state depended. As in the Middle East and the Aegean, royal tombs were loaded with the various trappings of power: treasures of jewels and bronze and even, in one case, a whole chariot with its horse and driver.

Shang rulers were supported by a nobility as well as a priesthood. As in the Middle East, the nobility consisted of trusted warriors, who followed the king into battle, riding in chariots and wielding spear and bow. In return for their loyal service, they expected, and received, gifts of land and valuables.

During the eleventh century B.C.E., a tribe from the northwest, specialists in breeding and deploying horses, overwhelmed the Shang and established the Zhou dynasty (to 221 B.C.E.). Coming to power as conquerors, they asserted their legitimacy by claiming to rule by the special will, or "mandate," of Heaven—a claim that would be repeated by Chinese rulers over the next 3000 years. The Zhou monarchy was precarious, however, unable to control a powerful nobility obsessed with war. The conflicts between these warlords culminated in the period of the Warring States (c. 450–221 B.C.E.), which overshadowed the last years of the weakened Zhou dynasty.

Despite weak kings and restive nobles, China flourished under the Zhou dynasty. Over the 800-plus years of its tenure, the population grew and commerce flourished, as did the many schools of philosophy that sprang to life. Several philosophical schools prescribed political goals strikingly absent from the Zhou regime: a strong central government, the rule of law, and a well-trained, selfless, and peaceable class of government officials. This last recommendation was particularly dear to Confucius.

Those noisy schools of thought would be silenced by the short-lived Qin dynasty (221–206 B.C.E.). The Qin came to power amid the chaos of late Zhou rule, about the time that iron replaced bronze in the

WHO'S WHO

In China and India

Chandragupta Maurya (r. 321–298 B.C.E.) carves out an empire in northern India.

Asoka (r. 272–232 B.C.E.) grandson of Chandragupta; renounces war to take up good works and promote Buddhism.

Shi Huangdi (r. 221–210/209 B.C.E.) foremost emperor of brief Qin dynasty which gives China its name; launches the building of the Great Wall and has philosophical books burned.

region. The Qin crushed local warlords and restored order, establishing thirty-six territories, each commanded by trained officials loyal only to the emperor, chosen for their talent and their freedom from ties of clan and friendship. Throughout the country, standard systems were established for weights and measures, for writing, for the value of coins, and even for the width of the axle of each cart that traveled on the country's well-planned roads.

Also standardized was the life of the mind. A halt was called to the splendid profusion of philosophical thought of the late Zhou era—for that had been the classical age when Chinese thinkers produced a "Hundred Schools of Flowers" and Confucius and Lao Zi flourished. Only technical books and manuals were now permitted, friendly to imperial rule and housed in the imperial library. In 213 B.C.E. the first Qin emperor, Shi Huangdi (r. 221–210/209 B.C.E.), ordered burned the books he didn't like—any that did not concern such practical matters as agriculture, medicine, or magic. When scholars protested against this destruction, 460 of them were executed and thrown into a common grave.

Such tyrannical behavior must be weighed against Shi Huangdi's most famous achievement: the Great Wall which joined together a series of walls previously built by local magnates to ward off external enemies. Standing 25 feet (7.6 m.) high, 20 feet (6.1 m.) wide, and equipped with 25,000 towers, the Great Wall extends 1400 miles (2253 km.). Equally astonishing, in a different way, is Shi Huangdi's mausoleum. Within this vast tomb is buried, along with the Emperor's own body, an army of more than 7000 life-size statues of warriors made of terracotta and bronze (see p. 41). Soon after Shi Huangdi's death, Qin rule was replaced by the Han dynasty, who carried forward the achievements of their predecessors.

Aryans and Emperors in India

Spreading southeast into India from around 1750 B.C.E., Indo-European peoples establised a new civilization in the Ganges River valley. These newcomers conquered the survivors of the Indus civilization, which had probably begun to fail even before the newcomers arrived, as well as the indigenous peoples of northern India. These Indo-Europeans called themselves "Aryans." The ancient connotations of the word were "honor" and "liberty," but in modern history its association with Nazi racial theory has lent it an unfortunate meaning. The same word is echoed in "Iran," the region settled by the Indo-European peoples who eventually came to be known as the Medes and Persians.

The Aryans were relentless warrior-charioteers who worshiped war gods such as the storm god Indra, who also conquered with horse and chariot. Memories of the age of Aryan conquest are stored in the later epic poems *Mahabharata* and *Ramayana*, classics of world literature. The civilization that emerged, a blend of the customs of Aryans and natives, is notable not only for its epic literature but also for its religious creativity. This creativity is displayed in the literature of the Vedic age, which followed the conquest. That age is named for the *Vedas*, or hymns, which were its first cultural product, and which culminate in the *Upanishads* with their yearning for other-worldy enlightenment. The Vedas were transmitted orally for more than a thousand years until writing was reinvented on the subcontinent.

The guardians of this tradition at once religious, literary, and ethnic were the brahmans, or priests, who formed an elite social class. In the pattern of social hierarchy that the brahmans prescribed, they themselves occupied the first rank. Below them in descending order were the classes of warriors, merchants, farmers, and laborers, and, in last place, the servile "untouchables," those with no social identity whatsoever. Within each category, females were ranked as inferior to males.

This brahmanic system did not exist in reality. But a hierarchical social structure far more complex did develop in which every individual belonged by birth to a particular social unit, or *jati*, loosely grouped within the brahmanic categories. That identification strictly limited his or her opportunities for social mobility or advancement—more so than the barriers that separated the classes of most other societies. People lived, intermarried, and even ate with members of their caste and no other. Originating in the Vedic age, these boundaries solidified into the **caste** system that in modern times so troubled observers from the more democratic nations of the West.

The sub-continent of India resisted unification; its civilization developed in the Vedic period without a centralized state structure. But by around 300 B.C.E. Chandragupta Maurya (r. 321–298 B.C.E.) had founded the Mauryan Empire in northern India; a true Golden Age emerged. Chandragupta was a near-contemporary of Alexander the Great (see below), whose followers had occupied and then left the Indus region. Chandragupta conquered the lands vacated by the Greeks, and established an empire extending from the Himalayan passes to the Bay of Bengal.

Chandragupta's achievement was overshadowed by that of his grandson Asoka (r. 272–232 B.C.E.), one of the most renowned of India's rulers (see *Witnesses*, p. 33). After some initial military ventures which he later regretted, Asoka, a convert to Buddhism, instituted the "Law of Piety." Renouncing war and promoting peace, he followed its enlightened precepts over his reign's last three decades. Out of respect for animal life, he ate only vegetables. He built inns, parks, hospitals, and veterinary clinics. His agents traveled extensively, supervising local administrations and guaranteeing the equitable treatment of his subjects. He himself traveled frequently and widely to ensure the observance of his laws. These he had inscribed in stone on tall limestone pillars erected throughout his dominions for all to view. Asoka's empire endured only fifty years after his death.

THE BIRTH OF THE WEST

A century before the ascendancy of Shi Huangdi in China or Asoka in India, a European empire had displaced the Persian Empire, marking the first entry of a Western power into the contest of nations. This empire was the creation of an obscure Balkan prince known to history as Alexander the Great (356–323 B.C.E.). By the time of his death, a little more than two centuries after Cyrus the Great swept to power, Alexander had established his supremacy in his native Macedonia, in mainland Greece, and over the ancient nations of the Middle East. But Alexander's Empire was grounded in more than his matchless talent and the might of his army. It had as its foundation the whole civilization of classical Greece. That civilization had evolved quietly over the previous four centuries.

Greece, Europe, and the West

In the age of the Sumerians and Egyptians, or that of the Hittites and Assyrians, there was no "Greece." The Mycenaeans who dominated the Aegean region during the second millennium B.C.E. spoke a language now known to be an early form of Greek. After the close of Mycenaean civilization and the interval of the Dark Ages, there emerged a new and distinctive Greek-speaking civilization. That civilization was called "**Hellenic**" by its contemporaries and, later, "Greek," by the Romans and their successors. Influenced by the traditions of neighboring Africa and Asia, which in turn it would dramatically and radically transform, Hellenic civilization would even more profoundly influence the later civilizations of Europe and of the Islamic world.

What we call "Western Civilization" today has its roots in ancient Greece, although the Greeks, at first, did not see themselves as "Western"—and indeed made no distinction between "West" and "East." Southeastern Europe belonged to the same cultural world as western Asia and northeastern Africa. Indeed, although the nation we call Greece belongs (apart from its islands) to the European mainland, ancient Greece included settlements on the coast of Asia Minor, as well as colonies throughout the Mediterranean and Black Sea regions. The poet Homer was born on the Asian, not the European, shore of the Aegean. The *Iliad*, Homer's epic tale of the siege and destruction of Troy, shows no conception of the Asian enemy as alien. The Trojans (as the poet imagined them) lived in a Greek city, worshiped Greek gods, and shared Greek funeral customs and concepts of personal honor.

About 300 years after Homer composed his epic *Iliad*, the Greeks' first historian, Herodotus (485–425 B.C.E.), wrote the Western world's first history. Like Homer, Herodotus viewed the Greek realm as part of the Near East. His inquiry into the origins of his people opens with a leisurely tour of the civilizations of the eastern Mediterranean. But it is with Herodotus that the "West" first distinguishes itself from the "East." He identifies as the critical event of his age the Persian Wars fought in the first decades of the fifth century B.C.E., in which a few Greek cities opposed that great empire. Persian armies twice crossed over the barrier of the Aegean between Asia and Europe, and were twice repulsed by the Greeks. When the tiny armies of the defiant Greek cities vanquished the hordes of the Persian imperial army, the ways of the "West" (as Herodotus and his contemporaries saw these events) triumphed over those of the "East." This bloody war fought with iron weapons was not only a political struggle, but a war between competing visions of human society and aspiration.

The civilization that Herodotus knew was a relatively young one, by the standards of the ancient world, although it had its roots in the much older one of Mycenaea. With the destruction or decline of Mycenaean centers after 1200 B.C.E., the elaborate palace communities, the advanced skills of a multiplicity of artisans, the ability to write were all lost. In the villages of mainland Greece, only a few potters and smiths continued to ply their trade. Their manufactures were used only by the local population of farmers and fishermen, for trade had ceased. And those farmers and fishermen faced starvation.

This period of poverty and chaos, known as the "Dark Ages," lasted four centuries. Then, in about 800 B.C.E., the dawn lifted on a scattering of small cities both on the mainland and, across the Aegean, on the western shore of Asia Minor. In most of these cities, the traditional form of government, monarchy, had been abandoned. Instead, networks of wealthy landowners ruled the city, their comfortable farms occupying the best valley land outside the city walls. These aristocrats made laws and debated them, decided for war or peace, and settled disputes among the citizens. In due course they created formal councils and assemblies and sometimes even juries, with rules for their selection: in effect, a constitution.

These cities were not democracies in the modern sense of the term. Many people (women, children, and slaves) were excluded from political life. Freedom belonged not to the individual but to the community. Yet even with these limitations, the political life of these Greek cities was remarkably free—with citizens and their leaders devoted to the Greek way of life and hostile to kings, and wary of tyrants. The chasm between civic life in Greece and in any Mediterranean or Middle Eastern land was enormous. It was dramatized by the response made by the Spartans when ordered to prostrate themselves before the Persian king Xerxes. To do so was to submit, and this they would not do.

To protect their way of life, many Greek cities were willing to go to war against any power that threatened. The threat eventually came from the Persians—ironically, of all the great imperial powers the most tolerant, the most adaptive, the most favorable to the development of human potential. Yet there remained a crucial difference between the two counterposed civilizations. The vast empire of Persia sought to grow, whereas the small cities of Greece sought to remain free.

The Persian Wars, the struggle between Greeks and Persians (which took place mainly from 499 to 479 B.C.E., then dragged on for another thirty years) began when some of the Greek cities on the shore of Asia Minor rose in rebellion against Persian overlordship, which had been imposed by Cyrus the Great in his great sweep through the region. The mainland Greek city of Athens, aided by Eretria, sent an armed fleet to assist the rebels—an act that would rankle with the Persians even after they had subdued the uprising and wooed back the allegiance of the rebel cities.

Determined to punish Athens for aiding the rebels, King Darius decided to establish, at least theoretically, his sovereignty on the Greek mainland. He sent agents to the Greek cities demanding earth and water, the material symbols of submission to his rule. Many Greek cities capitulated. They saw no danger of effective intervention by the distant monarch and wished to avoid a potentially disastrous conflict. From Athens and Sparta, Darius received a quite different response: they murdered his emissaries and set about preparing for war.

The spectacle of these two small cities, with their correspondingly small armies, preparing to fight the massed armies of the world's greatest empire seems amazing even now, 2500 years later. The shrewd Athenians and Spartans could have had no illusions

Battles of Kadesh and Marathon

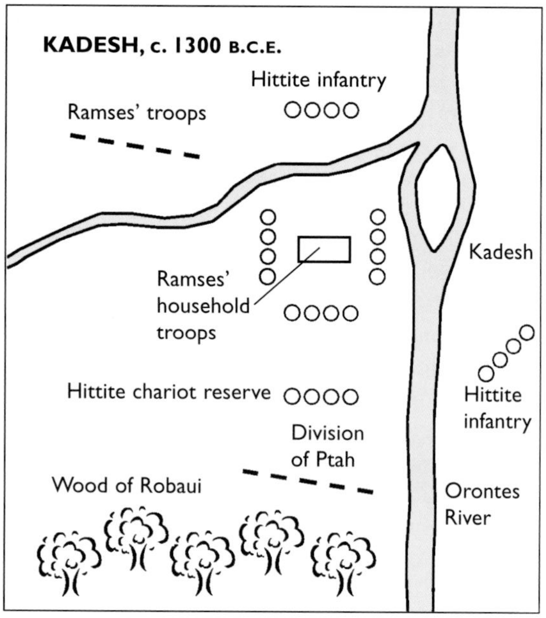

KADESH, c. 1300 B.C.E.

Hittite infantry
Ramses' troops
Kadesh
Ramses' household troops
Hittite chariot reserve
Hittite infantry
Division of Ptah
Wood of Robaui
Orontes River

A typical war chariot at Kadesh

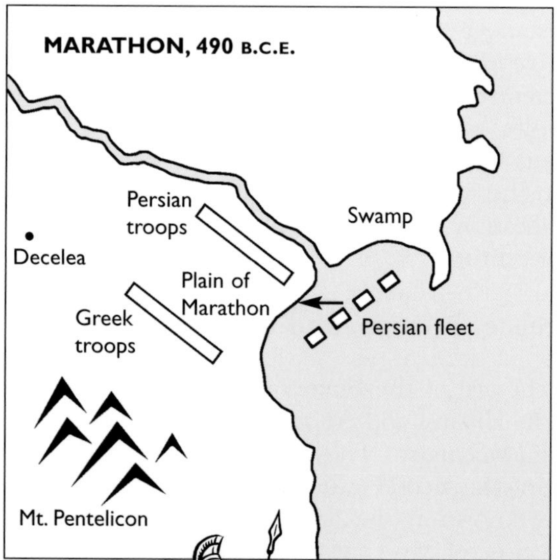

MARATHON, 490 B.C.E.

Persian troops
Swamp
Decelea
Plain of Marathon
Greek troops
Persian fleet
Mt. Pentelicon

A typical hoplite at Marathon

about their own strength relative to the Persians. The audacity of their stance compels admiration. Even more astonishing is what happened in 490 B.C.E. at Marathon, a village on the Attic peninsula of mainland Greece, where the Athenians, with an army of only 10,000 citizens, plus 1000 allies, turned back some 25,000 Persian soldiers. The defenders had better weapons and armor; moreover, they were fighting to defend their homeland—always an advantage. Finally, they had Miltiades, a steel-nerved adventurer whose strategy was to invite a Persian assault at the center of the Greek line in order to smash the enemy between its heavy and dangerous wings (see battle plan).

Ten years later, at the instigation of Darius' successor, Xerxes, the Persians returned, more determined than before to conquer Greece and punish Athens. This time they crossed the Hellespont by a bridge of linked, contiguous ships (engineered by their cooperative Phoenician subjects, trade rivals of the Greeks) and marched south through Macedon and Thessaly toward the lands dominated by Athens and Sparta. A small Spartan force of 300 crack citizen troops plus 700 of their allies resisted the advancing Persians at the pass of Thermopylae, fighting until they were all slain. The poet Simonides (c. 506–467 B.C.E.) composed their epitaph:

Tell them in Lacedaemon [Sparta], passer-by:
Carrying out their orders, here we lie.

Still the Persians continued their march on Athens, where the cagey statesman Themistocles (c. 528–462 B.C.E.), recognizing impending and irresistible disaster, had persuaded the citizens to flee to the offshore island of Salamis. The Athenians abandoned their city and temples to sack and to the torch. The Greek fleet bottled up their Persian opponents in the narrow channel between island and mainland and destroyed more than half of the Persian ships by ramming them with the iron-tipped prows of their warships (triremes) as described in *Witnesses* opposite. Xerxes watched, despaired, and turned home. The army he left behind was defeated at Plataea the following year. Although sporadic fighting would continue until 449 B.C.E., with Athens leading the resistance against Persian domination, the Persians no longer posed any serious threat to the Greeks.

From City-State to Empire

Over the next generation, Athens did not merely lead the anti-Persian alliance but effectively dominated it. The coastal city and island states that had formerly been co-equals were absorbed, briefly, into an Athenian Empire. Based on naval power first amassed by Themistocles and later extended by Cimon, the son of Miltiades, this alliance was meant to be a permanent bulwark against the menacing despotism to

WITNESSES

Greeks at War

Although the Greek poet Homer could imagine a peaceful world (see the Witness box, p. 42), the Greeks were not peaceful; nor did they become less violent as they became more civilized as the creators of magnificent works of science, philosophy, and literature. In these two passages, the tragic playwright Aeschylus and the historian Thucydides describe two incidents from the wartorn fifth-century B.C.E., one of the most glorious periods—in terms of cultural achievement—in human history.

The Persian defeat at Salamis (480 B.C.E.), according to the playwright Aeschylus (c. 480 B.C.E.):

First the floods of Persians held the line,
But when the narrows choked them, and rescue
hopeless,
Smitten by prows, their bronze jaws gaping,
Shattered entire was our fleet of oars.
The Grecian warships, calculating, dashed
Round, and encircled us; ships showed their belly:
No longer could we see the water, charged
With ships' wrecks and men's blood.
Corpses glutted beaches and the rocks. ...
... never in a single day
So great a number died.

(Aeschylus, *Persians*, 411–421, 431–432; eds. D. Grene, R. Lattimore, trs. S. G. Benardete, 1992)

Describing revolution at Corcyra in northwestern Greece, Thucydides diagnoses human nature as prone to violence and treachery (c. 420 B.C.E.): During seven days ..., the Corcyraeans were engaged in butchering those of their fellow-citizens whom they regarded as their enemies: and although the crime imputed was that of attempting to put down the democracy, some were slain also for private hatred, others by their debtors because of the monies owed to them. Death thus raged in every shape; and, as usually happens at such times, there was no length to which violence did not go; sons were killed by their fathers, and suppliants dragged from the altar or slain upon it; while some were even walled up in the temple of Dionysus and died there.

So bloody was the march of the revolution, and the impression which it made was the greater as it was one of the first to occur. Later on, one may say, the whole Hellenic world was convulsed. ... The sufferings which revolution entailed upon the cities were many and terrible, such as have occurred and always will occur, as long as the nature of mankind remains the same. ... In peace and prosperity states and individuals have better sentiments, because they do not find themselves suddenly confronted with imperious necessities; but war takes away the easy supply of daily wants, and so proves a rough master, that brings most men's characters to a level with their fortunes.

(Thucydides, *Peloponnesian War*, 3:81–82; ed. J. Crawley, 1951)

the east. Called the Delian League (478–404 B.C.E.), because its combined treasure was originally stored on the island of Delos, it became increasingly dominated by the Athenians, who found it a valuable source of revenue. Athens, which at Marathon had heroically defended its own freedom, became (it seemed to onlookers) the exploiter and oppressor of other once-free cities.

With the diminished Persian threat, Athens' allies became restive, and Sparta, in particular, cast a worried eye on the magnificence of its former friend. With its wealth and maritime allies, Athens had the advantage at sea and (it seemed) could be defeated only by an opponent with a comparably strong navy. Sparta, with its dominion over much of the Peloponnesus (the southern Greek peninsula) and alliance with other major cities, possessed a reputably unbeatable army and an impregnable position. Over nearly thirty years these two antagonists hammered each other in a war that was punctuated by internal disasters on both sides (such as an outbreak of plague in Athens described in *Witnesses*, p. 53), periods of truce, and outbursts of atrocities. This was the Peloponnesian War (fought intermittently 431–404 B.C.E.). It closed the century in which Greece achieved the highest cultural attainments of its history.

The two major cities of Greece had exhausted themselves in the Peloponnesian War and were now vulnerable to foreign aggression. As normality seemed to return, a power emerged to the north that would challenge the cities that once had faced the might of Persia. The new player in the game of Greek—and eventually world—politics was Macedonia.

Cities that had refused to sacrifice their autonomy even to other Greeks (let alone Persians) soon bent to the superior power of Philip II (r. 359–336 B.C.E.) of Macedon. To the Greeks, Macedonia was a crude and backward land, and Philip hateful simply by virtue of being a king. But that despised monarch ruled a unified nation and marched at the head of the most up-to-date army of the day. He was unstoppable. From the outset of his reign until his assassination twenty-three years later, he conquered all the cities of Greece: oligarchies and democracies alike.

Philip's ambition had been to conquer Greece. That of his son and successor, Alexander, was to conquer the world. He began with the Persians. Once, the Persians had amassed a huge army in a vain attempt to breach the Aegean and conquer Greece. Now, with his army of Macedonians and Greeks, Alexander would pay the Persians a return visit.

Astoundingly, Alexander won. His forces overran Asia Minor and the Middle East, pushing beyond the Himalayan passes to the shore of the Indus; they reached deep down the Nile River into southern Egypt. They combined the strength of the Greek phalanx where soldiers were organized in row upon tight row, as shown in *How Many?* on p. 128 with the machinery that the Persians had borrowed from the Assyrians and a tactical genius that exploited each geographical advantage, adapted to each variation in terrain, and boldly attacked fortifications that were believed impregnable.

Just as Persia had absorbed all that the Assyrians and the Hittites before them had once ruled, and more, Alexander absorbed all the realms of the Persians, as well as the whole of Greece. By Alexander's death in 323 B.C.E., the empire he had created was the largest ever known. It contained a greater diversity of communities and languages than had any previous state. It would exert an enduring cultural influence upon successor states—Rome, Byzantium, Islam (see Chapters 5 and 8)—and their modern descendants.

Conclusion

THE CONTEST FOR EMPIRE AND THE MEANING OF THE WEST

During the first 3000 years of civilization, armies and empires reigned. One armed state after another would emerge to dominate, and sometimes destroy, its neighbors. From Africa to Asia, from the Bronze Age to the Iron Age, kings led their armies in an endless struggle for power, sometimes winning a brief ascendancy for a century or more. With Alexander the Great, Europe for the first time entered the contest for ascendancy.

Alexander's conquests mark a new ascendancy for Europe—one that had been foreshadowed by Greek victories in the Persian Wars. Ironically, those earlier victories represented not a claim for empire but a claim for freedom—a refusal to bow to power expressed also in the proud words of the Spartan emissaries to King Xerxes, with which this chapter opened.

New political and cultural principles were introduced into the heritage of the West by the Greeks who had withstood the advancing might of the Persian Empire. These principles were in tension with the lust for empire. In the political sphere, they asserted the right of human communities to independence and self-determination. In the cultural sphere, they included high ethical and intellectual standards which more than once in the later history of the West would present a challenge to those who sought world domination at all costs.

REVIEW QUESTIONS

1. Why were most ancient states ruled by kings? What were the sources of kingly power? Why was warfare so important for ancient rulers?

2. Where did the first Bronze Age kingdoms develop? What kind of state did the pharaohs create in Egypt? How did Egypt differ politically from Mesopotamia?

3. Who were the Indo-Europeans? What states did they create in Europe and the Near East? What was Mycenean culture like? Why did it disappear? What resulted from the rivalry between Hittite and Egyptian Empires?

4. Why did the Bronze Age empires collapse? How did the decline of Egyptian and Hittite power affect Syria and Palestine? Describe the development of the Israelite kingdoms.

5. Why were the Assyrians so successful in building an empire? What benefits did the Persian Empire bring to the Near East? How did the brahmanic system affect Indian society?

6. How were the political, social, cultural, and intellectual outlooks of the Greek city-states different from those of Near Eastern empires? Why were the Persians unable to conquer Greece? Why was Macedon able to impose its rule on the Greeks?

SUGGESTED RESOURCES

Power and Civilization

Ferrill, Arther, *The Origins of War: From the Stone Age to Alexander the Great* (London: Thames and Hudson, 1985). A study of changing military strategy, tactics, organization, logistics, and technology from the Neolithic era to the conquests of Alexander the Great.

O'Connell, Robert L., *Ride of the Second Horseman: The Birth and Death of War* (Oxford: Oxford University Press, 1995). A survey of human experience of war, from the Ice Age to the present.

Raaflaub, Kurt & Nathan Rosenstein, *War and Society in the Ancient and Medieval Worlds: Asia, the Mediterranean, Europe, and MesoAmerica* (Cambridge, MA: Harvard University Press, 2000). A multi-authored work that studies the interface of war and society from the third millennium B.C.E. through about 1000 C.E. in the Asian, European, and American regions of early civilization.

Bronze Age Kingdoms in Egypt and Mesopotamia

Crawford, Harriet, *Sumer and the Sumerians* (Cambridge: Cambridge University Press, 1991). A review of social and technological developments from 3800 through 2000 B.C.E..

Johnson, Paul, *The Civilization of Ancient Egypt* (London: Weidenfeld and Nicolson, 2000). The whole 3,000-year course of Egyptian history, highlighting the simplicity and effectiveness of its theocratic government, the role played by an esoteric system of hieroglyphic writing in maintaining the privileged order of priests and scribes, and the cultural effects of the high status of women.

Postgate, J. N., and Nicholas Postgate, *Early Mesopotamia: Society and Economy at the Dawn of History* (London/New York: Routledge, 1994). Integrates historical and archaeological data drawn from specialist literature; scholarly yet readable.

Robins, Gay, *Women in Ancient Egypt* (Cambridge: Harvard University Press, 1993). An introduction to the history of women of all classes in ancient Egyptian society and culture.

Timeline of Egyptian military technology:
www.anthro.mankato.msus.edu/prehistory/egypt/military/tech.html

Bronze Age Kingdoms in the Aegean and the Near East

Mallory, J. P., *In Search of the Indo-Europeans: Language, Archaeology, and Myth* (New York: Thames & Hudson, 1989). An introduction to the history of the Indo-Europeans and the problematic history of Indo-European studies.

Sandars, N. K., *The Sea Peoples: Warriors of the Ancient Mediterranean, 1250–1150 B.C.* (London: Thames & Hudson, 1985). An account of migrating peoples known as Land and Sea Peoples, arguing that disparate groups combined to cause the collapse of Bronze Age civilizations in the eastern Mediterranean.

Vermeule, Emily, *Greece in the Bronze Age* (Chicago: University of Chicago Press, 1972). A classic survey of evidence and reconstruction of civilization of Bronze Age Greece.

Iron Age Empires of the Middle East

Aubet, Maria Eugenia (trans. Mary Turton), *The Phoenicians and the West: Politics, Colonies, and Trade* (Cambridge: Cambridge University Press, 1993). Shows how recent archaeological research has changed our understanding of the relationship of Phoenicia and its colonies to local Iron Age communities.

Brinkman, John A., *Prelude to Empire: Babylonian Society and Politics, 747–626 B.C.* (Philadelphia: University Museum, Babylonian Fund, 1984). A history of Babylonia, when Babylon regained political and military eminence after a period of Assyrian domination.

Bronze/Iron Age Kingdoms in East/South Asia

Basham, A. L., *The Wonder that was India: A Study of the History and Culture of the Indian Subcontinent before the Coming of the Muslims*, 3rd ed. (London: Sidgwick & Jackson, 1985). A survey of the civilization of classical India, prehistory to end of first millennium C.E., covering state, society, everyday life, religion, arts, language, and literature.

Xueqin, Li (trans. K. C. Chang), *Eastern Zhou and Qin Civilizations* (New Haven: Yale University Press, 1985). Covers 1500 years of Chinese history from 1700 through 200 B.C.E., discussing the shift from stone to bronze to iron, the development of a complex strictly ranked society, and the unification of the Chinese state.

Sun Tzu, *The Art of War* (earliest known guide to warfare, from ancient China): **http://eawc.evansville.edu/anthology/artwar.htm**

The Birth of the West

Burn, A. R., *Persia and the Greeks: The Defense of the West, c. 546–478 B.C.*, 2nd ed. (Stanford: Stanford University Press, 1984). A lively, detailed military history of the war between the Persian Empire and the Greeks, based on literary and archaeological evidence.

THE GREEK *POLIS*

1000 | 900 | 800 | 700 | 600 | 500 | 400 | 300 | 200 B.C.E.

Rulers, Nations, and War

Greek Dark Age, c. 1200–800

Archaic Age, c. 800–500

Classical Age, c. 500–323

Hellenistic Civilization, c. 323–31

Greek colonization, c. 750–600

Persian Empire, 550–323

Alexander's Empire, 334–323

Early and Republican Rome, c. 550–27

- Peisistratus, tyrant of Athens, comes to power, 546
- Persian invasion repelled at Marathon, 490
- Pericles presides in Athens, 443–429
- Athens surrenders to Sparta, ending Peloponnesian War, 404
- Thebes defeats Sparta at Leuctra, 371
- Thebes defeats Sparta at Mantinea, 362
- Philip II defeats Athens, allies, at battle of Chaeronea, 338
- Alexander becomes king of Macedon, 336
- Death of Alexander, 323
- Deaths of Aristotle, Demosthenes, 322

Society, Politics, and Ideas

- Homer's *Iliad*, c. 750, *Odyssey*, c. 725
- Hesiod's *Works and Days*, c. 700
- Alphabet used to write Greek, c. 700
- Spartan constitution established, c. 700
- Draco of Athens commits laws to writing, 621
- Solon is archon in Athens, 594/3
- Greek mercenaries carve names on statue of Ramses II, 591
- Aegina issues first Greek coin, the drachma, 575
- Cleisthenes reforms Athenian constitution, 508
- Common treasury of Delian League removed to Athens, 454
- Pericles' "funeral oration," 431
- Socrates arrested, tried, executed, 399

Beyond the West

Zhou dynasty, c. 1027–221

Chinese warring states, 450–221

Assyrian domination, c. 900–612

Chaldeans, 612–539

Qin dynasty, c. 221–206

Scythians, 800–550

- Phoenician maritime hegemony, after 900
- Chandragupta Maurya of India, r. c. 321–298
- Asoka of India, 272–232
- Shi Huangdi of China, r. 221–210/209

CHAPTER

3

THE GREEK *POLIS*

The New Politics of Ancient Greece

1000–300 B.C.E.

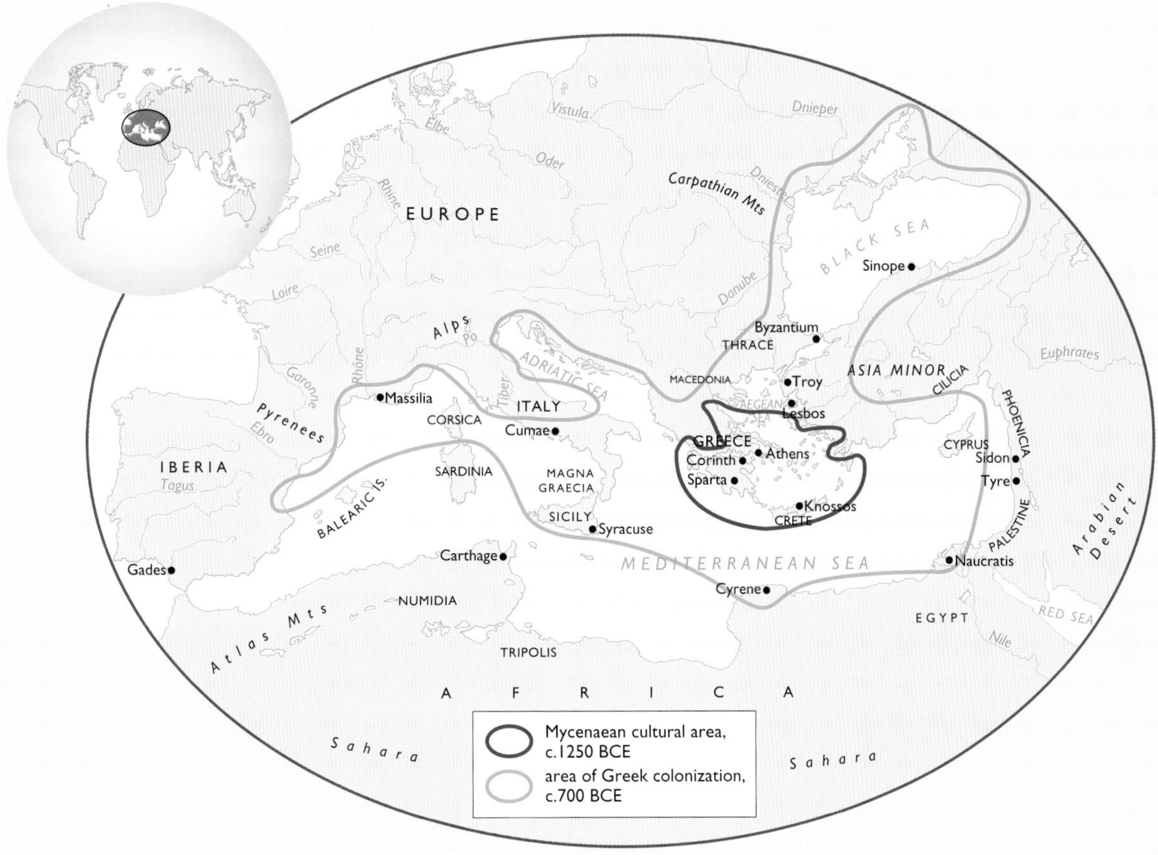

KEY TOPICS

- **The Formation of the *Polis*:** Within small cities formed around religious sites, Greeks depose their kings, construct public buildings, organize public spaces, and invent a new kind of politics.
- **Justice and the *Polis*:** The Greeks form a concept with a momentous future: the purpose of the community is to achieve justice for its members—or at least for some of them. This ideal was achieved in some Greek cities to a higher degree than anywhere else in the world before the advent of modern times.
- **Private Life of the *Polis*:** In the Greek house and *polis*, women have a small place, and men have all the rest. Men participate in many types of private association, and they alone are admitted to public life.

The Obedience of Socrates *One short, ugly, and unassuming man commanded the intellectual life of Athens when it was still the leading city of ancient Greece: the philosopher Socrates. In 399* B.C.E.*, Socrates was arrested, charged with "impiety," convicted, and sentenced to death. He had lured the young, it was said, from their reverence for the old gods and values.*

Socrates' friends begged him to escape, but he refused. He had been judged by the laws of the city. These laws were sacred: they enshrined the principle that the task of the human community is to establish justice. Socrates took from the prison guard the offered cup of poison, drank it, and died. That final act of obedience to the rule of law was the last lesson he had to teach. Socrates' reverence for the laws of his city is a key to understanding the achievement of Greek civilization. Greek civilization centered around the ***polis*** (plural *poleis*) or city-state. The Greek *poleis* were the cradles of the Western world.

THE FORMATION OF THE *POLIS*

Despite relentless poverty, the consequence of unyielding soil, the Greeks showed evidence early on of energy, inventiveness, and genius. By the end of the period called the Greek "Dark Ages" (c. 1200–800 B.C.E.), they had thrown off the yoke of kings and priests, created rich new literary and visual forms, wandered abroad to live and trade, and developed at home new ways to govern and defend themselves. During what is called the "Archaic" age of Greek civilization (about 800 to about 500 B.C.E.), they gave birth to the *polis*, and became the first **citizens** of the Western world.

Rich and Poor in a Poor Land

The *poleis* emerged toward the end of the Greek "Dark Ages," which followed the collapse of Mycenaean centers in c. 1200 B.C.E. Dark Age villagers lived in isolation, producing clothing and pottery only for their own use, using the crude implements forged by the smith to cook, to fight, to hunt, and to plow. Clustered in small communities bounded by craggy hill and rocky coast, they turned inward upon themselves. In the disparate intonations of the local dialects they told stories about their gods and what they remembered about their past. At once barred and yet sheltered from the world beyond the hill, they were loyal to their village, its people, its speech, and its way of life. Although they spoke different dialects—Dorian, Ionian, Aeolian—they thought of themselves as Hellenes (our word "Greek" is a legacy of the Romans' *Graecus*), and the Greek-speaking world as **Hellas**. Even as Greek civilization developed in distinct poleis, it was unified by its common language.

The Greek villagers labored hard and ate little. The land they worked was stingy—thin, rocky, depleted by overuse. While every Greek farmer wished for a son who would take over the right to toil on his land, he did not want many sons. There was not enough land and not enough food. The only remedy for poverty was work, advised the poet Hesiod (c. 700 B.C.E.) in his account of village life entitled *Works and Days*:

> *Work! Work, and then Hunger will not be your companion ...*
> *Let there be order and measure in your own work*
> *until your barns are filled with the season's harvest.*
> *Riches and flocks of sheep go to those who work.*

Some villagers owned more and better land than others—not much more, nor much better. These privileged proprietors may have been the descendants of Mycenaean kings or tribal chiefs. They were the ancestors of the aristocrats who would lead the transformation of Greece from a backwater of Mediterranean civilization into a paragon of political and cultural innovation. Wealth gave the greater landowners prestige and power. They settled disputes among the villagers, there being no law beyond their judgments. These decisions concerned what a modern lawyer would call civil cases such as disputes about land or livestock. Criminal matters were handled without benefit of court, by sword and dagger. The victim or the victim's family demanded compensation for the crime, in the form of treasure or the life of the perpetrator. Crime and criminal were apparent to all, and vengeance was swift and exact.

Village society of the Greek Dark Ages had no great kings ruling from vast palaces. Some landowners bore the title of "king"; but these "kings" were tillers of the soil and masters of herds, more like the war chiefs of Neolithic towns than the monarchs of Babylon or Persia to the east. Landowners also served as priests, performing the sacrifices of chosen beasts to satisfy ever-hungry deities. But unlike the priests of their forbears, they did not live in temple complexes managing the wealth of the gods or demanding tribute from fearful worshipers. The poverty of the Greeks could not support priests and kings. Poverty was a tyrant to the Greeks. It was also their liberator.

The Homeric epics, the *Iliad* and the *Odyssey*, depict the meager authority of the Greek "kings" in the years between the Mycenaean collapse and the appearance of the *polis*. In the *Iliad* (composed about 750 B.C.E.), the Greek war effort against the rival kingdom of Troy is headed by a squad of loosely leagued petty kings without clear channels of command. Agamemnon, the acknowledged chief, must bully his colleagues into action, or gather them for long debates in order to arrive at consensus.

The *Odyssey* (composed about 725 B.C.E.) describes the experiences of Odysseus, one of the heroes of the *Iliad*, on his journey home from the Trojan War. Both Homer and Odysseus fear the world lying beyond the boundaries of Greek culture: it is ruled by dagger-toothed monsters and one-eyed giants, vengeful deities and seductive cannibals, witches who cast spells and an angry cosmos armed with destructive storm and hungry whirlpool. When the hero, naked and scarred, finally reaches his home (more a large farmhouse than a palace) together with his son Telemachus and aided by his great bow he must massacre the uncouth princes who have occupied the premises. This king has no greater authority over his nobles than that exercised by his bow.

The Coming of the Archaic Age

It was the ordinary potter who created the first harbinger of the flowering of Greek culture—a simple vase. This was a pot of graceful contour, bare of decoration except for a few plain lines. Its style is known as "Proto-Geometric," as it anticipated the more richly decorated Geometric style that would follow (see *Windows On*, p. 61). The understatement of this object is profound yet wholly original and breathtakingly lovely. These qualities would characterize the artistic and intellectual products of the civilization that crystallized in the Archaic age that now opened.

Two centuries earlier, around 1000 B.C.E., Greeks pressed by hunger had ventured out in tiny fishing vessels in search of more fertile land to the east, across the Aegean Sea. They established Greek-speaking communities on the Aegean islands and along the western shore of Asia Minor. There, they continued to worship the same gods, remember the same heroes, follow the same customs, and speak the same language as their fellow Greeks on the mainland. Language, in particular, was the line of demarcation between these transplanted Greeks and the **barbarians** in whose midst they lived. To the Greeks, a "barbarian" was simply a person who could not speak Greek but

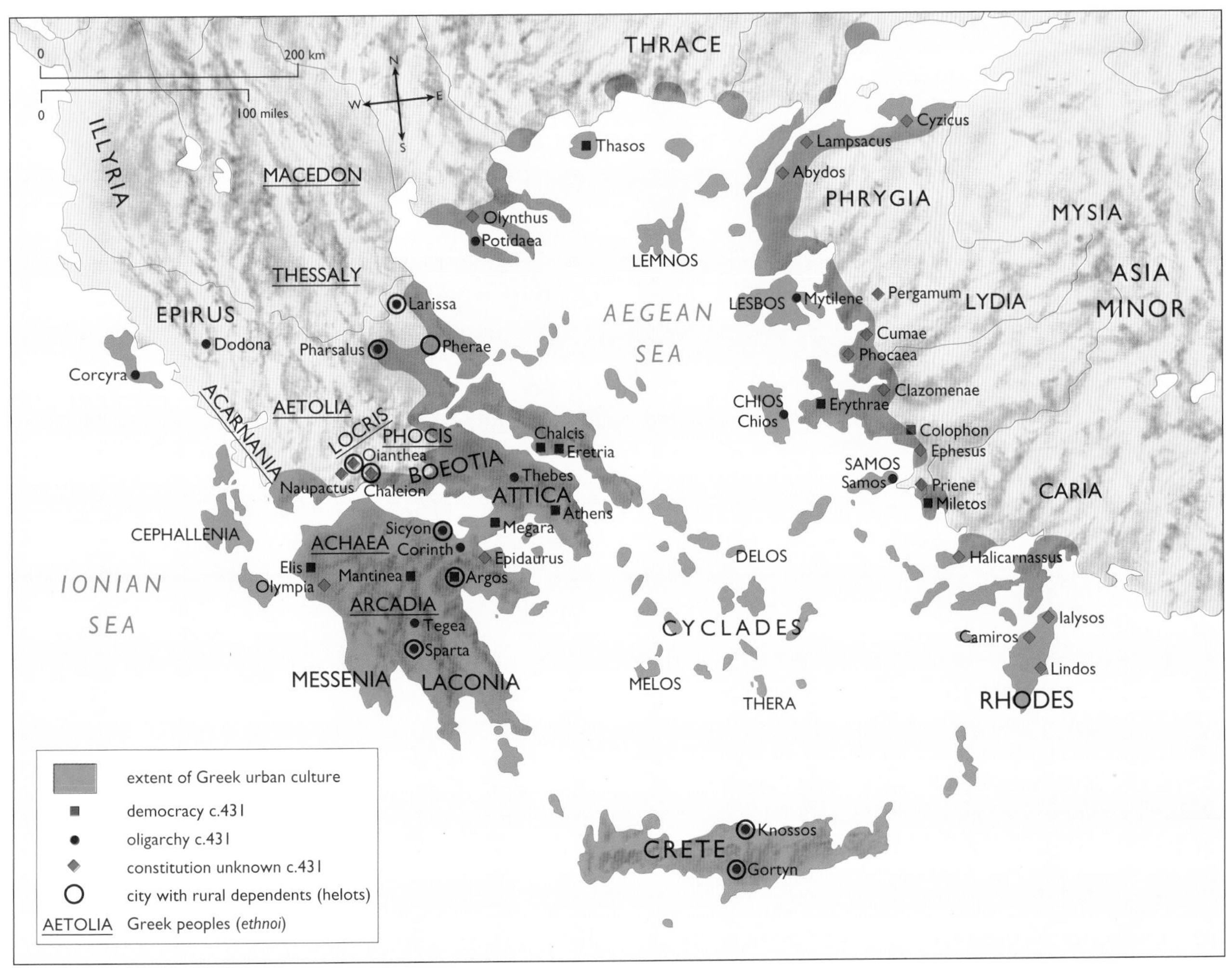

***Map 3.1* Cities of the Greek Homeland:** *Centuries after the destruction of most of the Mycenaean cities on the Greek mainland in c. 1200* B.C.E., *new centers, or* poleis, *arose amid the villages and farms of the Greek-speaking* ethnoi *("peoples"). No longer ruled by kings, the* poleis *developed new forms of government—most notably democracy, oligarchy, and tyranny.*

barked meaningless (to them) syllables or chirped "bar-bar" like mindless birds. Whereas, for them, a civilized person was distinguished by the ability to speak the language in which a great literature had been created.

Although the Greeks of Asia Minor shared a language distinct from that of their "barbarian" neighbors, they spoke different dialects of Greek. Reflecting the pattern of settlement that prevailed in the homeland, these dialects were distributed with Dorian in the south, Aeolian in the far north, and Ionian in between (see Map 2.3). The Ionian dialect came to dominate in Asia Minor and set the standard for Greek-speaking settlers there. The Ionian culture that subsequently developed in that region over the next few centuries was not only thoroughly Greek but more advanced than that of the mainland. Here the *polis* was born and developed.

A *polis* generally developed when one or several villages coalesced around a common religious center. The cult celebrated a local deity (usually a goddess) as patron, and built for this deity a wooden temple on a high hill, called the *acropolis*. At the foot of that hill was a flat, clear area: the ***agora***. Here people brought goods to market for exchange, wealthy landowners listened to civil disputes, and citizens gathered together for debate.

The Greek *polis* was an association of people united by place, by custom, by principle. It was not primarily an administrative or commercial center like the cities of Egypt or the Middle East, centered on palace or temple. The Greeks of the *polis* were rooted in the land they owned, on which they labored. They united to carry on a distinct way of life: to celebrate their principal gods, to decide between war and peace, to organize for mutual defense. The Greek *polis* was a gathering of those who defined and pursued shared goals—a group of people rather than an institution. The language used by contemporaries in referring to the *poleis* is significant: not Athens, but "the Athenians" opposed the Persians at Marathon; not Sparta but "the Spartans" supported **oligarchy** throughout Hellas. The Greek city was not a place, but a people.

The emergence of hundreds of *poleis* during the Archaic age enriched the Aegean world (see Map 3.1). The number of inhabited sites on the mainland, which had been reduced to a fraction of their level during the Mycenaean civilization, now began to rise rapidly, and their populations increased. By 700 B.C.E., the population of Attica (the region surrounding and including the city of Athens), had increased more than sevenfold from its low during the Dark Ages. On the peripheries of the zone of *polis* formation, social organization was by tribe and clan grouped into *ethnoi*. These communities considered themselves Greek and interacted with the *poleis* throughout the period. But social and cultural leadership belonged to the *poleis*.

Council, Assembly, and Phalanx

The people ruled the *polis*. Not all of them, sometimes only a very few; yet some consortium or committee drawn from the people organized city life. The primacy of the people resulted from the demotion of kings, which had occurred before the opening of the Archaic age (see Chapter 2). Ghosts of the earlier institution of kingship persisted in the organization of some *poleis*. Sparta retained the office of "king" and had in fact two kings simultaneously (probably reflecting an earlier alliance between two villages). They were generals who did not rule.

In Athens, one of the nine "leaders" (or archons) of the community was called the "king archon." He performed religious functions only—the vestige of a king who was the vestige of a priest. The priesthood itself, as a separate and privileged social class, had disappeared. Although the Greek world knew both priests and priestesses, these were either ordinary citizens performing special rites on ceremonial occasions, or inspired oracles attached to particular deities, public places, and temples. They did not constitute a priesthood such as that which had dominated Sumer or managed the Egyptian temple complex at Medinet Habu.

In the absence of monarchs, the Greek people devised for themselves a primitive machinery of government, or constitution. Their assembly, the first political institution of the early *polis*, had origins in earlier times. Even among Neolithic peoples, some sort of assembly probably met to approve actions proposed by a warlord. In early Hittite society, the assembly elected the king, although later the monarchy was hereditary, as in neighboring states (see Chapter 2). Homer describes in the *Iliad* assemblies held by the Achaean leaders (as he named the war chiefs now understood to be the kings of Mycenaean cities) in the struggle against Troy. In the Archaic age Corinthians, Thebans, Athenians, and citizens of other *poleis* practiced in their assemblies, in the *agora*, the skills of argument and debate, which would henceforth indelibly mark Greek culture.

The assembly was too large a body to examine a serious problem in depth. In Athens, the place set aside for the assembly could hold up to 6000. For this reason, some kind of guiding committee or council was formed to discuss issues in more detail. Nearly everywhere this more select body was made up of major landowners—men (never women) of the traditional nobility who firmly established themselves as a ruling elite. In some *poleis*, another criterion for admission to the council was advanced age. By the mechanisms of assembly and council, the *poleis* made decisions without the authority of monarch or priesthood.

The citizens also needed to develop a system of defense. In other societies, war was the responsibility

WINDOWS ON

The Evolving Vase

Octopus vase, from Mycenae, 1200–1125 B.C.E.

Proto-Geometric amphora, c. 950 B.C.E.

Hellenic civilization can be traced by observing the evolution of vases which served as useful utensils, ritual objects, prized works of art, and objects of trade. A Mycenaean vase (above) from the pre-Hellenic period features strong organic forms in its depiction of octopi and fish.

After the disappearance of Mycenaean centers in the twelfth century B.C.E., Athenian potters slowly began to create Proto-Geometric vases, typically stern and bare (above right).

Two centuries later, crowded linear patterns spread over the surface of this Athenian Geometric krater *from the early Archaic age (below right).*

From flourishing Corinth in the later Archaic period comes this krater *(below left), depicting in black-figure terms part of a marriage procession. Black-figure describes pottery in which the decoration is black on a red background. In contrast, the later red-figure pottery from the sixth and fifth century B.C.E. was decorated with red on a black background* *(see p. 63).*

(above: Metropolitan Museum of Art; upper right: Kerameikos Museum, Athens; below right: Louvre, Paris; below left: Vatican Museum, Rome)

Geometric krater, from Athens, c. 800 B.C.E.

Black-figure krater, Corinth, c. 560 B.C.E.

To continue your investigation of this topic, please go to www.prenhall.com/king for the related WINDOWS on the WEB activity

HOW MANY?

Citizens, Slaves, and Prices

6000 men: number who could stand in the place set aside for the assembly in Athens.

700 government jobs in Periclean Athens.

300 Scythian slaves: constituted the Athenian police force.

1 drachma: wages paid to a day laborer

200–300 drachmas: cost of a strong adult slave.

1 mina = 100 drachmas
1 talent = 6000 drachmas.

of kings. In the Dark Ages wars were fought by heavily armed aristocrats, often in single combat. The Greeks of the Archaic age, however, made war the responsibility of the people. In doing so, they transformed the methods of warfare. Whereas other armies of the time depended on cavalry and lightly-armed infantry, the Greeks developed the **phalanx**: a block of men, standing shoulder to shoulder, packed solidly for rows, defended by a wall of shields held by each soldier over his own left side and his comrade's right. These soldiers of the phalanx were genuine "citizen soldiers," called **hoplites**, after the newly devised double-gripped shield (*hoplon*) that each held. The success of the formation (which spelled life or death for the community) depended on the willingness of each man to fight and thereby sustain the courage of his neighbor. The *polis* was the assembly of its people. The phalanx was the *polis* at war.

Only fairly prosperous male citizens could be hoplites; for the soldier had to pay for the expensive bronze armor that gave the phalanx its muscle. Despite this restriction, the phalanx was much less exclusive than the old **aristocracy** which was made up of wealthy landowners. Men of middling prosperity served as hoplites, assuming new risks which brought new privileges—full citizenship and full participation in the state. Poorer men, too, might fight for the *polis*. They served as light infantry and archers, and, in those *poleis* that developed navies, as sailors and oarsmen. They were counted as citizens, like the hoplites, but were generally not admitted to the highest offices.

Battles between hoplite armies, scheduled between sowing time and harvest, were quick and decisive. The forces faced each other on the level, fertile ground in dispute, which then became the prize of the victor. The loser fled. Such wars occurred regularly in Greece, from the first imperial conquests of the Spartans, in the eighth century B.C.E., to the constant battering of city against city in the fifth and fourth centuries B.C.E. which ended in the Macedonian conquest. The phalanx maintained its dominance throughout this period, the tactics of war changing only in the fourth century B.C.E. under the generalship of Epaminondas from Thebes, Philip II of Macedonia, and Philip's son Alexander the Great.

The hoplite soldier was one of the first exports of Archaic Greece. Because too many men competed to feed their wives, children, and extended families from the thin soil of Greece, younger or disinherited sons and orphaned boys often sold their services abroad, to the kings of the Middle East. Some of those in the employ of the Egyptian pharaoh Psammetichos II (r. 595–589 B.C.E.) carved their names (like modern graffitists) on the legs of a colossal statue of Ramses II at Abu Simbel on the Nile River in southern (Upper) Egypt (591 B.C.E.). Greek mercenaries serving in armies throughout the Mediterranean region learned and profited much from wealthier and more advanced civilizations.

Colonization, Commerce, and Manufacturing

Overpopulation—or hunger—also impelled some Greeks to emigrate from the mainland and found colonies overseas. This period of colonization (extending from about 750 to 600 B.C.E.) resulted in the Greek domination of the northern rim of the Mediterranean as far west as Spain, as well as the coasts of the northern Aegean and Black seas as shown on Map 3.2. These regions became part of Hellas—as the Greeks referred to their own civilization—as had the earlier settlements on the west coast of Asia Minor.

Like its "mother city" or ***metropolis*** (the "mother" *polis* that established a colony), the Greek colony was from inception a *polis*—a self-contained political unit, a community of new citizens acting autonomously and aiming at economic self-sufficiency. The parent city recruited the colonists, funded the expedition, provided the necessary ships, and secured the good will of the patron god or goddess. Once the migrants were replanted on new soil, the parent city's function disappeared. The homeland was remembered fondly, and maintained its cultural influence, but the new *polis* claimed full autonomy.

Most of the colonies were coastal, just as most of the *poleis* of the Greek mainland were close to the sea. A lively exchange of goods developed among these settlements, a commercial advance to match the urban one. Olive oil and wine, staples of the Mediterranean diet, flowed out from areas of abundant production. Potters shipped their vases to the ports of the Middle East, Egypt, Italy, and the western Mediterranean. There, merchants bought and sold slaves and purchased the mineral resources Greece craved: amber and tin from the west and north, copper from Cyprus, and iron from Asia Minor. To feed their growing cities the Greeks imported wheat from the regions of the Black Sea, Sicily, and Egypt. From the more advanced civilizations to the east and south came luxury goods: fine ivories and elaborate metalwork, rugs and cushions, spices and perfume. Knowledge and skills, other gods and customs, the secrets of astronomy and mathematics, the techniques of coinage and the alphabet, all found their way back to Greece with the trading ships and returning mercenaries.

Ingots of precious metals were already used as a medium of exchange in the seventh century B.C.E. Around 650 B.C.E. stamped coins were first introduced, probably in Lydia (Asia Minor). These "croesids" (so named after King Croesus, r. 560–546) were circulated by the Persians, who after overrunning Lydia and capturing Croesus, imitated them with their own gold "darics" (after the monarch Darius). Around 575 B.C.E., Aegina became the first Greek *polis* to issue a stamped silver drachma (called a "turtle," after the city mascot on its face). Soon other Greek *poleis* minted their own coins stamped with figures relating to their city's myths and traditions: Corinth its "colts," for example, and Athens its "owls." These coins eased the exchange of goods in both local and international markets. Daily purchases were made in obols, a bronze currency; in the fifth century, a worker's wage reached a drachma per day (literally a "handful" of obols). The value of a ship's cargo or a nobleman's fortune was measured in minas and talents (respectively 100 and 6000 drachmas).

Like coinage, writing was an important commercial tool, as the merchants who brought the Phoenician alphabet to Greece clearly recognized. Now Greek producers could track inventories, as had the Mycenaean scribes. The new alphabet, extended to include vowel signs, was much simpler to learn than the old Mycenaean system of writing based on the graphic representation of syllables (see Chapter 1). The ordinary merchant, or even his intelligent slave assistant, could record transactions, send business letters, and report the various sights seen on a commercial venture.

Merchants occupied an uncomfortable place in Greek society. They were the agents of the commerce that brought wealth to Greece and fueled its achievements. Yet they were perceived as outsiders in the *polis*, which was understood as a community of farmers. Few farmers turned from the land in order to engage in the world of commerce. The great landowners almost never did so. Those who engaged in manufacture and commerce—working "seated and in the shade," as the historian Xenophon (c. 430–c. 354 B.C.E.) sneered—were looked down upon by the landowners. The ideal state, chided the philosopher Aristotle (384–322 B.C.E.), cannot allow its citizens to "live a mechanic or a mercantile life (for such a life is ignoble and inimical to virtue)."

Most merchants were foreigners, immigrants to the *polis* who formed a separate class of resident noncitizens, the "**metics**." Metics supported the *polis*, in Athens paying an annual head tax (twelve drachmas for men, six for women) and serving in the army. They could own personal property, but not land or houses. They could appear in law courts, but could not represent their own interests. Nor could they become citizens—the most serious liability of all—or hold office or join in the deliberations of the assembly. Barred from public life (for Greeks, the life that mattered the most), many Athenian metics settled in the commercial neighborhood of the port of Piraeus not far from the city. There they established workshops employing artisans, most of whom were slaves.

Slavery burgeoned in Greece as the *poleis* grew larger and required non-farm labor. At first, slaves

Working in Classical Greece

Clay statuette: *Fundamental to Greek life was agricultural work. In this figure from Boeotia, sixth century B.C.E., a man is plowing with the aid of two oxen.* (Louvre, Paris)

Red-figure cup: *The laborers shown in this red-figure Athenian cup, c. 480 B.C.E., are heating and hammering bronze in order to produce a statue of a man, who is also shown, on the far left, headless, but otherwise just like his fabricators.* (Staatliche Museen, Berlin)

were recruited from the ranks of abandoned children and captive peoples. These first slaves were mostly women, who spun and wove cloth, carted water, and doubled as concubines. Later, as the slave trade developed, slaves were bought and sold in auctions, held in the *agora* as they were for other commodities. Here a strong adult worker from Syria or Thrace might cost 200 or 300 drachmas, a child less than 100. Those who wished a slave's services on a limited basis might rent one from a slaveowner. Slavedealing was an acceptable occupation for an Athenian citizen, even though other commerce was despised. Many reputable gentlemen grew wealthy on income from the rented labor of their slaves.

Slaves were the engine of the Greek economy. Unskilled slaves loaded and unloaded ships; skilled ones produced the commodities of trade. Intelligent slaves were employed as record keepers, scribes, accountants, managers, bankers, and entrepreneurs. Slaves worked alongside metic and citizen workers in building the Parthenon and Erechtheum in Athens, and 300 Scythian slaves armed with bows and arrows constituted the Athenian police force. (The Scythians were a largely nomadic people who settled successively but temporarily in Asia Minor, southern Russia, and north of the Black Sea.) The Greeks did not subscribe to the notion that the slave was incompetent or untrustworthy. Yet the slave was considered the property of an owner, not because of his or her race (slaves in Greece were generally "barbarian" but resembled their masters in many racial characteristics), but because of his or her "nature." To Aristotle, a slave was an "instrument," ranking in the family hierarchy between children and inanimate objects. Slaves were naturally inferior, for "some people are marked out from the moment of birth to rule or to be ruled."

Most slaves worked in commerce, industry, and construction, supervised by metics. Others were servants; a rich man might require a staff of fifty, and even a poor citizen wanted one or two. More rarely, slaves were farmhands. Greece never employed the large contingents of agricultural slaves employed in the Roman Empire or in the United States before the Civil War. The worst fate for a slave was to be sent to work in the mines, where they worked prostrate for hours on end to extract ore, endured the terrible heat of smelting, which was done on the spot, and suffered appalling living conditions. The silver which enriched the *poleis* relied on the work of the slaves.

By contrast, some of the slaves who rose in commerce and industry to manage banks or businesses became wealthy enough to buy their own freedom. Yet in Greece, freed slaves (like metics) hardly ever acquired the political rights of native-born citizens. Membership in the *polis* was too precious a privilege, its citizens felt, to share with non-Greeks and other supposed inferiors.

The Cityscape

The spirit of the *polis* pervaded its physical structure. At its center stood *acropolis* and *agora*, the city's heart, combining the religious, political, and commercial strivings of the citizenry. Those at Athens are shown on p. 65. Scattered about the *agora* were a variety of public buildings: shrines, temples, fountains, storehouses, meeting houses, and ***stoa***, or free-standing colonnades, sometimes called "porticos." On market days this commercial center would also contain temporary structures, such as the tables on which bankers counted out their coins. Such variety was typical of the Greek city. Regularity in the pattern of streets or the shape of houses was not esteemed by city builders until a much later date (see Chapter 5).

Shrines were everywhere, within the city and out in the country, in public spaces and interspersed among urban dwellings, wherever custom and tradition demanded recognition for some encounter of the human with the divine. A shrine consisted of an altar and a bit of sacred land marked by boundaries—a gate or wall or simple stone markers. Often the shrine became a temple, the most important architectural innovation of the Greeks (see Chapter 4). Temple building accompanied the establishment of the *polis*. Nearly forty temples had been constructed by 600 B.C.E., nearly ninety more in the next century.

Other prominent features of the Greek city were **gymnasiums** and stadiums. These were open spaces, placed as nature dictated at the center, in the suburb, in residential zones, or wherever a flat, clear space could be found to allow physical training and exercise, unadorned except by groves of trees and a sprinkling of shrines. The theater, a Greek invention, was initially another open space where singers and dancers performed in celebration of some god. This unpaved, flat, and roughly circular surface was often located at the foot of a hill on which spectators sat to view the proceedings. In time, stone seats for the audience were constructed or carved out of the native rock.

Acropolis and *agora*, shrine and temple, gymnasium and stadium and theater—these were the main structures of the *polis*. Private houses were nondescript, a jumble of rooms, bundled together along a disorderly network of streets. The great palace architecture of the Minoans and Mycenaeans, long forgotten, could offer no pattern for rich man's house or council building. Also forgotten were the great walls and gates of Mycenae. Almost as an afterthought, the Greek citizens threw a circuit of walls around the mass of their buildings, but these were only lightly fortified, if at all, and played little part in defining the *polis*.

In the featureless houses of the *polis* lived people of all classes, intermixed: rich and poor, citizen and

The Agora and Acropolis

Plan of the Athenian agora: *The citizens of Athens shopped, did their banking, talked about the news or the latest ideas, and sacrificed to the gods in the market zone or agora—the physical center of civic life. They also attended religious rituals on the Acropolis (below).*

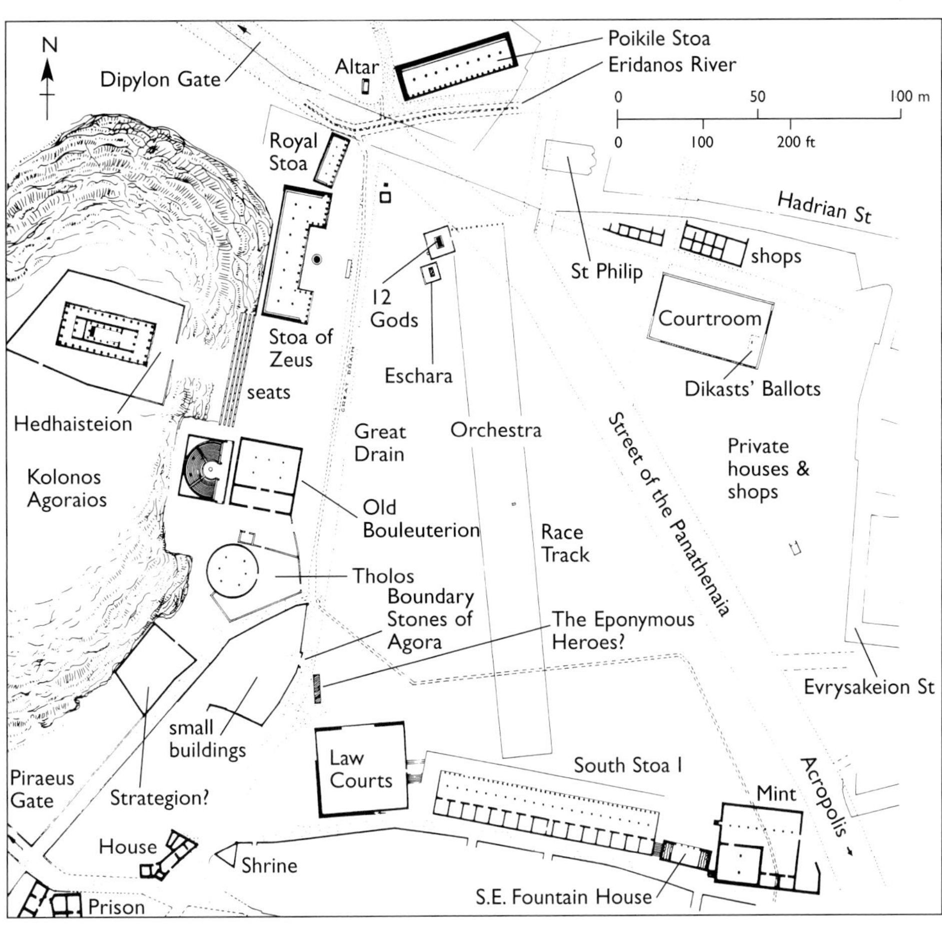

Plan of the Acropolis, Athens *(below)*: *The Parthenon (1), Erechtheum (2), Propylaia (3), and Temple of Athena Nike (4), whose reconstruction, 447–420 B.C.E., marked a high point in Athens' development as a major city.*

foreigner, free and slave. The total population was small. A population of 4000 or 5000 free men and women was common, and few cities exceeded 40,000. To these figures should be added at least an equal number of foreigners and slaves. Athens at its peak in 431 B.C.E. was the largest city by far, having a combined urban and rural population of 310,000. This number comprised 172,000 free men and women (of whom less than half lived in Athens and its harbor town of Piraeus), 28,000 metics (concentrated in Piraeus), and 110,000 slaves. Of this total, approximately 15 percent—between 40,000 and 50,000 adult males—were citizens who directed the course of both city and empire. The remaining 85 percent—slaves, foreigners, children, and women—had no voice in Athenian public life.

The free male citizens of the Greek *polis* were those whom the philosopher Aristotle had in mind when he asserted that "man is a political animal," or an animal capable of living in a city. Communities of no more than 100,000 citizens—not too small and not too large—should join, Aristotle advised, for "the purpose of living the good life after the manner of a political community." Nothing was more crucial to that ideal of the good life than justice. In pursuit of that preeminent value, the *polis* took form.

JUSTICE AND THE *POLIS*

Like modern cities, the Greek *polis* included rich people and poor ones. In the ancient world no fabric of laws or values had limited the right of the wealthy and powerful to exploit subordinates. The *polis*-dwelling Greeks were the first people in the Western world to formulate such a notion—that of ***isonomia***, or "equality before the law." That guarantee in no way implied the leveling of social classes, and it never extended to non-citizens. Yet it was a lofty principle which, from the Archaic through the next age, the Classical (about 500 to 323 B.C.E.), prevailed in many of the *poleis*, notably in Sparta and Athens. Extracts from Greek writings on law and justice are given in *Witnesses* on pp. 67 and 70.

Law and Tyranny

On a sparse diet of barley and lentils varied with figs, grapes, and garlic, the Greek peasant struggled to survive. The poorest men owned the least land (about one-third of the arable land around Athens in the Archaic period). They were often the victims of those who owned the most (those of the hoplite class or better, who together possessed two-thirds of the land).

Map 3.2 Greek Colonization and Trade: *"Hellas" consisted of the Greek-speaking world. At first, Hellenes lived on the mainland of modern Greece, clustering in and near their distinctive* poleis. *Later, those* poleis *sent out colonists, who created new cities loosely related to their "mother cities" or* metropoleis *in the homeland. The Greek cities established around the Mediterranean region, concentrated in the Aegean, participated in a lively trade network. "Hellas" embraced all its cities, colonies, and ventures—all sites of Greek culture, even when not located in Greece.*

Resources were slight, population pressure was great, and the wealthy would not yield to the demands of the poor: to release them from their debts, to give more seed or lend more tools, or to give up their own land. The magistrates to whom the poor man turned for justice were landowners, too, and more inclined to protect the interests of the rich than to defend the poor from exploitation.

In earlier societies, poor peasants locked in conflict with rich landowners often sank into serfdom—dependents often immobilized by debt who owed the landowners produce and service. In Greece at least a few of the peasants were able to climb into the political class, the circle of those who debated the issues of state and made decisions. These few achieved this status because rich and poor alike came to agree that the *polis* should guarantee its citizens "equality before the law."

The principle of equality before the law was established only after long social conflict. Especially in the early days of the *poleis*, there was strife between the various classes or factions within Greek society: the nobly born (the *aristoi*, "the best," from which term derives our word "aristocracy"), the wealthy few (the *oligoi*, from which comes the English "oligarchy"), and the people (the *demos*, from which the English "**democracy**"). In any *polis*, one of these groups asserted itself as dominant. At the peak of its development, Corinth was an oligarchy, Athens a democracy. In the late Archaic age, social conflict often led to **tyranny**.

Tyranny was a distinctively Greek phenomenon. It meant the rule of an illegitimate ruler, the tyrant, who seized power and held it by violence. Thus it was quite different from monarchy: the rule of a legitimate king (however ruthless), descended from a royal lineage. Both forms of rule were autocratic (with power concentrated in a single figure), but whereas monarchy can be seen as legitimate because right to rule inheres in the figure holding power, tyranny is not.

Tyranny was a new force in Greek politics. In early Greece the term implied innovation and energy in state-formation, and even had a "democratic" tinge—the tyrant, though himself an aristocrat, often came to power with the support of the *demos*, the ordinary people. In some cases tyrants were prudent and competent rulers whose policies benefited the people.

During the sixth century B.C.E., tyrants ruled Corinth and Athens. In Corinth, the tyrant Cypselus expelled the arrogant noble clan of the Bacchiadae, redistributing their wealth to satisfy the urgent land hunger of the *demos*, who propelled him to power.

WITNESSES

On Law and Justice, I

The publication of law codes was important for the citizens of the Greek poleis, *as it was for other ancient communities. The poet Homer describes a scene in which justice is being exercised by acknowledged public authorities. The poet Hesiod paints a stark contrast between the unjust—those whose "verdicts are crooked"—and the just, who "know neither hunger nor ruin." The historian Herodotus reports the conversation of a Greek exile to the Persian king, in which the former explains the mystery of the Spartans' courage: it is because the law is their master.*

Elders adjudicate in a scene on the shield of Achilles (c. 750 B.C.E.):

The people were assembled in the market place, where a quarrel
had arisen, and two men were disputing over the blood price
for a man who had been killed. One man promised full restitution
in a public statement, but the other refused, and would accept nothing.
Both then made for an arbitrator, to have a decision;
and people were speaking up on either side, to help both men.
But the heralds kept the people in hand, as meanwhile the elders
were in session on benches of polished stone in the sacred circle ...
The two men rushed before these, and took turns speaking their cases,
and between them lay on the ground two talents of gold, to be given
to that judge who in this case spoke the straightest opinion.

(Homer, *Iliad*, 18:497–504, 506–508; ed. R. Lattimore, 1951)

Hesiod on prosperity for those who do justice (c. 700 B.C.E.):

Justice howls when she is dragged by bribe-devouring men
whose verdicts are crooked when they sit in judgment.
Weeping and clothed in mist, she follows through the cities
and dwellings of men, and visits ruin on those
who twist her straight ways and drive her out.
But those who give straight verdicts and follow justice ...,
live in a city that blossoms, a city that prospers.
Then youth-nurturing peace comes over the land, and Zeus
who sees afar does not decree for them the pains of war.
Men whose justice is straight know neither hunger nor ruin,
but amid feasts enjoy the yield of their labors.

(Hesiod, *Works and Days*; ed. R. Lattimore, 1960)

Damaratus explains to Xerxes how Spartans obey the law (c. 450 B.C.E.):

So ... the Spartans, when they fight singly, are as good men as any in the world, and when they fight in a body, are the bravest of all. For though they be free men, they are not in all respects free; Law is the master whom they own, and this master they fear more than your subjects fear you. Whatever it commands they do; and its commandment is always the same; it forbids them to flee in battle, whatever the number of their foes, and requires them to stand firm, and either to conquer or die.

(Herodotus, *Histories*, 7:104; ed. G. Rawlinson, 1924)

Cypselus then spurred an economic renewal which established Corinth as the foremost commercial center in Greece, destroying Athenian preeminence, if only temporarily. Under Cypselus and his successors, Corinth also minted its own coins, supported poetry and the arts, began a major project of temple construction, and launched a famous festival celebrated with athletic games. The commercial class that benefited from these projects became the sturdy core of a new ruling class. This ruling class, or oligarchy, survived the tyrant, his son Periander (c. 628–588 B.C.E.), and his grandnephew Psammetichus, whose assassination in about 586 B.C.E. closed the chapter on tyranny in Corinth.

After having failed twice to make himself tyrant, Peisistratus of Athens (c. 605–527 B.C.E.) succeeded on his third attempt, around 546 B.C.E. Like Cypselus, he enjoyed the support of the *demos*, whom he favored with many benefits. Without changing existing political structures, this tyrant exiled all his aristocratic rivals and critics, confiscated their lands, and distributed plots of land from this store of confiscations to poorer citizens. He improved the city's water supply and developed new sources of revenue from customs duties and the city-owned silver mines at Laurium. Moreover, he was an active promoter of cultural life, in ways that benefited not only Athens but the whole of Greece.

Poetry was the main form of cultural expression in sixth-century Greece. The epic of wandering minstrels and the lyric of the leisured nobility were chanted or sung to private audiences in rich men's homes. Peisistratus democratized poetry by providing public settings for its recitation. He elevated two festivals, in particular, to state holidays: the Great Panathenaea for Athena, the city's patroness, and the City Dionysia for Dionysus, the god of wine and unrestrained revelry. The Panathenaea featured the public recitation of Homer's verse. Under Peisistratus, not only did Homer become the poet of Athens and all of Greece, but the words of his epics were transcribed, possibly for the first time, using the alphabet recently arrived from Phoenicia. Originally, the Dionysiac festival had been celebrated in the country with lively and ribald song and dance. Now relocated to the center of Athens, it was transformed into a public performance, from which developed the drama, both tragic and comic (see Chapter 4).

After Peisistratus' death in 527 B.C.E., his sons Hipparchus (assassinated in 514 B.C.E.) and Hippias continued his policies. Deposed in 510 B.C.E., Hippias took refuge in Persia, which welcomed disgruntled Greek leaders. In 490 B.C.E. he returned with the Persian invading force, hoping a Persian victory would lead to his reinstatement. The battle, at Marathon, turned against him and his Persian armies, and the founders of the new government established after his deposition were victorious.

The Greek tyrants made some positive contributions to the *poleis* in the Archaic age; they mustered public support, fostered public institutions, and nurtured public values. The irony is that, in so doing, they created the state, a political organism distinct from the personal rule and will of a monarch or any other single individual. Though popular at first, the tyrant was ultimately hated. Nowhere did a tyrant succeed in establishing a dynasty lasting more than three generations. In these formative years of the political life of the West, the Greeks collectively made a momentous decision: they chose to be governed not by rulers but by laws. The future of the *polis* would lie in the hands of the legislator.

Lawmakers of Sparta and Athens

During the Archaic age, legislators shared the stage with tyrants. Sometimes competently, always autocratically, tyrants ruled the people of the Greek *poleis*, elevating their own agendas above any existing political customs or values. Legislators, by contrast, forged the laws by which the citizens, or one group of citizens, ruled a *polis*. Those laws pertained both to criminal and to civil matters—to murder, assault, and feud, but also to transactions in the marketplace and the relations of masters and servants. Of the political structures, or constitutions, created by such legislators, the most famous are those of Sparta and Athens.

Sparta The earliest lawmaker was said to be Lycurgus of Sparta, a figure wrapped in legend. Whether or not he actually existed (possibly during the seventh century B.C.E.), he is credited with the creation of institutions that existed for many centuries. According to tradition, succeeding lawmakers bestowed upon Spartans the "Great Rhetra," or "enactment." This brief and cryptic document underlay the principles of the Spartan constitution. In the seventh century B.C.E., Sparta had achieved victory in a series of wars (begun the previous century) waged for the domination of the adjacent and fertile region of Messenia.

Victory brought its burdens. Having conquered hundreds of thousands of free Messenian peasants, the Spartan citizens found it necessary to keep them captive. Over nearly 350 years they pursued a policy of suppression and terror, reducing the conquered Messenians to **helots**, near-slaves, of the state. The helots were forced to labor on plots of land assigned in equal proportion to the handful of Spartan citizens called the "peers" or "equals." The poet Tyrtaeus (fl. c. 685–668 B.C.E.) described the helots' labors: "Like donkeys worn out with huge burdens, compelled by a terrible necessity, they bring to their masters a half of all the fruits of the earth."

The "Great Rhetra" defined the institutions Sparta needed in order to survive as a permanently armed garrison state. Like other Greek *poleis*, it was ruled by a council of thirty men, five annually elected executives, and an assembly of all the citizens. The novelty of the Spartan constitution lay in its mirroring of Spartan society. Elsewhere in Greece the citizenry included landowners and peasants and artisans. In Sparta, all citizens were equal by law, and all were soldiers. Distinctions between rich and poor were erased among the citizen "peers" or "equals," who jointly ruled the oppressed helots and the loosely allied citizens of neighboring *poleis*. These neighbors (to whom were left the functions of manufacture and trade, as those of agriculture were left to the helots) possessed a limited form of citizenship: they were expected to fight in the Spartan army, but had no political rights.

From around 550 B.C.E., the Spartan "equals" subjected themselves to a harsh regime, organized according to ancient structures of tribe and brotherhood. From age seven to age fifty, Spartan males lived with their comrades in military camps—not in private households with their wives and children. At age thirty, they were admitted to the assembly and allowed greater freedom to visit their marital homes. Meanwhile, they ate in common eating clubs, slept in barracks, and passed their days (when they were not at war) in drill, singing, and dancing—the sum total of their cultural activity. Engaging neither in agriculture nor commerce, their business was warfare. Intellectual, domestic, and economic life were subordinated to the needs of a male society perpetually ready for battle. This manner of life was expected to instill the virtues necessary so that Spartans might behave as the poet Tyrtaeus, spokesman for the city's militarist values, advised:

For no man ever proves himself a good man in war
Unless he can endure to face the blood and the slaughter,
go close against the enemy and fight with his hands.

Sparta's constitution made it, by the mid-sixth century, the most powerful *polis* in Greece. What kind of system was it? The Greeks considered Sparta an oligarchy, and indeed the city supported oligarchies among its allies and occasionally intervened to impose them elsewhere. But it also fitted other descriptions. It was democratic, in that the Spartan citizens accepted a leveling of condition, and became true "equals" in duty to the state and in submission to its laws. It was communistic in that property ownership was a right subordinated to the needs of the community: all shared in the produce of the land (worked by others), owned by no individual (at least not before the fourth century B.C.E.). It was aristocratic, in that the Spartans ruled as a nobility over the intimidated helots and neighboring cities. It was imperialistic, in that it depended on the subjugation of another people. It was totalitarian, in that all rights were subordinated to nationalist and militaristic goals. This curious society has been much admired by the philosopher Plato (c. 427–347 B.C.E.), among other fantasizers of ideal commonwealths. But was it just? It was—but only for the "equals," a restricted and ever-shrinking class. In contrast, the Athenian lawmakers—Draco, Solon, Cleisthenes—came closer to organizing a truly just society.

MUST READS

The World of the Greek poleis

Herodotus	*History*
Thucydides	*History of the Peloponnesian War*
Aristotle	*The Constitution of Athens*
Xenophon	*Oeconomicus (The Housholder)*
Plutarch	*Lives*, especially of *Lycurgus, Themistocles, Pericles*
Arrian	*Life of Alexander the Great*

Athens During the seventh century B.C.E. nine magistrates called archons ruled Athens, all of them members of the landowning class. These men (who comprised the council called the Areopagus) laid down the laws—and they were the laws, for outside of their personal judgment and memory there was no repository of the principles of justice. In about 621 B.C.E. the lawmaker Draco first organized this body of legal custom and had the laws inscribed on stone for the benefit of a *demos* who wanted to know them and, apparently, knew how to read. The publication of laws, wherever it occurs, is a landmark. It records the moment when people are given the means of knowing the otherwise mysterious rules by which they are governed. As the later playwright Euripides wrote, "When the laws are written down, weak and rich men get equal justice; the weaker, when abused, can respond to the prosperous in kind, and the small man with justice on his side defeats the strong." Draco's legacy to the small man of Athens was knowledge of the laws, and thus the possibility of justice.

Those of Draco's laws that survive concern criminal acts—principally homicide, the pressing legal issue of early societies. They define transgressions and assign punishments—of such severity that later political writers gave the name "draconian" to a very harsh punishment. Draco's achievement, however, pales next to that of Solon (c. 640–559 B.C.E.), an aristocrat and archon who, responding to the pleas of the *demos*, managed to rebuild Athenian society on new principles (see *Witnesses*, p. 70). If he had not done so, Athens might have become another Sparta, dedicated to the repression of a subject serf population.

WITNESSES

On Law and Justice, II

These passages on law and justice give evidence again of the immense importance for the Greeks of the ideal of justice. The archon Solon explains how he managed to balance the demands of competing factions in Athens, protecting both. The philosopher Socrates, in prison, refuses to allow his friends to secure his freedom, lest he violate the laws of the city that had reared him. The philosopher Aristotle argues that the human being is perfected by law and justice—without which he is "the most unscrupulous and savage of animals."

Solon explains his just settlement of factional struggles between rich and poor in Athens (c. 594/3 B.C.E.):

I gave the people as much privilege as they have a right to:
  I neither degraded them from rank nor gave them free hand;
and for those who already held the power and were envied for money,
  I worked it out that they also should have no cause for complaint.
I stood there holding my sturdy shield over both the parties;
  I would not let either side win a victory that was wrong.

(Solon, *Greek Lyrics*, 2e, 20; ed. R. Lattimore, 1960)

In prison, Socrates imagines that the personified Laws of Athens call upon him to obey them, and not, by escaping, to evade a sentence of death (360 B.C.E.): You, Socrates, are breaking the covenants and agreements which you made with us at your leisure, not in any haste or under any compulsion or deception, but having had seventy years to think of them, during which time you were at liberty to leave the city, if we were not to your mind, or if our covenants appeared to you to be unfair. You had your choice, and might have gone either to Lacedaemon or Crete, which you often praise for their good government, or to some other Hellenic or foreign State. Whereas you, above all other Athenians, seemed to be so fond of the State, or, in other words, of us her laws (for who would like a State that has no laws?), that you never stirred out of her: the halt, the blind, the maimed, were not more stationary in her than you were. And now you run away and forsake your agreements. Not so, Socrates, if you will take our advice; do not make yourself ridiculous by escaping out of the city.

(Plato, *Crito*, trans. Benjamin Jowett)

Aristotle argues that humans are excellent creatures when embracing justice, but evil when lacking it; and for this reason they should belong to a state (c. 330 B.C.E.): Therefore the impulse to form a partnership of this kind [that is, a state] is present in all men by nature; but the man who first united people in such a partnership was the greatest of benefactors. For as man is the best of the animals when perfected, so he is the worst of all when sundered from law and justice. For unrighteousness is most pernicious when possessed of weapons, and man is born possessing weapons for the use of wisdom and virtue, which it is possible to employ entirely for the opposite ends. Hence when devoid of virtue man is the most unscrupulous and savage of animals ... Justice on the other hand is an element of the state; for judicial procedure, which means the decision of what is just, is the regulation of the political partnership.

(Aristotle, *Politics*, 1.1.12, 1253, 32–38; ed. H. Rackham, 1932)

When Solon was elected chief archon in 594 B.C.E., the poorest peasants of Attica were in danger of slipping into serfdom. Each year they borrowed seed and tools. If they could not repay the value of that debt, they lost possession of their land, mortgaged to wealthy landowners. Driven deeper into debt, the least fortunate of these mortgaged life itself to satisfy their creditors: they sold their children, their wives, and themselves into slavery. Many were resold abroad. These lost Athenians were recovered by Solon. He issued a call for their return, sent agents abroad to identify and reclaim them, and provided funds for the purchase of their freedom.

As a further step in his policy, called the "lifting off of burdens," Solon cancelled existing debts—thereby abolishing the quasi-serfdom of the poor peasant.

Witness to his success (as he announced in the verses he later composed) was the "Black Earth" herself, freed of the stones inscribed with notices of debt which had pierced her surface:

> *I took away the mortgage stones stuck in her breast,*
> *and she, who went a slave before, is now set free.*

Next on Solon's agenda was a program to rebuild the economy. He promoted the export of oil and wine, which could be produced in surplus and sold abroad for cash; but he discouraged the export of wheat, for shortages of this grain meant famine. He invited artisans to relocate to Athens. The excellent work of Athenian potters soon invigorated the ceramic industry, in particular, and the influx of these and other skilled artisans allowed Athens to reestablish the commercial primacy it had yielded to Corinth. To encourage the use of all native talent, Solon directed that each man must teach a trade to his son. If he did not, his son would have no moral or legal responsibility to sustain his parent in old age.

To prevent a recurrence of the pernicious war between rich and poor, Solon revised the Athenian constitution to give the less privileged a voice in the political process. "I stood there holding my sturdy shield over both the parties," reflected Solon, referring to the rich and poor; "I would not let either side win a victory that was wrong." He classified the citizenry into four grades from the richest to poorest. At the top were the "men of five hundred bushels" (in annual yield of wheat); next, the "three hundred-bushel men," or horsemen; third, the "two hundred-bushel men" or "men of the line," wealthy enough to arm themselves as hoplites; fourth, the simple, even landless, "workers." Previously, the top rank of these social groups had held exclusive power.

With wealth, not birth, as the determinant of social status, the old aristocratic system gave way. Solon opened the archonship to men of the second rank, and apparently created a council of 400 persons to be drawn from all ranks except the lowest. By this constitution, Solon did not institute full democracy, in the modern sense, but he came close to doing so.

Solon enacted his revolutionary program swiftly. His work completed, he performed a last notable deed: he resigned, before he himself might be tempted to become a tyrant, or before the *demos* might desire to make him one. Both the Roman dictator Julius Caesar and the first President of the United States, George Washington, also declined the crowns offered them. But they did not renounce power so decisively as did their Athenian predecessor.

Two generations later (the interlude marked by Peisistratus' tyranny), the aristocrat Cleisthenes (fl. c. 508 B.C.E.) carried Solon's work of social reconstruction forward in the direction of democracy. Whereas for Solon the great threat to the Athenian *polis* was greed, for Cleisthenes it was the ancient authority of clans, brotherhoods, and tribes. These groups promoted the rule of the great aristocratic families. To counter the power of clan and tribe, Cleisthenes devised a wholly new system of social organization. Its basic unit was the *deme* (from the

***Map 3.3 Athens, its Allies and Enemies, c. 430* B.C.E.:** *Athens was the only major city of Attica, a triangular region projecting to the southeast from central Greece. By 500* B.C.E.*, the city dominated the region. Fifty years later, as center of the Athenian Empire, it dominated constellations of mainland, overseas, and island cities as well. The capital city was itself a democracy that had been reorganized by Cleisthenes (c. 508* B.C.E.*) so that representatives to its council were chosen from a social cross-section without regard to earlier tribal solidarities.*

Greek *demos*), or village. Before Cleisthenes, a young Athenian was registered in a *phratry*, or brotherhood, to which he belonged by virtue of birth. Now he would be registered in a deme by virtue of residence. Cleisthenes thus removed from the realm of politics the dimensions of kinship and hereditary rights, and approached closer to his ideal of *isonomia*—equality before the law.

The next step was to reconstitute the traditional tribe (of which there were four) according to new principles. The *polis* was divided into thirty regions or "thirtieths," each formed from several contiguous demes. These thirtieths were then grouped into three zones of ten thirtieths each: those of the plain, those of the city, and those of the coast. From the thirty divisions, ten new "tribes" were assembled to replace the four traditional ones, each consisting of three thirtieths in all and one from each of the three geographical zones—thus attaining a balance of rich plain dwellers, poor hill dwellers, and the middling sort of the coasts in each tribe. Each of the 10 tribes chose by lot 50 representatives to a council of 500 citizens (an expansion of the one Solon presumably created of 400), and served as a governing committee of that council for one-tenth of each year.

Cleisthenes' redefinition of the tribe was, in fact, a masterly act of social restructuring. In the world's first democracy, men could no longer claim the right to rule others by reason of blood and association. Tribes were composed of citizens from demes that varied in wealth, background, and interest, and politics was open to a process of decision-making based on argument and debate rather than origin and custom.

A final ingredient to the democratized constitution was **ostracism**, possibly another invention of Cleisthenes. This device, which was first used in 487 B.C.E., answered the need of citizens who recognized that a *polis* in which the *demos* ruled was vulnerable to seduction by tyrants. To forestall the rise of any tyrant, each year the citizens would assemble to vote whether there was a man in Athens dangerous to the state. They did so by inscribing a name on a shard of pottery, or *ostrakon*, the most available form of stationery—hence the term "ostracism." Whoever won this prize of unpopularity (some years, there was no candidate) would be exiled for ten years, whether or not he had committed any crime.

Justice in the Classical Age

During the Classical age—from about 500 to 323 B.C.E.—the Greek *poleis* flourished, at first, under the constitutions forged by legislators of the Archaic age; then they declined from the impact of war and misrule. The experience of Athens, in particular, traced a spectacular trajectory to glorious fruition and then to inglorious old age.

Athens was fortunate in its leaders. Solon originated the concept of the responsibility of the *polis* to its citizens. Cleisthenes created the structure by which citizens could rule the *polis*. Over the following (fifth) century, a series of leaders guided Athens. Aristides, Xanthippus, and Themistocles were leaders of the Athenian state in the critical years following the Battle of Marathon in 490 B.C.E. After 480 B.C.E., the general Cimon policed the seas and secured the primacy of Athens in the Aegean. Toward mid-century, the democrats Ephialtes and Pericles held sway. Ephialtes was assassinated, and in 443 B.C.E. Pericles (c. 495–429 B.C.E.) assumed the leadership of Athens, now the foremost state of the Greek world.

Under Pericles the Athenian democracy and the Athenian Empire reached their maximum development, as shown on Map 3.3. The democracy matured to such an extent that any Athenian citizen might aspire to a one-year term on the Council of Five Hundred. Annual selections by lot filled 700 government positions (not counting places on the 600-man juries)—enough jobs to give every citizen a chance to hold public office at least once in his lifetime. Public officials and jurors received salaries, which ensured that the poor as well as the rich could participate in government. The archonship was still restricted to men of the three highest classes by wealth, but archons were now selected by lot, in order to ensure the most open selection and widest distribution of the honor. Moreover, the archonship was now only an honor, its authority having been transferred to the more broadly based council. Real leadership was exercised by a board of ten generals, elected by popular vote each year. It was to this office that Pericles was reelected by the will of the *demos* every year from 443 to 429 B.C.E.

The citizens of Athens reaped other material benefits during Pericles' administration. In 454 B.C.E., the Athenians had removed the treasure of the Delian league to the capital at Athens, ostensibly to protect it. There Pericles tapped it at will, not only for the costs of defense but also for the private use of Athens. The Persians had destroyed the Athenian temples in 480 B.C.E.; shouldn't the monies gathered to rebuff the Persians be used to rebuild them, and more splendidly? The temples were magnificently rebuilt: the Parthenon and Erechtheum, both dedicated to the patron goddess Athena and each adorned with a statue of this deity; the temple to Nike, goddess of Victory; the Propylaea, or entrance gate to the Acropolis on the west. The ruins that stand on the Acropolis today still impress the viewer with the genius of their makers and the noble spirit of the civilization that produced them. A reconstruction of the Acropolis is shown on p. 65.

The leader of this democratic yet imperialistic *polis* was an idealistic aristocrat. Pericles was the friend of artists and thinkers: Sophocles the dramatist and Phidias the sculptor, Herodotus the historian, Protagoras the sophist (a teacher of philosophy or rhetoric noted for clever argumentation), Anaxagoras the philosopher, and Aspasia, Pericles' learned mistress. An imperious strategist at times, yet a democrat at heart, Pericles never boasted in public but led from the background. No document records his own words, but the contemporary historian Thucydides (c. 471–400 B.C.E.) may have been present at the speech Pericles gave in 431 B.C.E., and he reported its unforgettable message (see *Witnesses*, right).

In this speech, known to later generations as his "Funeral Oration," Pericles commemorated the dead of the first year of the Peloponnesian War by celebrating the city for which they had died—its independence, its democratic system, its encouragement of individual expression, its love of beauty and wisdom. Athens was, he maintained, the center of Greek culture, home to poets and philosophers, historians and sculptors, the focus of all discussion. It was by its example, he proclaimed, the "school," or "educator" of Hellas, the universe of Greek *poleis*.

Of Pericles' Athens, however, we may ask the question: Was it just? For the citizens, yes: this group, which included rich and poor, city and country-dweller, idler and artisan, attained an unprecedented level of political privilege. But excluded from the citizenry was more than half the population of Attica: foreigners, slaves, women, and children. Also excluded were the residents of the subject cities of the Athenian Empire. Any assessment of Athenian democracy must recognize the injustice suffered by the great number of the excluded. Nevertheless, the achievement of true political equality for much of the Athenian citizenry was unprecedented.

When Pericles delivered the "Funeral Oration," the Peloponnesian War had already begun. The Athens that surrendered to Sparta a generation later, in 404 B.C.E., was a ghost of the city that Pericles celebrated. Sparta stripped Athens of parts of her walls and her ships. It tried to smother her political institutions, imposing, briefly, an oligarchical government; called by the unhappy Athenians the rule of the "Thirty Tyrants," soon rejected in favor of a revived democracy. In the post-war period, Athenian democracy reached its zenith while Athenian power diminished. The citizens voted themselves ever-expanding government services, collected regular pay for government jobs, and sued each other in the law courts. They ignored the impending threat to the city's autonomy—the growing power of Macedonia, which loomed larger after the mid-fourth century.

Sparta, meanwhile, in the very flush of victory lost its heart as a military power. In 371 B.C.E., it was beaten decisively (at Leuctra, in Boeotia), in the aimless struggle among the *poleis* that filled these years after the Peloponnesian conflict. The victorious city was Thebes, a newcomer to the first rank of the *poleis*. Theban success was owed to the innovations of her military commander Epaminondas (c. 418–362 B.C.E.), the first Greek captain to do something new with the phalanx since its creation some four centuries earlier. Massing his hoplites at fifty deep on one wing, he crushed the Spartan troops, heretofore thought invincible. Over four hundred out of seven

WITNESSES

Pericles

In his "Funeral Oration" for the dead fallen in war, Pericles clarifies the reasons for the greatness of Athens—for which her citizens are proud to die (431 B.C.E.*).*

[O]ur system of government does not copy the institutions of our neighbours. ... Our constitution is called a democracy because power is in the hands not of a minority but of the whole people. When it is a question of settling private disputes, everyone is equal before the law; when it is a question of putting one person before another in positions of public responsibility, what counts is not membership of a particular class, but the actual ability which the man possesses. No one, so long as he has it in him to be of service to the state, is kept in political obscurity because of poverty. ...

Then there is a great difference between us and our opponents, in our attitude towards military security. ... Our city is open to the world, and we have no periodical deportations in order to prevent people observing or finding out secrets which might be of military advantage to the enemy. This is because we rely, not on secret weapons, but on our own real courage and loyalty. There is a difference, too, in our educational systems. The Spartans, from their earliest boyhood, are submitted to the most laborious training in courage; we pass our lives without all these restrictions, and yet are just as ready to face the same dangers as they are. ... Our love of what is beautiful does not lead to extravagance; our love of the things of the mind does not make us soft. We regard wealth as something to be properly used, rather than as something to boast about. As for poverty, no one need to be ashamed to admit it: the real shame is in not taking practical measure to escape from it. ... Taking everything together then, I declare that our city is an education to Greece. ... This, then, is the kind of city for which these men, who could not bear the thought of losing her, nobly fought and nobly died. Its greatness derives from the freedom of its citizens, which permits them to excel in many enterprises, and suits them to respond flexibly to any crisis that might arise. Pericles contrasts that freedom and flexibility with the rigor and regulation of Spartan society.

(From Thucydides, *Peloponnesian War*, 2:36, 39–42; ed. R. Warner, 1954)

WHO'S WHO

Lawmakers of Athens

Solon (639–c. 550 B.C.E.) lawgiver who "lifted burdens" from the Athenian poor and established a representative council that limited the arbitrariness of the archons.

Cleisthenes (c. 570–c. 507 B.C.E.) developed a new system of social organization for Athens based on place of residence, not clan allegiance, and thus promoted the development of democracy.

Pericles (c. 498–429 B.C.E.) presided for a generation over the Athenian city and Empire, under whose patronage and leadership it reached a cultural pinnacle.

hundred Spartan soldiers was killed at Leuctra (not to mention the devastation of allies and auxiliaries), including hundreds of Spartan officers. The humiliation was repeated in 362 B.C.E. at Mantinea. The "equals"—that privileged group of Spartan citizens—had, during the three centuries of their ascendancy, admitted no new families to their ranks. In the preceding century, their number had plummeted from about 5000 to 1000. The losses at Leuctra and Mantinea delivered a blow that crippled Sparta.

Thebes held the stage only briefly. For three years it had held, as hostage, a young prince who learned military arts there. In 359 B.C.E., this young man, Philip, became the second Macedonian king of that name. He promptly undertook a program of conquest, seizing cities around the northern Aegean and in Euboea, east of Athens. At Chaeronea, in 338 B.C.E., he smashed Athens and her allies, who had rallied too late to stop his advance. Athens had apparently forgotten what it had understood clearly in the years before Marathon—that life under a foreign master would crush her own identity. She rushed to support Philip, and in an act of great irony, made this foreign monarch a citizen.

City by city, region by region, Philip absorbed the once proud and autonomous *poleis*. Henceforth, although the Greek cities continued to exist, they never regained the quality of public life that they had known when free. Under Philip's son Alexander the Great Greece would be swept back into the world of monarchs and empires.

PRIVATE LIFE OF THE *POLIS*

In their public life, the ancient Greeks sought *isonomia* (equality before the law) and access to justice for rich and poor (though they did not generally, as in Sparta, eliminate social distinctions among citizens). The private life of the Greek *polis*, in contrast, was characterized by a great inequality between male and female. Women were subordinated to men to an extraordinary degree. Even the domestic space that they occupied was clearly separated from the open and public space occupied by men.

The Household: Woman's Place

The public life of the *polis* was based on distinctive patterns of private life, whose fundamental unit was the ***oikos***, or household. The need to preserve the *oikos* in an environment of continuing scarcity was the overwhelming concern of its head, always a male. This need triggered the anxiety that underlay the social organization of the *polis*.

The *oikos* consisted of a man, his wife and children, and related and unrelated dependents including slaves. The philosopher Aristotle defines these household members in his *Politics*, in a descending hierarchy from free adults to children and slaves to animals and even tools: a continuous system of superior and inferior being headed by a dominant male, since "the male is by nature superior and the female inferior, the male ruler and the female subject."

The *oikos* was **patrilineal** in origin and purpose, and **patriarchal** in character. A patrilineal family traces its foundation to a male forebear on the father's side. It considers as descendants only males. Female offspring are valued insofar as they marry men whose families, also patrilineal, are useful friends or allies to her family of birth (her natal family). In patrilineal families, all individuals (including children of both sexes) are asked to conform to the need for survival in the male line. Patrilineal families may also be patriarchal. In a patriarchy, not only is the bloodline traced through the father's ancestors, but power within the family and over all its members is exercised by a senior male.

The elevation of the male head-of-household in Greek society was matched by a derogation of the woman. The attitude is apparent in the works of Greek philosophers and poets. Aristotle may have spoken for common opinion when he stated that "we should look upon the female state as being as it were a deformity, though one which occurs in the ordinary course of nature." The tragedian Aeschylus, in his *Eumenides*, denied women's role even in reproduction. The god Apollo explains to the goddess Athena:

> *The mother is no parent of that which is called her child, but only nurse of the new-planted seed that grows. The parent is he who mounts.*

For Homer, women were valuable as sexual objects and as artisans: like the seven women the king Agamemnon offered the warrior Achilles, "the work of whose hands is blameless, ... who in their beauty surpassed the races of women." The poet Hesiod

Working Women

Greek pottery: *Shown here are characteristic forms of women's work. This detail from a* lekythos *or flask by the Amasis painter, c. 540 B.C.E. (above), shows women spinning and weaving at home. On this three-handled black-figure water jar* (hydria) *by the Priam painter, c. 520 B.C.E., women are shown carrying water from the fountain in jugs (below).* (top: Metropolitan Museum of Art; below: Museum of Fine Arts, Boston, William/Francis Warden Fund)

Priam painter, Black-figure hydria, c. 520 B.C.E.

described Pandora, the first woman, according to Greek mythology, as "an evil for mortal men," the "tempting snare" from whom descends the race of "wicked womenfolk." The great misogynist Simonides of Amorgos compared women to pigs, dogs, asses, horses, and monkeys, finding worthwhile only the woman who was like a bee, thrifty and productive: "To her alone no blame is attached, ... She grows old cherishing a husband who cherishes her, ... She does not take pleasure in sitting among the women / when they are discussing sex."

Nevertheless, women did have their champions. For Plato, capable women were suitable candidates for political rule. The ruling class of "Guardians," in the ideal state he outlines in his *Republic*, includes women who are expected to procreate more exceptional leaders. Here his views reflected to some extent the social reality of Sparta, which he admired, where women had somewhat greater freedom than in other cities and participated fully in athletic training. The tragedians portrayed female characters of extraordinary depth and power. Aeschylus created the magnificent but wily and dangerous Clytemnestra, and Sophocles the courageous Antigone. Euripides depicted giants of womankind: the implacable Medea, driven by insane jealousy to kill her children; the love-wracked Phaedra rejected by her stepson Hippolytus; the eloquent Hecuba, weeping for Troy and for her slaughtered grandson Astyanax.

Such commanding women may have reigned in tragic theater, but they were nowhere to be found in Classical Greek society. The sharp divergence between the dramatic portrayal of women and their actual social role defies explanation. Perhaps some women, though confined to a domestic role, impressed at least some men with their high capacity, and the tragic playwrights and poets report this rare and exceptional woman. Or perhaps the tragedians echo a tradition of female leadership (dating back to Mycenaean times) wholly lost by the Classical age in which they wrote. Whatever the explanation of the discrepancy between literature and life, the status of women in Classical Greece was low.

Generally, girls were married young (at about age fifteen, soon after attaining puberty) to considerably older men (about age thirty) chosen by their families. This age difference, which strengthens the imbalance of power within the family, is characteristic of patriarchal families. The wife's duties included obedience to her husband, who made most decisions of family life. They also included childbearing. Over her twenty to thirty years of fertility (if she did not die young in childbirth), a woman was expected to give birth to several children, including a male heir.

Although subordinate to her husband, a woman held some authority as a result of the useful labor she performed. Examples of tasks are shown here on the flask and water jar. In peasant families, she sowed and harvested, ground grain, carried water, milked and herded, gathered and stored surpluses. In wealthy families, she was a manager of household supplies, of tools and wardrobe, of slaves. In all households, she was the producer of textiles, performing the tasks of spinning, weaving, and embroidering, which from earliest times had been a female province.

Engaged in such labor, a woman spent her life first in her father's household and then in her husband's: each in turn was her "lord." She could not choose to remain single and live in her own house, or even at home. She could be divorced by her husband (though she could not, under any circumstances, choose to divorce him). In that case, she would be returned, with her dowry, to her father's house.

Just as the wife in a Greek household was subordinate to her husband, children were the subjects of their parents, and especially of their fathers, from the very moment of birth. The father had exclusive power to decide whether or not a child was to be accepted into the household. A child might be unwanted because resources were scarce, or because the family already numbered sufficient children or children of that sex. The unwanted child would then be "exposed"—left unprotected in a public place.

Often, the exposed child died. Sometimes he or she was claimed by other adults. Childless couples might take abandoned children into their households. Families who needed hands to assist with domestic tasks, or managers of workshops or brothels equally in search of inexpensive labor might also take them in. In none of these cases was a child "adopted,"in the modern sense. As the child was transferred from his or her original family to another one, his or her status sank from family member to subordinate. It is likely that most of the abandoned children who survived were enslaved.

The father who decided to expose his child thus condemned his own offspring to death, servitude, or slavery. These destinies more often greeted girls than boys. Female infanticide may account for the unnaturally high ratio of males to females in the population, while the practice of feeding girls less than boys may have resulted in girls' greater rate of natural death in childhood. Girls were also exposed more often than boys, though abandoned boys, as well as girls, were pressed into sex slavery—sometimes undergoing first the further humiliation of castration (a procedure which, in the absence of antibiotics, was also extremely dangerous). The plentiful supply of abandoned children meant that fewer foreign slaves were required. Slavedealers kept watch over the usual places of abandonment.

Along with evidence of infanticide and abandonment, there is evidence that many children were treasured by their parents. That sentiment is known from literary sources in which parents' love for children is described. Parental love is also documented by the gravestones whose inscriptions express the grief of fathers and mothers at the loss of their young children. Children were carefully reared. Mothers generally nursed their own babies. As was the near-universal custom in the ancient Mediterranean region,

Women's Lives

Life and death: *Confined to their houses, the wives and daughters of Greek citizens led quiet lives. Here we glimpse some moments, as on this grave stele (above) depicting a lady and her maid studying her jewels, Athens, late fourth century B.C.E.; and on this stone relief from the "Ludovisi throne" (below) where a woman emerging from the bath is robed by her servants, Rome, fifth century B.C.E.* (above: National Archaeological Museum, Athens; below: Museo Nazionale delle Terme, Rome)

Girl playing the lyre: *In leisure hours, a woman might sing to the lyre, a stringed instrument which accompanied the recitation of "lyric" poetry, another Greek innovation. Such musical activity was considered respectable for women in ancient Greece; not so the flute. Women flute-players were often slaves or prostitutes who entertained men at banquets and drinking parties.* (Antiken Sammlungen, Munich)

children were swaddled (wrapped tightly in cloth) at birth, parents probably believing they were protecting their infants. Nurseries were equipped with a variety of toys, feeding bowls, potties, and all the other cheerful paraphernalia found wherever children are cherished and protected.

Loving parents often had to face the sorrow of natural infant death. The mortality rate in ancient Greece ranged around 30 to 40 percent for the first year of life. Children were helpless before infection, to which inadequate nutrition left them even more vulnerable. Epidemic disease (or "plague") ravaged the very young. On average, each female would give birth to five or six children, of whom only two or three might reach adulthood. Life expectancy (about forty-five for men, thirty-six for women) was low largely because of the toll of death on the very young. A male who reached thirty years of age might hope to live to fifty or sixty. But most men had already died by age thirty, and even more women, due to frequent childbirth.

Since adults often died young, families were frequently disrupted by the death of a mother or father. A complete nuclear family, often posed today as the ideal basis of human society, was rare in ancient Greece. A mother's death most often meant the father's remarriage and the children's adjustment to a stepmother. A father's death meant the dissolution of the family, the removal of the children to another household of their father's ancestral line, and the loss of the mother, who returned to her natal family. These were normal, not exceptional, dislocations.

One particular form of family disruption was unique to Greece. It was triggered by the phenomenon of the *epikleros*: the surviving member and sole daughter of a household whose patriarch had died. All household wealth devolved to her. Being a woman, however, she could not inherit. According to Greek law and custom, she must be married to another male of the same line: her father's brother, cousin, nephew. The choice was not hers, nor even his. She was to marry the male closest to her in biological relationship, immediately and without exception. This practice was observed even when it required the new husband first to divorce his own wife.

The obligatory marriage of an *epikleroi* was only one Greek institution in which the economic concerns of the household impinged upon the lives of women. Another was the custom of the dowry. In Greece, as in most ancient civilizations, a woman was married to a man only upon payment of a dowry. In accepting it, the groom's parents assumed the burden of protecting a new family member. The ability to provide a dowry established capacity for marriage. The dowry institution assumes that the woman will not inherit, in her own right, household property, which is reserved for her brothers.

In the urban household of citizen families (specifically in Athens, the city for which evidence is available), women were strictly segregated from men. All women—the wife and mother, her husband's female relations, the female slaves, together with children of both sexes—lived in the *gynaeceum*, or "women's quarters." This set of rooms, sealed with a locked door, was physically remote from those in which adult men slept, ate, and met with their fellows. It was remote, too, from the *agora*, where men met to discuss the news or do the shopping—for men shopped, while women stayed at home.

The *gynaeceum* enfolded the lives of women. It was here that the endless spinning, weaving, sewing, washing, and mending were accomplished. Here women prepared food and planned meals, although they did not usually join the male household members at mealtimes. Children were raised in the *gynaeceum*, surrounded by the conversation and the concerns of women. That setting was limiting but appropriate for girls, whose destiny it was to reenact the lives their mothers lived. What were the effects on the men who shaped the public life of Greece of an early childhood spent exclusively in the company of their mothers and their maids?

Women were, however, permitted to leave their homes to participate in the religious festivals that dotted the calendar. They danced and sang and carried ritual objects in processions. Often their activities were gender related: girls might carry baskets of wool or dolls representing babies as symbols

WITNESSES

Women's Lives

Like the ideal woman envisioned in the Hebrew Bible (see Witnesses, chapter 1, p. 17), Greek women were expected to please their husbands by tending the household. This ideal is expressed in the third passage by the philosopher and historian Xenophon. As in all ancient societies, women also fulfilled expectations in their roles as mothers. That role occasions the more complex images of women as mothers offered in the first two passages by the poet Homer and the playwright Euripides. Homer's Andromache is poignantly aware of her own and her child's vulnerability if her warrior husband can no longer protect her. Euripides' Medea has been abandoned by her husband, and imagines she will be forced to leave her children—whom she will in fact, in the end, destroy.

Andromache, wife of the Trojan hero Hector, begs him to remain home and not lead the fighting, for her sake and her son's (c. 750 B.C.E.):

[She] stood close beside him, letting her tears fall,
and clung to his hand and called him by name and spoke to him: "Dearest,
your own great strength will be your death, and you have no pity
on your little son, nor on me, ill-starred, who soon must be your widow;
for presently the Achaians, gathering together,
will set upon and kill you; and for me it would be far better
to sink into the earth when I have lost you ...
... you are father to me, and my honoured mother,
you are my brother, and you it is who are my young husband.
Please take pity upon me then, stay here on the rampart,
that you may not leave your child an orphan, your wife a widow. ...
(Homer, *Iliad*, 6:405–411, 429–432; ed. R. Lattimore, 1951)

Thinking she must leave her children, Medea laments (c. 431 B.C.E.):

... I am going in exile to another land
Before I have seen you happy and taken pleasure in you,
Before I have dressed your brides and made your marriage beds
And held up the torch at the ceremony of wedding. ...
What was the purpose, children, for which I reared you?
For all my travail and wearing myself away?
They were sterile, those pains I had in the bearing of you.
Oh surely once the hopes in you I had, poor me,
were high ones: you would look after me in old age,
and when I died would deck me well with your own hands;
A thing which all would have done. Oh but now it is gone,
That lovely thought. For, once I am left without you,
Sad will be the life I'll lead and sorrowful for me.
And you will never see your mother again with
your dear eyes, gone to another mode of living.
(Euripedes, *Medea*, 1024–1027, 1029–1039; eds. D. Grene, R. Lattimore, 1951)

Xenophon's householder explains to his wife how she is to keep order in the household (c. 390 B.C.E.): How good it is to keep one's stock of utensils in order, and how easy to find a suitable place in a house to put each set in. ... And what a beautiful sight is afforded by boots of all sorts and conditions ranged in rows! How beautiful it is to see cloaks of all sorts and conditions kept separate, or blankets, or brazen vessels, or table furniture! Yes, no serious man will smile when I claim that there is beauty in the order even of pots and pans set out in neat array. ... There is nothing, in short, that does not gain in beauty when set out in order. ...
(Xenophon, *Oeconomicus*, 8:18–19; ed. E. C. Marchant, 1923)

of their roles, whereas boys engaged in athletic contests. Some festivals were especially linked to women. The "maenads" were women ("madwomen") whose wild and uncontrolled dancing celebrated the god Dionysus. For the Great Panathenaea, selected girls wove a new robe to be worn by the image of the patron goddess Athena. At the Thesmophoria, celebrating the fertility goddesses Demeter and Persephone, women set up their own city, for three brief days near the *agora*, from which men were excluded. There they performed magic rituals to ensure fertility. But these festal occasions were brief interruptions in a life spent almost entirely within the home.

Beyond the Household: Male Space

If the household environment of the *gynaeceum* seems limiting, so, too, do other elements of the private lives of the Greeks: their food, their clothing, their schooling. Of the latter, girls received none beyond the knowledge of the language and customs of their people, transmitted by the women of the household. Older boys went to school, accompanied by a slave called a **pedagogue**, to a master who taught music, gymnastics, and the essential tools of reading and writing (see Chapter 4).

Both men and women wore simple clothing: a tunic or a robe, longer or shorter, variously gathered and fastened. Only the wealthy dyed their clothes (their choice restricted to only a few colors, including the costly Phoenician purple), and few people even washed them more than occasionally. An adult might own only one or two such costumes. A set of clothes might cost as much (in current values) as a personal computer or a used car. The Greeks ate as simply as they dressed, consuming a sparse diet of porridge, porridge, and porridge, enriched with goat cheese, a few olives or figs, as well as an occasional piece of meat.

While women were isolated in the private household, men moved in the public realm, where they might

Gender Wars

Amazons and Greeks: *The struggle between Greek heroes and the female Amazon warriors was a central theme of Greek art, adorning no less a monument than the Parthenon in Athens. Here is a battle scene from the monument of Mausolus of Caria. This relief was possibly by Scopas, a great Greek sculptor of the fourth century* B.C.E. (British Museum, London)

participate in a variety of wholly male organizations. The oldest of these were the ancestral tribes and phratries, networks of men related by blood or by hereditary ties originating in military comradeship. Each newborn son was registered in a phratry, already admitted by virtue of blood and gender to a social network long before he was able to recognize its import.

The other male networks that pervaded Greek society were based on friendship. The action of Homer's *Iliad* revolves around one such friendship: that between Achilles and Patroclus. Slain by the Trojan hero Hector, Patroclus is honored by Achilles. Such male friendships flourished in a military setting, where young men trained together and fought together, united in danger and victory.

In Crete and Sparta, where Archaic military customs survived into the Classical age, young men in arms lived together and were encouraged to form deep ties, possibly homosexual ones. These were also the ties that inspired the fighters in the Sacred Band of Thebes (fourth century B.C.E.). "A band that is held together by the friendship between lovers is indissoluble and not to be broken," wrote the moralist Plutarch (c. 46–120 C.E.), "since the lovers are ashamed to play the coward before their beloved, and the beloved before their lovers, and both stand firm in danger to protect each other." Elsewhere, too, military training and exploits were the setting for important male associations.

The gymnasium was another setting for such relationships—similar in kind because athletics were viewed in part as a preparation for war. From adolescence through old age, Greek men exercised at the gymnasium. Here they also conversed and debated matters of public or intellectual interest—as Socrates instructed young boys in the interlude between games in Plato's dialogue *Lysis*. In the same way, schools were a setting for close relationships among groups of boys and men—both the grammar schools of Athens and the philosophical schools launched by that city's great philosophers Plato and Aristotle.

Achilles and Penthesilia: *In another struggle between a hero and an Amazon, the sculptor Exekias shows the Greek Achilles and the Amazon queen Penthesilea on a black-figure amphora, c. 540* B.C.E. (British Museum, London)

Preeminent among the all-male gatherings of Greek society was the drinking party, or **symposium**. Some of the earliest and finest Greek poetry to survive consists of drinking songs, composed by men engaged in that pastime during leisurely evenings. In private homes, the business of conversation, eating, and drinking (and sexual play with prostitutes or boys) took place in a special "men's room," which respectable women did not enter. Spartan citizens ate together, apart from wives and children, in eating clubs, which continued in another milieu the camaraderie of military exercise. An Athenian drinking party is depicted in Plato's brilliant dialogue entitled the *Symposium*. Here unfolds a rich complex of ideas that might be heard where men, by themselves, sat together in fellowship and freely conversed.

The Greek city can in some ways be seen as a club to which only men belonged. From Homer to Plato, a portrait emerges of an essentially masculine culture. Anthropologists also point to elements of civic ritual that denote a high valuation of the masculine, almost amounting to an obsession with male potency. Before every Athenian house, for example, there stood a "herm," a monument to the god Hermes consisting of the head of the god mounted on a square stone pillar from which projected at the mid-point a swollen, erect phallus. Participants in the festal processions that celebrated the god Dionysus carried huge and prominent terracotta penises. Actors in the comedies of Aristophanes probably also sported oversized leather phalluses, which they tapped or swung or raised as suggested by the script. Perhaps this phallic display is not surprising in a culture whose deities—notably the supreme Zeus—regularly engaged in seduction, adultery, incest, and heterosexual, homosexual, and pederastic rape. This behavior was unashamedly depicted with precision and grace on the exquisite painted vases sold in local and international markets.

Alongside the glorification of unrestrained male sexuality, Greek art celebrated men's power over women. The band of sculpted reliefs on the west side of the Parthenon in Athens, now nearly destroyed, depicts the legendary victory, at the time of the city's foundation, of the Athenian hoplites over the mythical female warriors known as Amazons. Amazons shunned the company of men and constructed their own nation, which they defended by their own prowess. In the Parthenon scenes, as in numerous other portrayals of battles against Amazons—on the frieze of the Temple of Apollo at Bassae, on the throne of Zeus at Olympia, on the Athenian treasury at Delphi, and elsewhere—these fierce women are not merely defeated: they are mangled, humiliated, and annihilated. Two examples are shown on p. 79.

The hostility to women expressed in Greek art and literature, and the importance given to the relationships between men, point to the widespread practice of homosexuality in Greece. The patterns of homosexual relationships differ, however, from those familiar in Western society today. In Greece, older men formed relationships with adolescents over twelve and not yet twenty. These relationships, although deplored by some, were generally seen as beneficial for both parties. It was believed that the young, having been deprived of close relationships with their own fathers, were guided by their older lovers toward understanding and high achievement. When the young man himself entered full adulthood, he in turn would seek an adolescent male companion. These homosexual liaisons in no way were seen to interfere with the heterosexual pursuits of marriage, fatherhood, and household management.

Neither homosexual relationships nor marriage, moreover, ruled out heterosexual relationships with prostitutes and *hetaerae*, or "courtesans." Prostitutes were generally slaves who also performed the roles of servant and entertainer. The *hetaerae*, often foreigners, were elegant and brilliant women who could offer to men companionship of the sort not provided by wives, who were confined by the social limits of the *gynaeceum*. Pericles and Alexander the Great had relationships with *hetaerae*. Pericles' mistress Aspasia was a constant companion, an intellectual who composed speeches and debated issues of philosophy. When she was tried for the grave crime of "impiety," he defended her tearfully before the jury, and in defiance of his own laws, he had his son by her legitimated.

The private life of the Greeks was ordered in a way that best supported their public life. The isolation and subordination of women was complemented by the intricately layered networks linking together the men who created the world's first democracies and laid the bases for later Western political theory. The "people" who were served by those political institutions and theories, however, were defined in markedly narrow and exclusionary terms—a definition restricted by class, by ethnic origin, and by gender. Such deep contradictions must be confronted in any consideration of the achievement of the ancient *polis*.

Conclusion

THE GREEK *POLIS* AND THE MEANING OF THE WEST

Planted on sparse soil and cultivated by hungry men, the Greek *polis*—though it granted justice to some and not to all—was a remarkable achievement. For the Greek experiment has nourished later attempts of Western civilization to create a just society. In modern times, it continues to underlie that quest wherever it occurs, in the West and in the wider world.

REVIEW QUESTIONS

1. How did Greek Archaic age society differ from that of the Mycenean age? How do you define the Greek *poleis*? What roles did the assembly and the phalanx play in the *poleis*?

2. Why did the Greeks consider farming superior to commerce or manufacturing? How did they view slavery? What work did slaves do in Greek society?

3. Did tyrants play a positive or negative role in the development of Greek cities? What did Draco, Solon, and Cleisthenes do for democracy? Why did Sparta develop a unique form of government and society?

4. Why did Pericles call Athens "the school of Hellas"? Was Athens a true democracy under him? What groups were excluded from Athenian citizenship? Why were they excluded?

5. What roles were Greek women allowed to play in public life? How subordinate were Greek women to their fathers and husbands? What was the *gynaeceum*?

6. Why can the Greek city be seen as an exclusive club to which only males were allowed to belong? How important was friendship among Greek males? Contrast the portrayal of males and females in Greek sculpture.

SUGGESTED RESOURCES

The Formation of the *Polis*

Hanson, Victor David, *The Other Greeks: The Family Farm and the Agrarian Roots of Western Civilization* (Berkeley: University of California Press, 1994). Argues that the real Greek innovation—which explains much about the Greek state and civilization—was the family farm, the nursery of concepts of individual rights.

Kurke, Leslie, *Coins, Bodies, Games and Gold: The Politics of Meaning in Archaic Greece* (Princeton: Princeton University Press, 1999). Traces the cultural symbols linked to the emergence of coinage in the Greek Archaic Age, building an ideological basis for the egalitarian *polis* system.

Murray, Oswyn, *Early Greece*, 2nd ed. (Cambridge, MA: Harvard University Press, 1993). Masterful account of the emergence of the *polis* system, and the patterns of cultural and social life that it supported.

Guide to classical Athens: society, economy, culture, politics: **http://www.fhw.gr/chromos/05/en**

Justice and the *Polis*

Cartledge, Paul, *Agesilaus and the Crisis of Sparta* (Baltimore: Johns Hopkins University Press, 1987). A detailed but readable critical history of the career of Agesilaos, king of Sparta during the height of its imperial expansion and its eclipse.

Davies, J.K., *Democracy and Classical Greece*, 2nd ed. (Cambridge, MA: Harvard University Press, 1993). Recent and authoritative study of how—and to what extent—democracy emerged in fifth-century Greece.

Hunter, Virginia J., *Policing Athens: Social Control in the Attic Lawsuits, 420–320* B.C.E. (Princeton: Princeton University Press, 1994). Fascinating exploration of how Athenian society regulated itself by community moral "policing" through the gossip of women and slaves, and the infliction of private as well as public punishments.

Kagan, Donald, *Pericles of Athens and the Birth of Democracy* (New York: Free Press, 1990). One of many studies of the fifth-century Greek world by a leading U.S. expert, focused on the critical Athenian leader Pericles as the creator of the democratic ethos.

Sealey, Raphael, *Demosthenes and his Time: A Study in Defeat* (Oxford: Oxford University Press, 1993). Studies the unraveling of the Athenian democratic paradigm and the world of the *polis* as Macedonia reached for and seized power in the fourth century.

Wood, Ellen, *Peasant-Citizen and Slave: The Foundations of Athenian Democracy* (London, New York: Verso, 1988). A controversial study of the Athenian citizenry. Argues that Greek slavery has been over-stressed and that Athenian agriculture and democracy were not based on slavery, but rather on the free peasantry.

Private Life and the *Polis*

Blundell, Sue, *Women in Ancient Greece* (Cambridge: Harvard University Press, 1995). A recent overview of a topic largely ignored until 1975, but now addressed in an abundance of studies.

Cohen, Edward, *Athenian Economy and Society* (Princeton: Princeton University Press, 1992). A detailed examination of economic practices in Classical Athens, demonstrating the presence of a market economy. Discusses the cultural practices and assumptions that underpinned Athenian business and finances.

Garland, Robert, *The Greek Way of Life: From Conception to Old Age* (New York: Cornell University Press, 1990). An imaginative account of the life-cycle of Classical and Hellenistic men and women, which discusses changing attitudes toward various phases of life.

Golden, Mark, *Children and Childhood in Classical Athens* (Baltimore: Johns Hopkins University Press, 1990). A persuasive reconstruction using archeological and documentary evidence of the lives of one of the most overlooked groups in Greek society—young children.

Halperin, David M., John J. Winkler, and Froma I. Zeitlin, eds., *Before Sexuality: The Construction of Erotic Experience in the Ancient Greek World* (Princeton: Princeton University Press, 1990). Fifteen authors examine Greek sexuality in relation to myth, law, medicine, and language, in order to comprehend how it functioned in a cultural context fundamentally different from our own.

Pomeroy, Sarah B., *Families in Classical and Hellenistic Greece: Representations and Realities* (Oxford: Clarendon Press, 1997). With a superb command of sources, Pomeroy studies the Greek family across centuries and regions, including patterns of inheritance and the meaning of death and work.

Everyday life in ancient Greece: **http://www.ibiscom.com/ancientgreece.htm**

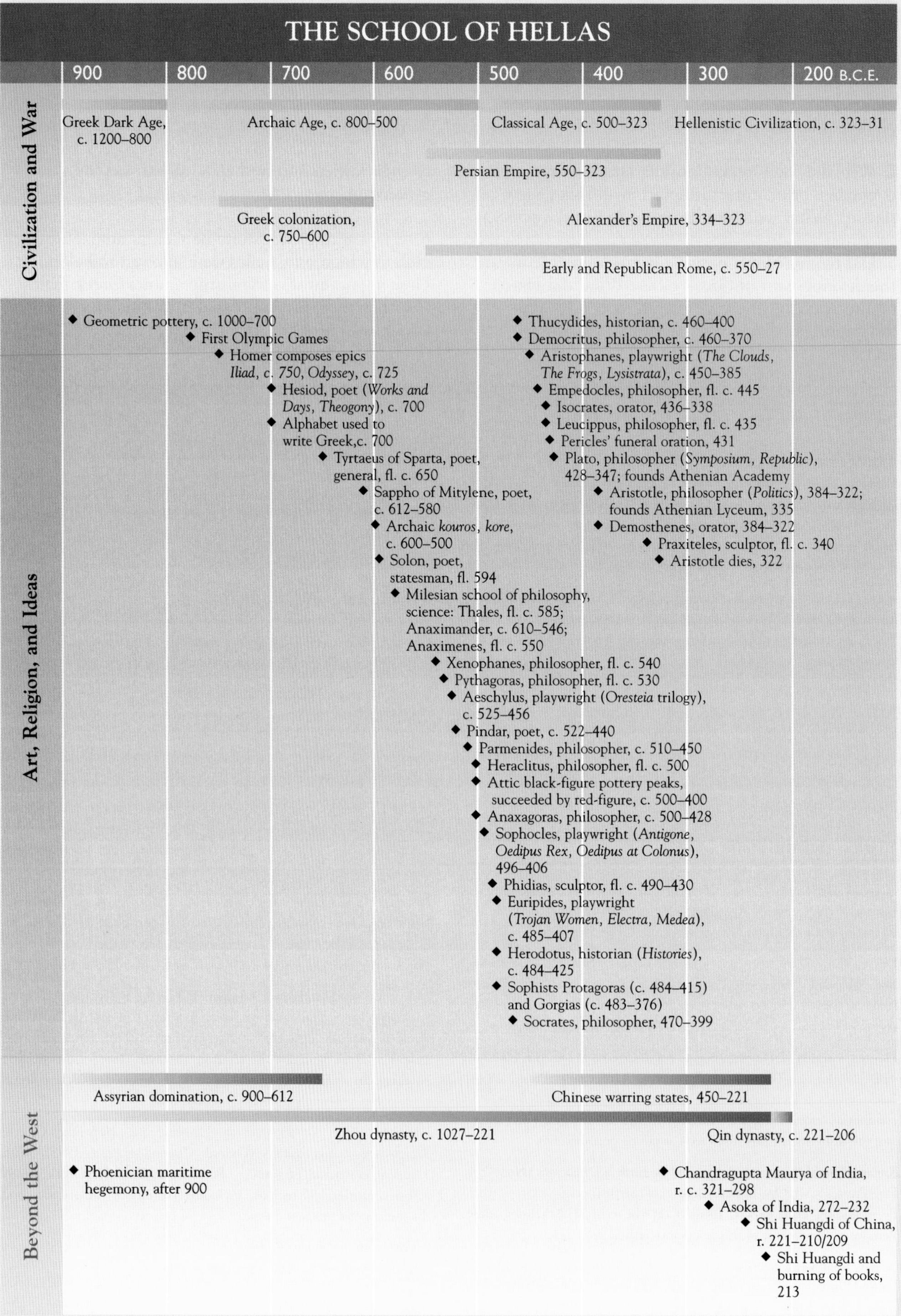
THE SCHOOL OF HELLAS
900
800
700
600
500
400
300
200 B.C.E.
Civilization and War
Greek Dark Age, c. 1200–800
Archaic Age, c. 800–500
Classical Age, c. 500–323
Hellenistic Civilization, c. 323–31
Persian Empire, 550–323
Greek colonization, c. 750–600
Alexander's Empire, 334–323
Early and Republican Rome, c. 550–27
Art, Religion, and Ideas
◆ Geometric pottery, c. 1000–700
◆ First Olympic Games
◆ Homer composes epics Iliad, c. 750, Odyssey, c. 725
◆ Hesiod, poet (Works and Days, Theogony), c. 700
◆ Alphabet used to write Greek,c. 700
◆ Tyrtaeus of Sparta, poet, general, fl. c. 650
◆ Sappho of Mitylene, poet, c. 612–580
◆ Archaic kouros, kore, c. 600–500
◆ Solon, poet, statesman, fl. 594
◆ Milesian school of philosophy, science: Thales, fl. c. 585; Anaximander, c. 610–546; Anaximenes, fl. c. 550
◆ Xenophanes, philosopher, fl. c. 540
◆ Pythagoras, philosopher, fl. c. 530
◆ Aeschylus, playwright (Oresteia trilogy), c. 525–456
◆ Pindar, poet, c. 522–440
◆ Parmenides, philosopher, c. 510–450
◆ Heraclitus, philosopher, fl. c. 500
◆ Attic black-figure pottery peaks, succeeded by red-figure, c. 500–400
◆ Anaxagoras, philosopher, c. 500–428
◆ Sophocles, playwright (Antigone, Oedipus Rex, Oedipus at Colonus), 496–406
◆ Phidias, sculptor, fl. c. 490–430
◆ Euripides, playwright (Trojan Women, Electra, Medea), c. 485–407
◆ Herodotus, historian (Histories), c. 484–425
◆ Sophists Protagoras (c. 484–415) and Gorgias (c. 483–376)
◆ Socrates, philosopher, 470–399
◆ Thucydides, historian, c. 460–400
◆ Democritus, philosopher, c. 460–370
◆ Aristophanes, playwright (The Clouds, The Frogs, Lysistrata), c. 450–385
◆ Empedocles, philosopher, fl. c. 445
◆ Isocrates, orator, 436–338
◆ Leucippus, philosopher, fl. c. 435
◆ Pericles' funeral oration, 431
◆ Plato, philosopher (Symposium, Republic), 428–347; founds Athenian Academy
◆ Aristotle, philosopher (Politics), 384–322; founds Athenian Lyceum, 335
◆ Demosthenes, orator, 384–322
◆ Praxiteles, sculptor, fl. c. 340
◆ Aristotle dies, 322
Beyond the West
Assyrian domination, c. 900–612
Chinese warring states, 450–221
Zhou dynasty, c. 1027–221
Qin dynasty, c. 221–206
◆ Phoenician maritime hegemony, after 900
◆ Chandragupta Maurya of India, r. c. 321–298
◆ Asoka of India, 272–232
◆ Shi Huangdi of China, r. 221–210/209
◆ Shi Huangdi and burning of books, 213

CHAPTER

4

THE SCHOOL OF HELLAS

Poetry, Ideas, and the Arts in Ancient Greece

800–300 B.C.E.

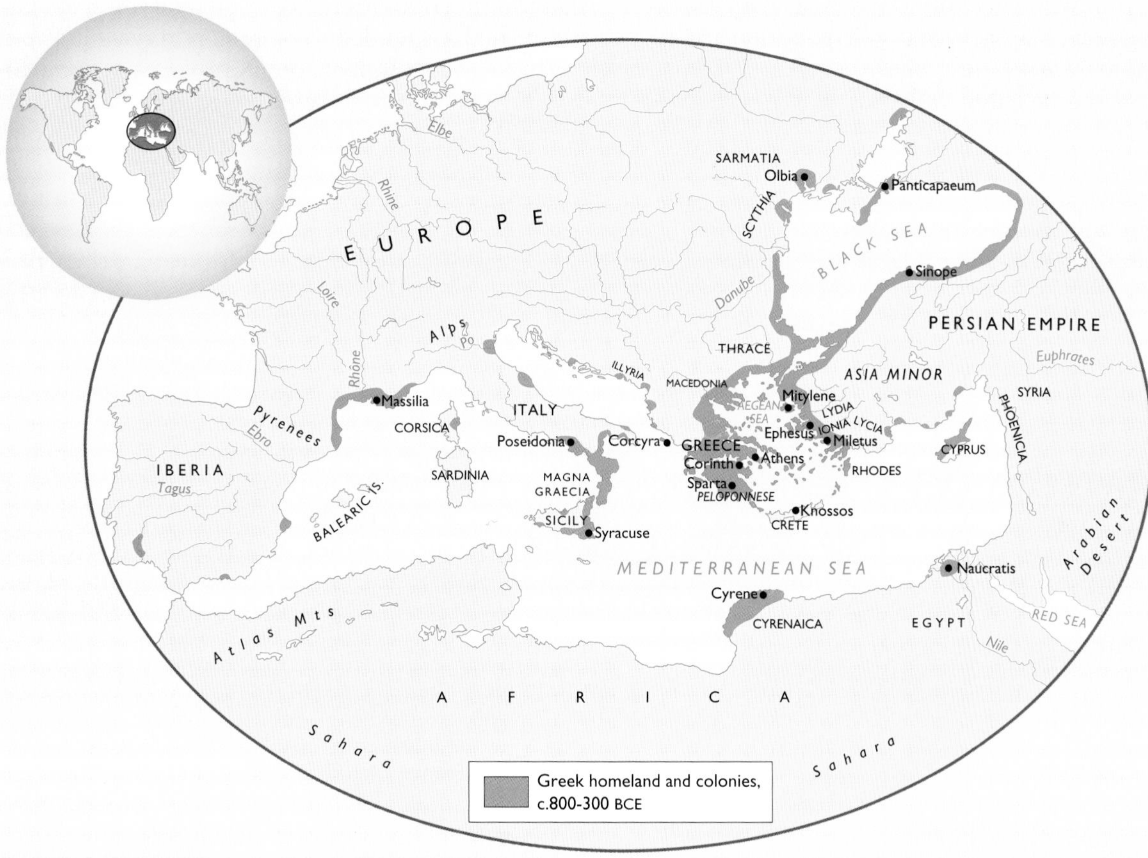

KEY TOPICS

◆ **The Birth of the Greek Gods:** Before the formation of the *polis*, Greeks describe the loves, the sorrows, and the strivings of their gods and goddesses in tales called myths, which are retold in works of stone and song.

◆ **Discovering Humanity:** The Greeks turn their sights from the immortals to mortals—themselves—and seek to understand the human condition in epic, lyric, and dramatic poetry.

◆ **To Know and to Love to Know:** Greek thinkers strive to understand everything that is; they create science, social science, history, rhetoric, education, and philosophy, culminating in the work of Plato and Aristotle—the foundations of subsequent Western thought.

*The **Life of Reason** "Intelligence, above all else, **is** man," wrote the philosopher Aristotle. Reason makes human beings human. The life of the mind is the true source of happiness. Aristotle died in 322* B.C.E., *the year after Alexander the Great succumbed to disease and drink in the heart of his Asian empire. The philosopher's claim that the mind's activity is life, that reason is the distinctively human quality, is the product of several centuries of Greek thought whose originality was nurtured by the world of the* polis.

Centuries before Aristotle wrote down these words, unnamed storytellers of the Dark Ages had transformed the religious fears and otherworldly visions of preliterate Greeks into myths that even today form part of the imaginative legacy of Western civilization. Later, poets and artists of the Archaic and Classical ages turned to considering the place of the human being on earth and the nature of earth itself. Their deep and imaginative seeking stimulated the development of philosophy, which was distinguished by the **rationalism**—acceptance of reason as supreme authority in the determination of truth—that has come to mark Western thought, but a few steps removed from the choral dances of heroes and the birth of the gods.

THE BIRTH OF THE GREEK GODS

The life of reason envisioned by Aristotle originated in the world of myth created by the Greek imagination before the onset of the Greek tradition of poetry or philosophy. The omnipresence of the gods, their immunity to death, the supremacy of the sky god all preconditioned later Greek thought, while the worship of the gods established the framework, as well, of Greek art and customs.

Myths and Mythmakers

Myths are stories that humans invent to explain their experiences. Over the centuries, the Greek myths were told by the old to the young and by mothers to children, and sung by wandering bards to avid listeners. In the seventh and sixth centuries B.C.E., when singing and storytelling gave way to books and alphabets, poets wrote the myths down. Some of those works still survive. Mythology reveals what the Greeks thought of their gods and the universe.

For the Greeks, the essence of the gods was that they were **immortal**, "deathless," free from the ordinary law of nature that applied to all other creatures, and in particular to humans. Gods could also traverse great distances instantaneously, hear human appeals over such distances, and disguise themselves magically. Aside from these distinctions, the Greek gods and goddesses resembled mortals. They were **anthropomorphic**, meaning they looked and behaved like humans, but to an extreme degree, possessing exceptional beauty and great sensitivity. Greek deities set a standard that human worshipers longed to achieve.

In the myths humans often encountered gods. The gods appeared to mortals in person, disguised as other men and women or wrapped in supernatural mists or clouds. Thus disguised, they aided mortals or punished them. They seduced, raped, and kidnapped mortal men, women, and children, and fathered or mothered half-divine offspring who were nearly as remarkable as their supernatural parents.

Greek deities thus differed markedly from those of neighboring civilizations in Asia and Africa. The gods of the East tended to be remote, invisible, often monstrous: multi-limbed or multi-breasted, animal-headed. Such awesome beings were approached only by professional priests, who alone knew how to communicate with them, and how, by elaborate ritual, to appease these unfathomable divinities. By contrast, Greek priests did not form a separate professional class. They performed a minimal role, and their rites required only an open-air altar, a special rock or tree, or a space set aside as sacred. Their gods demanded simple sacrifices: the offering of a cup of wine or a sacrificial beast, whose flesh was then given to the hungry worshipers to eat.

The presence of immortal gods did not stimulate in the Greeks, as it did in the Egyptians, an obsession with death and with the afterlife. The dead were dead. Their souls (for they did have souls, the Greeks believed) sometimes lingered in the vicinity of the grave, and demanded offerings of food and drink. That duty accomplished, the living preferred to celebrate life. With song, games, and dance they celebrated their deities in themselves.

The Greek gods were a motley group, an assortment of deities recruited from the numerous different peoples of the region. Some had been worshiped by the indigenous peoples who dwelled on the Greek mainland before the Indo-European speakers arrived from the north early in the second millennium B.C.E. Some were the gods of those newcomers. Some were the gods of neighbors on the eastern rim of the Mediterranean, of the Hittites and their successors in Asia Minor, of the Phoenicians and Babylonians in the Near East, and of the Egyptians. The names of these gods were changed as they entered the Greek pantheon.

These multitudinous deities promoted the fertility of the earth or represented the forces of nature: thunder, sky, and water. Zeus hurled his thunderbolts and lived on mountaintops, lofty and powerful. Poseidon roared and roiled the fearful waters of the oceans and rivers. Goddesses, too, had their distinct functions and attributes. Athena was, paradoxically, the goddess

WITNESSES

Who the Gods Are

The profound understanding that the Greeks developed of human nature was complemented by their view of the gods. The gods were deathless; human beings would die. That stark opposition encouraged the Greeks to conceive both of the mightiness of the powers beyond human control, and the nobility of human efforts to achieve greatness in the face of death. Here Pindar summons his listeners to "rival the Immortals," while Homer attributes to the supreme god, Zeus, an extraordinary conception of his own power.

The poet Pindar explains the difference between the immortal gods and humans destined to "run"—that is, to die (c. 460 B.C.E.):

There is a race of men
and a race of gods,
but both received the breath of life
from the same mother.
It is only power in all things
that separates us;
for men are as nothing,
while the brazen heavens remain forever
the secure abode of the gods.
Still, through the power of mind
or the strength of our bodies
we can rival the Immortals,
though we know not
what destiny awaits us in day or night,
what race fate has decreed
we shall run.

(Pindar, *Nemean VI*, 1–16; eds. S. Spyridakis, B. Nystrom, 1985)

Zeus declares that he is the greatest of the gods:

"Hear me, all you gods and all you goddesses: hear me
while I speak forth what the heart within my breast urges. …
Come, you gods, make this endeavor, that you all may learn this.
Let down out of the sky a cord of gold; lay hold of it
all you who are gods and all who are goddesses, yet not
even so can you drag down Zeus from the sky to the ground, not
Zeus the high lord of counsel, though you try until you grow weary.
Yet whenever I might strongly be minded to pull you,
I could drag you up, earth and all and sea and all with you,
then fetch the golden rope about the horn of Olympos
and make it fast, so that all once more should dangle in mid air.
So much stronger am I than the gods, and stronger than mortals."

(Homer, *Iliad*, 8:5–6, 18–27; ed. R. Lattimore, 1951)

of war and of wisdom, also of handicrafts. Because she was a virgin goddess, her temple in Athens was called the Parthenon, after the Greek for "virgin," *parthenos*. Aphrodite was the goddess of love and beauty; Artemis, of the moon and hunting. Demeter and her daughter, Persephone, were associated with grain and fruitfulness. However, all these female deities, including the supposedly virginal Athena and Artemis, were versions of the fertility goddesses long revered by humankind—as were the numerous nymphs, dryads (minor deities), "seasons," "fates," and "Muses," who breathed life into the human imagination. These deities of the earth, of its unknown depths and of its surface fruitfulness, appealed to worshipers with their promise of abundance.

From their various origins, the gods and goddesses of sky and storm and earth came to live together in the Greek imagination and to reign supreme over mortals, but not in equality. The gods of the conquerors edged out the gods of the conquered. The male sky god Zeus claimed precedence over the many female deities who had reappeared in the Archaic age as the patron goddesses of the new *poleis*. These changes resulted in a reorganization of the society of the gods into a hierarchy of male over female, sky over earth. That reorganization was accomplished before the Dark Ages and is codified in the words of Homer and Hesiod, the first Greek poets known to us.

In the *Iliad* and the *Odyssey*, the two epic poems ascribed to him, Homer gave the Greek deities their lasting definition. He named them, sketched their personalities, and plotted their relationships to each other and to the supreme and exalted Zeus. They were one "family" and lived together on Mount Olympus (in northern Greece), where "in the tall sky" the mother of the earthly hero Achilles, seeking help for her son, found Zeus "sitting upon the highest peak of rugged Olympus." The gods spent their endless days feasting and playing, quarreling and making love, and observing the life of mortals.

Of this pack of spoiled, child-like deities, Zeus was supreme. In Homer's narrative of the Trojan War (see Chapter 2 and *Witnesses*, left) it is Zeus who holds a golden balance beam to decide whether the Greeks or their opponents will win. Achilles, steeling himself to reenter the battle he had spurned in anger, draws from his chest of precious possessions the splendid cup he used to pour libations to Zeus alone. When Zeus is challenged by his brother god Poseidon, he sends Poseidon a stern message of his superiority:

I am far greater than he is
in strength, and elder born.

WHO'S WHO

The Deathless Gods

The Greeks thought of their gods descending in generations (like their human families), beginning with Uranus.
**M. = married*

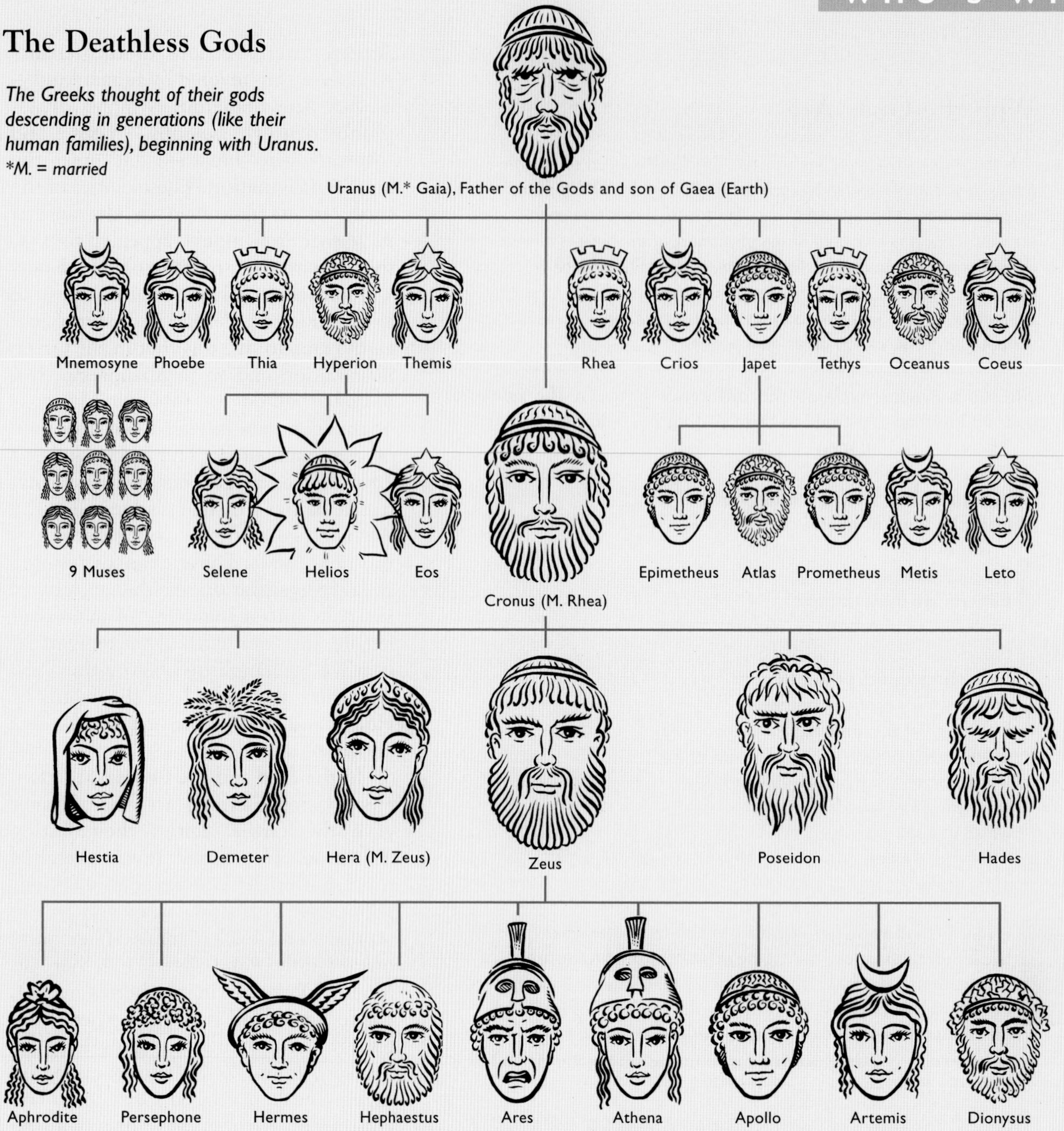

Uranus (M.* Gaia), Father of the Gods and son of Gaea (Earth)

Mnemosyne Phoebe Thia Hyperion Themis Rhea Crios Japet Tethys Oceanus Coeus

9 Muses Selene Helios Eos Epimetheus Atlas Prometheus Metis Leto

Cronus (M. Rhea)

Hestia Demeter Hera (M. Zeus) Zeus Poseidon Hades

Aphrodite Persephone Hermes Hephaestus Ares Athena Apollo Artemis Dionysus

And when the Olympians display too great partisanship for the mortals on the Trojan plain, Zeus calls an assembly and announces that he alone is in charge.

> *Now let no female divinity, nor male god either,*
> *presume to cut across the way of my word, but*
> *consent to it*
> *all of you…*

he thunders, and threatens grave reprisals if they disobey: "So much stronger am I than the gods, and stronger than mortals."

Homer's younger contemporary Hesiod (fl. c. 705 B.C.E.), a very different poet, enlarged the Greeks' conception of the gods by describing their origins and history. For this purpose, he borrowed from the literature of a non-Greek and pre-Homeric people—the Hittites—two epic myths of creation. These described the struggles of the gods for supremacy and the eventual triumph of a chief deity. Hesiod adapted this Hittite legend to Greek concepts and characters in his *Theogony*, or "Birth of the Gods."

Here Hesiod tells the story of "how the gods and the earth came into being, the rivers, the boundless sea with its raging swell, and the glittering stars, and the wide sky above," and "of the gods born of them to whom death never comes." Earth, or "Gaia," and Sky, "Uranus," were formed from the void of the beginning of things—Chaos itself. From the marriage of Earth and Sky there descended over generations all the races of gods and humans as shown in *Who's Who* on p. 86. Aided by his mother, Rhea, Zeus overturned his father, Cronus, and defeated his rivals to achieve supreme universal power. From the material of Greek myth and Hittite cosmology—study of the universe—Hesiod supplied the missing foundations of Greek theology.

Worshiping the Gods

In Greek religion, as in all ancient religions, the gods were fearsome beings whose good will was sought through the offering of gifts, especially that of a creature sacrificed on an altar (see Chapter 1). The temple was the house of the god, awesome and sacrosanct. Designed more as a residence than as a place of worship, the temple contained a statue of the resident god or goddess in an inner room, or *cella*. In temples of the eighth century B.C.E., the *cella* was approached through a porch supported by two columns—an arrangement that suggests the megaron of the Mycenaean kings and may have been modeled on it.

Over the next few centuries the Greek temple would develop into what may be the most influential building type in the history of Western architecture. Just as the institutions of the Greek *polis* have shaped the modern West, so the forms and decorative elements of the Greek temple have shaped its visual, constructed world.

The most distinctive feature of the temple is the column, which soon began to be used in rows to form a colonnade, often running around the entire building. The first columns were made of wood—the walls being of mud-brick. Later, the Greeks began to construct temples of stone, including the white marble with which parts of Greece are richly endowed. Several different styles of column evolved: the simple Doric; the taller Ionic, with its scrolled capital; the elegant Corinthian, with its intricately carved capital of acanthus leaves. Each type of column supported its own style of entablature, including a projecting cornice and a frieze, which might be decorated with relief carvings of gods, goddesses, and mortals illustrating the central myths of the community. Some of the finest examples of Greek sculpture to survive are remnants of temples.

The artistry of the decoration was matched by the mathematical precision that informed every part of the building. Proportions were carefully calculated to achieve the greatest sense of harmony and serenity. This included the use of optical tricks, or refinements, such as the slight swelling in an apparently straight column which prevents it from looking concave.

The Parthenon in Athens is the most famous of all Greek temples. An earlier temple to Athena, begun under the tyrant Peisistratus, was partially completed when the Persians destroyed all the buildings on the Acropolis in 480 B.C.E. From 443 to 429 B.C.E., Pericles drained vast sums from the Athenian treasury to build the new one. The sculptor Phidias (fl. c. 490–430 B.C.E.), one of the first artists known by name, erected in its interior a huge gold and ivory statue of the goddess. Carved in **relief** on the temple surfaces were scenes of Athena's birth; her foundation of the city of Athens; mythical battles between Greeks and barbarians, Athenians and Persians; and the solemn processional of the Great Panathenaea, the festival in honor of the goddess. Although the Parthenon was badly damaged in 1687 C.E. by a

WITNESSES

Achilles

Achilles, the hero of Homer's epic Iliad, *has a choice of a long and prosperous life in obscurity, or a brief life of heroic achievement. Here he ponders those possibilities, recognizing the advantages of the former choice. In the end, however, he will choose glory and death—and thus set a standard of heroism for all subsequent Western culture (750 B.C.E.).*

The hero Achilles wonders whether to go home (c. 750 B.C.E.):

"Fate is the same for the man who holds back, the same if he fights hard.
We are all held in a single honor, the brave with the weaklings.
A man dies still if he has done nothing, as one who has done much.
Nothing is won for me, now that my heart has gone through its afflictions
in forever setting my life on the hazard of battle. ...
. . . . For not
worth the value of my life are all the possessions they fable
were won for Ilion, that strong-founded citadel, in the old days
when there was peace, before the coming of the sons of the Achaians; . . .
. . . . Of possessions
cattle and fat sheep are things to be had for the lifting,
and tripods can be won, and the tawny high heads of horses,
but a man's life cannot come back again, it cannot be lifted
nor captured again by force, once it has crossed the teeth's barrier.
For my mother Thetis the goddess of the silver feet tells me
I carry two sorts of destiny toward the day of my death. Either,
if I stay here and fight beside the city of the Trojans,
my return home is gone, but my glory shall be everlasting;
but if I return home to the beloved land of my fathers,
the excellence of my glory is gone, but there will be a long life
left for me, and my end in death will not come to me quickly.
And this would be my counsel to others also, to sail back
home again. ..."

(Homer, *Iliad*, 9: 318–322, 400–403, 405–418; ed. R. Lattimore, 1951)

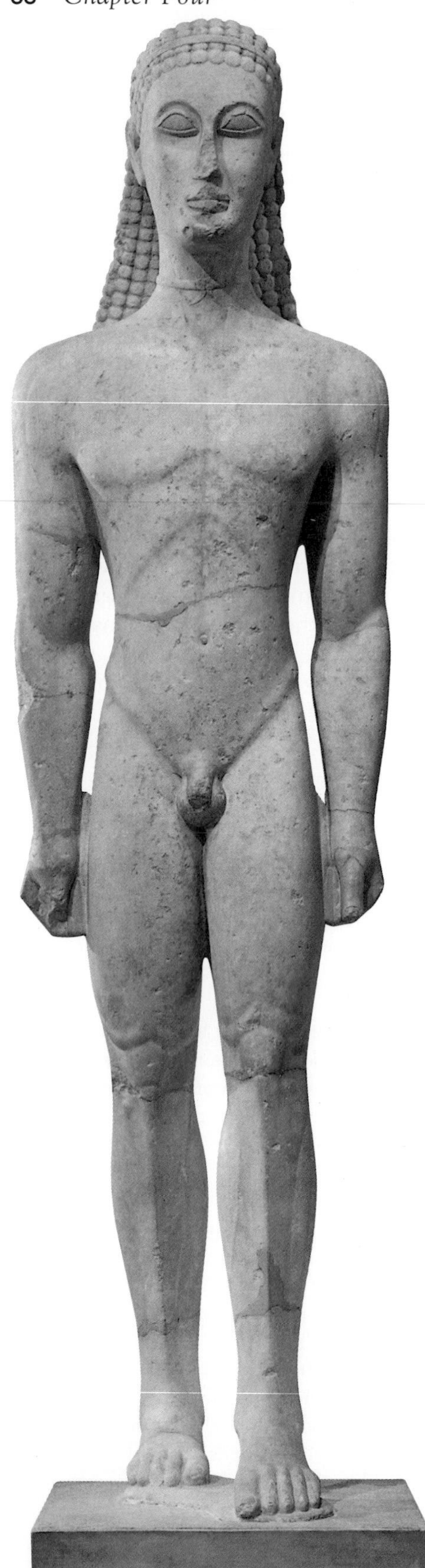

The Beauty of Man

Greek sculpture: *Lamenting the carnage underway in distant Troy, the old men of Argos who form the chorus of Aeschylus' tragedy* Agamemnon *weep for the "young men in their beauty," dead on the field of battle. Greek sculptors, most of them anonymous, labored to depict the beauty of the nude body and profound spirit of the knowing, heroic male. Here (left) is an example from Attica c. 600 B.C.E. of the* kouros *genre developed during the Archaic age. The term* kouros*, which is from the Greek word for "boy," denotes a type of standing male figure, typically carved in marble and usually commemorative in nature.* (Metropolitan Museum of Art)

Egyptian sculpture: *The Greek* kouros *was inspired by the Egyptian relief, c. 2500 B.C.E. (above) and free-standing sculpture. The* kouros *differs from the Egyptian relief in its solid and more lifelike qualities.* (Egyptian Museum, Cairo)

Venetian bomb, which exploded the gunpowder stored there by Turkish occupiers, it still stands after more than 2400 years, an elegant composition of horizontal and vertical lines (not one of which is absolutely straight), simple and perfect in its beauty.

The rationality of the Greek temple forms mirrored the rationality of the society of the gods as Homer and Hesiod depicted it, imposing poetic discipline upon the riotous throng of deities inherited from Greek prehistory. Yet in the minds of the Greek people the unknown still held its terrors. A manic irrationality counterbalanced the rational spirit of Greek religion. Dreams and omens, visions and possessions reminded people of the awful power of the divine. Many sought to defeat their enemies or woo their lovers with charms, amulets, and wax figures pierced with pins. In 413 B.C.E. the Athenian general Nicias lost a whole fleet, his men, and his own life during the Peloponnesian War because the dreadful omen of an eclipse of the moon delayed his retreat from the harbor of Syracuse in Sicily.

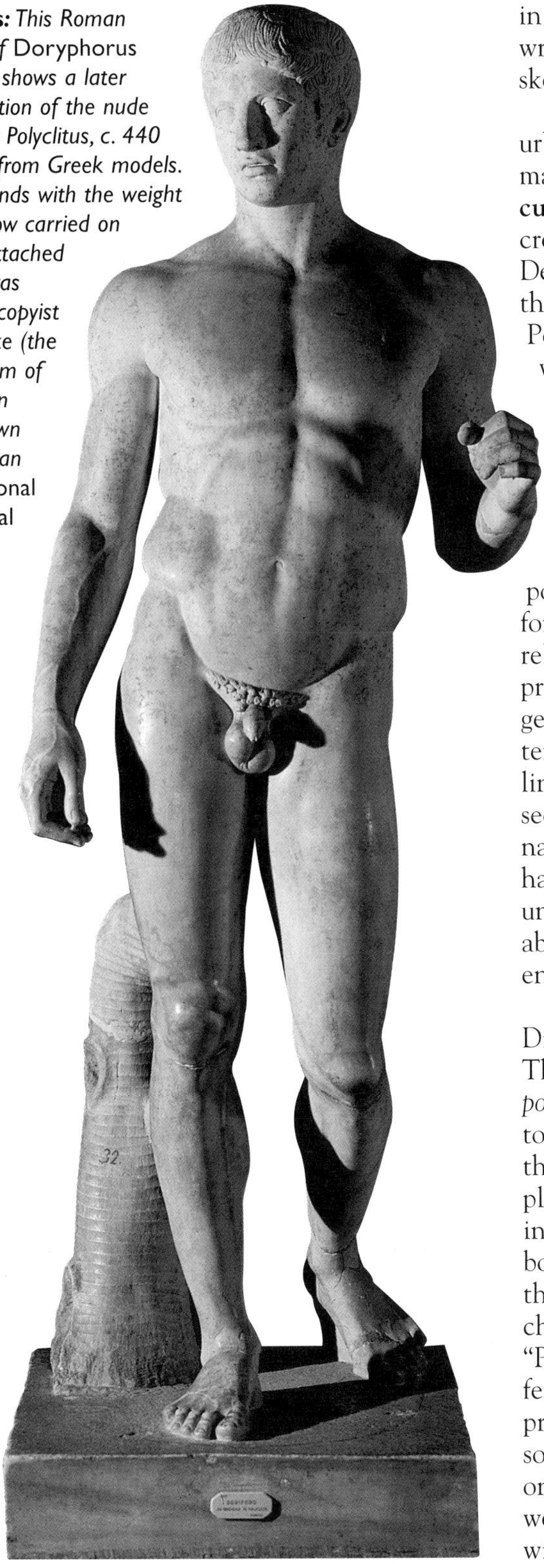

Doryphorus: *This Roman marble copy of* Doryphorus *(Spearbearer) shows a later Classical rendition of the nude male figure by Polyclitus, c. 440 B.C.E., derived from Greek models. This figure stands with the weight of the body now carried on one leg. The attached "tree trunk" was added by the copyist because bronze (the original medium of the statue) can stand on its own more easily than marble.* (National Archaeological Museum, Naples)

Communities feared the "pollution" (called *miasma*) caused by the spilling of blood or other impious acts, which placed them at risk of divine vengeance. A case of pollution required that acts of purification be performed by the responsible individual or even by the whole city. Trials for "impiety," as in fifth-century Athens, protected the city from the wrath of the gods against a community harboring skeptics, atheists, and religious nonconformists.

In the rural villages, especially, but also among urban sophisticates, the gods of the underworld had many worshipers, who sought in a variety of **mystery cults** to gain contact with the fundamental forces of creation, of spirit, of life itself. The adherents of Demeter, foremost of the earth mothers, reenacted in their ritual observances her grief for her child, Kore or Persephone, who had been snatched into the underworld by Hades and whose release in springtime signified both an abundant harvest and a resurrection of the dead. Pilgrims streamed to Eleusis outside Athens, the center for this cult which promised its initiates secret knowledge (hence "mystery").

Other mystery cults introduced from Asia also appealed to the spiritually hungry and socially dispossessed—especially to women, whose opportunity for religious experience in conventional Olympian religion was limited. Fertility was largely a female principle, because of the primal association of women, generation, and birth. Mystery religions often centered on such themes, and highlighted goddesses linked to sexual and agricultural reproduction. Many seekers were attracted to the Orphic movement, named after the legendary musician Orpheus, who had sought to recover his wife, Eurydice, from the underworld. Orphism consisted of a cluster of ideas about the immortality of the soul and promised enhanced, renewed, or eternal life.

Two gods who came late to the Greeks, Apollo and Dionysus (imported respectively from Asia and Thrace, northeast of the zone of mainland Greek *poleis*) won considerable attention. Although known to Homer, these new gods became fully established in the Greek pantheon shortly after his time. The temples of Apollo, a god associated with prophecy, with intellect, with law, with profound beauty of spirit and body, became pan-Hellenic cult centers: the nearest thing in the history of Greece to an established church. Apollo's priestess at Delphi (known as the "Pythia," or "pythoness" because Apollo killed a giant female snake there) uttered, from a deep trance, prophecies in scrambled verse which were regularly sought and pondered in the various *poleis*. Inscribed on the shrine, according to contemporary witnesses, were two statements summing up official Greek wisdom: "Know yourself," and "Nothing in excess." In contrast, excess was actively encouraged in the worship of Dionysus (also known as Bacchus), a fertility god associated with wine. Having partaken liberally of this liquid, his adherents (generally women) danced and ran in the open air, on hilltops, possessed, they believed, by the spirit of the god.

The disturbingly frenzied character and the great popularity of the Dionysian cult induced statesmen to civilize it—to mitigate its excess and to incorporate it into the normal cycle of urban religion. In Athens, Peisistratus organized the worship of Dionysus in the regular festivals known as the City Dionysia. At these festivals were performed songs and dances imported from village celebrations—notably the "goat dance," from which derives the Greek *tragoedia* and our word "**tragedy**." Soon the singing and dancing evolved into the chorus of tragic theater. And so, ironically, from the primitive rites of the god Dionysus evolved that form of poetry and thought that has, in the history of the West, most poignantly explored the universal predicament of all humans: to be alive but destined ultimately to die.

DISCOVERING HUMANITY

The poets who explored the grip exerted by the gods on human consciousness also examined, in the epic, lyric, and dramatic forms that they created, the depths of human nature. The cultivation and visual representation of the body also furthered that examination. The Greek inquiry into human nature began at the same point as the Greek study of the divine. It began with Homer and Hesiod.

Homer and Hesiod

Why did the Greeks treasure Homer? In delightful Olympian scenes, he portrayed their beautiful and immortal gods. He reminded them of their glorious, long-gone, and nearly forgotten Mycenaean past, naming the heroes they saw as ancestors. He took them to the battlefield where Achaean (or Greek) and Trojan heroes pierced, pounded, impaled, and slaughtered each other, models of skill and valor. Homer made war the business of life and the matter of history: henceforth, war was the theater in which human excellence would be tested and would triumph. Amid the clangor and tumult, he depicted for the first time in literature, in the figure of the Achaean hero Achilles, the struggles and contradictions of human existence.

The *Iliad*, as its author states in his opening line, is about the anger of Achilles, who has been dishonored by the supreme commander of the Achaean army, Agamemnon. The latter has taken away Achilles' concubine Briseis—perhaps for good reason—but Achilles' skill had won her fair and square. Achilles withdraws from the battle to sulk, and consequently the Achaean forces are desperately weakened and forced to retreat. Agamemnon and his commanders beg Achilles to return to the battle, but he will not. He plays the lyre and sings, considering whether a quiet life at home contemplating his fields would not be preferable to the life of battle (see *Witnesses*, p. 87).

Achilles stands aloof from the conflict until his companion, Patroclus, is slain by the Trojan leader Hector. Now he will act, but he is a different man from the one who spurned Agamemnon. He acts knowing that he has chosen death over life. His sole purpose is to exact his revenge and meet his destiny with dignity. He avenges Patroclus' death by slaying Hector. He then drags the body in the dust, seven times around the walls of Troy, buries Patroclus magnificently, then tempers his anger and returns the body of his slaughtered foe to King Priam, Hector's father. In the span of the *Iliad*'s more than 16,000 lines, the war has neither started nor closed, Achilles' life has neither begun nor ended, but a human personality has grown to understand the meaning of life and the purpose of death.

Until they were written down in the sixth century B.C.E., the verses of Homer were kept alive by the *rhapsodes*, traveling bards or minstrels whose special craft was the recitation of these myth-laden stories from prehistory. The poet Hesiod, who is believed to have been active a generation after Homer, may have been, briefly, one of these wandering *rhapsodes*. Steeped in that poetry, Hesiod stood one day on the summit of Mount Helicon, not far from his farm, and experienced a vision of the Muses. They inspired him, as he tells us, to become a poet.

Like Homer, Hesiod grappled in his verse with the meaning of human existence. But he did so in terms of his own daily life and that of other struggling farmers, crafting a quite different heroic ideal—the heroism of the ordinary. Unlike the *Theogony*, which addressed cosmic issues, his *Works and Days* addressed social ones. It describes the burdens borne by human beings who labor in the face of certain death and the cruel injustice of the powerful. The ordinary farmer, not the valiant warrior, is Hesiod's hero. The limits of human experience are touched by those who spend their days plowing and harvesting and who crave, as the fruit of their labor, justice:

This is the law Zeus laid down for men,
but fish and wild beasts and winged birds
know not of justice and so eat one another.
Justice, the best thing there is, he gave to men. ...

Lyric Poets: Personal and Civic Lives

A century after Hesiod, in the seventh century B.C.E., a new group of poets emerged as the leaders of Greek thought. These were poets of the emerging *poleis*. While not ignoring war or labor, their verse focused more often on their personal concerns as men—and one woman—forging an existence in a complex society. Their experiences were as varied as the cities where they lived and the circles of their friends. To express their new outlook, these authors created a new form of poetry, called "lyric." Brief and expressive, it was composed to be sung to the lyre, a small stringed instrument, in small gatherings, instead of chanted, like Homer and Hesiod's verse, to the public. Those earlier bards were addressing the nation of the Hellenes, all those who spoke Greek. The newer poets wrote for each other and for people like them: the leisured, cultivated aristocrats of the cities.

Archilochus (714–676 B.C.E.), from the Aegean island of Paros, is one of the earliest of the lyric poets whose work is extant. Illegitimate son of an aristocratic father and a slave mother, Archilochus lived on the fringes of fine society—an adventurer and mercenary, given to outrageous behavior. His poetry displays his aversion to traditional codes and values. One verse sounds an unheroic note, which must have seemed discordant in a world imbued with the warrior ethos of the *Iliad.* Part of an expedition that joined battle with some fearsome Thracians, Archilochus turned and ran:

Some Thracian has the shield I left behind,
My trusty shield—I had to—in a wood.
Well, I have saved my life; so never mind
That shield; I'll get another just as good.

Archilochus' intensely personal tone is soon heard again in two other poets, one male and one female, who were both well-born citizens of Mitylene, on the Aegean island of Lesbos: Alcaeus (fl. 620 B.C.E.) and Sappho (c. 612–c. 580 B.C.E.). A prominent citizen, Alcaeus portrays in his verse the concerns of the male aristocrat: his hatred for his political rivals, his fascination with the paraphernalia of war, and his delight in the comradeship of the *symposium,* or drinking party, where words and ideas flow freely.

Sappho may epitomize the circle of aristocratic women in Mitylene—but we have no way of knowing whether that is so. Her voice is unique, and her figure solitary, the only female poet of antiquity from whom more than a few scraps of verse survive ... and only a few more, at that. Sappho wrote of love and beauty with a passion unsurpassed for 2000 years. Perhaps her isolation from the concerns of war and politics left her free to explore these themes. She makes clear her distaste for the usual business of men: "Some say the fairest thing on earth is a troop of horsemen, others a band of foot-soldiers, others a squadron of ships. But I say the fairest thing is the beloved."

No man in Greek antiquity described the experience of love like Sappho: "When I even see you, my voice stops, my tongue is broken, a thin flame runs beneath all my skin, my eyes are blinded, there is thunder in my ears, the sweat pours from me, I tremble through and through, I am paler than grass, and I seem like one dead." To some, the emotional impact of these lines is greater because the words are probably addressed to another woman, one of Sappho's pupils.

The poet headed an informal school for upper-class girls, sent to learn the refinements of song and dance and manners (for these were the substance of Greek education at that time). They came to Sappho, who admired their beauty, nourished all, and loved some, then lost them to new, young husbands. So Sappho, poet of Lesbos, is the world's most famous Lesbian, and the reason why that term is used to describe women whose sexual desires are for other women. The idea has seemed variously repulsive, unimportant, or titillating to later readers, who agree, nevertheless, on the poet's brilliance.

The outlook of Tyrtaeus (fl. c. 650 B.C.E.) of mainland Sparta, in contrast, is resolutely male. Active as a general and a poet during the Messenian wars (c. 640–630 B.C.E.), Tyrtaeus was the architect of a warrior code for that city's aristocrats. Sparta could survive only if the "equals," the elite citizen class, maintained her military readiness at a constant pitch of ferocity. Tyrtaeus' words spurred them on to this state, as in this celebration of heroic death:

The youth's fair form is fairest when he dies.
Even in his death the boy is beautiful,
The hero boy who dies in his life's bloom....
More sacred than in life, more beautiful by far,
Because he perished on the battlefield.

In Tyrtaeus' verse, Homeric values are refashioned for the life of the *polis.* In the sixth century B.C.E., Athens' first known poet (and great statesman), Solon, follows Hesiod in exploring the theme of justice. Solon held that the moral force of justice would

MUST READS

A Sampling of the Greek Classics

Homer	*Iliad, Odyssey*
Hesiod	*Theogony, Works and Days*
Pindar	*Odes*
Aeschylus	*Prometheus Bound, Agamemnon*
Sophocles	*Antigone, Oedipus Rex*
Euripides	*Trojan Women, Hippolytus*
Aristophanes	*Clouds, Lysistrata*
Plato	*Apology, Symposium*
Aristotle	*Nicomachean Ethics, Poetics*
Demosthenes	*Orations*

WINDOWS ON

Worthy Maidens

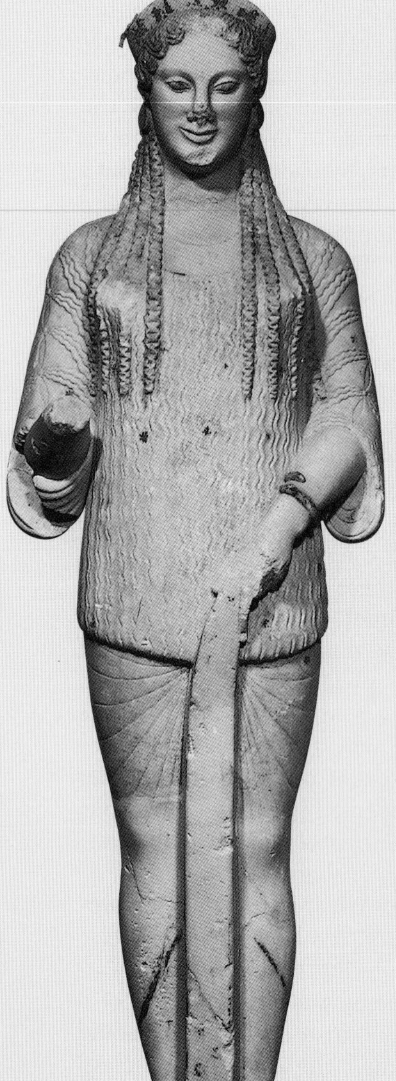

Kore, c. *510* B.C.E.

Caryatid, *Erectheum, Acropolis, Athens,* c. *420–410* B.C.E.

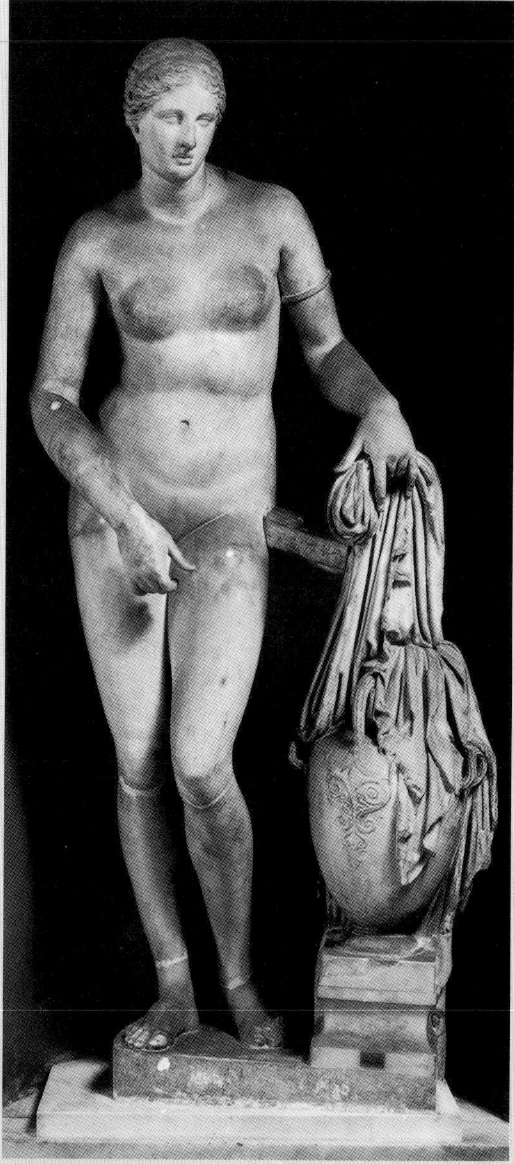

Cnidos Aphrodite *(Imperial Roman copy of Greek original)*

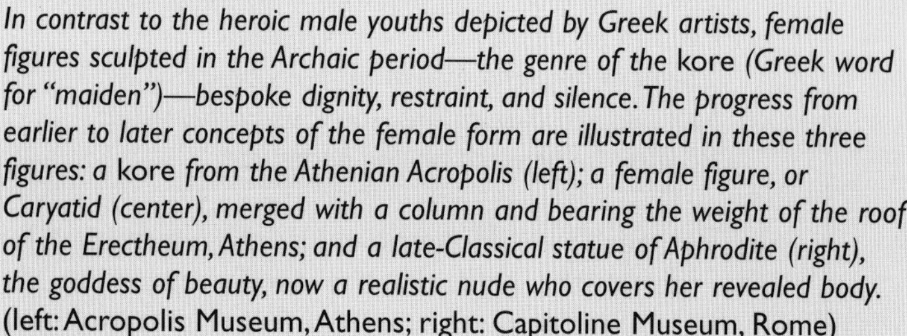

In contrast to the heroic male youths depicted by Greek artists, female figures sculpted in the Archaic period—the genre of the kore (Greek word for "maiden")—bespoke dignity, restraint, and silence. The progress from earlier to later concepts of the female form are illustrated in these three figures: a kore from the Athenian Acropolis (left); a female figure, or Caryatid (center), merged with a column and bearing the weight of the roof of the Erectheum, Athens; and a late-Classical statue of Aphrodite (right), the goddess of beauty, now a realistic nude who covers her revealed body. (left: Acropolis Museum, Athens; right: Capitoline Museum, Rome)

To continue your investigation of this topic, please go to www.prenhall.com/king for the related WINDOWS on the WEB activity

not permit the powerful to crush the powerless. Evil men "go on stealing, by force or deception each from the other, nor do the solemn commitments of Justice keep them in check ...," but Justice keeps track, "and in her time she returns to exact a full revenge."

Tragedy and Comedy: The Myth Transformed

With Solon, the inward gaze of the lyric poets turned outward again. Employing lyric verse to probe the soul of the city, he anticipated the Athenian poets who would, soon after his death, create dramatic tragedy and further the Greek exploration of the human spirit. These writers studied anew the body of myth preserved by the epic poets Homer and Hesiod. They not only retold the tales; they asked bold and horrifying questions about the human and divine players.

It was from the ritual dance and song of the Dionysiac festival that drama evolved, during the sixth century B.C.E. The dancers (ordinary citizens who diligently rehearsed for weeks) constituted the chorus, and the open space on which they danced, at first only a section of the *agora*, was called the *orchestra*. Poets composed the music as well as the words, and taught and directed the performers (always men, even for female characters). The chorus master managed and funded the project. Funding a dramatic production was one of the two principal ways (the other was the outfitting of a ship) in which the rich were expected to support the state.

On the slopes around the orchestra sat the spectators—a large audience including most of the citizen population. This audience listened carefully enough to be able to vote for the best performance of the several offered over three days. Ordinary citizens thus acted as literary critics and judges as well as observers. Later centuries saw the construction of spectator seating, and a stone building that served as set and backdrop. From the beginning, the performers wore costumes, including special shoes which elevated them above their ordinary stature and brightly colored masks with exaggerated features.

Tragedy According to Aristotle, the first tragedies were entirely choral—the events described or related by groups of singers. Who wrote these dramas is uncertain; however, the first recorded winner of a form of tragedy (in c. 534 B.C.E.) was a playwright named Thespis (in whose memory actors are sometimes called "thespians"). Thespis was the first to introduce an actor—the author himself—who broke away from the chorus of singers and dancers to deliver spoken individual lines. Once a separate actor appeared, so did the possibility of dialogue. Two generations later, the poet Aeschylus (c. 525–456 B.C.E.) introduced a second actor: now two characters could interact with each other, as well as an individual character with the chorus. That innovation allowed the dramatic confrontations of tragedy as we know it. At Greek tragedy's fullest development, no more than three speaking actors shared the stage.

With this skeletal cast of characters but with extraordinary power of language, the tragic poets reopened ancient myths. Aeschylus explored the story of Agamemnon, the leader of the Greek forces at Troy, who had returned triumphant to his homeland only to be murdered by his faithless wife, Clytemnestra. She held against him the grievance that he had sacrificed their young daughter, Iphigenia, like a beast on the altar in order to win the favor of the goddess Artemis for his military venture. The story and its consequences over two generations are told in a series of three plays—a "trilogy"—which would have been performed in a continuous sequence at the Dionysia. The trilogy is called the *Oresteia* (so named after Orestes, Agamemnon's son, who will avenge his father), and consists of the *Agamemnon*, the *Choëphoroe* ("Libation Bearers), and the *Eumenides* ("Furies").

These brief plays probe such problems as the justice of war; competing public and private claims on the individual's conscience; the nature of monarchy, tyranny, and democracy; the duties of children to father and mother, of parents to children; the rival loves of mother and nurse; and the forgiveness of sin. One unforgettable scene from the *Agamemnon* gives a taste of the whole. Clytemnestra, having lured Agamemnon into his bath, trapped him in his luxurious robe, and slaughtered him, appears proudly to proclaim the deed with terrible "I" sentences announcing both strength and guilt: "I stand now where I struck him down. ... Thus have I wrought, and I will not deny it now. ... I struck him twice."

The strength of Antigone, heroine of Sophocles' play of that name, is of a different sort. Following Aeschylus in the sequence of tragic authors, Sophocles (496–406 B.C.E.) was the popular victor of as many as twenty-four dramatic contests. Where Aeschylus interested himself in broad and multiple themes, Sophocles focused intensely on individual human characters. In *Antigone*, he draws on a Theban cycle of legend alluded to, but not recounted, by Homer. Polyneices of Thebes, the exiled son of King Oedipus, has been killed, a traitor to his own city. The new King of Thebes, Creon, has ordered that he be left unburied. But Polyneices' sister Antigone insists on burying him so that his spirit may find rest.

Creon had ordained that death would be the punishment for burying a traitor. Didn't she know the law? asked Creon. Not the gods but a man had made that law, Antigone responded:

Nor did I think your orders were so strong
that you, a mortal man, could over-run
the gods' unwritten and unfailing laws. ...

So not through fear of any man's proud spirit
would I be likely to neglect these laws. ...
I knew that I must die. ...

Creon has Antigone sealed up alive. She hangs herself. In this tragedy, tremendous and irreconcilable forces clash, shown as male and female polarities: the claims of the state on its citizens as against those of the gods, the claims of human and divine law, the claims of love.

Euripides (c. 485–407 B.C.E.), in his lifetime the least popular of these three tragedians, had a darker vision. His genius was recognized after his death when, in a bleaker age, spectators and readers more readily confronted the harsh truths he projects. Euripides was skeptical about the gods, pessimistic about the future, outraged by war, tormented by the pain inflicted by some humans upon others, especially upon the weakest, and obsessed with untangling the inner workings and secrets of the human mind. With such heavy thoughts he retired young to the island of Salamis, not far from Athens, to live as a recluse, with only the company of his library. Later he moved even farther away, to Macedonia, in the north, where he composed the last of his ninety-two plays, named a prizewinner after its author's death.

Euripides ransacked the material of myth for themes to develop in his original way. He developed, for instance, the legend of the hero Jason, who sailed with his loyal band of companions, the Argonauts, to retrieve the magical Golden Fleece from a distant city bordering the Black Sea. From this material Euripides fashioned the portrait of the ferocious Medea, Jason's spurned wife, who took her revenge on her disloyal husband by murdering their children. From the stories of Theseus, legendary king of Athens, he crafted the tortured triangle of that hero, of his wife, Phaedra, her desperate and unrequited love of her stepson Hippolytus, and Hippolytus' punishment of death as ordered by his vengeful father.

Moved by the massacre (in 415 B.C.E.) of the residents of the island of Melos by leaders of his own city, Euripides elaborated from the Trojan legend the drama of the *Trojan Women*. Slavery was the fate awaiting the women and children of a captured city; death, that of its men. Euripides requires his audience to listen to the pain of the captured. The prophetess Cassandra and Hector's wife, Andromache, are both carried away to degradation. Hector's son Astyanax is hurled from the city walls, his cries echoing offstage. The boy's grandmother, Hecuba, is left on stage to stroke his dead body—and to make the audience realize the dimensions of tragedy beyond even death.

Comedy While Euripides composed his painful dissections of human feelings, the comic playwright Aristophanes (c. 450–c. 385 B.C.E.) turned a cynical eye on Athenian society. Although **comedy** developed later than tragedy, it also derived from the worship of Dionysus. It evolved from the Dionysiac processions characterized by sexual play and costumes equipped with oversized phalluses, lest the god's association with fertility and the absurd be missed. By 486 B.C.E., comic drama had emerged from this carnival. By mid-century, it had its own festive season, the Lenaea, to match tragedy's Dionysia.

It was the purpose of Greek comedy to point out the defects of public life. This mission Aristophanes pursued with relish. His works are the only complete comedies to survive from Ancient Greece. They are hilariously funny—full of slapstick, puns, lewd asides, and sheer craziness. They are also biting critiques of the Athenian world during the years when it slid into brutality and thoughtlessness.

Aristophanes blamed the decay of Athens on a failure of culture. The elevated values of the old aristocracy were being undermined by the war frenzy of the masses, the vulgarity of thick-witted politicians, and above all, in his view, the dangerous novelties of a new generation of unprincipled teachers. In *The Clouds*, Aristophanes mocked the Sophists (among whom he wrongly numbered Socrates) for seducing the Athenian young away from the traditional values of piety, reverence, and fitness. These teachers taught the young to worship not the gods, but the Clouds—evanescent things, having no permanent form and tempting the mind to wild fantasies.

Athenian theater flourished for a century, during which many hundreds of plays were performed. The

HOW MANY?

The First Athletic Competitions

4	The period of years between each set of games (an Olympiad)
1	The number of events (the stade) in the earliest known athletic competition at Olympia (776 B.C.E.)
210	The length of the track in yards (192m) for the earliest track event (the stade)
500	The number of gallons of olive oil in the amphora awarded to the winner of the stade
600	The value in drachmas of 500 gallons of olive oil, equivalent to about two years' wages for a mason or carpenter
393	The date (C.E.) of the abolition of the games
1	The number of female spectators (the Priestess of Demeter)
0	The number of female competitors

plays of only four authors survive—those of Aeschylus, Sophocles, Euripides, and Aristophanes. Of the approximately 300 plays they wrote, there survive today 7 by the first, 7 by the second, 19 by the third, and 11 by the fourth. The whole body of Greek drama still extant fits on a very small bookshelf. Yet is is the matrix of all subsequent theater in the West, and it has influenced all of Western literature.

The Perfect Body

While Greek playwrights explored the human condition, their compatriots aimed to perfect the human body through an activity they found equally important: gymnastics. Gymnastic exercise helped build bodies that were healthy, powerful, and beautiful. These goals were achieved principally by men. (In Sparta, an exception, women also engaged in physical training.) The cultivation of perfect male bodies, delectable to the gods, was a central to Greek culture.

Gymnastics were a part of the daily routine of all those who had the leisure to engage in them. After a morning of work, the citizen would put in several hours of physical training: running, jumping, wrestling, and the throwing of spear or discus, all of which disciplines were performed in the nude. Some activities are shown in *Windows On* on pp. 96–7. Such athletic activity was considered desirable for all, and essential for the leader of the state.

Gymnastic training formed a major part of education, constituting half of the elementary curriculum. (The other half was "music," or poetry, an academic subject which included what would today be called grammar and literature as well as metrics and music. In the fourth century, the two most famous schools of philosophy, the Academy and the **Lyceum**, were founded adjacent to two of Athens' suburban gymnasia.

In their striving for physical perfection, Greek athletes competed vigorously, engaging in a struggle—a struggle to win, psychologically akin to the struggle of the tragic hero who combats an overwhelming destiny. The athlete's striving also related to the Greek pursuit of war. War and games were both athletic encounters. To lose the first was to suffer death. To lose the second was to suffer shame. To win, in either case, was glorious. Winning or losing spelled the meaning of the individual's existence.

Gymnastics and war were related in another way. The former prepared a man for the latter. Citizens who kept fit through gymnastics constituted a citizen army ready to defend the *polis*. Pericles pointed out in his "Funeral Oration" that Athenian males kept themselves in a state of readiness for war through their pleasant sports activities—in contrast to the dour Spartans who insisted on a conventional military drill. Gymnastics were a civic version of war.

The central role gymnastics would play in Greek civilization at its zenith was prefigured in Homer's *Iliad*. When Achilles has vanquished Hector and returned to the Achaean camp, he organizes a festival of funeral games for his martyred beloved, Patroclus. Chariot races, boxing, wrestling, running, dueling, archery: these sports absorbed the Achaean contestants as much as battle, which they closely resembled. To the reader unfamiliar with the role played by gymnastics in Greek culture, the devotion of more than 600 lines of verse to these activities is unfathomable.

Games in honor of Patroclus were not only mock battles but also sacred rites. Like song and dance, athletic performance was a mode of worshiping the gods. About the time that Homer described the funeral of Patroclus (the traditional date is 776 B.C.E.), athletic contestants from different cities met at Zeus' sacred city Olympia. These games were the first to be called "Olympic" and were the ancestors of today's Olympic Games. Other athletic festivals were launched by rival cities; for example, the Isthmian games were sponsored by Corinth in honor of its patron god, Poseidon. The games were ceremonies of worship, in honor of which the Greeks agreed to a holy truce for the protection of participants and spectators.

The winner (often a Spartan, whose whole life was dedicated to the culture of the body) became a hero whose achievement honored his family and, even more than that, his *polis*. He won valuable trophies in recognition of his victory, and when he went home he was guaranteed a lifetime of free meals at public expense. A sixth-century winner from Sybaris, in Italy, was able to construct a shrine to Athena with a fraction of his prize money.

Wealthy winners, or their families, might also hire a poet to commemorate a victory. Pindar (c. 522–c. 440 B.C.E.) specialized in writing odes for athletic heroes. These odes say little about the race. Instead, they celebrate as divine gifts the spiritual and physical prowess of the hero—and heap disgrace on the unfortunate losers, who receive "no glad home-coming":

They, when they meet their mothers,
Have no sweet laughter around them, moving delight.
In back streets, out of their enemies' way.
They cower; for disaster has bitten them.

The idealization of the male body that underlies the Greek sports culture is also fundamental to the evolution of its art. When the crude products of Dark Age artisans gave way to a new generation of pottery, its decoration consisted of the simplest and most austere lines (see Chapter 3). This Proto-Geometric style was followed by increasingly complex but still mainly linear decoration, which often included angular, highly stylized representations of human beings. This is known as the Geometric style.

Many of the pots in Geometric style were unearthed near Athens' Dipylon Gate. Crafted in the eighth century B.C.E., these colossal vases (nearly as

WINDOWS ON

Excellence through Struggle

Wrestling, boxing, and athletics: *The importance in Greek culture of athletic competition cannot be overstated. Those who had leisure to do so exercised daily in the gymnasium. Athletic competitions were held at religious festivals, an indication of their universal meaning. The relief above shows wrestlers in competition c. 500* B.C.E. *(above), while a black-figure amphora of 530* B.C.E. *(below) shows boxers competing as its main image, with a smaller image of wrestling above.* (above: National Archaeological Museum, Athens; below: British Museum)

Black-figure amphora, 530 B.C.E.

Black-figure amphora, Panathanaic, end of 6th century B.C.E.

Here are scenes of men racing (above), and of a Spartan girl engaging in races–called the Heraia—specifically designated for women. The central image, from the later Hellenistic era, is of a young rider on a racing steed. (above: Metropolitan Museum of Art; center: National Archaelogical Museum, Athens; below: British Museum, London)

Bronze jockey of Artemision, Hellenistic, 2nd-century B.C.E.

Bronze figurine, late-6th century B.C.E.

To continue your investigation of this topic, please go to www.prenhall.com/king for the related WINDOWS on the WEB activity

tall as an adult human) were funeral objects, ordered by wealthy patrons who wished to make drink offerings to the spirits of their dead. Accordingly, they often depicted funerals. These pots represent an early step toward establishing the human form as the proper subject of the visual arts.

That development presaged a dramatic change in the style of pottery decoration. During the seventh century, when the potters of Corinth temporarily took the lead away from Athens in ceramic art, the vase surface erupted in a riot of plant and animal forms: pouncing lions, bellowing cattle, devilish monsters. The motifs were Eastern, copied from the ivories and metalwork of Egyptian, Assyrian, and Phoenician luxuries that passed through the port of Corinth. In the sixth century, the Athenians responded with ballets of black figures painted on a reddish background.

These Athenian figures were different. They were fully formed human beings, engaged in the full range of human acts from farming to weaving to dancing to love. The painted dramas continued to be produced in the Classical age, yet were more refined and detailed in the red-figure pottery (developed about 530–480 B.C.E.). On these pots, the artist inscribed the outlines of the figures in the red clay and painted the background black—thus reversing the black-figure procedure. The surfaces of these pots became the screen for varied images of contemporary life: scenes from the gymnasium and the *symposium*, war and athletics, domestic and farm work, sexual activity of all varieties, amusements innocent and lurid. Some are shown on the cups illustrated on p. 63 and p. 99.

Meanwhile other artisans began to carve from stone, or cast in bronze, freestanding statues of the human figure. The first such statue-type to emerge in Greece—of the young male nude, the ***kouros***, or boy—belongs to the Archaic age. It is the commonest form of sculpture, and sets the pattern for all successive forms. Once introduced, the pattern sparked imitation: *kouroi* (plural of *kouros*) date from the seventh century B.C.E., when the genre was new, but five times as many—157—are known from the sixth century B.C.E. The *kouros* was based on Egyptian models, transformed with an unmistakably Greek face as shown on p. 88. Bones and muscles appear to move beneath the surface, the legs seem to bear weight and walk, the torso to fill with breath and the statue with life.

The female counterpart of the *kouros* was the statue of the ***kore***, or young woman as seen in *Windows On*, p.92. This, too, derived from Eastern models and was given new life by Greek artists. The *kore* statue, like the *kouros*, enjoyed growing popularity in ancient Greece: 35 are known from the seventh century B.C.E., and 144 from the sixth century B.C.E. Both were remarkable innovations in the history of sculpture. But the *kouros* exceeded the *kore* as an artistic creation. His nude figure was individualized, whereas her clothed figure tended toward the anonymity of the sculpted women, called caryatids, that served as columns to hold up the roof of a temple porch. He, not she, was seen as the prototype of human beauty: for the Greeks, the beauty of men was tantamount to beauty itself.

From the *kouros* and *kore* figures of the sixth century B.C.E. developed the realistic yet refined sculpture of the fifth and later centuries. Anonymous artisans and even some masters whose names are known—Phidias, Praxiteles, Scopas—created both freestanding and relief sculpture in stone and bronze, some life-size and some larger than life-size. In their surviving works, and in copies made by the Romans, we find eloquent testimony to the Greeks' reverence for the dignity and grace of the human being.

TO KNOW AND TO LOVE TO KNOW

By the sixth century B.C.E., to the Greek cultural world of myth and art, poetry and games, entered a series of thinkers who yearned to understand the universe. They came from all over the Greek world, as shown on Map 4.1. The first philosophers began to seek the foundations of reality in matter or spirit, while the first historians sought to explain human events, looking at cultures and individuals (rather than the gods) as motive forces. Professional speakers and teachers redefined the scope of useful knowledge and perfected the skills by which to learn how to succeed in human affairs. Orators helped communities decide matters of law and custom, and war and peace, while the philosophers of the Classical age, building on the achievement of their predecessors, probed the nature of the cosmos and the state, the natural world and the soul, the realms of ethics, language, and art.

Presocratic Knowers and Seekers

One group of Greek thinkers thrust the gods aside and rejected myth as the explanation of things. These are called the **Presocratics**, for they predate the figure of Socrates, the teacher of Plato, the teacher of Aristotle, who was to inaugurate a new phase in the history of thought. From the work of the Presocratics derives—to give only the short list—science and philosophy, theories of law and government, history, ethics, and psychology. There being no professions yet of science and philosophy, these thinkers were called "knowers," "knowers of many things," and "the wise."

The Presocratics began to make their mark in the sixth century B.C.E., one century after Archilochus, two after Homer, and in the same part of the Greek world: the Ionian coast of Asia Minor and its islands, whose cities had extensive contacts with Middle Eastern cultures. Their investigations were continued first by the Greeks of Italy, and only in the late fifth century B.C.E. by mainland Greeks.

Paideia: Transmitting Greek Culture

Red-figure cup: *In early Greece, "education" consisted of learning to farm, or hunt, or to craft tools, weapons, or pots. With the use of the alphabet in a more sophisticated society, it became necessary to transmit Greek language and values to new generations—a mission summed up in* paideia, *meaning not merely education in the modern sense but also acculturation. Among the propertied, it became common to send boys to study with a grammar-master. Scenes from Greek education are depicted on this fifth-century* B.C.E. *cup by the sculptor Douris where, from right to left in the first half (above), a boy learns to play the lyre, then reads from a manuscript page held by the master while his pedagogue waits. In the second half (below), the boy learns to play the flute and to write, watched, again, by the pedagogue.* (Staatliche Museen, Berlin)

Xenophanes of Colophon (in Asia Minor; fl. c. 540 B.C.E.) waged a relentless attack on the mythic conception of reality as he journeyed for sixty-seven years around the Greek world to recite his poems and share his wisdom. His poetry was different from the lyric, the epic, the tragic, or the comic: it was about the nature of reality, of human life, and of the gods. Xenophanes dismissed as absurd the multifarious gods and goddesses of myth. Foolish mortals believe "that the gods are born, and that they have clothes and speech and bodies like their own"; "But if cattle and horses or lions had hands, or were able to draw with their hands and do the works that men can do, horses would draw the forms of the gods like horses, and cattle like cattle. . . ."

Although Xenophanes rejected the deities of Olympus, he detected a spiritual substratum to all of reality: deity itself. "One" existed who was omniscient and omnipotent, commander of the universe which was regulated for the good: "one god, greatest among gods and men, in no way similar to mortals either in body or in thought" (see *Witnesses*, p. 100). The monotheism of Xenophanes is an exception to the polytheism of the Greeks.

While Xenophanes challenged the assumptions of polytheism, the three thinkers of the **Milesian school** (so called because they were all citizens of Miletus, in Asia Minor) invented what we call science. These were Thales (fl. c. 585 B.C.E.), Anaximander (c. 610–546 B.C.E.), and Anaximenes (fl. c. 550 B.C.E.). Their school was not an institution with a building, deans, and janitors, but simply a gathering of those who conversed about the same kinds of things.

The Milesian sages all rejected mythic explanations of the origins and causes of things, and sought better ones. Thales proposed that water was the universal medium: from it, he thought, all matter had been formed, and it continued to sustain the life of all earthly creatures. He was thus what we call a **materialist,** one who believes that reality itself is formed of an original material substance.

Anaximander and Anaximenes also named fundamental substances, but different ones, as the fabric of creation. For Anaximander, that substance was the *apeiron*, or "the Boundless": an infinite and nonperceptible primal mass in never-ending motion within which the universal opposites of heat and cold and wet and dry worked to generate the first creatures. For Anaximenes, the first substance was air, alternately thinning and thickening as pulled by opposing universal forces; from this derived both matter and spirit. Working without laboratories or textbooks and not thinking to conduct experiments, these theorists nevertheless approached the conclusions of modern scientists—that certain universal substances underlie all matter, whose interactions cause change and form.

According to Pythagoras (fl. c. 530 B.C.E.), the nature of things was determined not by a material substratum but by fundamental spiritual and logical relationships. Pythagoras was born on the Aegean island of Samos but worked in Croton (Italy) in the late sixth century B.C.E. As a religious leader, Pythagoras instructed his followers to observe strictly a number of rituals and taboos, and taught the transmigration of human souls after death. He was also an inspired mathematician, profiting from the work of Babylonian and Egyptian predecessors. Pythagoras is most famous for generalizing an ancient theorem for calculating the hypotenuse of a right angle—a theorem still named after him "Pythagorean."

Investigating the relations between numbers and musical harmonies, Pythagoras found that the fourth, fifth, and octave of a musical note were produced by plucking a lyre string respectively three-quarters, two-thirds and one-half the length of the string producing the initial sound. The relations between the lengths of the lyre string can thus be expressed in ratios that add up to ten—a number that Pythagoras represented as a figure controlling both number and shape, the spatial expression of a perfect number reflecting the underlying structure of the universe.

Heraclitus of Ephesus (in Asia Minor; fl. c. 500 B.C.E.) believed the key to the structure of the universe is change itself. Life is a constant struggle between opposite forces that are always shifting, yet always the same in the constancy of their oppositions, and therefore a check on what would otherwise be chaos. The universe is a never-ending fire, in which is found the unity of the opposites, the oneness behind antagonistic substances.

Responding to Heraclitus' theory of change, Parmenides of Elea (in Italy; c. 510–c. 450 B.C.E.) posited a single spiritual reality at the heart of the universe. What Parmenides calls "IT," or being, is an unmoving, perfect, eternal spiritual center completely removed from nonbeing, which cannot exist: for if **IT IS**, then that which is not, is not. Parmenides' intense consciousness of Reality itself would have a long future in Western thought. Presented in a long poem, much of which survives, his ideas are remarkable as an early exercise in purely abstract thought—pure reason. An extract is given in *Witnesses* above.

The Milesians had been materialists, for whom reality had a substantial, material basis. Pythagoras and Parmenides were idealists, for whom reality existed in an abstract realm, apart from matter. In the following generation materialism returned in the persons of Empedocles (fl. c. 445 B.C.E.; from Acragas in Sicily), Anaxagoras (c. 500–c. 428 B.C.E.; from Clazomenae in Asia Minor), Leucippus (fl. c. 435 B.C.E.; from Miletus in Asia Minor), and Democritus (c. 460–370 B.C.E.; from Abdera in northern Greece). Empedocles posited four basic elements (earth, air, fire, and water) from which all natural things were composed. These were subject to change and mixture through the powerful force of two principles of unification and disintegration: Love and Strife.

For Anaxagoras, the universe was made up of small and countless "seeds" governed by the rule of "mind." Those "seeds" are a foreshadowing of atomic theory, while that "mind" is reminiscent of Parmenides: "All other things have a portion of everything, but Mind is infinite and self-ruled, and is mixed with nothing but is all alone by itself." Anaxagoras' claim (inspired by the sight of a falling meteor) that the sun was a huge burning rock as big as the Peloponnese got him into trouble with the authorities, who charged him

WITNESSES

Presocratic Thinkers on Reality

What is real? The Greeks were the first thinkers to pursue an answer to that question through rigorous reasoning that has survived in written form. Here two of those early philosophers posit their visions of the real, and they are similar. For Parmenides, the real is Being itself, "entire, immovable and without end"; for Xenophanes, it is God, all of whom at once "sees," "thinks," and "hears."

Parmenides—Being is that which is immovable and without end (c. 470 B.C.E.): One way only is left to be spoken of, that it *is*; and on this way are full many signs that what *is* is uncreated and imperishable, for it is entire, immovable and without end. It *was* not in the past, nor *shall* it be, since it *is* now, all at once, one, continuous ... Nor shall I allow you to say or to think, "from that which is not"; for it is not to be said or thought that it is not . ... for if it came into being, it is not, nor if it is going to be in the future. So coming into being is extinguished and perishing unimaginable.
(Parmenides, no. 347; from G. S. Kirk, J. E. Raven, *Presocratic Philosophers*)

Xenophanes—The one, supreme god (c. 530 B.C.E.): One god, greatest among gods and men, in no way similar to mortals either in body or in thought.

Always he remains in the same place, moving not at all; nor is it fitting for him to go to different places at different times, but without toil he shakes all things by the thought of his mind.

All of him sees, all thinks, and all hears.
(Xenophanes, nos. 173, 174, 175; eds. G. S. Kirk, J. E. Raven)

Map 4.1* *The Geography of Thought, c. 750–320 B.C.E.: *The poets and orators, scientists and philosophers, historians and dramatists who created the monuments of thought that make ancient Greece memorable came from all over the Greek world—from Asia Minor in the east to Sicily in the west. An extraordinary number, however, came from Athens, whose political institutions and civic life nurtured imagination and creation.*

with impiety. He was living in Athens at the time, a friend of Pericles, whose political enemies aimed to strike at their adversary by discrediting the philosopher. Anaxagoras was forced to flee.

What Anaxagoras called "seeds," Leucippus and his follower Democritus called "atoms." These were infinite in number and form, unchanging in substance, hurtling and crashing through a void—not exactly what modern science has to say about the atom, but in its time a revolutionary concept. In this view of the universe Anaxagoras' controlling "Mind" had no place. The Democritean cosmos is irrational, and the tiny volatile atoms govern themselves and it.

History, Sophistry, and Oratory

While the inquiries of the Presocratics gave birth to philosophy and science, their rational method spurred the development of new groups of thinkers. Historians, Sophists, and orators turned the skeptical methods of the Presocratics to the problem of the past and present conduct of human society.

History Herodotus (c. 484–425 B.C.E.), whose distinction between "West" and "East" has already been noted, was the first major Greek historian. He traveled throughout the Mediterranean to gain insight into the peoples who affected the dramatic confrontation between Persia and Greece. Scythian burial customs, the astronomical lore of the Babylonians, courtly practices of the Persians—all were important to him.

In these researches, Herodotus invented a new discipline, the one that is practiced in the volume now before you: history. History, however, did not mean to him what it means now. In Greek, the word *historia* meant simply "inquiry": history originally was not the answer to a question but the process of seeking the answer. Why bother to seek? Herodotus announced his purpose in the opening words of his *History:* it is to preserve "from decay the remembrance of what men have done" and to prevent "the great and wonderful actions of the Greeks and the Barbarians from losing their due [measure] of glory."

Herodotus displays a skepticism reminiscent of Xenophanes. But whereas the latter simply scoffed at the absurd figures of the gods, Herodotus dutifully reported, but went on record as doubting, supernatural explanations. In response to the story that in the topmost chamber of the highest tower in Babylon a god slept with a woman provided for his comfort, the historian remarked: "but I do not believe it." When Xerxes' ships were wracked by storms, Herodotus wrote, "At length the [priests], by offering victims to the winds, and charming them with the help of conjurers, while at the same time they sacrificed to Thetis and the Nereids, succeeded in laying the storm four days after it first began." Then he added: "or perhaps it ceased of itself."

The goal of Thucydides (c. 460–c. 400 B.C.E.), the other renowned Greek historian, was similar to that of Herodotus: to understand the beginning and consequences of a war. But the men, and the wars, were

Thucydides

The historian Thucydides, most famous for his reporting of political struggle and violence (see Chapter 2, p. 53), is also an accurate observer of events caused by no human agency. Here is an excerpt of his famous description of the plague (its nature is controversial) that descended on Athens in 430 B.C.E, the year after Pericles delivered his funeral oration for the first year's dead (see p. 73).

Not many days after [the Lacedaemonian invasion of] … Attica the plague first began to show itself among the Athenians. It was said that it had broken out in many places previously …; but a pestilence of such extent and mortality was nowhere remembered. … It first began, it is said, in the parts of Ethiopia above Egypt, and thence descended into Egypt and Libya. … Suddenly falling upon Athens, it first attacked the population in Piraeus … and afterwards appeared in the upper city, when the deaths became much more frequent. All speculation as to its origin and its causes, if causes can be found adequate to produce so great a disturbance, I leave to other writers, whether lay or professional; for myself, I shall simply set down its nature, and explain the symptoms by which perhaps it may be recognized by the student, if it should ever break out again. This I can the better do, as I had the disease myself, and watched its operation in the case of others. As a rule, … there was no ostensible cause; but people in good health were all of a sudden attacked by violent heats in the head, and redness and inflammation in the eyes, the inward parts, such as the throat or tongue, becoming bloody and emitting an unnatural and fetid breath. These symptoms were followed by sneezing and hoarseness, after which the pain soon reached the chest, and produced a hard cough. When it fixed in the stomach, it upset it; and discharges of bile of every kind named by physicians ensued, accompanied by very great distress. In most cases also an ineffectual retching followed, producing violent spasms, which in some cases ceased soon after, in others much later. Externally the body was not very hot to the touch, nor pale in its appearance, but reddish, livid, and breaking out into small pustules and ulcers. But internally it burned so that the patient could not bear to have on him clothing or linen even of the very lightest description; or indeed to be otherwise than stark naked. … The body meanwhile did not waste away so long as the distemper was at its height, but held out to a marvel against its ravages; so that when they succumbed, as in most cases, on the seventh or eighth day to the internal inflammation, they had still some strength in them. But if they passed this stage, and the disease descended further into the bowels, inducing a violent ulceration there accompanied by severe diarrhoea, this brought on a weakness which was generally fatal. … By far the most terrible feature in the malady was the dejection which ensued when any one felt himself sickening, for the despair into which they instantly fell took away their power of resistance, and left them a much easier prey to the disorder; besides which, there was the awful spectacle of men dying like sheep, through having caught the infection in nursing each other. This caused the greatest mortality. On the one hand, if they were afraid to visit each other, they perished from neglect; indeed many houses were emptied of their inmates for want of a nurse: on the other, if they ventured to do so, death was the consequence …

(Thucydides, *Peloponnesian War*, 2:47.3–51.5; trans. R. Crawley)

different to the extent that, for a second time, history was invented anew. The Persian war was for Herodotus an epic confrontation between freedom and slavery. For Thucydides, the struggle between Athens and Sparta called the Peloponnesian War was a doomed and meaningless battle (though perhaps inevitable) between peoples already corrupted in spirit whose only outcome could be catastrophe. "Love of power," he grimly pronounced, "operating through greed and through personal ambition, was the cause of all these evils." Human psychology, he believed, was the motor that drove history forward.

The disaster unfolds, in Thucydides' presentation, in a series of intensely dramatic scenes. A social revolution in Corcyra, a Corinthian colony, is described in all its murderous and soul-destroying horror (see *Witnesses*, p. 53). The debate between the islanders of Melos and the Athenians who wished to dominate them displays the cold logic of power and ends in the enslavement of men, women, and children.

The departure of the Athenian fleet for adventures in Sicily is depicted as the tragic escapade of men who should have anticipated, but did not, the devastation that lay ahead. Every one of the survivors of the battles that followed faced incarceration and death by exposure, starvation, and disease. All these horrors are foreshadowed by paired events which occurred soon after the outset of the war. The first was Pericles' uplifting funeral speech for the first dead. The second was the plague that struck Athens shortly afterward and which, over three years, ravaged its population, killing one-third of its troops and Pericles himself, and leaving survivors demoralized. Thucydides' description is given in *Witnesses*, above.

The historian who wrote of these tragedies was scrupulous in his testing of sources and relentless in his pursuit of evidence. More than Herodotus, Thucydides rejects supernatural or even implausible explanations for events, seeking the springs of action in the decisions of the human minds that controlled the course of history. These he framed in speeches which he claimed were based on words that he heard or which had been reliably reported to him, but which he may have crafted to sound as though they had been uttered. In composing these speeches, he added the skills of the artist to those of the historian.

Thucydides was an Athenian of prominent family, distantly related to Miltiades, the hero of Marathon. He fought as a soldier in the war until 426 B.C.E. when he was exiled from his own city. From that distant vantage point, Thucydides was able both to describe war realistically and to understand its power to determine the future of human beings. His commitment to analyze the course and meaning of war has this defect: that he recognizes no history except the history of antagonistic states. For centuries to come, in the tradition of Herodotus and Thucydides, history was understood to be the history of empires and kingdoms and cities and the men who ruled them.

The Sophists Thucydides probably learned to write his chilling speeches from a new breed of specialist, the "Sophists." The original meaning of the Greek word *sophistes* was "expert" or "wise man," but it soon came to mean one who knew about, or talked about, or peddled wisdom. The Sophists were makers of speeches, and speech-making played a central role in Greek life. Like the bards of the Archaic age who traveled from city to city to recite the epics of Homer, the Sophists journeyed about the Greek world to display their talents, even addressing crowds of spectators at athletic festivals. They announced their arrival in each new locale with an elaborate speech, which was an exemplar of their eloquence and a form of job résumé: an invitation to the listener to employ the speaker. For the Sophists not only made speeches but taught others to make them—for a stiff fee.

The students who flocked to the Sophists did not aspire to knowledge, as did those who gathered around Thales or Pythagoras. They were often the sons of ambitious Greek citizens who aimed to participate in political life. Without training, they could not debate in the assembly, or defend friends or accuse opponents. The ability to make persuasive, dynamic speeches was a prerequisite of power. To gain that skill, many turned to the Sophists.

The Sophists taught another useful skill: that of devising deceitful or manipulative arguments. In addition to teaching the technique of building an argument, they also taught the technique of subverting their opponent's—to the dismay of cultural conservatives like Aristophanes and sticklers for the truth like Socrates. The willingness of the Sophists to adjust facts for practical ends was based on a profound transformation of values—just as their critics had feared. Many of them were atheists. Neither the Olympian gods and their myths nor the gods of the earth and their grip on natural forces impressed the Sophists. Their standards of behavior were eerily modern. "Is this action useful?" they might ask, not "Is it right?"; "Will this idea produce the desired response?" not "Is this the truth?"

The Sophist Protagoras of Abdera, in northern Greece (c. 484–c. 415 B.C.E.), came to Athens in the mid-fifth century B.C.E. and joined the brilliant circle around Pericles, which also included Aspasia, Anaxagoras, and Socrates. The philosopher Plato provides a full portrait of him in the dialogue entitled *Protagoras*. In addition, two of Protagoras' telling statements survive. The first expresses not merely skepticism about the existence of the gods, but sheer indifference to the possibility that they might exist: "Concerning the gods I cannot know either that they exist or that they do not exist, or what form they might have, for there is much to prevent one's knowing: the obscurity of the subject and the shortness of man's life." The second statement announces that truth and falsehood are not absolutes fixed by nature or the gods but relatives determined by the human mind: "Of all things the measure is man, of things that are that they are, and of things that are not that they are not." If man is the measure of all things, Protagoras' opponents feared, then standards of truth and falsehood, right and wrong, fall away.

It was said that to teach a young man such wisdom, Protagoras might charge 1000 drachmas: a worker's wages for three years. On such fees the Sophist Gorgias of Leontini, in Sicily (c. 483–376 B.C.E.), became rich. Gorgias claimed to be able to argue any case either way and to vindicate the unjust as well as the just cause. He demonstrated this in a piece of rhetoric entitled the *Encomium of Helen*. Here he argued the innocence of the woman blamed for embroiling the Greeks in the Trojan War: she was the victim of persuasion—in the same way that the Sophists' audience was a victim of their eloquence. No one can resist the power of speech, "which by means of the finest and most invisible body effects the divinest works," and must be acknowledged "a powerful lord" by the Greeks, who otherwise acknowledged none.

In his book *On Non-Being*, or *On What is Not*, Gorgias parodied the Presocratic thinkers whose ideas were often reported in books entitled *On Being*, *On Nature*, or *On What Is*. Here he announces the unknowability of anything for certain—a stance that leaves a Sophist with a clear field: "Nothing exists… even if it exists it is inapprehensible to man… even if it is apprehensible, still it is without a doubt incapable of being expressed or explained to the next man." With the possibility of rational knowledge of nature thus discarded, nothing is left but tissues of words. Of these, the Sophists were masters.

The Sophists' desertion of fixed standards of moral goodness or rational truth has been much lamented. Yet their achievement was considerable. By broadening the definition of what there was to know and what was worth knowing, they paved the way for many learned disciplines: the humanities and social sciences; the studies of language and meaning, of society and politics and of human behavior. The Sophists, finally, were the first professional educators, and very popular ones. Young men left the gymnasium and the stadium to attend to the sparkling words of the Sophists. These schools resemble ours far more closely than did the "school" of Thales or even the "school" of Plato. Under such instruction, young men were trained to assume leadership in their cities.

Oratory The elaboration by the Sophists of the discipline of prose composition paved the way for the professional orators who flourished in Athens in the last century of her independence. The long-lived Isocrates (436–338 B.C.E.), a speechwriter and (in the Sophist tradition) a teacher of oratory, was an elegant stylist, whose prose set a standard of Greek rhetoric. His speeches circulated in writing as models for composition. Demosthenes (384–322 B.C.E.) was a fierce and effective orator who spoke often in the law courts and councils of Athens during the years when her democracy reached its peak.

During the three generations between the end of the Peloponnesian War (404 B.C.E.) and the Greeks' defeat at Chaeronea by Philip of Macedon (338 B.C.E.), which brought an end to their independence, even the poorest Athenian citizens could participate in government. Only a few of them had received the education that was the privilege of the old aristocrats, or the expressive training offered by the Sophists. To present a defense or bring a suit, they required the services of an orator. Most of the surviving speeches of the fourth-century B.C.E. orators are private commissions of this sort. Others, however, deal with the tremendous issues of foreign policy the Athenians faced as the power of Macedon loomed ever larger.

To that threat Isocrates and Demosthenes had two different reactions. Isocrates' views are outlined in a famous speech entitled *Panegyricus*, in which he urges the Greek states to unite under Macedonian overlordship and turn to fight the still-mighty Persian Empire: "It is much more glorious to fight against the King for his empire," he chided, "than to contend against each other for the hegemony [of Greece]."

Demosthenes urged resistance to the Macedonian advance in a series of speeches delivered between 351 and 338 B.C.E.: three called the *Olynthiacs*, occasioned by the capture of the city of Olynthus, and four called *Philippics*, directed against the Macedonian king. While Philip advanced in summer and winter alike, intent on the domination of Greece, Demosthenes argued, Athenians thought only of their bribes and perquisites. There might still be a chance, he thundered in 351 B.C.E.: "If you will adopt this principle now, though you did not do so before, and if each citizen who can and ought to give his service to the state is ready to give it . . . , if, put bluntly, you will become your own masters and each cease expecting to do nothing himself while his neighbor does everything for him, then, God willing, you will recover your own, get back what has been frittered away, and turn the tables on Philip." The plea didn't work, and Philip advanced exactly as Demosthenes had forecast.

Philosophers—Lovers of Wisdom

By the time of Isocrates and Demosthenes in the fourth century B.C.E., the world of myth had diminished. Both of these men were heirs to the pragmatism of the Sophists, the realism of the historians, the skepticism of the Presocratics, as both men were shaped by the events that led to the collapse of the free *polis* in Greece. Also shaped by these cultural and political circumstances were the three men—Socrates, Plato, Aristotle—whose achievement it is to have invented philosophy: the "love of wisdom" or "love of truth," a ceaseless striving to know.

The new "**philosophers**" (*philosophoi*) asked the same questions as had their predecessors, especially the Presocratics, called "the wise" (*sophoi*): What is the universe made of? Is it substance or spirit, being or nonbeing? Is it one or many? Does it change? Is it in motion? What causes it to change or move? What causes it to stop? Is there any order in the cosmos? How do we know what it is—or anything that we know? Are there gods? What do they do? What meaning does human existence have in the cosmic system? What is the purpose of human life? What is the best form of state?

Socrates Socrates (470–399 B.C.E.) asked questions and wouldn't give answers. Claiming to know nothing, he challenged those who claimed to know everything or even something, and thus to be wise. Socrates did not give speeches or take fees for lessons (as his opponents falsely charged) and he attacked the Sophists for doing so. He sauntered to the *agora* and the gymnasium, as though he had nothing of importance to do, and engaged in conversation with the young men of Athens. He wrote nothing himself.

Socrates' method can be observed in the dialogues written by his pupil Plato. In his dialogue with Meno, Socrates asks that gentleman what virtue is. Meno responds that there are many kinds of virtue: the virtue of a man, of a woman, and many others. Gracefully, Socrates recoils from the spate of words: "I seem to be in luck. I wanted one virtue and I find that you have a whole swarm of virtues to offer." The implication is clear: Meno hasn't the slightest idea, in spite of his costly sophistic education, what virtue is.

A second Platonic dialogue, the *Symposium*, describes a drinking party at which the guests each give extemporaneous speeches in honor of love. The poet Agathon, the host, gives the most exquisite, his language sporting the excesses of contemporary drama and sophistic oratory. Then Socrates is asked to speak. He begins by praising Agathon's presentation, which he could never, he demurs, hope to equal. But, he

Plato's "Allegory of the Cave"

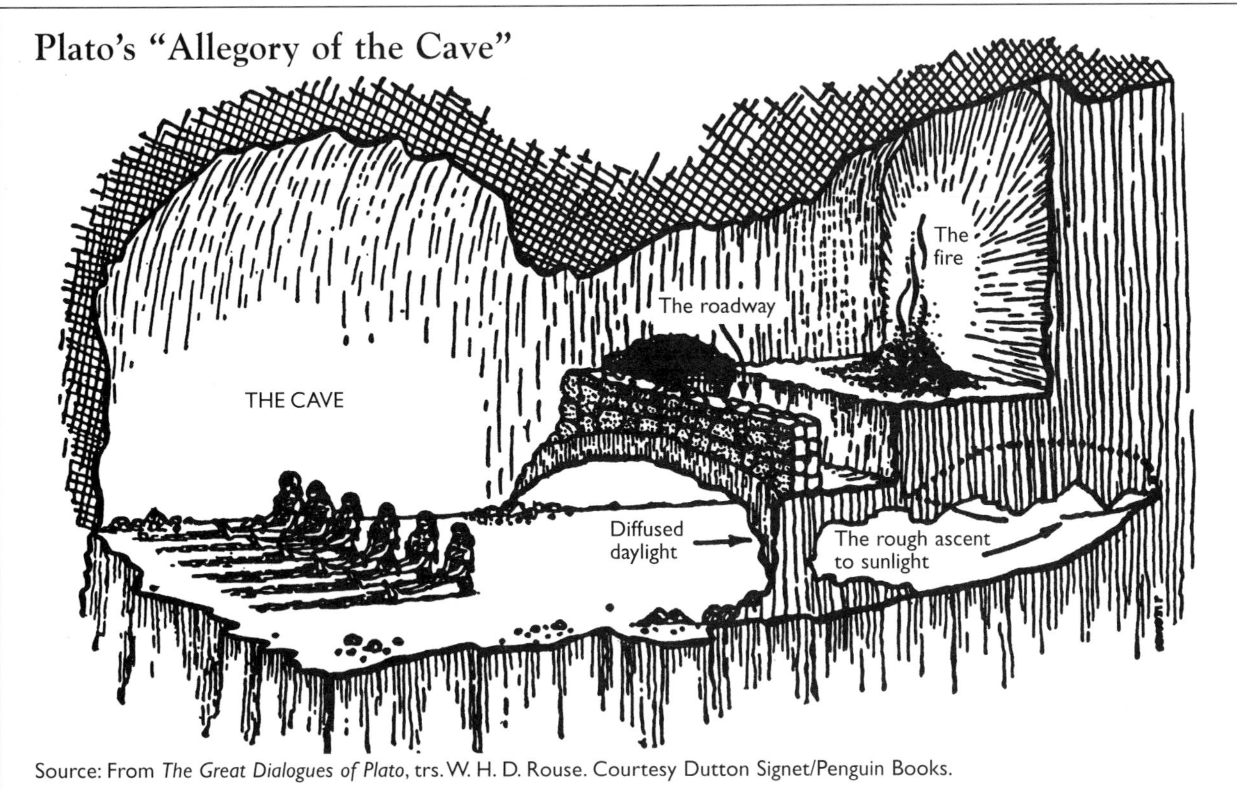

Source: From *The Great Dialogues of Plato*, trs. W. H. D. Rouse. Courtesy Dutton Signet/Penguin Books.

wonders, was it his job to speak beautifully about love (as Agathon had done), or to speak the truth? None of those, he implies, who had spoken had approached the real issue, which was the nature of love. Again, Socrates exposes the ignorance of others as a necessary step to finding what is actually the case.

Searching after truth is often dangerous, and for Socrates it was fatal. In 399 B.C.E. he was accused of "impiety": of having neglected religious duties and corrupted the young of Athens. The accusers demanded the death penalty. Socrates defended himself with the same kind of reasoning that had so charmed the gentlemen of the gymnasia and street corners. He was found guilty by a vote of 281 to 220. By a second and more emphatic vote of 300–201, the jury condemned him to death by poisoning. His friends proposed to bribe the jailors. Socrates refused. He died a martyr, at the hands of a democracy and by majority vote, to the principle of truth.

Plato Socrates' death shocked his younger friend Plato (428–347 B.C.E.). Plato's earliest works describe the trial and death of his mentor, and nearly all the later ones memorialize him. They are composed as dialogues between Socrates and his friends or acquaintances, dramatic reenactments of the open-air conversations in which the older man dazzled his hearers for nearly fifty years. Plato was both philosopher and dramatist, perpetual student of the questing Socrates, and pioneer of new regions of thought.

Plato believed that ultimate truths really existed and could be known. These were the Ideas of things: supernatural like the gods, unchanging like the "It" posited by Parmenides, invulnerable to the destructive criticism of the Sophists, apprehensible by the mind like the truths that Socrates sought behind meaningless chatter. To know these Ideas was the supreme purpose of life. The philosopher would be led by love of the beautiful: beyond beautiful things to the idea of the Beautiful and the Ideas themselves, formers and sustainers of the universe. Only philosophers were capable of the pure apprehension of Ideas. Ordinary people (as Plato explained in his "allegory of the cave" in the seventh book of his *Republic*), quoted in *Witnesses* on p. 106 saw only the shadows of images of things, like the fleeting and distorted images cast by a campfire on the wall of a cave.

Such lofty thinking did not blind Plato to the realities of life in the world. Believing that the philosopher should act and not just observe, he journeyed to Syracuse on the island of Sicily in 387 B.C.E., to guide the political education of the heir to the tyrant of that city. He opposed the Sophists' notion that, all things being relative, the ideal of justice was, too. In the *Republic*, he outlined an ideal state where justice was administered by carefully chosen philosopher-kings, male and female—for women, Plato held, were capable of excellence. Later in life, sobered by his experience of the decline of the *polis*, he wrote in his *Laws* a more sour sketch of how political life should be ordered. Never did he despair of justice, but he did despair of human benevolence.

On his return from a last, disheartening expedition to Sicily, Plato purchased a small park just outside Athens, where he founded a school: the "Academy." Not only a group of thinkers but also the institution in which they worked, Plato's Academy is the ancestor of academies, research institutes, and universities,

Plato and Aristotle on the Nature of Knowing

Ancient Greek philosophy culminates in the work of Plato and Aristotle, teacher and student, whose works in their sum outline the branches of philosophical thought to be pursued by Western thinkers for the next 2,400 years. In these passages, Plato presents his "allegory of the cave" to show that human beings think they know the truth when they in fact see only shadows of truth; and Aristotle speaks of the importance of knowledge: "the activity of our intelligence constitutes . . .complete happiness."

Plato—Humans, like prisoners in a cave who see only shadows, know nothing of reality (c. 380 B.C.E.): Picture men dwelling in a sort of subterranean cavern with a long entrance open to the light on its entire width. Conceive them as having their legs and necks fettered from childhood, so that they remain in the same spot, able to look forward only, and prevented by the fetters from turning their heads. Picture further the light from a fire burning higher up and at a distance behind them, and between the fire and the prisoners and above them a road along which a low wall has been built, as the exhibitors of puppet shows have partitions before the men themselves, above which they show the puppets. ... See also, then, men carrying past the wall implements of all kinds that rise above the wall, and human images and shapes of animals as well, wrought in stone and wood, and every material, some of these bearers presumably speaking and others silent. ... Then in every way such prisoners would deem reality to be nothing else than the shadows of the artificial objects. ...
(Plato, *Republic*, 7:514–515; ed. P. Shorey, 1982)

Aristotle—The greatest happiness lies in pursuing the life of the mind, since "intelligence *is* man" (c. 335 B.C.E.): [The activity of the mind] is not only the highest—for intelligence is the highest possession we have in us, and the objects which are the concern of intelligence are the highest objects of knowledge—but also the most continuous: we are able to study continuously more easily than to perform any kind of action. ... Again, study seems to be the only activity which is loved for its own sake. For while we derive a greater or a smaller advantage from practical pursuits beyond the action itself, from study we derive nothing beyond the activity of studying. ... [I]t follows that the activity of our intelligence constitutes the complete happiness of man. ... In other words, a life guided by intelligence is the best and most pleasant for man, inasmuch as intelligence, above all else, is man. Consequently, this kind of life is the happiest.
(Aristotle, *Nicomachean Ethics*, 1177–1178; ed. M. Ostwald, 1985)

and of the people who teach there, perform experiments, and pursue research. There Plato taught for nearly forty years, surrounded by friends and students (women as well as men, so long as they met the high prerequisites). Disciples carried on his work for nine centuries thereafter, until the Academy was suppressed by the Emperor Justinian (in 529 C.E.).

Aristotle A dozen years after Plato's death another school, the Lyceum, was founded by his restive student Aristotle (384–322 B.C.E.). Born at Stagira, in northern Greece, Aristotle grew up in the swelling shadow of Macedonia. There his father, Nicomachus, became physician to King Philip II. The young Aristotle moved to Athens in 367 B.C.E. to study at Plato's Academy. On the founder's death in 347 B.C.E. (and at a time when persons tinged with Macedonian relations were unwelcome in Athens), he moved to the court of the tyrant Hermeias of Atarneus (in Asia Minor), another of Plato's students. Three years later, Aristotle journeyed to Mitylene, on the island of Lesbos, off the coast of Asia Minor, where he befriended Theophrastus, who was to be his eventual successor. It was another short stay. From 342 B.C.E., Aristotle was in Pella, the capital of Macedonia, serving as tutor to the future world conqueror Alexander the Great. In 335 B.C.E., with Athens now under Macedonian control, he established there his new philosophical school, rival to the nearby Academy.

The Lyceum resembled a modern research institute. It received a subsidy, in the form of a huge gift (800 talents) from Alexander. It provided office, library, and laboratory space, and areas for teaching, spirited lunches, and private contemplation. Aristotle often taught as he walked the paths and arcades that crossed the property; hence he and his followers were called "Peripatetics," meaning "walking about." At the Lyceum Aristotle systematized the branches of Western philosophy.

Aristotle's approach to knowledge was different from that of Socrates and Plato, in that it was based on observable phenomena. To this end, he collected and classified data: thousands of species of marine life; 158 constitutions of Greek cities. From such a wealth of material, Aristotle established the study of biology and politics. On the basis of his data, he proceeded to theoretical statements. Like the modern manipulator of a database, Aristotle understood that classifying information made certain kinds of knowledge possible.

Upon the basis of classified data about the political structures of the Greek states, Aristotle established in his *Politics* forms of government that are still in use: monarchy, aristocracy, and democracy. Reared when the Greek *polis* was a vital reality, he argued that the city was a community of households, and superior to both family and individual: "For the whole must necessarily be prior to the parts." Individuals are

The Anatomy of Virtue and Vice

Extreme/Excess = Vice	Mean/Moderation = Virtue	Extreme/Deficiency = Vice
Confidence	Courage	Fear
Self-indulgence	Self-control	Insensitivity
Extravagance	Generosity	Stinginess
Vanity	Honor	Small-mindedness
Anger	Gentleness	Apathy
Boastfulness	Truthfulness	Self-deprecation

Source: Aristotle, *Nicomachean Ethics*, 2: 6–7

not unimportant: but what is good "for a nation and for states is nobler and more divine."

On the issues of change, motion, and the universe, Aristotle synthesized in his works on physics and metaphysics the insights of his Presocratic predecessors into a model of his own. Distinguishing matter from form, motion from rest, what was "lower" from what was "higher," being from becoming, cause from effect, he hypothesized a universal system, which was directed by its own laws to rational and worthy ends. It had a creator, too: the one God, life and thought itself, "a living being, eternally most good; and therefore life and a continuous eternal existence belong to God; for that is what God is." (See *Witnesses*, p. 106).

The human mind, according to Aristotelian psychology, shared in the eternity and rationality of the divine. This was not to say that the human being was all mind. Aristotle saw that human life consisted in a balance of good things: citizenship in a just city, the enjoyment in moderation of wealth and leisure and food and sex and friendship and other pleasures. In his *Ethics* he outlined his ideal: that virtue lies in moderation, in the choice of the mean between extremes of behavior. Nevertheless, the final happiness of the human being lies in the contemplation of truth, the absorption of his or her mind into the one eternal and incorporeal mind. Life is the activity of the mind: "Intelligence, above all else, is man."

Here in the fourth century B.C.E. Greek thought reaches its culmination. The *polis* had nurtured an explosion of intellectual life. The result was the elevation of reason as the one distinctively human quality. Over four centuries, Greek minds had explored the meaning of human existence, wandering far from inherited myths and memories to create vast systems of thought which have since then been modified and criticized but never cast aside.

These systems of thought endured, but the world of the *polis* was dying. In 323 B.C.E., Alexander died and Athens reverberated with anti-Macedonian feeling—boding ill for Aristotle, with his Macedonian connections. On the verge of being charged with the same crime of "impiety" that had threatened Anaxagoras and killed Socrates, he fled to the Macedonian stronghold of Chalkis—saving the Athenians from the charge, he commented wryly, of sinning a second time against philosophy. The next year he died. In this same year Demosthenes, encouraging a Greek revolt, was condemned to death by Alexander's successors, fled Athens, and committed suicide. Hereafter in the Greek-speaking world, the theater would flourish, gymnasia would stand in every city, the verses of Homer and Hesiod would be pounded into the heads of schoolchildren, and philosophers would philosophize. But the greatest era of creation was over.

Conclusion

THE LIFE OF REASON AND THE MEANING OF THE WEST

Pericles called Athens the "school of Hellas." By that statement he meant that his city's advanced and refined culture set a standard for the whole Greek-speaking region. Although Athens dominated Classical culture, other cities also contributed to the astonishing flowering of science and philosophy, poetry and rhetoric, pedagogy and scholarship achieved by Greek civilization. Over the course of four centuries, Greek poets and thinkers had expanded their intellectual world through the elaboration of myth, the exploration of the human condition, and the analysis of the natural and supernatural world about them—the latter analysis resulting in the rejection of the same mythic vision with which the cultural journey began. As a result of this inquiry, by the end of the Classical era the foundations of all subsequent Western thought had been laid.

REVIEW QUESTIONS

1. What qualities did the Greeks ascribe to their gods? How important were temples in Greek religion and culture? What were the rational and irrational features of Greek religion? Which was the more influential of the two?

2. Why was Homer so important to the Greeks? What did the lyric poets write about? Who was Sappho and why was she unique?

3. What were the origins of Greek drama? Who were the main Greek dramatists, and what themes did they prefer to portray? What was the purpose of Greek comedy?

4. Why were gymnastic exercise and athletics so important to the Greeks? How were these activities related to warfare? How did the idealization of the male body influence developments in Greek art?

5. Why did the pre-Socratics decide to break with traditional Greek beliefs? How did historians Herodotus and Thucydides use pre-Socratic methods? Were the Sophists a positive or negative influence on Greek society?

6. Why was Socrates executed? How did Socrates' death influence Plato? What did Plato consider to be the supreme purpose of life? How did Aristotle's approach to knowledge differ from that of Socrates and Plato?

SUGGESTED RESOURCES

The Birth of the Greek Gods

Burkert, Walter, *Greek Religion: Archaic and Classical* (Cambridge, MA: Harvard University Press, 1985). A thorough account of rituals, religious organization, deities, beliefs of Greek religion from the Neolithic to the Classical period. Discusses mystery cults, mythological narratives, philosophical religion, and death ritual.

Dodds, E. R., *The Greeks and the Irrational* (Los Angeles: University of California Press, 1951, 1973). Eight classic lectures on the irrational and subconscious in Greek life, literature, religion, and philosophy, from Homer to the Hellenistic period.

Easterling, P. E., and J. V. Muir, eds. *Greek Religion and Society* (Cambridge, MA: Harvard University Press, 1985). A thoughtful, wide-ranging collection of essays on the cultural meaning of Greek religion. Discusses poetry, death beliefs, temples and other sites of worship, religious festivals, divination, art, and the challenge to Greek religion posed by the Sophists.

Garland, Robert, *Introducing New Gods: The Politics of Athenian Religion* (Ithaca: Cornell University Press, 1992). Not all gods, or myths, were ancient; here the process is explored by which new gods and their cults were introduced to the surprisingly modern world of fifth-century Athens.

Lefkowitz, Mary R., *Women in Greek Myth* (Baltimore: Johns Hopkins University Press, 1986). Countering recent feminist interpretations of Greek mythology as fiercely misogynist, this amply documented study contends that Greek myths present, in their context, a balanced view of women's personalities and capacities.

Discovering Humanity

Morgan, Catherine, *Athletes and Oracles: The Transformation of Olympia and Delphi in the Eighth Century* B.C. (Cambridge: Cambridge University Press, 1990). A fascinating study of the connection between athletics and religion forged in the early years of the development of Greek culture, which continued to nurture Greek ways of understanding the world into the Hellenistic era.

Pickard-Cambridge, A. W., John Gould, and David M. Lewis, eds. *The Dramatic Festivals of Athens* (Oxford: Clarendon Press of Oxford University Press, 1988). Detailed descriptions of actors, choruses, audiences, and settings of Athenian tragedy, comedy, mime, and song.

Poliakoff, Michael D., *Combat Sports in the Ancient World: Combat, Violence and Culture* (New Haven: Yale University Press, 1987). The Greek gymnasium was a training ground equally for the disparate activities of philosophy and war. Here Poliakoff examines the ways in which Greek athleticism was centrally related to the defensive strategy of the *polis*.

Stewart, Andrew, *Art, Desire, and the Body in Ancient Greece* (Cambridge: Cambridge University Press, 1997). Considers the Greek fascination with the naked body as an expression of Greek society and mentality.

Ancient Olympic sports:
http://www.perseus.tufts.edu/Olympics/sports.html

To Know and to Love to Know

Barnes, Jonathan, *The Presocratic Philosophers* (London: Routledge & Kegan Paul, 1982). A survey of Presocratic writings, going from Hesiod to the Atomists, with essays on each major author or school. Contains useful summaries and analyses of Presocratic arguments.

Kerferd, G. B., *The Sophistic Movement* (Cambridge, MA: Cambridge University Press, 1981). Brief and readable, the best introduction to the history, philosophy, politics, and reputation of the Sophists. Argues that the Sophists have been neglected and are a key movement in the history of Greek philosophy.

Lateiner, Donald, *The Historical Method of Herodotus* (Toronto: University of Toronto Press, 1992). A sophisticated but accessible study of Herodotus as a creative historian. Discusses his selection and organization of material and structure and patterns of interpretation.

Robb, Kevin, *Literacy and Paideia in Ancient Greece* (Oxford: Oxford University Press, 1994). Fascinating study of how Greek civilization evolved, first before all others in the world, but only slowly over four centuries, from an oral to an alphabetic mode of communication and thought.

Vlastos, Gregory, *Socrates: Ironist and Moral Philosopher* (Ithaca: Cornell University Press, 1991). A riveting, erudite study of Socrates' style and moral philosophy.

About Sappho and her poetry:
http://www.sappho.com/poetry/historical/sappho.html

Plato's *Dialogues*: discussion, biography, bibliography, links:
http://www.plato.evansville.edu

Aristotle: discussion, biography, bibliography, links:
http://www.knuten.liu.se/~bjoch501/philosophers/ari.html

PART TWO

THE ORIGINS OF THE WEST

From Roman Dominion to the New Peoples of Europe (300 B.C.E.–1300 C.E.)

Greek dominion over the Mediterranean world, the achievement of Alexander the Great, yielded within two centuries to the sterner domination of Rome. As a republic (c. 500-27 B.C.E.), Rome extended its control over the Mediterranean region, while developing social and political institutions that would endure in the Western world. As an empire, it brought peace and prosperity, at first, to its subjects; later, it increasingly brought exploitation and war.

Before the western zone of the Roman Empire succumbed to invasions by nomadic tribes in 476 C.E., its civilization had matured to embody in art and literature the accumulated vision of the ancient Mediterranean world. And although Roman might had dispersed the Jews of Palestine, Christianity, an offshoot of Judaism, became the official religion of the Empire. As it did so, however, the frontiers, defended by an enormous and non-Roman army, began to fail.

As Germanic tribes settled in the western parts of Europe that were once Roman, a Christianized Rome lived on in the Greek-speaking, eastern zone of the Empire, centered at Constantinople (formerly Byzantium). This eastern Roman or Byzantine Empire endured until 1453. It was then overcome by a Turkish people, the Ottomans, who had adopted the religion and civilization of Islam.

Islam arose in the seventh century C.E., the creation of the Arab prophet Muhammad. Expanding across North Africa and the Middle East, and into Asia and Africa, Islam developed an advanced civilization that built upon the achievements of Greece, India, and China.

As the three successors of Rome (European kingdoms, Byzantium, and Islam) established themselves, other civilizations prospered in Asia, Africa, and the Americas. By the end of the first millennium C.E., the human species had expanded to inhabit the whole of the globe except Antarctica, and advanced civilizations flourished on five out of the seven continents.

OUR SEA

400 | 350 | 300 | 250 | 200 | 150 | 100 | 50 B.C.E. | 1 C.E.

Alexander's Empire, 334–323

Hellenistic Civilization, 323–31

Early and Republican Rome, c. 550–27

Roman Empire, 27 B.C.E.–476 C.E.

Rulers, Nations, and War

- Legendary founding of Rome, 753
- City of Rome formed on seven hills, c. 600
- Expulsion from Rome of last Etruscan king, 510
- Battle of Marathon, 490
- Celts from north of the Po attack Rome, c. 386
- Intermittent war between Rome and Samnites, 343–290
- Alexander crosses Hellespont, 334
- Alexander the Great dies, 323
- Rome dominates Italian peninsula, 275
- Three "Punic Wars" (with Carthage), 264–146
- Parthian kingdom established in Iran; pressures Seleucid dominions, 247
- Rome defeats Carthage at battle of Zama, 202
- Antiochus IV Epiphanes occupies Jerusalem, 167
- Carthage and Corinth destroyed, 146
- Tiberius Gracchus assassinated, 133
- Gaius Gracchus made Tribune, 123
- Suicide of Gaius Gracchus, 121
- Caesar, Pompey and Crassus the first "Triumvirate," 60
- Caesar elected consul, 59
- Caesar conquers Gaul, 51
- Caesar crosses Rubicon, joined by Mark Antony; Cicero, Cato, Pompey flee, 49
- Caesar vanquishes Pompey at Pharsalus, 48
- Julius Caesar assassinated, 44
- Cicero assassinated by Mark Antony, 43
- Mark Antony defeats Brutus, Cassius at Philippi, 42
- Mark Antony and Cleopatra flee Actium, 31
- End of Ptolemaic Dynasty in Egypt, 30
- Roman Senate bestows title "Augustus" on Octavian, 27

Religion, Ideas, and Society

- Codification of Hippocratic corpus begins, c. 430
- Greek translation of Hebrew Bible — the "Septuagint" — begins, c. 250
- Mathematician and inventor Archimedes killed when Romans take Syracuse, c. 212 B.C.E.
- Cynic, Stoic, Epicurean schools of philosophy join Peripatetics, Academicians, c. 200s
- Eunus leads Sicilian slave revolt, 135
- Spartacus' slave revolt crushed, 71
- Ptolemy's *Almagest*, 150

Beyond the West

Zhou dynasty, c. 1027–221
Warring states, 750–221

Qin dynasty, c. 221–206

Han dynasty, c. 206 B.C.E.–220 C.E.

- Chandragupta Maurya of India, r. c. 321–298
- Asoka of India, 272–232
- Shi Huangdi of China, r. 221–210/209
- Shi Huangdi and burning of books, 213

CHAPTER

5

OUR SEA

The Mediterranean World in the Hellenistic and Early Roman Eras

300–27 B.C.E.

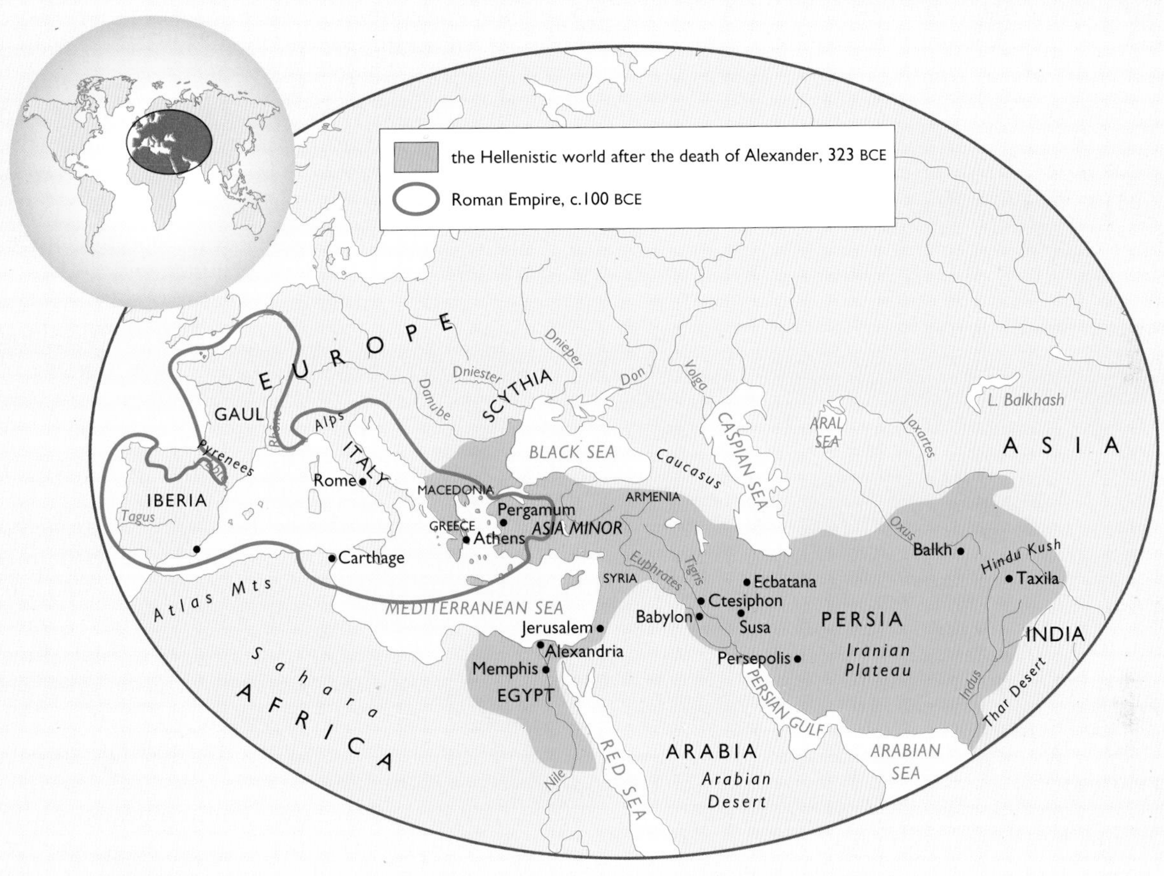

KEY TOPICS

- **Around the Mediterranean:** Alexander the Great's successors form Greek kingdoms in the eastern Mediterranean; further west, Carthage and Etruria link ancient civilizations with simpler societies on their borders.
- **Becoming Greek:** The Greek presence transforms Mediterranean culture, making it "Hellenistic" and a haven for scholars, scientists, and philosophers.
- **Rome: From Village to Nation:** A village on the Tiber river grows, rebels against Etruscan overlords, and constructs unique social and political institutions.
- **Rome: From West to East:** Rome expands on the Italian peninsula, then to the west, then to the east, and makes the Mediterranean a Roman sea.
- **Rome: From Republic to Empire:** Competition and war lead to the extinction of the Roman Republic and the elevation of an emperor to rule the Roman world.

Caesar's Words and the Roman Sea

Following his successful campaign in Asia Minor in 47 B.C.E., *the Roman general Julius Caesar (100–44* B.C.E.*) described his achievement in a single sentence:* Veni, vidi, vici *("I came, I saw, I conquered"). These three short Latin words convey the unrelenting efficiency of the Roman advance. Over the past three centuries, Rome had grown from village to* **cosmopolis**, *the chief city of the Mediterranean world. The Roman Empire encircled the Mediterranean sea, once dominated by older Middle Eastern and Greek civilizations. By the opening of the Common Era, that sea was Roman, and the Romans called it* mare nostrum, *"our sea."*

AROUND THE MEDITERRANEAN

Before Caesar, there was Alexander the Great (356–323 B.C.E.); the Roman conquest of the Mediterranean lands rested on the Macedonian Greek conquest. Alexander's swift advance through the eastern Mediterranean conveyed much of the surrounding territory into the hands of Greek-speaking Macedonian rulers, whose struggles and policies dominated the remaining autonomous cities and nations of the region. The leading powers of the western Mediterranean, though independent in their development, were also linked to eastern centers. The whole of the Mediterranean grew together to form a unified civilization, its unity the unexpected and remarkable fruit of a remarkable military conquest.

Hellenistic Civilization and the Eastern Mediterranean

Alexander and his successors reshaped the eastern Mediterranean politically, reorganizing boundaries, displacing rulers, and establishing cities (see Map 5.1). And they did so culturally, planting Greek customs and language. This civilization, beginning with Alexander and extending up to 30 B.C.E. and the onset of Roman domination, is called "**Hellenistic**"—unlike the pre-Alexandrian age known as "Hellenic."

Alexander came to the throne in 336 B.C.E., over the body of his murdered father, Philip II. He commanded a superb army based on the fast and flexible Macedonian phalanx, whose soldiers were equipped with spears longer and deadlier than those of the traditional Greek hoplite. This army consisted of 15,000 disciplined infantrymen, 25,000 light-armed auxiliaries and mercenaries, and 5000 cavalry, Alexander's "Companions." With the army marched a staff of secretaries, sages, and philosophers, servants of a prince who slept each night with the text of the *Iliad* (annotated by his tutor, Aristotle) under his pillow.

In 334 B.C.E., Alexander crossed the Hellespont, the narrow straits between Europe and Asia, through which the Persian King Xerxes had passed, seeking dominion over the Greeks, nearly 150 years before. Now Alexander intended to subdue Persia. In a series of battles from Asia Minor to Mesopotamia—at the Granicus River, at Issus, at Tyre, and at Gaugamela—Greek tactics outweighed greater Persian numbers. When Alexander's troops were checked at the Phoenician city of Tyre, which resisted their siege for seven months, the Persian king Darius III eventually sought an honorable peace. Alexander's highest-ranking general, Parmenion, sent a message that if he were Alexander, he would accept. "And I, too," answered Alexander scornfully, "if I were Parmenion." Alexander went on to take Tyre. By 331 B.C.E., he had conquered all that Darius possessed—including the mother, wife, children, and treasure of that monarch, who was butchered by his own guard.

From 330 to 324 B.C.E., Alexander marched across the Iranian plateau, east to the Himalayas and over the Khyber Pass to the Indus River. He had traversed 22,000 miles (35,420 km.) and won every battle along the route when on June 10, 323 B.C.E., at the age of thirty-two, he died of fever and drink in the heart of his empire. He had made no arrangements for the transfer of power. "Let the job go," he reportedly gasped on his deathbed, "to the strongest."

After Alexander's death, his generals struggled mightily for this prize. They eventually split it into three portions, over which they and their descendants reigned. To the south, a dynasty of kings named Ptolemy ruled Egypt, as the pharaohs had done before. To the east the Seleucid dynasty ruled an empire comprising Syria, Babylon, and Persia. The Antigonids ruled Macedonia to the north, dominating the Greek mainland.

The Ptolemies pressed the 7 million peasants who farmed the Nile valley to the limit of their capacity. Their overseers managed systems of irrigation and drainage, and experimented with new crops, crop rotation, and fertilizers, in order to maximize their master's profits and their own chances for promotion. Some of the profits were creamed off by **tax farmers**, private agents who paid themselves what they could from the sums demanded of the peasants. Sporadic rebellions by the exploited peasants were suppressed by the Ptolemies' Greek mercenaries.

The Ptolemies held monopolies on essential commodities (salt, oil, cloth, papyrus), which they protected with tariff barriers (tax duties on imports and exports). Trade flourished, nevertheless. Ships throughout the Mediterranean docked at the new capital, Alexandria, which was dominated by a 328-foot (100 m) high lighthouse, the Pharos.

Founded by Alexander himself (whose tomb there was a tourist attraction), Alexandria was the world's largest commercial center, teeming with merchants, bureaucrats, and artisans. By the first century B.C.E. it counted one million inhabitants from diverse national, cultural, and racial origins. Here were Syrians and Egyptians, Jews and Greeks, living in elegant town houses and crowded tenements. These surrounded public buildings approached by paved avenues and illuminated at night. The Ptolemies established botanical gardens and a zoo, the world's largest library and first **museum**, or "temple of the Muses," an institute of scientific research.

Hellenistic Egypt thrived longer than its sister kingdoms. At its peak in the third century B.C.E., it declined in the second, dwindled to the status of a Roman dependency, and ceased to be in 30 B.C.E. with the suicide of Cleopatra VII, the last of the Ptolemies.

Embracing more nations and peoples than Egypt, the lands of the Middle East proved a greater challenge to the Seleucids. Still, these Macedonian rulers did manage to impose order on a tumultuous empire and protected the trade caravans that wound their way toward Asia across desert and plateau. Pressed from the east by the Parthians (an Asian people from the Caspian region), and from the west by the Ptolemies, their empire had shrunk by 100 B.C.E. to a slim corridor on the Mediterranean's eastern coast (Syria–Lebanon). A Roman army under the general Pompey devoured that remnant in 63 B.C.E. Macedonians of the Antigonid dynasty dominated mainland Greeks. Other Greek *poleis* pursued their own civic lives under Antigonid domination until, after 167 B.C.E., Rome seized Macedonian Greece.

Adjacent to the Seleucid and Antigonid realms, several independent kingdoms and city-states emerged. On the coast of Asia Minor, King Attalus I (241–197 B.C.E.) created his city-kingdom at Pergamum, which rivaled Alexandria as a center of culture. Rising from the huddle of commoners' houses, the hallmark buildings of a Greek *polis*, including a theater, a temple, a library, and not one but three gymnasia, climbed the hill to the royal palace complex on the ridge. The plan is shown on p. 114, the ruins on p. 115. There stood the altar of Zeus "the Savior," its 400-foot (122 m.) frieze celebrating the victory of Olympian gods over primal "Giants," and of the Greeks over the barbarians. When the last Attalid king died childless in 133 B.C.E., he willed his prosperous kingdom to Rome, which still had to fight until 129 B.C.E. for it.

The island state of Rhodes flourished nearby, a center for banking and for the study of rhetoric. It acted as the policeman of the eastern Mediterranean, purging the seas of pirates. Over its busy harbor

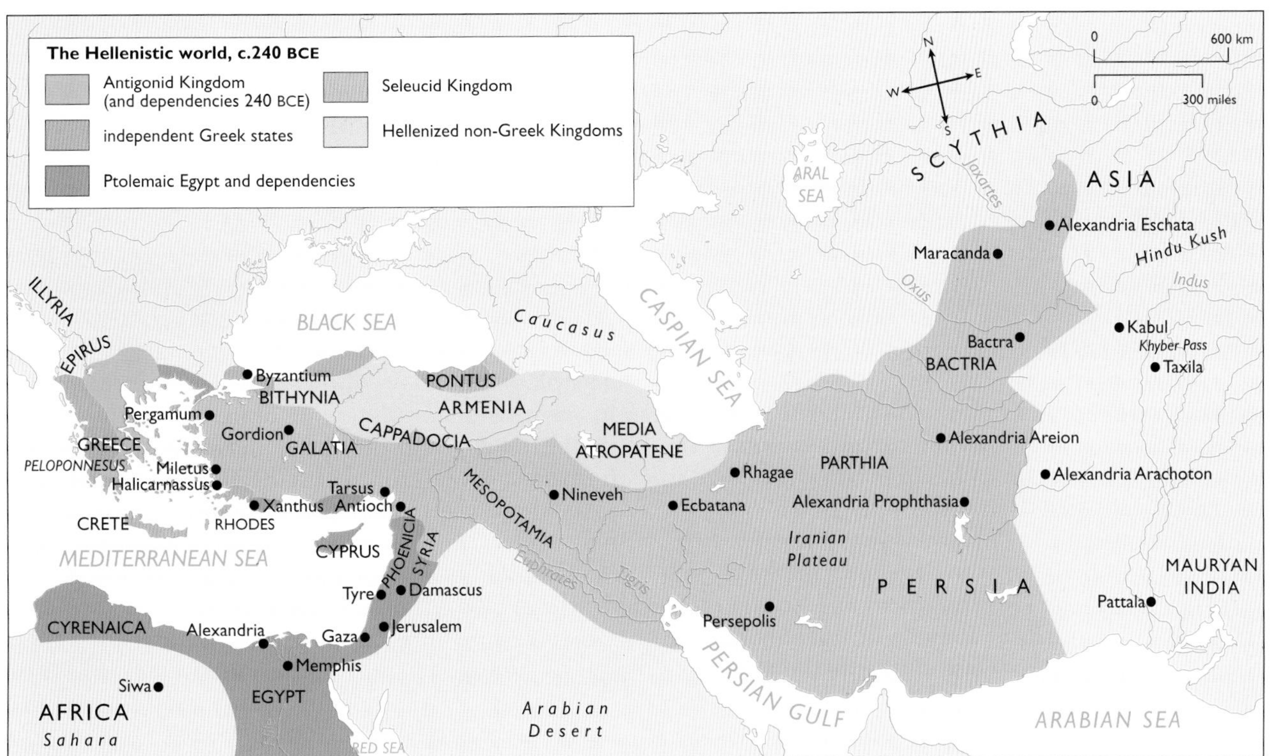

Map 5.1 Persia, Greece, and Alexandrian Successors, 334–240 B.C.E.: *The multinational empire of Persia had twice invaded Greece when, in 334 B.C.E., Alexander of Macedon crossed the Hellespont, vanquished Darius III, and dismembered the Persian state in just three years. Upon Alexander's death in 323 B.C.E., his generals and their descendants competed for his empire. By 276 B.C.E., the Antigonid, Seleucid, and Ptolemaic dynasties ruled, respectively, Macedon and Greece, the Near and Middle East, and Egypt until Roman expansion absorbed them all during the last two centuries B.C.E. By that time, Greek values had already penetrated the whole Mediterranean region and forged Hellenistic civilization.*

The City-Kingdom

Plan of Pergamum: *Near the coast of Asia Minor, King Attalus I created his city-kingdom at Pergamum (third-second century B.C.E.)—one distinguished enough to challenge Athens and Alexandria for preeminence in architecture, sculpture, and learning. The city contained the buildings of a Greek* polis *with three gymnasia and domestic buildings lower down the hill and a royal palace complex on the ridge. This plan of the upper city shows the palace, theater, and Altar of Zeus.*

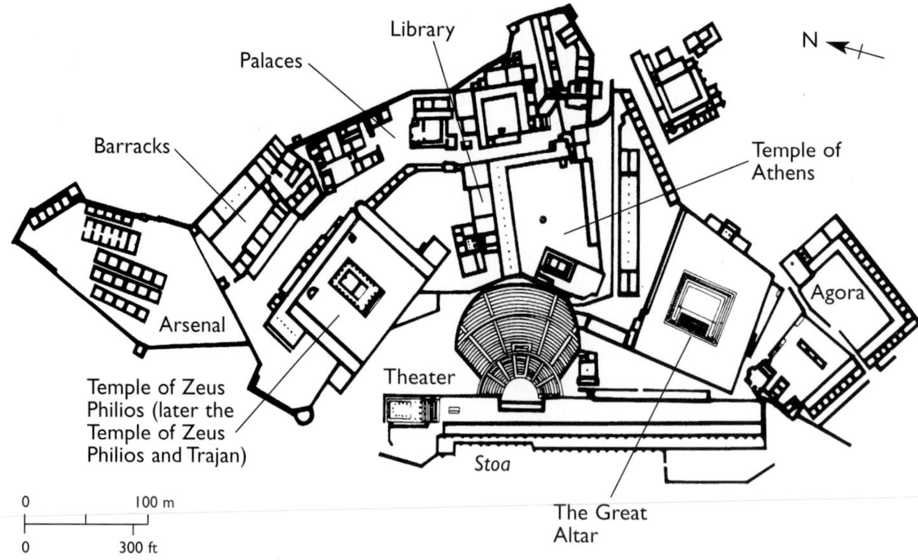

towered the Colossus, a statue 120 feet (33 m.) high of the sun god Helios. The earthquake that destroyed the Colossus in 226 B.C.E. also weakened the city. A much later earthquake, in about 155 C.E., ruined it. No longer a commercial center, it became a provincial Roman capital.

In the eastern reaches of Iran (Persia), the Parthians established an independent kingdom in the third century B.C.E.. Grown prosperous from the caravan traffic across the region, the Parthians pushed westward to the Euphrates River in 129 B.C.E., leaving only Syria and Palestine under Seleucid rule.

The interior of Asia Minor, including its Black Sea rim, was never completely tamed: not by Alexander, not by the Seleucids, and not by Rome. Here reigned the semi-Hellenized kings of Bithynia, Pontus, and Cappadocia, and the more isolated Galatians, descendants of Celtic invaders who had crossed from Europe in 278 B.C.E.

The Western Mediterranean and Beyond

While eastern Mediterranean lands had produced one great civilization after another, the inhabitants of the western Mediterranean gathered in tribes and lived in villages, dwarfed by their eastern neighbors.

By the time of the Alexandrian conquest, however, this area had begun to develop. The flourishing centers at Carthage (North Africa) and Etruria (central Italy) were engaged actively in trade, both with the more sophisticated East and with the promising hinterlands of Europe and North Africa. Through these connections, the western Mediterranean, too, was brought into the circle of advancing civilization.

Founded by Phoenicians from Tyre around 800 B.C.E., Carthage soon surpassed its mother city as a commercial center and controlled the north African shore of the Mediterranean. Spanish minerals and other European exports passed through Carthage, which guarded the Mediterranean at its narrow mid-point, across from Sicily. The light-skinned Berbers of North Africa, the native peasantry exploited by the Carthaginians, were little affected before the latter's arrival by the encroachment of civilization. To the east lay Ptolemaic Egypt, and the burgeoning Kushite kingdom up the Nile valley.

In southern Italy and Sicily, the Greek colonies (called Magna Graecia, or "Greater Greece," by the Romans) struggled for autonomy against Carthage across the sea and Etruria to the north. There, in the region between the Tiber and Arno rivers, the Etruscans by 800 B.C.E. had created a vigorous city-state civilization based on their iron resources, manufacturing skills, and fertile soil. While metalworkers produced tools and ornaments, engineers developed techniques of drainage and construction, anticipating Roman expertise in these areas.

Etruria's cities were federated in a league ruled by a monarch who was also a priest, general, and judge. A committee of magistrates advised him, while prosperous aristocrats dominated a population of **serfs**. The pleasurable lives of those aristocrats are depicted in painting and sculpture. Women participated fully in the revelry and are often shown alongside their husbands, proud and self-sufficient—a posture that scandalized the Greeks. Descent in Etruscan society may even have been traced through the female line.

The life-loving Etruscans were also obsessed with death. They arranged their elaborately sculpted sarcophagi in huge cities of the dead, whence their spirits descended to a grim afterworld inhabited by demons. To ward off the malice of these demons, Etruscan priests called "augurs" were engaged to determine whether conditions were favorable for any venture. They did so by inspecting the livers of sacrificial beasts or by tracking the phenomena of thunder and lightning. They encircled cities and sacred places with ritual boundaries, and occasionally sought to appease angry deities with human sacrifices—the victims obtained through duels of mortal combat.

The origins of Etruscan civilization are uncertain. Had the Etruscans come from Asia Minor, as Herodotus maintained? They were more advanced than their Italian neighbors, and they spoke a different, non-Indo-European language, which has never been fully deciphered. It was written in the Greek alphabet, which the Etruscans borrowed, with other customs, from their Greek trading partners. Among these, the Etruscans adopted many of the Greek anthropomorphic gods—including Zeus, Hera, and Athena. They constructed temples (mostly of wood), adorned on one face, in the Greek style, with columns, pediments, and frieze, but otherwise enclosed, in accord with their own ideal of sacred spaces. Just as the Etruscans learned much from the Greeks, they transmitted many of their traditions to Rome: their gods, the forms of their temples, the elaborate rules of augury, their engineering techniques and architectural innovations (notably the arch), their sacred boundaries and bloody sacrifices, the possibility of female autonomy.

Much of Europe was inhabited by less-advanced farming peoples or nomads: on the Italian peninsula, by the Oscans, Umbrians, Venetians, and Latins; north of the Alps and on the Iberian peninsula, by the Celts; to the east of the Celtic homelands, by the Germans of northern Europe. Still farther east lived the Scythians of the Crimean region, who traded with the Greek settlements on the Black Sea, exchanging their fine metal ornaments and their slaves for manufactured goods.

The Greeks, Persians, Phoenicians, and Etruscans who ringed the Mediterranean all participated in commerce, as did the neighboring peoples on the margins of civilization. Trade boomed in the century following Alexander's death, encouraged by the outpouring of Persian treasure. Greek coins circulated throughout the region, while bankers at Rhodes converted currency and bullion and issued letters of credit. The commodities of ancient commerce—slaves and pots, incense and perfume, spices, ivories, gems, wine and olive oil, copper and tin, papyrus and glass, silver and gold, and above all, wheat—flowed across the Mediterranean. They were carried by ever-larger ships which docked in well-designed harbors funded by adroit entrepreneurs. Caravan routes connected the Nile and the Red Sea, traversed mainly by camel trains. Routes to India, both across Afghanistan and up the Persian Gulf, were heavy with traffic. From at least the second century B.C.E., caravans traveled east and west on the Silk Road.

Not only goods but also people circulated through these prosperous regions. Travel was a popular activity for an adventurous elite, who were equipped with well-written guidebooks. Explorers probed the Caspian Sea and the Indian subcontinent, the shores of the Indian Ocean and Persian Gulf, the islands of the Atlantic, the upper Nile and Sudan regions, and the west coast of Africa. In the fourth century B.C.E., Pytheas of Massalia, a Greek colony (Marseille), circumnavigated distant Britain, encountering icy fog so dense that the elements of nature fused in a nameless mass: "The earth, the sea, and all the elements are held in suspension; and this is a sort of bond to hold all together, which you can neither walk nor sail upon." He had reached, he thought, the end of the inhabited world.

The whole Mediterranean world—European, African, and Asian–was now very nearly one: an **oecumene**. The region tended naturally to unity by its

Pergamum: *This photograph shows a southwesterly view of Pergamum from the top of the theater to the lower town and surrounding terrain. The theater was a prominent building in the upper city and emphasized the theatricality of the whole setting.*

geography, its climate, and its access to the sea. Its political unity was the culmination of the spread of civilization from the nuclei of Mesopotamia and Egypt in the third millennium B.C.E. Between Alexander's death in 323 B.C.E. and Cleopatra's in 30 B.C.E., it became culturally unified as well.

BECOMING GREEK

The Hellenistic civilisation that flourished in the Mediterranean *oecumene* was characterized by the vigorous growth of city life and an enormous outpouring of literary, philosophical, and scientific work. Eventually, when the Hellenistic states succumbed to Rome over the last two centuries B.C.E., the culture of that new participant in the world of nations was indelibly stamped by the ideas and forms of Hellenistic civilization.

Hellenistic Cities

During this period the Greek city entered a new phase of development. Political life proceeded on a local level as it had before—though the loss of autonomy and the constant surveillance by Macedonian overlords left the citizens to debate only such peripheral issues as the funding of theater construction or the hiring of schoolteachers.

Beyond the boundaries of the Greek homeland, new Greek cities sprang up. Alexander founded as many as seventy cities, while the Seleucids founded nearly eighty colonies, settled by Greek subjects. These new communities were named for towns in faraway Macedonia (Pella, Edessa, Amphipolis) or for the conquerors (Alexandria, Seleucia, and Antioch—of which there were several, named for Seleucid kings called Antiochus). Storehouses of Greek culture suspended in alien territory, these cities possessed many familiar institutions: councils and assemblies and magistrates, the trappings of democracy. A royal governor represented the monarchy and limited political activity to the purely local level.

Professional architects planned the new cities, following the principles introduced by the fifth-century Greek town planner Hippodamus. The new planned cities, in

Etruscans at War and at Leisure

Men at war *(above): Fed by contacts with Greek cities and the eastern Mediterranean region, Etruscan art conveyed deep emotion. This handle of an Etruscan bronze chest from Praeneste, fourth century B.C.E., is composed of two soldiers carrying their dead comrade between them—the functional verticals and horizontals serving to emphasize both the contrast and the links between the survivors and the fallen.* (National Museum, Villa Giulia, Rome)

Man and wife: *In this Etruscan sarcophagus (coffin) from Veii, c. 520 B.C.E., a man and his wife recline together on their marriage bed, the woman wrapped in her husband's protective presence. The sculpted bed forms the lid of their sarcophagus, so that their love and their death are combined in one monument.* (National Museum, Villa Giulia, Rome)

HOW MANY?

City Sizes

Sumerian	10–40,000
Indus	c. 40,000
Athens	100–200,000
Carthage	100–200,000
Rome	c. 1 million
Alexandria	c. 1 million
Provincial cities	10–20,000

contrast to the older, haphazardly constructed *poleis*, were organized in a rectangular grid of streets encompassing all the key components of city life: *agora* and temple, gymnasia and theaters, residences, harbors, and docks. These impressive monuments, set in their checkerboard frame, proclaimed throughout the region the dominance of Greek culture.

The major Hellenistic cities were multiethnic, multiracial, and multicultural. Amid such diversity, participation in the *oecumene* displaced identification based on city or nation. Place of origin and native customs mattered less than wealth, which mattered a great deal. An elite of leisured town dwellers, their wealth derived from land or investments, funded the buildings and temples, games and theatrical performances that graced urban life. Beneath them in the social hierarchy thrived merchants and bankers, physicians and intellectuals, and skilled artisans. Members of these trades and professions, as well as groups of foreign nationals or coreligionists (i.e. worshipers of the same gods) formed associations providing companionship and social benefits from pooled funds.

Alongside the rich and well-heeled lived masses of the poor and unfree, whose conditions worsened in the centuries after Alexander. Daily wages declined for the ordinary laborer, and slaves and serfs were subjected to new burdens. Peasant and slave revolts disturbed city and countryside and the sleep of monarchs. While Hellenistic society softened national and racial distinctions to an unprecedented degree, the gap between rich and poor became all the more pronounced.

Women in the Hellenistic World

Upper-class women enjoyed unusual freedom in the Hellenistic city—especially in Egypt, where, although they were not considered equal to men, women enjoyed greater respect than in other parts of the ancient Middle East. Cosmopolitan influences eroded the traditional Greek attitude toward women. Greek society was previously based on the *oikos* (household) and the *polis*, in both of which women played a subordinate role. In the Hellenistic world of autonomous individuals, those constraints no longer operated.

In particular, the consorts of rulers now acquired a high status. Among the Macedonian queens whose personalities influenced events was Olympias, the mother of Alexander, executed for political maneuverings. Other Macedonian queens supported religious innovations, founding cults and building temples. Most of these queens owed their station to marriage. However, the most famous of them, Cleopatra VII (69–30 B.C.E.), became queen of Egypt in her own right, first sharing the throne, successively, with two of her brothers (whom she married in turn, as was the custom). Seductive and clever, she secured her own sovereignty through alliances with Julius Caesar and Mark Antony, Roman general and statesman who fought under Caesar in Gaul (54–50 B.C.E.).

Several women won fame as poets, artists, and philosophers during the Hellenistic age. Late in the fourth century B.C.E., Erinna of Telos composed an exquisite 300-line poem, later entitled *The Distaff*, in memory of a friend who had recently married and died. The first well-authenticated female poet since Sappho, she managed to achieve a rudimentary education. Eurydice of Hierapolis (western Anatolia) somehow gained her education: already a mother "of young and lusty sons," she "by her diligence attained to learn letters, wherein lies buried all our lore," as we read in her epitaph.

Elite women were avid readers of love poetry and romances, and attended theatrical performances of the genre called "New Comedy" (to distinguish it from the "Old Comedy" of Aristophanes), in which the dilemmas of ordinary private life took center stage. The playwright Menander (c. 343–c. 292 B.C.E.) wove play after play around such matters as dowry and inheritance, marital and extramarital sex.

Yet patriarchal families still limited women's options, and those limits began in infancy. Hellenistic families were small, often numbering only one or two sons, and rarely including more than one daughter. That pattern suggests that infanticide, especially of females, was widely practiced. As one contemporary observed, "Everyone, even a poor man, raises a son; everyone, even a rich man, exposes a daughter." Another instructed his wife by letter: "If you chance to bear a child and it is a boy, let it be; if it is a girl, expose it." Of the families who migrated to Miletus in Asia Minor from Athens around 228–200 B.C.E., statistics survive for 79; among them were 118 sons and 28 daughters. Delphic inscriptions referring to some 600 families and dating from the next century reveal that only six reared more than one daughter. The absent women form a bleak, silent chorus on the Hellenistic stage.

WITNESSES

Roman Women

One of the first expressions that history offers of the organized protest of women against government is reported here by Livy, who describes the demonstration of wealthy Roman women against the restrictions upon them under the Oppian Law, and the speech made by the revered statesman, Cato the Elder, urging against any accommodation to women's taste for luxury, and presumptions against the state (195 B.C.E.).

During the Second Punic War, men and women were barred from the ostentatious display of wealth. When the war ended in 201 B.C.E., rich men resumed their habits of luxury, but women continued to be barred by the Oppian Law from that behavior. Six years later, they protested:

The matrons, whom neither counsel nor shame nor their husbands' orders could keep at home, blockaded every street in the city and every entrance to the Forum. As the men came down to the Forum, the matrons besought them to let them, too, have the luxuries they had enjoyed before. ...

The consul Marcus Porcius Cato (the Elder) spoke against their plea for the repeal of the Oppian law, and warned against female claims for sovereignty:

If each man of us, fellow citizens, had established that the right and authority of the husband should be held over the mother of his own family, we should have less difficulty with women in general; now, at home our freedom is conquered by female fury, here in the Forum it is bruised and trampled upon, and because we have not contained the individuals, we fear the lot. ... Our ancestors did not permit women to conduct any—not even private—business without a guardian; they wanted them to be under the authority of parents, brothers, or husbands. Even now let them snatch at the government and meddle in the Forum and our assemblies. ... If they are victorious now, what will they not attempt? As soon as they begin to be your equals, they will have become your superiors.

Other speakers took the other position, and the women persisted in their protest. The Oppian Law was repealed.
(Livy, 34:1–8; eds., trs. M. R. Lefkowitz, M. B. Fant, 1982)

The Mixing of Cultures

Greek colonists and expatriates transplanted their own way of life into foreign lands. In particular, the world of the eastern Mediterranean was transformed by the Greek rituals of athletic exercise and the simplified but still powerful Greek language. At the same time, voyaging Greeks grafted some of the political and religious institutions of the East onto their own cultural traditions.

In gymnasia constructed in the cities of the eastern Mediterranean, men exercised in the nude, as they had in Athens or Corinth, and barbarian newcomers who wished to attach themselves to the Greek elite were pressed to adopt that custom—a sign of Hellenistic culture. The gymnasium developed into a new form: originally merely an open field, it was now a complex of exercise rooms, baths, and stadium.

The native inhabitants also needed to learn Greek—the common tongue, or **koine**, of the Mediterranean world, which had largely displaced the earlier Aramaic language. Its distribution is shown on Map 5.2 below. In Egypt, peasants continued to speak their ancestral language, but Greek was used among

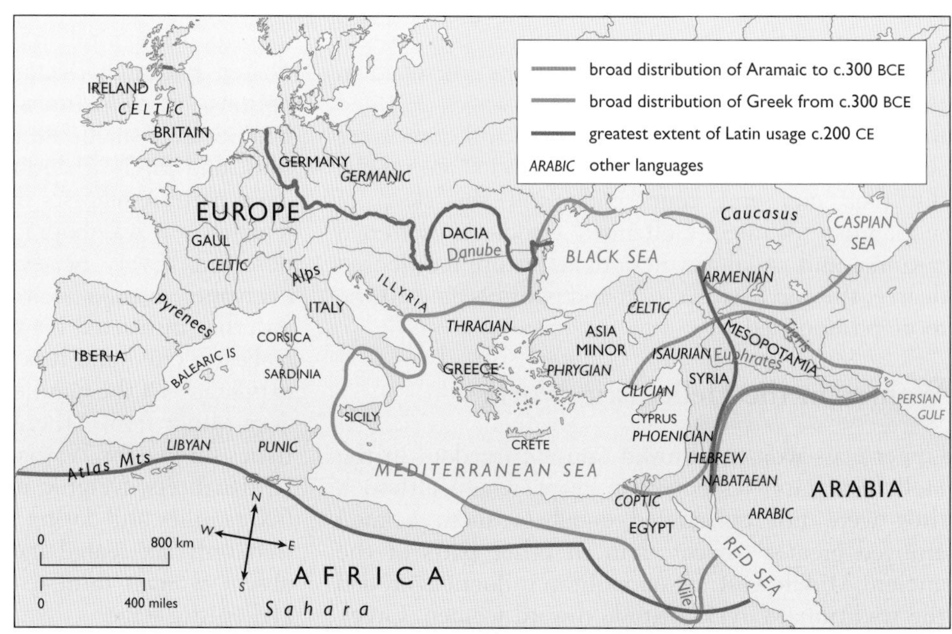

Map 5.2 Transnational Languages of the Mediterranean World, 1000 B.C.E.–300 C.E.: *The hybrid cultures of the ancient Mediterranean world adopted three successive languages as a means of communicating across political boundaries. Aramaic was the dominant language in the early first millennium B.C.E.; Greek dominated from the third century B.C.E.; Latin held sway from the first century B.C.E. until the third century C.E., when it would yield again to Greek in the eastern Mediterranean while flourishing in western Europe until c. 1800 C.E..*

the elites. In the first century B.C.E., the Roman author Cicero remarked that Greek was known everywhere: it was read "in nearly all nations."

Hellenization also entailed the translation into Greek of works of literature of the subject cultures and the writing of their history in that language. The priest Manetho of Egypt (fl. 280 B.C.E.) wrote a Greek history of his nation that remains an authoritative record of its dynasties and rulers. The Babylonian priest Berossus did the same for his nation. Around 250 B.C.E., the ruler of Egypt is said to have commissioned in Alexandria a board of Jewish scholars (seventy, as legend has it) to translate scriptures into Greek. The text is the *Septuagint*, or "the book of seventy." While such writers remained Egyptian or Babylonian or Jewish, they were now also Greeks.

The elite members of conquered peoples gave their children Greek names, wore Greek clothing, and adopted Greek models for ritual and worship. At the same time, Greek leaders borrowed customs from the people they ruled. The result was a hybrid civilization defined by Greek language and culture, but open to the diversity resident in native populations.

Among the customs adopted by the conquerors was the characteristic eastern form of government: absolute monarchy. Although the Macedonians had always lived under a monarchy, they found alien the veneration of kings practiced in the lands they occupied. Nevertheless, Alexander quickly adopted this custom, assuming the Persian title "king of kings" and the Egyptian "pharaoh." From 327 B.C.E. onward, he ordered his visitors to prostrate themselves before him, in the Persian custom; and in 324 B.C.E. he announced to the Greeks of the mainland the news of his deification—where it was received with consternation. "If Alexander wishes to be a god, we grant that he is a god," read a Spartan decree. "Let him be the son of Zeus and of Poseidon too, if he wishes it," snapped Demosthenes. After his death, Alexander was worshiped as a god by Greeks and Asians alike.

Greek expatriates readily acquired the religious beliefs of their hosts—the Olympians having failed as deities because they were too much like mortals, because they offered no chance of salvation, because their authority had been challenged by the speculations of the philosophers and the criticism of the Sophists, because they found no worshipers when uprooted from the *polis*. In contrast, the deities of the Middle East promised life and renewal. The dead and reborn gods of the ancient Caananites still lived in the cults of the Phoenicians, Syrians, and Egyptians.

The process of syncretism, or blending of diverse religious traditions, intensified in the Hellenistic period (see Chapter 7). The Greek Zeus became identified with the Egyptian Amon-Re and the Babylonian Baal, while the Egyptian mother-goddess Isis stood for several female deities of the Middle East and for the Olympians Hera and Demeter. The Macedonian pharaoh Ptolemy I (d. 282 B.C.E.) concocted a new god, "Sarapis," a version of the Egyptian Osiris. The temple of Sarapis in Alexandria, which housed a mechanical model of the god, was in its time a huge attraction.

Neither the old gods of the East nor the Olympians of the Greeks could win the allegiance of the Jews. Released from their Babylonian exile in 538 B.C.E., they had returned to their homeland, their religious faith matured by the experience of exile. There they rebuilt the temple in Jerusalem and forged the textual and ritual foundations of the Jewish religion. Rigorous followers of scriptural law, they shunned alien customs. Above all, they feared losing their young to the seductive customs of the Greeks, epitomized by the gymnasium and its idealization of the nude male human form.

The Seleucid King Antiochus IV Epiphanes ("the god made manifest") (d. 164 B.C.E.) was determined to bring Judaea (as the Greeks called the Jewish homeland) to heel and compel the Jews to accept Greek cultural supremacy. Supported by Jewish Hellenists, he occupied Jerusalem in 167 B.C.E. Antiochus intended to establish a gymnasium and school in Jerusalem and to rename the city after himself, Antioch. He ordered the Jews to eat pork (prohibited by their law) and forbade them to possess the Torah, their sacred scriptures, or circumcise their sons (a time-honored custom signifying their membership in the Jewish community). He set up a statue of Zeus in the temple, and burned there in sacrifice an offering (to the Jews detestable) of pigs: the "abomination of desolation."

In response, Mattathias and his sons, of the priestly family of the Hasmoneans, took to the mountains with a handful of supporters to oppose the Seleucid regime with "guerrilla" tactics. In December 164 B.C.E., Mattathias' eldest son Judah, called Maccabee ("the Hammer"), celebrated the first Hanukkah: a Jewish festival created (without scriptural authority, some later complained) to mark the recovery and purification of the temple. Judah was slain, and his brothers felled in turn until the survivor, Simon, reached an agreement in 142 B.C.E. with Antiochus' successor, Demetrius II, after Simon became High Priest. Judaea was granted a fragile autonomy in the Seleucid empire.

Books, Science, and Philosophy

While some Jews struggled against Hellenization and others made their peace with it, educated Greek elites strove to extend and preserve their cultural heritage. The Hellenistic era saw an explosion of creative work in literary and technical fields and the creation of institutions in which the products of the human imagination could be studied, reflected upon, and transmitted to later generations.

Such an institution was the library at Alexandria, which held a matchless collection, properly catalogued, of more than 500,000 papyrus rolls (the bound book wasn't yet invented), and housed a community of scholars who studied the literary works of Greece. The poet Timon of Phlius (c. 320–c. 230 B.C.E.), mockingly described their enterprise: while consuming the wealth of Egypt, he wrote, they "scribbled" on papyrus "in the bird-coop of the Muses."

Pergamum's library (about 200,000 rolls) ranked second to Alexandria's. Egyptian rulers were so envious of its collection that they banned the export of papyrus to Pergamum. That city's scribes learned to prepare sheepskin to make writing material. Known as "Pergamene paper," or parchment, this would remain in use in Europe throughout the Middle Ages.

Hellenistic artists created huge monuments in honor of their monarchs. They also provided the aristocrats and middle classes with more modest sculptures and paintings to adorn their gardens and houses. Whereas Classical artists had aimed to depict ideal beauty, their Hellenistic successors depicted exactly what they saw: the ordinary and the weird, the beautiful and the deformed; human bodies asleep, at play, drunk, or dying. An example is shown below. Even wealthy patrons learned to accept realistic portraits which revealed defects.

The scholars of the Hellenistic world preserved the intellectual heritage of antiquity for later generations. They studied, commented upon, and edited the Classical Greek texts and created supplementary texts such as chronologies, dictionaries, bibliographies, and textbooks. They divided each of Homer's epics into the twenty-four books that still constitute modern editions. They compiled the works of poets and playwrights and drew up lists of the "best" works. Their copying and recopying of these chosen texts ensured their later survival. With few exceptions, those that did not win the attention of Hellenistic scholars are lost to readers today.

The heart of a Hellenistic education lay in the reading of the corpus of literary works prepared by these scholars—a different enterprise from Greek education in the Classical era. It was more strictly literary, though it took place in the traditional setting (the gymnasium), which now functioned more like a modern school. In alien lands, the institution of the school preserved Greek culture and transmitted it to subsequent generations of children, who were enduringly stamped with the Greek world-view.

In these schools, children (including some girls) aged seven to fourteen learned letters, syllables, and words, by repetition. Older boys aged fourteen to eighteen mastered the core curriculum of Classical works. Graduates who wished for a higher education (there being as yet no university) traveled to Athens, Rhodes, or Cnidus (in Asia Minor) or Cos (in the Aegean Sea) to study philosophy, rhetoric, or medicine with the scholars and physicians in those centers.

While Hellenistic teachers perpetuated knowledge, Hellenistic scientists, mathematicians, and physicians were engaged in expanding it (see *Who's Who*, p. 122). Aristotle had established the method of systematic observation that first made science possible. Now increased contacts with the "barbarian" sciences of Babylon and Egypt stimulated Greek thinkers, many of whom enjoyed the patronage of monarchs. In this environment, science prospered in the two centuries after Alexander.

Hellenistic Science The greatest scientific achievement was in astronomy. Eudoxus of Cnidus (c. 390–c. 340 B.C.E.) showed that the planets moved in circular patterns on distinctive paths. Heraclides of Pontus (c. 390–310 B.C.E.) learned that the earth rotated on its own axis, and that Mercury and Venus both revolved around the sun. Aristarchus of Samos (c. 310–230 B.C.E.) proposed that the planets revolved around a fixed sun,

***Lysippos,* Apoxyomenos, *c. 320* B.C.E.**

The Hellenistic Vision

A range of feeling: *Like Etruscan art, Hellenistic art expressed strong emotions—but the former represented the daily range of sentiments in a restrained key, while the latter tended to the loud representation of extreme feeling, often of unusual persons or dramatic moments. The Roman copy of a bronze Greek original of an athlete scraping his arm (left), the* Apoxyomenos *by Lysippos, c. 320* B.C.E.*, can be contrasted with earlier representations in Greek art (see pp. 88, 92). The later artists highlighted individual personalities in a manner the earlier ones avoided and indeed would not have understood.* (left: Vatican Museums, Rome) beyond which stood fixed stars. His views lost out to the more geocentric, or earth-centered, hypothesis. Centuries later, Nicholas Copernicus (1473–1543) would revive Aristarchus' theory and open the doors of modern science (see Chapter 17).

The distant fixed stars posited by Aristarchus interested Hipparchus of Nicaea in Anatolia (fl. 161–126 B.C.E.), who produced a catalogue of 850 of them and "left the heavens as a legacy to all mankind." Hipparchus calculated within a second of the modern figure the length of the lunar month and contributed to the bizarre readings of planetary motion by which Hellenistic scientists tried to "save the phenomena"—that is, to explain erratic planetary motion so as to preserve the principle of the earth's centrality. Hipparchus' work would be continued by Ptolemy (c. 90–168 C.E.), whose codification of that geocentric system (in the *Almagest*, around 150 C.E.) was orthodox astronomy until Copernicus.

The mathematician Euclid (c. 325–250 B.C.E.) outlined the fundamentals of plane geometry in his *Elements*, which would remain the standard text for the next 2000 years. Eratosthenes of Cyrene in modern Libya (c. 285–194 B.C.E.) applied mathematics to the study of geography. He calculated the circumference of the earth (which he knew to be round) at a nearly accurate 25,000 miles (40,250 km.). His plan of the world is illustrated in *Windows On*, p. 123.

The mathematician and engineer Archimedes of Syracuse (c. 287–211 B.C.E.) calculated the value of *pi* (the ratio of the circumference of a circle to its diameter) and invented integral calculus. In a more practical vein, he invented the water screw—a device consisting of a screw inside a cylinder—which made possible the irrigation of dry land and the pumping of ship holds or mines, and also the compound pulley, which powered various other devices. Archimedes was famous for his role in the defense of Syracuse against the Romans in 213–211 B.C.E. It was his gamut of machines that kept the Romans at bay, including a system of mirrors that intensified the sun's rays and caused them to set the invaders' ships afire. When the city was taken, the command was given to take Archimedes alive. But he had already been murdered by a common soldier, annoyed by the scientist's imperturbability in the presence of Roman power. In accordance with his own wishes, Archimedes' grave was marked by a cylinder enclosing a sphere, accompanied by an inscription defining the ratio between their two surfaces and volumes—a discovery he considered his greatest achievement.

Other Hellenistic scientists studied the ills of the human body. In the second half of the fifth century B.C.E., Hippocrates of Cos (c. 460–c. 358 B.C.E.) had pioneered the science of medicine based on meticulous observation and careful record-keeping. From about 430 to 330 B.C.E., his followers produced what moderns call the Hippocratic Corpus: a collection of about sixty treatises on surgery and gynecology, dietetics and epilepsy, diagnostics, and more.

Hellenistic physicians extended the work of the Hippocratic school. Herophilus of Chalcedon in northwestern Anatolia (c. 330–260 B.C.E.) dissected corpses to explore the sensory nervous system, understood the function of the brain, learned that the arteries carried blood, and identified the ovaries of females. Erasistratus (c. 315–240 B.C.E.) from Ceos in the Aegean described the function of the heart, distinguished between sensory and motor nerves, and challenged the Hippocratic theory that health was governed by the interaction of four qualities, or "humors"—a theory that still prevailed for many centuries. Despite the empirical work of physicians, ordinary people placed their trust in magic, not science, and illness was treated with potions, charms, and prayers to the healing god Asclepius.

Hellenistic Philosophy Philosophy was still centered in Athens: the birthplace of democracy, now in its twilight years the home of philosophers. The followers of Aristotle (called "Peripatetics," meaning "walking about," based on Aristotle's habit of teaching while strolling around the Lyceum school) and Plato (called "Academics, after Plato's founding of the Academy), continued their studies until Emperor Justinian closed both schools in the sixth century C.E. Aristotle's student Theophrastus of Eresus in Anatolia

A Gaul slays himself over his dying wife: *Desperate action and emotion reach a climax in this marble copy of a Hellenistic group, late third century B.C.E., portraying a Gaul committing suicide rather than surrender. The Gaul has already killed his wife to prevent her becoming a slave.* (Museo delle Terme, Rome)

WHO'S WHO

Hellenistic and Roman Authors, Scientists, Philosophers

ASTRONOMERS

Eudoxus (c. 390–c. 340 B.C.E.) claimed planets move in circular patterns on distinctive paths.

Heraclides (c. 390–310 B.C.E.) showed that earth rotates on own axis.

Aristarchus (c. 310–230 B.C.E.) proposed that planets revolve around fixed sun.

Hipparchus (fl. 161–126 B.C.E.) compiled catalog of stars.

MATHEMATICIANS

Euclid (c. 325–250 B.C.E.) outlined fundamentals of plane geometry.

Eratosthenes of Cyrene (285–194 B.C.E.) applied mathematics to study of geography.

Archimedes of Syracuse (287–211 B.C.E.) calculated value of *pi* and invented calculus.

SCIENTISTS

Hippocrates of Cos (c. 460–c. 358 B.C.E.) pioneered science of medicine based on observation.

Herophilus (c. 330–260 B.C.E.) studied nervous system.

Erasistratus (c. 315–240 B.C.E.) described function of heart.

PHILOSOPHERS

Diogenes (412–323 B.C.E.) founded Cynic school.

Epicurus (341–270 B.C.E.) founded Epicurean school.

Zeno (335–263 B.C.E.) founded Stoic school.

WRITERS

Plautus (254–184 B.C.E.) comedy playwright.

Terence (c. 195–159 B.C.E.) comedy playwright.

Cicero (106–43 B.C.E.) orator and author.

(371–288 B.C.E.) pioneered the scientific approach that characterized the later Peripatetics. The thinking of the Academy evolved from Plato's idealism, to a skepticism that refused to accept virtually any statement as unarguably true, to a mysticism ("Neoplatonism") based on the primacy of the Light, the Good, the One—easily identified with the Christian God or with the principal deity of some pagan religions. Skepticism also developed independently, its views summed up in the writings of Sextus Empiricus in the second century C.E.

The philosophers Diogenes, Epicurus, and Zeno founded respectively the new Cynic, Epicurean, and Stoic schools. Diogenes of Sinope in northern Anatolia (c. 412–323 B.C.E.) proposed to live without possessions or responsibilities, in order to avoid the hypocrisy of the merchant or politician; in short, he lived "like a dog" (for that is what "cynic" means), and advised others to do so too.

Epicurus (341–270 B.C.E.) proposed that people should pursue what they were inclined to pursue anyway—pleasure. But that true pleasure consisted in tranquility, intellectual pursuits, the company of friends. All these were to be found in withdrawing from the maelstrom of society. Safe from the torments of competition and desire, the Epicurean sage was also safe from the more distant sources of unease: the fear of the gods, the fear of death. "Death, the most terrifying of evils," he wrote, "is nothing to us; for as long as we exist death is not present with us, and when death comes then we no longer exist."

Just as death lost its fearsomeness for the Epicurean, the cosmos itself threatened no ills. It was nothing but a flash of hurtling atoms let loose in a void (here Epicurus was influenced by Democritus), without malice because without meaning. The gods, if they existed at all, did nothing. Realizing these truths, the individual could achieve a tranquil state marked by the absence of distress and desire. Epicurus defined this ideal in 300 volumes of tortured prose, lost except for fragments, and preached it to his disciples in his pleasant Athenian garden.

The most successful of the schools of Hellenistic philosophy, Stoicism, presented a moral ideal, offered a cosmic theory, and championed the dignity of the human spirit and unity of the human race. Its founder, Zeno (335–263 B.C.E.), and his followers urged the individual to seek his own destiny and happiness, as Epicurus did—but to do so by pursuing "virtue," the habitual practice of acts worthy of a true gentleman, or statesman. The steady cultivation of virtue would allow the good man to rise above all emotions through the greater development of the inner self.

According to Zeno, that inner self contained a divine spark, a fragment of the fire that governed the cosmos, a force identified with reason. The wise man who lived according to virtue also lived in harmony with the cosmos, ordered and purposeful in its design. Since each individual possessed that spark initially to the same extent, no person was by nature greater than any other; conversely, no person could be considered, by nature, a slave. All human beings were equal, and

The Worlds of Eratosthenes and Archimedes

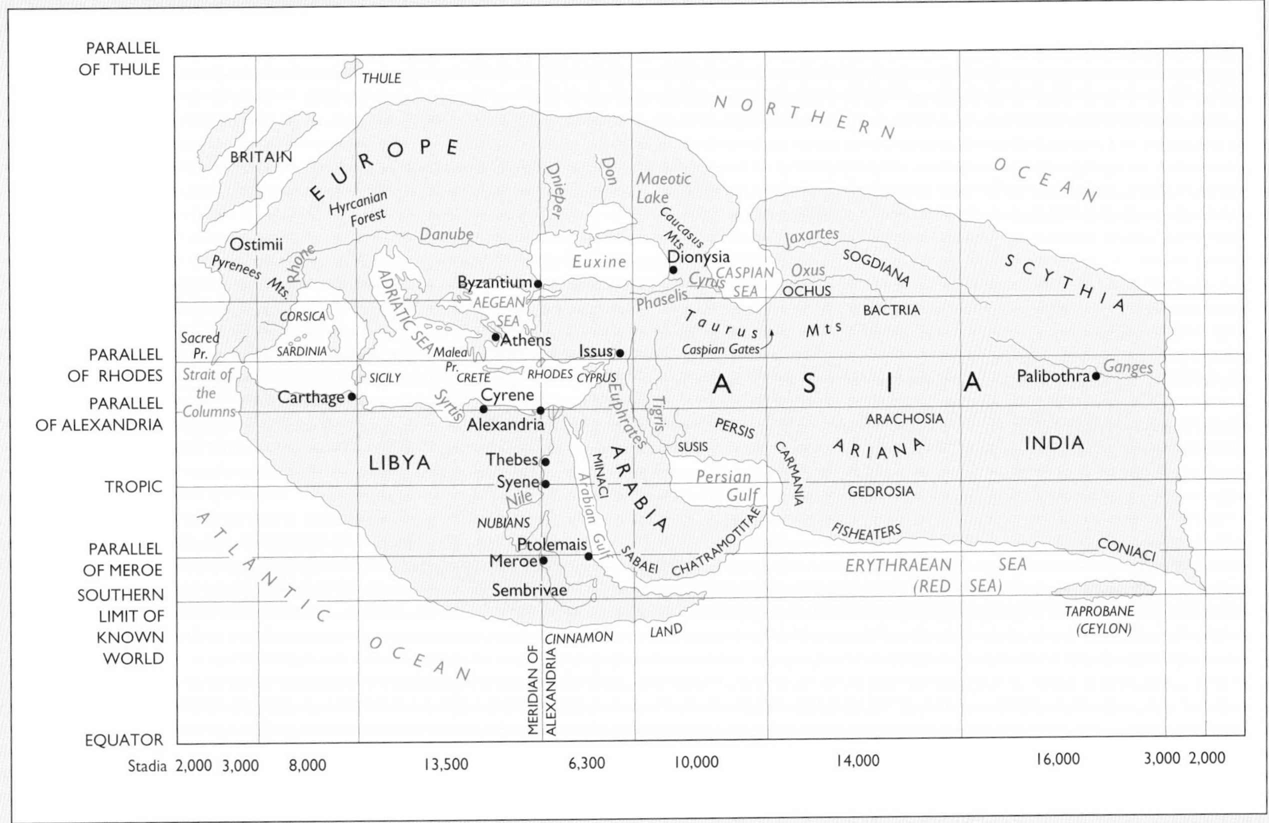

Eratosthenes, plan of the world, c. 215 B.C.E.

At the height of Hellenistic civilization in the third century B.C.E., when infant Rome was embarking on its first foreign ventures, scientists made remarkable progress toward understanding their world in mathematical and mechanical terms—progress that would soon slow down and not resume again in the Western world for eighteen centuries. Among those scientists were Eratosthenes of Alexandria, whose plan of the world (above) testifies to his capacity to extend his thoughts beyond the obvious and tangible, and Archimedes, bold mathematician and inventor of many machines, whose discovery of the principle of specific gravity is alluded to here in this later German woodcut. Legendarily, it was when Archimedes was in his bathtub, and noted how his body displaced the water, that the solution for the problem came to him.

Archimedes in his bath, sixteenth-century German woodcut

To continue your investigation of this topic, please go to www.prenhall.com/king for the related **WINDOWS** on the **WEB** activity

society should recognize their universal partnership, or "brotherhood." Zeno delivered these admonitions from the *stoa*, or arcaded, free-standing porch in the *agora* at Athens—whence the term "Stoic."

While Hellenistic culture flourished, the political framework that initially supported it proved less durable. Alexander's empire began to dissolve as soon as he died. By 100 B.C.E., it had collapsed. Nevertheless, the cultural achievements of the Hellenized world survived. Above all, its synthesis of intellectual and artistic vision—a synthesis derived from earlier civilizations but systematized by Greek methods and communicated in the capacious prose of that highly developed language—remained to stimulate later civilizations. Perhaps this was the true achievement of Alexander the Great.

ROME: FROM VILLAGE TO NATION

While Greeks, Macedonians, and Phoenicians dominated the Mediterranean in the last five centuries B.C.E., a small village near Italy's west coast grew, rebelled against Etruscan masters, devoured Italy, and conquered the Mediterranean world. As Rome expanded, the Romans developed a complex society and government, capable of absorbing new citizens and governing very large populations.

Early Days

According to a legend, very old and surely false, the city of Rome was originally founded by the Trojan refugee Aeneas, son of the goddess Venus by the noble Anchises. Two of his descendants, twin baby boys named Romulus and Remus, were abandoned in the wilderness by a jealous uncle who usurped their inheritance. There, they were nurtured by a she-wolf and survived to establish the city on one of the seven hills clustered near the easiest ford of the river Tiber. Romulus killed his brother Remus, gave his name to the settlement, and became its first king.

So much for legend. At about the time Romulus is supposed to have killed Remus, in 753 B.C.E., a village community formed around the Palatine Hill, one of seven on which the city would be built. Near the base of this hill was an open space called the Forum, where cattle grazed and men assembled to decide the relative merits of war or peace. Other communities developed on the remaining hills (see Map 5.3). By about 600 B.C.E., the seven hills had coalesced into a single town. Its inhabitants now thought of themselves as Romans, distinct from neighboring Latin tribes from whom they originated and whose language they spoke. Their small city was situated in Italy's central triangular plain, called Latium, which is formed by the Apennine Mountains as they wander from the Tyrrhenian Sea on the west coast to the Adriatic on the east, south to the toe of the Italian boot and across the straits to Sicily. Unlike the Greek *poleis*, which developed in isolation created by the physical barriers of mountains and sea, Rome lay exposed to its neighbors. Consequently, the Romans learned to cooperate with peoples from other nearby cities—while learning also how to defend themselves.

Kings ruled Rome in its earliest days: seven, according to tradition, between 753 and 509 B.C.E. The legendary Romulus was followed by three other kings of Latin or Sabine origin (the Sabines being a neighboring Italian people), and then by three Etruscan kings. From the Etruscans, the Romans learned to build temples and worship anthropomorphic gods (gods with human qualities and form); how to map the skies and inspect the prophetic livers of sacrificed beasts; and how to drain swamps and organize magistracies. They erected on the Capitoline Hill a temple to Jupiter, Juno, and Minerva (the Greek Zeus, Hera, and Athena) and walled their city.

Around 500 B.C.E., Rome detached itself from both Etruria and the monarchy. The Etruscans were expelled, or simply left. Rome now became a republic: a state governed by a body of its citizens. Those governors were the wealthy landowners, called **patricians**, a small elite of men who ruled the other Romans, the **plebeians**, or commoners.

Family and Society in Early Rome

Roman society was rooted in the ancient social organizations of tribe, clan, and family, which subordinated women, children, and slaves to one dominant male householder.

A Roman was a member of a tribe and a clan as well as of a family. Clan identification remained strong in Rome into the late Republic, at least among the landowning classes. The name of a Roman male citizen had three components: the name of the individual (Gaius, Quintus, Publius, etc.); the name of the clan (Julius, Cornelius, Fabius); and the name of the family within the clan. Gaius Julius Caesar, the general and dictator, had the personal name Gaius, the clan name Julius, and family name Caesar.

Identification with the clan was fostered by the worship of ancestors, the basis of Roman religion (see Chapter 7). The father of each family was the priest of the family cult, which venerated the ancestral spirits (a patrician holding the heads of his ancestors is shown on p. 127). Wax masks or (later) sculpted busts of these forebears were displayed in the household, adjacent to the central hall or *atrium*. These were silent participants in household rites and were carried in religious processions to honor the dead and cement their bonds with the living. When a Roman noble died, male family members went in a procession to the funeral wearing these ancestral masks, and in

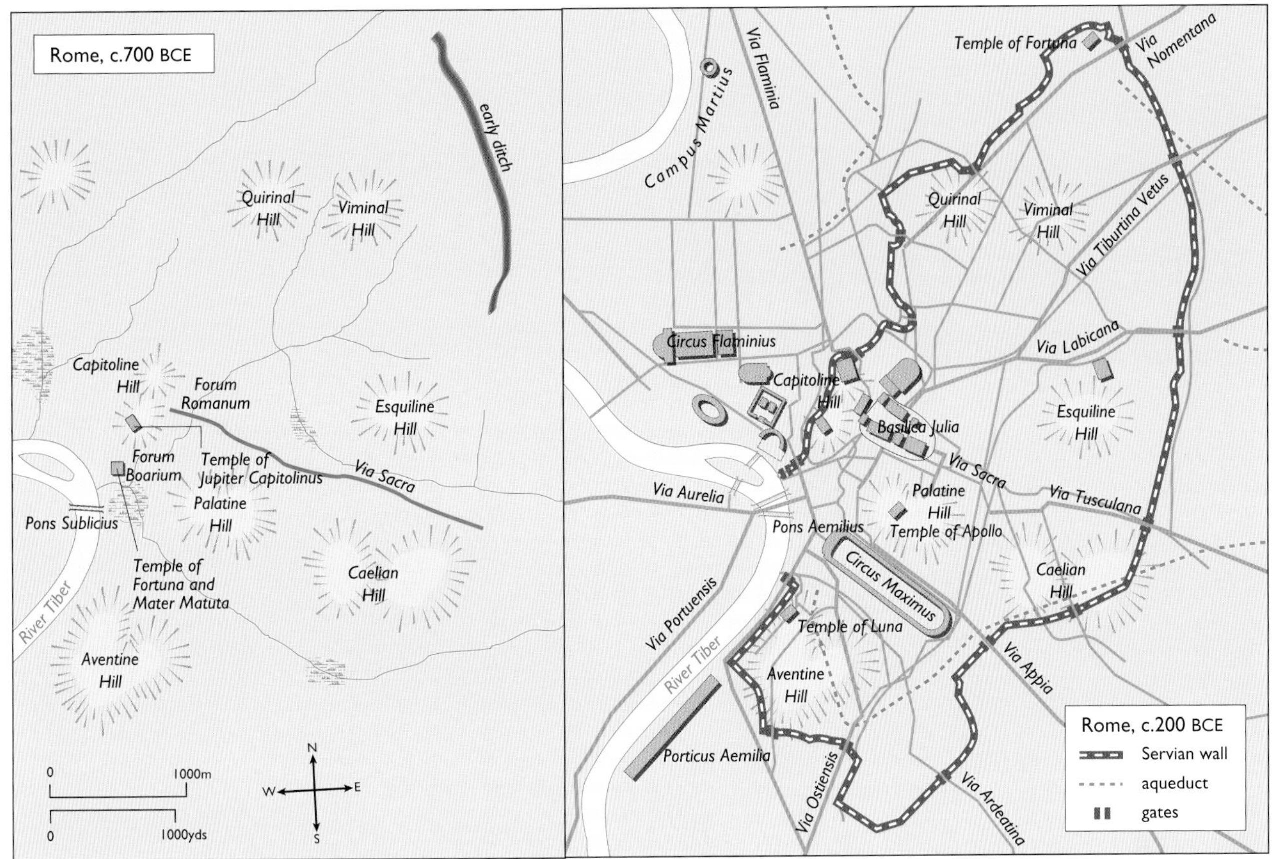

***Map 5.3* Rome before the Empire (c. 700–200 B.C.E.):** *Rome enjoyed a favorable location: a cluster of seven hills, excellent for defense, on the banks of the Tiber River, a conduit of trade and information. Originally a village clustered around the* Forum Boarium *(a field for the grazing of cattle), by the third century B.C.E. it had grown into a considerable town, equipped with walls, gates, streets, and public buildings.*

ghostly array listened to a kinsman or friend deliver an oration commemorating the achievements of the deceased and his forebears.

The father of each family, the *paterfamilias*, held absolute power over other family members who lived under his protection, literally under his *manus* or hand. He determined whether an infant was to live or not, ceremonially raising an accepted child from the ground where it was placed for his judgment. He governed his wife and children, relatives and slaves, with absolute authority, holding over each household member the power of life and death. A wife caught in adultery, a disobedient child, he could sell into slavery, or even kill.

Fathers fostered close ties with their children, who imitated and obeyed these fearsome elders. Education, conducted primarily by fathers and mothers, consisted in the inculcation of one virtue, that of ***pietas***. Quite different from our "piety," this was a selfless regard for the father and ancestors and a determination to protect and continue the lineage. "I ... sought to equal the deeds of my father," reads an epitaph expressing the values of *pietas*; "I maintained the glory of my ancestors, my honors have ennobled my stock."

A Roman girl bore only one name: the feminine form of her father's clan name. Thus Julia was the daughter of Julius, Pompeia of Pompeius. All daughters bore the same name, but might be distinguished with the addition of "second" (*secunda*) or "third" (*tertia*). Sons received individual names, but bore the same clan and family names as their fathers: thus Lucius, son of the general Publius Cornelius Scipio (236–183 B.C.E.), was called Lucius Cornelius Scipio. Names reflected the close ties the Romans made between fathers and daughters, and fathers and sons.

The mission of the family was to preserve itself in the male line and to transmit property down through the generations. Originally, property descended to sons only, and only to those born of legitimate marriages. Aside from gifts, daughters received only a dowry, which was always managed by a male: husband, father, brother, or guardian. Childless men might adopt sons of their peers so as to have a legitimate male heir, or bequeath the inheritance to **agnates** (male relatives in the paternal line). Sons or agnates inherited not only property, but also the responsibility to perpetuate the "sacred things" of each family—a religious obligation. If there were no surviving sons or agnates, the responsibility fell to the freed slaves of the family, who adopted the family name and identity.

The mothers of early Rome transmitted community values to their children. Unlike Greek women, Roman women were never sequestered in separate rooms from male family members. Yet, though respected for their maternal role, they received little

WITNESSES

The Irresistible Roman Advance

During the last two centuries B.C.E.*, Rome became a power recognized not only in Italy but throughout the Mediterranean world. The first of these passages (from the Biblical book of Maccabees) indicates how the Jews at this time perceived the Romans, remarkable both for their many conquests and for their republican form of government. The second, by the Roman historian Sallust, imagines how the increasingly arrogant behavior of the Romans must have appeared to a ruler of an eastern kingdom.*

The fame of Roman power and governance reaches Judas Maccabeus, leader of Jewish resistance to Greek overlords, in Judaea (c. 160 B.C.E.): Now Judas heard of the fame of the Romans, that they were very strong and were well-disposed toward all who made an alliance with them. ... He had been told of their wars and of the brave deeds that they were doing among the Gauls. ... what they had done in the land of Spain. ... They also had defeated Antiochus the Great, king of Asia, who went to fight against them with one hundred twenty elephants and with cavalry and chariots and a very large army. He was crushed by them. ... Yet for all this not one of them has put on a crown or worn purple as a mark of pride, but they have built for themselves a senate chamber, and every day three hundred and twenty senators constantly deliberate concerning the people, to govern them well.
(1 Maccabees, 8:1–13)

In the words of the historian Sallust, King Mithridates of Pontus describes the corruption and cruelty of Roman rulers to a potential ally, King Tigranes of Armenia (c. 30 B.C.E.): The Romans have one inveterate motive for making war upon all nations, peoples, and kings, namely, a deep-seated desire for domination and riches. Therefore they first began a war with Philip, king of Macedon, after pretending to be his friends. ... When Antiochus came to his aid, they craftily diverted him by conceding Asia to him, and then, after Philip's power had been broken, Antiochus was stripped of all the territory this side of Taurus and of 10,000 talents. Next Perseus, Philip's son, ... they took under their protection ..., and then those masters of craft and artists in treachery caused his death from want of sleep, since they had compacted not to kill him. Eumenes ... they ... [transformed] from a king into the most wretched of slaves [and] led his son Aristonicus in triumph like an enemy because he had sought to occupy his father's throne and took possession of Asia. Finally, on the death of Nicomedes, they snatched away Bithynia, although [his widow Queen] Nysa ... unquestionably had a son. ...
(Sallust, *Histories*, 4, fragment 69; trs. M. Reinhold, N. Lewis)

public recognition and only limited freedom. Given by their fathers to their husbands at an early age (as young as twelve), women of the early Republic lived under the rule—the *manus*—of their new masters. Their property passed entirely into his ownership.

Eventually the Romans evolved alternative forms of marriage, which allowed the wife greater freedom to move in society and to own property. Free marriage became more common among the upper classes in the later Republic. In this arrangement a woman still received a dowry, which was administered by a male; but the male was her father or his agent, rather than her husband. In effect, the woman often gained control of the administration of that dowry as though it were her own property. Ownership of property gave elite women greater status within their families.

Affluent households also included slaves. These victims of war, abandonment, and sale worked largely as farmhands and household servants. Their numbers swelled enormously during the period of Rome's military expansion. Many were high-status slaves from Greece or farther east, equipped with desirable artisan or intellectual skills. Their wares and services could be sold at a profit. Their masters might even establish them in shops and allow them considerable independence. Less gifted slaves worked as agricultural laborers on the expanding farms (the ***latifundia***, or "broad fields") of wealthy Roman and other Italian landowners. Domestic and skilled slaves were often granted their freedom in recognition of their services, or were allowed to purchase it. The freeing of a slave, or **manumission**, was practiced throughout antiquity but especially in Rome, where freedmen enjoyed unique privileges. Adopting the clan name of their masters, they practised the ancestor cult of their former proprietors. They acquired limited political rights, and their descendants inherited full citizen status. A freedman's son could vote even when a non-Roman Italian landholder could not.

A wealthy Roman householder also exercised authority over his "clients"—people farther down the social scale who depended on him in various ways. The reciprocal ties between patron and client were hereditary and enduring. The patron defended his clients in legal matters, interceded for them with the public authorities, and advised them in private and public affairs. The client visited his patron regularly and contributed toward the cost of a wedding, or an election bid, or a ransom. Poor clients climbed to the mansions planted on the hills of Rome to greet their patrons, collect a cash handout, and accompany them to meetings in the Forum. A patron's importance was indicated by the magnitude of this client escort.

The Organization of Power

Early Romans devised a system of councils and assemblies able to provide effective government and to adapt to changing circumstances. As in Britain today, their constitution was unwritten: a body of accumulated laws and customs. The organization of the army, mirroring that of government and society, involved the participation of all adult male citizens.

Under the Republic, Rome came to be ruled by elite landowners. Its Senate (literally "a gathering of old men"), which had advised the ancient kings, was made up at first exclusively of patricians. When the last kings left, the Senate remained to formulate policy for the young state. It continued to meet for more than one thousand years until its obliteration in the sixth century C.E.

Executive power resided in the magistracy of the consulate. Two **consuls** were elected each year to preside over the Senate and to head the army. For that purpose they were granted ***imperium***: the right to rule absolutely outside Rome itself, over Roman soldiers and subject peoples.

In the early Republic, the *censor* (one of two elected every four, later five, years, each serving only eighteen months) administered the *census*—a regular count of the population, providing data necessary in constituting the army, the assemblies, and the Senate. In addition, the censor established eligibility for the Senate, and could eject any person from that body for improper behavior. The one-year office of *praetor*—of which there were eight by the end of the Republic—consisted of administering justice, and serving as a general and/or provincial governor. Like the consulate, this office conferred *imperium*.

In time, two other offices were added: those of *quaestor* and *aedile*. The quaestor was a financial officer, while the aedile administered temple properties and managed the provision of public entertainments and entitlements. In an emergency, the consuls, advised by the Senate, could choose a *dictator*, who possessed extraordinary powers for a period limited to just six months.

Priests, also considered part of the government, held their title for life; they were charged to ensure scrupulous adherence to Roman traditions. The *pontifex maximus* (the chief priest, literally the "greatest bridge-maker" between human beings and the gods) had to be of patrician descent and to observe certain ritual laws. Such requirements of class and ritual purity were also applied to other priestly ranks, such as the augurs, and the vestal virgins.

All these officials were elected by the "Centuriate Assembly." That body included all the citizens of Rome down to the very poorest. But it was dominated absolutely by the wealthiest because of its voting procedure. The citizen population gathered and each man took his place in one of 193 "centuries" (from *centum*, a hundred—because each originally included 100 men), which were grouped in turn into six classes. The first century of the first class contained the wealthiest men in Rome; the last century, comprising the sixth and lowest class, contained the poorest. Voting proceeded century by century, from the top down. If the first ninety-eight centuries voted unanimously in the affirmative or negative, a majority was reached and the voting stopped—even though the poorer citizens had not yet voiced their will.

The centuriate organization of the assembly derived from the centuriate organization of the army. When the army

The living dead—patrician with heads of ancestors: *The Roman virtue of* pietas, *connoting not "piety" but rather reverence for ancestors, and the practice of honoring them through the* mos maiorum, *the "customs of our ancestors," attest to the deep bond held by Roman citizens with those from whom they were descended. Wealthier Romans kept wax masks of these forebears in their homes, and paraded with them through the streets on the occasion of a funeral. Later, they commissioned artists to sculpt lifelike busts of their ancestors, greatly increasing the production of realistic portraiture that was a characteristic genre of Roman art. Here a prominent Roman holds the busts of two of his forefathers, c. 15 C.E.—the living and the dead all equally captured in stone.* (Palazzo dei Conservatori, Rome)

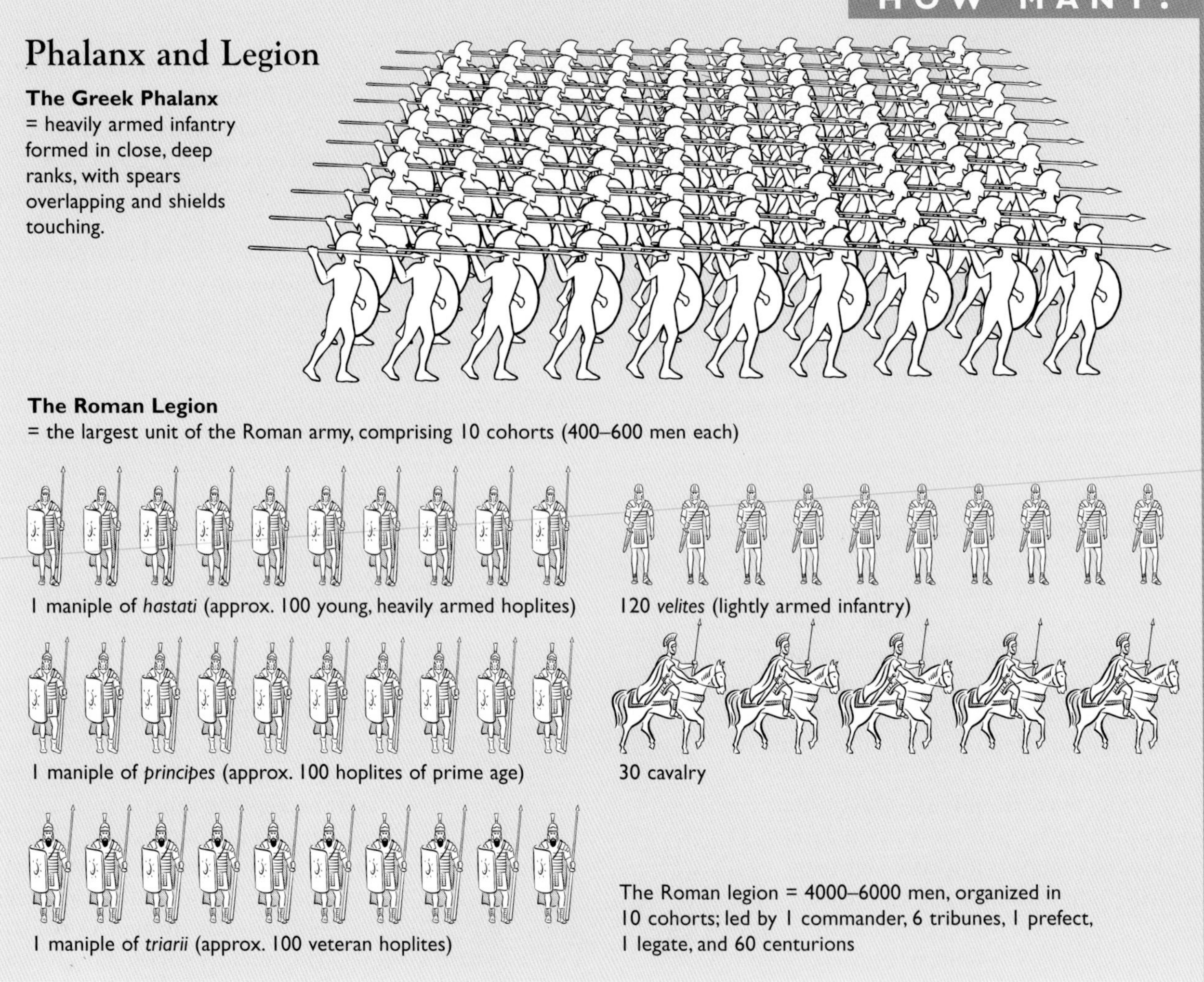

assembled for battle or review on the Field of Mars (the war god), immediately outside the city, it was ordered into centuries. As in the hoplite armies of Greece and Etruria, each warrior's wealth determined his place in the military system. Those who could afford to equip themselves with helmet, breastplate, spear, and shield held the highest rank, and were deployed in the first centuries. The remaining citizens eligible for war, outfitted to the extent of their fortunes as light infantrymen armed with javelins or daggers or as skirmishers, filled the remaining centuries. The very poorest citizens were not enlisted in the army. They were called the **proletarians** ("bearers of children"), because their only service to the state was to reproduce and thereby provide new generations of citizens.

Thus the Roman citizenry arrayed in the Centuriate Assembly resembled the Roman army arrayed for battle (with the exception that the proletarians were recognized as citizens, but not as soldiers). The military organization was adapted to a political one. And the military origin of the assembly explains why wealth played a decisive role in the political system. The wealthy who formed the first lines of battle—and took the greatest risks—were those who voted first, and held the greatest power, in the assembly.

The Roman army took the field organized into legions. The legion was subdivided into smaller units: "maniples" or "cohorts." Its organization is shown in *How Many?*, above. Participants were recruited from those aged between seventeen and forty-six, and served for sixteen (later twenty) years. By the time of Hannibal's invasion of Italy in 218 B.C.E., the Romans could mobilize more than 100,000 men, including legionaries and lighter-armed auxiliaries recruited from the non-citizen population.

Plebeian Gains

From the first days of the Republic, plebeian Romans pressed for increased representation in government and enhanced social freedoms. Even wealthy plebeians were barred from the Senate, from public office, and from marriage with patricians.

Wealthy patricians belonged to the higher ranks of the Centuriate Assembly, and so did some wealthy plebeians. Beginning in the fifth and fourth centuries, plebeian leaders launched what later historians have dramatically named the Struggle of the Orders. It was not until the end of the third century B.C.E., however, that the barriers to a dramatic plebeian advance dissolved and plebeians gained their true objectives. The wealthiest plebeians would now merge with the patrician order to form a powerful new ruling class: that of the office-holding "nobility."

The plebeian advance began with the clever tactic of secession, which they employed several times over two centuries. Plebeians withdrew from the city, refusing to bear arms (the most powerful card they held), swore mutual loyalty, and established their own temple, temple administrators (the *aediles*), and priesthood. They created two new powerful magistrates (later ten) called *tribunes*. The tribunes were granted the status of sacrosanctity: dedicated to the gods, they were considered holy, and anyone who laid a hand on them could be summarily killed without fear of divine or human justice. Thus protected from patrician vengeance, the tribunes could veto actions of the patrician magistrates deemed injurious to their emerging social order.

Plebeian leaders also demanded the publication of the laws. In about 450 B.C.E., patrician magistrates acceded to this demand and codified the laws. They may also, as later authors assert, have inscribed them on twelve tables, which were placed in the Forum for all to consult. The originals of these Twelve Tables do not survive, but they were in the minds of generations of Romans who, as schoolchildren, were required to memorize them. Excerpts contained in later historical works depict early republican Roman society and its already sophisticated concepts of law.

Plebeian leaders created a new assembly paralleling the Centuriate Assembly, in which their votes had greater weight: the "Tribal Assembly." This was based on an ancient tribal assembly, and it featured a majority of plebeians. The new assembly contained the same Roman population that constituted the Centuriate Assembly but was divided into "tribes"—at first twenty, later thirty-five. Crucially, the system of voting was different. One tribe voted at a time (the order of voting being decided by lot). A majority of eleven (later eighteen) voting yes or no controlled the decision. Patricians were excluded from the assembly (only because tribunes could only convene plebeians), leaving a body called the Plebeian Council, presided over by a tribune. The Plebeian Council was a very powerful body that could exercise a nearly democratic force in the republican machinery. In 287 B.C.E. this council obtained the right to pass laws binding on all Romans.

In the meantime, plebeian leaders also gained access to the high magistracies leading to the consulate. Eventually, plebeians served alongside patricians as consuls, praetors, and quaestors. As the first two titles conferred *imperium*, plebeians as well as patricians could lead the Roman army in battle and, eventually, rule provinces and the empire itself. Plebeians who won election to the city's chief offices became members of the "senatorial order," and becoming a Consul conferred nobility on their family.

By the time the plebeian order had achieved these goals, Rome itself had grown from a village to a nation. It would soon be an empire.

ROME: FROM WEST TO EAST

Without having any preexisting plan to do so, in the fourth century B.C.E. Rome began a career of military conquest that would result in its domination of all of the Mediterranean region. Its conquests began in Italy, extended south and west, especially to Carthage and Spain, then east to the kingdoms of the successors of Alexander as shown in Maps 5.4 and 5.5. As it progressed, the Roman advance became unstoppable, driven not so much by a need for self-defense as by the zeal to conquer. The engine of conquest transformed not only the conquered territories, but also the values of the conqueror (see *Witnesses*, p. 126).

Italy, Carthage, and the West

At first, Rome looked only to secure its position in Italy and to defend itself against possible aggressors.

Once they had expelled the Etruscans, the Romans subdued the neighboring Aequi and Volsci tribes then struck back at their old Etruscan neighbors by seizing one of their foe's principal towns, Veii. Thereafter, Etruscan power diminished as Roman power expanded. The next challenge came from a new quarter. In 386 B.C.E., the Celts (called Gauls by the Romans) who dwelled north of the river Po (in northern Italy) invaded Rome, sacked the city, and terrorized its people. Rallied by the patrician consul Marcus Furius Camillus (the conqueror of Veii, d. 365 B.C.E.), the Romans counterattacked. They drove off the Celts and laid the foundation of their empire.

The victorious Camillus, acting as dictator, constructed a ring of protective walls around Rome and reorganized the army. He discarded the phalanx formation (see p. 128) for the more flexible maniple, whose soldiers held javelins—lighter than hoplite spears. Rome was now ready for war.

Assisted by a league of Latin tribes, Rome subdued central Italy. By 300 B.C.E., Rome had disbanded the league and asserted dominion. According to the geographer Strabo (c. 64 B.C.E.—after 21 C.E.), the Latins were "struck with amazement" at Roman military strength, by which "all became subjects."

At this stage Rome was a gentle conqueror. She extended to her Latin allies some of the privileges of citizenship. In addition, Latins were invited to form colonies in lands newly conquered by Rome, In these they were autonomous and gained full citizenship rights. Rather than crush a vanquished people, the Romans welcomed them into their fellowship.

In three terrible wars from 343 to 290 B.C.E., the Romans defeated the Samnites, a hill-people of southeastern Italy. These, too, were incorporated into the

***Map 5.4* Roman Expansion in Italy, 500–80 B.C.E.:** *In 500 B.C.E., Rome was a small town subject to Etruscan kings which was situated on a peninsula shared with native tribes and Carthaginian and Greek strangers. By 275 B.C.E., Rome had gained its independence and established direct territorial control in the center of the peninsula and on the western coast. Over the next two centuries, Rome had engulfed Italy, its dominion made visible by the network of roads that radiated from Rome across the entire region. By 90 B.C.E., free Italians were made Roman citizens.*

growing Roman Empire by the strategies of alliance, colonization, and grants of partial citizenship. The Greek cities of southern Italy, not waiting for a Roman attack, preemptively declared war. They had hired the forces of King Pyrrhus of Epirus, on the Greek mainland, who arrived with a well-trained army of 25,000 men and 20 war elephants. He overpowered the Romans in 280 and 279 B.C.E., but only after suffering severe losses himself and by unleashing the fury of his awesome beasts. This was a "Pyrrhic" victory—one achieved with such damage that it is tantamount to defeat. Pyrrhus went home, having accomplished little. The Greek cities soon accepted Roman hegemony.

By 264 B.C.E., Roman power extended from the Po River to the toe of Italy, jutting deep into the central Mediterranean. The only other major power in the region, the Carthaginians, took notice. After a clash between the two forces in Sicily, Carthage declared war on Rome. Three wars were required to decide who would hold sovereignty in the western Mediterranean, and to achieve the destruction of the city of Carthage. In these Punic Wars, as they were called (after the Latin name for the Carthaginians, *Punici*–or "Phoenicians"), Rome waged an epochal struggle. At the outset, Rome was an Italian power and could have remained only that. With the end of the Wars, Rome controlled the western Mediterranean. In the course of these wars, the Romans more than once launched and lost their navies, sacrificed the lives of thousands of citizens and allies, and saw generals thought invincible lured into ambush, blinded by mist, or tricked by decoy armies.

Four brilliant Carthaginian generals of the same clan, the Barcids, led the assault on Rome in the first two Punic wars: Hamilcar, his son-in-law Hasdrubal, and his sons Hannibal and (again) Hasdrubal. The most famous was Hannibal (247–183/182 B.C.E.), who launched the second Punic War when he invaded the Italian heartland after crossing the seemingly impregnable Alps. With thirty-seven elephants and a massive infantry force, he won victory upon victory as he descended from the Po to the south. Arrayed against him were Rome's finest leaders, who found that the African could not be defeated in a head-on battle. Only Quintus Fabius Maximus succeeded, by harrying the enemy, in stemming Hannibal's advance.

The consul Publius Cornelius Scipio (236–183 B.C.E.), who had been stationed in Spain, slipped across the straits between Sicily and Africa, and marched on Carthage. The desperate citizens recalled Hannibal. His Carthaginian forces met the Romans at Zama, not far from the capital, in 202 B.C.E. Undefeated in Italy, Hannibal lost the war at home. The victorious Romans stripped Carthage of its territories, its wealth, and its international prestige. Rome had triumphed in the west, and Scipio acquired another surname: Africanus, the conqueror of Africa.

There was no need for a third Punic War (149–146 B.C.E.), except in the minds of Rome's elder statesmen, who feared a resurgence of Carthaginian power. Marcus Porcius Cato, called "the Elder" (234–149 B.C.E.), former consul, as well as censor, author, and moralist, harangued the Senate regularly with the pronouncement "Carthage must be destroyed." It was an already weakened Carthage that faced the Roman army sent to execute that mission in 149 B.C.E. The besieged citizens resisted, starving and unarmed, for three years. In 146 B.C.E., the remaining Carthaginians were captured or killed, the city burned to the ground, the ground itself spread with salt to prevent its renewal. The triumphant Roman general was another Scipio, called Aemilianus, and surnamed (like his adoptive grandfather) Africanus.

The first Punic War (264–241 B.C.E.) gave the Romans Sicily, the fertile island off Italy's toe. The second (218–201 B.C.E.) gave them Spain and a foothold in Africa. The third (149–146 B.C.E.) opened all of North Africa to Roman domination. From these new lands, Rome was immeasurably enriched. Both Sicily and Africa were breadbaskets, producers of wheat, which the Romans needed in quantity. Spain's lodes of ore and, above all, its silver mines were an unimaginable treasure which, once discovered,

WITNESSES

Defenders of the Roman Ideal

The roster of Roman heroes includes those notable for their self-control or self-sacrifice, as well as those known for their record of military successes. Among them are Cato the Elder, whose self-restraint is commended by the later Greek biographer Plutarch; Tiberius Gracchus, whose efforts to improve the conditions of the Roman poor are described also by Plutarch; and the orator Cicero, who at great personal risk publicly denounced the dictatorship of Mark Antony.

Plutarch describes the virtues of the statesman Cato the Elder (c. 80 C.E.): He gained, in early life, a good habit of body by working with his own hands, and living temperately, and serving in war ... For his general temperance ... and self-control, he really deserves the highest admiration. For when he commanded the army, he never took for himself, and those who belonged to him, above three bushels of wheat for a month, and somewhat less than a bushel and a half a day of barley for his baggage-cattle. ... Yet, though he seemed thus easy and sparing to all who were under his power, he on the other hand showed most inflexible severity and strictness in what related to public justice, so that the Roman government never seemed more terrible, nor yet more mild, than under his administration.
(Plutarch, *Lives*; trs. Dryden, rev. A. H. Clough 1875)

When Tiberius Gracchus advocated a program for land reform to requisition lands from the rich and redistribute them to the poor, the rich launched a campaign against him (c. 80 C.E.): But they had no success. For Tiberius ... was quite invincible. Whenever the people crowded around the rostra, he would take his place there and speak on behalf of the poor. "The wild beasts of Italy," he would say, "have their own dens as places of repose and refuge, but the men who fight and die for their country enjoy nothing more in it than the air and light, having no houses or settlements of their own, they must wander from place to place with the wives and children. The army commanders areguilty of a ridiculous error when they exhort the common soldiers to defend their sepulchers and altars, for not one among so many Romans has an ancestral altar or tomb. They fight and die to maintain the luxury and wealth of other men. They are called the masters of the world, but they have not one foot of ground to call their own."
(Plutarch, *Lives*; trs. Dryden, rev. A. H. Clough 1875)

Cicero denounces Mark Antony's dictatorship (43 B.C.E.): But today, this very day that now is, this very moment when I am speaking, defend your conduct during this very moment, if you can. Why is the Senate surrounded by a belt of armed men? Why are your henchmen listening to me sword in hand? ... Why do you bring Ityreans, the most barbarous of all tribes, into the forum armed with arrows? He says he does so as a guard. Is it not better to perish a thousand times than to be unable to live in one's own city without an armed guard? But believe me, there is no protection in that—a man must be defended by the affection and good will of his fellow-citizens, not by arms. The Roman people will take them from you, will wrest them from your hands—may it be while we are still safe! ... The name of peace is sweet, the thing itself is a blessing. But between peace and slavery there is a wide difference. Peace is liberty in tranquility; slavery is the worst of all evils—to be repelled, if need be, not only by war but even by death.
(Cicero, *Second Philippic*, 112–119; ed. N. M. Bailkey, 1996)

were brutally seized from the region's barbarian inhabitants for the benefit of Rome.

Rome also looked north. Roman armies seized Cisalpine Gaul (the region between the Po and the Alps), completing the conquest of the Italian mainland. Then they reached over the Alps, where they met new nations of barbarians: Germans and Britons. The general Gaius Julius Caesar mastered Gaul (modern France, Belgium, and the Rhineland) by 51 B.C.E. after eight years of battle and maneuver. He encountered the Germans but did not pursue them, and crossed to Britain but did not stay. Rome had tasted the possibilities of the north, and would return under the emperors to export its version of peace.

Greece and the East

Meanwhile, richer prizes awaited Rome in the eastern Mediterranean: first in Greece, and then beyond, in the Middle East and Egypt.

Even before the victory at Zama, the Romans had peered across the Adriatic toward Greece, where two city leagues (the Aetolian and the Achaean) struggled with the Macedonian kingdom to the north. The leagues now invited the Seleucid king in Syria to assist them against Macedonia. Persuaded by her allies (the island state of Rhodes and the little Pergamene monarchy), who were fearful of Seleucid aggression (and annoyed with Macedonia for its support of Carthage during the second Punic War), Rome then intervened.

Over seventy years, the Romans fought four Macedonian wars. At first they did not seek domination over Greece. Instead, they proclaimed the liberation of the Greek cities, intending that a system of competing powers would check the Macedonian kings. But the Greek states were unruly, and Rome had begun to develop a taste for conquest. At Pydna, on the frontiers of Macedonia, in 168 B.C.E., the Roman legions under Lucius Aemilius Paullus (henceforth "Macedonicus"; d. 160 B.C.E.) defeated the Macedonian king, Perseus. All of Greece was subsequently swept into Roman hands, the conquerors announcing their power unambiguously by the wholesale enslavement in a single day of 150,000 inhabitants of Epirus. The point was underscored in 146 B.C.E. by the obliteration of the city of Corinth.

The Romans had crossed several barriers in absorbing Greece, mental as well as real. Hitherto, Rome had waged wars to defend its interests. Henceforth, it would fight to extend its empire. When the Romans faced the Greeks, moreover, they faced a people of superior culture. The civilization of the vanquished would profoundly change the thought and values of the victors.

Beyond Greece, the Near East beckoned. The king of Pergamum sought protection from the king of Pontus on his eastern flank, and from his Seleucid neighbor to the south—the latter squeezed by Parthian newcomers pressing from Iran. Rome imposed order, making clients of the Egyptian Ptolemies and fencing in the Seleucid monarchs. When in 168 B.C.E. Antiochus IV (the opponent of the Maccabees) approached Alexandria with hostile intent, the Roman legate drew his sword and marked a circle around the king in the sand, commanding him to disavow his ambitions before stepping beyond it. Thus the new masters of Egypt publicly humiliated one of the great kings of the East.

Gnaeus Pompeius Magnus (106–48 B.C.E.; anglicized as Pompey) completed the job of subduing this region. By 63 B.C.E., he had crushed Pontus, abolished the Seleucid Empire, and reorganized Judaea as a Roman province. In 30 B.C.E., Egypt fell to Octavian, Caesar's heir and Rome's future emperor (Augustus). Rome had come full circle: clockwise, from Carthage, through northwest Africa and Spain, Gaul and Greece, Asia Minor and the Middle East, and, returning to Africa, to Egypt. The Mediterranean was now a Roman sea.

The Roman sweep of the Mediterranean was startling. Who was this new Western power? How could it unseat the established masters of that world? A Greek taken hostage after Pydna undertook to explain the Roman phenomenon to his countrymen. This was Polybius of Megalopolis (c. 200–c. 118 B.C.E.) in the Peloponnesus, subsequently tutor and companion of Scipio Aemilianus, the son of Polybius' captor. His history of Rome from 220 to 146 B.C.E. (of which only parts survive) is a portrait of irresistible state power. Her leaders' virtue, her military genius, her balanced constitution, he proposed, allowed Rome to outstrip all competitors and resist normal patterns of growth and decay, which otherwise prevailed in the world of nations.

When Polybius arrived in Rome to become the pet of high-society intellectuals, Greek influence could be felt everywhere. Greek New Comedy played in the theater, rewritten for a Roman audience by the playwrights Plautus (254–184 B.C.E.) and Terence (195–159 B.C.E.). Greek philosophy grabbed the attention of bright adolescents, who journeyed to Athens to study at the source. Stoic philosophers brought to Rome the tenets of the school that most meshed with that city's spirit. Teachers of rhetoric, fixtures of every major Hellenistic city, founded schools in Rome where future senators mastered new skills. In noblemen's homes Greek schoolmasters, captive slaves, taught Romans the international language of culture. At aristocratic houses the witty and elegant gathered to discuss new books and to consult the rolls from captured libraries. Greek statues graced the halls and gardens of the wealthy.

Many Roman leaders deplored the conquest of the Roman aristocracy by the Greek imagination. None did so more angrily than Cato the Elder (234–149

B.C.E.), who as censor attempted to stem the tide of what he considered immoral Greek values. Greek philosophy must go, he argued: "Theirs is a vile race, and an unruly one," whose literature may be worth looking at, but not closely. When the lectures of the Greek philosophers Carneades and Diogenes took Rome by storm, Cato expelled them from the city—this though he sent his son to study philosophy in Athens.

ROME: FROM REPUBLIC TO EMPIRE

Cato was probably right. Rome could not expand and conquer (whatever Polybius thought) without becoming transformed itself. By the end of the Republic, the experience of empire-building had transformed Roman institutions, Roman values, and the Roman people. The city that had begun its career by renouncing monarchy became the capital of a world empire, and subject to an emperor.

Changing Social Patterns

The provinces the Romans conquered they governed badly. Whether the lure was bushels of wheat or bars of silver, or statuary and libraries, greedy and corrupt governors milked the wealth of subject territories. So blatant was this theft that Rome established a court system—the Extortion Court—specifically to try officials charged by provincials with such crimes. However, the jury designated to hear those charges was generally made up of senators, with the same interests as the accused governors. In such an environment, corruption was the norm and honesty the exception. Writing in the fifth century C.E., when Roman depredations had long gone unchecked, Saint Augustine of Hippo (354–430 C.E.) concluded that empires were only "robbery on a grand scale."

Even had the provincial governors been honest, their subjects would have suffered from Roman rule. Rome lacked the machinery to administer an empire. A mere twenty or thirty magistrates, together with the Senate and the assemblies, ruled the city, Italy, and the Empire. The jobs of provincial administration (tax-collecting, road-building, importing, exporting) were auctioned to Roman entrepreneurs rich enough to undertake large projects. These men were *publicans*, who performed public services on commission. Some took only modest profits, but others equaled the worst of their senatorial counterparts and mercilessly bled the provinces.

Publicans belonged to the class of *equestrians*, which gained prominence in the late Republic. In earlier years, equestrians were men wealthy enough to

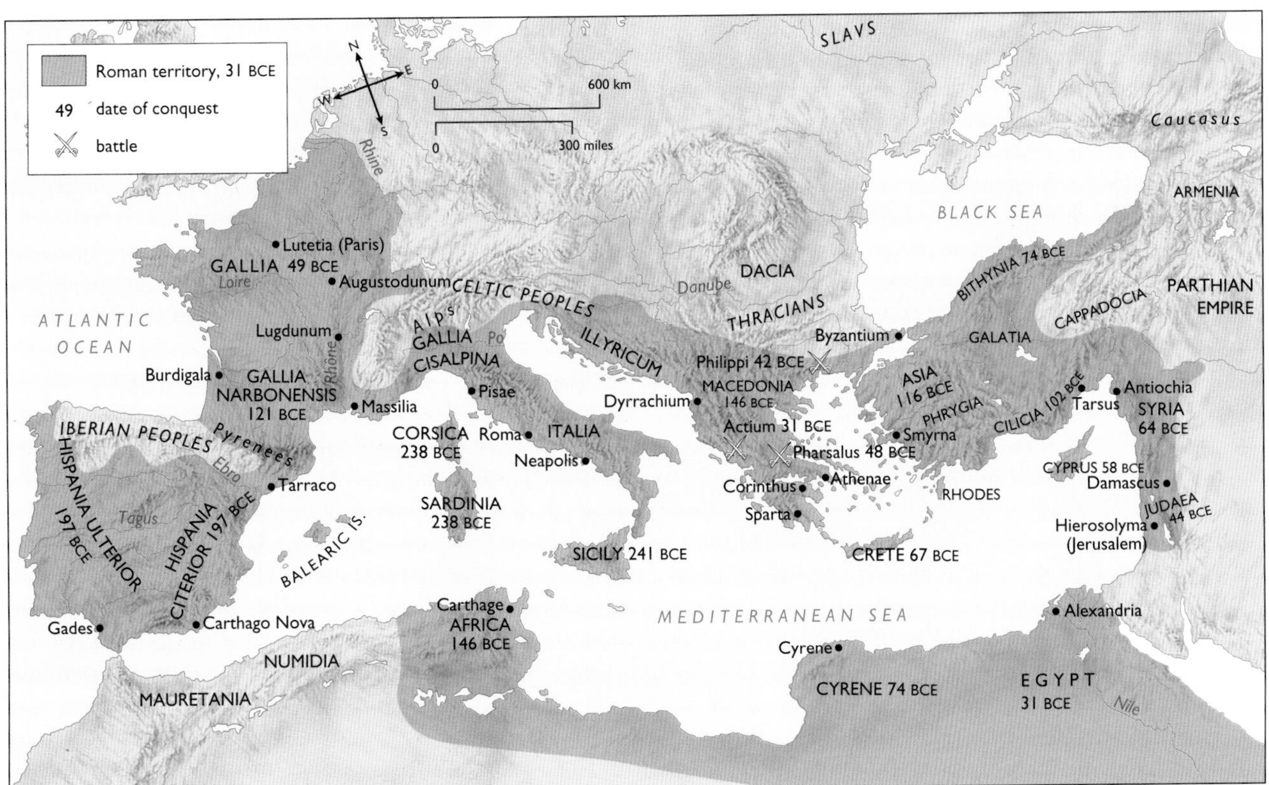

Map 5.5 Roman Imperialism in the Republican Era, 264–31 B.C.E.: *Having absorbed much of Italy by 264 B.C.E., Rome proceeded to confront other Mediterranean powers over the next two centuries. Its victories were hard-won but astonishing. By 100 B.C.E., Rome held most of the western Mediterranean region as well as the Balkans, Greece, and parts of Asia Minor. By 31 B.C.E., it had acquired the ancient centers of civilization in the Near East, Egypt, and parts of North Africa. It was a republic, but at the same time it was an empire.*

be rated with the cavalry in the Centuriate Assembly. Later, a minimum requirement of 400,000 *sesterces* (a *sestertius* coin equalled a quarter of a *denarius*) established eligibility for equestrian status. Equestrians were often as wealthy as the aristocracy whose sons formed the senatorial elite. Unlike the aristocracy, equestrians did not seek political office or a place in the Senate. The aristocracy who did so were barred from engaging in commerce, and it was commerce that interested the equestrians. They were a nonpolitical class of moneymakers, who profited from moneylending, trade, and public contracting.

During the late Republic, independent subsistence farmers, who had fought in the legions that won Rome her empire, were declining in number and prosperity. In some areas they were swallowed up by the large landowners: Roman senators and equestrians, and the Latin and other Italian aristocracy. Big men advanced at the expense of the small because they were able to take advantage of the burgeoning numbers of slaves: a consequence of empire.

The slave population swelled with imports of human cargo from conquered territories: 20,000 at one blow from Africa in 256 B.C.E.; 25,000 from Agrigentum, Sicily, in 262 B.C.E.; 150,000 from Epirus in 167 B.C.E.; 1,000,000 allegedly seized in Gaul by Julius Caesar. Laboring on Sicilian and Italian *latifundia*, this slave force was an unwilling army, rarely freed (unlike domestic and artisan slaves), impelled by force.

The slave hordes of the *latifundia* often rebelled—twice in such numbers that seasoned troops were deployed to suppress them. In 135 B.C.E., Sicilian slaves rebelled under the Syrian-born Eunus, amassing an army of 70,000 men before they were crushed in 131 B.C.E.. In 73–71 B.C.E., the Thracian gladiator Spartacus led a polyglot army of 90,000 desperate slaves on raids up and down the Italian peninsula. The general Marcus Licinius Crassus (d. 53 B.C.E.) destroyed the rebels, underscoring the message with a mass crucifixion of 6000 survivors along the Appian Way, the highway to Rome.

Small farmers who could not compete with the large plantations mortgaged their land, gave up in despair and, landless, migrated to Rome. Here perhaps they might become part of the floating mass of unemployed slum-dwellers, the **plebs**. This urban proletariat lived to eat and be entertained. In order to achieve this goal, they sold the one commodity they possessed: their vote. The capital belonged to the idle poor, the very rich, and the slaves.

A man of the plebs was not welcome in the army. He could not be disciplined, commanders feared. But with fewer small farmers, it was necessary to find a new social group from which to recruit soldiers. A solution was discovered by the general and consul Gaius Marius (c. 157–86 B.C.E.), an equestrian from a family that had never before held high office (thus that rarity, a "new man"). Marius brought into his army a new breed of men: the old proletarians. Men of this class had once made up one-half the population of old Rome: poor men without property or patrons, lumped as a mass into the last of the 193 centuries of the Centuriate Assembly. The proletarians whom Marius admitted to his army had one overriding loyalty: to the general who gave them a job, a mission, and the promise of a fat bonus upon retirement.

Returning soldiers expected that bonus: a piece of land to compensate for years of military service abroad. Marius' promises unleashed from his veterans a pressing demand for land, when most available land had been gobbled up by the large landowners to be cultivated by slaves or entrepreneurial tenant farmers.

To some extent, a serious program of colonization could meet this demand. Retired soldiers settled in the Po Valley, on the island of Sicily, or in North Africa. Far from Rome, they retained their citizenship, and served as a permanent reserve garrison in subject territory. Colonization was a useful but insufficient tool. To provide the veterans with land, it became necessary to take it from somebody else.

MUST READS

The Career of the Roman Republic

Polybius *The Histories*

Livy *The History of Rome*

Plutarch *Lives*, especially of *Tiberius and Gaius Gracchus*, *Julius Caesar*

Sallust *The Conspiracy of Catiline*

Cicero *Orations*, *On the Republic*

The Last Century of the Republic

During Rome's early expansion within Italy, new lands acquired from conquered neighbors were designated as "public land." Over the years, public land had been absorbed by large landowners or tenants who had made it their own. Those holdings could be reclaimed by the state and distributed in small allotments to retired soldiers—or they might be given to the landless poor of the city of Rome, who might repeople the class of smallholders. The latter proposal, called the "Agrarian Law," was the idea of Tiberius Sempronius Gracchus (d. 133 B.C.E.). It sparked the revolution that ended with the dismantling of the Republic.

The extraordinary lives of Tiberius and his brother Gaius Sempronius Gracchus did much to shape the history of the last phase of the Roman Republic. According to legend, their mother, Cornelia (the daughter of the elder Scipio Africanus and sister of Aemilius Paullus, victor at Pydna in 168 B.C.E.), when asked to display her jewels, pointed to her two sons and replied, "These are my jewels." A cultivated matron and known author, Cornelia raised and educated her sons herself. The monument eventually erected for her in Rome noted not only her parentage (as was usual) but her maternity (which was unprecedented): "Cornelia, daughter of Africanus, [mother] of the Gracchi." That monument rightly awards their mother some of the credit for the achievements of the Gracchi brothers.

It was while serving as a tribune in 133 B.C.E., that Tiberius Gracchus proposed the "Agrarian Law." An aristocrat himself, his aim was conservative: to bolster the peasant population, which had borne the burdens of Rome's expansion by being unable to compete with large slave-owners. His proposal angered his peers in the Senate, for whom land redistribution was anathema—even if it involved only public land and the appropriations were modest. Their refusal to sacrifice their property or their privilege would ultimately spell their demise as a political class.

Another tribune, a puppet of the senatorial elite, vetoed Tiberius' proposed law. Tiberius then unprecedentedly called for a special election to unseat the dissenting tribune, which secured passage of the law. He further appropriated for the use of the land commission set up by his law (whose members were people he could trust—himself, his brother, and his father-in-law) the treasury of the kingdom of Pergamum, recently willed to Rome. Finally, Tiberius outraged his opponents by (against all precedent) running for reelection. Incited by the Senate, a mob stabbed him to death. It was the first of the political assassinations of this troubled era.

Ten years later (123 B.C.E.), Tiberius' brother Gaius (d. 121 B.C.E.) became tribune and undertook a still more radical program. Continuing Tiberius' land distributions, he also ordered the distribution of cheap grain to the plebs, planned colonization programs for veterans, and proposed the extension of Roman citizenship to Latins, and of Latin rights to Italians. He introduced a reformed system for tax collection in Asia and for the prosecution in Rome of corrupt provincial governors. Opposition to some of these measures gathered force, and in 121 B.C.E. the Senate enacted a *senatus consultum ultimum*, or "Final Decree," which authorized the consul to impose martial law and destroy anyone perceived as an enemy of the state. In the fighting that followed, Gaius committed suicide to escape the shame of execution.

With their broad vision, bold programs, and tragic deaths, the Gracchi brothers opened a new era of republican politics. Henceforth, those who refused to surrender privilege in order to heal the pain of Roman society called themselves the **Optimates**, the "best." Those who courted the masses were known as the **Populares**, the "popular" or "people's" party. The rigidity of the Optimate position and the ruthlessness of the Popular leaders hastened the downfall of the Republic.

The laws of the Gracchi and the governance, while consul, of Marius cost senators some of their privileges (and, in some cases, their lives). They regained their privileges when Lucius Cornelius Sulla (c. 138–79 B.C.E.), once Marius' lieutenant, established himself as Dictator for the Reconstitution of the Republic, a post he held from 82 to 80 B.C.E. Posting the names of his opponents in the Forum, Sulla invited their murder and saw to the confiscation of their wealth. These **proscriptions**, as they were called, resulted in the butchery of some 10,000 men and the redefinition of the ruling class.

Julius Caesar

A general with an army behind him had great power—more so if it were an army of landless men whose futures depended on the skill and success of their leader. In the last half-century of the Republic (up to 31 B.C.E.), generals held sway. Crassus and Pompey—two of Sulla's lieutenants who between them had vanquished the slave Spartacus, cleared the Mediterranean of pirates, suppressed rebellion in Spain, and acquired a large chunk of the Middle East, dominated Rome for the next generation. They were soon joined by Julius Caesar (100–44 B.C.E.), the greatest general of all.

From 65 to 59 B.C.E., Caesar served as aedile, chief priest, praetor, governor of Spain, and consul. In 60 B.C.E. he joined forces with Crassus and Pompey to form the First **Triumvirate**, an unofficial alliance dedicated essentially to their mutual advantage. On stepping down from the consulship in 59 B.C.E., he assumed command of the armies in Cisalpine and Transalpine Gaul. By 50 B.C.E. he had subdued these regions. Meanwhile, the "First Triumvirate" had crumbled: Crassus died fighting the Parthians in 53 B.C.E., and Pompey betrayed Caesar's policies to become the darling of the Senate. Fearful that Caesar would return to Rome as a conqueror, the Senate, early in 49 B.C.E., appointed another general to succeed him in Gaul and ordered him to lay down his arms. Defying that command, Caesar led one of his legions across the Rubicon River at the southern boundary of his province, in an act tantamount to a declaration of war. Pompey and the senators fled, abandoning the state treasury, which Caesar found useful when he occupied the capital.

Caesar pursued Pompey and vanquished his superior force at Pharsalus, in Macedonia, in 48 B.C.E. Pompey then fled to Egypt, where he was murdered by order of the Ptolemaic king, and Caesar proceeded to rule the empire as Perpetual Dictator. This title he preferred to that of king, which he refused, placing the proffered crown instead on a statue of the god

Jupiter. Caesar reformed provincial administration, extended citizenship to deserving provincial elites, provided free grain and entertainment to the urban plebs, opened the Senate to eager equestrians, settled his veterans on colonial and public land, and in these and other ways seriously addressed the social problems that had first prompted the Gracchi brothers in their heroic attempts at reform. Caesar was a brilliant administrator as well as a brilliant general. But the Republic was dead.

Among the senators who had opposed Caesar and championed Pompey were the younger Marcus Porcius Cato (95–46 B.C.E.), great-grandson of Cato the Elder, and Marcus Tullius Cicero (106–43 B.C.E.), orator, author, and (though a timid man) dedicated republican. Cato possessed high principles, honed by a superior education in the Greek classics and Stoic philosophy. The best advocate the Optimates could put forward, he was self-righteous, nostalgic for the old Republic, and committed to protecting the authority of the senatorial order. After Pompey's defeat, Cato commanded an army that faced Caesar and lost at Thapsus (North Africa) in 46 B.C.E. Rather than submit to the enemy, he killed himself at Utica—considered the most eloquent suicide of the age.

Cicero, a moderate, had feared Caesar's return in 49 B.C.E., but was reconciled with the general, who bore no grudge against his former opponent. Cicero spent the next five years far from the Forum, writing his celebrated works: *On Duties*, *Tusculan Disputations*, *On the Orator*, *The Republic*, *On the Nature of the Gods*. In these treatises and dialogues, he distilled the Roman outlook on society and politics in prose that would become a standard of composition for two millennia. In these works, too, he translated into Latin the key concepts of Greek philosophy. It was in Ciceronian Latin that Greek thought first won the attention of Europe's philosophers in the age of the Renaissance. His numerous orations and more than 900 letters taught later generations to think and feel like Romans. This dedicated intellectual was an unlikely martyr. A martyr he became.

Caesar died on March 15, 44 B.C.E., stabbed twenty-three times by conspirators led by Marcus Junius Brutus (c. 85–42 B.C.E.). Caesar's lieutenants Marcus Antonius (83–30 B.C.E; anglicized as Mark Antony) and Marcus Aemilius Lepidus (d. 13/12 B.C.E.), intent on vengeance, seized command of Rome. The murderers dispersed. Antony and Lepidus were joined by the adolescent Gaius Octavius (63 B.C.E.–14 C.E.), renamed, according to Caesar's will (adopting him as son and heir), Gaius Julius Caesar Octavianus (anglicized as Octavian). The three formed the Second Triumvirate, dedicated like the first to the promotion of its members and the mastery of Rome.

At the top of the Second Triumvirate's agenda (though Octavian regretted it) was the assassination of Cicero. For that scholar had stood in the Forum on fourteen occasions after Caesar's murder and with piercing eloquence denounced Mark Antony as a traitor to Rome, as quoted in *Witnesses* on p. 131. Those speeches he called Philippics: an allusion to Demosthenes' orations against Philip of Macedon. Cicero was slain by Antony's soldiers while attempting, reluctantly and too late, to flee. Antony ordered his head and hands (with which he had spoken and written the *Philippics*) to be nailed to the rostrum in the same Forum where he had delivered his orations.

The Second Triumvirate defeated Caesar's assassins in Spain and Greece, then turned on each other. Lepidus was pushed aside. Octavian and Mark Antony fought a duel to the death, the latter aided by the last Ptolemaic monarch, Caesar's one-time lover Cleopatra. Losing their nerve during the naval battle of Actium (off the Greek coast) in 31 B.C.E., Mark Antony and Cleopatra fled to Egypt, and Octavian won the field. The next year, the two fugitives were both suicides. After 27 B.C.E., Octavian ruled Rome: not as consul or dictator, but as Caesar Augustus. He had made the Roman sea his own.

Conclusion

THE ROMAN SEA AND THE MEANING OF THE WEST

With the conquests of Alexander the Great, the Greek world engrossed the whole of the eastern Mediterranean world. The Hellenic culture of the Greek Classical age blended with local cultures to produce Hellenistic civilization. To the west, Carthage and Etruria emerged as new centers of civilization related to the ancient Middle East and open to the Hellenistic synthesis. In Etruria's shadow, Latins centered at Rome won independence from Etruscan domination and began to forge the institutions that constituted the Roman Republic. From the fourth to the first century B.C.E., Rome extended its sovereignty throughout Italy, North Africa, and the regions of the Alexandrian conquest, and claimed the Mediterranean Sea as *mare nostrum*, "our sea."

The whole product of civilization that had accumulated on the shores of that sea became part of the Roman heritage, which passed in time to other Europeans who carried forward the cultural tradition of the West. A fusion of the successive strata of the Asian, African, Greek, and Latin imaginations, that heritage was to outlive both the Roman Republic and the Empire.

REVIEW QUESTIONS

1. What were the consequences of Alexander's conquests? Which main states evolved from his empire after his death? Which were the centers of western Mediterranean civilization at this time?

2. What were the main characteristics of the Hellenistic Age? To what extent did Greek culture merge with that of the eastern Mediterranean? How did women's lot improve in the Hellenistic Age?

3. What were the main achievements of Hellenistic science? How did Stoic and Epicurean philosophies differ? In what ways did Hellenistic culture survive the collapse of Hellenistic kingdoms?

4. What role did the family play in Roman society? Why was the *paterfamilias* so important? What was the status of women, children, and slaves in the early Roman Republic?

5. Name the main Roman magistrates. How were they chosen? What role did theSenate play in Roman government? What did the plebeians gain from the "Struggle of the Orders"?

6. Why did Romans refer to the Mediterranean as "Our Sea" by the first century B.C.E.? How did the possession of an empire affect Roman society and politics? What role did Caesar play in the destruction of the Republic?

SUGGESTED RESOURCES

Around the Mediterranean

Green, Peter, *Alexander of Macedon 356–323 B.C.: A Historical Biography* (Berkeley: University of California Press, 1992). Portrays Alexander as a brilliant but brutally single-minded general, a man capable of patricide or the massacre of civilians.

Horden, Peregrine & Nicholas Purcell, *The Corrupting Sea: A Study of Mediterranean History* (Oxford: Blackwell, 2000). Studies the interaction between people and the environment in the Mediterranean region during prehistory, antiquity, and the Middle Ages.

Alexander the Great on the web:
http:/ancienthistory.about.com/msubalexander.htm?once=true8
http://www.pbs.org/mpt/alexander/index.html

Becoming Greek

Canfora, Luciano, *The Vanished Library: A Wonder of the Ancient World* trans. Martin Ryle; Berkeley–Los Angeles (University of California Press, 1990). Imaginative and elegant reconstruction of the Hellenistic intellectual world, and particularly of the legendary library at Alexandria created by the Ptolemies to hold all the world's books.

Green, Peter, ed., *Hellenistic Culture and Society* (Berkeley–Los Angeles: University of California Press, 1992). Sixteen essays examining Hellenistic civilization, confirming its originality and worthiness as a successor to classical Greece.

Snowden, Frank M., *Before Color Prejudice: The Ancient View of Blacks* (Cambridge, MA: Harvard University Press, 1983). Argues that black people were culturally assimilated and color prejudice was unknown.

Archimedes: inventions, problems, and solutions:
http://www.mcs.drexel.edu/~crorres/Archimedes/contents.html

Rome: From Village to Nation

Bradley, Keith R., *Slavery and Society at Rome* (Cambridge: Cambridge University Press, 1994). Examines Roman slavery as a social institution from the last two centuries of the Republic through the first two of the Empire, noting comparisons with later slave systems.

Dixon, Suzanne, *The Roman Family* (Baltimore: John Hopkins University Press, 1992). Scholarly synthesis of the latest views on law and marriage, household and servitude, women and children, and life-cycle stages in Roman society.

Mitchell, Richard E., *Patricians and Plebeians: The Origin of the Roman State* (Ithaca: Cornell University Press, 1990). A controversial account of the patricians as a hereditary religious elite, de-emphasizing the patrician/plebeian struggle.

Watson, Alan, *The Spirit of Roman Law* (Athens GA: University of Georgia Press, 1995). An intellectual framework of lawmakers in Rome, from around 451 B.C.E. to around 235 C.E.

Rome: From West to East

Harris, William V., *War and Imperialism in Republican Rome, 327–70 B.C.* (Oxford: Clarendon Press of Oxford University Press, 1979). Argues that Rome was consistently aggressive and imperialistic, a once-revisionist view now generally accepted.

Kallet-Marx, Robert, *Hegemony to Empire: The Development of the Roman Imperium in the East from 148 to 62 B.C.E.* (Berkeley: University of California Press, 1996). Argues that Roman influence in Greece, and Greek influence on Rome, was exerted at first without any real conquest or intention to rule; the idea of empire developed only gradually.

Keppie, Lawrence J. F., *The Making of the Roman Army: From Republic to Empire* (Totowa, N.J.: Barnes & Noble Books, 1984). A lively account of Roman military institutions and traditions to 50 C.E.

Rome: From Republic to Empire

Crawford, Michael, *The Roman Republic*, 2nd ed. (Cambridge, MA: Harvard University Press, 1993). Excellent overview, stressing Roman expansion and the crisis of the last Republican century.

Dupont, Florence, *Daily Life in Ancient Rome*, trans. Christopher Woodall (Cambridge, MA: Blackwell, 1994). Lively reconstruction of life in Republican Rome—how it felt to live in Roman public spaces, amid the cultural symbols that made Rome what it was.

Rawson, Elizabeth, *Intellectual Life in the Late Roman Republic* (Baltimore: The Johns Hopkins University Press, 1985). Analyses the arts, rhetoric, mathematics, medicine, law, geography and ethnography, philosophy, and theology.

Wallace-Hadrill, Andrew, *Houses and Society in Pompeii and Herculaneum* (Princeton: Princeton University Press, 1994). A revisionist history of Pompeii and Herculaneum, based on archaeological evidence.

Julius Caesar, resources: **http://www.virgil.org/caesar**

PAX ROMANA

50 B.C.E. | 1 C.E. | 50 | 100 | 150 | 200 | 250 | 300 | 350 | 400 | 450 | 500 C.E.

Rulers, Nations, and War

Roman Republic, c. 500–27 B.C.E.

Roman Empire, 27 B.C.E–476 C.E.

Byzantine Empire, 476–1453

- Julius Caesar assassinated, 44 B.C.E.
- Cicero assassinated, 43 B.C.E.
- Roman Senate bestows title "Augustus" upon Octavian, 27 B.C.E.
- Augustus dies; Julio-Claudian emperors to 68 C.E.
- Roman invasion of Britain, 43 C.E.
- Flavian dynasty: Emperors Vespasian and sons Titus and Domitian, 69–96 C.E.
- Five "good" emperors: Nerva, Trajan, Hadrian, Antoninus Pius, Marcus Aurelius, 96–180 C.E.
- Roman assemblies cease to legislate, 98 C.E.
- Roman victory over Dacians, 106
- Trajan's Forum and celebratory column, 113
- Empire reaches greatest extent under Trajan
- Severan Dynasty, 193–235
- Diocletian becomes emperor, 284
- Empire split, West assigned to Maximian, 284–86
- Diocletian and Maximian retire from power, 305
- Emperor Constantine establishes power in Italy, 312
- Constantine dies, 337
- Theodosius, called "the Great," becomes emperor, 379
- Visigoths seize, sack Rome, 410
- Attila the Hun invades West, 451
- Vandals seize, sack Rome, 455
- Odoacer, leader of Visigoths, deposes emperor, seizes power in Rome, 476

Religion, Ideas, and Society

- Cicero, statesman, philosopher, 106–43 B.C.E.
- Lucretius, poet, philosopher, c. 94–c. 55/51 B.C.E.
- Vergil, poet, 70–19 B.C.E.
- Horace, poet, 65–8 B.C.E.
- Augustus' legislation on marriage and family, 18 B.C.E–9 C.E.
- Altar of Peace built, 13–9 B.C.E.
- Jesus of Nazareth born, c. 4 B.C.E.
- Jesus of Nazareth crucified in Jerusalem, 30 C.E.
- Quintilian, rhetorician, c. 35–c. 100 C.E.
- Plutarch, historian, moralist, c. 46–c. 120 C.E.
- Tacitus, historian, c. 55–c. 120 C.E.
- Nero launches persecution of Christians, 64 C.E.
- Great Fire in Rome, 64 C.E.
- Seneca, philosopher, dies by suicide, at command of Nero, 65 C.E.
- Rebellion in Judaea suppressed; burning of Temple in Jerusalem, 66–70 C.E.
- Galen, c. 129–199 C.E.
- Suppression of Simon "Bar-Kokhba" revolt in Jerusalem; expulsion of Jews, 132–35
- Ptolemy, astronomer; Almagest, 150 C.E.
- Plotinus, 205–270 C.E.
- Caracalla extends Roman citizenship to free subjects of Empire, 213
- Porphyry, philosopher, 225–305 C.E.
- Emperor Aurelian constructs new set of walls for defense of Rome, 271–75
- Diocletian issues Edict on Prices, 301
- Edict of Milan grants toleration to all religions, 313
- Theodosian Code promulgated, 383

Beyond the West

Han dynasty, 206 B.C.E–220 C.E.

- Ezana of Aksum's conquests, c. 350

Maya civilization, c. 300–900

Gupta dynasty, c. 320–550

CHAPTER

6

PAX ROMANA

Society, State, and Culture in Imperial Rome

27 B.C.E.–500 C.E.

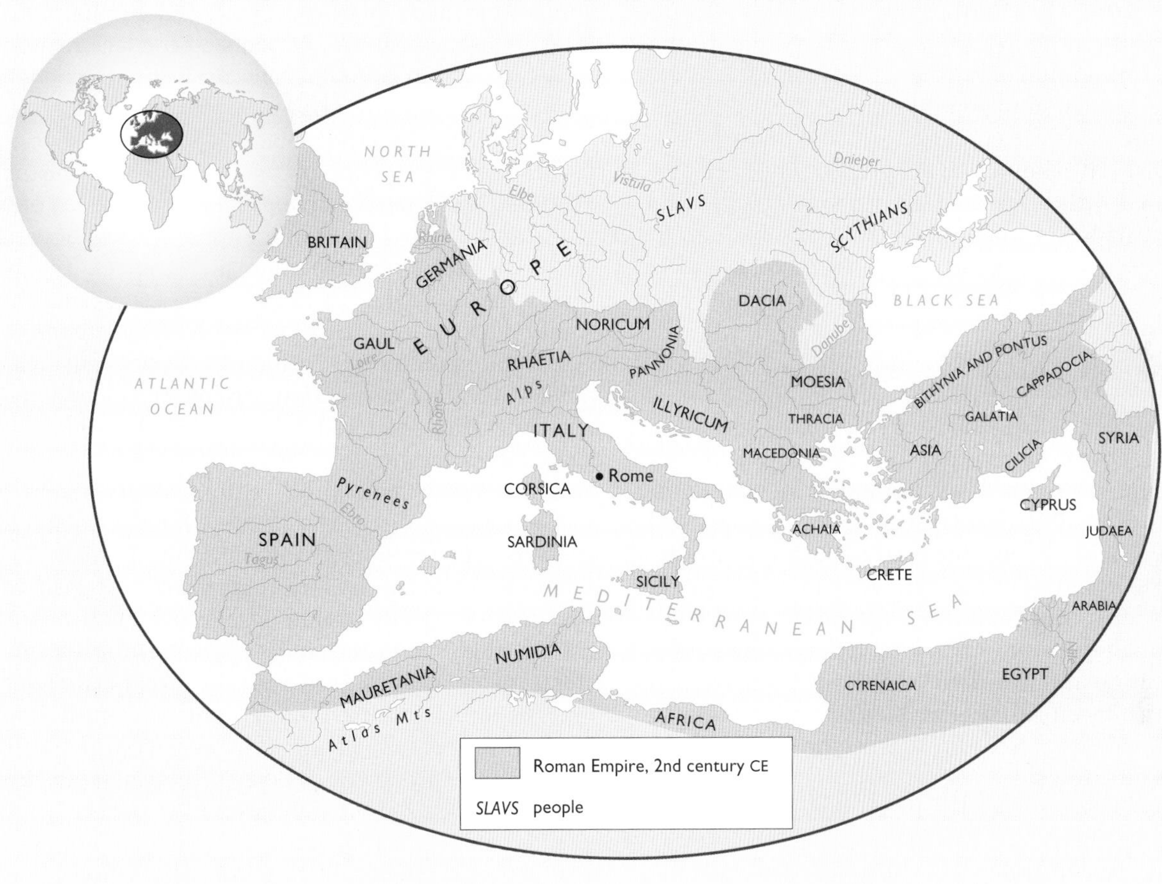

KEY TOPICS

- **The New Imperium:** Rome enjoys two centuries of peace under emperors from Augustus to Marcus Aurelius, who head an ever-expanding bureaucracy and army.
- **Upper Classes and Other Classes:** Republican institutions wither, the old nobility decays, equestrian and freedman classes prosper—while ordinary Romans, often unemployed, are entertained and fed at the expense of the Roman state.
- **The Culture of Imperial Rome:** Greco-Roman culture reaches its zenith and then declines, in part due to the loss of political freedoms under imperial rule.
- **Holding the Frontier:** Emperors Diocletian and Constantine reorganize the Empire as a quasi-totalitarian state, while the promise of Roman peace fades in a world on the brink of collapse and permanently at war.

***Peace, Roman Style** At the limit of the inhabited world, reports the historian Tacitus (c. 56–118 C.E.), a rebel chieftain rallied his followers to defy Rome in the name of freedom. The Romans had pacified Britain, he charged, by devastating it. "To robbery, butchery, and rapine, they give the lying name of 'government'; they create a desolation, and call it peace."*

Tacitus' narrative, composed in about 105–110 C.E., dramatizes the nature of Roman power, both creative and destructive (it is further quoted in *Witnesses* on p. 141). During the 500 years of the Republic, Rome acquired an empire. In the 250 years following Augustus' ascension to power in 27 B.C.E., that empire reached its zenith. It conferred upon its subjects the *pax romana* ("Roman peace"), purchased by conquest and secured with bloodshed. Over the next 250 years the peace failed. Rome's power was insufficient to stave off devastation in the land of its origin, or transformation in the eastern lands it had conquered.

THE NEW IMPERIUM

Octavian, later called Augustus (r. 27 B.C.E.–14 C.E.), conferred peace, order, and beauty upon the city and empire of Rome. His testimony is quoted in *Witnesses* on p. 141. His leadership also inaugurated an unprecedented concentration of authority in one person. He became "prince," the first among formerly equal citizens, and "emperor," the latter word itself (the Latin ***imperator***) taking on enlarged and ominous meaning from the nature of his rule. The Roman *imperator*, henceforth, was no mere general, wielding *imperium* in conquered lands, but the ruler of the Mediterranean world.

Augustus was succeeded first by members of his own family, then later by outsiders who acceded to imperial power by the will of the army or the Senate, by violence, or simply by luck. From Augustus' death in 14 C.E. until the middle of the third century, these rulers shaped the administration of an imperial monarchy. The principal emperors are listed in *Who's Who* on p. 144.

Augustus, the First Citizen

After Caesar's assassination in 44 B.C.E., Octavian waged war: first against Caesar's murderers, then against fellow triumvirs Mark Antony and Lepidus, now his rivals. After the battle of Actium in 31 B.C.E. and the deaths of Antony and Cleopatra, Octavian consolidated his control of Egypt, Greece, Syria, and Asia Minor. In 29 B.C.E., he returned to Rome, having established his leadership out of the ruins of the Republic. The Senators celebrated, but with some anxiety. Would he become dictator, like Caesar? Or king, like the other rulers in the Mediterranean region? Or would he, like his predecessor Sulla, having reorganized matters in Rome, retire in order to concentrate on writing his memoirs? Octavian chose another course altogether.

Octavian took his time and established his authority gradually. The army was behind him, and during the civil wars he had obtained an oath of allegiance from all Italians. Employing the extraordinary powers granted him as military commander, he reduced the number of senators from 900 to 600 (during most of the Republic the number had stood at 300)—thus eliminating many of those appointed by his great-uncle Julius Caesar. And he reduced the legions from 60 to 28. Then in 27 B.C.E., he went before the Senate and announced that he had restored the Republic.

Octavian allowed the Senate (unconvinced that his intentions were so benign) to name him "Augustus" ("revered") and, later, **princeps** ("first citizen"). These were titles of respect, not offices of the Republic; and they were more valuable than mere offices. By the time of his death the "Principate" was established; an empire directed by a "first citizen" who still acknowledged the validity of republican forms, but with increasingly less conviction. In effect, Octavian—now Augustus—had not restored the Republic but created a monarchy.

Octavian assumed other titles which permitted him covertly to direct the organs of government. In 23 B.C.E., he surrendered the consulate (which gave him military authority, the *imperium*) bestowed on him in 27 B.C.E. by a grateful Senate. He accepted instead the *maius imperium* ("greater authority"), which meant that as proconsul, or provincial governor, he held authority over other proconsuls and could intervene in those provinces governed by the Senate. He now controlled both military and political institutions throughout the Empire.

The Senate's further grant of tribunician powers—as a patrician, he could not hold the office of tribune—reaped other benefits. He could initiate or veto legislation in the Senate and popular assemblies; he was immune from arrest or punishment; and he enjoyed the popular support generally accorded tribunes, traditionally the advocates of the people. As chief priest, he associated himself with the sacred rituals of republican Rome. He appointed priests conscientiously and saw to the construction of temples. Among them was one dedicated to his preferred deity, Apollo, whose temple and enormous statue he erected beside his modest palace on the Palatine Hill. Another he constructed for his adoptive father Caesar, who had recently been declared a god.

As Augustus laid the foundations of the imperial monarchy, an inattentive observer might have accepted the fiction that the Republic had indeed been temporarily restored. After a generation of civil war, the Senate and assemblies again met, issued

Imperial Power in the Words of Emperor Augustus and Tacitus

These passages provide two different views of Roman rule in the first century of the Empire. In the first, Augustus, the first of the emperors, describes his own significant achievements as a liberator, conqueror, and benefactor of the Roman people. In the second, in words imagined by the historian Tacitus, the leader of a British rebellion describes the Romans' insatiable greed and lust for conquest.

The emperor Augustus describes his achievements (c. 14 C.E.): 1. At the age of nineteen, on my own initiative and at my own expense, I raised an army by means of which I liberated the Republic, which was oppressed by the tyranny of a faction. ... 3. I waged many wars throughout the whole world by land and by sea, both civil and foreign, and when victorious I spared all citizens who sought pardon. ... About 500,000 Roman citizens were under military oath to me. ... 15. To the Roman plebs I paid 300 sesterces apiece in accordance with the will of my father; and in my fifth consulship, I gave each 400 sesterces in my own name out of the spoils of war; ... in my eleventh consulship I made twelve distributions of food out of grain purchased at my own expense. ... These largesses of mine reached never less than 250,000 persons. ... 17. Four times I came to the assistance of the treasury with my own money, transferring to those in charge of the treasury 150,000,000 sesterces. ... 20. I repaired the Capitol and the theater of Pompey with enormous expenditures on both works, without having my name inscribed on them. I repaired the conduits of the aqueducts which were falling into ruin in many places because of age. ... 34. In my sixth and seventh consulships, after I had put an end to the civil wars, having attained supreme power by universal consent, I transferred the state from my own power to the control of the Roman senate and people. For this service of mine I received the title of Augustus by decree of the senate. ...

(Augustus, *Res gestae divi Augusti*, nos. 1, 3, 15, 17, 20, 34; ed. N. Lewis, M. Reinhold 1966)

In words supplied by the historian Tacitus, Calgacus, leader of rebellious Britons, calls for resistance to Roman imperialism (c. 105–110 C.E.): When I consider the motives we have for fighting and the critical position we are in, I have a strong feeling that the united front you are showing today will mean the dawn of liberty for the whole of Britain. You have mustered to a man, and all of you are free. ... Out of sight of subject shores, we kept even our eyes free from the defilement of tyranny. We, the most distant dwellers upon earth, the last of the free, have been shielded till today by our very remoteness and by the obscurity in which it has shrouded our name. Now, the farthest bounds of Britain lie open to our enemies; and what men know nothing about they always assume to be a valuable prize. But there are no more nations beyond us; nothing is there but waves and rocks, and the Romans, more deadly still than these—for in them is an arrogance which no submission or good behaviour can escape. Pillagers of the world, they have exhausted the land by their indiscriminate plunder, and now they ransack the sea. A rich enemy excites their cupidity; a poor one, their lust for power. East and West alike have failed to satisfy them. They are the only people on earth to whose covetousness both riches and poverty are equally tempting. To robbery, butchery, and rapine, they give the lying name of "government"; they create a desolation and call it peace.

(Tacitus, *Agricola*, no. 30; ed. H. Mattingly, rev. S. A. Handford 1970)

decrees, and held elections. Over the next five centuries, however, these republican gestures were to fade to mere vestiges. They were already failing by the end of Augustus' reign. The Senate had usurped many functions of the unruly plebeian assemblies which had supported the Gracchi and later revolutionaries. Under Augustus, senatorial decrees acquired the force of law. The assemblies, ceding that function to the Senate, ceased to legislate after 98 C.E. Elections for the higher magistrates were also shifted from the assemblies to the less democratic Senate.

As republican institutions withered, Augustus created imperial ones. Secretaries, drawn from his own vast ranks of slaves and freedmen, kept accounts of his personal fortune—much greater than the ancient "Treasure of Saturn," the store of public wealth administered by the Senate (Saturn was father of the Roman gods). He placed the army under his control. Each of its 250,000 to 300,000 soldiers swore a personal oath to him. A separate Praetorian Guard of nine citizen **cohorts** kept close watch over Italy and Rome and in the immediate vicinity of the ruler.

In the provinces, imperial interests were managed by officials called procurators who were drawn from the secondary elite of the equestrian order (see Chapter 5). Newly created officials called prefects took responsibility for five key tasks: to head the ruler's personal military guard (the Praetorian Prefect); to manage the city of Rome (the Urban Prefect); to head the city's seven semi-military cohorts of police and fire forces; to monitor the city's grain supply; and to rule Egypt, Rome's breadbasket. Although the Urban Prefect was of senatorial status, all the other officials were equestrians.

His claim to have restored the Republic was a fiction, yet Augustus could legitimately claim many impressive achievements. Shortly before he died he described these in his *Res gestae* ("My Deeds"). "At the age of nineteen, ... I raised an army by means of which I liberated the Republic," claimed the aged emperor. He distributed largesse to the Roman plebs, funded the public treasury, built temples, and repaired aqueducts. He provided for shows in which gladiators fought (in the public arena for the entertainment of spectators) or wild beasts were butchered by the thousands. He drove out pirates and expanded the frontiers, established colonies of army veterans, and appropriated for Rome the wealth of the Nile.

His contemporaries loved Augustus for having restored peace. "The civil wars were ended after twenty years," wrote the historian Velleius Paterculus; "foreign wars suppressed, peace restored, the frenzy of arms everywhere lulled to rest. . . ." Cultivating that association, Augustus constructed the "Altar of Peace" in the Roman Forum. In this monument imperial imagery commingles with the sacred, expressing in stone the lofty message of an old man who, in his youth, had ravaged the people of Rome and murdered the leaders of the expiring Republic. One of the reliefs is shown below.

Emperors Good and Bad: Augustus to the Severi

Augustus saw his children and grandchildren die, and outlived two of his appointed heirs: his trusted comrade and son-in-law Marcus Vipsanius Agrippa (c. 63 B.C.E.–12 C.E.), and his beloved nephew, Marcus Claudius Marcellus (c. 42–23 B.C.E.). As he approached his own impending demise, the matter of succession loomed. By now there was no thought of relinquishing power; the Republic would never be truly restored. Augustus must be followed by another Augustus, of his extended family, if not of his own blood. The mantle fell on Tiberius (r. 14–37 C.E.): the son of Augustus' consort, Livia, by her first husband, a member of the Claudian clan.

To cement the relationship, Augustus grudgingly adopted Tiberius as son and heir, merging the ancient Julian and Claudian clans, his own and his wife's. In 14 C.E., upon Augustus' death at age seventy-six, Tiberius became emperor. Efficient, surly, and autocratic, Tiberius scaled down the citizen assemblies, bullied the Senate, and hoarded gold and silver for the imperial treasury. He also held the frontiers Augustus had attained and supervised his provincial administrators. If his personality had not been so frosty, and if his sexual eccentricities had not been so offensive, he might have been better liked. He was not, upon his death, made a god. Instead, the populace rejoiced, shouting "Into the Tiber with Tiberius."

The new emperor was Gaius (r. 37–41 C.E.), called "Caligula," or "little boot," a nickname from the days when he was an endearing child. As an adult, he was dangerous and probably insane. The soldiers of the Praetorian Guard murdered him, designating as successor the one surviving adult male of the Julio-Claudian line: the scholar Claudius (r. 41–54 C.E.). This elderly man, seemingly inept and chronically ill, nevertheless saw to the conquest of Britain, the construction of the lighthouse at the port of Ostia, and the creation of an imperial bureaucracy. He, too, was murdered: by his fourth wife, Agrippina (15–59 C.E.), a great-granddaughter of Augustus.

Agrippina promoted her own son Nero for the imperial title, even murdering Britannicus (Claudius' son by a previous marriage) to assure Nero's future. Her maneuvers met with due reward: Nero had her murdered, his soldiers ripping open the womb from which Nero had sprung. As mad as Caligula, Nero (r. 54–68 C.E.), let the now well-oiled machinery of empire churn on while he declaimed, strummed his lyre, and even leaped into the arena to contend, like the gladiators, with savage beasts. When a great fire destroyed much of Rome in 64 C.E., he blamed it on the Christians, thus launching the first major persecution of what was then a despised sect. Four years later, having aroused the opposition of the Praetorian Guard, he fled Rome, accompanied by his concubine and his nurse. These loyal servants assisted him to commit suicide and avoid assassination.

Imperial Power

Altar of Peace: *The emperors employed cultural as well as political strategies to announce and bolster their power, as seen here in objects associated with the successful emperors Augustus, Vespasian, and Trajan. In the marble-relief on the* Ara Pacis *("Altar of Peace"), Rome, 13–9 B.C.E., a mother goddess is surrounded by images of abundant fertility—the fruits of the peace won by Augustus.*

Imperial Philanthropy: *This detail from a relief on the triumphal arch erected in honor of Trajan in Benevento, 114–117 C.E., shows the emperor distributing gifts of food to the children of the poor.*

Five emperors had now reigned as descendants, if only indirectly, of Julius Caesar. Now the last of the Julio-Claudian dynasty was dead. In the absence of a legitimate heir to power, the legions were all too ready to provide for the succession. The four armies dispersed through the provinces selected four generals in turn as emperor in the single year 68–69 C.E.. As each emperor claimed the throne, only to be replaced by the next strong man, senators and ordinary citizens trembled in Rome.

The end of the "Year of the Four Emperors" found the last of them, the experienced and sensible Titus Flavius Vespasianus (r. 69–79 C.E.; anglicized as Vespasian) alive, secure, and in charge.

In the remaining ten years of his life, Vespasian enlarged the Senate with recruits from the provinces, favored skilled equestrians over freedmen in the bureaucracy, enriched the treasury, and tamed the dangerous security force Augustus had created, the Praetorian Guard. A relief after Caligula and Nero, this prudent penny-pincher shunned the glossy attributes of power. As he died, his whispered last words mocked the pretensions of his deified predecessors: "My, I think I am becoming a god." Vespasian had already arranged for the succession of his sons: his family or anarchy, he had warned the Senate. Vespasian's sons reigned in turn: Titus briefly (r. 79–81 C.E.), quickly followed by Domitian (r. 81–96 C.E.). Fascinated by his own power, Domitian was obsessed with possible conspiracies directed against him by the senators, whom he bullied and persecuted. Spies and informers, paid from the imperial purse, identified potential conspirators. Domitian compelled the Senate to participate in the prosecution of these alleged enemies of the state—and even to condemn the books they wrote. Jointly emperor and senators purged the ranks of the Senate, sending many to their deaths for "treason." Ironically, the autocrat who called for this bloodletting did not escape the fate he most feared. He, too, was murdered, by conspirators who had escaped the notice of imperial spies. The Senate moved quickly to appoint the next emperor in 96: a senator like themselves, an old man with no sons, the gentle and capable Nerva (r. 96–98 C.E.).

With Nerva began a series of five emperors who succeeded each other by a nondynastic principle over nearly a century (from 96 to 180 C.E.). Each appointed his successor during his lifetime. Nerva named the general Trajan (r. 98–117 C.E.). Trajan appointed his own cousin Hadrian (r. 117–138 C.E.). Hadrian reluctantly named the dutiful Antoninus (r. 138–161 C.E.), commanding Antoninus to adopt as his sons and joint successors the latter's nephew Marcus (later called Marcus Aurelius; r. 161–180 C.E.) and also Lucius Verus, the son of the candidate Hadrian would have preferred. Under these rulers, the Empire reached its maximum extent, its frontiers were fortified, trade flourished, the treasury swelled, the fusion of Greek and Roman culture was accomplished, and the city of Rome became more beautiful than ever. The Senate relaxed, unaware that its power had evaporated. The *pax romana* reached its zenith.

Marcus Aurelius was a philosopher as well as an emperor, and he ruled capably and diligently. Yet all his mental prowess could not avert the problems that befell Rome in the late second century. Barbarian tribes gnawed at Italy's northern frontier, while armies returning from the East brought a deadly plague to the capital—which could not be halted. Lucius Verus died in 169 C.E., and Marcus Aurelius proposed his own son Commodus to replace him.

It was a terrible mistake. An unstable megalomaniac who wished to be a gladiator, Commodus (r. 180–192 C.E.) became emperor on Marcus Aurelius' death in 180 C.E. and retained power for twelve years before he was strangled by an assassin. Two emperors reigned briefly, then the army intervened with its own candidate: the Punic general Septimius Severus (r. 193–211 C.E.). Severus was able, in a reign of nearly twenty years, to reassert Roman military strength at vulnerable border points and to rebuild the treasury, depleted by Commodus' excesses.

Severus was succeeded by three members of his Afro-Syrian family. The Severan dynasty ended in 235 C.E. with the murder of Alexander Severus and

WHO'S WHO

Principal Players in the Imperial Roman Succession

	Emperor	Dates	Reign
1	Augustus	63 B.C.E.–14 C.E.	27 B.C.E.–14 C.E.
2	Tiberius	42 B.C.E.–37 C.E.	14–37 C.E.
3	Vespasian	9–79 C.E.	69–79 C.E.
4	Antoninus Pius	86–161	138–161
5	Marcus Aurelius	121–180	161–180
6	Commodus	161–192	180–192
7	Septimius Severus	c. 145–211	193–211
8	Diocletian	245–313	284–305
9	Constantine	c. 285–337	312–337

his mother—the partner, if not the mastermind, of his reign and mother (so she claimed) of the "Armies, Senate, Fatherland, and whole Human Race."

Inside the Imperial Monarchy

By this time the Roman Republic was forgotten, its revival out of the question. For the second time in the history of the West, monarchy had replaced a government where the citizens—at least some of them—had ruled. Before his death in 323 B.C.E., Alexander had reintroduced monarchy to the world of the Greek *polis*. Augustus reintroduced it to Rome. For now, the experience of self-government was lost except in the books that recorded its history. Until the end of antiquity in the West, emperors ruled.

The emperor went through the formality of presenting his decrees to the Senate, which promptly approved them. Still sporting togas trimmed in purple, like their predecessors of republican days, the new class of senators was a shadow of the old. The old nobility had been ravaged by revolution and purges. Equestrians or provincials, the new senators were loyal to the monarch who promoted them. The emperor now ruled with the advice of a council of bureaucrats, mostly equestrian. From that class also came the officers of the army—from which, beginning in the mid-third century C.E., senators were barred.

Imperial administration lay in the hands of secretaries, accountants, and other bureaucrats who handled finances, letter-writing, minutes-taking, and record-keeping. Augustus' office staff was composed of his own slaves and freedmen. Claudius created a more elaborate bureaucracy, also staffed with freedmen of his household. Later emperors replaced Claudius' freedmen with equestrians. This bureaucracy was subdivided into departments like those of a modern state: finance, foreign affairs, domestic administration. As republican institutions deteriorated, this civil service managed the business of empire.

Law was a central concern of the Roman people. In the Republic, schoolboys had memorized the laws, legendarily inscribed on the Twelve Tables. Prospective senators were amateur lawyers who began their careers by testifying as character witnesses, defending family members, clients, or friends, or prosecuting a defendant charged with a private or public crime. Summaries of the legal issues involved in these cases and records of the precedents they established became the basis of later Roman law. To these were added senatorial edicts and laws voted in the assemblies. Private citizens called **jurisprudents** (men learned in the law but holding no official magistracy) advised private persons.

Under the emperors, law and lawmaking changed. New laws originated with the emperor and his council, not the Assembly or the Senate (who still ratified them). The jurisprudents were now professionals in the imperial bureaucracy, whose documentation and analysis of past decisions constituted a system of law. Imperial jurisprudents began the process of codification under Hadrian. Under Marcus Aurelius this resulted in a textbook of Roman law: the *Institutes*. Later experts under the Severan rulers created original new theories about the relation of civil law (***jus civile***) to the "law of nations" (*jus gentium*) and the "law of nature" (*jus naturale*) (see Chapters 17, 19). Modern thinkers would draw on these concepts to argue that some rights are universal and inalienable—the concept underlying all democratic constitutions.

The final codification of Roman law was achieved in the sixth century under the emperor Justinian in the *Corpus juris civilis* (*The Collected Civil Law*) which became a source of much of the law of the modern West (see Chapter 8). In this body of law as developed over the next 1000 years is distilled Rome's contribution to the world in the area of government.

The growing sophistication of the legal system coexisted with ancient patterns of monarchy. The emperors were worshiped as gods—in Rome only after their death (at first) but in the eastern provinces while living. The custom of king worship was a continuation of Hellenistic custom, in which kings were worshiped as benefactors: providers of protection, food, relief from taxes, or a new set of walls. They acquired surnames such as "savior" or "doer of good deeds" or "the god made manifest."

In Rome, the worship of the ruler was introduced tentatively. After his death, Julius Caesar was declared a god, a designation plausible to his subjects because his family was thought to be descended from the deities Mars and Venus. Still, some Romans resisted—as did Cicero, who scoffed at the **deification** of a man who had been buried by his family in the ordinary way. Such scruples soon disappeared. Augustus was worshiped in the East during his lifetime, and deified by the Senate at his death—one senator solemnly attesting that he had seen the deceased ascend to heaven. Domitian was addressed in his lifetime as "lord and god." The divinity of later emperors was celebrated in temples and sanctuaries throughout the realm. In the ceremony of **apotheosis**, the deification of a deceased emperor was announced by the release to the heavens of an eagle caged above the funeral pyre. Astonishingly, this rite continued to be practiced even for Christian emperors.

Under Augustus, all subjects and citizens swore loyalty to the emperor, pledging their own persons and calling down upon their children and their descendants "utter ruin and utter destruction" if they violated that pledge. The monarchization of Rome implicit was accomplished by the time of the Severan emperors. Individuals might act freely in their personal or economic lives. Only the emperor was free to participate in the political realm. The Empire—Augustus' new *imperium*—bestowed a hollow peace on Rome: one disguising the loss of civic freedom. It was a sad benefit to confer upon a people whose history had begun with the expulsion of a tyrant.

UPPER CLASSES AND OTHER CLASSES

In the social realm, as well as the political, the imperial regime brought both advantages and drawbacks. On the one hand, the old senatorial elite suffered terribly under the emperors, both from direct and concerted repression and from a long-term waning of influence. On the other, a new elite of equestrian entrepreneurs found a role in the imperial bureaucracy alongside its already established position in commerce and public contracting.

Social opportunities also improved for other, less privileged Romans. The status of elite women, of children, and of slaves improved slightly. The ranks of "freed" persons, male and female, increased, and also fed the rolls of new citizens, once their own children, one generation removed from slavery, claimed their right of full citizenship. Now extended to larger and larger groups outside Rome and even outside Italy, citizenship meant little politically—the right to vote being meaningless under an increasingly authoritarian monarchy. But it did enhance status and bestow commercial privileges. And for those citizens who lived in the capital, it also conferred the right to free grain and free and lurid entertainments.

Senators and Equestrians

The emergence of the imperial monarchy most severely affected the members of the old senatorial order. While members of this elite faced declining opportunities, other Romans of the equestrian order actually experienced a rise in status.

The Senate's deliberations, debates, and divisions still filled the long hours, but the conclusions were predetermined: they would be those that the master wished. The memory of their decimation during the years of civil war discouraged any senatorial initiative. To defy the emperor was to be vulnerable to a charge of *laesa maiestas*, "injured majesty": it was considered a capital crime even to criticize the ruler.

The demoralized nobility embarked on its own extinction: unable to resist the advance of imperial power, the senators were not even able to reproduce themselves. Their population dwindled. Few married, or they divorced; or if they married, they remained childless. The practice of celibacy may have caused this sterility, or more probably the widespread practice of birth control, or the equally widespread exposure of unwanted infants.

To staunch the hemorraging of the senatorial ranks, Augustus proposed over the period from 18 B.C.E. to 9 C.E. a package of laws extending special privileges to upper-class fathers of children. Acknowledging that children were a financial burden—boys requiring an expensive education and allowances commensurate with their rank, girls needing dowries—Augustus offered cash bonuses, tax exemptions, and opportunities for political advancement to aristocratic fathers. Conversely, childless men were penalized, and unmarried heirs heavily taxed. Elite women with three or more children were fully emancipated—free, that is, to handle all property transactions without a male guardian as intermediary. Augustus' legislation extended to the private sexual behavior of the upper classes as he attempted to promote traditional models of family life as shown in *Witnesses* on p. 146. Heretofore adultery (defined exclusively as the wife's violation of marriage vows) had been punished within the family, at the discretion of the *paterfamilias*. Now it became a crime: one that implicated many upper-class matrons and their partners. Married men who engaged in sex outside marriage were free of the charge of adultery, so long as their lovers were of a lower social class. Any male, married or unmarried, who engaged in sex with an unmarried woman of the elite was guilty of *stuprum*, or "fornication": a new criminal offense. Augustus' moral zeal was unrelenting. He exiled his daughter and his granddaughter, both bearing the distinguished clan name of Julia, for adultery.

Augustus' pro-family legislation failed. Augustus himself died with no direct heir of his own blood, as did many of his successors. Domitian and Septimius Severus attempted to revive Augustus' legislation, with equally poor results. Their attempts could not promote the biological survival of the nobility or check its flight from politics. Its place would be filled by new men filtering up from lower social ranks.

Family Values in Imperial Rome

How people in the past felt about their families and loved ones is difficult to assess —even in the case of the Romans, for whom we have rich literary, historical, and legal sources. The four excerpts here give a glimpse of the private world in a society that sometimes seems very like, sometimes very remote, from our own. In the first, the historian Suetonius describes the laws made by Augustus to promote and preserve families. The second reveals the sentiments of an upper-class author, Pliny the Younger, towards his wife. The third, by the poet Juvenal, reflecting the sophisticated lives of elite Romans, mocks women and marriage both. The fourth is from the law codes issued by the much later emperor Theodosius, whose Christian outlook is displayed in legislation against the sale of children.

The emperor Augustus tries to strengthen families with new legislation (c. 9 C.E.): He revised existing laws and enacted some new ones, for example, on extravagance, on adultery and chastity, on bribery, and on the encouragement of marriage among the various classes of citizens. Having made somewhat more stringent changes in the last of these than in the others, he was unable to carry it out because of an open revolt against its provisions, until he had abolished or mitigated a part of the penalties. ... When the knights even then persistently called for its repeal at a public show, he sent for the children of [the popular hero] Germanicus and exhibited them, some in his own lap and some in their father's, intimating by his gestures and expression that they should not refuse to follow that young man's example. And on finding that the spirit of the law was being evaded by betrothal with immature girls and by frequent changes of wives, he shortened the duration of betrothals and set a limit on divorce.
(Suetonius, *De Vita Caesarum*, 34; trans. J. C. Rolfe, 1920)

Pliny the Younger writes lovingly to his wife (c. 100 C.E.): Never have I chafed more impatiently under my engagements which have prevented me from accompanying you on your journey to Campania to convalesce and from following immediately after you. For at this moment I particularly want to be with you; I want to believe the evidence of my eyes and see what you are doing to look after your strength and your little self, whether in fact you are enjoying to the full the peace and the pleasures and the richness of the place. ... I beg you therefore all the more earnestly to be kind to my fears and to send me a letter, or even two letters, every day. While I am reading it, I shall worry less: when I have finished it, my fears will at once return.
(Pliny the Younger, *Letters*; ed. R. H. Barrow, 1949)

Satirist Juvenal urges a friend not to marry (c. 120 C.E.):
... Postumus, are you *really*
Taking a wife? You used to be sane enough ...
Why endure such bitch-tyranny when rope's
  available
By the fathom, when all those dizzying top-floor
  windows
Are open for you, when there are bridges handy
To jump from? Supposing none of these exits
  catches
Your fancy, isn't it better to sleep with a pretty boy?
Boys don't quarrel all night, or nag you for little
  presents
While they're on the job. ...
(Juvenal, *Satire* 6)

The law code under Emperor Theodosius bans the sale of children (383 C.E.): XI.xvii.1: A law shall be written on bronze or waxed tablets or on linen cloth, and posted throughout all the municipalities of Italy, to restrain the hands of parents from infanticide. ... [I]f any parent should report that he has offspring which on account of poverty he is unable to rear, there shall be no delay in issuing food and clothing, since the rearing of a new-born infant can not tolerate a delay. ... XI.xvii.2: We have learned that provincials suffering from scarcity of food and lack of sustenance are selling or pledging their children. Therefore, if any such person is found who is sustained by no substance of family possessions and is supporting his children with hardship and difficulty, he shall be assisted through our fisc before he becomes a prey to calamity. ... For it is repugnant to our customs to allow any person to be destroyed by hunger or rush forth to the commission of a shameful deed.
(Theodosian Code, 11:27:1–2; ed. N. Lewis, M. Reinhold, 1966)

Equestrians, meanwhile, who under the Republic had performed valuable services as publicans and entrepreneurs, now participated in the imperial bureaucracy and council, and in intelligence and diplomatic and fiscal services. They might be employed as accountants in the provinces, or hold one of the prefectures created by the emperor, or serve as officers in the army. From Italians and provincials of equestrian rank the emperors also replenished the ranks of the Senate.

Wives, Mothers, and Children

The senatorial and equestrian orders made up the class designated *honestior* ("more honorable") by Roman law (see Chapter 5). Women of this social class were granted extraordinary freedom in the early Empire—resembling in their status, but exceeding in privilege, even the upper-class women of the Hellenistic East. The form of marriage by which a woman passed from her father's to her husband's authority—marriage with *manus*—had been replaced by a form of free marriage. Women who married remained theoretically under the authority of their father or guardian, who retained supervision of the dowry wealth that wives brought their husbands. Thus women possessed (if only through male relatives) an independence conferred by wealth that they had not known in earlier eras. Augustus' "law concerning children," moreover, liberated elite women who had borne at least three legitimate children from all restrictions of guardianship.

Romans developed a concept of companionate marriage similar to the modern one, in which spouses are seen as loving partners. The biographer Plutarch (c. 50–120 C.E.) considered married love the highest form of friendship. The author Pliny the Younger (c. 61–112 C.E.) vividly expressed in his letters to his wife his great affection for her (see *Witnesses*, p. 146)—an affection implicit in his sharing with her the drafts of his works, for her comment. A greater respect for wives may explain the extension of the concept of the family to include relatives on the wife's side (cognates) as well as those in the male or agnate line.

Old restraints and new freedoms characterized the lives of upper-class wives. On the one hand, they were largely confined to their homes, where they were still expected to spend much of their time spinning—and in epitaphs and letters, many women were congratulated for their excellent work with wool! On the other hand, some matrons were active in public life, attending banquets and literary readings, where they might even discourse on philosophy or recite their own poems. Less gifted women might accompany their husbands to the games and races and mock battles in the Colosseum, proclaiming their status in society with the brilliance of their jewels.

A widow was expected to wait ten months after a spouse's death before remarriage (widowers didn't have to wait at all). The widow who renounced remarriage was more greatly honored. Such women were rare. More is heard of the lively widows preferred as lovers by young aristocrats.

During the Empire, divorce was easy and common. Either partner could divorce the other by repudiation: one merely informed the other of the step. Upon divorce, women (or their families) reclaimed their dowries. Among the ranks of the divorced were Julius Caesar, Pompey, Cicero, Augustus, Tiberius, and Nero; and divorce reached epidemic proportions in the generations thereafter. Some women, remarked the philosopher Seneca (c. 3 B.C.E.–65 C.E.), reckoned the year not by the names of the consuls (as was traditional) but by those of their husbands.

The wives and mothers of emperors, often echoing the pattern of Hellenistic queens, enjoyed fame and power. Livia, Augustus' wife for fifty-two years, received the title "Augusta" and was deified by her grandson Claudius. She helped groom her son Tiberius for power. Agrippina, wife and murderer of Claudius, promoted her own son Nero. Trajan's wife, Plotina, may have engineered the succession of his cousin Hadrian, a great favorite of hers whom she continued to advise. Her influence was acknowledged in Hadrian's funeral oration for the dynamic empress: "She often made requests of me," declared the emperor, "and I never once refused her anything."

The four Julias of the Severan dynasty—the wife of Septimius Severus, her sister, and her two daughters—were stalwart women. The first survived her husband to wield the power behind the throne of their son Caracalla—after the latter had murdered her other son as she held him in her arms. This capable woman managed the treasury, attempted government reform, encouraged religious tolerance, and patronized both philosophy and law. After her son Caracalla's assassination in 217 C.E., she starved herself to death. She was soon avenged by her sister, who engineered the succession in turn of her two grandsons: the bizarre Elagabalus (who took the name of the Asian solar deity he favored) and the docile Alexander Severus, both closely monitored by their mothers.

The efforts of highly placed mothers for the advancement of their sons is one small part of the story of family life in imperial Rome. Similar behavior is found in nonimperial families. The mother of Saint Augustine (354–430 C.E.), Monica (a devout Christian, who also achieved sainthood), groomed him for a career in the civil service, praying both for his soul and for his professional success. The author Seneca discoursed on philosophy with his mother, Helvetia, who had been forbidden by her husband to study that lofty subject. Such glimpses of maternal initiative suggest, at least among the elite, close ties between mothers and sons.

Among the elites, nurses, too, may have played a significant role in the lives of young Romans. The nurse began as a wet nurse: a woman who, having recently borne a child herself, was lactating and available to provide nourishment to other women's infants. She did so, if she were free, for a price. More often, she was a slave. Frequently, she was Greek-speaking, which was desirable, as the child would thereby easily learn the language considered, for its cultural value, superior to Latin.

Wet nurses often stayed with the household for years, continuing to nurture and support the young children whom they had once nourished. With what feelings the nurse contemplated the child who was her social superior, who had replaced her own offspring (by compulsion of poverty or slavery) in her life, can only be guessed. In a few cases, adult Romans expressed their profound affection for the nurses who had raised them.

Upper-class Roman men treasured their daughters. They became close to their daughters' husbands, and often preferred the children of their daughters to

WINDOWS ON

Private Lives

Not only the deeds of emperors, but also the personal relations of ordinary people are recorded in Roman monuments. This tomb sculpture (left) shows a freedman (center) with his wife and child (left). The child is called her father's "delight" in the inscription below the figures. This relief (right) of a well-known merchant depicts the merchant's shop, with five standing clerks (including one woman, a slave, shown in profile) and two seated customers. The funerary relief (below right) shows a man holding a portrait bust. (left: Deutsches Archaeologisches Institut; right: Uffizi, Florence; below, Villa Albani, Rome)

Funerary relief of Sextitius Selprimus, Rome, first century C.E.

Funerary relief, Rome, first century C.E.

Funerary relief, Rome, mid–1st century C.E.

To continue your investigation of this topic, please go to www.prenhall.com/king for the related WINDOWS on the WEB activity

On Education and Oratory

Whereas Cicero, Livy, and Virgil were deeply immersed in politics during the last years of the Republic, cultural life in the first century of the Empire became more detached from the political realm, and at the same time both more varied and more legislated. The orator Quintilian became a schoolmaster, who taught young Romans the fundamentals of rhetoric and wrote a book on the topic, the source of the first of the first passage here. His contemporary, the historian Tacitus, laments the loss of political freedom that had permitted the originality and spontaneity of an older generation of orators.

Quintilian on children's potential to learn (c. 90 C.E.): I would, therefore, have a father conceive the highest hopes of his son from the moment of his birth. If he does so, he will be the more careful about the groundwork of his education. For there is absolutely no foundation for the complaint that but few men have the power to take in the knowledge that is imparted to them, and that the majority are so slow of understanding that education is a waste of time and labor. On the contrary, you will find that most are quick to reason and ready to learn. ... Those who are dull and unteachable are as abnormal as prodigious births and monstrosities and are but few in number. ... But, it will be urged, there are differing degrees of intellectual ability. Undoubtedly, I reply, and there will be a corresponding variation in actual accomplishment; but that there are any who gain nothing from education, I absolutely deny.

(Quintilian, *The Elements of Oratory*, 1:1–3; eds. N. Lewis, M. Reinhold 1966)

Tacitus explains why oratory flags when dictators rule (c. 90 C.E.): Great oratory is like a flame: it needs fuel to feed it, movement to fan it, and it brightens as it burns. At Rome too the eloquence of our forefathers owed its development to the same conditions. For although the orators of today have also succeeded in obtaining all the influence that it would be proper to allow them under settled, peaceable, and prosperous political conditions, yet their predecessors in those days of unrest and unrestraint seemed to accomplish more when, in the general ferment and without the strong hand of a single ruler, a speaker's political wisdom was measured by his power of carrying conviction to the unstable populace. ... [A]s long as the constitution was unsettled, so long as the country kept wearing itself out with factions and dissensions and disagreements, so long as there was no peace in the Forum, no harmony in the senate, no restraint in the courts, no respect for authority ... the growth of eloquence was doubtless sturdier just as untilled soil produces certain vegetation in greater luxuriance. But the benefit derived from the eloquence of the Gracchi did not make up for what the country suffered from their laws, and too dearly did Cicero pay by the death he died for his renown in oratory.

(Tacitus, *Dialogue on Oratory*, 36–40; eds. N. Lewis, M. Reinhold 1966)

those of their sons. The harsh paternal authority of the early Republic had faded. Boys, too, were freer of the paternal yoke in the imperial centuries. A father could not sell into slavery a son he had acknowledged as his own, and the killing of a son was seen as murder, the equivalent of killing a parent. Still, the boy remained economically subject to his father for many years, not acceding to full adulthood until his father's death—an event sometimes anxiously awaited as the springboard to financial and personal autonomy.

As in Greece, there were more boys than girls, more men than women—that different sex ratio indicating the widespread elimination of females in all classes, by exposure, by the preferential feeding of males, and as a result of young women's death in childbirth or as a result of abortion. Throughout the Empire, it was rare for a family to have more daughters than sons. Children of both sexes born out of wedlock, ill, or deformed, were regularly exposed. Indeed, children must have been exposed in quantity to explain the widespread childlessness of adults, to which both histories and epitaphs of the rich and poor attest. The high incidence of child mortality is not sufficient to do so.

"Exposure" consisted of abandoning children in public places: typically, on heaps of garbage or dung. Here they might die of hunger and cold. Alternatively, they might be picked up by ordinary folk or professional slavedealers. In the former case, the "adopted" child became an **alumnus** of the family—not a true child but a valued servant trained in the skills necessary to assist the household economy. Epitaphs testify to the great number of these *alumni* (more often male than female), many cherished by their surrogate parents. The child's status was theoretically determined by that of his biological mother—free or slave—but was often unknown because of the silence of the dungheap. If a slave, or presumed a slave, the child could be freed (manumitted), but never, having begun life in the womb of a slave, legally adopted. If picked up by the slavedealer, a foundling of either sex would be sold as a servant or laborer or to the brothel manager as a prostitute.

The lot of children improved in the later Empire. Domitian prohibited the castration and prostitution of children. From the reign of his successor, Nerva, until that of Septimius Severus, a system of relief for poor children, funded by the profits on low-interest loans, maintained at least 5000 children at a time in some 40 Italian cities. By the late third century, the abandonment of a child was considered an act of murder. In the late Empire, under Christian influence, infanticide and abortion were harshly condemned.

The condition of children, especially their vulnerability to abandonment, touches on two other aspects of private life in Rome: misogyny and homosexuality. The lesser value of women is witnessed by the presumed rate of female infanticide. The hatred of women (expressed in the literature of the aristocracy) reached a peak in the imperial centuries at the same time, ironically, as they achieved their greatest freedom. Meanwhile, the practice of male homosexuality (so central to Greek culture) became more prevalent—reflecting, among other factors, the easy availability of young male slaves and *alumni*.

Freedmen, Slaves, and the Poor

The circumstances of birth determined to which half of Roman society a child would belong. The few children of the legitimate marriages of members of the elites belonged to the class of *honestiores* (the "more honorable"). The many children of the legitimate marriages of the poor, the children of concubinage relationships, and the children of slaves all indiscriminately belonged to the class of the *humiliores* ("more humble"). From the second century, these two social groups acquired legal definition, adding to the preexisting social distinctions between free and slave, citizen and noncitizen. *Honestiores* and *humiliores* were treated differently in civil and criminal cases. Penalties such as torture, condemnation to the mines, crucifixion, or consignment to the wild beasts of the arena were reserved for humbler folk.

The *humiliores* included three groups: freedmen (and freedwomen), slaves, and the plebs (poor but free citizens). Of these, freedmen held the highest position in Roman society. It was a class made up of freed slaves who, uniquely in the ancient world, became citizens without taint in the second generation. Freedman status lasted only a generation; even then the freedman had only partial citizen rights. A freedman's children and grandchildren were free to enter into Roman society at any level to which their skills could bring them. They could intermarry with other Roman citizens. By the second century, many senators and equestrians numbered among their family, a mere one or two generations back, a freedman ancestor—and in the previous generation a slave.

Freedmen were numerous and powerful. Although they constituted only about 5 percent of Rome's total population, they were especially visible because their industry and zeal rewarded them with wealth and status. Their numbers swelled from the rapid rate of manumission—explainable perhaps by the fact that highly motivated freedman artisans were more valuable to upper-class families than slaves. So common became the practice of manumission that the slave population in the city of Rome declined rapidly. Augustus attempted to stem the tide of manumissions (although he also opposed the abuse of slaves). Yet the freedman population continued to grow, filling the ranks of the shopkeepers and artisans and their collegial organizations.

Since few women practiced as artisans or had any trade beyond spinning and weaving, they were less likely to be manumitted. However, a freedwoman who subsequently bore at least four children gained the legal status of a freeborn woman and economic independence. For women of both classes, high fertility opened up an avenue to higher economic status.

Freedmen continued after manumission to have special ties to former owners, resembling the traditional Roman tie between client and patron. They took on the clan name of those owners, and visited them on a daily basis to offer their homage. Should the noble family die without heirs, it was the family's freedmen who were pledged to carry on the worship of its ancestors. If a noble family faced extinction because of a lack of children, a possible remedy was to adopt the child of a family freedman—but not the freedman himself, or the freedwoman, for he or she had been born a slave. The freedman, indeed, might have to free his own child, if that child were born to a slave concubine, and await grandchildren if he wished for progeny with full citizen status. A freedman lived more often with women in concubinage than in legitimate marriage, whether the woman was slave, freed, or freeborn.

The possibility of manumission offered hope to skilled slaves. Most urban slaves were artisans, producers of goods for local consumption and export. They received an allowance from their masters (rather than a wage) in compensation for their labor. While city slaves looked to manumission, the slaves who had worked on the land were replaced by poor tenant farmers called ***coloni***. Rome still housed many slaves—some working as domestic servants in the houses of the rich or imperial families, others pressed into prostitution or trained as gladiators. But increasingly their offspring joined the society of freedmen.

Legislation introduced by Augustus, Claudius, Domitian, Hadrian, Antoninus Pius, and others attended to the protection of slaves. If sick and neglected by their masters, they were to be manumitted; if they were mistreated, their masters would be charged before the urban prefect of Rome. They were not to be castrated for use in brothels, sold into prostitution or into the gladiatorial schools, nor executed by the sole judgment of their masters without a confirming investigation by the proper authorities.

Still the condition of a slave was low. Slaves called as witnesses were examined under torture: how else could one guarantee the truth of their testimony?

Lives of Slaves and Masters

Underlying the patterns of social life was the institution of slavery. Here the philosopher Seneca, with a very modern outlook, notes that "slavery" can be seen as an existential, as well as a social condition (no great consolation to the slave). Pliny the Younger tells the story of a wealthy man's murder by his slaves, which, without comment, raises questions about the justice, or at least the viability, of the institution of slavery.

Philosopher Seneca discourses on slavery, and finds character to be the real determinant of the human condition (c. 60 C.E.): Remember, if you please, that the man you call slave sprang from the same seed, enjoys the same daylight, breathes like you, lives like you, dies like you. You can as easily conceive him a free man as he can conceive you a slave. ... Treat your slave with compassion, even with courtesy; admit him to your conversation, your planning, your society. Here the genteel will protest loudly and unanimously, "Nothing could be more degrading or disgusting!" ... "What is the upshot? Am I to bring all slaves to my table?" No more than all free men. But if you imagine I would exclude some because their work is dirty, that muleteer for example, or that cowhand, you are mistaken. I value them not by their jobs but by their character; a man gives himself his own character, accident allots his job. ... "He is a slave!" But perhaps a free man in spirit. "He is a slave!" Shall that count against him? Show me a man who is not; one is a slave to lust, another to greed, another to ambition, all to fear. ... Voluntary slavery is the meanest of all.
(Seneca, *Moral Epistles*, no. 47; ed. M. Hadas 1956)

Pliny the Younger narrates the incident of slaves who killed their master (c. 90 C.E.): Here is the terrible story ... of how Larcius Macedo, a man of praetorian rank, was treated by his slaves. To be sure, he was a haughty and cruel master, who remembered too little—or rather, only too well—that his own father was once a slave. He was bathing at his villa near Formiae. Suddenly slaves surrounded him, one seized him by the throat, another struck him in the face, another pommeled him on the chest, the stomach, and even, shocking to relate, on the private parts; and when they thought he was lifeless, they threw him onto the hot floor, to see if he was alive. He, either unconscious or pretending to be, lay stretched out and motionless, giving the impression that death was complete. Then, finally, they carried him out as if he had fainted with the heat. Faithful slaves received him, and his concubines rushed up, wailing and shrieking. ... [H]e opened his eyes and moved his body to show, since it was now safe, that he was alive. ... He himself was with difficulty kept alive a few days, and did not die without the consolation of revenge.
(Pliny the Younger, *Letters*, 3:14; eds. N. Lewis, M. Reinhold 1966)

Stewards of households or villas were almost always slaves: unlike free citizens, they could, under torture, be made to confess to embezzlement. Slaves, unable to contract legitimate marriages, could have neither wives nor children. Female slaves more often escaped the horrendous conditions of the fields and the mines, but in other ways they suffered as much as males. Their skills were largely limited to domestic tasks and textile production. Consequently, their labor was less valued. Market values reflect that fact. Female slaves cost less: in the time of Emperor Diocletian (243–313 C.E.) about two-thirds to three-fourths the price of a man.

Roman households had fewer female than male slaves. Those few were considered sexually available to their masters (as were, indeed, young males). They were frequently (perhaps because of their many pregnancies) sold away from the master's family. If so, they were forced to leave their own children—who were considered slaves, whatever the status of their fathers, having been carried in the womb of a slave. Many were sold into prostitution, or to the inns and cookshops whose unskilled female servants were amateur prostitutes. Taverns and brothels were the bleak reservoir of unfree Roman women.

One class of Roman citizens enjoyed untrammeled freedom, if little wealth. These were the Roman citizens who made up the city's underclass: the plebs, meaning "people," or even "mob." As in the Republic, citizenship gave the plebs the right to vote, however meaningless that might now be. The plebs had done little but grow since the time of the Gracchi, when cheap, subsidized grain was first made available. Now the grain was free, and the citizens were no longer motivated to work—an activity considered better left to lower status people: slaves and freedmen. Some 200,000 to 250,000 male citizens received the daily gift of grain, which supported (when one adds women and children) more than half the urban population of about one million.

Not only did the plebs count on the distribution of grain, but they insisted as well (if the rulers wished no riots) on increasingly gaudy and frequent entertainments. Their idleness left them available for the many entertainments offered throughout the year. Performances of mime and the chariot races in the Circus Maximus were especially popular. So were the blood sports: gladiatorial combats often pursued to the death and "hunts" in which wild beasts, kept hungry for the occasion, tore at each other or at the bodies of condemned men and women sent into the arena. Did a people who had gained world leadership because of an exceptional capacity for violence require staged displays of contrived violence to retain their sense of control?

Such events were the prime attraction of the Colosseum, shown below, which was erected in 80 C.E. on the site of the hated Nero's palace. They continued to fascinate the Romans into the Christian era. "He saw the blood and he gulped down savagery," wrote Saint Augustine of one of his contemporaries who became a leader of the new church. For the urban poor, such pleasures were counted among the chief benefits of living in Rome. "The people which once bestowed imperium, fasces [symbols of authority], legions, everything, now forgoes such activities and has but two passionate desires: bread and circus games," observed the satirist Juvenal (c. 60–130 C.E.).

The dispossession of the plebs, stripped of an active political role, like the humiliation of the senators, served the interests of the imperial monarchy. At the same time, the regime's patronage of equestrians, the promotion of freedmen, and the easing of the reins on some of the most disadvantaged—women, children, and slaves—made the epoch of the *pax romana* one of social opportunity as well as of decline.

THE CULTURE OF IMPERIAL ROME

Roman culture reached its apex in the era of the *pax romana*. The city of Rome acquired new spaciousness and splendor, befitting its status as the foremost city of the civilized world. The system of roads, sewers, and aqueducts begun in the Republic now served ample domestic residences, both utilitarian and palatial, and numerous public buildings: baths, colonnades, and amphitheaters, all embellished with statues, arches, and columns. Digesting the inheritance of Greek literature, Roman literature flourished. Trained in Greek and Latin letters, in rhetoric and philosophy, educated Romans enjoyed Latin epics and plays, treatises and speeches, in which Greek forms were adapted to Roman cultural requirements. Yet this florescence was increasingly tinged by a tone of despair, reflecting political demoralization and the threat of invasion by hostile tribes.

Buildings and Waterways

During its first four centuries, Rome was a modest city. Its circuit of walls, embracing the seven hills, was intersected by the Sacred Way, which led from the Forum to the temple of Jupiter on the Capitoline Hill. In the last decades of the Republic, the city's spaces expanded, boasted more buildings and sprouted adornments. Scattered throughout the open spaces were Greek statues, both originals brought from Greece and Sicily and copies made by Roman artisans. The great fire of 64 C.E. destroyed much of the city's center and created space for more building ventures, among them the Colosseum.

Intensive building began with Pompey and Caesar. The former added a theater seating 40,000 people, and the latter began improvements to the Forum. Augustus completed Caesar's projects and added a panoply of temples to the city's fabric. He boasted that he had found Rome a city of brick and left it a city of marble. Already the largest city in the Mediterranean world, Rome became the most splendid.

The emperor Trajan added his own forum, adjacent to those areas already constructed, which overpowered them in grandeur. Completed between 109 and 113 C.E., it consisted of a covered area bounded by a **basilica**, or public assembly hall, and two libraries—one dedicated to Latin and the other to Greek texts. The semicircular plans of the latter echoed the form

Roman Monuments

The Colosseum: *Under the emperors, Rome sprouted arches and columns, temples and theaters, palaces and bathhouses. The Colosseum, built 72–80 C.E. on the site of the hated Nero's palace, housed many of the gladiatorial contests and races so popular with members of all classes. The interior of the surviving structure shows the basement pens and passageways.*

Temple of Mars Ultor: *From the Roman Forum, a complex built up from republican through imperial times, are shown (left) the ruins of the Temple of Mars Ultor, late first century* B.C.E., *and a drawing (below) depicting how the Temple would have appeared.*

of the scrolls within. They were adorned with busts of great authors of the past. The central space of Trajan's Forum was punctuated by a marble column almost 90 feet (27 m.) high, commemorating the emperor's campaigns in Dacia (modern Romania), the culmination of Rome's military expansion.

While temples and palaces beautified the city (see above and pp. 170 and 171), the Romans' genius for practical building works and their synthesis of form and function were best displayed by their system of aqueducts and sewers shown on Map 6.1. This system was almost as old as Rome itself. Some of the sewers, including the famous Cloaca Maxima, began as Etruscan drainage tunnels. The first aqueducts, which piped fresh water from the countryside to the city, dated from the fourth century B.C.E. By the reign of Augustus, eleven had been constructed. His lieutenant Agrippa added three more, along with 700 basins and 500 fountains. Agrippa also upgraded the sewers, which he explored, it is said, by boat.

Hundreds of miles of aqueducts brought water into the city, supplying public drinking fountains and baths; the overflow was diverted into the sewers. The baths, which contained a series of pools at different temperatures, were more than an aid to cleanliness. They were social and recreational centers.

Baths, aqueducts, and sewers, the Forum, and the Colosseum served all groups in the population. In contrast, domestic building reflected the gulf between *honestiores* and *humiliores*. The urban poor lived in tenements several stories high, shoddily built, inadequately supplied with light, air, heat, or water (only the ground floor benefited from the public water supply), vulnerable to fire. Each tenement building generally featured, on the ground floor, shops open to the street. Above were warrens of apartments consisting of featureless rooms without baths or kitchens. In the fourth century, Rome is said to have contained more than 46,000 of these tenements, in contrast to fewer than 2000 homes of the rich.

The wealthy lived in private town houses similar to the ones shown in *Windows On* on p. 155. These were one story high and built around a central courtyard, called an **atrium**, lit by a roof opening. Stables and storage rooms, servants' rooms and baths, dining rooms and bedrooms served the functions of the household. One house was not enough; a rich man might own several. "Say where I may call upon you, say in what quarter I may look for you," the poet Martial implored one of his wealthy patrons, as the latter circulated among his establishments.

A City, an Empire, a World

Other nations had boundaries, wrote the poet Ovid, but Rome was "*urbs et orbis idem*"—at the same time one city and the whole world. During the early Empire, Rome had a population of about one million—superseding Alexandria as the largest city in the Mediterranean world. Of its residents, many were non-Roman and even non-Italian foreigners. About 400,000 were slaves.

In the time of Augustus, Italy had a population of four or five million Roman citizens, plus two to three million slaves. At Rome's zenith (around 200 C.E.), the population of the whole Empire—slave, citizen, and free—was about 50 million. Although most lived on the land, we know more about those who dwelled in cities. The Roman Empire was a network of cities, at whose center stood the capital city itself.

The Hellenistic cities of the East—such as Alexandria, Antioch, Carthage, Ephesus, Smyrna, and Pergamum—were nodes of Roman power. To these established centers were added new cities in Italy and in the western provinces of Europe and Africa. In these latter regions, veteran colonies or army camps might form the nuclei of cities where none had existed before. New or old, the cities of the Empire modeled themselves on Rome. The Greek cities added Roman basilicas and baths to their centers, already packed with gymnasia, theaters, and marketplaces. The new cities of the Empire were equipped with amphitheaters, forums, and temples, basilicas, baths, and aqueducts funded by the local aristocracy or by imperial largesse. Each city (a large one counted between 100,000 and 200,000 citizens) had its own magistrates and justice system, its own assembly, elections, and charter.

The Empire adopted the Hellenistic commercial system, itself derived from ancient patterns of trade. Pots from Greece, Italy, and now Gaul traveled throughout the Mediterranean. So did olive oil from Spain, Italy, and Greece; wheat from Sicily, Egypt, and the Black Sea; wine from Gaul, Italy, and Greece; minerals from Spain and Britain; spices and perfumes, ivory and silk from the Middle East, India, and China.

Neither the commodities nor the techniques of production changed under the Empire. Yet the volume of trade increased. A web of paths and roads and sea routes, shown on Map 6.2, linked large and small localities into one Eurasian world—prefiguring the global village we inhabit today. On land and by sea, camels and sailboats directed by Roman, Greek, Arab, Persian, Indian, and Chinese entrepreneurs carried goods east and west across the great expanse from Spain to the Far East. Roman merchandise and coins reached the interior of Arabia, India, the Malay peninsula, Vietnam, China. A representative of emperor Marcus Aurelius reached the Chinese court in the second century.

Most commerce was seaborne. Indian and even Chinese ships traveled the Red Sea; from Red Sea and Persian Gulf ports, more than 100 ships per year loaded with goods from the Mediterranean and the African and European hinterlands took sail for India. Within two or three months, a ship could travel from Rome to Carthage, Alexandria, Antioch, or Ephesus. More ships carried more goods around the Mediterranean and nearby waterways in the late Republic and early Empire than at any time for the next 1000 years. (From the third century Italy's exports decreased as its colonies became more self-sufficient.) The commercial system of the late Roman world endured into the modern era, when it was outpaced by new systems centered on the Atlantic and Pacific oceans.

Land travel was slow (20 to 40 miles [32–64 km.] per day was an achievement) and not always safe. The roads themselves, however, were excellent. Roman roads linked the capital to the farthest outposts of the Empire, facilitating rapid communications and the transport of armies and military supplies.

Roman infrastructure: *In addition to freestanding monuments, Roman engineers designed aqueducts, roads, and bridges that extended throughout the empire, structures unsurpassed until recent times, as beautiful as they were functional. Seen here is the splendid aqueduct bridging the River Gardon, known as the Pont du Gard, near Nîmes, France.*

Pont du Gard, Nîmes, late first century B.C.E.

WINDOWS ON

Lifestyles of the Wealthy: Villa and Townhouse

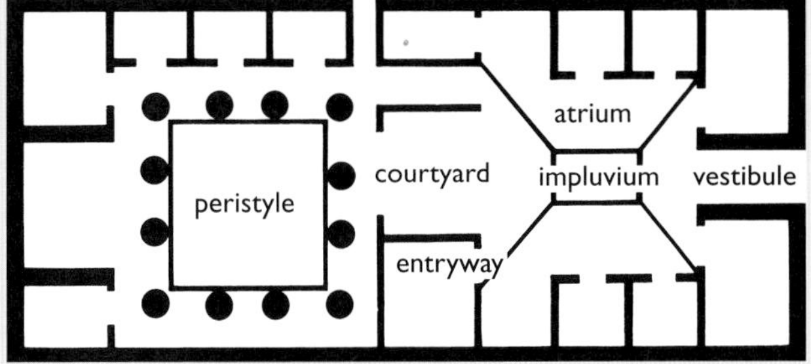

Patrician townhouse plan

Wealthy Romans developed luxurious styles of townhouses and country villas that were closer to the lifestyles of rulers than to the dismal dwellings of the poor. Shown here are a plan of a patrician townhouse (above) and the atrium of one of the fine houses of Pompeii (left).

House of the Silver Wedding atrium, Pompeii, early first century C.E.

Bedroom, Boscoreale villa, near Pompeii, first century B.C.E.

This reconstruction drawing (right) of a villa complex shows the magnificent main residence and the simpler farm buildings beyond its garden walls. The owner may also have had a house in a neighboring town. This bedroom (above right) at Boscoreale shows the fine furniture and rich wall paintings that decorated such buildings. (Metropolitan Museum of Art)

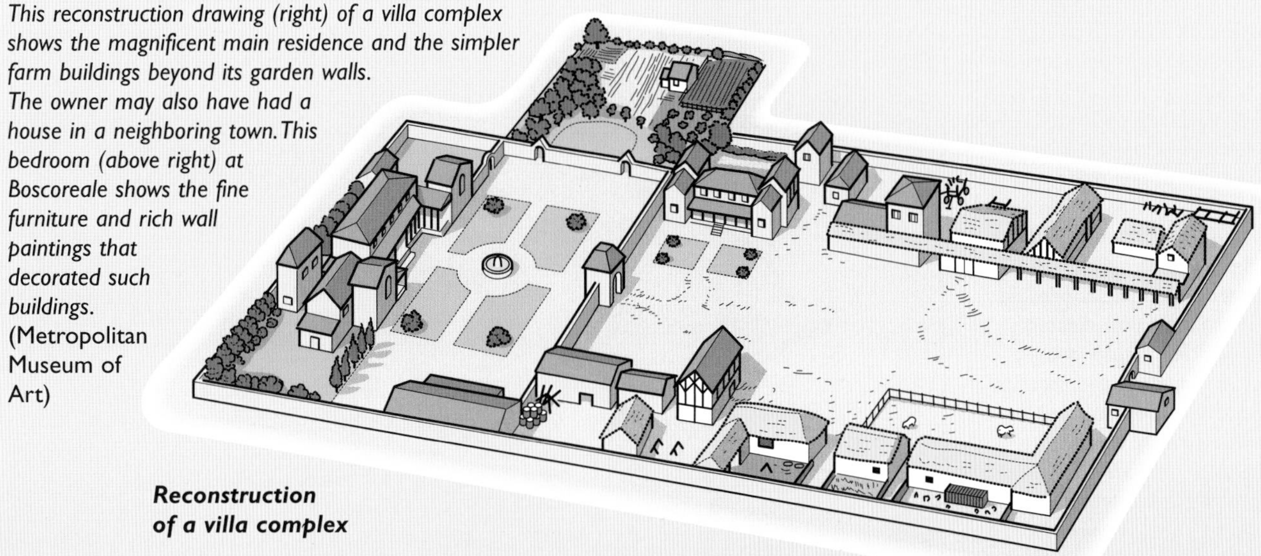

Reconstruction of a villa complex

To continue your investigation of this topic, please go to www.prenhall.com/king for the related WINDOWS on the WEB activity

Road-building, too, was a legacy from the Etruscans. By 312 B.C.E. a road had been constructed leading south from Rome to Capua (later to Brindisi); it was named the Via Appia, or Appian Way, after the censor Appius Claudius, who supervised the project. More than 800 years later, the historian Procopius of Caesarea in Anatolia described how the stones were smoothed, made flat and shaped, and joined together without mortar: "And they were fastened together so securely and the joints were so firmly closed," he marveled, "that they give the appearance … not of being fitted together, but of having grown together."

The Via Appia was joined by the Via Flaminia, begun around 220 B.C.E., which crossed the Apennines to the Adriatic, and by the Via Aemilia, from Rimini to Piacenza along the western edge of the Po plain. In 20 B.C.E. Augustus set up at one end of the Forum a stone column called the Golden Milestone. The bronze plaques attached to it announced the distances from Rome to all the main cities of the Empire.

The network of roads carried information and armies, travelers and merchants. It bound together capital and satellite cities, Greek east and Latin west, center and periphery. Building on earlier unities of the Hellenistic kingdoms, Rome had achieved a greater unity, due to its unusual aptitude for absorbing the people it conquered. That pattern began with the absorption of Latin and Sabine tribes in the early Republic. In the late Republic, all Italians gained full citizenship, and in the early Empire, citizenship was extended to the elites of many provincial towns. Rome's outreach culminated in 212 C.E., when the Emperor Caracalla (the better to collect his taxes) bestowed citizenship on every free male within the Empire's boundaries. Now one could be just as Roman in Syria or Spain as in the Po Valley or Rome itself.

The leaders of Rome came from all over the Roman Empire. The historian Livy was from the northern Po Valley. The writers Seneca, Martial, and Quintilian all came from Spain, as did the emperors Trajan and Hadrian. The Emperor Septimius Severus was African; so were the writers Fronto and Apuleius, and the Christians Tertullian and Saint Augustine. Country of origin was forgotten in the *orbis* of Rome. A Latin, or political, dimension had been added to the Hellenistic notion of *oecumene* (see Chapter 5), the community of the inhabited world.

HOW MANY?

Population Statistics

Rome (early Empire) 1 million (of which 400,000 were slaves).

Italy 4.5–5.5 million possessing Roman citizenship plus 2–3 million slaves.

Empire (around 200 C.E. at zenith) 50 million (including slave, citizen, and freeman)

Constantinople (c. 530) 300–400,000 (Asians, Slavs, Jews, and Romans)

Baghdad (c. 9th century) 300–500,000

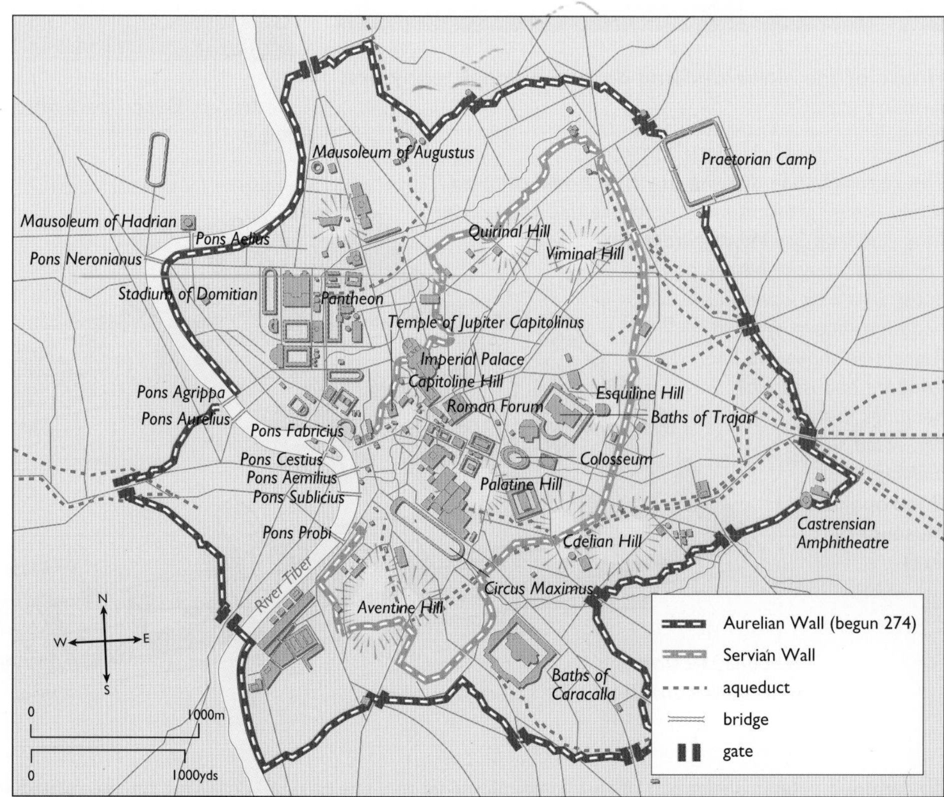

***Map 6.1 Imperial Rome, 27 B.C.E.–300 C.E.:** Under the emperor Augustus, who boasted that he had transformed a city of brick into a city of marble, Rome was at the same time a great metropolis and the capital of the Empire: "urbs et orbis," a city and the whole world. Already a populous center of government and trade, and the repository of monuments plundered from around the Mediterranean world, the city under the emperors became star-studded with theaters and baths, temples and arches, markets and libraries, palaces and racecourses. It was served by an intricate network of roads and aqueducts and protected, when dangers mounted in the third century C.E., by a huge circuit of walls (see also Map 5.3).*

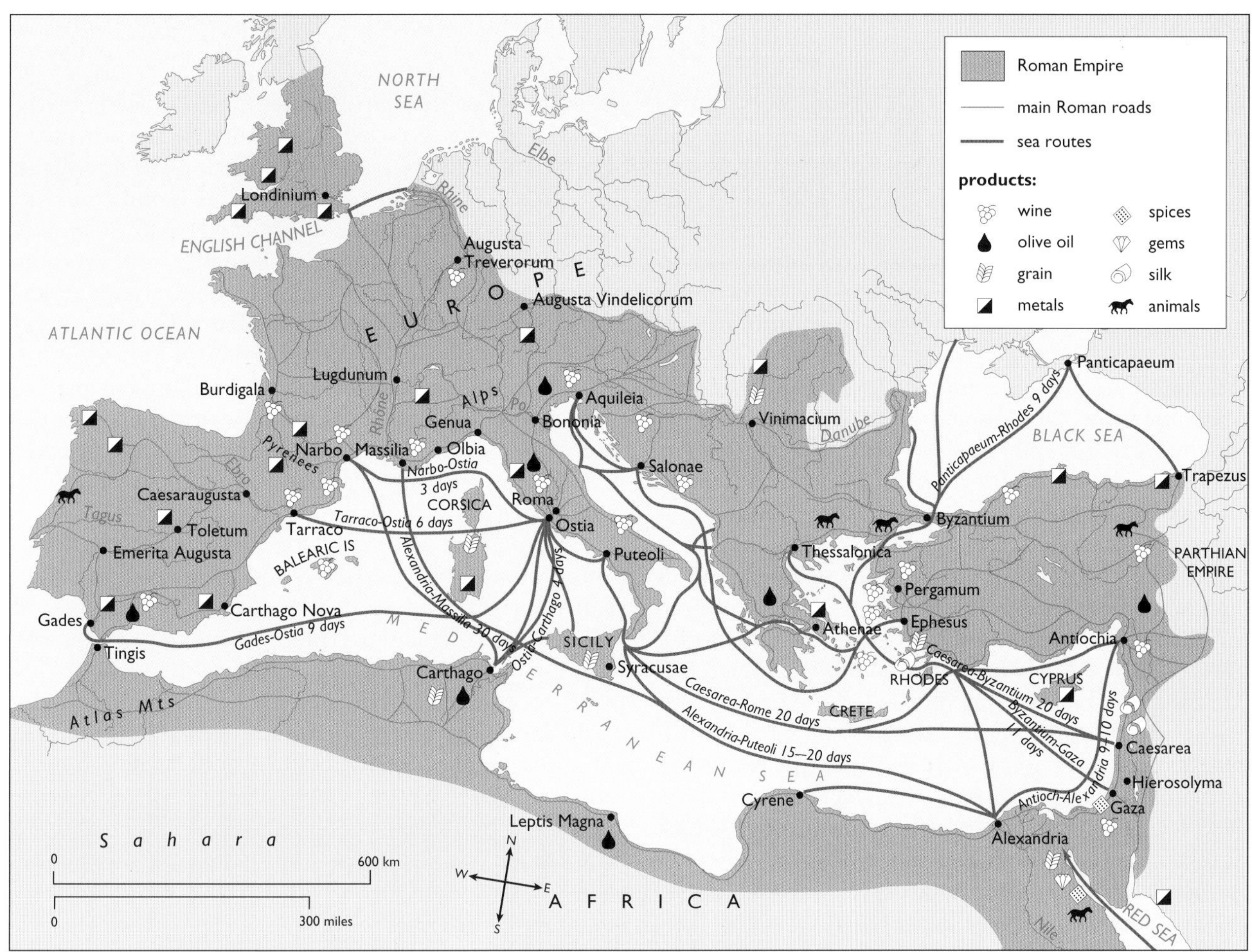

***Map 6.2 The Roman Trade System (c. 200 C.E.):** From Britain in the northwest, to the fringes of the African Sahara in the south, to India in the east, the jumpoff point for more remote trading ventures to Southeast Asia and China, Roman ships and Roman merchants journeyed on their mission to supply necessities (wheat, olive oil) and luxuries (perfumes, spices, gems, and textiles) to the center of the Empire—and incidentally brought variously news of other cultures, and deadly epidemic diseases. Encompassing the earlier trade empires of western Asia and the western Mediterranean, the Roman trading system foreshadows the one that developed during the European Middle Ages, to be dominated successively by Arabs and Italians.*

Roman Literature in Florescence and Decay

A universal culture based on a common literature was the earlier achievement of Hellenistic civilization, which now became the Roman as well, and was exported to all the new provinces of the West. Children of the elites were taught by nurses and pedagogues, and sent to school to learn to read and write from the grammar teacher, who was generally Greek and often a slave. Learning (first in Greek, then in Latin, even for Romans) was by memorization and repetition, enforced by frequent beatings.

Classic works of literature were used as spellers and as textbooks of geography, history, religion, music, and science. Students bound for high positions went on to study rhetoric and even philosophy. This training marked the student as an educated and cultured person who, from whatever region he came, could converse freely anywhere in the Empire with anyone of his class. Such an education conferred status.

While only the wealthy achieved the fine veneer imparted by the schools of rhetoric and philosophy, even ordinary people learned the rudiments of reading and writing. In sculpture, the educational level of the elite man would often be represented by a scroll. The literate commoner would be represented holding tablets on which were recorded prices and inventories. Literacy among artisans and shopkeepers is witnessed by graffiti found in ancient ruins. It is also indicated by the epitaphs that these commoners left behind—more than 100,000 of them, mostly from the first two centuries C.E. Planted along the roads outside the city walls, these inscriptions begged the reader to attend to the story of the person who spoke from the grave.

Greek literature flagged in the late Hellenistic period, but revived in the early Empire as shown in *How Many?* on p. 158. Strabo the geographer (64 B.C.E.–21 C.E.), Plutarch the biographer and moralist (c. 46–c. 120 C.E.), Ptolemy the astronomer (d. 180 C.E.), Galen the physician (129–199 C.E.), the Neoplatonic philosophers Porphyry (225–c. 305 C.E.) and Plotinus (205–270 C.E.); all these created works which would be studied for centuries. Strabo distinguished for later ages the regions of Europe, Asia, and Africa, while Ptolemy's *Almagest* codified ancient astronomical knowledge. Galen's medical works (twenty-one volumes survive) in their Latin and Arabic versions dominated the Middle Ages and Renaissance, the same eras that responded to the Neoplatonist identification of God with the One, the Good, the Beautiful, the Light. Plutarch narrated in his forty-eight extant *Lives* the accomplishments of the great leaders of Greece and Rome. Pairing forty-four of these biographies in twenty-two pairs, in which a Greek hero was matched with a Roman one, he claimed the parallelism of Greco-Roman culture.

The early Republic had produced little in the way of literature. Most authors were Greeks of Italian or Sicilian background, or Romans who dutifully followed Greek models. Much of this early literature is lost. Roman literature began a steady development in the second century B.C.E., when Cato the Elder wrote about agriculture and composed a book of maxims for his son. In the following century, the poet Lucretius (c. 94–c. 55/51 B.C.E.) expressed the principles of Epicurean thought in six books of luminous Latin verse entitled *De rerum natura* ("On the Nature of Things"). The same century was graced above all by Cicero (see Chapter 5), both a transmitter of Greek learning and an original Roman thinker. Cicero's enormous production of treatises, dialogues, letters, and orations opens up the richest period of Latin literature: the Golden Age.

Golden Age and Decline The great confidence in the future stimulated by Augustus' achievements set the stage for the supreme literary work of the Golden, or Augustan, Age. Three of the finest writers of this era were all identified with Augustus: the poets Horace (65–8 B.C.E.) and Vergil (70–19 B.C.E.) and the historian Livy (59 B.C.E.–17 C.E.). The low-born Horace was bankrolled by Augustus through his agent Maecenas (c. 70–8 B.C.E.), an equestrian aesthete and full-time literary patron. At a secluded villa purchased with Maecenas' money, Horace composed his famous *Odes* celebrating Roman life and character. Vergil celebrated the Roman state with religious fervor in his epic *Aeneid*, retelling the story of the city's supposed founding by a son of Troy. In his fourth *Eclogue*, Vergil proclaimed Augustus as savior in messianic language which Christian scholars later took as evidence that Vergil was "a soul Christian by nature." Livy celebrated the deeds of the ancients, whose virtues set the ideal still admired by Romans, though no longer practiced. The achievement of these authors was to forge a tradition distinctively Roman, even though built on forms established by Greek predecessors.

After the death of Augustus, the refined Latin prose of the early Empire continued to sparkle in literary works for two more centuries, but the spirit of literature changed greatly. As the future clouded over, authors concentrated on practical matters and on digesting the lessons of the past. That practical orientation is illustrated in such works as Columella's *On Country Life*, a twelve-volume guide to farm management; or Pliny the Elder's *Natural History*, an encyclopedia of more or less true information; or even Quintilian's *The Elements of Oratory*, on proper rhetorical training. Reflection on past history is evidenced in the brilliant but painful *Histories* and *Annals* of Tacitus, grieving the loss of the Republic; or his exquisite *Germania* and *Agricola*, covert exercises, disguised as anthropology and biography, on the meaning of liberty.

Curiously it was the historian Tacitus, rather than the professional rhetorician and educator Quintilian (an imperial employee), who diagnosed the cultural disease from which the Empire suffered: it was the decline of oratory, directly related to the loss of political freedom (see *Witnesses*, p. 149). Taught in the schools by the tedious recitation of mock orations on absurd set topics, rhetoric had become a stale relic of the age when Cicero, at imminent risk of his life, delivered his *Philippics* in the Forum. Because there was no opportunity to speak the truth, Tacitus argued, the one literary genre in which Rome had especially excelled died with the coming of the Caesars.

The other literary genres met their own deaths following the demise of oratory. After the second century, few new Latin works were considered fit to be numbered among the "classics." Great works in Latin were yet to be created: but they were Christian, and the import of their message was to despair of Rome and to trust in God. The flow of Roman eloquence, which had coursed freely under Augustus, had slowed to nothing and left barrenness behind.

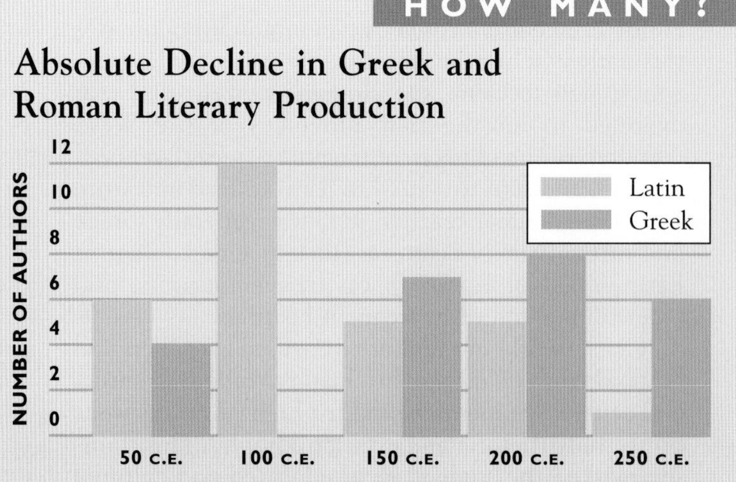

Authors in Loeb, Oxford, and Teubner Libraries (assigned to period by date of death minus ten years).

Source: R. MacMullen, *Corruption and the Decline of Rome* (New Haven–London: Yale University Press, 1988).

According to Tacitus, the present sterility was a direct outcome of the loss of freedom instituted by Augustus himself. While acknowledging that Augustus brought an end to the lawlessness that followed Julius Caesar's power grab, Tacitus maintained that the price for the restoration of order, monarchy, was too high. "Thenceforth," concluded the embittered writer, "our bonds were tighter."

A spiritual aridity characterized Roman culture even as the Empire basked in peace, grew in wealth, and reached its peak years of growth. People sought out new and more satisfying forms of religious experience (see Chapter 7), and new philosophical consolations. Such a collapse in the realm of spirit may explain the grim words of the Stoic philosopher Seneca (tutor and adviser to Nero who eventually, on that despot's order, took his own life) on the ready availability of freedom: "Look at that precipice—a descent to freedom; that sea, that river, that well—at the bottom of each there is freedom. That stunted, parched, unfruitful tree; freedom hangs from its branches. Your neck, your throat, your heart—escape-routes from slavery, all of them. ... If you are looking for a way to freedom, any vein in your body will do."

The spiritual impoverishment of late Roman culture is expressed in this dismal equation of death with liberty and slavery with life. Meanwhile, Rome came to face a problem more severe than the loss of freedom: that of survival.

HOLDING THE FRONTIER

During the *pax romana* of the first two centuries C.E., the Roman Empire reached its maximum extent. Its borders were secure, trade flourished; the lives of city dwellers, even including plebs, were enhanced by comforts and refinements, while those of the peasants, never easy, were not evidently harsher. Then, in the third century, the tide turned. A deep and persistent crisis took hold. Prosperity faded; poetry and philosophy languished. The borders could be held only by enormous efforts involving a desperate reorganization of the army, the economy, and the machinery of the state. Thenceforth, until the final collapse of authority in the Western Empire in the late 400s, although Rome survived, it bled. A new city took form in the Greek-speaking eastern zone of the Empire, which was to transmit some remnants of Roman culture into the next age. In the western, Latin zone, the old city of Rome fell to invaders, who plundered and consumed it. The survival of Roman civilization rested insecurely in the hands of the expanding Christian Church.

Defending the Boundaries

In the second century C.E., Rome's dominion included all the lands of the Mediterranean as well as much of western Europe beyond the Alps. By the third century, its extensive borders were at risk.

The first major setback to Roman expansion came under Augustus. Roman armies plunged northeast into Europe, where in 9 C.E., the troops of the general Publius Quinctilius were slaughtered by the horsemen of the German leader Arminius (Hermann), a former Roman "auxiliary" commander (a foreign commander in the service of Rome), who ambushed them in the Teutoburg Forest (near Osnabrück). Varus committed suicide. Legions XVII, XVIII, and XIX of Augustus' twenty-eight legions were lost, an enduring reproach to Roman ambition.

Augustus' successor, Tiberius, assumed the inglorious task of holding a frontier with less ambitious dimensions. He labored to secure the line formed by the Rhine and Danube rivers, slicing across Europe from the North to the Black Sea. Claudius acquired Britain in 43 B.C.E., a task previously attempted by Caesar in 55–54 B.C.E.

The need to secure the lower Danube brought Trajan to Dacia, in the Balkans, to discipline that people's rebellious king. The vicious wars of 101–102 C.E. and subsequent treaties of 105–106 C.E. reduced the Dacian king to client status. Roman settlers arrived to colonize the area, achieving the domestication of that region (where today the Romanian language, descended from Latin, is still spoken). A further benefit was the profit from the Dacian gold mines, which poured into Rome and into Trajan's pockets. Trajan's Column in the Roman Forum shown on p. 161 commemorates his Dacian victory, depicted with splendid narrative detail in carved reliefs winding upward along the length of the monument.

Trajan also confronted the Parthians, who had overrun Iran and now pushed against the Empire's eastern border. Roman armies seized Arab caravan routes, quarreled over Armenia, and invaded Mesopotamia, where they seized (for a while) the town of Ctesiphon, capital of Parthia, and set up a puppet prince. The Empire reached its greatest extent in 117 C.E., as shown on Map 6.3. But what Trajan had acquired in remote eastern lands, some of his successors abandoned.

Not so Trajan's cousin and chosen successor, Hadrian, who adopted a different strategy. His aim was to hold the forty-three provinces that his predecessors had won—as much as could be prudently conserved. Parthia was forgotten for the moment. In the rest of the East and on the African coast, it was necessary only to maintain a stable position.

To the north, Hadrian adopted a militantly defensive position. Where his predecessors had warred with the fierce Celts in the remotest north of Britain, Hadrian retreated southward and built a mammoth wall across the island, through what are now the northernmost counties of England. The ruins of Hadrian's Wall still stand. Along the Rhine and

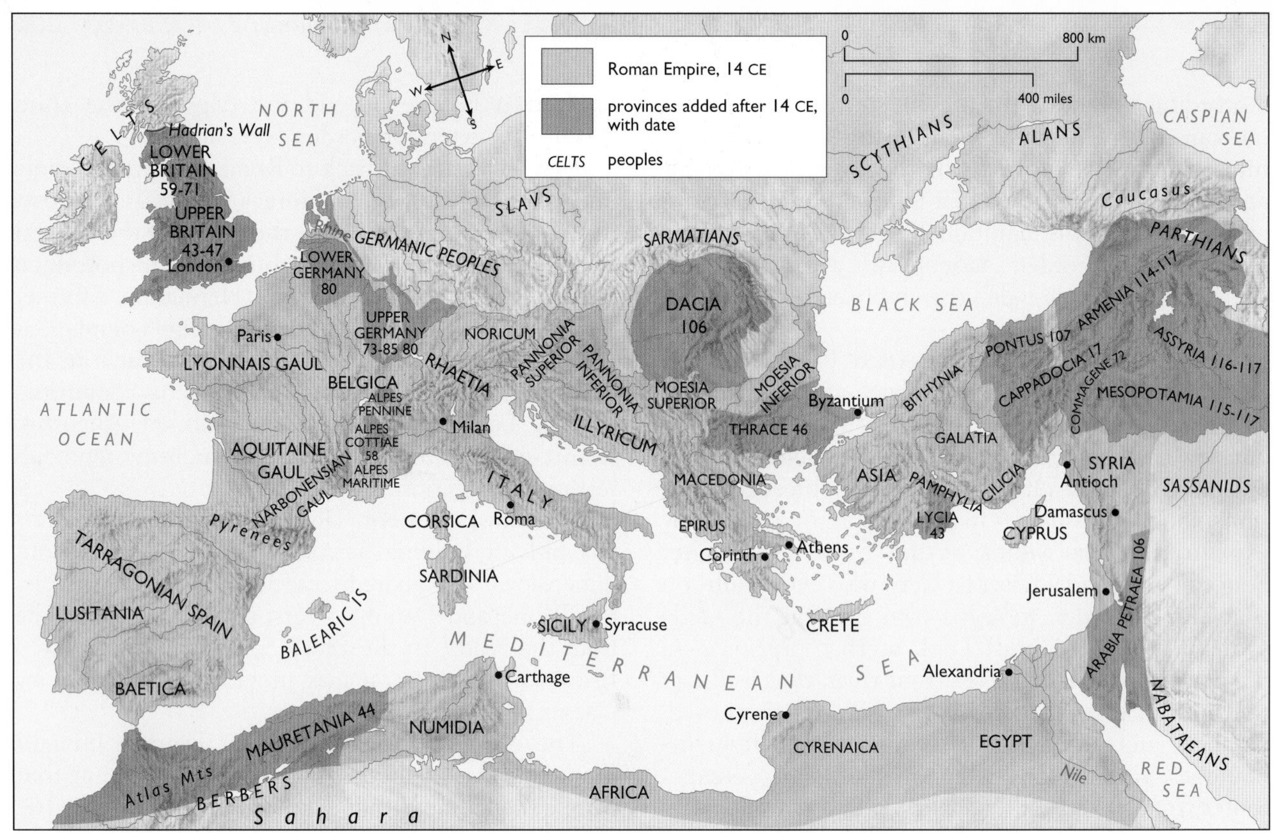

Map 6.3 The Roman Empire at its Apex, 117 C.E.: *By the time of Emperor Trajan's death in 117 C.E., the Roman Empire had reached its greatest limit. Later emperors chose to defend, garrison, or even contract the frontiers, rather than continue to press against irresistible forces—the German tribes in northern Europe, and the Parthians and Sassanids in Iran—or unbridgeable obstacles—the Atlantic ocean and the African Sahara.*

Danube line, he ordered permanent fortifications built and garrisoned. To all the frontiers he sent troops, which he inspected regularly, keeping them out of war but war-ready. One war Hadrian could not avoid was in the troublesome province of Judaea. There, a rebellion under the Jewish leader Bar-Kokhba in 132–135 C.E. was suppressed with horrific slaughter.

Hadrian's strategy of holding the frontier became permanent. It was pursued by prudent sacrifices of land, generous alliances with alien peoples, and the outpouring of military personnel from the center to the periphery of the Empire. Whereas the task of the Empire during its first two centuries was to acquire more provinces, its task over the next three centuries was to defend them. The task proved impossible.

Redefining the Army

To hold the frontiers required the reorganization of the army, the institution on which the Roman system was based and in which the state of Rome itself was most clearly reflected. Its increasing size is outlined in *How Many?* on p. 162.

From the time of the early Republic, Rome's army was composed of legions of four to six thousand citizens of the appropriate census classes, commanded by officers from the nobility. Backing up the legions were auxiliary forces (foreign troops in the service of Rome). In the late Republic, after the innovations of Marius and the extension of citizenship to all Italians, the legionaries were drawn from poorer census classes, and the auxiliaries from more distant and alien regions. Meanwhile, the army gained political importance. It helped boost such figures as Marius and Sulla, Pompey and Caesar, who acquired political power because of their military strength (see Chapter 5).

During the civil wars, the legionary forces of Octavian and Mark Antony swelled from about 80,000 to more than 400,000. After the defeat of Antony and Cleopatra at Actium in 30 B.C.E., Octavian (now Augustus) demobilized, retiring almost half the legionaries with cash bonuses or grants of land. The remaining soldiers were organized in 28 legions (5500 to 6000 men each), reduced to 25 legions after the disaster at Teutoburg. An equally large force—150,000 men—was provided by auxiliaries organized in cohorts of about 1000 men each. In addition, each army marched with a supply train and machines for sieges and defense. The legionaries served twenty years, after which they retired with the usual bonuses. Auxiliaries served twenty-five years, receiving at discharge a grant of citizenship which allowed foreign-born sons to enter the legions.

The army of the early Republic cost nothing: each citizen supplied his own food, weapons, and armor. Not so under the Empire. Feeding, transporting, and paying its legions and auxiliaries was the biggest charge on the Roman treasury. The imperial systems

Narrative in stone: *Completed in Rome in 113 C.E., the column built to celebrate the conquests of the emperor Trajan soared nearly 100 feet high, circled by 23 spirals that extended more than 200 meters and displayed 2500 figures—a panorama that documents the scale and complex organization of Rome's imperial expansion. The lower bands of spiral relief depict the imperial troops advancing along the Danube river, with a Roman camp shown in the top band of the column.*

of coinage and taxation were structured to manage the giant military machine. The biggest drain was in coin. Caesar doubled the pay of common soldiers, and Augustus raised pay for centurions (non-noble officers) and provided legionaries with bonuses on discharge of 3000 *denarii* (75,000 *sestercii*): more than ten times the annual pay of 225 *denarii* (5625 *sestercii*). Domitian raised the annual figure to 300 *denarii*, and Septimus Severus to almost 500 *denarii*. Praetorian guards were paid more than twice that. These figures reflect a high rate of inflation and an increased dependence on the military.

By Hadrian's reign (117–138 C.E.), the army was no longer seen as a mobile striking force but was largely stationed in semi-permanent positions on the frontier. Roman soldiers became builders of camps and designers of fortifications, engineers and farmers, who sometimes neglected the business of war in the quest for maximum security. Augustus' twenty-five legions were distributed in this way: three in Spain, eight on the Rhine, seven on the Danube, four in Syria, two in Egypt, and one in Africa (the III Augusta legion, stationed there for more than 300 years). The greater stability of Africa and Egypt is indicated by the smaller number of legions needed to hold it. The volatility of the Rhine–Danube line to the north and northeast, on the other hand, and the weakness of the Syrian border are reflected in the heavy arming of those regions.

Towns sprang up around the semi-permanent army camps planted on the frontiers. The towns supported magistracies and law courts, commerce and theaters, baths and games. The language spoken in these communities was the rough Latin of the average soldier. That uncouth figure was a principal agent of Romanization in the European part of the Empire. Veterans were also effective agents of Romanization in the colonies they peopled upon retirement. At the same time that the legions were a Romanizing force, the army itself became less Roman and increasingly "barbarized," as its soldiers acquired the language and customs of the people among whom they settled and with whom they intermarried. By the late Empire, legionaries were no longer recruited primarily from Rome or even from Italy: after 300 C.E., fewer than 20 percent came from Italy. Auxiliaries were recruited not merely from non-Italian but even from alien communities: from the warlike peoples on the fringes of the Empire, kin to the tribal peoples who threatened the frontier. By the last years of the Empire, whole groups of foreign peoples were allowed to penetrate that boundary and settle within it. At that point, invasion was scarcely necessary. Rome itself had become the home of European peoples who roamed the forests and grasslands beyond the zone of civilization.

Managing the Crisis

In the last two centuries of the Empire, the emperors scrambled to manage the economic and military crisis as indicated in *Witnesses* on p. 163. Some of them responded brilliantly, flexibly reinventing the administrative machinery to deal with new realities, just as their predecessor Augustus had done. Even these heroic efforts at adaptation, however, were unsuccessful.

In the fifty years between the death of Alexander Severus and the reign of Diocletian (284–305 C.E.), at least eighteen men held the title of emperor. One of these, Aurelian, constructed, in 274 C.E., a new set of walls around Rome to secure it—an act that demonstrated at the same time his prudence and the grave collapse of order. By such desperate measures, these near-forgotten emperors attempted to stem the tide of barbarian invasion, the decay of civic institutions, and the decline of the rural economy. The plain-speaking but brilliant Diocletian managed—but just barely—to keep in check the inner strains and external stress that beset the Empire.

Never had the army been more important. It did not merely protect the state. Rather, the state existed to support the army, as all other objectives rolled into the single imperative of defense. The auxiliary forces,

HOW MANY?

Army Organization

The Roman army that had conquered Carthage, Greece, and the eastern Mediterranean lands numbered only a few tens of thousands of soldiers recruited from among Roman or Italian citizens. That army quintupled in size during the Civil Wars. Once normalcy had been restored, Augustus demobilized many of the legionaries—reducing the force, after the Teutoburg disaster, to 25 legions—while recruiting many "auxiliary" soldiers from non-citizen provincials and tribal peoples of the frontier. Under his successors, who established fixed maximum borders for the Empire and planted soldier garrisons to defend them, the overall force rose to a maximum of about 500,000—a vast army not to be seen again in Europe until the eighteenth century. The maintenance of that force (whose annual pay had doubled since the days of Augustus) drained the wealth of the Empire.

ARMY SIZE AT VARIOUS POINTS:

Before Julius Caesar's death (44 B.C.E.) about 80,000 Roman legionaries

Under Octavian and Mark Antony (during Civil Wars 43–31 B.C.E.) about 40,000 Roman legionaries

Under Augustus (after Teutoburg 9 C.E.) about 150,000 Roman legionaries, plus about 150,000 auxiliaries

Around 400 C.E. about 500,000 total forces

adept in the skills required to deal with the barbarians, now mattered more than the legions. Heavy cavalry edged out infantry in importance, foreshadowing medieval styles of warfare. German recruits prevailed in both the mobile cavalry forces that accompanied each emperor and the troops stationed on the frontier. By 400 C.E., 500,000 men were serving in arms—a force nearly double that of Augustus' army, exceeding even the peak numbers of the civil war years.

To fund the army, the state became a machine for the generation of tax revenues, waging a relentless raid on the meager resources of the poor. "No man shall possess any property that is tax-exempt," read the Theodosian Code of 383 C.E.. New methods of land assessment increased the flow of revenues from the countryside. The sums due the government, based on an annual budget, were announced on a regular schedule. Ceilings were established for prices and wages in order to control inflation, which was driven by the debasement of the currency. A negative side effect of price fixing was to dim initiative, thus contributing to the already plummeting volume and value of trade.

Roman coins, prized throughout the ancient world, were used to carry on trade and to pay taxes. Under Augustus, the metal content (gold, silver, bronze, copper) was fixed for the various coins: the *aureus*, the *denarius*, the *sestertius*, the *as*, and the *dupondius*. Upon these standardized coins were stamped the emperor's profile and a variety of symbols of his achievements. The value of these splendid coins began to deteriorate in the third century, as the emperors allowed the currency to be debased and as inflation ate at its value. Quality coins fell out of circulation, to be melted down or simply hoarded, while the corrupt currency continued to circulate. This tendency, together with the Western Empire's negative trade balance with the East led, especially in the West, to the near-disappearance of coins and a slide into a barter economy.

The cities suffered economic decline. That decline put pressure on the **decurions**—the elite class in the outlying cities who were responsible for municipal functions. Once the decurions had been the proud patrons of civic life. By ancient custom, they funded public monuments and services: theatrical performances, council halls, shipbuilding, roads and bridges, athletic games, and even the statues by which their own accomplishments were publicly commemorated. The decurions were also responsible for collecting taxes and feeding the Roman treasury. Whole families were assigned municipal responsibilities on a hereditary basis. The decurions could not escape these obligations, nor could their sons—except by fleeing altogether, a remedy they chose as Rome continued to decline. From fourth-century Antioch a mournful voice complained, speaking of the citizen elite, that "we used to be six hundred ... but now we are sixty."

Seeking relief, decurions fled the cities; some of the cities, fearful of depredations, relocated to more secure hilltop sites, well fortified with walls and towers. In the countryside, great tracts of land lay waste, abandoned, the result of rapid depopulation, the erosion of the soil, and the devastations of the army. Overburdened peasants were required to guard—and pay taxes on—the land abandoned by their neighbors. The great landowners alone remained prosperous, living on the accumulated produce of their tenants, who were by now for the most part hopelessly in debt. In exchange for the right to farm the land and to claim the master's protection, these tenants, the *coloni*, willingly surrendered much of their freedom. They were the immediate ancestors of the serfs of medieval Europe.

The emperors, too, withdrew from urban society to their court, where they spoke mainly with their officials and advisers and slaves. These made up a small council, the chief members of which were called *comites*, or "companions" (in medieval times, "counts"). From this court emanated all public decrees. An elaborate ritual developed to enhance the

Crisis and Response in Late Imperial Rome

By the fourth and fifth centuries C.E., *Roman institutions were crumbling. Emperors Diocletian and Theodosius attempted to stave off crises by issuing regulatory edicts, such as those excerpted here: Diocletian's capping prices, and Theodosius's restricting the mobility of rural workers and municipal officeholders. Yet Roman institutions weakened nevertheless, inviting the invasion of tribal peoples, whose devastation of the city of Rome is lamented in the third passage by the Christian author Jerome.*

In his "Edict on Prices," the emperor Diocletian explains why the state must intervene to protect citizens from the avarice of profiteers (301 C.E.): Avarice boundless and frenzied, with no consideration for humankind, multiplies its spreading grasp like wildfire, not by years or months or days but every hour and minute. Since the unrestrained madness of lust will take no thought for the common welfare, since only necessity ... can check the seething and torrential avarice of unscrupulous exploiters ... in view of this situation we who are protectors of humankind have resolved that justice should intervene as arbiter ...
(Diocletian, "Edict on Prices"; ed. M. Hadas 1956)

The law code promulgated under the emperor Theodosius issues certain restrictions on the semi-dependent peasants (called *coloni*) and on the class of municipal officeholders (called *decurions*) (383 C.E.): 5.17.1.1: Coloni ... who meditate flight must be bound with chains and reduced to a servile condition. ... 5.19.1: There is no doubt that coloni do not have the right to alienate the fields that they cultivate [or] ... transfer them to others without the advice and knowledge of their patrons. 12.1.13: Since ... the municipal councils are being left desolate by those persons who are obligated to them through birth status... we order all municipal councils to be admonished that if they should apprehend any persons with less than twenty terms of service in governmental offices ... they shall drag such persons back to the municipal councils.
(Theodosian Code, 5.17.11, 5.19.1, 12.1.13; ed. B. Tierney 1973)

Saint and scholar Jerome, quoting Vergil, describes Rome plundered by the tribe of Visigoths (410 C.E.): A terrible rumor has arrived from the West. Rome is besieged. ... The City is taken which took the whole world. It had perished of famine before it died by the sword, and only a few captives were found. The fury of the hungry sought out horrible food; men tore each other to pieces; a mother did not spare her infant at the breast and ate what she had brought forth a little before. ...

What tongue can tell the slaughter of that night?
What eyes can weep the sorrows and affright?
An ancient and imperial city falls. ...

(Jerome, Letter 127,12; trs. J. Hillgarth, 1986; Vergil, *Aeneid*, 2.361–365, 369; trs. Dryden)

figure of the emperor, who was displayed, bejeweled, like a deity on earth. Diocletian was no longer *princeps*, "first citizen;" he was, and was addressed as, *dominus*, or "lord." He was an absolute monarch who ruled not by persuading but by dominating—hence the naming of this phase of the Empire as the "Dominate," as opposed to the earlier "Principate." He and his successors resorted to terror to enforce their domination; like Valens (376–378 C.E.), who, it was said, held "death at the tip of his tongue."

More and more, the emperor resembled an eastern monarch of the age before the Greeks. Indeed, he established himself in the East, more secure than the unstable West, which was vulnerable to tribal pressures. Diocletian appointed Maximian to police that region as a partner equal to himself and with the same title: "Augustus." Each Augustus had a lieutenant designated his heir, each one entitled "Caesar." By this organization of four rulers, two senior and two junior (called the tetrarchy, or "rule of four"), Diocletian aimed both to secure all zones of the Empire and to ensure an orderly succession. He stepped down, as he had said he would, in 305 C.E., and waited for the planned succession to take place. The plan failed. The two caesars and several others vied to be sole monarch. Chaos once again ruled, east and west.

Constantine's City and *The City of God*

The Emperor Constantine, called "the Great" (r. 312–337 C.E.), once again united and pacified the Empire—if briefly. He governed it now from a new city in the Eastern Empire, "Constantinople." The Empire survived by changing its character: it was now led from a Greek-speaking Rome ensconced in the eastern Mediterranean.

As the legitimate successor of Maximian, Diocletian's partner in the West, Constantine had battled his way to power by 312 C.E.. By 324, he had succeeded in ousting his co-ruler, abandoned the tetrarchy, and claimed sole authority. Nevertheless, Constantine preserved much of Diocletian's imperial reorganization. He followed Diocletian toward the east, establishing his new capital in the old Greek city of Byzantium on the Bosporus. Grandly renamed Constantinople, after himself, it reflected the changing image of the Empire, now a repressive state under an absolutist king.

Constantine was the first Roman emperor to become a Christian. His formal conversion took place only on his deathbed, but in spirit he had already embraced Christianity much earlier than this. In 313, his Edict of Milan extended toleration to all religions, including Christianity and Judaism, thus ending the terrible persecutions that Diocletian had instituted toward the end of his reign for the security of the realm. Constantine followed the endless discussions of theologians over various fine points of doctrine: the humanity of Christ, the motherhood of Mary, the possibility of free will (see Chapter 7). When he died in 337, the Empire had already become more Christian than pagan.

Under Constantine's successors—with one exception, Julian (r. 361–363)—Christianity continued to flourish. With the accession to the throne of Theodosius (r. 380–395), Christians rejoiced; for Theodosius (whom they called "the Great") did what two centuries earlier would have been inconceivable: he made Christianity the official religion. The very religion that had been seen as a threat to the Empire was now its refuge. So severe and pathless was the crisis that confronted Rome that the army was not sufficient to rescue it. The peace imposed by Roman power from the time of Augustus and maintained by its legions had disintegrated. It could not be reestablished by military means.

The "New Rome" planted at Constantinople would endure on the foundations laid by Diocletian and Constantine for one thousand years more (see Chapters 10, 11). But the old Rome, and the whole western sector of the Empire, decayed and fell prey to hungry newcomers—Visigoths, Ostrogoths, Vandals, Huns, and Franks. In 410, the Visigoth king Alaric I invaded Italy and sacked Rome. A contemporary description is given in *Witnesses* on p. 163. In 451, the Huns rammed through northern Italy, spreading desolation. One by one, the garrisons that had held the frontier gave way—as they did on the Danube border, when the soldiers ceased to be paid and "the military units were abolished together with the frontier." In 455, Rome was sacked again, by the Vandals. In 476, the Germanic warrior Odoacer deposed the reigning western emperor and declared himself king of Italy. "Rome fell to the Goths in the 1164th year after its foundation," was the terse comment of the English scholar the Venerable Bede (c. 673–735), writing when Rome was only a memory.

Long before Odoacer captured Rome, the western Empire was dead. Saint Augustine (who died during the Vandal invasion of North Africa in 430) had pronounced it doomed in 410, when the capital was sacked by the Visigoths under Alaric. It was this catastrophe that impelled Augustine to write his monumental work *The City of God.* In that work, he dissected the inadequacies of Roman paganism and the Roman state: the "city of man," which compared unfavorably to the community of believers gathered in the "city of God." His analysis would lead the way to later understandings of human society and the state by such diverse thinkers as Hobbes (English political philosopher, 1588–1679), Hegel (German philosopher, 1770–1831), and Darwin (British naturalist, 1809–1882).

Like Tacitus, Augustine exposed what he saw as the fraudulence of the great Empire: it was a bloodstained arena where the strong destroyed the weak, "a sea wherein men devour one another in turn like fish." Far from benefiting its citizens, the megalithic state torments them with crime, sedition, and war, "from the occurrence of which states are rarely free, from the apprehension of them never." An organization designed for the hoarding and spending of wealth, the business of the state is robbery, and that of large states (in Augustine's unforgettable judgment), "robbery on a grand scale." In Rome, "the lust for possession . . . triumphed in the persons of a few men of exceptional power, only to reduce and exhaust the remainder and, ultimately, to impose upon them the yoke of servitude." While the state may confer certain cultural benefits, it does so at an enormous cost in the spilling of human blood: "its victories are deadly or at any rate deathly."

Conclusion

THE ROMAN PEACE AND THE MEANING OF THE WEST

Observing the ruins of the crumbling Empire, Augustine argued that true peace (peace of the spirit, peace for eternity) was to be found only in communion with a transcendent God. Many, over the next two thousand years, would agree with him. But the Roman Peace—Augustus' *pax romana*—was not, though it failed, a meaningless episode in the building of the West.

The Roman Peace was actually a permanent condition of war, waged hot and cold on the borders of Empire far from the center. There, over five centuries, Roman emperors struggled to save Roman institutions by transmuting and subverting them. As they struggled, and though they lost, Roman generals and soldiers, landowners and poets and, eventually, bishops (see Chapter 7), brought the products of ancient culture to the peoples of Europe and planted the Latin language in fields far from Rome before French, German, or English were born. By their agency, and protected by the formidable power of the imperial state, a bridge was built between the ancient Mediterranean and unformed, unsettled Europe. Across that bridge, the cultural heritage of the ancient world traveled north to nurture that civilization that we call the West.

REVIEW QUESTIONS

1. How did Augustus lay the foundations for an imperial monarchy? What were the main achievements of his rule? What changes in government, law, and religion showed that Rome was an absolute monarchy by the third century B.C.E.?

2. How did Roman society change under the Empire? Why did the senatorial elite decline? How did the position of upper-class women improve?

3. What groups made up the *honestiores* and the *humiliores*? What role did freedmen play in Roman society? What benefits did the plebs enjoy under imperial rule?

4. What were the benefits of imperial Roman civilization for the city of Rome and the Empire? How did commerce and the network of roads help to unite the Empire?

5. How did the Greeks influence Roman literature? When was the Golden Age of Latin literature? Why did Roman culture sink into a decline in the two centuries after Augustus?

6. How did the Roman army change under the Empire? What problems did the Empire face in the third and fourth centuries C.E.? How did Diocletian and Constantine try to solve these problems? What was the ultimate significance of the *Pax Romana*?

SUGGESTED RESOURCES

The New Imperium

Campbell, J. B., *The Emperor and the Roman Army, 31 B.C.–A.D. 235* (Oxford: Clarendon Press of Oxford University Press, 1984). Discusses the means by which the emperor maintained the support of the army, without which he could not rule.

Millar, Fergus, *The Emperor in the Roman World, 31 B.C.–A.D. 337* 2nd ed. (Ithaca, 1977: Cornell University Press, 1992). A massive account of the emperor's nonmilitary functions, stressing the personal nature of his activities, the general acceptance of imperial authority, and the role of subjects in initiating petitions to which the emperor responded.

Zanker, Paul, *The Power of Images in the Age of Augustus* (Ann Arbor: University of Michigan Press, 1988). Studies the visual imagery of the Roman state and identity under Augustus.

Chronology of Roman History, Trojan War to Byzantine Empire (Forum Romanum):
http://www.geocities.com/Athens/Forum/6946/history.html

Upper Classes and Other Classes

Ariès, Philippe and Georges Duby, eds., *A History of Private Life*, vol 1: *From Pagan Rome to Byzantium*, trans. Arthur Goldhammer (Cambridge, MA: Belknap Press of Harvard University Press, 1987). These essays discuss family structures and private life, domestic architecture, and the presuppositions underlying private life.

Evans, John K., *War, Women, and Children in Ancient Rome* (London: Routledge, 1991). Surveys the effects of imperialism on the status of propertied women, working women in towns and the countryside, and ties between parents and children.

Saller, Richard P., *Personal Patronage under the Early Empire* (Cambridge: Cambridge University Press, 1982). A study of the crucial role of patronage in Roman politics and society up to the third century C.E., with comparisons to patronage relations in China.

Treggiari, Susan, *Roman Marriage:* Iusti coniuges *from the Time of Cicero to the Time of Ulpian* (Oxford: Clarendon Press of Oxford University Press, 1991). Exhaustive study of legal and other sources yields a comprehensive understanding of the functioning of marriage in the various social classes of the Empire.

Yavetz, Zvi, *Plebs and Princeps* (Oxford: Oxford University Press, 1988). An account of how Julio-Claudian emperors gained the support of the plebs through grain supply, entertainments, and clemency.

Diotima: materials for the study of women in antiquity:
http://www.stoa.org/diotima

The Culture of Imperial Rome

Boatwright, Mary Taliaferro, *Hadrian and the City of Rome* (Princeton: Princeton University Press, 1987). A solid and readable study of city planning and construction in imperial Rome, emphasizing the emperor Hadrian's building program and administrative reforms.

Mellor, Ronald, *Tacitus* (London: Routledge, 1991). Thorough presentation of the thought and craft of the great first-century historian which makes a persuasive case for Tacitus as moralist, psychologist, and political analyst, as well as literary artist.

Sullivan, J. P., *Literature and Politics in the Age of Nero* (Ithaca: Cornell University Press, 1985). An insightful study of the profound influence of patronage and politics on literature during Nero's reign.

Holding the Frontier

Burns, Thomas S., *Barbarians within the Gates of Rome: A Study of Roman Military Policy and the Barbarians, ca. 375–425 A.D.* (Bloomington: Indiana University Press, 1995). Studies a critical half-century where Roman policy changed step by fatal step—fatal for the survival of the Empire—from allowing Germans to fight in Roman armies to allowing them to fight under their own kings, upon whom Roman leaders, in turn, became dependent.

Cameron, Averil, *The Mediterranean World in Late Antiquity, A.D. 395–600* (London: Routledge, 1993). Excellent up-to-date overview of the two centuries of Roman disintegration, including ample consideration of both the eastern and western zones of empire.

MacMullen, Ramsay, *Corruption and the Decline of Rome* (New Haven: Yale University Press, 1988). MacMullen argues that the collapse of the Roman Empire in the north and west was due to an erosion of moral standards, which led more people in authority to use their positions solely for private profit, at the expense of the common good.

Southern, Pat & Karen Ramsey Dixon, *The Late Roman Army* (New Haven: Yale University Press, 1996). How the Roman army and its managers from Septimius Severus to the last throes of the Empire addressed multiple crises by adjusting systems of funding, recruitment, fortification, and tactics until it could fend off disaster no longer.

The destruction of Pompeii, 79 C.E.:
http://www.ibiscom/pompeii.html

PAGAN, JEWS, AND CHRISTIANS

500 B.C.E. | 400 | 300 | 200 | 100 | 1 C.E. | 100 | 200 | 300 | 400 | 500 C.E.

Rulers, Nations, and War

Roman Republic, c. 500–27 B.C.E.

Roman Empire, 27 B.C.E–476 C.E.

Byzantine Empire, 476–1453

- Alexander the Great conquers Judaea (Palestine), 333 B.C.E.
- Pompey's troops occupy Jerusalem, 63 B.C.E.
- Herod "the Great" takes charge in Judaea, 37 B.C.E.
- Emperor Caracalla extends Roman citizenship to free subjects of Empire, 213
- Visigoths sack Rome, 410
- Attila the Hun invades West, 451
- Vandals sack Rome, 455
- Visigoth Odoacer, deposes emperor, seizes power in Rome, 476

Ideas, Religion, and Society

Christian persecutions, 64–311 C.E.

- Humans sacrificed in Rome to appease gods in Second Punic War, 216 B.C.E.
- Antiochus IV's occupation of Jerusalem triggers Hasmonean revolt (Maccabees), 167 B.C.E.
- Augustus' legislation on marriage and family, 18 B.C.E.–9 C.E.
- Altar of Peace built, 13–9 B.C.E.
- Jesus of Nazareth born, c. 4 B.C.E.
- Jesus of Nazareth dies, c. 30 C.E.
- Paul's journey to Damascus, c. 33 C.E.
- "Great Fire" in Rome; Persecution of Christians begins, 64 C.E.
- Paul dies in Rome, c. 67 C.E.
- Jerusalem Temple destroyed by Roman soldiers under Titus, 70 C.E.
- Gospels of Christian New Testament, c. 70–100 C.E.
- Masada stormed; mass suicide of Jewish occupants, 73 C.E.
- Final defeat of "Bar Kokhba" revolt, dispersion of Jews of Jerusalem, 135
- Martyrdom of Justin, Christian apologist, c. 165
- Christian persecutions in Lyon (Gaul), 177
- Martyrdom in Carthage of noblewoman Perpetua, 203
- Manichaean movement begins, c. 240
- Plotinus, exponent of Neoplatonism, dies, 270
- Emperor Aurelian erects temple to to "unconquerable sun" (*Sol Invictus*), 274
- Diocletian issues Edict on Prices, 301
- "Great Persecution" of Christians under Emperor Diocletian, 303–11
- Edict of Milan grants toleration to all religions, 313, 323
- Council of Nicaea, resulting eventually in Nicene creed, 325
- Ambrose, Bishop of Milan excommunicates Emperor Theodosius, 390
- Emperor Theodosius I outlaws pagan practices, 392
- Christian theologian St. John Chrysostom's (c. 354–407) *Sermons Against the Jews*, 400

Beyond the West

Zhou dynasty, c. 1027–221

Qin dynasty, c. 221–206

Han dynasty, 206 B.C.E.–220 C.E.

Maya civilization, c. 300–900

Gupta dynasty, c. 320–550

CHAPTER

7 PAGANS, JEWS, AND CHRISTIANS

Religions around the Mediterranean

500 B.C.E.–500 C.E.

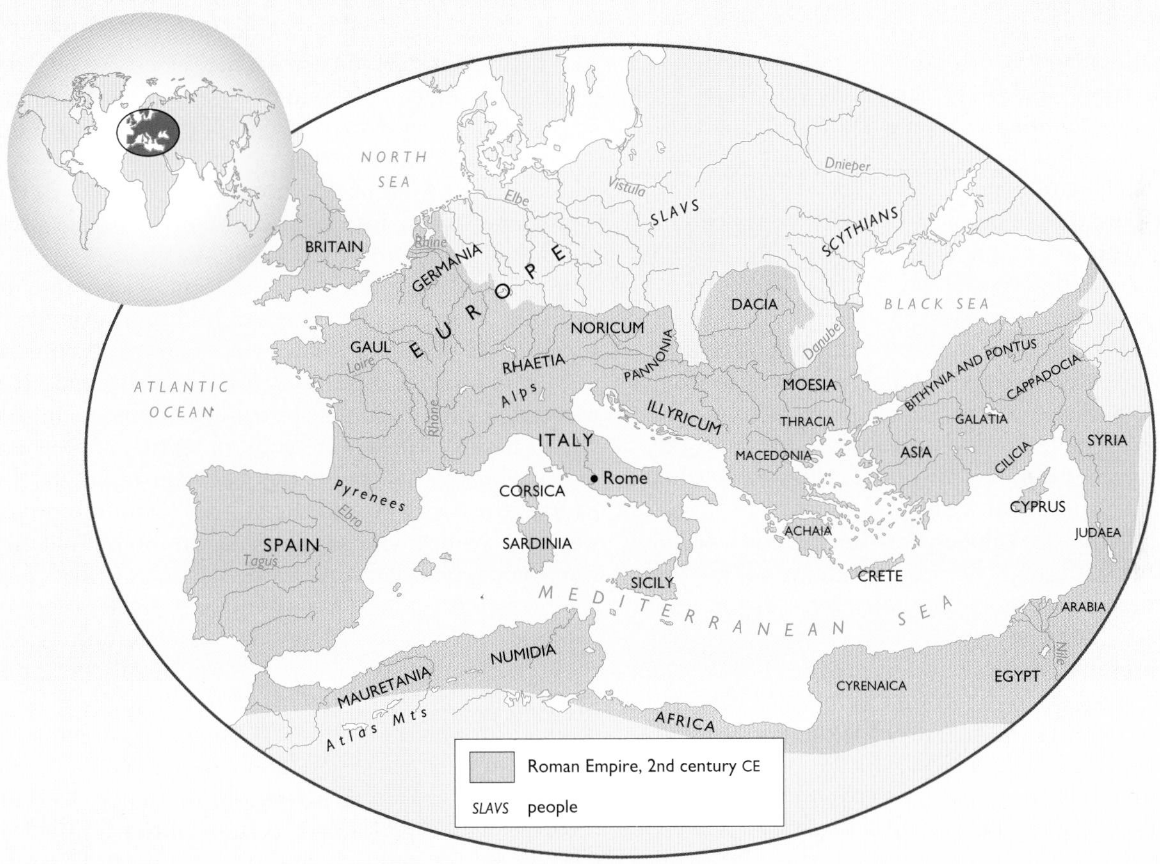

KEY TOPICS

- **Roman Gods:** As Rome expands, the gods of household and state are joined by the Greek Olympians, Asian fertility goddesses, solar deities, and "mystery" religions.
- **Judaism in Transition:** As Palestinian Jews suffer the destruction of the Second Temple, failed revolution, and expulsion from Jerusalem, they scatter and reorganize under their **rabbis**.
- **Origins of Christianity:** Meanwhile, Jesus of Nazareth lives and dies, and becomes the focus of a movement offering salvation through faith in a crucified savior.
- **Progress of Christianity:** The early Church matures into a complex institution, nurtured by its leaders' genius and its followers' courage; when Rome falters, the Church takes its place.

The Unknown God In Athens, where the latest intellectual fad caused tongues to wag and where every new god found a worshiper, there stood one altar—in case any deity had been slighted—to the "unknown god." Here Paul of Tarsus, a follower of the crucified teacher Jesus of Nazareth, preached a sermon around the midpoint of the first century C.E. "What therefore you worship as unknown, this I proclaim to you. The God who made the world and everything in it ... does not live in shrines made by human hands, nor is he served by human hands, as though he needed anything, since he himself gives to all mortals life and breath and all things." The god who was unknown to the Athenians, Paul told his audience, was the Jewish God, revealed in Jesus.*

The doctrine Paul preached gave birth to Christianity: the religion that today has more followers than any other on the globe and that has fundamentally shaped the experience of the Western world. Unknown to the Athenians of the first century, it would go on to triumph throughout the Roman Empire before that power fell in the West. It triumphed for several reasons: because it responded to human needs not addressed by ancient polytheistic religions; because it reached populations broader than those responding to its parent religion, Judaism; and because, as it developed within Rome's harsh bosom, it adopted the principles of organization established by that once-successful state.

The polytheistic religions of the ancient world—many of which found their way to Rome itself—will be the first concern of this chapter. Within that polytheistic universe, Judaism developed, insisting on the awesome presence in the cosmos of only one God, whose action in the world was revealed in sacred Hebrew scripture, and who made moral demands on his worshipers. From Judaism, finally, emerged Christianity, which added to the monotheism, the scriptural tradition, and the ethical principles of its parent religion the figure of Jesus the Christ, or Savior, or Messiah. With its promise of **salvation** and eternal life, and with the support of some of the greatest minds and most effective leaders of the era, Christianity flourished in the fading Roman world.

ROMAN GODS

Like most other ancient peoples, the Romans were polytheists who revered gods of earth and sky and the spirits animating their natural world. The evolution of Roman polytheism is as outlined in *Who's Who* on p. 172. At first, Roman villagers worshiped the deities of their households and fields. As Rome developed, its citizens embraced the gods of the peoples they conquered and imitated. Later, Romans experimented with exotic cults that promised salvation to troubled souls, or looked to elevated philosophies that offered a different path toward the same spiritual peace. By the fourth century, with Christianity ascendant, the Romans who still worshiped many gods were called pagans: "country-dwellers." These simple villagers clung to ancestral ways when most urbanites had abjured polytheism and embraced the one God of ancient Israel and the new church.

Ancestral Ways

The religion of the early Romans was simpler than that of the Christians or Jews, simpler even than that of other Indo-European peoples. Common to most Indo-European groups was a powerful sky god: the Greek Zeus, the Hindu Indra, the Persian Ahura Mazda, the Viking Odin (see Chapter 1). An anthropomorphic deity, with human forms and human attributes, he caused storms, thunder and lightning, and ruled the other deities, approximating, in some cases, the one God of the monotheistic faiths. In the Greek and Viking traditions especially, a rich body of myth grew up around thundering sky gods.

In the earliest days, before Rome's exposure to Etruscan customs, the Romans did not worship a supreme sky god. Nor did they conceive of their gods in human form, or develop a mythology. Instead, they worshiped a multitude of spirits: mystic forces embedded in nature. There were gods, or spirits, of plowing, of harvest, of the boundaries between farms, of the hearth, the doorway, and the granary. Most important were the beings who safeguarded the household and were worshiped daily in the domestic cult: the *lares* (deified spirits of dead ancestors) and *penates* (gods of the household stores). Each day the family honored these deities with ritual acts and sacrificial offerings.

The important role of the household in Roman religion mirrors the role of the *paterfamilias*, its head, in Roman society. The religion of the Roman state was the religion of the household writ large. Certain rites had to be performed, certain duties fulfilled, if the community was to thrive. The Latin word for religion—*religio*, meaning a bond between humans and gods—connotes the scrupulous fulfilment of obligation, the union of human beings in their duty to the divine. If all due rites were paid to the deities, there would be peace with the gods, among the gods, and among human beings: "the peace of the gods." If not, all was at risk. No public business was to be undertaken, no war prosecuted unless proper deities had been consulted and rituals conducted.

Among the Etruscan religious practices the Romans inherited was that of divination. Some Etruscan priests predicted future events by examining the livers of sacrificed beasts. Others examined the movements of birds or other natural phenomena.

Another Etruscan religious concept was that of sacred space. The boundaries of Etruscan cities were marked with special rituals, and their temples, although modeled on those of the Greeks, were erected in a reserved spatial realm defined by ancillary buildings.

The Romans borrowed and blended these features of Etruscan ritual with their worship of the spirits of the granary and the hearth. Accordingly, the early Romans marked the boundary of their city with a sacred ritual to ensure its protection by spirits. Until the practice was abolished by Christian emperors, the young men of the city, stripped naked, ran the circuit of Rome in a ritual that promised security and abundance. On festal days (of which there were about 100 each year), public business was not to be conducted. State priests published a calendar of these days to prevent infractions, which would anger the gods.

Roman religion was greatly concerned with the preeminent business of war. One god's function was to announce whether the city was at war or at peace. This was Janus, the god of the city's doorways. The door of his temple was open in peacetime and closed

WITNESSES

Faith and Skepticism in Roman Religion

The Romans regarded religion very seriously, taking care to show due reverence to the gods by observing all obligations and following rituals meticulously; in return, they expected that the gods would protect their households and city. Those attitudes find expression in the passages by Livy and Plutarch, later historians describing behavior dictated by traditional religion: the self-devotion to the gods (exemplified by the sacrifice of P. Decius Mus), and the guardianship of the purity of the Vestal Virgins. In contrast, the third passage by the poet and Epicurean convert Lucretius is wholly skeptical. For Lucretius, the atomic "science" of Epicurean philosophy was a consolation to human beings who need no longer fear the afterworld or the vengeance of the gods.

To save Rome, P. Decius Mus devotes himself to the gods of the underworld (340 B.C.E.): In the confusion of this movement Decius the consul called out to Marcus Valerius in a loud voice: "We have need of the gods' help, Marcus Valerius. Come therefore, state pontiff of the Roman people, dictate the words, that I may devote myself to save the legions." The pontiff bade him don the purple-bordered toga and, with veiled head and one hand thrust out from under the toga and touching his chin, stand upon a spear that was laid under his feet and say as follows: "Janus, Jupiter, Father Mars. ..., ye gods in whose power are both we and our enemies, ... I invoke and worship you, ... that you may prosper the might and the victory of the Roman people, ... and visit the foes of the Roman people ... with fear, shuddering and death. As I have pronounced the words, even so ... do I devote the legions and auxiliaries of the enemy, together with myself to the divine Manes and to the Earth." ... He then girded himself ..., and vaulting, armed, upon his horse, plunged into the thick of the enemy. ...

(Livy, *History of Rome*, 8.9.4–10; eds. N. Lewis, M. Reinhold, 1966)

Plutarch describes the punishment assigned to a Vestal Virgin (one of the priestesses assigned to guard the perpetual flame of Rome), who has broken her vow of chastity (c. 110 C.E.): [A Vestal who] has broken her vow of chastity is buried alive ... [under] a little mound of earth ... [where] a narrow room is constructed, to which a descent is made by stairs; here they prepare a bed, and light a lamp, and leave a small quantity of victuals, such as bread, water, a pail of milk, and some oil. ... The culprit herself is put in a litter, which they cover over, and tie her down with cords on it, so that nothing she utters may be heard. They then take her to the Forum; all people silently go out of the way as she passes, and such as follow accompany the bier with solemn and speechless sorrow; and, indeed, there is not any spectacle more appalling, nor any day observed by the city with greater appearance of gloom and sadness. When they come to the place of execution, the officers loose the cords, and then the Pontifex Maximus [the chief priest] ... brings out the prisoner, ... and placing her upon the steps that lead down to the cell, turns away his face with the rest of the priests; the stairs are drawn up after she has gone down, and a quantity of earth is heaped up over the entrance to the cell. ... This is the punishment of those who break their vow of virginity.

(Plutarch, "Life of Numa" in William Stearns Davis, ed., *Readings in Ancient History*, 1912–13)

The poet Lucretius explains why mortal humans need have no fears; the world is ruled by the forces of nature alone, and there are no gods who have power over us (c. 55 B.C.E.):

This fright, this night of the mind, must be
dispelled
not by the rays of the sun, nor day's bright spears,
but by the face of nature and her laws.
And this is her first, from which we take our start:
nothing was ever by miracle made from nothing.
You see, all mortal men are gripped by fear
because they see so many things on earth
and in the sky, yet can't discern their causes
and hence believe that they are acts of god.
But in all this, when we have learned that nothing
can come from nothing, then we shall see straight
through
to what we seek: whence each thing is created
and in what manner made, without god's help.

(Lucretius, *De rerum natura*; trs. F. O. Copley 1977)

in wartime. War was undertaken only after consulting with religious experts such as diviners—called augurs or *haruspices* (singular *haruspex*)—who studied the movements of birds, clouds, and wind, and the organs of sacrificed beasts to judge whether the time was auspicious for battle, as shown on p. 172. *Fetial* priests were responsible for the ethics of war. Because Romans were not to fight except in self-defense, it was the fetials' duty to determine whether a proposed war was legitimate or not (they generally thought it was). When the time came for battle, Roman priests accompanied the army and exhorted the deities of the enemy city to flee before the attack. With terrifying gravity, the priests proclaimed those alien gods doomed if they did not defect to the victor.

The priests who performed such rituals were elected from among the "fathers," those heads of families who belonged to the order of patricians. Organized in groups, each responsible for a different element of the Roman cult, the priests established the calendar, supervised worship, and authorized the building of temples or the admission of new deities. Chief of all the priests was the *pontifex maximus*, a title that has lived on as the Latin name for the head of the Roman Catholic Church.

In addition to the male priests drawn from the patrician crust of Roman society, a group of six patrician women was charged with the performance of one important duty. That duty was to tend the flame (rekindled every March) that burned on the communal hearth in honor of Vesta, the patron goddess of the city. The women designated for this task (mostly young girls from leading families) were required to be virgins at the time of their selection and, by law, to remain so until they resigned their office (permissible after age forty), or died. These were the vestal virgins: the pure "daughters" of the city of Rome. The punishment was severe for those vestals discovered to have broken their vows: they were buried alive. It happened only rarely—for the last time during the reign of the emperor Domitian. "There is no spectacle in the world more terrifying," wrote the moralist Plutarch (46–120 C.E.), "and in Rome no day of comparable horror (see *Witnesses*, p. 169)."

Besides the six vestals, other women also participated in the Roman cult. As in Greece, religious celebration was one of the avenues for female participation in public life. Women danced, prayed, adorned their houses, and joined in processions. The annual worship of Ceres, the goddess of grain, for example, could be celebrated only by women. During the Second Punic War, these rites were canceled; so many women were in mourning for lost husbands and sons that there were not enough available to serve the goddess.

The Greeks of the southern Italian peninsula worshiped the Olympian gods of their homeland: Zeus, Apollo, Athena, Ares, Hermes. These cults became

A Temple for all the gods

The Pantheon *(left, right): By the second century C.E., Roman building techniques had matured considerably, as seen in the Pantheon, Rome, the temple to all the gods erected under the emperor Hadrian, c. 118 C.E. Built of marble, brick, and concrete, the most prominent feature of this temple was the enormous dome, its expanse pierced in the center by a round window (oculus) that admitted light to the spacious interior. This interior was captured in 1740 (facing page) by the Italian painter Giovanni Paolo Pannini.* (facing page: National Gallery of Art, Washington D.C. Samuel H. Kress Collection)

known to the Romans both directly from the Greeks resident in Italy and indirectly from the Etruscans, who had absorbed Greek customs in earlier centuries. The Romans soon adopted these deities, who looked and behaved like human beings. They built a temple on the Capitoline Hill to Jupiter, Juno, and Minerva (the Roman designations for the Greek gods Zeus, Hera, and Athena), which became the center of Roman religious life. In the temple consecrated to these three gods were deposited the books of prophecies announced by the Cumaean sibyl (from Italian Cumae), one of Rome's revered female prophets.

The anthropomorphic gods of hearth and household now encountered the anthropomorphic gods of a kindred yet very different people. The temples of the indigenous and the imported deities shared the same sacred zone: those dedicated to Janus and Vesta stood adjacent to those dedicated to Jupiter or Apollo. Native Roman traditions merged with adopted Greek ones, and Greek myth was Romanized.

New Religious Impulses

This early Roman religion—a mixture of Greek imagination, Etruscan practice, and ancestral Roman cult—faced a severe challenge during the last years of the third century B.C.E., in the Second Punic War, when the Carthaginian general Hannibal ravaged

Sacrifice and prophecy: *In Roman as in many ancient polytheistic cultures the sacrifice of an animal on the altar was a central religious ritual. Also important for the Romans was the practice derived from the Etruscans: the expert examination of the sacrificed beast's entrails for signs that predicted favorable or unfavorable outcomes for intended actions. These ritual events are depicted in this first century bowl, showing a bull being sacrificed.* (Louvre)

The sacrifice of a bull, first century B.C.E.

Italy (see Chapter 5). While wives, widows, and orphans were left at home alone to till the land, virtually all adult males were enrolled in the army. Routs, massacres, and retreats followed from encounters with the African general, along with a mounting death toll among the Romans and their Latin allies. In 216 B.C.E., the Carthaginians trapped and butchered a Roman force of 60,000; only 10,000 men escaped. Reaching deep into their past for a suitable response to this seemingly inexplicable disaster, the Romans sacrificed human victims to appease the gods for the last time in their history—two men and two women (according to the historian Livy), Greeks and Celts, buried alive in the cattle market.

When Hannibal's forces paraded outside the gates of Rome, some Romans, gripped by fear, sought strength in new forms of religious experience. Foremost among these was the cult of Cybele: the *Magna Mater* (Great Mother). In 204 B.C.E., a Roman delegation brought back from Pessinus (in Asia Minor) a black stone sacred to Cybele. Her cult and that of her dead and reborn consort Attis were celebrated each spring with orgiastic rites, performed by castrated male priests, the Galli (a profession barred to Roman citizens until the reign of the emperor Claudius, r. 41–54 C.E.).

Around the same time, the Greek god Dionysus (or Bacchus) began to be celebrated in Rome. As the god of wine, this deity was worshiped with noisy and orgiastic festivals (known as Bacchanals) that grieved the senatorial fathers who had already bent their principles to the arrival of the Great Mother.

Rome's further conquests in the East meant that more and more foreign religious cults found their way back to Rome. Traditionalists distrusted their exotic message and sometimes bizarre practices—especially since they often appealed to slaves, who could participate as equals in cultic rites and even become priests. The historian Sallust (86–34 B.C.E.) lamented that greed had driven morality from Rome and replaced it with "pride, cruelty, neglect of the gods, and total materialism." It was the neglect of religion, Cicero maintained, that had brought the civil wars upon the Romans. But these voices could not prevail against the appeal of exotic cultural forms that appeared to offer certainties about this world and the other. Compared to these, the Roman cults of hearth and house seemed irrelevant.

WHO'S WHO

The Evolution of Roman Polytheism, 500–100 B.C.E.

500 B.C.E.

Household Gods
Lares and *Penates*

State Religion
Pontifex maximus, *rex sacrorum*, *flamines*, Vestal Virgins, augury and prophecy

Romanized Greek Gods
Jupiter, Juno, Minerva, Diana, Apollo

Foreign Deities
Cybele, Isis, Mithras

100 B.C.E.

The man who once had consented to Cicero's murder came later to defend, like him, the worship of the ancient gods. Augustus believed that traditional worship would help preserve the "customs of our ancestors," the virtues that had made Rome great. As *pontifex maximus*, he revived the Roman cults and oversaw a program of temple construction. Yet even as he defended traditional religion, Augustus, too, was a religious innovator. He chose as his personal deity Apollo—among the Greeks, the god of the intellect, and patron of the rational approach to human existence, but also (as a result of Hellenistic syncretism) assimilated to the sun gods of eastern cults.

Augustus' patronage of Apollo encouraged later emperors to choose a personal god, and served to break down the solidity of the ancient Roman tradition. So did the creation of a priesthood dedicated to Augustus' imperial cult, which was practiced after Augustus' death in the Hellenistic lands where king-worship was an established practice (see Chapter 6). Just as Augustus, as restorer of the Republic, sealed its death sentence, so Augustus, champion of ancestral virtues, helped open the path to the unrestrained syncretism of the imperial centuries.

Later Roman Religion

In the early Empire, the religious traditions of the Mediterranean world continued to fuse. To be sure, the official cults of the Greek *poleis* and the Roman state remained distinctive, as did Judaism. Otherwise, the deities of West and East were interchanged to such an extent that their ethnic origins were forgotten. This process of syncretism (the blending of diverse religious traditions) resulted in the elevation of some deities to near universal status. One example of this is the amalgamation of Sarapis from the Egyptian Osiris with various other deities of the ancient East. The syncretic process flourished under Roman rule, which tolerated all forms of religious expression that were not perceived as threatening to the power of the state.

Not only did ancient cults blend by the process of syncretism, but ancient "mystery religions" found new popularity in Rome during the early Empire. These promised a secret knowledge or special experience of the divine realm which could lead to individual illumination. The mystery religions appealed especially to the swollen populations of the cities of the Hellenistic and Roman eras.

In earlier antiquity, religion tended to be communal: the household, the village, the city gained by the worship of specific gods. In later antiquity, religion tended to become personal: the individual hoped to experience the benefits of worship and was more willing to risk his or her personal security to gain that benefit. The former kind of religious system was ideally suited to peasant communities, with their strong ties to the land. The latter suited the cities, where diverse populations were offered many religious options, where individuals often felt isolated amid the crowd and were vulnerable to promises of salvation, and where the boredom of the rich and the desperation of the poor both sought remedies in devotion.

The goddess Isis attracted many worshipers over the centuries, especially women. She was understood as the universal and compassionate mother, often depicted with her consort Osiris (sometimes Sarapis) or holding her infant son Horus, as shown on p. 174. Her priests were a regular clergy, robed in white, who daily administered rituals of purification. They baptized new initiates, who were thereby cleansed from sin and expected to pass through a final judgment by Sarapis and enter into eternal life. There are elements here of belief and ritual that anticipate mature Christianity.

People also worshiped the Sun, which had been personified as a deity by the Egyptians and the Hittites, among others. In late antiquity, the worship of the Sun gained such popularity that it almost became a universal religion—in the place not long after to be filled by Christianity. Augustus' worship of Apollo, in this era a Sun deity, has been noted. Hadrian's Pantheon (built c. 118 C.E. to celebrate all the gods) especially exalted the Sun, the light of which shone through the special opening in the building's huge domed roof.

In the third century C.E. the Severan emperors and their wives also worshiped the Sun. The emperor Aurelian (r. 270–275 C.E.) made sun worship the central feature of the state religion, erecting a temple to Sol Invictus, the Invincible Sun (in 274 C.E.). The emperor Constantine (r. 312–337 C.E.) worshiped the Sun until his victory over a rival claimant to the Empire at the Battle of the Milvian Bridge (312 C.E.), which he believed was due to Christ's favor. The birthday of Sol Invictus was celebrated annually on December 25 (approximately at the winter solstice). The same date served as the birthday of the god Mithras, and would be adopted by Christians for the celebration of the birth of their Savior.

The Persian deity Mithras was one of the many solar gods of the imperial era. Brought home to Rome by Pompey's troops, Mithras became a favorite among the Roman soldiers, who worshiped him in barracks, garrisons, and frontier camps. A heroic champion against evil (a reflection of his Zoroastrian origins), Mithras appealed to those who often faced danger and death. The faithful (exclusively male) gathered to worship their deity in his temple, in the center of which was a sculpted image of the god slaying a bull, from whose body all living things were thought to be created. Initiation involved progress through seven stages, including a ritual washing in the spilled blood of a sacrificial beast. Full members participated in communal meals at which consecrated bread and wine were consumed. Through these they gained unity with the god, and hoped for an eternity in Heaven. In these practices, there were prefigurations of Christianity.

While many Romans sought to enrich their lives through religion, others looked to magic. Religion involved reverence for the gods and the performance of required duties or rituals. Magic offered control over divine spirits and natural forces with the aim of increasing personal power. Magic manipulated the supernatural realm and could (it was believed) arrange love affairs, cure diseases, tell the future, and even murder an enemy.

Magic was the science of the unlearned. For the learned, astrology offered an opportunity to penetrate (so they thought) otherwise unknowable secrets of the universe. Astrology used the knowledge of the motion of the stars and planets to predict the future and understand the present. As the planets circled the earth, they also (apparently) influenced earthly events. They did so according to their position in the sky relative to the earth, to the other planets, and to the signs of the zodiac (a set of twelve constellations each at the zenith during a different period of the year). Astrologers could use their knowledge to forecast the future, as magicians could use their charms and incantations to shape it.

Other religious beliefs derived from the learned traditions. The ancient Zoroastrians had seen the universe as a stage for a struggle between gods of Good and Evil (see Chapter 1). That **dualism**, which supported such religious beliefs as immortality and the Devil, survived into later antiquity and beyond. It influenced some Jewish authors of the last centuries B.C.E. and reemerged in the theology of the Persian prophet Mani (216–276 C.E.). Mani preached that the struggle between the forces of Light and Darkness would be decided by a Savior (whom he identified with Jesus). Mani's teachings survived in the Manichean religion, which had many adherents—including the young Saint Augustine before his conversion to Christianity—during the first few centuries C.E. Mani was crucified as a heretic by the Zoroastrians.

The Neoplatonists were the late successors to Plato, the great Athenian philosopher (see Chapter 4). They developed a secular theology that appealed to the skeptical intellectuals of the late Empire. The Egyptian-born Plotinus (205–270 C.E.) envisioned a transcendent force of the One, or First Principle: being that exists beyond number, thought, motion, or time. From the One there radiates all of existence, in ever-widening circles, to its farthest limit: the Many, creatures locked in time and space. Nearest to the One is the Universal Mind; and immediately below it, Universal Soul. The individual human being can hope, through the cultivation of his own soul or mind, to reach the One in an experience of intimate union. Plotinus' philosophy, developed for oral instruction, is recorded in the six books of *Enneads*, by his pupil Porphyry of Tyre (234–305 C.E.).

In the last Roman centuries, philosophy became an alternative to religion, more a guide for existence than a method for the rational investigation of the cosmos. That tendency could already be seen in the work of Lucretius, Cicero, and Seneca. These were popularizers, whose aim was to make available to literate but practical Romans the visions of the ancient philosophers—all of them Greek. Lucretius' enormous verse exposition of Epicurean philosophy, *On the Nature of Things*, assured his compatriots in moving and insistent tones that they need not fear death. On the one hand, the universe itself would never die, as all substance was eternal. On the other, humans would die without consequence, with no prospect of afterlife or punishment or pain, since all souls were mortal.

The eclectic Cicero drew on all the philosophical schools. In *De natura deorum* he encapsulated the Academic, the Peripatetic, the Epicurean, and the Stoic views of the nature of the universe, the role of the gods, and the role of the human being. In his *Tusculan Disputations* and *On Duties* and other works, he explored Greek insights into the interactions of human society and the predicaments of the soul.

Divine Mothers

***Isis and Horus** (left): Just as Roman religion was syncretistic, readily absorbing the deities and beliefs of other religious traditions practiced in the Mediterranean world, so also was Christianity, which grafted Greek, Roman, and other ancient ideas and practices onto the original stem of Judaism. The worship of the Egyptian goddess Isis (left), the loving mother of Horus, was widely practiced in Rome, as shown in this sculpture c. 1400 B.C.E.* (Schimmel Collection, New York)

***Virgin and Child** (right): When Jesus, the central figure of emerging Christianity, became paired in artistic representations with his mother Mary—as shown in this apse mosaic from Hosias Loukas, Greece, c. 1020 C.E.—the resulting image could resemble those of the Greeks, Romans, or Egyptians.*

Seneca's moral essays and letters popularized Stoicism (see Chapter 5)—of all the ancient philosophies the one most congenial to the Romans. He chided his readers about the emptiness of their lives, and nudged them to a deeper understanding of humanity. Each person had within him or her a spark of the divine fire, Seneca wrote reassuringly: "God is near you, he is with you, he is within you. ... A holy spirit indwells within us, one who marks our good and bad deeds, and is our guardian. ..."

The second-century emperor Marcus Aurelius retold in his diary all that ancient philosophy could offer as a guide to daily life, to the encounter with evil and with chance, and to the imminence of death. That the emperor's work *To Himself* (later referred to as his *Meditations*) seems weak testifies to the exhaustion of the intellectual tradition begun with Thales, Anaximander, and Anaximenes (see Chapter 4). For spirits in search of nurture, the two monotheistic faiths—Judaism and Christianity—offered more.

JUDAISM IN TRANSITION

On returning to Judah after 538 B.C.E. from their exile in Babylon, the Jews reorganized the life of their community under new leaders in accord with their ancient traditions. Over the next several centuries, they lived under the Persians, the Greeks, and the Romans in turn, struggling to maintain their unique religious and cultural identity. At some points, that struggle became violent. And the era ended in violence, in 135 C.E., two generations after the Temple at Jerusalem was destroyed for the last time. Thenceforth, Jewish faith and culture would survive only in exile, in scattered communities around the ancient Mediterranean and beyond, under the guidance of learned teachers, **rabbis**, whose knowledge of scripture constituted a standard for daily life (see Map 7.1).

The Jewish State Under Foreign Overlords

When Cyrus the Great of Persia destroyed the Babylonian Empire in 539 B.C.E., he allowed the thousands of Jews exiled there to return to their land of Judah. Governors and priests led the restored community in the crystallization of a Jewish way of life based on the sacred writings of the **Torah**. Among these towered Nehemiah (d. 415 B.C.E.) and Ezra "the Scribe" (fl. c. 458 B.C.E.). Nehemiah, an effective administrator, oversaw the building of the walls of the city that Nebuchadnezzar had demolished. Ezra organized the compilation of Hebrew writings (probably some part of the Pentateuch, the first five biblical books—perhaps only Deuteronomy). From a wooden pulpit, he read the law aloud and stirred the Jewish people to commit to the covenant with an almighty God that it defined. With that determination (as distinct from the already long history of the Jewish people) the history of Judaism begins.

Alexander's conquest of 333 B.C.E. shook the newly formed Jewish community. The Ptolemies of Egypt invited Jews to settle in Alexandria, and ruled Judaea (as it was known to the Greeks) benevolently. Later, the Seleucid rulers of Syria challenged the Ptolemaic presence in Judaea, and Antiochus III (r. 223–187 B.C.E.) finally unseated the Egyptians and took command of the region. The Jewish hero Mattathias, of the Hasmonean clan, along with his sons, successfully resisted the Hellenizing crusade of Antiochus IV Epiphanes. By 142 B.C.E., his last surviving son, Simon, held the title of high priest over an autonomous Jewish state within the fading Seleucid Empire.

After 63 B.C.E., authority seeped from the high priest Hyrcanus to his adviser, Antipater (an Idumaean or Edomite, whose people—related to the Jews but traditionally hostile to them—had been recently converted to Judaism). Herod, one of Antipater's sons, gained supremacy in 37 B.C.E. and ruled an expanded Judaea until his death in 4 B.C.E. A generous patron of building and the arts, Herod (called "the Great") was known for both his exceptional brutality and his great competence. He was the last person to command an autonomous Jewish state until the twentieth-century leaders of Israel. Herod's successors were titular rulers until 70 C.E., when the Second Temple, which Herod had rebuilt and adorned, fell to Roman conquerors, who destroyed it. A description is given in *Witnesses* on p. 177.

Herod's successors were rulers in name only, for Rome now controlled Judaea. Just as external politics had introduced the Jews to the Greeks, so they introduced the Jews to the Romans. During the years of Hasmonean rule in Judaea, the Roman presence loomed in nearby Asia Minor, Syria, and Egypt. In 63 B.C.E., Pompey reached Jerusalem and entered its temple, penetrating to the inner sanctum known as the Holy of Holies, heretofore the unique prerogative of the high priest on the holiest day of Yom Kippur.

Roman procurators and tax-collectors ruled Judaea. Herod's successors followed Roman directives as they clung to remnants of their autonomy: Herod even built a temple in Samaria for the celebration of the imperial cult, as well as an athletic complex (hateful to some Jews) in Jerusalem. Nevertheless, the Jewish community flourished. As of the census of 48 C.E., there may have been as many as 2 million Jews within Palestine and 7 million within the Empire; a large proportion, perhaps as much as 15 percent of the population of that cosmopolitan state was Jewish.

Under Roman rule, the high priest in Jerusalem and the members of the Sanhedrin, or council, avoided politics and concerned themselves with strictly religious matters. Of these there were many.

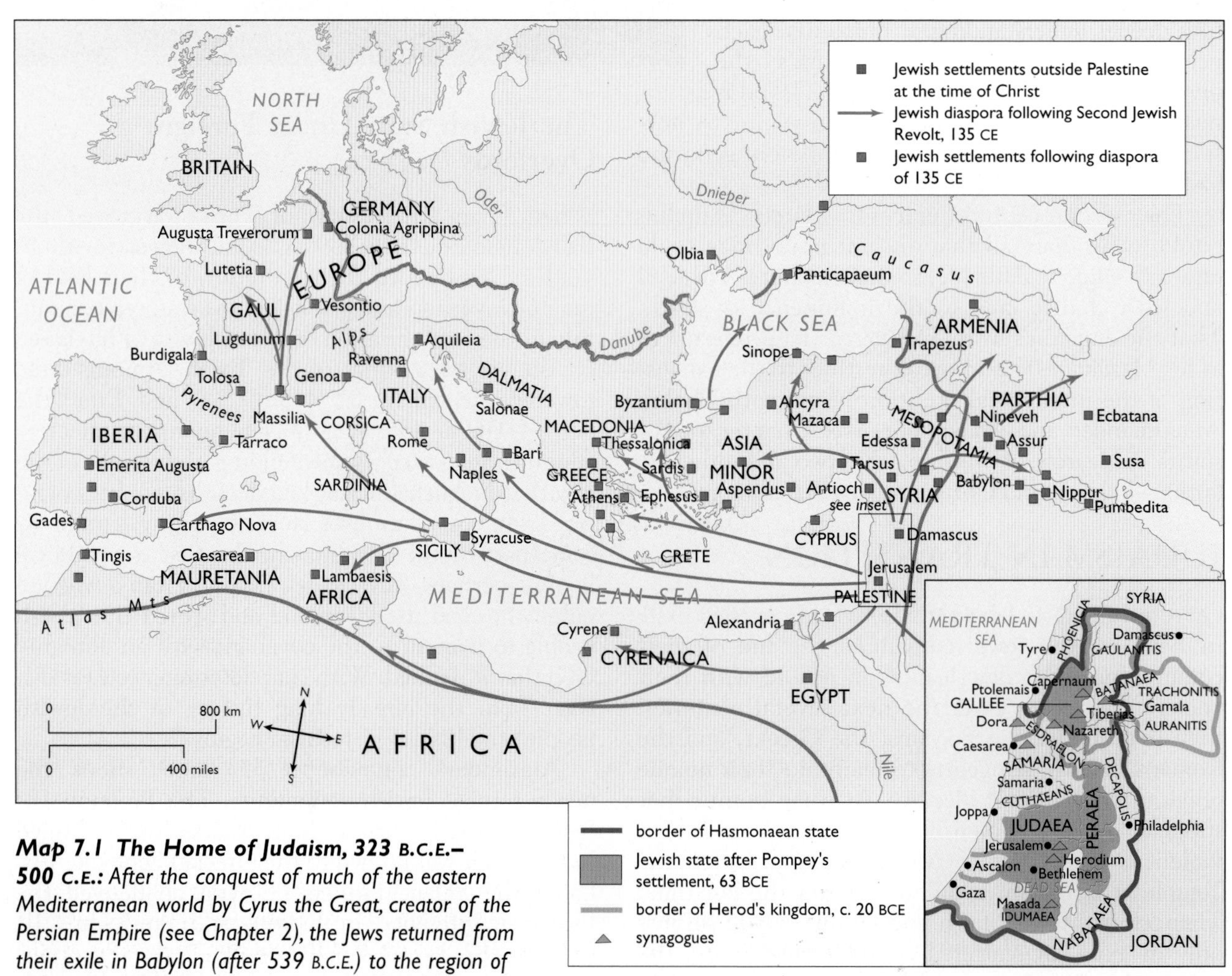

***Map 7.1 The Home of Judaism, 323 B.C.E.–500 C.E.:** After the conquest of much of the eastern Mediterranean world by Cyrus the Great, creator of the Persian Empire (see Chapter 2), the Jews returned from their exile in Babylon (after 539 B.C.E.) to the region of Judah, which would later be known to the Greeks and Romans as Palestine. Over the next centuries, the Temple in Jerusalem would be rebuilt (the Second Temple) and the religion of Judaism formed around it. Meanwhile, Jewish communities also flourished in Babylon, in Ptolemaic Egypt, Asia Minor, the Aegean, and Italy—the communities of the Diaspora, or "dispersion."*

WITNESSES

Jerusalem Destroyed, and Lamented

The Temple in Jerusalem, built by Solomon around 960 B.C.E. (see Chapter 1), had represented the center of the world for the Jews, and also the site for ritual and sacrifice. It was destroyed by the Babylonian king Nebuchadnezzar in 587 B.C.E., and a second temple was built to replace it when the large community of Jews who had been exiled to Babylonia were liberated by the Persian King Cyrus and returned to Jerusalem. It was destroyed again by a Roman army in 70 C.E., a loss that would transform Jewish life forever. In the first passage, the historian Tacitus describes the Roman destruction of the Second Temple. The second is a prophet's lamentation for the destruction of the First Temple by Nebuchadnezzar.

When Vespasian, who had been conducting the war against the Jews, returned to Rome in 70 C.E. to become emperor, he left his son Titus to pursue the siege of Jerusalem—which ended in the storming and burning of the temple: Titus pitched his camp before the walls of Jerusalem, and displayed his legions in battle order. The Jews formed their line close under the walls. ... The temple had its own walls, like a citadel. ... The founders had foreseen frequent wars because of differences from other peoples, and had prepared for protracted siege. ... It is recorded that the besieged, of every age and both sexes, amounted to 600,000. All who could bore arms. ... Men and women showed equal perseverance: they feared life more than death if they should be forced to leave their country. ...

About the fifth hour of the following day the Jews were overpowered and shut up in the inner court of the temple, whereupon Titus withdrew, resolved to attack the following dawn with his whole force and gain the temple. ... [At this point] one of the soldiers, awaiting no order and feeling no dread at such a deed but yielding to some demonic impulse, snatched a brand from the burning timbers and ... hurled the fire through a little golden door which gave access to the rooms around the sanctuary on the north. As the flames shot up the Jews raised a cry worthy of the disaster and scurried to the rescue. ...

[Titus] Caesar was unable to restrain the frenzy of his soldiers, and the fire got the upper hand. With his officers, he stepped in and saw the holy of holies and its contents. ... One of the men who had made his way in ... thrust a brand into the hinges of the gate. At once, a flame shot up from the interior and Caesar and his officers withdrew; now there was no one to prevent those outside from spreading the fire. And so, against Caesar's wishes, the temple was burned down.
(Tacitus, *Histories*, 5.11; ed. M. Hadas 1956)

Once before the destruction of the temple in 70 C.E., Jerusalem had been devastated—when it fell to the Babylonian king Nebuchadnezzar in 587 B.C.E. On that occasion, a prophet lamented its downfall:

How lonely sits the city
  that once was full of people!
How like a widow she has become,
  she that was great among the nations!
She that was a princess among the provinces
  has become a vassal.

Her foes have become the masters,
  her enemies prosper,
because the Lord has made her suffer
  for the multitude of her transgressions;
her children have gone away,
  captives before the foe.

Jerusalem remembers,
  in the days of her affliction and wandering,
all the precious things
  that were hers in days of old.
When her people fell into the hand of the foe,
  and there was no one to help her,
the foe looked on mocking
  over her downfall.
(Lamentations, 1:1,5,7)

During the Hasmonean and Herodian eras, two parties of Jewish thought emerged with different views of the relative value of written and oral tradition and with different outlooks upon the law and worship: the **Sadducees** and **Pharisees**.

Sadducees, Pharisees, and Essenes The wealthy Sadducees (the term derives from Zadok, high priest under David) were prominent in the Sanhedrin and dedicated themselves to the performance of the Temple cult. They recognized the written Torah as final and authoritative, resisting new ideas which, as they saw it, threatened the timelessness of the ritual performance. Because many of them came from the elite of Jewish society, they were inclined to support the balance of power established between foreign overlords and the native rulers.

The Pharisees (the term means "separated" or "distinct"), their natural opponents, differed from the Sadducees above all in their recognition of an oral tradition of law, handed down from Moses, that had validity alongside scripture. Holding that the observance of the law, more than the practice of the Temple cult, was central to Judaism, they developed a liturgy for worship in the synagogue based on scriptural readings and prayer. They closely examined points of law, often by disputations, foreshadowing some aspects of post-Temple Judaism. Some Pharisees

MUST READS

Great Books of the Bible

Old Testament	New Testament
Genesis	Gospel according to St. John
Book of Job	Acts
Psalms	Letter to the Romans
Isaiah	Revelations
Lamentations	
Ezekiel	

accepted the idea of an afterlife for the pious and of the **resurrection** of the body, perhaps influenced by Greek and Zoroastrian thought. In addition, the Pharisees elaborated the concept of the **Messiah** as an ideal future leader who would bring the reign of divine justice to the earth. That concept was an extension of what can be read in the Hebrew Bible about the Messiah (meaning "one who is anointed"); references are striking but few.

Associated with the Pharisees were the scribes and rabbis, or teachers. The scribes were laymen learned in scripture, who could define the conduct required by a strict reading of biblical law. The rabbis, the heirs of the Pharisees, were learned men who read and commented upon the Torah in the synagogues of the Jewish world, in Judaea and beyond. Their activity marked the emerging importance to the Jewish community of the **synagogue**—a place of study, assembly, and prayer, as contrasted with the Temple in Jerusalem, which was a holy place for ritual acts and sacrifice. Two great rabbis taught in Herod's reign: Hillel (c. 30 B.C.E.–10 C.E.) and his contemporary Shammai (c. 50 B.C.E.–30 C.E.), forerunners of a great tradition. The rabbis preserved the tradition of Pharisaic observance of the law when the high priests and Sadducees were no more, and Judaism was guided by its teachers.

Contemporaries of the Sadducees and the Pharisees were the Essenes (the term means "holy" or "pious"), members of one of the Jewish **sects** that flourished in the Herodian age. Highly disciplined, ascetic observers of the law, they withdrew into wilderness communities to pursue a religious life and, expecting the imminent arrival of the Messiah, to prepare for a cosmic war to ensue—similar to the Zoroastrian prediction of a conflict between the Children of Light and the Children of Darkness.

The most famous Essene community was at Qumran, near the northern tip of the Dead Sea. In 1947, scrolls from Qumran that recorded the community's sacred work and apocalyptic vision were found buried in caves. Among these Dead Sea Scrolls, a fragment of which is illustrated on p. 179 were copies, mostly fragments, of nearly all the canonical books of Hebrew scripture, the oldest still extant.

Resentment of Roman power simmered in the Jewish community of the Herodian age. In the countryside, especially, some rebels plotted the random assassination of Roman officials and collaborators. Such groups gathered force and men, setting the stage for the great rebellions of the first two centuries C.E.—the most serious ones the Romans would experience—and their terrible consequences.

The Revolts and Rabbinical Judaism

The first of these rebellions resulted in the destruction of the temple refounded by Nehemiah. The second resulted in the devastation of Judaea.

Rebellion first broke out in 66 C.E., triggered by the Roman desecration of the Temple. To suppress the revolt, the emperor Nero sent his experienced general Vespasian. Jewish leaders seized the Temple, and Vespasian prepared to besiege the city. In 68 C.E., Nero killed himself, and the Empire was claimed by four successors in turn. Returning to Rome to claim the imperial title for himself, Vespasian left his son Titus to complete the siege of Jerusalem.

Titus stormed the Temple heights, and, failing to weaken the walls with his formidable war machines, burned the gates. The fire spread. The complex was obliterated, and Roman soldiers sacked Jerusalem. The destruction of the Second Temple was the second great national tragedy of the Jewish people, comparable to their long-ago captivity in Babylon (see *Witnesses*, p. 177). Refugees from Jerusalem streamed into the countryside, north to Galilee, east to Mesopotamia, and south to Egypt, where they did not forget their suffering or the principles for which they stood.

The Roman army had seized all Jewish fortifications they encountered en route to Jerusalem. When they came to Galilee, in the north of the Jewish state, the defending Jewish general Joseph, or Josephus (37–c. 100 C.E.), quickly sized up the strength of the Roman force sent against him and surrendered. Soon he was to be found amid the councils of the Roman leadership. Detested by many of his coreligionists for his apostasy, Josephus nevertheless performed a valuable service for them, recording the narrative (flawed by some self-protective inaccuracies) of Jewish life in this age and of the inexorable Roman advance.

One flawed story he tells is the tragic one of Masada. A group of Zealots (a faction that fervently resisted the Roman presence) and their families had taken refuge there, in Herod's fortified mountaintop palace, south of Jerusalem near the Dead Sea. Well-supplied, this rump of the Jewish resistance was able to hold out for three years. In 73 C.E., the Romans stormed the citadel and found almost all the belligerents dead. The men had killed their wives and children and then themselves. They had chosen suicide before submission to Rome. Only a handful of women and children survived, hidden in a cistern.

WINDOWS ON

Ancient Jewish Life

Practices and beliefs very different from those of the Romans and other ancient polytheists characterized the ancient and still-living religion of Judaism. From its earliest formation, Judaism was a religion of the "book," the "Bible," the name taken from the Greek word for book. The Dead Sea Scrolls (top) are the earliest extant portions of the Bible read by first-century Jews (in this case, those belonging to the ascetic community of Essenes at Qumran).

The stone relief from the Arch of Titus in Rome (center) depicts a procession of Roman soldiers carrying the Menorah, the seven-branched candelabrum borne in the Hanukkah celebration to commemorate the Maccabean revolt against Greek overlords.

The fresco (below) is from one of the synagogues around which Jewish worship centered, especially after the fall of the Second Temple in 70 C.E.. It depicts the wheeled Ark of the Covenant (carrying the sacred books) shattering and scattering pagan idols.
(top: Israel Museum, Jerusalem; below: National Archaeological Museum, Damascus)

Dead Sea Scrolls

Arch of Titus, Rome, c. 81 C.E.

Wheeled Ark of the Covenant, Dura-Europos, Syria, c. 245 C.E.

To continue your investigation of this topic, please go to www.prenhall.com/king for the related **WINDOWS** on the **WEB** activity

The Roman repression of the revolt of 66–70 C.E. was severe, but its severity did not prevent recurrences. In 117 C.E., during Trajan's reign, Roman troops brutally suppressed a concerted rebellion of the Egyptian Jews, with huge losses on both sides. Trajan's successor, Hadrian, who was determined to discipline the Jews, introduced unprecedented forms of discrimination against them—including a ban on circumcision, central to the Jewish way of life. Like Antiochus IV Epiphanes, whose attempts to Hellenize Jewish culture had been thwarted by Maccabean resistance, Hadrian attempted to Romanize the Jews. Above all, he insisted on their participation in the imperial cult, from which they had been previously excused.

Hadrian's behavior provoked a last rebellion in Palestine (as Judaea was called after 70 C.E.): that of Simon, dubbed Bar Kokhba, or "Son of the Star," by the rabbi Akiba ben Joseph. When the revolt was suppressed in 135 C.E., Bar Kokhba was executed, Akiba (according to legend) horribly tortured to death, and many other of the rabbinical leaders martyred. On the site of ruined Jerusalem stood Hadrian's new capital of Aelia Capitolina. This was a Roman city to which, except for one day a year, Jews were not even admitted. Judaea was ravaged, and more than half a million people were killed. Jews were now a minority in their homeland. The history of Judaism would develop henceforth primarily outside the Jewish homeland.

The **Diaspora**, or "scattering," of the Jewish people had begun long before Bar Kokhba's rebellion. The Assyrians deported the Ten Lost Tribes from Israel. The Babylonian king Nebuchadnezzar deported a large number of Jewish people to Mesopotamia. When they were permitted to return to Judaea (Judah) by Cyrus the Great, some stayed. These formed the nucleus of the Babylonian community of Jews which grew eventually to equal and exceed the Palestinian remnant.

After the death of Alexander and before the arrival of the Romans, many Jews had migrated to Egypt, North Africa and the Arabian peninsula, to Asia Minor, and even to Europe. In Roman times there were sizable Jewish communities in Athens and Corinth, in Greece; in Rome and Milan, in Italy; in Córdoba and Gades, in Spain; in Marseille and Lyon, in Gaul; in Cologne and Ratisbon, on the fringes of the German wilderness. In these remote places, Jews were united by their allegiance to the Torah and, once it was formulated, to the **Talmud**.

The Torah had been completed before the Herodian era. But the literary product of Jewish experience continued to grow. The Talmud was the creation of the rabbis, who took command of the destiny of Judaism after the destruction of the Second Temple and the devastation of the Bar Kokhba rebellion. The **Mishnah** was a legal casebook that commented upon orally transmitted law, put together by the patriarchs of the Sanhedrin (in Jabneh and Usha, in Galilee) during the second century C.E. **Midrash** consisted of stories and sermons elaborating biblical material. The Talmud consisted of these and of further *Halachah* (laws) and *Agada* (narratives), as well as more informal discussions about proper Jewish life, and a miscellany of folklore, science, literature, and history, recording the experience of a people frequently challenged desperately by events but never left spiritless.

The Talmud was compiled in the third and fourth centuries C.E., first by the rabbis of Palestine (the *Palestinian Talmud*) and more than a century later, independently, by those of Mesopotamia (the *Babylonian Talmud*). These works were the basis for the forged unity of the Jewish people, homeless and stateless, dispersed over three continents. The Talmud was the creation not of priests, but of scholars equipped with knowledge and intelligence. As a result, the Jewish hero henceforth was neither king nor conqueror, but student. The people he led were not a nation but—more resourceful, more lasting—a spiritual community.

After the catastrophes of 117 and 135 C.E., the Jewish population of the Empire, though diminished, remained a vigorous presence and—after Hadrian's decrees lapsed—were allowed to practice their religion undisturbed. When Caracalla extended Roman citizenship to all free subjects of the Empire in 212 C.E., the Jews enjoyed, alongside polytheists, all the privileges of that status. With the exception of Hadrian, moreover, the emperors did not insist on Jewish participation in the imperial cult. Constantine's Edict of Milan of 313 C.E. extended toleration to all religions, specifically naming Judaism among those encompassed by the new decree.

Yet the attitude of many Romans toward Jews was highly critical. Roman authors often made negative allusions to the Jews, as when Tacitus (c. 55–120 C.E.) complained: "Most Jews were convinced that ... those who came forth from Judaea should possess the world." Nonetheless, many Romans—including some of the elite and many women—were attracted to Judaism. These converts supported the local synagogues, studied the Torah, observed the Sabbath, and accepted the dietary restrictions. For such adherents, the learned Philo of Alexandria (c. 20 B.C.E.–45 C.E.), or "Philo Judaeus" (Philo the Jew) harmonized Plato and the *Septuagint* (the Greek version of the Bible read outside Palestine). Philo argued that Greek philosophy and Judaism could be reconciled, that philosophy preceded and supported theology.

The uneasy coexistence of Romans and Jews was threatened by the emergence of a new religious community, Christianity. Persecuted at first, then favored, it insisted upon and won preeminence within the Roman world. Christian preeminence was to spell new disadvantages for Judaism.

ORIGINS OF CHRISTIANITY

The Christian religion originated when Rome was at its zenith. Roman emperors, generals, and nobles knew nothing of the lives of the people of Judaea, a province of the Empire. Those people suffered under Roman domination while believing that, one day, a servant of their one God would redeem them. In the reign of Augustus, a man was born among them whom a few followers at first, but ultimately most of the Roman world, acknowledged as that redeemer. The religion that came to be known as Christianity formed around the singular figure of Jesus of Nazareth. Propelled by the Greek-speaking Jew Paul of Tarsus, Christianity spread beyond Judaea and the eastern shores of the Mediterranean, reaching all the way to imperial Rome itself.

Jesus of Nazareth

Christianity developed from the message preached and enacted by Jesus (4 B.C.E.–c. 30 C.E.), a Jew from Nazareth in Galilee. His parents observed Jewish law and ritual and he himself was learned in scripture. These facts are known from the accounts of Jesus' life in the **Gospels** of the Christian **New Testament**.

The Gospels were compiled in the latter part of the first century C.E., more than a generation after Jesus' death. They are not scientific biographies but interpretative narratives, based on oral reports and lost earlier sources. They were written in the Greek of the *oecumene*, rather than the Hebrew or vernacular Aramaic of the Palestinian region. On the whole, they are acknowledged as giving fairly sound evidence about many of events. The authors identified as Mark, Luke, Matthew, and John (in the order of the composition of their works) transmitted a living faith based upon a real historical figure: the Jew Jesus.

When Jesus was about thirty years old, the Gospel authors report, he met one of the self-appointed holy men who were a feature of late Hellenistic Judaism. The visionary was his cousin John, called "the Baptist" because he ritually blessed his followers as they washed in the river Jordan, symbolizing their renunciation of sin. In the tradition of the prophets of Israel, John denounced the ways of the world and called his listeners to repent or turn away from guilty lives.

Jesus was one of those baptized by John. God himself acknowledged the event, according to the Gospels: "And just as he was coming up out of the water, he saw the heavens torn apart and the Spirit descending like a dove on him. And a voice came from heaven, 'You are my Son, the Beloved; with you I am well pleased.' " From this moment, Jesus' mission begins. For the next three years (probably 27–30 C.E.), he traveled through Judaea, Samaria, and Galilee, gathering disciples, performing miracles of healing, and preaching to crowds of followers.

Jesus' central message was similar to John's: the Kingdom of Heaven was coming, in which God would reign on earth as in heaven, punish those who had strayed from his way, and gather up the true believers in his love. His worshipers should pray for the coming of that kingdom, which Jesus made it his mission to announce: "Then Jesus went about all the cities and villages, teaching in their synagogues, and proclaiming the good news of the kingdom. ..." In his **parables**, or instructive stories, Jesus likened the kingdom of God to a variety of familiar and organic things that were joyously capable of growth: a mustard seed, sprouting grain, little children.

Jesus' announcement to the faithful of the coming of the Kingdom of God was a message well within the framework of Hellenistic Judaism. His idea of who the faithful were, however, was new and surprising. They were not the powerful, but the weak; not the rich, but the poor; not the wise, but the ignorant; not only those who were strong or healthy, but those who were sick and disabled; not only men, but women; not only adults, but children; not the established, but the homeless and the lost. According to the Gospel writers, Jesus proposed a revolution in the valuation of the human being: one implicit in Judaism, but unknown in all the polytheisms of the ancient world.

According to Jesus, the meek would inherit the Kingdom of God, and he called the meek to be his disciples. The disciple Peter was a fisherman, and Matthew a despised tax-collector. Jesus conversed with prostitutes and women considered unclean, with children (generally ignored in antiquity), with **Gentiles** (non-Jews avoided by faithful Jews), and with Samaritans (who had lapsed from **orthodoxy**). Those whom others condemned Jesus recommended as models of behavior: the prostitute who loved more than the Pharisee, the Samaritan who tended with compassion an injured and abandoned man ignored by two members of the Judaean elite.

Jesus also healed the sick: a stream of the blind and paralyzed, limping and bleeding, dying and dead. The figure of the healer endowed with special spiritual powers was often lionized in the Hellenistic era. Yet Jesus was different: he healed by forgiving sins and admonishing demons of madness and despair. It was not magic but faith, the Gospel authors claimed, that healed the sick who knew Jesus.

Just as he elevated faith over magic, Jesus placed love over law, subtly shifting emphasis in the values established by scriptural tradition. That tradition centered on law: God's gift of the commandments and the community's obedience to them. The tradition also distinguished itself among ancient religions by an emphasis on acts of love and mercy. Jesus does not depart from his tradition when he speaks of the great power of love. Yet he takes a small but significant step in placing love before and above the law, which was the cornerstone of Jewish life.

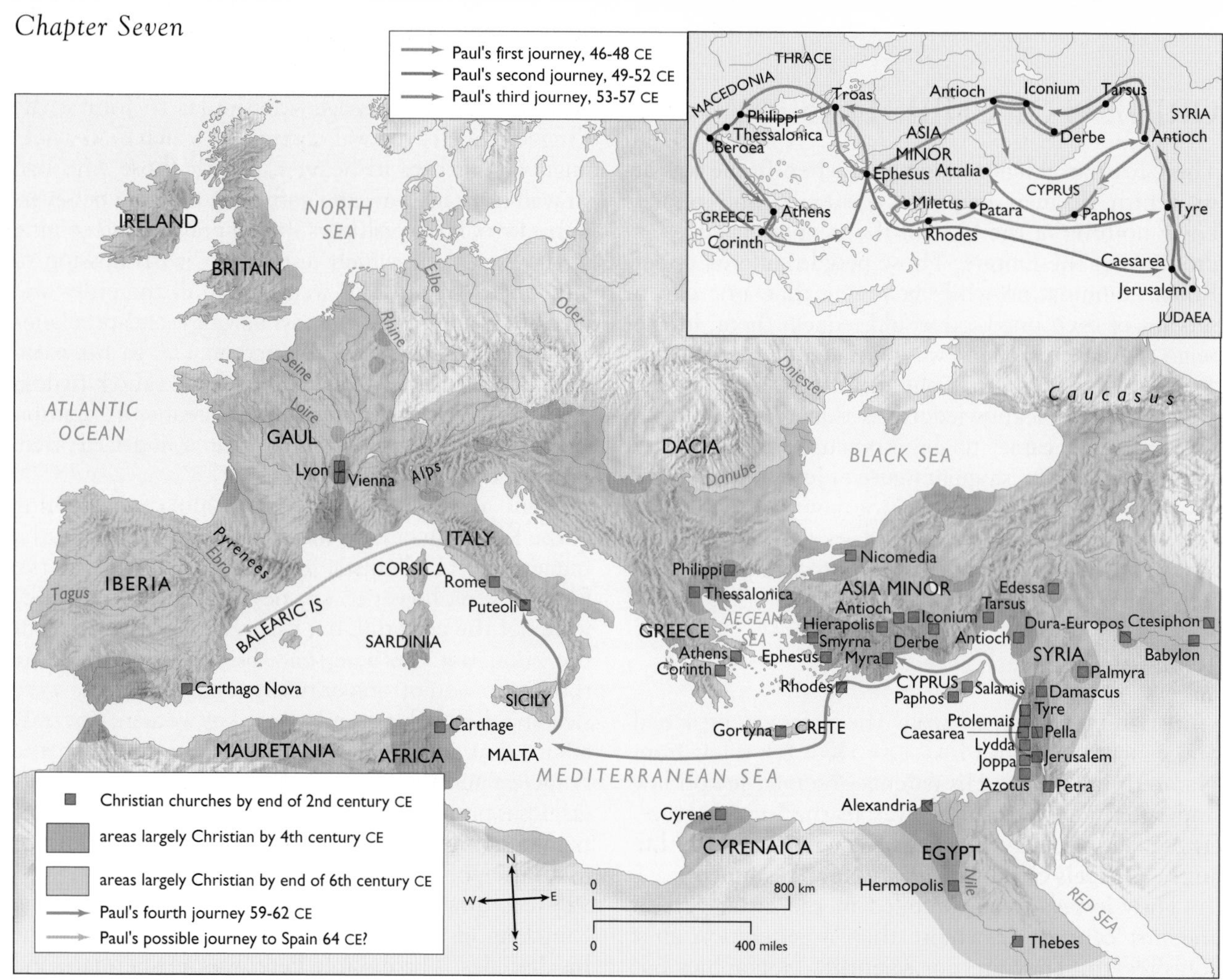

Map 7.2 The Growing Christian Realm, 30–c. 500 C.E.: *When Jesus was crucified, the "church," or assembly of followers, was resident in Jerusalem. Among their enemies was the rabbinical student Saul or (to use his Greek name) Paul. Following his experience of conversion on the road to Damascus, Paul became a promoter of the new beliefs. In Antioch, his converts first came to be known as "Christians." Over the approximately thirty years of his missionary career, Paul added many Christians to the church, which subsequently made significant progress within the borders of the Roman Empire as that state reached its height in the second century C.E. By 313 C.E., Christianity was a tolerated religion, and by 600, when the Roman state in the west had been disrupted, it was the official religion of the majority of those living within the former boundaries of the Empire.*

Jesus' ministry extended from his baptism until his last entry to Jerusalem, where he had gone to celebrate the holiday of Passover, five days before his death. The events of that last week are laden with meaning for Christians—and also for Jews, on whom these same events inflicted a legacy of pain.

On the day he entered Jerusalem (according to the Gospel accounts), Jesus was greeted by crowds of ordinary people who hailed him—an ordinary man—as the Messiah. For four days he preached in Jerusalem, visited the Temple, and talked with his disciples and friends. The evening of the fifth day, Thursday, was the start of the Passover feast. Jesus celebrated it with his twelve closest disciples in the room of a house lent by a friend. In the course of the ritual meal, Jesus warned his followers of his impending death. He then blessed the bread and wine, which were the staples of the Passover feast, and distributed them to his disciples with the message to take and eat and drink: "This is my Body, which is given for you. Do this in remembrance of me. ..." (Luke 22: 19), "Drink from [this cup], all of you; for this is my Blood of the new covenant, which is poured out for many for the forgiveness of sins" (Matthew 26: 27–28).

These words predicted Jesus' imminent death and influenced the ritual by which later Christians would remember him. This meal—Jesus' last, called by Christians the Last Supper—was later seen as the institution of the Eucharist, the central act of Christian worship. It is re-created regularly in churches of all sorts: Roman Catholic; Eastern, Russian, and Armenian Orthodox; and many Protestant churches.

The Gospels report that Judas Iscariot, one of the disciples present at the Last Supper, had already agreed to point Jesus out to his enemies. Later that evening, after Jesus had gone into the Garden of Gethsemane to pray about the grim destiny that he foresaw, Judas pointed him out to the guards—with a kiss—according to Matthew and Luke. Jesus was brought before the Sanhedrin. Seen as a danger to the Jewish community, he was sent before the Roman procurator, the governor of Judaea, who alone could condemn a man to death. The procurator, Pontius Pilatus, or Pilate (known as a harsh judge of upstart leaders and fomenters of riot), condemned Jesus to be tortured and crucified. The execution occurred at midday, on Friday.

That Jesus of Nazareth was crucified during Pontius Pilate's procuratorship in Judaea (26–36 C.E.) is a secure historical fact. It is also exceedingly probable that some Jews, including some Jewish leaders, urged his death—although most others played no part at all in these events, and some were his enthusiastic followers to the last. For centuries, the crucifixion story was a source of anti-Semitic prejudice among some groups of Christians, who blamed all Jews for the death of one man whom they recognized as both innocent and divine. Matthew notoriously invites that conclusion when he portrays the cruel Pilate saying self-righteously, "I am innocent of this man's blood," and the crowd responding, "His blood be on us and on our children!"

Because they shaped the narrative of Jesus' mission during a time of hostile relations between Jews and Christians, the Gospel writers encouraged their gentile converts to blame the Jews as a whole. That interpretation of the events of the last days of Jesus' life is now rejected by most Christians and churches, including the largest, the Roman Catholic church.

Jesus was crucified on Friday, and buried in a tomb a follower had prepared for himself. Christians believe that on the following Sunday morning (celebrated as Easter) he was resurrected: that he rose bodily from the dead, walked the earth again, and thereafter returned to God. The Gospel accounts testify to the resurrection: an angel announces that Jesus has risen; the resurrected Jesus invites his skeptical follower Thomas to touch the wound in his side, as proof that it is really he, restored to life.

It was reported that fifty days after the Passover at which he had eaten his Last Supper (on the day of the Jewish feast of Shavuot, or Pentecost), a startling experience shook Jesus' followers. They were gathered in Jerusalem, reflecting on the meaning of their departed master's life, when "suddenly from heaven there came a sound like the rush of a violent wind, and it filled the entire house where they were sitting. Divided tongues, as of fire, appeared among them, and a tongue rested on each of them. All of them were filled with the Holy Spirit and began to speak in other languages..." (Acts 2: 2–4).

The disciples believed that they had been sent the divine force of the Holy Spirit as consolation for the loss of Jesus. This event is recorded in a fifth book of the Christian New Testament, the Acts of the Apostles. The Acts also records other occasions on which early Christians (as the followers of Jesus were soon called) were visited by the Holy Spirit. Most dramatic among those occasions was the experience of the tentmaker Paul of Tarsus (d. c. 67 C.E.), the one most responsible, after Jesus himself, for the creation of the Christian religion.

Paul's Mission

Paul's achievement was to spread the news of Jesus' ministry and to elucidate its meaning to the Jews of the Diaspora as well as, even more significantly, to non-Jews. By expanding the Christian mission beyond the small Jewish communities of the Mediterranean world to gentile populations, Paul added success.

Paul was a Jew (born Saul) from one of the Diaspora communities of Asia Minor. A faithful observer of the law, he studied in Jerusalem with the eminent rabbi and Pharisee Gamaliel. Initially, Paul was an enemy of the early followers of Jesus, "breathing threats and murder against the disciples of the Lord," according to Luke (Acts 9: 1). As an enemy of the infant Christian sect, he had watched the stoning of Stephen, the first **martyr** (one who willingly suffers for a belief) of the church. Rioters had laid their robes at Paul's feet, while he stood by and "approved [of Stephen's death]" (Acts 8: 1).

Committed to eradicating the **heresy** (religious doctrine at variance with accepted doctrine), as he saw it, spread by Jesus' followers, Paul visited the various communities of Jews. It was on such a mission (around 33 C.E.) to the Jews of Damascus, in Syria, that Paul experienced (as recorded in Acts 9: 3–8) the profound vision that changed his life. He fell prostrate on the road, struck blind, and heard a voice say: "Saul, Saul, why do you persecute me?" Taken into the town, he was reluctantly tended by a Christian. Soon he could see again, and he, too, became a converted Christian. No more a persecutor of the new sect, Paul now became its greatest advocate.

In the 40s C.E., Paul set out on a series of three missionary expeditions, extending over twenty years, which took him and the new faith from Jerusalem to Rome. He preached first to the Jews of Syria, Cyprus, and Asia Minor, and then increasingly to the Gentiles of the Near East and Greece. The letters he wrote to the churches he founded (the Epistles) form a substantial part of the New Testament. They helped nurture the Christian communities at Ephesus, Colossae, and Galatia, all in Asia Minor; at Corinth, Philippi, and Thessalonica, in Greece and Macedonia; and eventually in Rome.

By the time Paul undertook his journeys, the followers of Jesus were known as Christians: followers, that is, of "the anointed one," *Christos* in Greek, the equivalent of the Jewish "Messiah." But these early Christians considered themselves Jews. The disciples in Jerusalem insisted upon strict observance of Jewish

The Christian Way

Ruler and Redeemer: *By the end of the fourth century* C.E.*, the Roman Empire was a Christian empire. The heroic ideal of classical antiquity, exemplified in the early first-century statue of the emperor Augustus of Prima Porta (right) had yielded to a new ideal of the silent and mysterious redeemer, Jesus Christ—as shown in this sixth-century* C.E. *mosaic from Ravenna (left). Even the medium makes a difference—the three-dimensional stone sculpture describing the worldly ruler, but the flat, glistening mosaic surface more suitably portraying the incarnate God.*
(right: Vatican Museums, Rome)

Augustus of Prima Porta, early first century **C.E.**

law as part of the obedience to the new creed. That requirement was a barrier to the recruitment of Gentiles to the new religion—which, by the authority of Jesus himself, claimed a mission to the non-Jew. "Go therefore and make disciples of all nations," Jesus had commanded in the account of the Gospel author Matthew (28: 19). His disciple Peter, instructed in a vision that what was unclean by Jewish law could be sanctified by God, opened the infant church to gentile converts. Paul advanced that venture when he found the Jews of the Diaspora hostile to his message but the Gentile adherents of the synagogues accessible. These he converted in great numbers. By Paul's death, around 67 C.E., the church was becoming more Gentile than Jewish.

The mission to the Gentiles was the key to Christianity's ultimate success. It was facilitated by the compromise Paul made with the Jerusalem Christians on the matter of Jewish law. The requirements of the law included dietary rules, ritual procedures, and the all-important bodily sign of circumcision. Gentile adherents were reluctant to assume the full burden of the law that devolved by birth onto the Jew. Paul persuaded the Jerusalem church to agree to this formulation: that new converts should be required only to abstain "from things polluted by idols and from fornication and from whatever has been strangled and from blood" (Acts 15: 20). In other words, they did not need to follow all the requirements of Jewish law in order to become Christians. Paul was required to give proof of his own orthodoxy by undergoing a rite of purification.

While Paul acted as a negotiator between the different worlds of Gentile and Jewish Christians, he was also elaborating a theology—still fundamental to Christian belief—centered on the issue of law, its relation to sin, and the abrogation of both by Jesus the Christ. All the requirements of the law, according to Paul, were satisfied by the death of the man who was also the Son of God: he had expiated the sins of humanity. Moreover, his resurrection carried the promise of eternal life to all those who accepted the expiation of sin effected by his supreme sacrifice. That acceptance was an act of faith, the expiation or righting of all wrongs. The followers of Jesus the Christ (although by no means free to act immorally or licentiously) were freed from the law because they were "justified," or made righteous, by faith—a concept that would later become central for the sixteenth-century German Protestant reformer Martin Luther. "Therefore, since we are justified by faith," wrote Paul, "we have peace with God through our Lord Jesus Christ" (Romans 5: 1). In the love of Jesus Christ is the Christian's assurance of eternal salvation: "Who will separate us from the love of Christ? Will hardship, or distress, or persecution, or famine, or nakedness, or peril, or sword? ... For I am convinced that neither death, nor life, nor angels, nor rulers, nor things present, nor things to come, nor powers, nor height, nor depth, nor anything else in all creation, will be able to separate us from the love of God in Christ Jesus our Lord" (Romans 8: 35, 38–39).

Paul's supreme confidence in the love of God withstood the trials of danger and persecution. In 58 C.E., he returned to Jerusalem. There he preached in Hebrew (instead of the Greek of his missionary journeys) to an angry crowd. Accused of blasphemy in bringing a Gentile into the forbidden part of the Temple, he was remanded to Roman authorities and detained at Caesarea, the Roman administrative capital on the Mediterranean coast. Two successive Roman governors avoided making any decision about him. Paul insisted on bringing his case to Rome—an appeal which, as a Roman citizen, he was entitled to make. Transferred to the capital, he spent at least two years in prison. According to Christian tradition, he was condemned following a trial probably instigated by rivals in the Jewish Christian community in Rome, and executed around 67 C.E. He left behind him the germ cells of the world's most influential religion.

PROGRESS OF CHRISTIANITY

When Paul was a student in Jerusalem, and watched Stephen become the first martyr of a new faith, a few followers of Jesus, who still thought of themselves as Jews, formed the small matrix of the Christian Church. When Paul died, small communities of Christians, many of gentile origin, practiced their new faith amid the Greek and Jewish communities of the Mediterranean east. Over the next few centuries, the Christian churches grew in members, in moral force, in intellectual power, and in political status. By the time the western Roman Empire was weakening, Christianity was rooted, east and west, as the dominant religion of the Roman people and the official faith of an empire. Its expansion is shown on Map 7.2 and in *How Many?* on p. 192.

The Early Church

The early Christians were mostly Greek-speaking city-dwellers of the eastern Mediterranean world: artisans and laborers and household slaves. Paul took note of the humble status of his flock when he wrote to the Christians of Corinth: "Not many of you were wise by human standards, not many were powerful, not many were of noble birth. But ... God chose what is weak in the world to shame the strong; God chose what is low and despised in the world ... so that no one might boast in the presence of God" (I Corinthians 1: 26–29). The second-century polytheist Celsus (fl. c. 175–181 C.E.) mocked the low estate of the new Christians: "Let no one educated, no one wise, no one sensible draw near. ... But as for anyone ignorant, anyone stupid, anyone uneducated, anyone who is a child, let him come boldly."

The humbler members of society may have been attracted to Christianity because of its universalism: all who accepted baptism in Christ were considered equal. "For in Christ Jesus you are all children of God through faith. ... There is no longer Jew or Greek," wrote Paul, "there is no longer slave or free, there is no longer male and female; for all of you are one in Christ Jesus" (Galatians 3: 28).

The promise that there was "neither male nor female" in the new religion must have attracted women, who were among the most loyal early Christians. Already in the first generation (as narrated in Acts), the churches thrived under the protection of female patrons. In Philippi, Paul and Luke stayed in the house of Lydia (apparently a widow), "a worshiper of God" and a "dealer in purple cloth" (Acts 16: 14). Having heard Paul's message, this evidently wealthy woman was baptized with her whole household. Aquila and Priscilla, a Jewish couple expelled by the emperor Claudius from Rome, became Paul's converts. He stayed with them in Corinth, where they helped establish the church there. The wife is noted as much as the husband by Paul, who, in his letter to that community, sends greetings from them in Asia: "Aquila and Prisc[illa], together with the church in their house, greet you warmly in the Lord" (I Corinthians 16: 19).

Elsewhere Paul recommends to the Roman church the deaconess Phoebe: "I commend to you our sister Phoebe, a deacon of the church at Cenchreae, so that you may welcome her in the Lord ..., for she has been a benefactor of many and of myself as well" (Romans 16: 1–2). The tradition of female participation continued into the fourth century, when Christianity had won wide support among upper-class women—not least among them Helen (d. c. 328), the mother of the emperor Constantine.

Charity did not begin with Christianity. In the Greek *poleis* and in the Roman Republic, wealthy patrons had supported poor suppliants or clients. Such patrons also funded public benefits in their cities: they paid for theatrical and athletic spectacles, religious festivals, ships, and palaces, statues to adorn public spaces and grain to feed the hungry in times of scarcity. Professionals, artisans, and laborers gathered in guilds, and other groups organized by their ethnic or religious allegiances pooled their resources to provide mutual support and alms to the desperate.

These Greco-Roman benevolent institutions were exceeded by those of the Jews, who sustained the needy in their communities. The systematic and generous philanthropy of the early Christians continued

The Christian basilica: *Christians required a new space in which to worship God, and the Christian basilica was developed that combined the architecture of the Roman law courts with the traditions of the Jewish synagogue. The great basilica of Santa Maria Maggiore, Rome, c. 440 C.E., is flanked by two aisles, the majestically proportioned nave clearly suggesting the grandeur of the basilican style of architecture.*

these earlier traditions. The churches aided the poor and sick, widows, orphans, and children (working to make abandonment, abortion, and infanticide illegal) and slaves (who were urged, nonetheless, to accept their status as legitimate).

The main goal of worship in ancient religious practices was to make a human or animal sacrifice to a deity on an altar. The altar could stand independently, or within a temple, which was understood as the house of a god. Among early Christians, who worshiped in private houses or even, when endangered, in underground catacombs, altar and sacrifice gave way to common prayer and celebration. Once Christianity became a legal religion, it required a new physical space: not one to house its deity (whose house was "not made with hands") but one that could accommodate a community joined to give thanks for Jesus' life, death, and resurrection. Christians adapted a kind of building already in existence: the Roman basilica. Originally designed as a place of assembly for judicial or commercial purposes, the basilica became the fundamental unit of Christian architecture.

The basilica provided a large central space lit by high windows—an example is shown on p. 186. The rectangular, vaulted building developed side aisles and focused attention on the eastern end of the longitudinal axis, where stood an altar backed by a sunlit apse. The spaciousness, the height, the clear orientation, and the light operated to provide an ideal place for worship, subordinating the individual to the group and to an ideal beyond them all. By the fourth century, Christian churches in basilican form had been erected all over the Empire. In some areas, almost the only buildings constructed were ecclesiastical.

The fourth-century basilicas of Saint Peter and Saint John Lateran in Rome and the Church of the Holy Wisdom (Santa Sophia) in Constantinople were built under Constantine's direction. His mother, Helen, built a church on the alleged site of Jesus' ascension (the Mount of Olives) in Jerusalem and another on the presumed site of Jesus' birth in Bethlehem—discovering in the excavations (according to legend) the cross on which he died. Soon every major city had a church. Within them developed the **liturgy** of Christian worship (much of it borrowed from Judaism), the performance of sacraments, the vocabulary of ceremony, vestments, and accessories that would characterize mature Christianity.

The first churches were informal gatherings of the faithful. They were led by elders or "presbyters" and deacons: the former charged with the spiritual guidance of the community, the latter with the administration of charity. As larger Christian communities formed, leaders called bishops presided over all the churches in a city and surrounding area. Possessing greater authority because of their social status or learning, they took precedence over local leaders in the institution of the church. The bishops imitated the secular government in administrative style and court ritual. As bishops (always men) asserted control over local communities, women were relegated to supportive roles in the institution of the church.

Persecutions and Controversies

While Christian communities grew, distaste for the new sect remained strong among the Roman elites. They found the Jews more like themselves in that they worshiped the god of their ancestors. Christians, by contrast, all converts at the outset, and without ancestral authority, were seen as peculiar and secretive. And worse: Christians engaged (so Roman critics believed or found it convenient to believe) in magic, incest, drunkenness, and cannibalism. As one Christian writer put it: "They gather together ignorant persons from the lowest dregs, and credulous women, easily deceived as their sex is, and organize a rabble of unholy conspirators, leagued together in nocturnal associations and by ritual fasts and barbarous foods, not for the purpose of some sacred rite but for the sake of sacrilege—a secret tribe that shuns the light, silent in public but talkative in secret places."

They seemed, according to Tacitus, to be possessed by a "baneful superstition" and to have a "hatred of the human race"—in fact, because they avoided the company of their pagan neighbors, for fear of being infected by their beliefs. In the second century, the aesthete Celsus (in his *On True Doctrine*) expounded the Greco-Roman case against Christianity, and in the fifth century, the philosopher Porphyry (in his vitriolic *Against the Christians*, 448 C.E.), both vaunting the humane values of late pagan thought against what they saw as Christian incivility.

Persecution Avid dislike of Christians periodically erupted in persecution. Judaism had bequeathed to the world as models of martyrdom the Maccabees, the zealots of Masada, and the faithful rabbis of the days of Bar Kokhba. Beginning in the first century C.E., Christian martyrdom had increased spectacularly by the third century, when thousands of Christians went to their death rather than participate in the imperial cult. Two accounts are given in *Witnesses* on p. 188. The sacrifice of these convinced Christians helped to energize the survivors. "Nothing whatever is accomplished by your cruelties," the theologian Tertullian (c. 160–c. 240 C.E.) boasted to Roman oppressors. "We multiply whenever we are mown down by you; the blood of Christians is [like] seed."

Tertullian was right: martyrdom was indeed stupendously successful. The spectacle of Christians so committed to their faith that they chose to die rather than make the slightest compromise with the demands of the secular world impressed even highborn Romans. The martyrs' courage affirmed these Romans' own stoic values—as when the theologian

WITNESSES

Christians to the Lions

The Roman persecution of Christians began in the first century C.E., *continued intermittently for more than 200 years, and peaked under the emperor Diocletian— yet Christianity still grew. As the African theologian Tertullian commented, the blood of martyrs, whose self-sacrifice inspired confidence and recruited new followers, was the "seed" of the Church. These passages describe two impressive incidents where Christian witnesses willing to die for their faith defied persecution: the martyrdoms of the bishop Polycarp and the noblewoman Perpetua.*

Polycarp, Bishop of Smyrna, declining to compromise with power or to flee it, is burned alive, a martyr to the Christian faith (c. 155 C.E.): And when finally he was brought up, there was a great tumult on hearing that Polycarp had been arrested. ... The proconsul ... tried to persuade him to deny [the faith], saying, "Have respect to your age"—and other things that customarily follow this, such as, "Swear by the fortune of Caesar; change your mind; say, 'Away with the atheists!' " [by which he meant the Christians].

But Polycarp looked with earnest face at the whole crowd of lawless heathen in the arena, and motioned to them with his hand. Then, groaning and looking up to heaven, he said, "Away with the atheists!" [by which he meant his persecutors].

But the proconsul was insistent and said: "Take the oath, and I shall release you. Curse Christ."

Polycarp said: "Eighty-six years I have served him, and he never did me any wrong. How can I blaspheme my King who saved me?" ...

But the proconsul said: "I have wild beasts. I shall throw you to them, if you do not change your mind."

But [Polycarp] said: "Call them. For repentance from the better to the worse is not permitted us; but it is noble to change from what is evil to what is righteous. ..."

And when he had said these things and many more besides he was inspired with courage and joy, and his face was full of grace. ... The proconsul was astonished, and sent his own herald into the midst of the arena to proclaim three times: "Polycarp has confessed himself to be a Christian." When this was said ... the entire crowd ... shouted with uncontrollable anger. ... Straightway then, they set about him the material prepared for the fire. ... And with his hands put behind him and tied, like a noble ram out of a great flock ready for sacrifice, a burnt offering ready and acceptable to God, he looked up to heaven and said: "Lord God almighty, ... I praise thee, I bless thee, I glorify thee, through the eternal and heavenly High Priest, Jesus Christ, thy beloved Servant, through whom be glory to thee with him and Holy Spirit both now and unto the ages to come. Amen." And when he had concluded the Amen and finished his prayer, the men attending to the fire lighted it. ...

(The Martyrdom of St. Polycarp, Bishop of Smyrna, c. 155 C.E., as told in the letter of the Church of Smyrna to the Church of Philomelium, 9:2–15:1; ed. J. Richardson 1970)

The noblewoman and martyr Perpetua, slaughtered by beasts in the arena at Carthage on 7 March 203, chronicled her imprisonment (during which she gave birth to a child) in her own words. Here, in the last passage of her memoir, she describes the vision she experienced (in which she becomes a man and vanquishes her enemy) the day before her execution: ... I saw in a vision that Pomponius the deacon had come hither to the door of the prison, and knocked hard upon it. And I went out to him and opened to him. ... And he said to me: Perpetua, we await thee; come. And he took my hand. ... At last with much breathing hard we came to the amphitheatre, and he led me into the midst of the arena. And he said to me: Be not afraid; I am here with thee and labour together with thee. And he went away. And I saw much people watching closely. And because I knew that I was condemned to the beasts I marvelled that beasts were not sent out against me. And there came out against me a certain ill-favored Egyptian with his helpers, to fight with me. ... And I was stripped, and I became a man. ... And there came forth a man of very great stature, so that he over-passed the very top of the amphitheatre, ... bearing a rod like a master of gladiators, and a green branch whereon were golden apples. And he besought silence and said: The Egyptian, if he shall conquer this woman, shall slay her with the sword; and if she shall conquer him, she shall receive this branch. And he went away. And we came nigh to each other, and began to buffet one another. ... And I rose up into the air and began so to smite him as though I trod not the earth. But when I saw that there was yet delay, I ... caught his head, and he fell upon his face; and I trod upon his head. And the people began to shout, and my helpers began to sing. And I went up to the master of gladiators and received the branch. And he kissed me and said to me: Daughter, peace be with thee. And I began to go with glory to the gate called the Gate of Life.

And I awoke; and I understood that I should fight, not with beasts but against the devil; but I knew that mine was the victory.

Thus far I have written this, till the day before the games; but the deed of the games themselves let him write who will.

(Perpetua, from J. Geary ed., *Passion of Perpetua*, 1989, 83–89; ed. W. H. Shewring, 1931)

Justin confronted his persecutors at his own martyrdom (c. 165 C.E.): "You indeed may be able to kill us, but you cannot harm us."

Nero blamed the Christians for the Great Fire of 64 C.E., which marked the beginning of his downfall. To appease the Roman populace, he sent hundreds of Christians into the arena to be slain by gladiators or hungry beasts. During a later persecution, Tertullian angrily remarked, "If the Tiber reaches the walls, if the Nile does not rise to the fields, if the sky doesn't move or the earth does, if there is famine, if there is plague, the cry is at once: 'The Christians to the lions!' "

Around 110 C.E., the emperor Trajan cautioned the author Pliny the Younger, governor of Bithynia, in Asia Minor, not to act too zealously to pursue Christians: if they superficially conformed to the Roman state cult, they were to be left alone. Yet later in the same century, the high-minded Marcus Aurelius permitted the slaughter of Christians in the arena of Lyon in Gaul (in 177 C.E.). Men should be willing to face death, reflected the philosophical emperor, but not "out of crude obstinacy, like the Christians." In the arena at Lyon women, too, faced death willingly—going to their crucifixion, wrote an observer, in an ecstasy of union with Christ.

Around 249–50 C.E., the emperor Decius (r. 249–251 C.E.) commanded every suspected Christian to perform at least once the sacrificial rites of the imperial cult. In 303 C.E., Diocletian and his caesar, or deputy, Galerius launched the Great Persecution, in an attempt to stamp out the new faith, which had by now been adopted by a fifth of the Empire's population and was seen as an enemy of old Roman values. The persecution lasted eight years, raging most fiercely in the east, where it consumed some 3000 believers. Its aim was to root out the new faith: to suppress its churches, its clergy, its followers.

Controversy and Heresy The persecutions extended over nearly 250 years and consumed perhaps 100,000 victims. Nevertheless, martyrdom did not weaken the Church. Neither did the controversies it carried on through its spokesmen—theologians and scholars later collectively given the name "Fathers of the Church". The Church faced three opponents: the Roman world (which stood for polytheism and for the learned tradition); the Jews (from whom the Christians had sprung); and heretics (dissenters from the emerging orthodoxy of the Church). Out of these controversies the Fathers evolved the doctrines that still underlie Christian theology.

The Fathers attempted to build a bridge between Christianity (perceived as a sect followed by illiterates) and the high Classical tradition. One of them was Justin of Neapolis, in Samaria (c. 100–c. 165 C.E.), martyred around 165 C.E. and thus known to history as Justin Martyr. Justin wrote two *Apologies* for Christianity against the intellectuals who assailed it. Portraying the new faith as reasonable, he invited his enemies to join the community of those who sought peace. As for the Classical tradition that Christians were accused of undervaluing, he revered it and proposed to enlist the learning of the past in the service of the future: "Whatever things were rightly said among all men are the property of us Christians."

Clement of Alexandria (c. 150–c. 215 C.E.) headed a Christian school in which Classical learning was studied as a tool for the advancement of the new faith. His pupil Origen of Alexandria (c. 185–c. 254 C.E.), a philosopher in the Platonic tradition, defended the Christian church against the Roman advocate Celsus. Origen's defense provided at last a rational foundation for the tenets of the new religion, sophisticated enough to interest its detractors. Justin, Clement, and Origen (all writing in Greek) established the Christian approach to Classical culture and to the intellectual life generally. Although the anti-intellectual alternative was voiced—most succinctly by Tertullian, who thundered, "What has Athens to do with Jerusalem?", that is, philosophy with faith—it was these scholars' formulation that endured. While Christians rejected the paganism of the Roman world, they embraced, enlarged, and transmitted its culture. Their decision to do so would help to shape the development of civilization in the West.

By the end of the first century C.E., most Christians were Gentiles. The Jews themselves, led by the rabbis who now guided their community, had expelled Jewish Christians from their fellowship. Before the two religions parted course, Christians had taken much from the Jews: the idea of the Sabbath, the priests' vestments, and the chants and hymns of the choir. Most important, they adopted the whole of the Hebrew Bible, which formed the **Old Testament**

WHO'S WHO

Fathers of the Church

Clement of Rome, late 1st century C.E.; bishop of Rome c. 88–101

Justin Martyr (Justin of Neapolis), c. 100–c. 165 C.E., Rome

Tertullian, c. 155/160–after 220 C.E., Carthage (modern Tunis)

Origen, c. 185–c. 254 C.E., Caesarea (coast of modern Israel)

John Chrysostom, c. 347–407 C.E., Antioch

Jerome, c. 347–419/420 C.E., Palestine (Bethlehem)

Augustine, 354–430 C.E., Hippo (modern Annaba, Algeria)

companion to their own scriptures, the New Testament. The Jewish foundation of Christianity was an incontrovertible fact recognized thereafter, if reluctantly, by the official church. That debt did not preclude opposition to Judaism and even active anti-Semitism in the Christian community.

Justin established the case for Christianity against Judaism in his *Dialogue with Trypho*. He was not alone: several early Christian writers wrote similar books. The tone became angrier around 400 C.E., when the eloquent Saint John Chrysostom (c. 354–407 C.E.) delivered in Antioch eight *Sermons against the Jews and Gentiles*. Accusing the Jews of the murder of Jesus, Chrysostom's fierce diatribes provide many of the arguments that supported anti-Semitism in later centuries (see Chapters 24, 25, 28).

As they defined their position vis-à-vis pagan and Jewish communities, Christian intellectuals faced new opponents on another flank: heretics within their own ranks. In its early years, Christianity could have followed a different course from the one firmly established by the end of the fifth century. Each of these other possible directions came to be labeled a "heresy" by the thinkers who battled to establish Christian principles about the nature of God, of Jesus, and of the human being.

Gnostics believed that they had received a special *gnosis*, or "knowledge," which set them apart from other worshipers. Montanists (followers of the second-century C.E. prophet Montanus) revered inspired prophets within the church, whose utterances they saw as authoritative. In both cases, an inequality of status was admitted to the Christian community. Christian leaders rejected this notion: all were equally sinners, they argued, all equally saved by the crucifixion and resurrection of Christ. Knowledge of God came from his revelation of himself in scripture and in the person of Jesus, God's Son.

In the fourth century, a new crop of heresies arose. These revolved around the nature of Jesus and his mother, Mary. If Jesus was the son of God, how could he also be human? If he was human, how could he also be God? The Arians (followers of the priest Arius [c. 260–336 C.E.]) believed Jesus was a human being, godlike, but separate in nature from the divine. The opposition to the Arians was led by another bishop, Saint Athanasius (c. 295–373 C.E.), who endured persecution and exile before his formulation of the nature of Jesus—that he was both fully human and fully divine—triumphed as the central tenet of Christian orthodoxy. The Athanasian position was hammered out at a council of the leaders of the church, held in Nicaea, in Asia Minor, which was called by the emperor Constantine in 325 C.E. Its resolution was eventually enunciated in the Nicene Creed, still recited by most Catholic Christians today. These two positions were differentiated linguistically by a single letter: the "i" in the Greek word defining the nature of Christ. For the Arians, Christ's nature was similar to that of God: *homoiousios*. For the Athanasians, it was identical: *homoousios*. Subsequent councils ratified the Athanasian principle.

Although the Arian doctrine had been defeated, Arian worshipers persisted in what was seen as their error. It never completely disappeared. In the meantime, yet another movement emerged—that of the Monophysites, who believed that Christ had only one nature (*monophysite* means "one nature"), which was divine. The Nestorians (followers of the bishop Nestorius [d. c. 451 C.E.]) upheld a more complex view: that Mary, a mere human being, could have given birth only to Jesus' human nature, which was a kind of shell enclosing his divine nature. These positions were duly debated and rejected.

Two more bishops lent their names to heresies defeated in the fourth century: Donatus (d. c. 355 C.E.) and Pelagius (fl. 380–410 C.E.). The former refused to acknowledge as effective certain sacred rites (called **sacraments**) when performed by members of the clergy who had, during the persecutions, momentarily repudiated their faith rather than face martyrdom. The orthodox response was that the sacraments were effective whatever the moral condition of the officiating clergyman.

Pelagius argued that human beings exercising their free will (although aided by divine **grace**) could work their own salvation. The orthodox retorted that all human beings were sinful and could be saved only by the gift of grace bestowed upon those who accepted Jesus' sacrifice. In both of these heresies, the issue was not so much the nature of God, or Jesus, but the nature of the human being.

The Triumph of Christianity

The councils, the debates, the books, and the sermons together constructed the edifice of Christian theology. It was based on the Bible, both Old and New Testaments. It honored and acknowledged the preceding Jewish tradition. It saw human nature as basically good but utterly debased by sin and in need of divine rescue. It saw God as omnipotent, and Jesus as fully God yet fully human.

The difficult relationship between an omnipotent God and God incarnate in Jesus was articulated in the central and difficult doctrine of the **Trinity**: the notion that God was threefold (or triune, "three in one"). In God were included the persons of the Father, the Son, and the Holy Spirit. All were in God, all were eternal, and each, when acting separately, was wholly God. The trinitarian concept is complex and rests on intricate philosophical reasoning. But it remains fundamental to Christianity.

The culminating statement of the doctrine of the Trinity was the work of Saint Augustine (354–430), arguably the most important and most brilliant of

Christianity Victorious

Christianity did not became the religion of the Roman Empire overnight, but by a series of steps, each involving a conscious decision. Three of those decisions are highlighted in these passages. In the first, Emperor Constantine makes Christian worship legal. In the second, Emperor Theodosius establishes Christianity as the official religion of the Empire. In the third, the scholar Augustine makes a personal decision—in contrast to the preceding official ones—in favor of Christianity.

The emperor Constantine and his associate Licinius issue the Edict of Milan (313 C.E.), permitting free Christian worship: We, Constantinus and Licinius the Emperors ... give both to Christians and to all others free facility to follow the religion which each may desire. ... [and decree that] no one who has given his mental assent to the Christian persuasion or to any other which he feels to be suitable to him should be compelled to deny his conviction, so that the Supreme Godhead ..., whose worship we freely observe, can assist us in all things with his wonted favour and benevolence. Wherefore ... it is our pleasure that all restrictions which were previously put forward in official pronouncements concerning the sect of the Christians should be removed, and that each one of them who freely and sincerely carries out the purpose of observing the Christian religion may endeavour to practice its precepts without any fear or danger. ...
(From S. Ehler, J. Morrall eds., *Church and State through the Centuries*, 1954)

The Code of the emperor Theodosius I establishes Christianity as the sole official religion in the imperial capital of Constantinople, and assigns penalties for pagan practices (392 C.E.): *Theodosian Code, 16.1.2 (380):* It is Our will that all the peoples who are ruled by the administration of Our Clemency shall practice that religion which the divine Peter the Apostle transmitted to the Romans. ...

Theodosian Code, 16.10.25 (435): We interdict all persons of criminal pagan mind from the accursed immolation of victims, from damnable sacrifices, and from all other such practices that are prohibited by the authority of the more ancient sanctions. We command that all their fanes, temples and shrines, if even now any remain entire, shall be destroyed by the command of the magistrates, and shall be purified by the erection of the sign of the venerable Christian religion. ...
(*Theodosian Code*, 440, 476; ed. C. Pharr)

Torn between dissatisfaction with his past life and doubts about Christianity, Augustine hears the message that will resolve his uncertainties and lead to his conversion (c. 400 C.E.): I was saying these things and weeping in the most bitter contrition of my heart, when, lo, I heard the voice as of a boy or girl, I know not which, coming from a neighboring house, chanting, and oft repeating, "Take up and read; take up and read." Immediately my countenance was changed, and I began most earnestly to consider whether it was usual for children in any kind of game to sing such words; nor could I remember ever to have heard the like. So, restraining the torrent of my tears, I rose up, interpreting it no other way than as a command to me from Heaven to open the book, and to read the first chapter I should light upon. ... So quickly I returned to the place where Alypius was sitting; for there I had put down the volume of the apostles, when I rose thence. I grasped, opened, and in silence read that paragraph on which my eyes first fell—"Not in rioting and drunkenness, not in chambering and wantonness, not in strife and envying; but put ye on the Lord Jesus Christ, and make not provision for the flesh, to fulfil the lusts thereof." Nor further would I read, nor did I need; for instantly, as the sentence ended—by a light, as it were, of security infused into my heart—all the gloom of doubt vanished away.
(Augustine, *Confessions*, 1: 19–20; ed. J. G. Pilkington 1896)

the Christian Fathers. He has already been encountered as the author of the massive *City of God*. His *Confessions*, an autobiography (the first) constructed as a lengthy prayer, reveals an understanding of the human psyche that has left its mark on later generations. An extract is given in *Witnesses* above. His *On the Trinity*, his commentaries on Scripture, and his many other works form a monument of Christian doctrine fed by the preceding centuries of debate and illumined by Augustine's peerless originality, literary style, and power of expression. Moreover, he was a master of Latin—which by the fifth century had become the international language of the West, as Greek was of the East.

In the early years of the Empire, learned Romans used Greek as well as Latin. Greek reigned supreme in the eastern Mediterranean, where the various elites nevertheless mastered Latin as the language of politics and administration. By the fourth century, the Empire had split into Latin and Greek zones, centered respectively at Rome (and later Milan or Ravenna) and Constantinople. This process of separation was under way precisely during the years of the formation of Christian theology. Its creators, the Church Fathers, became distinguished as Greek- or Latin-speaking, Eastern or Western. The early Fathers were Greek-speaking. The cantankerous Tertullian (who died a Montanist heretic), a Latin author, was the first of a series of Latin-speaking Fathers who created the Latin tradition that would over the next centuries serve as the crucible of Western thought.

Constantine's Edict of Milan (313) declared Christianity a legal religion in the western Roman Empire. A decree of 323 extended that order to the

HOW MANY?

Converts to Christianity

Year	Number of Christians	Percent of population
40	1,000	0.0017
50	1,400	0.0023
100	7,530	0.0126
150	40,49	0.07
200	217,795	0.36
250	1,171,356	1.9
300	6,299,832	10.5
350	33,882,008	56.6

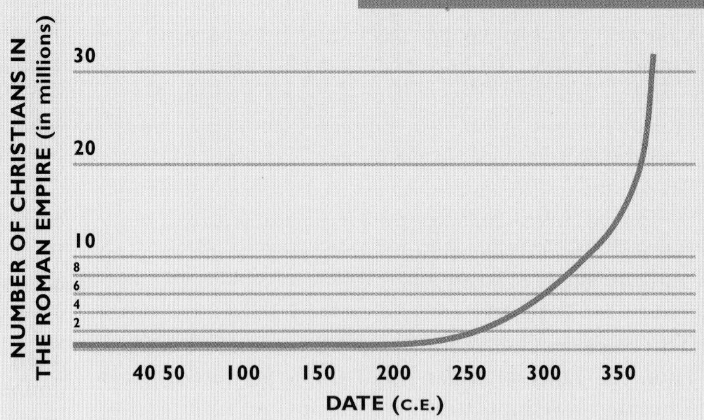

NUMBER OF CHRISTIANS IN THE ROMAN EMPIRE (in millions)

DATE (C.E.)

This projection of the extraordinary growth of Christianity is based on figures relating to the urban populations within the Roman Empire in the period 40–350 C.E., assuming a total population of 60 million people.
Source: Philip F. Esler, *The Early Christian World* (Routledge, 2000).

East. Within a century, Christianity was elevated to the status of an official religion. It had pursued an extraordinary path from target of persecution to object of tolerance to identification with the state.

In the middle of the fourth century, the emperor Julian (r. 361–363), known as "the Apostate," attempted to stem the tide of Christian expansion and to restore the glory of pagan philosophy. Although he was raised as a Christian, his youthful training was overwhelmed by his later Classical education and his resentment of the Christianizing members of Constantine's family, who had slaughtered all those of his own family except himself. He outlawed Christian teaching of the Classics and restored to the Senate house in Rome the statue of the pagan god of Victory.

Julian was the last non-Christian emperor of the ancient world. In 382, the emperor Gratian (the first emperor not to bear the ancient title of *pontifex maximus*) removed the restored statue of Victory from the Senate. In 391, Theodosius ordered the destruction of the pagan temples of Alexandria, the center of the late imperial culture; in 392, he banned all pagan sacrifices throughout the Empire. In 391, (possibly Christian) mobs in Alexandria burned the city's great library and in 415 a Christian mob murdered Hypatia (370–415), female philosopher and mathematician. Justinian (r. 527–565) closed the schools of pagan philosophy and decreed that only baptized Christians could be citizens.

As the Empire became more Christian, the Church grew more like an empire. The power of church leaders increased. Because they were all male, their advancement entailed the exclusion of women from public roles in the churches. In the East, the Christian hierarchy was subordinated to the emperor. In the West, where public governance was fading, the bishops were in command. In 390, the bishop of Milan, Saint Ambrose (c. 340–397), had banned the emperor Theodosius from the sacraments of the Church (an order of excommunication), and forced him to do penance to lift the ban. By the fifth century, the bishop of Rome (now called "**pope**," from *papa*, or "father," and *pontifex maximus*) played the role of the emperor. Pope Innocent I (r. 401–417) negotiated with the Goth Alaric; later, Pope Leo I (r. 440–461) persuaded the Hun Attila in 451 to halt his Italian campaign and spare the city of Rome.

When the Empire faded, the Church was there in its place; as one scholar has written, the Church "outthought it, outwrote it, and outlived it." The Unknown God, born in Galilee and preached by Paul to Athenian bystanders, had won.

Conclusion

Roman Gods, the One God, and the Meaning of the West

It was Paul's genius that plucked the Unknown God, one of many, from the pantheon of the Greco-Roman world, and persuaded his audience that he was the one God of the universe. Belief in the one God, inherited from his worshipers in ancient Judaea and adopted by the followers of Jesus of Nazareth, separates the later fully developed Western civilization from the ancient world that gave it birth. As much as the culture of Greece and Rome, itself the bearer of the culture of still earlier civilizations, the beliefs and traditions of the first monotheistic religions, Judaism and Christianity, helped form the West.

REVIEW QUESTIONS

1. Who were the first Roman gods? How did the Etruscans and Greeks influence Roman religion? What role did women play in Roman worship?

2. How did syncretism influence Roman religion? Why did religion became more personal in later antiquity? What were some of the popular cults in the later Roman centuries? Contrast the influence of magic and philosophy on Roman beliefs.

3. Why can Judaism be said to have begun in the fifth century B.C.E.? How did the Jews fare under Roman rule? How did the focus of Judasim change after the destruction of the second temple?

4. How reliable are the Gospel accounts of Jesus? What was new and surprising about Jesus' message? How did Paul of Tarsus influence the development of early Christianity?

5. Why did Christianity triumph throughout the Roman Empire? Why did the Roman state persecute Christians for so long? How did the early Church deal with heresy?

6. What did the term "pagan" mean? How did the status of the Church change in the century after the Edict of Milan? How did the decline of the Roman Empire in the West affect the pope's position and the papacy?

SUGGESTED RESOURCES

Roman Gods

Athanassiadi, Polymnia & Michael Frede, eds., *Pagan Monotheism in Late Antiquity* (Oxford: Clarendon Press, 2000). Studies of late ancient pagan monotheism, a literary tradition that was the context for the development of Jewish, Christian, and Islamic monotheism.

Dzielska, Maria, *Hypatia of Alexandria,* trans. F. Lyra (Harvard: Harvard University Press, 1995). Reconstruction of the life of the fabled mathematician, philosopher, and teacher, a pagan scholar caught in the conflicts among Alexandrian Christians, tragically murdered in 415.

Liebeschuetz, J. H. W. G., *Continuity and Change in Roman Religion* (Oxford: Oxford University Press, 1979). Surveys Roman religious attitudes from the early republic to the reign of Constantine; examines the relation between religion, morality, and politics in Latin literature.

Dictionaries of Greek and Latin mythological characters (Forum Romanum and Oracle):
http://www.geocities.com/Athens/Forum/6946/mythology
http://www.geocities.com/Athens/Oracle/5545/index.html

Judaism in Transition

Feldman, Louis H., *Jew and Gentile in the Ancient World: Attitudes and Interactions from Alexander to Justinian* (Princeton: Princeton University Press, 1993). Interactions of Jews and gentiles especially in the diaspora, exploring the Jewish community's ability to attract converts through the fifth century of the new era.

Lieu, Judith, John A. North, and Tessa Rajak, eds., *The Jews among Pagans and Christians in the Roman Empire* (London: Routledge, 1992). Examines Jewish interactions with other groups under Roman rule, including Jewish proselytizing, diaspora, Christian views of Judaism.

Segal, Alan F., *Rebecca's Children: Judaism and Christianity in the Roman World* (Harvard: Harvard University Press, 1986). A controversial study of the common origins of rabbinic Judaism and Christianity.

Timeline of Jewish history (University of California Davis):
http://www.philo.ucdavis.edu/zope/home/bruce//RST23/chart.html

Origins of Christianity

Chilton, Bruce, *Rabbi Jesus: The Jewish Origin of Christianity* (New York: Doubleday, 2000). Based on recent archeological research, recreates world of first-century Palestine and situates Jesus within the social customs, political world, and religious controversies of the Jewish community—and especially that of Galilee, with its own tradition of personal communication with God.

Meeks, Wayne A., *The Origins of Christian Morality: The First Two Centuries* (New Haven: Yale University Press, 1993). Explores how Christian ethics, like Christian theology, developed in the context of pagan and Jewish philosophy and practice, and responded to the real, largely urban world which sheltered the first Christian communities.

Segal, Alan F., *Paul the Convert: The Apostolate and Apostasy of Saul the Pharisee* (New Haven/London: Yale University Press, 1990). Argues that Jewish history can be illuminated by examining Paul's writings.

Watson, Alan, *Jesus: A Profile* (Atlanta: University of Georgia Press, 1998). A controversial examination of the Gospels, depicting Jesus as a charismatic individual who demanded personal faith from his followers.

Progress of Christianity

Brown, Peter, *Authority and the Sacred: Aspects of the Christianisation of the Roman World* (Cambridge: Cambridge University Press, 1996). This examines the work of Christian leaders as negotiators between the new faith and traditional ways of dealing with the supernatural.

Hopkins, Keith, *A World Full of Gods: Pagans, Jews, and Christians in the Roman Empire* (London: Weidenfeld & Nicolson, 1999; New York: Free Press, 2000). A bold historiographical experiment mixing fictional characters, speculation, and scholarship, the author asks but does not quite answer why Christianity prevailed over pagan rites, mystery cults, Gnostic rivals, Greek philosophy, and Hellenized Judaism.

MacMullen, Ramsay, *Christianity and Paganism in the Fourth to Eighth Centuries* (New Haven: Yale University Press, 1997). Shows that Christianity did not triumph suddenly and neatly over paganism, but prevailed only after a long period of interaction, in which paganism resisted the Christian advance and Christianity became to some extent assimilated to pagan practices and outlooks.

Salisbury, Joyce E., *Perpetua's Passion: The Death and Memory of a Young Roman Woman* (New York–London: Routledge, 1997). Raised in a wealthy, still-pagan household, the young mother of an infant son, Perpetua enthusiastically welcomed martyrdom in a famous moment that is here placed solidly in the context of the magical and mystical passions of the third century.

Chronology of the early church:
http://www.gospelcoom.net/chi/EARLYF/earlychs.shtml

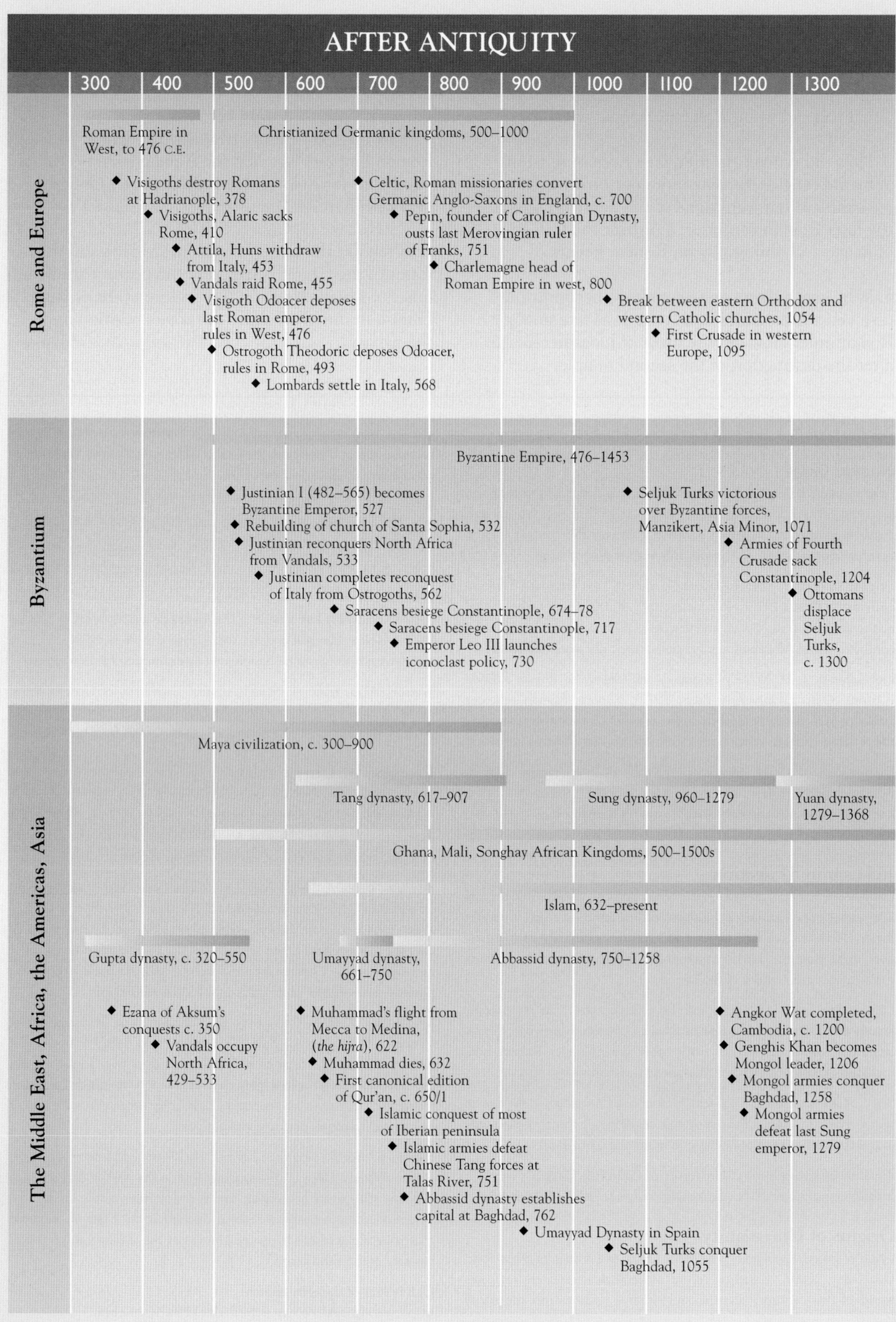

AFTER ANTIQUITY
300
400
500
600
700
800
900
1000
1100
1200
1300
Rome and Europe
Roman Empire in West, to 476 C.E.
Christianized Germanic kingdoms, 500–1000
◆ Visigoths destroy Romans at Hadrianople, 378
◆ Visigoths, Alaric sacks Rome, 410
◆ Attila, Huns withdraw from Italy, 453
◆ Vandals raid Rome, 455
◆ Visigoth Odoacer deposes last Roman emperor, rules in West, 476
◆ Ostrogoth Theodoric deposes Odoacer, rules in Rome, 493
◆ Lombards settle in Italy, 568
◆ Celtic, Roman missionaries convert Germanic Anglo-Saxons in England, c. 700
◆ Pepin, founder of Carolingian Dynasty, ousts last Merovingian ruler of Franks, 751
◆ Charlemagne head of Roman Empire in west, 800
◆ Break between eastern Orthodox and western Catholic churches, 1054
◆ First Crusade in western Europe, 1095
Byzantium
Byzantine Empire, 476–1453
◆ Justinian I (482–565) becomes Byzantine Emperor, 527
◆ Rebuilding of church of Santa Sophia, 532
◆ Justinian reconquers North Africa from Vandals, 533
◆ Justinian completes reconquest of Italy from Ostrogoths, 562
◆ Saracens besiege Constantinople, 674–78
◆ Saracens besiege Constantinople, 717
◆ Emperor Leo III launches iconoclast policy, 730
◆ Seljuk Turks victorious over Byzantine forces, Manzikert, Asia Minor, 1071
◆ Armies of Fourth Crusade sack Constantinople, 1204
◆ Ottomans displace Seljuk Turks, c. 1300
The Middle East, Africa, the Americas, Asia
Maya civilization, c. 300–900
Tang dynasty, 617–907
Sung dynasty, 960–1279
Yuan dynasty, 1279–1368
Ghana, Mali, Songhay African Kingdoms, 500–1500s
Islam, 632–present
Gupta dynasty, c. 320–550
Umayyad dynasty, 661–750
Abbassid dynasty, 750–1258
◆ Ezana of Aksum's conquests c. 350
◆ Vandals occupy North Africa, 429–533
◆ Muhammad's flight from Mecca to Medina, (*the hijra*), 622
◆ Muhammad dies, 632
◆ First canonical edition of Qur'an, c. 650/1
◆ Islamic conquest of most of Iberian peninsula
◆ Islamic armies defeat Chinese Tang forces at Talas River, 751
◆ Abbassid dynasty establishes capital at Baghdad, 762
◆ Umayyad Dynasty in Spain
◆ Seljuk Turks conquer Baghdad, 1055
◆ Angkor Wat completed, Cambodia, c. 1200
◆ Genghis Khan becomes Mongol leader, 1206
◆ Mongol armies conquer Baghdad, 1258
◆ Mongol armies defeat last Sung emperor, 1279

CHAPTER

8 AFTER ANTIQUITY

New Peoples of Europe and Other Peoples of the World

300–1300 C.E.

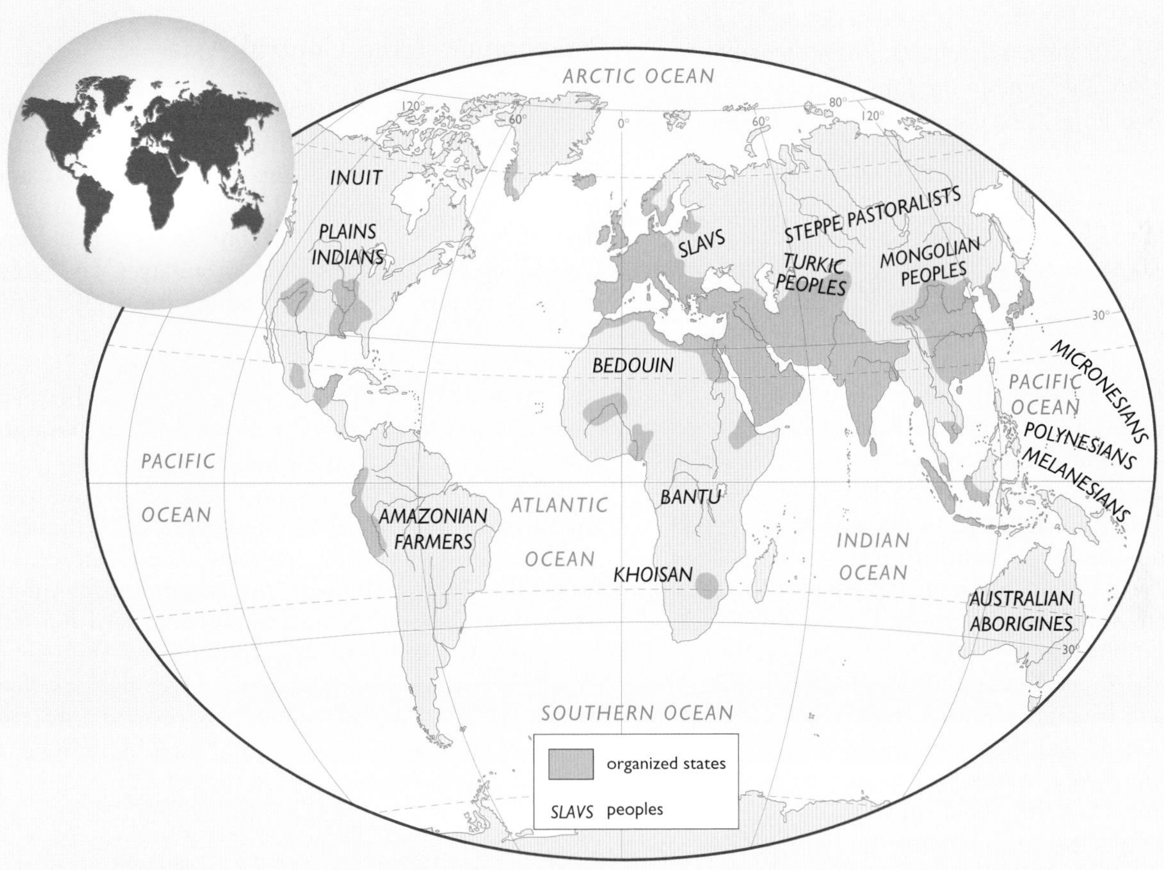

KEY TOPICS

- **The "Triumph of Barbarism and Religion":** Nomadic peoples pressure the ancient civilizations and ultimately overcome Rome in the Western Empire.
- **Byzantium: The Enduring Empire:** At a new capital established at Byzantium—now Constantinople—Roman and Greek traditions endure, and commerce and Christianity flourish.
- **Islam: From Arabian Desert to World Stage:** Islam expands across North Africa, the Middle East, and Asia, and develops a civilization as influential as those of Greece, India, and China.
- **Beyond the West:** Peoples travel across the oceans to inhabit the whole of the globe except Antarctica, and advanced civilizations flourish on five of seven continents.

The Conversion of Clovis *"If you grant me victory over these enemies ...," promised the Frankish king Clovis (r. c. 481–511), "I will believe in you and be baptized in your name." So, according to legend, he prayed to his wife's protector Jesus Christ during a desperate moment in battle. He had invoked his own gods, but they had not responded: "and therefore I believe that they possess no power, since they do not help those who obey them." Until then, Clovis had resisted his Christian wife's pleas that he should renounce his forest idols. Now Clovis won the battle and kept his promise. He was the first important convert the Roman Church made among the peoples considered "barbarian." Over the next several centuries, the nations of Europe would emerge from the tribal peoples who had come to the fore in Rome's last days. Their kings, like Clovis, became Christian.*

The civilization of the West took form in a Christianized Europe during the thousand years after antiquity known as the Middle Ages. The conversion of Constantine (see Chapter 7) was decisive for the Christianization of the Roman Empire as it entered its twilight years. Similarly, the conversion of Clovis (along with 3000 of his troops) was crucial to the Christianization of Europe, as Roman power, Roman institutions, and Roman memories waned.

During the centuries after Clovis' conversion, in regions on the fringe of the ancient Mediterranean world and already imbued with its ancient traditions, new cultures formed as Germanic peoples settled and laid the foundations of Europe. The eastern sector of the old Empire, centered at Constantinople, recreated itself as the Byzantine Empire. In the Middle East, the founders of Islam, the world's third major monotheistic religion, forged their own distinctive civilization. Meanwhile, well-rooted civilizations flourished in Asia, as did newer kingdoms and empires in Africa and the Americas, and the world's peoples explored every habitable region of the globe.

THE "TRIUMPH OF BARBARISM AND RELIGION"

The eighteenth-century historian Edward Gibbon (1737–1794) held that Rome's decline was accomplished by "the triumph of barbarism and religion." What Gibbon saw as an explanation for Rome's collapse (which it was not) may be seen as simply a description of what occurred: Rome was gone, the descendants of barbarians (as the Romans, and Gibbon, called them) ruled, and Christianity thrived. Roman disintegration in Western Europe, together with the Arabic conquest of the Mediterranean, mark the end of antiquity. After its close, "barbarism" and religion triumphed.

Roman collapse and tribal invasion are features specifically of the Empire's western zone. The eastern region, ruled from Constantinople, though embattled and diminished, as will be seen, continued the Roman tradition in Greece and the Balkans, in Asia and in Africa, even as Roman authority in the west evaporated. Farther west and north, in contrast, Celtic, Germanic, and other tribal peoples admired, imitated, and then engulfed the civilization of Rome.

Newcomers from Central Asia

The tribal peoples who engulfed Europe came from the margins of Eurasia's civilized core. They were prestate, pre-urban and preliterate. Before they came into contact with advanced Mediterranean civilization, they existed only at a Neolithic level of culture (see Chapter 1). They lived in villages and grew crops, or roamed as nomads tending the herds of animals who fed them. The elites of the advanced civilizations, especially the Greeks and the Chinese, sneered at them. They were wrong to do so. The "barbarians" they despised were dangerous and hungry and held the future in their hands.

Like the tribal peoples who harassed Rome from the third century C.E., the first founders of civilization were originally nomadic peoples (see Chapter 1). From the fourth through the second millennium B.C.E. they swept into western and southern Europe, Mesopotamia and Iran and India, from the Asian steppes or the Arabian peninsula. Over the next few millennia, more waves of nomads pressed into the newly civilized regions of Asia and the Mediterranean

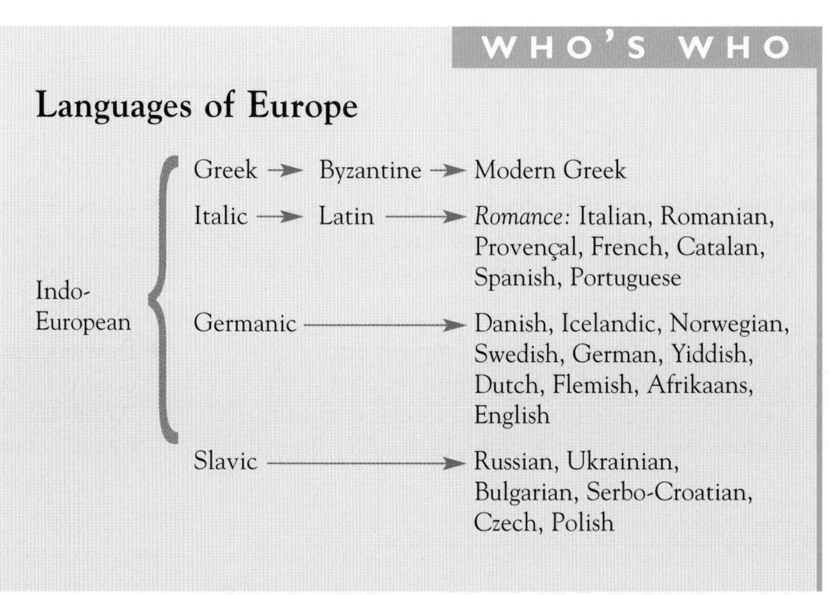

Roman and German Leaders

The column of Marcus Aurelius: *The spectrum of relations between the Romans and the Germanic peoples who invaded the Western Empire is hinted at in this relief from the column of Emperor Marcus Aurelius, 121–180 C.E., depicting Roman soldiers beheading German prisoners.*

world. Searching for a better place to live, they followed the gradient of the great steppes downward toward land that was warmer and wetter, or where rich, walled cities lay ready for sacking.

Among them were the Celts. By 500 B.C.E., the Celts had settled down in central and western Europe: in Switzerland, Germany, and Austria, in modern France and Belgium. As time went on, they moved north into Ireland and Britain and south into Spain and Portugal. Their languages (of the Indo-European family) have left traces in Breton, Gaelic, and Welsh still heard in parts of France and Britain. The Celts built villages and grew crops, practicing an ancient religion under the guidance of their priests, or *druids*. The druids (some of whom may have been women) practiced magic, wrote a language as yet undeciphered, presided over ritual sacrifices of human beings and beasts, and preached the resurrection of the body. They advised the chieftains and educated their sons.

In 390 B.C.E., the Celts of Gaul (modern France) attacked northern Italy, burned the infant city of Rome, and fell before the counterassault of the patrician general Camillus. A century later, they were rebuffed in Asia Minor by the kings of Pergamum, who celebrated in sculpture their victory over the Celtic invaders. A contingent of the same Gauls founded the nation called "Galatia" in the interior of Asia Minor, where, three centuries later, the apostle Paul founded a church.

The Romans pacified many of the Celtic territories. Resistant at first, the Celts of Spain and Gaul eventually yielded to Roman rule, adopting the customs and language of their overlords. The Celts of Britain, conquered last, were less completely Romanized. They often rebelled against the foreign presence—as they did in 60 C.E. under the fierce Queen Boudicca of the Iceni tribe. The Roman emperor Hadrian constructed his famous wall (c. 120 C.E.), shown on p. 198, to define the frontier between the zones of Roman domination and of unconquered natives. In 407 C.E., no longer able to hold that frontier, Roman armies abandoned Britain. Soon the British were overrun by new Germanic peoples, while Roman customs and language were forgotten. But Roman walls, roads, and camps—even baths and foundations of villas—still remain, witnesses to the Roman conquest.

Meanwhile, tribes speaking Germanic languages (another Indo-European branch) and living on the shores of the Baltic Sea moved into central Europe. In their migrations, their tribal divisions multiplied. Those in the north would develop the Nordic dialects, ancestral to the modern Scandinavian tongues. They, too, would migrate, but later, as the feared Vikings:

Flavius Stilicho: *The Germanic Vandal general employed by the Romans, Flavius Stilicho is represented in Roman dress on this ivory panel from Monza, Italy.*

Frontier Defenses

The Great Wall of China: *The crisis caused by the movements of nomadic steppes peoples, which triggered equally vast movements by other peoples, developed from the first century C.E. and affected both China in the east and Rome in the west. The Great Wall of China was the famous achievement of Shi Huangdi (r. c. 221–210 B.C.E.), who ordered the joining together of previously built walls to defend China against foreign incursions. The Great Wall extends 1400 miles (2253 km.) and is studded with many towers which served as signaling stations, warning of the approach of enemies.*

Hadrian's Wall: *Three centuries after the building of the Great Wall of China, the Roman emperor Hadrian (76–138 C.E.) sponsored the building of a wall from west to east across the narrow neck of the northern part of England. Hadrian's wall both consolidated Roman possessions and provided a strategic defense line, with a small fort every mile, and 12 substantial garrison posts across the 73-mile (118 km.) span of the frontier.*

east to Russia, and west to France, England, Ireland, and Iceland. The German peoples who settled in southern Russia spoke Gothic. Those who moved into western Europe gave birth to modern German.

By 300 C.E., German tribes were arrayed along the Roman frontier marked by the Rhine and Danube rivers: Franks and Alamanni, Vandals and Goths (split into western Visigoths and eastern Ostrogoths), Burgundians, Saxons, Lombards, and others. The historian Tacitus, who admired the freedom of the Germans while he scorned their simplicity, named tens of these tribes, describing their outlandish costume, surly drinking bouts, and untarnished strength.

Tacitus also described German society, in meticulous detail (see *Witnesses*, p. 204). The knotted coiffure he described as characteristic of the tribe called the Suebi, for instance, adorns a skull archaeologists unearthed in the German state of Schleswig. Modern archaeologists and anthropologists have explored buried villages and bogs (which have yielded human remains, perhaps of sacrificial victims) that provide tangible evidence of German tribal customs.

Germans were grouped by tribe (the "**folk**"), clan, and family. Ten or twenty families formed a clan, and groups of clans lived together in villages. A number of these were grouped for military or judicial purposes as the "hundred." German men were warriors and herders, counting their wealth in booty and in cattle. They left agriculture to women and to prisoners of war, who used a simple wooden plow to score the heavy northern soil. Women were responsible (as elsewhere) for spinning and weaving, but they also accompanied their menfolk into battle, goading them on to feats of valor. A German husband could have several wives and some concubines. German laws witness that the chastity of German women (much admired by Tacitus) was honored, and its violation harshly punished.

Laws were customary and unwritten. Fixed remedies of vengeance or compensation were set for different categories of crime. Each individual had a price: the **wergeld**. Women, children, old men, and warriors in their prime were assigned wergelds according to their perceived usefulness to society. Rather than taking vengeance on a murderer, the victim's family might instead accept the wergeld in compensation. These payments reduced the overall level of violence in the community.

Chiefs or kings, who were elected by an assembly of the folk for their perceived strength and courage, administered this legal system. Often the king came from a distinguished or "royal" family. Around him clustered a band of elite warriors united to him by oaths of loyalty. The Romans called this band the *comitatus*, or group of companions. These companions foreshadow the vassals of later European kings, who swore oaths of loyalty to their rulers. In addition to his personal band, the king could call on all his tribesmen to fight. All were joined to him, as to the tribe, by pledges of loyalty.

Across the Asian steppes dwelled other peoples, who threatened China, India, and Rome. These included Scythians and Sarmatians near the Black Sea, and Parthians near the Caspian—from where they descended to take over Persia from the Seleucid kings. In central Asia roamed the Altaic- or Turkic-speaking tribes of future conquerors: Huns, Mongols, Turks. From these descended the Kushans, who briefly established rule in the Indian Punjab in the early centuries C.E. Of the same origin were the Hsiung-Nu (the Huns), who prompted Shi Huangdi, in the third century B.C.E., to build the Great Wall as a defence against intruders. Later the Huns turned west to dislodge the Goths from the Dnieper-Danube region and to push into the rich lands of Italy. The Mongols would eventually erupt west, east, and south, to dominate the Eurasian core and shape the future of Russia, China, and western Asia.

Romanization, Invasion, and Rule

Tribal peoples positioned close to the Roman frontier learned to be just like Romans. For centuries, they lived as admiring neighbors, trading their coarse wares for Roman handicrafts and learning to use iron tools and weapons and to haul their belongings in wheeled carts. Often German warriors were recruited as auxiliary soldiers. Some of these Roman-trained warriors returned to their people to lead rebellions against their old commanders. One such was Arminius ("Hermann"), who defeated Varus in the Teutoburg forest in 9 C.E.. Other Germans spent time within Roman boundaries as captives, slaves, or visitors.

Admiration turned to desire. The wealth of Rome was a magnet, especially to people who were starving. The Germans asked the emperors for permission to cross the frontier. Often they were permitted to do so, settling on wasteland or collecting cash subsidies from a state in need of capable mercenaries. If the Romans told the newcomers to stay out, they came anyway: groups of 20,000 to 100,000, who would then form part of the populations they conquered.

After 300 C.E., the accumulated energy of these roaming and expanding populations spilled over the barriers of the Roman frontier, as indicated on Map 8.1. The Huns were the catalyst. Expelled from China, these expert horsemen and bowmen pushed westward across the steppe. After arriving in south Russia in 355, they went on to ravage the Ostrogothic kingdom, between the Don and Dnieper rivers, around 376. The neighboring Visigoths asked the Roman emperor Valens at Constantinople for permission, which he granted, to cross the Danube and take refuge within imperial borders. An extraordinary step had been taken in admitting a whole people across the frontier. Imperial agents abused and cheated the migrants, offering to supply the starving refugees with dog meat at the price of one woman or child per dog. The Visigoths rose up in protest, destroying the imperial forces at Hadrianople (modern Edirne, in Turkey) in 378. The battle marked the first serious encounter between Romans and newcomers in which the newcomers won. Other such encounters would follow.

Over the century, waves of expanding peoples—migrants, raiders, and conquerors—pounded the western Empire. The Visigoths left the Balkans and pushed on into Italy itself, where the emperor now huddled behind the walls of Ravenna in northern Italy on the Adriatic, protected by swamps and fortifications. The emperor Honorius employed his Vandal commander-in-chief, Stilicho (r. 359–408), portrayed on p. 197 as a bulwark against the Visigoths. When Stilicho was murdered, on his master's instructions, in 408, Honorius (r. 384–423) was left on his own to address the threat of invasion.

In this he failed utterly. The Visigoth king Alaric (r. c. 395–410), having been refused permission to occupy Austria, proceeded, in 410, to attack Rome. "Rome, the mistress of the world," wrote the contemporary Christian heretic Pelagius, "shivered, crushed with fear, at the sound of the blaring trumpets and the howling of the Goths." The invaders left the city with booty of gold and silver, bolts of silk, jewelry, and portable household furnishings. Resettled in southern Gaul in 418, these restless people soon crossed the Pyrenees and occupied northern Spain.

The Huns, who had driven the Ostrogoths and Visigoths from the Danube Valley, now stormed westward to forage for food and treasure within the boundaries of the Roman Empire. Stopped near Troyes, in Gaul, in 451, their young chief Attila (r. 435–453) turned back to raid northern Italy the following year. There he was met by Leo I, the Roman pope, and a delegation, whose offers of tribute (added to the Huns' own difficulties with famine and disease) caused the invaders to withdraw to the north in 452.

The Vandals invaded next, also driven by hunger. Under their king, Gaiseric (r. 428–477), they swept into Spain, arriving ahead of the Visigoths. Their ultimate goal was prosperous Africa, Rome's breadbasket. Despite attempts to keep from the invaders either boats or knowledge of shipbuilding, the Vandals commandeered the craft they needed, and in 429 all of them, numbering more than 80,000, sailed across the Straits of Gibraltar to North Africa. Over the next ten years they struck across the Mediterranean coast of Africa to Carthage, which they captured in 439, establishing a kingdom that lasted almost a century thereafter. From their North African base, they attacked Rome by sea in 455. It was the second time in fifty years that the capital was looted.

Twenty-one years later, the German commander Odoacer (r. 476–493) rebelled with his troops against his employer, the incompetent Western emperor Romulus Augustulus, whom he deposed. Odoacer then proceeded to Rome and, in 476, gave himself the title of "king." The Roman state in the west had been a ghost for nearly a century. Odoacer's coup merely made absolutely plain the deterioration that was already accomplished. The eastern emperor, Zeno, commissioned Theodoric (r. 493–526), the king of the Ostrogoths (who had by now migrated to the west) to unseat Odoacer. Theodoric accomplished this feat in 493, sealing the usurpation with the murder of Odoacer and his son. Romans no longer ruled the Empire in the west.

Europe Transformed

The Romans still didn't know they had lost. Nor did the conquerors realize they had won. Rome itself still

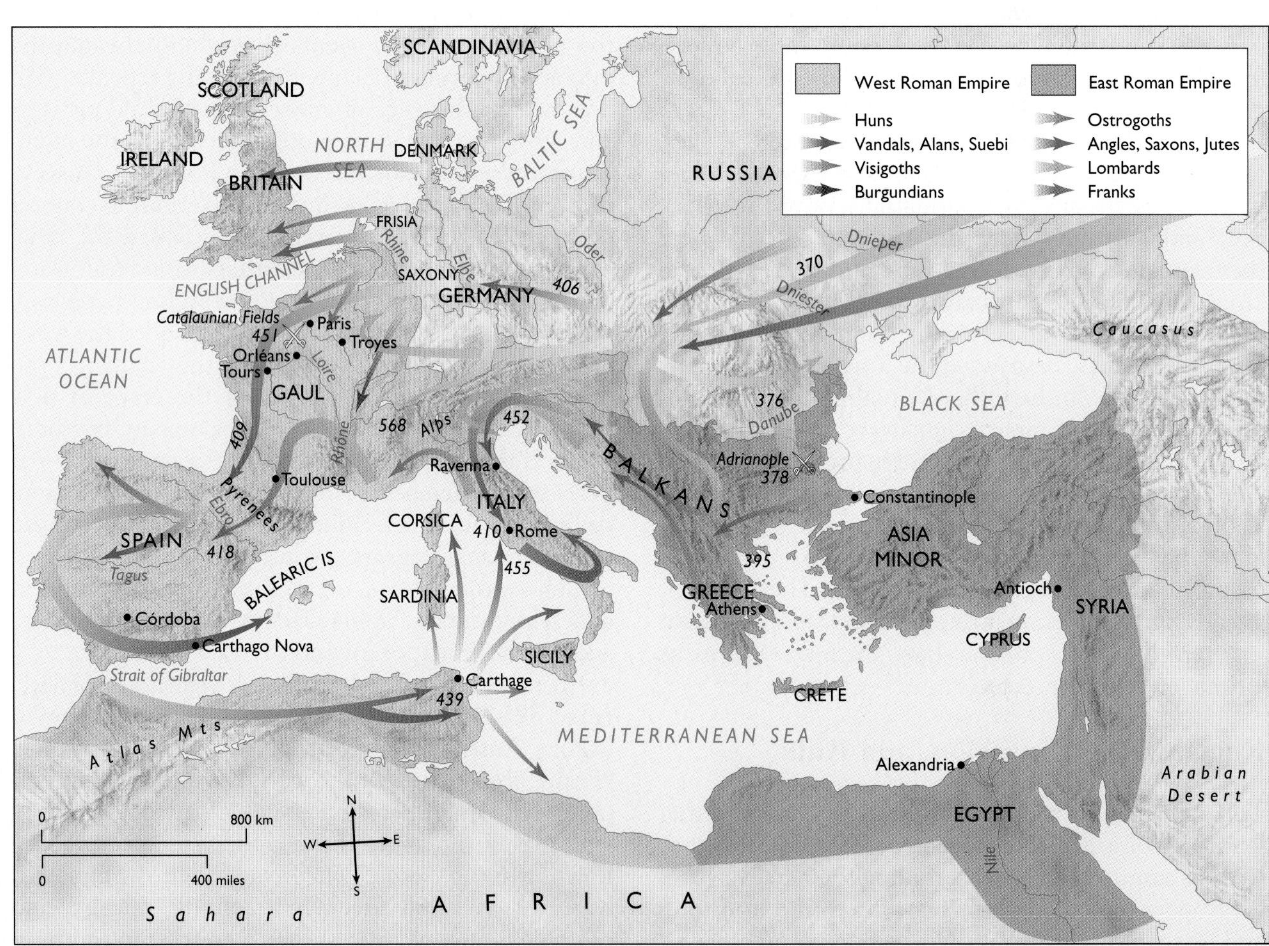

Map 8.1 Migrants, Raiders, and Conquerors, 100–800 C.E.: *Beginning in the first century C.E., nomadic peoples of the central Asian steppes began to expand both west and east, disrupting civilization in both the Mediterranean region and in China. China resisted determinedly, and had attained some stability by around 600. In the west, the movement of Asian peoples triggered the dispersion first of Germanic, and then of Slavic peoples, which was to cut western Europe off from the Mediterranean and the Eastern Roman Empire centered at Constantinople, and to result in the failure of Roman rule in the west. (Compare Map 6.3, p. 160, showing the region when Rome, governed from its single capital, held unquestioned dominion over the region; and Map 8.2, p. 205, showing the position of successor kingdoms to western Rome.)*

stood amid the splendid, crumbling monuments of its youth. Italy lived as before. Although bishops and popes now guided a thoroughly Christianized world, the great landowners still called their leaders "senator" and studied Greek and Roman classics in the libraries of their villas. Theodoric prudently enlisted the senators in his service. Among them were the cultivated Romans Cassiodorus and Boethius.

Cassiodorus (c. 490–585) recorded Theodoric's correspondence, and wrote in elegant Latin a *History of the Goths* (now lost, except for a later abridgment). Having served the Ostrogoths for more than thirty years, he retired in 538 to found a monastery in southern Italy, and to copy the manuscript books that were the legacy of the Roman way of life.

His colleague in Theodoric's service, Boethius (c. 480–524), was accused of treason, imprisoned, and eventually executed. The author of a treatise on music and translator of important works of Aristotle and Plato, Boethius composed in prison his *Consolation of Philosophy*. In this last product of Roman thought, the ghostly figure of "Philosophy" visits the tormented Boethius in his cell. Boethius recounts his miseries, and she diagnoses the disease: he had sought the Highest Good in pleasures, advancements, and wealth, where it could not be found. That supreme reward, which alone could satisfy the longing of the human soul, was to be found only in the mind. Boethius' work announces a turn toward the inner life, which would be a hallmark of the thought of the medieval age to come.

WHO'S WHO

Conquerors of Rome

Arminius (Hermann; d. 19 C.E.) German chief; defeats Roman general Varus in the Teutoburg forest in 9 C.E., destroying three legions and halting the conquest of Germany.

Alaric (r. 395–410) leader of the Visigoths; attacks and sacks Rome in 410, provoking in response Saint Augustine's explanatory *City of God*.

Attila (r. 435–453) leader of the Huns; ravages Germany, Gaul, and northern Italy in 451–452, before being persuaded to turn back.

Gaiseric (r. 428–477) leader of the Vandals: leads the force that sweeps through Spain to North Africa in 429, takes Carthage in 439, and attacks Rome in 455.

Odoacer (r. 476–493) Visigothic king; deposes Western emperor Romulus Augustulus and rules as king at Rome.

Theodoric (r. 493–526) "the Great," king of the Ostrogoths; with blessing of Eastern Emperor Zeno crosses the Alps and retakes Italy from Odoacer (r. 488–493), whom he assassinated, and reigns as king at Rome.

Germanic Kingdoms The Ostrogothic kingdom in Italy lasted from Theodoric's accession in 493 until the emperor Justinian's reconquest of Italy, completed finally in 562—to be followed only a few years later by the new invaders, the Lombards. The Vandal kingdom in North Africa was also relatively short-lived: from the 429 invasion until Justinian's reconquest of that region in 533. By the end of the sixth century, these kingdoms had all vanished, while the Visigoths held Toulouse, in southern Gaul, and then Spain from 418 until the Arab conquest in 711.

In the meantime, other peoples to the north had penetrated Roman frontiers to establish a second generation of kingdoms. The Lombards, arriving in 568, founded a kingdom in northern Italy that lasted for two centuries. As Roman authority waned in Britain, German-speaking Saxons, Angles, and Jutes from across the Channel invaded, destroying churches and monasteries as they progressed, zealous champions of their ancient polytheistic culture. By 700, Christian missionaries from Ireland and Rome had converted the descendants of these invaders—who were a church before they were a nation. Their story was told by the contemporary scholar and saint Bede (c. 673–735), called "Venerable," in his *Ecclesiastical History of the English People*. Meanwhile, Germanic Burgundians infiltrated southeastern Gaul, and Franks moved into the north.

In 481 or 482, the vigorous leader Clovis took charge of the Frankish kingdom. Its turbulent career would be described by Bishop Gregory of Tours (538–594) in his *History of the Franks*. Clovis and his descendants, called "Merovingians" (after their patriarch Merovech), ruled until 751, when Pepin, the king's minister, deposed the last of them and assumed the royal title. Pepin's line was "Carolingian," after his father Charles (Carolus in Latin) Martel (i.e. "the Hammer"; 688?–741). In 732 Charles Martel had driven Arab Muslim invaders back at Poitiers—the high-water mark of their penetration of western Europe. Pepin's son was also called Charles: Charles "the Great," or Charlemagne (r. 768–814).

Germanic newcomers settled among Roman citizens gingerly, displacing but not crushing the natives. They occupied one-third to two-thirds of the land, and governed their own people by Germanic law—which was often codified and committed to writing in the Latin of the vanquished Romans. The Romans, meanwhile, maintained their own laws and customs. The two societies dwelt side by side, at first neither intermingling nor intermarrying. Eventually, they blended. They used as a common language the simple Latin of late Roman times, which absorbed some Germanic words and concepts—except in distant

Britain, more resolutely Germanic in speech. In Spain, Portugal, France, and Italy (as well as Romania and parts of Switzerland) the rough provincial Latin of the Roman inhabitants developed into the **Romance** languages spoken in these countries today.

Arians and Catholics Some of the tribal peoples who descended on the western Empire were already Christians: Arian Christians (see Chapter 7). The Goth Ulfilas (c. 311–382) had learned this heresy in Constantinople, where he was consecrated bishop in 341. When he returned to his people, he brought the new religion and a new alphabet. He translated parts of the Bible into Gothic and adapted the Greek alphabet to write it down. Gothic Arianism spread to neighboring peoples. The kingdoms of the Vandals, the Ostrogoths, and the Visigoths were all Arian.

The Romans, in contrast, were staunch catholics. They adhered, to the key Christian doctrines, notably those proclaimed in the Nicene Creed (see Chapter 7); and they were obedient to the bishop of Rome, the pope. The Anglo-Saxons of Britain and the Franks of northern Gaul were both converted from polytheism to Latin catholicism. These tribes, especially the Franks, became the allies of the Church in the Christianization of Europe. When the Roman popes despaired of Byzantine aid against the Lombards in the eighth century, they called on the kings of the Franks to defend the faith. Thus, a long tradition of Church–state interdependence was born in the West.

***Protecting ancestral graves:** This tomb guardian figure, c. 386–534 C.E., was crafted by the nomadic Asian Mongols, later raiders of Europe.* (Inner Mongolia Museum, Hahehaote)

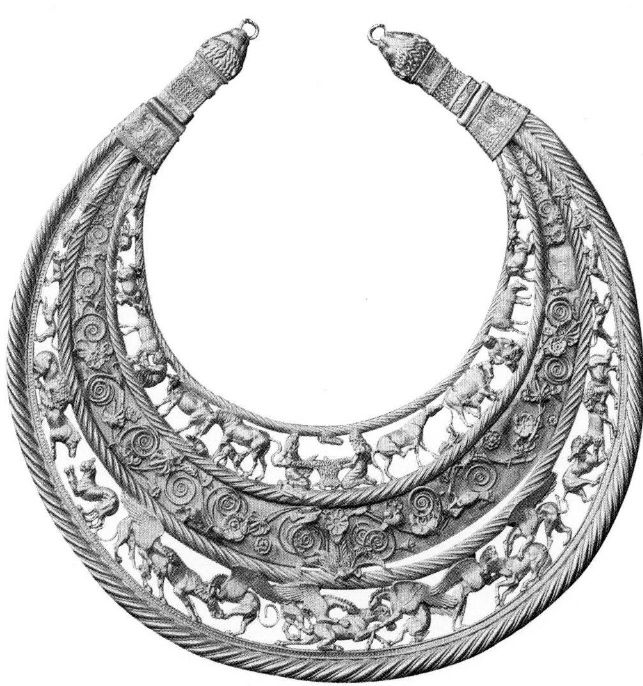

The Fringes of Civilization

***The Wild and the Tame:** Not only the great civilizations, but also peoples on the fringes of civilization produced artifacts of great beauty. This pectoral, or necklace, by a Scythian craftsman, fourth century B.C.E., depicts in the first band foals and calves feeding and a man milking sheep. In contrast, the lower band shows wild animals—boars, lions, and winged beasts—attacking each other.* (Historical Museum, Kiev)

The Task of Preservation As newcomers settled in the world that had been Roman, Roman intellectuals tried to keep Roman literature alive. As Christian converts, they had at first shied away from the body of Classical works forming the foundation of the Greco-Roman curriculum. It was laden with allusions to a pagan world now repudiated, whose religious and sexual customs were equally repugnant. But by now these converts had made their peace with the Classics, which they read, copied, abridged, and raided. The great task of preservation began.

Although the literature of the past was prized, it was no longer understood. As the task of preservation progressed, complexity of thought declined. A curtain had dropped between the new world of Germanic kingdoms and Christian orthodoxy and the old world of elevated language, erudition, and empire. The *Etymologies* of the Spanish scholar-bishop Saint Isidore of Seville (c. 560–636), an encyclopedia of the "origins" of things, contained shreds and fragments of the whole ancient literary tradition. It had lost the coherent vision of antiquity and exemplifies the

A King's helmet: *Excavated from a trove of grave-goods at Sutton Hoo on England's east coast, c. 660 C.E., was this Saxon helmet. With other objects like hinged clasps and brooches, it was buried in a ship under a mound which served as a memorial to an East Anglian king.* (British Museum)

process of intellectual decay. The conquest had done its work. "Barbarism" won, and a chasm yawned between past and present.

The debasement of literary culture paralleled a loss of population, a decline of urban life, the collapse of commerce, the disappearance of currency, an increase in lawlessness, and a deep isolation: these features characterized a period once called the "Dark Ages." It is called so no longer. Historians now recognize that the deep changes of the sixth through ninth centuries laid the foundations of modern European culture. The period was more one of transition than of decline, as the focus of European life shifted from the Mediterranean to the forested interior of western Europe. The shift from oil (the fruit of the olive consumed throughout the Mediterranean) to butter (processed from the milk of Europe's cows) marked a new departure in Western civilization.

BYZANTIUM: THE ENDURING EMPIRE

As Rome languished in the west, Rome in the east, centered at Constantinople, flourished and would endure for a millennium to come. Thoroughly Roman before it became detached from the Latin West, the eastern Empire sought for two centuries to reestablish the western domain. Then it turned inward and eastward, and spoke only Greek. Now known as the Byzantine Empire, it was to survive confrontation with the forces of Islam, as well as its own internal religious conflicts, until 1453. During that time, it was the center of a commercial network linking interior regions of Russia and western Asia with Mediterranean ports, and the principal home of the preservation of ancient Greek culture.

The Eastern Empire to the Autocracy of Justinian

The split between West and East began early. The Latinization of the eastern Mediterranean had never been so thorough as the Latinization of North Africa or Western Europe. The emperor Hadrian had encouraged Greek culture to reassert itself. After Commodus, many Roman emperors were of eastern origin. These and other factors encouraged the break between the two halves of the Empire.

The two men who rescued Rome from its third-century depression were also those who precipitated the divorce between West and East. Both were Latin-speaking Westerners. Diocletian divided the administration of the Empire between the two regions. Constantine established an eastern capital at Constantinople (formerly Byzantium). With the death of Theodosius the Great in 395, imperial unity broke down irrevocably. His sons ascended to separate western and eastern thrones. The division between East and West had been a cultural reality since the second century and an administrative one since the third. Now it was absolute. A century and a half later, while the Ostrogoths ruled Italy, in the east Justinian (r. 527–565) was to establish the full autocracy of the Byzantine emperor. He is shown with his retinue on p. 207.

Justinian the Autocrat The pharaohs of ancient Egypt and the Persian "king of kings" had pointed the way to autocracy. Earlier Roman emperors revived such claims, and Diocletian especially, seeking to impose order, exalted himself as "lord." But with Justinian the evolution of the emperor's role from "first citizen" to absolute monarch reached its culmination. In establishing this autocracy, Justinian was motivated at least partly by an incident early in his reign that challenged his authority.

Justinian often attended the horse races at the Hippodrome in Constantinople. In 532, the audience began a riot against his repressive regime. These were the Nika riots, so named after the shout "*nika!*" (meaning "win!") so often heard at the races. After the trauma of this rebellion (suppressed by his versatile agent Belisarius, c. 505–565, who trapped and massacred the insurgents), Justinian was now even more committed to autocracy.

His partner in this venture was his wife, the intelligent Theodora (c. 497–548). Unusually for a queen,

WITNESSES

The Coming of the Germans

The culture and society of the Germans differed markedly from those of the Romans, as the Roman historian Tacitus expertly notes in his ethnography—the first of its kind—of those tribal nations, of which some extracts are given in the first passage. The different values of the Germans, captured in Tacitus's narrative, is also recognized in their laws and customs, as in the excerpts from the laws of the Salian Franks.

The Roman historian Tacitus describes, with some amusement and with some admiration, the customs of the Germans (c. 105–110 C.E.):

7. They choose their kings by birth, their generals for merit. These kings have not unlimited or arbitrary power, and the generals do more by example than by authority. If they are energetic, if they are conspicuous, if they fight in the front, they lead because they are admired. But to reprimand, to imprison, even to flog, is permitted to the priests alone. ... They also carry with them into battle certain figures and images taken from their sacred groves. And what most stimulates their courage is, that their squadrons or battalions, instead of being formed by chance or by a fortuitous gathering, are composed of families and clans. Close by them, too, are those dearest to them, so that they hear the shrieks of women, the cries of infants. ...

11. About minor matters the chiefs deliberate, about the more important the whole tribe. Yet even when the final decision rests with the people, the affair is always thoroughly discussed by the chiefs. They assemble, except in the case of a sudden emergency, on certain fixed days, either at new or at full moon; for this they consider the most auspicious season for the transaction of business. ... When the multitude think proper, they sit down armed. Silence is proclaimed by the priests, who have on these occasions the right of keeping order. Then the king or the chief, according to age, birth, distinction in war, or eloquence, is heard. ... If his sentiments displease them, they reject them with murmurs; if they are satisfied, they brandish their spears. The most complimentary form of assent is to express approbation with their spears.

14. When they go into battle, it is a disgrace for the chief to be surpassed in valour, a disgrace for his followers not to equal the valour of the chief. And it is an infamy and a reproach for life to have survived the chief, and returned from the field. To defend, to protect him, to ascribe one's own brave deeds to his renown, is the height of loyalty. The chief fights for victory; his vassals fight for their chief ...

(Tacitus, *The Agricola and Germania*; trans. A. J. Church and W. J. Brodribb, 1877)

The laws of the Salian Franks, written down beginning in the seventh century from oral traditions, assign monetary penalties, graded according to the social status of victim and perpetrator, for assault and murder; note especially the heavy punishment assigned to the murderer of a male child, or a woman capable of bearing children:

Title XIV. Concerning Assault and Robbery: 1. If any one have assaulted and plundered a freeman, and it be proved on him, he shall be sentenced to 2500 denars, which make 63 shillings. 2. If a Roman have plundered a Salian Frank, the above law shall be ordered. 3. But if a Frank have plundered a Roman, he shall be sentenced to 35 shillings ...

Title XVII. Concerning Wounds: 1. If any one have wished to kill another person, and the blow have missed, he on whom it was proved shall be sentenced to 2500 denars, which make 63 shillings. 2. If any person have wished to strike another with a poisoned arrow, and the arrow have glanced aside, and it shall be proved on him: he shall be sentenced to 2500 denars, which make 63 shillings. 3. If any person strike another on the head so that the brain appears, and the three bones which lie above the brain shall project, he shall be sentenced to 1200 denars, which make 30 shillings. 4. But if it shall have been between the ribs or in the stomach, so that the wound appears and reaches to the entrails, he shall be sentenced to 1200 denars-which make 30 shillings... 6. But if a freeman strike a freeman with his fist so that blood does not flow, he shall be sentenced for each blow—up to 3 blows to 120 denars, which make 3 shillings.

Title XXIV. Concerning the Killing of Little Children and Women: 1. If any one have slain a boy under 10 years ... he shall be sentenced to 24000 denars, which make 600 shillings ... 3. If any one have hit a free woman who is pregnant, and she dies, he shall be sentenced to 28000 denars, which makes 700 shillings. 6. If any one have killed a free woman after she has begun bearing children, he shall be sentenced to 24000 denars, which make 600 shillings. 7. After she can have no more children, he who kills her shall be sentenced to 8000 denars, which make 200 shillings.

("The Salic Law," in Ernest F. Henderson, *Select Historical Documents of the Middle Ages*, 1910) especially in ancient times, she began life near the bottom of the social ladder (her father was reported variously to be a circus bear-trainer or a horse-stable owner) and descended further. If not actually a prostitute when Justinian met her, she was engaged in no respectable trade. In later life, perhaps recalling her origins, she founded a hostel for reformed prostitutes. Theodora was an active empress, whom Justinian consulted frequently. She is famous for her advice to him during the Nika riots. If he wished to flee, she said, "yonder is the sea, and there are the ships." She herself would stay, regardless of risk; "purple [the color of royalty] makes an excellent shroud."

Freed from the poverty of her youth, Theodora enjoyed the opulence of the imperial court, where she was served, witnesses report, by as many as 4000 attendants. The luxury, the rituals, the obeisance of courtiers matched the claims of imperial status. Access to the emperor was controlled by slaves and eunuchs (thought to be asexual and therefore trustworthy). Intrigues abounded. These, and observations about the private lives of the principals, are recorded in the scandalous and elegant *Secret History* of the court historian Procopius (c. 500–565).

Justinian's civil servants were highly educated men from middling or immigrant backgrounds. They formed a bureaucracy which collected taxes, governed the provinces, and watched the treasury, enriched by the profits from state monopolies such as that of the luxury fabric silk. Justinian's bureaucrats were expected to labor ceaselessly in the interests of the emperor, emulating Marinus of Syria, adviser to Justinian's predecessor Anastasius (r. 491–518), who even at night kept "a pen-and-ink stand hanging beside his bedside, and a lamp burning by his pillow, so that he could write down his thoughts on a roll."

Church and State Justinian was head of the church as well as of the government. In these roles, he followed the examples of his predecessors Constantine and Theodosius the Great, who had called councils, debated with bishops, and refereed dogmatic squabbles. Now that pattern of ecclesiastical leadership became fixed. In a law of 535 Justinian announced that the state possessed two powers, both granted by God: those pertaining to the priesthood and those pertaining to politics—meaning that the emperor was empowered to lead the church as much as the state.

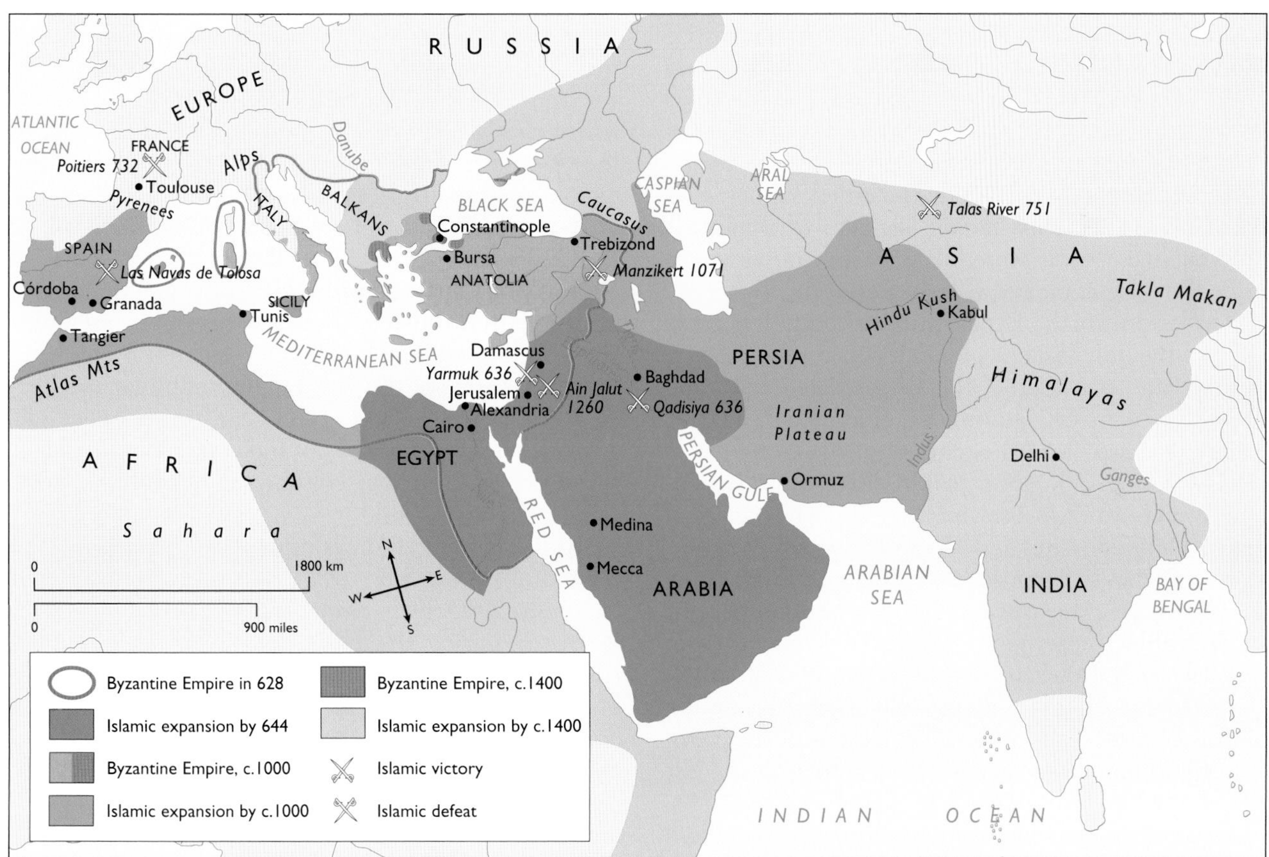

Map 8.2 Byzantium and Islam, 500–1400: *By 500 C.E., the eastern half of the Roman Empire was on its way to becoming the Byzantine Empire: Greek-speaking and eastward-facing, though solidly rooted in its Roman past. After 632, the new Islamic civilization that began to form in the Near and Middle East, across North Africa, and into Spain, challenged Byzantium militarily and economically. The period from 800 to 1453 saw the still greater expansion of Islamic civilization, which reached into regions beyond its Mediterranean origin. At the same time, after some recovery in the ninth century, Byzantium gradually deteriorated to the position of a weak state on the fringe of Islam, and it fell to the assault of Turkish Muslims called Ottomans.*

Byzantium and Islam

Basilica of Santa Sophia: *Christian Byzantium and Islamic caliphates nurtured grand architectural projects and exquisitely decorated interior surfaces, the latter affected by cultural norms—for Islam forbade the representation of human or animal figures in religious contexts, whereas these were essential to the didactic purposes of Christian art. The most impressive building of Justinian's reign was Santa Sophia in Constantinople (Istanbul), built 532–537. The four minarets were added when the basilica was converted into a mosque with the Turkish capture of the city in 1453 C.E.*

Byzantine Christianity was different from that evolving in the West. The East had concurred in the orthodox definition about the human and divine natures of Jesus the Christ crystallized by the Council of Nicaea in 325. Yet it always tended to emphasize the Christian Savior's universal and divine qualities more than his human and concrete ones. It was Jesus as *Logos* ("the Word of God") rather than Jesus of Nazareth (the man) who won the allegiance of the Eastern church. It is this disembodied Christ who floats on the brilliant mosaic surfaces of Byzantine monuments: an all-powerful ruler of the universe more than the compassionate healer of the Gospels.

Under Justinian, Byzantine Christianity became not just the only legal religion but a colossal force permitting no opposition. Officials pressured Jews and pagans to convert. Justinian's chief legal adviser, Tribonian (c. 470–544), architect of the *Corpus Iuris Civilis* (see below), was a striking exception: he was quietly permitted to remain a pagan. The heretical sects of Monophysites and Nestorians established separate churches in Egypt and the Middle East; later they would welcome the arrival of Islam as a counterweight to Byzantine repression. Procopius' skeptical voice raised a lonely protest against the tether of conformity: "I consider it a mark of insane folly to investigate the nature of God and of what kind it may be." We scarcely comprehend human affairs, he argued; "far less of anything that pertains to the nature of God."

Pagan thought, like pagan worship, was suppressed under Justinian. In 529, he closed down the Academy and the Lyceum in Athens, the schools that had been opened 900 years before by Plato and Aristotle. Meanwhile, in Constantinople there flourished the Christian school founded by the emperor Theodosius II (r. 408–50) in 425, with a staff of eight professors of Greek and Latin rhetoric, ten of Greek and Latin grammar, one of philosophy, and two of jurisprudence. Here and at Alexandria and Gaza (in Palestine), orthodox Christian doctrine was taught by Christian teachers, along with the standard curriculum of the Greco-Roman world. The unemployed professors of the ancient pagan schools went into voluntary exile among the Monophysites and Nestorians, or to Persia, where they discoursed on philosophy at the court of the king of the Sassanids (ethnic Persian rulers of the region since the third century C.E.).

Buildings and Laws In addition to his work of establishing Christian orthodoxy, Justinian undertook more practical projects, including his ambitious building program. He had fortifications rebuilt around the shrunken cities of the late Empire and near the perilous frontiers. He had hostels constructed near **pilgrimage** sites, and hospitals and orphanages to meet the needs of Christian conscience. Above all, there were churches to build.

Justinian's most important enterprise was the rebuilding, from 532 C.E., of Constantine's church of "holy wisdom," Santa Sophia, shown above, destroyed during the Nika riots. Justinian's renovations (funded by treasure snatched from the Vandals of North Africa) made Santa Sophia the largest domed church of the age. Viewing the completed monument, Justinian exclaimed (referring to the First Temple of the Jews): "Solomon, I have outdone you!" Under Turkish rule, it was redesigned as a mosque.

Larger than its nearest rivals, Alexandria and Antioch (Rome had shrunk to about 30,000 by the late sixth century), Constantinople under Justinian was at its peak, the foremost city of the eastern Empire. A center of international trade as well as church and government, it was home to a population of between 300,000 and 400,000 Asians and Slavs,

Jews and Romans, both Latin- and Greek-speaking. A fifth-century document catalogues its major features: among them 14 palaces, 4388 residential houses, 8 public and 153 private baths, 2 theaters, not counting the Hippodrome; 20 public and 120 private bakeries, and 14 churches, all guarded by 65 night-watchmen and 560 firemen.

More lasting than any building was the great law code compiled at Justinian's direction: the whole legacy of Roman experience of the administration of justice. The collection and analysis of the law had been the ongoing concern of the great jurists of the second and third centuries. Two earlier codes had been gathered under Diocletian, and Theodosius II had seen to the publication of the Theodosian Code of 438. Yet the job needed to be done again: new legislation needed to be ordered, contradictory or out-of-date laws eliminated, and the relevant commentaries of legal experts organized in a useful way.

The *Corpus Iuris Civilis* ("The Collected Civil Law") consisted of four parts: the *Code*, a revised compilation of laws, the preface to which is quoted in *Witnesses* on p. 208; the *Digest*, containing summaries of the opinions of the classical jurists; the *Institutes*, a legal textbook; and the *Novels*, a compilation of the new laws issued after 533, when the *Code* was completed. Justinian left no monument to his achievement more important for the history of the West than the *Corpus Iuris Civilis*, in which he proclaimed the primacy of law above even emperors: "the subordination of sovereignty under the law is a greater thing than the imperial power itself." This acknowledgment of the superior authority of law is a rare statement of monarchical principle.

Roman law was written in Latin. Justinian was by birth a Latin speaker, and Latin remained during his reign the official language of the Byzantine court. But in the *Corpus Iuris Civilis*, Latin had its last day in the East. Soon the language of imperial administration, of the church, and of scholarship would be Greek.

Justinian's jurists achieved more than his generals. A year after suppressing the Nika riots, Belisarius set

Justinian and his retinue: *The splendid mosaics in San Vitale, Ravenna, crafted c. 547 show the Byzantine emperor Justinian with his retinue. Justinian in fact never went to Ravenna, but the mosaic was intended to serve as his substitute and as an important visual reminder of his power.*

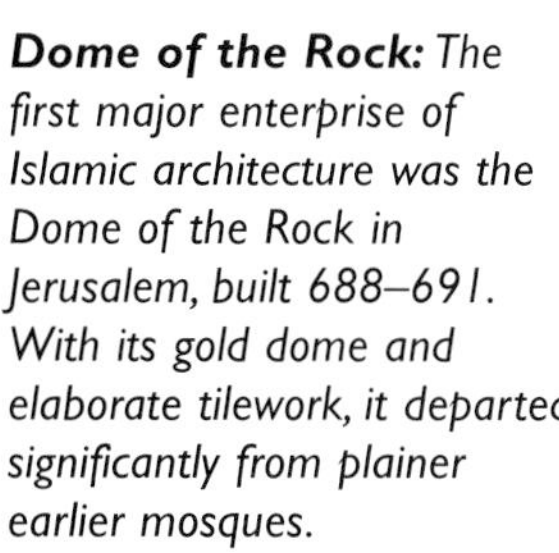

Dome of the Rock: *The first major enterprise of Islamic architecture was the Dome of the Rock in Jerusalem, built 688–691. With its gold dome and elaborate tilework, it departed significantly from plainer earlier mosques.*

out to reconquer the western half of the Empire, accompanied by his staff historian, Procopius, who would report the entire operation in his *History of the Wars of Justinian*. At first, all went well. Belisarius reconquered North Africa from the Vandals in 533, and he and another general, Narses (c. 480–574), reconquered much of Italy between 535 and 561. The African mission achieved its goals. The wealth seized from Carthage and Rome by the Vandals was recovered, and the native, Romanized elites welcomed Byzantine overlordship. This arrangement would endure about a century, after which Africa was absorbed into the new power of Islam. The Italian reconquest, in contrast, was bloody and troubled. In the end, only Ravenna, Rome, and Sicily were securely held for Byzantium. The rest of Italy succumbed in 568 to the invading Lombards.

Byzantium after Justinian

These losses in the west were followed by devastating losses in the north and east. The Byzantine Empire would never again be so large as it was under Justinian. Slavic peoples seized the Balkans in the sixth and seventh centuries, while nomadic Bulgars and Avars ravaged the northern frontier. Persians, under Sassanid leadership, threatened Byzantium's eastern flank from 609 to 622. Then the still more powerful force of Islam challenged the bastions of the Empire. Armies of **Saracens** (as Muslim Arabs were called by the Greek-speaking Byzantine chroniclers) swept away Byzantine defenses in Egypt, Palestine, and Syria, and besieged Constantinople regularly from 674 to 678 and again in 717. The defenders sprayed or pumped "Greek fire" (a flammable brew of petroleum, sulfur, and pitch) on enemy ships, saving the capital from capture. But the borders of the Empire were shrinking.

Three hundred and fifty years later, Islamic armies would return—not the Saracens as before, but the Seljuk Turks, who had seized power from the caliphs of Baghdad. Turkish armies defeated Byzantine forces decisively at Manzikert, Asia Minor, in 1071, removing much of that region from Byzantine domination. Emperor Alexius I Comnenus (r. 1081–1118) asked the pope for help, and brought on his head the avalanche of the Crusades. Soldiers poured out from western Europe ready to fight the "infidel" who had captured the holy sites in Jerusalem. A century later, in 1204, the Crusaders turned on their Christian brethren in Constantinople. When a Byzantine regime was restored later in the same century, it had fewer than two centuries more to endure. Ottoman Turks, manning the first warships ever to be mounted with guns, seized the last remnant of the Roman Empire in 1453. Today Istanbul—as Constantinople was renamed in 1930—is the major city of the modern nation of Turkey.

WITNESSES

The Byzantines in Charge

These two passages give brief glimpses into the exercise of imperial power in Byzantium. In the first, the sixth-century Emperor Justinian explains the importance of the monumental compilation of law called the Corpus Iuris Civilis, *completed under his direction. In the second, the daughter of a later emperor, the twelfth-century conqueror Alexius, explains how he delegated the tasks of ordinary government to his mother.*

In the preface to the *Institutes*, a part of the *Corpus Iuris Civilis* containing the codification of Roman law, the emperor Justinian explains the nature of the whole work (c. 540): In the name of Our Lord Jesus Christ ... to the youth desirous of studying the law. ... Having removed every inconsistency from the sacred constitutions hitherto inharmonious and confused, we extended our care to the immense volumes of the older jurisprudence, and have now completed a work of which we once despaired. When this had been done, we [ordered the completion of] ... a book of Institutes. ... Receive then these laws... and show yourselves so learned ... that ... you may have ability to govern such portions of the state as may be entrusted to you.

(Justinian, preface to the *Institutes*; ed. M. Hadas 1956)

Anna Comnena, chronicler of the reign of her father, the emperor Alexius, describes his entrusting civil power to his mother, her grandmother Anna Dalassena (c. 1120): My father reserved for himself the waging of wars against the barbarians, while he entrusted to his mother the administration of state affairs, the choosing of civil servants, and the fiscal management of the empire's revenues and expenses. ... For my grandmother really had the gift of conducting the affairs of state. She knew so well how to organize and administer that she was capable of governing not only the Roman Empire but also every other kingdom under the sun. ...

(Anna Comnena, *Alexiad*; ed. P. Thiébaux 1987)

During the centuries from Justinian's reign in the sixth century until the collapse of the Byzantine Empire in the fifteenth, the cities of the Empire weakened and failed. The profits of trade drained eastward, and coins fell out of circulation. The concern with security was obsessive, as "fortifications replaced men." Alexandria and Antioch withered, and lesser cities disappeared altogether. Constantinople itself declined: hit by plague in 542 and by other disasters thereafter, its population decreased in the eighth century to fewer than 50,000 residents. Two centuries later it had regained some prosperity and had a

HOW MANY?

Comparative City Sizes and Plans, c. 800–1000

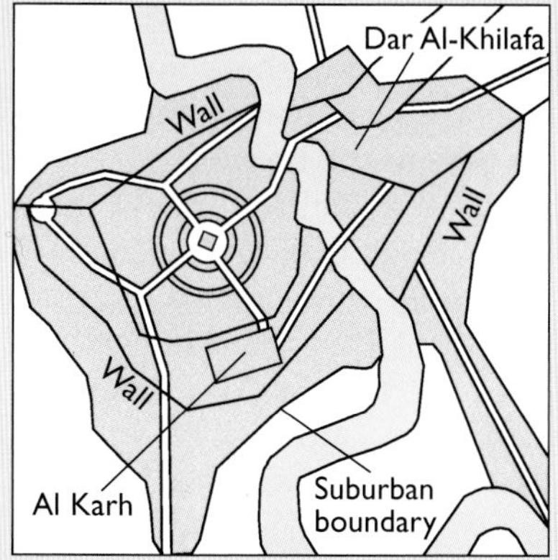

Baghdad, Iraq *300–500,000*

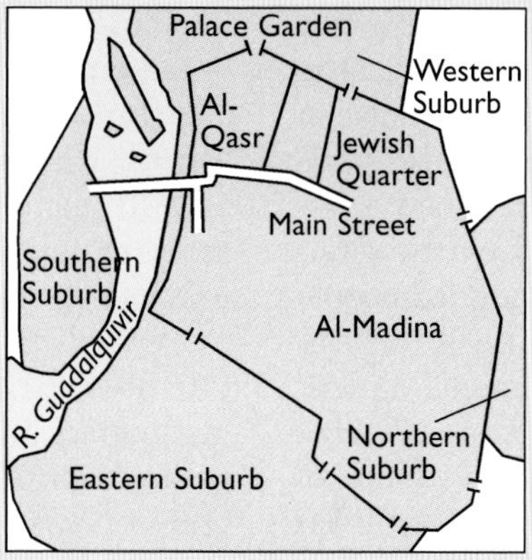

Córdoba, Spain *500,000*

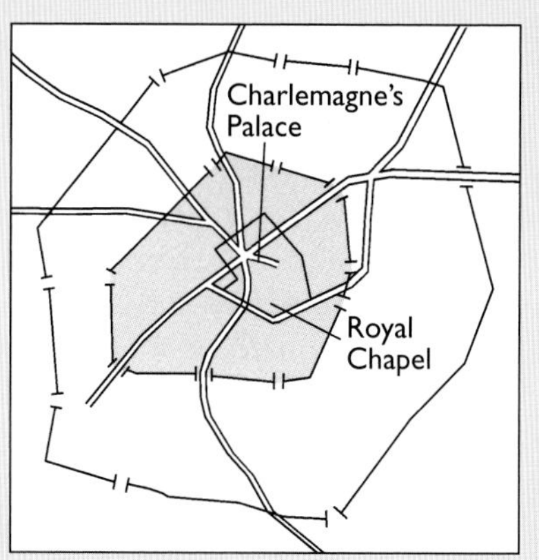

Aachen, Germany *2000–3000*

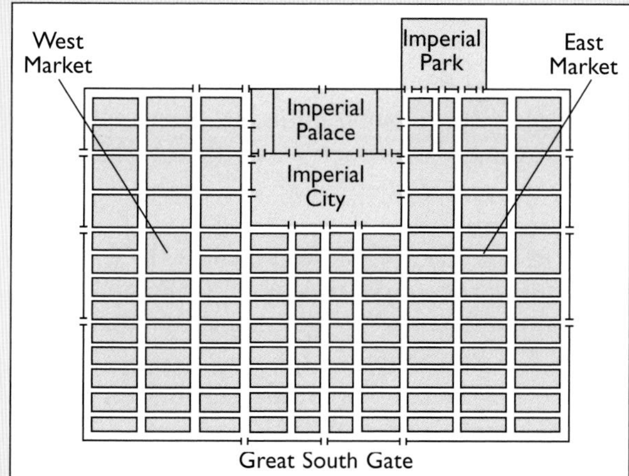

Chang'an, China *1,000,000*

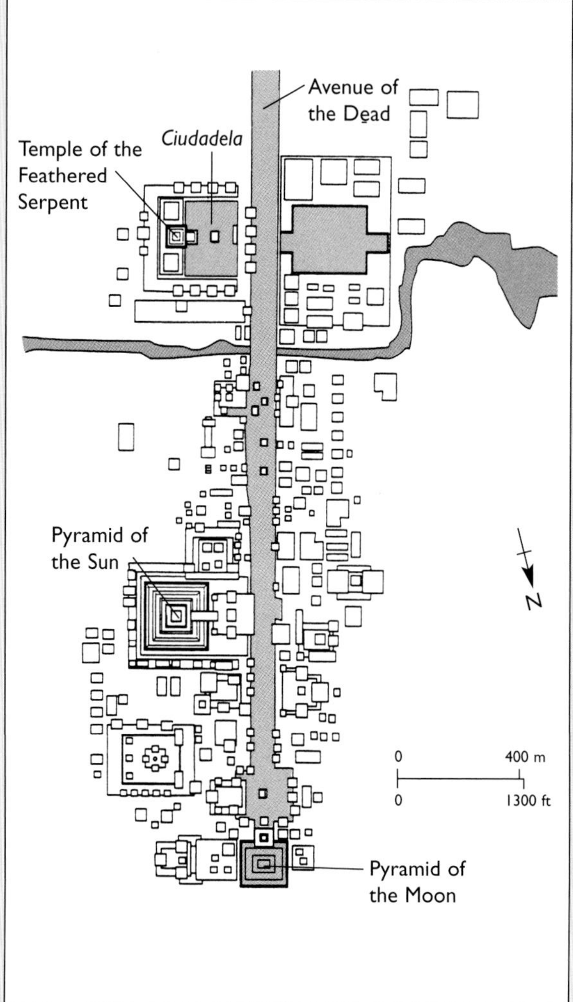

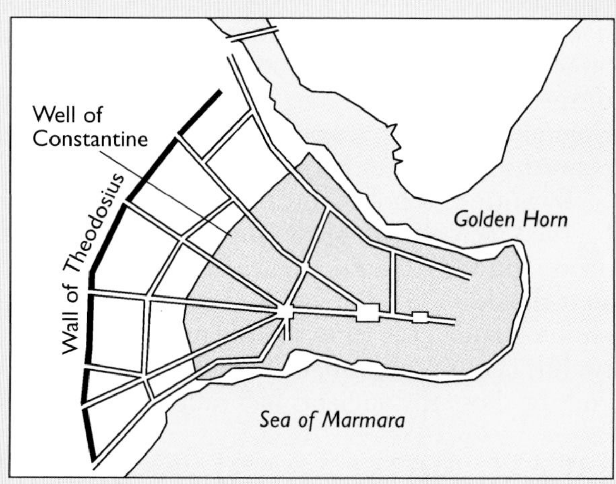

Constantinople (modern Istanbul), Turkey *300–400,000*

Teotihuacán, Mexico *100,000*

population of several hundred thousand; but the city that fell to the Turks in 1453 was a small mercantile center whose population had again shrunk to 50,000.

The Iconoclastic Controversy and the Emperor Irene An early religious crisis greatly influenced the culture of Byzantium. In 730—precisely when Islam threatened Byzantium with annihilation—the puritanical Emperor Leo III (r. 717–741) launched a war on the holy images, or icons, treasured by the pious as aids to devotion. Leo and other like-minded people in the Eastern church condemned the use of icons as a violation of the Second Commandment, against idolatry. Their opponents considered icons valuable means of apprehending the divine. The policy of **iconoclasm** (meaning "the smashing of images") was ultimately reversed. Yet it created irreparable tensions with the West and encouraged the eventual and enduring rift between the Roman Catholic and Eastern Orthodox churches (see Chapter 10).

The decision, in 787, by the Council of Nicaea to restore icons to homes and churches was prompted by Irene (r. 780–802), mother of the future emperor Constantine VI and regent during his minority (780–91). This determined woman wanted to rule herself, rather than yield to her son. On being proclaimed emperor in 790, Constantine confined his mother to house arrest. When she seized power in 797, Irene ordered her son captured, blinded, and killed; she then ruled in her own right for five years. The Frankish king Charlemagne is reported to have proposed marriage to her in 802, intending perhaps to reunite the eastern and western remnants of ancient Rome. That possibility alarmed high officials in Constantinople, who deposed Irene in 802. She died in exile a year later.

Court scribes, not having dealt before with a female ruler, referred to Irene as "emperor," a ruler in her own right; the term verbally differentiates her from "empresses," who were merely consorts. Despite the exalted status achieved by Irene and by Theodora and other empress-consorts, for most women conditions under Byzantine domination resembled those of Hellenistic or Roman society. Women could still be executed for adultery, be summarily divorced, testify in court only about matters concerning children and family, and lose guardianship of their children upon remarriage. These were the measures of women's legal and sexual status. The boundary of a woman's life remained the walls of her home.

Scholarship, Male and Female Amid conflicts and crises both internal and external, Byzantine scholars kept ancient knowledge alive. Many of the best manuscripts of Greek philosophy and literature—nearly the whole of what is now known, barring the papyrus fragments recovered in modern times from Egypt—were produced in Constantinople. That achievement was the work of earnest bishops, committed teachers, and leisured aristocrats, whose Greek was native and natural. For these scholars, there was no need for the kind of "Renaissance" (or "rebirth") that occurred later in the West. However, some authors or books became more fashionable than others, and occasionally fits of editorial enthusiasm saw to the purging of "errors" that had crept into the text.

Although the goal of Byzantine scholarship was more to preserve the wisdom of the ancients than to develop new learning, one or two exceptional individuals did flourish in this age. Michael Psellus (1018–1096), author of treatises on science and mathematics, rhetoric, law, and history, wrote compellingly of his discovery of the works of the ancient philosophers: "Having found philosophy extinct in its practitioners, I revived it by my own efforts. ...Since, however, I heard it said that Greece had achieved great things in philosophy, ... [a]fter reading some commentators on this science, I learned from them the road to knowledge: one referred me to another, the inferior to the superior ... and so, finally, to Aristotle and Plato."

At least two women joined in the intellectual life of Byzantium. The poet Icasia (b. c. 810) sparkled briefly in court circles before she retired to spend the rest of her life in a convent. Of even higher social position was Anna Comnena (1083–1153), the eldest daughter of the emperor Alexis I Comnenus.

Comnena wrote a biography of her father in fifteen books (an extract is given in *Witnesses* on p. 208): a significant historical work, based on Classical models and contemporary sources. Strikingly, Comnena says nothing about women's inner experience in the Byzantine milieu. Her record would surely have been interesting. This Byzantine princess mastered Classical literature clandestinely, while confined within her house. As a child she cherished hopes of deposing her brother and succeeding her father on the imperial throne. She was forced instead to spend her mature years, like Icasia, in a convent. Comnena wrote not a word of those constraints as she penned the record of her father's achievements.

Byzantine scholarship discouraged innovation. Learned men copied, memorized, edited, commented upon, and stored classic texts. Within two centuries after the death of Justinian, leadership in science and philosophy had passed to the Islamic world. After the twelfth century, philosophy found a home in Europe, built by those the ancients had called "barbarians."

ISLAM: FROM ARABIAN DESERT TO WORLD STAGE

As Rome faded in the west and revived in new guise in the eastern Mediterranean, in that region where the world's first civilizations took root there emerged a new faith and a new culture: that of Islam, the third to develop of the world's monotheistic religions. Shaped at first by the Arab prophet Muhammad and his followers, it spread by force and by persuasion throughout the main centers of ancient Eurasian civilization and to farther regions beyond. Many non-Arabs were converted to Islam, which offered its followers the spiritual experience of a transcendent God while providing moral principles.

The Formation of Islam

When the western Empire yielded to the Ostrogoths, what had been one world became two. Soon it would become three. Less than a century after Odoacer seized Rome, in the city of Mecca, on the Arabian Peninsula not far from the Red Sea, was born the creator of a new religion and a new world civilization: Muhammad ibn Abdullah (c. 570–632). His followers were called Muslims ("those who submit"), and the faith they followed Islam ("submission" to God's will). Islam was the third child—after Byzantium and western Europe—of the Roman world. The three were united by their common past, rooted in the history of the ancient Mediterranean; and by their common monotheism, rooted in scripture.

By trade, Muhammad was a merchant who journeyed with the caravans of the Arabian desert north of Syria. By birth, he was a worshiper of the many gods of his homeland, although he learned much from Judaism and Christianity. When Muhammad was about forty, he had a vision in which the angel Gabriel (the same who appeared to the Virgin Mary in Luke's Gospel account) appeared to him and made known to him the will of the one God, called (in Arabic) Allah. By this experience Muhammad was transformed into the prophet of Allah—called simply the Prophet by Muslims. The record of his communion with Allah is the substance of the ***Qur'an*** (the word means "reading" or "reciting"), the holy book of Islam.

After some initial setbacks, the new monotheism Muhammad espoused made rapid progress. Muhammad's first converts were members of his immediate circle: his wife, Khadijah; his friend, Abu Bakr; and a Meccan merchant, Umar. These were his supporters in the city of Mecca, where, at first, the Prophet had mostly enemies. So hostile was the reception to his new gospel that in 622 Muhammad fled from Mecca to Medina, 240 miles (386 km.) distant. The flight, which marks the first year of the Islamic calendar, is called the *hijra*.

In Medina, the new religion planted its roots. Muhammad enrolled enough enthusiastic believers in the one God to take control in Medina and to enable a return in 630 to what would become the Muslim holy city of Mecca. The Ka'ba, the city's central temple, was cleansed of its idols. The ancient black stone it housed, revered in local polytheism, became the holy object that every Muslim hoped someday to touch; according to legend it had been given to Adam on his leaving paradise. Modern Muslims still strive to make, someday, a pilgrimage to Mecca. During the prayers that are said five times every day, they turn their faces to the city of Muhammad's birth.

When Muhammad died in 632, Islam spread among the Arabic nomads of the Sinai peninsula, the Bedouins. Bedouin society was based on the groupings of family, clan, and tribe similar to those encountered among the early Greeks and Romans, the nomads of the steppes, and the villagers of the north. These small groups gathered under the authority of leaders called sheiks. They created vibrant poetry in the language that became the classic language of Islam, and

WITNESSES

The Civilization of Islam

Among the controversial principles of Islam is that of jihad, *or holy war. The obligation of* jihad *is described here from the Islamic scripture, the Qur'an, which also contains many other ethical and spiritual principles that are the foundations of Islamic civilization. That civilization was richly productive during the period that European historians call the "Middle Ages" of scholars, scientists, and philosophers. Among the greatest of these is Avicenna, an excerpt of whose* Autobiography *is given here.*

The Qur'an prescribes *Jihad*, the Holy War for Islam, an obligation of the whole community (c. 640): When you meet those who are infidels, strike their necks until you have overwhelmed them, tighten their bonds, and then release them, either freely or for ransom, when war lays down its burdens. Those who are killed in the path of God, he does not let their good deeds go for nothing.
(Qur'an, XLVII, 4/4–5; ed. N. Lewis, 1983)

More than for conquest, Islamic civilization is known for its great achievements in the sphere of the philosophy of science. Here Avicenna (980–1037) describes the early training that helped make him one of the foremost Islamic thinkers: By the time I was ten I had mastered the Koran [Qur'an] and a great deal of literature, ... [There followed training in philosophy] ... [then] ... I took to reading texts by myself ... [mastering logic, geometry and astronomy] ... I now occupied myself with mastering the various texts and commentaries on natural science and metaphysics, until all the gates of knowledge were open to me. Next I desired to study medicine, and proceeded to read all the books that have been written on this subject. ... At the same time I continued ... to study and dispute on law, being now sixteen years of age.
(Avicenna, *Autobiography*, ed. C. Brand, 1969; trs. A. J. Arberry, *Avicenna on Theology*, 1951)

worshiped many gods and imagined the interventions of genies, or *jinns*. To the Bedouins, Islam offered a novel political, social, and ethical ideal.

Arab herdsmen were important agents in the commercial system of the ancient world, conveying by camel caravans the goods of Asia from Indian Ocean ports to depots on the Mediterranean coast. In their journeys, they encountered Jewish and Christian, Monophysite, Nestorian, and Zoroastrian believers in a transcendent God. All had an impact on the concepts of Islam, a religion of high ethical content and great depth, numbering today more than 900 million adherents.

The faith of Islam centers on the Qur'an. About the length of the New Testament, it was committed to writing around 650 or 651, within a generation of the Prophet's death. In 114 *suras* ("chapters"), it enjoins absolute obedience upon its followers to the will of one single God, called Allah, as revealed through his prophet Muhammad: "God, there is no God but he, the living, the self-subsistent." Islam accepts the messages of the Hebrew Bible and the Christian New Testament, and reveres the earlier prophets Isaiah and Jeremiah, the patriarchs Abraham and Moses, and, as witnesses, Jesus and Mary of Nazareth.

Islam requires its followers to adhere to the Five Pillars of Islam. These are (1) to accept with conviction the core principle of the faith, that there is no God but Allah and that his prophet is Muhammad; (2) to pray five times each day; (3) to fast during daylight hours in the holy month of Ramadan; (4) to give alms to the poor; and (5) to go at least once in a lifetime as a pilgrim to Mecca and visit the Ka'ba.

Islam provided rules governing virtually every aspect of life: commerce, family life, personal behavior. These rules banned usury and set high standards of fairness in economic life. They forbade gambling and the consumption of all pork and alcohol. They granted women and children protections unknown in earlier pagan society.

Still, women enjoyed fewer opportunities than men. Although they could own property, they could not divorce their husbands (who could obtain divorce at will) and were severely punished for violating premarital virginity or marital chastity. Men were limited to four wives (plus as many concubines as they chose). Respectable women were to be veiled in public, a practice in Middle Eastern society going back to the Assyrians (see Chapter 1). Although most women were powerless to change their condition, the wives, daughters, and sisters of Islamic rulers were often able to wield considerable influence.

The **mosque** is the Islamic place of worship and the central building of an Islamic city. It generally consists of a court with fountain for ritual purification, a hall of prayer, and one or more towers, called minarets, from which the call to prayer is issued. Decorated with intricate metalwork, mosaic floors and walls, and sinuous columns, some mosques rivaled the great cathedrals of medieval Europe (see Chapter 10) in architectural splendor. Nowhere in a mosque is the human form represented. According to Islam (as in Judaism), the work of God as creator of humanity must not be imitated by human hands.

Unlike most religions of the late ancient world, Islam had no priests. Instead, religious experts called *'ulamâ* emerged. These were not priests, but preachers, judges, teachers, and other experts in the Muslim tradition, who extracted from the implications of the words of the Prophet a theological system. In every locality, a *qâdî* served as a judge in civil and criminal cases and as arbiter of all disputes. He represented at once Islamic orthodoxy, political authority, and social and economic custom. Law, as announced by the *'ulamâ* and the *qâdî*, reflected the principles of Islam in every action of the lives of the faithful.

Some Muslims did not accept the interpretation of tradition provided by the *'ulamâ*. Among these were the **Shiites** (who would be counterposed to the **Sunni** respecters of the mainstream tradition). The Shiites were followers of Muhammad's son-in-law Ali, the fourth **caliph** (a ruler understood to be a successor of Muhammad) of the Arab Muslims. Groups of Shiites survived in independent communities, where they resisted the secularizing tendencies of governments. They were concentrated for the most part in Persia, as they are in modern Iran. Another group of Muslims were the Sufi: ascetics and mystics, whose inner conviction and charismatic healing inspired many converts and assisted in the worldwide diffusion of Islam.

The first Muslims spread the faith by "holy war," or **jihad** (see *Witnesses*, p. 211). Within a few generations, however, Islamic policy shifted from coercion to toleration. Practitioners of other faiths in conquered territory were not forcibly converted, although these **infidels** had to pay a burdensome tax. Freedom from that tax, along with the possibility of full participation in Islamic society, encouraged many to acquiesce willingly to conversion and to adopt the Arabic language and culture of their conquerors. Christians and Jews in Islamic lands were generally not harassed. As "people of the book" (the Bible), they even enjoyed the respect of Muslim leaders as children of Abraham and co-worshipers of the one God.

Arabic Expansion under the Caliphs

The beliefs and customs of Islam gained a large following in part because of its political structure and military prowess. Immediately after Muhammad's death began the first dynasties of caliphs who flourished for three centuries before stumbling on to extinction another three centuries later. The caliphs provided direction and pursued the conquests that made Islam a religion not of Arabs alone, but of many other peoples of Africa and Asia.

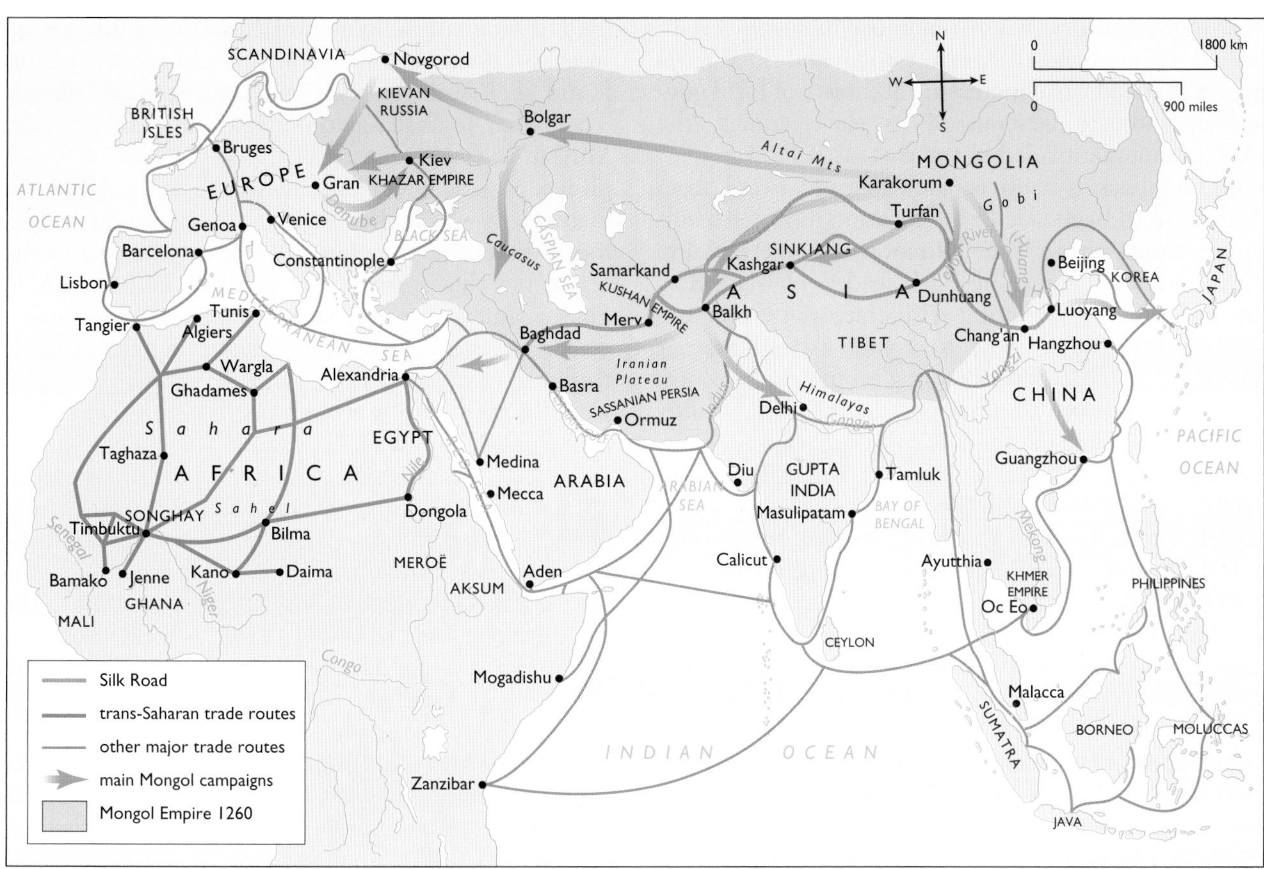

***Map 8.3 Africa and Asia: Pathways of Trade, to 1300 C.E.:** As Byzantium and the first Islamic caliphates faced each other in the Mediterranean region, African nations and cities crystallized, stimulated by trade opportunities with both the Mediterranean zone of Islamic civilizations, reached by trade pathways (followed by camel caravans) across the Sahara, and the Asian one, reached by water routes across the Indian and Persian oceans.*

Muhammad's friend Abu Bakr was the first leader of Islam (from 632 to 634) after the Prophet himself. He rallied the leaders of the Arabian cities, and compelled the compliance of desert sheiks. By the time of his death, just two years after Muhammad's, the Arabian Peninsula was united. Earnest Muslims were ready to spread the new faith.

Under the second caliph, Umar (r. 634–644), Bedouin Muslims seized much of the territory once dominated by the Persian emperor: Mesopotamia, Iran, Syria, Palestine, and Egypt. Some of this territory was grabbed from the weakened Byzantine Empire (including the holy site of Jerusalem in 638); the rest from the Sassanid dynasty (the ethnic Persian rulers of the region since the third century C.E.). The conquerors learned from the conquered. Byzantine and Sassanid administrative systems became the model for caliphal government. The still vital Zoroastrianism of the Persian regime seeped into Islam, as it had into Judaism and Christianity.

Umar and his two successors, Uthman and Ali, were all assassinated: in 644, 656, and 661, respectively. A struggle then ensued between Sunni traditionalists and Shiite followers of Ali, with the victory going to the former. The Umayyad dynasty quickly established its authority from its capital, Damascus, and ruled throughout the lands of Islam from 661 until 750. Under their leadership, Islam became a far-flung civilization, centered on flourishing cities and bountiful courts.

The conquests resumed. Umayyad armies swept victoriously through North Africa, the Iberian peninsula, and, in Asia, the Caucasus region and Indus Valley. They met resistance at two points of entry to the European continent. Byzantium saved itself, rebuffing naval expeditions sent against Constantinople in 674–678 and 717. In 732, Charles Martel turned back the attempt to penetrate the Frankish kingdom. Islam had extended into Europe for the moment as far is it might. In Asia, it held the frontier against Chinese expansion. In 751, at the Talas River, near Samarkand, Islamic forces fought and won a decisive victory against the expansive force of Tang China.

By that year, the Umayyad dynasty had fallen to Abu al-Abbas (r. 750–754), who claimed to be the successor of Muhammad. To prove it, he marched out of Persia to Damascus and murdered all but one of the surviving males of the Ummayad clan. The Abbasid caliphate would now govern the lands of Islam until the tenth century, when separatist dynasties established themselves in North Africa and Iberia. Its power sapped by the increasing authority of local governors and the generals of its slave armies, the Abbasid remnant ruled in the east until 1258.

The Abbasids removed the capital eastward, from Damascus to Baghdad. This relocation mirrored a cultural change within Islam. No more did an Arab elite dominate foreigners. The Arab leaders of Islam now merged with the surviving aristocracies of Persia and the Mediterranean shore to create a new international ruling class in which all Muslims, Arab or not, found opportunity to advance. The resulting multi-ethnic and multinational society required a giant, centralized administrative system—comparable to those created earlier by the Persians, Macedonians, and Romans. Under the caliph and his chief counselor, the grand vizier, hereditary governors ruled the many Islamic provinces.

The Mediterranean, which once the Romans called "our sea," was now Islamic. The commerce of the ancient world continued to flow through the cities of the eastern Mediterranean coasts and at other nodes farther east and south. Here the caliphs and their governors established their courts, where artists and writers, physicians and philosophers pursued their callings.

Foremost among these cities was Baghdad, a center of international trade founded in 762 and called the "city of peace." A plan is shown in *How Many?* on p. 209. The city was polyglot, multireligious, multi-ethnic: Arabic, Persian, and Aramaic were spoken; Jews, Christians, and Zoroastrians coexisted with Muslims; Syrians and Turks, Greeks and Arabs competed for advancement. Reaching, in the ninth century, a population of between 300,000 and 500,000, Baghdad was the largest city in the Fertile Crescent; the largest in the Mediterranean since Rome and Alexandria, now in their fading glory; the largest in the world outside China.

Islamic Civilization

As they tended to their empire-building, the Umayyad and Abbasid caliphs also nurtured Islamic civilization. As early as the eighth century there rose in Jerusalem the mosque called the Dome of the Rock, shown on p. 207 and in Damascus the Great Mosque, blending the borrowed forms of Byzantium and Persia in a new Islamic architectural language. The Arabic poetic tradition flourished in new urban and court settings. The collection of classic stories entitled in English *The Arabian Nights* had been written by the time of the Abbasid Harun al-Rashid (r. 786–809). In 802 Harun al-Rashid sent his royal contemporary Charlemagne an elephant named Abul Abaz as a pet: a creature as strange to that Frankish king as the refined culture of the caliphate.

The ancient schools and libraries of the pagan world that had been shut down by Christian emperors found shelter in Antioch and Damascus and Persia. There they revived again under Umayyad patronage. Muslim scholars translated the key works of Greek philosophy, science, and medicine into Arabic, a medium in which they fueled an intellectual flowering. Resident at the courts of the caliphs and in the academies that sprang up at Córdoba and Seville, in Spain; Cairo and Damascus, on the Mediterranean coast; and Baghdad and Bukhara, farther east, Islamic thinkers from the ninth through twelfth centuries were the most daring and productive in the world.

Scholars in Damascus and Baghdad studied Aristotle's works when these were still unknown in western Europe. From the tenth through twelfth centuries, a series of Arab philosophers wrote commentaries on Aristotle which digested and explored the Greek thinker's understanding of the cosmos, the soul, and logical method. Notable among these was Al-Farabi (d. 950); Ibn Sina (980–1037), called Avicenna in the West (who claimed to have read Aristotle's *Metaphysics* forty times) whose autobiography quoted on p. 211; and Ibn Rushd (1126–1198), called Averroës. The death of Averroës at the close of the twelfth century marks the end of Islamic leadership in philosophy. The torch would be passed to the university professors of once-laggard western Europe.

During the same period, Arab thinkers also developed the ancient Greek legacy in science and medicine. Al-Kindi (c. 800–c. 870) performed experiments with light and heat, color and optics, perfumes and drugs. Al-Razi (c. 865–932), called Rhazes in the Latin-speaking West, wrote a classic treatise distinguishing smallpox and measles. Avicenna established the medical curriculum which endured until displaced by Western medical science in the nineteenth century.

Other Islamic thinkers explored the astrological and agricultural treatises of Indian scholars. It was from India that Islamic mathematicians imported the system of numerals we use today: one through nine plus zero—a system based on powers of ten (today's decimal system) which permitted complex calculations. These "Arabic" numerals, formed in their distinctive hand, were borrowed by the West after 1300 and replaced (generally) the more cumbersome Roman numerals. Arab mathematicians also invented the advanced mathematics that is known by its Arabic name as algebra.

From China came an invention as important for the history of thought as the philosophy of Greece or the mathematics of India: paper. Among the captives taken by the Muslims after the Battle of Talas, in central Asia in 751, were Chinese artisans skilled in paper-making. Their instruction made possible the wide availability of paper, and of knowledge, throughout Islam and the West.

Islam Becomes Global

After the tenth century, when its culture achieved its zenith, the political unity of Islam was shattered. Independent caliphates ruled in Spain, North Africa, and Persia. Meanwhile, new peoples arrived from the Asian steppes: successively Seljuk Turks, Ottoman Turks, and Mongols. They fought for the caliphs as foreign mercenaries. Then they took charge.

The Seljuk Turks, a pastoral people originally from northern Persia led by a dynasty of that name, conquered Baghdad in 1055. Imposing their dominion over the eastern wing of Islam, they pushed west to the Mediterranean and into Asia Minor, where, at Manzikert in 1071, they inflicted defeat on the Byzantine army. Two centuries later, Seljuk authority weakened, enabling a renegade Turkish band called "Ottoman" after their leader, Uthman, to claim leadership in 1300, and to pursue further conquests in Asia Minor and Europe. In the meantime, the Mongols, another group of Asian tribespeople, had penetrated the Middle East from the 1220s. In 1258 they captured Baghdad, ravaging the city (and killing its last caliph). Mongol rule put an end to Islamic theocracy. The caliphs still presided as religious leaders and judges under non-Arabic Seljuk and Ottoman overlords, who became Muslims themselves.

While eastern Islamic lands once ruled by Arab caliphs fell to the Turks and the Mongols, Islam itself spread peaceably to other regions of the world. Muslim traders touring the commercial centers of the Mediterranean Sea, the Indian Ocean, and the African Sahara brought with them their law, their faith, and their way of life. Through their activity, and that of Sufi mystics who acted as missionaries, Islam spread from the Mediterranean shore across the Iranian plateau into India and the East Indies; across North Africa to western Sudan and south along the east African coast; across the Mediterranean to European Spain and the Balkans. Its expansion is shown on Map 8.2.

Thus, long before Christianity, Islam became a global religion. Most Muslims live in south and southeast Asia, far from the Saudi desert. Indonesia has the world's largest Muslim population: about 150 million. Another 300 million live in Pakistan, Bangladesh, and India. More than two-thirds of the world's Muslims live outside the Middle East where Islam began. More than four-fifths are non-Arabs. Yet five times a day, they pray in that Semitic tongue to the God of the Arab prophet Muhammad.

BEYOND THE WEST

While the civilizations of Islam, Byzantium, and Europe were forming, different cultures and civilizations developed in Africa, in Asia, and in the Americas as indicated in *Witnesses*, p. 216. These emerged independently of the traditions in the Fertile Crescent and around the Mediterranean. Neither "ancient" nor "medieval", they exist in a timeframe apart from the Western one. Yet it is important to understand their career in the first millennium C.E., for the West—which increasingly meant Europe—would soon confront these distant and alien worlds.

African Tribes, Cities, and Kingdoms

As civilizations formed in Egypt and Mesopotamia, most native Africans developed the skills of farming and herding animals typical of the Neolithic era (see Chapter 1). During an unusual period of very high moisture in the Sahara and to the south, bringing greater fertility to the land, these peoples increased in population and prosperity. One African community, bordering southern Egypt, achieved an advanced level of civilization.

The black African civilizations of Kush, Meroë, and Aksum developed immediately to the south of Egypt as ruled by native pharaohs, Greek Ptolemies, and Roman emperors. The kingdom of Kush, which had emerged by 1000 B.C.E. along the upper Nile, sent rhinoceros horns and leopard skins, ebony and ivory, and mercenaries and slaves north to Egypt in exchange for Egyptian linen and payprus. From the pharaohs, Kushite monarchs learned the skills of statecraft, pyramid construction, and hieroglyphic writing. Kushite society was hardy enough, when Egyptian society deteriorated, to take over the senior civilization. Its king Piankhi and his successors ruled Egypt for a little over a century as the Twenty-Fifth Dynasty (c. 719–663 B.C.E.), until overrun and defeated by the Assyrian Empire.

Defeated in Egypt in 663 B.C.E., the former pharaoh Tanutamon reestablished Kushite civilization at the new capital of Meroë, where it flourished into the fourth century C.E. This region enjoyed fertile, well-watered soil and a position on the trade routes that led to the Red Sea and the commercial network beyond. Most important, it possessed rich deposits of iron ore which the Kushites learned to exploit—leaving a litter of furnaces and slag heaps for archaeologists to discover and admire. From Meroë's iron factories, knowledge of iron-working spread to other regions of Africa. Africa proceeded to the Iron Age without pausing for the Bronze.

Around 350 C.E., Emperor Ezana (r. 320–350) of neighboring Aksum (modern Ethiopia) destroyed the city and temples and storehouses of Meroë. His people (mostly Christian) were a mixture of African Kushitic-speakers and Semitic-speaking Arab migrants from across the Red Sea. The merchants of Aksum were intermediaries in trade between western and eastern Asia. Indian ships sailed to African Red Sea ports, where Aksumite merchants exchanged for their goods the products of Syria, Palestine, Egypt,

WITNESSES

Africa and Asia: Glimpses of the World beyond the West

These three passages give brief glimpses of other non-Western civilizations that flourished from late antiquity into the period of the European Middle Ages: those of East Africa, Buddhist India, and Japan. In the first passage, a traveler describes how an African king is revered by his subjects. In the second, a Chinese pilgrim searches for Buddhist sacred writings in India. In the third, a famous woman author describes in her fictional Tales of Genji *the competition among the ladies of the court for the favor of the emperor.*

The learned Ibn Battuta (1304–1368), an Arab Muslim who chronicled his travels, describes his encounter with an East African chief: The ceremonial at the [public] session of this king is as follows. He takes his seat on a platform carpeted and decorated with silken fabrics; to right and left of him are the men-at-arms, those nearest him holding swords and shields, and next to them the bowmen; in front of them to the right and left are the chamberlain and the officers of government and the private secretary. ... When the sultan takes his seat they cry with one voice *Bismillah*, and when he rises they do the same, so that all those in the audience-hall know the moment of his rising and the moment of his sitting.

(Ibn Battuta, *Travels 1325–1354*; ed. H. A. R. Gibb, 1986)

The Chinese monk Fa-Hsien (fl. 399–414) searches for traces of the Buddha and the Buddhist sacred writings during his journey to India (402 onwards): [In Patna.] Here, in the mahayana monastery, [Fa-Hsien] found a copy of the Vinaya ... rules—those which were observed in the first Great Council, while Buddha was still in the world. ... He further got the transcript of the ... sarvastivadah rules,—those which are observed by the communities of monks in the land of Ts'in; which also have all been handed down orally from master to master without being committed to writing. ... In consequence (of this success in his quest) [Fa-Hsien] stayed here for three years, learning Sanskrit books and the Sanskrit speech and writing out the Vinaya rules.

(Fa-Hsien, *A Record of Buddhistic Kingdoms, an Account of his Travels in India and Ceylon (399–414) in search of the Buddhist Books of Discipline*; trs., ed. J. Legge, 1965)

Lady Murasaki's (978–1014) *Tale of Genji* describes the intrigues of the Japanese court and the deadly business, managed by women behind the scenes, of inheriting the throne: In a certain reign there was a lady not of the first rank whom the emperor loved more than any of the others. The grand ladies with high ambitions thought her a presumptuous upstart, and lesser ladies were still more resentful. She survived despite her troubles ... [and] bore the emperor a beautiful son, a jewel beyond compare.

With the birth of the son, it became yet clearer that [the mother] was the emperor's favorite. The mother of the eldest son began to feel uneasy. If she did not manage carefully, she might see the new son designated crown prince. ...

(Murasaki Shikubu, *The Tale of Genji*, 11th century; trs. E. G. Seidensticker, 1985)

and Mesopotamia. Ethiopians traded overland as well, west across the Sahara to the gold- and salt-producing regions of the western Sudan. When the Aksumite kingdom declined around 800, its people left behind *stelae*: tall needle-shaped monuments crafted in stone using skills the original Arab settlers had brought from their homeland, as shown on p. 223.

Once a hospitable pasture, the Sahara had become, by the third millennium B.C.E., dry and waste. Its inhabitants dispersed southward, to the grasslands that stretched west to east across the continent, and farther south, to the rain forests of the center. Carrying with them their farming skills and iron tools, these Negroid migrants drove before them weaker tribes, hunters and gatherers still, who took refuge in remote pockets of the interior. Many of these migrants were ancestors of modern speakers of the Bantu languages that predominate today in sub-Saharan Africa. They lived in small communities dominated by "big men," leaders of extraordinary wealth in wives, children, and cattle, who could therefore command local obedience.

Caucasoid Arabs and Berbers (now Muslim) dwelling far to the north on the Mediterranean shore took control of the Sahara. Though a desert, the Sahara served as a highway (its main vehicle the camel caravan) from the African interior to Mediterranean and Indian Ocean ports. The caravans journeyed to the Sudanese kingdoms in western Africa, in the grasslands south of the Sahara called the Sahel, where resources of gold, other minerals, and agricultural products encouraged the successive growth, after 900, of three native African civilizations.

These were the three kingdoms of Ghana, Mali, and Songhay, which from about 500 through the 1500s dominated in turn the region between the Niger and Senegal river valleys of the western Sudan. Ruled by revered and powerful kings, who claimed to be in touch with a multitude of deities, these autonomous African states developed advanced administrative machinery and military strength. Exchanging Saharan salt for gold and other goods, Arab traders brought these commodities to Mediterranean ports to exchange them in turn for Asian and European products. A by-product of trade was religious conversion; Islam became securely planted as the religion of the western Sudan.

On the east African coast of the Indian Ocean (from modern Somalia to Mozambique), cities established by native Bantu migrants during the first millennium C.E. participated in the brisk trade that developed after 1100 between the Mediterranean zone, India, and east Asia (see Map 8.3). Islamic Arab merchants acted as intermediaries, whose architecture and language left their stamp on African civilization—especially on the Swahili language, which predominated in the region. Arab trading ships sailed the Indian Ocean, following the prevailing winds, in a pattern that intensified as India also became drawn into the sphere of Islamic civilization. The commercial sector of the east African coast stimulated the growth of interior kingdoms, like that of Zimbabwe, which supplied ivory and other tropical products to merchants for re-export to distant ports.

Unity and Disunity in India

Soon after 200 B.C.E., the northern Indian Empire established by Chandragupta Maurya fragmented (see Chapter 2). For 500 years thereafter, the Indian subcontinent possessed no single unified state. Instead, many regional kingdoms and principalities developed, whose elites practiced diverse forms of a religion now called Hinduism and shared a sacred literature recited orally on ritual occasions and recorded in classic Sanskrit (accessible only to a literate and exclusive few). Amid this diversity of political and cultural forms, commerce flourished. The merchants of India exported fine cotton cloth, pearls and exotic woods (teak and sandalwood), iron and copper, gold and silver. They transshipped spices and silks from eastern Asia to ports on the Red Sea and the Persian Gulf, and overland to Mediterranean depots. The prosperous coastal cities of India, in turn, were a lure to the fleets that set out from Arabia and Africa across the Indian Ocean.

Around 320 C.E., the Gupta dynasty established a unified Indian state in the same part of India—the Ganges River valley—that had given birth to the earlier Mauryan Empire. Gupta kings ruled a belt of territory extending from the Indus in the west to the Bay of Bengal in the east. Their empire lasted about two centuries, falling prey in the fifth century C.E. to nomadic invaders, the Huns. By the mid-sixth century the Guptas had retreated to their homeland on the Ganges and abandoned the west to the invaders. Thenceforth, until the establishment of the Muslim Mughal Empire after 1526, India was once again the home of multiple states and kingdoms, no one of which dominated the whole of the subcontinent. Despite political disunity, cultural life (which had reached a new height under Gupta patronage) continued to flourish all the same in a true golden age.

In the first millennium C.E., Indian culture achieved its classic stage. Brahman scholars preserved and studied ancient Sanskrit literature (see Chapter 1). Respected teachers of that Vedic tradition, called *gurus*, taught the male children of the three upper castes of Indian society. Girls of the elites often learned to read and write, and some composed literary works (see p. 218). Indian sages wrote on law and political theory, in which they distinguished between just and unjust conquest and exhorted kings to rule justly. Astronomers determined that the earth rotated on its axis and calculated the length of the solar year, while mathematicians calculated the value of *pi* and laid the basis for the decimal system of numbers.

Hinduism also flourished in the post-Mauryan period. The caste system became increasingly complex as new peoples and occupations were assigned their niche in the hierarchy and as the Brahmans exercised their dominance. The gods of the northern region, now a vast pantheon composed of Aryan and non-Aryan deities, spread to the south as well. Among the populace below the elite, religious devotions increased in form and earnestness, as temple-building proceeded vigorously and worshipers undertook frequent pilgrimages to offer homage to their gods. Of the many deities revered in ceremony and incarnated in sculpture, two stood out: Shiva, the storm god, creator and destroyer of the universe; and Vishnu, whose incarnations as Rama and Krishna were the subject of epics. The fertile goddesses of earlier antiquity returned, usually represented as consorts of male deities. Hinduism dominated Indian culture from the Mauryans in the fourth century B.C.E. until the arrival of the Muslim Moghuls in the sixteenth century. It overshadowed the Buddhist and Jain traditions, while at the same time absorbing the ideas of these faiths.

Meanwhile, Buddhism, which had prospered under the patronage of the Mauryan king Asoka, splintered thereafter into many sects, among which two main branches emerged: the "Greater" and "Lesser Vehicle," Mahayana and Hinayana. The Hinayana, closer to the original form of Buddhism, traveled on Indian trade routes to Ceylon (modern Sri Lanka), the East Indies (the Malaysian archipelago and Indonesia), and Indochina. The Mahayana tradition, a more popular form of Buddhism, would have been in some ways unrecognizable to the founder. It admitted numerous deities (including the Buddha himself), centered around temple worship and rituals, and featured leaders called *boddhisattvas*: holy men committed to the service of humanity. Missionaries carried Mahayana Buddhism to China, Korea, and Japan, where it flourished after India itself had settled back into its native Hinduism.

Asian Arts

An Indian woman writing: *As Islam and Christianity, eastern or Roman, determined the course of the development of the arts in the Mediterranean region and in Europe, in Asia secular as well as religious matter informed architecture, sculpture, painting, and the decorative arts. This sculpture, tenth-eleventh century, is from Khajurāho, the capital of a small central Indian kingdom, and shows a woman engaged in writing.* (Indian Museum, Calcutta)

A Chinese view of Spring: *This Chinese landscape executed in ink and light color on silk was painted by Guo Xi in 1072 during the Sung dynasty.* (National Palace Museum, Taipei)

China and its Neighbors

China, once it was unified by the Qin dynasty, remained a centralized state for nearly 2000 years. Its political history is the history of a sequence of dynasties interspersed with briefer periods of fragmentation and discord. After the death of the last Qin emperor, Shi Huangdi, the Han dynasty ruled (with a brief interruption) for more than 400 years (206 B.C.E.–220 C.E.)—contemporary with Rome at its height. Han emperors (ruling, as they believed, by the mandate of heaven) reinforced the northern frontier, pressured by nomadic peoples whom they called "barbarians." At the same time, they extended China's boundaries west into Mongolia and Tibet, south into Vietnam, and northeast to Korea.

Han, Tang, Sung, and Yuan Dynasties Han rule was marked by economic well-being and cultural resurgence. Under the Qin, China had become the most populous nation in the world. Under the Han, population continued to increase to about 60 million—comparable to that of the Roman Empire. Foreign trade flourished, not only east (to Korea and Japan) and south (to north Vietnam), but west across Eurasia, traveling on the Silk Road through central Asia to the Mediterranean shore. Imperial agents supervised the silk industry, and the cloth served—as did coins or measures of grain—as a unit of value.

The great profits of foreign trade reflected domestic commercial and technological success. Canals joining the two river systems of the Yellow (Huang He) and the Yangzi reached the capital at Chang'an and made commerce safe and easy through the country's central corridor. Public granaries collected surpluses to cushion the impact of famines. Under the Han, the tax burden was less onerous and the justice system less harsh than under the Qin. Inventions included the wheelbarrow, the water lift (for irrigation), the stirrup, and paper. Made from rags, bark, and other cheap materials, paper soon spread throughout Asia, the Islamic world, and Europe.

Whereas the Qin had promoted the "legalist" school of philosophers as the most supportive of the imperial mission, Han emperors embraced Confucianism. The old books—those that had escaped burning by Shi Huangdi in 213 B.C.E.—were taken out of hiding, copied, and studied. Thereafter the precepts of Confucius became the official doctrine of the Chinese state.

Confucian works formed the body of knowledge that state officials were expected to master. Bureaucrats were required first of all to be scholars, trained in the Confucian body of ideas. "Exceptional work demands exceptional men," declared the emperor Wu Ti (r. 141–86 B.C.E.). "We therefore command the various district officials to search for men of brilliant and exceptional talents, to be our generals, our ministers, and our envoys to distant states." These scholarly paragons, trained in special schools, took rigorous examinations to qualify for government service: "Parents, however much they love a child," wrote a later poet, cannot ensure his future; "only the examiner can bring the youth to notice. ..." As a consequence of this strict training, Han officials and the Han state were the most efficient anywhere.

Confucianism was primarily an educational program which embodied high ethical ideals. It was not a religion, although in popular practice some sacrifices were offered to the ancient sage, and his memory was venerated. This popularized form of Confucianism coexisted with the religions of Han China, primarily Taoism and Buddhism. Taoism continued to attract adherents, with its nature mysticism and magical adjuncts and vague promises of immortality. Buddhism, a newcomer, also won many adherents, converted by Indian missionaries.

Japanese Buddhist temple complex: *This photograph shows the Buddhist temple complex at Horyuji, Nara, Japan, 670 C.E., one of the earliest Japanese Buddhist temple complexes. Surrounded by a wall, it included a lecture hall (Kodo) and a pagoda.*

Interest in Buddhism resulted in a classic work of contemporary description. Around 400 C.E., the Chinese scholar Fa-hsien journeyed to India. There he remained for ten years, in the company of Buddhist monks and scholars, copying their sacred texts, which he translated from Sanskrit into Chinese. Other scholars wrote history. The courtier Sima Qian (c. 145–85 B.C.E.) chronicled 3000 years of Chinese history in his *Records of the Grand Historian*. Ban Zhao (c. 32–102 C.E.) (a woman, the daughter and sister of historians) helped write a history of the reigning Han dynasty. She also wrote a treatise on female decorum, *Lessons for Women*, amid whose bleak prescripts she included a plea for the education of girls.

Nearly four centuries of political disorder followed the fall of the Han in 221 C.E., as a series of short-lived regimes (the "Six Dynasties") ruled different parts of China and nomadic peoples invaded through the northern frontier to settle in old Han centers. Confucian culture, in temporary eclipse, along with the centralized empire it supported, was overshadowed by Buddhism, which traveled along the trade routes from India. Taoism also resurged during this period of disunion.

By the late sixth century C.E., China was reunited under the brief Sui dynasty (581–618). For three centuries thereafter, the Tang dynasty (618–907) ruled a reconstituted China. Emperor T'ai-tsung (626–49) reformed the imperial administration and pushed the boundaries of China westward. His successor, the Empress Wu (r. 649–705), continued his work for more than fifty years, holding not only the title of ruler but (at least during the last fifteen years of her reign) real power in her own hands. China's westward movement finally halted in 751, when, at the Talas River, Arab Muslims defeated the armies of Empress Wu's grandson.

The Tang capital at Chang'an was a planned city, holding a million people, with another million in the immediate suburbs—by the eighth century C.E., the world's largest city. The imperial complex of office and palace occupied a precinct of several square miles in the north of the city, reached by a ceremonial road. From here, Confucian scholars governed the great expanse of China, while the emperor and his court enjoyed a luxurious way of life in the palace. "Behind those vermilion gates meat and wine go to waste / While out on the road lie the bones of men frozen to death," wrote the poet Li Po (701–762), who had lived at court before his own impoverishment and disgrace. The rest of the city housed residences, temples, gardens, and marketplaces where merchants from many nations exchanged their goods. Yet Chang'an was vulnerable. It was sacked, pillaged, and burned during the invasions that accompanied the destruction of the Tang regime in 907.

Anarchy reigned again until the establishment in 960 of a new imperial dynasty: the Sung (960–1279).

MUST READS

Travellers, Founders, and Commentators

Sima Qian (c. 145–c. 85 B.C.E.)	*Records of the Grand Historian*
Ban Zhao (c. 32–102 C.E.)	*Lessons for Women*
St. Augustine (354–430)	*City of God*
Boethius (c. 480–524)	*Consolation of Philosophy*
Procopius (c. 500–565)	*Secret History*
Gregory of Tours (538–594)	*History of the Franks*
Isidore of Seville (c. 560–636)	*Etymologies*
The Venerable Bede (c. 673–735)	*Ecclesiastical History of the English People*
The Qur'an	
The Arabian Nights	
Anna Comnena (1083–c. 1153)	*Alexiad*

The Sung set a new standard of government efficiency. Managed from the capital at Kaifeng, its bureaucracy was fed by about 200 graduates each year from Confucian schools. They represented the top 20 percent who succeeded in the elaborate examination system, now the only method by which a young man, even a prosperous one, could secure a government position.

Commerce thrived under the Sung. The growing fashion for tea drinking, begun in the eighth century C.E., necessitated the circulation of that product, as well as the development of fine porcelain (to which Westerners would give the name "china"), which joined silk as a major export commodity. The abacus, a Chinese invention, facilitated commercial transactions, and a water-powered bellows improved iron production. Continuing a pattern that had begun under the Tang, the center of Chinese prosperity and culture shifted southward. The cultivation of rice (a southern crop) edged out millet (the northern staple).

Other Chinese innovations included the compass, facilitating navigation on the high seas; the block printing press, permitting the publication of both books and money; and gunpowder, used for firework displays and not (until the fourteenth century) for military use. Cartography, medical research, and literature flourished. Some 5000 poets composed during the Sung centuries, while painters depicted the region's striking landscapes. A revived Confucianism dealt with metaphysical issues as well as politics and morals. Some women received an education from their fathers and brothers—an asset valued for its future usefulness in raising their sons. Many Chinese women found that their position declined as marriage options narrowed. Among the elite, girls were made to bind their feet from an early age so that they would remain small and render the mature woman more sexually desirable—and less mobile.

The last Sung emperor died in 1279 in the final standoff between Chinese troops and Mongol armies. The Mongols were fierce steppe nomads who had, for 3000 years, menaced the Eurasian civilizations. In the thirteenth century, these herders of sheep and goats, survivors of the stark cold of their high plateau, mounted their shaggy horses to ride off in three directions: to China, where they successfully established the brief Yuan dynasty (1271–1368); to Islamic western Asia, where they settled in modern Afghanistan, Iraq, and Iran; and to Russia, where (called the "Golden Horde") they ousted the princes of Kiev and ruled for more than two centuries. By 1259 their vast empire reached from Asia Minor to the Pacific Ocean.

The Mongol armies were the best on earth at that time. Exceptionally mobile, organized in disciplined units by decimal principles, skilled in reconnaissance, spying, and communications over long distances, they could sustain themselves in the field on long campaigns, their reserves of horses providing milk, blood, and meat. From the Chinese, they learned to make catapults and incendiary missiles. From the Turkic-speaking, Muslim Uighur, their neighbors on the central Asian plain, they learned to write. From their native customs they developed one of the great premodern law codes, the Yasa, which dealt sensibly with criminal, commercial, and civil matters. It ensured that the Mongols' ferocious conquest led to effective political settlement.

Gifted leaders were the key factor in the initial success of the Mongol advance. Raised in conditions severe even for a Mongol, the warrior Temuchin was appointed chief by his fellows in 1206 with the title of "universal leader," or Genghis (or Jenghiz) Khan (1167–1227). Genghis was the first leader of the Mongol invaders who seized much of Asia in the thirteenth century. His grandson Kublai (r. 1260–1294), the fifth Great Khan, completed the conquest of China. In 1267 Kublai Khan removed the Mongolian capital from the western outpost of Karakorum (its ruins situated in the modern Mongolian People's Republic) to the vicinity of modern Beijing. There, in 1275, he welcomed the Venetian merchant Marco Polo and his companions. Polo's account of his Chinese journey is the first landmark of the western European encounter with Asia. Meanwhile, although China succumbed to the Mongols, the Mongols did not disturb the refined patterns of Chinese customs and governance. Chinese influence continued even under these alien rulers to spread powerfully to the neighboring peoples of east and southeast Asia.

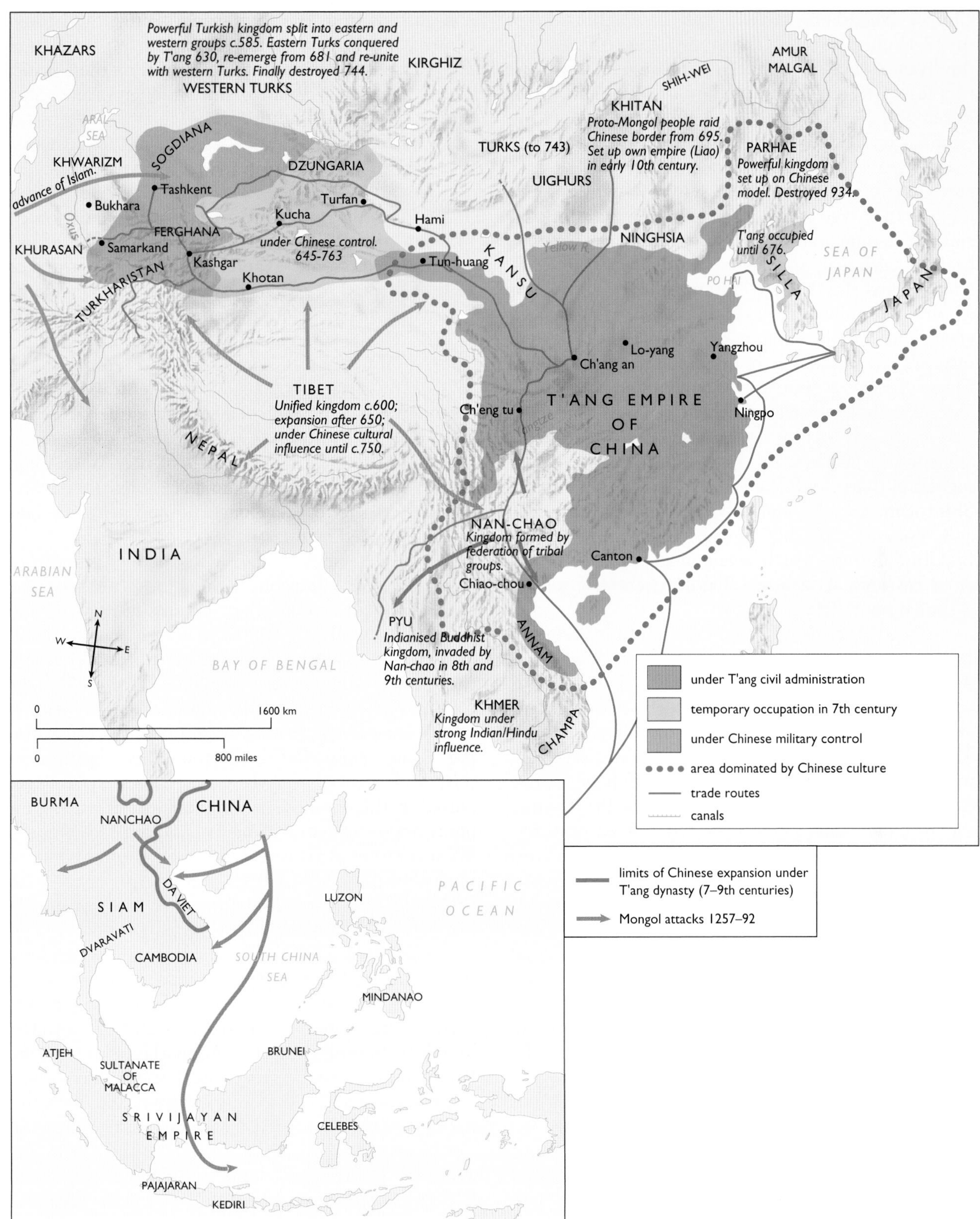

Map 8.4 The Chinese world, seventh to eighth centuries: *While in western Europe, after 500 C.E., Roman civilization was in retreat under the pressure of invasions by warlike Germanic, Islamic, Magyar, and Viking peoples, the Chinese empire proceeded, in fits and starts, to expand its influence in east Asia. This map of China under the T'ang dynasty shows the area directly dominated by China, and the areas under its military, cultural, and economic influence. The inset map shows T'ang expansion into the rich trading zone of the south China sea and, ominously, some centuries later, the path that would be taken by Mongols originating in central Asia when they swept into and came to dominate the empire.*

China's Neighbors in Asia and the Pacific From the first centuries C.E., Chinese influence transformed the lives of the simple hunting, fishing, and farming peoples of Korea, Japan, and north Vietnam. Both Korea and Japan formed independent states on the Chinese model. Korean institutions adhered strictly to Chinese patterns. Confucianism was deeply entrenched, and the Chinese system of writing, and for centuries even its language, was employed for official documents and laws. By contrast, Japanese civilization, although permeated by Chinese influence (transmitted by Korean intermediaries), was not wholly determined by it. Here warrior nobles from great court families dominated, their lives of leisure inspiring an abundance of literary and artistic works. These aristocrats circulated around an emperor alternately revered and resisted, whose claim to legitimate rule was buttressed by his supposed descent from an ancient sun goddess. In Japan, Buddhism was more successful than Confucianism. Originally the home of **Shintoism**, a traditional polytheism of nature spirits and ancestor worship, Japan developed a rich Buddhist culture which accommodated native religious customs. A Japanese Buddhist temple complex is shown on p. 219.

In north Vietnam, Chinese overlordship shaped a culture based on Chinese patterns, which informed its government, arts, religion, and language. In other parts of Indochina, Indian culture—brought by merchants and missionaries, not conquerors—had a great impact. The greatest religious center of the region was Hindu, not Confucian or Buddhist; this was the huge temple complex at Angkor Wat, built in the twelfth century C.E. by Cambodian kings. Even when freed from foreign domination, the kingdoms of Indochina remained within either the Chinese or the Indian cultural zone.

Off the Asian coasts on Pacific islands and archipelagoes lived peoples isolated from the advanced civilizations of the mainland. Beginning as long as 35,000 years ago, but according to other models perhaps only 5 to 6,000 years ago, migrants from southeast Asia ventured into the Pacific Ocean to settle in island homelands: the East Indies (including the Malaysian and Indonesian archipelagoes) and the Philippines, Australasia and Melanesia, Micronesia, and Polynesia (collectively Oceania). Meanwhile, other Asian peoples crossed the Siberian land-bridge to the Western Hemisphere, where they continued migrating throughout its two vast continents (see below, and Chapter 16). As a result, by about 1000 C.E. the habitation of the globe had reached its zenith. People were planted in all parts of the globe where the human race still makes a home.

Inhabitants of Indonesia, poised between the Indian and Pacific oceans, supplied Indian and Arab traders with spices and other exotic products from at least the first millennium C.E. Inhabitants of the Philippines began to come into contact with advanced civilizations from the fourteenth century, and those of Australia did so from the seventeenth (see Chapter 16). But those on the remote islands of the Pacific, wholly isolated, remained until modern times at a Stone Age level of culture.

American Migrations and Civilizations

Asian hunters migrated across the land-bridge between Siberia and Canada as long as 36,000 years ago, although some experts argue only in the last 20,000 years. They were in pursuit of the big game herds that wandered the tundra of North America. As the glaciers of the last Ice Age receded, they continued to move southward and eastward. In Mesoamerica (modern Mexico and Central America) and in northwest South America around 7000 years ago, some of the natives learned to cultivate maize (corn) and potatoes, the staples of the Amerindian diet. Population increased, languages multiplied, and organized societies developed around religious cult centers, headed by priests.

Map 8.5 shows the early development of Amerindian civilizations. The oldest, that of the Olmecs, began to take shape around 1200 B.C.E. and reached its height by 400 B.C.E. These people inhabited the fertile southeastern tail of Mexico. Although the Olmecs did not develop cities, they did have lively commercial networks and a system of writing. Olmec society had priests, who supervised the building of large pyramidal earth mounds as worship centers, and aristocrats, whose rich possessions were buried in their tombs. Its farmers lived in huts, grew maize and beans, and made clay pots and tiny statues. We do not know who created the most stunning monuments of the Olmec world: giant human heads, with lifelike features carved of stone and looming up to 9 feet (2.7 m.) tall on the flat lowlands.

After Olmec civilization faded, soon after reaching its zenith, other cultures flourished in Mesoamerica and elsewhere in the Americas. Temple complexes high in the Andes (modern Peru) and the artifacts found in the villages of the Adena-Hopewell culture (in the midwestern United States), the multistory residences (or pueblos) of the southwest, and the ceremonial mounds of native Mississippian farmers all testify to the presence of advanced societies in the Western Hemisphere long before the arrival of European conquerors after 1492. The more advanced peoples of Meso- and South America used metal and developed writing, formed stratified societies and practiced elaborate religious rites. These were the precursors of the most brilliant of the early Amerindian civilizations: the Mayan, which began to form in the Yucatán peninsula (modern Mexico and Guatemala) in the last three centuries B.C.E. It flourished later during a "classic" phase, from about 300 to 900 C.E., which paralleled the formative years of western

WINDOWS ON

A Roundup of World Monuments

***Stonehenge, England, c. 2100–2000* B.C.E.**

The monumental architecture of peoples very remote from the Western or Mediterranean world is also deserving of attention. Great structures, wonderfully expressive by their massive size and simple forms, were created by the Neolithic inhabitants of ancient Britain, the Mayans of the Americas, and the Ethiopians of Aksum. Here are shown Stonehenge (right) on Salisbury Plain in England; the stepped pyramid at Tikal (below) in present Guatemala; and an Aksumite pillar in East Africa (below right).

***Tikal, Guatemala, before 800* C.E.**

Aksumite pillar, East Africa, fourth-fifth century

To continue your investigation of this topic, please go to www.prenhall.com/king for the related **WINDOWS** on the **WEB** activity

Map 8.5 A World Apart: Amerindian Cultures and Civilizations, to 1000: *By the year 1000, the Western Hemisphere was home to hundreds of Amerindian societies ranging in development from Stone-Age cultures to civilizations possessing writing and advanced metallurgical skills, and speaking vernaculars belonging to more than twenty unrelated language families. Though the classical Mayan civilization had passed its zenith by 1000, the Mayan and Andean cultural zones continued to be centers from which high skills were diffused to surrounding areas. In those two zones, the Aztec and Inca civilizations would emerge in the fifteenth and sixteenth centuries, on the brink of the era of European (particularly Spanish) conquest (see Chapter 16).*

European civilization, and endured through a decline that extended into the seventeenth century. Its descendants survive to this day in Yucatán.

Heirs to Olmec civilization, the Maya developed an efficient agricultural system involving extensive irrigation projects to produce the maize that was central to their diet and way of life. Maize surpluses permitted the development of elites: nobles, priests, warriors, merchants, and artisans, whose responsibilities were not directly related to agricultural production. This complex society supported a rich intellectual and artistic life.

The Maya invented an ideographic system of writing which has recently been deciphered—the only natives of the Western Hemisphere to do so. The Spanish invaders found many Mayan writings—and destroyed many. Bishop Diego de Landa (c. 1524–1579), whose eyewitness account of the Spanish conquest of Yucatán in the 1500s survives, reported seeing many books written in their strange (to him) characters: "And, as they contained nothing in which there was not to be seen superstition and lies of the devil, we burned them all … which [the natives] regretted to an amazing degree, and which caused them affliction."

Despite the efforts of the conquerors to destroy them, quantities of Mayan writing exist.

The Maya developed a calendar based on the 365-day solar year that was more accurate than the one then used in Europe. They possessed advanced mathematics which included the concepts of place value and the all-important zero. They built bustling cities and huge stepped pyramids on the high inland plateau of Yucatán as shown on p. 223. They left traces of their artistry in stone and plaster sculpture and vivid murals featuring, alongside scenes of gaiety and celebration, other scenes of violence and victory and human sacrifice. Organized in a grid pattern encompassing homes for rich and poor as well as temples, courts, and markets, their central city of Teotihuacán housed a population, around 600, of some 125,000. Its largest structure was the mammoth Temple of the Sun, larger than the pyramids of Egypt. Smaller step-pyramids abounded, in the capital itself and at scattered sites obtruding from the cover of jungle foliage. The Maya's cities mysteriously disappeared, along with most other vital features of their civilization, after around 900. But their heritage lived on in later Amerindian cultures, such as the Aztecs defeated in every way by Cortés (see Chapter 16), and among their distant posterity, who survived the later Spanish conquest despite its cruelties, and even today preserve their identity.

Conclusion

THE ANCIENT WORLD, ITS LEGACY, AND THE MEANING OF THE WEST

By the end of the first millennium C.E., the human species had made an appearance in every part of the globe hospitable to human life. Advanced civilizations were established on five of the seven continents—all but solitary Australia and frigid Antarctica. From their centers travelers, peddlers, refugees, conquerors, and slaves carried the arts of civilization to human communities around the planet. Of these communities, those of Europe were among the poorest—lacking the sophistication and wealth of the Byzantine, Islamic, and Chinese empires, the formidable strength of the Mongols. But they stood poised for an explosion of cultural energy that would soon boost them to the front rank of nations.

Today Europe encompasses, among others, the nations of Great Britain and France, Belgium and the Netherlands, Spain and Sweden, Hungary and Poland, Russia and Italy. In the years following the disintegration of Rome, Europe was a backwater, and these nations did not exist. They would emerge over the centuries that extend between antiquity and the era of European mastery: the period Europeans call the Middle Ages.

Those years after antiquity—the Middle Ages—begin with the "triumph of barbarism and religion" and end with the transformation of Europe in the era of the Renaissance and the Reformation. They span almost one thousand years. During those years Europe would create the civilization called "Western": grounded in the experience of antiquity yet profoundly original. The elements of which it was formed were preeminently two, both ancient in origin: a religious tradition rooted in Judaism and developed as Christianity; and a cultural tradition deriving from Greece and elaborated by Rome. Those two distinct traditions blended throughout the early history of the West, whenever Christian intellectuals embraced with renewed vision the Greco-Roman heritage. They did so at peak moments, the first of which occurred as early as the eighth century C.E.

A Frankish king presided over that cultural renewal, the leader of one of the warrior tribes who had penetrated Roman defenses, and a successor to Clovis with whose momentous conversion this story began. The king was Charles the Great (in French, Charlemagne; in Latin, Carolus Magnus). And the renewal is named, after him, the Carolingian Renaissance. Its makers reached back into the past whose experience was concretized in church liturgy and in libraries. These scholars gathered at the king's court in Aachen (in modern Germany; Aix-la-Chapelle in French) with their leader Alcuin of York (c. 732–804), director of the palace school. They organized the copying and distribution of books, so that new generations could learn to preach the word of God and manage the business of the king.

In the libraries of the Frankish kingdom trained monks copied the works of Cicero and Seneca and others. They did so in a clear and lucid script (the Carolingian minuscule) which is the ancestor of the type used in the printed books of the Western world. More, they punctuated the text (as the Romans never had) for sense, and adorned the margins with splendid and ebullient paintings called "**illuminations**." Their manuscripts (the word means "written by hand") were bound between hard covers and were the first true books. Scattered over Europe, these books were the principal source of subsequent Western thought. Barbarism and religion may have triumphed, but the legacy of Greece and Rome, poured by the careful and loving hands of Christian monks into the vessels of their books, was never lost.

REVIEW QUESTIONS

1. How true is it to say that the collapse of the Roman Empire in the West was the result of "the triumph of barbarism over religion"? Who were the barbarians? Did the barbarians intend to destroy the Roman Empire?

2. To what extent was the Byzantine Empire a continuation of the Roman Empire? What role did the Church play in Byzantium? What was Justinian's greatest achievement?

3. What are the five pillars of Islam? How did Islam become a global religion? What were the main achievements of Islamic civilization?

4. How did Kush influence civilization in other parts of Africa? What role did Aksum play in trade between Africa and other regions? How did Islam spread in West and East Africa?

5. How did the political history of China differ from India in the first millenium C.E.? What role did Confucianism play in the Chinese state? How did Chinese civilization come to influence other parts of East Asia?

6. What evidence is there for advanced societies in the Western Hemisphere before the Europeans arrived? What was the agricultural foundation for Mayan civilization? Why were the Maya the most brilliant of early Amerindian civilizations?

SUGGESTED RESOURCES

The Triumph of Barbarism and Religion

Wallace-Hadrill, J.M., *The Barbarian West: 400–1000* (New York: Barnes & Noble, 1998). Useful overview of the different groups of tribal peoples settled in Europe and their interactions during the whole of the late ancient and early medieval periods.

Wells, Peter S., *The Barbarians Speak: How the Conquered Peoples Shaped Roman Europe* (Princeton: Princeton University Press, 1999). Uses a range of archeological evidence to reconstruct the culture of the Celtic and German peoples as they observed and responded to the Roman advance.

Byzantium: The Enduring Empire

Evans, J. A. S., *The Age of Justinian: The Circumstances of Imperial Power* (London: Routledge & Kegan Paul, 1996). A history of the reign of Justinian, with attention to the theological issues that split the empire and left deep divisions after Justinian's death.

Haldon, J. F., *Byzantium in the Seventh Century: The Transformation of a Culture* (Cambridge: Cambridge University Press, 1990). A survey of Byzantine culture, society, and state in the seventh century C.E., including the consolidation of Christianity, the background to the iconoclastic controversy, the development of Byzantine institutions, and the response to the rise of Islam.

Holum, Kenneth G., *Theodosian Empresses: Women and Imperial Dominion in Late Antiquity* (Berkeley: University of California Press, 1982). A study of the role of empresses in eastern Roman political life, c. 376–451, and in the controversy over the status of the Virgin Mary.

Treadgold, Warren, *A History of the Byzantine State and Society* (Stanford: Stanford University Press, 1997). Overview, especially good on the processes of Christianization and related cultural change.

Byzantine civilization, sources, and links:
http://members.nbci.com/romaioi
Byzantine women: **http://members.nbci.com/romaioi/women.htm**

Islam: From Arabian Desert to World Stage

Armstrong, Karen, *Islam: A Short History* (New York: Modern Library, 2000). Synopsis of the whole history of Islam, from the flight of the prophet Muhammad to encounters with the West in the modern era.

Bulliet, Richard W., *Islam: The View from the Edge* (Cambridge: Cambridge University Press, 1993). An interesting synthesis of Islamic social history, arguing that local developments are, in the final analysis, more important than central political history.

Lewis, Bernard W., *The Arabs in History*, 6th ed. (Oxford: Oxford University Press, 1993). A classic account emphasizing earlier periods (Arabia before Islam, conquests, the Islamic Empire, civilization).

History of Islam, with timeline, and discussion of current events in Islamic world: **http://members.nbci.com/romaioi/women.htm**

A brief chronology of Islam (Northpark University):
http:/campus.northpark.edu/history/WebChron/Islam/Islam.html

Beyond the West

Chaudhuri, K.N., *Trade and Civilization in the Indian Ocean: An Economic History from the Rise of Islam to 1750* (Cambridge: Cambridge University Press, 1997). Compact history of the trade networks across the Indian Ocean, demonstrating the lively mercantile interactions of Asians, Arabs, and others.

Fairbank, John King, *China: A New History* (Harvard: Belknap Press, 1992). Comprehensive, up-to-the-minute history of China from antiquity to the present.

Keay, John, *India: A History* (New York: HarperCollins, 2000). A comprehensive historical portrait of the many peoples and civilization of India from the ancient Harappan culture to modern times.

Munro-Hay, S. C., *An African Civilization: The Axumite Kingdom of Northern Ethiopia* (Stanford, CA: Stanford University Press, 1989). A solid introduction to the ancient Aksumite Kingdom, based on recent archaeological discoveries, literary evidence, and inscriptions.

Sharer, Robert J., *The Ancient Maya*, 5th ed. (Stanford, CA: Stanford University Press, 1994). The standard account of the first mature American civilization.

Introduction to the civilization of India:
http:/www.interknowledge.com/india/index.html

A brief history of China, with timelines (University of Maryland): **http:/www-chaos.umd.edu/history/toc.html**

A guide to major Mesoamerican civilizations (University of Minnesota):
http://www.harappa.com/har/har0.html
http:www.angelfire.com/ca/humanorigins/index.html

PART THREE

The West Takes Form

Medieval Society, Politics, Economy, and Culture (500–1500)

Peasants and nobles created the society of the European Middle Ages. As Roman institutions crumbled and waves of invaders destroyed communities, medieval peasants devised new patterns of agricultural work and life, generally on the manors, or large estates, of noble landholders. The nobles, as an elite group of military men, warded off invaders and struggled among themselves for power.

Amid the bounds of mainly local authority, the first European kingdoms emerged, and kings employed violence and persuasion to assert their authority over nobles. The Crusades sent knightly armies east to the Levant (Palestine and Syria, on the eastern Mediterranean shores), while knights who stayed home at court developed the rituals of chivalry. In the late medieval centuries, which were gripped by famine and plague, peasant rebellions against landholders were frequent.

Providing cohesion to the disparate communities of Europe was the Catholic Church, centered in Rome under the pope, whose authority was at its height around 1300 after a process of reform, centralization, and resistance to the encroachments of secular rulers. A powerful Church summoned Christians to respect celibacy, the priestly administration of the sacraments, and the examples of saints and martyrs; and it disciplined those who strayed from orthodoxy. Providing access to libraries and schools, the Church trained most of Europe's intellectuals, who elaborated a rational system of theology and laid the foundations for modern philosophical, political, legal, and scientific thought.

As monarchical and ecclesiastical institutions crystallized, a new social group and setting emerged: merchants and towns. By 1300, towns stretching from the Mediterranean to the North Sea coasts housed artisans, merchants, bankers, and entrepreneurs. By 1500, their commercial ventures, extending to Africa, the Middle East, and Asia, made Europe rich and ready to expand.

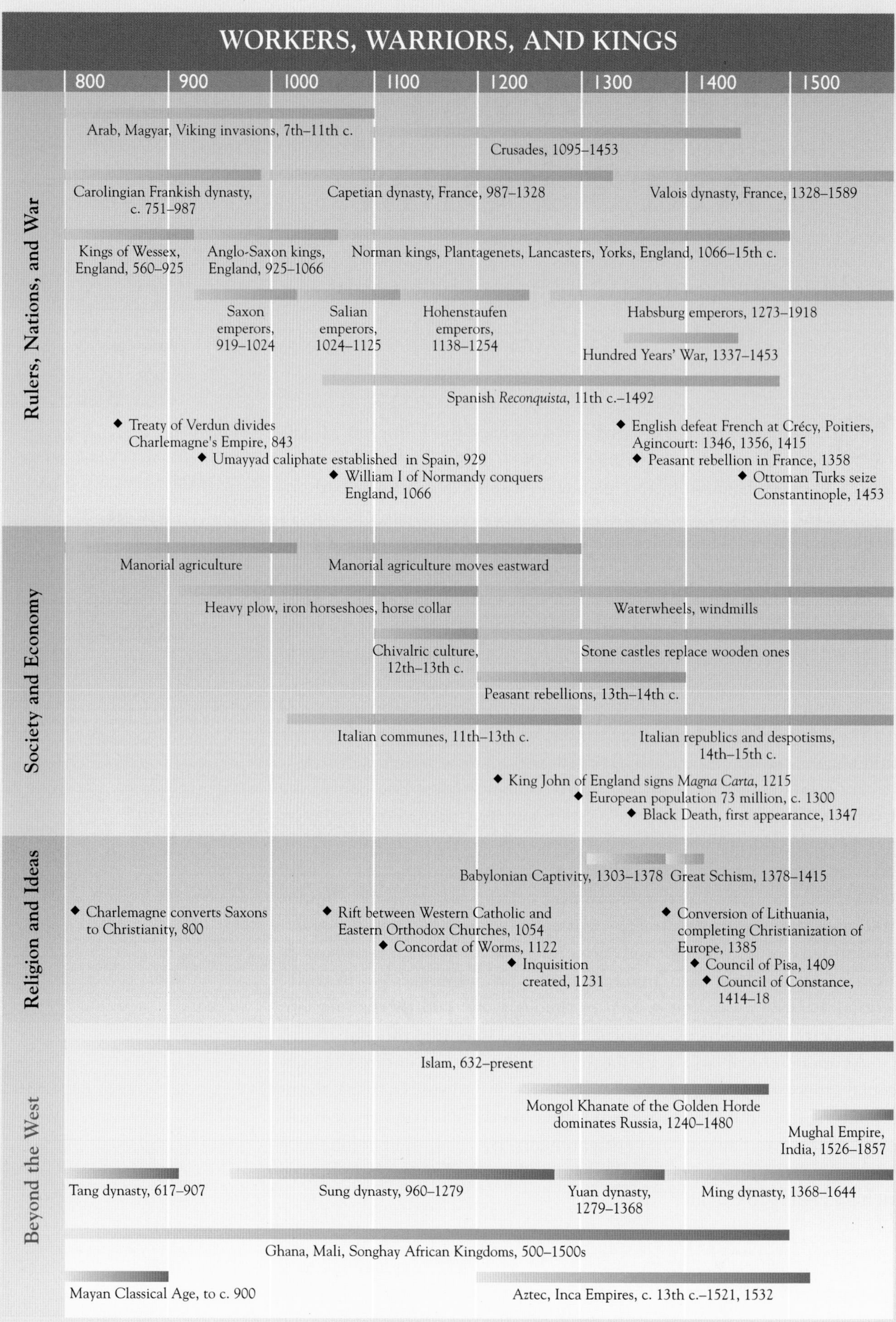

WORKERS, WARRIORS, AND KINGS
800
900
1000
1100
1200
1300
1400
1500
Rulers, Nations, and War
Arab, Magyar, Viking invasions, 7th–11th c.
Crusades, 1095–1453
Carolingian Frankish dynasty, c. 751–987
Capetian dynasty, France, 987–1328
Valois dynasty, France, 1328–1589
Kings of Wessex, England, 560–925
Anglo-Saxon kings, England, 925–1066
Norman kings, Plantagenets, Lancasters, Yorks, England, 1066–15th c.
Saxon emperors, 919–1024
Salian emperors, 1024–1125
Hohenstaufen emperors, 1138–1254
Habsburg emperors, 1273–1918
Hundred Years' War, 1337–1453
Spanish Reconquista, 11th c.–1492
◆ Treaty of Verdun divides Charlemagne's Empire, 843
◆ Umayyad caliphate established in Spain, 929
◆ William I of Normandy conquers England, 1066
◆ English defeat French at Crécy, Poitiers, Agincourt: 1346, 1356, 1415
◆ Peasant rebellion in France, 1358
◆ Ottoman Turks seize Constantinople, 1453
Society and Economy
Manorial agriculture
Manorial agriculture moves eastward
Heavy plow, iron horseshoes, horse collar
Waterwheels, windmills
Chivalric culture, 12th–13th c.
Stone castles replace wooden ones
Peasant rebellions, 13th–14th c.
Italian communes, 11th–13th c.
Italian republics and despotisms, 14th–15th c.
◆ King John of England signs Magna Carta, 1215
◆ European population 73 million, c. 1300
◆ Black Death, first appearance, 1347
Religion and Ideas
Babylonian Captivity, 1303–1378
Great Schism, 1378–1415
◆ Charlemagne converts Saxons to Christianity, 800
◆ Rift between Western Catholic and Eastern Orthodox Churches, 1054
◆ Concordat of Worms, 1122
◆ Inquisition created, 1231
◆ Conversion of Lithuania, completing Christianization of Europe, 1385
◆ Council of Pisa, 1409
◆ Council of Constance, 1414–18
Beyond the West
Islam, 632–present
Mongol Khanate of the Golden Horde dominates Russia, 1240–1480
Mughal Empire, India, 1526–1857
Tang dynasty, 617–907
Sung dynasty, 960–1279
Yuan dynasty, 1279–1368
Ming dynasty, 1368–1644
Ghana, Mali, Songhay African Kingdoms, 500–1500s
Mayan Classical Age, to c. 900
Aztec, Inca Empires, c. 13th c.–1521, 1532

CHAPTER

9 WORKERS, WARRIORS, AND KINGS

Politics and Society in the Middle Ages

800–1500

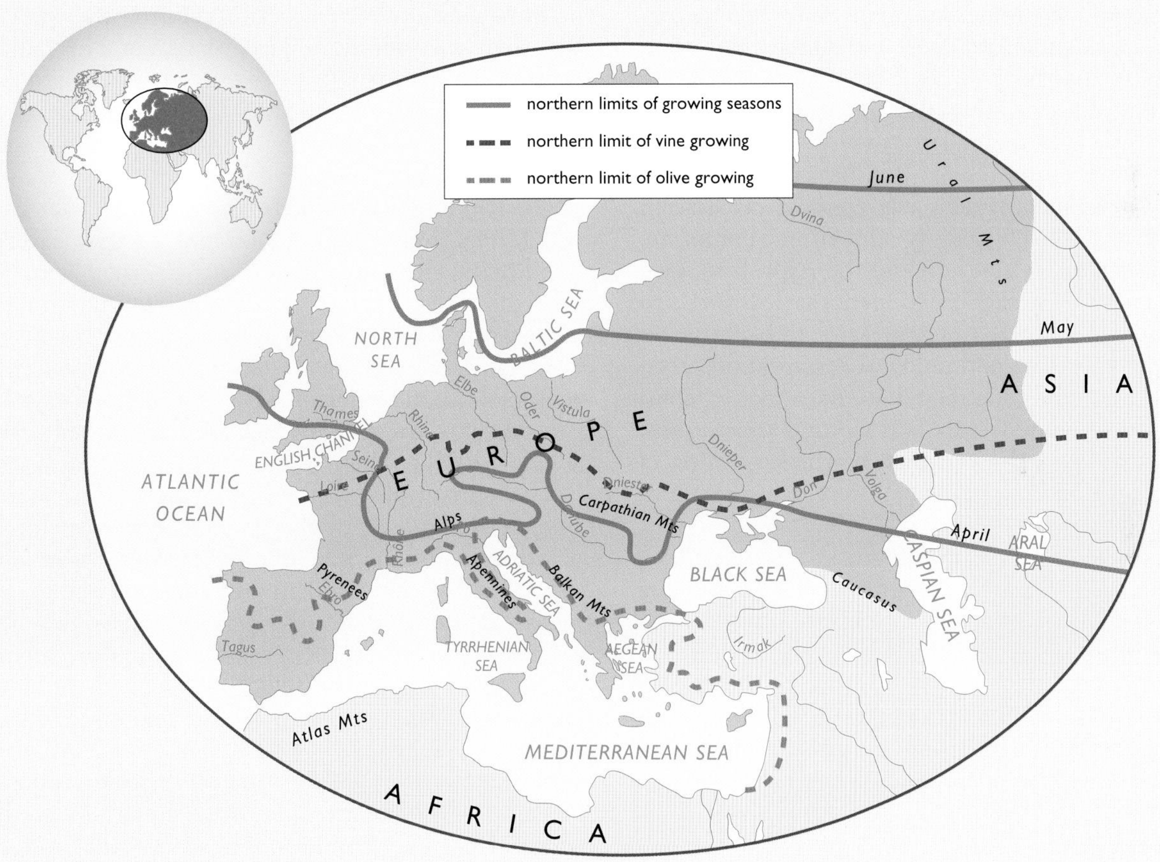

KEY TOPICS

- **Workers:** Medieval workers plow dense soil, fell forests, build village communities, and rebel against lords and kings.
- **Warriors:** European nobles fend off invasion, hunt and joust, and venture eastward to reclaim Jerusalem; at court, in schools of chivalry, they learn good manners and fall in love.
- **Kings:** Kings struggle to secure domains and exert authority over their nobles; the most successful monarchies create the framework for the modern states of Europe that would soon reach out to dominate the world.

Piers, the Plowman *The peasant hero of* The Vision of Piers Plowman *(probably by the fourteenth-century English poet William Langland, c. 1330–c. 1400) bewailed in eloquent verse the world's injustice and his own poverty: "I have no penny," he cried, when Hunger asked for an offering, "to buy pullets, nor geese nor pigs," but only the food of the poor—cheese, beans, grain. The poor, Piers lamented, are like "prisoners in cells ... charged with children and overcharged by landlords."*

What they may spare in spinning they spend on rental,
On milk, or on meal to make porridge,
To still the sobbing of the children at mealtime.

The fictional Piers represents many millions of workers who could not always feed themselves or their children; for hunger haunted Europe during much of the Middle Ages (as it did most people in all regions of the world before modern times). Yet, over the seven centuries from the age of Charlemagne to that of the Renaissance, a new and vigorous civilization emerged. It devised systems of agriculture appropriate to the damp, heavy soil north of the Alps. It molded the social groups needed to perform its work, to defend its boundaries, to create laws and administer justice. As its social and political organizations crystallized, Europe reconstructed its networks of commerce and generated ideas and cultural institutions. Thanks to these achievements, by the beginning of the sixteenth century, Europeans were in a position to dominate the world stage.

The foundations of this greatness were laid, to a great extent, by members of three social groups: the agricultural workers known as serfs and peasants; the warriors, who constituted the class of nobles; and the kings, who consolidated their authority and forged the framework of the modern nations of Europe. (The contributions of other—**clergy**, scholars, and merchants—will be examined in later chapters.)

WORKERS

Of the achievements of the Middle Ages, those in farming were the earliest and most fundamental. They were accomplished by peasants, who made up 90 percent or more of all Europeans. These workers invented the techniques of medieval agriculture, felled forests for settlement, and built stable village communities. They also launched rebellions, increasingly frequent, of those who worked against those who commanded.

Serfs, Peasants, and Poverty

In the early Middle Ages, until about 1200, most peasants became serfs, dependent laborers on their masters' lands. After that time, many serfs in western Europe were able to win their freedom. In the east, the process worked in reverse; there, by the late Middle Ages, after about 1300, many previously free peasants were enserfed.

As in antiquity, peasants had to struggle to produce the minimum necessary for survival. The soil was stubborn and unpredictable. To yield crops, it had to be loosened with a stick or a plow—a wooden or iron blade that scratched or sliced or turned the earth and was drawn by human or animal power. Even when soil was manipulated in this way, it still needed enrichment—from decayed plant matter or manure dropped by animals or spread by workers. It needed watering, by nature or by human artifice, by rain or flood. At times the earth was stingy. The rains did not come, or they washed away the topsoil, or the sun did not warm the growing crops. At such times during the Middle Ages there was **famine**, and the peasant and his family might starve to death. If they survived, they might fall victim, in their weakened state, to an **epidemic**.

Nature imposed these hardships of stubborn soil, bad weather, and disease. Human beings imposed others. Landholders, whose extensive properties protected them from the starvation and, to some extent, the disease that threatened the ordinary laborer, added to the peasants' suffering. The landholder might lend seed or lease tools to the peasant in exchange for a share of the crop. The price for that assistance was high: one-third or one-half of the yield. In good years, the peasant paid his due. In bad years, he fell into debt. Then he was likely to become a serf.

The agricultural economy of medieval Europe was characterized largely by the phenomenon of serfdom. A serf was neither free nor slave. Many were the descendants of late Roman peasants and slaves. By the last centuries of the Roman era, many peasants had already fallen into a desperate condition, forced into dependency by the relentless demands of landholders and tax collectors. These oppressed smallholders of late antiquity were called *coloni*, in Latin, or "settlers"; they were peasants who had surrendered their freedom in order to gain the right to stay on the land and farm it. Unlike slaves, they could not be sold, or even removed from the land they had bargained sacrificially to win. But neither could they leave and seek a different occupation, or richer soil, elsewhere. Meanwhile, slaves escaped their servitude. Amid chaos and disintegration, they ascended, ironically, to the condition of serfdom.

As invasions hammered Europe and public institutions disintegrated, thousands of former slaves and formerly free peasants turned to landholders, with whom they made contracts of serfdom. They and their descendants, they promised, would labor on the great man's land and contribute to his stores specified "dues," defined as quantities of crops and animals or labor service. In exchange, they and their

WINDOWS ON

Plow and Field

January page of a calendar showing plowing, eleventh century

The heavy plow, which could dig deep and turn over dense northern soils, was the key to medieval agriculture. This illustration (above) from a manuscript calendar shows a plow drawn by four oxen.

Compare this with a modern sketch of the medieval mechanism (below).

The ridges and furrows arrayed in strips characteristic of medieval agriculture are revealed in this aerial photograph of an English field at Padbury (right).
(top: British Library, London; right: Cambridge University Collection, England)

Padbury, England

To continue your investigation of this topic, please go to www.prenhall.com/king for the related **WINDOWS** on the **WEB** activity

descendants, they were assured, could count on certain services performed by the lord. He would protect their right to the land, provide justice, and defend them from invaders. The promise of protection lured peasants to surrender their freedom and assume the dues and burdens of serfdom.

Although most medieval peasants became serfs, some remained free, and some who had been serfs won their freedom. Free status persisted where the lords were not so powerful. In parts of what is today Germany, or in the sparse, hilly land on Europe's northern fringe, there were few great landowners, and free ownership of land by peasants remained common. In modern France and England, in contrast, where powerful lords dominated nearly all available land, serfdom advanced swiftly. But in these lands the early establishment of governmental authority and an official administration of justice made possible its equally quick decline. After about 1200, French and English serfs were able to sell a surplus or market a skill. They purchased their freedom and were serfs no longer. Farther east, even in those areas where the free ownership of land had previously been common, peasants subsequently were pressed into serfdom.

Working the Land

During the early Middle Ages, the serfs of northern Europe worked soil that was more difficult to till, but also more fertile, than the land around the Mediterranean. A series of innovations in plowing and managing the soil made European agriculture productive.

North of the Alps, the soil demanded a different pattern of land cultivation from that common in the ancient civilizations ringing the Mediterranean Sea. The Mediterranean climate was warm, the soil thin, but easily cultivated with a lightweight plow, the terrain hilly. Here the olive tree and vine were the major crops, while grain was imported from fertile Egypt and Sicily. To the north, the climate was cool and wet, the soil heavy, damp, and deep, the land a forested plain from the Atlantic shore eastward into modern Russia. Once the forests were cleared, that rich and well-watered plain was suitable for growing grain. The peasants of this region developed new techniques to meet the demands of climate and topography.

By about 1000, they had developed a heavy plow, called the moldboard plow, the key to Europe's future prosperity. Drawn by a pair of yoked oxen or a team of horses, this powerful implement pierced the tough skin of the northern soil, sheared the grass at the roots, turned the sliced soil, and mounded it alongside the deep furrow (see *Windows On*, p. 231). The deep cultivation of the soil accomplished by the heavy plow permitted the intensive cultivation of grains. By the beginning of the fourteenth century, thanks to this invention, grain yields had climbed to a peak that would not be surpassed until the eighteenth.

To mill the grain, serfs used human or animal power, but also that of waterwheels (and later, windmills), described in *Witnesses* on p. 235. Although known to antiquity and in the east, waterwheels were first fully exploited by medieval peasants. On the land of the monks of Saint Germain-des-Prés (in modern Paris) as early as the ninth century, 59 water-driven mills were operating. In 1086, the agents of King William the Conqueror of England counted 5624 mills in 34 English counties. Later in the Middle Ages the wheel's power was used for brewing, fulling of cloth, and papermaking. The last of these processes, though invented by the Chinese and spread by Muslims, was mechanized only by Europeans.

Oxen are strong but slow workers; horses are brisk and dependable. But the ancients, who harnessed their horses the way they yoked their broad-shouldered oxen, never were able to utilize horsepower effectively. The horse hauling a full load was strangled by his harness. By the ninth century medieval peasants had learned to employ a device imported from the Asian steppes—a rigid, padded collar. Equipped with such a collar, the horse could pull heavy loads without choking. At about the same time, peasants began to equip their beasts with another device, also Asian in origin—iron shoes nailed to the hoof. Now teams of horses with armored hoofs and hitched in teams could work faster than the cheaper, clumsier ox. Energetic horses freed human labor, which could now be applied to tasks requiring skill and intelligence. And peasants who lived scattered about within an ox's stroll of their fields began to cluster in villages, where they developed a rich rural culture that persisted well into modern times.

Another useful innovation was neither a machine nor a device but a method—that of **fallowing.** Peasants learned that planting the same crops on the same fields year after year inevitably resulted in the impoverishment of the soil. Leaving one-half of the soil idle, or fallow, for a season enriched it. This practice allowed nutrients to be reintroduced through the normal processes (which people then lacked the scientific knowledge to understand) of the decay of vegetable matter and the interaction of elements in the soil with those in the air.

In some regions, peasants developed a more refined fallowing process, the three-field system, as shown on p. 233. They left only one-third of the land fallow. They planted a second third in winter with a staple but soil-depleting grain, and the final third in the spring in an alternate crop (often one of the legumes, whose roots release soil-enriching nitrogen, such as peas, beans, alfalfa, acacia, and peanuts). The peasants' collective decision to leave one-third of their land fallow won them better yields and more robust health. These fallowing techniques were possible only for those peasants of northern Europe who dwelled on the region's great plain. In the Mediterranean climate,

The Three-Field Cycle

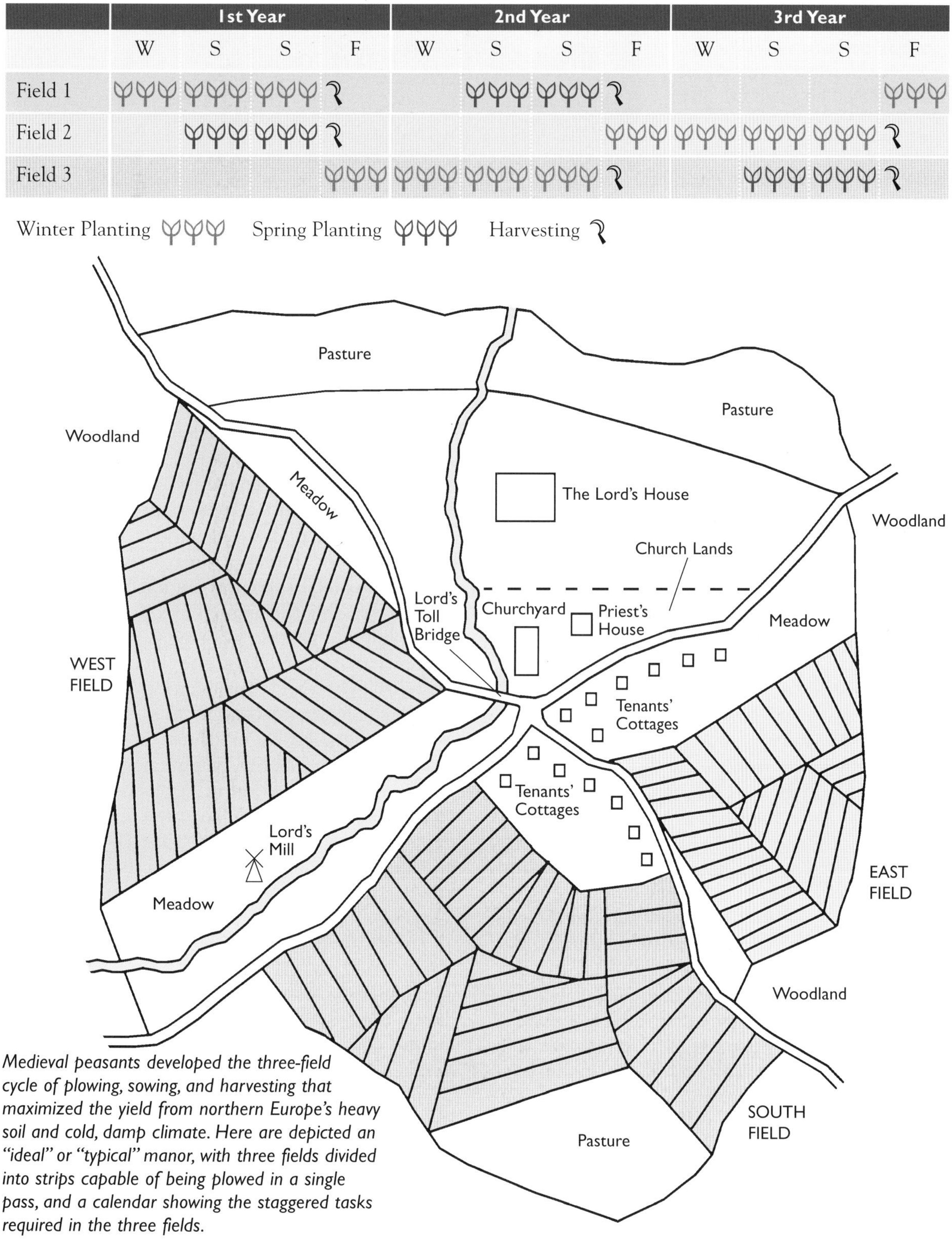

	1st Year				2nd Year				3rd Year			
	W	S	S	F	W	S	S	F	W	S	S	F
Field 1	ΨΨΨ	ΨΨΨ	ΨΨΨ	ʔ		ΨΨΨ	ΨΨΨ	ʔ				ΨΨΨ
Field 2		ΨΨΨ	ΨΨΨ	ʔ				ΨΨΨ	ΨΨΨ	ΨΨΨ	ΨΨΨ	ʔ
Field 3				ΨΨΨ	ΨΨΨ	ΨΨΨ	ΨΨΨ	ʔ		ΨΨΨ	ΨΨΨ	ʔ

Winter Planting ΨΨΨ Spring Planting ΨΨΨ Harvesting ʔ

Medieval peasants developed the three-field cycle of plowing, sowing, and harvesting that maximized the yield from northern Europe's heavy soil and cold, damp climate. Here are depicted an "ideal" or "typical" manor, with three fields divided into strips capable of being plowed in a single pass, and a calendar showing the staggered tasks required in the three fields.

there was insufficient rainfall for a spring crop of legumes to supplement the winter yield of wheat.

This rich soil and these technical innovations made Europe a producer of grain sufficient not only to sustain population levels but even to support population growth. By 1300, Europe had achieved a prosperity that would not be surpassed for centuries.

Manor, Village, and Household

The rotation of fallow and cultivated land, and of grain and legume crops, characterized a medieval plantation, often called a **manor**. Although there was no "typical" manor, most in the prosperous regions of western Europe possessed—in addition to open

Peasant labor: *The biblical Adam and Eve are depicted in this stone relief from the façade of the cathedral in Modena, Italy, early twelfth century. They have just been expelled from the Garden of Eden and are now at work, hoeing.*

fields—forest, common grazing lands, a manor house with the lord's demesne, or private land, and one or more parish churches and peasant villages.

The lord's house was normally the largest structure on the manor. Often it was fortified and called a **castle**. In the early years, the castle was a plain wooden tower. By the thirteenth century, it was an imposing stone pile (if the proprietor was wealthy) containing a spacious hall and kitchen, for feeding large numbers of people, a private chapel, and various bedchambers. In some cases the manor "house" was actually a monastery, inhabited by a community of monks (see Chapter 10). The Church controlled a significant portion of the land of Europe. Its monasteries governed that land much as did the medieval lord. Monks, pledged to poverty under the rule of their abbot, warehoused crops and directed the labor of serfs. The great monastery of Bobbio, in northern Italy, for instance, had 650 serfs in its employ.

The other structures on the manor formed the village: the one-roomed houses of the serfs, the church, and a mill to grind essential grain. Around these stretched blocks of land divided according to purpose: first, common land for the grazing of the animals of all members of the community; second, forest reserved for the lord and his peers and for the peasants' pigs, who rooted for nourishment on its floor; and third, open fields, the pattern for medieval cultivation.

The requirements of the plow encouraged the patterning of the land into great open fields, divided into long, narrow strips. These strips, visible in the photograph in *Windows On* on p. 231, were as long as possible, so that a plow could move in one direction without turning, and as narrow as the swath the plow cut through the soil. An individual serf might have the right to the produce of various strips of land scattered over the fields—some in fallow, some in grain, some in low, wet land, some in high, light soil.

While certain strips were assigned to each peasant for the sustenance of his household, others were reserved to the lord of the manor for the stocking of his storehouses. But all were worked by teams of peasants who cooperated in providing the tremendous labor demanded by the heavy plow. This organization of agricultural production was adapted to the needs of the laborers and the nature of their tools.

The manorial organization of agriculture prevailed in the level and well-ordered lands of northwestern Europe—France, England, and western Germany. On the northern, eastern, and southern fringes of Europe's central plain—among the Celtic peoples of Iceland, Ireland, Scotland, and in northern Scandinavia, in Spain, the Balkans, Russia, and eastern Europe—this system failed to gain a foothold. These areas continued to suffer invasions, or remained outside the zone of Latin Christianity longer, or were too hilly for the use of the plow. Here free peasants on lone farms or in scattered hamlets scraped what they could from the soil or tended sheep and goats.

A manor was a community of laborers subject to the rule of the lord or the abbot, and his agent, the steward. These masters demanded contributions in kind of plant or animal produce, as well as labor dues, which consisted of farming the lord's demesne, building and mending the manor's roads and walls, clearing forest, hauling goods, or personal service. The goods and services required of the laborers varied from master to master and from manor to manor. So did the style of the landholder's exactions—fair and equitable in some cases, abusive in others.

Some of the laborers on the manor were engaged in work other than farming. A prosperous manor had its own blacksmith, who made the few necessary iron implements: plowshares (the part of the plow that cuts the furrow) and hoes, hammerheads and chisels, knives and pots. The miller was another key figure, one whose honesty was critical: Did he return in flour all the grain that was brought to the mill, less the small share that was his pay? The steward might be a member of the lesser nobility, but occasionally he was drawn from the peasant population. He might exercise his considerable power for his own advancement as much as for the benefit of the landholder.

The manor had to clothe itself as well as feed itself. In medieval Europe, as nearly everywhere else, women performed the work of producing textiles—generally wool or linen—for clothing. Peasant wives, grandmothers, and daughters carried on the perennial tasks of spinning and weaving and sewing. On small manors they worked in their huts. On larger manors, they produced textiles for the use of the whole population in a central workshop called the *gynaeceum*, or "women's quarters"—a term derived from the Greek word for the women's quarters of a citizen's house (see Chapter 3). That earlier gynaeceum, too, had among its other functions the responsibility for textile production.

Serf women also assisted with farmwork—even with the heavy plowing, although they more often

WITNESSES

Country Life

The moments of medieval rural life sketched here give some idea of its variety and dynamism. The first passage shows Frankish King Charlemagne ordering an inventory of his manors. The second depicts a waterwheel in operation. The third describes an uprising of discontented peasants.

Charlemagne orders his stewards to make an inventory of his manors (c. 800): We desire that each steward shall make an annual statement of all our income, ...; of the pigs, of the rents, of the obligations and fines; ... of the mills, of the forest, of the fields ...; of the hay, firewood, torches, planks and other kinds of lumber; of the waste lands; ... of the wool, flax and hemp; ... of the hens and eggs; of the geese; ... of the colt and fillies. They shall make all these known to us, set forth separately and in order, at Christmas, so that we may know what and how much of each thing we have.
(Charlemagne, *De Villis*; trs., ed. J. H. Robinson, 1904)

A monk describes the working of a waterwheel which provides power to mill grain and full cloth: The stream first hurls itself impetuously at the mill where ... it strains ... to crush the wheat beneath the weight of the millstones, then to shake the fine sieve which separates flour from bran ... One by one it lifts and drops the heavy pestles, the fullers' great wooden hammers. ... How many horses would be worn out, how many men would have weary arms if this graceful river, to whom we owe our clothes and food, did not labour for us. ...
(From J. Gimpel, *The Medieval Machine: The Industrial Revolution of the Middle Ages* 1976)

The peasants of northern France rise up in revolt (1358): They banded together and went off, ... unarmed except for pikes and knives, to the house of a knight who lived near by. They broke in and killed the knight, with his lady and his children, big and small, and set fire to the house. Next they went to another castle and did much worse; for, having seized the knight and bound him securely to a post, several of them violated his wife and daughter before his eyes. Then they killed the wife, who was pregnant, and the daughter and all the other children, and finally put the knight to death with great cruelty and burned and razed the castle. They did similar things in a number of castles and big houses, and their ranks swelled until there were a good six thousand of them.
(Froissart, *Chronicles*; ed., trs. G. Brereton 1968)

gathered hay or carefully gleaned the scattered kernels of grain left behind by teams of male harvesters. They brought their babies with them into the fields, or let their toddlers run on the **common** while they and the older children watched the sheep or fed the chickens. Back in the village, they brewed ale from barley, milled grain, baked bread, cooked and preserved foods by salting or drying, and tended small garden patches of vegetables and herbs. Their housekeeping tasks were minimal because their huts had dirt floors, no windows, few implements other than the cooking pot, and scarcely any furniture beyond a table and some stools.

In these rude huts the peasant family gathered after work for the brief leisure before sunset and sleep. They ate a supper of bread—of wheat, if they were fortunate—which was the largest part of their diet, perhaps accompanied by a soup or stew of vegetables flavored with garden herbs; only the rich had spices. Peasants in the north drank beer; in the south, wine. Occasionally they ate cheese from sheep, goats, or cows. They ate meat rarely, and then most often pork or mutton from the superfluous or elderly beasts slaughtered before the onset of winter, when no fodder could be spared to feed them. In those unlit evenings they may have told stories to entertain each other, creating and transmitting the folk traditions of Europe. They slept together, parents and children—generally not on a bed, an expensive item of property. Children alert enough to do so witnessed the sexual relations between their parents or others in pairings of which no record remains.

In this casual manner, children learned all the things they needed to know for the course of their short lives. The death toll was especially high in the first year or two of life. Those who survived infancy were quickly integrated into peasant existence. They followed their mother in her work until they were old enough to perform small tasks, such as feeding the chickens, rounding up the sheep, carrying messages. By eight or nine, boys and girls learned the ways of adult work from, respectively, their fathers and mothers. Adolescence as we know it today—a time of turmoil when the young person constructs his or her future social identity—did not exist. Childhood flowed into adulthood as skills matured and strength grew. Adult lives were scarcely longer than the course of childhood, as life expectancies hovered around 30 or 40 years, much like in Ancient Greece—barely half that of the modern North American or European (although those who survived infancy and epidemic might live into old age).

The flowing continuity of peasant life unfolded in a regular sequence from generation to generation. The rhythm of the seasons determined the framework of plowing, sowing, maintaining, harvesting, and storing from spring to autumn, and, in the harsh winter, of making and repairing tools to prepare for the spring. The celebrations of the church punctuated the rhythms of agricultural life. Saints' days littered the calendar, numerous enough to serve the same purpose as modern weekends. On these days, work ceased, and the villagers gathered for festivals as boisterous as their stores of food and drink allowed.

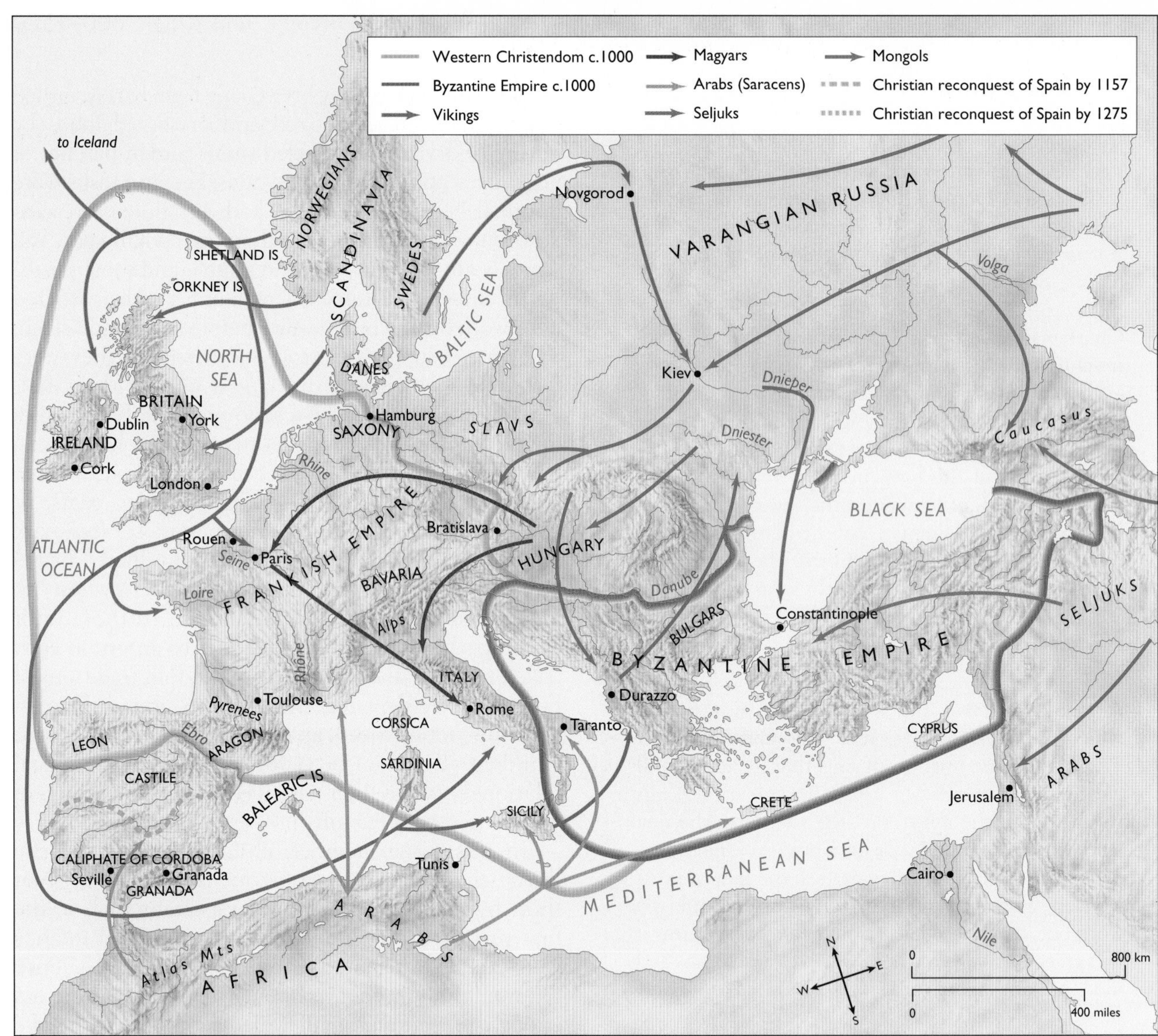

Map 9.1 Settlement and Invasion, 700–1300: *From 500 to 1000, Romanized and Christianized Europeans settled down to cultivate their lands. Beginning around 700, they were beset by waves of invasion from the north, east, and south: by Vikings originating in Scandinavia; by Magyars and Mongols originating in central Asia; and by Arabs originating in North Africa. By 1000, many of the invaders were absorbed into the European culture, and Europeans themselves began a steady advance outward from their center: south into the Iberian peninsula in the first phase of the "Reconquest"; eastward through Germany, then east and north into the Slavic regions on the Baltic sea.*

In a world where even the landholder was generally illiterate, the medieval serf received no schooling. The manor priest, often as ignorant as the peasants, offered little instruction but performed the rituals that led the way from birth to death. Knowledge and poetry, customs and beliefs, and the fruits of experience lived in songs and stories told by mothers to children, who matured rapidly and might die swiftly, but not before they had repeated the stories and sung the songs to the next cohort of the young. From generation to generation, that wisdom and that ignorance survived, distilled in adages and tales and in the melodic fragments that have inspired much of the Western musical tradition. These folk traditions would yield to the printed book and, in the nineteenth century, to mass education, and many, apart from those recorded by scholars, would disappear.

Expansion, Crisis, and Protest

Parallel with the seemingly changeless pattern of village life, many changes were, in fact, taking place. After around 1200, western Europe experienced dynamic growth, underwent economic crisis, suffered the devastations of the plague, and saw frequent outbreaks of peasant rebellion.

The biggest change was the increase in population, as indicated in *How Many* on p. 237. The productivity of the land, tended by the plow and nursed by fallowing, and greater prosperity, meant that people live a longer; that healthier mothers, fertility enhanced by ample diets, gave birth to more children; and that children more often survived. From around the year 700, when Rome had withered but Charlemagne had not yet begun his work of cultural renewal, to around

HOW MANY?

European Population Growth, 700–1500

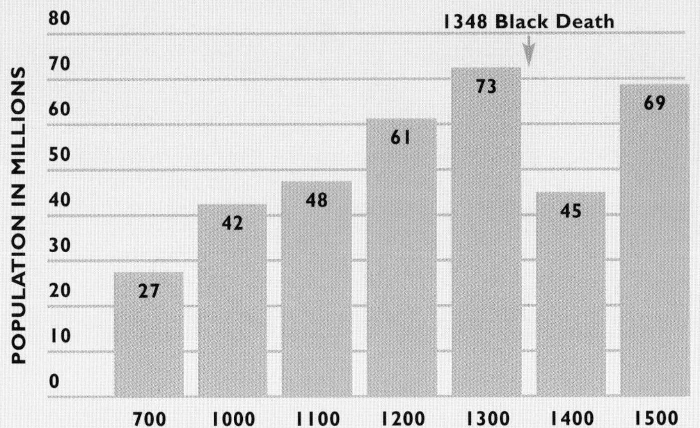

The European population sagged from a high during the Roman Empire around 200 C.E. to a low during the seventh to ninth centuries. It then surged forward around 1000 to a new peak just before the onslaught of the Black Death. Having then lost a third to a half of its population, and still vulnerable to new outbreaks of plague, the European population recovered slowly and had not yet reached its pre-plague high before the end of the Middle Ages.

Source: B. H. Slicher van Bath, *The Agrarian History of Western Europe, A.D. 500–1850* (New York: St. Martin's Press, 1963).

the year 1300, when medieval Europe reached the height of its prosperity, its population grew from approximately 27 million to 73 million. The growth of the advanced European centers is impressive. Between the arrival of William the Conqueror (1066) and the plague called the Black Death (1347–1351), the combined population of England, Scotland, and Wales tripled, reaching a peak of between 5 and 6 million. During that time, France grew to 20 million persons, not far short of its population at the outbreak of the French Revolution in 1789 and one-half its population in 1940 at the beginning of World War II. Even the poorer eastern regions experienced population growth. Poland, for instance, grew dramatically from 1.25 million to 3.1 million between 1340 and 1580. This increase in population was largely due to the labor and initiative of the peasant.

Territorial expansion followed upon population growth. Prodded by their lords, the peasants of western Europe undertook the enormous task of clearing for cultivation the forests and swamps of the eastern region. At the beginning of the Middle Ages, most of Europe was wilderness. Only the fields within the boundaries of the old Roman Empire were regularly cultivated. Many of these reverted to waste during the years of invasion. Around 800, the emperor Charlemagne launched an eastward migration with the conquest of German Saxony and its forced conversion to Christianity. Around 1000, Europeans completed the conquest of the soil within the western region and began pushing the boundary of the zone of settlement to the Elbe River and beyond to the Oder in eastern Germany. Claiming the wilderness for the plow was the epic tale of medieval agriculture, and the peasant was its hero.

The explosive growth of western Europe halted around 1300. The years that followed brought cycles of famine and disease. The most serious famine was the prolonged one of 1315–1317, in part the result of an epochal cooling of the climate. In these years, cold, wet winters were followed by cool, sterile summers. Famine paved the way for disease, culminating in the terrible onslaught of the Black Death, which ravaged Europe from south to north in 1347–1351 and would recur in every generation until the eighteenth century.

The Black Death took so many lives that a labor shortage developed in some regions, benefiting, ironically, the peasants who survived. They could now negotiate a good price for their labor. Many bargained for freedom, and won. Others began to dream of bettered conditions, and some began to risk their lives to fight for them. While hopes of change swept through their communities, peasants armed with their simple tools revolted against their lords—most dramatically in France and England.

In 1358, peasants in parts of France rebelled against the imposition of ever-higher taxes and other burdens. Tales of rape and torture, murder and cannibalism reached the royal court in Paris, which was itself threatened by an urban revolt (see *Witnesses*, p. 235). In 1381, English peasants, aroused by the peasant priest John Ball (d. 1381), joined in an uprising that flourished in the southeast region of that kingdom. Most peasant rebellions had as their objective the amelioration of farmers' contracts with their lords, rather than the dismantling of the apparatus of lordship. Ball reached further, preaching the equality of all people, in an age unready for such claims. He urged the confiscation of church lands and their redistribution to peasants, and the abolition of serfdom. For his revolutionary activity, Ball was imprisoned several times; but his message found an audience.

In June 1381, an angry mob under the peasant leader Wat Tyler (d. 1381) marched on London, where the king resided, plundering the mansions of the privileged that lay in their way. They released Ball from prison. The king and his retinue met Tyler and his men for negotiations, in the course of which Tyler was slain. By mid-July, Ball was hanged, his corpse mutilated in judicial revenge, and his protest silenced.

Clasped in the rhythms of nature, slaves of the soil and servants of the landholders, the peasants produced the first wealth that fueled Europe's expansion. By the end of the medieval era, a few began to ask a fundamental question—silenced at the time, but not forever: By what right do some rule, compelling others to obey?

Nobles Armed for War

Fighting with the lance: *War was a nobleman's job. Until the nineteenth century, the possession of a sword announced elite status—an attitude inherited from the Middle Ages when only noblemen could afford armor, weapons, and horses. On these pages are images of armed nobles. The eleventh-century Bayeux Tapestry colorfully depicts the Norman conquest of England (1066). The section shown reveals the defining characteristics of medieval knights: they are armored, they ride horses, and they wield long spears called* ***lances****.* (Bayeux Tapestry Museum, by special permission of the City of Bayeux)

WARRIORS

The masters of the land (apart from clergy) constituted, according to region, between 1 percent and 10 percent of the population. These were the nobles of Europe, those men who possessed the tools of war and the skill to use them. Their military skills enabled them to snatch the greater part of the power, status, and wealth that could be accrued in a world bereft of cities and schools and dominated by chaos. They seized command of great chunks of Europe's land, claiming them by birthright, by the commission of a higher lord, or by simple force. These lands they defended from invaders as warlike as themselves. Once possessed of Europe's land, they guarded their wealth and strove to pass it undiminished to their heirs. Like other elite groups, they developed their own code of values and sponsored a cultural program suited to their position. These were the values of chivalry and a culture of the court.

Nobles, Knights, and Lords

Over some five centuries, as the Roman state died and no new one could take form, Europe suffered recurrent invasions of warriors from the east, south, and north, as Map 9.1 shows. In this vacuum of authority, the first European nobles performed the single most essential governmental function: that of defense. Granted the right to do so by kings, or claiming that right by virtue of their strength, they assumed judicial and other administrative functions as well. The lands they possessed they also governed, claiming the obedience and dues of their serfs. Nobles without land did not govern, but they did fight, offering their skills and their counsel to lords greater than they and forming part of these great lords' households and retinue. In time, nobles took steps to secure heritable title to their lands within their branch of their family.

The medieval nobles were the counts or "companions" of the chiefs of the Germanic tribes that spread through Europe. As kings emerged from the welter of tribal chiefs, their counts acquired control of whole regions ("counties") on their behalf, where they administered justice and executed royal decrees. As a reward for such services, they were granted land; for money—if there was any available—was of no use where there was little commerce. Other nobles were assigned to hold border areas, or marches, and were entitled "marquess" or "marquis." Others, called "dukes," were usually rulers of small regions, not quite kingdoms. Beneath the duke, marquess, and count (in England, an earl) were their loyal supporters, who followed them in battle and formed the lesser ranks of the nobility: viscounts, barons, and **knights**.

From duke to knight, all of these nobles were essentially warriors, and all fought on horseback. Beginning in the eighth century, they adopted a distinctive mode of warfare. It depended on the development of the stirrup, an invention of the nomads of the great Asian plains, which reached western Europe around 730. With his feet in stirrups, the horseman more easily held his seat. He could withstand a thrust from a mounted opponent attacking even at full force. Instead of throwing his spear at his enemy, he could hold it firmly under his armpit, knowing that the powerful momentum of horse and rider would give his spear's (or lance's) piercing tip a more deadly power. From the eighth through the fourteenth centuries, cavalry outstripped infantry, and the mounted warrior, or knight, ruled the land.

The knight rode to war on his horse and wielded, as his chief weapon, not the sword of the Romans but a lance, a long sharpened wooden spear held extended as he charged into battle. The power of a charging horseman armed with a lance was formidable—the medieval equivalent of a modern tank with blasting guns. Squadrons of knights encountering each other in this way fought until they were unhorsed, or their lances splintered or were wrested from their hands. A vest of interlinked chains—"chain mail"—might protect them from the assault of the lance (later in the Middle Ages, plate armor offered more protection). If captured alive they were generally ransomed. Payment was made to the victor by the vanquished knight's family, lord, or friends.

An unknown knight: *This stone effigy shows an unknown knight in armor, from Dorchester Abbey, England, c. 1295–1305. He is wearing chain mail and a surcoat, and is drawing his sword.*

Knights fought in wars, and even when there was no war. They honed their skills in the uncleared forests, the nobleman's preserve. Their dogs and hawks helped these idle soldiers track deer and wild boar in a perpetual war against nature (one effect of which being that nobles dined excessively on meat). Alternatively, knights without real wars to fight might engage in mock ones. Tournaments, staged in times of peace by noblemen or kings, were more than sporting events; they were a form of controlled warfare. Groups of knights attacked each other in a melee that resembled the chaos of battle. In the joust, the predecessor of the duel, one knight faced another in personal combat, the outcome of which might decide an important issue. Only toward the end of the Middle Ages did the lance and sword of the knight begin to yield—though it survived in the ritualized tournament—to the longer range and fearful power of the projectile crossbow, longbow, and gun.

Nobles in general were fighters. Many, in addition, held land. A few held high judicial and administrative authority, granted by a ruler. These three sources of noble privilege—military service, land tenure, and administrative authority—were distinct but intersecting. Only a few nobles possessed all three assets, while many boasted only their military standing.

Men considered noble because of their military role actively sought to acquire land, the major source of wealth in the Middle Ages. They might possess it absolutely, in freehold, or might have the right to use and dispose of the products of the land granted to them by another noble, a king, or an agent of the Church. Although that right was not equal to possession, noble tenants often achieved the same end by making the right itself permanent and heritable by their descendants. Thus nobility, originally the professional order of military experts, came to be, in effect, a class of hereditary landholders.

From the twelfth century, as professional jurists in Italy began the task of recovering and reinterpreting Roman law for medieval social conditions, a technical language was fitted to the arrangements of noble land tenure. Land held by a noble in **usufruct** and granted by another noble, or a king or an agent of the Church, was often called a **fief**. The nobleman receiving the fief was then called the **vassal** of the person or institution granting it. In exchange for the fief, he owed military and administrative services. Sometimes the fiefholder was wealthy and powerful; granted a large and lucrative fief, he was obliged in return to administer this large territory, and his military obligation consisted of supplying a company of men. But sometimes he was only a knight or baron, whose small fief required him to provide his lord merely with "aid and counsel": personal military service and free advice.

The understanding between lord and vassal was between two persons of similar status who each

Noblewomen at war: *Noblewomen, as well as noblemen, often defended castles. This manuscript illumination by G. Boccaccio,* Des Clercs et nobles femmes, *France, c. 1470, depicts, in a fanciful way, such an event.* (Spencer Collection, New York Public Library; Astor, Lennox, Tilden Foundation)

expected to gain an important benefit. The lord acquired a soldier, adviser, loyal supporter. The vassal acquired land, the right to rule that land, and to take the yield from the labor of its serfs. The relation between lord and vassal was wholly distinct from that between lords and serfs, where the two parties were of widely different social status. The interlocking arrangements between lords and serfs and lords and vassals, demonstrated in the passages in *Witnesses*, below, are sometimes called (but with too great an implication of formal organization) the "**feudal** system" or "feudalism."

These terms are now best avoided because they give an impression of symmetry and order to social relationships that were quite unsystematic and forged, in fact, in an environment of radical disorder. Medieval society was not so much a hierarchy as a web of interlocking rights and obligations; or, as one scholar has colorfully expressed it, not so much a layer cake, in which each social stratum retained a separate identity, as the English dessert called a trifle—"its layers ... blurred, and the sherry of accepted values soaked through."

WITNESSES

Vassals and Serfs

In the turbulent Middle Ages, individuals of all social levels might seek security and protection from powerful men. Rural laborers entering into such a contract might become serfs; modest landowners seeking out a patron became the "vassal" (the "boy") of that "lord" (the master of land and people). These two excerpts show a landowner assuming vassal status in the ninth century; and another winning freedom from servitude in the more prosperous thirteenth century.

A charter of Louis the Pious grants privileges to a faithful vassal (815): A certain faithful man of ours, named John has come before us and commended himself to us; and he has asked our permission to occupy and take possession of whatever our father and we ourselves have granted to him, together with possession of whatever he or his sons have occupied and possessed in the past. ... And all these things he and his sons shall hold as a gift from us; they and their posterity shall hold them from us free from rent and free from all molestation.
(From R. C. Cave, H. C. Coulson, *A Source Book for Medieval Economic History*, 1936)

Richard, Abbot of Peterborough, frees a serf (1278): Let all know that we have manumitted and liberated from all yoke of servitude William, the son of Richard of Wythington whom previously we have held as our born bondman, with his whole progeny and all his chattels, so that neither we nor our successors shall be able to require or exact any right or claim in the said William, his progeny, or his chattels. But the same William with his whole progeny and all his chattels will remain free and quit and without disturbance, exaction, or any claim on the part of us or our successors by reason of any servitude, forever.
(From J. H. Robinson, *Translations and Reprints from the Original Sources of European History*, 1897)

The desire to make land tenures heritable encouraged the reorganization of noble families. After about 1000, noblemen increasingly defined their kin on the male side alone. By emphasizing that agnatic lineage, they limited the numbers of claimants to property, and assisted them in preserving it intact for male heirs. Often only one son—generally the eldest, in the system known as **primogeniture**—was designated to inherit the bulk of landed property, while the others were assisted in gaining positions in the Church or as landless retainers of other nobles. Daughters were excluded from inheritance in those noble families adopting an agnatic definition of lineage. They were assigned a **dowry** in lieu of an equal share of the inheritance, sufficient to make them eligible to marry a man of acceptable rank, or to enter the religious life, for which a fee was required.

Noblewomen served the interests of their families by marrying or not marrying, as instructed. Unmarried, they could assist their families with prayers from behind convent walls, or even gain prominence as abbesses. Married, they served as links to other noble families whose political and military support could be vital. If the alliance formed by the marriage was no longer useful, the marriage could be dissolved (assuming cooperative clerics could be found to arrange this) and the young woman remarried to a more promising husband. Although women appear to have been much disadvantaged by these arrangements, in fact some noblewomen gained considerable authority under certain circumstances: as proprietors of noble courts; as **regents** (or political guardians of their minor sons); and as surrogate rulers in the absence of their husbands. Blanche of Castile was one such regent: from 1226 until 1236, she competently ruled France until her son Louis IX (destined to be one of the most effective of the French kings) ascended the throne. Women could not rule in their own right; but as surrogates for their husbands, they often demonstrated a complete capacity for leadership.

The administrative authority conferred with land tenure varied considerably. Noble landholders collected dues in goods and labor from their serfs. In addition, sometimes for fees stipulated in ancient contracts, they approved marriages, served as guardians for orphans and widows, and supervised the inheritance of land tenures upon death. The extent of a lord's right to rule varied. The knight who administered a manor could certainly punish a serf for theft, and could issue orders about the use of the mill or the

Dover Castle: *Castles began as defensive positions erected in the tumultuous ninth and tenth centuries when invasions were a constant threat. They began as mere mounds of earth; then they were constructed as mounds of earth topped with wooden towers. By the twelfth century, castles were built of stone, and those of the wealthier nobles were sometimes luxurious complexes which housed the lord, his family, and his many retainers. This photograph (left) shows Dover Castle in England, which was begun in the Norman period.*

maintenance of the road. A high-ranking nobleman with extensive lands might possess the right of "high justice," the right to punish wrongdoing with death. This right was symbolized by the presence on the manor of a gallows.

A great nobleman on his lands resembled a king in his kingdom—particularly at a time when kingdoms were tiny and kings frail. Such nobles housed their own retainers, who followed them in battle, and might ignore kings altogether when it suited them to do so. These great lords expressed their power in their castles. Originally built of wood, by the eleventh century of stone, these fortified structures featured a central tower, or keep, and outbuildings, the complex protected by ditches, moats, and gates. As indicated in the photograph of Dover Castle shown above. A garrison of their knights guarded the tower. When invasion threatened, nobles and peasants and animals sheltered within the strong walls and there survived the passing of the storm—or suffered sack and massacre if the castle were taken by force. By 1300 or 1400, castles sometimes resembled great stone cities, centers of administration as well as bulwarks against invasion. As kings became more powerful in the late Middle Ages, the noblemen's proud towers were sometimes razed by royal overlords who sought to draw all authority into their own hands.

Courts and Courtly Culture

Although they did not yet value reading and writing, the European nobility nevertheless developed a refined cultural code. As invasions ceased and prosperity increased, the courts of the higher nobles were sites for the nurturance of chivalric values, the sentiments of loyalty and love, and high standards of decorum. Elevation of thought and sentiment characterized the courts of the later Middle Ages, even while these most privileged people lacked all the basic comforts that are now taken for granted.

Beginning in the 1100s, with the encouragement of the Church, of leisured noblewomen, and of the poets and storytellers who loitered about the great courts, the young noblemen who wandered from court to court in search of employment and adventure were challenged to learn something new. They were asked to become gentlemen, observers of the code of **chivalry**. "Chivalry" was a set of values proposed to soften aristocratic culture, otherwise centered on war and acquisition. It held rough warriors to standards of behavior enforced by sentiments of loyalty and honor. It designated certain groups worthy of protection—widows, orphans, noblewomen, clerics, noncombatants—and decreed that certain places and times—churches and holy days—were not to be violated by bloodshed. It insisted that noblemen loyally serve their lords and, equally, their ladies. For the first time in European history, women were raised to high status, in theory at least, and deemed worthy to receive special attention from men.

Noblemen who subscribed to the code of chivalry were considered to be "gentle" (hence our word "gentleman") and to exhibit "gentility." In time, gentility required medieval noblemen and noblewomen to adopt the forms of modern behavior embraced by the name of "civility." Customs now generally accepted as signs of proper behaviour in the Western world, such as using a handkerchief, deferring to another person at table or in a doorway, bowing, or shaking hands, derive from the patterns of behavior invented at the medieval court.

Chivalric values and the postures of civility coexisted with a still unrefined style of life. Life in a castle was more comfortable than life in a serf's hut; yet (by our standards) it was rude. Most of the activities of daily life took place within the great hall: a vast room, poorly lit, barely heated, and sparsely furnished. When times were good and the hunt was productive, food was ample—and so was drink. But amenities were few and privacy nonexistent. Until late in the Middle Ages, food was consumed without forks, only with knives and fingers; napkins evolved even later. The lord's family had separate sleeping quarters, but other courtiers found a bench or stretch of floor in the hall on which to spend the night.

In this austere setting, entertainers amused the company and celebrated the manners and exploits of their patrons. By the twelfth century, wandering poets called minstrels or troubadours sang epics of the exploits of heroic nobles in war or in love. This oral culture is reminiscent of early Greece when Homer composed his epics from the fragments of earlier poetic traditions. But the medieval epics were quickly written down, and their composers were master craftsmen (and occasionally craftswomen), concerned with the accurate transmission of their work.

Courtly Love The romantic love celebrated by the poets of the Middle Ages was a new phenomenon, called courtly love because it was cultivated in the grander courts of western Europe. Its nature is explained in *Witnesses* on p. 243. Courtly love was limited to members of the aristocracy and limited, in its life span, to the eleventh to thirteenth centuries (though its legacy endures today). It was characterized by the longing of a young man for an unattainable woman. The man was typically a younger son without property of his own, who sought advancement at court. The woman might be unattainable because she was socially superior to the longing knight, because her virginity could not be violated, or because she was already married. Most of the love relationships encompassed by the phenomenon of courtly love were adulterous, many were unconsummated, and many were fictitious. Far more real were the forgotten sexual encounters between noblemen and lower-class women, victims of rape rather than objects of adoration, and rarely the subjects of poems.

Why and how did the phenomenon of courtly love become established? And why is it important? Among several possible answers, historians often mention these. In an era of frequent warfare, the husbands of high-ranking noblewomen were absent for long periods, and vassals resident at their courts may have been tempted to think about obtaining their master's wife as a precious prize. Or perhaps the values of courtly love controlled and civilized the lustful impulses of vassals at court, bringing them to heel in obedience.

Courtly love is important because of its influence on all subsequent literature in the European languages. And this literature has shaped the Western tradition of romantic love. The yearning and the courting which were celebrated by a small social elite of the high Middle Ages, have for several centuries been accepted by ordinary people as the normal course of events leading to a sexual relationship—with the significant difference that the relationship now often includes marriage. Thus, the experience of love as it is understood in the Western world was first explored by the medieval nobility.

Women enthusiastically promoted courtly love. The wives, mothers, and daughters of great noblemen encouraged the knights of their courts to listen to the troubadours, staged the contests of love that the cult encouraged, and were often the objects of the romantic obsessions of their vassals. Queen Eleanor of Aquitaine (c. 1122–1204), who was married in turn to the king of France and the king of England, was the granddaughter of a man who was not only a patron but a poet himself. She grew up amid the courtly games of love and knew them intimately.

Women and Power Courtly love intrigues might amuse a medieval noblewoman whose experience was much harsher. For most of their lives noblewomen were pawns in the political strategies of fathers and husbands. They were married, sometimes at young ages, to the nobleman or king with whom their father considered an association most advantageous. With puberty, they were expected to give birth, for all the years of their fertility—perhaps twenty-five, if not cut short by death in childbirth, the commonest cause of death for women of childbearing age.

Noblewomen did not breastfeed their own infants but employed wet nurses. As a result, they did not experience the contraceptive effects of lactation and could expect to face a rapid cycle of pregnancy, birth, and new pregnancy. The burden of reproduction was inevitable because of the social assumptions of European noblemen. Although a nobleman's wife brought him fine properties or valuable alliances, her most important function was to produce a male heir—one who survived the perils of childhood. If a wife failed to do so, her husband might renounce her, with or without the approval of the Church.

Although noblewomen were powerless to choose husbands, homes, and way of life, the circumstances of medieval life often gave them power. When their husbands were away, women acted as their surrogates and were accorded due respect. If the family castle were attacked while her husband was away at war, the noblewoman defended it, directing the troops and standing in the zone of the battle, as depicted in the manuscript illumination on p. 239. If her husband were held for ransom in another lord's prison, she could call his retainers to meet to give counsel, to reaffirm their loyalty, and to raise funds. Most notably, noblewomen could rule lands for years after the death of their lords, while a young heir grew to adulthood. Young kings, too, often learned their leadership skills from a mother who, as regent, governed the kingdom after the death of the monarch.

WITNESSES

Noblewomen as Mothers and Lovers

Most medieval women—like most women throughout history—were mothers. Did they feel towards their children as mothers do today? The first two passages here suggest that they did. The first is by a ninth-century noblewoman who wrote a book to advise her exiled son, because she could not herself be with him. The second is by a prominent twelfth-century cleric, who fondly remembers his mother's affection for him. In contrast, the third passage concerns the passionate love between adult men and women, which medieval elites considered as existing only outside the institution of marriage.

The ninth-century noblewoman Dhuoda opens the book of advice written for her exiled son William: Having noticed that most women in this world are able to live with and enjoy their children, but seeing myself, Dhuoda, living far away from you, my dear son William, filled with anxiety because of this, and with the desire to be of aid to you, I am sending you this little manual, written by me, for your scrutiny and education, rejoicing in the fact that, though I am absent in body, this little book will recall to your mind, as you read it, the things you are required to do for my sake.
(From K. M. Wilson, *Medieval Women Writers*, 1984; trs. J. Marchand)

Abbot Guibert of Nogent (12th century) praises his mother: Yet you know, Almighty One, with what purity and holiness in obedience to you she raised me, how greatly she provided me with the care of nurses in infancy and of masters and teachers in boyhood, with no lack even of fine clothes for my little body, so that I seemed to equal the sons of kings and counts in indulgence. ...
(From J. F. Benton, *Self and Society in Medieval France: The Memoirs of Abbot Guibert of Nogent, 1064–c. 1125*)

In the words of Andrew the Chaplain (12th century), a nobleman explains to a noblewoman the nature of courtly love: But I am greatly surprised that you wish to misapply the term "love" to that marital affection which husband and wife are expected to feel for each other after marriage, since everybody knows that love can have no place between husband and wife. ... For what is love but an inordinate desire to receive passionately a furtive and hidden embrace? But what embrace between husband and wife can be furtive, I ask you, since they may be said to belong to each other. ...
(Andreas Capellanus, *Art of Courtly Love*; ed. J. J. Parry, 1941)

It was a fortunate mother who was able to nurture her young son at home. Many noblewomen saw their sons leave home at an early age to live in other households, as the passage reproduced in *Witnesses* above reveals. The child might be sent there to learn courtly graces and skills away from parental interference. In the early Middle Ages, especially, he often served as a hostage—his father having guaranteed a certain course of behavior by sending his child to live with a skeptical and possibly hostile lord. If the father failed to keep his promise, the child might be put to death, paying the price of his parent's duplicity. In such ways mothers often lost the company of their young sons. Their daughters more often stayed home, to learn from their mothers the skills of managing the intricacies of an aristocratic household until their own marriages.

In addition to the skills of conversation, household management, and defense, noblewomen acquired the traditional skills of textile production. Like peasant women on the manor, noblewomen spun thread and wove cloth. Whereas peasants wove the crude fabrics worn by ordinary folk, however, the lady created the fine tissues worn at court—embroidered and embellished or interwoven with silver or gold—and the bright banners held by knights in battle or a joust. One product of medieval women's needlework is the Bayeux Tapestry. When Duke William of Normandy ventured across the English Channel in 1066 to win the throne of England, the events of the conquest were recorded (tradition holds) by his wife and her companions on an embroidered strip of cloth (not, in fact, a tapestry) 230 feet (76 meters) long.

Defending the Kingdoms and the Faith

It was the nobleman's job to fight. It was a job he performed regularly, as medieval Europe was wracked by virtually constant warfare interrupted by respites of peace. Much of the fighting was internal, disruptive, and unnecessary, as nobles or kings competed with each other for land or advantage. Other warfare was necessary to defend the newly emerging communities of Europe against outsiders. Still other campaigns were fought to defend the interests, as it was thought, of Christians by rescuing the Holy Land from newly arrived Turkish overlords, or wresting the Iberian peninsula from Muslim rule, or completing the conversion of the peoples of Europe to Christianity.

Invaders The first struggles pitted young European communities against invaders from east, south, and north. From 500 to 700, while the memory of Roman rule was still vivid, Celts, Romans, and Greeks tried in vain to fend off Gothic and Vandal, Lombard and Frankish, Angle and Saxon invaders. Once settled, these erstwhile invaders in turn wheeled around to face new intruders: Avars (eventually destroyed), Slavs, and Bulgars, who settled down on Europe's eastern periphery. From 700 to 1000, new generations of combatants arrived to continue the onslaught.

The first of these were the "Moors," North African Muslims of mixed Arab and Berber descent (see Chapter 8). In 711 they moved northward into the

Noble Couples

Count Dirk II of Holland and his wife, Hildegard, 940–970

European noblemen were deeply concerned with the continuation of their lineage. Their wives, noblewomen of equivalent birth and fortune, were partners in a conjugal unit upon which the future of the lineage depended. These images give a hint of the solidarity that could be achieved by the noble couple. This manuscript (above) shows Count Dirk II of Holland and his wife Hildegard jointly donating a book to the Egmont monastery.

This sculpture (right) shows the crusader knight Hugo I of Vaudémont locked in a single stone block with his wife.

(top: Koninklijke Bibliothek, The Hague; right: Musée des Monuments Français, Paris)

Hugo I of Vaudémont and his wife, after 1163, Church of the Cordeliers, Nancy, France

To continue your investigation of this topic, please go to www.prenhall.com/king for the related WINDOWS on the WEB activity

Iberian peninsula (modern Spain and Portugal), which they quickly conquered. A century later, Arab invaders called, Saracens by contemporaries, struck at the southern coastline of Europe. They seized the island of Crete in 824 and thus confronted the Byzantine lords of the Aegean Sea. Three years later, Arabs conquered Byzantine outposts on the island of Sicily, effectively curtailing Greek influence in the western Mediterranean. Arab raiders had already helped themselves to numerous Mediterranean islands lying between Italy and Spain. From these posts they could contemplate further movements toward the mainland. The possession of these Mediterranean bases stimulated trade, which at first profited the conquerors but eventually benefited even the Europeans, whose ships traveled the ancient sea.

After 899, eastern Europe was attacked by the Magyars, ancestors of modern Hungarians who spoke a rare (non-Indo-European) Finno-Ugric language. These nomads raced across the Eurasian steppe as had the Germanic tribes and Huns before them. The Magyars' advance was stopped only by the combined forces of the Frankish king Otto I (r. 936–973) at the Battle of Lechfeld (in southeastern Germany) in 955. Like the Bulgars and the Slavs, the Magyars retreated a little eastward, settled and stayed.

In the 800s and 900s, the Vikings, or "Northmen," descended from the Scandinavian lands (modern Norway, Denmark, and Sweden). The Vikings were traders who roamed the Baltic and North seas and founded commercial depots on their coasts. When circumstances changed, they adapted easily to piracy. Spurred by poverty and overpopulation, they sailed swiftly along the shores of Europe in their elegantly designed long, shallow boats. Darting up rivers, deep into the centers of developing civilization, they raided, burned, and pillaged monasteries and villages, raping, kidnaping, and sometimes killing the inhabitants.

In time, the Viking incursions changed in nature. Instead of small groups of raiders, large armies arrived, headed by rulers seeking permanent settlement. In 911, one of these won from the cowering king of France a duchy of his own at the mouth of the river Seine—later known as Normandy. Another settled with his followers in a large section of eastern England (later designated as the Danelaw), and collected tribute from Anglo-Saxon peoples who had settled there not so long before. Others, mostly from Sweden and known as Varangians, journeyed down the Dvina and Dnieper river systems to settle in the western part of European Russia, where they established a capital at Kiev.

When the pressure of Viking incursions waned, European nobles proceeded to wage war against each other. These were profitable battles for clever landholders. They could build up their territorial holdings, their retinues, and their status. Over the generations, men of little property became great lords, and great lords fell to insignificance.

Crusaders Other noble warriors took part in a series of wars that would span three centuries and more, far from the European homeland. These were the Crusades (see Map 9.2), fought in the name of the cross on which Jesus had died in Jerusalem (and which pilgrims to that city used as an emblem on their clothing). Several circumstances combined to launch these wars of conquest. The embattled emperors of Byzantium, their own territories falling like dominoes to Turkish invaders, had requested assistance from the West. A newly vigorous, reformed papacy sought to extend the realm of **Christendom** and to arouse the faith of its followers. Italian traders, sparsely outfitted and meagerly supplied, sought to gain a presence in a Mediterranean dominated by Arab competitors. Landless knights, the younger sons of Europe's now-established nobility, sought land, adventure, and opportunities for advancement.

The event that triggered the first Crusade was the fall, in 1071, of the city of Jerusalem—holy to Christians, Muslims, and Jews—to the Seljuk Turks. An Asian people who had usurped the sovereignty of the Arab caliphs of Baghdad in 1055, the Seljuks had then advanced westward and northward. After their victory over the Byzantine army at Manzikert in 1071, they went on to conquer much of Asia Minor, the buffer between the Byzantine capital at Constantinople and the centers of Islamic civilization.

With Constantinople now endangered, the pope saw an opportunity to play a larger role in the eastern Mediterranean. In 1095 Pope Urban II issued a call to the nobility of Europe—not to defend the Byzantine remnant of the Roman Empire, but to recapture Jerusalem itself, as a Christian act meriting the remission of all sins. "God wills it!" shouted his followers. Large crusader armies set out under nobles ready to profit from any opportunities that battle afforded. In 1099 they captured Jerusalem, where they massacred both Muslim and Jewish inhabitants. Seizing the coastal strip that forms part of the modern nations of Syria, Lebanon, and Israel, the crusaders established states on a European model which would endure into the thirteenth century in the midst of a Greek, Turkish, Arab, and Islamic world.

When the crusader state of Edessa fell to the Turks in 1144, Church leaders launched the Second Crusade (1147–1148). It failed to achieve any useful end. The recapture of Jerusalem in 1187, by Saladin, the king of Egypt and Syria (r. 1186–1193), precipitated the Third Crusade (1189–1192), which was headed by three of Europe's monarchs: Frederick Barbarossa of the Holy Roman Empire, Philip Augustus of France, and Richard I, "the Lion-Hearted," of England. Little was accomplished. Jerusalem remained lost (although the theoretical right of pilgrims to visit that capital was assured), along with most other crusader possessions.

The major beneficiaries of the first three Crusades were the Italian trading cities who ferried supplies to

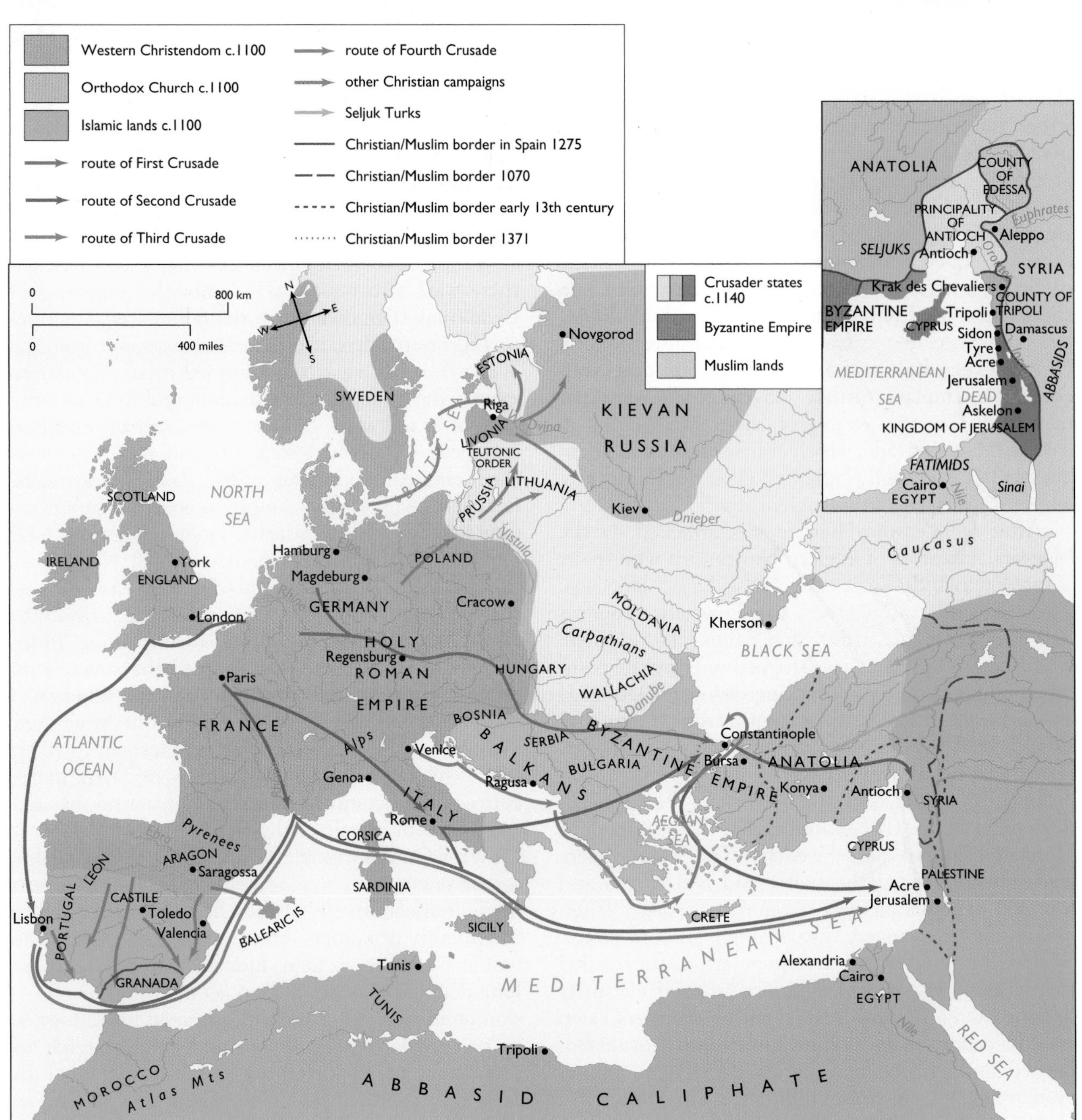

Map 9.2 Seljuk Advance and the Crusades, 1071–1204: *The Seljuk Turks, having defeated Byzantine defenders of Anatolia (Asia Minor) in 1071 at Manzikert, soon dominated the Near East and threatened Constantinople. European armies traveled east in successive ventures—the Crusades—beginning in 1096 and continuing into the fifteenth century. The first arrivals established a Latin Kingdom in the Near East which endured only a few generations, but had tremendous impact on European culture and commerce. In 1204, crusaders traveling eastward to recapture Jerusalem were diverted by Venetian paymasters to the conquest of Constantinople.*

the troops. One of these, Venice, was the principal actor in the Fourth Crusade (1202–1204), which the Venetians diverted in 1204 to serve their own interests. With a ruthlessness at odds with every Christian precept, Venice employed the crusader army to capture, sack, and control Constantinople, the home of Eastern Orthodox Christianity and purported ally of the western European force. The result was—as Venice intended—to enhance its own commercial foothold in the eastern Mediterranean.

A bizarre variation on the crusading idea was the so-called Children's Crusade (1212), in which thousands of children, aged between ten and fourteen, set off to retake Jerusalem themselves. Virtually all its little soldiers died or were taken into slavery long before reaching the east. Later Crusades gave opportunity for glory to eager noblemen, kings, and popes, but failed to reassert the dominance of Latin leaders. The whole crusade movement closed painfully and finally in 1453, when the Ottoman Turks (successors to the Seljuks) overran the region and seized Constantinople. Its magnificent church of Santa Sophia was converted into a mosque. The crusading spirit was not dead; it would reemerge in various guises in later European ventures against non-Christians all over the globe (see Chapter 16).

Although the Crusades did not succeed in their original objective—the permanent conquest of the Holy Land for Christendom—they had enormous consequences for the development of Europe. Knights and kings had contact with a world outside Europe, and learned much from an alien and in many ways superior culture. Italian ship captains and sailors took command of the Mediterranean Sea, and brought the luxury goods of Asia back to European ports while they mastered the techniques of international commerce. With the Crusades begins the opening up of Europe to the outer world which has continued steadily since that time.

By 1300, crusading zeal had slackened, while the nobility of western Europe had reached the zenith of its military prowess. Another great conflict—the Hundred Years' War (1337–1453)—absorbed the attention of the knights of France and England intermittently over the last years of the Middle Ages. It caused great devastation in France, while leaving the political situation little changed. England, the aggressor, possessed considerable French territory at the beginning of the struggle, only a foothold at its close. In 1453, devastated France set about to repair its wounds and reform its monarchy. The English then entered upon the debilitating Wars of the Roses (1455–1485), which saw rival claimants to the throne and their noble supporters savage each other over two generations, until in that country, too, rebuilding began.

One outcome of the Hundred Years' War was to retire the weapons and tactics of medieval warfare, and with them the assumption of knightly invincibility. They were surpassed on the battlefield in three signal contests all won by massed English infantrymen equipped with their native longbow. At Crécy in 1346, at Poitiers in 1356, and at Agincourt in 1415, the English defeated superior numbers of French. That third victory conveyed a lesson that the new French king, Charles VII (r. 1422–1461), at last absorbed. Before the curtain was drawn on the war in 1453, he had constructed a national army on the basis of infantry and artillery units. Between the English tactical innovations and the French model of military organization, modern warfare took root from the last stale conflict of the Middle Ages (see Chapter 15).

KINGS

In the early Middle Ages, warrior nobles had seized leadership at a time when chaos and invasion prevailed, often overshadowing the petty kings of Europe. Over the next five centuries kings emerged as sovereigns of the new nations of Europe. Seeking to maximize their own authority, these powerful leaders also sought to bring order to the fragmentary and quarreling communities of their region. They cobbled together orderly states by enlisting the cooperation of nobles and commoners. In doing so, they borrowed the administrative methods of the Roman Church, which shared the goal of bringing order to Europe, or availed themselves of the skills of its prelates. Most of the modern nations of Europe originated from the ordered domains of medieval lords who compelled others to regard them as kings. What follows is a survey of the progress of monarchy in the core regions of Europe—France, England, and the German lands—and on its periphery.

Charlemagne's Empire

Charlemagne (r. 768–814) was the greatest figure of the Carolingian dynasty which had seized power over the Frankish kingdom from the Merovingian dynasty installed by Clovis. He has already been introduced as the architect of the ninth-century cultural renewal called the "Carolingian Renaissance," a key moment in the formation of Western civilization (see Chapter 8). Had he accomplished nothing more, this Charles would have deserved his title Charlemagne, or "Charles the Great." Other accomplishments as significant in the realm of politics, however, secure him that honor. Charlemagne harnessed the might of his nobles, choosing able men—as many as 250 counts—and supervising them systematically. He sent out to the far reaches of his domain special agents who scrutinized the performance of the nobles and listened to appeals from the aggrieved. His treasurers and secretaries kept careful records of the people and products in his own domains. Decrees specified just how the harvest should be counted, and under what circumstances serf women should work.

Like others whom history has deemed "Great," Charlemagne was also a conqueror. He extended the limits of the Frankish kingdom deep into Italy, down to the Pyrenees, and east beyond the Rhine into the land the Romans had called "Germany," the home of still-pagan Saxon tribes whom he forcibly converted to Christianity. Charlemagne's empire at its height comprised much of modern Italy and Germany, and all of modern Belgium, the Netherlands, Austria, and Switzerland, in addition to buffer zones, or marches, in northern Spain and eastern Europe.

Charlemagne's interventions in Italy won him the support of the Church, which could no longer rely on the protection of the emperor in the east. In 774 Charlemagne assisted the pope, Adrian I, by conquering the kingdom of the Lombards and so releasing the papacy from their domination. In 799, he came to the assistance of Pope Leo III, the near-victim of a Roman conspiracy, and had him reinstated. On Christmas Day, 800, in Rome, Leo crowned Charlemagne "emperor of the Romans"—a title better than that of king, for as emperor he became the successor to the successors of the great Augustus. This revival of the Western Empire would be the basis of the concept, still to mature, of a Holy Roman Empire, a Christianized European simulacrum of ancient Rome.

At the time of his death, Charlemagne ruled vast territories from which many of the future states of western Europe would be carved. On his death in 814, his empire descended to his one son, Louis the Pious (r. 814–840), and then to his three grandsons. Their squabbles over the division of that inheritance, begun even before the death of their father, fractured the unified state Charlemagne had erected. These disputes were resolved in the Treaty of Verdun, one of Europe's earliest, in 843. By its terms, Charles the Bald (r. 843–877) received the western zone, consisting largely of parts of modern France; Louis the German (r. 817–875) received the eastern zone, consisting largely of parts of modern Germany; and Lothair (r. 843–855) received the narrow ribbon of territories running between the two. Those territories included parts of modern Belgium, the oft-disputed provinces of Alsace, Lorraine, and Burgundy, and patches of northern and central Italy. Each heir received a slice of the empire Charlemagne had built, and now was no more.

France: The Patient Capetians

In the western zone of Charlemagne's empire, the developing kingdom of France, his descendants struggled for 150 years to hold power. When the last Carolingian king died in 987, the nobles bypassed his available Carolingian descendants and elected one of their own company to succeed to the throne. Their choice was deliberate: a weak king posed no threat to lords intent on expanding their own power.

The man they chose was Hugh Capet (r. 987–996), whose realm consisted initially of the minuscule territory called the Ile de France ("island of France") in which sat the then obscure town of Paris. Hugh soon died, but he had a son, and so on for fourteen successions—an unequaled example of dynastic success. The sheer biological tenacity of these Capetian kings was perhaps the most important ingredient of their achievement. Confounding the expectations of the great lords, Hugh Capet's descendants held the monarchy for more than 300 years.

With the conquest, in 1202–1204, of the duchy of Normandy and other territories, the reigning Capetian, Philip II (called "Philip Augustus"; r. 1179–1223), was now master of a state that was beginning to look like France and was the leading nation of Europe. Paris was a populous city, with paved streets and new wall, a royal fortress (the Louvre), a partially completed cathedral (Notre Dame); and it was home of one of Europe's first and most influential universities. These achievements must be credited to Philip Augustus, who also centralized royal administration and finances.

The successors of Philip Augustus continued to expand the territory, efficiency, and prestige of France. In 1302–1303, his great great-grandson Philip IV (called "the Fair"; r. 1285–1314) presided over the first Estates-General, one of the representative assemblies that are the ancestors of modern Western congresses and parliaments. Philip's ruthless acquisition of some of the wealth of the Church for the royal coffers (his nickname refers to his good looks, not to any sense of fairness) enhanced both his financial and his political position. His three sons succeeded him in turn, the last of the Capetian line. Their cousin, the first of the Valois dynasty, ascended the throne as Philip VI (r. 1328–1350) in 1328.

The first century or so of Valois rule was dominated by the Hundred Years' War with England, which brought foreign occupation and the devastation of the countryside. Yet postwar recovery came swiftly under Charles VII. That vacillating young man had received his crown through the efforts of Joan of Arc (see Chapter 10), but lived to reorganize France's army, its finances, and its relationship with

WHO'S WHO

Kings, Queens, and Peasants

Alfred the Great, King of Wessex (849–899) scholar and patron who held off the Danes during the Viking invasions and laid the foundations for the English monarchy.

Otto I the Great, Emperor (912–973) established the Holy Roman Empire in Germany and met the Magyar onslaught at Lechfeld (955).

William I (the Conqueror) of England (1027–1087) led a successful invasion of England in 1066 and established the Norman monarchy, the foundation of modern English governance.

Eleanor of Aquitaine (1122?–1204) divorced and remarried; a political pawn who grew powerful enough to gain both respect and hatred; mother of two kings of England, Richard I and John.

Philip IV the Fair, King of France (1268–1314) asserted royal power against the papacy.

John Ball and Wat Tyler (died 1381) peasant rebels in England.

Ivan III the Great, Grand Duke of Moscow (1440–1505) threw off Mongol domination; reined in the nobles and pronounced Moscow to be the "Third Rome."

Ferdinand II, King of Aragon (r. 1479–1516) and Isabella, Queen of Castile (r. 1474–1504) as joint rulers, they completed the Reconquest, expelled the Jews, and sent Columbus westward across the Atlantic.

Crowning the king: *Medieval kings gradually elevated themselves above their noblemen by military power, financial maneuvering, and deft use of symbols and rituals. Yet by the end of the Middle Ages nobles and even commoners began to resist by asserting rights and creating new constitutional principles. This fourteenth-century manuscript shows the coronation of a king, with ecclesiastical and secular lords. The vessels near his shoulder held the oil with which he was anointed.* (Master and Fellows of Corpus Christi College, Cambridge, England)

Rome. His son Louis XI (r. 1461–1483) continued in the tradition of his most effective predecessors: he expanded the territory of France, fending off neighbors and enemies alike, centralized the bureaucracy, increased the flow of revenue, and encouraged industrial and commercial growth.

England: The Heritage of Conquest

The building of the English nation was a task already begun by the descendants of Angle, Saxon, and Danish invaders over the five centuries before 1066. In that year, Duke William of Normandy (in modern France; r. 1066–1087), himself a descendant of Viking raiders, invaded the island; within about five years he had made the kingdom his own. William and his successors asserted royal authority, establishing systems for the collection of taxes, the summoning of armies, and the administration of justice. By 1500, despite the long disruption of the Wars of the Roses, tiny England was one of the best-managed nations in Europe.

During the chaotic 400s, the Saxons, Angles, and Jutes, all northern Germanic peoples, had overrun Britain, destroying the remains of Roman settlement and undoing the process of Christianization. Saxon kings proceeded to form their own miniature kingdoms (Wessex, Essex, Sussex, and Mercia); they accepted Christianity in the sixth and seventh centuries as a result of two waves of missionary effort, from, respectively, Ireland and Rome.

In the late ninth century, the king of Wessex ("West Saxony") remained as the one strong Anglo-Saxon leader in a land largely occupied by Danes. King Alfred (r. 871–899), called the Great, not only ruled the nation that was the germ of modern England and began the process of reconquest from the Danes but also, like Charlemagne, instituted a cultural revival, patronizing scholars and furthering education. A Latin scholar himself, he translated into English such fundamental works as Boethius' *Consolation of Philosophy* and the *Pastoral Care* of Pope Gregory the Great (c. 540–604), a manual outlining the duties of priests. In doing so, he helped to create what would become the language of Chaucer (c. 1345–1400) and Shakespeare (1564–1616).

Under Alfred's leadership, a unified English kingdom took form (neatly organized into administrative units called "shires"), with one established religion and one accepted code of law. The Danes were confined to a region in northern and eastern England called the Danelaw. Alfred's England was the first nation of Europe since Rome to achieve such integration. Although the unity would be disturbed after Alfred's death (899), it would soon be regained under a new line of kings.

Alfred's successors continued the struggle against invaders. For a brief period in the eleventh century, the Danish monarch Cnut (or Canute; r. 1016–1035) dominated the English kingdom. After several years of instability, the Anglo-Saxon king Edward (r. 1042–1066), called "the Confessor" in recognition of his exceptional piety, regained the kingdom.

On Edward's death in 1066, two claimants for his throne presented themselves simultaneously: his brother-in-law Harold (who immediately resumed the endless job of repelling invaders from the north) and his kinsman William, Duke of Normandy. According to William, Harold himself had sworn to uphold his claim. When Harold showed no sign of stepping aside, William promptly launched an invasion of England. Harold had no sooner defeated a combined force of English rebels and Norwegians at Stamford Bridge in the north when he was summoned to Hastings on the Channel coast in the south to meet the Norman army. He was crushed. The Normans and their descendants have held the throne of England (apart from 1649–1660; see Chapter 15) ever since.

William was not only a successful soldier but an efficient ruler. He seized the lands of virtually all the English lords and parceled them out to his own followers. As he did so, he reorganized the conditions of land tenure on the Norman model, so that most of the major lords owed obedience directly to the king. His officials compiled a systematic inventory of English land, down to the number of cattle on each manor (called the Domesday Book, presumably because there was no appeal against it, just as there would be none on Doomsday). The Norman knights who acquired land tenures by William's actions owed allegiance directly to him. Boldly, William had managed to establish structures of authority linked to landholding, ensuring that in England power remained centered in the king.

William's successors continued to centralize systems of law. Royal officials travelling to local courts established the supremacy of royal justice and created the **common law**. Compounded of both customary and Roman elements, common law was the law that would be enforced by the king's courts. It came to override local custom and became common to all inhabitants. It has had a continuous history from the twelfth century to the present.

Equally fundamental was the Norman monarchy's reordering of finances. From every corner of England, officials brought taxes due the king to the Exchequer, the office of the treasurer at Winchester (later relocated to Westminster, in London). There, a method of accounting was employed that was meaningful even to the illiterate stewards of the day. Wooden sticks notched to indicate the amount tendered were split in two, one half remaining with the royal treasurer, the other returning with the local representative. These sticks, called "tallies," performed essentially the same function as multi-paged carbon forms do today. An unbroken record of these transactions extends from the twelfth century onward.

William's conquest of England gave the king ascendancy over the nobility, making England the first European state to balance the principles of centralization of power and local governance. Some 150 years later, in 1215, the barons of England who were restive under the autocratic King John (r. 1199–1216), compelled that monarch to sign an agreement known as *Magna Carta* ("Great Charter"). It too aimed at a balance between the power of the king and the prerogatives of his nobility.

Although the *Magna Carta* was concerned only with regulating the relations between kings and lords, this medieval document stated principles that would later be brilliantly developed for wider purposes. It stated for the first time the guarantee that lies at the heart of the Anglo-American concept of freedom: that "no free man shall be arrested, or imprisoned, or deprived of his property, or outlawed, or exiled, ... unless by legal judgment of his peers or by the law of the land." Two other principles developed from clauses of the *Magna Carta* gained prominence in the seventeenth century, when the revolutionary movements began that yielded the English constitution and its offspring in the United States. These are the principles that the king was not to pass laws without consulting those who would be compelled to obey them; and that the king was subject to the law of the whole land. The *Magna Carta* did not create a modern democracy. But it

WITNESSES

Kings at Work

In contrast to later periods, in the turbulent Middle Ages many people looked to kings to administer order and justice. The first two passages praise the English King Henry II and French King Louis IX for doing just that. The third argues that a harmonious world can only be achieved by obedience to a powerful monarch.

The chronicler William of Newburgh describes the ascension of Henry II of England (1154): In the year 1154, Henry ... came into England ... [and] received there his hereditary kingdom, ... was consecrated king with the holy oil, while all the people throughout the kingdom exclaimed, "Long live the king!" Having experienced the unhappiness of the former reign in which so many evils had arisen, all hoped for better things from the new king, especially since ... a great zeal for justice seemed to possess him, and since he already gave the appearance of a great leader in his very first acts. ... Especially did he take care of the public order, and that the strength of the law might be felt again in England. ...
(From E. P. Cheyney, *Readings in English History drawn from the Original Sources*, 1935)

The thirteenth-century French King Louis IX administers justice (c. 1280): In summer, after hearing mass, the king often went to the wood of Vincennes, where he would sit down with his back against an oak, and make us sit all around him. Those who had any suit to present could come to speak to him without hindrance from an usher or any other person. The king would address them directly, and ask: "Is there any one here who has a case to be settled?" Those who had one would stand up. Then he would say: "Keep silent all of you, and you shall be heard in turn, one after the other."
(Jean de Joinville: "The Life of St. Louis," *Chronicles of the Crusades*; ed. M. R. B. Shaw 1963)

The Florentine poet Dante argues that a powerful monarch is necessary for the good of the world (1310/1316): A single kingdom. ... should have one king who rules and governs it. If not, not only do those living in the kingdom not achieve their goals, but the kingdom itself also falls into ruin. ... The whole human race is ordered to one end, ... [and] should have one ruler or sovereign who can be called the "Monarch" or "Emperor." And so it is evident that for the world's well-being there is necessary a Monarchy or Empire.
(Dante, *Monarchia*; ed. P. G. Ricci, 1965, trs. M. L. King 1997)

enunciated assumptions that would become essential to modern democratic constitutions.

John's grandson Edward I (r. 1272–1307) extended the principle of consultation. It had been commonplace for the king to consult with the lords of his realm (who constituted a *curia*, or court) in a session called a *parliamentum* (literally, a session for "talking together"). John had run into trouble when he failed to do this. Three times in the reign of John's son Henry III (r. 1216–1272), the parliament met with enhanced membership, including elected representatives of the knights of each shire and, twice, with representatives of the town (called burgesses). Henry's grandson Edward remembered this practice and turned it from a device for managing a crisis to a feature of government for preventing one. Edward's Model Parliament of 1295 is an important landmark in the development of that assembly. Not long after his death, the knights and burgesses assembled in London in what became the House of Commons, while the great lords continued to meet together in what came to be called the House of Lords. Both chambers of Parliament continue to sit to this day.

From Henry II (who ascended in 1154) through Richard III (who was killed in 1485), members of the Plantagenet, Lancaster, and York branches of William the Conqueror's family ruled England in turn. The 1300s and 1400s were occupied by their struggles for supremacy, accompanied by conspiracy, murder, and warfare. During the same period, the English kings fought in France in the Hundred Years' War. Despite the turbulence of this era, English institutions—the monarchy and system of shires, the common law, the courts of justice, and Parliament—all survived. By the end of the Middle Ages, England was a small kingdom compared to populous France. But it was well organized and prepared to assume an important role in the world of nations that would follow.

The Empire: Two Romes in Conflict

Although Charlemagne's empire was split up after his death, the idea of a Western European Empire—a successor to Rome—lived on. Charlemagne's grandson Lothair, ruler of the central kingdom, retained the title of emperor. But the further partitioning of this middle kingdom under his successors left a power vacuum in this region, and during the tenth century, the eastern Frankish kingdom (modern Germany) asserted its own right to be considered the heir to Rome. In this it received, at first, the support of the papacy; but conflict soon emerged between these two powers. The Rome of the popes had political and territorial ambitions over and above its spiritual role as the seat of Latin Christendom, while the new secular, or temporal, "Rome" of the German emperors not only competed with the Church in the political realm but also assumed some ecclesiastical powers. Its claims to supremacy are expressed in the titles that came in the thirteenth century to preface that of "Empire": "Holy" and "Roman."

During the one hundred years or so following Charlemagne's death in 814, the eastern Frankish kingdom had suffered both from repeated invasions from the east and from political fragmentation within its boundaries. In the absence of a strong central monarchy, the German dukes managed the defense of their own lands and ultimately took it on themselves to elect their kings. When Louis (called "the Child"), the last of Charlemagne's descendants to rule this kingdom, died in 911, the dukes elected as king one of the weakest of their number, Conrad of Franconia (r. 911–918). On his death, seeing the losses incurred by Conrad's ineffectiveness, they elected the strongest: Henry the Fowler, Duke of Saxony (r. 919–936). Henry's successors included the most brilliant ruler of the century, Otto I, victor over the Magyars at Lechfeld, who was crowned emperor by the pope in 962. In 1024, the imperial election went to a different Conrad, founder of the Salian line, which reigned until 1125, through the whole period of papal reform (see Chapter 10), which was to present a challenge to imperial ambitions.

In the absence of a dynastic monarchy, in which power descended on hereditary lines, no unified government or generalized system of law took hold in the imperial lands. The ruler was never able to subordinate the dukes and other great nobles whose interests tended to undermine the structure of government power. Instead, the German emperors looked to the Church as a source of loyal and skilled administrators. These could serve the emperor as the territorial lords could not. The choice was logical, but it had a flaw. Beginning in the eleventh century, the popes opposed the control of clerical offices to further the interests of a secular state. The tension between empire and papacy mounted. It climaxed in 1076, during the reign of Henry IV (r. 1056–1106) when the pope forced the Emperor to yield on the issue of the appointment of clergy by secular rulers.

No longer permitted to exploit the expertise of the clergy for political purposes, Henry's successors sought other ways to consolidate their power. In the German lands, they won the cooperation of territorial lords and free cities. They aimed at center the empire, however, in Italy, where imperial sovereignty might be established, rather than in Germany, where all such attempts seemed to fail. These were the ambitions of Frederick I and II, two rulers of the Hohenstaufen dynasty which held the imperial title from 1138 to 1254. The former tried but failed to establish his sovereignty in northern Italy. The latter did establish a power base in southern Italy, where he had been born and where, as the son of a German father and a Sicilian mother (of Sicily's Norman royal house), he had a cosmopolitan background suitable for this polyglot, ethnically mixed region. But after his death the papacy and its allies among the northern Italian city-states threw off the German imperial yoke.

By the mid-fifteenth century, the Habsburg family had gained preeminence as the imperial rulers of the German lands. In 1477, the future emperor Maximilian (r. 1493–1519) married Mary, the heiress to the rich duchy of Burgundy and attached county of Flanders. Their son Philip married Joanna, the heiress to the Spanish kingdoms of Aragon and Castile and became Philip I of Spain. Their eldest son, Charles, not only inherited Spain, which he ruled as Charles I from 1516, but also became emperor, as Charles V, from 1519 until his death in 1556. With title to Spain, the Netherlands, Burgundy, and the German realm, he was the greatest monarch on the continent.

The moment of imperial supremacy in Europe soon passed. The Habsburg realms were divided in two, with Spain going its own way and the German Habsburgs continuing the tradition of the empire. The failure of the empire to assume a strong role in the post-medieval world began with its foundation. Although it was medieval Europe's dominant political structure, the empire never achieved the organizational sophistication of little England or the wealth and muscle of France. Despite the luster of the "Roman" name, these monarchs were unable to concentrate power in their hands or to establish a single dynasty that ruled by hereditary right, or to disenfranchise the other territorial lords of the huge Germanic domain. By the eighteenth century the empire was something of a joke—in the scornful but apt judgment of the French writer Voltaire (1694–1778), it was "neither holy, nor Roman, nor an Empire." In 1806, it ceased to be.

The European Core and Periphery

As Map 9.3 indicates, the German lands and the kingdoms of England and France constituted the core regions of western, Christian Europe in the Middle Ages. Here lordship was most developed, the manorial system was most deeply entrenched, and the foundations of modern monarchical states were laid. Around the periphery of this European core, other political units were forming. But they followed courses tied to their differing origins and circumstances.

Stretching northeastward from France along the English Channel and North Sea were the Low Countries of Flanders and Holland (in modern Belgium and the Netherlands). Already in late antiquity, cloth made by the people of Flanders was a valuable commodity of international trade when Europe had scarcely any other. Later, the towns of the Low Countries were pioneers in international commerce in the northern European waterways. Alternately subject to the kings of France and to the emperors of the German lands, these areas did not develop their own monarchies during the Middle Ages. Instead, their flourishing towns were subject to the local governance of secular or ecclesiastical lords.

Along the northwestern rim of Europe, Ireland and Scotland (inhabited by peoples of Celtic origin) and Iceland (settled by the Vikings during the ninth and tenth centuries) retained their ancient organization by clan and tribe—and would do so into recent times. The Scandinavian homelands, as has been seen, gave birth to the Viking raids and migrations, while developing their distinctive culture. In this era the Viking sagas were compiled—the last European folk epics—and the Norwegian, Danish, and Swedish people established monarchies of their own.

The Swedish Varangians, who had expanded into Russia from the early 800s and vanquished the resident Slavs, established their capital at Kiev. Christianized by Byzantine missionaries, Kievan Russia grew wealthy from trade with Constantinople. The Kievan state fell to the Mongol invasion that hammered Asia and Europe in the thirteenth century. Organized as the Khanate of the Golden Horde, the Mongols dominated Russia from 1240 to 1480.

In the fourteenth century, Ivan I (r. 1328–1341), the native prince of Moscow, gained the confidence of Mongol overlords and succeeded in undermining their governance. Under his rule, the Grand Duchy of Moscow emerged as the center of Russian civilization and the germ of the modern state of Russia. A century later, Ivan III (r. 1462–1505), called "the Great," won independence from Mongol domination and gained sovereignty over the other Russian princes. Married to the niece of the last Byzantine emperor (whose realm had fallen to the Turks in 1453), he pronounced Moscow the successor to Constantinople as the central Christian **see**—the "Third Rome." His grandson Ivan IV (1533–1584) pursued the imagery further, naming himself head of the Eastern Orthodox Church and taking the title of *Tsar* ("Caesar").

Among some of Russia's neighbors, too, Christianization led to the development of young monarchies. Soon after the year 1000, in Poland, Hungary, and Bulgaria, kingdoms were established. The Baltic lands, extending from Denmark to Russia along the Baltic Sea, were a special case. Still pagan in 1000, this last European frontier became the special mission of the order of Teutonic Knights, who slowly established Christian worship and Western governance in the region. The most concerted resistance to conversion came from Lithuania, which expanded after 1300 to include parts of Russia, Belarus (Byelorussia), and Ukraine. Once joined to Poland by dynastic ties in 1383, Lithuania at last accepted Roman Catholic Christianity and joined its neighbors in becoming part of European Christendom. Deep in eastern Europe, the culture of Prussia, Lithuania, Latvia, and Estonia was Western.

Although it had been Christian before the Middle Ages began, Mediterranean Europe did not form independent monarchies as early as other parts of western Europe. The unification of Italy achieved by the Romans in the first century B.C.E., then shattered in the fifth century C.E., would not be restored for fourteen hundred years. During the Middle Ages, Italy was an ever-shifting patchwork of jurisdictions. The kingdom established by the Lombards and taken over by Charlemagne gradually withered after the ninth century. The Byzantine outposts at Ravenna and in southern Italy and Sicily were lost to that Empire in the Middle Ages. In this vacuum of authority, territorial lords and local towns took charge.

In the eleventh century, the new island city of Venice in the northeast retained a titular loyalty to Byzantium. To the interior, the areas of Lombardy and Tuscany were the home of flourishing towns. These were ruled by a consortium of local lords and urban merchant elites, who were amassing the capital that would launch the European commercial revolution. Some were also creating political institutions that would help shape the modern state system. Across the center of the peninsula stretched the belt of the Papal States. Patched together from donations fictitious and real and ruled, sometimes directly, sometimes only nominally, by the pope, the Papal States lasted until 1870. The last vestige of these holdings, today's Vatican City, is an independent state within the boundaries of Italy's capital at Rome. Southern Italy and Sicily formed yet another region, heavily influenced by its Greek and Arab populations, ruled successively by Norman, German, French, and Spanish monarchs. Its cultural variety made it a fertile source

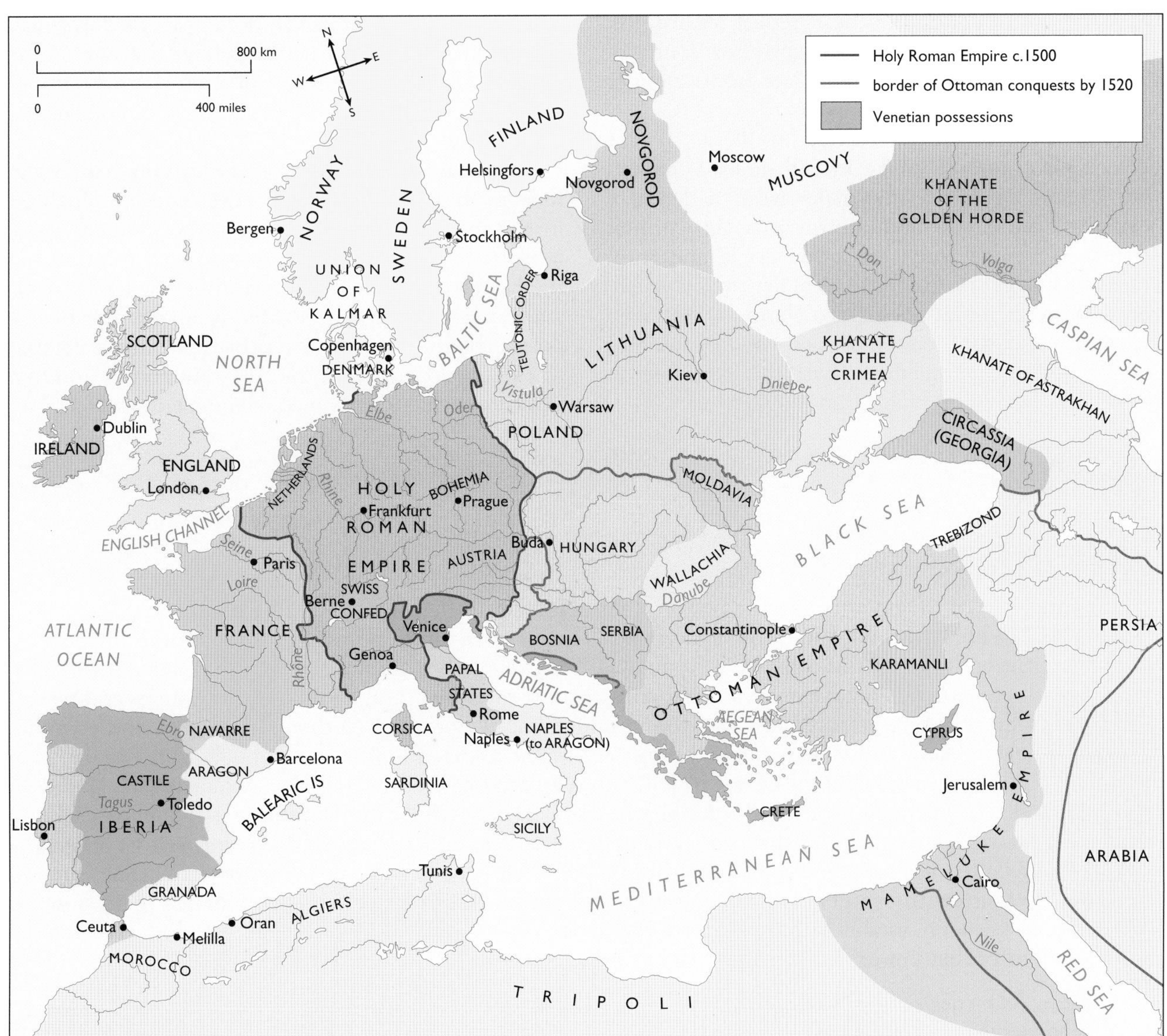

Map 9.3 European States in 1453: *The process of state-building that had occupied European monarchs and other territorial rulers during the Middle Ages produced a constellation of kingdoms, principalities, and city-states very different in 1453 (the year Constantinople fell to the Ottoman Turks) than it had been in 500 (see Map 8.1, p. 200) or during the later phase (beginning in the eighth century) of invasion (see Map 9.1, p. 236).*

of innovations in thought and literature that helped shape the civilization of late-medieval Europe.

To Italy's east, the small states of the Balkan region broke free of Byzantium during the era of the Crusades, then became subject to the Ottoman Turks from the late fourteenth century. To the west, the Iberian peninsula was the setting for a dramatic confrontation of Arabic and European cultures. There, from the fifth century, Visigothic invaders had established a unified kingdom under their Arian Christian monarchs (converted to Catholic Christianity by 600). The Visigoth kingdom was home to an early medieval civilization that flourished when the rest of Europe had reached a cultural nadir. The promising career of the Visigothic realm was cut short in 711 C.E., when Islamic invaders from North Africa conquered nearly the whole of the peninsula. The only Christian settlements that survived were Léon and Asturias, far to the north in the shadow of the Pyrenees Mountains. Charlemagne established the region just south of the Pyrenees as a Spanish "march," or frontier buffer state, the germ of the later kingdom of Aragon.

The Islamic state established in Iberia in 711 became a separate caliphate in 929 under Umayyad rule. Islamic Spain was the major western depot of Mediterranean trade and an unsurpassed cultural center. At a time when the crude noble and royal courts of Europe to the north kept records, if at all, through the labors of one or two clerics, the Islamic cities promoted the creation of poetry and music, philosophy and law and medicine with the participation of Muslim, Jewish, and Christian scholars.

By 1100, the Christian states in the north of Spain had begun the enormous task of "*Reconquista*," the reconquest of the whole peninsula from Islamic rule. Led by the kingdom of Castile (founded in 1035), this project succeeded, by 1252, in bringing most of the Iberian lands under a variety of Christian dominions. The final Islamic stronghold of Granada fell to Christian forces in 1492. It did so after a concerted offensive mounted by the two monarchs of Aragon and Castile, respectively Ferdinand (r. 1479–1516) and Isabella (r. 1474–1504), whose marriage permitted their joint rule from 1479 and the concentration of military strength needed for that purpose. The royal pair clinched their military victory with a cultural show of force: a purge of all non-Christian elements. They expelled from the kingdom all unconverted Muslims and Jews (whose leaders were closely identified with the Muslim regime). This accomplished, they proceeded to persecute with notorious cruelty, through the arm of the Spanish **Inquisition**, those converts whose loyalty to the Catholic faith and the new monarchy was subject to any doubt.

In about 1000, medieval civilization had begun to form in a cluster of small states and principalities in the west of Europe. By 1300, the foundations of modern England and France were well formed, and the Holy Roman Empire was still regarded as an overmastering state. By 1500, nearly all the regions of Europe had formed the bases of their modern states, and were participants in the Western civilization that was the product of the medieval experience.

Conclusion

POWER, PRIVILEGE, PROTEST, AND THE MEANING OF THE WEST

The privileges of the nobility and the power of kings forged in the Middle Ages would shape the social and political life of the West into the modern era. They emerged in response to the conditions of chaos and destitution left after the collapse of Roman authority. Together, nobles and kings provided security and developed Europe's fundamental judicial and governmental institutions. By 1500, the states and territories of Europe were prepared to foster the development of European culture, technology, and economy—a development that would enable the tiny continent to extend influence throughout the globe.

The whole edifice of medieval society rested, however, on the labor of its workers—mostly serfs bound to the land. They benefited from the order Europe's leaders created. At the same time they suffered, subject to the vagaries of nature, the exactions of landholders, and the restrictions imposed by rulers. Peasants rebelled against the weight of authority, but their rebellions were everywhere, in time, suppressed. In fourteenth-century England, one of the last of these medieval uprisings culminated in the confrontation between established power and the masses of human beings who questioned the very foundations of that power. The revolutionary priest John Ball asked:

> *When Adam delved [dug] and Eve span,*
> *Who was then the gentleman?*

This verse must have sparked the imagination of peasants who, like Piers the Plowman, struggled to feed their children as the lords of the earth accumulated wealth and power. The extinction of aristocratic privilege and royal power was already anticipated in these words.

REVIEW QUESTIONS

1. Who were the serfs? Why did so many peasants in Europe become serfs? What particular innovations increased agricultural productivity in the early Middle Ages?

2. What was a medieval manor? What role did serf women play in the medieval manor? How did the Black Death benefit those peasants who survived it?

3. Why did a warrior nobility emerge in medieval Europe? What were the main features of a "feudal" society? What role could women of the nobility play in the Middle Ages?

4. What type of warfare absorbed the energies of the medieval nobility? Why did the popes launch the Crusades? How did the Crusades influence European development?

5. How did medieval kings lay the foundation for the modern nations of Europe? Why does Charlemagne deserve the title "the Great"? What was significant about his coronation as emperor by the pope?

6. How did the kings of France expand the authority of the French state? What was the significance of the *Magna Carta* for English institutions? Why did the Holy Roman Empire fail to become a unified state?

SUGGESTED RESOURCES

Workers

Génicot, Léopold, *Rural Communities in the Medieval West* (Baltimore, MD: Johns Hopkins University Press, 1990). An overview of village economy, legal structures, and parishes in medieval Europe.

Hanawalt, Barbara A., *The Ties That Bound: Peasant Families in Medieval England* (Oxford/New York: Oxford University Press, 1989). A study of the medieval English peasant household, kinship ties, childhood, marriage, old age and death, neighborhoods, and brotherhoods.

Moore, R.I., *The First European Revolution* (Basil Blackwell, 2000). Argues that Europe underwent its first and most important transformation 1000–1300, when masses of people were recruited by competing elites into the political process.

Rösener, Werner, *Peasants in the Middle Ages* (New York: Polity Press, 1996). A study of Central European peasants, including house and farmyard, clothing, labor, sociability, kinship, relationships with lords, legal status, rebellions, and the late medieval crisis.

TeBrake, William H., *A Plague of Insurrection: Popular Politics and Peasant Revolt in Flanders, 1323–1328* (Philadelphia: University of Pennsylvania Press, 1993). The individuals involved in peasant revolts in a key, highly urbanized region of medieval Europe.

Warriors

Bartlett, Robert, *The Making of Europe: Conquest, Colonization, and Cultural Change, 950–1350* (London: Penguin, 1994). Shows how backward Europe expanded from center to periphery and created a common culture by the fourteenth century, poised for expansion.

Duby, Georges, *The Chivalrous Society* (Berkeley: University of California Press, 1992). Essays on nobility, kinship, knighthood, and other topics.

Madden, Thomas F., *A Concise History of the Crusades* (Totowa, NJ: Rowman & Littlefield, 1999). Clear and up-to-date overview, examining why the crusaders left Europe to fight in the Middle East, and how the conflict affected the Byzantine and Islamic East.

Poly, Jean-Pierre and Eric Bournazel, *The Feudal Transformation, 900–1200* (New York: Homes & Meier, 1991). An analysis of the development of European society, mainly France. Discusses lordship, serfdom, peace movements, church, kingship, heretics, and women.

Reynolds, Susan, *Fiefs and Vassals: The Medieval Evidence Reinterpreted* (Oxford: Oxford University Press, 1994). Bold and controversial reconceptualization of property rights and law in medieval Europe, arguing that the formal rules of "feudalism" derived from academic and legal texts, and never existed until monarchical centralization encouraged them, in real life.

Rosenthal, Joel T., *Patriarchy and Families of Privilege in Fifteenth-Century England* (Philadelphia: University of Pennsylvania Press, 1991). Examination of kinship patterns among noble, gentry, and mercantile families in England, highlighting wider kin networks, the importance of patriarchy, and the condition of widows.

Kings

Abulafia, David, *Frederick II: A Medieval Emperor* (London: Pimlico, 1992). A landmark biography, balancing the weaknesses and strengths of this remarkable medieval monarch.

Douglas, David C., *William the Conqueror: the Norman Impact Upon England* (London: Eyre & Spottiswoode, 1964, rpt. 1977). A classic biography, focusing on Norman institutions' influence on England.

Howell, Margaret, *Eleanor of Provence: Queenship in Thirteenth-Century England* (Malden, MA: Blackwell, 1998). Portrays the life of a medieval queen, consort of Henry III, who was enmeshed in politics, war, and diplomacy, and who powerfully influenced, even as she struggled with, her even more important son, Edward I.

Kantorowicz, Ernst H., *The King's Two Bodies: A Study in Medieval Political Thought* (Princeton: Princeton University Press, 1957; rpt. 1998). A classic study of medieval kingship, important not only for the understanding of that era but for that of later Western political formations.

Lewis, Andrew W., *Royal Succession in Capetian France: Studies on Familial Order and the State* (Harvard: Harvard University Press, 1981). A study of kingship, comparing royal and noble models of family.

Pennington, Kenneth, *The Prince and the Law 1200–1600: Sovereignty and Rights in the Western Legal Tradition* (Berkeley and Los Angeles: University of California Press, 1993). Traces how European jurists developed concepts of common law roughly universal in Western Europe, which understood that the powers of sovereigns were limited both by the rights of subjects and the demands of natural (and divine) law.

ORB: the OnLine Reference Book for Medieval Studies (Medieval Academy, Kalamazoo): **http:orb.rhodes.edu/default.html**

King René d'Anjou's tournament book, in English—how to conduct a medieval tournament (Princeton): **http://www.princeton.edu/~ezb/rene/renehome.html**

Eleanor of Aquitaine, extraordinary medieval queen, brief biography: **http://www.womeninworldhistory.com/heroine2.html**

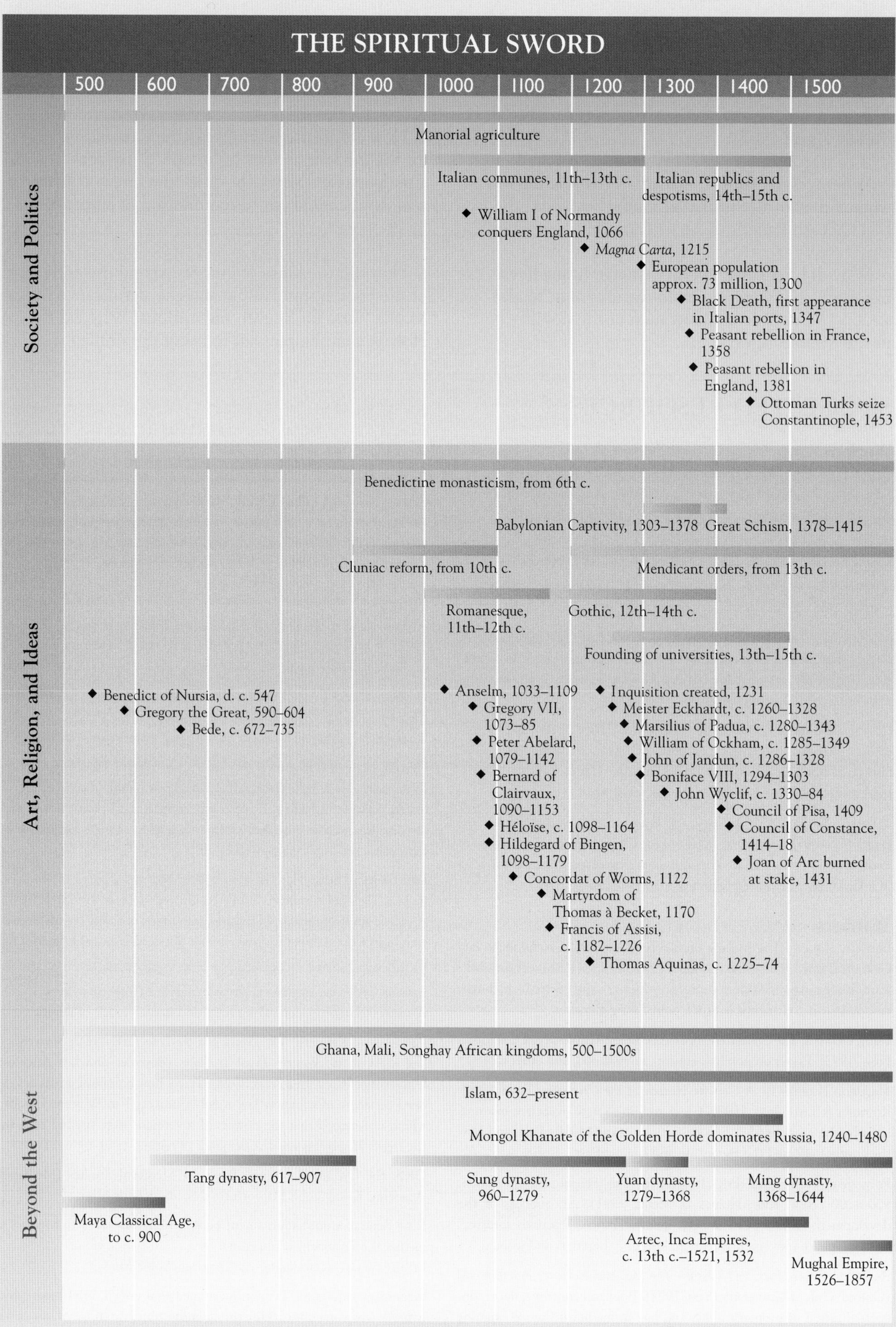
THE SPIRITUAL SWORD
500
600
700
800
900
1000
1100
1200
1300
1400
1500
Society and Politics
Manorial agriculture
Italian communes, 11th–13th c.
Italian republics and despotisms, 14th–15th c.
William I of Normandy conquers England, 1066
Magna Carta, 1215
European population approx. 73 million, 1300
Black Death, first appearance in Italian ports, 1347
Peasant rebellion in France, 1358
Peasant rebellion in England, 1381
Ottoman Turks seize Constantinople, 1453
Art, Religion, and Ideas
Benedictine monasticism, from 6th c.
Babylonian Captivity, 1303–1378
Great Schism, 1378–1415
Cluniac reform, from 10th c.
Mendicant orders, from 13th c.
Romanesque, 11th–12th c.
Gothic, 12th–14th c.
Founding of universities, 13th–15th c.
Benedict of Nursia, d. c. 547
Gregory the Great, 590–604
Bede, c. 672–735
Anselm, 1033–1109
Gregory VII, 1073–85
Peter Abelard, 1079–1142
Bernard of Clairvaux, 1090–1153
Héloïse, c. 1098–1164
Hildegard of Bingen, 1098–1179
Concordat of Worms, 1122
Martyrdom of Thomas à Becket, 1170
Francis of Assisi, c. 1182–1226
Thomas Aquinas, c. 1225–74
Inquisition created, 1231
Meister Eckhardt, c. 1260–1328
Marsilius of Padua, c. 1280–1343
William of Ockham, c. 1285–1349
John of Jandun, c. 1286–1328
Boniface VIII, 1294–1303
John Wyclif, c. 1330–84
Council of Pisa, 1409
Council of Constance, 1414–18
Joan of Arc burned at stake, 1431
Beyond the West
Ghana, Mali, Songhay African kingdoms, 500–1500s
Islam, 632–present
Mongol Khanate of the Golden Horde dominates Russia, 1240–1480
Tang dynasty, 617–907
Sung dynasty, 960–1279
Yuan dynasty, 1279–1368
Ming dynasty, 1368–1644
Maya Classical Age, to c. 900
Aztec, Inca Empires, c. 13th c.–1521, 1532
Mughal Empire, 1526–1857

CHAPTER

10 THE SPIRITUAL SWORD

Religion and Culture in the Middle Ages

500–1500

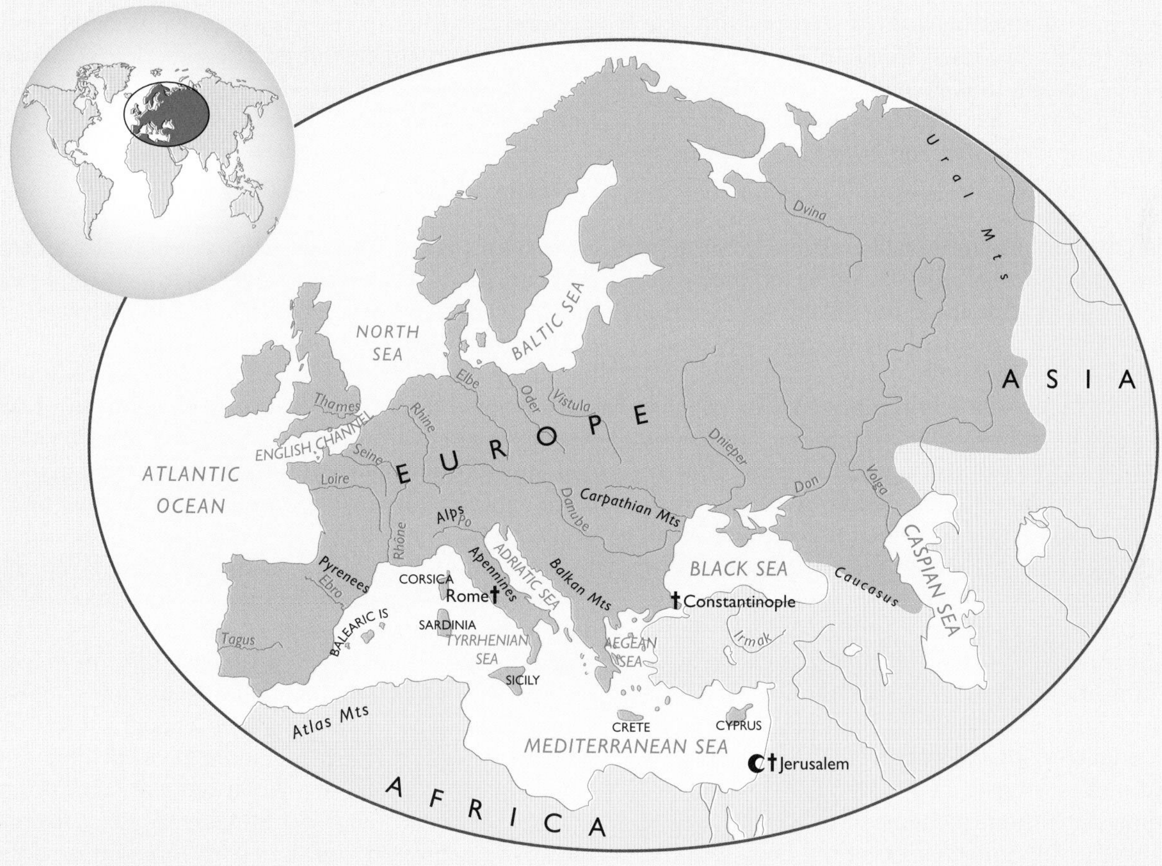

KEY TOPICS

- **Renunciation of the Body:** The Church demands the renunciation of the body, exalts saints and martyrs, and promotes monasticism as the ideal pattern of Christian life.
- **Church and State:** As the Church accumulates property and its clergy accumulate skills, it guards its autonomy against nobles and monarchs, while defining itself against other monotheisms.
- **The Church and the People:** The rhythms and rituals of the Church define the lives of ordinary Christians, while some among them become mystics, saints, or heretics.
- **The Mind's Road to God:** Schools and universities nurture developments in philosophy, theology, medicine, and law—all fundamental to Western thought about nature, politics, and God.

*P**ower and spirit** "Pardon me," Saint Catherine of Siena wrote to the lethargic Pope Gregory XI in 1376, for "what I have said to you and am saying; I am constrained by the Sweet Primal Truth to say it. His [God's] will ... demands that you execute justice. ... Since He has given you authority and you have assumed it, you should use your virtue and power; and if you are not willing to use it, it would be better for you to resign what you have assumed. ..."*

With these words, a holy woman rebuked the Pope, the head of the Roman Catholic Church and spiritual leader of the majority of European Christians of her time. She was summoning him to return with the papal court to Rome, understood to be the proper home of the Church, from Avignon, where a flourishing papacy enjoyed special favors from the French king. Both Saint Catherine and Pope Gregory, who is portrayed on the ivory book cover on p. 259 were figures of vast authority—possessors of different but equally mysterious and formidable powers. They represent two extremes of the meaning of medieval Christianity—she represented the inward spirit of the believer, while he represented the institutional structures of the Catholic Church.

Medieval Europe was overwhelmingly Christian: it was, indeed, Christendom, a civilization defined by the creed liturgy, and institutions of the Latin church. The Church constrained individuals, it battled with kings and waged war with enemies, it corrected social ills, it influenced the patterns of Western thought. The charisma and the decisions of some popes swayed millions of people. The values and ideas of Christianity shaped the inner lives of Europeans of all social groups. At the same time, the doctrines and decrees of the clergy, a hierarchy of Christian professionals, shaped political, educational, and charitable institutions.

Christianity's impact on inner lives and their social behavior is the first theme of this chapter. The Church taught the renunciation of the body and the disciplining of the will. As its institutions developed through a process of internal self-examination and reform, the Latin church confronted the kings and princes of Europe and demanding that they, too, the lords of the earth, acknowledge ecclesiastical supremacy. Meanwhile, church intellectuals developed an all-encompassing theology which absorbed and Christianized the philosophical traditions they had inherited from antiquity as well as those of neighboring Islamic and Jewish cultures. In so doing, they elaborated methods of argument and proof that would outlast even the propositions they articulated. The great edifice of theological thought created and developed by medieval clerics, ironically, prepared the West for its breakthroughs in rational, **secular**, and scientific thought. Some of the important figures of the period are listed in *Who's Who* on p. 280.

RENUNCIATION OF THE BODY

Medieval Christianity's great success may be due in part to its radical departure from Classical values in insisting upon the separation of spirit from flesh and the renunciation of the body. As early as the first century C.E., Christian theologians embraced the principle that the body must be renounced for the sake of the spirit's salvation. In forging this ascetic ideal over the next few centuries, Christianity diverged from both Judaism and Islam, the two other world monotheisms. The institution of **monasticism**, which matured in western Europe from the fifth century C.E. (somewhat earlier in the Greek-speaking East), both limited and institutionalized the practice of asceticism. Monasticism in turn shaped the social and intellectual lives of medieval Europeans.

Origins of Christian Asceticism

Early Christian thinkers developed a radically ascetic program. It prized virginity over marriage (and certainly over any sexual relations outside marriage). It exalted martyrdom, the willingness to die rather than renounce the faith. It canonized saints, or holy persons, revered after their deaths in recognition of the heroic sacrifices they had made or the miracles they had apparently worked while alive. Virginity, martyrdom, sanctity all involved the denial of the needs of the body.

Jesus himself was no enemy of the body. He acknowledged the urgent human need for food, as he demonstrated in the miracle of the loaves and fishes, when he fed thousands of his listeners from one meager meal. He commanded his disciples in the wheatfields to pick and eat, even though it was the sabbath (when Jews were forbidden to work). He welcomed women followers, a violation of ancient norms that construed women as irremediably sensual creatures, and expressed willingness to forgive the violation of sexual limits.

In these respects, Jesus did not, as his later followers did, advocate a renunciation of the body. Yet Jesus did demand sacrifice, a renunciation of the worldly delights bought with wealth and power. To the rich man who had fulfilled all the commandments, he assigned one further task—to surrender all his wealth. To the powerful Sadducees and Pharisees he proclaimed that the meek, not the powerful, would inherit the earth. Moreover, he submitted to the ultimate renunciation of the body when he offered up his body unprotestingly to torture and crucifixion.

The importance of bodily renunciation became more prominent with the Christian missionary Paul of Tarsus. Paul distinguished sharply between body and spirit, insisting that the latter was superior to the former. The spirit turned to God, he said, but the flesh rebelled. "For I know that nothing good dwells … in my flesh," lamented Paul; "I see in my members another law at war with the law of my mind. … Wretched man that I am! Who will rescue me from this body of death?" Paul inherited from Greek thought the split between body and spirit, and introduced to Christianity a new hierarchy—the overwhelming superiority of spirit to body.

Paul's understanding of pure spirit and deceitful flesh profoundly influenced early Christian thought and practice. In quest of the higher good of the spirit, Christians renounced their homes, families, and ordinary comforts. A few deeply committed disciples fled to the deserts of Egypt and the Middle East to live in isolation. Here these hermits made amends for past sins by abusing their bodies and practicing an asceticism which they believed would prepare them for perfect communion with God.

Christian hermits were generally male, but Christian women also sought to approach God through the renunciation of the body. In antiquity women were understood as sexual beings—those who through sexual union gave birth to new generations. Women who rejected that sexual role implicitly declared themselves to be wholly transformed and ready for perfection. The spirituality and holiness of these virgins brought glory to the whole Christian community. Saint Ambrose, an early Church Father, described them as "gardens heavy with the scent of flowers, like shrines filled with solemn worship, like altars that touch their priests with holy awe." Many widows, too, embraced the celibate life. Often groups of these women established female religious communities, including one at Bethlehem, Jesus' birthplace. Their way of life was considered "above nature, and beyond common human living," a realm beyond marriage and childbirth, wealth and property.

The Bishop of Assisi and Francis of Assisi: *In this fourteenth-century fresco from the Basilica of Saint Francis of Assisi, the Bishop of Assisi covers the nakedness of Francis (later Saint Francis of Assisi) after he stripped off his clothes and hurled them at his father whose values he rejected.*

Forms of Sainthood

Gregory the Great: *Medieval sainthood took many forms. This image from an ivory book cover, tenth century, shows Gregory the Great (Pope Gregory I) seated at his writing-desk and receiving the word of God from the dove on his shoulder.* (Kunsthistorisches Museum, Vienna)

The assumption that virginity brought one closer to holiness applied to men as well as women. The same men who encouraged women to deny their bodies also struggled themselves with the demand of celibacy. Saints Ambrose and Jerome urged virginity upon all male aspirants to the holy life. Saint Augustine detailed in his *Confessions* the difficulties he had faced in submitting to its demands: "Make me chaste," he cried to God in one anguished moment, "but not yet."

Martyrdom The willingness to suffer for one's religious beliefs defined martyrdom—the surrender to death in witness of faith. Like hermits and virgins, Christian martyrs—created by persecutions under Roman emperors—elevated spirit over body. In imitation of Jesus, they sacrificed their flesh for the sake of their own souls and the spiritual welfare of the church. In appreciation of their sacrifice, Christian communities revered the martyrs, who, they believed, were made holy, or "sanctified," by their ultimate sacrifice. Many of these martyrs were among the first Christians to be proclaimed saints, or canonized.

After death, the bodies of the saints became holy objects. Believers began to worship at their graves, or to treasure their material remains—pieces of clothing or even bodily **relics**, such as bones or portions of their persecuted flesh. Special tombs were built for their remains, which were believed to have special properties, including that of immunity to decay. The reverence for the lost personality easily slipped toward the worship of his or her bodily remains. Sometimes that worship seemed to work miracles, which were interpreted as the signs of sanctity. Even in the absence of a miracle, Christians believed that the deceased saint now lived close to God, and that, having once had bodily form, he or she could serve as an intermediary between the human world of the flesh and the eternal realm of spirit. If approached rightly, it was believed that saints would intercede with God for aid or forgiveness. Thus, paradoxically, a part of the body—despised in life—became, in death, an object of veneration.

These attitudes toward the bodies of particular individuals were new. The ancients generally viewed corpses as unclean and capable of polluting the precincts in which they were laid. For that reason, Greeks and Romans preferred to bury their dead outside the city walls. Christian reverence for the bodies of the holy reversed popular attitudes toward death. For the ancients, the body was beautiful in life but terrifying in death. For Christians, the body was detestable in life, but in death (the pure death of the believer) it was glorious. By about 500 C.E., European Christians, who now buried their dead close about their places of worship at the center of their communities, revered the saints and treasured their bodily relics.

Monasticism and the Christian Mission

By the fourth century C.E., the impulse for holiness had found a new means of expression. The persecutions had ended, and with them the opportunity for martyrdom. The ascetic life still beckoned, but the response to that call shifted. Men began to explore the spiritual life not as isolated individuals, but in groups, as monks. During the early medieval centuries, monks living in communities founded throughout Europe enriched the Church's liturgy, read, copied, and stored books, taught children, treated the sick, and housed the superfluous members of noble families. Monasticism attracted many thousands of people during the Middle Ages, becoming one of that era's foremost institutions.

While the ascetic ideal remained central to monastic life, it was not the only purpose served by communities of holy men (and women). In his two *Rules* for monks, Saint Basil of Caesarea (c. 330–379) stressed the humanity of the communal life and the centrality of study to the monastic mission. Cassiodorus (already encountered as the secretary of the Ostrogoth king Theodoric), in his monastic retirement at Vivarium, on Italy's "heel," devoted himself to transcribing numerous religious manuscripts. He gathered there one of the world's foremost libraries, which would one day help to reinvigorate intellectual life.

Most important for the development of monasticism in western Europe was the work of the Roman nobleman Benedict of Nursia (c. 480–c. 550). As his native Italy was being devastated by Justinian's reconquest, Benedict defined monastic life as a rational alternative to the turmoil of the secular world. Basil, Cassiodorus, and Benedict, established the main features of life in a monastery: study and contemplation, prayer and chant, and, in some cases, productive work in service to the poor and ill of the community.

Saint Benedict's compact *Rule for Monks* outlined in seventy-three chapters the organization of the Christian community. He called it a beginners' guide, and it served more to restrain excess than to demand any sacrifice. An extract is given in *Witnesses* on p. 266. He reduced the demands of early monastic life to three, which each and every monk must vow to assume—poverty, chastity, and obedience. Thenceforth, those who took monastic vows were considered "regular"—meaning they followed a rule, or *regula*. They were distinct from the priests and bishops, who were called the secular clergy because they lived in the *seculum*, the world.

Monastic communities formed under the *Rule* of Saint Benedict sprang up throughout Europe. They formed in the old Roman lands, as many Christians left the decaying cities to join communities of their fellow believers in searching for an indestructible truth. In the new lands wrested from the wilderness or from invasion, the monasteries served as fortresses of established culture.

Monasticism took root with special success on the remote island of Ireland, recently and profoundly converted to Christianity through the efforts in part of Saint Patrick (c. 390–c. 461). Here a particularly strict form of monasticism arose under the *Rule* of Saint Columban (543–615). This Irish saint demanded absolute obedience and ceaseless austerities: "Let [the monk] come weary and as if sleep-walking to his bed, and let him be forced to rise while his sleep is not yet finished." In the seventh century, Irish missionaries helped convert the Anglo-Saxon peoples and exported to the Continent their high standards of dedication and intellectual life.

As *Windows On* on p. 261 shows, the main task of the monks was the glorification of God in communal worship. Seven times a day (including twice in the night), Benedictine monks assembled in their chapel to chant liturgical prayers and Old Testament psalms. They chanted in simple but expressive melodies, derived from Jewish practice and Greek theory, which

The Monastery and the Monastic Day

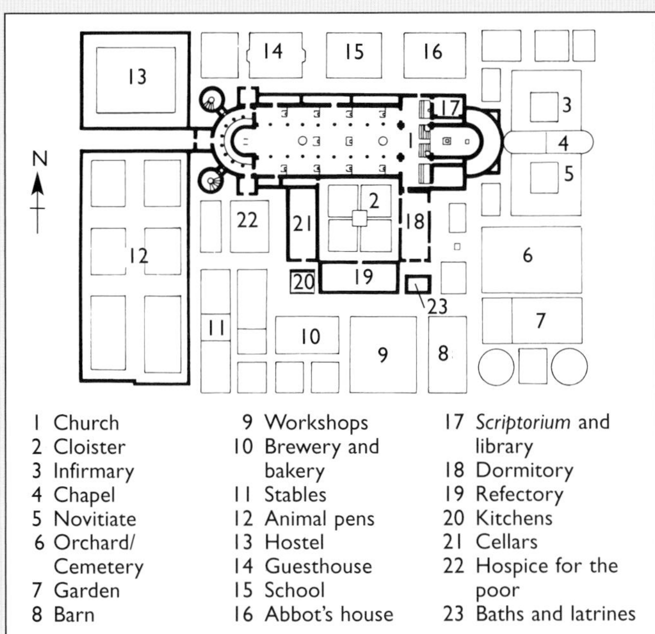

Plan of the Monastery of Saint Gall

The medieval monastery was a complete world, whose facilities provided for the monk's needs and whose rituals structured his mental universe. The plan of the monastery of Saint Gall in Switzerland is shown (above), together with a reconstruction (below) of how it might then have looked. The monks' day was divided between periods for divine service (song and prayer in the chapel), for work (manual, administrative or intellectual), and for meals and sleep, as shown in the daily plan (right).

A Summer's Day for a Medieval Monk	
MIDNIGHT	Sing *Matins* in church
	Sleep
6 A.M.	Sing *Prime* in church
	Eat breakfast
	Study or manual labor
9 A.M.	Mass in church
10 A.M.	Meeting of the Chapter (council of monks)
11 A.M.	High Mass in church
12 NOON	Dinner
	Rest
2 P.M.	Sing *Nones* in church
	Work
4 P.M.	Sing *Vespers* in church
	Work
6 P.M.	Supper
7 P.M.	Sing *Compline* in church
	Sleep
The winter schedule was adjusted to the hours of daylight	

Reconstruction of the Monastery of Saint Gall

To continue your investigation of this topic, please go to www.prenhall.com/king for the related WINDOWS on the WEB activity

later evolved into increasingly complex patterns. Called plainsong or Gregorian chant, because it was linked to the work of Pope Gregory I, "the Great" (r. 590–604), the monastic chant of the Latin church is the origin of the formal tradition of Western music.

When not performing the central duty of worship, Benedictine monks were expected to work—their duties including housekeeping, study, teaching, medical service, and hard physical labor in the fields. Amid the poverty and disruption of medieval Europe there was no way for a community of Christians to sustain life except by farming. As conditions improved, the monks employed others to grow their food—serfs attached to the monastic lands or ordinary men pledged to the monastery but not full members of the community. One effect of the Benedictine labor requirement, even when it was no longer strictly observed, was to establish the principle of the dignity of work. If the Christian served God even as he labored, then labor itself was sanctified.

There was also mental work to be done. The European monasteries were the chief repositories of books that had survived the collapse of Roman authority in the west—and such repositories were the only link between the European wilderness and ancient culture. The more learned monks studied and, more importantly, copied these works. Their reverence for these Latin texts, which they did not always understand, is visible in the brilliant illustrations with which they decorated the margins, the chapter-opening capital letters, and the title pages of their books. Those illustrations, called miniatures or illuminations, were the major form of artistic expression in early medieval Europe. The copyists and illuminators were trained in the monastery schools—which for centuries, with few exceptions, were the only ones in Europe.

Convents Monasticism was not exclusively male. Female monasteries, or convents, were also established throughout Europe. Their residents, called nuns, were often unmarried or widowed noblewomen. Although some women entered the conventual life unwillingly, many others found in convents the opportunity for education and spiritual enrichment. Both types appear in *Witnesses* on p. 278.

Like monks, nuns also took vows of poverty, chastity, and obedience and passed their days in prayer and work (see the illustrations on this page and p. 263). An abbess governed their convent, usually a woman of great authority: "noble in wisdom and holiness, as well as noble by birth," wrote one advisor.

Cloistered Nuns

Nuns singing: *The convent was a complete world for medieval nuns. They are shown singing in this fifteenth-century psaltery of Henry VI.* (British Library, London)

Claricia, by herself: *Like monks, nuns copied and illustrated manuscript books. The initial letter Q can be seen in this manuscript, c. 1200, by the nun Claricia. On the tail of this letter Claricia has represented herself as a female scribe.* (Walters Art Gallery)

In the early Middle Ages, monasteries often consisted of a male and a female house adjacent to each other, administered by an abbess. In these "dual monasteries," the prominent role of the abbess, truly parallel to the abbot of all-male institutions, underscored the equality (later lost) of the male and female monastic mission. Yet there were fundamental differences. Because only men could be priests, and only priests could administer the sacraments, female convents required the services of these professionals from a neighboring monastery or church.

Abbesses might be women of great skill and even great learning. An outstanding example was Hildegard of Bingen (1098–1179), renowned as a scholar, a visionary, a composer, and a leader. Founder of her own convent (in 1150), she wrote a play, a treatise on natural science and medicine (as understood in that day), and her important *Scivias*, describing the visions that presented themselves to her inner senses. "I do not hear these things ... with my external ears," she wrote, "nor do I perceive them by the thoughts of my heart, nor by any combination of my five senses—but rather in my soul, with my external eyes open, so that I ... alertly see them by day and by night." The spirit itself commanded her to record them: "For the benefit of mankind, do not relinquish your pen! Write down what your inner eye has seen and your inner ear has heard. ..."

Places of Refuge Increasingly, monasteries served as a refuge for upper-class noblemen. Repentant or elderly nobles often retired to monasteries, believing that the cloistered life was the only alternative to certain damnation. Thus one nobleman stated in the charter by which he donated his property to the monastery he entered: "Acknowledging the enormity of my sins and ... fearing the dread condemnation of the reprobate, ... I fly to the harbor of safety."

Guda, by herself: *This self-portrait of the nun Guda appears in an illuminated manuscript,* Homilia super Evangilia, *late twelfth century. Here Guda describes herself as a scribe, artist, and sinner.* (Stadt-und-Universitätsbibliothek, Frankfurt)

Monasteries also provided a refuge for children. The monastic life was an alternative career for those not destined to share in the inheritance of property. In the early Middle Ages, it was common for families to commit to monasteries very young children, along with a monetary donation. This system of "offering up" or oblation of children to a religious house benefited both parties. It gave the monasteries a steady stream of novice monks or nuns, who could easily be trained to monastic service. It gave noble families a means of reducing family size and future claims on inheritance. At the same time, it conferred upon these families the spiritual benefits accrued from the prayers of their children, who now worked for their parents' salvation.

There is no way of knowing how many children disliked the monastic life, from which they would never escape, or how many were cruelly denied all possibility of choosing their own destiny. But many such children later thrived, among them the Anglo-Saxon scholar Bede (c. 672–735), called "the Venerable." A skilled historian, prolific writer, and fertile thinker, he produced a study of chronology that promoted the now nearly universal method of dividing the calendar from the presumed date of the birth of Jesus. Bede had no regrets about his childhood: "I have spent all my life in this monastery," he wrote, "applying myself with all my might to the study of the Scriptures; and ... it has always been my delight to learn or to teach or to write."

Monastic Reform and Transformation

Along with a steady supply of high-ranking novices, monastic institutions received a steady influx of wealth—partly from benefactions, or charitable donations, and partly from the products of their lands. That wealth posed a problem for an institution based on the principle of renunciation. Monks were pledged to poverty, yet the monasteries in which they lived became wealthy. By the late Middle Ages, the Church controlled a considerable portion of all the land of Europe.

This wealth nourished corruption. Monks accustomed to fine food and drink, luxurious surroundings, the company of the powerful, and dazzling ritual displays abandoned the regimen of simple duties and plain food. During the troubled ninth and tenth centuries, when they were isolated in remote houses within a world beset by invasion and disorder, the monks became lax in performing even basic duties. Critics recalled the essential mission of monasticism, its renunciation of the body and the world. Pressure for reform swelled, spearheaded by determined abbots. Map 10.2 shows the centers of monastic reform.

An early program of reform took place in the Abbey of Cluny, in eastern France, which was founded in 910. In 927, its abbot, Odo (879–942) launched a reform movement that would have repercussions beyond his own monastery, or order, or age. First, he reestablished strict standards within his own community, insisting on the performance of constant communal prayer (exceeding the Benedictine guideline, which called only for intermittent prayer service). Then he agreed to supervise other houses that petitioned him for help in achieving the same goals. Soon, reformed monasteries, all linked by a common submission to the authority of the abbot at Cluny, who in turn was directly responsible to the pope, spread throughout the region. These in turn attracted new patrons and their benefactions. Cluny became the center of medieval monasticism, and from there flowed an energy for reform that reached Rome.

Patrons rushed to associate themselves with the greater purity of the reformed Cluniac order. Their donations enriched its monasteries, whose residents readily prayed for the souls of the great men and women whose endowments they enjoyed. With that newly acquired wealth, several Cluniac monasteries rebuilt their churches in the first major architectural style of the Middle Ages: the **Romanesque**.

A Romanesque church resembled the basilican style of church begun in early Christianity. These included a long hall, or nave, often flanked by side aisles, surmounted by a flat or tunnel-vaulted roof, and climaxed (usually in the east) by a semicircular or polygonal **apse** or an **ambulatory**, a curved aisle behind the altar, used originally for processions. To this plain and stately format, the Cluniac builders added elaborate sculptural embellishment. The columns and capitals supporting the upper interior walls of the nave and the moldings surrounding the round-arched windows and doors on the exterior were decorated with intertwined plant, animal, and human

Romanesque Style

Poitiers Cathedral: *Romanesque architecture was dominant in Europe from the ninth to the twelfth century and derived from ancient Roman precedents. The style was characterized by massive architectural forms, as shown here in this view of the west front of Poitiers Cathedral, c. 1130–1145.*

Autun Cathedral: *Romanesque style is also characterized by its energetic, expressive sculptural decoration, as in this scene of the torment of souls in hell from the* ***tympanum*** *(drum), part of the facade decoration of Autun Cathedral. Saint Bernard criticized the ebullience of Romanesque style, which he feared would distract monks from their studies:*
". . . what is that ridiculous monstrosity doing? what is that deformed beauty and that beautiful deformity? those unclean monkeys? those ferocious lions? . . . on all sides one sees such a rich and amazing variety of forms that it is more pleasing to read the marbles than the manuscripts."

forms. These decorative forms were united by complex themes reflecting the main preoccupations of the era—salvation and damnation and the Last Judgment, the majesty of Jesus Christ as judge, the giant confrontation of the human and divine. Such carvings also decorated cathedrals, as shown in the figure above and on p. 264.

The impassioned saints, the grinning demons, the florid patterns of Romanesque sculpture were symptomatic of the problem with the Church, charged a new generation of critics. They argued that the elaborate sculptural decoration of Cluniac churches distracted people from true religion. New twelfth-century reform efforts included those of the Carthusians and the Cistercians, both in France. The Carthusian reform laid new austerities on the monks, who were to maintain strict silence and live and sleep in a solitary cell (in which they were to keep, ready at hand, parchment, pen and ink, and ruler; for every Carthusian was required to be a scholar). The Cistercian order aimed to return to the original simplicity of the Benedictine ideal. Its churches were denuded of adornment, and the requirement to do manual work was strictly enforced. The special mission of the Cistercians was to clear and reclaim the wastelands that still littered the surface of Europe.

The Mendicant Orders Reform efforts culminated in the thirteenth-century innovation of the **mendicant** orders,which transformed monasticism by creating an alternative to it. Mendicant friars—called "brothers," rather than monks—pledged themselves to service in a world that was no longer poor, no longer exclusively rural, and no longer simple. The growth of cities of a vigor unimaginable in the days of Benedict called for radically new forms of Christian mission. It was a young Italian, the son of a wealthy cloth merchant, but later known to the world as Saint Francis of Assisi (c. 1182–1226) who first defined that new venture. Francis began by giving away his possessions to the poor, whereupon his father disowned him. According to legend, Francis then stripped himself of all his finery in the market square of his native town of Assisi and, wearing a cloak donated by the bishop of Assisi, journeyed forth in poverty to seek God, as illustrated on p. 259. Francis urged that poverty was central to true reform. For twenty years, he and his loyal followers devoted themselves to "spiritual poverty." They wandered from village to village and town to town, begging for food, offering service, and preaching in their "lofty poverty" a gospel focused on the humility of Jesus. With neither monastic house nor endowment, the Franciscans were the pioneers of a form of Christian devotion adapted to thirteenth-century life—mobile and urban—just as Benedictinism had suited those of the sixth.

Among the followers of Francis of Assisi was a young noblewoman, Clare, who was converted by him and founded a female order, the "Poor Clares," the counterpart of Francis' own order of Franciscans. (The "Clares," however, remained cloistered and could not follow the mendicant life of their Franciscan brothers.)

Not long after Francis' death, the Franciscan movement began to encounter a familiar obstacle: wealth. The stupendously rich merchant leaders of the Italian cities respected the deep spirituality of the Franciscans. Their generous gifts flowed into an order that had, at the outset, neither treasury nor administrative center. These soon appeared, causing a rift among the Franciscans.

The "Conventual" Franciscans became managers of wealth, and adjusted Francis' rule—the pope concurring—to suit its new condition. The friars who refused to compromise and maintained strictly their founder's injunction to poverty were called "Observant" or "Spiritual" Franciscans. The absolute standard of poverty, though it accorded perfectly with scripture, implicitly challenged the practices of property management essential to the institutional Church, which made it a dangerous idea in the eyes of that organization. The pope declared the Observants heretical. Many were burned at the stake.

Before these internal tensions weakened the Franciscan mission, a contemporary of Francis of Assisi, the Spanish nobleman Dominic Guzmán of Castile (c. 1170–1221) inaugurated another movement of itinerant friars. Like Francis, Dominic saw that a new form of Christian service was required to meet the needs of the society of his day. He, too, pledged his followers to poverty. But Dominic had a further mission: to teach orthodox Christian doctrine and to prevent the spread of false or heretical views. Dominicans became not only teachers but also inquisitors—agents of the church in the identification and prosecution of heresy.

The launching of the Inquisition in the thirteenth century marks the culmination of a period of change in the medieval church. The Catholic Church, rooted in Rome, where once Senate and emperor had held sway, and led by an effective hierarchy of clerical administrators, had become an institution of unprecedented power. Establishing policy and issuing decrees, church leaders now often found themselves in conflict with kings and princes whose claims for authority they sought to control.

CHURCH AND STATE

While monasticism evolved with changes in medieval society, the relations of the Church with the political powers of Europe also shifted. In the early Middle Ages, the institutions of the Church performed the functions abandoned by the Roman state. Lords and princes availed themselves of churchmen's skills of management and literacy, with the effect that many of the higher clergy became attached to the interests of secular rulers. Under church leadership, Europeans battled with Muslim Turks in the Crusades for access to the Holy Land (see Chapter 9), and defined their differences with the Eastern church and with their own Jewish populations. The Catholic Church acted like a state, or provided aid to the rulers of states, while those rulers employed churchmen as their secretaries and advisers. Thus, by the twelfth century, political and ecclesiastical functions were thoroughly intertwined.

Beginning around 1000, the papacy had led an extensive reform movement which established the independence of the clergy from secular government and society. Now, as the Middle Ages reached maturity, the powerful papacy forgot its original mission and warded off efforts to restrict its power by subordinating the pope to the authority of representative councils. As the institutional Church grew in wealth and power, the needs of the ordinary Christian were often forgotten.

WITNESSES

Monastic Life and Mendicant Spirituality

Monasticism was a primary institution of the medieval world, offering stability to its members, and solace and services to those beyond its doors. Benedict, the author of the first passage, lays down guidelines for a meaningful life in religious community. Seven centuries later, some observant Christians sought a different kind of spiritual experience—not of stability and labor, but of service in the world, and a more passionate connection to God and his creation. Francis of Assisi, the pioneer of this later "mendicant" movement, is the author of this prayer of praise to God, closely identified with nature.

Benedict sets limits on work and wealth for monks (c. 536): Idleness is the great enemy of the soul, therefore the monks should always be occupied, either in manual labor or in holy reading. The hours for these occupations should be arranged according to the seasons .... But if the conditions of the locality or the needs of the monastery, such as may occur at harvest time, should make it necessary to labor longer hours, they shall not feel themselves ill-used, for true monks should live by the labor of their own hands, as did the apostles and the holy fathers. ...

The sin of owning private property should be entirely eradicated from the monastery. No one shall presume to give or receive anything except by the order of the abbot; no one shall possess anything of his own, books, papers, pens, or anything else; for monks are not to own even their own bodies and wills to be used at their own desire, but are to look to the father [abbot] of the monastery for everything.
(St. Benedict, *Rule*, c. 536; eds. O. J. Thatcher, E. H. McNeal, 1905)

Francis of Assisi exalts God in nature (13th century):

Praise be to Thee, my Lord, with all Thy creatures,
Especially to my worshipful brother sun,
The which lights up the day, and through him dost Thou brightness give;
And beautiful is he and radiant with splendour great;
Of Thee, most High, signification gives.

...

Praised be my Lord for our sister, mother earth,
The which sustains and keeps us
And brings forth diverse fruits with grass and flowers bright.
(St. Francis, "The Canticle of the Sun"; ed. P. Robinson, 1906)

Popes and Kings: The Era of Cooperation

By the fourth century C.E., when the Roman world was turning Christian, the bishops of the great ancient cities of Rome, Constantinople, Alexandria, and Antioch had gained preeminence over all others. Of these, only Rome lay in the Latin-speaking west. The bishop of Rome represented special authority

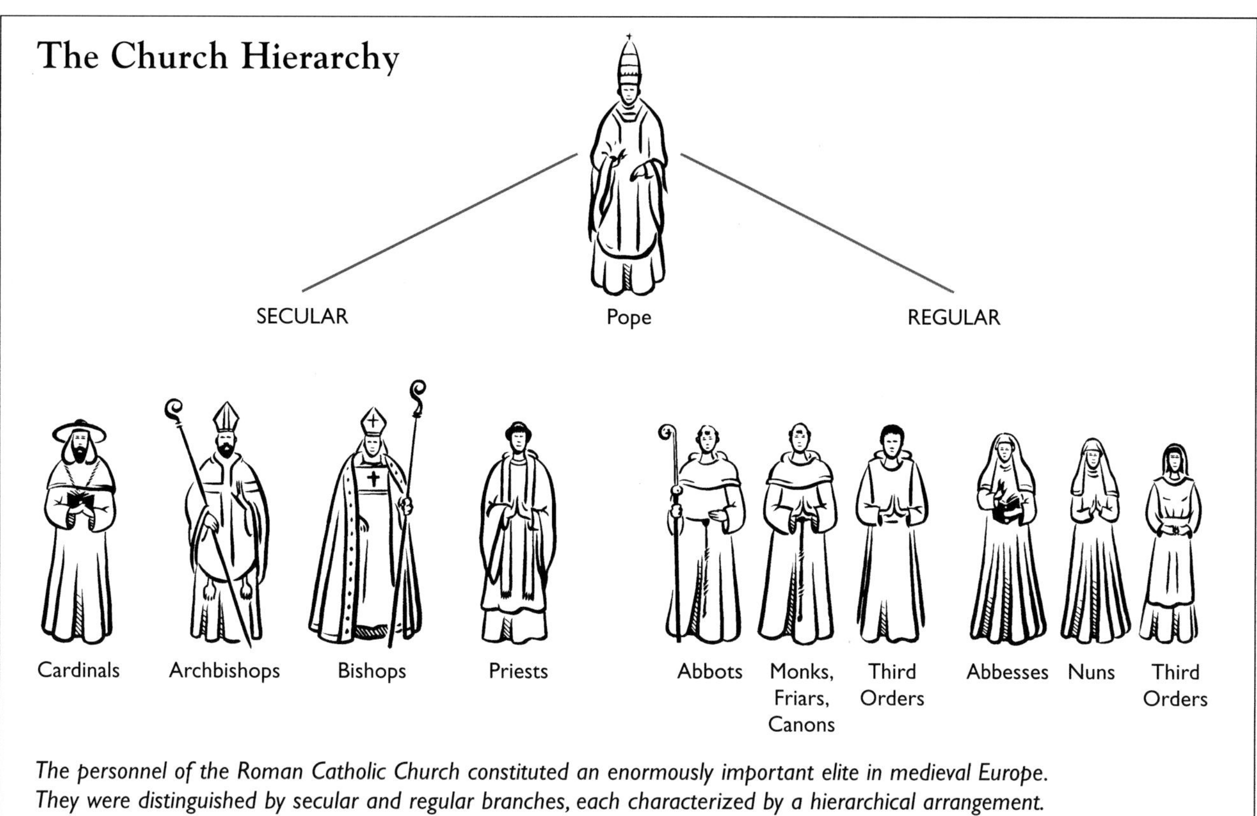

The personnel of the Roman Catholic Church constituted an enormously important elite in medieval Europe. They were distinguished by secular and regular branches, each characterized by a hierarchical arrangement.

because of the association with Saint Peter, one of Jesus' twelve disciples, who was believed to have been executed in that capital during Nero's persecution. Jesus had granted Peter authority over the church, it was thought, when he pronounced these words: "You are Peter [in the original Aramaic phrase, *Caipha*, meaning "rock" and in Latin translation *Petrus*, or rock] and on this rock I will build my church." Peter transferred that authority (it was believed) to all subsequent bishops of Rome. In time, these prelates assumed the title of "pope," meaning "father." They also assumed the functions of rulers, as Roman authority crumbled and no one was left in charge.

The emergence of the papacy as a major institution began with the Roman bishop Leo I (r. 440–461), called "the Great," later canonized. Amid the many crises of the fifth century, the figure of Pope Leo towers. He was a serious theologian, a prolific author, and a dauntless leader. When Attila the Hun swept into northern Italy in 452 intent on conquest (though weakened by sickness), Leo and a small delegation of churchmen conferred with him. According to legend, it was the pope's pleas that deflected the bellicose chieftain from his path.

At the end of the next century, another pope later called "Great" led the Church. Gregory (r. 590–604), the son of a Roman senator, grew up in an Italy devastated by the Gothic wars and beset by Lombard invasions. As a scholar, Gregory encapsulated Christian teachings in works that were easily mastered by a barely literate clergy. More, he established the role and duties of priests and bishops in an environment where secular authority had practically vanished. These two achievements helped prepare the West for the great isolation that prevailed in the early Middle Ages, and helped extend Christian institutions to the farthest reaches of Europe (it was Gregory's mission that finally achieved the conversion of Anglo-Saxon England). By the time of his death, the principle that the pope was head of the Church not only in Rome or in Italy but in the whole of Latin-speaking Europe had been clearly asserted.

Yet the popes had to concern themselves especially with Italy, lest the Church be swallowed up by the conflicts that boiled there after the Lombard takeover. They sought the protection of the Eastern emperor, who still controlled footholds in Sicily, the south, and Venice. When that aid became undependable, the popes sought military aid from another secular ruler, Pepin, the king of the Franks, who was both strong and a Catholic. In 754 and again in 756, Pepin was invited into Italy to dispel the Lombard threat to Rome. Pepin's son and successor, Charlemagne, twice went to Italy to secure the pope's safety.

By 800, the papacy had acquired, through Frankish intervention, control over a belt of territory (in addition to smaller, scattered possessions) running from sea to sea across central Italy. This region, called the Papal States, enabled the papacy to both feed and defend itself. Meanwhile, Italy, which had already experienced invasion by the Gauls, the Ostrogoths, the Huns, and the Lombards, had learned to expect periodic irruptions of armies led by northern kings over the Alpine frontier.

In the ninth and tenth centuries, the Church at Rome continued to work with the emerging monarchs of the European nations for their mutual benefit. The pope expected priests to be supported by the secular power. At the same time, he expected secular rulers to respect the autonomy of the Church—its property, its personnel, and its laws. Secular rulers, in turn, helped select church leaders in their own lands and employed clergy (for years the only literate persons in Europe) in their own administrations. This symbiotic relationship of Church and state endured until about 1000. Thereafter, it changed, as both Church and state sought to expand their power.

The Militant Church

After the millennium year 1000, a confident Church within a confident Christendom, no longer fearful of persecution or invasion, began to show its strength, as indicated on Map 10.1. It struck out against Islam in a series of holy wars, the Crusades, and defined its position relative to European Jews and Eastern Orthodox Christians. Christian society then turned aggressively on its fellow monotheists in confrontations supported and sometimes led by the Church. Opening the door to an era of intolerance, these events witness the readiness of the Church to assert its authority within Europe and beyond.

The Crusades were fought by European knights against Turkish dominion of lands considered holy (see Chapter 9 and Map 9.2). But it was the newly powerful papacy that instigated and orchestrated these wars. The First Crusade (1095–1099) was triggered by an appeal to the pope from the Byzantine emperor, under threat from the Seljuk Turks. The pope, Urban II (r. 1088–1099), saw several good reasons to hurl an army of European knights against the Muslim Turks, whose advance put Christian pilgrimage routes to the Holy Land at risk. A foreign war, moreover, would mobilize Christian sentiments in the west, would channel the aggression of western warriors in a useful direction, and might possibly result in the recovery of Jerusalem, the Holy City, which had been occupied by Seljuk Turks in 1071. In 1095, at Clermont (in France), Urban exhorted the people to join the Crusade. Thousands of poor pilgrims and armored knights set out from the European heartlands. Europe had begun to expand its authority, impelled in part by the leadership of the Church.

Military Orders One sign of the aggressive posture of Christianity in the crusading era was the birth of military-monastic orders. Two of these were inspired by the need to provide security and medical care for the pilgrims who flooded the Holy Land after its conquest in the First Crusade. They were the Hospitallers (the "Knights of the Order of the Hospital of Saint John") and the Templars ("Knights of the Temple"). Members of these orders took monastic vows but wore arms and led a military life.

Both orders were expelled from the Holy Land after the Turks reconquered the region in the thirteenth century. The Hospitallers relocated to the islands of Cyprus, then Rhodes, and finally Malta. The Templars returned to Europe, immensely wealthy from their activity as protectors of Crusader treasure. Their control of thousands of castles and manors in France aroused the greed of the French king, Philip IV (r. 1285–1314). He accused the Templars of abominable crimes, tortured and executed their leaders, and confiscated property. In cooperation with the French monarchy, the Church dissolved the order.

A third order, the Teutonic Knights, established themselves in the thirteenth century in the German lands of eastern Prussia. Their mission was to Christianize the last pagan territory of Europe—a form of crusade itself, though in a different geographical arena. The Teutonic Knights dominated the Baltic area from Gdansk (in modern Poland) to Estonia, and presided over the colonization of the region by German settlers. They were dissolved in the sixteenth century during the Protestant Reformation.

Intolerance The era of the Crusades occasioned a shift in the Church's relationship with Islam (see Chapter 8). Islamic society had successfully absorbed both Christians and Jews, because they considered them, like themselves, "people of the book," cobelievers in one God and in his prophets, from Abraham to Moses to Jesus—albeit not Muhammad. In Islamic regions both communities were tolerated, although they were required to pay special taxes. Christians were less tolerant toward Islam, but had little opportunity to confront it in the early Middle Ages. After 1000, that confrontation began on several fronts. In Spain, Christian leaders began the long "Reconquest" of the Iberian peninsula from Moorish domination. In the Mediterranean, the navies of Pisa and Genoa, with papal aid, swept aside Saracen fleets and raided North African cities. In the south of Italy, Norman knights supported by the pope wrested Sicily from Saracen hands. Then, beginning with the First Crusade, Christian soldiers faced the Muslim Turks in a struggle over what both considered holy land.

At the same time, Christian relations with Judaism also became more hostile. Officially, the Church viewed Judaism as the matrix from which Christianity had been born. For this reason, it was stipulated that Jews were not to be harmed or forcibly converted to Christianity. Despite that official stance of grudging toleration, ordinary Christians sometimes behaved differently. The First Crusade opened

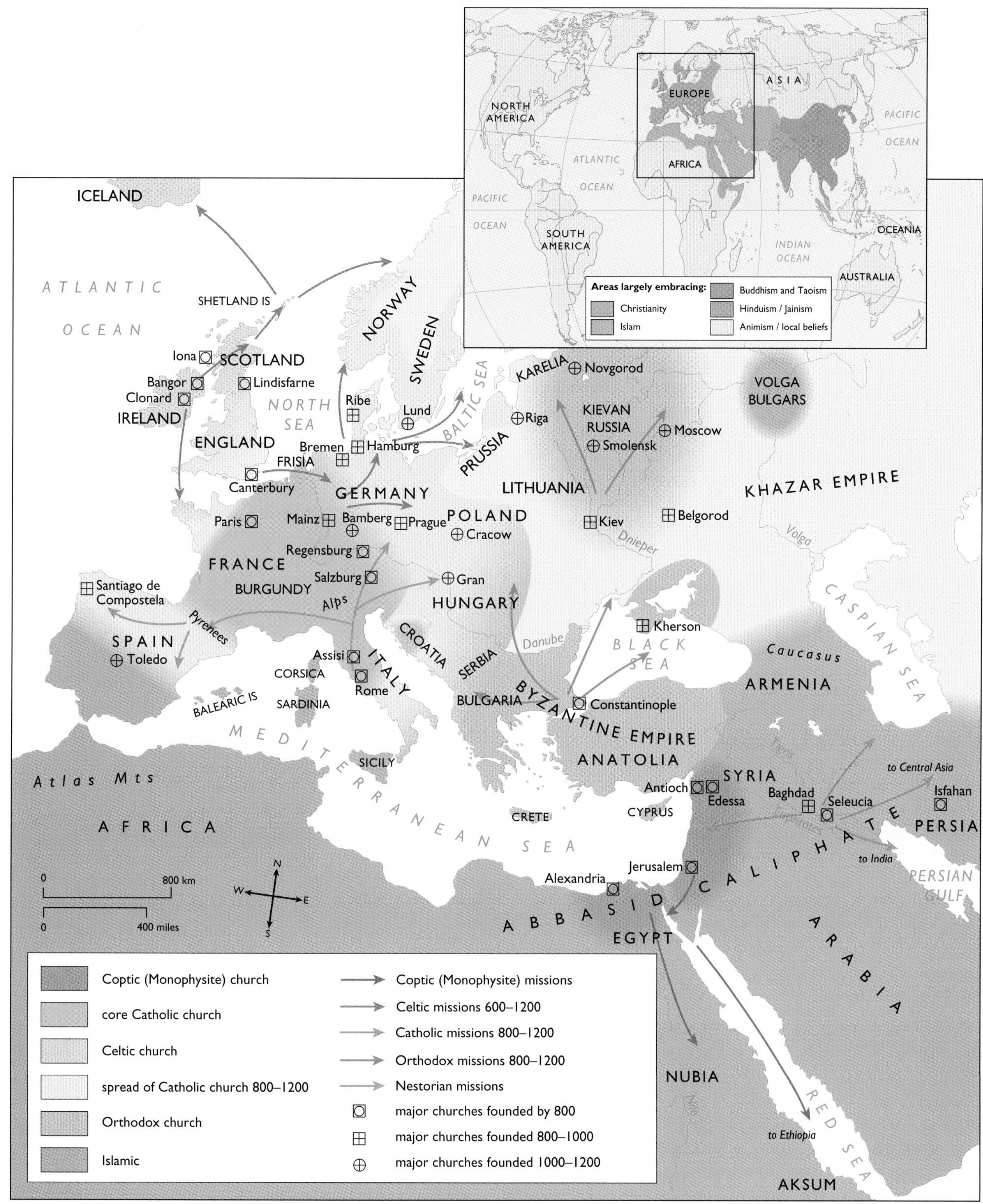

Map 10.1 Christianity and other World Religions, to 1500: *Over many centuries, Christianity spread from Constantinople and Rome; from Celtic Ireland, Anglo-Saxon England, and the eastern Frankish kingdom; from Moscow and Novgorod. As Christianity expanded from its Mediterranean homeland to touch the remotest boundaries of Europe, it took its place as a major actor among the matured religious systems of the world.*

with massacres of Jews in the German Rhineland, an expression, at this exceptionally intense moment, of endemic hostility toward neighbors perceived as alien. Anti-Semitism broke out frequently thereafter, as Jews continued to be stigmatized in popular culture and even in learned treatises as monstrous, greedy, and bloodthirsty. Throughout medieval Europe rulers expelled Jews from their lands—from England in

WITNESSES

Papal Supremacy, Clerical Reform, and Conciliar Resistance

What kind of an institution would the Church become? Who would be in charge? These questions pressed urgently from the eleventh through the sixteenth century. These three passages contain three different claims to authority. In the first, the pope asserts his authority even over the emperor, the greatest of secular rulers. In the second, a church official reports to his superiors about the lax behavior of some cathedral canons, who will be required to reform. In the third, a council of prelates and scholars announces that it has its "power directly from Christ," and can therefore exercise it even over popes.

Pope Gregory VII insists on papal supremacy (1075), decreeing:

1. That the Roman church was founded by God alone.
2. That the Roman pontiff alone can with right be called universal.
3. That he alone can depose or reinstate bishops.

. . .

8. That he alone may use the imperial insignia.
9. That of the pope alone all princes shall kiss the feet.
10. That his name alone shall be spoken in the churches.
11. That this is the only name in the world.
12. That it may be permitted to him to depose emperors.

. . .

19. That he himself may be judged by no one.

(Gregory VII, *Dictatus papae*, 1075, 1:121–125; ed. E. F. Henderson, 1892)

Eudes de Rigaud describes the lax obedience of the clergy (1248): We visited the Chapter of Rouen [attached to the cathedral], and found that they talk in choir contrary to rule. The clergy wander about the church, and talk in the church with women, during the celebration of divine service. The statute regarding the entrance [of lay folk] into the choir is not kept. The psalms are run through too rapidly, without due pauses. ... Moreover, the clergy leave the choir without reason, before the end of the service already begun; and, to be brief, many other of the statutes written on the board in the vestry are not kept. The chapter revenues are mismanaged.

(Eudes de Rigaud, "Register of Visitations," 1248; ed., trs. G. G. Coulton, 1892)

Decree of the Council of Constance, claiming authority even over popes (1415): This holy synod of Constance, constituting a general council, does hereby ordain, ratify, enact, decree, and declare the following:

First, it declares that ... it has its power directly from Christ, and that all persons of whatever rank or dignity, even a Pope, are bound to obey it in matters relating to faith and the end of the Schism and the general reformation of the Church of God in head and members.

Further, it declares that any person of whatever position, rank or dignity, even a Pope, who contumaciously refuses to obey the mandates, statutes, ordinances, or regulations enacted or to be enacted by this holy synod, or by any other general council lawfully assembled, ... shall, unless he repents, be subject to condign penalty and duly punished. ...

("Decrees of the Council of Constance," 1415; trs. L. R. Loomis 1961)

1290 (under Edward I); from France in 1306 (under Philip IV); from Spain, horribly, in 1492 (under Ferdinand and Isabella); from Portugal, on the Spanish model, in 1497. The Jewish communities migrated: from the Iberian peninsula to the eastern Mediterranean and North Africa; and from the north, eastward to the German and Slavic lands of Europe, where great numbers lived until the Holocaust of the twentieth century (see Chapters 24, 28).

When the crusading era opened, the Roman Church had split from the Eastern Orthodox Church, whose official leader, or patriarch, reigned in Constantinople under the protection of the Byzantine Empire. As early as the fourth century, doctrinal and philosophical differences could be observed between western (Latin-speaking) and eastern (Greek-speaking) leaders of the church. Thus, their respective churches developed, quite early, separate intellectual traditions. From the fifth through the seventh centuries, the Catholic Church often appealed to the Eastern emperor for political support but in vain. In the eighth and ninth centuries, finding itself increasingly isolated, it turned instead to the Frankish king. That era coincided with the episode of iconoclasm in the Eastern Church, decried by the popes (see Chapter 8).

Relations between the two churches foundered irremediably over a single clause in the formulation of the Nicene Creed. The Western Church insisted that the Holy Spirit (one of the three members of the Trinity) proceeded from the Father *and* the Son. The Eastern theologians insisted that the Spirit proceeded from the Father only. In 1054, leaders of the two churches excommunicated each other. The rift endures. The break with the Eastern Church left the pope the unrivaled Christian leader in the west.

In the meantime, Byzantine missionaries had brought their form of Christianity to the Slavic peoples of Europe inhabiting the eastern part of the continent from the Baltic to the Balkans. Byzantine missionaries reached Bulgaria in the ninth century, and Russia in the tenth. In the 860s, the missionary Saint Cyril (c. 827–869) devised from Greek characters an alphabet (named, after him, Cyrillic) in which to write the Slavic language (which heretofore had had no written form). Thereafter the saints' lives could be read by the new converts, just as the beautiful icons representing their faces could be venerated. Among the Slavic practitioners of Eastern Christianity were the ancestors of modern Russians. After Constantinople fell to the Ottoman Turks in 1453, the independent Russian Church preserved the Eastern Orthodox tradition.

Reform and Confrontation

As it proceeded to distinguish itself from other faiths, the Catholic Church undertook a thorough self-examination, inspired by the monastic reform begun at Cluny. In the same way that the Cluniac abbots insisted on monastic discipline, the Church in Rome (beginning shortly before 1100) announced stringent standards of personal behavior for the secular clergy. They were to remain strictly celibate (abstaining completely from sexual contacts) and to fulfill their pastoral responsibilities. Church offices were not to be sold or conferred upon relatives, friends, or favorites. Above all, authority was to be centered at Rome, and church personnel and funds were to be strictly reserved for the purposes of the Church.

The papal reform effort placed the Church at loggerheads with secular rulers on matters regarding the selection, appointment, and **investiture** of bishops—investiture being the process by which an office, either secular or ecclesiastical, was conferred. A new bishop was invested by being given the ring and staff that symbolized his clerical office. Because bishops and other church officials had both spiritual and temporal authority, confusion reigned as to who was entitled to appoint them and perform the ceremony of investiture. In the ninth and tenth centuries, the appointment and investiture of church officials had been the prerogative of secular rulers, but this right was now reclaimed for the Church by the papacy, who saw lay investiture of clergy as a major impediment to the establishment of church autonomy. The shift in policy especially affected the German emperors, whose political power rested on the bishops and lesser clerics, and who wanted able, skilled men to serve the interests of their state.

Also included in the papal reform agenda was the enforcement of moral standards with regard to the sexual behavior of the clergy and to the sale of church offices. In the early Middle Ages, celibacy had been thought desirable but not essential for the secular clergy. Many priests had concubines who acted virtually as wives, or engaged in other illicit forms of heterosexual behavior; homosexuality, too, appears to have been tolerated. Not only were the heterosexual alliances of priests increasingly considered improper, but they threatened church property, which might be lost to the illegitimate sons of errant priests. With church reform, celibacy became a requirement. Almost as common as the failure of priestly chastity was the sale of church offices, called **simony**, or their bestowal upon unworthy or juvenile relatives, called **nepotism**. These corrupt practices often resulted in the conveyance of church responsibilities to unqualified candidates who endangered both the effectiveness and the wealth of the Church. They, too, were now condemned.

One eleventh-century pope—one of the greatest in the history of the papacy—is particularly associated with the reform thrust of the mature medieval Church. Born Hildebrand, he was elected to the papacy as Gregory VII in 1073, having developed his reform program under the two previous popes. His principal target was the German emperor, Henry IV. In 1075, Pope Gregory wrote about his condemnation of lay investiture and his conception of papal authority in his register known as *Dictatus papae* ("The Pope's Decree"), quoted in *Witnesses* on p. 270. It declared, among other things:

> *That all princes shall kiss the feet of the pope.*
> *That he may be permitted to depose emperors.*
> *That he himself may be judged by no one.*

In 1076, Henry assembled his bishops and got them to declare their independence of the pope. Gregory responded by excommunicating Henry. The decree of **excommunication** was a sanction of utmost gravity, cutting the Christian off from the sacraments and ordinary social relations; and, when a monarch was excommunicated, releasing his subjects from allegiance to him. Thus it humiliated and incapacitated the German emperor, whose authority was fragile and whose barons now found it convenient to rebel. In the winter of 1077, in a hauntingly memorable scene, Henry stood for three days as a barefoot penitent outside the castle at Canossa, in Tuscany, where the papal party was en route to an assembly where the emperor's status would be discussed. The pope granted Henry **absolution**. For the moment, the papacy had outpaced in authority the secular monarchy.

The moment of reconciliation quickly passed. Years of papal-imperial conflict ensued; and in 1084 Henry IV succeeded in deposing his old adversary. Gregory died the following year, affirming, in the words of the psalmist, "I have loved justice and hated iniquity, therefore I die in exile."

The emperor's son and successor, Henry V (r. 1106–1125), continued to battle with popes. In 1122, he and the reigning pope, Calixtus II (r. 1119–1124) agreed to the Concordat of Worms (a city in the southwest of modern Germany), a landmark accord that settled at last the issue of lay investiture. The emperor guaranteed the free election of clergy and renounced any role in their investiture with ring and staff. The pope granted the emperor the right to be present at elections and to invest those elected with their lay responsibilities. In effect, this document described a new and enduring balance between church and secular powers—in the metaphor of the day, two "swords." The Church held the spiritual

Church and State

***Thomas à Becket:** The clashes between popes and emperors, bishops and kings, are represented vividly by the manuscript illumination (Ramsey Abbey, England, c. 1316) of the murder of Thomas à Becket, Archbishop of Canterbury and martyr of the English Church.* (Pierpont Morgan Library)

sword and authority in all matters pertaining to faith. The empire held the temporal sword and authority in all matters related to the security of the realm and the administration of justice among **laypeople**. The pope would choose his bishops, but the emperor might suggest his own candidates. The pope would invest the new cleric, then the emperor would charge him with his secular responsibilities. The principle had been announced—and would eventually prevail in the West—that Church and state were distinct.

The settlement at Worms was precarious, as soon became apparent in a different setting. King Henry II (1154–1189) of England had among his closest advisers the shrewd churchman Thomas à Becket (1118–1170). When, in 1162, Becket assumed the highest ecclesiastical office in the land, that of Archbishop of Canterbury, his behavior changed profoundly. No longer the cooperative royal servant, he was now the guardian of ecclesiastical rights. King and archbishop differed over the issue of punishing "criminous clerics"—churchmen accused of crimes, who were tried and convicted in church courts. Henry wanted them to be punished by secular authorities, to which Becket refused to assent. The king later charged Becket with financial improprieties while serving as his chancellor, and Becket went into exile rather than submit to trial in a secular court. The pope intervened, belatedly, on behalf of his archbishop. On Becket's return, he again offended the king, and Henry complained aloud of his troublesome prelate. In 1170, four of his knights—spontaneously perhaps, or too hastily responding to the king's instruction—slaughtered Becket in his own cathedral at Canterbury—murder compounded by sacrilege. England acquired in Becket a saint, and Canterbury became a pilgrimage site. Henry did **penance** and acknowledged church authority.

Pinturicchio, Pope Pius II at Ancona: *The papal role in fostering the Crusade effort is depicted by Pinturicchio in a fresco in Siena Cathedral, c. 1500, showing Pope Pius II assembling forces (in 1464) for a last vain attempt to reconquer the Holy Land from the Ottoman Turks.*

Born ten years before Becket's murder and made pope in 1198, Innocent III (r. 1198–1216) was a worthy successor to Gregory VII as an intellectual, reformer, and opponent of lay encroachment on ecclesiastical authority. Just as spirit reigned over body, he maintained, popes held rightful preeminence over secular princes—a belief he put into action on several occasions, one being when he excommunicated King John of England for interfering with the process of papal appointments. The principle of papal supremacy was acknowledged by the French, Spanish, and German monarchs, from whom Innocent demanded obedience.

At the opening of the fourteenth century, pope and monarch clashed again, this time in France. Here the issue was not investiture or judicial rights but money. King Philip IV (the Fair) planned to tap church wealth to restore the national treasury. In 1302 Pope Boniface VIII (r. 1294–1303) hurled at Philip the decree *Unam Sanctam*, which declared the supremacy of the Church over secular monarchs. Philip ordered his agents to depose the pope; they pursued him to Anagni, the town of his birth, where he had taken refuge, and proceeded to terrorize him. The townspeople rescued Boniface, but he died soon after, no doubt hurried along by his ordeal. The French king proclaimed the autonomy of the church in France from papal intervention. Philip IV's humiliation of Boniface in 1303, some two centuries after Pope Gregory's triumph over Henry IV in 1077, is a significant measure of the decline of papal authority in the later Middle Ages.

Popes and Councils

Following the death of Boniface, papal authority continued to wane. The next pope, Clement V (r. 1305–1314), was a Frenchman and Philip's puppet. He established himself and his court in the southern town of Avignon (then a papal possession, now part of France). Ordinary Christians were disheartened. For the first time, the head of the Catholic Church was no longer at Rome. Later critics of the papacy named the period of French residence (1309–1377) the "Babylonian Captivity" of the Church, recalling the image of the exile of the Israelites in Babylon in the sixth century B.C.E (see Chapter 2). It was the first phase of a period in which an increasingly corrupt and worldly papacy asserted its power in the face of mounting popular resentment.

During the Avignon years, and continuing a trend begun in the thirteenth century, the Church came to resemble a modern corporation. It employed an enormous staff of secretaries and treasurers and handled great sums of money. It reformed its administration, organized its bureaucracy, and improved its methods of accountancy. Presenting a model for growing monarchies to imitate, the papacy became the foremost monarchy in Europe. Some observers were impressed; others resented its political ambitions.

The Great Schism The pope belonged in Rome—so nearly everyone but the king of France believed. In 1377, persuaded by voices such as that of Catherine of Siena, Pope Gregory XI returned to Rome accompanied by his court and the College of Cardinals, high-ranking prelates whose unique privilege it is to elect popes. On Gregory's death in 1378, these cardinals (pressured by a Roman mob) elected his successor—an Italian—in Rome. Then, dissatisfied with their candidate, they repudiated him and elected a French pope, with whom they returned to Avignon. In Rome, however, the first candidate continued to reign, claiming supremacy and surrounded by a newly appointed College of Cardinals. The Church was now divided—in a state of **schism**.

Throughout Europe, nations, principalities, and cities now aligned themselves with one or the other pope. In 1409, at a council of clerical delegates and university theologians held at Pisa, the two then-reigning popes were deposed and a third was elected. Since neither of the deposed prelates recognized the authority of the council, they refused to step down. As a result, there were three popes. The scandalous "Great Schism," as the period of a divided church was called, lasted from 1378 to 1417. During those years, some Christians began to wonder whether they needed a pope at all.

Council of Constance The schism came to an end by actions taken at another council, held at Constance (in modern Switzerland) from 1414 to 1418 under the stern gaze of Sigismund, the Holy Roman Emperor (r. 1411–1437). The council's goals were three: to end the schism, to check the spread of heresy, to reform the Church. With nearly all the important leaders of the Church as well as university experts in theology and church law participating, it resolved the schism by deposing all three popes and electing (in 1417) the reliable Martin V (r. 1417–1431). It also, notoriously, condemned as a heretic the Czech scholar and visionary John Huss (c. 1372–1415), who was burned at the stake.

Before disbanding, those assembled at Constance decreed that the Church was to be governed not by the pope alone but by regularly held councils made up of persons like themselves (see *Witnesses* p. 270). Once the popes were solidly established at Rome, however, and getting ever richer, they resisted. A council was held beginning in 1431 (at Basel, in Switzerland), which degenerated into hostilities between pope and councilors. In 1437 another council convened—first at Ferrara, in Italy, then in Florence when Ferrara was struck by plague. It was dedicated to conversations with prelates from the Eastern Orthodox Church. Terrified at the Turkish advance, which was in its final stage, the emperor at Constantinople had sent that delegation hoping that reconciliation would yield western military assistance for his embattled capital. Despite a compromise, the rift between the two churches was not healed. Constantinople fell in 1453. In the west, the conciliar movement faded under the eagle eye of a now-potent pope.

In the century following the elevation of Martin V at the Council of Constance, the papacy became increasingly powerful, wealthy, and corrupt. The centralized bureaucracy collected taxes from every corner of Christendom. The wealth funded the rebuilding of Rome, the creation of a fine library at the Vatican, the defense of the Papal States, a network of ambassadors and agents, and even the preparations for a last futile Crusade. The popes, the cardinals, and the bishops, well compensated for duties they left others to perform, promoted their friends, nephews, and illegitimate children to lucrative offices. The Catholic Church had strayed far from the example of simplicity and sincerity presented by the biblical Jesus. To many, it seemed to have abandoned ordinary Christians, and especially those that Jesus had especially recommended: the poor and the forgotten.

THE CHURCH AND THE PEOPLE

Most people at this time were unaware of the papacy's accumulation of wealth and power, or the scandalous behavior of the various popes. Their knowledge of the Church was based only on the rhythms and rituals of the Christian year and their acquaintance with the parish priest. Even the dedicated lives of the monks and nuns in nearby monasteries and convents seemed remote to ordinary villagers and townsfolk. A few, however, lived extraordinary lives. Craving a deeper religious experience, they were drawn to **mysticism**, or to heresy, or to the movements of pious lay people that flourished in the later Middle Ages.

The Pattern of Christian Life

Most medieval Christians knew the tenets of the Church only as told them by a village priest—often a peasant like themselves, uneducated and unaware. Those who lived in the towns and cities that developed after 1000 knew the priest of their immediate neighborhood or parish, the bishop and semimonastic **canons** of the cathedral, and the friars who preached in the market squares and begged in the streets. The wealthy nobleman was tended by his own priest or chaplain, who officiated in the private chapel of his castle. In village, city, or castle, the priest celebrated the **mass** by which Christians experienced union with the Deity, and administered other sacraments by which they received the grace of God and some assurance of salvation.

Only an ordained priest could officiate at the mass, in which bread and wine—the elements—were believed to be transformed into the body and blood of Christ. Worshipers consuming those transformed elements (by 1300, only the bread called "the host" was offered to the **laity**) were believed to be in communion with Christ. This ritual event, called the Eucharist, was one of the seven sacraments of the Church.

A sacrament in the Catholic and Orthodox churches is a ritual act conveying grace to the worshiper. Four others mark stages in human life—baptism, which incorporates a child into the church; confirmation, by which a child affirms his or her faith; marriage, which joins male and female in a legitimate relationship; and anointing, or extreme unction, which prepared a dying person for eternity. The other two sacraments are ordination, by which a man is made a priest; and penance, which follows a person's confession of their sins. The priest assigns an act of penance to be performed in order to atone for a particular sin and obtain absolution, the forgiveness of that sin.

The crucified Jesus: *The central event of the Christian religion is the crucifixion of Jesus, represented frequently over the medieval centuries in every available medium. Here is shown an ornate crucifix from fourteenth-century France.* (Musei Civici, Padua)

To medieval Christians (and to some Christians today), penance and absolution were matters of supreme importance. Those whose sins had been confessed and absolved looked forward to life after death in Heaven. Those who died burdened with serious sins would be doomed to Hell, a place of eternal punishment. These were the poles that defined the universe of the medieval Christian. The faithful were instructed about these destinies in words and forms, in the preachers' sermons and in the stone and wooden sculptures and stained-glass windows of the churches. Fears of Hell were somewhat lessened, however, by the possibility of spending some term of the afterlife in Purgatory.

From late antiquity to the thirteenth century, the concept of Purgatory gradually developed as a third realm to which the soul might be temporarily consigned. Here the Christian who was not entirely sinless could expiate his or her sins and still eventually achieve admission to Heaven. He or she could be helped along by the intercession of the saints or of the Virgin Mary, or by the prayers of the faithful still on earth. Some careful planners left bequests in their wills to pay for the performance of masses for the welfare of their souls in Purgatory. These could help. But the Christian who wished to gain Heaven and avoid Hell must attend mass, receive the sacraments, confess, and receive absolution for sins. Thus priests were the gatekeepers of salvation.

Guidebooks called "penitentials" assigned punishments to those who had sinned. In the early Middle Ages, an adulterer or murderer might be assigned a long and difficult penance—years of fasting on bread and water, for instance, or confinement. In the later period, available acts of penance also included gifts to the Church for the building of a hospital or a chapel—attractive alternatives to persons of middling wealth, just as great noblemen of earlier times had found it beneficial to found a monastery.

A form of penance popular with repentant sinners throughout the period was the pilgrimage (which for knights could take the form of a Crusade). A long and hazardous journey to Jerusalem or a somewhat shorter one to the Shrine of Saint James of Compostela (in Spain) or that of Saint Thomas à Becket at Canterbury (in England) or to Rome might atone for a mountain of sins. At these sites, the penitent could revere the body or part of the body—the relic, sometimes only a knucklebone or a tooth—of a saint, who could intercede with God for forgiveness of sins.

The many sins were classified in seven categories: pride, envy, anger, greed, lust, gluttony, and a spiritual apathy dangerous to the soul called sloth. Although all were evil, the emphasis in the confessional often fell on lust—illicit sexual desire and sexual misconduct. Confessors asked adult men and women about adultery and prostitution, male adolescents about masturbation, and females about secret pregnancies. They asked husbands and wives whether they had performed intercourse only for the purpose of procreation, and if they had done so according to acceptable guidelines established by church scholars. They queried women about obedience to parents or husbands, and men about homosexual behavior. Homosexuality was considered not only a sin but, in some regions and periods, a crime punishable by death. Yet it was common in the exclusively male community of the monastic clergy.

Baptism was expected to follow birth promptly. The death of an unbaptized infant condemned the soul of the unfortunate to a zone on the margins of Hell, called limbo—and threatened survivors with contamination. Clerical experts also condemned abortion and infanticide; abandoned infants were considered a responsibility of the Church. The dying were to confess their sins, making a "good death" so that they might enter Heaven or, at least, Purgatory. Those who died unbaptized or excommunicate or as a result of suicide were denied burial in sacred ground.

Marriage was considered not only a sacrament of the Church but also a secular institution involving the transfer of property between families. For those who bestowed or received wealth in a marriage agreement, the moment when the contract was signed or when the bride was conducted to her husband's house might be considered the moment of marriage. The Church attempted to bring marriage customs under its jurisdiction. It insisted on the equal importance of the man's and the woman's intention to marry. Each had to consent freely to the arrangement, and it was their freely exchanged words, when followed by consummation, that were regarded as establishing the marriage. Around the beginning of the thirteenth century, it became the custom for this exchange of vows to be conducted in front of or inside the church building and to receive the blessing of a priest. However, the marriage ceremony was not wholly standardized until the sixteenth century, when both Protestants and Catholics insisted on church control of the institution.

Although the Church regulated the lives of most Christians, it especially controlled those of women. Clerical authors considered women—in the pattern of Eve, who had led Adam to sin in the Garden of Eden—to be the origin of all sin (see *Windows On*, p. 277). From this assumption emerged a clerical and long-enduring misogyny. Women's bodies were condemned for luring men into vice. The monastic reformer Odo of Cluny exclaimed: "How can we desire to embrace such a sack of dung?" Women were deceitful, lustful, incapable of reason. They had to be confined to domesticity and to carefully guarded chastity. A special target of preachers and confessors, women were portrayed as an ever-present danger. Summing up the Church's view of women, a cleric warned, "Woe unto this sex, which knows nothing of awe, goodness, or friendship, and which is more to be feared when loved than when hated!" Of that sex also, ironically, was the Virgin Mary, revered by medieval Christians, and the subject of many works of prayer and art, as illustrated on p. 175.

As it battled against the dangers posed by women, as it was believed, to the health of the soul, the medieval Church also struggled with the relics of paganism—the customs and beliefs surviving among European communities from the days before Christianization. Many of the attributes of ancient gods had become attached to revered saints. The old legends and rituals were gradually assimilated into Christian practices. As late as the eighteenth century, in some quiet villages and enclaves, people who were nominally Christian displayed vestiges of pre-Christian religious behavior—evident in their faith in charms or spells or special objects—despite the rigorous intervention of priests and inquisitors.

If the Church intruded in many ways upon the lives of Christians, it also provided services that were otherwise unavailable. The Church cared for the ill, the poor, the hungry, the widowed and orphaned. In the early Middle Ages, monasteries served as hospitals and hostelries in the absence of any others. With the expansion of urban life, later in the Middle Ages, the Church expanded its mission, establishing hospitals and orphanages and homes for abandoned wives and destitute widows. Here the pious and the saintly, by their concern, their labor, and their donations, might give expression to charity.

HOW MANY?

630 Saints

SAINTS' BIRTHPLACES

	Century of Saints' Death				
	11th	12th	13th	14th	15th
British Isles	19	20	10	2	2
Low Countries	8	11	6	1	2
France	23	37	24	11	7
Italy	26	35	79	74	53
Iberia	11	13	12	3	9
Scandinavia	1	9	1	3	0
Holy Roman Empire, Switzerland	32	27	22	7	4
Eastern Europe	7	0	4	5	4
Non-European	1	1	1	1	2
Total (630)	128	153	159	107	83

SAINTS' PROFESSIONS

	Century of Saints' Death				
	11th	12th	13th	14th	15th
Popes, cardinals	4	3	4	2	3
Bishops, archbishops	31	42	28	8	7
Abbots, abbesses, priors, prioresses	34	49	26	14	20
Lesser clerics	19	18	35	32	18
Tertiaries	5	0	8	15	5
Lay people	35	41	58	36	30
Total (630)	128	153	159	107	83

Source: D. Weinstein & R. M. Bell, *Saints and Society: The Two Worlds of Western Christendom, 1000–1700* (Chicago: University of Chicago Press, 1982)

Extraordinary Christians

Although the lives of ordinary people were saturated with Christian meanings and regulated by Christian instruction, some individuals found even this degree of religiosity inadequate to their spiritual needs. They yearned for a deeper, more complete experience of God. Some of them were later canonized as saints, whose holy works could transfer holiness to those who revered them. Some were mystics, who sought in the interior self a union with the divine. Some were heretics, who urged that God be sought outside the norms and boundaries of Catholic orthodoxy. Some lived outwardly normal lives in the world while they privately devoted themselves to a higher standard of devotion than did their neighbors. Men, women, laity, and clergy, these extraordinary Christians added to the rich texture of medieval life.

During the Middle Ages, the pattern of sainthood shifted, as *How Many?* on this page indicates. In the early Christian centuries, martyrs, theologians, and missionaries were canonized. In the high Middle Ages, many saints were healers and feeders; their care for the poor and the abandoned was understood as the sign of their sanctity. At the same time, female saints became more numerous. The percentage of women among the saints rose from just under 10 percent around 1100, to 15 percent around 1250, to 24 percent by 1300, to 29 percent for the fifteenth century.

Female sanctity differed from male sanctity. Female saints tended more than males to explore the inner life. They engaged in mystic contemplation, experienced divine visions, struggled with demons, and uttered prophecies. More than men, too, they engaged in extreme forms of asceticism. They confined themselves to cells, had themselves whipped, tormented their bodies, drank pus from the festering wounds of lepers, and starved themselves.

WINDOWS ON

Female Spirituality

Berthold Fürtmayr, The Tree of Life and Death, _Salzburger Missale, c. 1481_

Radegund dining, kneeling, and praying, late eleventh century

Eve and Mary represented for medieval people the polar possibilities for women: wicked Eve, who brought damnation upon humankind, or holy Mary, who almost redeems Eve's wickedness. Depicted in this miniature of the Garden of Eden (left) are these two figures of female possibility.

In this manuscript (right) is depicted the eleventh-century holy woman Radegund, a follower of Mary. She is seen here kneeling in her chapel, sitting at table reluctantly with her husband, and (below) abandoning her husband's bed in order to pray on the hard floor.

(left: Bayerische Staatsbibliothek, Munich; right: Médiathèque François Mitterrand, Poitiers)

To continue your investigation of this topic, please go to www.prenhall.com/king for the related WINDOWS on the WEB activity

WITNESSES

Holy Women

For women as well as men, the religious life could offer a refuge, or an opportunity for study and spiritual development; and for some, whose commitment was shallow, a stress-free life with opportunities for indulgence and sociability. In the first passage, the seventh-century queen Etheldreda deliberately chooses a religious life over a secular one. In the second, the fourteenth-century mystic Beatrice of Nazareth describes in vivid and sensual language her relationship to God. In the third, the fourteenth-century English poet Geoffrey Chaucer sketches as a fictional character a shallow and self-centered nun.

Etheldreda marries King Egfrid and becomes a nun (7th century): King Egfrid married Etheldreda, a daughter of Anna, King of the East Angles. ... Although she lived with him for twelve years, she preserved the glory of perpetual virginity, which fact is absolutely vouched for by Bishop Wilfrid of blessed memory, of whom I made enquiry when some people doubted it. He said that Egfrid promised to give estates and much money to anyone who could persuade the queen to consummate the marriage. ... For a long time Etheldreda begged the king to allow her to retire from worldly affairs and serve Christ the only true King in a convent. And having at last obtained his reluctant consent, she entered the convent of the Abbess Ebba, king Egfrid's aunt. ... A year later she was herself made Abbess of Elge [Ely], where she built a convent and became the virgin mother of many virgins vowed to God, displaying the pattern of a heavenly life in word and deed.

(Bede, *History of the English Church and People*, Bk. 4, Ch. 19, 660; ed. L. Sherley-Price, 1955)

Beatrice of Nazareth describes the experience of loving God (14th century): At times love throws off all restraint, it surges forth with such power and sets the heart beating so fast and furious that it feels wounded through and through, and those wounds are constantly reopened, each day more searing and painful than the last. The veins seem to open, the blood to run out, the marrow to wither. Bones crack, the chest explodes, the throat is parched. One's face and limbs burn inwardly with the sovereign rage of love. Sometimes it is as though an arrow were passing through the heart and into the throat, causing loss of consciousness; at other times it is like a fire that consumes everything in its vicinity. Such is the violence to which the soul is subjected, such is the effect on it of unrestrained and pitiless love, which wants and devours all things.

(Beatrice of Nazareth, *The Seven Kinds of Love*, 14th c.; ed. E. Petroff, trs. E. Colledge, 1986)

The English poet Geoffrey Chaucer describes a different kind of nun—aristocratic, vain, and shallow (c. 1387–1400):

Full well she sang the services divine,
Intoning through her nose, becomingly;
And fair she spoke her French, and fluently,
After the school of Stratford-at-the-Bow,
For French of Paris was not hers to know.
At table she had been well taught withal,
And never from her lips let morsels fall,
Nor dipped her fingers deep in sauce, but ate
With so much care the food upon her plate
That never driblet fell upon her breast.

(Chaucer, *Canterbury Tales*, The Prioress, c. 1387–1400; trs. J. U. Nicholson, 1934)

Besides caring for the needy, medieval saints and other holy men and women peered deep into themselves, where they found a spiritual life and an openness to God not possible in the busy and practical world. Their mysticism belongs to a distinct kind of religious experience encountered in many religions. The Buddha and his followers in quest of Nirvana participated in mystical experiences, as did the Muslim Sufis, whose insight was so compelling a force in the spread of Islam.

In Christian mysticism, the worshiping self was understood to merge with the reality of God. As Saint Bernard of Clairvaux (1090–1153), a leading exponent of the mystical knowledge of God, described: "For in a certain way you lose yourself, as if you were not." Another mystic was the German Dominican Meister Eckhardt (c. 1260–c. 1328). Female mystics were active, too: the deep passion of Elizabeth of Schönau and Mechthild of Magdeburg probably informed the work of Eckhardt. The female recluse Julian of Norwich (1342–d. after 1416) explored the meaning of a God who contained both female and male principles: "God almighty is our kindly Father, and God-all-wisdom is our kindly Mother, ... which is all one God, one Lord." The mystical experience of Beatrice of Nazareth is described in *Witnesses* on this page.

Prophets, unlike mystics, concerned themselves with the state of affairs on earth and within Christendom. Their inner experience and deep convictions led them to critique the present and predict the course of things to come. A burst of prophecy accompanied the crossing of the millennium in the year 1000. Later prophets were self-appointed critics of the secular world, such as Joachim of Fiore (c. 1130–c. 1201). This nobly born, former Cistercian abbot predicted the imminent end of his age and the birth of a new one which would be guided by genuinely spiritual monks (the corrupt priests of his day having been ousted) in a universal sabbath for the human race. Joachim's ideas, which were judged heretical, continued to circulate long after his death, in a popular book entitled *The Everlasting Gospel.*

Heresy and Unorthodoxy Among the prophets, mystics, and saintly people were those whom authorities labeled heretics, deviants from orthodox belief. The first heresies dated from the earliest centuries of the church—those of the Arians and Pelagians, Montanists and Nestorians, which proposed alternate formulations of the Church's creed. Medieval heresies were different. They opposed the Church itself. Their centers are shown on Map 10.2.

The heretics called Waldensians took their name from Peter Waldo (d. c. 1184), a merchant of Lyons, who gave up all his possessions (about 1176) and pledged himself to a life of poverty. His followers, too, embraced a simple life, similar to that later followed by the Franciscans. Unlike the Franciscans, who did not so plainly challenge church institutions and were able to persuade the pope to approve their order, the Waldensians challenged the doctrine of Purgatory and saw no need for priests. In 1211, eighty of the faithful were burned in Strasbourg, inaugurating a persecution that would extend for centuries.

Even more critical of the mainstream Church were the Albigensians, centered at Albi, in France. Their views can be traced to the Manicheanism of the early Christian era. Repudiating the Church and the priesthood, the Albigensians—also called Cathars—rejected the flesh, and with it marriage and procreation. They believed that the Christian's aim, attainable only by an elite few, was to achieve a perfect purity in this life as a condition of salvation. The "perfect" who succeeded in meeting these stern demands constituted a kind of alternate priesthood, who could bestow the yearned-for "consolation," a bestowal of sacred grace. Despite the extraordinary demands of this faith, it won widespread support in the south of France, especially from the nobility, a few of whom became converts. It was so successful that in 1208 the Church in Rome launched a crusade against

Map 10.2 Religious centers and centers of heresy, to 1500: *The great events of Christian history in western Europe were also events that influenced the political, social, and cultural lives of Europeans. The sites of reform initiative, of conflict between rulers and prelates, of pilgrimages and councils, of the centers of heresy and intellectual life, are all major landmarks in the fascinating development of Western civilization.*

the heretics—one of several, culminating in one led by the French king, Louis VIII, in 1225–1226. That war resulted in the near-extermination of Albigensian adherents and won the region for France. But it failed to eradicate the heresy. Dominican friars set themselves to that task as agents of the Inquisition, begun by papal order in 1231 precisely for this purpose.

A century later, John Wyclif (c. 1330–1384), one of Catholic orthodoxy's most formidable opponents, was born in England. He studied and taught at Oxford University, seldom leaving its precincts before 1381 (although he acquired a number of ecclesiastical benefices), just three years before his death. This churchman and scholar denied papal claims to earthly authority and attacked the Church's priestly and sacramental structure. Worse, as the official Church viewed it, his message was heard with interest by king and Parliament. Still worse, it reached the common people, including artisans and merchants, among whom it gained a significant following.

Wyclif believed that Scripture was the source of all truth and that even ordinary human beings, if enlightened by the Holy Spirit, could understand it. Since the only Bible available in the Middle Ages was a fourth-century Latin translation, Wyclif translated it into English. As growing numbers of the laity could read the English, the effect of his translation was electrifying. Wyclif inspired many followers, called "Lollards" (from the Middle Dutch word *lollaerd*, "mutterer," applied to various pious but heretical groups who "muttered" their prayers). The Lollards endured long after Wyclif's death, despite intense persecution, up to the time of the Protestant Reformation (see Chapter 14). Wyclif himself was admonished to silence in 1378, and died a few years later. In 1428, his body was exhumed and burnt—a posthumous punishment for heresy.

Far from England, in the section of the Holy Roman Empire called Bohemia (the modern Czech Republic), the schoolmaster John Huss (c. 1372–1415) read Wyclif's books and began to spread his message. Huss preached to the people and wrote learned books against the clergy and for the right of the laity to take communion in both kinds (both the wine, normally reserved to the clergy, and the bread). His message won a large following among the Bohemians, who, from 1388, had available a Czech translation of the Bible and whose desire for religious reform mingled with their nationalist ambitions. Alerted by the Archbishop of Prague, the pope excommunicated Huss and ordered him to stand trial for heresy. Huss traveled to the town of Constance to present his case before the council of the Church then meeting there. Although he had been promised a safe-conduct by the emperor Sigismund himself, the document provided was merely a passport. When Huss arrived in Constance, he was condemned as a heretic, imprisoned, and tortured. Finally he was burned at the stake and his ashes scattered on the waters of the Rhine, lest any relic remain for followers to revere. Even so, the Hussite movement survived and even thrived, until—like Lollardy and Waldensianism—it merged with the many strands of the Protestant Reformation (see Chapter 14).

Many heretics were women. They were attracted to the Albigensian and Lollard messages, and even to other, more extreme, movements. Why the inordinate appeal of **heterodoxy** among those who, for the most part, were the patient bearers of culture and transmitters of the mainstream Catholic faith? It is possible that heterodoxy gave opportunities for personal expression that orthodoxy did not. Such was probably the explanation for the career of Marguerite Porete.

The Flemish Marguerite Porete (?–c. 1310) expressed in more than 60,000 words some deeply heretical notions. Excerpts from her book *The Mirror of Simple Souls* were examined by scholars at the University of Paris, who found much to condemn in her notions of the annihilation of the soul and its

WHO'S WHO

Hildebrand, as Pope Gregory VII (r. 1073–1085) the engineer of the papal reform of the Church and opponent of Henry IV, Holy Roman Emperor.

Thomas à Becket (1118–1170) saint and martyr, friend then critic of Henry II, King of England.

Dominic of Castile (c. 1170–1221) sainted Spanish founder of the mendicant order named after him, and champion of orthodox Christian doctrine.

Francis of Assisi (1182?–1226) sainted Italian founder of the mendicant order named after him, and advocate of absolute Christian poverty.

William of Ockham (c. 1285–1349) skeptical English philosophical thinker who urged systematic investigation of things of this world and reverence for the absolute power of the divine; wielder of the logical Razor; opponent of the papal monarchy.

John Wyclif (c. 1330–1384) English professor, translator of the Bible, advocate of church reform and lay piety.

Catherine of Siena (1347–1380) Italian saint who urged the restoration of the papacy to Rome.

John Huss (c. 1372–1415) Czech teacher, translator of the Bible, advocate of church reform and lay piety; burned at Constance as a heretic.

Joan of Arc (c. 1412–1431) peasant visionary; savior of French military during Hundred Years' War; taken captive, tried, and burned as a witch and heretic; canonized 1920.

identification with the divine: "Now this soul is a blank, because it sees its nothingness by fullness of divine knowledge, which makes it a blank, makes it a void. ..." Into this void comes God, who "sees himself in the Soul ... by means of his divine majesty." In another time and place Porete might have been thought a mystic, or even a saint; instead, she was burned at the stake.

Joan of Arc (c. 1412–1431) also defied orthodox norms and suffered condemnation for heresy. A pious and illiterate girl from the French countryside, she grew up during the Hundred Years' War between France and England. In 1429, Joan presented herself to the uncrowned king of France, Charles VII, and announced that she had been sent by God to defeat the English. Fully armed and dressed as a man, this seventeen-year-old girl fought with the French forces at Orléans, and so inspired them that within three days they had lifted the seven-month-long siege of that city. Subsequently, she stood by King Charles at his coronation in Rheims. In 1430, she was captured and remanded to the enemy—Charles making no attempt to win her release. Handed over to the Inquisition in Rouen (who, though French, supported the English), Joan was imprisoned, tortured, intimidated, and, in the course of a ten-week-trial, interrogated, chiefly over the nature of the "voices"—of saints, she maintained—that had guided her actions. In the end, the court condemned her as a heretic and a witch and had her burned in the market square of Rouen. Five hundred years later, in 1920, the Church declared her a saint.

Other women were inclined by their religious yearnings to join communities of the faithful. By the late Middle Ages, however, female monasticism was in serious decline, hemmed in by ecclesiastical regulations and avoided by women seeking greater scope for their spiritual lives. Some women were attracted to heresy or a solitary mysticism, but others wanted to devote themselves to a communal Christian life without taking vows. Many chose to live in lay communities, where they supported themselves and others, performed Christian service, and engaged in prayer and study. From the end of the twelfth century, beginning in the Low Countries, women called Beguines congregated in such communities, called *béguinages*; later, Beguine houses were established in the various towns of the prosperous German Rhineland. Between 1250 and 1350, about 100 of them were founded in Cologne, housing about 1,000 women. Those in Strasbourg housed about 600. The movement of these pious laywomen anticipates other lay movements, involving both men and women, of the late Middle Ages. Of these perhaps the most influential called themselves the "Brethren of the Common Life."

Followers of the Dutch reformer and mystic Gerhard Groote (1340–1384) joined together as the "Brethren of the Common Life" to foster a simpler, more sincere piety than was found, they felt, in the official Church. Their brotherhood was part of the larger movement of the *devotio moderna*, or "New Devotion." The Brethren supported the education of young people bound for clerical service, and influenced scholars of the next generation. Their views are most fully expressed in *The Imitation of Christ*, which may have been written by the shadowy Thomas à Kempis (1379–1431), who was associated with them. In some ways their beliefs approximate those of the followers of Wyclif and Huss, deemed heretical, and anticipate some aspects of the Protestant Reformation.

THE MIND'S ROAD TO GOD

While Christianity dominated the lives of ordinary people and, even more, those of saints and religious reformers, it also ruled the lives of intellectuals. Rather than through mystical experience or a pious, communal life, they sought a road to God built on thought and reason.

Christian rationalism was developed further in medieval Europe than in any other culture. It nurtured the tradition of high medieval philosophy. It opened the paths to modern science and political thought, in which the West would make major contributions. It was cultivated in the schools and universities of the Middle Ages, wholly new institutions which grew up in the shelter of the monastery and the cathedral.

School and University

It was thanks to the Church that the practice of reading, reflecting, and writing survived in medieval Europe. Christianity was based on a written tradition, and the Church required trained experts to guide the faithful in the worship of God. Clerics were virtually the only literate people in the early Middle Ages. (Our word "clerk" derives from "cleric," or "churchman.") They learned to read and write in schools created for the purpose of training servants of the Church.

For centuries, the principal schools in Europe were monastic schools. At first, they taught only monks, many of them child oblates. Their curriculum consisted of learning to read and write Latin, using fragments of the books drawn from monastic libraries. In time, the monastic schools also taught persons destined for the secular clergy. After 1000, new schools were formed for this purpose, attached to the cathedrals of some larger cities, especially in northern France (Laon, Rheims, Paris). Their graduates would become priests and bishops themselves, or advisers and secretaries to kings. The purpose of monastic education was thus different from that of the cathedral schools. The monks wished to preserve the Christian tradition and to reflect upon its meaning. The cathedral schools wished to develop skills of rational analysis for men who needed to accomplish things. From these schools developed the intellectual movement called **Scholasticism**.

Scholasticism can be identified by its characteristic method of reasoning, evidenced in the **disputation**, which derived from the circumstances of medieval education. Instruction in medieval schools was oral, as books were scarce. The presentation of arguments developed a form suited for oral delivery, the disputation. A kind of structured debate, the disputation required each of two participants to present arguments for or against a proposed statement, or thesis. The disputation required mastery of language and knowledge, the ability to speak and think quickly and sharply, and psychological qualities of determination and combativeness. It was a superb training ground for the mind—the intellectual counterpart of the medieval tournament.

The method of reasoning used in oral disputation or in written books was **dialectic**. In the dialectical method, a problem was proposed, arguments pro and con presented and evaluated, and a conclusion reached. At the close of the argument, medieval authors would often add the triumphant words "*quod erat demonstrandum*," abbreviated Q.E.D., meaning "which was the thing that had to be proved," and was now resolved. This dialectical method of reasoning was pursued in virtually every subject matter—philosophy, theology, law, and medicine, the premier disciplines of the age.

Peter Abelard In Paris, a quarrelsome teacher named Peter Abelard (1079–1142) cultivated an even bolder critical style. Abelard attracted students from all over Europe, who flocked to hear penetrating critiques of other men's ideas from the man who considered himself "the only philosopher remaining in the world." Abelard's challenging notion of truth is illustrated in his *Sic et Non* ("Yes And No"). Here a series of controversial views from the Church Fathers are presented and assessed by arguments pro and con. No conclusion follows. Abelard deliberately left these matters open to trouble later thinkers and inspire further exploration. A critical thinker rather than a builder of systems, Abelard is representative of the first phase of Scholasticism.

Abelard is also known for his involvement with Héloïse (c. 1098–1164), one of the most tragic love stories of the era. The niece of Fulbert, the cleric with whom Abelard boarded, Héloïse became Abelard's student and then his lover. When she got pregnant, she refused to stay with him, which would have cut short his promising intellectual career. Learning of the clandestine marriage performed at Abelard's insistence over Héloïse's objections, Fulbert had Abelard seized, beaten, and castrated. Thus mutilated and shamed, Abelard sought refuge and peace in a monastery. Letters exchanged between Abelard and Héloïse—perhaps genuine, although their authenticity cannot be proved—testify to their continuing love. But Abelard refused to have further personal relations with Héloïse, who became abbess of the convent he founded. While the story reveals much about Abelard, it is also a record of the experience of an educated woman. Her story is known not only from the letters, but from one of the most absorbing books of the era, Abelard's own autobiography, one of the earliest in the Western tradition.

MUST READS

Books to Remember

Benedict of Nursia (c. 480–c. 550) *Rule for Monks*

Peter Abelard (1079–1142) *Sic et Non (Yes and No)*

Hildegard of Bingen (1098–1179) *Scivias (Visions)*

Joachim of Fiore (c. 1130–c. 1201) *Everlasting Gospel*

St. Thomas Aquinas (c. 1225–1274) *Summa Theologica (Compendium of Theology)*

Marguerite Porete (?–c. 1310) *Mirror of Simple Souls*

Universities Abelard helped establish Paris as a center of learning. It would soon become the site of one of Europe's foremost universities. In earlier civilizations there had been centers of learning—Plato's Academy and Aristotle's Lyceum in Athens, the Museum at Alexandria, and the schools of Byzantium. Centers of Islamic civilization, including Córdoba, Damascus, and Baghdad, housed similar places of learning. In western Europe, medieval universities established the pattern for the institutions of higher education still functioning in the modern world. Map 10.2 shows the principal intellectual centers.

The word "university" originally meant a guild, or an association of professors or students. They banded together to establish who was eligible to teach, then to set standards for instruction—the courses offered, when and how often professors would teach, what subjects needed to be mastered for a student to be certified at an elementary or advanced level. The medieval institution did not at first have its own campus or buildings. It was a group of persons in search of, or ready to provide, knowledge, and who, to that end, agreed to certain regulations.

Universities were exclusively for men. Most developed from monastic and cathedral schools, and as such were clerical institutions—and the clergy (except for cloistered nuns, who did not attend schools) were all male. (Universities did not begin to admit women until late in the nineteenth century.) The religious origins of the university are visible even today. They are seen in the "quad" or quadrangle, reminiscent of the cloister, and in the style of academic robes still worn at official events. They live on also in the titles of the degrees awarded (Bachelor and Master of Arts, Doctor of Philosophy), which marked the attainments of the clerical scholar.

The University of Paris was officially established by royal charter in 1200. The two major universities in England, Oxford and Cambridge, soon followed. In the thirteenth and fourteenth centuries, several universities were founded in the sprouting cities of north Italy, and both the medical school at Salerno and the law school at Bologna were even older than the University of Paris. In the fourteenth and fifteenth centuries, universities sprang up rapidly throughout the German lands (where fourteen were established between 1386 and 1506) and throughout central Europe. When Europeans settled in the Americas after 1500, they brought the university tradition with them.

One characteristic of the medieval university that distinguished it from the monastic and cathedral school, was the granting of degrees. Degrees were granted to those who had completed a prescribed sequence of courses and public demonstrations of mastery. They were offered in four subject areas: the elementary area of arts (including language, logic, and philosophy) and the advanced areas of law (**canon** or civil), theology, and medicine. Of these, the greatest was theology, considered to be the culmination of the other disciplines, on whose intellectual foundations it was firmly grounded. The medieval schools and universities saw no contradiction between matters of faith and the life of the mind.

The Age of Faith and Reason

The Middle Ages has often been called the "age of faith." But it was just as surely an age of reason. The example of the eleventh-century philosopher and saint Anselm illustrates very well how the profound faith of medieval people could be joined to a relentless rationalism.

Saint Anselm (c. 1033–1109) already believed that God existed when he set out to prove it. Yet belief was not enough—enough for salvation, perhaps, but not for him. He wanted to understand: "I believe," he proclaimed in his famous formulation, "so that I may understand." Anselm searched for the mind's road to God. The result of his intellectual quest is the "ontological proof" (ontology is the study of the nature of existence) of the existence of God.

It works like this: (1) I have in my understanding a concept of God—that is, of "a being than which nothing greater can be conceived." (2) But it cannot be that a being "than which nothing greater can be conceived" exists *only* in the understanding. (3) If it existed only in the understanding, I could conceive of a being that is greater: a being that exists also in reality. (4) But it is impossible that there can be a conception greater than the conception of "a being than which nothing greater can be conceived." (5) Therefore that being exists not only in the understanding but also in reality, and that being is God. (6) God, furthermore, cannot be conceived not to exist; for if I conceive of being whose nonexistence is possible, then I could also conceive of a being greater still (one which could exist), and this latter being would truly be God. For medieval thinkers, reason and faith meet perfectly in this proof; for the correspondence between their interior, mental life and what existed in fact in the external world seemed to them to be absolute.

Anselm and his many successors shaped the mental world of the Middle Ages and of the modern West. A variety of circumstances prepared Europeans to take the lead in critical, rational thought after the twelfth century. First, Europe was defined by Christianity, a religion based on a book, the Bible, inherited from Judaism and extended by its own authors, which invited constant study and reflection. Second, the Fathers of the Church in the first centuries C.E. chose to embrace the whole of the Classical tradition, Greek and Latin, and to synthesize it with Christian doctrine. Third, monasticism from the start deemed as a preeminent objective the collection, transcription, and study of books and reliably transmitted the linguistic skills necessary to pursue this objective. Fourth, in its universities Europe provided a place for the prolonged study that intellectual creation requires. Finally, in the twelfth and thirteenth centuries, contacts with Arabic, Greek, and Jewish cultures provided materials and insights that stimulated several centuries of creative thought. Of these, the most important was certainly the recovery of the works of Aristotle.

The Aristotelian Revival The works of Aristotle, studied throughout antiquity, were still available during the Middle Ages in Constantinople (in their original Greek) and at the major centers of Islamic culture (where they were read both in Greek and in Arabic translation). Aside from the simpler logical works, they were not well known in western Europe. Beginning in the twelfth century, Jewish and Christian scholars based in Spain, in southern Italy, and in Constantinople began to acquire Aristotelian texts and translate them from the Greek and the Arabic into a serviceable, technical Latin. In addition to this flood of Aristotle, translations of three of Plato's dialogues reached the Christian West.

Not only did Christian Europeans acquire Aristotelian texts, but they read some of the Islamic and Jewish works that had been based on the Greek philosophical tradition. Of these, the scientific and philosophical works of Avicenna and Averröes were central to the development of scholastic thought. They focused on problems raised by the combined Platonic, Aristotelian, and Neoplatonic tradition—within a monotheistic framework—about the meaning of "essence" and "existence," the status of the individual soul, the rule of freedom or necessity, the relation between God and nature. More strictly Aristotelian was the work of the Jewish philosopher and physician Maimonides (Moses ben Maimon) (1135–1204). Forced by persecutions to leave Córdoba, then under Moorish domination, he lived in Egypt as a physician in the royal court and leader of the Jewish community. His *Guide for the Perplexed* (written in Arabic around 1204) contained a synthesis of ancient and theistic ideas. These were important issues for Christians who wished to make sense of the universe in which they lived without denying the truths taught them by faith.

Through the filters of Islamic and Jewish philosophy, and directly from the Greek, as well, the ideas of Aristotle reshaped the mental world of Christian Europe. Previously, the text that was the mainstay of their study was the Bible—rich in literary image and meaning, but poor in the abstract ideas that appealed to masters of disputation. Aristotle provided books on logical method, which became the new basis for arguing and proving propositions. Moreover, Aristotle provided a complete system of **metaphysics** (the study of the essential nature of reality), physics, political theory, and ethics that, however alien in origin, could be attached to fundamental Christian conceptions. Aristotle's understanding of a just ruler or of sexual moderation agreed with Christian notions of goodness and virtue. Aristotle's Prime Mover (an unmoved force which moves the universe) could be identified with God, and the whole of his metaphysical and physical model could be employed to explain a God-driven universe. The university professors, now voracious consumers of Aristotle, became the ancestors of our scientists and political theorists, ethicists, and logicians, as well as of our philosophers and theologians.

Saint Thomas Aquinas Perhaps the best known of these scholastic thinkers is Saint Thomas Aquinas (c. 1225–1274). An Italian nobleman and Dominican friar, Thomas wrote (among other works) two very large books establishing Christian theology on a systematic philosophical basis which are still read today by those capable of appreciating the author's vast understanding: the *Summa theologica* ("Compendium of Theology"), and the *Summa contra gentiles* ("Compendium against the Gentiles," an argument against the pagan construction of reality, quoted in *Witnesses* on p. 285). Thomas envisions a completely rational universe run by a rational God, in which the experience of the senses provides reliable knowledge and evil is not a force in itself but the absence of the good. Like Anselm and Maimonides, he presented important proofs of God's existence, which could be known through reason. Although his ideas were once suspected of heresy, they are now considered official doctrines of the Catholic Church and one of the grandest structures of thought in world history.

The English scholar and bishop (of Lincoln) Robert Grosseteste (c. 1175–1253) took Aristotle in a different direction—toward the consideration of the phenomena of the natural world—thus opening the road to modern scientific thought, based on mathematics rather than dialectic, and informed by a direct reading of Greek texts. Grosseteste saw God as light, and understood knowledge to be a form of illumination. But his theory of light was scientific as well as mystical: Grosseteste saw light as the basis of the whole of the physical universe, and experimental optics ("optics" is the scientific investigation of light and vision) as the key to its understanding. His approach (continued by his equally renowned student Roger Bacon, c. 1214–1294) identifies him as an early practitioner of the scientific method.

Another Englishman, the Franciscan William of Ockham (c. 1285–c. 1349), opened the final phase of medieval Scholasticism. By the fourteenth century, Aristotelianism and its implications had been well digested, and reaction set in. Was the God of creation and of revelation really so rational? Were the truths of faith and reason truly harmonious? Ockham's response to such questions was skeptical, and his answers disclose a waning of faith in cosmic or ecclesiastical or political order. His thinking had tremendous impact on later philosophy, theology, and politics (see Chapters 14, 15).

In the field of philosophy, Ockham was an **empiricist**, accepting the reality of things as perceived by the senses—a position essential for the development of science. Opposing the tendency toward unnecessary elaboration in the explanation of phenomena, he insisted on a principle not original with him but called ever afterward "Ockham's Razor"—that one should not postulate the existence of a greater number of factors than will suffice to explain a phenomenon. The rule can be judiciously wielded in many areas even today.

In theology, Ockham insisted on the dignity, power, and unknowability of the divine. By what right did men dictate to God how he conducted the business of the cosmos? God's will and power were alike absolute and undisclosed to humankind except through the actions of his creatures. Ockham's insistence on the unlimited power of the divine would be echoed in late mysticism and heresy, but even more powerfully in the theology of the Protestant reformers (see Chapter 14).

Ockham's daring views were suspect to church officials, particularly because he was a professed supporter of the Spiritual Franciscans (as opposed to the Conventual Franciscans), who were deemed heretical. In 1328, he was condemned by a papal inquisition at Avignon, whereupon he fled to Munich (modern Germany) with the aid of the emperor Louis of Bavaria. He was then joined by other heterodox intellectuals united in their opposition to what they saw as papal tyranny: John of Jandun (c. 1286–1328) and Marsiglius of Padua (c. 1280–c. 1343). Ockham and his fellow exiles helped lay the intellectual groundwork for the burgeoning of state power of the coming centuries.

In Munich, under imperial protection, Ockham dedicated himself to philosophical work and to destroying the theory of papal supremacy. Undeterred by a 1328 order of excommunication, Ockham declared the interfering Pope John XXII (r. 1316–1334) a heretic. Where the pope had claimed supremacy even in temporal affairs, Ockham argued the autonomy of the secular state. At the beginning of the Middle Ages, Saint Augustine had proclaimed the failure of the state and the triumph of the kingdom of God. At its close, Ockham declared church power fraudulent and hailed the supreme authority of the secular ruler. The circle had been completed.

The Glory of Gothic

Ockham challenged the earlier medieval assumption that the mind's activity could lead the seeker to God. The same assumption had reached full and public expression in a new style of architecture which emerged late in the twelfth century, when Scholasticism was reaching its innocent heights.

WITNESSES

Schools and Scholars

By the thirteenth century in medieval Europe, Christian thought had developed in a markedly rational direction under the influence of a renewed study of Roman law and Greek (especially Aristotelian) philosophy. Students, mostly clerics, flocked to study this new synthesis of scriptural truths and logical methods at centers called "universities." These passages variously reflect the nature of the scholarly pursuit at such institutions. The first describes the not-always admirable behavior of university students in thirteenth-century Paris. The second shows a teacher announcing his plans for the semester, promising "to teach you faithfully and in a kindly manner." The third exemplifies the style and substance of the work of the philosopher, saint, and university professor Thomas Aquinas, for whom what was true and what was reasonable must necessarily coincide.

The cleric and bishop Jacques de Vitry skeptically describes student life at the new university in Paris (early 13th century): Almost all the students at Paris, foreigners and natives, did absolutely nothing except learn or hear something new. Some studied merely to acquire knowledge, which is curiosity; others to acquire fame, which is vanity; others still for the sake of gain, which is cupidity and the vice of simony. Very few studied for their own edification, or that of others. They wrangled and disputed not merely about the various sects or about some discussions; but the differences between the countries also caused dissensions, hatreds and virulent animosities among them, and they impudently uttered all kinds of affronts and insults against one another.
(Jacques de Vitry, *Letters*, 13th c.; ed. N. Downs, 1959)

Odofredus explains to his students at the university of Bologna how he intends to teach them the *Corpus Juris Civilis*, or Compendium of Civil Law (c. 1250): If you please, I will begin the *Old Digest* on the eighth day or thereabouts after the feast of St. Michael [September 29] and I will finish it entire ... in the middle of August or thereabouts. The *Code* I will always begin within about a fortnight of the feast of St. Michael and I will finish it ... on the first of August or thereabouts. ... And so all scholars including the unskilled and novices will be able to make good progress with me, for they will hear their text as a whole, nor will anything be left out, as was once done in this region, indeed was the usual practice. ... For it is my purpose to teach you faithfully and in a kindly manner. ... And if any law is deserving of a review by reason of its fame or difficulty, I shall reserve it for an afternoon review.
(Odofredus, c. 1250; ed. L. Thorndike, 1944)

The philosopher and saint Thomas Aquinas explains that the truth uncovered by reason is in harmony with the truth taught by faith (1258–1260): Now, although the truth of the Christian faith which we have discussed surpasses the capacity of the reason, nevertheless that truth that the human reason is naturally endowed to know cannot be opposed to the truth of the Christian faith. For that with which the human reason is naturally endowed is clearly most true; so much so, that it is impossible for us to think of such truths as false. Nor is it permissible to believe as false that which we hold by faith, since this is confirmed in a way that is so clearly divine. Since, therefore, only the false is opposed to the truth, as is clearly evident from an examination of their definitions, it is impossible that the truth of faith should be opposed to those principles that the human reason knows naturally.
(St. Thomas Aquinas, *Summa contra gentiles*, 1258–1260; ed. A. Thompson, 1980, trs. A. Pegis, 1955)

Gothic style—Abbey Church of St. Denis: *Gothic architecture is full of light and apparently weightless, in comparison to the Romanesque. Where Romanesque was characterized by intricate sculptural forms, Gothic is characterized by harmonious compositions in stained glass, their effect wrought by light and color, as revealed in the apse and ambilatory of the church at St. Denis. Begun in 1140, the church pioneers Gothic style.*

Arising in the cities, adjacent to the schools and universities, marketplaces and courts it would challenge the earlier Romanesque style and stand as arguably the greatest artistic achievement of the mature Middle Ages.

The **Gothic** style (so named by some various eighteenth-century critics, who disapproved of it) replaced the round arch, inherited from antiquity, with a pointed arch. This is composed of two intersecting arcs that appear to soar upward, like the trees of northern forests, to the source of light and grace. Another characteristic of the Gothic style was the presence of light, achieved by allotting less space to wall and more to window. The windows, generally pointed like the related arches, were glazed with hundreds of tiny panes of richly colored glass conveying the narratives and messages of scripture.

A third characteristic of the Gothic was the accentuation of clear, daring structural elements. As the style developed, the wall thinned, the light intensified, and builders learned to brace this weaker structure with graceful external supports called flying buttresses, which added to the lace-like beauty of the whole. Just as the purpose and presence of these supports were acknowledged without embarrassment, the structural forms of the interior—pillars, columns, ribs—were boldly highlighted. It was as though the builder's aim was to clarify the process of building, just as the aim of the whole Church was to clarify for people's edification the nature of God's creation.

Romanesque had suited monasticism at its height: brooding and mysterious. Gothic suited an energized Europe: vibrant with change, daring in vision, refined and logical, pursuing a road to God expressed in stone and light surging powerfully and elegantly upward. "The very world," wrote a contemporary, "had shaken herself and cast off her old age and [was] clothing herself everywhere in a white garment of churches."

Conclusion

THE MEDIEVAL CHURCH AND THE MEANING OF THE WEST

In our secular modern world, it is easy to forget the Christian contribution to the formation of Western civilization. But that contribution is profound. Guided by leaders of exceptional talent, the Church shaped the values, institutions, customs, ideas, and styles of the Middle Ages over the course of one thousand years. Those values, which once fed nearly all of Europe's people, have not been obliterated, but reside still in the consciousness of those who are building the modern world—even those who reject the moral codes and doctrinal formulas of Christianity. Just as Saint Catherine of Siena summoned Gregory XI to be mindful of his duties, so the Christian past summons the heirs to Western civilization to be conscious of their standards of thought and behavior. It is, even today, a spiritual sword.

REVIEW QUESTIONS

1. What does "Christendom" mean? Why did Christianity stress the renunciation of the body? How did this attitude differ from those of ancient Greeks and Romans?

2. What features of monastic life did Basil, Cassiodorus, and Benedict establish? What opportunities did convents provide for women who became nuns? What were the mendicant orders?

3. How did the papacy become a major institution? How did the crusading movement affect Christian and Jewish relations? What issues divided the Western from the Eastern Church?

4. How did papal reform efforts in the twelfth century affect the Church's relations with lay rulers? Why was the metaphor the "two swords" used to describe the balance of authority between church and state? How did the Great Schism arise? How strong was papal authority in the late 1400s?

5. How important were the sacraments in medieval Christian life? How did the Church seek to control women's lives? What social services did the medieval Church provide?

6. What was Scholasticism? How were medieval universities different from the earlier monastic and cathedral schools? Why were the Middle Ages an age of reason as well as an age of faith?

SUGGESTED RESOURCES

Renunciation of the Body

Brown, Peter, *The Body and Society: Men, Women, and Sexual Renunciation in Early Christianity* (London: Faber, 1990). A study of early Christian attitudes toward sexuality and the body.

Johnson, Penelope D., *Equal in Monastic Profession: Religious Women in Medieval France* (Chicago: University of Chicago Press, 1991). A social history of French nunneries, focusing on their organization, the social origins of the nuns, relations with bishops, and monasteries.

Lawrence, C.H., *The Friars: The Impact of the Early Mendicant Movement on Western Society* (New York: Longman, 1994). Discusses the importance of the new orders of mendicant friars in medieval religious experience and society.

St. Benedict's *Rule for Monks*: Order of St. Benedict gateway page and texts: **http://www.osb.org/rb**

Church and State

Brentano, Robert, *A New World in a Small Place: Church and Religion in the Diocese of Rieti, 1188–1378* (Berkeley–Los Angeles: University of California Press, 1994.) Meticulous, original study of how church, religion, and society are transformed by the arrival of the Franciscans in one small Italian diocese under the rule of its enterprising bishops.

Morris, Colin, *The Papal Monarchy: The Western Church from 1050 to 1250* (Oxford: Oxford University Press, 1989). Discusses the investiture controversy, the structure of ecclesiastical government, and church–state relations.

The Church and the People

Brundage, James, *Law, Sex, and Christian Society in Medieval Europe* (Chicago: University of Chicago Press, 1987). An examination of the development of canon law and theology on sexual morality from early Christianity to the 16th century.

Bynum, Caroline Walker, *Holy Feast and Holy Fast: The Religious Significance of Food to Medieval Women* (Berkeley: University of California Press, 1987). An original exploration of the importance of food, food imagery, and fasting among medieval religious women.

Clark, Anne L., *Elisabeth of Schönau: A Twelfth-Century Visionary* (Philadelphia: University of Pennsylvania Press, 1992). Explores how the literary works of a twelfth-century mystic (often ignored in favor of Hildegard of Bingen) illuminate women's relationships to the male-dominated social, religious, and intellectual worlds.

Geary, Patrick, *Living with the Dead in the Middle Ages* (Ithaca, NY: Cornell University Press, 1995). Explores the nature of popular piety by tracking the "exchange and interaction between the living and the dead" in the early to high Middle Ages, when the reverence for saints called for the possession of part or whole of the bodies of the saints.

Little, Lester K., *Religious Poverty and the Profit Economy in Medieval Europe* (Cornell: Cornell University Press, 1978, rpt. 1983). Argues that monastic reform and religious dissent emphasized the moral value of voluntary poverty in reaction to growth in urban economy.

Weinstein, Donald, & Bell, Rudolph M., *Saints and Society: The Two Worlds of Western Christendom, 1000–1700* (Chicago: University of Chicago Press, 1982). A statistical study of the lives of 864 saints, revealing patterns relating to their social status, gender, geographical distribution, and motivation.

HildegardofBingen.org, for materials on the most famous of the medieval women saints:
http://www.uni-mainz.de/~horst/hildegard

The Mind's Road to God

Cobban, Alan B., *The Medieval English Universities: Oxford and Cambridge to c. 1500* (London: Scholar Press, 1988). An examination of the origins, governing structure, curriculum, and student life.

Clanchy, M.T., *Abelard: A Medieval Life* (Malden, MA: Blackwell, 1997). Comprehensive and up-to-date biography of this key figure in the making of scholasticism, the most important intellectual expression of the Middle Ages and the medieval Church.

Radding, Charles M. & William W. Clark, *Medieval Architecture, Medieval Learning: Builders and Masters in the Age of Romanesque and Gothic* (New Haven: Yale University Press, 1994). Argues that the two successive styles of Romanesque and Gothic were analogous to developments in medieval philosophy.

Siraisi, Nancy, *Taddeo Alderotti and His Pupils: Two Generations of Italian Medical Learning* (Princeton: Princeton University Press, 1981). A learned discussion of the reception of Aristotle and Greco-Arabic science in the medical faculty of the university at Padua.

Works by/about philosopher Robert Grosseteste (funded British Academy): **http://www.grosseteste.com**

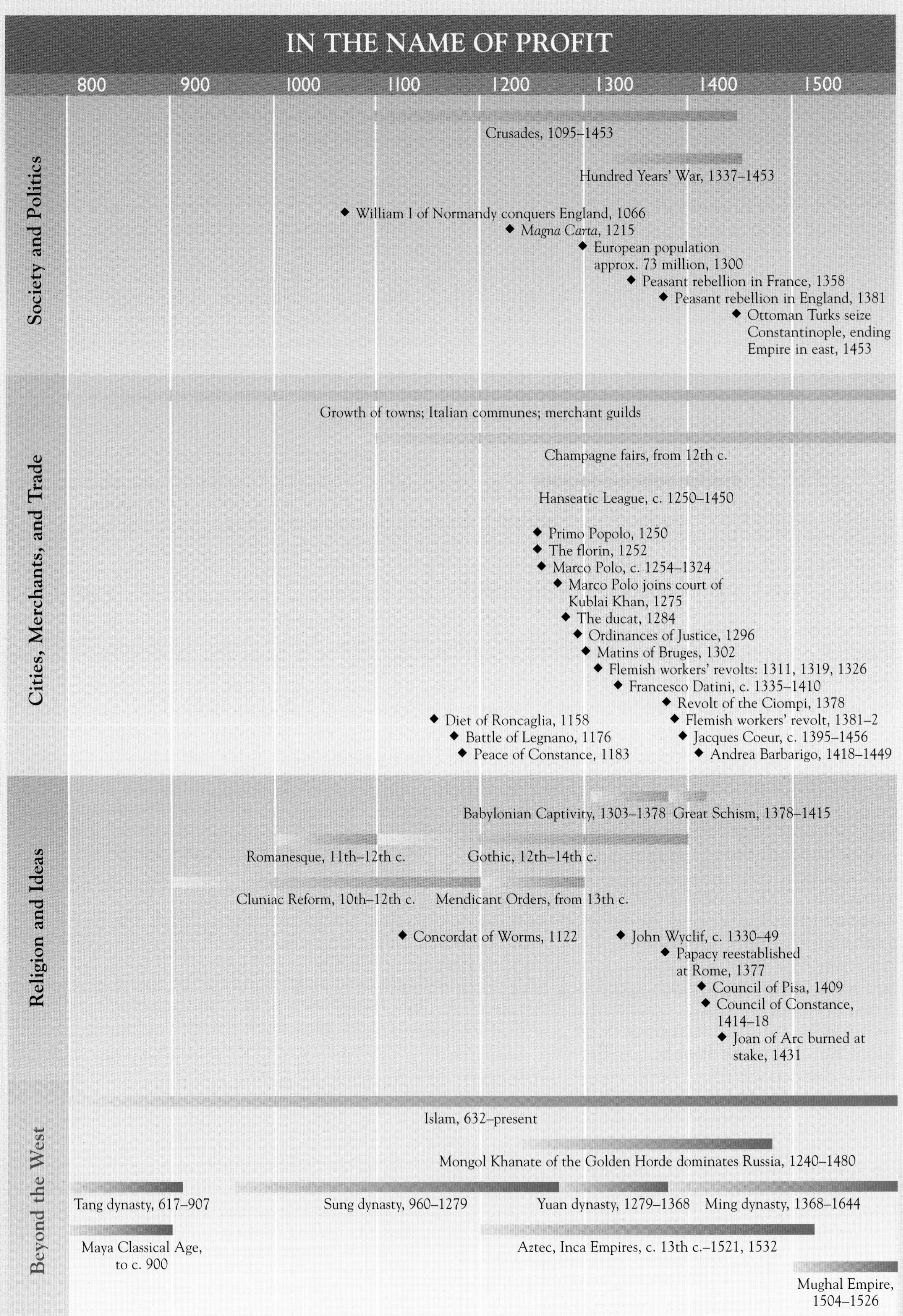
IN THE NAME OF PROFIT
800
900
1000
1100
1200
1300
1400
1500
Society and Politics
Crusades, 1095–1453
Hundred Years' War, 1337–1453
William I of Normandy conquers England, 1066
Magna Carta, 1215
European population approx. 73 million, 1300
Peasant rebellion in France, 1358
Peasant rebellion in England, 1381
Ottoman Turks seize Constantinople, ending Empire in east, 1453
Cities, Merchants, and Trade
Growth of towns; Italian communes; merchant guilds
Champagne fairs, from 12th c.
Hanseatic League, c. 1250–1450
Primo Popolo, 1250
The florin, 1252
Marco Polo, c. 1254–1324
Marco Polo joins court of Kublai Khan, 1275
The ducat, 1284
Ordinances of Justice, 1296
Matins of Bruges, 1302
Flemish workers' revolts: 1311, 1319, 1326
Francesco Datini, c. 1335–1410
Revolt of the Ciompi, 1378
Flemish workers' revolt, 1381–2
Jacques Coeur, c. 1395–1456
Andrea Barbarigo, 1418–1449
Diet of Roncaglia, 1158
Battle of Legnano, 1176
Peace of Constance, 1183
Religion and Ideas
Babylonian Captivity, 1303–1378
Great Schism, 1378–1415
Romanesque, 11th–12th c.
Gothic, 12th–14th c.
Cluniac Reform, 10th–12th c.
Mendicant Orders, from 13th c.
Concordat of Worms, 1122
John Wyclif, c. 1330–49
Papacy reestablished at Rome, 1377
Council of Pisa, 1409
Council of Constance, 1414–18
Joan of Arc burned at stake, 1431
Beyond the West
Islam, 632–present
Mongol Khanate of the Golden Horde dominates Russia, 1240–1480
Tang dynasty, 617–907
Sung dynasty, 960–1279
Yuan dynasty, 1279–1368
Ming dynasty, 1368–1644
Maya Classical Age, to c. 900
Aztec, Inca Empires, c. 13th c.–1521, 1532
Mughal Empire, 1504–1526

CHAPTER 11

In the Name of Profit

Cities, Merchants, and Trade in the Middle Ages

1000–1500

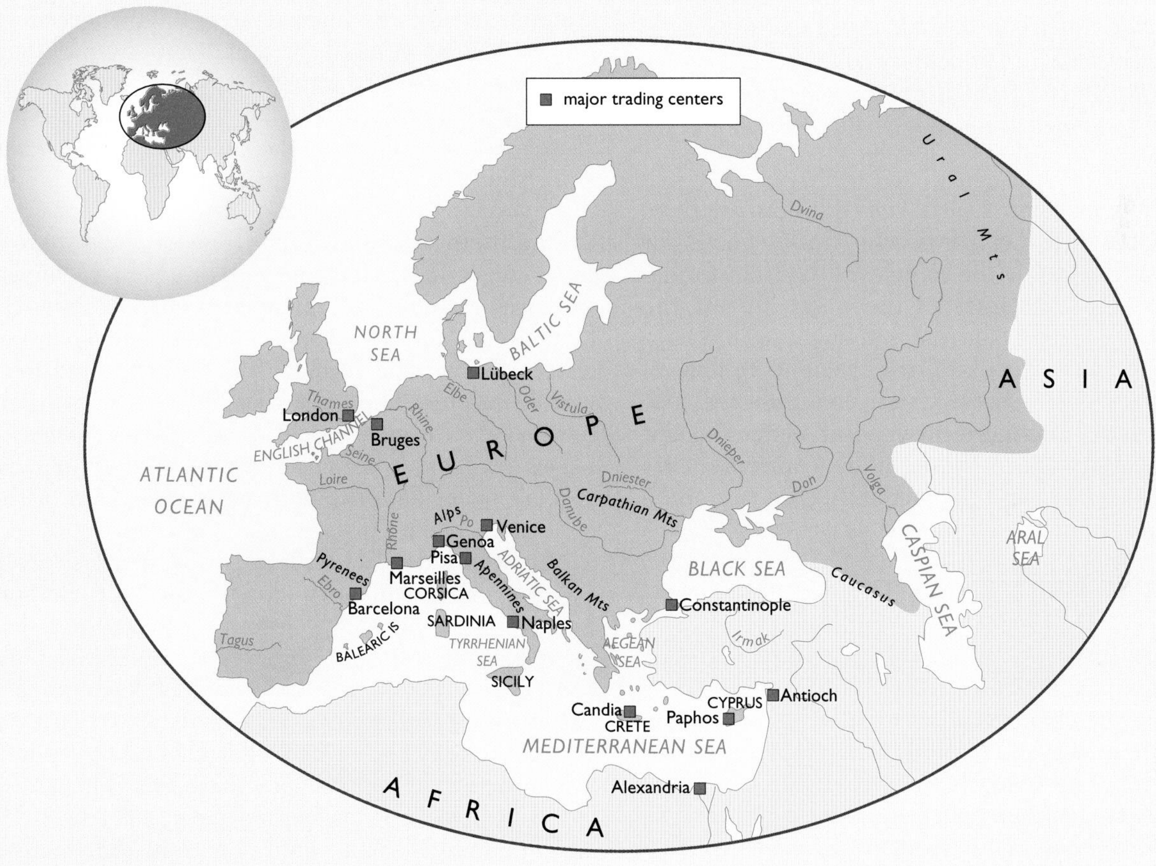

KEY TOPICS

- **Money and Merchants:** Money circulates once again in Europe as itinerant traders yield to the enormous power of merchant princes commanding fabulous wealth.
- **Cities and Towns:** Towns begin to form around the nucleus of a Roman core, or cathedral or castle complex, and strive for self-government and economic autonomy.
- **Artisans and Entrepreneurs:** Merchant and artisan guilds control standards and access to materials, while tensions result in unsuccessful rebellions against merchant elites.
- **The World of Commerce:** Italian merchants gain preeminence in the Mediterranean, and develop new technological skills in shipping as well as commercial accounting methods.

The creed of Francesco Datini *It was the custom of Francesco Datini (c. 1335–1410), merchant of Prato, to head the records of his transactions with the invocation "In the name of God and of profit." "Money is all the help you have," said another Tuscan merchant. "It is your defense, honor, profit, and adornment." "Florins are the best of kin," the kind who never give you any trouble, wrote the Sienese poet Cecco Angiolieri (c. 1260–1312) speaking of the newly minted gold coins that Western entrepreneurs used to buy more than their share of the world's luxuries. These statements breathe a spirit distant from church and manor. Beginning around 1000, Europeans began to sell, acquire, hoard, spend, and crave in a project of economic expansion that has lasted into this century. By 1500, their activity had propelled Europe all the way from last place to first in the race for the world's goods.*

It was money that fueled the transformation of Europe, and the merchants who traded goods for money were certainly the vehicles of that transformation. As they concentrated their activities at the intersections of key trade routes, they caused towns to form and ripen into cities, the dynamic centers of commerce. Within those cities, and gathered into **guilds**, **artisans** produced the goods that were bought and sold, while the great international **entrepreneurs** of the age forged new commercial techniques and a new mental world.

MONEY AND MERCHANTS

Merchants made the profits that transformed Europe from a commercial backwater to a commercial superpower. A merchant sells a commodity for a price greater than its cost to him (rarely her). His profit is the difference between the two amounts. Early in the Middle Ages that merchant was merely a peddler who carried his goods in his saddlepack, traveling from village to village. It was a precarious living. Often he was the target of bandits and marauders.

Later, the merchant was typically a dealer traveling with a group of other dealers who shared risks and costs. Eventually, he might even be a merchant prince, directing the buying and selling operations of a host of agents located throughout Europe, Africa, the Middle East, and Asia. The career of one merchant is described in *Witnesses* on p. 293. From the peddler's slim profit margin to the international entrepreneur's fat one came wealth that circulated, slowly at first, in small streams of silver coins, and later, torrentially, in gold **florins** and **ducats**. Those currents expanded the possibilities that life could offer even the humblest peasant.

Economic Crisis and Recovery

Even before incursions of tribal raiders and settlers overwhelmed the Roman west wealth had begun to seep away to the east. The economy of the late Roman Empire slumped into a downturn which, in the western zone, proved irreversible (see Chapter 6). Gold and silver leaked to the depots of Constantinople, Antioch, and Alexandria, to be exchanged for the fine products of Asia—oils and perfumes, spices, silk, ivory, and other exotic products. In its declining years, the Roman economy sank under the weight of a serious trade imbalance. Commerce slowed dangerously in the west, to revive only after a lapse of centuries.

The early Middle Ages saw a near-eclipse of trade. Bandits and pirates roamed at will, unchecked by Roman legions or auxiliaries, endangering merchant shipments by road or water. Roads and bridges were no longer maintained and fell into disrepair. Water routes became even more dangerous after 700, when Arab ships claimed the Mediterranean, and in the ninth and tenth centuries, when Vikings prowled the northern seas and rivers (one of their ships is shown on p. 302). Merchant enterprises in the imperiled cities dwindled and merchants quickly dispersed. By the ninth century, even the names of merchants or references to trade have virtually disappeared from written records. The trade that did exist must surely have suffered from political disarray—there were no judges available to enforce contracts and no financial officials to regulate the **minting** of new coins or the conversion of currency.

Already drained of **bullion** by the reckless spending on foreign luxuries during the late Empire, Europe, under its newly formed principalities, lost its remaining currency reserves to hoarding. Gold coins were stored as treasure or melted down to make the gorgeous objects that warriors displayed on their person (belt buckles and sword hilts) and that priests displayed on their altars (crucifixes and reliquaries). The little wealth that Europe possessed was frozen and immobilized, unavailable for trade. Small silver coins of little value were sufficient until the thirteenth century, when the florins and ducats of the great Italian cities established gold and silver as different standards of value.

Barter As coins disappeared, trade was conducted by means of barter: things were exchanged for things—so many chickens for so much grain, a percentage of the crop to pay the Church's **tithe**, or tax, the use of the lord's mill for a sack of flour. Such trade was almost purely local. Neither chickens nor sacks of flour were transported over large distances. Medieval peasants saw the boundaries of their own manor or village as the limit of their economic world.

If small sums were measured in chickens and sacks of barley, large sums were measured in land. Even a king paid an administrator in this way, by giving him the use of a certain quantity of land for a period of time. In exchange for the land given him in usufruct, as this arrangement was called, the recipient often owed the lord or king who had granted it specified services—military, advisory, managerial (see Chapter 9). On the land-user's death, the gift might become hereditary, his heir continuing to owe services, in theory at least, to the lord who conferred the benefit (or to his descendants). In the same way, the serf on the manor was rewarded for his labor by the right to use land that he did not own.

In this economic setting, where most trade was by barter and most payment was in land use, a few daring men traveled about buying and selling their wares—no more than could be carried in one wagon or two saddlebags. From the Mediterranean ports of Italy, Spain, and southern France, these peddlers journeyed north to the local markets of the interior. The first traders of the medieval West were Syrians and Jews with close ties to the Levant, the chief marketplace of Mediterranean civilization. They traveled "from the East to the West and from the West to the East by land as well as by sea [from the] land of the Franks" to Egypt and Constantinople, according to an Arab geographer of the ninth century.

Quinten Massys, A Moneylender and his Wife: *The conflicting demands of spiritual and worldly matters is illustrated in this fifteenth-century painting of a woman distracted from perusing a religious text by her husband weighing coins in a balance.* (Louvre, Paris)

The disruption of maritime trade in the west, following the Islamic conquests and new prohibitions against the Jews caused many thousands of these merchants to vanish eastward across the Mediterranean to more welcoming lands.

By the tenth century, some Europeans, dislodged from the soil by population pressure or misfortune, had learned of the great profit to be gained from buying things cheaply and selling them dearly. Among these were Vikings, or Norsemen (kin to the raiders who beset monasteries and villages), who packed up the produce of their farms and villages, once the harvest was in, and journeyed through the various ports of the North Sea in order to sell it. From such enterprising traders came the makers of the medieval towns and, ultimately, the great merchants of the later Middle Ages.

Fairs In the absence of permanent markets, traveling merchants brought their goods to depots where, for a few days or a few weeks a year, an open-air market was held. In the twelfth century, the count of Champagne, one of the greatest landholders in the Frankish lands, realized how he could profit from inviting a great confluence of these merchants to buy and sell in his territory. The county of Champagne

Masaccio, Resurrection of Tabitha: *The frescoes painted by Masolinoda Panicale and his more talented assistant—who was known by his sobriquet Masaccio—for the wealthy Felice Brancacci in the church of the Carmine in Florence described incidents from the life of disciple Peter as though they had occurred in a contemporary Florentine setting. Shown here is a detail of two fashionably dressed merchants engaged in conversation in a medieval street setting. Peter heals a disabled beggar to the left.* (Church of Carmine, Florence)

WITNESSES

Wandering Merchants and Flourishing Towns

The individual initiative and willingness to assume risk displayed by the earliest medieval merchants helped build up a trade network and, in time, an urban grid which, by 1300, supported a vital, prosperous economy. These passages describe, first, the solitary ventures of an eleventh-century merchant and, second, the enormous wealth of the merchants of early fourteenth-century Florence, who had formed themselves into several specialized guilds to further their interests.

The profitable journeys of merchant Godric of Finchale (1070): At first, he lived as a chapman [peddlar] ..., going on foot and carrying the smallest wares; then he travelled abroad, first to St. Andrews in Scotland and then for the first time to Rome. On his return, ... he began to launch upon bolder courses, and to coast frequently by sea to the foreign lands that lay around him. Thus ... he traded in many divers wares and ... made great profit in all his bargains, and gathered much wealth in the sweat of his brow; for he sold dear in one place the wares which he had bought elsewhere at a small price.

(Reginald of Durham, *Life of Godric of Finchale*, 1070; ed. G. G. Coulton, 1918)

The chronicler Giovanni Villani describes the business enterprises of Florence (1335–1338): The workshops of the *Arte della Lana* [wool guild] were 200 or more, and they made from 70,000 to 80,000 pieces of cloth, which were worth more than 1,200,000 gold florins. ... And more than 30,000 persons lived by it. ... The *fondachi* [businesses] of the *Arte di Calamala* [finished cloth guild] ... were some twenty, and they imported yearly more than 10,000 pieces of cloth, worth 300,000 gold florins. ... The banks of moneychangers were about eighty. The gold coins which were struck amounted to some 350,000 gold florins and at times 400,000 [yearly]. ... There were then in Florence 146 bakeries.

(Giovanni Villani, *New Chronicle*, 1335–1338, Bk. XI; eds. I. Raymond, R. Lopez, 1955)

was ideal for this purpose, lying just at the point where river boats traveling up the Rhone, Saône, and Seine Rivers could go no farther. Saleable goods could be unloaded from the boats and brought directly for display at the Champagne fairs.

Six fairs were held annually at various towns of Champagne, in addition to others elsewhere in France and nearby Flanders (in modern Belgium and northeastern France). At the midpoint of the main axis of European trade from the North Sea to the Mediterranean, which led on to Russia and Constantinople respectively, they served until the fourteenth century as Europe's greatest clearinghouse. In the following century, international fairs were held in Geneva (in modern Switzerland), Frankfurt, and Nuremberg (both in Germany). By this time, new and revitalized cities had also become centers of trade.

The great fairs, such as those in Champagne, were international markets. Here the goods of the east were available as well as European goods such as salt, metals, food, and wool. They were distinct from the local markets and fairs in which villagers exchanged the products of their farms. The two economies persisted side by side—the local economy of the manor, and the long-distance economy of the merchants.

The Flow of Money

Having purchased goods at the fairs of western Europe, itinerant merchants returned to the depots where they had acquired the eastern goods offered in exchange, and sold the European products for cash. Some of that cash they exchanged immediately for new commodities to carry back to the interior of western Europe. Some of it was not used for purchases but was taken back to Europe, and so a small trickle of coin began to circulate from center to center; in time the trickle broadened into a stream of silver. That stream, flowing like blood through the body, would revive the European economy. Nobles with ready cash spent it on new luxuries; serfs with cash—acquired by extra labor—could purchase their own liberation. While coin worked its swift magic, however, its abundance alarmed the guardians of Christian morality, who read in Scripture that the poor were destined to inherit the earth.

The silver coins that circulated among European markets were of various kinds. Each type needed to be measured for conversion into the units of currency minted by other communities. A new figure—the moneychanger—took his place at the fairs. Merchants with currency of diverse origins came to the moneychanger to have their metal tested and their coin weighed. Kings and the great lords took an interest in guaranteeing the quality of coin produced in their domains.

The moneychanger was often a moneylender as well. If so, he was often a Jew. Jewish merchant communities had formed in England and France and the German lands, from which their trading ventures extended into eastern Europe. Where their services were especially valued they were protected by local authorities, and allowed to possess property. Some converted to Christianity and merged with the local population. But many kept their ancient faith, building synagogues and continuing, under their rabbis, a long tradition of learning and remembrance. By the twelfth century, Jews in the small English city of Lincoln had a stone-built community house. In the German city of Cologne at about the same time, there were forty-eight Jewish households.

The reason why Jews were the main moneylenders in the Middle Ages (at least before 1300) was that the Christian religion prohibited **usury**. "Usury" was defined as lending money at interest, since charity required lending to any in need without charge. Since the prohibition against usury is in the Old Testament (Leviticus 25:35–37; Deuteronomy 23:19–20) it applied, theoretically, to both Jews and Christians. But Jews, although they did not take interest within their own community, were compelled to take it from others in order to earn a livelihood, being barred from most occupations in the Christian community—dealing with "others" as they were not permitted to deal with "brothers." Another group that felt free to trade usuriously were the merchants of Lombardy, in northern Italy (so named because it had earlier been occupied by the Lombards). Lombard merchants, though professed Christians, disregarded church law against lending money at interest and seemed fearless of the associated punishment. Their example may have encouraged other Christian merchants to lend money.

Church law condemned not only usury but also overcharging. Theologians posed the abstract rule of the "just price," a price for commodities that fairly rewarded the seller for his labor but did not unfairly burden the buyer in his need. Their speculations about the costs of labor and materials and the factor of risk foreshadow later economic theories of capitalism and socialism (see Chapters 21, 25).

By the thirteenth century, Italian merchants had overcome their reluctance to lend money at interest or take high percentages of profit—if not their sense of guilt. Having encountered banks in their journeys to the Middle East, where these institutions were well established, they became not merely moneychangers or moneylenders but bankers—possessors of great wealth, exchangers of vast sums, engineers of currency conversion on a large scale. While worrying at times whether they could manage to do so, these men hoped to serve both God and profit.

The Worth of Wealth

Bankers were among the vanguard of businessmen who, in an era overshadowed by the Christian preference for poverty, lived according to the principle of the peerless worth of wealth. They were at odds with the norms of medieval society in other ways as well. While most Europeans were knit together by their common village life or their dependency upon a lord, town dwellers were, at first, socially undefined. They did not belong to one of the three main groups of medieval society: they did not fight, they did not plow the fields, they did not lead the faithful to salvation. They made things, bought things, sold things—tasks little known to earlier medieval society. But in the construction of Western society these men (and a few women) who were without lords or masters, these kings of account books and warehouses, were as important as the canniest monarchs and emperors. Three examples of outstandingly successful merchants will display their outlook.

Datini and Barbarigo One of the leading merchants of fourteenth-century Italy was Francesco Datini (c. 1335–1410) of Prato, a small town near Florence. He spent his youth apprenticed to an Italian businessman in Avignon, where the papal court was located for much of the fourteenth century. In about 1385, he returned to Prato a rich man and joined its guild of silk merchants. He then set up a business in Florence, dealing not only in silk but in all sorts of other items from Europe and beyond, including leather from Córdoba, Spain, wheat from Sicily, cloves from the East Indies. Rather than travel himself, he had agents in the cities where his business was done. Datini shared profits with these agents, but always retained the senior position. With the fortune he made from his investments, he bought houses and farms in the Tuscan countryside outside Florence. His extraordinary command of detail is witnessed by the extensive records that survive—574 books of accounts and 153,000 other business records.

Two generations later, a struggling Venetian nobleman, Andrea Barbarigo (1418–1449), rescued his family fortunes from the morass into which they had fallen as the result of a single disastrous shipwreck.

WHO'S WHO

Merchant Princes

Francesco Datini, "the Merchant of Prato" (1335–1410), tireless entrepeneur, whose 574 books of accounts and 153,000 business records, as well as a volume of letters, still survive to tell of the scope of his commercial ventures.

Andrea Barbarigo (1418–1449), Venetian nobleman and businessman who rescued his family's fortunes through his commerce in woolen and cotton cloth from the Mediterranean to Britain.

Jacques Coeur (c. 1395–1456), citizen of Bourges, enriched by extensive trade in luxury goods with Egypt and Syria, managed by a staff of 300 agents stationed in several French cities, made him the king's banker and adviser.

Barbarigo acquired woolen cloth from England and the Netherlands, oil from Valencia, in Spain, and cotton cloth from Asia, all of which he sold in Venice at a neat profit. Like Datini, he stayed home and directed the operations of his business, engaging agents abroad with whom he shared his profits, never allowing too great a portion of his assets to be involved in any single venture.

Jacques Cœur Barbarigo's contemporary Jacques Cœur (c. 1395–1456) was born to a commercial family in the French city of Bourges. He began his career in 1427, voyaging to the eastern Mediterranean and establishing the trade connections that would make him one of the richest men of the age. Obtaining a papal dispensation that permitted him to trade with non-Christians in Egypt and Syria, Cœur transported, by his own fleet of four **galleys** and three smaller vessels, the high-profit goods that were the staple of Mediterranean commerce—silks and spices, armor and furs, feathers and ivory. One of his galleys is depicted on p. 303. A staff of 300 supervised warehouses at Marseilles, Paris, Tours, and other French centers, and arranged for the sale of his merchandise throughout northwestern Europe.

Unlike Barbarigo and Datini—both citizens of independent city-states—Jacques Cœur belonged to a nation just emerging from the Hundred Years' War under a monarch striving to forge a modern centralized state. When Cœur undertook his first ventures, the French king, Charles VII, was a desperate refugee from his own capital city. In later years, as France struggled free of foreign domination, Cœur stood by the now-confident king, a trusted servant who provided much of the money needed to pursue these aims. Grateful for Cœur's support and acumen, the king drew him into royal service, made him a member of the council, conferred upon him the insignia of nobility, promoted his children, and made him master of the royal mint—a position both sensitive and lucrative.

Meanwhile, Cœur was the universal moneylender at the French court. He lent to the king, the queen, the nobles, building up good will and dangerous resentment at the same time. When the king's mistress Agnès Sorel died in childbirth, in 1450, Jacques Cœur was accused of having poisoned her. After a cycle of torture and forced confession, the merchant paid a huge fine, suffered the confiscation of all his wealth, and was banished from France. The king used Cœur's money to recapture the stubborn English stronghold in the French city of Bordeaux. Cœur died fighting the Turks on the Aegean island of Chios, a captain in the papal navy.

Before his fall from power, Cœur had built a mansion in Bourges befitting his wealth and circumstances. From the front, it looked like a commercial house, with warehouse facilities on the ground floor. From the back, it looked like a castle. The architecture expressed the ambivalence of a merchant's place in late medieval society: imbedded in, yet aloof from, the world of knights and nobles.

The merchants and bankers of the Middle Ages were the first agents of Europe's great expansion over the coming centuries. Their activity radiated out from the towns and cities in which they gathered to live, to bargain, and to profit.

CITIES AND TOWNS

During the late Roman Empire, the once-populous cities of western Europe bled and dwindled (see Chapter 6). People left them in order to avoid taxes and responsibilities and even honors, which came at a heavy price. City walls, now mere shells, enclosed areas too large for the population that remained. Yet these shrunken cities would revive in the three centuries after 1000, and new cities would emerge alongside them. These European towns fostered the growth of institutions that were the foundations of modern civilization.

Urban Decline and Revival

The city of Rome itself typified this urban decline. From about a million at the height of the Empire, the population of Rome dropped to less than half that in the mid-fifth century, then to about 50,000 after Justinian's devastating war against the Goths a hundred years later. In the thirteenth century, its population numbered scarcely 35,000. The whole population of the city could have found seats in the Colosseum. By the fourteenth century it had fallen even further, to about 20,000.

Beyond the Alps, in Gaul, Britain, and elsewhere, Roman towns wasted to ruins. "The work of giants moldreth away," wrote one Anglo-Saxon poet of the decline of a Roman outpost in Britain: roofs collapsed, towers crumbled, gates were breached, "battered ramparts ... shorn away and ruined." Opportunists salvaged the well-dressed stones from ancient crumbled buildings to build their new cathedrals and fortifications. Beyond the limits of Rome's former rule, there were not even ruined cities. Instead, there was only a virgin wilderness of dense forest and swampy wasteland.

From this depressing landscape, there began to arise, in the eleventh century, an urban civilization. Cities emerged in various places: within the shells of the old Roman centers, amid the wastelands of central and eastern Europe, around the castles of the great lords, as shown on p. 297. Wherever they emerged, they introduced new energies, opened new possibilities, and presented new challenges to a world in which warriors, workers, and kings had just managed to achieve stability.

Many cities developed around the households of bishops, who remained in the old Roman centers as imperial authority declined, representatives of the now-mighty Church. This household consisted of the bishop, his secretaries and clerks, servants and artisans, priests and canons (members of a cathederal chapter or collegiate church) who sang the daily offices, and, in time, the students and teachers of the cathedral school. The bishop's extensive church property was farmed by serfs for the benefit of the whole household. This land was a natural focus for a weekly or monthly market for the exchange of local produce, where surplus crops were traded with the community just like for any landlord.

Merchants from distant places occasionally came offering rare and expensive goods. Some of them settled together, forming a commercial community not far from the cathedral precincts, content to live under the rule of the bishop. Other merchants followed, as did landowners who wished a house in town and peasants from nearby villages who had escaped from serfdom or bought their freedom with the profits of their labor. Originally, the merchants' "town" was very much distinct from the bishop's nearby "city." In time they drew together, and the same wall expanded to enclose them both.

Burgs Other cities formed around the fortified castles of the European countryside. These offered to local villagers a reliable defense against raid and assault. They had other advantages as well. They held stores of grain in case of a protracted siege, and the local lord or prince provided justice. These advantages attracted merchants fearful of insecurity and disorder. Some merchants ceased to wander, settled down, and built their houses and shops outside the castle walls in a development called a *suburbium*—the first **suburbs**—meaning "below [that is, outside] the walls."

A fortified place that served as a mercantile center was called *bourg* in French, *burg* in German, *borgo* in Italian, and *borough* in English. In time the word came to signify the city that grew straggling outside its walls. Its residents were called **burghers** or *bourgeois*. In these fragile merchant settlements began the career of the European ***bourgeoisie***—a class of enterprising merchants, bankers, and long-distant traders. Like the residents of the cathedral city, they would in due course erect a stone wall with ramparts and gates around their new settlement, absorbing the smaller circle of fortification that was the original burg. While merchant colonies tended to cluster around the bishop's see in areas once under Roman domination, the burg-centered city was more typical in

HOW MANY?

The Functions of Medieval Towns

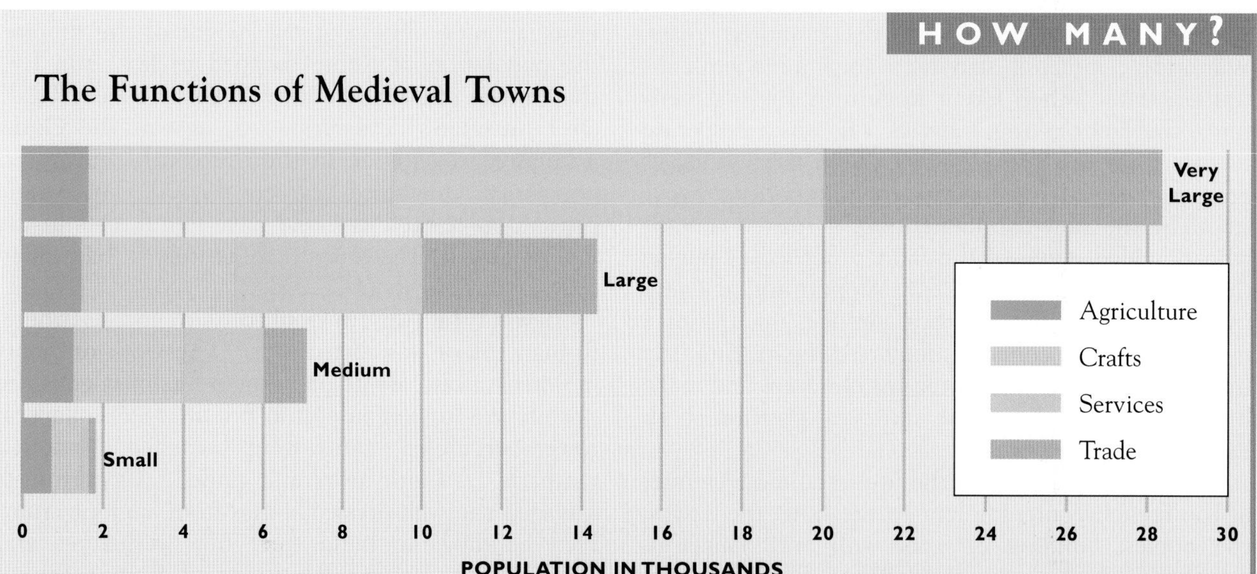

This is a schematic representation of the kinds of functions performed in four sizes of medieval towns: very large (c. 28,000); large (c. 14,000); medium (c. 7000); and small (c. 2000). The small size, to modern eyes, of even "very large" towns should be noted. Europe's great vitality came from its numerous, interlinked, but modest commercial centers, most of them less than one mile in diameter. The tasks represented here are "trade" (buying and selling); "services" (inns and taverns, banking, professional services); "crafts" (artisan production such as shoes, textiles, wood and metal work); and agriculture. The agricultural function becomes increasingly less important as town size grows, and the trade function—the central activity of a commercial society—increases at the most rapid rate of all four functions as town size expands from "small" to "very large." The "trade" function of a small town is virtually invisible. For a medium town, it might absorb 1000 (15%) of 7000 residents; of a large town, 4000 (29%) of 14,000 residents; of a very large town, 8000 (again 29%) of 28,888. The "service" function also increases notably, from 29% to 36% to 40%. The "craft" function declines from 43% to 29% as town size increases from medium to very large.

Source: Norman J. G. Pounds, *An Economic History of Medieval Europe* (London: Longman, 1974), p. 255, fig. 6.7.

How Cities Grew

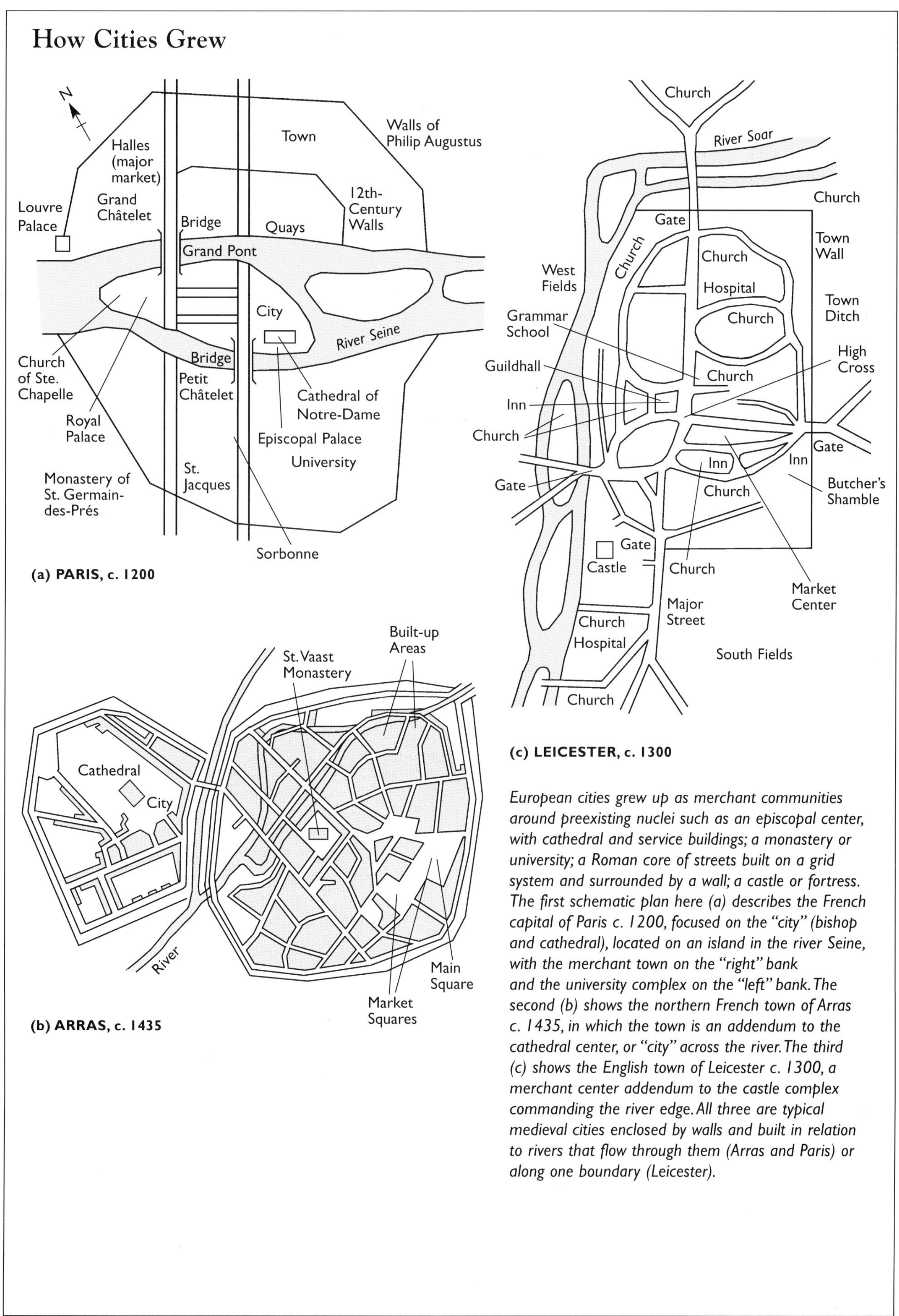

European cities grew up as merchant communities around preexisting nuclei such as an episcopal center, with cathedral and service buildings; a monastery or university; a Roman core of streets built on a grid system and surrounded by a wall; a castle or fortress. The first schematic plan here (a) describes the French capital of Paris c. 1200, focused on the "city" (bishop and cathedral), located on an island in the river Seine, with the merchant town on the "right" bank and the university complex on the "left" bank. The second (b) shows the northern French town of Arras c. 1435, in which the town is an addendum to the cathedral center, or "city" across the river. The third (c) shows the English town of Leicester c. 1300, a merchant center addendum to the castle complex commanding the river edge. All three are typical medieval cities enclosed by walls and built in relation to rivers that flow through them (Arras and Paris) or along one boundary (Leicester).

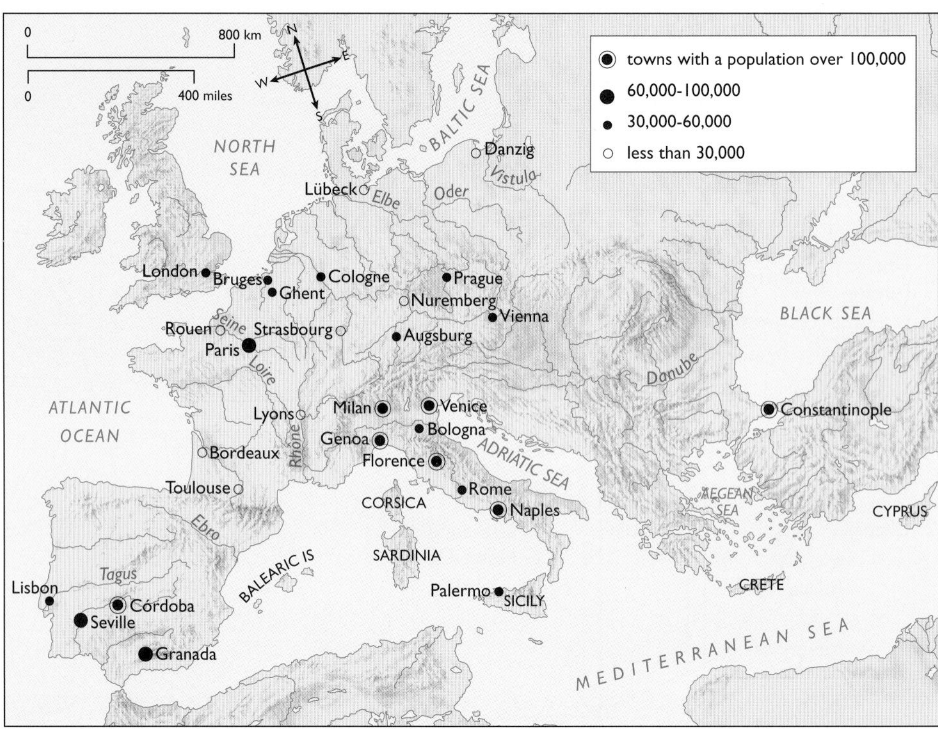

Map 11.1 Towns Large and Small, c. 1350: *From the shells of old Roman cities, around cathedrals and castles, amid farmlands newly cleared for the plow, after 1000 European merchant communities expanded and established thriving towns. Note that around 1350, the largest towns outside Islamic Spain (Córdoba) and the Byzantine Empire (Constantinople) were in northern Italy. As the chart below shows, most towns in Europe were small.*

northern and central Europe. The great cloth towns of Flanders, for instance—Bruges, Ghent, Ypres, Lille, and others—began as burgs.

New towns Some towns were created wholly new. They might be planted in rural areas by a nobleman wishing to cultivate new soil. The peasant farmers attracted to these areas were granted personal freedom and a charter establishing civic autonomy. They formed a kind of rural bourgeoisie, to whose settlements commerce and industry eventually migrated. The proliferation of "new towns" marks the effects of the growth of commerce and urbanization on even the rural landscape. Their presence is especially conspicuous in central and eastern Europe, areas opened up by colonization efforts after about 1200.

The cities formed within Roman walls soon outgrew the original enclosure and new rings of walls of greater dimensions had to be built. In prosperous cities, this process occurred more than once. Dynamic Florence extended its walls repeatedly. The ancient Roman ring was replaced by a larger medieval one, which was also outgrown and replaced in the fourteenth century by a third set of walls. Those walls, 5 miles (8 km.) in circumference, and capable of housing its maximum population of some 100,000, stood until the 1860s. Likewise in 1240, neighboring Pistoia built its third and final circuit of walls, which mark the maximum growth of the medieval town.

Cities that formed as merchant colonies outside fortified sites were also encircled by walls—in this case brand-new. At first these were mere mounds of earth or wooden palisades, in the north at least, but soon the art of building in stone was learned from the Mediterranean south. Whatever the type of town, eventually all of its constituent parts—merchant quarter, lord's castle, cathedral precinct—were united in a common whole and ringed by a common stone circuit of wall.

By 1200, much of western Europe (and, to a lesser extent, eastern Europe) was speckled with cities constructed within Roman walls or around castles, or sprung up at a crossroads or ford or confluence of waterways. The framework of cities by now far surpassed that during the Roman occupation. Although western Europe had as yet no huge metropolises, such as Constantinople and Baghdad, its web of small and densely-packed centers constituted an urban network of great productive capacity and flexibility. By 1300, as much as 10 percent of the population of western Europe lived in cities. After that time few new towns were founded, and existing towns rarely extended their walls farther.

Towns and their populations are indicated on Map 11.1 and *How Many?* on p. 299. Cities remained small throughout the Middle Ages. At their peak, around 1300, many numbered between 10,000 and 20,000 persons. Only the giant Italian cities of Florence, Milan, Genoa, Naples, and Venice reached 100,000, while the largest northern cities, Paris and London, housed only about 80,000 and 40,000 persons respectively (the latter expanded over the 12,000 that William the Conqueror found in 1066). Of the 50 or so major German towns around 1400, 35 had populations of 10,000 or less. Of the 15 that exceeded that figure, Cologne was the largest, with 30,000, followed by Lübeck, with 25,000, and Strasbourg, Nuremberg, and Danzig (modern Gdansk, in Poland), with about 20,000. Other major cities in this era included Prague (in today's Czech Republic), which reached 30,000 to 40,000; Ghent and Bruges (in Belgium), with 60,000 and 45,000 respectively; Toulouse, Bordeaux, Rouen, and Lyons (in France), which surpassed 25,000. Barcelona, in Christian Spain, reached about 35,000, while in Islamic Spain, Seville and Granada exceeded 50,000, and Córdoba half a million. Cities with populations over 20,000 generally engaged in long-distance commerce as well as the manufacture of goods. Smaller towns tended to produce for local markets, and agriculture played a significantly larger role than manufacture in their economy.

The Bourgeoisie The first townspeople—the burghers, or bourgeoisie—were undoubtedly the children or descendants of serfs. They could scarcely have come from any other class of medieval society. Yet by virtue of having detached themselves from the land, they had become free. Serfs who managed to escape to a city, and who remained there unreported for a term of "a year and a day," were generally protected by city law and not returned to serfdom. Moreover, they were considered not only free but (legally at least) equal; there were no differentiations in the status of freemen. That fact lent meaning to the German proverb "*Stadtluft macht frei*," that the air of the city makes one free. The towns were havens of freedom and autonomy, to the extent that those concepts could be understood in a hierarchical society.

The societies of free men in the burgeoning cities promptly sought charters from the lords who held dominion over the land—whether noble, king, or Church—defining their special standing in medieval society (see *Witnesses*, p. 300). Kings especially found it useful to protect the cities whose merchants had access to ready cash. City charters established the privileges and exemptions of the urban community, along with its obligations. The townspeople might be granted the privilege of creating and administering their own laws, or of commuting to money payments the labor and military service owed the lord, or of being exempt from the gate and road tolls that the nobility exacted everywhere, which were grave impediments to trade. They sought the precious privileges also sought by territorial lords—to hold a market, to mint coins, to collect tolls.

Once freed from subjection to overlords and from irksome dues and services, the burghers of the medieval cities proceeded to establish their own

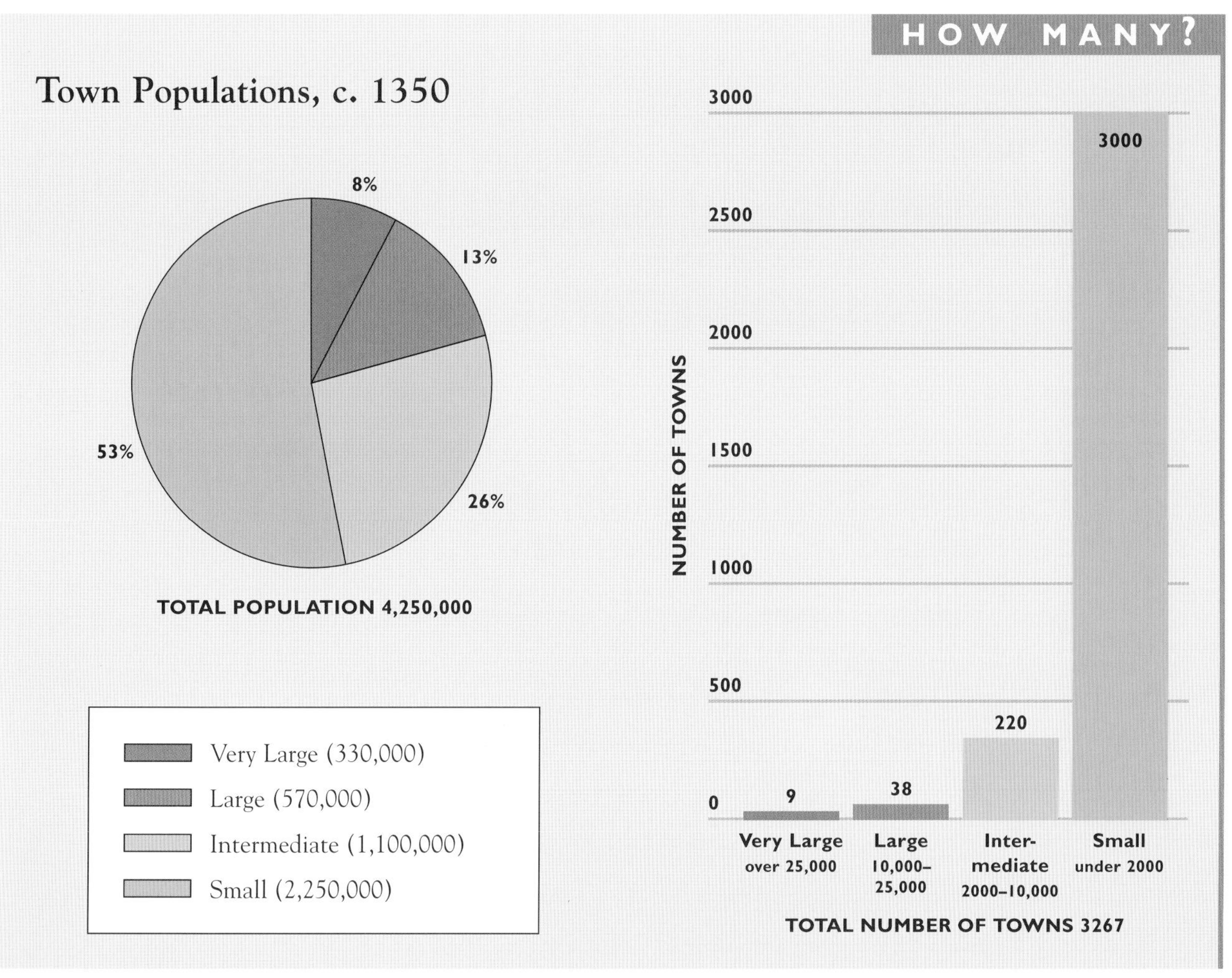

WITNESSES

Town Statutes and Troubles

The nodes of medieval economic life were the towns, which were carved out of a rural landscape by the energy of the merchant citizens aided by legal charters granted by feudal overlords, who sometimes lost all authority over the townspeople. In the first passage, the Count of Flanders grants a charter to the town of St. Omer, a charter that is particularly generous in freeing the citizens of taxes and toll liabilities, a great boost to commercial development. The second describes the citizens of the self-governing commune of the Italian city of Volterra swearing mutual loyalty. The third is a report by a hostile witness of the revolt of the commune of the merchants of French Laon against their overlord, the bishop, who was supported by members of the nobility.

William Clito, Count of Flanders, grants a Charter offering valuable tax relief to the town of St. Omer, 1127: I, William, by the grace of God, Count of Flanders, not wishing to reject the petition of the citizens of St. Omer ... grant them the laws written below, and command that those laws remain inviolate. 1. First that to every man I will show peace, and I will protect and defend them with good will just as I do my other men ... 9. All who dwell within the walls of St. Omer, or who dwell there in the future, I make free from *cavagium, i.e.*, from head-tax, and from suit of court ... 11. Moreover they have asked the king of France and Ralph of Peronne that wherever they go in their lands they may be free of toll, transit dues, and passage; I wish this to be granted to them ... 13. As I wish the citizens of Flanders to be free henceforward from all customs [taxes], I shall require from them no *scot*, or *taille*, or forced loan.
(From J. M. Kemble, *The Saxons in England*, 1965)

Oath of the citizens of Volterra to obey their magistrates, meet in assembly, and to rise to defend the city: I ... swear on the holy gospels of God to observe and fulfill and never violate by fraud each and every order which the consuls [chief magistrates] or podestà [judge] of Volterra should have me obey. ... Likewise, if I should hear the great bell sound once the call to assembly I shall come to the public meeting without arms, and I shall remain in good faith until the end of the meeting. ... Likewise, if I should hear the two great bells sounding the call to assembly I shall appear at the designated place armed. ...
(*Volterra Statutes*; eds. J. Mundy, P. Reisenberg, 1958)

Abbot Guibert of Nogent describes the revolt of the commune of Laon against the bishop and his noble allies (1166): The next day, ... behold there arose a disorderly noise throughout the city, men shouting "Commune!" and again through the middle of the chapel of the Blessed Mary ... citizens now entered the Bishop's court with swords, battle-axes, bows and hatchets, and carrying clubs and spears, a very great company. As soon as this sudden attack was discovered, the nobles rallied from all sides to the Bishop. ... In this rally Guiimon ... , an aged nobleman of handsome presence and guiltless character, armed only with shield and spear, ran out through the church and as he entered the Bishop's hall, was the first to fall, struck on the back of the head with a battle-axe by a certain Rainbert, who was his fellow-citizen. ... Next the outrageous mob attacking the Bishop and howling before the walls of his palace, he with some who were succoring him fought them off by hurling of stones and shooting of arrows.
(Guibert of Nogent, *Autobiography*, 1166; ed. C. C. Swinton Bland, 1925)

systems of government. As a **commune**, a sworn community constituting in their whole a power equivalent to lordship, they created codes of law that dealt amply with distinctively urban crime (such as theft and vandalism), and other urban problems, such as the role of transients and foreigners. They devised methods of proof other than the duels and ordeals that elsewhere characterized the administration of justice. They devised punishments specific to the urban context, notably public executions that took place in the town square.

Town leaders created their own officials, usually called mayors or "consuls," in imitation of ancient Rome. They elected a representative council, which might in turn have an elaborate system of standing and special committees. These officials, councils, and committees attended to city finances, levied taxes, warehoused emergency supplies of water and grain, initiated and supervised public works, saw to the relations between laity and clergy, and provided for the ill, the widowed, and the rootless young.

Commercial Zones

Commerce in western Europe radiated out from two principal zones: one centered on the North Sea and one on the northern Italian plain. The first included those cities with access to North Sea routes, especially those of modern Belgium, the Netherlands, Germany, and England. The second included those poised on the Mediterranean coast, on the tributaries of the Po River, or on Alpine passes to central and northern Europe. The commercial system ruled by these cities flourished into the seventeenth century.

Commerce in the North The cities of modern Belgium and the Netherlands in the low-lying lands along the North Sea were among the first outside Italy to spring into activity. As early as the time of Charlemagne, cloth-makers of this region produced an especially fine "Frisian" wool (of which Charlemagne was proud to send a sample to the Caliph Harun-al-Rashid, in exchange for the elephant the latter had tendered as a gift). Frisian cloth was one of the few manufactures traded at that time. The region was also enriched by the commercial activity of the Norsemen, who established merchant colonies there in the ninth and tenth centuries. As these enterprising northerners discovered that commerce yielded wealth more safely and reliably than raiding, they extended their network northwestward to Iceland, eastward to Russia, and from there southward to Constantinople. All of these contacts invigorated the economic life of the Netherlands. After 1000, the Viking depots of this northern region yielded their primacy to the flourishing centers at Bruges, Ghent, Ypres, and elsewhere.

The Hanseatic League After 1200, with the opening up of eastern Europe and the continued extension of trade avenues, commercial networks around the North and Baltic seas reorganized for long-distance ventures. A group of port cities leagued together for the more effective transport of goods and the security of their merchants. This alliance, which united northern Europe into one economic unit between about 1250 and 1450, was known as the Hanseatic League (*hansa* means guild or company). It had its own flag, was governed by its own laws, and exercised diplomacy with foreign governments.

At its peak in the fourteenth century, the League included some eighty cities and extended from Bruges in the west to Novgorod (in Russia) to the east. Between lay the German towns of Hamburg, Lübeck, Rostock, Danzig, and others. Across this system flowed the exchange of goods: English wool to Flanders, where it was woven into cloth, some of which was traded for the raw materials of Scandinavia and Russia (furs, amber, herring, hunting falcons, and timber) and the fine goods and gold coin brought from the larger market of Constantinople.

Hanseatic commerce had brought prosperity to the cities of southern Germany, most notably Nuremberg. Nuremberg exchanged its armor and swords, wrought

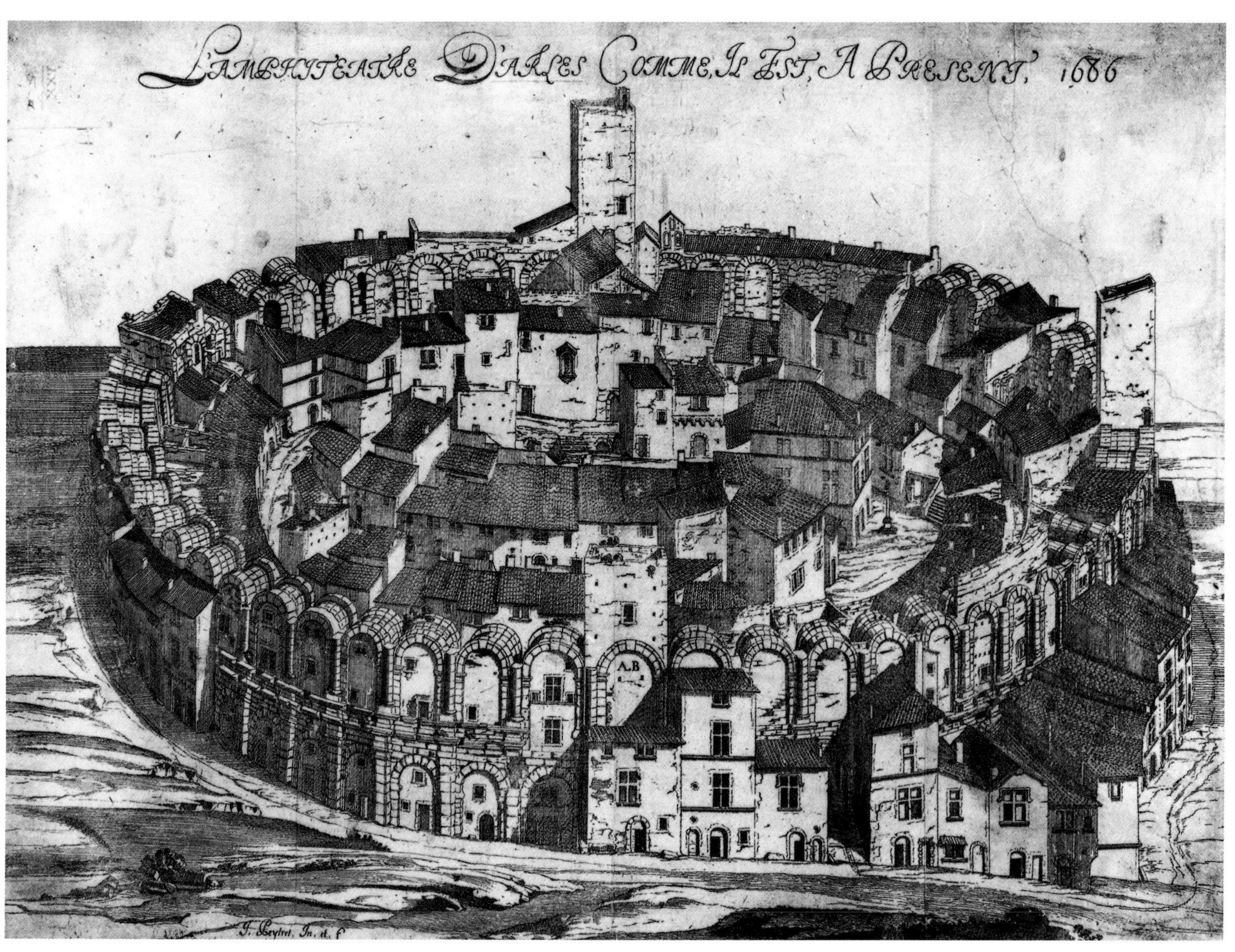

Medieval Town: *Many medieval European towns took form within the walls of old Roman settlements—as was clearly the case of medieval Arles, shown here in an engraving of 1686. Arles was built within the remains of the colosseum that Roman settlers had built in antiquity. The structure that had served as an arena for games and races was transformed into city walls.* (British Library, London)

Ships and Shipbuilding

The Arsenal: *Ships and shipbuilders made it possible for Italian merchants to dominate Mediterranean trade after 1100. This plan shows the Venetian "Arsenal" as it stood around 1560, Europe's largest shipbuilding operation until modern times.*

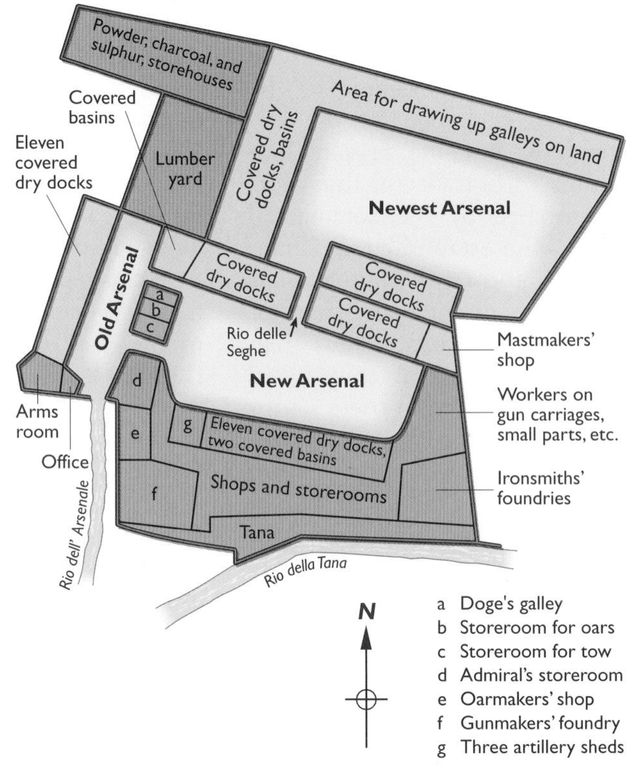

Viking ship: *As trade routes developed, so ships were built to transport money and goods back and forth across the Old World. This Viking ship from Oseberg, early ninth century, was capable of swift, accurate navigation of stormy northern waters.* (University Museum, Oslo)

from metals mined in the region, for the goods of eastern Europe and northern Italy. By 1500, Nuremberg had become the foremost trading city of the German lands. Nearby Augsburg and Frankfurt were also energized in this way.

London was one of the outlying ports of call for Hanseatic merchants. Their market in that city flourished until the end of the fifteenth century. Here English merchants mingled with foreigners and participated, from their remote corner of Europe, in the commercial web that reached from their own Thames River to the Mediterranean Sea. A twelfth-century observer was struck by the exotic wares that reached the London market: "The Arabian sends gold. ... The Scythian brings arms, and from the rich fat lands of Babylon comes oil of palms. ... the men of Norway and Russia [send] furs and sables; nor is China absent with purple silk."

Commerce in Italy Nowhere in Europe, however, was there a greater concentration of flourishing towns and cities than in northern Italy. Despite urban depopulation and the splintering of authority throughout the region, some city traditions lingered from the ancient Roman era. Milan, Lucca, Padua, Florence, and others descended from cities once inhabited by toga-clad senators. These cities revived early—soon after 900—and steadily progressed. Venice led them all.

Sailing ship: *Ships sailed from the Islamic Middle East to China and back, transporting silks and spices to ports such as Alexandria where the Europeans bought these luxury goods. Such a ship is shown in this manuscript illumination from Al-Hariri's* Tales of Fiction, *1237, showing the stitched planking of the vessel, Arabs manning the rigging, and the faces of Arab passengers at the portholes.* (Bibliothèque Nationale, Paris)

A ship of Jacques Coeur: *This round galley of the fifteenth-century merchant prince Jacques Cœur is depicted on stained glass.* (Bourges Museum, France)

Never a Roman city, Venice had its origins in the chaos of the early medieval invasions. Refugees from northeast Italy, not trusting even in their walled fortifications, fled from the mainland to settle on the sandbars and marshes and shifting islets of the Adriatic lagoon. Here they fished. After 900, they began to sell their catch and supplies of salt as well, which they farmed on the shores of the abundant sea around them. They carried these cheap commodities to nearby coastal settlements and to inland villages on the tributaries of the Po River, In exchange they acquired the grain they could not grow in their watery domain.

By 1000 the Venetians had formed a government (theoretically under Byzantine rule) and a fleet. With their ships they brought to Constantinople the plain but useful products of the west—wine and wheat, timber and salt, and (though the trade was officially forbidden to Christians) slaves from the Slavic settlements on the eastern Adriatic coast. From

Constantinople they sailed home with the sumptuous fabrics produced in Byzantine workshops and spices from far Asia. Back in Europe, nobles and kings awaited hungrily these luxurious imports.

The Venetians soon outstripped their masters in Constantinople and dominated the trade routes of the Adriatic. By the fourteenth century, their administrative and market center on the island of Rialto had become the greatest emporium in the west. "Merchandise flows through this noble city even as water flows from the fountains," wrote the chronicler Martino da Canale, "and the salt water runs though it and round it and in all places save in the houses and the streets. ... You may find within this fair town many men ... who buy and sell, and money changers and citizens of all crafts, and therewith mariners of all sorts, and ships to carry them to all lands and galleys to lay low their enemies."

Late in the eleventh century, Genoa and Pisa burst into activity, equipped with their own war galleys, with which to join in the Italian infiltration of Mediterranean trade. Their fleets traveled to Arab ports from Tripoli (modern Libya) to Morocco on the North African coast, which they opened up by force even before Urban II launched the First Crusade in 1095. The military support of Genoese and Pisan warships was essential to the conquest of Jerusalem and the surrounding territory, which was the chief result of this Crusade. Afterward, the Genoese and Pisans, like the Venetians, established merchant colonies of their nationals in Constantinople and throughout the eastern Mediterranean.

After 1100, the towns of Lombardy fed by Pisa and Genoa on the west coast of Italy and by Venice on the east, began to swell with people and products. Watered by the broad Po River, the fertile Lombard plain produced amply the agricultural goods that could be exchanged for the new commodities brought by merchants from the coasts. Towns and cities sprang up densely along the river banks, along the Italian rim of the Alps, just to the north, and the slope of the Apennines to the south. From the northernmost centers, such as Milan, which edged out the other contenders for eminence, merchant caravans crossed the Alps by passes now cleared of bandits and properly maintained. Once over the mountain barriers, they sought the river valley routes to the interior. These Lombard merchants soon became a well-known presence in the commercial centers of western Europe.

Urban Revolution in Northern Italy

In Italy, particularly, the burgeoning of mercantile centers had important political consequences. The nascent Lombard towns joined together to defend themselves, when central authorities were too weak to do so, and to advance their special interests against those of their masters. Some northern Italian cities developed republican patterns of government, and a few managed to retain these for a century or more. None survived Venice, whose republic did not fall until 1797—to the French conqueror Napoleon (see Chapter 20), who boasted that he would ravage Venice as Attila the Hun had intended to ravage Rome, and did so. The precedent of self-government that the Italian republics posed to the nations of modern Europe did not go ignored.

The Lombard towns were not only numerous, but populous—numbering in the range of 10,000 to 25,000 inhabitants. There were no powerful kings in northern Italy, and the cities, welcoming within their walls the nobles of the countryside, became centers of authority. Merchant leaders (who lived rather like lords) joined forces with noble town dwellers (who dabbled in trade). These alliances—sometimes amiable and sometimes tense and perilous—served to gain control over both city and region and to construct a politics ruled by law and administered by representatives of the governing elite. From as early as the 1080s until 1138, sixteen Italian towns declared themselves independent communes, ruled not by bishops or lords but by sworn associations of merchant and noble citizens.

The Lombard League In 1167, these towns joined together to form the Lombard League. Its purpose—unlike that of the Hanseatic League—was to provide a common defense. The threat that rallied the cities was the power of the Holy Roman Emperor, who periodically asserted his claim to the overlordship of northern Italy, dating back to the times of Charlemagne. The now-sophisticated leaders of the Lombard cities believed that both their autonomy and their profit margins were threatened by the prospect of rule by a monarch insensitive to the needs and aspirations of urban populations.

The man whose ambitions so threatened the Lombard merchants was the emperor Frederick I, called "Barbarossa" ("red-beard"), of the Hohenstaufen dynasty. Determined to execute the imperial claim to rule as king in Italy, Barbarossa (r. 1152–1190) entered Italy six times. He declared his sovereignty at the **Diet** (assembly) of Roncaglia in 1158; then, backed up by a knightly army, he attempted to place imperial agents in the rebel Italian cities. In a convincing show of force in 1162, he razed Milan to the ground. Formed in response to these acts of aggression, the Lombard League was ready when Barbarossa marched south to Italy in 1174, and defeated him at Legnano in 1176. In the peace treaty of 1183, the League gained a historic victory for the Italian cities and delivered an early challenge from self-governing peoples to the principle of monarchy.

Guelfs and Ghibellines The Peace of Constance of 1183, which established peace between the Italian cities and the Holy Roman emperors, did not entirely settle the hostility between them. For centuries, emperors claimed Italy as their own, while the Italian cities—after their rare moment of cooperation in the Lombard League—struggled separately for economic and political autonomy. When imperial designs for expansion spelled danger, however, they found it useful to join forces, especially with the Empire's greatest enemy, the papacy (see Chapter 10).

Supporters of the imperial party in Italy were called "Ghibellines," and those of the papal party "Guelfs." Although alliances shifted, Italy's nobility tended to be Ghibelline, and the merchants of its major commercial cities tended to be Guelf. The pope, who now headed a great bureaucracy needed bankers and tax-collectors, and the merchants obliged.

During the thirteenth century, Florence was the preeminent Guelf republic. As a reward for their city's loyalty to the Guelf cause, Florentine bankers were commissioned as papal agents. Throughout Europe they collected the rich tax revenues destined for Rome, and skimmed their due percentage from the top. The wealth they brought to Florence stimulated the city's already-thriving industry of cloth production and refinishing, described in *Witnesses*, p. 293, and *Windows On*, p. 306.

In 1250, some of the city's foremost merchants led the citizenry in a revolt against local noble magnates, aligned with the Ghibellines. In 1250 they formed a republic, called the "Primo Popolo," or the "First People's Government." Two years later the Florentines celebrated their triumph by minting the first gold coin to rival Byzantine currency in Mediterranean commerce. Named after the city of its birth, the florin, along with its cousin the ducat, first minted in Venice in 1284 (and named after the *dux*, or *doge*, who presided over the city's republican institutions), replaced the coins of Constantinople and Islam as the principal currency of western Europe for the purchase of costly commodities. General purchases were still made with silver coins.

After further wrangling, the Florentine republic was finally constituted in 1267 as a Guelf merchant state, run by an oligarchy of prominent citizens. Establishing laws that protected the interests of merchant rulers against noble landholders in 1296, the new government gave orders to tear down the towers of the nobles (built for defence against rival families) which dominated the city. When the jagged skyline posed by the fortified towers of a hereditary aristocracy fell to the discipline of law imposed by a merchant elite, Europe was on the threshold of a new age. Commercial growth would lead to political and social transformation.

ARTISANS AND ENTREPRENEURS

Cities and towns were the sites of commercial growth and political innovation in the Middle Ages. They were also home to the workers and businessmen whose activity made both happen.

Some of the goods sold at a profit by European merchants were grown from the soil, fished from the sea or rivers, or mined from the earth. But the most profitable goods were produced by the artful labor of human hands. Those laborers were skilled craftspeople, or artisans. Some artisans sold their own products in their own workshop, generally the front room of their homes. Others worked for merchants

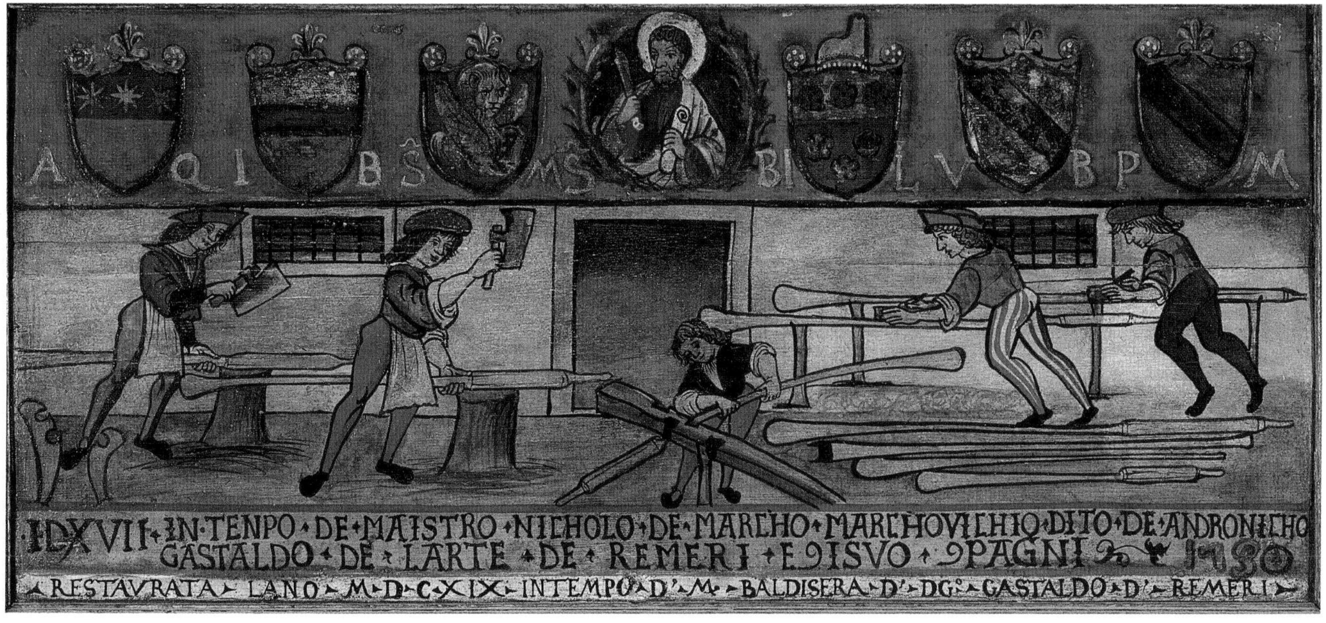

Oar makers at work: *Guilds existed for the production of goods as various as cloth and oars; oars and other wooden components are shown in this fifteenth-century painting of a medieval guild sign.* (Museo Correr, Venice)

WINDOWS ON

The Florentine Wool Cloth Industry, Thirteenth Century

Spinning the thread

Weaving the cloth

Florentine wool workshops were a prototype of modern industrial production. Tasks were subdivided and performed by human labor, as shown here: spinning the thread (distaff and wheel), performed mostly by women (above); weaving cloth, horizontal loom (left); combing and fulling the woven cloth (below). (For dyeing see p. 309).

Combing the cloth

Fulling the cloth

To continue your investigation of this topic, please go to www.prenhall.com/king for the related **WINDOWS** on the **WEB** activity

who organized large-scale industrial enterprises. These merchant entrepreneurs, their artisan employees, and independent **master** artisans often struggled to be heard in the medieval city; and sometimes struggled to exclude the others from power.

Medieval Industry: Textiles, Mining, and Shipbuilding

It was the productive capacity of the expanding medieval cities that made them formidable. Unlike the cities of Greek and Roman antiquity, which considered commercial and industrial functions inferior to political and military ones, medieval cities were engines of production.

The most important product of European manufacture was cloth. The textile industry produced the wealth that powered Europe's commercial achievements during the period from 1000 to 1300, and centuries later stimulated the industrialization of modern Europe (see Chapter 21). Its modest origins gave little sign of this great outcome. In the early Middle Ages, cloth was produced at home, by serf women and noblewomen. On the larger manors, women workers were gathered into a central workshop, the *gynaeceum*. Much of the cloth made in such home workshops was crude. After 1000, while households continued to produce cloth for local use, the new towns and cities became centers of textile production. As quality improved with the concentration of textile production in the towns, cloth became Europe's most important export, the basis for its emerging preeminence.

Linen was the first fabric produced in Europe of a quality fine enough to serve as a commodity of long-distance trade. It was processed from flax, which grew in marshy regions of the Low Countries, an area that won an early primacy in textile production. Burghers and nobles might wear undergarments of linen or spread their beds or tables with sheets of the fine fabric—hence even today, the shelves on which sheets and tablecloths are stored are called "linen closets" even though few people still use linen for those purposes. A tenth-century Arab geographer saw especially fine samples of this fabric in Naples and wrote that the like could not be found in any other country: "There is no craftsman in any other workshop in the world who is able to manufacture it."

Silk was even more of a luxury than linen. Originally imported from Asia via depots in Syria, Constantinople, or Egypt, this luxury textile was, by the late Middle Ages, being domestically produced—in Italy at Lucca and later in Venice, Florence, Bologna, and Milan, and in south-central France in Lyons. The nobility and high clergy were among the first attracted to silk, but soon the town dwellers of Italy and northern Europe developed an appetite for splendidly woven and decorated silks. Few consumers

WITNESSES

Commercial Contracts

Essential to the growth of trade was the development of tools of credit. In the first excerpt, an individual receives a loan from another and promises to return the amount with a sum of interest buried in the final payment. In the second, a sedentary partner contributes twice the amount of the active partner in a colleganza contract, while they agree to share all profits from the venture equally, "without fraud and evil device." Both contracts have the effect of rewarding the lender without utilizing the term "interest," considered to be usury, and against church law.

A contract explicitly mentioning interest equivalent to 20 per cent per year, forbidden by church law (Genoa, July 16, 1161): I, Embrone, have taken in loan from you, Salvo of Piacenza, £100 Genoese, for which I shall pay you or your messenger ... £120 within in one year; but if I wish to pay the aforesaid £100 and accrued interest before the next feast of the Purification, you must accept them and for that purpose have your messenger in Genoa. If I do not so observe [these conditions], I promise you, making the stipulation, the penalty of the double.

(From R. Lopez, I. Raymond, eds., *Medieval Trade in the Mediterranean World*, 1955)

A Venetian *Commenda* agreement between a seagoing merchant and a passive partner (Venice, August, 1073): I, Giovanni Lissado of Luprio, ... have received in *collegantia* [partnership commitment] from you, Sevasto Orefice, ... £200 [Venetian]. And I myself have invested £100 in it. And with this capital ... we have [acquired] two shares ... in the ship of which Cosmiro da Molino is captain. And I am under obligation to bring all of this with me ... to Thebes ... Indeed, by this agreement and understanding of ours I promise to put to work this entire [capital] and to strive the best way I can. Then, if the capital is saved, we are to divide whatever profit the Lord may grant us from it by exact halves, without fraud and evil device. ... And if all these goods are lost because of the sea or of [hostile] people ... neither party ought to ask any of them from the other; if, however, some of them remain, in proportion as we invested so shall we share.

(From R. Lopez, I. Raymond, eds., *Medieval Trade in the Mediterranean World*, 1955)

could afford this fine product, but those few yielded large profits for manufacturers and merchants.

Medieval industry was based not upon these luxury fabrics, however, but upon a humbler textile: wool. Sheared from the coats of English and Spanish sheep, processed and refined in Flemish, Italian, and, later, English workshops, wool furnished the peasant's tunic and the patrician's robe, and it traveled to foreign markets to fetch a tidy profit for Western merchants. Matted, filthy clumps of raw wool were transformed into gold by European workers and merchants, and by the bankers who financed the industry.

Once the raw wool reached the hands of artisans, it underwent a series of operations: cleaning, combing, spinning, weaving, fulling (shrinking and thickening for expensive cloth), dyeing, and finishing, as shown in *Windows On*, p. 306. Some of these tasks, such as weaving and dyeing, required considerable skill, while others, such as cleaning and spinning, were menial. Often these unskilled tasks were performed in nearby country villages, where women especially were available at low wages to prepare the thread for city weavers.

So many women were spinners that they became permanently identified with that labor. The word "**spinster**," which today signifies a woman who has never married, recalls the medieval woman (especially the young unmarried girl or dependent widowed relative) who spent much of her life spinning. She twisted the fibers between her fingers, adding one fiber at a time to a thread that gradually increased in density and length. By the thirteenth century, an early form of spinning wheel (probably invented in India) was available, powered by a hand crank. But it was not always used. Armies of women workers continued to wind and twist raw fiber into thread with their tools of **distaff** and **spindle** which were everywhere the symbols of the female gender.

Weavers made up perhaps the largest group of urban craftworkers. By the high Middle Ages, most of them were men, who displaced women as the looms grew in size and capacity. From the thirteenth century, the mammoth horizontal loom replaced the simple vertical ones traditionally used in home workshops. The new loom stretched a **warp** as long as 164 feet (50 meters), across which the **woof**, or weft, progressed, thrown by a pedal-operated **shuttle**.

Spinning and weaving were the principal operations of cloth production. The cloth was also fulled and beaten to make it thick, then stretched into proper shape. The fabric's nap was raised with teasing, using a spiky plant called a teasel, then shorn smooth. Last, it was colored in any of a number of bright hues by one of the many available vegetable and animal dyes, which penetrated the fibers with the aid of the metallic compound alum (aluminum potassium sulfate), another commodity essential to the industry, also used as an astringent and in dyeing and tanning.

After textiles, the most important European industries were the mining of metals and production of metal goods. Iron was mined throughout Europe, as were tin, lead, and copper. Silver mined in remote mountains of northern Germany helped build that region's prosperity. Southern German cities specialized in metal products, as did Milan—above all in the manufacture of armor and weapons—as one recent historian has observed, an "illustration of the inferiority of the west in every craft except those of war." Outside of these metalworking centers, the craft was practiced at a more basic level in every European city or town, where blacksmiths labored to produce tools. Even remote manors boasted a blacksmith (his skill perhaps shared by several villages), who supplied the plowshares and hoes agricultural production.

Shipbuilding was an increasingly important industry. The poet Dante (1265–1321) visited Venice's famous dockyard, the Arsenal, which he described:

... the winter through
there boils the sticky pitch to caulk the seams
of the sea-battered bottoms. ...

The operation Dante described was Europe's largest industrial enterprise. Founded in 1104, the Venetian Arsenal (the word, derived from Arabic, testifies to contacts with Islamic) grew at its height in the early sixteenth century to enclose 60 acres (24 hectares) of the city's land, as shown on p. 302. Here were built and launched the Venetian merchant and war fleets which dominated the Mediterranean, outstripping Muslim, Byzantine, and other Italian competitors.

Guilds and Their Functions

The Arsenal was huge, and it was unique. Most medieval production, by contrast, took place in a small workshop, usually within the master's home, where artisans labored to produce the modest commodities needed in daily life—barrels, bread, shoes, and the like. These simpler artisans joined "craft guilds," distinct from the "merchant guilds" that developed earlier in the period of commercial revival.

The great entrepreneurs—those who got raw fiber or metallic ores into the hands of workers, who transported finished cloth or brought tools and arms to markets in Europe and abroad, who invested in workshops, equipment, and mines, or funded expensive commercial ventures, who managed the exchange of high-quality goods across the boundaries of county, country, or continent—probably belonged to the town's merchant guild, which represented the interests of merchants rather than artisans. This body was known by different names all over Europe—"guild" and "hansa" most common in the north, "brotherhood," "company," or "society" in Italy.

Management and labor—a guildmaster supervises the dyeing of cloth: *By the thirteenth century specific craftsman's guilds began to emerge. These guilds issued regulations that covered everything from protecting the welfare of deceased members' families to ensuring quality of production. This fifteenth-century Flemish manuscript illumination shows a guildmaster of the dyer's guild supervising men dyeing cloth.* (British Library, London)

At first, merchant guilds were undifferentiated by the merchandise they sold. In time, especially in larger cities, an early merchants' association did become differentiated by industry. In Florence, the more elite merchants belonged to one of seven "major" guilds. These included the bankers, cloth merchants, spice dealers, and goldsmiths. Their status was distinct from the retailers, who sold cheaper commodities in local markets, and from artisans such as bakers, brewers, and blacksmiths. They were called the *popolo grasso* (the "fat people") because of their wealth and social prominence.

The members of merchants' or upper guilds were those who negotiated city charters with the leaders of medieval society and thus became the city's governors. The urban elite became a "patriciate"—not a nobility, with its ancestral military associations, but an urban ruling class. As it assumed near-permanent control of the higher offices and responsibilities of leadership, the patriciate became hereditary and jealous of its authority, and especially in Venice rarely permitted new men to break into their circle. These men, the source of much of the city's wealth through donations or forced loans, were also the main patrons of building and the arts.

The lesser traders and artisans produced what they sold, performing both functions within the walls of their own house. They gathered in the craft guilds.

Their roster varied from city to city, but bakers, brewers, and barrelmakers generally figured among them, along with makers of purses and hats, and even physicians and **notaries** (the trained professionals who drew up deeds, contracts, wills, and other types of important documents).

These guild members worked not for a wage but for the profit on the goods they produced. They were both capitalists, who invested in workshop, tools, and materials, and laborers, equipped with special skills. Skill was critical in the medieval industrial system, the success of which rested on the performance of each individual worker. To assure the high quality of the products, the craft guilds insisted on rigorous observance of minimum standards in manufacture.

Guilds also concerned themselves with quantities—the exact weight and measure of goods sold, and the precise value of coin tendered. Together with the town governments, they helped overcome the weakening of standards that had occurred throughout Europe after the disappearance of Roman authority. Of particular concern to the towns was the minting of reliable coins, especially silver, in which virtually all wages and most local purchases were paid. Eventually towns were equally careful about gold, used in long-distance transactions and standardized, from the late thirteenth century, by the Florentine florin and Venetian ducat.

Guilds regulated the training of new workers. Training began with **apprenticeship**, in which a young boy was apprenticed to a guild master—one who had established his credentials and been admitted to the guild. The period of apprenticeship was from seven to fourteen years. At the end of that term, the apprentice would become a journeyman, so called because he worked by the day (in French, *journée*). When the journeyman could demonstrate his superior skills—in some towns by completing a "masterpiece"—he might be admitted to the guild as a master, but only if the guild approved of the person and was willing to accept new members. By the later Middle Ages, entrance to a guild was often limited to the sons of masters (and, until her remarriage or death, to his widow and her new husband). The craft guild was far from being the ancestor of the modern labor union, as it is often wrongfully described. It protected the interests of the owner-employer, not the worker.

In return for their members' compliance with tough standards, the guilds bestowed upon them the privilege of monopoly. Non-members could not engage in the trade except as apprentices or journeymen. Prices were set at a level considered "just." That regulation limited competitive practices such as price-cutting, and prevented the free floating of prices in accord with shifts in supply or demand. Workshops were small, and guild rulers kept them that way, limiting the amount of equipment, such as looms and furnaces, that any master might have. Such restrictions prevented one master from too far outstripping the others and breaking the fellowship of the guild circle.

If guild regulations assured quality of production, they also discouraged competition and may have prevented or retarded the development of new and more productive modes of manufacture. During the last two centuries of their existence—into the 1700s—the guilds' effect on the pace of commerce was chilling.

Guilds served other functions besides economic ones. They were a kind of "brotherhood" (although they did enrol some women), with a sense of solidarity, of common purpose and identity, similar to other overlapping communal and confraternal gatherings so frequent in medieval society (see Chapter 12). In the towns, in fact, guilds served many of the functions performed elsewhere by the village community or the protective church. Members gathered for banquets, assumed the responsibility to fund civic or religious festivals, staged processions and plays. They pooled funds for the funeral expenses of members and their families, and insured the protection of members' widows and orphans. Above all, the personal associations made through the guilds yielded practical benefits and were emotionally sustaining.

Diversity and Conflict

Commercial expansion resulted in the diversification of economic activity and the increased likelihood of conflict. Workers skilled and unskilled, merchants small and great, entrepreneurs local and international, patrician managers and subordinate laborers were arrayed against each other by their social and political interests even as they labored together, increasing the wealth of their cities and of Europe.

While the guilds functioned to ensure conformity and standardization within each craft, the number of enterprises in the medieval towns and cities mushroomed. Florence's 14 "minor" guilds numbered twice as many as the "major" guilds and encompassed a broad range of occupations. By the late Middle Ages, Cologne had a population of about 30,000 and as many as 45 guilds. Those enrolled in the woolen cloth industry were most numerous, but the city also supported 122 master goldsmiths. In 1292 Paris had 130 regulated professions, including 22 each in textiles and metallurgy and 18 in foodstuffs and consumable materials such as firewood, and employed more than 5000 artisans. In 1322, the French city of Toulouse counted 177 butchers, while Milan, with a population of about 75,000, counted 300 bakeries. Little Carcassonne (in France), with a population of 9500 in 1304, boasted 63 notaries.

Working Women Most women worked in medieval Europe, even in the cities, dominated though they were by the jealous guild structure and male-oriented patriciates. They worked as "butchers, chandlers, ironmongers, net-makers, shoe-makers, glovers, girdlers, haberdashers, purse-makers, cap-makers, skinners, bookbinders, gilders, painters, silk-weavers and embroiderers, spiciers [dealers in spices], smiths and goldsmiths. ..." They entered these trades as laborers, after an apprenticeship with a female instructor, usually arranged by a father or his surrogate. Or they gained entry as the wife, daughter, or widow of a master. In addition, women were often vendors of goods produced in family workshops, as shown on this page. Some women labored as prostitutes, a profession considered legal and necessary throughout most of Europe; many of them were organized in guilds, with an exclusively female membership. At the lowest level of the pay scale, women worked for a small daily wage as spinners of thread.

The most privileged female worker was the wife or widow or daughter of a guild master in the northern European cities. These women engaged in skilled and high-status work. They often supervised other workers as well—daughters, apprentices, journeymen—and so gained habits of authority. Although barred by law from buying and selling goods, or handling money without the approval of husband or guardian, women often circumvented such regulations. Because they generally worked in the home,

Going to market—a woman selling fish: *Like the husband-and-wife bankers shown on page 291, medieval merchants and artisans often produced or sold goods from workshops or shopfronts located in homes. This manuscript illumination from 1385 shows a woman selling fish from a shopfront.* (Österreichische Nationalbibliothek, Vienna)

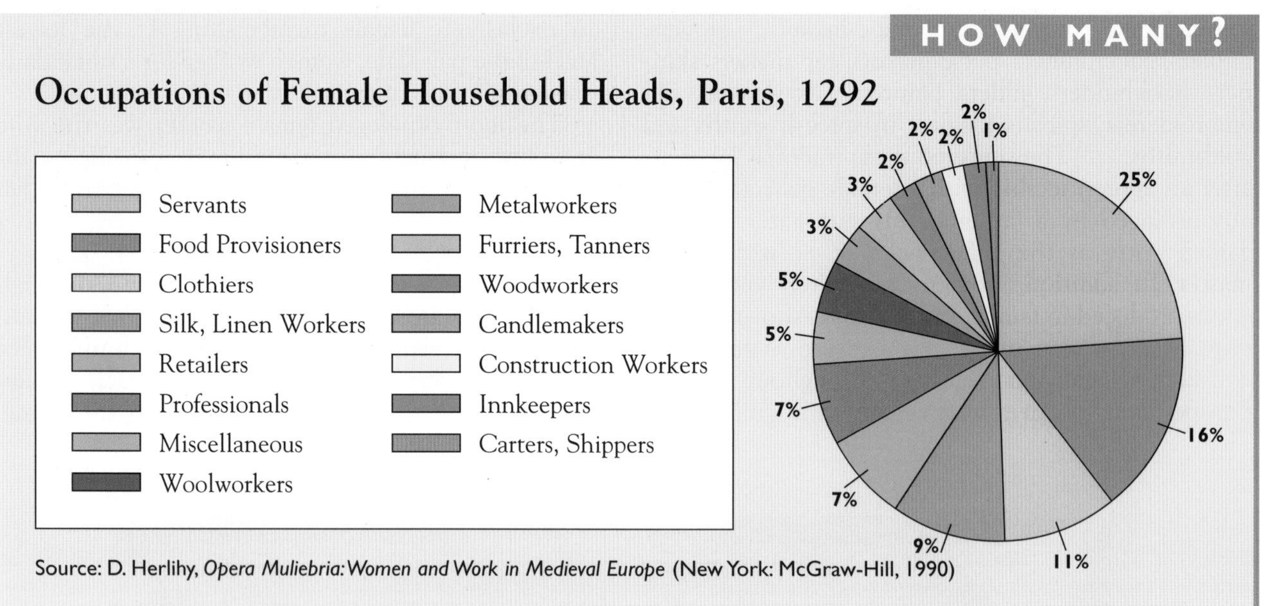

Occupations of Female Household Heads, Paris, 1292

Source: D. Herlihy, *Opera Muliebria: Women and Work in Medieval Europe* (New York: McGraw-Hill, 1990)

they could tend to a variety of other household needs as well as to the rearing of their children.

In some trades—especially in luxury garment trades such as gold-spinning and silk-weaving, the embroidery of bags and gloves and headdresses—the guild may have been dominated by women. In others, such as weaving or dyeing, women were enrolled in guilds because of their connection to male members. Most often, these women were widows, who maintained the family enterprise until the maturity of a male heir, or who married an ambitious journeyman until they took over the master's role.

Women workers generally accepted the marginal roles assigned to most of them in medieval cities. Male workers consigned to such positions, on the other hand, often seethed with resentment, and that resentment sometimes exploded into riot or rebellion. The level of conflict rose in the later Middle Ages as the wealthier merchants consolidated their positions and excluded lower-level artisans from important civic roles. In the later thirteenth century, unrest between merchants and artisans broke out in seven of the most important cities of northern Italy and in five of those in Flanders, as well as in Barcelona and smaller Spanish and French towns.

These revolts were not democratic revolutions. The rebellious laborers sought access to guild membership or privileges, not the recognition of principles of political equality or civil rights. Those who gained admittance to guilds, or who were permitted to form their own guilds, could well be ready to exclude others from the same privilege. Yet the language of rebellion was not forgotten, and the clamor of medieval workers for economic rights would echo in the revolutions of later centuries.

Workers' Revolts Toward the end of the fourteenth century, weavers in Cologne challenged patrician dominance and won changes in the political constitution. Indeed, weavers' revolts were then commonplace in the textile-producing towns of Germany. The Parisian merchant Etienne Marcel, fired by the stress of war as well as by social and political resentments, led a revolt of fellow citizens against the government at about the same time as the peasant Jacquerie of 1358 (see Chapter 9).

Flanders and the Netherlands were densely studded with cloth-producing cities where a large labor force was harshly subordinated to a jealous patriciate. Not surprisingly, throughout the fourteenth century Flemish workers joined in major revolts. In 1302, workers turned on the French allies of their patrician masters in an event dubbed the "Matins of Bruges" (a "wake-up call," alluding to the *matins*, or early morning prayers, of medieval monks). It was followed up two months later with a stunning victory at Courtrai over an army of knights. In 1311 and 1319 in Ghent and in 1326 in Bruges, cloth weavers banded against their city governments. In 1381, workers from Ghent, Ypres, and Bruges defied the count of Flanders, only to be crushed the following year. The artisan leaders of these movements were heroes in the eyes of their contemporaries and forerunners of the champions of later revolutions.

The *Ciompi* In 1378, the wool workers of Florence rose up against guildmasters and governors in the most famous workers' revolt of the age.

The Florentine system of textile production was the most advanced in Europe. Merchants imported in quantity fine English wool and beautiful dyes, from which the highest-quality cloth could be made. They processed the raw wool in a series of steps that anticipate the mass production patterns of modern times. They controlled the whole process of production through a network of agents, owning and directing it

Petrus Christus, A Goldsmith in his Shop: *This painting from 1449 shows a goldsmith (possibly Saint Eloi, the patron saint of goldsmiths) at work in his home workshop. Note the elegantly dressed couple come to examine the artisan's elegantly crafted and highly expensive goods—and the mirror that reflects the life of the town outside.* (The Metropolitan Museum of Art, Robert Lehman Collection, 1975, 1.110)

themselves. The wool was washed in the Arno River, transferred to the countryside for spinning, brought back to an army of urban pieceworkers for weaving, sent out to workshops for dyeing and to the fulling mills for further processing, and finally sent to the central factory for packaging prior to export. The process involved many transfers of goods and a hierarchy of personnel, from the supervisors and skilled workers down to the ordinary laborers, called the *ciompi* ("people of God").

In Florentine society, where wealth was power, the *ciompi* ranked lower even than the members of smaller guilds. In 1378, encouraged by a faction of dissident patricians, but led by one of their own, the woolcomber Michele de Lando, the *ciompi* seized the Florentine government and made Lando chief executive, or *gonfaloniere* (literally, the "standard-bearer"). The *ciompi*'s demand was reasonable—they wished to be admitted to the guild structure, which provided access to government. In response, the guild structure expanded to add three new guilds of wool workers to the twenty-one existing guilds. By this modification, the common workers of Florence became eligible for political office. Having achieved this end, Lando resigned from office.

Within a few weeks, the rebellion was suppressed. Some constitutional changes remained in place until 1382, when disgruntled conservatives from the "minor" guilds joined the elites in restoring the old guild structure, and the control of a narrow oligarchy of "major" guildsmen was asserted. The aspirations of the common workers were defeated. Of the *ciompi* leaders, 161 were executed. Lando himself died in peace and obscurity.

The social unrest of the late Middle Ages left workers where they were before—with those who produced the goods having little share of the wealth and power they had helped to create.

THE WORLD OF COMMERCE

As cities grew and production expanded, European commerce reached the ports of the eastern Mediterranean and the remote depots of Asia and Africa, as Map 11.2 shows. This expansion of trade, which some historians call a "commercial revolution," was a major step toward European economic primacy in the Old World.

By the end of the Middle Ages, Italian merchant venturers had achieved that primacy. And although the Italians would soon lose control of the Mediterranean, European supremacy in trade was maintained by their Spanish, Dutch, English, and French successors, who shifted the economic activity westward to the Atlantic Ocean. The tools and methods they would employ were those developed by Italians in the Middle Ages.

Italy and the Old World Commercial System

In 1000, the Eurasian trade network was essentially the same as it had been since antiquity. The major ports of the eastern Mediterranean were world depots, exchanging goods from Middle Eastern civilizations, Africa, Europe, and south and east Asia. This network had been dominated in turn by the Phoenicians, the Greeks, the Carthaginians, and the Romans, who established their supremacy in the Mediterranean in the first millennium B.C.E. As Rome's economic supremacy declined, Constantinople—the capital of the Eastern, or Byzantine, Empire—took charge. The Arab caliphates soon challenged Constantinople, their ships dominating the Mediterranean from about 700 to about 1000.

Thereafter European, and especially Italian, convoys swept Arab fleets aside and took command of what had once been the Roman sea (see Chapter 5). Italian merchants established residential colonies at key points on the Mediterranean. Nor did their supremacy end at the Mediterranean shore but reached out across the belly of Eurasia, pressing forward by land as well as by sea in the tireless quest for profit.

Byzantium and the Arabs In the seventh and eighth centuries Arab conquests in the Middle East, North Africa, and Spain posed a threat to Byzantium. After that, the Mediterranean was dotted with Arab vessels warily avoiding and sometimes confronting the Byzantine fleets, which held their own in the Aegean region and the approaches to the Black Sea. In the ninth and tenth centuries, as Viking raiders terrified northern Europe, Arab forces further extended their realm. They not only seized Crete and Sicily, but grabbed footholds in southern Italy, and attacked Marseilles and the Christian Spanish city of Barcelona.

Constantinople was a major Mediterranean port as well as an imperial capital. Byzantine ships sailed regularly to the Black Sea and Asia Minor and toured the Aegean islands, southern Italy, and the Adriatic shores. The city exported wine and oil and the lustrous silk fabrics made in government-run workshops from raw silk acquired from Asia. It imported ordinary wheat to feed its population as well as spices, papyrus, and exotic luxury items. Facilitating this commerce were the splendid gold coins that marked Byzantine authority and prestige on the Mediterranean Sea—the bezants, successor to the Roman solidus.

Paradoxically, the Arab irruption into Mediterranean trade produced a net gain for Europe, because it brought Europeans into contact, gradually, with the outside world. Islamic explorers, merchants, and sailors knit the Middle East to Africa (including regions south of the Sahara, previously unexplored by advanced Mediterranean cultures), to Russia (from which Islamic silver currency and goods made their way to the North Sea), and to India and East Asia. One observer listed, among the products arriving from distant suppliers, ostriches and panthers, gems and papyrus, armor and slaves, ermine and musk, combs and pomegranates, cuirasses and jasmine ointment, pistachios and pearls—commodities for consumers who lacked nothing. The words *bazaar* and *arsenal*, *admiral* and *risk*, all Arabic in origin, suggest the significant impact of Islamic control of international commerce at this time.

In 762, Abbasid caliphs transferred their capital from Damascus to Baghdad. Located on the Tigris River the new capital thus had access to the Persian Gulf, which led to the Indian Ocean. From here Islamic traders swept across the Indian Ocean and beyond to the ports of India, Sri Lanka, Malaysia, Vietnam, and China. One of their ships is illustrated on p. 303. According to a tenth-century chronicler, the caliph announced, on the founding of Baghdad,

"Here is no distance between us and China. Everything on the sea can come to us."

Some things came from China overland by the old Silk Road, its stretch across the Middle Eastern plateau kept clear of raiders by the Abbasids as it had been earlier by the Sassanids and Parthians (see Chapter 8). The road reached west to the Mediterranean shore, where merchants transshipped the raw fiber and luxury fabrics to other ports.

Meanwhile, Islamic merchants extended their African ventures. From the Middle East, ships sailed the Persian Gulf to the eastern shore of Africa to take on cargoes of ivory, feathers, exotic woods, and slaves. From North Africa, merchants traveled overland into the sub-Saharan interior. They were lured by unimaginably rich deposits of gold mined in the western Sudan and managed by the kings of Ghana, Mali, and Songhai (see Chapter 8). The gold-starved Byzantine merchants, whose bezants flowed at a dangerous rate to eastern depots, snapped up this precious commodity, paying a heavy toll to the Arab traders who hauled it from the remote African interior.

The Varangians Both Constantinople and Islam profited from trade with the Varangians, centered at Kiev (modern Ukraine). In the ninth century, these descendants of Viking invaders had established themselves in fortified communities called *gorods* along the Dvina and Dnieper river valleys. The most famous of these—Novgorod—flourished for centuries as the easternmost port of call of Hanseatic ships. Even in the early Middle Ages, the Varangian settlements connected the bleak desert of northern Europe to the flourishing civilizations of western Asia.

From their *gorods*, Varangian overlords collected tribute from the Slavic peoples who had settled in

WITNESSES

Faraway Places

In the medieval world, merchants traveled far to obtain the valuable luxury goods desired by the wealthy and powerful at home. In the first passage, King Richard of England, while on crusade in the Holy Land, captures a whole caravan of merchant goods. In the second, a Florentine merchant describes the journey to China for his fellow merchants. In the third, the Venetian merchant Marco Polo describes the prosperity of Beijing, where he spent many years serving the Chinese emperor.

Forces led by King Richard of England capture a merchant caravan in the Holy Land, 1192: By this defeat the pride of the Turks was entirely cast down, and their boldness effectually repressed; whilst the caravan, with all its riches, became the spoil of the victors. Its guards surrendered to our soldiers ... and stretching forth their hands in supplication, they implored for mercy, on condition only that their lives should be spared. They led the yoked horses and camels by the halter, and offered them to our men, and they brought mules loaded with spices of different kinds, and of great value; gold and silver; cloaks of silk; purple and scarlet robes, ... besides arms and weapons of divers forms; coats of mail, ... costly cushions, pavilions, tents, biscuit, bread, barley, grain, meal, and a large quantity of conserves and medicines; basins, bladders, chess-boards; silver dishes and candlesticks; pepper, cinnamon, sugar, and wax; ... an immense sum of money, and an incalculable quantity of goods, such as had never before ... been taken at one and the same time, in any former battle.

("Geoffrey de Vinsauf's Itinerary of Richard I and Others, to the Holy Land"; trs., ed. H. G. Bohn, *Chronicles of the Crusades*, 1848)

Francesco Pegolotti advises merchants traveling to Cathay [China] (Florence, 1310/1340): The road leading from Tana to Cathay is quite safe both by day and by night, according to what the merchants report who have used it—except that if the merchant should die along the road, ... everything would go to the lord of the country where the merchant dies. ... It is reckoned that from Tana to Sarai the road is less safe than all the rest of the journey. But should there be sixty men [in the caravan], [even] when the road is in its worst condition you would travel as safely as [if you were] in your own home.

(From R. S. Lopez, I. W. Raymond, trs., *Medieval Trade in the Mediterranean World*, 1955)

***The Book of Ser Marco Polo the Venetian* (1298) concerning the kingdoms and marvels of the east—the city of Cambaluc (Beijing):** You must know that the city of Cambaluc has such a multitude of houses, and such a vast population inside the walls and outside, that it seems quite past all possibility. There is a suburb outside each of the gates, which are twelve in number; and these suburbs are so great that they contain more people than the city itself. ... In those suburbs lodge the foreign merchants and travellers ... who have come to bring presents to the Emperor, or to sell articles at Court, or because the city affords so good mart to attract traders. ... To this city are brought articles of greater cost and rarity, and in greater abundance of all kinds, than to any other city in the world. For people of every description, and from every region, bring things (including all the costly wares of India, as well as the fine and precious goods of Cathay [China] itself with its provinces). ... As a sample, I tell you, no day in the year passes that there do not enter the city 1000 cart-loads of silk alone. ...

(Marco Polo, *The Book of Ser Marco Polo the Venetian*, 1298; trs. H. Yule, ed. G. B. Parks, 1929, modernized)

the region during the late Roman period. Having no productive agriculture of their own, the Varangians seized the produce of the Slavs, as well as furs and skins, honey and amber. They also took human beings as tribute from the Slavs. (In most European languages, the word for "slave" is derived from "Slav.") The slave trade was central to the development of Russian commerce. Loaded with such goods, Varangian river rafts floated downriver to the Black Sea and on to Constantinople, or eastward via the Volga to the Caspian Sea and the Islamic center at Baghdad. Until the mid-eleventh century, these traders were pagan, so no Christian proscriptions barred either the slave trade or commerce with Muslims. By the tenth century, the profits of this trade had enriched Kiev, the center of Russian civilization until the Mongol onslaught in the thirteenth century (see Chapter 9). Hoards of Greek and Arab coins were stored in Russia and Scandinavia.

From the seventh through the tenth centuries, western Europeans contributed little to the international commercial system that thrived on the Mediterranean and stretched to Africa and Asia. But Arab, Jewish, and Syrian merchants visited the Mediterranean ports of Spain, France, and Italy, and some penetrated to the fairs of the interior. Here they acquired the few, cheap, bulky goods the West had to offer—salt and fish, raw wool and some finished linen, timber, tin, and iron. European elites in turn bought luxuries from the east, in the small quantities that they could afford with their few silver coins and their ever-diminishing treasure of gold. These luxuries included spices, perfumes, medicinal herbs, silk, and other luxury fabrics.

The Italians By the eleventh century, Italian fleets had begun to claim their piece of Mediterranean commerce. Venetian ships hugged the Adriatic shores en route to and from Constantinople, while Pisan and Genoese raids announced the intent of their merchants to gain footholds in both North Africa and the Middle East. After the Crusades began in 1095, Italian ships carried armies and supplies to the eastern Mediterranean and planted colonies of their nationals in the region. The Italian presence became so great that a considerable fraction of the population of Constantinople consisted of resident Italian merchants.

Although the Crusaders failed to hold Jerusalem, by the thirteenth century the Mediterranean was dominated, as in Roman days, by people speaking Romance languages. Genoese merchants emerged as the major presence in the northern Aegean, carrying cargoes of alum from Asia Minor to supply the cloth workshops of Florence and other textile-producing centers. The Venetians controlled trade with Egypt and Syria, having secured bases in the Aegean, especially Crete. Spices were their chief cargo, especially pepper, prized and expensive, the importation of which remained in Venetian hands into the sixteenth century. These two Italian giants became fierce rivals in the thirteenth and fourteenth centuries, as they competed for control of markets in the Black Sea and access to Russia, and were often at war. A final war in 1379–1380 resulted in a hard-won victory for Venice.

The Italian grip on Mediterranean commerce was tight, but their merchants generally halted at the eastern Mediterranean. There, Asian products, brought by Arab or Jewish intermediaries, were purchased for shipment to the west. In 1271, Marco Polo (c. 1254–1324) accompanied his father and uncle, both Venetian merchants, on a trip to Asia, including China, which the older men had visited a few years earlier (becoming among the first Europeans to do so). There Marco lived for seventeen years (1275–1292), working for the emperor Kublai Khan, which he describes in *Witnesses* on p. 315. Those eventful years included a three-year stint as governor of Yangchow, a city with a population of more than one million. Of this city, Marco later wrote: "It surpasses in grandeur, wealth and beauty, every other city in the world." In a Genoese prison, after his return to Italy in 1295, Polo dictated his memoirs. His experience marked Europe's first reliably documented encounter with cultures beyond the Mediterranean and pointed the way to future such ventures.

But Italian hegemony in the Mediterranean was to face a new challenge in the fifteenth century, when Constantinople fell to the Ottoman Turks. By 1300 the Ottoman Turks, a new power in Asia Minor, named after their dynasty of rulers, were advancing aggressively toward Constantinople. In 1350, they seized Nicaea, the last Byzantine foothold in Asia Minor. Soon they arrived on the Balkan peninsula, overwhelming the Serbs at Kosovo in 1389. In the following century, they absorbed the whole of the Balkans and the islands of the Aegean, then reached to Syria and Egypt to the south, and toward Vienna to the north. In 1453, they captured Constantinople, the fortress city once believed to be impregnable. Rome had truly died with the seizing of its last eastern outpost. An Islamic nation had established itself in southeastern Europe. Italian supremacy in the Mediterranean was doomed.

Venice proceeded cheerfully to do business with the "heathen" Turks despite papal condemnation. Yet Ottoman fleets continued to expand in the Aegean, the Adriatic, and the Mediterranean, gobbling up Italian islands and depots. Control of the pepper trade slipped to the Portuguese, who had begun to probe the Atlantic shores of Africa and opened up an oceanic trade link to Asia. Soon those nation states of Europe with windows on the Atlantic would snatch commercial leadership from the Italians and build an even greater engine for generating profits.

The Tools of Trade

Although they would come to surpass their Italian predecessors, the merchants of northern Europe were greatly indebted to these pioneering traders who had developed both the tools and methods of commercial success.

Ships Over some three centuries, the Italians became master shipbuilders and sailors. Their ships—no bigger than the 130-foot (40-m.)-long grain transports of ancient Rome—had a rudder (a northern European invention of about 1200), which afforded precision in steering; articulated sails, which permitted the exploitation of winds from any direction; and improved charts, which guided adventurous sailors through unfamiliar territory.

Two types of vessel emerged: the swift longship, or galley and the heavier, capacious round ship. The galley was powered by oars (manned by ordinary laborers or condemned criminals) and supplementary sails and could race through seas ridden with pirates or enemy fleets. But much of its interior was occupied by the crew and the rowing decks, so little space remained for cargo. These fast, safe ships were operated only by the larger and wealthier cities, and they carried mainly luxury goods. The round ship was cheaper, slower, and spacious. It carried a smaller crew, including, for security, a few crossbowmen. Its vast hold could accommodate such bulky goods as wheat and alum, metals and wool, salt and timber. The humble round merchantman, relying entirely on sail power, was true ancestor of the ships that later carried Europeans to the Americas.

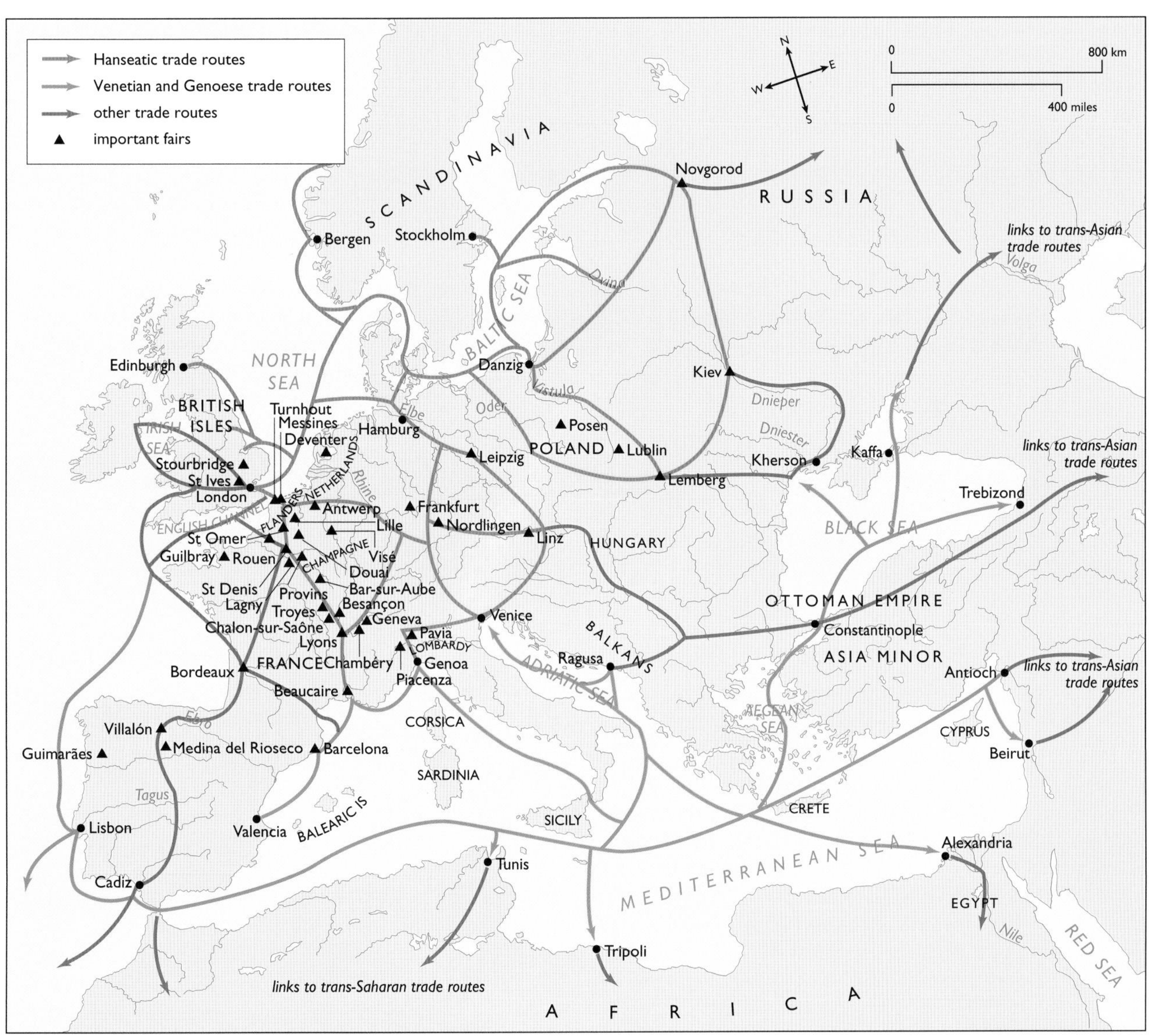

Map 11.2 Trade Networks, to 1500: *Money and goods streamed back and forth across the underbelly of the Old World, transported by Chinese, Arab, Byzantine, and western European ships. By the close of the Middle Ages western Christians had achieved dominance, Venetians foremost among them, but the basis for the emergence of other powerful European dynasties and merchant families was already laid.*

Venice developed the greatest fleets of the late Middle Ages, edging out the Genoese and the latecomer Florentines (who acquired Pisa and Livorno, on the coast, in the early 1400s). Her Arsenal could complete four or five galleys every two years, supplying her merchant complements of seven to ten galleys for the routes to Syria, Egypt, and Flanders. Her "great galley," introduced in 1290, was immense: 120 to 150 feet (37–46 meters) long, it carried a crew of up to 200, its oarsmen arrayed on 25 to 30 benches each side in banks of two or three. The mightiest ships of the west, these were used in long voyages until the mid-sixteenth century, when sails displaced oars.

Law and Bookkeeping Together with merchants, goods, and ships, other important components of the economic expansion were notaries and lawyers, who created the culture that supported the mechanisms of trade. Building on the expertise of canon (that is, church) lawyers, civil lawyers explored the Roman legal tradition for precepts applicable to commerce, while notaries drew up the documents that met the standards so developed. Merchants, too, learned to read and sign contracts and to keep records of inventories and transactions. In the commercial centers of Europe, but especially in Italy, a new secular and commercial culture began to flourish.

Merchants faced a variety of problems, three of which were solved by the creation of new contractual forms. First, they needed to be able to transfer funds without actually exchanging large quantities of currency. Second, they needed to raise capital for merchant ventures. Third, they needed to charge interest—though the practice was forbidden by the church—on such capital loans.

The bill of exchange solved the first problem. This performed the function of the modern check or its equivalent. A merchant in one city instructed his agents in another to release a specified sum in the currency of that locality to another merchant. The

WITNESSES

How and How Not to Succeed in Business

As important for business as buying and selling itself are certain intellectual or cultural traits acquired by merchants, which allow them to make prudent judgments. The first of these passages consists of a merchant's advice to other merchants about careful record-keeping. The second sternly condemns a fellow merchant for attempting too much, and ending up in bankruptcy.

Benedetto Cotrugli's advice on business methods (Naples, 1458): The pen is an instrument so noble and excellent that it is absolutely necessary ... to merchants. ... And when you see a merchant to whom the pen is a burden ..., you may say that he is not a merchant. And [a good merchant] not only must be skilled in writing but also must keep his records ... methodically. ... Mercantile records are the means to remember all that a man does, and from whom he must have, and to whom he must give, and the costs of wares, and the profits, and the losses, and every other transaction on which the merchant is at all dependent. ...

Therefore the merchant ought to keep three books, that is, the ledger ..., the journal ..., and the memorandum. ... And the ledger ought to have its alphabetical [index] through which one may quickly find any account written in the said ledger. ...

In the journal you shall reconstruct methodically all [your] capital, item by item, and you shall carry it forward in the ledger. ... And when you have finished writing the said ledger, you shall settle all accounts opened in it, extract from them all balances ... to the debit or likewise to the credit. ...

In the memorandum you ought to note every evening or morning before you leave your home everything you have traded and transacted on that day because of your commerce. ... And you should further note that you ought to keep always with you a small notebook ... in which you shall note day by day and hour by hour even the minute [detail] of your transactions, so that later you may at your best convenience create accounts in the memorandum book or the journal ... then carry them forward into the ledger daily. ...

And therefore I warn and encourage any merchant to take pleasure in knowing how to keep his books well and methodically. ... Otherwise your commerce will be chaos, a confusion of Babel—of which you must beware if you cherish your honor and your substance.

(Benedetto Cotrugli, *On Commerce and the Perfect Merchant*, 1458; eds. R. Lopez, I. Raymond, 1955)

Chronicler Francesco da Molin describes the bankruptcy of a wealthy Pisan merchant (1584): He had built up much credit by his many business transactions, but in truth it was based on his reputation alone and not upon his capital, for this market and the city of Venice are naturally very much inclined to love and trust in appearances. Hence, heaping business upon business, his reach exceeding his grasp, he suffered the fate of almost all those who want to be bigger than other men. With his fall came the fall of the bank, because its creditors ... all wanted to be satisfied at the same time. The bank kept going for a few days, ... but in the end the crowd of creditors increased and the bank collapsed and failed, to the detriment of numberless people and great damage to this market.

(Francesco da Molin, *Compendio ... delle cose che reputero degni di venerne particolar memoria*, 1584; eds. D. Chambers, B. Pullan, 1992)

second merchant, rather than collecting the funds, could acquire credit with the agent for the purchase of goods which he could then exchange elsewhere. The bill of exchange also served to provide short-term credit, and permitted merchants to exploit differences in currency values between markets.

With such documents in circulation, little currency changed hands. Instead, merchants kept records of transactions in "money of account," a theoretical currency. Medieval commerce conceived of value abstractly and exchanged instruments of credit as comfortably as in the modern world.

To raise capital for commercial ventures, merchants developed a variety of partnership arrangements. In a true partnership, the parties pooled their capital, shared risks, and divided profit in proportion to their contributions. In other varieties of partnership, such as the one cited in *Witnesses* on p. 307, a passive party contributed all or part of the capital and received a stipulated share of the profit, but did not travel with the merchandise. He was in fact an investor, rather than a merchant.

To circumvent the prohibition against charging interest, merchants levied extra charges by building interest charges invisibly into the bill of exchange; payment to the distant merchant would correspond to the value of the merchandise in foreign currency plus an additional percentage. They also concealed interest in loan contracts. The investor was repaid not merely the amount advanced, but an additional amount ostensibly in compensation for risk or for services. Such mechanisms had precedents in Byzantine, Islamic, Roman, Greek, and Babylonian practices. But by 1300, Italian merchants, lawyers, and bankers had made these practices much more sophisticated.

By the early fourteenth century, the merchants who watched revenues flow in and expenditures spill out had elaborated from Arab models a new method of keeping track of them—double-entry bookkeeping. Still in use today (its principles still underlie computerized systems), this method of accounting revolutionized commercial practice. Linked credit and debit entries were posted in a journal in columns aligned side by side, with cross references to other ledgers or customers' accounts, as required, and with an alphabetical index at the end. These detailed ledgers enabled merchants to gain their virtual monopoly of western Europe's foreign trade.

Fifteenth-century handbooks taught merchants commercial practices. The *Compendium of Arithmetic* (1494) by Luca Pacioli, a friar and mathematician, contained a section on accountancy. Francesco Pegolotti's *Practical Business Methods* advised on currencies and measures and how to get by abroad. The importance of good penmanship was emphasized by Benedetto Cotrugli in *On Commerce and the Perfect Merchant* (1458). "The pen is an instrument so noble and excellent that it is absolutely necessary ... to merchants ... And when you see a merchant to whom the pen is a burden or who is inept with the pen, you may say that he is not a merchant (see *Witnesses*, p. 318)."

These handbooks taught merchants how to succeed in business with diligence and precision. With these attitudes, commercial instruments and fine sailing ships and skilled navigators, merchants introduced Europe to the world and its wealth, the taste of which awakened ardent appetites. Europe would now be integrated into a world economy, which it would one day dominate in the name of God, and of profit.

MUST READS

Books to Remember

Luca Pacioli	*Summa de arithmetica (Compendium of Arithmetic)* (1494)
Francesco Pegolotti	*Pratica della mercatura (Practical Business Methods)*
Marco Polo	*Milione* ("Million," memoirs of his journey to China) (c. 1298)

Conclusion

MERCHANTS, MONEY, AND THE MEANING OF THE WEST

Kings and emperors, priests and scribes, peasants, prophets, and poets made the ancient world. Those who prayed, those who fought, and those who plowed created the civilization of early medieval Europe. But among the later developers of that civilization were also European merchants, who teased a profit from the sale of goods, who opened the dikes and floodgates of an agrarian economy to the rush of cash, who built cities that were monuments to entrepreneurial ingenuity and greed. They accumulated the wealth, and—just as important—they developed the techniques and mental habits that enabled the West to breach the borders of Europe and explore the world. The quest for profit was the dynamo that powered the expansion of Western civilization after 1500.

REVIEW QUESTIONS

1. Why did trade revive in the tenth century? Why did Jews and Italians dominate early moneylending and banking?

2. Why did cities begin to revive in the eleventh century? How was the growth of cities linked to the revival of commerce? Who were the bourgeoisie? Why did they became an influential force?

3. How did cities help to change medieval society? Why was the urban revival so important in Italy? What role did Italian cities play in the conflict between the Empire and the papacy?

4. How was the textile industry linked to the growth of cities? Why was wool the most important medieval textile? How important were women in the textile industry?

5. What were the guilds? How did the guilds operate to regulate craftsmanship and trade? How did the guild structure affect working women and unskilled laborers?

6. What important role did Arabs play in international trade? How did the Italians gain such widespread control of Mediterranean commerce? How did merchants get around the Church's prohibition against charging interest?

SUGGESTED RESOURCES

Money and Merchants

Cipolla, Carlo M., *Before the Industrial Revolution: European Society and Economy, 1000–1700*, 2nd ed. (New York: Norton, 1980). Argues that the Middle Ages be treated as part of a longer preindustrial economy.

Hodges, Richard, *Dark Age Economics: The Origins of Towns and Trade, A.D. 500–1000* (New York: St. Martin's Press, 1982). Argues that noncommercial exchange among elites was channeled through trading centers, comparable to those in precolonial Africa and Asia.

Lopez, Robert, *The Commercial Revolution of the Middle Ages, 950–1350* (Englewood Cliffs, NJ: Prentice Hall, 1971). An account of Europe's transformation from underdeveloped periphery to economic center.

Cities and Towns

Clarke, Helen & Björn Ambrosiani, *Towns in the Viking Age* (New York: St. Martin's, 1991). Uses archeological evidence to reconstruct the history of commercial towns from Ireland to Novgorod from late Roman times to the eleventh century.

Hohenberg, Paul M. and Lynn Hollen Lees, *The Making of Urban Europe, 1000–1994*, 2nd ed. (Cambridge: Harvard University Press, 1995). Unique history of the whole span of European urbanization from the first significant commercial settlements to recent times.

Jones, Philip, *The Italian City-State: From Commune to Signoria* (Oxford: Clarendon Press of Oxford University Press, 1997). An authoritative and up-to-date synthesis.

Nicholas, David, *The Growth of the Medieval City: from Late Antiquity to the Early Fourteenth Century* (Addison Wesley Longman, 1997). A recent synthesis by an expert in the highly urbanized region of Flanders.

Medieval English towns, town histories, study of office-holding, links (ORB): **http://orb.rhodes.edu/encyclop/culture/towns/towns.html**

Artisans and Entrepreneurs

Epstein, Steven A., *Wage Labor and Guilds in Medieval Europe* (Chapel Hill: University of North Carolina Press, 1991). Original study of the apprenticeship system that developed within the framework of medieval guilds and prepared the way for modern wage labor.

Herlihy, David, *Opera muliebria: Women and Work in Medieval Europe* (Philadelphia: Temple University Press, 1990). A thoughtful reconstruction of the kinds of women's work in medieval society.

Howell, Martha C., *Women, Production, and Patriarchy in Late Medieval Cities* (Chicago: University of Chicago Press, 1986). An examination of women workers in Leiden and Cologne.

Mazzaoui, Maureen Fennell, *The Italian Cotton Industry in the Later Middle Ages, 1100–1600* (Cambridge: Cambridge University Press, 1981). A study of cotton in the 12th-century, and Italy's role as bridge between Islam and the West.

Swanson, Heather, *Medieval Artisans: An Urban Class in Late Medieval England* (Oxford: Basil Blackwell, 1989). Examines craft production, the place of artisans in municipal government, relations between artisans and the merchant class, and political subordination.

The World of Commerce

Abu-Lughod, Janet L., *Before European Hegemony: The World System, A.D. 1250–1350* (Oxford: Oxford University Press, 1989). A view of the medieval world as an interdependent, decentralized world system made possible by the decline of a previous world system.

Crosby, Alfred W., *The Measure of Reality: Quantification and Western Society, 1250–1600* (Cambridge: Cambridge University Press, 1997). The European habit of quantification is identified as the precondition for Europe's later expansion and world dominance.

De Roover, Raymond A., *Money, Banking, and Credit in Medieval Bruges: Italian Merchant-Bankers, Lombards, and Money-Changers* (Cambridge, MA: Medieval Academy of America, 1948). A landmark study in the origins of banking.

Larner, John, *Marco Polo and the Discovery of the World* (New Haven: Yale University Press, 2000). Discusses the pivotal role of Polo's book for later geographical thought and exploration.

Mueller, Reinhold, *The Venetian Money Market: Banks, Panics and the Public Debt, 1200–1500* (Baltimore: Johns Hopkins University Press, 1997). The second and final volume of a comprehensive study of the financial system of Venice, examining the trajectory from moneychanging to banking, bank failures, and bank underwriting of government functions through public loans.

Francesco Datini, merchant of Florence, brief biography and images (Istituto Datini):
http://www.istitutodatini.it/schede/datini/eng/fdatini.htm

PART FOUR

THE WEST EXPANDS

The Self, the State, the World (1200–1750)

From 1200–1750, Europe's unique urban civilization fostered wealth and innovation. The precocious cities of northern Italy, in particular, nurtured the artists and intellectuals who created the brilliant cultural movement of the "Renaissance." Drawing on the literary and artistic legacy of the ancient world, they laid the foundations for the modern development of European thought and expression, an enterprise aided by the new technology of the printing press.

As the Renaissance reached its zenith, criticism of clerical corruption, ecclesiastical finances, and the sacramental system of the Roman Catholic Church exploded into the rival movement of the Protestant Reformation. Diversified into a spectrum of beliefs and institutions, Protestantism spread rapidly, sometimes supported, and sometimes suppressed by powerful emerging states. In response to Protestant advance, the Catholic Church reaffirmed its authority, rededicating itself to its mission at home and abroad.

As the coherence of medieval civilization yielded to these disruptive cultural currents, the European monarchies claimed a new sovereignty over that of the modern nation state. Their rulers possessed, or hoped to possess, absolute power. To assert that claim, they fielded huge armies, equipped with guns and cannon, ordered in squares, rows, or columns, and drilled to fire on command. Some theorists defended the monarch's divine right to rule, a right proclaimed in ritual and images; others proposed the countervailing notion of the rights of citizens.

European civilization was content no longer, after 1500, to remain within its borders. Venturing across the unknown Atlantic, explorers, conquerors, entrepreneurs, and Old World refugees opened two new continents to European settlement. Others traded in Asia and Africa amid civilizations that, for now, thought little of these western visitors who would soon deem themselves lords of the world.

CITY LIFE

1200 | 1250 | 1300 | 1350 | 1400 | 1450 | 1500

Rulers, Nations, and War

Capetian dynasty, France, 987–1328

Valois dynasty, France, 1328–1589

Norman kings, Plantagenets, Lancasters, Yorks, England, 1066–1485

Spanish *Reconquista*, 11th c.–1492

Habsburg emperors, 1273–1918

Hundred Years' War, 1337–1453

- Constantinople, falls to Ottoman Turks, 1453
- Sack of Rome, 1527

Society and Economy

Italian communes, 11th–13th c.

Italian republics and despotisms, 14th–15th c.

Plague endemic in Europe, 1347–1720

Hanseatic League, c. 1250–1450

- The florin, 1252
- Marco Polo joins court of Kublai Khan, 1275
- The ducat, 1284
- European population approx. 73 million, 1300
- Ponte Vecchio, Florence, 1345
- Black Death strikes Europe, 1347–52
- Dondi clock, 1364
- Streetpaving begins in Nuremberg, 1368
- Revolt of the Ciompi, 1378
- Public brothel opened in Frankfurt, 1396
- Execution of Savonarola, 1498
- Venetian *ghetto*, 1516

Art, Religion, and Ideas

Babylonian Captivity, 1303–78

Great Schism, 1378–1415

- Jews expelled from England, 1290
- Jews expelled from France, 1306
- Dante's *Divine Comedy*, c. 1308–14
- Boccaccio's *Decameron*, 1353
- Christine de Pisan's *Book of the City of Ladies*, 1405
- Council of Constance, 1414–18
- Jews expelled from Spain, 1492
- Michelangelo's Sistine chapel, 1508–12
- Machiavelli writes *Prince*, 1513

Beyond the West

Sung dynasty, 960–1279

Yuan dynasty, 1279–1368

Ming dynasty, 1368–1644

Mughal Empire, 1526–1857

Aztec, Inca Empires, c. 13th c.–1521, 1532

Ghana, Mali, Songhay African kingdoms, 500–1500s

- Voyages of Zheng He, China, 1405–1433
- Dias at Cape of Good Hope, 1488
- Columbus reaches West Indies, 1492
- Cortés conquers Mexico, 1519–21
- Magellan sails the world, 1519–22
- Pizarro conquers Peru, 1531–39

CHAPTER

12

CITY LIFE

Public and Private Life in the Late Medieval Cities

1200–1500

KEY TOPICS

- **The Urban Landscape:** The medieval city's space and distinctive forms—gates, walls, bridges, and buildings—shape the awareness of townspeople, who move for the first time to the steady pace of mechanical clocks.
- **Public Life:** Merchants, artisans, foreigners, prostitutes, and the poor throng into cities, which are the setting for dynamic public rituals and for the devastations of bubonic plague.
- **Private Life:** The requirements of childbirth and childrearing frame women's experience, in the city as elsewhere; so does (among the elites) the dowry system, which channels wealth from females to males.
- **The City and the Book:** City people have time to read, while writers, like the Frenchwoman Christine de Pisan or the Italian Dante Alighieri, often write about city life.

*U**rbanity*** *As soon as towns began to spring up in medieval Europe, the "city slicker" began to mock the "country bumpkin." The poet and scholar Brunetto Latini (c. 1220–1294), an advocate of urban life, commended the town-dweller who rides "in a stately manner," and urged newer arrivals to emulate his poise:*

> *. . . . . . Guard against moving*
> *Like a man from the country;*
> *Don't squirm like an eel, go self-assuredly*
> *Through the streets and people.*

Town-dwellers developed customs, speech, and perceptions, superior (as they saw it) to those of peasant villagers. To be of the city was to be "urbane"—well-mannered, polished, and sophisticated.

The citizens' prejudice had some basis in fact. Although the culture of western Europe first took form in monastery, castle, and village, its later development was conditioned by life in the city. Amid the packed **urban** landscape and busy public life, townspeople inhabited a very different world from that of the peasants, monks, and mounted warriors outside the walls.

The previous chapter traced the development of towns in their commercial aspects. But what was life like within these towns? Visually, the town presented a marked contrast to the fields and villages that surrounded it. As the illustrations opposite show, the urban landscape was marked by gates, towers, and steeples, twisting roads and welcoming open spaces, public and private buildings, and the crowded districts of the poor. Here, city people carried on their public life of celebration, service, and suffering, and their private lives of marrying and child-rearing. The mental world of the city, so different from the court or university, would also powerfully shape Western civilization.

THE URBAN LANDSCAPE

Like most medieval towns, the German city of Nuremberg in the fifteenth century was encircled by a wall, shown on p. 325. Entry to the town was through one of four huge gates—as few as two in smaller towns, or as many as eight in larger ones. Heavy chains and iron clamps secured these gates at night or in time of danger. If these could not deter an intruder, there was an extra barrier: the portcullis. "Vertical bars and drop gates fitted with needle-sharp bronze spikes can be thrust down upon invaders," reports the scholar and poet Conrad Celtis (1459–1508) "and, throwing them to the ground, pierce their bodies through." Its portcullis shut, the town was an island, secure from the assaults, the business, and the ways of the outside. All who came to the city passed through the ferocious barrier of the city gate.

That gate and the wall it sealed marked the boundary between city and country—never absolute, for goods and people flowed regularly across that limit, yet still distinct. Outside the walls lay the country landscape, a gentle undulation of cultivated fields, striped by the plow. Within was a boisterous chorus: crowded, noisy, and in motion. Within the stone circle of walls, city people moved faster than the folk in the country. Time was short and space was tight, and both were worth money.

Time and Spaces

Church bells tolled and clocks chimed to measure the working day for medieval town dwellers. Similarly, the rich patterns of buildings, streets, and open spaces shaped their consciousness.

Work began at dawn for town dwellers, summoned by the ringing of church bells. They rang at intervals all day until the toll of curfew at nightfall. Bells called people to prayer or to face an emergency; they marked the opening and closing of markets, sent

Urban Forms

From the Tower to London Bridge: *This fifteenth-century view of London shows the city wall and royal Tower in the foreground. In the background is London Bridge with its many houses spanning the River Thames.* **(British Library, London)**

civic officials to their deliberations, and announced executions. The spaces of time that stretched between the tolling of the bells were a commodity to be saved, and certainly not wasted.

During the fourteenth century clocks replaced bells in the larger and wealthier cities. A town clock was installed in Florence in 1325, Milan in 1335, and Geneva in 1353. In 1370, the French king, Charles V, ordered that all the bells of Paris coordinate with the clock at the royal palace. By this ruling the musical bells were subordinated to the modern tempo of mechanical motion. The precise partitioning of time coordinated with the psychology of the merchant, for whom the new machines imposed on the flow of natural rhythms time that was measured, orderly, and precise. The clock was an instrument, commented an English monk, "by which the people rule themselves."

Regulated by the arithmetic of passing hours, the town dweller's mentality was also shaped by the visual grammar of urban forms: the city's compact mass of buildings and its streets. Again, Nuremberg is typical; by the fifteenth century the perimeter of its wall enclosed more than 500 streets and thousands of buildings. Both individuals and corporations (guilds and **confraternities**, church and government councils) organized the construction of buildings of wood, brick, or stone. Few still stand that are older than the thirteenth century, but their outlines can be deduced from documents or later structures that do survive.

The halls of the guilds declared the success of those who labored to produce and sell. That is the boastful spirit observed in the lines of the Cloth Hall of Ypres and of Orsanmichele in Florence. Not far from the guildhall was the market square, the nerve center of the medieval city. The "haymarket" or "fishmarket" or "flowermarket" provided a space to buy and sell, but also to dance or to repent, to shout down a leader or welcome a guest, hear a sermon or plot a rebellion.

Nuremberg within its walls: *This woodcut from Hartmann Schedel's* Liber Chronicarum, *1493, shows the sloped roofs of tightly packed buildings mounting the hill from city gate to castle.*

Church and Town Hall Towns were also centers of the life of the spirit. Throughout a medieval city were scattered the buildings that marked the presence of the Church. At or near the center stood a cathedral or another large church. Built with the love and labor of citizens for the glory of God, cathedrals and churches were also built for the glory of the prosperous bourgeoisie, who provided the materials, appointed the masters, and paid the bills, and whose family and guild chapels intruded upon the sacred space, alongside those of nobility and important clergy, lining the nave and encircling the high altar.

The great cathedrals represented only a fraction of church construction. Churches proliferated as the population grew, each serving the surrounding neighborhood, or parish, and most dedicated to one or another of the saints. The 200,000 residents of thirteenth-century Milan were divided into 115 parishes: no inhabitant was expected to journey far to hear mass. In the parish church and adjacent churchyard citizens were baptized, married, and buried, and here they settled the contracts that made up the web of commerce, sworn to by witnesses on sacred relics.

Monasteries and convents stood at the edge of the city or just beyond its walls. Convents housed mostly wealthy women, along with their servants. Whereas traditional monasticism was rural in origin, but found a place in the city, the mendicant orders of the Franciscans and Dominicans embraced an urban mission from the start. As part of the core of city life, they staked out their claim at once to the cheap land on the city's fringe.

In Paris, the Dominicans and the Franciscans found homes in the then-suburban expanses of the Left Bank, around the nucleus of the growing university. In Nuremberg, the Franciscan complex had been built outside the circuit of the walls that stood at the time of its foundation, but hugged the inner perimeter of the expanded late-medieval walls. In the same way, in Florence, the Franciscans, Dominicans, and Augustinians established their orders beyond the city walls, to be eventually encompassed within a still-larger circuit. They occupied, as at Paris, the sparsely settled areas of the city where dwelt the poor and restive masses who particularly responded to their message.

Not far from the commercial zone of market and guildhall and the ecclesiastical centers of monastery and cathedral stood the imposing public buildings that housed the government. The councilors of Siena explained the need for such grand structures: "It is a matter of honor for each city that its rulers and officials should occupy beautiful and honorable buildings. … This is a matter of great importance for the prestige of the city." The patricians of Bruges deliberated in

***Ambrogio Lorenzetti,* The Effects of Good Government in the City and the Country:** *This fresco (Palazzo Pubblico, 1338–1339) by the Italian artist Ambrogio Lorenzetti encompasses a peaceful country landscape and well-regulated urban scene, clearly contrasted and separated by the city's walls and gates.*

the Old Hall; those of hilltop Volterra, Italy, in the Palazzo dei Priori (Priors' Palace); those of Florence in the Palazzo del Popolo ("palace of the people"; now called the Palazzo Vecchio, or "old palace"); those of Venice in the Doge's Palace (the Doge was the title of the city's elective presiding head), adjacent to the Piazza and the basilica of San Marco: "the most beautiful square in the world," pronounced one of the city chroniclers, "and ... the most beautiful church in the world."

Houses Not to be outdone by Church, corporation, or council, the town's leading merchants proclaimed their status by building themselves houses as splendid as their considerable fortunes would allow. The ordinary merchant lived comfortably, though he shared his premises with commercial bustle and the business of strangers. His house might have shop and warehouse on the ground floor, hall with kitchen and pantry on the second, and bedchambers on the third, furnished with multiple beds for master's family and servants alike. Beds were shared by parents and children, masters and servants, merchants and workmen, occasioning a kind of interaction among diverse groups unacceptable—even unthinkable—today.

Fireplaces provided heat on every floor of multistory houses, served by chimneys (an improvement on the hole in the roof of peasant establishments). This heating system was so improved over those of earlier periods that it made city life comfortable, whereas hitherto winter was only "a period of stupefied hibernation." The new fireplaces not only took smoke out of a room, but could be modified to radiate heat into the room before taking it out of the building. Windows still lacked glass, but were closed against the elements by oiled cloth or parchment; at night, shutters protected the house against harsh cold and unlawful entry. Likewise, hefty doors locked or barred at night, kept out cold and strangers.

Floors were strewn with rushes—green in summer, dried into hay by winter—food for fire. Walls were finished with plaster or wood paneling and, in affluent homes, hung with tapestries. These added color and texture while protecting against drafts. The toilet? A chamber pot, emptied the next morning from the window, or a shed over a ditch in the rear

garden—next to the neighbor's property line—served the purpose. Better-equipped homes had a privy near the bedrooms, from which a chute conducted waste to a pit in the cellar.

An ordinary burgher's house was usually built as part of a row of attached houses, backed by a series of gardens or a common green. The grand houses of important merchants were mostly free-standing. The thirteenth-century Florentine moralist Brunetto Latini admired the houses of the grand burghers of France, "great and spacious and painted, their fair chambers wherein they have joy and delight," and the splendid gardens adjacent to them. These homes set a new standard of luxury and, still more novel, of privacy—featuring that most precious of innovations, a private bedroom, at least for the master of the house and his wife.

The town houses of urban patricians and those of ordinary merchants differed not only in scale and elegance, but even in function. The ground floor of the average tradesman's or master craftsman's house was devoted to his trade. It included a shop or workshop, perhaps also an office for bookkeeping and a storeroom. By contrast, the residence of a rich merchant was dedicated to the display of wealth rather than its production, and kept separate from the workshop. Cosimo de' Medici (1389–1464), for example, Florentine financier and unofficial ruler, built his splendid palace apart from his place of business, the family's famous bank, left behind in the heart of the old town. The divorce of home life and work life begins with these great merchants, the first commuters of the western world. (An exception was Venice, where the ground floors of the great merchants' palaces opened onto dank canals and were used for loading and unloading).

The Italian writer Leonardo Bruni (c. 1370–1444) had in mind the palaces of rich merchants when he described their "entrance courts, halls, pavements, banquet halls … [and] the curtains, arches, the paneled ceilings and richly decorated hung ceilings … beautiful chambers decorated with fine furniture, gold, silver and brocaded hangings and precious carpets." He claimed that in Florence (which included some of the richest men in Europe), such buildings were found in every street and neighborhood: "Just as blood is spread throughout the entire body, so fine architecture and decoration are diffused throughout the whole city (see *Witnesses* on p. 331)."

Nearby, in crowded houses near the center of town or in cave-like recesses under the walls, lived the small craftsman or aspiring journeyman, the poor worker and his family, the destitute widow and her children (if they had not been dispatched as servants

WINDOWS ON

Walls, Halls, and Towers

Aigues Mortes, France, thirteenth century

Medieval towns were often sited to provide a clear view of the surrounding countryside, for defense purposes. The thirteenth-century walled city of Aigues Mortes (right) in northern France, is symmetrically proportioned, which the flat landscape allows. By contrast, another walled French town of around the same period, Carcassone (below) is sited on a plateau and the walls are built to fit its shape.

Public buildings in the Gothic style added grandeur to medieval cities. The great vaulting structure of Westminster Hall (opposite) in London accentuates the beauty of windows intricate with tracery. In the flamboyant Gothic style, Brussels Town Hall has ornate turrets, high windows, balconies and small bell towers. The tall tower bears a shrine, upon which sits Archangel Michael, the patron saint of the city.

Carcassone, France, twelfth to thirteenth centuries

Westminster Hall, London, 1397–1399

Brussels Town Hall, Belgium, fifteenth century

To continue your investigation of this topic, please go to www.prenhall.com/king for the related WINDOWS on the WEB activity

or laborers). The poorest of these inhabited a miserable space in tenements. Others occupied a room in a rich man's house, or a lean-to shack thrown against cathedral walls, or a small room adjoining the master's workshop. They paid rent drawn from daily wages to live in these places without the merest amenities: "For a poor man who has no money," wrote one twelfth-century author, "does not sit by a fire, nor sit at a table, rather he eats on his lap."

Houses of rich and poor alike were jumbled together, without zoning restrictions or social or stylistic barriers. Public and private, ecclesiastical and municipal buildings stood side-by-side, as did the grand and the tiny, the ornate and the plain. New buildings required little advance planning or cash investment: no installations for sewerage, electricity, or telephones were needed. Space could easily be extended upward by adding a new story, or outward by tearing down a wall. Cities could increase quickly in area and density, as space was emptied or filled. The medieval town dweller saw no impropriety in the haphazardness of such construction, the juxtaposition of shacks and palaces, warehouses and cathedrals. In 1300 still a hodgepodge lined with the faceless tenements of the poor and punctuated by the towers of the great, Florence became in the fourteenth century one of the first cities to impose order on the medieval cluster of forms.

The vigorous interplay of buildings and towers, of private and public, of sacred and civic, of urgent chimes and bells created a world full of energy.

On the Street

The pathways of urban life were the network of streets, bridges, and rivers, snaking past the imposing buildings in the shadow of the towers. Townspeople worked, governed, prayed, and slept indoors, but city life was lived in the streets. Narrow, winding, and dirty, the city streets knit together miscellaneous structures in an integrated system.

City streets were meant for pedestrians, who could walk across even the largest cities in twenty or thirty minutes. Begun as cattle paths or the beds of ancient streams or the contours of hill and valley, they formed organic patterns—except where the tight grid of a preexistent Roman town imposed an abstract order. Often they grew in a starfish or web pattern, as arterial roads led out from the center to the city gates. Streets were wide enough to accommodate the tradesman's wagon but no wider. Sometimes they shrank to narrow tunnels almost entirely covered by the projecting upper stories of the buildings on either side.

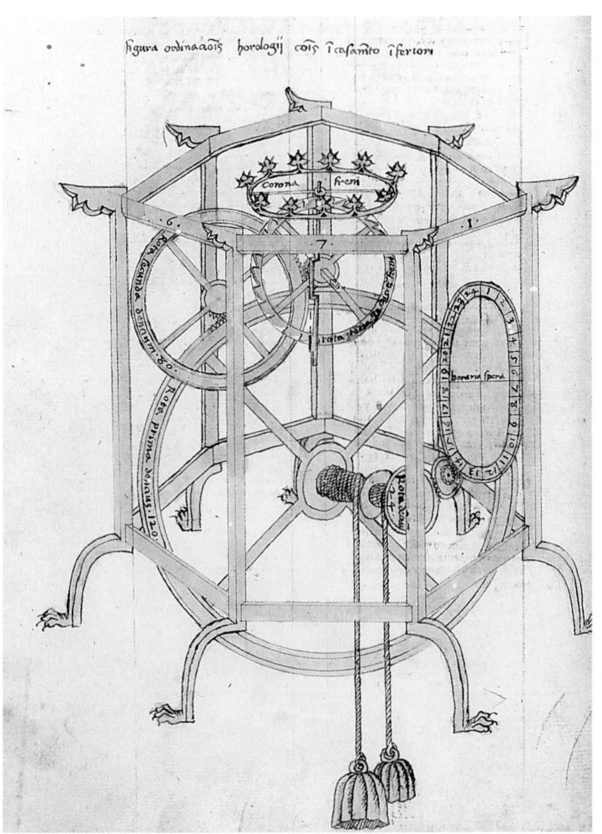

City Time

Dondi's clock *(left and right)*: *The mechanism of the Paduan Giovanni de' Dondi's astronomical clock (1364) is known from the author's own detailed descriptions, available in several surviving manuscripts which provide the earliest-known illustrations of mechanical clocks. A modern reconstruction is shown here (left), together with a sketch of the mechanism (right) from one of the Dondi manuscripts, fourteenth century.* (left: Smithsonian Institution, Museum of American History; right: Bodleian Library, Oxford)

WITNESSES

The Splendors of Florence and Venice

By the fifteenth century, some leading cities had become extraordinarily wealthy, powerful, and beautiful, developing in each case a unique architecture and sense of space appropriate to its location, its governance, the taste of its elites, and its mercantile activities. Here two renowned authors describe their own cities of Florence and Venice, the first stressing the buildings and street system of the former, the second the unique situation of the latter, a series of linked islands afloat in a lagoon in the Adriatic Sea.

Leonardo Bruni praises the buildings of Florence (1404): What in the world is so splendid and magnificent as the architecture of Florence? ... In other places perhaps one or at the most two streets in the entire city are filled with important buildings, while the rest of the town is so devoid of architectural distinction. ... But in our city there is really no street, no quarter that does not possess spacious and ornate buildings. ... The sort of careful scrutiny that brings shame to other cities only serves to raise the esteem held for Florence, for behind the walls of the buildings of Florence there are no fewer ornaments and no less magnificence than there is outside; nor is any one street better decorated or more handsome than another, but every quarter shares in the beauty of the city. Hence, just as blood is spread throughout the entire body, so fine architecture and decoration are diffused throughout the whole city.
(Leonardo Bruni, "Panegyric," 1404; eds. B. Kohl, J. Witt, 1978)

Marino Sanudo describes the glories of Venice (1493): The city of Venice is a free city, a common home to all men, and it has never been subjugated by anyone, as have been all other cities. ... This city, amidst the billowing waves of the sea, stands on the crest of the main, almost like a queen restraining its force. It is situated in salt water and built there, because before there were just lagoons, and then, wanting to expand, firm ground was needed for the building of palaces and houses. These are being constructed all the time; they are built above the water by a very ingenious method of driving piles, so that the foundations are in water. Every day the tide rises and falls, but the city remains dry. At times of very low tides, it is difficult to go by boat to wherever one wants. The city is about 7 miles in circumference; it has no surrounding walls, no gates which are locked at night, no sentry keeping watch as other cities have for fear of enemies; it is so very safe at present, that no one can attack or frighten it. For it takes pride of place before all others, if I may say so, in prudence, fortitude, magnificence, benignity and clemency. ... To conclude, this city was built more by divine than human will.
(Marino Sanudo, "Laus urbis venetae," 1493; eds. D. Chambers, B. Pullan, 1992)

As the rivers along and across which cities grew became incorporated in the urban fabric, they needed to be crossed by bridges. On some of these bridges rose towers and churches, **hospitals** and shops, homes and schools. Paris's Pont au Change ("Commerce Bridge") once sheltered about 120 moneychangers and goldsmiths, while Florence's Ponte Vecchio ("Old Bridge"), built in 1345 and still preserved today, was designed from the first to house shops. Rents from bridge residents, along with donations received from passersby, paid for maintenance and new construction. Cheaper bridges made of wood were vulnerable to fire and flood and were replaced by durable stone wherever funds allowed. London Bridge was reconstructed in stone by 1209; Venice's splendid Rialto Bridge only in 1588.

Sanitation Paving the streets eased traffic and helped control the filth of the city. Road paving began in Paris as early as 1185, but only the streets that led to the city gates were so improved. Lübeck, in Germany, paved its main streets in 1310; Nuremberg hers from 1368; Florence paved them all between 1235 and 1339, which made that city "more clean, and more beautiful, and more healthy," reports her leading chronicler, Bruni. English municipalities set standards for the maintenance of roads, policing those laborers who neglected to dig down to lay a proper substructure. Unchecked, such lazy workers would lay new pavement over old layers to such a height, supervisors complained, that one had to step down in order to enter home or church.

Water for washing and bathing was hauled from nearby streams, drawn from public wells, collected from rainwater in cisterns, or, in some cases, piped in from distant sources. The water-starved hill towns of Italy built aqueducts to bring in water, which was then dispersed through wells and fountains. Not only useful amenities, these were civic focal points and often very imposing—as was Perugia's Fontana Maggiore ("Great Fountain"), completed in 1278, which was adorned with reliefs by the sculptor Nicola Pisano (c. 1220–c. 1278) and his son Giovanni. Public bathhouses abounded: there were 12 in Nuremberg, 15 in Frankfurt, 17 in Augsburg; 26 in Paris. Medieval townspeople bathed regularly—in contrast to their descendants in the sixteenth through eighteenth centuries, who feared that water might spread infection and preferred perfume and powder (if they could afford such luxuries) to soap and water.

In patrician houses, washbasins of copper and even silver held water for washing. Most people wore heavy wool garments which they rarely washed, but servants and professional laundresses washed linens for bed and table in large cisterns—or, illegally, in the wells and rivers. It was the merchant's responsibility to clothe his servants and apprentices decently (as it was a husband's to clothe his wife). One London tailor was sent to prison on a charge of ill-treatment, which included that of having forced a boy to sleep in a bed "foule shirtyd & full of vermin."

Although city leaders knew about the value of cleanliness, they did not always achieve it. Bruni praised Florence for its excellence in this regard: "Surely this city is unique and singular in all the world because you will find here nothing that is disgusting to the eye, offensive to the nose, or filthy under foot." Any other city, in contrast, "is so dirty that the filth created during the night is seen in the early morning by the population and trampled under foot in the streets. Really can one think of anything worse than this?"

The omnipresence of the privy, the coexistence of humans with animals destined for work and for slaughter, and the insufficiency of paving made sanitation an intractable problem. Through open gutters flowed dirty water from kitchen and tavern, animal dung, the refuse of dyeing vats, the entrails of butchered animals, the heads of fish and the corpses of dogs, cats, and horses: an accumulation horrible to see and worse to smell. The waste products of the butcher and—worse—the dyer flowed into rivers and canals: as at Antwerp, where citizens complained that the polluted water of the canals killed thirsty horses. Official street sweepers and overseers, hired rakers, carters, and scavengers labored to reduce the mountains of dirt. Pigs ran loose, to glean what they could from the wondrous leavings in the street. The Italian writer Petrarch (1304–1374), usually deferential, berated the ruler of Padua: "This city ... so outstanding in its many glories, is being transformed—with you looking on and not stopping it, as you easily could—into a horrid and ugly pasture by rampaging herds of pigs!"

Fire and Crime Fire was a worse menace than vagrant pigs or open dungheaps. Every town knew this purgative killer and mindless agent of urban renewal. Most houses were built of wood, and filled with flammable furnishings—even including the paint on the walls. If one house burned, an entire district was at risk. Rouen burned six times within twenty-five years; and in a single year—1188—fire attacked the French cities of Rouen (again), Troyes, Beauvais, Provins, Arras, Poitiers, and Moissac. A conflagration in Florence in 1304 destroyed 1700 buildings, another in Nuremberg in 1340 more than 400. Lübeck was burned to the ground in 1157, and in Padua, in 1174, 2614 houses—three-quarters of the residences—were destroyed. In an attempt to prevent such calamities, city governments issued regulations prescribing fireproof materials and stipulating the hours when fires could be lit. Firefighting systems were organized. But where no means existed for the conveyance of water, they could do little.

Municipalities also struggled with accident and evildoing. Watchmen toured the unlit streets at night, charged to pursue and arrest suspected felons. Bruges, with a population (before the Black Death) of some 35,000, maintained a police force of 27. In 1422, the English city of Coventry hired 24 constables for a population of some 5000, and giant London, in 1461, employed 285 watchmen. To police its population of about 100,000, Venice required several government agencies: magistrates called the "gentlemen of the night" performed this service at the local neighborhood level. In smaller towns, the duty of "watch and ward" (as it was called in England) was passed in rotation to all male burghers. The streets belonged to everyone.

PUBLIC LIFE

In this urban complex of buildings and streets, diverse groups of people lived together observing their separate customs. At the same time, the whole city engaged in public celebration and suffered together in times of calamity, as all benefited from the institutions of public charity that aimed to ameliorate the conditions of the least fortunate urban dwellers.

Foreigners, Friends, and Outcasts

Because of the diversity of the city's population, life within its walls offered ample opportunity for violence and disorder. Just as rich and poor crowded together, workers and merchants, slaves and servants, men without roots and women without families, so also—especially in the case of larger cities—did members of different national groups: the French, Flemish, and Germans in London and Novgorod; Turks, Slavs, Germans, and Greeks in Venice and Genoa. These outsiders gathered in closed communities under their own leaders and laws. Germans representing the towns of the Hanseatic League (see Chapter 11) formed a stable community at London's Steelyard, while the Greeks and Dalmatians of Venice formed autonomous societies centered on two churches called respectively "Saint George of the Greeks" and "Saint George of the Slavs."

Jews Regarded as strangers wherever they settled, Jews were the ethnic community most widely encountered in European cities. Gathering in the shadow of the town synagogue, they maintained their own social and religious customs while sharing wherever possible in the surrounding cultural world. This was not always possible. As Christian Europe developed its own merchants to carry on functions for which Jewish traders were once valued, resentment swelled against perceived "outsiders." Native Christians blamed the Jews in their midst for accidents or disasters, or held them guilty of imaginary and horrible crimes. Although sporadically, and fiercely, persecuted in the spate of massacres that accompanied the Crusades, Jewish communities fared relatively well in medieval Europe into the twelfth century. Then economic resentments and psychological fears took over. Their status in the centers of trade and industry began a downturn that would last for centuries.

Jews were subject to special restrictions. An Avignonese law of 1243 proclaimed that "Jews or whores shall not dare to touch with their hands either bread or fruit put out for sale. ..." In Lübeck, a chronicler commented, there were no Jews; "there is no need of them either." In Florence in 1463, a limit of 70 was placed on the number of Jews that were allowed in the city—"to prevent any large concentration ... or a greater number than is necessary"—and all adult members of the community were required to wear a distinguishing sign: a yellow "O," which "shall be worn on the left breast, over the clothing in a visible place. ..." Nevertheless, all religious practices were permitted, in this decree, and religious and scholarly books might be "possessed, read, studied, and copied."

Many Jewish communities suffered doubly during the Black Death: not only from the disease itself but also from the fury of Christian neighbors, as described in *Witnesses* beneath. Having already been expelled from England and France (in 1290 and 1306, respectively), Jews were driven from many cities, victims of the notion that they had caused the disease. In 1349, they were expelled from Nuremberg, where the whole

WITNESSES

Jews and Medieval Cities

The communities of Jews scattered throughout Europe's towns and cities were occasionally tolerated, as official pronouncements said they must be. They were also occasionally, but horribly, persecuted, often by mobs made unsteady by crisis conditions, or sometimes instigated by those who would profit most by their rivals, or their creditors', removal. In the first passage, Pope Gregory X urges the toleration of the Jews. In the second, a chronicler reports the vicious massacre of the Jewish population of Strasbourg.

Pope Gregory X (1271–1276) clarifies the Church's official policy of toleration toward the Jews of Europe: The Jews ... ought not to suffer any disadvantage in those [privileges] which have been granted them ... we therefore admit their petition and offer them the shield of our protection through the clemency of Christian piety. ...

We decree moreover that no Christian shall compel them or any one of their group to come to baptism unwillingly. ... Moreover no Christian shall presume to seize, imprison, wound, torture, mutilate, kill, or inflict violence on them. ... In addition, no one shall disturb them in any way during the celebration of their festivals, whether by day or by night, with clubs or stones or anything else. ...

Since it happens occasionally that some Christians lose their Christian children, the Jews are accused by their enemies of secretly carrying off and killing these same Christian children and of making sacrifices of the heart and blood if these very children. ... And most falsely do these Christians claim that the Jews have secretly and furtively carried away these children and killed them, and that the Jews offer sacrifice from the heart and the blood of these children. ... We decree, therefore, ... that Jews seized under such a silly pretext be freed from imprisonment, and that they shall not be arrested henceforth on such a miserable pretext, unless—which we do not believe—they be caught in the commission of the crime. We decree that no Christian shall stir up anything new against them, but that they should be maintained in that status and position in which they were in the time of our predecessors, from antiquity till now.

(Pope Gregory X, *Letter*; ed. B. Tierney, 2e, 1973)

Jacob von Königshofen on Strasbourg's Jewry (1349): In the matter of this plague the Jews throughout the world were reviled and accused in all lands of having caused it through the poison which they are said to have put into the water and the wells ... and for this reason the Jews were burnt ... from the Mediterranean into Germany, but not in Avignon, for the pope protected them. ...

On Saturday ... they burnt the Jews on a wooden platform in the cemetery. ... Many small children were taken out of the fire and baptized against the will of their fathers and mothers. And everything that was owed to the Jews was cancelled, and the Jews had to surrender all pledges and notes that they had taken for debts. The council, however, took the cash that the Jews possessed and divided it among the working-men proportionately. The money was indeed the thing that killed the Jews. If they had been poor and if the feudal lords had not been in debt to them, they would not have been burnt. ...

(Jacob von Königshofen, *Chronicle*, 1349; eds. J. Ross, M. McLaughlin, 1949)

City People

Massacre of the Jews of Cologne: *The persecution of the Jews of Cologne is shown in this illustration from a contemporary chronicle, the* Liber Chronicarum Mundi, *Nuremberg, 1493.*

Jewish quarter and synagogue were immediately razed. The Jews of Basel (in modern Switzerland) were herded together on an island in the Rhine and burned, while the town council, to drive the point home, prohibited their future resettlement in that city for 200 years. Some 2000 Jews of Strasbourg (now in France) were burned—purely to free the lords from debt, suggests a contemporary witness. "The money was indeed the thing that killed the Jews. If they had been poor and if the feudal lords had not been in debt to them, they would not have been burnt." Jews could save themselves by converting, but they usually resisted that act, which would result in their destruction as a people and as a faith. Parents condemned to death reportedly hurled their children into the flames to prevent their being seized and baptized into an alien religion.

The Jews of the German lands suffered many massacres during the plague years. Persecutions surged again in the fifteenth century, as illustrated above. After 1424 in Cologne, and 1435 in Rhineland Speyer, no Jews were allowed. Between the effects of plague and persecution, the Jewish population of the Iberian peninsula was reduced to one-fourth its former size; then from 1492 to 1496 all Jews were commanded to convert or to leave. The Inquisition notoriously persecuted those Jews who had converted, if they lapsed into the observance of Jewish rituals.

With the significant exception of the Spanish Inquisition, the Church urged restraint upon the Christian population with respect to the Jews in their midst (see *Witnesses* on p. 333). The Jews were to be able to practice their religion freely, and to enjoy limited rights in society. Eventually, it was believed—on the eve of the Apocalypse—their conversion would be accomplished. In the meantime, they were to be unmolested. Ordinary Christians, however, did not always accept the policy officially formulated. It was in vain that the Church pointed out that Jews, too, died of the plague; common people held them responsible. If a child died or disappeared under mysterious circumstances, people blamed the Jews. Such "ritual murder" charges became "blood libels" when Christians accused Jews of using the blood of these allegedly kidnapped and murdered children. One such fantastic charge was that they mixed the blood with the unleavened bread, or matzoh, used during the Jewish holy days of Passover.

Jews suffered wave upon wave of persecution, despite Pope Gregory X's ruling in 1272 that "no Christian shall presume to seize, imprison, wound, torture, mutilate, kill, or inflict violence on [the Jews]," or "compel them or any one of their group to come to baptism unwillingly." Later Clement VI, reigning (1343–1352) during the plague years, rebuked those who shed "the blood of Jews, whom Christian piety accepts and sustains." European **anti-Semitism** developed in the communities of medieval Europe, even as the Church forbade physical attacks against Jews and deplored the accusations of ritual murder, often with the participation of churchmen.

City governments found it useful to make Jews welcome when their services as moneylenders or pawnbrokers or physicians were needed. Yet they did not include Jews fully as members of society. In time, in addition to requirements of special dress, some cities allocated special neighborhoods for Jewish residents. The first organized precinct of this sort was the **ghetto** of Venice, founded in 1516—the one from which the word "ghetto" originated.

The Venetian dialect word "ghetto" (derived from *gettare*, "to cast") originally designated an iron foundry, the site of which became the locus of the Jewish community newly permitted to stay within city limits. Ghetto residents (there were as many as 5000 at its height) had frequent and sometimes cordial relations with Christian merchants, scholars, and patricians. Within their walls, they freely followed their own rites (requiring the importation and preparation of special foods in order to observe the dietary laws). Yet those walls were also a prison: the gates were locked at nights and during certain Christian holidays, purportedly for the security of ghetto residents. Over later centuries, ghettoes were established in other cities, eventually becoming a commonplace of Jewish social life within European Christendom.

Prostitutes Prostitutes, like Jews, had a precarious place in the medieval town. One is depicted on p. 335. In some places, prostitutes were required to wear distinctive dress—a headdress or a telltale color—to set them apart from respectable citizens. Often their brothels were cautiously located outside the walls.

A Prostitute's Trade: *In the well-furnished bedchamber depicted in this sixteenth-century engraving after Lucas van Leyden, a client fondles a prostitute as she reaches for his payment.* (Warburg Institute, London)

Elsewhere, prostitution was openly acknowledged and even fostered. In Italy, public brothels were opened in Venice in 1360, in Florence in 1403, and in Siena in 1421. In Germany, Frankfurt led the way in 1396, Nuremberg by 1400, Munich by 1433, Memmingen (in Bavaria) by 1454, and Strasbourg by 1469. In France, Dijon opened its "Great House" in 1385, and Toulouse operated a municipal brothel from 1363 or 1372.

Nobles A considerably grander city enclave, found especially in Italy, was formed by the associations of noble clans. Members of the nobility who settled within the city during the period of formation and built their own houses there led their lives, as much as possible, as though they were still in the country and masters of all about them. In the close confines of the city, they carried on the feuds and fights that occupied them elsewhere. In Italy they even endowed their houses with fortified towers, always on the ready for an attack. Their towers afforded a view of the region, warehoused weapons, and sheltered dependents. Noblemen's towers soared over the roofs of burgher dwellings, creating a skyline of verticals anticipating modern skylines such as that of Manhattan in New York City. Eventually, municipal governments tore down the anomalous towers. Some 140 were dismantled in Rome in the 1250s, while in Florence, hundreds were sawn off to an altitude that matched the reduced status of nobles in a merchant republic. But in the little Tuscan town of San Gimignano, 13 towers survive today to bristle menacingly against the horizon.

Neighbors For most town dwellers the important associations were those of parish, neighborhood, and friendship. In Florence, the formula of "kin, neighbors, and friends" was routinely used to define the networks that mattered. The patrician Gino Capponi advised his sons to "stick together above all else with your neighbors and your kinsmen, and serve your friends within and without the city." A town's neighborhoods—Rome's thirteen *rioni*, Florence's sixteen *gonfaloni*, Venice's six *sestieri*, Nuremberg's eight *viertel*—actively fostered social life. In Genoa, clusters of people who hailed from the same country village reproduced the intimacy of their former life in a tightly packed urban colony. In Venice, wealthy people gave gifts to poor neighbors who shared the same courtyard. Especially among women, barred from the public communities of market or government, the neighborhood courtyard offered a buzz of news and advice among friends and neighbors.

The desperately poor belonged nowhere and to no group. The disabled or unemployed or those newly arrived from a famine-ridden countryside pressed into the city. Vagrants and migrants formed an underclass of shifting dimensions. In Nuremberg, out of a population of about 30,000 in 1449–1450, nearly one-third were refugees without permanent residence. In Florence, the wretchedly poor or "destitute," as distinguished from the working poor, made up nearly one-third of the population. These rootless folk worked if they found work, begged if they could not, and slept in the shadow of the houses of the wealthy.

The different kinds of people who inhabited the towns—foreigners and visitors, Jews, beggars, and prostitutes, friends, kin, and neighbors—enriched the experience of urban life, just as did the variety of its visual forms.

Special Days

The everyday activity of a medieval town often gave way to the heightened activity of special days, when work ceased and the streets filled with throngs of spectators and participants. From every parish, and courtyards, quarters, and wards, city people poured into central public spaces for the celebration of special events—religious festivals, public ceremonies, and executions.

The calendar of religious festivals supplied ample occasion for spectacle and display. Throughout Europe, religious dramas, originally produced in churches, later out of doors, were performed on various holy days. In England, the "mystery" plays celebrating

Corpus Christi (the feast of the "body of Christ") were among the most important. The feast of Saint Firmin was celebrated in Pamplona (Spain) by a parade of giant characters representing Moors and Normans and the running of bulls through the streets. A horse race marked the celebration in Florence of the festal day of Saint John the Baptist, its patron saint, and in Siena (the famous "Palio"), on the day after the Feast of the Assumption of the Virgin, in the city's huge Piazza del Campo.

The tournament, a ritual of the knightly class, was adapted for town use. In imitation of noblemen, common soldiers and rich merchants donned special tournament armor. Patricians formed special societies of urban chivalry—such as Bruges' "Order of the White Bear," whose pudgy mascot carved in stone adorns a niche of the patrician meeting house, the Poortersloge. The marriage of the son of the Doge Francesco Foscari in Venice in 1441 was celebrated by a tournament in which mercenary captains vied with each other to capture mock wooden castles.

When no celebration was in the offing, the townspeople might enjoy an execution. Venetians gathered to watch the hanging, caging, or decapitation of the condemned between the Columns of Justice in the Piazza San Marco. Here, in 1432, died the mercenary captain Francesco Carmagnola, trapped by the notorious Council of Ten (part of the Venetian government), who claimed to have found evidence of his collusion with the enemy. As momentous was the execution in Florence in 1498 of the Dominican leader and prophet Girolamo Savonarola (1452–1498), who was condemned for heresy. Criminals met their fate in Bruges before the market square's belfry, adorned with a statue of Saint Michael driving out Satan.

Piero della Francesca, Pregnant Madonna: *As depicted in this fresco by Piero della Francesca in Monterchi, Italy, c. 1410, the stature accorded the pregnant woman is suggested by the serene and dignified figure of the Virgin Mary, who is about to give birth to the Savior.*

On one occasion, the townspeople of Mons (France), temporarily short of local criminals, bought a condemned thief "for the pleasure of seeing him quartered"—at which event, reported a contemporary, "the people rejoiced more than if a new holy body had risen from the dead." The citizens of Nuremberg accompanied the targets of their judicial vengeance to a place beyond the walls, where the machines necessary to hang, burn, draw and quarter, behead, or drown the victim were masterfully assembled by the public executioner. Justice was then served, a historian observed, "amid the noise of the crowd and the smell of frying pork sausages from the butchers' stalls put up for the occasion."

Town dwellers also assembled to witness the ceremonial entrances of rulers and dignitaries. It was the custom for the kings of France, having been crowned and anointed at Rheims, to process through the whole city of Paris en route to the royal palace. In 1440 the entrance to Bruges of its Burgundian lord, Duke Philip the Good, was followed in full splendor by 136 Hanseatic merchants, 48 Spaniards, 40 Milanese, 40 Venetians, 12 Lucchese (citizens of Lucca), 36 Genoese, 22 Florentines, and scatterings of others. Great exits, too, attracted a crowd. The whole city turned out for the funerals, in Florence, of the English-born mercenary captain John Hawkwood (1394) and the chancellor Coluccio Salutati (1406); in Venice the burials of the doges were attended by the whole population. Witnesses of the funeral of King Charles VII of France in 1461 saw the procession of luminaries attired in deepest mourning: "and because of the great sorrow and grief they exhibited for the death of their master," wrote one of them, "many tears were shed and lamentations uttered throughout the town."

Other moments, sacred and political, were celebrated with a processional of ranked groups of citizens and corporations. In Bruges, on solemn occasions, the people bore the city's collection of saints' relics through the town and around the walls, followed by civic officials, mounted knights, and resident foreign merchants. For weeks during the year 1412, the citizens of Paris processed daily, seeking victory for their king, then engaged in the grim struggle of the Hundred Years' War. Those who marched or looked on wept "piteously, with many tears, in great devotion," while the rain poured down relentlessly, in what one contemporary described as the "most touching processions in the memory of men."

At Nuremberg, crowds gathered each May to view the imperial regalia, which had been deposited in the city for safekeeping in 1424: gilded and jeweled scepters, crowns, orbs, clasps, and stirrups, and sacred relics, including the lance that had opened Jesus' side (it was thought) and one of the nails that fixed him to the cross. Venetian processions celebrated the transcendent role of their own doge and state over both emperor and pope. The doge's preeminence was symbolized in objects known as the *trionfi*, or "triumphs"—a white candle, lead seals, banners, a sword, gold ring, ceremonial umbrella, and silver trumpets—the gifts (legendarily) bestowed upon the doge in 1177 by the then pope, Alexander III. Twelve times a year, for sacred feasts and state events, these *trionfi* were paraded through the Piazza San Marco in processions of unmatched splendor and a discipline elsewhere unknown, reported one observer, "in the best order imaginable."

In such public ceremonies, the town dwellers, who were united by their residence within the walls, by their ties to the producers and sellers of goods, by their neighborhood and family and group allegiances, were further bound together by the mutual experience of celebrating—not only the glory of the saints or the triumph of justice but the excellence of their own city.

Charity

The sense of unity experienced by the citizens expressed itself also in charitable activity. To a remarkable degree, medieval town dwellers cared for their neighbors, their associates, and even the most unfortunate of their fellow citizens.

From its earliest days, the Church had taken seriously Jesus' command to "feed my sheep"—to care for the sick, the hungry, and the deserted. To do so in an urban setting required the creation of new institutions. The urban public organized itself in a variety of corporations for pious purposes. The lay confraternity, an association of men and women linked by a common mission or obligation, combined spiritual observance and charitable service. The craft guilds had social and fraternal functions as well as professional ones, providing for the burial of members and their kin and the saying of penitential prayers for the souls of the departed. They also dispensed charity, helped construct public works, planned and produced mystery plays, and supported schools. Residential communities of holy women (see Chapter 10) or networks of pious laymen also dispensed charity and organized schools.

The great numbers of the poor made such charitable service necessary. To feed the poor, tend the ill, house the deserted wife or homeless widow, nurture the abandoned infant, or provide a dowry for a fatherless girl, townspeople created hospitals and asylums. Almshouses for the destitute and **hospices** for the aged were among the biggest public buildings of the medieval city. Foundling homes received the unwanted infants left at their doorsteps. Similar institutions welcomed women seeking refuge from neglectful husbands, engaged them in productive work, and prepared them for return to society.

Hospitals were the most conspicuous of these institutions. Built by pious lay donors or monastic foundations, the hospitals provided for the great numbers of the ill, who were cared for by volunteers from the lay confraternities or semireligious orders. Most German towns had two—one for "lepers" (victims of Hansen's Disease) and one for victims of other diseases; while populous Breslau, with 15, offered one hospital for every 2000 residents. Thirty hospitals, affording more than 1000 beds (each shared by several patients), served 90,000 residents of Florence, and the French city of Toulouse boasted 7 leprosariums and 13 general-purpose hospitals. An astonishing 200 hospitals in England tended exclusively to lepers.

Most hospitals housed only a dozen or so patients, but some were, by medieval standards, enormous. The Hôtel Dieu ("God's House") in Paris, begun in the 1190s, had by 1260 extended to include 375 feet (114 m.) of patient wards. The largest was Milan's Ospedale Maggiore (the "Greater Hospital"), begun in 1456 and completed in the seventeenth century. Consisting of a rectangular block about 920 by 350 feet (280 by 107 m.), it was divided internally into two wings, one for men, one for women, and was equipped with a latrine for each bed.

The people who funded this charitable activity were the same merchants whose aggressive profit-seeking built the cities, who were as deliberate in their giving as in their taking. Patterns of charity are revealed in their wills. While most made bequests to the traditional religious institutions of parish and monastery, of 660 persons making wills in Siena between 1205 and 1500, approximately 15 percent aided hospitals and confraternities. In Pistoia (Italy), philanthropists supported hospitals and religious organizations in preference to the traditional institutions of monastery and cathedral. Gifts to hospitals are a signpost of the concern medieval townspeople felt for those disadvantaged in the present world: a spirit one scholar has called "civic Christianity."

Plague

The medieval philanthropists who did so much to relieve those in pain were helpless against the greatest emergency of the Middle Ages: the plague. The plague known as the "Black Death" struck in 1347 and did not die out until the eighteenth century. It was the single greatest natural disaster in the history of the West. It was especially severe in towns and had an enduring effect on urban life. Map 12.1 shows the extent of the plague.

Originating in Asia, the plague was caused by a deadly bacterium, *Yersinia pestis*, and entered western Europe through busy Italian ports. Spread by the bite of an infected flea which lived in the hair of the black rat, it caused swellings or buboes (hence "bubonic," as one variety of the plague is termed) in the armpits and the groin of its victims. The accompanying hemorrhage turned dark; thus the name "Black Death." In an even more deadly variant form, pneumonic plague, the bacterium was airborne and highly contagious. Even before the advent of the plague, European peoples had been weakened—in body, in morale—by a sequence of poor harvests and famine (see Chapter 9). The population was thus especially vulnerable to the disease, which struck down from 25 to 45 percent of the inhabitants of Europe before 1400, wiping out whole generations, and stripping the crowded cities with special savagery.

In Italy, the disease took the lives of about two-thirds of the populations of Bologna and Venice, 30 to 40 percent of Pisa and Genoa, one-half of Orvieto and Florence. Sixteen times in the thirteenth and fourteenth centuries pestilence devastated Florence, as described in *Witnesses* on p. 340. Nearby Pistoia suffered twelve bouts of plague between 1313 and 1458. The onslaught of 1400 devoured half that city's population, and of the dead nearly three-fourths (1140 of 1625) were children. A chronicler of the first 1348 attack witnessed the massacre of the young of Siena: "And I, Agnolo di Tura, called the Fat, buried my five children with my own hands." The old were

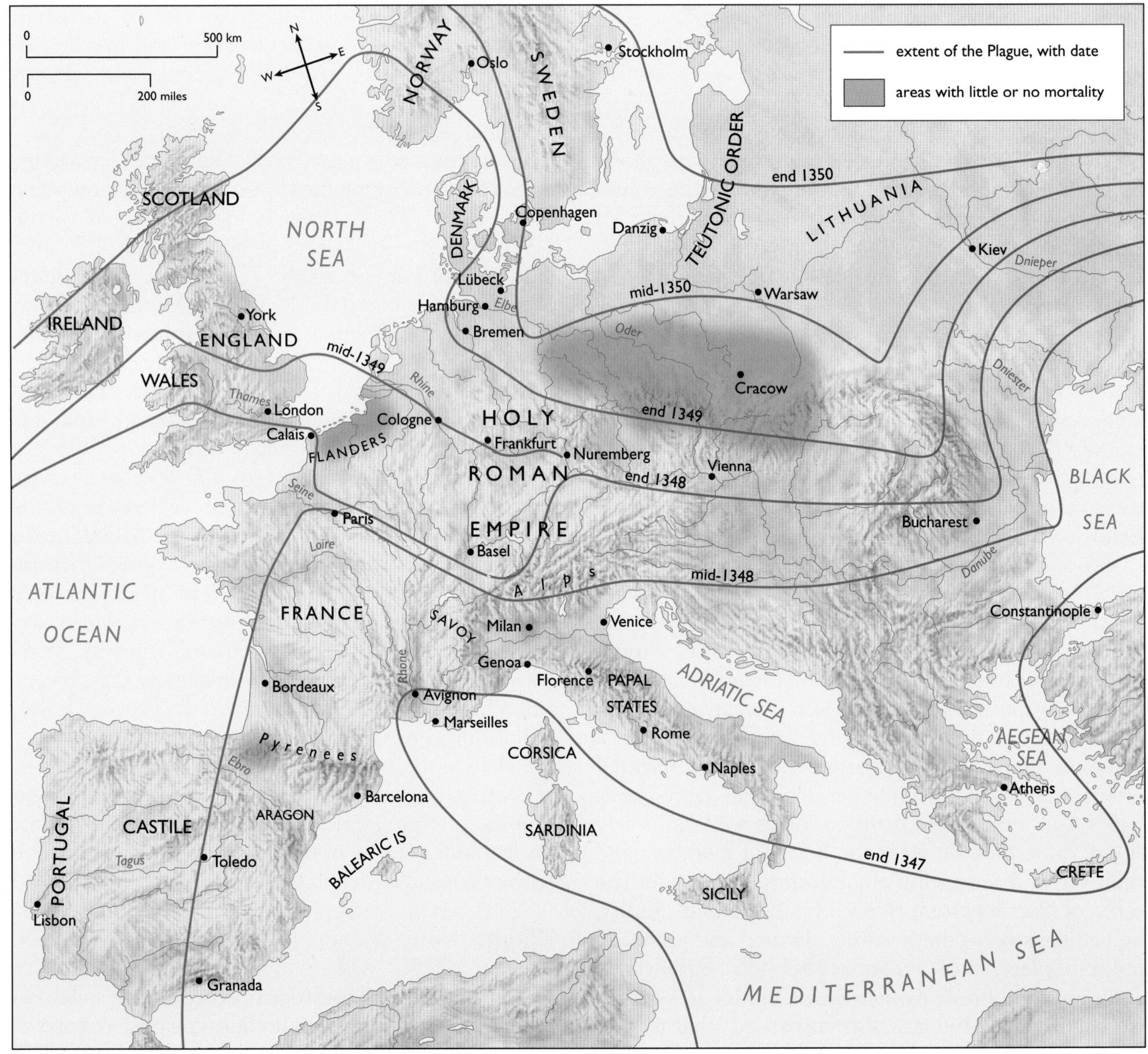

Map 12.1 The Progress of the Plague, 1347–1353: *Originating in Asia and extending to Constantinople by 1347, the plague bacillus invaded Italy in 1347–1348 and spread north, west, and east on the European continent through 1353. It would return sporadically and irregularly for centuries to come.*

also at special risk: 70 percent of the 52,000 plague victims at Siena in 1348 were elderly.

The plague traveled over the Alps from late 1348, and struck northern Europe with equal ferocity. England may have lost up to half her population—"in every parish a great multitude (see *Witnesses* on p. 340)." In France, Avignon, then seat of the papacy, lost more than 50 percent of its people, Paris one-third. In Flanders and the Netherlands the mortality rate was typically 20 to 30 percent. Most German towns lost 25 to 50 percent, but in little Bremen, 6966 individuals, known and identified, were lost: close to two-thirds of that population. Even remote parts of Europe were hard-hit. The plague wrought such havoc in Scandinavia that the king of Sweden proclaimed, "By it, most of our countrymen are dead." An Irish Franciscan described the siege of his country, while being himself "as if among the dead, waiting till death do come"; he left blank parchment ready for a future chronicler to record the outcome, "if by chance anyone may be left in the future, and any child of Adam may escape this pestilence and continue the work thus commenced."

Doctors could neither cure nor prevent the disease. The level of medical expertise can be gauged from the fact that Gentile of Foligno, a physician at the University of Padua, ascribed the plague to planetary motions which caused "poisonous material [to be] generated about the heart and the lungs." Yet medical services were sought and paid for, and many professionals dutifully tended the sick at great personal risk to themselves. One doctor described his experience with a patient in Lucca during the outbreak of 1373: "I cared for [this woman] with the greatest devotion, constantly, both day and night, six or eight times a day. She died of the worst kind of plague, and the most contagious: that involving spitting blood. This went on for four entire days. I would never have treated her for money, but for love alone."

Not all physicians were so devoted. Many escaped to the countryside or declined to serve. In Florence, so many young men of elite families now sought other and safer careers that the profession of medicine became the business of foreign immigrants. In Brescia in 1477, according to one chronicler, the ill perished because of lack of medical care: "The physicians were few in number, and nearly all succumbed while in service." In 1479, the Italian city of Pavia hired Giovanni Ventura as a municipal plague doctor. His contract specified that he must "treat all patients and visit infected places as it shall be found to be necessary," and that he would be suitably rewarded "according to how he shall behave himself." If he died in the course of his duties—"may God forbid it"—his heirs would be relieved of the obligation of restoring the salary he collected in advance. That salary was remuneration high enough, apparently, "to attract a doctor to a job which bordered on suicide."

Like the historian Thucydides (see Chapter 4), witness to a different but similarly lethal epidemic in ancient Athens, the poet and scholar Giovanni Boccaccio (1313–1375) described how moral values and human affection crumbled in the presence of ubiquitous death. In his account (which may have embroidered upon reality to some extent) terrified fathers abandoned their own children, daughters their own parents. Physicians neglected the sick, and gravediggers cast the carcasses of the lost into unmarked and unconsecrated graves. The devastation wrought by the Black Death is a reminder of how fragile is the shell of civilization, and how easily ruptured by crisis, tragedy, and dislocation.

From 1347 until 1720, the plague struck anew each generation of Europeans. City populations shrank markedly after the first onslaught, and each new episode eroded population gains (although slow net growth was achieved after 1500). The fear of disease darkened the urban landscape for centuries.

PRIVATE LIFE

Despite the devastating effects of the plague on family life, the family remained a vital organism for urban Europeans, a refuge against danger, the matrix of social values, the core community in a social world made up of interlocking rings of diverse communities. In western and northern Europe it was a nuclear family, centered on a married couple who together established a household independent of their elders. For women, especially, marriage was the central reality of life. Instructed by their fathers, the Church, and their husbands in turn, women carried on the business of the household and bore responsibility for the critical tasks of bearing and raising children.

Although marriage was common to all social classes, among the middle and upper classes it differed in involving the transfer of property. Thus it was a concern for merchants and tradesmen, for whom, like the nobility, the preservation of property across the generations was of the utmost importance.

Marrying for Love and Money

Today, young people generally marry because they are in love. In medieval Europe, they married to perpetuate the human species and, in some cases, to preserve family wealth. Marriage was a supremely serious matter, requiring proper behavior (as defined by the Church, by law, by families) of both spouses and obedience and diligence, particularly of wives.

The Church considered that a marriage had been constituted whenever a man and a woman expressed to each other words of consent. These words might be uttered in private, and the marriage would be valid whether or not the family approved, or whether a priest was present. Love, in its broader sense, was

WITNESSES

The Assault of the Plague

The epidemic of bubonic plague known as the "Black Death" struck Europe for several years beginning in 1347, and then recurred periodically for another 400 years. Two of those who witnessed its onslaught are represented, although their vivid descriptions must be understood as literary constructions and cannot be considered to be wholly accurate. They convey, nevertheless, a sense of the devastation of human life caused by the epidemic.

Giovanni Boccaccio, who survived the plague in Florence (1348), describes the disease and its effect on the people: In the year of Our Lord 1348 the deadly plague broke out in the great city of Florence, most beautiful of Italian cities. ... The plague had arisen in the East some years before, causing the death of countless human beings. It spread without stop from one place to another, until, unfortunately, it spread over the West. Neither knowledge nor human foresight availed against it, though the city was cleansed of much filth by chosen officers in charge and sick persons were forbidden to enter it. ...

At the onset of the disease both men and women were afflicted by a sort of swelling in the groin or under the armpits which sometimes attained the size of a common apple or egg. ... From these two starting points the boils began in a little while to spread and appear generally all over the body.

Afterwards, the manifestation of the disease changed into black or livid spots on the arms, thighs and the whole person. ... Like the boils, which had been and continued to be a certain indication of coming death, these blotches had the same meaning for everyone on whom they appeared. ... Neither the advice of physicians nor the virtue of any medicine seemed to help or avail in the cure of these diseases. ... The fact was that not only did few recover, but on the contrary almost everyone died within three days of the appearance of the signs. ...

More wretched still were the circumstances of the common people and, for a great part, for the middle class, for, confined to their homes either by hope of safety or by poverty, and restricted to their own sections, they fell sick daily by thousands. There, devoid of help or care, they died almost without redemption. A great many breathed their last in the public streets, day and night; a large number perished in their homes, and it was only by the stench of their decaying bodies that they proclaimed their death to their neighbors. Everywhere the city was teeming with corpses.
(Giovanni Boccaccio, *Decameron*, 1348–1353; trs. F. Winwar, 1955)

Henry Knighton observes the arrival of plague in England (1348): In this year [1348] and in the following one there was a general mortality of men throughout the whole world. ... Then that most grievous pestilence penetrated the coastal regions [of England] by way of Southampton, and came to Bristol, and people died as if the whole strength of the city were seized by sudden death. For there were few who lay in their beds more than three days or two and a half days; then that savage death snatched them about the second day. In Leicester, in the little parish of St. Leonard, more than three hundred and eighty died; in the parish of the Holy Cross, more than four hundred, and in the parish of St. Margaret in Leicester, more than seven hundred. And so in each parish, they died in great numbers. ...

During this same year, there was a great mortality of sheep everywhere in the kingdom; in one place and in one pasture, more than five thousand sheep died and became so putrefied that neither beast nor bird wanted to touch them. And the price of everything was cheap, because of the fear of death; there were very few who took any care for their wealth, or for anything else. ... After the aforesaid pestilence, many buildings, both large and small, in cities, towns, and villages had collapsed, and had completely fallen to the ground in the absence of inhabitants. Likewise, many small villages and hamlets were completely deserted; there was not one house left in them, but all those who had lived in them were dead. It is likely that many such hamlets will never again be inhabited. ... Moreover, both the magnates of the kingdom and the other lesser lords who had tenants, remitted something from the rents, lest the tenants should leave, because of the lack of servants and the dearth of things. ... They either had to excuse them entirely or had to fix them in a laxer manner at a small rent, lest ... the land everywhere remain completely uncultivated. And all foodstuffs and all necessities became exceedingly dear. ...
(Henry Knighton, *Compilation of Events in England, Book VI*; eds. J. Ross, P. McLaughlin, 1949)

understood to be at the center of family life, a bond of mutual affection making wife and husband equal partners in the act of marriage (although the wife nevertheless was expected to remain subordinate to her husband in practical affairs). The Church posed one model for the medieval household: the companionate model, the joining of spiritual equals.

Owners of property posed another: the patriarchal model. The family patriarchy was a miniature society in which the male "partner" exercised authority over wife, children, servants, and others. Its purpose was to preserve and transmit property from fathers to sons. Like the families of Greece and Rome, those of the medieval nobility were patriarchies. Merchants adopted the same pattern of family structure, husbanding their resources for the benefit of male heirs and the continuity of the lineage.

Husbanding resources meant restricting inheritance. In many regions of Europe, and consistently in England, only the eldest son inherited. Younger sons were provided for, where possible, by guidance into lucrative careers at royal courts, in knightly armies, or in the Church. Or they were sent out with their parents' blessing to "seek their fortune."

Daughters faced a different prospect. They were excluded from the inheritance lest they remove wealth from the father's lineage on marrying into that of a stranger. Instead, girls received when they married a set sum, a dowry, which was their only and final claim upon paternal wealth. Invariably less than an equal share of the **patrimony** (familial wealth), the dowry could, however, be a sizable sum of money, and might include clothing, jewelry, investments, and even land. At the death of the endowed woman, the dowry passed to whomever she designated: often to her children. In this way, dowry wealth was subtracted from her father's "line" and grafted upon her husband's.

What happened if the woman's husband died? If she was young enough to remarry, she returned to her father's house. Her husband's family was responsible for returning the dowry to the wife's family of birth, where it might be used a second time to purchase a good marriage. If she did not return to her father but stayed with her husband's family, the dowry, too, would remain with her and pass to her designated heirs.

Prudent fathers were torn between responsibility to a child and duty to the patrimony. They calculated carefully before assigning a dowry to a daughter, for the drainage of wealth could be ruinous: "girls do not make families but rather 'unmake' them," warned Marguerita Datini (wife of the merchant Francesco Datini, c. 1335–1410). Often the decision was made not to arrange for a daughter to marry but to send her instead to a convent. Convents also required a dowry of new entrants. But the conventual dowry was much smaller than the marital dowry. The parsimony of many fathers populated European convents with nuns whose piety was less than ardent.

Although theoretically the wife's property, the dowry was used and administered (but not owned) by her husband, who alone was viewed as competent to do so. A married woman is "a kind of infant," wrote an English lawyer; her husband, he continued, is "her prime mover, without whom she cannot do much at home, and less abroad." In Italy, it was commonly understood that no wife could make a contract without the consent of her husband. And the code of the German **duchy** of Saxony declared that "when a man takes a wife, he also takes all her goods into his power by right of guardianship."

Among less prosperous people, too, the destinies of male and female children were radically different. At an age as young as seven, a boy might be apprenticed to a craftsman to learn a trade or sent off to a wealthier family as a domestic servant—choices narrowing the range of future opportunities. Poor girls were also dispatched from the family as workers or servants—but with lower pay and status than their brothers. Girls also faced the further dilemma of marriage. To marry, they needed a dowry. If neither their father nor their employer provided one, they labored to accumulate one themselves. Without a dowry—with rare exceptions—a girl did not marry.

Towns had virtually no place for unmarried women (unless cloistered, or under religious vows). The proportion of unmarried women was well under 10 percent in the larger towns, probably less in smaller ones. These women needed to be disposed of in some way. Some girls were dowered by the town or by a benefactor. Some found in domestic service an alternative to marriage. Others—some burdened with illegitimate children—sought refuge in one of the many asylums medieval towns provided for the deserted and the widowed, reformed prostitutes and unwed mothers. Others might live with a family: their father's or someone else's. The "families" of the affluent included—in addition to those related by blood—servants and foster children, retired widows or widowers, apprentices and journeymen.

Domestic Duties Most households were led by a husband who commanded, while his wife obeyed and labored, as described in *Witnesses* on p. 342. Delineating the duties of a housewife in the fourteenth century, the anonymous "Goodman of Paris" advised a young woman to keep the fire smokeless and the bedchamber free of fleas. She was to see to her husband's comfort, "and I pray you keep him in clean linen, for that is your business." Husbands must labor hard in the world "and journey hither and thither, in rain and wind, in snow and hail, now drenched, now dry, now sweating, now shivering, ill-fed, ill-lodged, ill-warmed and ill-bedded." In these trials he would be sustained by thoughts of the care his wife would provide: "to be unshod before a good fire, to have his feet washed and fresh shoes and hose, to be given good food and drink. … And the next day fresh shirts and garments."

The housewife was expected to spin and weave, care for children and servants, purchase and store supplies, entertain guests, and tend the ill. "She takes care of the granary and keeps it clean, she takes care of the oil-jars …," wrote the popular preacher Saint Bernardino (1380–1444). "She sees to the salted meat … she sees to the spinning and the weaving [and] to the whole house." In childhood, advised an expert on household management, a girl should be taught "everything about the house, to make bread, clean capons, sift, cook, launder, make beds, weave French

WITNESSES

Family Life

The intimate relations between people of the past can't quite be comprehended by people living today, when women and children (in modern Western nations) have been liberated from the power of fathers and husbands. Yet parallels do exist. In the first passage, a wife is advised to stifle her complaints and allow her husband to remain "lord and master" of his household. In the second, mothers are urged to nurse and rear their own children. In the third, a widow advises her absent son about his health and his conduct far away from home.

***The Goodman of Paris* shows how a wife must yield to her husband (c. 1393):** And if you cannot move him [your husband] that he turn his wrath from you, take heed that you make not plaint thereof to your friends or to others, so that he may perceive it, for he will think the less of you and will remember it another time; but go you into your chamber and weep gently and softly in a low voice, and make your plaint to God; and thus do all wise ladies. And if perchance he be prone to wrath against another person less near unto him, do you wisely restrain him. ...

Whereof I say unto you that it behoveth good ladies, subtly, cautiously and gently, to counsel and restrain their husbands from the follies and silly dealings whereunto they see them drawn and tempted, and in no wise to think to turn them aside by lording over them, not by loud talk, by crying to their neighbours or in the street, by blaming them, by making plaint to their friends and parents, nor by other masterful means. For all this bringeth nought but irritation and the making of bad worse, for the heart of man findeth it hard to be corrected by the domination and lordship of a woman, and know that there is no man so poor nor of so small value that would not be lord and master when he is wed.

(*The Goodman of Paris*, c. 1393; ed. J. Adams, 1969)

Francesco Barbaro advises mothers to nurse their own children (1415): In pregnancy the same blood of which women are otherwise cleansed in their monthly effusions is held back. This time, following the laws of nature, the fetus is nourished by this blood until the time of birth arrives. Then, as in all animals who give birth, the nourishment of milk is supplied. For this, Nature has made breasts, which, like bountiful fountains, nourish the young child and help it to grow gradually in all its parts. Moreover, women have been given two breasts so that if they have twins they may easily suckle and nourish them together. All these things have been thus provided with great wisdom, but they still might seem to have been done in vain except that Nature has also instilled in women an incredible love and affection for their offspring. Here the special care and diligence of Nature can be observed, for while she has placed the nipples of other animals under their stomachs, in women she has affixed them on their breasts so that they may feed their children milk and fondle them with embrace at the same time, kiss them easily and comfortably, and, as they say, receive them to their bosoms.

Thus Nature has assigned to women the duty of bearing and rearing children not only by necessity but also with her singular goodwill and love. ... Therefore, women ought to consider it best, very honorable, and commendable to suckle their own children, whom they should nourish with great love, fidelity, and diligence; or they may commit this part of their duty to well-trained nurses who will esteem and care for the infants, not with a pretended enthusiasm nor out of mercenary consideration.

(Francesco Barbaro, "On Wifely Duties," 1415; eds. B. Kohl, J. Witt, 1978)

Alessandra Strozzi entreats her son to write often and to do as she says (1447): Do not wonder if I do not write to you often, as I am immersed in Caterina's affairs. I shall compensate for my silence when Matteo learns to write. You should not emulate me. Send me a letter with every courier, even if you say no more than that you and Niccolò are well. I do not know how you are conducting yourself in your affairs. God knows of my unhappiness when I learned that you could not come to see me while visiting Livorno; such displeasure can only be expressed orally and not in writing. May it please God that I see you again in good health before I die. Above all, my son, make certain to behave well so that, while last year you caused me so much grief by your poor behavior, now you may give me consolation. Consider well your position, and reflect upon all the benefits that Niccolò has rendered to you. You will then realize that you should kiss the earth on which he walks. You are more obligated to him than to your father and mother for all that he has done for you; no one else would have done the same. You should not be ungrateful to him for his past and present favours. I do not wish to say anything more, for you must be able to understand. You are not a little boy any more, as last July you were already 19. Above all, save some money. You will need it because your conditions are even worse than you think. Nor do I wish to say anything more in this letter. May God keep you from evil. ... And if you are the treasurer of your company behave honourably, keep your hands clean so that I may not suffer more pain than I already did in the past.

(Alessandra Strozzi, *Lettere di una gentildonna fiorentina del secolo XV ai figliuoli esuli*, 1447; ed. A. Molho, 1969) purses, embroider, cut wool and linen clothes, put new feet onto socks. ..." The wife who cheerfully met these expectations was genuinely appreciated. "These are so useful to us, so convenient, / That if they were lacking, the good order of life would be diminished," wrote the eleventh-century poet and bishop Marbode. "Of all the things that God has provided / For human benefit ... there is nothing lovelier, / Nothing better, than a good wife ..." More frequently encountered than such expressions of appreciation were attacks on woman's character. They were, claimed the anonymous fifteenth-century author of *Fifteen Joys of Marriage*, domineering, lascivious, flighty, demanding. Insatiable and devious, he continued, women make the putative joys of marriage the "greatest torments, pains, sorrows, and sufferings to be found on earth, than which no others are worse or more continuous, except the cutting off of one's limbs."

Women who did not meet a husband's expectations could be beaten—in moderation, moralists urged. A regional French law code stated the general principle: "Provided he neither kills nor maims her, it is legal for a man to beat his wife when she wrongs him—for instance, when she is about to surrender her body to another man, when she contradicts or abuses him, or when she refuses, like a decent woman, to obey his reasonable commands." Even if women were not physically abused, they were limited to the sphere of the household and (in artisan circles) the marketplace, and carefully supervised. In Italy, upper-class women lived virtually under house arrest, rarely leaving except, with chaperone in tow, to visit their peers or go to church. The "**honor**" or reputation of the family was at stake if a wife's chastity were suspect or a daughter lost her virginity.

Not only fathers and husbands, but magistrates and churchmen also kept a close watch on women's behavior. **Sumptuary** laws defined, among other levels of consumption, the limits of appropriate dress. Although these applied to men also, they chiefly targeted women. They admonished women to dress modestly and in accord with their social standing, lest those of lower social rank overreach themselves by sporting the furs, velvets, and jewels of the privileged. Observing that young women formerly dressed modestly, the Italian storyteller Franco Sacchetti (c. 1330–1400) complained that now they "go attired like common women, wearing caps, and collars and strings round their necks, with divers kinds of beasts hung upon their breasts." The purpose of much of this finery—especially the jewels—was to announce the status of the husband, whose property it remained. "The very goods which a man giveth to his wife, are still his own, her chair, her bracelets, her apparel, are all the goodman's goods. ..."

Those moralists who insisted on propriety in dress also defined the limits of women's sexual behavior. The fifteenth-century Sienese friar Cherubino forbade intercourse on Sunday, during Lent, on the day of taking holy communion, during menstruation (given to women by God "to humble you," Cherubino explained), pregnancy ("or else you are worse than beasts"), or lactation. Intercourse should not be too frequent (a risk to health); it should be performed face to face; without the use of hands or mouth to stimulate the genitals ("And you call this *holy matrimony?*"); without obscenity, visible nudity, violence, or insult.

Ejaculation outside the body, recognized by Cherubino as a method of birth control, was deemed a sin. As for "place," Cherubino is explicit: "You must come together in those generative parts, ordained by God for that purpose, for generation," and intercourse achieved with any other organs is considered to be a mortal sin: "You must not consent to so great a sin; rather let yourself be beaten, rather than be forced to do this. And if ... your husband batters you, submit with good will; for you would die a martyr, and you would go surely to eternal life."

Like the other sexual prohibitions imposed by church doctrine, this one was guided by the principle that sexual intercourse occurred only for the sake of procreation. "Coitus is only permitted for the sake of offspring," pronounced the fourteenth-century physician Bernard de Gordon. If its goal were not the generation of new life, it should not occur at all.

Childbirth and Childrearing

Caring for a newborn infant and rearing the young child were seen as a mother's responsibility, performed so as to meet the expectation of her husband, the Church, and society at large.

Most women faced a future of frequent conception, pregnancy, and childbirth. Elite women married in their adolescence, and poorer women in their mid-twenties. Once married, they experienced a cycle of childbirth and nursing and childbirth again. Poor women gave birth every twenty-four to thirty months on average, rich women as often as every year. Rich women were enormously fertile. The wealthier households of Italian cities, for instance, reared more than twice as many children as the poorest.

For a brief moment, the patrician woman who gave birth to a legitimate child was favored with an assortment of elaborate honors. Her bedchamber, for example, might be richly adorned with the finest textiles—linen and silks intricately embroidered with gold thread. Even to be pregnant won a woman recognition. In Piero della Francesca's (c. 1420–1492) painting of the pregnant Virgin (see p. 336), the lovely young woman proudly points to her belly in which she is carrying the infant Christ, signifying to her viewers not only the miracle of his conception but also the prestige enjoyed by the ordinary woman soon to bring forth life.

The realities of childbirth were, of course, somewhat less delightful than the attendant honors suggested. If the unborn child were illegitimate, the mother faced both shame and poverty. Even married women had much to fear in the painful and dangerous process of giving birth. Many women died in childbed, a factor that explains the relatively high mortality rates, compared to those for men, for the years from puberty to menopause.

If childbirth was full of risk, so was infant life. Infants and children died at an appalling rate, especially in the cities. In the countryside, the rate of mortality for children under five was 25 to 30 percent; in large cities, that figure climbed to 40 to 50 percent. In fifteenth-century Florence, of the children born to well-off families, 45 percent died before the age of twenty. The death of children figured sadly in the histories of many prominent families. Of the twenty-one children of the sixteenth-century Nuremberg patrician Konrad Paumgartner, only nine married and had children. From about 1400 to about 1600, sixty-five children were born into the Rorach family of Frankfurt. Of these, eighteen died before their fathers did, and only twelve married. Of the twenty children born to the first three wives of the fifteenth-century Florentine merchant Gregorio Dati, only five survived; of the six to which his fourth wife gave birth, three survived.

Did parents learn from the deaths of children not to hope and not to love too much? Perhaps; but some at least grieved each loss. The Florentine Alessandra Macinghi Strozzi wrote that the death of her son Matteo in 1459 caused her to suffer "the greatest pain in my heart that I have ever experienced." When Gregorio Dati's three-month-old son died in 1411, he wrote poignantly of the "very attractive baby boy" that "God was pleased to call the child very shortly to Himself," where he could now intercede with God for the benefit of his parents' souls.

Surplus Children Some children were unwanted. Measures were taken to control birth through contraception or abortion, measures that the Church vehemently condemned. Saint Bernardino (1380–1444) believed that these diabolic practices were so widespread as to result in the damnation of a great many souls: "I believe that very few of those in the married state will be saved. Out of 1000 marriages, 999 ... are of the devil." Friar Cherubino believed that some women tried to prevent conception or achieve abortion, and that when those attempts failed, "then

***Ghirlandaio,* Birth of the Virgin, 1486–1490:** *Ghirlandaio's lavish and stately depiction of the Virgin birth—which most certainly would not have happened in a luxurious palace decorated with a row of naked boys, or putti—reveals the characteristic feature of childbirth in pre-modern Europe. It was a collective event, and one which involved only women, and many of them. Here midwives and servants prepare to bathe (or to baptize) the infant, as neighbors arrive to observe and to pay their respects to the hero of the day: the mother, elevated in her bed, who surveys with lordly interest the care taken of the baby to whom she has just given birth.* (Santa Maria Novella, Florence)

when the creature is born, they beat it, and would want to see it dead, so that they can be free to go freely about their business, here and there."

Sometimes, in desperation, women did kill the infants for whom they could not care. Infanticide was considered a grave crime meriting the death penalty. It was the only crime other than witchcraft for which women faced capital punishment. Often infanticide went undetected, disguised as a case of "overlaying"—death caused when a sleepy or drunken parent or nurse rolled over in bed and suffocated a fragile child.

Unwanted children were more often abandoned than murdered. "How many infants ...," Boccaccio wailed, "are given over to the forests, how many to the wild animals and to the birds!" Although Boccaccio bemoaned the practice, abandonment was not considered sinful. In an era when poor families with too many children to feed faced starvation, and when wealthy families with too many heirs faced the dissipation of their wealth, it was considered a plausible method of family limitation. Often the abandoned babies were "found," and put to work as a servant or a prostitute, or foster child. The generally small size of poor families and the vast numbers of servants, some of them very young, can be explained in part by the practice of abandoning children.

One solution to the problem of child abandonment was the foundling hospital. Several of these institutions dedicated to the care of unwanted children were founded as early as the seventh and eighth centuries, in France, Germany, and Italy. Noteworthy foundling hospitals were established in Venice and Florence, in the fourteenth and fifteenth centuries. The task, however, was insuperable, and their resources were insufficient. The foundlings were very young, mostly female (more often unwanted than boys), and not yet weaned. These infants needed to be sent out to **wet nurses** in the country, as there was no adequate substitute for breastfeeding. Often they did not survive the experience. Death rates were around 50 percent at Florence's "Hospital of the Innocents" in the fifteenth century. In Lyons and Paris, foundling hospitals amounted to, in one critic's words, "a veritable system of social infanticide."

Like any other infants at this time, the abandoned babies in the municipal hospital needed to be breastfed for eighteen to twenty-four months. Other food and drink were often contaminated or indigestible, even if they could be fed to a nursling; human milk alone was suitable, giving adequate immunity. Most women must have spent much of their time nursing babies—especially poor women, since wealthy ones often avoided this task. The words of the Italian fifteenth-century physician Paolo Bagellardo imply that social distinction: "If the infant is a child of the poorer class, let it be fed on its mother's milk." Despite the fact that, as one pediatric historian has written, "almost every writer on the subject points out the desirability of maternal suckling," most elite women declined to nurse their babies as shown by the passage quoted in *Witnesses* on p. 342.

The wet nurses who sustained upper-class babies and foundlings entrusted to them were, of necessity, lactating women who had recently given birth themselves, who had consigned their own offspring (if it still lived) to another's care (perhaps for even lower pay). Employers (generally fathers or their agents) took great pains to select a suitable nurse. They considered the health, age, and character of the candidate, the magnitude of her breasts, and the consistency of the product. "It should be white, sweet to taste and free from any unnatural savour," counseled one expert, "not too watery and not too thick." A drop placed on a fingernail should be dense enough to hold its form. Milk was to be examined thus diligently because it was distilled, physicians believed, from the nurse's blood, and was thus imbued with her character. As much as her speech and behavior, it would shape, for better or worse, the character of the nursling.

Thus, in the medieval city, male heads of households made the decisions that framed the lives of women, whose behavior was strictly regulated, and of children, whose very existence was precarious. Their scrutiny was searching and their right to command unquestioned. The openness and vitality otherwise characteristic of the town did not apply to the intimacy of private life.

THE CITY AND THE BOOK

From the thirteenth century, urban households began to acquire books. Merchants and artisans and their wives learned to read, and reading encouraged them to think about more than their money and their shops. In the towns and cities of medieval Europe, for the first time since antiquity, laymen and even women learned to read and sent their children to school. As those institutions matured, the intellectual world of the medieval city began to produce great books of its own.

Learning and Literacy

The child's first teacher was his mother. Once weaned from the nurse the child was left, until the age of seven, in the care of his or her mother, from whom he acquired his basic knowledge of his own society and culture. From her, the child, male or female, received religious and moral values, and even, in elite circles, some reading and writing. But maternal education was insufficient to prepare townspeople for the tasks of business and government. These necessary skills were provided by schools.

In order to manage their accounts and plan their business ventures, medieval merchants needed, first, to know how to read. In the early Middle Ages that competence had been the prerogative of the clergy, who monopolized the few schools. The townspeople of Europe were the first to break the clerical monopoly on learning, recognizing the crucial value of education in formulating business transactions and keeping records.

By the thirteenth century, most European merchants could read and write. By 1500, the wives of many London merchants were literate also. In 1262, the Lübeck city council created the Saint James School to teach Latin to sons of citizens. In Paris around 1400, the moralist Christine de Pisan urged mothers of the artisan class to have their children "taught first at school by educated people so that they may know how better to serve God," before having them apprenticed to a trade.

In Italy, many children of townspeople attended some sort of school, if only, as in the case of some girls, to learn to sew. High rates of literacy resulted; for example, in Venice in 1587, one-third of all boys and a little more than one-tenth of all girls were literate. In the case of the boys, literacy was largely the fruit of attendance at **vernacular** "abacus schools" (so named after the device that facilitated high-speed arithmetical calculation). Those schools trained young boys to read and write, to do arithmetic, and to keep the books, as a commercial career required. These schools were set up, much like shops, by independent schoolmasters, who thrived only to the extent that their pupils learned. Such masters were numerous. In fourteenth-century Venice (with a population of about 100,000), between 130 and 165 teachers were laboring at any given time to inculcate a basic curriculum.

The masters ran their schools without the intervention of a "board of education" or any plan from above. Students went early in the morning to spend a long day, all year round. There were no readers or workbooks. The texts they used were the books that parents had at home: moral books, the Gospels, saints' lives, or tales of knights and dragons and battles. Boys also learned "abacus"—not the use of the ancient abacus itself but rather the practical mathematics imported from Arab centers in the thirteenth century. This study comprised arithmetic, algebra, and geometry, and used the numerals still known today as "arabic" rather than the clumsy Roman symbols they replaced. The student of abacus could convert currencies (which varied from city to city), calculate the inheritance due to each member of a family, or compute the annual profits and losses in his father's business.

Some cities established a "public" school, "for the common good." Quite different in purpose from the "abacus" school, these Latin "grammar" schools, staffed by one or two experts, offered an advanced

The City and the Book

Benozzo Gozzoli, Saint Augustine Given to the Grammar Master: *In this fresco by Benozzo Gozzoli (San Gimignano, Italy, 1465) Saint Augustine as a child is being taken to school by his parents, suggesting what that experience might have been like for a city boy.*

***Giovanni Boccaccio,* A Woman Copying a Manuscript:** *A few women did master literacy, as appears in this image in a fifteenth-century French manuscript of Boccaccio's* Le Livre des clercs et nobles femmes, *in which a well-dressed woman copies a book in a well-equipped study.* (Bibliothèque Nationale, Paris)

curriculum designed to prepare a select group of future managers and the sons of patricians. ("Grammar" included the formal study of Latin and Classical literature.) "Since the knowledge of grammar is the origin and foundation of all virtue and knowledge," read the founding document of the school of Lucca in 1371, "it is not only useful but necessary to locate a qualified man who will teach the young and guide their behavior." The city fathers of Treviso, Italy, asserted in 1524 that "nothing else can dignify and exalt a city so much as higher education." In wealthier households, a private tutor offered a similar curriculum. Status and wealth determined what training a boy would receive. Whether obtained in public, at a school, or in private, from a tutor, education was bought.

Class as well as gender limited education for girls. Girls of the middle classes did learn to read, as the figure above shows, but rarely at schools. Female instructors might train them in needlework, as well as the rudiments of reading and arithmetic. Upper-class girls might acquire a Classical education from their fathers, their brothers, or their brothers' tutors.

Although Latin learning among women was rare, city women of the elite classes were avid readers of works written in the vernacular languages of the people—works of devotion (approved by educators) and of romance (disdained). The latter could corrupt a young woman with thoughts of unregulated love or distract her mind from domestic duties. "If you have a female child," warned the fourteenth-century Florentine moralist Paolo da Certaldo, "set her to sewing and not to reading, for it is not suitable for a female to know how to read unless she is going to be a nun. …"

In time merchants' sons even went to the university. Their attendance at these temples of abstract thought marked a breakthrough: as recently as the thirteenth century, when the first universities were in their infancy, almost all students were "clerks," members of the clergy (if only the minor clergy), destined for jobs in church or royal **chanceries**. But the knowledge offered by the universities had a far wider appeal. Training in law and medicine (also studied by clerks) would open up lucrative careers. From university lecture halls came the skilled physicians and lawyers, the administrators, managers, letter-writers, and diplomats of a vigorous urban culture. After 1400, many of the patrician leaders of the larger cities possessed university degrees. The town clerks of Germany were now more likely to be laymen than clergy, university graduates from the burgher class.

The language of the university was Latin, and those young patricians seeking an academic degree necessarily mastered it. But such mastery was rare. Most literate townspeople read vernacular books. The greatest storytellers of the fourteenth century—

***Bartolomé Murillo,* Saint Anne Teaching the Virgin to Read:** *This seventeenth-century painting by Murillo shows the child Mary learning to read at the knee of her mother Saint Anne.* (Prado, Madrid)

the Englishman Geoffrey Chaucer and the Italian Giovanni Boccaccio—were avidly read by literate members of the merchant classes, who were their main audience. In the case of Boccaccio, whose *Decameron* was dedicated to a noblewoman, the targeted audience was not only bourgeois, but female: "Most gracious ladies," the narrator began.

Favorite Books

The favorite books of the town-dwellers were all about knights: courtly epics and romantic tales derived from the troubadour tradition. Shopkeepers and their wives delighted in tales of ancient Troy, of King Arthur and his comrades, of Charlemagne and Roland, according to legend the king's most trusted knight. The characters of chivalric romance spilled into daily life as merchants adorned the walls of their houses with tapestries and frescoes depicting scenes from the quest of the legendary Holy Grail (the lost chalice thought to have been used by Jesus), or named their daughters after literary heroines—Isolde and Guinevere. The popular French poem *The Romance of the Rose* (completed 1275–1280) provided both romantic fantasy and keen bourgeois observation—and more than a little hostility toward women.

Although they loved romances, city folk also treasured devotional books: collections of prayers and psalms, lives of the saints, works of moral admonition. In Italy, the *Flower of Virtue* (written between 1300 and 1323) served for leisure reading and instruction alike. It consisted of about forty chapters, each illustrating with a lively story a vice and its dangers or a virtue and its rewards. Sebastian Brant's monumental *Ship of Fools* of 1494 provided an encyclopedia of medieval characters and clever satire of contemporary greed and pettiness.

"How-to" books on manners and household management were also standard fare for the bourgeois reader. In Italy, and especially in Florence, patricians composed such works for their sons. These memoirs gave advice about making sound investments, weaving political alliances, and choosing a spouse, interspersed with memorable events of family history or lists of the birth and baptismal dates of offspring. The general tone is exemplified by Giovanni Morelli's admonition to his sons (in his memoirs composed between 1393 and 1421), after he had retold a cautionary tale of fiscal irresponsibility: "I decided to write this down ... as a warning that no one ... should ever divest himself of his property or rights either from fear, flattery, or any other motive."

Accumulated wisdom was also handed on to children by their mothers. Women who owned books (one historian has discovered as many as 186 laywomen who did in the fourteenth and fifteenth centuries) might bequeath them to their daughters in their wills. The Frenchwoman Christine de Pisan (1365–1430) addressed to her fatherless son a book entitled *Moral Instructions*. Though she dedicated no such work to her daughter, she nevertheless argued staunchly for the education of women. "If it were customary to send little girls to school and teach them the same subjects as are taught to boys, they would learn just as fully and would understand the subtleties of all arts and sciences. Indeed maybe they would understand them better. ..." Her own father, a royal physician and astronomer, had approved of her studies, although her mother, "who held the usual feminine ideas on the matter," wanted Christine "to spend her time spinning." She did not. Having received a rudimentary education from her father, she pursued her studies as a girl in the library of the king of France and as a wife and widow among her own books. She became the first professional female writer of the modern age.

Christine de Pisan and the *City of Ladies*

Christine de Pisan was not only a learned city woman, but an author who wrote about women and cities. Her *Book of the City of Ladies* (completed 1405) envisions the mystical building of a "city" of the mind in which the heroes are women. The story opens in the author's study, as she recalls the many (male) authors who had written disparagingly of the female sex. She wondered "how it happened that so many different men—and learned men among them—have been and are so inclined to express ... so many wicked insults about women and their behavior." So many books, and so much agreement: "it seems they all speak from one and the same mouth."

As Christine falls into despair, three celestial ladies—Reason, Rectitude, and Justice—appear before her. It is jealousy, resentment, and error that drive male authors to demean women, they explained. Why then, the author asks, do women not defend themselves from these slanders? That task, Lady Rectitude replies, is to be assigned to Christine. She must write a book in defense of women—and build a city that will be their fortress and their monument. Her mission will be to protect the good women of past, present, and future, and to house them forever. "Thus, fair daughter," explains Lady Reason, "the prerogative among women has been bestowed on you to establish and build the City of Ladies [which] will be extremely beautiful, without equal, and of perpetual duration in the world." This city will be their indomitable castle. Wielding the "pick of her understanding," Christine will build it herself, using the tools provided by her advisers: mortar, a ruler, and a balance, the instruments, respectively, of builders, mathematicians, and judges. Men have built the cities of the past; in heaven, God has His. Now there would tower also a city for women.

Yet that city exists only in the imagination. More popular than her *Book of the City of Ladies*, Christine's

Book of Three Virtues (also called *The Treasure of the City of Ladies*) describes the real settings of women's lives—court, city, village. *Three Virtues* outlines the duties appropriate to women in different social categories: royalty, the high nobility, and all the lower social orders—including women of the bourgeoisie, artisanry, and peasantry. In each category, women are enjoined to exemplary behavior and hard work, keeping to their own particular stations in life.

Wives of merchants should wear "handsome, fine, and modest clothing," and beware of dressing beyond their station. "It is very great folly," chides the first modern feminist, "to dress up in clothes more suitable for someone else. ... It is to [women's] advantage and it is their best course of action to wear their rightful clothing, each woman according to her own position." As for the wives of artisans "who live in cities and fine towns," far from tending to luxury, they face the omnipresent risk of descent into poverty. They must be "very painstaking and diligent if they wish to have the necessities of life," encouraging husbands and workers alike "to get to work early in the morning and work until late, for mark our words, there is no trade so good that if you neglect your work you will not have difficulty putting bread on the table."

Unlike city women of high and low estate, the hard-working peasant wife had no one to advise her. Christine de Pisan reaches out in particular to such women, deprived of the commerce and conversation of the city: "Listen, simple women who live in villages, in low country or in mountains, who cannot often hear what the Church prescribes to every person for his salvation. ... Remember our lessons addressed to you, if it happens to reach your ears, so that ignorance, which can deceive you through lack of knowing more, will not deprive you of salvation." For Christine, it is ignorance, above all other evils, that imperils women, but especially those who have not the good fortune to live in cities.

HOW MANY?

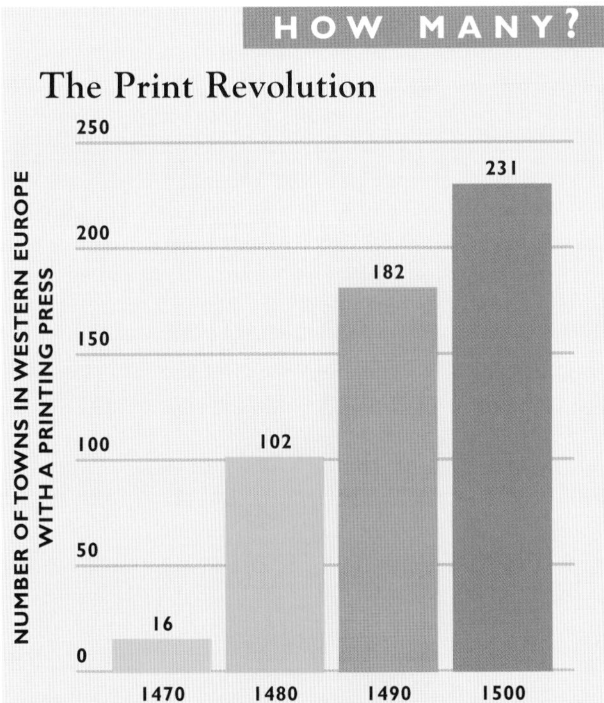

Medieval manuscripts rarely survive in large numbers. We know for instance that Wolfram von Eschenbach's Parvizal *was a popular work because over 80 copies have come down to us; about 60 copies of Chaucer's* Canterbury Tales *survive. With the advent of the printing press, however, came the bestseller. In the last three decades of the fifteenth century Thomas à Kempis's* De imitatione Christi (The Imitation of Christ) *passed through 99 editions of up to 200 copies each. At the beginning of the following century Erasmus's* Adagia *passed through 34 editions of 1,000 copies each.*

Sources: S.H. Steinberg, *Five Hundred Years of Printing* (Harmondsworth, Middlesex: Penguin Books 1955); W.T. Berry and H.E. Poole, *Annals of Printing: a chronological encyclopedia from the earliest times to 1950* (London: Blandford Publishing, 1966)

Dante the Florentine

Like de Pisan, the great Italian vernacular poet Dante Alighieri (1265–1321) was shaped by the life of the city. Dante was born into a substantial Florentine family during the time of that city's birth as a Guelf power, ruled by the party of the "people" (as opposed to the "fat ones," as ordinary citizens described the elite, or patriciate). But the Guelfs, once in power, split into the factions of "Whites" and "Blacks"—more moderate and more radical, respectively. Allied with the former, Dante was on the losing side when the Blacks seized control in 1301. Being absent from the city at the time, he prudently stayed away. His voluntary absence turned into unwilling exile, which lasted until his death.

Even before that turning point of his life, Dante had emerged as the city's foremost poet. From two sources of inspiration—the figure of Beatrice, a woman he loved who came to represent the salvation he craved, and the ideal of a Holy Roman Empire that would truly emulate the kingdom of Heaven—he derived the theoretical bases of his most important work, *The Divine Comedy*. This epic (c. 1308–1314) records Dante's spiritual loss and his self-discovery in the experience of exile and maps out his conception of the afterlife and the course of his own path to God. It is also concerned with the rise and fall of cities: his hopes for his own city of Florence, his despair over the condition of Italian cities in general, and his vision of the heavenly city, realm of perfection.

The shadow of Florence falls on this grandest of Dante's works and colors the poet's journey through the realms of the afterlife—Hell, Purgatory, and Heaven. In his voyage, he encounters many citizens of his native city. Passing through the circle of Hell

MUST READS

Books to Remember

Dante Alighieri	*Divine Comedy* (1314)
Giovanni Boccaccio	*Decameron* (1353)
Anonymous	*The Goodman of Paris* (around 1393)
Christine de Pisan	*Book of the City of Ladies* (1404–1405)

reserved for gluttons, Dante is hailed by Ciacco, a Florentine. Like all the dead, Ciacco is gifted with the ability to foretell the future; and at Dante's request he predicts the future course of internecine conflict in Florence and makes known to the poet the locations in the nether regions of Hell of other countrymen.

Dante goes on to encounter these Florentines: friends, enemies, and neighbors from the earthly city that had nurtured so much evil and so many evildoers. Faced with eternal torment, they think of themselves still as citizens of Florence. Among the heretics Dante encounters is the Florentine nobleman Farinata degli Uberti. Doubly imprisoned in Hell and in the tomb that will become at the end of time his eternal sarcophagus, Farinata remains proudly Florentine in his outlook despite God and fate: "Erect, / he rose above the flame, great chest, great brow; / he seemed to hold all Hell in disrespect."

Lower still in Hell and nearer its vortex, Dante is surprised to find Ser Brunetto Latini, one of his teachers, among the sodomites (as male homosexuals were termed). Dante learns from this prominent patrician and moralist of his own fate: he will be ground between the factions that struggled over the identity of the city. The conflict between factions that dominated Dante's Florence, as it later would Machiavelli's, is in the forefront of the poet's mind even as he plumbs the lowest depths of the afterworld.

In Purgatory and Paradise, there are more reminders of the urban world. The spirits Dante encounters still identify with their earthly cities and issue dire warnings about the danger of civic strife. The poet Vergil, Dante's companion and guide through Hell and Purgatory, encounters a fellow Mantuan: a near-contemporary of Dante's named Sordello. The compatriots greet each other affectionately: "O Mantuan," cries the latter, "I am Sordello / of your own country," and embraces Vergil. The encounter spurs Dante to reflect on his torn country, Italy, and his own city of Florence. Beset by factional strife, Florence had destroyed itself: "[you have] hacked your own limbs off, and sewed them on."

In Paradise, Dante meets his own ancestor, Cacciaguida, who recalls the city in a simpler age: "Florence, within her ancient walls secure … / lived in sweet peace, her sons sober and pure." Florence was then unbloodied by the factionalism that sent Dante into exile: "the red dye of division." Later Dante concludes that the only just community is that of Heaven: here there are no factions.

In *The Divine Comedy*, Dante looks back at Florence after a twenty-year exile begun in 1301. His love for his city and his resentment of its shortcomings permeate its pages. In the end, as Cacciaguida prophesies, Dante becomes a "party of [his] own"—a vigorous proponent of unity against factionalism.

Factionalism was a great defect of city life. Another was plague, which more harshly devastated populations in towns than in villages. Another was the pressing problem of poverty, more urgent in the urban than the rural setting.

Yet the life of the city, where time was short and precious, where opportunity and profits beckoned, offered intense pleasures. Not the least of these were those of the intellect. City life encouraged forms of thought different from those nourished in a monastic school or university. Town dwellers read with pleasure and studied for advancement. The world they created would produce great triumphs over the centuries to come.

Conclusion

CITY LIFE AND THE MEANING OF THE WEST

Within their walls, city people thought differently than country people, and moved faster. The rich visual forms of the city and the constant activity of its public life continually inspired them (even as their private lives were closely controlled by patriarchs and moralists). In this vital setting, there emerged a distinctively urban culture. Townspeople forged the culture of Europe as much as the monks in their abbeys, knights in their castles, and peasants in their crude huts. Moreover, it was the cities that gave birth to the ideas and the patterns of life that would rupture the fabric of medieval European culture, and set the West on the road to a new consciousness. Soon after Dante penned his *Divine Comedy*, and before Christine de Pisan created her visionary city, northern Italy, Europe's most urban region, would produce the cultural transformation that historians call the "Renaissance."

REVIEW QUESTIONS

1. What were the main public buildings in a medieval town? How did wealthy town dwellers' houses differ from those of ordinary burghers and the poor? How did poor town planning affect the shape of medieval cities and the way buildings were constructed?

2. How clean were medieval cities? How did medieval cities cope with fire and crime? Why was sanitation a problem?

3. Why could a medieval city's diversity lead to violence? Why were Jews sometimes treated with tolerance and at other times with intolerance?

4. What kind of public festivals did medieval towns celebrate? Why were public ceremonies important for town dwellers? What forms did charitable activity take in medieval towns? Why was charity so necessary?

5. What religious and secular functions did marriage fulfill in medieval life? How did the domestic roles of husbands and wives differ? Why was infant mortality so high?

6. Why was literacy on the increase in the thirteenth century? How important were class and gender in determining the education of a child? How did urban life influence the writings of Christine de Pisan and Dante?

SUGGESTED RESOURCES

The Urban Landscape

Brentano, Robert, *Rome Before Avignon: A Social History of Thirteenth-Century Rome* (New York: Basic Books, 1991). A lively description of city life in medieval Rome.

Brucker, Gene A., *Renaissance Florence*, rev. ed. (Berkeley: University of California Press, 1983). The classic portrait of this great cultural center, with investigations of the patriciate, the Church, social conflict, and the undergirdings of the Renaissance cultural explosion.

Le Goff, Jacques, *Time, Work, and Culture in the Middle Ages* (Chicago: University of Chicago Press, 1980). Eighteen essays are included, including the classic cultural study of time in history, "Merchant's Time and Church's Time."

Public Life

Geremek, Bronislaw, *Poverty: A History* (trans. Agnreszka Kolakowska; Cambridge, MA: Blackwell, 1994). Originally written in Polish in 1978 under Cold War conditions and first published in Italian, this classic work still vividly recreates the world of the poor from the Middle Ages into the early modern period.

Hanawalt, Barbara & Kathryn Reyerson, eds., *City and Spectacle in Medieval Europe* (Minneapolis: University of Minnesota Press, 1994). Twelve essays offering vivid accounts and explanations of public ritual events in English, French, Flemish, Spanish, and Italian settings.

Herlihy, David, and Samuel Kline Cohn, *The Black Death and the Transformation of the West* (Cambridge: Harvard University Press, 1997). A provocative overview of the plague and the role it played in creating modern Europe.

Karras, Ruth Mazo, *Common Women: Prostitution and Sexuality in Medieval England* (Oxford: Oxford University Press, 1996). A synthesis of the legal and social framework for prostitution in medieval England.

Stow, Kenneth R., *Alienated Minority: The Jews of Medieval Latin Europe* (Cambridge, MA: Harvard University Press, 1992). An overview of medieval Jewry in France, Spain, and Italy, from antiquity through the reign of Pope Paul IV.

Private Life

Atkinson, Clarissa W., *The Oldest Vocation: Christian Motherhood in the Middle Ages* (Ithaca: Cornell University Press, 1991). An interesting survey of medieval motherhood; treats motherhood both as an ideology and an institution.

Dean, Trevor & K. J. P. Lowe, eds., *Marriage in Italy, 1300–1650* (Cambridge: Cambridge University Press, 1998). Defines the Italian case of rules and patterns of marriage at a time when the family determined the destinies of children, especially daughters.

Hanawalt, Barbara A., *Growing up in Medieval London: The Experience of Childhood in History* (Oxford: Oxford University Press, 1993). This text reconstructs the condition of urban children, including apprenticeship, wardship, inheritance.

Herlihy, David, *Medieval Households* (Cambridge, MA: Harvard University Press, 1985). An introduction to the history of the domestic family, from the late Roman period to about 1500 C.E., concentrating on Tuscany.

Musacchio, Jacqueline Marie, *The Art and Ritual of Childbirth in Renaissance Italy* (New Haven: Yale University Press, 1999). A woman's birthing a child was one of the peak moments of her life, assessed here through the range and meaning of the objects that surrounded the ritual of birth.

Shahar, Shulamith, *Childhood in the Middle Ages* (London: Routledge, 1989). A survey of childhood from the Carolingian era to the 15th century, using anecdotal evidence and psychological theory.

The City and the Book

Hollander, Robert, *Dante: A Life in Works* (New Haven: Yale University Press, 2001). An intellectual biography of the poet reconstructed from an exhaustive reading of the whole gamut of his works.

Richards, Earl Jeffrey, ed., *Reinterpreting Christine De Pisan* (Athens: University of Georgia Press, 1992). Seventeen diverse essays about the work of Christine de Pisan and the origins of feminist thought.

Christine de Pisan, brief biography: **http://www.distinguishedwomen.com/biographies/pisan.html**

Bibliographies of women writers of the Middle Ages (University of Calgary): **http://www.ucalgary.ca/library/subjects/HIST/womenwriters.html**

Dante Alighieri on the Web: **http://www.greatdante.net**

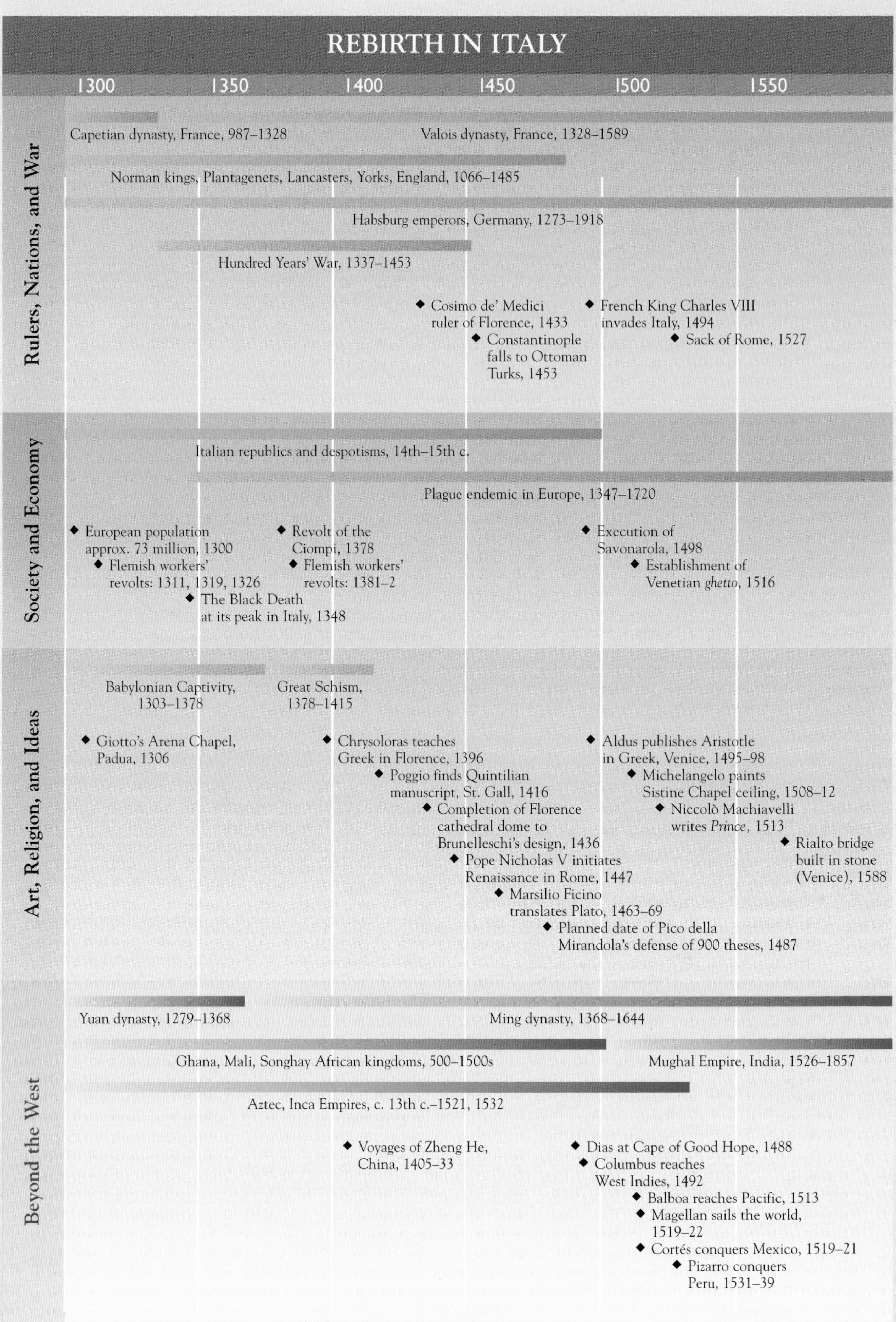
REBIRTH IN ITALY
1300
1350
1400
1450
1500
1550
Rulers, Nations, and War
Capetian dynasty, France, 987–1328
Valois dynasty, France, 1328–1589
Norman kings, Plantagenets, Lancasters, Yorks, England, 1066–1485
Habsburg emperors, Germany, 1273–1918
Hundred Years' War, 1337–1453
Cosimo de' Medici ruler of Florence, 1433
Constantinople falls to Ottoman Turks, 1453
French King Charles VIII invades Italy, 1494
Sack of Rome, 1527
Society and Economy
Italian republics and despotisms, 14th–15th c.
Plague endemic in Europe, 1347–1720
European population approx. 73 million, 1300
Flemish workers' revolts: 1311, 1319, 1326
The Black Death at its peak in Italy, 1348
Revolt of the Ciompi, 1378
Flemish workers' revolts: 1381–2
Execution of Savonarola, 1498
Establishment of Venetian ghetto, 1516
Art, Religion, and Ideas
Babylonian Captivity, 1303–1378
Great Schism, 1378–1415
Giotto's Arena Chapel, Padua, 1306
Chrysoloras teaches Greek in Florence, 1396
Poggio finds Quintilian manuscript, St. Gall, 1416
Completion of Florence cathedral dome to Brunelleschi's design, 1436
Pope Nicholas V initiates Renaissance in Rome, 1447
Marsilio Ficino translates Plato, 1463–69
Planned date of Pico della Mirandola's defense of 900 theses, 1487
Aldus publishes Aristotle in Greek, Venice, 1495–98
Michelangelo paints Sistine Chapel ceiling, 1508–12
Niccolò Machiavelli writes Prince, 1513
Rialto bridge built in stone (Venice), 1588
Beyond the West
Yuan dynasty, 1279–1368
Ming dynasty, 1368–1644
Ghana, Mali, Songhay African kingdoms, 500–1500s
Mughal Empire, India, 1526–1857
Aztec, Inca Empires, c. 13th c.–1521, 1532
Voyages of Zheng He, China, 1405–33
Dias at Cape of Good Hope, 1488
Columbus reaches West Indies, 1492
Balboa reaches Pacific, 1513
Magellan sails the world, 1519–22
Cortés conquers Mexico, 1519–21
Pizarro conquers Peru, 1531–39

CHAPTER

13

REBIRTH IN ITALY

The Civilization of the Italian Renaissance

1300–1550

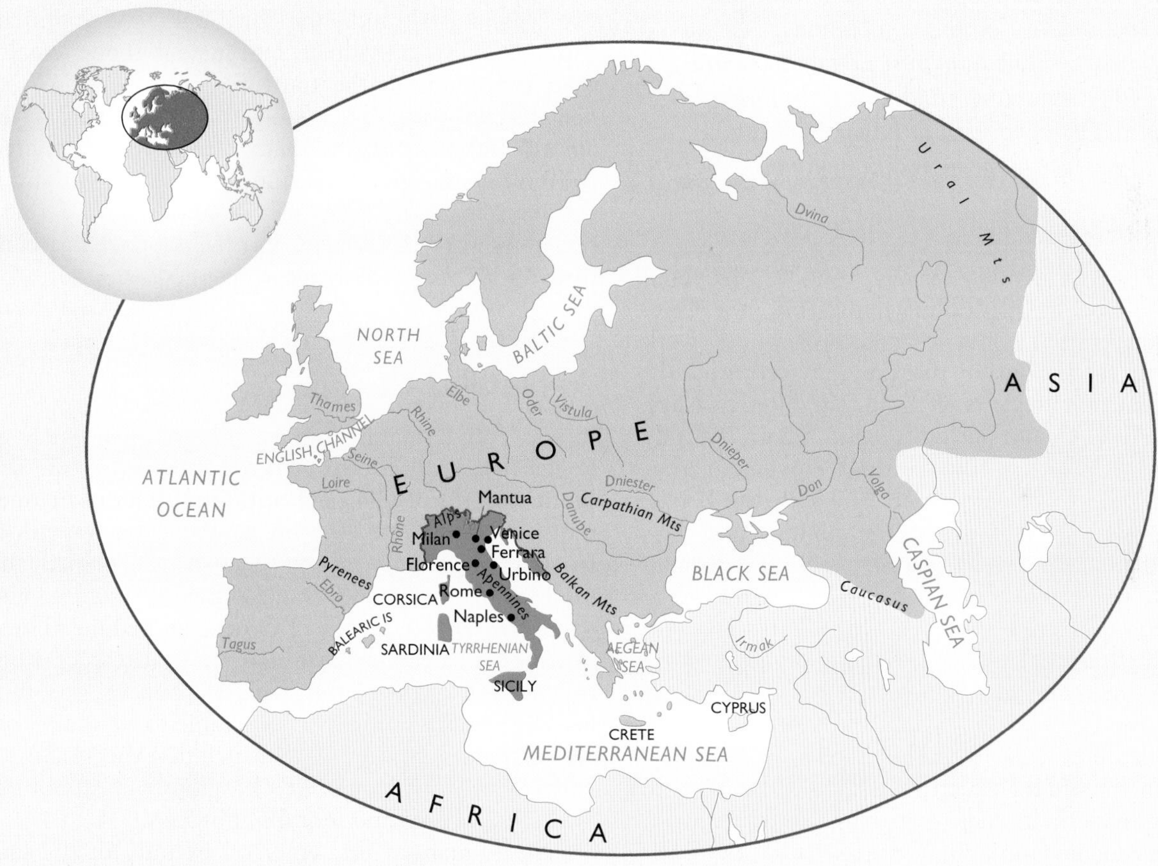

KEY TOPICS

- **The Rebirth of Classical Antiquity:** Intellectuals and artists renew links to ancient civilization, establishing modern Western culture on the classical as well as the Judeo-Christian heritage.
- **Italian Renaissance Settings:** The Renaissance develops differently in different settings: the republics of Florence and Venice; the despotisms of Milan and Naples; the courts of Ferrara, Mantua, and Urbino; and papal Rome.
- **Italian Renaissance Profiles:** Five dynamic figures—four male and one female—from three centuries have decisive influences: a painter (Giotto di Bondone), a philosopher (Pico della Mirandola), two humanists (Lorenzo Valla and Isotta Nogarola), and a political theorist (Niccolò Machiavelli).

Born Again *In 1416, the noted scholar Poggio Bracciolini (1381–1459) and his friends found, in a Swiss monastery, the long-lost complete text of a book by the first-century* C.E. *Roman orator Quintilian—the* Institutio oratoria *("The Training of an Orator"). Here, in the oblivion of a monastic library, wrote Poggio, intentionally confounding the author and the book, "he was being kept prisoner." The searchers found the "prisoner ... still safe and sound" amid a heap of valuable and neglected volumes, "though filthy with mold and dust ... in a sort of foul and gloomy dungeon at the bottom of one of the towers." At the sight of "countless books ... kept like captives and the library neglected and infested with dust, worms, soot," wrote one of Poggio's companions, "we all burst into tears." The humanist Leonardo Bruni (1370–1444) sent congratulations from Florence: "For Quintilian, who used to be mangled and in pieces will recover all his parts through you. ..."*

These fifteenth-century book hunters recovered Quintilian's work, Quintilian's mind, and, in a sense, Quintilian himself, only fragments of whose work had been known during the previous centuries. In effect, Quintilian was "born again." In different ways, other books of distant antiquity were "reborn" in Italy in the first phase of the cultural movement that historians call the **Renaissance**. Not only the books, but also the art and ideas, the politics and law, the thoughts and the values of Greek and Roman antiquity were "reborn" in the period 1300–1550 as Europeans created a new synthesis of ancient and Judeo-Christian cultures. In that combined heritage the subsequent cultural achievements of the West are securely rooted.

The people who lived during the Renaissance (the French word for "rebirth") did not use that term, or its equivalent in their own language (in Italian, *Rinascimento*; in German, *Wiederbelebung*), but considered their own era as one of "renewal" (in the scholars' preferred Latin, *renovatio*). This renewal, or rebirth, followed an age that most of them considered one of absolute darkness, a "Middle Age" that lay between the glorious past and their own era.

The "Renaissance" began in Italy, home to the most urbanized and commercialized society in Europe apart from Byzantium. In the thriving Italian cities, great wealth provided great opportunities for cultural expression and for the employment of artists and scholars to accomplish it. Here the rediscovery and rebirth of Classical antiquity was achieved. This achievement inaugurated a new phase in Western civilization, and set it on the road to modernity. Renaissance scholars' explorations of the past led them to examine contemporary concerns as well, better understood with the tools of Classical literature, they believed, than with those of medieval theology or philosophy. Those concerns were different in each city (in republics such as Florence and Venice; in large principalities such as Milan and Naples; in small ones such as Mantua, Ferrara, and Urbino; and at the papal court in Rome) and shaped by the interests of both creators and patrons.

In these various settings individuals of extraordinary genius—an unusually large group over a few brief generations—emerged to create the culture of the Renaissance. Of these individuals, profiles of five, whose careers were distinguished by great originality and significance, are examined toward the end of this chapter: one painter, one philosopher, two humanists, and one historian and political thinker. These individuals, four male and one female, span the era from the fourteenth through the sixteenth centuries. They and their contemporaries among Italy's artists, scholars, and patrons created the culture of the Renaissance that diverged from the main patterns of medieval culture and defined the framework of thought and feeling that has continued into the modern age.

THE REBIRTH OF CLASSICAL ANTIQUITY

It was the humanists above all—scholars such as Poggio Bracciolini—who led the drive to restore the literary world of Classical antiquity. Important ones are listed in *Who's Who* on p. 356. The humanists (mostly men, and mostly laymen) developed the capacity to read, understand, discuss, imitate, and value the written legacy of Greece and Rome. These skills were developed through the mastery of what they called, in Latin, the *studia humanitatis*, or "studies of humanity," roughly comparable to what are now called the humanities. These included the studies of Latin (and sometimes Greek) grammar, literature, dialectic, history, and moral philosophy.

The humanists first emerged in Italy in the late 1300s as an elite group of intellectuals charged with the administrative, diplomatic, and **rhetorical** functions of the cities and the Church. They became teachers as well, training humanists like themselves, both Italian and foreign, for literary and practical careers; and training the children of wealthy patricians and powerful rulers who were persuaded that the skills taught by the humanists groomed intelligent and capable leaders.

While performing their various official tasks, the humanists also labored to recover Classical texts and their forgotten meanings. Those texts, in turn, took on new life as the humanists employed these Classical forms in order to inquire about the cosmos, the self, and society.

***Vittore Carpaccio,* Saint Augustine in his Study, 1460–c.1526:** *Surrounded by his books, his pens, his votive candles, and a lap dog, in a magnificent Renaissance setting, the fourth-century saint, Augustine, attends to a voice or vision from the divine realm. The painting is intended to convey the humanist ideal of the fulfillment the scholar achieves in the pursuit of the life of the mind.* (Scuola di S. Giorgio degli Schiavoni, Venice)

Recovering the Past

The humanists gathered the books of the ancient Greco-Roman world to master its languages. The book-hunters, such as Poggio Bracciolini, exemplify those who learned to understand the ancient past. Like all humanists, they had a mastery of Latin and sense of history that gave them access to a culture distant from theirs in time and outlook. Fewer humanists acquired Greek, but their contributions, too, were essential.

Poggio found the manuscript of Quintilian's *The Training of an Orator* in the monastery of Saint Gall, in Switzerland, not far from the city of Constance, where high-ranking prelates gathered in council discussed church unity and the threat of heresy. But these were not the matters that concerned Poggio and his friends, secretaries in attendance on Pope John XXIII (an "antipope," deposed in 1415). In search of lost books, they scoured the libraries of venerable monasteries. In such expeditions not only Quintilian's work but those of other Roman authors were brought to light. Humanist book-hunters "rescued" Cicero from bondage, and "discovered" the theologian Lactantius, the philosopher Lucretius, the architect Vitruvius, the novelist Petronius, the grammarian Priscian, and the playwright Plautus.

In fact, this process of discovery was begun much earlier, as *How Many* on p. 379 shows. Two generations before the rescue of Quintilian, the poet Petrarch (Francesco Petrarca; 1304–1374) had already launched the recovery of antiquity: its texts, its artifacts and monuments, its mental world. Petrarch was the third of three fourteenth-century Italian authors, known to their fellow Florentines as the three "crowns" of literary culture. The others were Dante and Boccaccio (see Chapter 12). All three mined antiquity for models of excellence in human behavior and for insight into the purpose of human life. Of these, Petrarch especially understood the passions that moved those ancient figures and found in them an unsurpassed greatness of spirit. In the preface to his collection of biographies entitled *On Great Men*, Petrarch explained that only the ancients, not his contemporaries, were great. The lives of the latter are material for "satire, not history," he wrote; if they won fame, it was only because they were lucky.

So deep a bond did Petrarch feel with the men of antiquity that occasionally he spoke to them directly.

He addressed letters dated from "the world above" to Cicero, Seneca, Quintilian, Vergil, and Homer, in the realm of the dead. He apologized to Homer (see Chapter 4) for intruding on his time: "I realize how very far removed you are, and I fear lest it may be annoying to you to read so lengthy a letter in the dim light of the lower world." For this Renaissance author, the Greek poet seemed still to be alive.

Petrarch knew Homer by reputation only, for he could not read Greek. He had tried to learn it, without success. Greek manuscripts—including the works of Plato—sat on his shelves, admired but unread. Petrarch's friend the scholar and storyteller Giovanni Boccaccio (1313–1375) also longed to know Greek, but failed. During the 1390s, the visit of the Byzantine scholar and diplomat Manuel Chrysoloras (1350–1415) spurred in Italy the successful study of that ancient tongue. The Greek works that are read in translation today were first made available through the efforts of Renaissance scholars to learn a forgotten language.

Knowledge of Classical Greek had largely disappeared from western Christian Europe after the collapse of Roman hegemony; the modern Greek used by some Italian merchants in commercial dealings was quite a different language. Although some Greek works were known in Latin translation, original Greek texts were not studied in medieval Europe outside of Byzantium and Islamic Spain. If parts of Quintilian, Cicero, and Tacitus were "missing" during the Middle Ages—Latin works on history, on philosophy, on rhetoric—even more deeply "lost" were the tragedies, orations, histories, and dialogues of such Greek authors as Euripides, Demosthenes, Plato, and Thucydides. Like the Latin volumes, these were missing from the shelves of monastery libraries. Had they been available, few people in Europe could have read them.

Even the Latin of the ancients was difficult for medieval scholars. Classical Latin was fluent and complex, whereas contemporary Latin employed a workaday vocabulary and simplified grammar. It was suitable for contracts and treaties, brief communications, handbooks and dictionaries, summaries and lists. But the scribes of courts and abbeys could not fully comprehend the texts of the orator Cicero, let alone the elaborate prose of the historian Tacitus. Scholars based in Italy's busy cities, immersed in the flow of ideas and languages, would in time learn to write the Latin of Cicero, and understand the dense structure of Tacitus.

The culture and traditions of antiquity also were strange to medieval readers. The names of the gods and goddesses, heroines and heroes were perplexing, the names even of the rivers and mountains a mystery. Moreover, the dominance of Christian ideals and images posed a barrier to the understanding of the pre-Christian past. The ideals and the style of Classical Greece and Rome had vanished from memory. These ancient values were to be reborn (as forgotten books were recovered) through the efforts of the Italian humanists.

WHO'S WHO

Renaissance Humanists

Petrarch (Francesco Petrarca, 1304–1374) one of the earliest and foremost humanists; among his many works are letters to dead authors as well as poems.

Leonardo Bruni (1370–1444) papal secretary and chancellor of Florence; author of (among many other works) *Panegyric on Florence* and *On Studies and Letters*.

Poggio Bracciolini (1381–1459) papal secretary and chancellor of Florence; bookhunter; author of *On Avarice* and *On Nobility*.

Francesco Barbaro (1390–1454) Venetian nobleman and author of *On Marriage*.

Giannozzo Manetti (1396–1459) Florentine diplomat; defender of the "dignity of man."

Leon Battista Alberti (1404–1472) Florentine exile; architect and art theorist; author of (among other works) *On the Family*.

Lorenzo Valla (1407–1457) expert textual critic, who exposed the forged Donation of Constantine and argued for a new Christian ethic based on the principle of pleasure.

Isotta Nogarola (1418–1466) author of *Dialogue on the Equal or Unequal Sin of Adam and Eve*, letters and orations.

Marsilio Ficino (1433–1499) son of the physician of Cosimo de' Medici; philosopher, scholar, and translator of Plato.

Giovanni Pico della Mirandola (1463–1494) philosopher who argued the oneness of all truth; he sought to defend publicly the truth of 900 philosophical theses; silenced by a church commission.

The Humanist Program

Besides reading and rereading the Classics, the humanists taught others to read them as well. For those who found the reading difficult, they wrote commentaries. For those who could not learn Latin and Greek, they translated the originals into Italian, French, English, German, and Spanish. These translations provided the vernacular languages of modern Europe with a wealth of new concepts and images, forgotten forms and genres.

By making ancient ideas accessible to contemporary readers, the humanists were the first modern scholars. Through their labors, the surviving fruit of antiquity was transmitted to the modern world. They learned to write history from Classical authors, becoming the first secular historians of Europe. Their scholarly activity is the bedrock of modern literature, modern philosophy and theology, and even modern science.

Renaissance humanists were also creators of new values, suitable for a new age. They lived in a dynamic society centered on cities built on commerce and industry, and they served its leaders. They were secretaries to the merchants of Florence and Venice and to the princes of Milan and Ferrara. Or they were high-ranking patricians, who in their leisure time read and composed works for others to read. Or they were (less frequently) the sisters or daughters of those patricians. They were the teachers of these secretaries, these noblemen, and these merchants. The humanist culture of the Renaissance inevitably reflects the values of the elite society that nurtured it.

For medieval scholars, the residents of cloisters and universities, **contemplation** had been the ideal: quiet and solitary thought. Many humanists shared that outlook—among them Petrarch, who championed the superiority of the solitary life (although decidedly not the monastic one). More often, however, Renaissance humanists focused on the ideas necessary for the active life, and on the moral concerns of city-dwellers. They sought the kind of practical knowledge useful to men of affairs—merchants, bankers, politicians. These humanists admired the active more than the contemplative life. This dimension of their work had been labeled by later scholars "**civic humanism**"—humanism adapted to life in a city. "Civic humanism" was an important dimension, but only one dimension, of Renaissance humanism, which also pursued problems defined by medieval thinkers.

Philosophical Dimensions of Humanism

The perspective of the "civic humanist" is evident in Renaissance discussions of the nature of the human being. Traditionalists viewed human beings as sinful. The humanists countered that God created human beings "in His image and likeness" and declared them "good" (Genesis 1:26–27, 31): only a little less than angels. Herein the humanists proposed the notion of the "dignity of man", as shown in *Witnesses* on p. 358 and *Windows On*, p. 359. Behind the creation of that notion lay another kind of revolution: the humanist revolt against dialectic and the supremacy of Aristotelian metaphysics in favor of rhetoric and the espousal of Plato's ideas.

"How does man resemble God?" asked Florentine humanist, scholar, and statesman Gianozzo Manetti (1396–1459). The answer: in his activity. Human beings freely enjoy and manipulate the beauty that God has bestowed upon them and imitate the Creator in their own creations. Consider, urged Manetti, what men have produced: "all homes, all towns, all cities, finally all buildings in the world"; paintings, sculpture, arts, sciences, discoveries, "all the different kinds of languages and literatures." In such creativity lies the worth of humanity—its "dignity."

Manetti's views exemplify the strand of Renaissance thought that valued will over intellect, doing over knowing. If will precedes intellect, then the discipline of "rhetoric," which persuades people to do the good, is to be preferred to philosophy, which simply informs them of the truth. Truth acquires life only when communicated in the vivid language that can move the will. As Petrarch proclaimed, "It is better to will the good than to know the truth." Thus poetry, which teaches "other men to speak," wrote another humanist, is—rather than philosophy—the "most fertile mother of all knowledge."

The philosophy the humanists opposed was that of the medieval schoolmen: the clerics who taught theology and philosophy in the universities, and wrought the vast compendia ("summations" or *summae*) of all that was known. The intricate demonstrations of Scholasticism repelled the humanists. But they did not oppose all philosophy. Renaissance thinkers, in fact, rescued from ignorance (as they saw it) the two greatest of the ancient philosophers: Plato and Aristotle (see Chapter 4).

It was from Cicero that the humanists first learned of Plato's immense importance. Then, soon after 1400, the first generation of humanists trained in Greek (largely through the efforts of Chrysoloras) made direct contact with this most profound philosopher. A few years later, Greek scholars laden with books and skills began migrating to Italy from Constantinople, around the time of its fall to the Turks in 1453. Now the way was prepared for the heroic work of Marsilio Ficino (1433–1499): the publication of all of Plato's surviving works.

Son of the physician to Cosimo de' Medici (1389–1464), the de facto ruler of Florence, Ficino acquired the mastery of Greek (as well as the philosophical and humanistic disciplines) necessary for this massive enterprise. Between 1463 and 1469, he translated the text of Plato into Latin, adding his own valuable commentaries to some works. In 1484 the work was printed (thanks to the recent development of the printing press in Germany) for circulation throughout Europe. Ficino and friends recreated Plato's Academy in their gatherings and conversations. Its members discussed serious ideas at lively *symposia*, in imitation of Greek models, and regularly celebrated their hero's supposed birthday.

With the revival of Platonism came the rebirth also of Neoplatonism, a philosophical school of late antiquity. More mystical than Platonic philosophy, Neoplatonism speculated about the unity of the cosmos and the possibility for the human intellect of perfect identification with the divine. As they had in the early centuries C.E., such ideas both resembled and departed from orthodox Christian views of humanity, divinity, and the natural world. They would have a profound and lasting impact upon developments over the next three centuries in science and literature.

Unlike Plato, most of whose works were not read in medieval Europe, Aristotle had circulated in Europe since the twelfth century, in translations from the original Greek or from Arabic versions. These medieval translations, used by the schoolmen in constructing a Christian philosophy, the humanists scorned as incorrect and inelegant.

Now the translation of Aristotle was undertaken again—this time by humanists expert in Greek. Other scholars strove to rescue the master from Latin altogether. One Venetian humanist taught Aristotle in Greek, hoping "to converse" with Aristotle "as though he were alive and in our midst." Between 1495 and 1498, the printer Aldo Manuzio (also called, in Latin, Aldus Manutius; c. 1450–1515) published in five volumes all of Aristotle's works in the original Greek.

WITNESSES

Defining the Self

Among the many projects and themes of the humanists, one has fascinated contemporary and later audiences: that of the "dignity of man," the worthiness of the human being. The humanists Leon Battista Alberti and Giovanni Pico della Mirandola here address that issue. Alberti talks of the striving for excellence that he understands to be the main task of the human being. Pico creates a mythic creation story, based on the Biblical book of Genesis, to isolate a central characteristic of the human condition: free will, the freedom to choose how to act—and to bear the consequences of one's actions.

Leon Battista Alberti sees life as a race in which merit and effort win honor and glory—and idleness and incapacity win shame (1443): Let us suppose a great regatta were being organized in the harbor of Venice, a display of many ships with a multitude of participants. Suppose you were the captain of one of the ships. ... You would strive mightily to reach the goal, where the garlands and trophies of victory were stored and where the prizes and honors were given out to the winning contestants. You would want your ship to share with no more than two others in the first three prizes. ... The other participants in the race, however, would remain unknown. No one would speak of them. These contestants might perhaps have been better off if they had remained on land, taking no active part. They might have been judging, laughing, criticizing the slowness and tardiness of others as much as they liked instead of having, so to speak, shown only languorous enthusiasm in the race. As it is, they find themselves far from admired, indeed they are generally mocked. In the race of human life and the general contest for honor and glory, ... it is best to hope and desire and fight wholeheartedly for a place among the first, if not the first place. One must surpass entirely that obscure and forgotten crowd behind. One must struggle with all the force and cunning at his disposal for a certain fame and a measure of glory.

(Leon Battista Alberti, *On the Family*, 1443; from R. N. Watkins, 1989)

Giovanni Pico della Mirandola explains how each man determines his own nature (1486): *[After God had created all other creatures of sea and land, he turned to the creation of the human being, whose nature he left indeterminate, totally at the disposition of the individual's free will.]* At last the best of artisans ordained that the creature to whom He had been able to give nothing proper to himself should have joint possession of whatever had been peculiar to each of the different kinds of being. He therefore took man as a creature of indeterminate nature and, assigning him a place in the middle of the world, addressed him thus: "Neither a fixed abode not a form that is thine alone nor any function peculiar to thyself have we given thee, Adam, to the end that according to thy longing and according to thy judgment thou mayest have and possess what abode, what form, and what functions thou thyself shalt desire. The nature of all other beings is limited and constrained within the bounds of laws prescribed by Us. Thou, constrained by no limits, in accordance with thine own free will, in whose hand We have placed thee, shalt ordain for thyself the limits of thy nature. We have set thee at the world's center that thou mayest from thence more easily observe whatever is in the world. We have made thee neither of heaven nor of earth, neither mortal nor immortal, so that with freedom of choice and with honor, as though the making of thyself, thou mayest fashion thyself in whatever shape thou shalt prefer. Thou shalt have the power to degenerate into the lower forms of life, which are brutish. Thou shalt have the power, of thy soul's judgment, to be reborn into the higher forms, which are divine."

(Giovanni Pico della Mirandola, *Oration on the Dignity of Man*, 1486; from E. Cassirer, et al, 1989, trs. E. L. Forbes)

The Dignity of Man

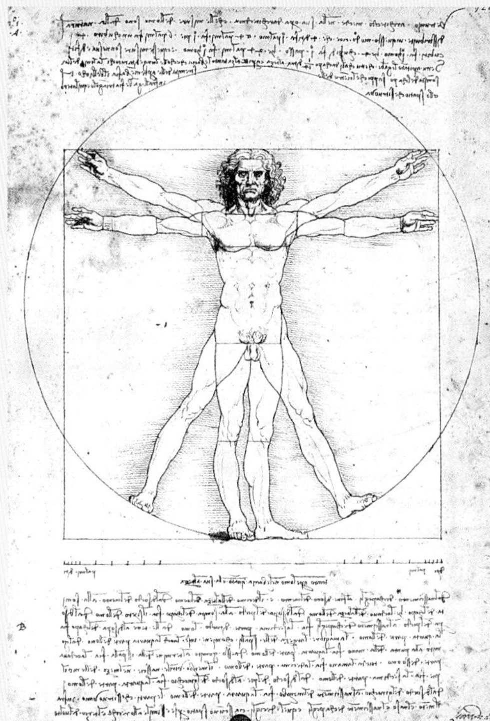

Leonardo da Vinci,* Man in a Circle and a Square, *c. 1485

Michelangelo,* Rebellious Slave, *1513

Piero della Francesca,* Resurrection, *Sansepolcro, 1450s

The notion of human dignity was realized in Renaissance art just as it was in Renaissance humanism, as can be seen in the few examples offered here.

Leonardo da Vinci's study of the human body (above left) shows the perfect figure defining the limits of the square and the circle, and of the perfect cosmos these inscribed figures represent.

In this late-1450s fresco of the Resurrection *(above) in the Town Hall at Sansepolcro, Piero della Francesca depicts Christ as a superb human form.*

The Rebellious Slave *sculpted by Michelangelo (left) for the tomb of Julius II has, as a human being, the consciousness of freedom that drives him to struggle free from the imprisoning block of stone.*

(top left: Accademia, Venice; right: Pinacoteca Comunale, Sansepolcro; left: Louvre, Paris)

To continue your investigation of this topic, please go to www.prenhall.com/king for the related **WINDOWS** on the **WEB** activity

Humanism and Society

The humanists also studied their own social world. As they did so, they adapted traditional concepts of moral virtue to the context of urban society. Moral philosophy was one of the disciplines of the "studies of humanity" promoted by the humanists. In their hands, moral philosophy turned to issues of pressing social concern: the limits of avarice; the determinants of social status; the goal of political action; the nature of the family; the role of women.

Poggio Bracciolini posed an economic ethos unthinkable in the Middle Ages in his **dialogue** *On Avarice*. Christianity, in theory, urged the value of poverty over wealth. Medieval preachers (not all of them, but those whom Poggio mocked) warned darkly about the evil of greed. But Renaissance culture was built on the Renaissance city; and the Renaissance city was built—if not on greed—certainly on credit, investment, interest, and profit.

The dialogue form, a favorite device of humanists based on the Classical genre, permitted an author to present two or more competing viewpoints and argue for each plausibly without committing himself to any explicit (or unpopular) point of view. Poggio uses the device to advantage, allowing different speakers to expound traditional and modern arguments about the acquisition of wealth. He programs one provocative speaker to counter the Christian consensus by pointing out the good side of greed. Unlike lust (always harmful, he maintains) greed is sometimes beneficial. "Avarice does not subvert the soul, upset the mind, or impede the study of literature and the acquisition of knowledge." Only the rich can benefit the communities in which they live. Without the wealth accumulated by ambitious men, willing to spend it, "No one would build churches or colonnades; all artistic activity would cease, and confusion would result ... if everyone were satisfied with only enough for himself. ... What are cities, states, provinces, and kingdoms, ... if not the workshops of avarice?"

Poggio's dialogue *On Nobility* boldly addressed a social issue of immense significance for centuries to come: by what right do some men rule over others?

WITNESSES

On Studies

A central concern for humanists was the structure of the curriculum of studies for young people. Should they be oriented towards practical, mercantile, clerical, or bureaucratic careers? Or curricula be aimed at broadening the mind and developing the character of young people, male and even (a daring project for the age) female? The humanists opted for the latter, developing the curriculum of the "studies of humanity," which we would today call, with some approximation, the "liberal arts." Here Pier Paolo Vergerio advocates such a program of studies for his pupils, and Leonardo Bruni does so for a prominent noblewoman.

Pier Paolo Vergerio advocates a liberal education and the value of books (c. 1404): We call those studies *liberal* which are worthy of a free man; those studies by which we attain and practice virtue and wisdom; that education which calls forth, trains and develops those highest gifts of body and of mind which ennoble men, and which are rightly judged to rank next in dignity to virtue only. For to a vulgar temper gain and pleasure are the one aim of existence, to a lofty nature, moral worth and fame. It is, then, of the highest importance that even from infancy this aim, this effort, should constantly be kept alive in growing minds. For I may affirm with fullest conviction that we shall not have attained wisdom in our later years unless in our earliest we have sincerely entered upon the search. ...

In [books] are contained the records of the great achievements of men; the wonders of Nature; the works of Providence in the past, the key to her secrets of the future. And, most important of all, this Knowledge is not liable to decay. With a picture, an inscription, a coin, books share a kind of immortality. In all these memory is, as it were, made permanent. ...

How bright a household is the family of books! ... In their company is no noise, no greed, no self-will; at a word they speak to you, at a word they are still; to all our requests their response is ever ready and to the point. Books indeed are a higher—a wider, more tenacious—memory, a store-house which is the common property of us all.

(Pier Paolo Vergerio, *De ingenuis moribus*, c. 1404; from W. H. Woodward, E. F. Rice, Jr., rev. ed., 1964)

Leonardo Bruni advises Battista Malatesta to gain knowledge and verbal proficiency (1424): To sum up what I have endeavoured to set forth. ... Proficiency in literary form, not accompanied by broad acquaintance with facts and truths, is a barren attainment; whilst information however vast, which lacks all grace of expression, would seem to be put under a bushel or partly thrown away. Indeed, one may fairly ask what advantage it is to profess profound and varied learning if one cannot convey it in language worthy of the subject. Where, however, this double capacity exists—breadth of learning and grace of style—we allow the highest title to distinction and to abiding fame. If we review the great names of ancient literature, Plato, Democritus, Aristotle, Theophrastus, Varro, Cicero, Seneca, Augustine, Jerome ... we shall find it hard to say whether we admire more their attainments or their literary power.

(Leonardo Bruni, *De studiis et litteris*, 1424; ibid, 1964)

Traditionally in Europe, the nobility was defined by ability to bear arms, a capacity linked to birth in a privileged order of warriors. Poggio urged a new standard. Only those who are virtuous—wise, learned, productive, committed—are noble. His arguments would reappear many times in the social revolutions of later centuries.

So would those that Alamanno Rinuccini (1426–1504) expressed in his dialogue *On Liberty*. Where Poggio argued that only the wise man is noble, Rinuccini argued that only the free man can be wise. Exiled by the Medici family which had trapped Florence in its snares (as he saw it), Rinuccini argued that despotism spelled the diminution of the human spirit. Liberty is "potential or capacity": only in freedom can human greatness realize itself in creative action.

Humanists also reexamined that institution fundamental to all other social forms: the family. Francesco Barbaro (1390–1454) advised young men about the selection of a wife in his treatise *On Marriage*. She was to be chosen for her virtue, a quality considered more important than beauty or wealth. Only a virtuous woman could competently perform her responsibilities: from unquestioning love and support of her husband to proper decorum and the competent administration of the household staff. The dialogue *On the Family*, by the humanist and architect Leon Battista Alberti (1404–1472) emphasized the critical role of the father. It was he who guided the destinies of all family members, the monarch of his own little kingdom.

These humanist experts on the family were hardly sympathetic to women's own claims for productive roles and for due recognition of achievement. Most humanists, like most intellectuals of the Middle Ages and later eras, largely ignored women. There were exceptions. The educator Vittorino da Feltre (1378–1446) counted at least one young woman among his pupils: Cecilia Gonzaga, daughter of the Marquis of Mantua, who at age ten entertained visitors with her recitations in Greek and Latin. Leonardo Bruni (1370–1444) and Lauro Quirini (c. 1420–c. 1475), in letters advising two women in their studies, assumed that intelligent women could master the same skills as intelligent men. For the most part, however, women made their own way.

Some women, prodigies of Renaissance culture, acquired the difficult skills that Bruni and Quirini outlined, and joined the ranks of the humanists. A handful, no more than a score, these learned women came mostly from ruling or patrician families—often that specialized in learning or even in learning specifically for women. Four women stand out: the Veronese noblewoman Isotta Nogarola (1418–1466); the Brescian Laura Cereta (1469–1499), daughter of a physician (see *Witnesses*, p. 375); the Venetian Cass-andra Fedele (1465–1558), from a family of cultivated citizens; Olimpia Morata (1525–1555), daughter of a Ferrarese court humanist and émigré spouse of a young German Lutheran. Authors of letters, poems, orations, and treatises, they rank with the male humanists of the day.

Humanists skilled in Latin and sometimes Greek, knowledgeable in the literature of the past and conscious of current affairs, reshaped the culture of Italy. But they were not the only creators of the Italian Renaissance. They were joined by other thinkers, by artists and musicians, and by their patrons. Important ones appear in *Who's Who* on pp. 366 and 369.

ITALIAN RENAISSANCE SETTINGS

The Italian cities, where the city clock set a brisk pace and gold reigned instead of kings, were the first home of the Renaissance (see Chapter 11, 12, and Map 13.1). Here the humanists who launched the revival of ancient learning were employed as secretaries, administrators, and teachers. Here princes and bureaucrats hired architects to create buildings reminiscent of those of the ancients; artists to breathe new life into the statues and paintings that filled those buildings; and poets, playwrights, and composers to educate a new generation in the refined tastes of a renewed culture.

These patrons invested their wealth in the new culture not simply to create beauty but also to advance their own interests. The brilliant creations of Renaissance scholars, artists, and writers lent legitimacy to the rule of city councils and upstart princes in a Europe elsewhere ruled by pedigreed noblemen and monarchs. The cities that had begun their careers as laboratories of civic freedom became the stage on which a prince, with a cadre of artists and intellectuals in tow, enacted his ambitions and displayed his power. In due course, the forms thus created in the small Italian cities would be adopted by the nobles and monarchs of the great nations of Europe to enhance their authority.

The following pages survey the manifestations of Renaissance culture in two independent cities, in a series of the greater and the lesser princely courts, and in the papal court at Rome.

Florence: Capital of the Renaissance

"What city, not merely in Italy, but in all the world, is more securely placed within its circle of walls, more proud in its [palaces], more bedecked with churches, more beautiful in its architecture, more imposing in its gates, richer in piazzas, happier in its wide streets, greater in its people, more glorious in its citizenry, more inexhaustible in wealth, more fertile in its fields?" So wrote one humanist chancellor of Florence in praise of his city. Though it measured little more than a mile (1.6 km.) across, Florence was the capital of Renaissance civilization in Italy.

Many reasons have been offered for the preeminence of Florence during the Renaissance. It was a city of merchants—confident and wealthy. It was large: with some 100,000 residents prior to the Black Death in 1348 (though it sank thereafter to less than half that size), one of the largest cities in Europe. It was conscious, if distantly, of a Roman past. It was a republic, with a record of a successful democratic revolution. In addition—and inexplicably—Florence and its environs produced more of the creators of Renaissance culture than any other single setting.

Beginning around 1300, the merchants of Florence diverted some of the profits from foreign trade, banking, and cloth manufacture to the beautification of their city. In a spate of constructive energy, they built, replaced, and refurbished churches, guildhalls, palaces, marketplaces, and bridges. Two central zones were carved out of the fabric of the medieval city: the area around the palace where the city magistrates met—the Palazzo della Signoria (now called the Palazzo Vecchio, "Old Palace"), and the complex surrounding the cathedral, or Duomo. These new urban centers, respectively political and ecclesiastical, lent majesty and purpose to the jumbled stone structures of Florence.

A piazza, or open square, was constructed in front of the remodeled Palazzo Vecchio—a clear statement of governmental power in a city where open space was rare. A new cathedral and freestanding *campanile*, or bell tower, were constructed on the site of the old cathedral, across from the baptistry, the older, freestanding building where all Florentine infants were baptized. The latter edifice was refurbished with three sets of sculpted bronze doors—two of which were executed in the fifteenth century by Lorenzo Ghiberti (1378–1455). The commission for the north

Map 13.1 Renaissance in Italy, 1300–1570: *From 1300–1570 in Italy, artists and intellectuals worked to fuse the Christian tradition (originating in antiquity but developed during the Middle Ages) with the Greco-Roman tradition in a movement fundamental for the later evolution of the modern civilization of the West: the Renaissance. This map shows the principal places that are associated with the named important figures.*

The Competition Panels

The Sacrifice of Isaac: *Shown here are the two panels, completed 1401–1403, submitted by Brunelleschi and Ghiberti in the competition for the commission to sculpt the bronze doors of the Florentine baptistry. While both represent "The Sacrifice of Isaac," Ghiberti's depiction (above right) is not only more fluent than Brunelleschi's (above left), but shows the would-be sacrificial victim Isaac as a magnificent human figure, honorable in his readiness to suffer without fear: another emblem of human dignity.* (Museo Nazionale [Bargello], Florence)

door was won by Ghiberti in a competition with Filippo Brunelleschi (1377–1446). Each contestant created a sample panel (see above) representing "The Sacrifice of Isaac," both of them powerful images in which the characters are treated naturalistically. But whereas in Brunelleschi's panel Isaac is shown crouching and twisted, with his father clutching his head, preparing to strike the blow, in Ghiberti's panel the boy is shown as a splendid nude, accepting his fate with Classical dignity; indeed, all the figures in Ghiberti's panel are depicted with the grace and restrained eloquence that would characterize Renaissance art. After completing the north door, Ghiberti went on to create the even more magnificent east door, known as the "Gates of Paradise."

Italian architecture had never quite abandoned Classical forms during the Middle Ages. Although many Gothic-style buildings were constructed, the Romanesque style persisted; and in Florence, by the late eleventh century, Classical motifs such as attached columns and pediments had begun to reappear. This process accelerated during the fifteenth century. Palaces displaying elements of Classical style—those of such leading families as the Medici, Rucellai, Strozzi, and Pitti—replaced the old houses in the city center. The Medici Palace shows the cautious approach of its architect Michelozzo (1396–1472). In its basic form—massive and somewhat forbidding, with roughly cut stone on the first story—it recalls the traditional forms of civic architecture. Yet the building's symmetry, the graceful arches of its courtyard, and its imposing cornice announce the presence of a Classical sensibility.

Churches, too, acquired new elements of Classical style. The Gothic church of Santa Maria Novella was given a Classically inspired façade by Leon Battista Alberti. The contrasting interior and exterior of the church illustrate the process by which the revived antique style of the Renaissance grew out of and overlaid earlier styles. The churches of San Lorenzo and Santo Spirito, designed by Filippo Brunelleschi, were fully conceived as Classical buildings.

The same architect erected over the cathedral crossing (of **nave** and **transepts**) the splendid dome which dominates the city's skyline. Spanning a space of 138 feet (42 m.) in diameter, it was an achievement of great technical, as well as artistic, ingenuity. With the completion of the Duomo (as cathedrals are called in Italy) in 1436, Florence was visually, as well as intellectually, a Renaissance city.

Inside these new and remodeled structures, a new style of painting portrayed the world in the language preferred by patrons of the arts whose tastes were Classical and whose vision of humanity was confident. Artists rendered human figures in three dimensions (not the traditional two), engaged in motion, seemingly inhabiting a real space behind the flat panels and frames in which they were contained. These figures stood in backgrounds familiar from contemporary life: kitchens, gardens, bedrooms, piazzas, and battlefields, as the Uccello's painting below shows. The recently invented science of **perspective** made this realism possible. Artists now knew how to represent three-dimensional bodies on flat surfaces. In subject matter, most Renaissance art remained religious, depicting scenes from the Bible and the lives of the saints, although subjects from Classical mythology and even portraits of living people were beginning to appear.

Patrons of the arts, the rulers of Florence also supported literature and humanism. They read the works of Dante, Petrarch, and Boccaccio. They hired humanists to teach their sons and, sometimes, their daughters. They supported the humanists in their first discoveries and creations, and funded chairs of humanist learning at the local university. Some of them even became humanists themselves: patrician amateurs rank among Florence's most distinguished intellectuals.

In their role as government officials, the city's merchant princes employed humanists to record their debates, to compose letters destined to be read in foreign assemblies, and to formulate documents fixing the terms of war and peace. The chancellors, or chief secretaries, of Renaissance Florence were among Italy's foremost humanists. Well rewarded by their employers, they were also among the city's wealthiest and most important citizens.

The heads of the Medici family, who directed Florence from behind the scenes from 1433 to 1494, were the city's leading patrons of arts and learning. Surrounding themselves with books, paintings, and monuments and philosophers, they thus claimed a legitimacy that they could not claim by birth.

Cosimo de' Medici (1389–1464), the first of his family to assume leadership in Florence, displayed his commitment to Classical scholarship by supporting Ficino's translation of Plato. He also commissioned the rebuilding of the church of San Lorenzo, as well as the monastery of San Marco (where he housed his own remarkable collection of books, making them accessible to the public and thus creating Europe's first public library), and his own family palace. In addition, Cosimo and his son Piero employed several of the sculptors and painters who created some of the most glorious treasures of Western art, including Donatello (1386–1466) and Fra Angelico (Giovanni da Fiesole; c. 1395–1455).

Lucrezia Tornabuoni (1425–1482), wife of Piero de' Medici (r. 1464–1469), was herself a talented poet and enthusiastic patron. Perhaps it was she who inspired her son Lorenzo in his adventures of the spirit. Lorenzo de' Medici (1449–1492), called "the Magnificent," wrote excellent poetry. The brisk lines

Renaissance Style: Perspective

Paolo Uccello, The Battle of San Romano: *Uccello was one of the first painters to apply the theory of perspective to his works. This panel painting, c. 1445, is more a study of how forms (human and equine bodies, ornaments and weapons) inhabit space than it is a depiction of a battle.* (National Gallery, London)

Renaissance Style: Myth

***Sandro Botticelli,* Primavera:** *Botticelli borrows figures and themes from ancient mythology in this painting, c. 1482, to depict a hauntingly lovely scene.* (Uffizi, Florence)

and charming rhymed pattern of one famous lyric passage by Lorenzo call up sensations of love's joy, the swift march of time, and death's advent:

Quant' è bella giovinezza,	How beautiful is youth,
Che si fugge tuttavia!	But it vanishes, utterly—
Chi vuol esser lieto, sia:	If you wish to be happy, be happy today;
Di doman non c'è certezza	Of tomorrow, there is no certainty.

Lorenzo brought a special flamboyance to the role of the Medici as directors of artistic endeavor. Like his father, Piero, and grandfather, Cosimo, Lorenzo promoted the major artists of the city (though he could not always afford to employ them)—among others, the remarkable Sandro Botticelli (1445–1510) and, in his youth, Michelangelo Buonarroti (1475–1564).

Influenced by the Platonism of Ficino's circle, Botticelli translated into form and color the pagan myths that the humanists unearthed from Classical literature. Even the esoteric messages found behind these myths by philosophers informed some of Botticelli's works. For example, in his renowned painting *Primavera* ("Springtime"), illustrated above, the lovely maiden at the center may represent a Christianized deity or a rational principle, perhaps "humanitas" itself, the human ideal. Contrasting with Botticelli's complexity is Michelangelo's statue of *David*, commissioned by the republican government that replaced the Medici after Lorenzo's death. In its simplicity, its heroic nudity, its confidence, it is a majestic statement of contemporary moral and aesthetic values, and perhaps the most remarkable monument of the age.

Reviewing the Medici family's enormous expenditures on **patronage** projects Lorenzo concluded that they amounted to an "incredible sum"—663,755 florins (at a time when a worker might earn 20 florins per year, or a university professor 100). It was well worth the expense to Lorenzo to acquire the glory reflected by the buildings and paintings and works of literature this money purchased. "Nor would I complain about this, for though many a man would like to have even part of that sum in his purse I think it gave great luster to the state and this money seems to be well spent and I am very satisfied."

Venice: "La Serenissima"

Unlike Florence, in which the rediscovery of Classical learning and art created a great cultural ferment, Venice adopted Renaissance ideals with caution.

Seeking to maintain a high standard of civic discipline, the rulers of "La Serenissima" ("the Most Serene" republic) imposed firm control on those who forged its intellectual culture. As a result, its humanists and its artists, the works they wrote, and even the subjects they painted, seem faceless compared to those of her sister republic. But even so, Venetian Renaissance art is graced with extraordinary beauty.

Venice's visual tradition was first Byzantine and then Gothic. As late as the fifteenth century, Venetian palaces along the Grand Canal boasted such features as quatrefoil (four-leaf clover-shaped) windows and balconies with lacy Gothic tracery—at a time when Classical forms had gained hold in Florentine architecture. The monuments to Venice's self-concept (the Doge's Palace, the basilica of San Marco, the showiest canal façades) posed an unashamed medley of forms—whimsical, exotic, echoes of ancient Constantinople or the French court. The element of fantasy in these forms was enhanced by Venice's physical setting, seemingly floating in mist and water, as described in *Witnesses* on p. 331. Eventually, however, Classical shapes began to rise above the Venetian Lagoon and along the canals—imposing new palaces and churches. Two of the latter, the churches of San Giorgio Maggiore and the Redentore, by Andrea Palladio (1508–1580), rank among the great masterpieces of Western architecture.

In painting, as in architecture, a Venetian Renaissance style evolved slowly. It was finally realized by Giovanni Bellini (c. 1430–1516), who achieved the transformation from Byzantine stiffness with a focus not on the manipulation of space and form, as in Florence, but rather on mood and feeling. The differences can be seen in Bellini's representation of the *Pietà*, shown on p. 367, which depicts the mourning over the crucified Christ by his faithful mother and his beloved disciple John. In Bellini's interpretation of this theme, Jesus has suffered not so much from his wounds as from the pain of knowledge. John turns away, a participant in the anguish of the Savior who now directs outward the wisdom yielded by the experience of death. Mary supports her dead son's hand and face with her own, united with him in body and in spirit. All three figures stand in an open sarcophagus in a ghostly landscape. Bellini's understanding of the central event of the Christian drama is quiet, contained, and profound.

Patronage in Venice was not confined to private or ecclesiastical commissions. The government commissioned works of art to adorn its public spaces: paintings of military victories or historical legend, or of the haughty lion with open book, a politicized symbol of Mark the Evangelist, the city's patron saint and one of its ubiquitous emblems. The walls of the city's *scuole* or "schools" (religious confraternities of non-noble citizens) provided a distinctive setting for some of the most charming paintings of the Renaissance, for example the painting by Gentile Bellini on p. 367.

While Venetian artists adapted themselves to the currents of Renaissance taste, the city's humanists were long bound to the particular ideology of its rulers. Two-thirds of the fifteenth-century Venetian humanists were themselves of noble birth and members of the inner circle of the city's ruling elite. These men promoted humanistic studies particularly of the type that bolstered the reputation of Venice. They themselves produced a respectable corpus of works defending the Venetian nobility, Venetian government, and Venetian values.

Typical of this group is Bernardo Giustiniani (1408–1489), a diplomat and humanist like his father, and the nephew of the city's first patriarch (its leading prelate), the revered ascetic Lorenzo Giustiniani (1380–1456). Giustiniani's *Origin of the City of Venice*

WHO'S WHO

Renaissance Artists

Giotto di Bondone (1267–1337) pioneer of Renaissance artistic style, famed especially for Arena Chapel frescoes.

Filippo Brunelleschi (1377–1446) pioneering architect of the dome of Florence cathedral and the Ospedale degli Innocenti.

Lorenzo Ghiberti (1378–1455) sculptor, winner of competition with Brunelleschi to design the bronze doors of Florence's baptistry.

Donatello (1386–1466) sculptor of *St. George*, *David*, and *Mary Magdalene*.

Fra Angelico (c. 1395–1455) Dominican monk, painter of several fresco cycles, including the *Annunciation*.

Giovanni Bellini (c. 1430–1516) one of the founders of a distinctive Renaissance style in Venetian painting, with a characteristic emphasis on feeling and color.

Sandro Botticelli (1445–1510) painter of lovely mythological scenes, especially *Primavera*.

Leonardo da Vinci (1452–1519) most versatile of Renaissance artists, a painter, sculptor, designer, inventor, scientific draftsman.

Michelangelo Buonarotti (1475–1564) painter, sculptor, architect, known especially for his frescoes in the Vatican's Sistine Chapel.

Raphael (Raffaello Sanzio) (1483–1520) painter known for his lush color and many lovely depictions of the Virgin Mary and Child; with Michelangelo provided the decoration of the Sistine Chapel.

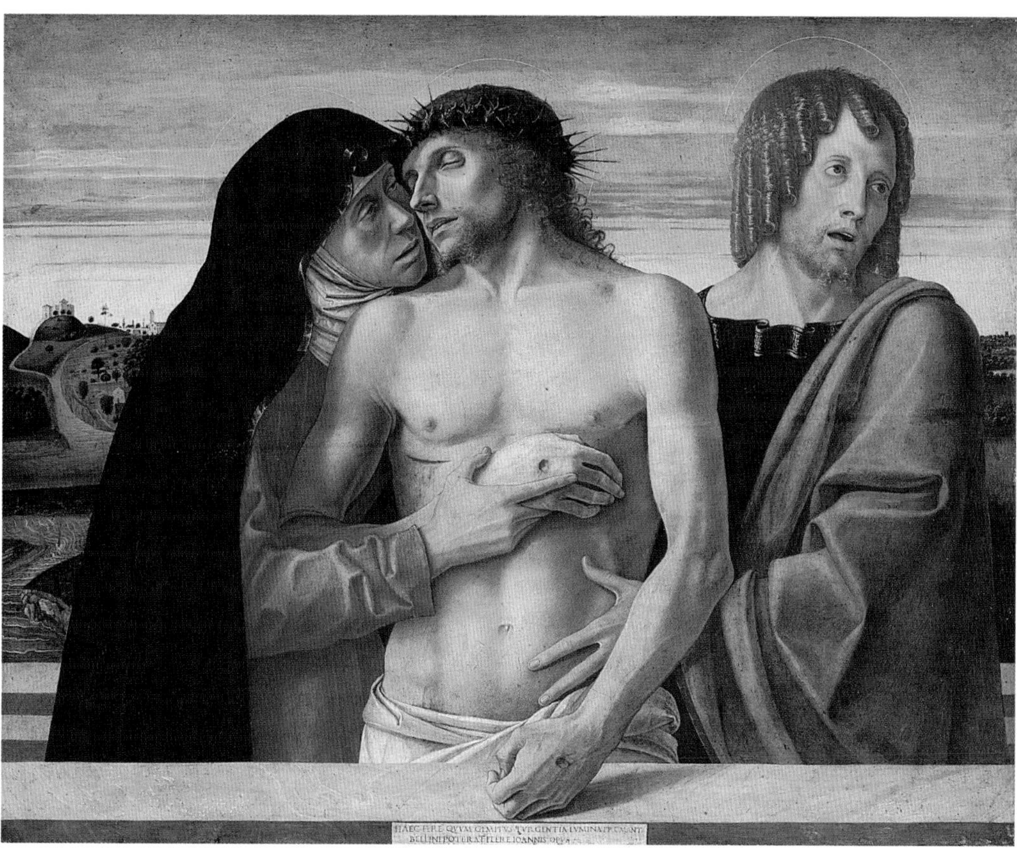

Views from Venice

***Giovanni Bellini,* Dead Christ with Saint John and the Virgin:** *The brothers Giovanni and Gentile Bellini provide different insights into the Venetian experience. This fifteenth-century painting is an intimate and expressive exploration of the emotions of those who first understood the meaning of Jesus' death.* (Pinacoteca di Brera, Milan)

Gentile Bellini,* Procession in the Piazza San Marco** *(above):** *This splendidly executed procession, 1496, is the best of official art—a precise rendering of the leaders of the Venetian state in their hierarchical order, framed by the resplendent space of the city's central square.* (Accademia, Venice)

is at once a fine specimen of humanist historiography and a hymn of praise to the city that both reared and exalted its author. Other humanists collected manuscripts—notably many from the Greek—and arranged for their transcription, circulation, and translation. Two priceless libraries were offered to Venice by foreigners: that of Petrarch (although the donation was never effected) and that of Cardinal John Bessarion (a treasure of Greek texts which form the basis of the city's National Library of Saint Mark).

The new craft of printing found a natural home in this city where learned men from the centers of Italy and Greece circulated more than anywhere else in Italy, and where a cultivated elite read, purchased, funded, lent, and borrowed books. In the 1460s and 1470s, the presses issued forth the Latin classics that had been so rare only two generations earlier. In the shop of the printer Aldo Manuzio, the Greek classics were prepared in unadorned clean type and with unprecedented accuracy.

In the sixteenth century, patrician intellectuals broadened the range of their endeavors to include official history and church reform; the theoretical discussion of mathematics, science, and metaphysics; and the collection of antiquities and rare books. In their "academies," special clubs where they gathered to discuss ideas and the arts, they cultivated the art of polite conversation. Countering this refined society of noble aesthetes was a swelling crowd of newcomers. Foreign and transient writers, editors, book-dealers, and teachers formed another stratum of intellectual life—one that spoke with a brusque voice disruptive of the smooth finish of Venetian culture. This circle included numerous "*poligrafi*," professional writers with sharp and dauntless pens ready for hire, and the female poets Veronica Franco (1546–1591) and Gaspara Stampa (c. 1523–1554). The elegant verse of these two courtesans (as high-status prostitutes were called) displayed not only the play of wit so prized in Venice, but the tension they were bold enough to express between male and female perspectives on love and meaning.

The republics of Florence and Venice were uniquely unfettered in their explorations of thought and form. The cities to be considered next were all centered around courts. Ruled by princes, these cities and city-states produced distinctive cultures, guided in each case by its rulers and their agents. Each would make a unique contribution to the civilization of the Renaissance.

Milan: Culture from Above

The Visconti family, who ruled Milan between 1287 and 1447, were among the first Renaissance despots to enlist intellectuals in their struggles for territorial aggrandizement. Giangaleazzo Visconti, despot, then Duke of Milan (r. 1385–1402) and Florence's fierce opponent, surrounded himself with poets and propagandists. The last of the Visconti died in 1447, and three years later the city surrendered to an illiterate mercenary captain of rare intelligence, Francesco Sforza (r. 1450–1466). This new Duke of Milan gathered about him a staff of well-trained secretaries who performed his intricate diplomacy and rewrote the history of his ascent to power, in prose and verse, in Latin and Greek.

Sforza's successors were less concerned with history and epic than with glamor and display, theater and the hunt. His son Ludovico "il Moro" (r. 1476–1505; called "the Moor," perhaps, because of his dark complexion) presided over a splendid court, adorned above all by the genius of Leonardo da Vinci (1452–1519), artist and scientist, in his own words, a "universal master of creating through his art all the qualities of the forms which nature produces. ..." Painter, sculptor, engineer, architect, and set designer, Leonardo executed all the kinds of commissions that a whimsical patron could make: altarpieces and guns, stage sets that swiveled and spun around, works of art designed for destruction before the next performance. Ludovico was also the patron of the Dominican monastery of Santa Maria delle Grazie, for which Leonardo painted *The Last Supper*.

Naples: Legitimacy for Kings

In 1442 Alfonso V, the first of a line of Aragonese monarchs, seized the throne of Naples, which had long been occupied by German emperors or Frenchmen of royal blood. Like the usurping Sforza dukes of Milan, the kings of Naples sought to establish legitimacy through the cluster of scholars and artists they patronized. Once established in Naples (he already reigned in Sicily and Sardinia), Alfonso of Aragon (r. 1435–1458), dubbed "the Magnanimous," purchased the loyalty of several of Italy's leading humanists. Their first assignment was to describe in the most flattering light the deeds of their king. On generous stipends—salaries double or triple those available from other patrons—these writers also produced works on moral philosophy, astronomy, history, and biblical scholarship, as well as translations from Greek to Latin and Latin to Italian, which filled the shelves of the court library. Alfonso's son Ferrante (r. 1458–1494), although less generous than his father, employed some of the finest musicians and performers in Europe.

Ferrara, Mantua, and Urbino: The Condottiere Courts

It was not only the rulers of important states like Naples and Milan who surrounded themselves with leading artists and scholars. In the smaller cities of Mantua, Ferrara, and Urbino, the Gonzaga, the d'Este, and the Montefeltro families cultivated equally brilliant courts. The founders of all these dynasties were or had been ***condottieri*** by profession—**mercenary** captains. Their ducal titles and literary and artistic patronage were meant to legitimize regimes won by usurpation. These petty monarchs built splendid palaces, adorning the rooms with beautiful frescoes, plasterwork, and paneling, dined to music provided by Europe's finest performers of that art, acquired libraries, and listened to the orations of their court humanists in a Latin they had absorbed from the best teachers of the age. Even more than the rulers of republican Florence and Venice, or the upstart despots of Milan and Naples, they are the models, culturally, for the great monarchs who would command Europe in coming centuries and, in their courts, define that continent's standards of taste.

Ferrara In 1429, the Ferrarese ruler Niccolò d'Este (r. 1393–1441) engaged the humanist educator Guarino da Verona (1374–1460) to bestow upon his adolescent son Leonello the polish of a Classical training. Guarino did so, establishing a school that also nourished many of the notable minds of the age. Guarino's circle soon expanded into the "Studio" of Ferrara, a still-flourishing university. Niccolò's successors followed his model of patronage, enhancing the d'Este library with ancient and humanist works and brilliantly illuminated manuscripts of vernacular works and translations.

Another of Niccolò's sons, Ercole (r. 1471–1505), married the daughter of the king of Naples, Eleonora of Aragon. A patron of the arts in general, she also amassed her own small collection of books, consisting largely of devotional works. An exception was the volume dedicated to her by the court humanist Bartolomeo Goggio, entitled *In Praise of Women*, a celebration of the whole female sex.

Eleonora's husband, Ercole ("Hercules"), commissioned costly dramatic and musical performances. He maintained a stable of musicians to create and perform serious sacred music: "two musical choruses of expert singers," a contemporary reports, "one of twenty-four young boys, and the other of more than that number of very expert professionals." Also on the d'Este payroll were the painters and architects who built and decorated their palaces—such as the Schifanoia palace, whose frescoes, although damaged, still convey the pleasure and elegance of life at the d'Este court. Great expanses of frescoed wall embellished the palaces of these petty Italian princes. Most are now unfortunately lost.

At the court of Ercole's son, one of Italy's most renowned poets, Ludovico Ariosto (1474–1533), enjoyed special favor. His epic *Orlando Furioso* is set against the background of a holy war between Charlemagne and the Saracens and portrays a magical world in which a knight is driven mad by thwarted love and maidens are rescued and honor saved by indomitable heroes both masculine and feminine.

WHO'S WHO

Renaissance Rulers, Patrons

Cosimo de' Medici (1389–1464) behind-the-scenes ruler of Florence.

Francesco Sforza (1401–1466) condottiere who fought his way to become Duke of Milan.

Lorenzo de' Medici (1449–1492) "the Magnificent" Cosimo's grandson; ruler of Florence.

Isabella d'Este (1474–1539) daughter of the Duke of Ferrara, wife of the Duke of Mantua and regent in his absence; a patron of great vision.

Nicholas V (r. 1447–1455) pope, promoter of Renaissance culture in Rome.

Mantua At Mantua, the Gonzaga family rivaled the d'Este of Ferrara in their artistic patronage. The Marquis Gianfrancesco (r. 1407–1444) hired the humanist Vittorino da Feltre (1378–1446) to educate his sons and daughter. In 1425 Vittorino created a school, called the "House of Joy," which had features anticipating modern educational trends. About 70 children in all (for the Gonzaga children were joined by those of Mantua's nobility and Italy's scholars) withstood early morning recitations of Vergil in the cold (which Vittorino found bracing) and long mountain hikes intended to prime the intellect.

Here Cecilia Gonzaga (one of the few women in Renaissance Europe ever sent to school) mastered Greek and Latin and failed to still the love of learning that Vittorino had aroused. She refused the husband her father had selected for her. When his death bought her freedom to do so, she entered a convent, in which shelter, if nowhere else, she might pursue the studies of her youth.

The most notable patron at the Mantuan court was Isabella (1474–1539), wife of Francesco Gonzaga, and daughter of Ercole d'Este and Eleonora of Aragon. Taught by renowned humanist tutors, she mastered a Classical curriculum as well as the skills of dance, lute-playing, and witty conversation. Isabella nurtured scholars and writers, studied maps and astrology, and had frequent discussions with the court librarian. Her *Studiolo* and *Grotta*, specially decorated rooms of the palace—the Grotta lined with intarsia, or inlaid wood paneling—suggest her refined taste, although the collection of works of art they once contained (an inventory of which occupies fourteen pages in a modern edition) has long since been dispersed. It included statues, boxes, clocks, marbles, lutes, dishes, gowns, playing cards, jewels, and gold, as well as paintings by outstanding artists, including the Gonzaga court painter, Andrea Mantegna (1431–1506). He and other painters produced allegorical paintings based on Classical schemes devised by Isabella in consultation with her humanist advisers. To fill her library, she dealt directly with printers, whom she bullied about the quality of parchment and design.

Urbino Emulating his colleagues in Ferrara and Mantua, the soldier-prince of Urbino, Federigo da Montefeltro (r. 1444–1482), portrayed with his wife in the portraits below, made his mountaintop fortress one of the most civilized courts in Europe. The wealth Federigo earned through the exercise of arms (an annual fortune of 60,000 to 80,000 ducats) he bestowed on the arts of peace. His enormous ducal palace was filled with gilded chests and chairs, silver objects, silk and velvet furnishings, and resident astrologers and physicians, painters, humanists, and musicians. A lover of books, the aging *condottiere* developed one of the finest libraries on the peninsula. By 1482, this library included 1100 volumes in Latin, Greek, Hebrew, and even Coptic (a language derived from ancient Egyptian), specially bound in velvet and leather.

The court of Federigo's son Guidobaldo (r. 1482–1508) was graced by his duchess, Elisabetta Gonzaga, and her ladies-in-waiting, who helped to create the kind of setting described in *The Courtier*, by Baldassare Castiglione who spent several years at Guidobaldo's court. While the ladies presided over after-dinner games, the learned and important conversed wittily and discoursed gravely. The type of the European courtier, who would flourish from this time until the French Revolution, was born not in France or England or any other of the nations of modern Europe, but in the diminutive court of Urbino.

Rome: Reclaiming the Ancient City

Like secular princes, popes also sought to enhance their status with literary and artistic projects. Traumatized by more than a century of crisis, Rome had reached its nadir by 1417, when Martin V was elected Pope, ending the Great Schism. His successors established their authority in that city, employing in this endeavor an army of the learned and accomplished. The first step was to revive Rome's Classical past. Later, the monuments of that past and the new forms they inspired were pressed into the service of the papacy, which was now celebrated in works of art and architecture of stupendous power and scale.

The many humanists who gravitated to Rome in the service of the pope searched intently for the material relics of the ancient city. They described and

Reflections of Power

***Piero della Francesca,* Portraits of Federigo da Montefeltro and Bianca Sforza:** *The rulers of the Italian court cities (including papal Rome) were also patrons seeking to aggrandize themselves. Reproduced here are Federigo da Montefeltro and his wife Bianca Sforza, c. 1465, whose stark profiles are elevated above the landscapes they dominate, in art as in life.* (Uffizi, Florence)

Michelangelo Buonarroti, Sistine Chapel ceiling: *The Sistine Chapel in the Vatican, Rome, was built in 1473 by Pope Sixtus IV, after whom it was named. The pope commissioned Michelangelo to paint the ceiling with frescoes of scenes from the Old Testament. Michelangelo, who worked on the ceiling and window lunettes between 1508 and 1512, had to lie on his back in cramped conditions on high scaffolding in order to paint the scenes.*

catalogued its ruins, while also establishing the historical context that gave these ruins meaning and significance. Meanwhile, the artists Donatello and Brunelleschi reconstructed the fabric of the city in drawings which measured, traced, and dissected what was left of Roman greatness.

With the elevation of Nicholas V to the papacy in 1447, Renaissance culture took root in the city. Nicholas ordered existing structures embellished, collapsed fortifications rebuilt, office complexes constructed for the secretaries, librarians, accountants, and clerks of the papal establishment. In many cases, enthusiasm triumphed over conservation. Cardinals built themselves palaces around the ancient city, carelessly erecting them on the layered ruins of past ages. While humanists peered into coverts for relics of the past and climbed ladders to read half-obliterated inscriptions, a frenzy of building tore at the remnants of old Rome, cannibalizing the very monuments that earlier generations had admired.

A humanist himself, Nicholas (r. 1447–1455) collected the volumes that today form the nucleus of the Vatican Library, one of the world's richest repositories of ancient, medieval, and Renaissance texts. He appointed a humanist as head of the library, and planned for its eventual housing in a new Vatican complex—a plan that would be realized by his successor Sixtus IV. Nicholas' successors, the humanists Pius II and Paul II, added to this treasury of books. The latter also collected antiquities—ancient bronzes, ivories, medals, coins, and cameos. Later popes added to that collection, while they erected odds and ends of ancient statuary on the Capitoline Hill and in the Vatican. Noblemen and bankers, cardinals and diplomats followed suit, littering their houses and gardens with statues and sarcophagi.

Amid this enthusiasm for all remnants of the Classical past, the monuments of Christian antiquity were joined to the papal cult. The figure of Saint Peter (who, according to tradition, was crucified in Rome) was enlisted in the network of ideas that propped up the Renaissance papacy. The popes derived their legitimacy from Jesus' commissioning of Peter, whom he dubbed the "rock" of his church. The Vatican complex on the west side of the Tiber, as planned by Nicholas V, was accordingly centered on the ancient basilica dedicated to Peter.

In 1475, Sixtus IV took up Nicholas' building program. His best-known achievement was the building of the chapel known, after him, as "Sistine" in the Vatican. The adornment of the chapel was eventually completed under Sixtus' successors by artists including Raphael (Raffaello Sanzio; 1483–1520) and Michelangelo Buonarroti. Raphael designed a set of tapestries depicting scenes from the lives of the apostles to cover the chapel's walls. They now hang in a gallery in the Vatican Museums. For the ceiling, Michelangelo executed the renowned cycle of paintings portraying the story of Creation, as well as various Old Testament figures; for the wall behind the altar, the overwhelming "Last Judgment," illustrated on p. 371. Michelangelo's concerns—about humankind, subject to death, about his own future—are compellingly expressed in smaller compass in his original design for the never-completed tomb of Pope Julius II (r. 1502–1513). The subject was to be the liberation of the soul: from its imprisonment in the body, in sin and death, to its redemption. Two struggling and dying figures, known as the "Slaves" or "Captives," represent the striving soul. Now dispersed in museums in Paris and Florence, these powerfully expressive sculptures are emblems of Michelangelo's spiritual yearnings and eloquent statements of the Renaissance concept of heroic humanity.

Michelangelo's vision was extraordinary, but he was only one genius among the many who peopled the age of the Renaissance. The wealthy and powerful people who wished to proclaim their status required the talents of many writers and artists of whom hundreds, gifted with exceptional boldness and originality, flourished over these two centuries.

ITALIAN RENAISSANCE PROFILES

The Florentine book-dealer Vespasiano da Bisticci (1421–1498) occupied the leisure hours of his retirement with a project that still amuses and enlightens modern readers: writing the *Lives of Illustrious Men*. His compilation profiles bankers and tyrants, architects and humanists, popes and courtiers. It portrays the abundant life of Renaissance society. Following Vespasiano's example in miniature, we will look closely at five of the exceptional creators of Renaissance culture.

The five chosen are Giotto (Florence); Lorenzo Valla (Rome); Isotta Nogarola (Verona); Giovanni Pico, Count of Mirandola; and Niccolò Machiavelli (Florence). They include one painter, one philosopher, two humanists, and one historian and political thinker; four men and one woman.

Giotto: Form in Space

Even his contemporaries recognized that the great artist Giotto di Bondone (1267–1337) surpassed his contemporaries in the depiction of real bodies in real space. Dante and Boccaccio celebrated him, and Petrarch bequeathed a painting by Giotto to the ruler of Padua, with this comment: "The beauty of this painting the ignorant cannot comprehend, but masters of the art marvel at it." The sixteenth-century biographer Giorgio Vasari explained Giotto's unique importance: "For after the many years during which the methods and outlines of good painting had been buried ... it was Giotto alone who ... rescued and

Form in Space

***Giotto,* The Meeting at the Golden Gate** *(left)**:** Giotto's ability to find expressive force by manipulating forms in space is signalled in this depiction of the intimate embrace of Anne and Joachim. This painting is one of a series of scenes from the life of the Virgin which Giotto painted in the Arena Chapel, Padua, 1305–1306.*

***Giotto,* Betrayal:** *The same ability to manipulate forms is seen in* Betrayal, *also in the Arena Chapel, 1305–1306. Here the kiss is a hostile and world-changing one—as Judas' kiss points to Jesus' crucifixion and resurrection.*

restored the art. ..." Scholars have debated whether Giotto was, strictly speaking, a medieval or a Renaissance artist, since his career unfolded precisely on the boundary between the two ages. But it is indisputable that his transformation of the concept of human form was fundamental to all later Renaissance innovations in painting.

Giotto altered the canons of painting. He uniquely understood the density of meaning that could be concentrated in the human form when it was free to turn in palpable space. Rooted in assumptions of the solidity, plasticity, and expressiveness of the human form, his style would remain authoritative until the days of the Impressionists in the late nineteenth century.

The sheer attractiveness of Giotto's sturdy figures derives from their expressive quality. Without their ability to communicate meaning, their compact masses—however clear the space they occupy and brilliant the color—would have been lifeless and without consequence in the art of the Renaissance. Giotto made these figures speak. Two scenes from the cinematic sequence lining the chancel walls of the Arena Chapel in Padua exemplify Giotto's special achievement.

The Arena Chapel was a modest church built for the Paduan merchant Enrico Scrovegni on the site of ancient Roman ruins. Between 1303 and 1305, Giotto transformed its interior into a compact encyclopedia of Christian truth with a series of compelling and moving frescoes. The blue ceiling, representing Heaven itself, is studded with portraits of the Evangelists and a central Christ, his hand held up to bless his saints. At one end, on slim panels framing the triumphal arch that surrounds altar and apse, the angel Gabriel tells the Virgin that she is to be the mother of Jesus (Luke 1:36–38). At the other, Christ is depicted in glory at the Last Judgment. Between these two events the side walls present forty-eight narrative scenes of the life of Mary, the mother of Jesus, and of her son's birth, ministry, and death.

Especially forceful is the scene of the reunion of Mary's parents, Joachim and Anne, before the gates of Jerusalem, illustrated on p. 373. Since their last meeting, Joachim had been exiled for his failure to beget a child. Anne in the meantime had received the God-sent message that she would soon give birth. These contrasting experiences are forgotten in the joyful rush of greeting. Their compact figures are charged with emotion, their heads, eyes, hands, even backs reaching for joining and consummation. These bearers of truth, these vehicles of divine expression, are for Giotto above all two human beings in love.

The embrace of Joachim and Anne contrasts with that portrayed lower on the same wall of Jesus and his betrayer (see p. 373). This is the moment when Judas identifies the Savior to his enemies by a kiss. Judas leans forward slightly to clasp Jesus in his arms, the taut folds of his robe sweeping up to engulf his victim. The assault of evil is counterposed to the positive stasis of good. Jesus stands firm, immobile in the tormented man's arms, supreme in dignity as his eyes lock with those of the traitor. His absolute calm is underscored by the chaos played out around him: torches and spears and the jumble of half-hidden faces of Roman soldiers charged to carry out the predestined arrest and execution.

In both these scenes, Giotto speaks with unprecedented insight. His aim is not only to display the narrative of Jesus' life and resurrection but to probe the human significance implicit in each encounter of that narrative. He portrays not just the skeleton of truth but its flesh and sinew; not so much religious truth, as the mysterious, glittering Byzantine icons, but human truth. For that weight of meaning, he devised bodies never seen before in paint and rarely even in sculpture, full of power and mass.

Valla and the Transformation of Values

Quite as original as Giotto, the humanist Lorenzo Valla (1407–1457) was considerably more shocking to contemporaries. He was born in Rome, the city whose masters, the papacy, he would challenge. The son and the nephew of lawyers, Valla developed to the maximum a lawyer's critical eye in a twenty-six-year career productive of bold and thoughtful works. These challenged squarely the conventional ethical and religious assumptions of his day.

While still a young man, teaching at the University of Pavia (near Milan), Valla published a dialogue *On Pleasure*, cited in *Witnesses* on p. 378. The very title was dangerous: for the prevailing ideal of Christian asceticism denied the value of pleasure. Valla's defense of pleasure was actually an insightful rereading of Christian doctrine. It is not the puritanical Christian who represses all desire who truly loves God and merits salvation, Valla argues, but the sinful, striving seeker of deeper meaning, fuller existence, paradisiacal joy. In a stroke, he rejects the ethics of the medieval confessional for the profound self-examination and transformation that later thinkers, both Christian and secular, would propose as the test of human authenticity and worth.

Valla's *On Pleasure* placed these bold notions in the mouths of his friends among the smart set of Pavia. Two years later, he prudently revised his work, altering the cast of characters (which now included two reputable clerics). Renamed *On the True and the False Good*, it exerted great influence—eventually upon the Protestant reformers Martin Luther and John Calvin (see Chapter 14).

Both Greek and Christian philosophers had generally agreed that virtue was intrinsically good and vice intrinsically evil. These central propositions Valla denied. Vice is to be avoided only because it makes its practitioner miserable: "Those who do not possess

WITNESSES

Women and Humanism

A few—very few—of the humanists were women; and they wrote about the paradox of being women and thinking beings at the same time. Isotta Nogarola confronts that paradox by grappling with the biblical story of the expulsion of Adam and Eve from the Garden of Eden; it was Adam's fault, she argues, attempting to free all women from the intolerable burden of Eve's prior act of disobedience. Laura Cereta defends her own anomalous position as a woman intellectual by striking out at other women whom, she believes, waste themselves on trivialities.

Isotta Nogarola excuses Eve from responsibility for the Fall by conceding women's innate ignorance and moral incapacity (1451–1453): Eve sinned out of ignorance and inconstancy, and hence you contend that she sinned more gravely, because the ignorance of those things which we are obligated to now does not excuse us. ... I would concede your point if that ignorance were crude or affected. But Eve's ignorance was implanted by nature, of which nature God himself is the author and founder. In many people it is seen that he who knows less sins less, like a boy who sins less than an old man or a peasant less than a noble. ... The same is true of imperfection. For when gifts increase, greater responsibility is imposed. When God created man, from the beginning he created him perfect, and gave him a greater understanding and knowledge of truth as well as a greater depth of wisdom. Thus it was that the Lord led to Adam all the animals of the earth and the birds of heaven, so that Adam could call them by their names. For God said: "Let us make mankind in our image and likeness, and let them have dominion over the fishes of the sea, and the birds of the air, the cattle, over all the wild animals and every creature that walks on earth," making clear his own perfection. But of the woman he said: "It is not good that the man is alone; I will make him a helper like himself." ... Therefore, it appears that Adam's sin was greater than Eve's.

(Isotta Nogarola, *On the Equal or Unequal Sin of Adam and Eve* 1451–1453; from M. L. King, A. Rabil, 2e, 1992)

Laura Cereta lambastes women who follow outlandish fashion instead of building their character (1487): I would pardon the morally hopeless and even people destined for a life of crime, whom wagging tongues are accustomed to castigate with obvious fury. But I cannot tolerate the gabbing and babbling women who, burning with wine and drunkenness, harm with their petulant talk not only their sex but themselves. These mindless women—these female counselors who emerge victorious from the cookshop jar after a prodigious vote among their neighbors—hunt down with their bilious poison those women who rise to greater distinction than they. The bold and undisguised passion these women have for destruction and disgrace, this hunger of theirs for calamity, which strives to smear even those who are completely above reproach, deserves to bring a worse disgrace on itself. ... Besides, these women, being idle with time on their hands and no interests of their own, occupy themselves with keeping watch over other people's business. ... Human error causes us to be ashamed and disgusted that those women who are themselves caught in a tangle of doubt have given up hope of attaining knowledge of the humane arts, when they could easily acquire such knowledge with skill and virtue. For an education is neither bequeathed to us as a legacy, nor does some fate or other give it to us as a gift. Virtue is something that we ourselves acquire; nor can those women who become dull-witted through laziness and the sludge of low pleasure ascend to the understanding of difficult things. But for those women who believe that study, hard work, and vigilance will bring them sure praise, the road to attaining knowledge is broad.

(Laura Cereta, Letter to Lucilia Vernacula, 1487; ed, trs. D. Robin, 1997)

quiet minds are always wretched; such are robbers, thieves, murderers, gamblers, tyrants. ..." As to the notion that virtue is its own reward, "I personally have never heard a sillier idea than this one," Valla's spokesman remarked in disgust.

Valla questions assumptions held sacred even today. Is it really praiseworthy, he asks, to die for your country? What does it matter to you, when you are dead? "You undergo death because you want your country not to die, as though in your death, your country did not become dead to you. For the man deprived of his eyes, light itself is a darkness, and for the man who is extinguished in death, all things are extinguished." From the radical vantage point of the lone individual, Valla boldly reexamines even the secular piety of patriotism.

A nasty academic quarrel compelled Valla to leave Pavia and seek employment as a secretary to Alfonso "the Magnanimous" of Aragon, who was struggling to win dominion over Naples. In Alfonso's court, Valla published a series of provocative books: which challenged prevailing Catholic belief in salvation through works. These included a biography of his patron; a gem-like dialogue entitled *On Free Will*; challenges to the authority of Aristotle and the ascetic ideal fundamental to monasticism; a guidebook to correct Latin usage; and the celebrated *Falsely-Believed and Forged Donation of Constantine*.

The "Donation of Constantine," a document generally accepted as valid by jurists and church scholars from the ninth century until Valla's day, supposedly recorded a gift from the emperor Constantine (306–337) to Silvester I (314–335), Bishop of Rome—and hence to subsequent popes. According to the "Donation," Constantine gave the head of the Roman Church authority over all other bishops and patriarchs in the West, dominion over the lands of the Church in Italy, and implicit supremacy even over all secular rulers in western Christendom. It thus supported papal ambitions as the Church took its place among the competing states of Europe. According to Valla, that gift had never been made.

In a model exercise of destructive criticism, Valla exposed the "Donation" as a medieval forgery. His minute humanist analysis of the text uncovered anachronisms, inconsistencies, and errors of fact. This exposé laid the groundwork for more profound challenges to papal authority in the following century. Valla charged the popes with boundless greed and ambition. "Indeed, I have never heard or read that any of you has been deterred from striving to increase his dominion," he wrote acidly. "And this passion, this desire for immense rule agitates and torments most intensely those who are most powerful."

That the powerful might retaliate against critics, Valla knew well. In the service of truth, he was willing to run higher risks than most other men. "Many have run the risk of dying in order to defend their country on earth; shall I be afraid to risk death in order to reach the celestial fatherland? ... One must defend the cause of truth, the cause of justice, the cause of God, with steadfast courage, great confidence, and undying hope. For he who has the ability to speak well should not be considered a true orator unless he also has the courage to speak."

Valla ended his life in—of all places—Rome, which was now hospitable to the humanists. At his death there in 1457, his mother commissioned his tomb. The sarcophagus bears a conventional sculpted likeness of Valla lying supine, a peaceful expression on his face—an ironic image for a man of such a fearlessly combative spirit.

Nogarola and the Defense of Eve

Something of Valla's anger is found in the figure of Isotta Nogarola (1418–1466) of Verona, an outstanding figure among the few women humanists of the Italian Renaissance. Tutored by a student of Guarino da Verona's hired by her mother (this was quite unusual!), she engaged enthusiastically, while still a young woman, in the exchange of letters and books so central to the life of humanism. Soon, however, she became disillusioned with the world and retreated to solitude and her studies. Unlike her medieval predecessors—the abbesses and mystics who flowered in the solitude of the convent—Nogarola did not embrace the religious life. Her solitude was that of the scholar, and not of the cloistered nun. She prefigures the women writers and thinkers of subsequent centuries whose careers took place in the world and not the cloister.

Images of Women

Antonio del Pollaiuolo,* Portrait of a Young Woman*: *Beautiful women were often portrayed in Renaissance art as angels, goddesses, or graces, and featured in portraits, as of this nameless woman, 1460s.* (Museo Poldi Pezzoli, Milan)

The incident that probably triggered Nogarola's withdrawal from the world was an act of slander. An anonymous detractor, in an obscene letter to his unnamed friend, alleged that she had committed incest, an act that would surely ravage a woman's reputation. The slanderer complained that "she, who sets herself no limit in this filthy lust, dares to engage so deeply in the finest literary studies," linking Nogarola's unnatural erudition (for so he viewed it) to the unnatural sexuality he alleged. A woman who attempted to enter the male preserve of humanist studies would be punished for her presumption!

Soon after this incident, Nogarola retired to her "book-lined cell" in her mother's house, where she continued her studies until her death. During these years, she engaged in a debate with the Venetian diplomat Ludovico Foscarini on the question often raised in these Christian centuries: Who was more responsible for Original Sin—Adam, who ate the forbidden fruit, or Eve, who persuaded him to do so? Eve, most authorities answered. In their answer is concealed the full weight of ancient and medieval misogyny.

Nogarola's discussion with Foscarini resulted in a dialogue of crucial importance in the history of feminist thought: *On the Equal or Unequal Sin of Adam and Eve* (see *Witnesses*, p. 375). Eve was a tremendous obstacle for women who wished to claim sexual equality. Theologians over the centuries had blamed her for submitting to the serpent and manipulating Adam, so bringing about humanity's fall from innocence. Nogarola confronts the issue directly, defending Eve and assigning the fault for the fall of Man to the first man, Adam. Yet even while she champions Eve, she deprecates women, basing her defense, paradoxically, on the supposed weakness of female nature. Created imperfect, Eve could not be held responsible for universal sin. God had made Eve ignorant; but Adam He had created perfect: "When God created man, from the beginning he created him perfect, and gave him a greater understanding and knowledge of truth as well as a greater depth of wisdom. ..."

The beleaguered Nogarola here conceded that woman was essentially inferior to man, and that all women were to bear the burden of the first defiance of God's law. She lived wrapped in the predicament of her sexual identity for the quarter-century of her voluntary solitude until her death. Her career illustrates some of the possible obstacles faced by a woman of the Renaissance who sought to participate in cultural life.

Pico della Mirandola's One Truth

While Nogarola explored the essential nature of "woman," the brilliant philosopher Giovanni Pico della Mirandola (1463–1494) brought to a climax Renaissance thinking about the nature of "man." Having mastered the traditional philosophical curriculum based on Aristotle, the young Pico thirsted for more than that relatively meager store of knowledge and added to it the study of the sage's Greek, Arabic, and medieval commentators; the works of Plato, Avicenna, and Averroes; and the medieval Jewish mystical books called the Kabbalah. At heart, he believed, all philosophies were one. The diverse tenets of all the philosophers were true, and could be united into one truth.

Above all a philosopher—a seeker of truth—Pico also participated in humanist discussions. With one friend (the Venetian Ermolao Barbaro, a formidable scholar in his own right), Pico held a famous debate on the issue of whether rhetoric or philosophy was the better road to truth. Barbaro had written Pico a letter lambasting the "barbaric" Latin of the medieval philosophers. In his response, Pico defended his calling, and not without a humanist's eloquence. The task

Masaccio, Expulsion from Eden: *More revealing of attitudes toward women is Masaccio's panel showing Adam and Eve, in the Brancacci Chapel, Florence, c. 1425. Adam is humbled by the consciousness of sin, his realization of its gravity signified by his holding his head. Eve, all emotion without understanding, bewails her condition.*

of a **rhetor**, he argued, is "to lie, to entrap, to circumvent, to practice sleight-of-hand." This "sheer mendacity" contrasts with the aim of the philosopher, "whose entire endeavor is concerned with knowing the truth and demonstrating it to others." At home in the highest society and a participant in convivial celebrations of the young, Pico wrote romantic sonnets and was occasionally in love: once he abducted a woman married to a lesser member of the Medici family. Pico also chose as his mentor the prophet Girolamo Savonarola (1452–1498), who was brought to Florence at Pico's urging. When Pico's body was laid to rest, it was clothed in imitation of Savonarola in the garb of a Dominican friar.

Before Pico's religious conversion and early death, he was involved in another scandal more serious than the one involving a Medici lady. He had called an international meeting of scholars to take place in Rome in 1487. Its task would be to bring into the harmony of the One Truth the disparate truths scattered over the spectrum of thought. To structure the debate, Pico proposed 900 theses—a gargantuan sum of philosophical propositions!

The audacity of Pico's project alarmed the Church. A commission examined his propositions for heresy and condemned seven of them, along with their unrepentant author. The judges decided that his 900 propositions were "in part heretical, in part they

WITNESSES

Rethinking Right and Wrong

The ethical questions raised by humanists occasioned a profound reevaluation by some authors of the nature of the human being. Whereas the religious and philosophical thought of the previous era assumed that human beings, rightly guided, would be motivated to pursue virtuous ends, here the humanist and philosopher Lorenzo Valla suggests that perhaps they are in fact motivated only by pleasure. The politician and theorist Niccolò Machiavelli suggests that they are moved only by power—or fear.

Lorenzo Valla presents the Epicurean argument that not virtue but pleasure motivates human activity (1431–1433): But now, having arrived at our conclusion ... we must speak in praise of pleasure. ... Not only the laws ... were framed for the sake of that expediency from which pleasure stems; cities and states were created for the same reason. In governing them, no prince, administrator, or king was ever chosen unless men expected great advantage from him. In addition to the arts that are called liberal, ... the innumerable other arts ... for instance, agriculture ..., architecture, weaving, painting, shipbuilding, sculpture, dyeing. In any one of these was there virtue? And what about the liberal arts? Do numbers or geometrical measurement or song shape the virtues belonging to rightful action? What about medicine, whose students seek nothing but the health of others and their own profit? ... And what is the aim of friendship? Has it been so sought for and so greatly praised by all ages and nations for any other reasons than the satisfactions arising from the performance of mutual services ..., and the joy arising from talking, listening, and doing other things in company? As for masters and servants, there is not doubt that their only is one of common advantage. What should I say about teachers and students? Those who teach cannot be devoted to their students without expecting from them remuneration or a portion of fame. ... Or let us advance to the most intimate relationship of all: what, finally, forms the link between parents and children if it is not advantage and pleasure? ... There is even less doubt concerning the love of man and wife and brothers and sisters. Marriage, in any case, and the union of male and female, seems to be born from the very womb of pleasure. ...

(Lorenzo Valla, *On Pleasure, De Voluptate*, 1431–1433; ed., trs. A. K. Hiett, M. Lorch, 1977)

Niccolò Machiavelli assumes that the prince will do what is necessary—not what is right—to gain and hold power (1513–1514): Many have dreamed up republics and principalities which have never in truth been known to exist; the gulf between how one should live and how one does live is so wide that a man who neglects what is actually done for what should be done learns the way to self-destruction rather than self-preservation. The fact is that a man who wants to act virtuously in every way necessarily comes to grief among so many who are not virtuous. Therefore if a prince wants to maintain his rule he must learn how not to be virtuous, and to make use of this or not according to need.

[Machiavelli lists some virtues considered desirable in princes: generosity, compassion, loyalty, courage, courtesy, piety, etc.] I know everyone will agree that it would be most laudable if a prince possessed all the qualities deemed to be good among those I have enumerated. But, human nature being what it is, princes cannot possess those qualities, or rather they cannot always exhibit them. So a prince should be so prudent that he knows how to escape the evil reputation attached to those vices which could lose him his state, and how to avoid those vices which are not so dangerous, if he possibly can. ... That is because, taking everything into account, he will find that some of the things that appear to be virtues will, if he practises them, ruin him, and some of the things that appear to be wicked will bring him security and prosperity.

(Niccolò Machiavelli, *The Prince*, 1513–1514; ed., trs. G. Bull, 1961)

savor of heresy; ... many ... are inimical to the Catholic faith and to the human race." Pico fled to France—but only after having penned a defiant *Apology*, dedicated to Lorenzo de' Medici, defending his original beliefs. Why were they deemed so dangerous? To a Christian tribunal (even in an age of clerical corruption), the great emphasis on the power of the human will and the corresponding denigration of faith and grace were profoundly shocking.

Captured and imprisoned, Pico was released at the intervention of Lorenzo de' Medici, and allowed to retire quietly to Florence for the remainder of the lightning burst that was his life. There he continued to write books—*On Being and the One*, *The Seven Days of Creation*—which maintained, as had his 900 impudent propositions, the oneness of all things.

In these works, Pico verged on a "new science, new logic, and new methods of research." He is best remembered today, however, not for these but for his *Oration on the Dignity of Man*. Pico had planned to recite this work as an introduction to the 900 theses whose publication so troubled the Church. Never delivered nor even published in Pico's lifetime, it won tumultuous fame in later centuries. For the work expresses a unique vision of the potential of the human being to create his own reality. That vision is among the key contributions of the Renaissance to present and future citizens of the globe.

By the sixth day of Creation, Pico wrote in his *Oration* (embroidering freely the account in Genesis of the creation of the world), God had already filled the heavens with stars and the earth with beasts. But He still longed to create a creature who could contemplate the splendor of the divine creation. For this purpose, He created Man, addressing him thus: "Neither a fixed abode nor a form that is yours alone nor any function peculiar to yourself have we given you, Adam." All other beings are assigned a precise nature. Man alone, granted perfect free will, may choose his own identity. "We have made you neither of heaven nor of earth, neither mortal nor immortal, so that with freedom of choice and with honor, as though the maker and molder of yourself, you may fashion yourself in whatever shape you shall prefer." Alone in the universe, the human being is free to create himself.

HOW MANY?

Bibliophilia

Monastic institutions were the repositories for learning during the early medieval centuries, but at the Renaissance, with the renewed interest in classical texts and the invention of movable type, the initiative passed to private collectors and secular educational institutions.

Date	Location/Collector	Number of volumes
1162	Durham Abbey	352
1331	Christ Church, Canterbury	1,850
1338	Sorbonne, Paris	1,722
1362?	Petrarch, humanist poet	???
1372	Charles V of France	910
1436	Niccolò Niccoli, librarian to Cosimo de' Medici	800
1490	Matthias Corvinus, king of Hungary	50,000
1576	Biblioteca de el Escorial	4,000
1604	Trinity College, Dublin	4,000
1642	Bibliothèque du Roi, Paris (basis of the Bibliothèque Nationale)	6,000
1655	Collection of the Fugger family, Germany	15,000
1727	Die Nationalbibliothek, Vienna	90,000
1837	British Library, London	240,000

Source: John L. Thornton, *The Chronology of Librarianship* (London, 1941).

Machiavelli's Hard Facts

While Pico ranked human beings as little lower than God, the politician and historian Niccolò Machiavelli (1469–1527) placed them closer to the beasts: just as fierce and dangerous, but greedier and more cruel. These assumptions he expressed in his most famous book, *The Prince*, as well as in other works, especially the *Discourses on Livy* (advocating a republican form of government), the *Art of War*, the *History of Florence*, and three remarkably cynical comedies. Machiavelli's negative vision of human nature was based on hard facts as he knew them in the years before and after 1500. His writings would inspire political theorists whose ideas would frame the modern notion of the state.

Born in Florence to a minor patrician family, Machiavelli witnessed in young adulthood the invasion of Italy—and his own city—in 1494 by the French king Charles VIII. The democratic regime instituted in Florence thereafter soon succumbed to the spell of the theocratic friar Savonarola. Upon the prophet's fall, at the age of twenty-eight Machiavelli procured a bureaucratic position in the city's reorganized republican government.

For the next fourteen years, as a committed servant of the republican state, he wrote the letters (thousands of them) for the Ten, the committee overseeing Florence's foreign policy in these tense years. He wrote communications to army captains and city governors, and dispatched reports from some thirty diplomatic missions, as foreign troops devoured the disunited Italian peninsula bit by bit. This experience fueled Machiavelli's dim view of human nature and his dynamic vision for the future: Italy could be rescued still, but only by extraordinary means—only under a ruthless prince who could unify the nation and expel the "barbarians."

The Prince is a handbook for the man who would undertake this mission (a passage from it is quoted in *Witnesses* on p. 378). Machiavelli's models were ruthless men, praised not for their kindness but for their efficiency and power. In the political emergency suffered by Italy in the early 1500s, it was these skills that were needed to establish a state. By this yardstick, cruelty could be counted a plus. Cesare Borgia was considered cruel, acknowledged Machiavelli; "nevertheless, this cruelty of his reformed the Romagna [a province of central Italy], brought it unity, and restored order and obedience."

The prince might need to compel obedience through terror. Posing the famous question "whether it is better to be loved than feared, or the reverse," Machiavelli concludes that it is better to be feared, given the nature of humankind. "One can make this generalization about men," he wrote: "they are ungrateful, fickle, liars, and deceivers, they shun danger and are greedy for profit." They must be forced to obey. Still, it is wise to avoid their hatred. This the prince can easily do "if he abstains from the property of his subjects and citizens and from their women"; above all, from their property, "because men sooner forget the death of their father [*padre*] than the loss of their patrimony [*patrimonio*]." The author presents such judgments with the ruthlessness of a surgeon, knife poised to salvage what he can of the suffering body of his nation.

The Prince expresses with matchless clarity Machiavelli's analysis of the condition of Italy and of humanity. It was written during the exile and enforced retirement in which the disgraced Machiavelli languished from 1512 until his death in 1527, and was addressed to the Medici, now hereditary dukes of Florence, by an author desperate to rejoin the world of action, in the hope of forgiveness and favor. In the isolation of his rural farm, he had turned to the studies that everywhere spurred the Renaissance imagination. At nightfall he withdrew to his study, and changed from his mud-stained country clothes to the "robes of court and palace":

> *And in this graver dress I enter the antique courts of the ancients where ... I taste the food that alone is mine, for which I was born. And there I make bold and speak to them and ask the motives of their actions. And they, in their humanity, reply to me. And for the space of four hours I forget the world, remember no vexation, fear poverty no more, tremble no more at death: I am wholly absorbed in them.*

Machiavelli's adult life was wholly enmeshed in the tragedy of Italy's decline. In poverty and isolation, accompanied only by his wits and the shades of ancient heroes with whom he conversed, properly attired, he watched Florence fall to the "barbarian" princes whom he hated more than he hated evil. The Italian Renaissance was not yet over, but it had reached old age.

Conclusion

THE ITALIAN RENAISSANCE AND THE MEANING OF THE WEST

The Renaissance was a peak moment in the history of the Italian people, equaled only by that of the Roman Empire. The patterns of high culture created in that resplendent era continued through the next three centuries—long after the Italian cities of the high Renaissance had succumbed to invasion, oppression, and lassitude.

Outside Italy, the Renaissance found a home in other nations. Exported over the course of two centuries by returning students and returning armies, by printed books and stolen paintings, the ideas and products of the Italian Renaissance continued to flourish, developing in two principal directions. First, the thinkers of the early Reformation—many of whom were humanists themselves—employed humanist methods and arguments in constructing their different vision of Christendom. Second, Renaissance thought, imagination, and manners found a richly receptive environment in the royal courts of the emerging national states, poised to extend their influence across the face of the globe.

The Renaissance, finally, has left its distinctive mark on the modern age, and up to the present day. Renaissance thinkers achieved a reintegration of ancient thought with the medieval tradition that constituted the rebirth, the reformulation, of Western culture. The two ancient traditions tributary to Western civilization—the Judeo-Christian and the Greco-Roman—were fused again, as they had been in late antiquity, and for the last time. From that melding descend the values fundamental to the West, even in an age when those values sometimes seem forgotten. They are neither Judeo-Christian nor Greco-Roman, but a combination of both.

REVIEW QUESTIONS

1. What does "Renaissance" mean? How were the works of Classical antiquity rediscovered? Which Classical figures and works most affected the development of Renaissance thought?

2. Define humanism. Who were some of the major scholars in the schools of civic humanism? How did Neoplatonism affect it? What role did women play in the humanist movement?

3. Why is Florence considered the Renaissance capital? Compare and contrast its influence with Venice. Explain the role of the Medici. How did architecture style change in the Renaissance?

4. Assess the roles in the Renaissance of the Visconti of Milan; Alfonso of Naples; the d'Este of Ferrara; the Gonzaga of Mantua; Federigo da Montefeltro of Urbino. What role did the papacy play in the development of the Renaissance?

5. Why is Giotto so critical in the development of Renaissance art? How did Valla change the concept of values? Why is Nogarola's work in the dialogues about Adam and Eve so critical in the history of feminist thought?

6. How did Pico della Mirandola change the philosophical concept of man? What were Machiavelli's "models" of successful rulers? How does he view human nature?

SUGGESTED RESOURCES

The Rebirth of Classical Antiquity

Baron, Hans, *The Crisis of the Early Italian Renaissance: Civic Humanism and Republican Liberty in an Age of Classicism and Tyranny*, rev. ed. (Princeton: Princeton University Press, 1966). Classic and groundbreaking work, which places humanism in the context of contemporary political and ideological struggles.

Grafton, Anthony, *Commerce with the Classics: Ancient Books and Renaissance Readers* (Ann Arbor: University of Michigan Press, 1997). How Renaissance readers read the classics—where they read them, how they thought about them—including major thinkers such as Alberti, Pico, Bude, and Kepler.

Grendler, Paul F., *Schooling in Renaissance Italy: Literacy and Learning, 1300–1600* (Baltimore–London: Johns Hopkins University Press, 1989). A comprehensive intellectual and social history of primary and secondary education in early modern Italy.

Hankins, James, *Plato in the Italian Renaissance* (Leiden: E. J. Brill, 1990). A careful reconstruction of how humanists read Plato and appropriated his ideas for modern European thought.

Ianziti, Gary, *Humanistic Historiography under the Sforzas* (Oxford: Oxford University Press, 1988). Careful study of a new dynasty's quest for legitimacy and the historians it commissioned to bestow it.

King, Margaret L., *Venetian Humanism in an Age of Patrician Dominance* (Princeton: Princeton University Press, 1986). Unravels the relationship between patrician and humanist thought that distinguishes Venetian humanism from Florentine or other humanisms.

Nauert, Charles G., *Humanism and the Culture of Renaissance Europe* (Cambridge: Cambridge University Press, 1995). Recent synthesis, that relates the dramatic achievements of Italian humanism to the humanist culture it engendered beyond the Alps.

Witt, Ronald G., *In the Footsteps of the Ancients: the Origins of Humanism from Lovato to Bruni* (Leiden-Boston: Brill, 2000). Pathbreaking study of early humanism in Italy, linking it to medieval French currents and the crucial contributions of participants in northern Italy's notarial culture.

Jacob Burkhardt's 1860 classic, The Civilization of the Renaissance in Italy, trans. S.G.C. Middlemore, 1878 (Boise State University): **http://www.idbsu.edu**

Francis Petrarch: works, bibliography, website links (Hanover College): **http://history.hanover.edu/early/pet.htm**

The Settings of the Italian Renaissance

Brown, Patricia Fortini, *Venice and Antiquity: the Venetian Sense of the Past* (New Haven: Yale University Press, 1997). Founded only after the Roman Empire dissolved in Italy, Venice created a complex series of relationships with its Byzantine, Roman, and local past, drawing on medals and inscriptions, works of art, and literary texts.

Brucker, Gene, *Florence: The Golden Age, 1138–1737* (Berkeley–Los Angeles: University of California Press, 1998). By the Florentine expert (bar none) on either side of the Atlantic, this work offers a rich and diverse story of the city—not just the wars and changes of regime, but the people in the streets, the enterprise of the merchants, the brilliant new visions of artists and thinkers—over a full six centuries.

Goldthwaite, Richard A., *The Building of Renaissance Florence: An Economic and Social History* (Baltimore–London: Johns Hopkins University Press, 1981). An extensive study of construction in Florence (1350–1550). Interweaves economic, social, and architectural history.

Martines, Lauro, *Power and Imagination: City States in Renaissance Italy* (New York: Knopf, 1972; rpt. Baltimore–London: Johns Hopkins University Press, 1988). A brilliant narration of the rise of the city states, and the use of humanism and the arts to glorify power.

Rowland, Ingrid D., *The Culture of the High Renaissance: Ancients and Moderns in Sixteenth-Century Rome* (Cambridge: Cambridge University Press, 1998). Imaginatively reconstructs the economic, civic, and religious life of Rome at the point when Renaissance culture burgeoned there, along with the evolving networks of patronage that made that flowering possible.

Italian Renaissance Profiles

Burke, Peter, *The Italian Renaissance: Culture and Society in Italy* (Princeton: Princeton University Press, 1987). Defines an "elite" of intellectuals and artists, and examines them (and their audience and patrons) in social context in an attempt to discover the reasons for the clustering of talent that characterizes the Renaissance.

Viroli, Maurizio, *Machiavelli* (Oxford: Oxford University Press, 1998). An up-to-date interpretation of Machiavelli's contribution, stressing his commitment to civic life and law.

Leonardo da Vinci homepage (Boston Museum of Science): **http://www.mos.org/sln/Leonardo**

Select list of links to websites for Renaissance and Reformation Studies (University of Toronto): **http://www.library.utoronto.ca/crrs**

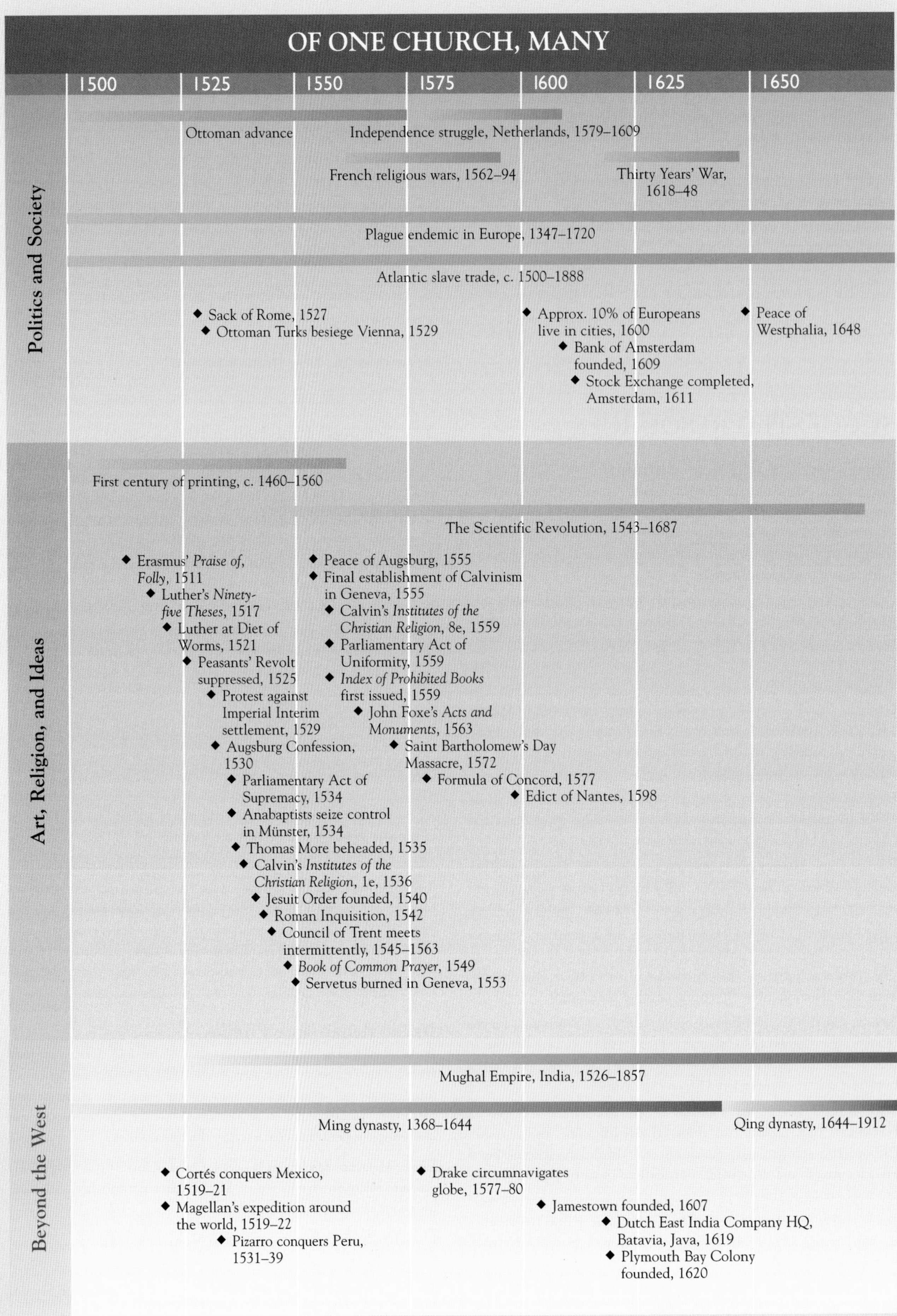
OF ONE CHURCH, MANY
1500
1525
1550
1575
1600
1625
1650
Politics and Society
Ottoman advance
Independence struggle, Netherlands, 1579–1609
French religious wars, 1562–94
Thirty Years' War, 1618–48
Plague endemic in Europe, 1347–1720
Atlantic slave trade, c. 1500–1888
◆ Sack of Rome, 1527
◆ Ottoman Turks besiege Vienna, 1529
◆ Approx. 10% of Europeans live in cities, 1600
◆ Bank of Amsterdam founded, 1609
◆ Stock Exchange completed, Amsterdam, 1611
◆ Peace of Westphalia, 1648
Art, Religion, and Ideas
First century of printing, c. 1460–1560
The Scientific Revolution, 1543–1687
◆ Erasmus' *Praise of, Folly*, 1511
◆ Luther's *Ninety-five Theses*, 1517
◆ Luther at Diet of Worms, 1521
◆ Peasants' Revolt suppressed, 1525
◆ Protest against Imperial Interim settlement, 1529
◆ Augsburg Confession, 1530
◆ Parliamentary Act of Supremacy, 1534
◆ Anabaptists seize control in Münster, 1534
◆ Thomas More beheaded, 1535
◆ Calvin's *Institutes of the Christian Religion*, 1e, 1536
◆ Jesuit Order founded, 1540
◆ Roman Inquisition, 1542
◆ Council of Trent meets intermittently, 1545–1563
◆ *Book of Common Prayer*, 1549
◆ Servetus burned in Geneva, 1553
◆ Peace of Augsburg, 1555
◆ Final establishment of Calvinism in Geneva, 1555
◆ Calvin's *Institutes of the Christian Religion*, 8e, 1559
◆ Parliamentary Act of Uniformity, 1559
◆ *Index of Prohibited Books* first issued, 1559
◆ John Foxe's *Acts and Monuments*, 1563
◆ Saint Bartholomew's Day Massacre, 1572
◆ Formula of Concord, 1577
◆ Edict of Nantes, 1598
Beyond the West
Mughal Empire, India, 1526–1857
Ming dynasty, 1368–1644
Qing dynasty, 1644–1912
◆ Cortés conquers Mexico, 1519–21
◆ Magellan's expedition around the world, 1519–22
◆ Pizarro conquers Peru, 1531–39
◆ Drake circumnavigates globe, 1577–80
◆ Jamestown founded, 1607
◆ Dutch East India Company HQ, Batavia, Java, 1619
◆ Plymouth Bay Colony founded, 1620

CHAPTER

14 OF ONE CHURCH, MANY

Protestant Reformation and Catholic Reform

1500–1650

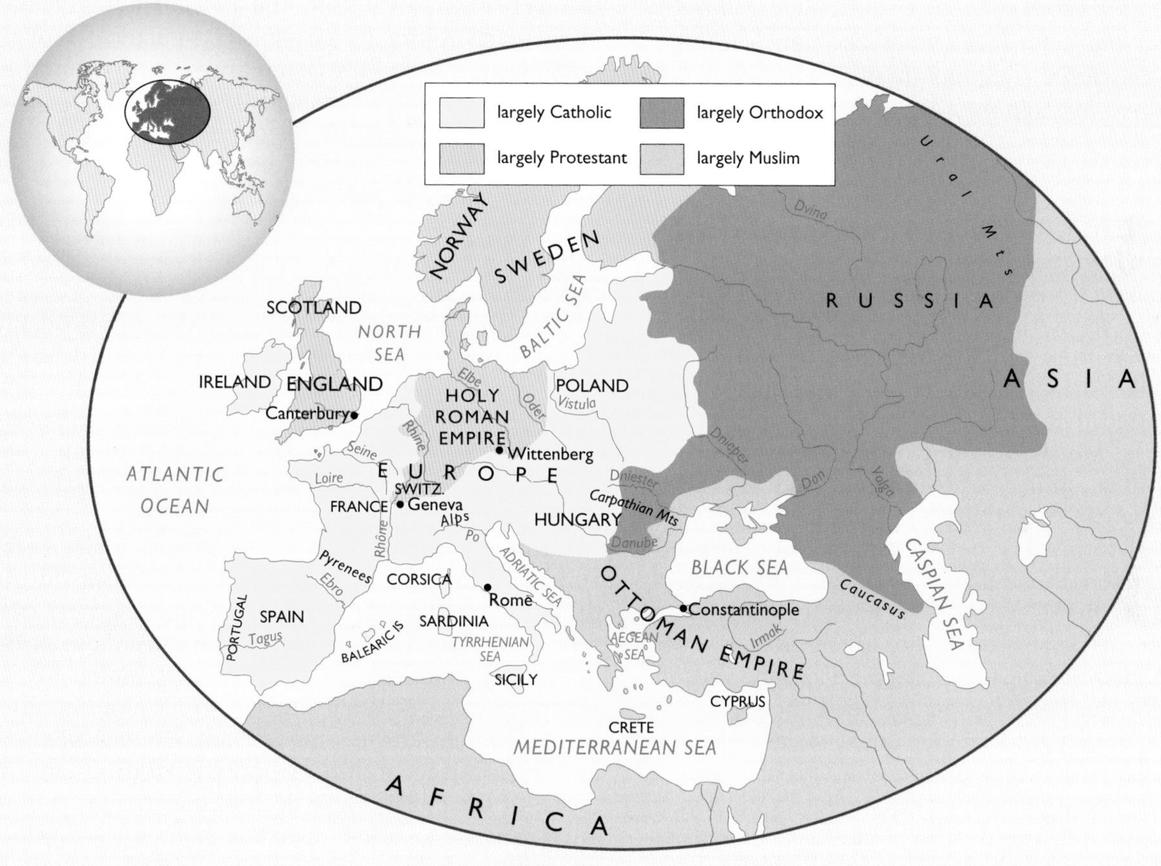

KEY TOPICS

- **Before the Reformation:** Clerical corruption and popular anxiety spark criticism of the Church, none sharper than that of Desiderius Erasmus.
- **Faith and Works:** Martin Luther insists on the worship of God alone, as prescribed by Scripture alone, with confidence in faith alone.
- **The Unfolding Reformation:** Lutherans, Calvinists, Anabaptists—now Protestants—seek new converts in Europe.
- **Protestantism and Society:** Fathers rule, and women must obey; the education of the young becomes a priority, the poor are neglected.
- **Catholic Reform:** The Catholic Church reaffirms papal and priestly authority, wins new advocates, and reconverts Protestants.
- **The Reign of Intolerance:** Hostility to Muslims and Jews persists, while Protestants and Catholics try and burn accused witches.

*"**Here I Stand ...**" In 1521, the German monk Martin Luther (1483–1546) was summoned to appear before the Holy Roman Emperor Charles V (r. 1519–1556). On a table before him lay his books, fearsome to the religious and secular leaders of Europe. He was asked to repudiate them, and recant—the order normally given to an identified heretic, permitting the accused to disown his views and escape punishment. Luther refused. "I am bound by the Scriptures I have quoted," he responded, according to German words inserted in the Latin notes of the session, "and my conscience is captive to the Word of God. I cannot and will not retract anything, for it is neither safe nor right to go against conscience. I cannot do otherwise. Here I stand, may God help me, Amen."*

At that point, Luther stood a good chance of being condemned to death—his views spurned and his memory erased. Instead, he survived to lead a revolution. That revolution, called today the Protestant Reformation, ruptured the monopoly of the Roman Church over the Christians of western Europe and, in turn, spurred that Church to its own reformation. It transformed European culture and society, formed in the era of a unified Christendom, and left many churches where once there had been one.

The Reformation developed in the sixteenth century, when the Italian Renaissance had already outlived its heroic phase (see Chapter 13) and as European settlers established themselves in the Western Hemisphere (see Chapter 16). The preconditions for the Reformation included the neglect or abuse of church leaders; the quest of lay men and women for religious assurance; the opportunism of rulers, and the intellectual currents set in motion by Renaissance humanism, which liberated its participants from the Church-dominated thought systems of medieval Scholasticism (see Chapter 10).

The Reformation began in 1517, when Martin Luther first issued a list of ninety-five objections to Roman church laws and practices. Once launched, Protestantism spread throughout many parts of Europe. In its various forms, it impacted profoundly upon society—on the family, on women and children, and on the poor. Catholicism responded to the Protestant challenge, generating its own reform program and charismatic leaders. Catholic and Protestant movements alike, at this volatile moment of change and readjustment, experienced a surge of intolerance—intolerance and bigotry toward outsiders, heretics, and dissenters, and those labeled as witches, victims of their neighbors' very deepest anxiety and insecurity.

BEFORE THE REFORMATION

Long before Martin Luther confronted the emperor and declined to recant, the preconditions for his revolt were forming. The failures of the Roman Church, and the anxieties of the faithful, formed one set of those preconditions. By 1500, corruption had diminished the Church in the eyes especially of educated elites. Both church leaders and secular rulers had stifled earlier movements for fundamental change. Many Christians were skeptical of the Church and uncertain of their own salvation. They were open to the new solutions proposed by reformers.

A second precondition of the Reformation was the emergence of humanism, the principal intellectual movement of the Renaissance. Humanist thinkers squarely challenged the dominance of the Church in the realm of ideas. Humanist critics, meanwhile, called for moral reform, although they hesitated to take action against the structures of the Church. They were overtaken by the flood of events.

Christendom at Risk

The two centuries from 1300 to 1500 saw the collapse of the Church's prestige, caused by the proliferation of corrupt practices within that institution, and the growth, among lay people, of extreme or bizarre beliefs and customs, at odds with the austere prescriptions of orthodoxy. By 1500, the Church and Christendom itself were in crisis.

From the election of Pope Martin V in 1417, which marked the end of the Great Schism, to the death of Pope Leo X in 1521, the year of Luther's trial for heresy, the Roman Church reached new peaks of worldly grandeur. At great cost, it undertook to rebuild the city of Rome and construct new churches and palaces amid the ancient ruins. To pay for these building projects and to support the lavish establishments of the clergy, papal agents collected taxes from all over Europe. These demands drained a struggling peasantry, while a few privileged men benefited. Wealthy clerics clustered in Rome and spent lavishly to further their ambitions and their comforts. The secretary of the German city of Augsburg wrote ominously in 1491 of his visit to Rome: "I see that everything here can be bought from top to bottom. Intrigues, hypocrisy, adulation are highly honored, religion is debased; ... righteousness sleeps."

The offices of the Church could indeed be bought, and not only in Rome. Among laymen and clergy, abuses were rampant. Wealthy men bought lucrative church positions for their nephews or sons (the abuses of simony and nepotism). Clergymen acquired several titles at once (the practice of **pluralism**). Or they collected incomes from positions they held as bishops while they resided elsewhere and delegated their responsibilities to less eminent substitutes (the abuse

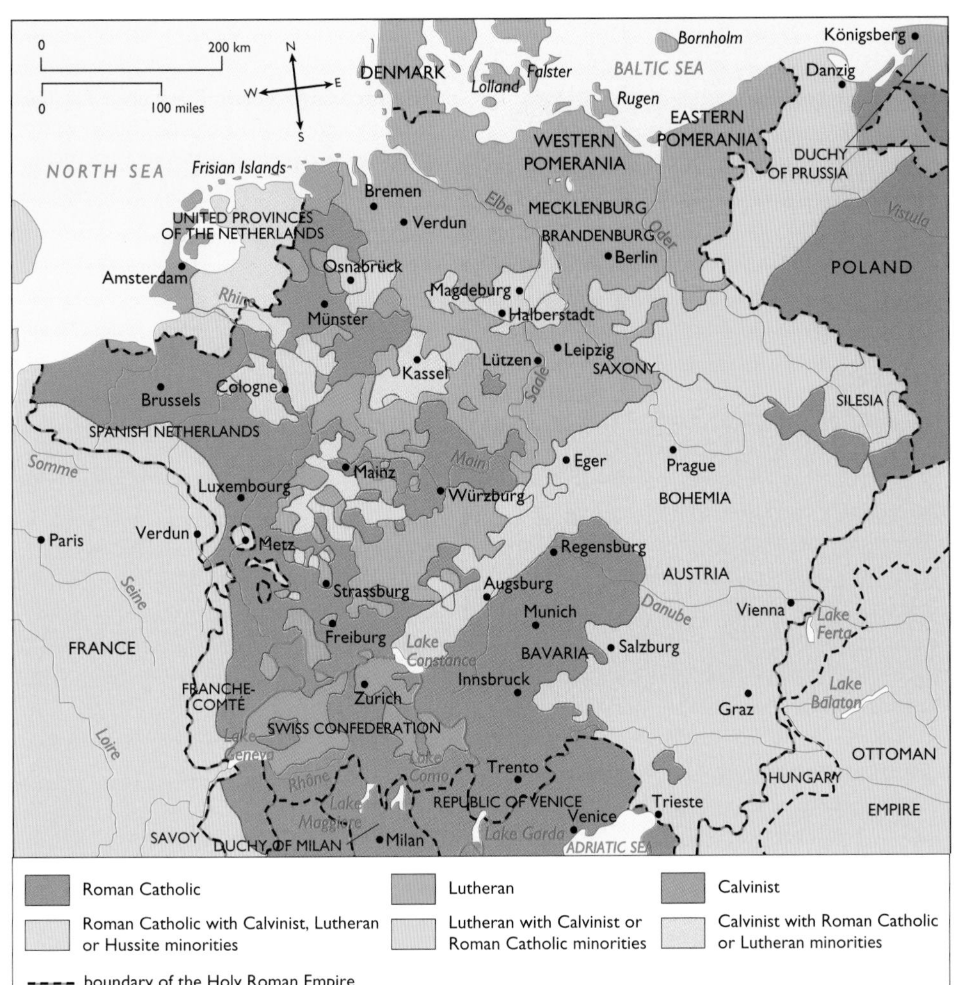

Map 14.1 German confessionalization, sixteenth to seventeenth centuries: *"Protestantism" was not a monolithic movement. Within the first 50 years after Luther's defiance of the Roman church, it flourished in several different varieties, mostly versions of either Lutheran or Calvinist theology. This map shows that the religious divisions of Germany in the century after Luther's revolt were nearly as numerous as the political divisions—and indeed they mirrored the religious preferences of the princes or city-states that dominated in each state.*

of absenteeism). Or they arranged for offices to be conferred on them or their kin in the future (the abuse of reservation). Or they paid to be nominated to vacant offices. The treasury in Rome, meanwhile, grew fat from collecting the annate, the first year's revenue from these ecclesiastical offices. Besides profiting from their official positions, priests, bishops, cardinals, and even the pope kept concubines, or surrounded themselves with courtesans and prostituted boys.

Male and female monasticism were also in decline. Even the mendicant friars, created in the last surge of monastic reform, often lived comfortable lives. Although monasteries and convents included many pious men and women, they also housed people who had no true vocation or calling for the religious life. At the same time, the friars who preached to ordinary lay people ranted at them for their sins and painted vividly the tortures of Hell awaiting the unrepentant. Receptive to and terrified by such tirades, Christians often feared that their sins would merit eternal damnation or prolonged suffering in Purgatory. To avert these destinies, they could repent and receive absolution and perform penance.

They could also earn or purchase an **indulgence**, a papal letter to those who had performed an especially worthy act (such as going on a pilgrimage or making a large donation). It granted remission from punishment for sins that had not been absolved at the time of death. This practice dated back to the early Middle Ages. It received new life in the mid-1400s when the Church decreed that indulgences could remit punishment for souls of the dead already in Purgatory, as well as those still alive who might someday find themselves in that state. After about 1500 the papal sale of indulgences accelerated. The proceeds were earmarked to pay for the building of the new Basilica of Saint Peter's and to fend off a feared invasion of the Turks.

The sale of indulgences was an extremely successful mode of fund raising because it tapped the fervent piety of the Christian public. Throughout the fourteenth and fifteenth centuries popular religious feeling had been increasingly intensifying. The number of shrines multiplied, especially those that promised miracles of healing, and the number of people going on pilgrimages likewise mounted. The use of the **rosary** as an aid in devotion and the recitation of prayers became popular. The collection and veneration of relics of the saints, a long-established practice, intensified around 1500, when the craze for relics also heightened. One famous and proud collector was Frederick III (r. 1486–1525), called "the Wise," the Elector of Saxony—later the protector of Martin Luther (an elector was one of the German princes entitled to participate in the election of the Holy Roman Emperor). Among his enormous collection of 19,000 relics were a straw from the manger in Bethlehem where Jesus was born, wood from the cross on which he had died, and the thumb of Saint Anne.

***The faces of reform:** The scholar Erasmus, a severe critic of the Catholic Church who nonetheless remained within its circle until his death, is depicted in a lithograph together with students, and prominent disciples.*
(Nederlands Geschiedenis)

These pious practices could not entirely allay people's anxiety about death or their fears of the afterlife. Skeletons figured often in paintings; references to the decay of the body appeared in poems; and the design and construction of tombs preoccupied many eminent patrons. Manuals of instruction in "the art of dying" sold well. Wealthy men and women made prudent bequests to religious communities to pay for special services for their own departed souls. For the first time, mourners clothed themselves in black and devised elaborate funeral rites.

While the higher clergy misbehaved and the pious sought comfort where they could, several reform movements developed to meet the spiritual needs of the faithful. The Waldensian, Wyclifite, and Hussite movements (see Chapter 10), all decreed heretical, distrusted the clergy and called for a deeper piety, more closely linked to the New Testament Jesus. In Italy, pious Christians joined in ritual processions to win the favor of the saints and met regularly in confraternities to worship, to do charitable service, and to perform works of penance. The Italian movements climaxed in an extraordinary four years in Florence, where the Dominican monk Girolamo Savonarola (1452–1498) persuaded the citizenry to make a "bonfire of the vanities"—to burn in public their mirrors, jewelry, works of art, books—as a sign of repentance.

The Low Countries (modern Belgium and the Netherlands) were the home of the "New Devotion," an anticlerical and anti-institutional movement of pious laymen and women influenced by the tradition of northern mysticism. Its practitioners believed that each individual should find his or her way to God through devotional reading and reflection. It was this mix of piety and books that characterizes the work of Desiderius Erasmus (c. 1466–1536), the leading intellectual of the day.

Christian Humanism

An education influenced by the "New Devotion" was one stimulus behind Erasmus' religious thought. Another, equally important, was humanism. Erasmus was the major communicator outside Italy of humanist scholarship (see Chapter 13). The dual ommitment to Christian piety and humanist learning that he exemplified is known as "Christian humanism." Although Christian humanists laid some of the groundwork for the Protestant Reformation, they stopped short of a commitment to that movement.

Erasmus Born in the city of Rotterdam (modern Netherlands), Erasmus considered himself, with reason, a citizen of the world. After spending six years in a Dutch monastery and taking holy orders, he went on to study and work in England, France, Italy, and Switzerland. He rejected the dogmatic, intolerant attitudes of his religious training, being drawn increasingly toward the scholarship of the humanists. In the early 1500s, he urged a return to the simple faith of the followers of Jesus, a set of beliefs that he called the "philosophy of Christ." The vast hierarchy of the Church, the panoply of rituals and sacraments, the worship (rather than merely reverence) of saints, the claim to forgiveness for sins through the performance of pilgrimages or the purchase of pardons—all these practices he considered unnecessary and a barrier to faith. His views reached a huge audience.

Erasmus wrote many works—sixty-five volumes—which underwent many editions and translations and were read widely throughout Europe. It was the invention of movable type that made this voluminous production possible. Perfected by John Gutenberg in the 1440s and 1450s in Mainz (modern Germany), the printing press revolutionized the dissemination of ideas. By 1500 printing presses could produce accurate and legible versions of religious and secular classics. In the past, all books had been copied by hand. They circulated in two or ten or thirty copies, each a little different because transcribed by a different writer. Only a classic, such as the orations of Cicero or the Bible, would be available in hundreds of copies—and their texts might differ significantly. After the invention of the printing press, identical copies of a single work could be purchased for a relatively modest price at one of the bookstalls that began to appear in towns. More than ever before, books could sway people's minds.

One of the bestsellers of the early 1500s was Erasmus' *Handbook of the Christian Soldier*. The book was written, the author explained, on the plea of a woman whose soldier husband's sins put him in danger of losing his soul. Erasmus offered as a remedy his own prescription for a Christian life. A person who imitated Jesus, he wrote, could achieve an experience of oneness with God. There was no need for saints or pilgrimages, popes or theologians, or even priests. Erasmus' recipe for piety plain and simple amounted to a frontal attack on the Roman Church—precisely what the author, who hoped to die in bed and not as a branded heretic, wished to avoid.

Erasmus' reputation as a troublemaker only increased when he wrote (in 1511) the *Praise of Folly*. "Folly" herself—an outlandish female personification of foolishness and irrationality—narrates this lively essay in self-praise, sharp satire, and Christian vision. She defends the "folly" of friendship and marriage, self-delusion, and even insanity against a spiritless and life-defeating rationalism. She pokes fun at schoolteachers and philosophers, bishops, cardinals, popes, priests, monks, and, most of all, theologians. She argues that religious experience, by which one deserts earthly concerns to dwell in the spirit of God, is a form of folly. The whole work is a witty exercise in indirection, a veiled but still devastating attack on a corrupt clergy and decadent Church.

Even more audacious than Folly's critique of the Church was Erasmus' edition of the New Testament (1516). In the fourth century, the whole Bible had been translated into Latin, in which version, later called the Vulgate, it circulated during the Middle Ages. But the Vulgate was occasionally inaccurate, argued Erasmus, who was influenced in this criticism by the Italian humanist Lorenzo Valla. It interposed meanings not justified by the literal text, and its inaccuracies, he believed, had led Christians astray. Erasmus' New Testament contained the authoritative Greek text and his own translation into Latin, together with his critical commentary. It could be seen as a scholarly exercise. Or it could be interpreted as an assault on the authority of the Church.

Erasmus wrote *The Education of the Christian Prince* for a privileged boy who would one day become a ruler—the future emperor Charles V. A young prince, rightly trained, argued the author, would mature to hate war, provide justice, and nurture the poor. As for ordinary children, Erasmus feared they might grow up ignorant and therefore vulnerable to the excessive formalism of the Church. The antidote he offered was, again, proper learning, and he wrote a treatise, *On Education*, advocating a rigorous yet humane course of study for the young.

Erasmus also produced a textbook: a collection of entertaining dialogues entitled *Colloquies*, designed to teach young people the rudiments of Latin as they discussed current issues. One of these dialogues, called "The Shipwreck," illustrates how Erasmus promoted his concept of true piety through his humanist work. On the bleak North Sea, sharp winds batter a little ship. The mast breaks. The captain tells his passengers that all is lost—it is just a matter of time. The voyagers pray to the saints, to whom they offer gifts of golden candlesticks or golden coin if they survive. A woman holding a child prays quietly to herself. A priest strips himself to his underclothes—so as best to be prepared to swim. The narrator of the story silently trusts to God. The mighty waves tear the ship to pieces, and the voyagers pile onto the lifeboat—which quickly sinks—or cling to splintered planks and fragments of mast. Only seven of the fifty-eight passengers find their way to shore. All those who tried to buy the favor of the saints perish. Among the survivors are the narrator, the mother and child, and the literally unfrocked priest.

This simple story unveils the false worship of saints, de-sanctifies the clergy, and depicts nature as an autonomous force not readily controlled by ritual. It amounts to a critique of contemporary religion, addressed to an unprecedently large public and energizing a whole generation of thinkers.

Erasmus' friends and correspondents, some of whom are depicted on p. 386, included many of Europe's leading intellectuals. Most important among these were his English colleagues John Colet (c. 1467–1519) and Thomas More (1478–1535), and the Spanish-born Juan Luis Vives (1492–1540), who worked in England and Louvain (or Leuven; in modern Belgium). Colet labored to introduce Greek as well as Latin studies to English education. He founded a school at Saint Paul's Cathedral in London, centered on the new humanist curriculum, reserving a few places for poor scholarship students. Vives, too, was a teacher, and briefly tutor to Princess Mary, King Henry VIII's elder daughter and future queen of England. He wrote groundbreaking works on liberal education, and specifically on women's education. The work of both Colet and Vives had a social dimension, in line with Erasmian principles: Colet was a pacifist, and Vives proposed for one Belgian town (Ypres) a complete program for poor relief.

Thomas More The lawyer (later saint) Sir Thomas More did much to promote humanistic scholarship, training his own children in the Classics (including his daughter, Margaret More Roper, an author in her own right). The author of letters, history, biography, and religious treatises, More is best known for his slim book ***Utopia***. In its pages he criticizes the social policies of contemporary England and proposes a wholly rational model society, which exists "nowhere" (the literal meaning of the Greek word *utopia*). Thomas More rose in the government of King Henry VIII to the lofty position of lord chancellor—then fell suddenly, later to be convicted of treason. His earnest Catholicism, which he would not relinquish to save his life, led him into fatal conflict with the king, who had broken with the Roman Church to solve some problems of his own.

In 1535, More was beheaded, a martyr and a Christian humanist. For the previous fifteen years, Erasmus had been maneuvering to avoid the same fate. Opposed in principle to all conflict, Erasmus especially feared conflicts caused by religious disagreement. These he could not avoid, although he did manage to die in his bed and not on the scaffold. His own works excited the controversy he so much deplored. They were condemned in country after country, burned or defaced. Yet Erasmus remained a Catholic. In his last years, he settled in Basel (Switzerland), which he found very congenial until it officially adopted Protestantism, whereupon he transferred swiftly to Catholic Freiburg (modern Germany)—returning to Basel only when close to death. Though he refused to join the new Protestant movement (hatched, as one observer put it, from the egg Erasmus laid), he could not disown his criticism of the Roman Church.

Erasmus and his colleagues, caught up in the furor of the first phase of the Reformation, were men whose intellectual outlooks were formed by the Renaissance.

***Hans Holbein the Younger,* Erasmus of Rotterdam, c.1523:** *Hans Holbein, the leading German artist of his generation, knew Erasmus from his youth. Both artist and author were actively involved in the printing houses, then in their dynamic first years. In 1523, Holbein painted Erasmus as a scholar in his prime at work in his study. In this later portrait, Erasmus is portrayed as the cosmopolitan senior intellectual of the age, as upstanding and elegant as the classically sculpted pillar next to which he stands, his hands, which had crafted so many books, lightly resting on a book on the edges of which appear words in Greek—"the Herculean labors"—and Latin—"of Erasmus of Rotterdam."* (Private Collection)

The two movements were very different in nature but were closely related and nearly contemporary—in Italy the Renaissance preceded the Reformation; in the north, the two movements coincided. The Renaissance was a cultural movement, fueled above all by the zeal to recover and relive the world of Classical antiquity. Its agents were intellectuals, mostly male, mostly lay people, and mostly from the middling and elite ranks of society. The Reformation was a religious movement which had enormous social and political effects. It was impelled by the spiritual needs of individuals and communities, as well as by the ambitions of opportunistic rulers and leaders. It had consequences for men and women, rich and poor, Protestants and Catholics, town dwellers and villagers, from every region of Europe. Erasmus was a Christian and a man of the Renaissance whose high principles opened the path to the Reformation, a revolution he had no desire to join.

The Erasmian blend of Renaissance humanism and Christian piety offered a promise of spiritual, educational, and social reform. However, its program was not sufficient for the challenges of that day, and so it ultimately failed. Religious tensions had already developed to the point that they called forth fundamental changes in the lives and beliefs of Christians. The unity of the one church and the one faith would soon be shattered.

FAITH AND WORKS

The following revolution had spiritual, social, and political dimensions of a magnitude Erasmus could not have imagined. The critical figure was the German monk and university professor Martin Luther, who struck at the heart of the Roman Church by questioning the whole apparatus of clergy, sacrament, and canon law. He insisted on a transformation of the individual personality resulting from a renewed commitment to the New Testament Jesus as the route to salvation (see *Witnesses*, p. 393). He stood by those beliefs before the Holy Roman Emperor, and survived to see his ideas transform Europe.

Luther's Message

For centuries, Christians had sought salvation, a reunion with God in Heaven after death, through a lifelong striving to do good deeds and avoid sin. They purged any sins they might commit through the sacramental process of confession, penance, and absolution, and thus achieved justification. Luther upset this understanding of the Christian's road to God. All people were immersed in sin, he believed, and no one could perform truly good works or avoid sinful acts. Every Christian seeking salvation must experience the forgiveness of God inwardly—the experience of faith, which itself conferred justification.

Like all conscientious Christians of his day, the young man Luther had sought assurance of salvation. He examined his conscience scrupulously: had he committed any deeds he had forgotten to confess? was there some secret sin, of which he was not even aware, that might spell his damnation? Luther was afraid of God and afraid for himself. The consequence was anxiety and despair.

While in his early twenties, Luther had joined the Augustinian order and had subsequently been ordained a priest. Later, he became a lecturer in philosophy at the University of Wittenberg, in Saxony (in modern Germany); and it was while teaching there that he found the solution to his predicament. He found it in the Epistles of Paul. "The just shall live by faith," wrote Paul (Romans 1:17); that is, they would receive from God the gift of righteousness. Luther argued that the Christian was reconciled with God, or justified, not by the performance of certain acts but by the reception of divine forgiveness: the grace of God.

The doctrine of "justification by faith alone" countered the Roman Church's assumption (later made official doctrine) that salvation could be attained by doing good works, aided by God's grace. According to the traditional outlook, sin was inevitable but could be erased by doing penance—more good works. In theory, sincere repentance was required before absolution would be granted. In practice, absolution was often granted in the absence of a repentant attitude upon the performance of a penance (such as the recitation of a prayer a certain number of times), or a donation to the Church, or the purchase of an indulgence.

This last practice seemed especially outrageous to Luther. How could the mere purchase of a letter release a sinner from punishment when God required true and perfect obedience? In 1517, aware of the approach of the indulgence salesman John Tetzel, a Dominican monk, Luther compiled a list of abuses in the contemporary Church as a series of theses, or propositions he would debate with any challenger. Luther's *Ninety-Five Theses* may not actually have been nailed to the door of Wittenberg's castle church, as legend has it. Nevertheless, they roused a clamor, as printed copies of the *Theses* flew to all parts of Europe. "No words of mine could describe the storm raised here by your books," wrote Erasmus, then in Louvain, a few months later.

Erasmus was horrified. Initially, he agreed with Luther's statements about indulgences, the bloated papacy, the excessive stress on rites and sacraments. But Erasmus feared the coming conflict and its consequences. He gradually distanced himself from Luther. In 1518, he expressed cautious approval of the German reformer's statements. In 1519 and 1529, he lamented their outspokenness. By 1524, he had rejected Luther's positions on faith and grace. These theological giants contended in a verbal duel, as Erasmus outlined his views in *On Free Will*, and Luther expressed his in the rebuttal entitled *On the Bondage of the Will*.

If human beings are not free to choose, Erasmus argued, then how can they be rewarded for good acts and punished for evil ones? Upon the freedom of the individual to make moral decisions hinges the individual's welfare and, ultimately, that of human society as well. In responding, Luther pointed to the omnipotence of God, who created the human actors of deeds good and bad. These human agents, if filled with the spirit of God, performed good acts; if not, they performed evil ones. With considerable psychological insight, Luther argued that those who did evil did not do so unwillingly but spontaneously. Such an impulse to do evil the individual "cannot, by his own strength, eliminate, restrain, or change." Although free will may operate in ordinary matters, in matters pertaining to God and salvation, "man has no free will, but is a captive, servant and bondslave, either to the will of God or to the will of the Devil."

By 1525, the profound implications of the concept of justification by faith emerged. It was in faith, rather than in works, that Christians found salvation and true liberty—a personal, interior liberty, and a liberation from the institutions of the old Church. For now each Christian was his own priest, equipped (increasingly) with a Bible translated into his own native language. Priests, bishops, monks, cardinals, nuns, and abbots, the whole splendid hierarchy of the Church, were useless. At the weekly Sunday celebration of Jesus' resurrection, not a priest but a **pastor** presided: a "shepherd," or minister, whose role was not to confer grace but to teach Scripture. Authority resided in Scripture alone, and the church consisted of a "priesthood of all believers."

The Confrontation

In the traditional Church, members of a professional priesthood saw to the spiritual growth of its adherents. Luther's concepts of justification by faith alone, of the bondage of the will, of the scriptural standard for truth, and of the priesthood of all believers challenged the status of those professionals. Prelates and theologians denounced Luther. Nevertheless, unlike John Huss and some others who had challenged the Church of Rome (see Chapter 10), Luther survived the attacks against him. Three circumstances explain his survival: his compelling message, his powerful personality, and the ambitions of the German princes and free cities, for whom conversion to the new faith meant liberation from Rome. As a result, Luther's revolt matured into a new religion.

The printing press which enabled the circulation of increasingly accurate texts also drove Luther's reform. New views now spread swiftly, in cheap and easily digested form. Luther's pamphlets could be understood by the sizable number of readers literate in the vernacular. Even those unable to read could understand the inflammatory cartoons mocking fat and greedy clergymen which were reproduced from woodcuts in pamphlets and single sheets. One is illustrated in *Windows On* on p. 391. The 30 tracts Luther wrote between 1517 and 1520 were distributed in 300,000 printed copies, each appearing in as many as 19 editions. By early 1519, his works had reached France, Spain, Italy, England, the Low Countries, and Switzerland. "I have never had such good luck with a book," the overjoyed Basel-based printer John Froben reported to Luther; he had only ten copies left.

In the single year 1520, Luther published three works that further eroded the universal authority of the Roman Church. In his *Address to the Christian Nobility of the German Nation*, he summoned local secular rulers to take charge of church matters (including social welfare and education) and participate in the reform movement he delineated. In his *Babylonian Captivity of the Church*, he denied the capacity of priests or popes to affect the relationship between individuals and God. In *On the Freedom of a Christian*, he argued that true human liberty was obtained through God's justification.

To these three angry and uncompromising pamphlets, the pope responded with an official letter or "**bull**": if Luther persisted, warned the pope, he would be excommunicated. Luther responded by burning the bull, along with the works of his adversaries, in full view of the faculty and students of Wittenberg University. Early in 1521, the pope excommunicated the rebellious monk. The emperor then summoned him before a Diet (a meeting of the imperial Reichstag, or parliament) at Worms. Upon examination Luther appeared to be guilty as charged. He refused to recant, in the memorable words quoted at the outset of this chapter.

In anticipation of Luther's arrest (which meant a likely heresy trial and death), his friends arranged his to escape. He took refuge for a year in a castle provided by the German prince of Saxony, Frederick the Wise. There Luther undertook a translation of the New Testament into German—in violation of church guidelines—so that it might be read by ordinary Christians. He subsequently completed a German translation of the whole Bible. His masterful translation helped mold the German language and encouraged Biblical translations into other vernaculars in the years that followed.

In only a few years, Luther had wrought a new theology and inspired a movement of peoples prepared to shed the customs of their childhood and of their ancestors for a different way of life. Luther explained how it happened: "I simply taught, preached, and wrote God's word; otherwise I did nothing. ... The Word did everything. ..."

Protestant Propaganda

Cranach the Younger, **The Last Supper of Lutherans, c. 1540**

The pope and clergy fleecing sheep, c. 1530

The early reformers fought their battles in print. In inexpensive pamphlets and broadsheets as well as traditional, sturdy volumes, they presented their case against the abuses of the old Church to ordinary people, especially of the towns, where literacy rates reached as high as 50 percent. Woodcut cartoons and narrative pictures had the desired effect on those who were not literate. In this engraving by Cranach the Younger (above left), Lutheran worshipers left and center receive the bread and wine of the Last Supper while Catholics, on the right, descend to hell; in the middle, Luther preaches the Word of God.

In the second of these scenes (above right) the pope and clergy are shown fleecing sheep, which stand for the ordinary Christian people.

On the title page of John Foxe's Acts and Monuments *(left) commemorating English Protestant martyrs, Protestant worshipers are depicted in the lower left vignette listening to and revering the Word of God (in Hebrew characters at top right), while Catholic worshippers in the right vignette, condemned to Hell in Foxe's eyes, hold rosary beads and march in mindless uniformity behind a clerical procession.*

(top right: Graphische Sammlung Albertina, Vienna; left: Folger Shakespeare Library)

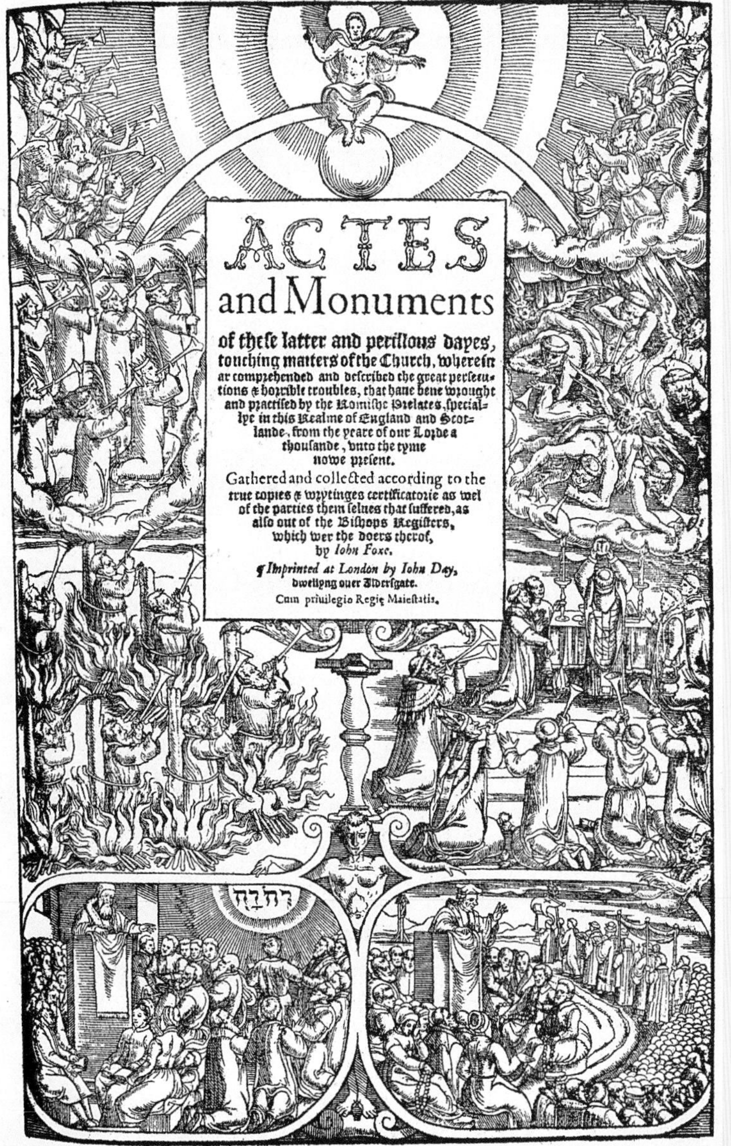

ACTES
and Monuments
of these latter and perillous dayes, touching matters of the Church, wherein ar comprehended and described the great persecutions & horrible troubles, that haue bene wrought and practised by the Romishe Prelates, speciallye in this Realme of England and Scotlande, from the yeare of our Lorde a thousande, unto the tyme nowe present.
Gathered and collected according to the true copies & wrytinges certificatorie as wel of the parties them selues that suffered, as also out of the Bishops Registers, which wer the doers therof, by *Iohn Foxe.*
Imprinted at London by Iohn Day, dwellyng ouer Aldersgate.
Cum priuilegio Regię Maiestatis.

John Foxe, **Actes and Monuments,** ***1563***

To continue your investigation of this topic, please go to www.prenhall.com/king for the related **WINDOWS** on the **WEB** activity

THE UNFOLDING REFORMATION

It took more than words to make this revolution. In 1522, with the climate of opinion in Wittenberg leaning towards reform, Luther returned to rebuild its form of worship and way of life. From there he and his associates oversaw the conversion of towns and their princes elsewhere in the Empire. Soon other leaders inaugurated independent reform movements in other parts of Europe—notably in the towns of Switzerland, under the leadership of Ulrich Zwingli and John Calvin. Meanwhile, rulers exploited Protestantism in order to promote their ambitions, elevating themselves as heads of the church within their own nations. Not only petty German princes, but also the kings of Denmark, Sweden, and England sought to enhance their authority by this route. Within a generation of its origin, the Reformation, now "Protestant," reinvented itself in disparate forms throughout much of Europe.

Wittenberg, Zurich, and Geneva

Luther's Wittenberg, Zwingli's Zürich, Calvin's Geneva: these were the three nurseries of the Reformation. In each, a reformer who was both an original thinker and a gifted leader, supported by committed disciples and a cooperative civic administration, led a whole community to exchange the yoke of tradition for a radically different form of religious observance.

Luther's colleagues in Wittenberg did not wait for him to return from exile before escalating their attack on Catholicism. They seized churches, smashed altars and images, and ousted uncooperative clergy. They opened the monasteries and convents, dispersing monks and urging nuns to marry. On Christmas Day, 1521, Andreas Karlstadt (c. 1480–1541) celebrated for the first time anywhere the Protestant communion instead of the Catholic mass. His call for the removal of images is quoted in *Witnesses* on p. 397.

Luther returned in 1522, reined in his associates, and led a more moderate transition to a reformed liturgy. Still, worship differed radically from the Latin mass. By 1526, it was performed in German, so that the whole congregation might understand it. It centered on the sermon, rather than on the ritual of the mass. Most crucially, the very meaning of the Eucharist was changed. In place of **transubstantiation**, the miraculous transformation of bread and wine into the body and blood of Christ, Lutherans (as they now called themselves) embraced the doctrine of the "real presence" of Christ in the elements (see below). Musically, too, the service was different. Instead of only listening to priest and choir, all joined in singing hymns, or "chorales," some of them composed, words and music, by Luther. The singers included women, whose voices had not previously been heard in the churches. Hymn singing would inspire later composers and spur new developments in Western music.

By the mid-1520s a leading clergyman of Zürich, Ulrich Zwingli (1484–1531), had started a revolution of his own. An admirer of Erasmus, Zwingli had pursued the logic of the humanist critique of medieval Christianity to the point of rebellion. Luther's ideas encouraged him further. In 1522, during the forty-day penitential fast of Lent, the Reformation in Switzerland was launched as, in Zwingli's presence, some of the city's most prominent men sat down ceremoniously to a meal of forbidden sausages.

In 1523, Zwingli composed sixty-seven articles summarizing his theological principles, based on the premise that Scripture contained the whole word of God. In 1524–1525, he and his followers purged the city's churches of the statues of saints and painted their figured walls white. In 1527, he had the splendid organ of the great cathedral removed and chopped to pieces in the belief that beautiful music promoted idolatry. Other old church practices which Luther continued—such as elaborate choral music—Zwingli banned.

Zwingli differed from Luther especially on the meaning of the Lord's Supper. For Zwingli, the event was simply a remembrance of the Last Supper, during which, stirred by symbolic representation, the believer experienced communion with God. For Luther, the bread and wine of the Supper were ("essentially and substantively") also the body and blood of Jesus. Thus he held to the doctrine of the "real presence" of Christ in the communion, while rejecting the Roman doctrine of transubstantiation. A Lutheran Last Supper is depicted in *Windows On* on p. 391. In 1527, Luther fired a bitter tract at Zwingli entitled "That These Words of Christ 'This Is My Body' Still Stand Firm Against the Fanatics." Zwingli responded in kind.

In 1529, the two combatants met in the German city of Marburg to settle the matter, which they were unable to do. By this time, other German and Swiss cities (including Basel and Strasbourg) had begun the process of reformation, and their leaders were present. Although no final agreement was reached, the stage was set for the Augsburg Confession of the following year. The terms of the Confession were composed by Luther's younger associate, Philip Melanchthon (1497–1560). The document was a moderate and minimal statement of the Lutheran position, which provided a point of focus for the diverse churches and communities that had begun to crystallize in central Europe. A later statement of Lutheran principles was reached in the 1577 Formula of Concord, endorsed by the majority of the electors, princes, dukes, and cities which by then had taken up the banner of reform.

Zwingli died in 1531, on the battlefield at Kappel (modern Germany) in one of the first wars of religion that would mark the century to come. The Zwinglian reform had made its particular contribution, but developed no further. The Calvinist movement which began soon after Zwingli's death, and borrowed much from the Swiss reformer's achievement, was quite another matter.

The French-born John Calvin (1509–1564) was on the road to reform himself when Luther's revolution broke. As a student in Paris, Calvin had been inspired by the Christian humanist Jacques Lefèvre d'Etaples, who enjoyed the patronage of the sister of the king of France, Marguerite d'Angoulême. But the royal court was less tolerant of Lutheranism, and in 1533–1534 Calvin found his life in danger for associating with reform-minded friends. It was around this time, when forced to flee Paris, that he decided Luther was right.

Once converted to the reform movement, Calvin moved swiftly. By 1536, he had written the first version of his *Institutes of the Christian Religion* outlining the basic arguments of Calvinist, or "Reformed," Protestant theology. Subsequent, larger editions were published until the final eighth one of 1559. The precepts of the *Institutes* were also contained in Calvin's

WITNESSES

Luther and Calvin Challenge the Church

Martin Luther and John Calvin both challenged the Roman Church fiercely and defiantly—but from different positions. Here Luther argues that faith in Jesus Christ confers a complete freedom upon the believer, who in his transformed condition acts upon his faith purely and uncompelled. Calvin argues, in contrast, that the human individual from birth has been predestined by an omnipotent God either towards salvation or damnation.

Luther defines the freedom of a Christian (1520): Man has a twofold nature, a spiritual and a bodily one. According to the spiritual nature, which men refer to as the soul, he is called a spiritual, inner, or new man. According to the bodily nature, which men refer to as flesh, he is called a carnal, outward, or old man. ... Because of this diversity of nature the Scriptures assert contradictory things concerning the same man, since these two men in the same man contradict each other, "for the desires of the flesh are against the Spirit, and the desires of the Spirit are against the flesh," according to Gal. 5 [:17].

First, let us consider the inner man to see how a righteous, free, and pious Christian, that is, a spiritual, new, and inner man becomes what he is. It is evident that no external thing has any influence in producing Christian righteousness or freedom, or in producing unrighteousness or servitude. ... It does not help the soul if the body is adorned with the sacred robes of priests or dwells in sacred places or is occupied with sacred duties or prays, fasts, abstains from certain kinds of food, or does any work that can be done by the body and in the body. The righteousness and the freedom of the soul require something far different since the things which have been mentioned could be done by any wicked person. Such works produce nothing but hypocrites. On the other hand, it will not harm the soul if the body is clothed in secular dress, dwells in unconsecrated places, eats and drinks as others do, does not pray aloud, and neglects to do all the above-mentioned things which hypocrites can do. ...

One thing, and only one thing, is necessary for Christian life, righteousness and freedom. That one thing is the most holy Word of God, the gospel of Christ.

The Word of God cannot be received and cherished by any works whatever but only by faith. Therefore it is clear that, as the soul needs only the Word of God for its life and righteousness, so it is justified by faith alone and not any works; for if it could be justified by anything else, it would not need the Word, and consequently it would not need faith.

(Martin Luther, *On the Freedom of a Christian*, 1520; ed. J. Dillenberger, 1961)

John Calvin insists that some are predestined to eternal life, and some to damnation (1559): Book II, Chap. i. Therefore original sin is seen to be an hereditary depravity and corruption of our nature, diffused into all parts of the soul ... wherefore those who have defined original sin as the lack of the original righteousness with which we should have been endowed, no doubt include, by implication, the whole fact of the matter, but they have not fully expressed the positive energy of this sin. For our nature is not merely bereft of good, but is so productive of every kind of evil that it cannot be inactive. Those who have called it concupiscence have used a word by no means wide of the mark, if it were added (and this is what many do not concede) that whatever is in man, from intellect to will, from the soul to the flesh, is all defiled and crammed with concupiscence; or, to sum it up briefly, that the whole man is in himself nothing but concupiscence. ...

Book III, chap. xxi. No one who wishes to be thought religious dares outright to deny predestination, by which God chooses some for the hope of life, and condemns others to eternal death. ... By predestination we mean the eternal decree of God, by which He has decided in His own mind what He wishes to happen in the case of each individual. For all men are not created on a equal footing, but for some eternal life is preordained, for others eternal damnation. ...

(John Calvin, *The Institutes of the Christian Church*, 1559, Bk. II, Ch. I, Bk. III, Ch. 21; from ed. H. Bettenson, 1950)

treatises, biblical commentaries, letters, and sermons, of which more than 2000 survive.

This great body of works presents a sternly consistent theology. Like Luther, Calvin insisted on the priority of Scripture, the omnipotence of God, and the power of redemptive grace, while challenging the authority of the priesthood, sacraments, and saints. More than Luther, he stressed the power of God to govern the universe and to determine the destiny of individual human beings. Central to Calvin's theology is the doctrine of predestination: that God has determined, prior to any human action, the destiny of each human being for good or evil, salvation or damnation (see *Witnesses*, p. 393). Luther, following Saint Augustine (354–430) agreed that God had such authority. But he would not agree to Calvin's imposing statement that "eternal life is fore-ordained for some [people] and eternal damnation for others," each person "predestined either to life or to death." It was a grim message, which, ironically, strengthened the confidence of those who believed themselves among the saved, or "elect."

After leaving France, Calvin settled in Geneva (modern Switzerland) in 1536. Except for a three-year interlude, he preached weekly until his death in 1564, creating of the bourgeois citizens of Geneva a righteous Christian society as he envisioned it. An extract from the Ordinances of 1547 is given in p. 397. In Geneva, Calvinism was a complete way of life, providing a model for other new Protestant communities as to how reform doctrine could be expressed in social arrangements. Preachers guided the behavior of all citizens, and a council, or consistory, scrutinized all lapses. While directing life in Geneva, Calvin coordinated an international Reformed movement, which was unsurpassed in winning new converts and initiating social change. "The Reformation of the church is God's work," a triumphant Calvin wrote to the Emperor Charles V, "and is as independent from human hope and intention as the resurrection of the dead."

The Progress of Protestantism

In 1529, the movement acquired a name. A minority of delegates to the Diet of Speyer, which had condemned the young Lutheran movement, issued a dissenting report in its defense. This was entitled the *Protestatio*, or "protestation"; thus the term "Protestant" was born. By 1555, equipped with a name as well as an identity, Protestantism claimed most of the autonomous cities of the Holy Roman Empire and many of its principalities (small states headed by hereditary rulers). It had also reached peoples in England, France, the Netherlands, Scandinavia, and eastern Europe, as shown on Map 14.2. The map of Protestantism would not achieve clear boundaries for another hundred years and after much bloodshed.

In reaching these boundaries, Protestantism advanced in diverse ways. It expanded city by city, principality by principality, community by community. Sometimes it was instituted by the collective decision of civic leaders. Sometimes it was imposed from above, by a ruler who was himself a convert, or who saw in religious conversion an opportune tool for advancing his interests. Sometimes it came from below, from groups of peasants or artisans for whom liberation from the traditional church promised social liberation also. Sometimes a charismatic figure reminiscent of Huss or Savonarola whipped the mass of the population into a frenzied enthusiasm for reform.

The early changes in Wittenberg and Zurich provided a model for Protestant conversion which many other communities imitated. The reform program in such cases was enacted gradually as decreed by the town council. A new ritual of communion and new beliefs concerning it replaced the celebration of mass. The sacrament of confession and absolution ceased to be performed, although baptism—which, like communion, was sanctioned by Scripture—was retained. The statues of saints vanished from the churches, and Friday and Lenten fasting was forgotten. Preaching based on Scripture and in the language of the people dominated the church service. Schools taught a new set of beliefs organized in question-and-answer form as a **catechism**; the congregation, including women, sang hymns. The monasteries and convents were emptied, and the brothels were shut down.

This was the pattern of reformation in the cities of the Holy Roman Empire, where, in the absence of an overarching system of authority, Protestantism had remarkable success. A majority of the sixty-five imperial cities became Protestant either permanently or for a period (as did a majority of more than 200 smaller towns). In some cases, former clergymen of the Roman Catholic Church, now Protestant reformers, initiated the change. They were supported by the burghers. The ruling council of the town then acted officially to mandate the change. Where the Protestant cause had broad appeal, no particular party or interest group is identifiable as the initiator of city-based reform.

In the principalities of the Empire, the reformation process depended on the prince. If he became a convert to the reform movement, he mandated the reform of all the churches in his domain. If he remained loyal to the old church, so must his subjects. As a result of these princely choices, Protestantism became the established religion, and other religions were either not tolerated or subjected to disadvantages. The same model was followed by whole nations—such as England and Sweden—which became Protestant because of decisions made by their monarchs. The people at large were not consulted, although the reform may already have won many individual converts.

Thus Protestantism spread like a quilt, patch by patch: one became Protestant if one lived in a Protestant city or principality or region. The process was not entirely smooth. It was especially rocky for the principalities of the Holy Roman Empire. In 1530 the Emperor commanded the Lutherans to re-convert to Catholicism. The Lutheran cities and principalities banded together in the League of Schmalkalden (the town in which they met) and raised an army. After years of negotiation and a brief war, the Emperor acknowledged the Protestants' rights in the Peace of Augsburg of 1555. The ruler's religion was to be the religion of his people—a principle later succinctly stated in the Latin phrase "*Cuius regio, eius religio*": "Whoever rules the realm, his religion shall also prevail." Protestant states gained equal rights with Catholic states and were allowed representation in imperial councils. By 1570, well over half of the inhabitants of the Empire were Protestant.

In a region officially Roman Catholic, Protestants of any variety (Lutheran, Calvinist, or one of the smaller **sects**) formed a minority. Or a minority Protestant community might coexist with an established Protestantism of another type. Often these minority Protestant communities, being denied the use of the regular churches, met for worship and governance in "conventicles": in small groups in members' homes or in some other setting. Minority Protestantisms existed most notably in France (officially Roman Catholic) and eastern Europe (officially Catholic or Lutheran). The Puritans of England were minority Protestants within a Protestant nation whose official religion was Anglican—neither Lutheran nor Calvinist, it was similar to Roman Catholicism but owing no allegiance to Rome.

A Protestant city was often multiconfessional. Although the majority adhered to a Lutheran or Calvinist agenda, practitioners of other religions

Map 14.2 The Christian Churches in Europe in the mid-Sixteenth Century: *By the mid-sixteenth century, the Reformation showed significant territorial gains. Central and eastern Europe had dissolved into a patchwork of churches, while the northern kingdoms of England, Scotland, Denmark, and Sweden had converted solidly to Protestant denominations. Roman Catholicism held its own in the Mediterranean south and much of France. Russia remained the bulwark of the Eastern Orthodox church, while Orthodox adherents shared the Balkans with a Catholic minority and Islamic converts.*

were tolerated (although not accorded the same legal rights as conformers): other Protestants, sectarians, Roman Catholics, Jews. Typical of this pattern of reform were cities such as Nuremberg, Basel, and Strasbourg (modern France).

Protestantism and Catholicism coexisted in two regions formerly part of the Holy Roman Empire that gained their political independence in this period: in the cantons of Switzerland and the northern provinces of the Netherlands. In these regions, the divisions of the early Reformation spurred violence. In time, however, the lack of religious uniformity promoted mutual tolerance and did not prevent cooperation for national objectives. When the northern provinces of the Netherlands united to gain their independence from Spanish Habsburg rule after 1579 (see Chapter 15), both Protestant and Catholic nobles participated in the struggle.

France France was not so fortunate. Protestant communities spread especially in its southern regions. They clustered around cities where merchant councils supported reform, as in the Empire, and around noblemen converted to the new faith for various personal and political ends. Sporadic war raged between the Protestant (called "Huguenot") and Catholic nobles until the last decades of the sixteenth century. The hostilities climaxed on the eve of Saint Bartholomew's Day (August 24) of 1572, when the principal representatives of both parties were gathered in Paris. The Catholic nobles sparked a massacre of their Protestant opponents. Smelling blood, a mob of Parisians took to the streets in pursuit of "heretics," slaying more than 3000 before the day dawned. The hysteria spread to the outer provinces, where many thousands more were slain on both sides. The Pope had a medal struck celebrating the massacre and the Catholic king of Spain rejoiced at the news.

After the Saint Bartholomew's Day Massacre, depicted on p. 411, some leading Frenchmen, deploring the effects of religious fanaticism, tried to restore political stability. Calling themselves the "*politiques*" (because their secular and purely *political* goal was to achieve order) they included both Catholics and Protestants. Among them was the Huguenot King Henry of Navarre (a region between France and Spain), who in 1589 succeeded to the throne of France as Henry IV (r. 1589–1610). After several years of Catholic resistance to his rule, he sagaciously converted to the majority faith in 1593, saying (according to some reports), "Paris is well worth a mass." Five years later, Henry issued the Edict of Nantes, which permitted his former coreligionists not merely freedom of worship but even freedom to arm themselves and to build and maintain fortifications against possible outbreaks of anti-Protestant violence. At least for a while, France peaceably contained both Protestant and Catholic communities.

England In England, as in France, Protestantism did not advance smoothly. There, it was the king, Henry VIII (r. 1509–1547), who initiated the break with Rome. He did so in order to divorce his first wife, Catherine of Aragon (daughter of the Spanish monarchs Isabella and Ferdinand), who had failed to produce a male heir, and take a new wife—a move the pope steadfastly forbade. The king then asserted his own supremacy over the Church in England.

With the cooperation of the high clergy and with a minimum of theological debate, Parliament passed the enabling legislation whereby the king displaced the pope as head of the Church. By 1534 there was an independent Church of England, though a Protestant creed for this church had not yet been established. Indeed, by this date very few English men or women were Protestant—including Henry himself. A staunch Catholic, he had previously written a rebuttal of Lutheran beliefs, for which a grateful pope had dubbed him "Defender of the Faith." Britain's Protestant monarchs have borne this ironic accolade down to the present day.

The king's will worked through his ministers and through Parliament. In 1533, Parliament passed the Act of Restraint of Appeals, and in 1534 the Act of Supremacy, which made the king the head of the Church. The Ten Articles issued by clerical convocation in 1536 and the parliamentary Six Articles of 1539 set guidelines for correct belief. Meanwhile, the king had dissolved the monasteries and confiscated their lands and wealth thereby doubling crown revenues. Until 1553, when the Catholic Queen Mary came to the throne the plundering of the churches and monasteries—beautiful and historic stained-glass windows, statues, bells, candlesticks, and vestments, things still sacred to many—proceeded with ravenous force.

Just how Protestant the Church of England would become was an unresolved issue on Henry's death in 1547. For the next decade, England rocked between Protestantism, Catholicism, and Protestantism again. In the reign of Henry's young son Edward VI, a Protestant orthodoxy was established based on the *Book of Common Prayer* (published 1549) and the Forty-Two Articles of 1553, the year of the young king's death. Henry's daughter Mary I, succeeding Edward, reestablished the Catholic Church and persecuted non-repenting Protestants. Responsible for the death of some 300 Protestants (and the exile of many others), she won for herself the epithet "Bloody Mary."

On Mary's death in 1558, she was succeeded by her half sister Elizabeth I (1558–1603), the third surviving legitimate child of Henry VIII (although some opponents questioned her legitimacy). In 1559, Parliament passed the Act of Uniformity, once again abolishing the Catholic mass and bringing back the prayer book of 1549 as a standard for worship

WITNESSES

The Progress of Protestantism

Protestantism progressed as diverse individuals in different settings and moved by greatly varied circumstances made a decision to substitute new beliefs and practices for old and familiar ones. These passages give a sampling of the kinds of decisions or assertions that were made. In the first, Luther's early associate Andreas Karlstadt moves to "cleanse," as he saw it, the churches of images of the saints that traditionally had been the prized objects of reverence. In the second, peasant rebels seize upon reform theology to justify their resistance to serfdom. In the third, the reformed church at Geneva—Calvin's Church—lays out regulations for daily life for members.

Andreas Karlstadt calls for the removal of images from churches (c. 1521): God's houses are buildings in which God alone should be glorified, invoked, and adored. ... Deceitful images bring death to those who worship and praise them. ... We could never deny that it is out of love that we have placed the so-called saints in churches. If we had not loved them, we would not have set them up where God alone should dwell and rule. Had we been opposed to them, we would have fled them rather than embraced them. Our deeds convict us of loving images. Have we not shown them the honour which we show exclusively to great lords? Why have we caused them to be painted and coloured, to be adorned with velvet, damask, silver, and golden robes? ... And offer them that honour and love that we do not willingly give our children, our wives, our parents, our most exalted princes and lords? Who can believe us when we say: We have not loved the idols, the carved and painted images? When our actions have betrayed us? God hates and is jealous of pictures ... and considers them an abomination, and proclaims that all men in his eyes are like the things they love. Pictures are loathsome. It follows that we also become loathsome when we love them.

Thus images bring death to those who worship or venerate them. Therefore, our temples might be rightly called murderers' caves, because in them our spirit is stricken and slain.

(Andreas Karlstadt, "On the Removal of Images," c. 1521; eds. B. D. Mangrum, G. Scavizzi, 1991)

God ordains freedom from serfdom, according to "The Twelve Articles of the Peasants" (1525): The Third Article: It has been the custom hitherto for men to hold us as their own property, which is pitiable enough, considering that Christ has delivered and redeemed us all, without exception by the shedding of his precious blood, the lowly as well as the great. Accordingly, it is consistent with Scripture, that we should be free and wish to be so. Not that we would wish to be absolutely free and under no authority. God does not teach us that we should lead a disorderly life in the lusts of the flesh, but that we should love the Lord our God and our neighbor. ... We are thus ready to yield obedience according to God's law to our elected and regular authorities in all proper things becoming to a Christian. We, therefore, take it for granted that you will release us from serfdom, as true Christians, unless it should be shown us from the Gospel that we are serfs.

("The Twelve Articles of the Peasants," 1525, no. 3; ed. J. H. Robinson, 1897)

Defining the Christian life: from Ordinances For The Regulation of the Churches Dependent Upon the Seigniory of Geneva (1547): *Blasphemy.* Whoever shall have blasphemed, swearing by the body or by the blood of our Lord, or in similar manner, he shall be made to kiss the earth for the first offence; [for the second and third offenses a monetary fine is assigned]; and for the last offence be put in the pillory for one hour. *Drunkenness* 1. That no one shall invite another to drink under penalty of [a fine]. 2. That taverns shall be closed during the sermon ... *Songs and Dances.* If anyone sings immoral, dissolute or outrageous songs, ... he shall be put in prison for three days and then sent to the consistory. ... *Games.* That no one shall play at any dissolute game or at any game whatsoever it may be, neither for gold nor silver nor for any excessive stake, upon penalty of [a fine] and forfeiture of stake played for.

(*Translations and Reprints from the Original Sources of European History*, 1898–1912; ed. George L. Burns)

and belief. Four years later, the moderate and mainstream Thirty-Nine Articles attempted to resolve religious discontents. The English state Church, which was later called Anglican, was thereby established; it posed a *via media* ("middle path"), Protestant in principle but not too distant in its ritual from Roman Catholicism.

Scotland and Ireland In neighbouring Scotland, Calvinist reformers led by John Knox (c. 1514–1572) won converts among both the populace and the nobility, who distrusted their Catholic Stuart queen Mary (r. 1542–1568) and her Catholic French relatives and allies. By the 1560s, much of the nation, including most of its powerful nobles, was Protestant; the monarch, Catholic. After Mary's flight to England and eventual execution by Elizabeth (in 1587), Protestantism was firmly established in Scotland.

Ireland, subject to English rule, remained Catholic during the sixteenth century, but Protestantism was forcibly imposed in the next. A 1641 uprising that was partly a peasant rebellion, partly a strike for national independence, and partly a religious struggle provoked a brutal English response. Oliver Cromwell's equally brutal raid followed in 1649–1650. The 1652 Act of Settlement which concluded this cycle of rebellion and repression not only sought to establish Protestantism as the official religion but expropriated most of the land of Ireland's Catholic natives. The Irish people and their priests have felt the repercussions of these events into the twentieth century.

Scandinavia and eastern Europe With reforming preachers at their side, the Scandinavian kings of Denmark (then including Norway) and Sweden imposed Lutheranism on the German model in the 1520s and 1530s. These were the first kingdoms—as opposed to principalities—to leave the Catholic fold. Here, as in England later, religious autonomy enhanced the authority of the monarch.

By contrast, the spread of Protestantism in eastern Europe, late in the 1500s, took place because of its appeal to aristocratic opponents of centralized monarchy. For a time, Poland became largely Protestant, as its powerful nobles inclined variously to Lutheran, Calvinist, and other reformed beliefs. Protestantism had similar attractions for the nobles of Hungary, while those of Bohemia (the modern Czech Republic), some descendants of the Hussites, easily inclined to the new faith. The Protestantizing tendency of eastern Europe lasted less than two generations. By 1648, these lands had nearly all been won back for the Catholic Church.

By 1555, Protestant communities were established in Germany, Switzerland, France, Belgium, the Netherlands, Scandinavia, England, and Scotland; and, by 1600, in Poland, Bohemia, Hungary, and Austria. By the time Protestantism had achieved these gains, however, it was already being challenged by competing radical sects and countered by a reformed Catholicism.

Radical Reform

Lutherans, Calvinists, and Anglicans were able to achieve political settlements for their adherents. Other Protestant groups were unable to do so. These alternative groups, or sects, constituted the "radical reformation" and were harshly repressed even by other Protestants. Radical Protestants remained critical of both secular and ecclesiastical power. These attitudes foreshadowed some of the views that would accompany political revolution in the seventeenth and eighteenth centuries.

In 1524 to 1525, the German peasants of Thuringia rose up in a revolt that was both a rebellion against oppressive landowners and a call for religious reform (see *Witnesses*, p. 397). The peasants' leader Thomas Müntzer (c. 1489–1525) declared that lords and princes, priests and monks were all "hypocrites and worshipers of men" in whom no further faith could be placed. "I tell you the time has come for bloodshed to fall upon this impenitent and unbelieving world." Müntzer's own blood was spilled at Frankhausen in 1525, along with that of 5000 of his 9000 supporters. Armed only with farming tools, they sang hymns ("as if they were insane," commented a chronicler) as they were slaughtered by soldiers sent to put down the rebellion.

Anabaptists Müntzer is often grouped with the Anabaptists, whose umbrella sheltered a variety of Protestant movements. Beginning in the 1520s, Anabaptist communities spread from Switzerland and the southern German region to the Netherlands and England in the west, and, somewhat later, to Moravia, Bohemia, Prussia, and Poland in the east.

Anabaptists pursued a strict Biblicism, testing each element of their life and belief against the model posed in Scripture. By that biblical yardstick, Anabaptists denied the validity of infant baptism. They believed that, like Jesus himself (baptized in his thirtieth year), the baptized convert to the Christian life should be a thinking, willing adult (including adolescents as young as twelve) who genuinely confessed an experience of faith. On the basis of this belief, they underwent, and required converts to undergo, a "second baptism"—the meaning of the term "Anabaptism." By contrast, Luther, Calvin, and the other mainstream reformers accepted the traditional Church's arguments for infant baptism. Those held that a Christian identity was obtained through birth into a Christian community because of the intent of the adults present. Like their Catholic counterparts, Protestant leaders were, however, horrified by a second rite of baptism performed on adult Christians.

Anabaptists shared more than a preference for adult baptism. They opposed all authorities, secular or ecclesiastical, who sought to limit the perfect freedom of individual conscience. Champions of religious liberty, skeptical of political institutions, they anticipated the position of the United States' Bill of Rights written some 250 years later, with its clear delineation between the realms of church and state.

In sixteenth-century Europe, Anabaptist views aroused great hostility, as was evident in an episode that occurred at the German city of Münster. In 1534 Anabaptists seized the marketplace and town hall, elected their own council, and expelled Catholics and Lutherans from the city. They held all goods in common, opened all houses to all, and burned all books but the Bible. This Anabaptist flock of about 10,000 was led by the charismatic worker John of Leiden, who established a "royal" court, complete with a harem of his fifteen wives, to preside over what he proclaimed to be the New Jerusalem. His reign was brief. In 1535 an army under Münster's bishop besieged, then stormed, the city. They tortured and executed John of Leiden and his followers, tore down the city walls, and returned the residents to Catholicism.

After Münster, the Anabaptist challenge subsided. Equally detested by Protestant and Catholic establishments, Anabaptist groups endured only in a few enclaves, where they appealed to other opponents of secular regimes. Among their best-known descendants are the Moravian Brethren and Mennonites (including the Amish) of North America.

Quakers Other "radical" movements that survived the sixteenth-century persecutions, or which sprang up thereafter, also met with harsh persecution. Inward-looking reformers known as **spiritualists** included the English Society of Friends, popularly known as Quakers (because early Friends sometimes trembled with religious emotion in their meetings). Quakers refused to fight in wars, to swear oaths in court, or even to pay conventional signs of respect to highly placed members of society. They believed that each individual possessed an inner light, an extension of God Himself within the human personality. Originally excluded from public office in England and despised in colonial North America, Quakers managed to survive despite repression and still thrive on both sides of the Atlantic.

Unitarians Another group of scripturally-based religious individualists were the anti-Trinitarians or **Unitarians**, a sect founded in the early 1500s by several theologians including the Spaniard Michael Servetus (c. 1511–1553), a physician who had discovered the pulmonary circulation of the blood, who was executed at Geneva with Calvin's approval, and the Italian Faustus Socinus (1539–1604). Unitarians denied the principle, shared by Catholics and mainstream Protestants, of the threefold nature of God, expressed mystically in the persons of Father, Son, and Holy Spirit. A Unitarian hymn places these provocative words in the mouth of God: "I am one! I am not three persons, but I am one! ... I alone am!" Their author was beheaded, as other Unitarians were viciously and mercilessly hounded and persecuted. In eastern Europe, Unitarianism found a welcome, where it was protected by libertarian nobles sympathetic to its anti-establishment agenda.

Radical reform could not compete with the mainstream Protestant reform movements instituted by city governments or princes. The conservative Protestants urged obedience to political authority—or at least cooperation with rulers and magistrates. For kings, princes, and city councils, church and state must be one and must be united in the interests of the secular order.

PROTESTANTISM AND SOCIETY

The Reformation transformed the lives of ordinary men, women, and children. Under Protestantism, the household, rather than the monastery, became the ideal Christian community. Here the values of orderliness, hard work, sexual morality, economic success, and (as usual) female subordination were cultivated. More schools were created to educate the young, who required literacy if they were to read Scripture and earn salvation. The poor, the grateful recipients of the medieval Catholic charity, had little to hope for from Protestant leaders and patriarchs.

The Family, Sexuality, and Women

Protestantism reshaped the family (see *Windows On*, p. 413). No longer considered by religious leaders to be inferior to contemplative celibacy, family life became the new social ideal. In the household, the dominant male enjoyed enhanced power, even greater than before. He was the chief intermediary between his dependents and God. He led prayers, read Scripture, and enforced moral discipline upon his wife and children, other female kin, and servants. "Every man must be in his own house ... a bishop," explained one prominent Protestant preacher, "not only giving good example, but teaching according to it, rebuking and punishing vice." The household was not merely a family, but a miniature church.

While the father took on pastoral duties, Protestant pastors, who had replaced presumably celibate priests, formed families and households of their own. By 1525, all of Luther's colleagues at Wittenberg had married. Luther himself, at age forty-two, married the twenty-six-year-old Katherina von Bora, a nun who had just been released from her convent. Protestant leaders elsewhere increasingly followed suit. "It is better to make a home and teach the Word of God to one's family than to mutter frigid prayers alone in a sanctuary," thundered the radical Protestant reformer Karlstadt.

Closing the convents was high on the Protestant agenda. Luther's pamphlet entitled *Why Nuns May Leave Cloisters with God's Blessing* asserted that only "blind and mad" bishops and abbots would condemn young girls to waste away in cloisters, for "a woman is not created to be a virgin, but to conceive and bear children." Yet some women preferred to stay in convents—among them the scholar and abbess Caritas Pirckheimer, a noblewoman of Nuremberg. When, in 1525, the city council ordered her to free her nuns of their vows, she protected those who wished to stay. Only one member of the community deserted willingly to Protestantism.

Closing the brothels was often one of the first things a city council did when it embarked on becoming Protestant. In the Middle Ages, prostitution was tolerated, even encouraged and regulated. Protestant reformers, aiming to establish high moral standards, viewed the brothel as an obstruction to the new program. They determined also to control sexual behavior, targeting illegitimacy and single motherhood, premarital sex, infanticide, and sodomy.

Tied to roles as daughters and wives, Protestant women were entirely subject to men and lost the option of the convent offered by the Roman Church. As wives, their duty was to bear and raise children, as Martin Luther himself declared: "Even if they bear themselves weary, or bear themselves out ... this is the purpose for which they exist." Unmarried women were at a disadvantage, where all women were understood to have as their destiny the tasks of childbearing, child-rearing, and household management. As under the old Church, daughters were to accept their parents' choice of spouse. Some Protestant reformers approved of divorce (never accepted by Catholics) for overwhelming cause—where there was adultery or impotence, abandonment or abuse.

The Protestant doctrine of the "priesthood of all believers" presumably granted women a new autonomy, in that they were free as individuals to forge their own relationship with God. In the early days of reform, some women benefited from that new principle. The wives of the early reformers participated in the Protestant **mission**, helping refugees, entertaining visiting pastors, organizing hospitals. One such was Catherine Zell (1497–1562), wife of the Strasbourg reformer Matthias Zell, who helped care for the refugees from the Peasants' War and urged toleration for Anabaptists and other sectarians.

Wealthy women might be patrons of reform. The queen of Navarre Jeanne d'Albret (r. 1555–1572), granddaughter of one king of France and mother of another (Henry IV), whom she raised as a Protestant, protected Huguenots in her realm while practicing a policy of religious liberty unique among European rulers of her day. Ordinary women often persuaded their husbands and sons to embrace Protestantism.

Women were especially active in the radical sects, many of whose leaders allowed women the role of prophet and martyr. About 300 women prophets are known to have existed in England in the 1640s and 1650s alone. Anabaptists welcomed female adherents, even to the priesthood. Spiritualists, who focused on the inner life, inspired by a spark of divine light, viewed women as the equals of men. The sixteenth-century spiritualist Ursula Jost, active in Strasbourg, had many visions of the coming end of the world, seventy-two of which were published. Margaret Fell, wife of the Quaker leader George Fox (1624–1691), announced women's right to preach in her 1666 pamphlet entitled *Women's Speaking, Justified, Proved, and Allowed of by the Scriptures*. The Quakers at first accorded women status equal to men, although they ultimately retreated from that liberal attitude during the eighteenth century.

Even so, there was fear of women becoming involved in matters thought better left to men. The low esteem in which the sects were held by established religions was partly due to the active role taken in them by women. The only church office that women were normally permitted to hold was that of deaconess (a position charged with supplying aid to the sick and the poor). Authorities placed limits on women's discussion of religious matters and even of their thinking about them. The council of the German city of Memmingen prohibited women from discussing religion while drawing water at the well, and King Henry VIII of England officially forbade women to read the Bible.

Reaching the Young

The Protestant emphasis on Bible-reading as the means of establishing a relationship with God triggered an educational mission. Each individual must learn to read. Building on the pedagogical work of the Christian humanists, Protestant reformers opened schools. Their work would ultimately promote the ideal of universal education even after its religious purpose was no longer central.

Beginning with Luther's own town of Wittenberg, schools were established to teach all children to read and to master the rudiments of Christianity. Luther himself created a shorter and a longer catechism by which to instruct both little children and adults in the faith. The shorter catechism was used in the Lutheran schools established throughout Protestant Germany. In 1530, the reformer assessed his achievement: "Our young people, girls as well as boys, are now so well taught in catechism and Scripture that my heart grows warm as I observe children praying more devoutly and speaking more eloquently of God and Christ than, in the old days, all the learned monks and doctors."

On the secondary and university levels, Luther's younger colleague Philip Melanchthon (1497–1560) introduced rigorous academic programs which incorporated the goals of Renaissance humanism along with those of Protestant reform. Melanchthon constructed a secondary school curriculum designed to prepare the young for entry to the advanced professional programs offered in the university. New universities were founded, equipped with theological faculties for the training of future Protestant leaders.

Little was expected of girls' education, as there was no possibility whatsoever of their continuing from elementary to secondary or university education. Girls' schools taught reading, along with morality, decorum, sewing, and singing. As a direct result of Protestant educational efforts, however limited, literacy rates among women rose.

Calvinists also instituted schools to prepare young Christians for the experience of divine grace. Children went to school in remote parts of Scotland and in the English Puritan communities in Massachusetts in North America during the early 1600s. The Geneva Academy, founded in 1559, trained young men from all over Europe to lead new Calvinist communities. In Strasbourg, Johann Sturm (1507–1589), one of the leading pedagogical thinkers of Protestantism, founded a secondary school informed by both humanist and reformed agendas, which came to be influential as a model throughout western Europe. The English Society for Promoting Christian Knowledge (founded in 1698) established fifty-four charity schools to teach boys arithmetic, reading, and writing, and to teach girls "to knit their stockings and gloves," to "learn to write and to spin their clothes."

Such Protestant educational ventures spawned the systems of public education that would be firmly established in some European countries by the end of the nineteenth century, and eventually through much of the world.

The Plight of the Poor

Saint Francis of Assisi (1181–1226) had awakened the conscience of Europe when he insisted that poverty was the key to the genuine worship of God. The true Christian, he maintained, voluntarily embraced poverty, and served the poor. Here Francis renewed the commitment to the poor made by Jesus in the Gospels and acknowledged by the early founders of the Christian churches. The Roman Church acted on that understanding by creating numerous charitable organizations, especially hospitals, orphanages, and asylums for prostitutes, widowed, and abandoned or abused wives. Beggars (who were numerous in many medieval towns) were seen as an opportunity for charitable giving.

The Protestant churches took a dimmer view of the poor, especially of beggars. Jesus loved the poor, they acknowledged, and Protestantism was rooted in Scripture. But Protestants insisted that Christians exert themselves mightily to escape from poverty, just as they were to exert themselves to seek the experience of grace. (Of course, such exertions could not in themselves win salvation for the Christian, who, in Protestant theology, was justified only by faith; but they prepared the spirit for the experience of salvation.) A poor person, especially an able-bodied and youthful male, had self-evidently not exerted himself very much. Protestant towns expelled beggars. At the same time, Protestantism did create institutions to deal with poverty to replace those funded by the Roman Church. Each town or parish had to wrestle with the problem of the local poor, creating workhouses or providing for outrelief.

WHO'S WHO

Precursors, Reformers, Radicals

Erasmus of Rotterdam (c. 1466–1536) Christian humanist who called for reform, but never left the Roman Church that condemned his books.

Gasparo Contarini (1483–1542) Venetian nobleman and humanist dedicated to the reform of the Roman Church; he signed with Melanchthon a moderate formulation on the issue of justification by faith repudiated by the papacy.

Martin Luther (1483–1546) defied papal excommunication and spearheaded the Protestant break from the Roman Church.

Ulrich Zwingli (1484–1531) architect of the Reform in Zürich (Switzerland), who opposed Luther's moderate stand on the sacrifice of the mass.

Thomas Müntzer (c. 1489–1525) adopting the scripturalism of radical Reform, led the Peasants' Revolt of 1524–1525.

Ignatius of Loyola (1491–1556) Spanish nobleman, he founded the Jesuit order on the principles of absolute obedience to the pope and the defense and expansion of the Roman Church.

Philip Melanchthon (1497–1560) Luther's scholarly adviser, author of the Augsburg Confession; mediated many controversies and created the pattern of Protestant higher education.

John Calvin (1509–1564) led the Reformed Church of Geneva, the capital of the European Calvinist movement.

Michael Servetus (c. 1511–1553) Spanish physician and opponent of the doctrine of the Trinity fundamental for both Protestant and Catholic believers; executed by order of the Genevan consistory.

John Foxe (1516–1587) author of *Acts and Monuments of these Latter and Perilous Days* (1563), the much-read account of English Protestant martyrs.

Charles Borromeo (1538–1584) reforming prelate of the Roman Church who attempted to form a model Christian commonwealth in the city of Milan over which he presided as Archbishop.

The peasants were one group of the poor who expected much from the Protestant reform when it first began. These tillers of the soil had been restive during the late medieval centuries, seeking relief from their ancestral dues to territorial lords and from the taxes owed the Roman Church. Expecting that liberation from priests and sacraments would lead to liberation from landlords and rulers, the German peasants, under Thomas Müntzer, mounted their rebellion. In their Twelve Articles published that year, they called for release from serfdom, access to fish, game, firewood, and common lands; modification of tenure, tax, and labor requirements; and the right of a community to choose its own pastor.

Luther at first sympathized with the peasants who had rebelled in the name of the reform, acknowledging their great hardship. The blame lay, he argued, with the lords and princes, the "blind bishops and mad priests and monks," whom he berated: "[you] flay and rob your subjects in order that you may lead a life of splendor and pride, until the poor common folk can bear it no longer." Still the proper remedy for that abuse, he argued, was not rebellion but a new spirit of kindliness on the part of the rulers, and forbearance on the part of the victims. "Suffering, suffering, cross, cross! ... For no matter how right you are," Luther counseled the peasant rebels, "it is not for a Christian to appeal to law, or to fight, but rather to suffer wrong and endure evil; there is no other way. ..."

These were Luther's calm pleas of May 1525. But his tone became harsher. In the end, the same Luther who had defied the authority of the Church could not bring himself to defy the authority of secular rulers, the guarantors of social order. In his treatise *Against the Murdering and Thieving Hordes of Peasants*, he condemned the revolt of the poor mounted in the name of Jesus. Anyone who could do so was invited to "smite, slay, and stab" the rebels. "It is just as when one must kill a mad dog; if you do not strike him, he will strike you, and a whole land with you." Protestant and Catholic princes and lords joined in crushing the revolt, with Luther's approval, in the process slaughtering thousands of rebels.

As Protestantism took form in its many settings, it supported political leaders, enforced moral guidelines, and bolstered the family, showing little indulgence for the poor and little support for women. The Roman Church, meanwhile, undertook its own reform.

CATHOLIC REFORM

Even before Luther, the clergy, intellectuals, and lay people of the Roman Church had urged reform. After the Protestant challenge, the papacy at last undertook a program of self-examination and self-discipline. Reenergized Catholic leaders now renewed their commitment to lead and serve the laity, to worship God wholeheartedly, to recover for the old faith those lost to Protestantism, and to lure to Catholic Christianity those who had never before encountered it, in Old and New Worlds alike. In all, the Catholic reformation, which is sometimes called the Counter-Reformation, amounted to a revolution as significant as the Protestant one.

Catholic Reform

Anonymous, The Burning of Girolamo Savonarola: *Catholic reform had many dimensions as represented in this and the next image. This anonymous painting, c. 1600, shows the execution of Savonarola, the Dominican reformer and prophet of Renaissance Florence.* (Saint Mark's Museum, Florence)

The Struggle for Change

From the late 1400s, when its moral prestige was at its nadir, both laity and clergy struggled to reform the Church of Rome. Christian humanists urged a return to the simplicity of the early church; fiery preachers called for repentance and social change; and church leaders sought to restore forgotten standards of responsibility. Eventually, galvanized by the desertion of millions of its flock, the Church heard the calls for renewal. Beginning in 1545, it undertook a serious program of reform.

Christian humanism was a strong current in Spain and France even before Luther's break with Rome. Its adherents translated and commented upon biblical and early Christian texts as part of a program for the renewal of what Erasmus had called the "philosophy of Christ." The Cardinal Francisco Ximénez de Cisneros (1436–1517), confessor to Queen Isabella of Castile (r. 1474–1504) from 1492 and founder of the Spanish University of Alcalá, exemplified this approach. A diligent scholar himself, he oversaw the production of a Bible, published after his death in

The Changing Church

***Caspar Crayer,* Saint Charles Borromeo Giving Communion to the Plague-stricken in Milan*:* *In this seventeenth-century Flemish painting, Bishop (later Saint) Charles Borromeo is depicted serving his flock during an epidemic of plague in Milan, while his attendant distributes coins.* (Musée des Beaux-Arts, Nancy, France)

1522, containing the complete text printed in parallel columns of Hebrew, Greek, Aramaic, and Latin. Such a tool for study conformed to the Erasmian program that aimed to return religion to its biblical source.

The home of the papacy as well as of the Renaissance, Italy bristled with humanists, saints, prophets, preachers, papal secretaries, and reformers of all categories. The episode of the Dominican monk Girolamo Savonarola revealed the intensity of religious feeling in Florence, the most culturally advanced city on the peninsula. Savonarola pressed Florentines of all social classes, intellectuals and artists among them, to repent of their sins, and reordered the government along republican lines consistent with his vision of a holy city. Denounced in 1498 for heresy, he was tried, condemned, and executed, as shown on p. 402. The deeper streams of spiritual yearning that he tapped would surface again in the turbulent century that followed.

More mild-tempered Christian humanists, often high-ranking clerics, were active in the early 1500s. A group of these formed the Oratories of Divine Love, voluntary associations of clerics seeking a more intense spirituality. Similar ideals inspired the creation of such new orders as the highly orthodox Theatines and the Capuchins, an austere offshoot of the Franciscans.

Some theologians explored dimensions of the problem of salvation that seemed to anticipate Luther. Others attempted practical reform programs on their own; among them was the bishop Gian Matteo Giberti (1495–1543), whose diocese of Verona became a model of Christian administration. Many of these men and movements gravitated to Venice in the late 1520s and 1530s, where they were joined by refugees from Rome (sacked in 1527 by imperial troops) and a variety of visitors from abroad who shared their ideals.

After the election of the reforming Pope Paul III (r. 1534–1549), Rome became once again a magnet

The Complutensian Polyglot*:* *Shown here is a page from* The Complutensian Polyglot Bible*, product of a Catholic committee of scholars, which provides Greek, Latin, and Hebrew versions of the same scriptural passage.*

for prelates intent on Christian renewal. The new pope elevated many reformers to the office of cardinal. In 1537, a group of these cardinals presented to him their *Proposal for the Reformation of the Church*, blasting simony, nepotism, absenteeism, pluralism, and clerical immorality and laxity. By then, both Luther and Calvin had broken away from the Catholic Church.

Briefly in the 1520s to 1540s, Catholic reform tilted toward heresy, as intellectuals and leaders reacted to Luther's challenge. In Venice, Protestant books rolled off the presses and were snapped up by visitors, students, patricians, professionals, and artisans. In Naples, a circle of aristocratic women and adventurous clerics gathered to study scripture with the Spanish mystic and follower of Erasmus Juan de Valdés (c. 1500–1540). Valdés' views, which approached the Lutheran doctrine of justification by faith, inspired a number of erudite noblewomen and Italian clerics, some of whom fled north in 1542 to find safety in Protestant lands.

Even the loyal papal servant Gasparo Contarini (1483–1542), prime mover of the 1537 *Proposal*, found that some Lutheran views made sense. Dispatched in 1541 to the German city of Regensburg to meet with representative Protestant leaders, he and Melanchthon came to a compromise agreement on the issue of justification. It was a dangerous moment for Contarini. His *Letter on Justification*, dispatched from Regensburg to Rome, came close to the Protestant formulation. He died the next year, having narrowly escaped being charged with heresy by the newly established (in 1542) Roman Inquisition.

At first, popes and cardinals had ignored the rebellion brewing north of the Alps. By the time they set in motion the machinery to counter Protestantism and initiate a Catholic reform it was almost too late. Nevertheless, over the next twenty years, the Church would prove itself more than capable of surviving and triumphing over its many problems.

Papal Reform

The Renaissance popes remembered the Council of Constance (1414–1418) all too clearly: it had pushed aside three popes (two were deposed, one resigned) and elected its own papal candidate. After Martin V's election in 1417, reigning popes avoided councils and pursued their own business: the waging of war, the rebuilding of Rome, the accumulation of wealth. Tentative steps toward reform were few and unsuccessful. The Fifth Lateran Council, which was called by Julius II (r. 1503–1513) and which met in Rome over five years from 1512, failed to address the question of papal reform. Its main achievements were to reaffirm the bull *Unam sanctam*, asserting the authority of the pope over secular rulers and to declare officially the doctrine of the immortality of the soul recently questioned by some university-based philosophers. The eloquent reform proposals of the Venetian reformers went unanswered. It was felt that Catholic reform would need to proceed from above, a course intimated by the Platonist scholar Egidio da Viterbo (1465–1532): "Man must be changed by religion, not religion by man." Any changes to be made would be required to respect the supremacy of the Church.

Finally in 1545, no longer able to remain deaf to the Protestant threat, the papacy summoned the council that would grapple with the serious problems facing the Church. The representatives at the Council of Trent (Trento, in northern Italy), which met intermittently in twenty-five formal sessions during the period from 1545 to 1563, undertook the complete reformulation of the Catholic position necessary if the Church were to withstand the explosive force of burgeoning Protestantism. Attendance was scant, and mostly Italian. Only thirty prelates were present at the opening session, sixty at the session where the decision was made on justification that closed the door to compromise with Protestantism, and only 255 at the closing sessions to approve and sign the various decrees. These numbers contrast sharply with the more than 1000 who had gathered at Constance in 1414.

These few delegates repudiated Protestant doctrines and reaffirmed Catholic ones. They reformed and strengthened the church hierarchy while at the same time reaffirming the primacy of the pope. They worked to establish religious uniformity and to stem the variants introduced by popular religion or overzealous mysticism or female activism. They created a new social discipline with regard to marriage, the family, and sexuality.

The matter of first importance was to counter the main Protestant tenets. Against the Lutheran doctrine of justification by faith, church leaders at Trent reaffirmed the effectiveness of good works for the soul's salvation, aided by divine grace transmitted through the sacraments. Where Protestants, following the Gospel accounts, reduced the sacraments to two (baptism and the Lord's Supper), the Catholic reformers reaffirmed the validity of all seven (penance, matrimony, confirmation, ordination, and extreme unction, in addition to those named above; see *Witnesses* on p. 407). Where Protestant reformers recognized the authority only of Scripture, Trent maintained the authority of church tradition, along with that of the Bible (in the approved Latin version), as a sound basis for doctrinal judgment.

Overriding the Protestant claims that the laity should receive the wine as well as the bread in the Eucharist, Catholic leaders reestablished the traditional boundary between laity and clergy which permitted lay people only the bread. They reaffirmed the requirement of clerical celibacy against the Protestant encouragement of clerical marriage. They restated the validity of the veneration of the saints, the efficacy of relics, the intercessory power of the Virgin Mary—all challenged by Protestant reform.

Catholic leaders listed and banned books that were thought to pose a threat to the conscience of the faithful. The list, called the *Index of Prohibited Books*, was first issued in 1559 and later regularly revised and reissued. It included prominently the name of Erasmus, who had never deserted the Roman Catholic fold. Thereafter, in Catholic Europe, all books published were required to gain the permission of church authorities. These books carried (and still do) the notation "*Imprimatur*" ("Let it be printed") as a sign of the approval. In addition to books, works of art fell under the scrutiny of ecclesiastical censors. The nudes painted on the walls and ceilings of wealthy cardinals' palaces were decorously clothed. Simony, nepotism, pluralism, absenteeism, and other such abuses of clerical office which had angered many for centuries were all condemned by the council. It subjected sainthood to more rigorous standards and redrew the guidelines for canonization. The pious lay movements and the spontaneous expressions of spirituality that had arisen in the late Middle Ages were now to be scrutinized by well-trained and well-coordinated church officials.

Another series of reforms inaugurated at Trent pertained to the institutions of marriage and the family. Prior to Trent, the role of the Church in constituting a legal marriage was minimal. A priestly blessing might play a part in the completion of a marriage, but it was no more important than other elements, such as the betrothal contract, the exchange of gifts, or the

Saint Peter's, Rome: *The grand façade and colonnade of the basilica of Saint Peter's in the Vatican City, seat of the pope, dominates Rome. Begun by the Renaissance pope Julius II in 1506, it was completed under Paul V in 1615.*

words of consent exchanged between the new spouses. It was the marriage itself that was considered to be sacramental in character. Church leaders at Trent established a standard form of marriage, to be performed in a church and by a priest, after due notification of all members of the community who might testify to any impropriety.

The decrees of the Council of Trent affected women's lives in various ways. By reaffirming the power of the priesthood to confer grace through the sacraments the delegates effectively kept women on the margins of the religious life. Confessors strictly regulated even saintly women, and priests supervised marital conduct and familial relationships. Women's sexual lives and relationships with family members were subjects for the questions of the confessor. Even those with a religious vocation were now under stricter control. Many of the spontaneous and informal communities that had flourished in the past were eliminated. Women were limited to the formal convents of one of the established orders, which, moreover, were tightly supervised and enclosed. Although, unlike Protestant women, Catholic women still had the option of the convent, they were confined in their cloisters and barred from the opportunities that their predecessors had enjoyed in the Middle Ages.

Catholic Revival

The reorganization achieved at Trent ensured the Church's survival in the face of the Protestant challenge. At the same time, committed Catholic leaders outside the Council sought not merely for survival but for revitalization. These men and women labored as much as the reformers at Trent to create the modern Catholic Church, leading their communities, serving the poor, the sick, and the ignorant, exploring the inner recesses of the spirit, recovering Catholics lost to Protestantism, and extending the mission of the Church beyond the borders of Europe.

Reforming bishops worked to reinvent the real mission of their office. They restored churches that had fallen into disrepair, set standards for the secular clergy and members of the religious orders, and intervened with secular authorities to protect the interests of the members of their dioceses. Whereas bishops presided over a whole community, other reformers served particular groups within that community, tending the ill, the poor, the ignorant, in hospitals, orphanages, institutes, and schools. In France, saints Francis de Sales (1567–1622) and Vincent de Paul (c. 1581–1660) organized charitable missions of this sort. They also promoted the work of Saint Jane de Chantal (1572–1641), the founder, together with Francis, of the Visitation Order of nuns, and Saint Louise de Marillac (1591–1660), Vincent's disciple, founder of the Daughters of Charity (also known as the Sisters of Charity). Lay women *dévotes* ("devout ones"), who remained unmarried but avoided the cloister, participated in these missions of teaching, nurturing, and nursing. They continued the medieval Christian mission to the poor at a time when most Protestant communities were engaged in reducing or abandoning it.

Education Like Protestants, Catholic leaders recognized that education was vital to the success of their church. In the parishes, weekly catechism classes provided training in basic literacy for all children. Religious orders established schools for able students and offered scholarships to the poor. Convents provided schooling for the daughters of the wealthy, even those without a religious vocation, with instruction in literacy, needlework, and Catholic piety as a preparation for marriage.

In 1535, in the north Italian city of Brescia, Saint Angela Merici (c. 1474–1540) created a new order named after the legendary martyred virgin saint Ursula. The women who joined Merici's Ursulines lived, at first, not in cloistered seclusion but in their own homes, gathering together for business meetings and prayers. They devoted their days to teaching the female children of the poor. Returned to the cloister by the legislation of the Council of Trent, the Ursulines have survived as a teaching order into modern times.

Even England, now officially Protestant, produced another pioneer of female Catholic education: Mary Ward. Inspired by the example of the Jesuits (see below), Ward (1585–1645) founded, in 1609, a society later called the Institute of the Blessed Virgin Mary. By 1628, her society was running a network of eight schools for girls on the Continent (none could be founded in England), especially in central Europe, where its lay women teachers were known as the Englische Fräulein ("English young ladies"). These schools offered a rigorous secondary education grounded in the classics and the Christian tradition.

Mysticism Other Catholics excelled in spiritual life. In Spain, saints Teresa of Avila (1515–1582; see *Witnesses*, p. 407, and *Windows On*, p. 413) and her student John of the Cross (1542–1591) were remarkable for their exploration of the inner life. Teresa's *Interior Castle* and John's *Dark Night of the Soul* describe the paths by which the soul achieves divine communion. The Spanish *Alumbrados*, or "enlightened ones," and the French Jansenists (followers of the doctrine of Cornelius Jansen, bishop of Ypres in Flanders, 1585–1638), both similar in some ways to the spiritualist vein in Protestantism (and similarly tending to heresy), assumed that each individual possessed an inner spark of divine light.

The Jesuits The Jesuit order (the members of the Society of Jesus) combined features of these elements

WITNESSES

Catholic Reform and Revival

The Catholic Church responded vigorously to the Protestant challenge by reaffirming its traditions and developing new forms of spiritual experience. In the first of these passages, the Council of Trent prelates reassert the validity of traditional Catholic practices. The second and third are the words of two representatives of a resurgent religious leadership: Ignatius of Loyola summons his followers to a renewed, absolute obedience to the Church; Teresa of Avila, explorer of the inner life, describes her spiritual vision.

Decrees of the Council of Trent reaffirm the validity of the sacraments in general and of the Eucharist in particular (1545–1563): *Decree on the Sacraments in General: Canon I.* If any one saith, that the sacraments of the New Law were not all instituted by Jesus Christ, our Lord; or, that they are more, or less, than seven, to wit, Baptism, Confirmation, the Eucharist, Penance, Extreme Unction, holy Orders, and Matrimony; or even that any one of these seven is not truly and properly a sacrament; let him be anathema. [note: *anathema* is a formal ecclesiastical curse of damnation.]

Canon IV. If any one saith, that the sacraments of the New Law are not necessary unto salvation, but superfluous; and that, without them, or without the desire thereof, men obtain of God, through faith alone, the grace of justification; ... let him be anathema.

On the Most Holy Sacrament of the Eucharist: Canon I. If any one denieth, that, in the sacrament of the most holy Eucharist, are contained truly, really and substantially, the body and blood together with the soul and divinity of our Lord Jesus Christ, and consequently the whole Christ; but saith that He is only therein as in a sign, or in figure, or virtue; let him be anathema.

Canon II. If any one saith, that, in the sacred and holy sacrament of the Eucharist, the substance of the bread and wine remains conjointly with the body and blood of our Lord Jesus Christ, and denieth that wonderful and singular conversion of the whole substance of the wine into the Blood—the species only of the bread and wine remaining—which conversion indeed the Catholic Church most aptly calls Transubstantiation; let him be anathema.

(*The Canons and Decrees of the Sacred and Oecumenical Council of Trent*; trs. J. Waterworth, 1848, ed. E. Weber, 1990)

Ignatius of Loyola counsels his companions to obedience (1541): *Rules for Thinking with the Church.* 1. Always to be ready to obey with mind and heart, setting aside all judgment of one's own, the true spouse of Jesus Christ, our holy mother, our infallible and orthodox mistress, the Catholic Church, whose authority is exercised over us by the hierarchy. ... 9. To uphold especially all the precepts of the of the Church, and not censure them in any manner; but, on the contrary, to defend them promptly, with reasons drawn from all sources, against those who criticize them. 10. To be eager to commend the decrees, mandates, traditions, rites and customs of the Fathers in the Faith or our superiors. As to their conduct; although there may not always be the uprightness of conduct that there ought to be, yet to attack or revile them in private or in public tends to scandal and disorder. Such attacks set the people against their princes and pastors; we must avoid such reproaches and never attack superiors before inferiors. The best course is to make private approach to those who have power to remedy the evil. ... 13. That we may be altogether of the same mind and in conformity with the Church herself, if she shall have defined anything to be black which to our eyes appears to be white, we ought in like manner to pronounce it to be black. For we must undoubtingly believe, that the spirit of our Lord Jesus Christ, and the Spirit of the Orthodox Church His Spouse, by which Spirit we are governed and directed to Salvation, is the same; ...

(Jesuits' "First Sketch," 1541; ed. J. C. Olin, 1990)

Saint Teresa of Avila describes a rapturous vision (1565): Our Lord was pleased that I should sometimes see a vision of this kind. Beside me, on the left hand, appeared an angel in bodily form, such as I am not in the habit of seeing except very rarely. Though I often have visions of angels, I do not see them. ... But it was our Lord's will that I should see this angel in the following way. He was not tall but short, and very beautiful; and his face was so aflame that he appeared to be one of the highest ranks of angels, who seem to be all on fire. They must be of the kind called cherubim, but they do not tell me their names. I know very well that there is a great difference between some angels and others, and between these and others still, but I could not possibly explain it. In his hands I saw a great golden spear, and at the iron tip there appeared to be a point of fire. This he plunged into my heart several times so that it penetrated to my entrails. When he pulled it out, I felt that he took them with it, and left me utterly consumed by the great love of God. The pain was so severe that it made me utter several moans. The sweetness caused by this intense pain is so extreme that one cannot possibly wish it to cease, nor is one's soul then content with anything but God. This is not a physical, but a spiritual pain, though the body has some share in it—even a considerable share. So gentle is this wooing which takes place between God and the soul that if anyone thinks I am lying, I pray God, in His goodness, to grant him some experience of it.

Throughout the days that this lasted I went about in a kind of stupor. I had no wish to look or to speak, only to embrace my pain, which was a greater bliss than all created things could give me.

(Teresa of Avila, *The Life of Saint Teresa of Avila by Herself*, 1565; ed. J. M. Cohen, 1957)

MUST READS

Books that Made the Reformations

Erasmus	*Praise of Folly* (1511)
Luther	*On the Freedom of a Christian* (1520)
Calvin	*Institutes of the Christian Religion* (1536)
Loyola	*Spiritual Exercises* (1541)
Foxe	*Acts and Monuments* (1563)

of Catholic revival while dedicating itself to a particular mission: to defend papal authority and combat the enemies of the Church. That mission was defined by the Jesuits' founder, the Spanish nobleman and priest Saint Ignatius of Loyola (1491–1556).

In 1521, a cannonball wound ended Ignatius's first career as a soldier and precipitated a spiritual crisis. To prepare himself for the religious life to which he was now committed, Ignatius undertook advanced theological studies at Paris, which he completed in 1535. From Paris, he set out with six companions, who had vowed to devote themselves to a life of mission. Their object was a pilgrimage to Jerusalem, a dangerous venture at the time, which was abandoned of necessity. Instead, the travelers stopped at Venice, then moved on to Rome in 1537, on the eve of the creation of the Roman Inquisition.

In 1540, Ignatius obtained papal approval of a new order, of which he became the first head, or General—the Society of Jesus. Enlisting sixty founding members (called "Jesuits") the order was directly responsible to the pope and committed to active service of the Church. In his *Spiritual Exercises*, published in 1541, Ignatius described his inner struggle to subordinate his will to divine commands. Now he joined his deep spirituality with a commitment to practical action in the world.

The Society of Jesus was organized on a military model, with absolute obedience as its first requirement (see *Witnesses*, p. 407). How else was the authority of the Catholic Church to be reestablished where critics and dissenters had overcome it? "Your superior is to be obeyed," Ignatius enjoined his followers, "not because he is prudent, or good, or qualified by any other gift of God, but because he holds the place and the authority of God." The *Spiritual Exercises* declared, "I will believe that the white that I see is black, if the hierarchical church so defines."

By Ignatius's death in 1556, more than 1000 Jesuits were living by such principles in their work as teachers and missionaries around the world. They set for themselves three main objectives: to develop committed Catholics in their western European homeland; to recover Protestant defectors in eastern Europe; and to win new converts in Asia, the Western Hemisphere (newly opened to Europeans), and Africa.

To achieve the first of these goals, the Jesuits created a network of prestigious schools offering a humanist education coupled with training in Catholic principles. An original, graded curriculum was designed to guide children from the earliest ages through their adolescence. By 1600 there were approximately 500 Jesuit schools. Although they admitted a few poor children on a scholarship basis, these Jesuit schools primarily enrolled the sons of the aristocracy and burgher elites, who were the future leaders of Catholic Europe.

Protestantism had won many adherents in Poland, Bohemia, Austria, and Hungary. The Jesuits won back these lands of central and eastern Europe by convincing their rulers that the Roman Catholic Church best supported their goal of national consolidation under the monarchy. In those regions, whose most revered saints included royal converts and the founders of nations, the Jesuit strategy was especially effective.

Jesuit Missions Abroad While they sought to return Europe to the Catholic fold, the Jesuits also faced the challenge of Christian expansion. In the New World, Theatine, Franciscan, Dominican, and Augustinian missionaries were already seeking Catholic converts among the native populations when the newly formed Jesuits joined their efforts. In Asia from the 1540s, Jesuit missionaries attempted to bring Christianity to non-Christian civilizations. The Jesuits pledged "to go, without complaint, to any country ..., whether to the Turk or other infidels, in India or elsewhere," and so they did, reaching India and many of the East Indian islands, Japan, and China.

Saint Francis Xavier (1506–1552), a Spanish nobleman and Ignatius's close associate, had already baptized thousands in the Portuguese colonies in India and the East Indies when, in 1549, he reached Japan, a place hardly known to Europeans. Establishing a Christian community there, he remained for two years before attempting to reach China. In this latter venture he died.

A generation later, the Jesuit Matteo Ricci (1552–1610) set off in Xavier's footsteps for the East. At the court at Beijing, he translated works of Western theology and learning, winning thousands of converts and some respect for Christianity. At the same time, impressed by the high cultural achievements of Chinese scholars, he learned their language and adopted their dress and customs. Ricci's mission, and the Jesuit endeavor in China generally, failed in the sense that it could not convert the population to Catholic Christianity. Yet the Jesuit adventure in Asia was not without effect. It formed the peaceful first chapter in the story of western Europe's interaction with the people of east Asia.

By 1600, Catholic reform had borne fruit. The institutional Church corrected the abuses that beset it, reaffirmed the authority of pope and priesthood, and commanded the obedience of Catholics. It established high standards of moral behavior for both clergy and laity, controlled the flow of books and ideas considered injurious to orthodoxy, and committed itself anew to wide-ranging programs of social service and education. Its missionaries won back to conformity whole regions of central and eastern Europe and assumed the task of extending Catholic Christianity throughout the globe.

THE REIGN OF INTOLERANCE

Both the Catholic and the Protestant movements were combative and exclusive. Both opposed groups deviating from their orthodoxies—radicals, dissenters, heretics, and presumed witches. Both demonized Turks, Jews, and Moors. And they battled each other ferociously. The abundantly creative period

WITNESSES

The Persecutions

The affirmation of religious beliefs by reformers and traditionalists brought with it a surge of persecution and violence—a continuation, but also an acceleration, of the suppression of heresy and rage against "infidels" that had marked European life since the eleventh century. These passages report a massacre by a Catholic mob of presumed false converts to Christianity, and the testimony of a Protestant woman who would be executed for her beliefs, as well as the moderate voice of Erasmus revealing the absurdity, brutality, and self-deception of Christian Europe's hostility to the Muslim Turks.

The chronicle of the massacre of *conversos* in Lisbon, Portugal (1506): Some men from the lower orders who were there hauled [a worshiping New Christian, or *converso*] out of the church by his hair and killed him and immediately burned his body. ... To this disturbance many people came, to whom a friar gave a sermon, to call them together against the New Christians. After this two friars came out of the monastery with a crucifix in their hands, shouting "Heresy! Heresy!" This made such an impression on many foreigners, [who were] ordinary people, sailors from ships ... of the same [social] condition and low quality, that, more than five hundred having assembled, they began to kill all the New Christians they found in the streets. They threw the dead and dying bodies onto, and burnt them on, a bonfire which they had made. ... In this business they were helped by slaves and serving-lads, who with great diligence carted wood and other materials to light the fire. On this Easter Sunday they killed more than five hundred people.
(Damaio de Gois, *Cronica de Don Manuel*, 1506; from ed. J. Edwards, 1995)

Anne Askew describes her examination for heresy, in which her responses elevate the authority of the Bible over that of the Church (1545): I [Anne Askew] was asked how I interpreted the passage in the Book of Acts which says that God dwells not in temples made with hands. I replied that I would not cast pearls before swine. Acorns are good enough. Did I say that five lines out of the Bible are better than five masses? Yes, I get something out of the Bible, nothing out of the masses. ... At the next examination ... I was asked, If Scripture says that the bread and wine are the body of Christ will you believe it? I replied that I believe Scripture. If Scripture says they are not the body of Christ will you believe it? I replied that I believe Scripture. I believe all things as Christ and the apostles did leave them. I was asked to sign a confession that the body and blood of Christ are in substance at the mass. I said, in so far as Holy Scripture doth agree unto. At the third examination ... I wrote out for them my confession of faith: The sacramental bread was left to us to be received with thanksgiving, in remembrance of Christ's death, the only remedy of our soul's recovery; and that thereby we also receive the whole benefits and fruits of his most glorious passion. I told them that if the bread is left in a box for three months it will be mouldy, so it cannot be God. I wish neither death nor fear his might. ...
(Anne Askew; ed. R. H. Bainton, 1972)

Erasmus reproves those who want to fight the "cruel" Turks, when Christians have been cruel (1530): Whenever the ignorant mob hear the name "Turk," they immediately fly into a rage and clamour for blood, calling them dogs and enemies to the name of Christian; it does not occur to them that, in the first place, the Turks are men, and, what is more, half Christian; they never stop to consider whether the occasion of the war is just, nor whether it is practical to take up arms and thereby to provoke an enemy who will strike back with redoubled fury. ... For however cruel the deeds of the Turks, the same deeds committed against his fellow by a Christian are still more cruel. What a sight it would be if men were confronted with paintings of the atrocities which Christians have committed against Christians in the last forty years! This is all I have to say to those who do no more than scream "War on the Turks! War on the Turks!"
(Erasmus; ed. E. Rummel, 1990)

Repressing Dissent

A scene of torture: *A suspected heretic is tortured by the Venetian state's inquisitorial Holy Office in this sixteenth-century drawing by Domenico Beccafumi. The tribunal's notaries kept meticulous records of the tortures.* (Louvre, Paris)

The sacrament of penance: *Another aspect of Catholic reform (and of the Protestant Reformation) was the repression of dissent. In this illustration from Luca Bertelli's* Typus Ecclesiae Catholicae *(Venice, 1574), a priest administers the sacrament of penance (rejected by Protestantism), while defeated "heretics" including John Calvin are punished by drowning.*

of the Protestant Reformation and the Catholic Counter-Reformation was also an age of intolerance. Yet before the reform era ended, many critics were pleading vigorously for the toleration of dissent and difference.

Excluding Outsiders

For Europeans, "outsiders" were those who lived beyond the borders of Christendom, or within them as non-Christians. The Moors of Spain and Portugal; the Turks in the Balkans, western Asia, and North Africa; the Jews scattered across the Continent; all were outsiders, and all were hated.

It was especially on the Iberian peninsula and the borders of southeastern Europe that Europeans confronted many non-Christians. The Iberian kingdoms that eventually became the nations of Spain and Portugal had completed their *Reconquista* by 1492, when the last Moorish stronghold, Granada, was seized (see Chapter 9). The king and queen of Aragon and Castile, Ferdinand and Isabella, had already begun an internal *reconquista*, an ethnic cleansing of Moors and Jews. Meanwhile, the Ottoman Turks, who had captured Constantinople in 1453, surged through the Balkan peninsula and threatened Vienna, gateway to western Europe, as illustrated on p. 424. These developments fueled old fears of Jews and of Moorish and Turkish Muslims.

The Spanish Inquisition In Spain such fears spurred the creation of a new Inquisition. As early as the thirteenth century the Church had appointed special inquisitors (generally Dominicans) to investigate charges of heresy. Around 1480, Ferdinand and Isabella established the distinct organization of the Spanish Inquisition to complete the ideological task of conquest of the Iberian peninsula. From that time, and even more intensively after the 1492 conquest of Granada and the merciless expulsion of all non-converting Muslims and Jews, this task was pursued in earnest.

The Inquisition targeted for special scrutiny the Moors and Jews who converted and remained in Spain. Called respectively the *Moriscos* and *conversos*, they formed a considerable population; many of the latter, moreover, were well-educated and prosperous and held high places in the Church and the royal bureaucracy. Perpetually under suspicion of false conversion, they were virtually exterminated over the next century. Most of the Moriscos were expelled. Those of Jewish descent (there may have been close to 100,000 around 1500) were suspected of continued Jewish observance despite conversion to Christianity and were the special targets of the Spanish Inquisition. Charged with heresy, they were forced to undergo the public humiliation of an ***auto-da-fé***, or "act of faith," confronted with their alleged crime,

***François Dubois,* Saint Bartholomew Day's Massacre:** *In this sixteenth-century painting, Catholic soldiers and citizens slaughter Huguenot (French Protestant) opponents, August, 1572, in Paris, perhaps encouraged by the regent queen, Catherine de' Medici.* (Musée des Beaux Arts, Lausanne, Switzerland)

and consigned to secular authorities for punishment and often execution. The Inquisition also had other targets: the *alumbrados*, Erasmian intellectuals, and actual Protestants. But the Jews were the Spanish Inquisition's main victims.

Spanish Jews, numbering in the hundreds of thousands in 1492, were all expelled or forcibly converted. Jewish communities elsewhere in Europe, where they existed, were also subjected to increasing restrictions. Venice, home of Europe's first ghetto, confined Jews to one locked section of the city and barred them from practicing certain professions. In other Italian cities, they lived in segregated communities and wore distinguishing marks on their clothing. In eastern Europe, especially Poland, Jews expelled from western regions in the Middle Ages had settled in villages and towns where they lived according to their own customs. Here they were taxed, watched, and sporadically persecuted. Throughout Europe, Jews were vulnerable to charges of the ritual murder of Christian children, products of a hysterical mythology that peaked in the age of the Reformation.

European intellectuals viewed the Jews ambivalently. A few, like the humanists Giovanni Pico della Mirandola (1463–1494) and Johannes Reuchlin (1455–1522), admired Hebrew scholarship and studied the mystical tradition called the Kabbalah. Others, however, vividly displayed their anti-Semitism. Some critics trounced Reuchlin for "Judaizing," and Luther in his old age wrote the vicious tract *On the Jews and their Lies*. Neither Erasmus nor Calvin departed cleanly from medieval anti-Judaism. Jews remained vulnerable to hostility, despite grudging acceptance by some.

The Turks European Christians were also afraid of the Ottoman Turks. During the fourteenth and fifteenth centuries, Ottoman armies pressed northward from the Middle East through Asia Minor, Greece, and the Balkans. The conquest of Constantinople in 1453 gave them a foothold in Europe of maximum strategic and commercial importance. At the battles of Kosovo (modern Serbia) in 1389, Belgrade (modern Serbia) in 1522, and Mohács (modern Hungary) in 1526, Turkish armies defeated Christian Serbs and Hungarians.

In 1529, a Turkish army stood outside Vienna. Only the hectic arrival of troops from both Catholic and Protestant German regions allowed the Austrian force of some 20,000 men to withstand the siege manned by some 200,000 Turks, whose heavy artillery repeatedly breached the fortifications. Turkish forces returned to Vienna the following year and again in 1683, to be repulsed eventually to a position only 50 miles (80 km.) short of its wall. Meanwhile Turkish and European navies clashed in a struggle for supremacy on the Mediterranean, climaxed by the victory of Spanish and Venetian galleys at Lepanto in 1571. But the victory was short-lived. Christendom was on the defensive.

The Balkan region of southeastern Europe lay under Turkish domination for some 500 years. There, most Christians (and Jews) practiced their own religion, lived under their own laws, and engaged in commerce during this period. But whereas Eastern Orthodox Christians enjoyed considerable freedom, western Catholic missionaries, usually Franciscans, suffered persecution, and many were martyred. Many natives of Bosnia and Albania found cogent reasons for conversion to Islam, and Christian boys throughout the Balkans were likely to be kidnapped, forcibly converted, and incorporated as military slaves into the elite Turkish janissary corps.

As Protestant-Catholic cooperation in the 1529 defense of Vienna demonstrated, Europeans were united in their fear and hatred of the Turks. Yet some contemporaries passed beyond this hatred sufficiently to query the behavior of Christians. Luther suggested that the repeated Turkish assaults were the just punishment of God for the sins of Christians, and should not be repulsed. Erasmus granted that the Turks committed atrocities—but so had Christian armies, and recently. "That is all I have to say to those who do no more than scream 'War on the Turks! War on the Turks!' " he wrote; let them remember that "the Turks are men" (see *Witnesses*, p. 409).

Sebastian Castellio (1515–1563), whose influential book *Concerning Heretics, Whether They Are to Be Persecuted and How They Are to be Treated* (1554) was published in 133 editions, called for toleration all around: "Let not the Jews or Turks condemn the Christians, nor let the Christians condemn the Jews or Turks, ... and let us, who are Christians, not condemn one another, but, if we are wiser than they, let us also be better and more merciful." The humanist and spiritualist Sebastian Franck (c. 1499–c. 1542) professed simply: "I have my brothers among the Turks, Papists, Jews, and all peoples," with whom "in the evening" of the Apocalypse he expected to enjoy eternity. But Europeans were not yet ready for the peaceful tolerance these pioneers recommended.

Witches and Martyrs

Intolerant of outsiders, Europeans also hated their neighbors. Within villages, towns, and nations, Catholics and Protestants, moderates and radicals persecuted each other, and waged wars along the fault lines of religious allegiance. Hostility toward those who were different, odd, or powerful resulted in fantasies of diabolic possession, and broke out in witch-hunts claiming the lives of tens of thousands of innocent victims, mostly women.

In the sixteenth and seventeenth centuries, martyrdom became as common as it had been in the early church. Missionaries in the Balkans, Asia, and the New World, Protestants in Catholic regions, Catholics in Protestant ones, and radical sectarians everywhere produced an abundant crop of new Christian martyrs—in addition to the Moors, Turks, and Jews that were killed by the Inquisition or by European armies. New rosters of martyrs fed new

WITNESSES

Witches

The persecution of witches, which was undoubtedly fueled by passions beyond the religious aroused by changing social patterns, is seen as part the history of religious persecution because the accused were identified as heretics who had surrendered themselves body and soul to the Devil. In the first of these passages, two Dominican clerics explain why they think that women are especially prone to witchery. In the second, an eyewitness describes the witch-hunt at Trier, in western Germany.

Heinrich Krämer and James Sprenger explain why women are especially prone to witchery (1486): *Question VI: Concerning Witches who copulate with Devils:* As for the first question, why a greater number of witches is found in the fragile feminine sex than among men; it is indeed a fact that it were idle to contradict, since it is accredited by actual experience, apart from the verbal testimony of credible witnesses. ...If we inquire, we find that nearly all the kingdoms of the world have been overthrown by women. Troy, which was a prosperous kingdom, was, for the rape of one women, Helen, destroyed, and many thousands of Greeks slain. ... And so with others. Therefore it is no wonder if the world now suffers through the malice of women.

And now let us examine the carnal desires of the body itself, whence has arisen unconscionable harm to human life. ... a woman is beautiful to look upon, contaminating to the touch, and deadly to keep. ... Let us consider also her gait, posture, and habit, in which is vanity of vanities. There is no man in the world who studies so hard to please the good God as even an ordinary woman studies by her vanities to please men. ... To conclude. All witchcraft comes from carnal lust, which is in women insatiable. ...

(Heinrich Krämer, James Sprenger, *Malleus maleficarum*, 1486; ed. M. Summers, 1928)

The canon of Linden, author of a chronicle of the city of Trier, describes the witch persecutions there of the late sixteenth century: Inasmuch as it was popularly believed that the continued sterility of many years was caused by witches through the malice of the Devil, the whole country rose to exterminate the witches. This movement was promoted by many in office, who hoped wealth from the persecution. And so, from court to court throughout the towns and villages of all the diocese, scurried special accusers, inquisitors, notaries, jurors, judges, constables, dragging to trial and torture human beings of both sexes and burning them in great numbers. Scarcely any of those who were accused escaped punishment. Nor were there spared even the leading men in the city of Trier ... [who] were swept away in this ruin. ... Meanwhile notaries, copyists, and innkeepers grew rich. The executioner rode a blooded horse, like a noble of the court, and went clad in gold and silver; his wife vied with noble dames in the richness of her array. ... This persecution lasted for several years; and some of those who presided over the administration of justice gloried in the multitude of the stakes, at each of which a human being had been given to the flames. At last, though the flames were still unsated, the people grew impoverished, rules were made and enforced restricting the fees and costs of examinations and examiners, and suddenly, as when in war funds fail, the zeal of the persecutors died out.

("The Witch Persecutions", from *Translations and Reprints from the Original Sources of European History*, 1898–1912; ed. George L. Burns)

WINDOWS ON

Women in the Era of Reform

Robert Crowley,* The Burning of Anne Askew, *from Confutation of Nicolas Shaxton, 1548

From* The Whole Book of Psalms in Four Parts, *1563

Different facets of women's participation in the Reformation era are illustrated here. The burning of the Protestant martyr Anne Askew, who abandoned her Catholic husband to pursue her faith, is shown in this illustration (above left). In this household scene (above right) is depicted the husband's supremacy over wife and children, accentuated in Reformation theology. Witches are shown burning at Dernburg, Germany, in a mid-sixteenth-century woodcut (below). The Catholic mystic Saint Teresa is shown in a sculpture by Bernini (left) experiencing the ecstasy of divine union, understood by many observers as an ecstasy of sexual climax.
(top left: British Library, London; top right: Private Collection)

Gianlorenzo Bernini,* The Ecstasy of Saint Teresa, *Cornaro Chapel, Rome, 1645–52

Witches burning, mid-sixteenth century

To continue your investigation of this topic, please go to www.prenhall.com/king for the related **WINDOWS** on the **WEB** activity

martyrologies, or biographical anthologies of these victims of official repression. An example is illustrated in *Windows On* on p. 391. These widely read works kept the memory of pain and persecution alive in the public mind.

The repressive capacity of early Protestantism is illustrated by the execution of Michael Servetus (c. 1511–1553), a Spanish physician. Among his other works, Servetus published anti-Trinitarian tracts, culminating in *The Restoration of Christianity*. Provocatively, he sent the unfinished manuscript to John Calvin, who refuted the arguments in the next edition of his *Institutes*. The two antagonists seemed drawn to each other: Servetus was determined to go to Geneva, and Calvin was determined to pounce on him if he did. They met at last, and Calvin prevailed. In 1553, Servetus was arrested, tried, convicted, and burned at the stake—a freethinking martyr to a revolutionary but intransigent Protestantism.

War created martyrs even more abundantly than did trials and persecutions. The Protestant Reformation ushered in an era of religious warfare that did not slow until 1648. In the lands of the Holy Roman Empire and in France, with effects extending throughout Europe, Protestants confronted Catholics on the field of battle. Religious warfare finally ended in the West only when markets and dominions replaced religion as the cause of conflict among nations.

Even amidst fighting, Protestants and Catholics agreed on one subject: witchcraft. Witches were diabolical and dangerous and should be suppressed. Today it is clear that there never was such a thing as a witch, in the medieval sense of the word: someone who has sworn a pact with the Devil, who can ride a broom, who cannibalizes children or causes plague as part of a systematic program of evil. But sixteenth- and seventeenth-century Europeans accepted the reality of witches. For about two centuries, beginning just before the Protestant revolt, the fear and distrust of witches became epidemic, as described in *Witnesses* on p. 412. This was the era of the great witch-hunt, resulting in the execution of 60,000 and the terrorization of the villages of Europe.

The story of the witch-hunt belongs here because it forms part of the history of the persecution of heresy. The witchcraft accusation touched tens of thousands of Europeans, mostly women, often the old eccentric or envied solitary or gifted but fallible healer. These unfortunates were charged with child murder, blasphemy, sexual liaisons with the Devil, and nocturnal broom-riding among other hideous and outlandish crimes. Like accused heretics, accused and unrepentant witches were tortured until they confessed—torture being a legal option in the investigation of heresy. Torture worked. Where torture was not used (or only rarely used, as in England), few confessions resulted, and few accused witches were condemned. Upon confession, victims were pressed to name their associates in diabolic activity. Like heretics, they were executed not by the Church but by the "secular arm" of the state.

The voices of learned men fanned the witch hysteria—the same humanists, lawyers, and physicians who promoted the study of the classics and the arts and sciences. German, French, and Italian writers produced comprehensive witch manuals, luridly illustrated, and two Dominican friars wrote an impressive *Hammer of Witches* (1487), a guidebook to the identification and conviction of diabolically possessed, baby-murdering, broom-flying deviants. At the same time, a few voices were raised on behalf of the accused. The physicians Johann Weyer (1515–1588) and Reginald Scot (1538–1599) argued in separate works that the witch accusation was illegitimate, and easily foisted upon depressed, aging women. The jurist Andrea Alciati (1492–1550) pointed to abuses in witch trials, and the essayist Michel de Montaigne (1533–1592) insisted that there be "sharp and luminous evidence" for witchcraft accusations: "It is putting a very high price on one's conjectures to roast a man alive for them."

Over the clamor of the witch-hunt, such voices of reason were heard at last. These enlightened critics resembled those others who cautioned against the persecution of the Jews or the Turks, or who were grieved by the slaughter and by the pointlessness of religious warfare.

Conclusion

THE PROTESTANT CHALLENGE AND THE MEANING OF THE WEST

Luther's bold stand at Worms was a revolutionary moment in the history of the West. It was the first step in a tortuous process that dismantled the cultural and religious monopoly of the Roman Church. It opened up an era of competition among churches for the consciences of Europeans, and of the redefinition of the Catholic mission. It was an era, also, of deadly intolerance, in which only a few dissonant thinkers called for mutual understanding. Amid these intersecting currents of thought and belief, the rulers of the states of Europe took advantage of religious turbulence to strengthen their positions. In the short term, the princes were the winners of the struggle for reform. Amid warfare and zealotry, which they turned to suit their purposes when they could, they began to build the nations of modern Europe.

REVIEW QUESTIONS

1. Which factors led to the decline of Church influence just before the Reformation? How did the writings of Erasmus, More, and other humanists contribute to the background of the Reformation?

2. What led Martin Luther to launch the Reformation? Describe the ninety-five theses, the concept of salvation, and the importance of doing good. How did the Church respond to Luther's attacks?

3. Explain the importance of Zwingli, Calvin, and predestination in advancing the Reformation. What factors enabled Protestantism to survive and evolve?

4. Summarize the progress of Protestantism in France, England, Scotland, Ireland, Scandinavia, and eastern Europe. Why did Henry VIII break with the Roman Catholic Church?

5. Why were some Protestant reforms labeled more radical than others? Why couldn't the more radical Protestant groups compete with the mainstream groups? How were Anabaptists different from other reformers?

6. How did the Protestant Reformation affect the status of women? How did it affect the family, education, the young, the poor? How did the Inquisition, the Turkish Empire, and witchcraft contribute to an age of intolerance?

SUGGESTED RESOURCES

Before the Reformation

Bossy, John, *Christianity in the West, 1400–1700* (Oxford: Oxford University Press, 1985). A survey of the principal beliefs and practices of the Christian people of Europe.

Halkin, Leon-E., *Erasmus: A Critical Biography* (Cambridge, MA: Blackwell, 1993). Comprehensive and up-to-date biography of Erasmus, forerunner of the revolution, by a leading Belgian scholar.

Faith and Works

Oberman, Heiko Augustinus, *Luther: Man Between God and the Devil* (New Haven–London: Yale University Press, 1989, orig. 1982). A compelling analysis focusing on Luther's apocalyptic vision.

Ozment, Steven, *Protestants: The Birth of a Revolution* (New York: Doubleday, 1992). Recent and reflective overview by a veteran Reformation historian, who asks why Protestant beliefs appealed to, and why in the end they could not overtake, the Catholic Church's hold on European Christians.

Martin Luther: biography, resources, and links (Michigan State University): **http://www.educ.msu.edu**

John Calvin: biography, resources, and links (Michigan State University): **http://www.educ.msu.edu**

The Unfolding Reformation

Scribner, Bob, Roy Porter and Mikuláš Teich, eds., *The Reformation in National Context* (Cambridge: Cambridge University Press, 1994). Thirteen essays surveying how and why Protestantism came, didn't come, or came and went, to twelve regions of Europe.

Tracy, James D., *Europe's Reformations, 1450–1650* (Totowa: Rowman & Littlefield, 1999). A careful examination of Europe's migration from a single faith to a multiplicity of confessions over two centuries, always attentive to continuities and complexities.

Protestantism and Society

Benedict, Philip, *The Huguenot Population of France, 1600–1685: The Demographic Fate and Customs of a Religious Minority* (Philadelphia: American Philosophical Society, 1991). An analysis of France's Protestant population, explaining the Huguenot community's ability to retain the majority of its members despite increasing persecution.

Mack, Phyllis, *Visionary Women: Ecstatic Prophecy in Seventeenth-Century England* (Berkeley–Los Angeles: University of California Press, 1992). Traces women's limited participation in the Reformation as prophets and visionaries.

Catholic Reform

Ahlgren, Gillian, *Teresa of Avila and the Politics of Sanctity* (Ithaca: Cornell University Press, 1996). Studies Teresa's carefully constructed works which aimed to protect women's visionary experience in a restrictive and persecuting age, and shows how she thereby became the one Spanish religious woman of the era promoted to sainthood.

O'Malley, John W., *The First Jesuits* (Cambridge, MA: Harvard University Press, 1993). Comprehensive account of the formation of the Society of Jesuits, understood in their social context.

The Reign of Intolerance

Briggs, Robin, *Witches and Neighbors: The Social and Cultural Context of European Witchcraft* (New York: HarperCollins, 1995; Viking; Penguin, 1996). A recent entry to the list of many excellent studies on European witchcraft, focusing on the nature of the victimized alleged witch.

Ginzburg, Carlo, *The Cheese and the Worms: The Cosmos of a Sixteenth-Century Miller*, trs. John A. and Anne Tedeschi (London: Penguin Books, 1980). A pathbreaking microhistory, the prosecution of an ordinary man with heretical views.

Gregory, Brad S., *Salvation at Stake: Christian Martyrdom in Early Modern Europe* (Cambridge MA: Harvard University Press, 1999). Probing account of the phenomenon of martyrdom suffered by the victims of both Catholic and Protestant states.

Grell, Ole Peter and Bob Scribner, eds., *Tolerance and Intolerance in the European Reformation* (Cambridge: Cambridge University Press, 1996). Essays examining the different contexts for incidents of tolerance and intolerance in all the regions of Europe, revealing no clear progression towards greater toleration on the continental level.

Peters, Edward, *Inquisition* (New York: Free Press, 1988; Berkeley: University of California Press, 1989). A survey of the law, procedures, and practice of the Inquisition, focusing on the persecution of heretics in Spain, Italy, and the New World. Seeks to dispel the heavy layers of myth surrounding the Inquisition.

John Locke, A Letter Concerning Toleration, 1689 (University of Tenn Martin): **http://www.utm.edu/research/iep/text/locke/tolerat.htm**

ABSOLUTE POWER

1500 | 1550 | 1600 | 1650 | 1700 | 1750 | 1800

Rulers, Nations, and War

French religious wars, 1562–94

Thirty Years' War, 1618–48

Anglo-Dutch Wars, 1652–74

Seven Years' War, 1756–63

Independence struggle in Netherlands, 1579–1648

War of Spanish Succession, 1701–14

Polish partitions, 1772, 1793, 1795

Elizabeth I in England, 1558–1603

English Civil War, 1642–51

Peter the Great in Russia. 1682–1725

Frederick the Great in Prussia, 1740–86

Philip II in Spain, 1556–98

Louis XIV in France, 1643–1715

Maria Theresa in Austria, 1740–80

- Fall of Granada, 1492
- Peace of Augsburg, 1555
- Treaty of Câteau-Cambrésis, 1559
- Defeat of Spanish Armada, 1588
- Henry IV assumes throne of France, 1589
- Peace of Westphalia, 1648
- Execution of King Charles I, 1649
- English Restoration, King Charles II, 1660
- Glorious Revolution, 1688
- Peace of Utrecht, 1713
- Treaty of Paris, 1763
- U.S. Constitution ratified, 1788
- French Revolution begins, 1789

Society and Economy

Plague endemic in Europe, 1347–1720

Atlantic slave trade, c. 1500–1888

- Expulsion of Jews from Spain, 1492
- Peasants' Revolt suppressed, 1525
- Spanish "New Laws" prohibit Amerindian slavery, 1542
- Approx. 10% of Europeans live in cities, 1600
- Bank of Amsterdam founded, 1609
- Stock Exchange completed, Amsterdam, 1611
- London's population tops 500,000, 1700
- Southern U.S. slave population tops 700,000, 1790
- London's population 1,000,000

Religion and Ideas

First century of printing, 1460–1560

The Enlightenment, 1685–1795

The Scientific Revolution, 1543–1687

- Erasmus' *Praise of Folly*, 1511
- Luther's *Ninety-Five Theses*, 1517
- Loyola's *Spiritual Exercises*, 1541
- St. Bartholomew's Day Massacre, 1572
- Jean Bodin's *Six Books of the Commonwealth*, 1576
- Edict of Nantes, 1598
- Thomas Hobbes' *Leviathan*, 1651
- Newton's *Mathematical Principles of Natural Philosophy*, 1687
- John Locke's *Letter on Toleration, Essay Concerning Human Understanding*, and *Second Treatise on Civil Government*, 1689–90
- Rousseau's *Social Contract*, 1762

Beyond the West

Mughal Empire, India, 1526–1857

Ming dynasty, 1368–1644

Qing dynasty, 1644–1912

- Columbus' first voyage, 1492
- Magellan sails the world, 1519–22
- Cortés conquers Mexico, 1521–2
- Chinese officials allow Portuguese trading, Macao, 1557
- Drake circumnavigates globe, 1577–80
- Jamestown founded, 1607
- Dutch East India Company, Batavia (Jakarta, Java), 1619
- Plymouth Bay Colony founded, 1620
- Dutch acquire Malacca from Portuguese, 1641
- East India Company founds port, Calcutta, India, 1690
- British control Dutch Cape colony, 1795
- Ireland incorporated into the U.K., 1800

CHAPTER

15 ABSOLUTE POWER

War and Politics in Early Modern Europe

1500–1750

KEY TOPICS

◆ **Power and Gunpowder:** The emerging nations of Europe gain new strength—and face mounting costs—as guns outpace swords, infantry displaces cavalry, and the demand grows for drillmasters and engineers.

◆ **War Games:** Wars fought increasingly for plain political advantage culminate in a struggle between France and Great Britain in the global struggle of the Seven Years' War.

◆ **An Age of Kings:** Kings aim to rule absolutely in Spain, France, England, Prussia, Austria, and Russia; in England, however, Parliament imposes limits on monarchy.

◆ **Mirrors for Princes:** Artists and intellectuals celebrate kings; some thinkers propose a social contract and the rights of citizens, which will in time undo the absolutist pretensions of kings.

The Perfect Prince *Around the beginning of the sixteenth century, the Italian duke Cesare Borgia (1475–1507) was engaged in acquiring for himself a large chunk of central Italy. To bolster his authority in the city of Cesena, he decided to rid himself of the agent he had placed in charge of it. He waited for the right moment; "Then, one morning, Remirro's body was found cut in two pieces on the piazza ..., with a block of wood and a bloody knife beside it." The brutal message had its intended effect, keeping the citizens, at least for a while, "appeased and stupefied."*

This incident was narrated by Niccolò Machiavelli (1469–1527) in his handbook for the perfect prince (see Chapter 13). For Machiavelli, the concern of a prince is to gain and hold power—by any means necessary. He should crush enemies, rather than forgive them; inflict cruelties as necessary, swiftly and all at once. His subjects need not love him; better that they fear him, since "fear is strengthened by a dread of punishment which is always effective." Such a prince might possibly, Machiavelli thought, save Italy.

Machiavelli's prince never came. Hopelessly fragmented, Italy fell to nations beyond the Alps. Those nations embodied new dimensions of power, not seen since the days of the Roman Empire—enough to consume each other and to dominate much of the rest of the world. Their ascension owed much to their ambitious kings, who exemplified the principles that Machiavelli proposed.

The period from 1500 to 1750—often called the "early modern" era—saw a great concentration of power in Europe: the power of armies, of states, and, above all, of kings. Changes in military organization and funding, as well as terrible new weapons, made their progress possible and their ambitions urgent. (*How Many* on p. 428 shows the growth in army size and casualties.) Those ambitions erupted into a series of wars, fought at first in the name of religion and later for ***raison d'état***, "reason of state." The kings and princes who profited from these wars—who taxed their subjects, reined in their fractious nobles, and compelled ordinary men to fight—not only expanded their states but maximized their power. In several states, they reached for absolute power, which would allow them to execute law without the restraint of parliament or peerage. As monarchs gathered power, abetted by prime ministers, advisers, and **courtiers**, intellectuals developed theories of monarchy justifying the power of kings to the people who had none.

POWER AND GUNPOWDER

Machiavelli's hypothetical prince was armed with acute intelligence and supreme force of will. The states of Europe armed themselves with new weapons and new military methods. By 1500, armies that depended on the force of their **infantry** had supplanted armies of mounted knights. Lance and sword gave way to **arquebus** and **pike**, then to **musket** and **bayonet** (see p. 419); the cavalry charge, to rows and columns of uniformed soldiers; the simple medieval wall, punctuated by gates and towers, to elaborate systems of fortification, designed to foil the force of cannon fire. Military leaders—now required to be management experts as much as battle chiefs—forged armies that performed on the battlefield with the precision they learned on the drill field.

Knights and Guns

On late medieval battlefields, ordinary foot soldiers had already proved themselves a match for mounted knights. In Flanders, in 1302, a mob of urban workers smashed an army of French cavalry. Afterwards, the fragments of the noble warriors' expensive arms and armor littered the "Field of Golden Spurs," as the disaster was expressively named. In 1346, at Crécy, and 1415, at Agincourt, two battlefields of the Hundred Years' War, English peasants armed with longbows, made from the flexible wood of their native yew trees, mowed down heavily armed knights.

Within a century, the advent of guns clinched the triumph of infantry over cavalry. Basically, the gun is an iron tube in which gunpowder—a mixture of potassium nitrate, sulfur, and charcoal—is exploded to fire a missile. The Chinese and the Arabs had used gunpowder since the eighth century C.E., mainly for fireworks. The Mongols who attacked Sung Chinese fortifications early in the thirteenth century exploded gunpowder-packed bamboo stalks, the ancestor of the first guns. When Mongol armies swung westward to Poland and Hungary in 1240, Europeans first experienced the deadly might of gunfire. Soon European ironworkers—who honed their skills making swords and horseshoes, metal plowshares and great church bells—learned to manufacture guns.

Around 1400, the Ottoman Turks employed German and Hungarian metalworkers to construct the cannon they fired in their advance through the Middle East and the Balkans. Cannon fire figured in the Ottoman victory at Constantinople in 1453. Europeans soon surpassed the Turks, however, developing gun technology to an extraordinary degree. Guns would be the premier tool of European explorers, conquerors, and merchants as they penetrated other continents of the globe.

In the short run, guns prompted the creation of tougher suits of armor for mounted knights. In the long run, they spelled the death of knighthood. No cavalry force could withstand the direct assault of a battery of guns, although as late as the twentieth century some were still trying to. Ordinary foot

The Tools of War

The cannon: *From the mid-fifteenth century, innovations in weapons changed the nature, costs, and social implications of warfare. The most dramatic changes affected the cannon, as shown here in* Four Books of Knighthood, *1528.*

soldiers armed with better and better guns formed the heart of the modern army, replacing mounted warriors as these had once replaced the ancient legion and phalanx. In the sixteenth and seventeenth centuries, ranks of arquebusiers surrounded a core of pikemen (soldiers armed with long spears). In the eighteenth, lines or columns of musketeers—their more accurate weapons fitted with bayonets which made the pike obsolete—fired in unison, in precise rhythm on command, to halt an enemy charge.

At first, guns could not fire straight or very far. The main use of the new weaponry was in big guns, used to batter down gates and walls. Huge cannon, finely adorned by the talents of engravers and sculptors, were dragged by beasts or before the besieged town or castle. Firing ball after ball, they eventually breached the defenses. The greedy horde of soldiers then swarmed in to sack, rape, and burn. Among the first to use these tactics was the French king Charles VII (r. 1422–1461), who, in 1450, drove the English from their strongholds in France at the close of the Hundred Years' War.

Siege warfare had long figured in human conflict—as testified by the protective circuit of walls that ringed some of the most ancient communities. But now the siege became newly destructive. Innocent populations, trapped within their walls, hearing the cannon fire, awaited in fear the ending that must come as walls gave way to explosive force.

Responding to the challenge of cannon fire, military engineers designed a new type of fortification. The long, exposed **curtain walls** of medieval castles and towns were vulnerable to bombardment. The squat walls of the new-style fortifications, equipped with projecting **bastions** and thickened by earthworks, as shown in the illustration on p. 420, withstood cannon fire painlessly. The triangular bastions distanced the battle from the town within, and enabled crossbowmen, **musketeers**, and riflemen to rain missiles upon attackers from two sides at once. These fortifications required fat purses and master designers—among the first of whom were Leonardo da Vinci and Michelangelo. The craft of military engineering developed sophistication as the demand for fortifications increased, and was advanced by the experience of battle.

Although the development of land warfare was crucial, much of the fighting took place at sea. Europe's expanding dominion in the world, linked together by oceans and rivers, owed much to its naval power. Here, too, firepower proved its value, giving European navies an incontestable advantage over those of other civilizations precisely when the stakes of shipborne commerce peaked. Cannon mounted on shipboard or below deck could defend merchant convoys or fight all-out naval battles.

Guns and fortifications were expensive, as were the accoutrements of the new mode of warfare. Soldiers and sailors required not only weapons, but helmets and armor, ammunition and cannonballs, powder flasks and water canteens. Armies traveled with baggage wagons and construction gear, bringing in their wake servants, wives, mistresses, children, and spare horses. In the Greek *polis* or ancient Rome or medieval Europe, the soldier came to fight bearing his own equipment. Now the principality or nation supplied that equipment. The machinery of revenue collection strained to meet the cost of outfitting forces that numbered, by 1600, tens of thousands of men.

Military Organization

The use of guns and the greater reliance on infantry constitute major changes in methods of warfare.

The gun: *The gun, which later developed to become a musket with bayonet, was also an important innovation (shown here in a 1508 drawing).*

***The castle:** The curtain walls of medieval castles, which were incapable of withstanding cannon fire, were replaced by massive fortifications like at Deal Castle in the sixteenth century, specially designed to face artillery attack from all angles.*

But these were only part of what some scholars have called the "military revolution" of the early modern period. Military organization also developed, as gifted leaders forged the modern, professional army.

Italy Modern warfare first unfolded in Italy, where war was a paid profession. Unlike the armies of the north, which consisted of native noblemen and their peasant auxiliaries, those of the Italian cities consisted of hired warriors, paid with cash. Managing these hired, or mercenary, armies were generals called *condottieri* ("contractors"), one of whom is depicted in *Windows On* on p. 432. The *condottieri* were strategists, economists, and engineers, as well as soldiers. They were experts at recruiting troops, keeping them paid, pitching camp, and retreating in the face of danger. They fought to fulfill their contracted terms with their paymaster state. They aimed to spill as little blood, and to face as few battles, as possible. Thus Italian warfare was an efficient tool of statecraft, but it was not especially deadly.

It was on the shrewdest of such *condottieri* that Machiavelli modeled his prince (although he deplored the use of mercenary soldiers, who he thought would always fight less well than natives). Such men as Cesare Borgia (the son and agent of Pope Alexander VI) and Francesco Sforza (1401–1466, who in 1450 became Duke of Milan) battled their way to eminence and, in the case of the latter, even to sovereign power. Their skills of military organization lifted them far above the ranks of ordinary men and close in line to the thrones of hereditary monarchs.

Switzerland Among the mercenaries hired by the combative Italian states were soldiers from Switzerland. In that mountainous southwestern zone of the Holy Roman Empire, local regions called **cantons** had been engaged, since the late thirteenth century, in a struggle for independence. This struggle encouraged the development of native military skills. Swiss soldiers, like the hoplites of ancient Greece, fought on foot and side by side, mutually supporting each other. Armed with pikes and arrayed in tight squares from which their weapons bristled, they could withstand the cavalry charges led by the Empire's noblemen. The ordinary male citizen of a Swiss canton was nearly always of necessity a soldier. When the Swiss finally won their independence in 1499, these disciplined infantrymen sold their skills abroad.

Sweden Far to the north, Sweden's King Gustavus II Adolphus (r. 1611–1632) led the way in creating a national standing army, rather than a knightly or mercenary one. Sweden was then a small and rather poor country whose role in European affairs before the seventeenth century was minimal. That role was changed with the outbreak of the Thirty Years' War. Gustavus Adolphus intervened in that conflict in 1630 to protect Protestant interests and to secure a footing on the south shore of the Baltic Sea. The supreme performance of his disciplined troops and mobile cannon won fame for Sweden, whose hymn-singing soldiers were forbidden by their pious king to pillage or rape—a unique prohibition in that era.

England A generation later, the Englishman Oliver Cromwell (1599–1658), a leader of Parliamentary opposition to the king, organized the New Model Army, which defeated the Royalist forces in 1645. He personally led the military unit known as the Ironsides, men who as he said, "had the fear of God before them." Forming tight squares, their unflinching pikes projecting at set angles like a deadly, mechanical porcupine, his soldiers set a new standard for disciplined warfare.

France Also contributing to the military revolution was France. In the mid-1400s King Charles VII reorganized the French army, building up a strong artillery and de-emphasizing the role of knights (who had once been so shamefully vanquished by England's bowmen). As knights became less important, the power of the nobility (which often challenged that of the monarch) could be curtailed. Charles ordered the castle towers of feudal strongholds cut down and extended his mandate into every pocket of regional power, seeking to create a national spirit and a national military organization.

Despite Charles's efforts, the French military remained a motley combination of individual units recruited by semi-independent generals. Then, in the later 1600s, King Louis XIV (r. 1643–1715) thoroughly reconstituted the army as an instrument of state policy. Its captains and generals became part of a hierarchy arrayed under the king's personal authority. Its soldiers wore standard uniforms, drilled and marched, and were provisioned by a central office. By the early 1700s, intensive recruiting had resulted in an increase from 100,000 to 400,000 men, making the French army the largest in Europe.

Prussia It was in Prussia, however, that the professionalization of the early modern army reached its zenith. Prussia was a new state, formed by the Great Elector Frederick William (1640–1688) from two non-adjacent territories—the imperial electorate of Brandenburg and the Polish duchy of Prussia. Geographically fragmented (it included several other small territories) Prussia required a powerful army for its defense. Its first ruler, the Great Elector Frederick William, made military values and needs the linchpin of his political strategy. Prudently providing for all other state expenses from the modest resources of his private purse, he dedicated all tax revenues to the maintenance of the army, while recruiting nearly the whole of the Prussian aristocracy—called the *Junkers*—to lead it. By these methods, he built the army up to 40,000 men, enormous for its time and for the size of the principality, which then numbered 1.5 million inhabitants. His successors in the next century raised that total to 200,000, one-half that of the army of France, with a population more than ten times that of Prussia.

By the eighteenth century, the miscellaneous cavalry contingents of the Middle Ages had been replaced by the modern army.

War and Diplomacy The eighteenth-century army centered on an infantry force armed with smooth-bore muskets, descendants of the earlier arquebus, which were transformed into spears by affixing a sharp dagger or bayonet. The infantry faced an enemy who had already been ravaged by artillery teams with mobile, increasingly accurate cannon. Salaried soldiers wore centrally-issued uniforms, slept in barracks, and drilled regularly the maneuvers that they would be called upon to perform in battle. Officers of noble origin learned the art of command at military academies such as those in Paris, Saint Petersburg, or Turin (modern Italy). Conducting a siege, according to King Frederick II, the Great, of Prussia (r. 1740–1786), was a craft "like that of carpenter or clock-maker." Battle itself—unlike the whirling charges of mounted warriors or the relentless pressure of a siege—was a formal, choreographed event in which two bodies of men faced each other across an open field and fired precisely on command.

***Titian,* Charles V on Horseback, 1548:** *The Italian painter Titian (Tiziano Vecellio) painted this portrait of the Holy Roman emperor Charles V on horseback after the latter's victory in 1547 over Protestant armies at Mühlberg. The portrait evokes the energy and magnificence of the Roman emperors, to whom Charles, at this date the ruler in name of much of Europe, wished to think himself equal.* (Prado, Madrid)

Why did they fire? Because they were drilled to load, aim, and shoot in unison, and paid to do so—however meagerly and irregularly. Certainly, they did not fight for glory or territory, or for their faith; in the eighteenth century, religious differences did not spark wars. Nor did they fight from patriotism, a sentiment not yet invented. But if patriotism was not yet born, national and dynastic interests were very much alive. European wars were fought in the service of those interests, as rulers jostled for prestige, for land, and for power. To win those ends, they tolerated devastating losses of life and property, and incurred huge expenses borne by the citizenry.

Then, as now, talk was the main alternative to war. By the fourteenth century, especially in Flanders and Italy, the medieval herald, who conveyed messages between leaders, was beginning to develop into that of the modern **ambassador**. The ambassador also represented a state or ruler at the courts or assemblies of another. He brought information; conveyed messages of sympathy or congratulations; and presented terms for the settlement of disputes. Two are portrayed on *Windows On* on p. 432.

Even in the midst of hostilities, the ambassador enjoyed promises of personal security from all parties. By the sixteenth century, ambassadors were based in the main European centers and conducted negotiations between states. Those negotiations, constituting what is called **diplomacy**, prepared the peace treatises that followed upon war, or prevented war altogether. In 1619, an experienced Spanish diplomat advised that wars were no longer a test of strength, like a bullfight, to be decided by "mere battles"; "rather they depend on losing or gaining friends and allies, and it is to this end that good statesmen must turn all their attention and energy."

The citizens of *Utopia*, the ideal "nowhereland" envisioned by the sixteenth-century English writer Thomas More, did not go to war. If necessary, mercenaries were dispatched to do so. Utopian ambassadors arranged for a settlement of differences even at great financial cost. When diplomacy failed, Utopian policy called for the assassination of the enemy leader—an atrocity resorted to only to prevent the worse one of war. Europe was not yet so civilized.

WAR GAMES

Three centuries of war trace the shifts in the political configuration of Europe after 1500, as shown by Maps 15.1 and 15.2 and *How Many?* on p. 428. Cities and principalities lost to nations competing for dominance. Each sought security, territory, commercial advantages, and a share in the balance of power maintained by national leaders. Equipped with the latest military technology, rulers and statesmen employed war to reconfigure the map of Europe, playing a game that dealt its winners status, wealth, and power.

In the first phase of early modern warfare from 1500 to 1648, the enmity between two great players—France (successively under Valois and Bourbon rulers) and the House of Habsburg (Holy Roman Emperors, whose domains included Austria, Styria, Carinthia, Tyrol, the Netherlands, and Spain) stoked the fires of religious conflict. By the end of the Thirty Years' War, religious issues had waned, outpaced by political objectives. In the second phase, from 1648 to 1763, France again played a central role. Having emerged from the Thirty Years' War the most powerful nation in Europe, France ceded that title, in 1763, to the new dynamo on the world stage, Great Britain.

Wars over Faith and Turf, 1500–1648

From 1500 to 1648, religious controversies and territorial disputes between rival dynasties saw Europe in a nearly constant state of warfare. By 1500, Italy was overrun with Spanish, German, and French soldiers—"barbarians," they were called, but barbarians in such numbers as to overwhelm the once-proud Italian city-states. At the same time, the Protestant Reformation created the issues that precipitated warfare between Protestants and Catholics, especially in the Holy Roman Empire and in France. Religious differences also figured in a war for independence in the Netherlands and in a civil war in England, although these conflicts also had political dimensions. From 1618 to 1648, much of Europe became involved in the Thirty Years' War, fought largely on German soil. At its outset, religious issues were prominent. By its close, religious factors had been overshadowed by the contest between the dynasties of France and the German lands: the Bourbons and the Habsburgs.

The trends in international politics characteristic of the early modern era first emerged in Italy, where the experience of city-states prefigures that of the nations beyond the Alps. Intermittently at war, some of the principal Italian states, including Milan, Naples, Rome, Venice, and Florence, had arrived at an agreement by the Peace of Lodi in 1454. This truce aimed at maintaining a balance of power among contending nations. Within a generation, however, the five participants were at war again. Soon they looked for assistance to the nations on the far side of the Alps. Beginning in 1494, France, the Empire, and Spain sent their armies. Where the Italians had sought helpers, instead they stirred up conquerors.

The process of conquest rolled on for fifty years more on the slippery battlefronts of the Italian Wars (1494–1559). At the end, by the Treaty of Câteau-Cambrésis in 1559, the Spanish and allied imperial forces had bested the French and seized control of the peninsula. Of the major Italian states, only four remained independent: the two republics of Venice and Genoa, and the two principalities of Savoy and Tuscany (the region of which Florence was capital), now under the Grand Dukes of Tuscany, descendants of the Medici family of Renaissance days. Italy was mortally wounded, but the political system of balanced competitive states which it pioneered set the pattern for relations between European nations until World War I in the twentieth century.

As cities and nations contended on Italian soil, north of the Alps a series of conflicts arose as a consequence of the Protestant Reformation (see Chapter 14). Within the Empire, Protestant and Catholic princes and states maneuvered against and fought each other, as did Huguenot, Catholic, and *politique* nobles in France. In the German lands these wars lasted until 1555, when they ended with the Peace of Augsburg. War in France continued until the reign of Henry IV (1589–1610), drawing to a close with his conversion to Catholicism in 1593 and his issuing, in 1598, of the Edict of Nantes. These conflicts, ending in territorial settlements for Protestants and Catholics and some hope of reconciliation, belong to the history of the Reformation. Although religion figured in other conflicts in the Netherlands, the Empire, and England, these were essentially struggles between competing nations and interests. The first was the Dutch war of independence against Spain, begun officially in 1579 (though fighting dated from 1568). The second was the Thirty Years' War (1618–1648), which began as a struggle between Protestant and Catholic rulers in the Empire, and ended as a European-wide conflict in which religious identification had lost political significance. The third was the English Civil War (1642–1651).

In the seventeen provinces of the Netherlands, in 1566, discontent with Spanish rule, especially among Protestants, gave way to full-scale protests and to riots. The Spanish responded by sending the Duke of Alba at the head of an army, to subdue these unruly subjects and administer the Inquisition. "Everyone must be made to live in constant fear of the roof breaking down over his head," ordained the Duke.

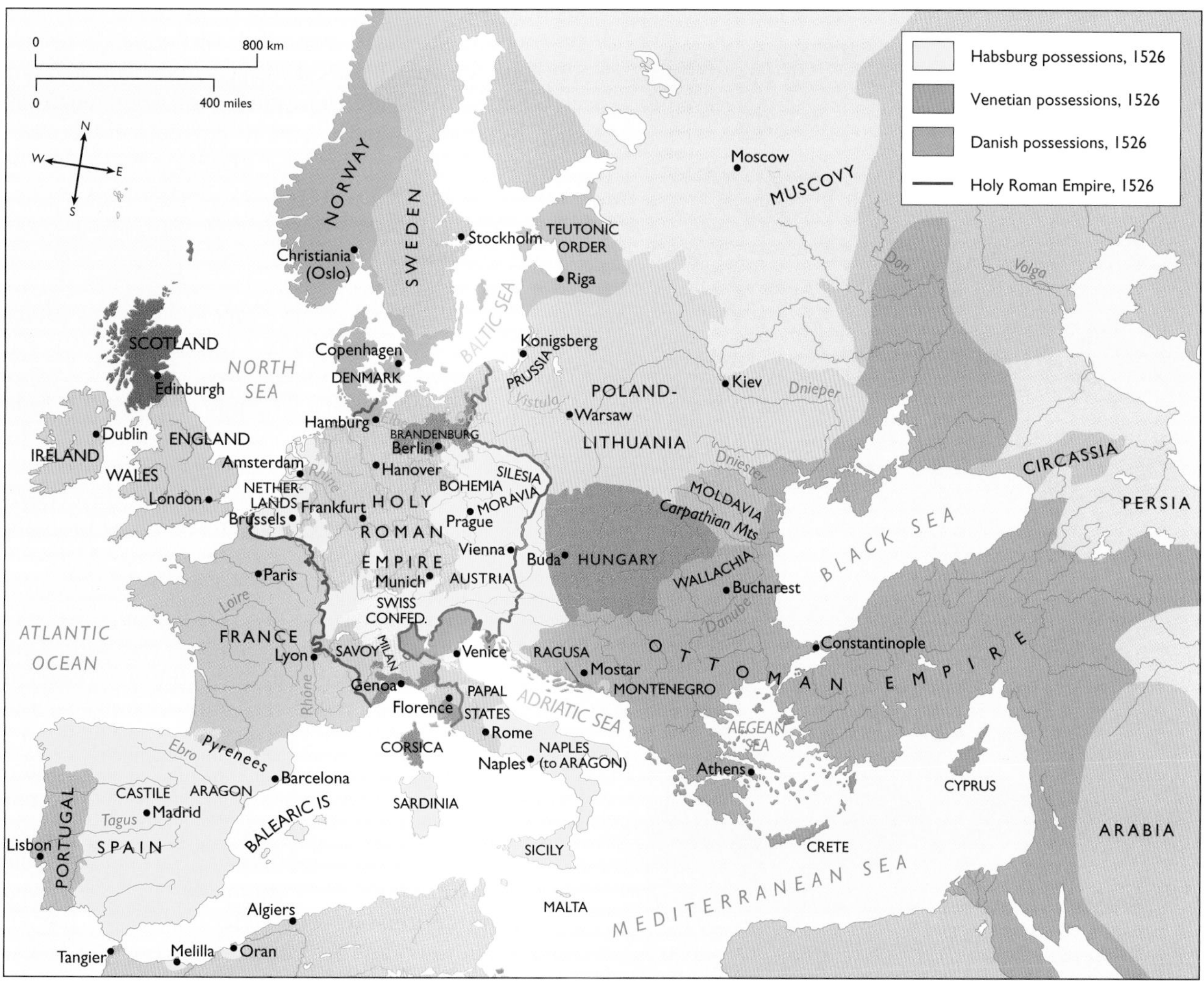

Map 15.1 The European States in 1526: *The map of Europe in the early 1500s was dominated by the House of Habsburg, with possessions in Spain, the Netherlands, southern Italy, and central Europe. Northern Italy and the German-speaking center of Europe were fragmented into hundreds of cities and principalities. To the east, the duchy of Muscovy was being transformed into Russia, bordering on the great expanses of Poland and Lithuania. The Ottoman Empire pressured Europe from the southeast.*

His Council of Troubles, set up to track down heretics, sentenced thousands of Protestants to death, and ordered the confiscation of many noble estates. In the face of this tyranny, Catholics and Protestants of all classes united in armed revolt.

In 1578, the more moderate Duke of Parma, sent by the Spanish to reestablish obedience, rallied the support of the largely Catholic southern provinces. These ten provinces returned to Spanish dominion calmly, and after 1713 to the Austrian Habsburgs. The seven largely Protestant northern provinces, led by Holland and Zeeland, formed the Union of Utrecht in 1579 and declared independence from Spain in 1581. Their leader was Prince William I, called "the Silent," of the House of Orange (1533–1584). Previously appointed *stadholder*, or lieutenant-governor in Holland, by the emperor Charles V, he had already begun, in the 1570s, to direct military and naval operations against Spanish rule.

The United Provinces, as they were called after 1579, were supported by England, which sent several thousand troops to assist in the struggle. It was partly to stop this support that Spain launched, in 1588, its fearsome Armada. Although the Armada boasted formidable guns, its ships were cumbersome. The sleeker, swifter English vessels, fitted with excellent guns, chased the Spanish fleet from the English Channel into the North Sea—and into oblivion. As England stood poised to enter into Continental power struggles, it perceived its success in this incident as providential.

Dutch and Spanish armies struggled until 1609, when the Twelve Years' Truce provided for a division between Catholic south and Protestant north. Dutch independence was officially recognized in 1648, and the new federal Dutch Republic took its place in the political arena. The Dutch had already greatly expanded their maritime ventures (see Chapter 16), which flourished as the English became involved in their Civil War. Emerging from that struggle, the English Parliament responded to Dutch competition by issuing the Navigation Act of 1651. This act (subsequently reissued several times) limited the shipment of goods to England to English-owned ships or the ships of the region of origin. The Navigation Acts challenged the Dutch carrying trade, the source of that Republic's wealth, and provoked war between these two Protestant powers—the First Anglo-Dutch War of 1652–54, followed by two others before 1674—who not long before had cooperated in resisting the Spanish.

War in Action

The Turkish army at Mohacs, 1526: *This miniature painting depicts the Battle of Mohacs, in Hungary, on the campaign road to Vienna in 1526. In it, Suleiman I, "the Magnificent," is shown directing his Turkish army from behind a row of cannon.* (Topkapi Museum, Istanbul)

The Thirty Years' War Sparked by rebellious Protestant nobles, the Thirty Years' War developed into a general European melee involving at least seventeen sovereign powers. The war was fought largely on German soil between, on the one hand, the Habsburg dynasty (both its Austrian and Spanish branches) and, on the other, the German Protestant princes and their allies, both Protestant (Denmark, Sweden, the United Provinces) and Catholic (France). The Habsburgs stood for a strong central European empire, backed by the Roman Catholic Church. Their opponents, both Protestant and Catholic, wished for political and religious reasons to preserve the autonomy of the states composing the Holy Roman Empire—now a nearly vaporous entity.

Coursing through several phases—Bohemian, Rhineland, Dutch, Swedish, and French—as different generals and interests came to the fore, the conflict was finally settled in 1648 by the Peace of Westphalia. That treaty provided for a balance of power between the main contenders (the Habsburg and French Bourbon powers) and associates. Granting virtual sovereignty to the component German states, it dictated the effective death of the Holy Roman Empire (although the Empire lingered in name until 1806) and created a power vacuum in central Europe, threatening danger to come. Finally, the treaty recognized existing religious differences, thereby signaling the end of religious warfare in Europe.

What was indisputably accomplished by thirty years of battle was the devastation of Germany: its people, of whom perhaps 20 percent died; and its towns, its commerce, its blighted economy, its ruined fields, as the woodcut below and the passage reproduced in *Witnesses* on p. 427 testify. From the German perspective alone, this may have been the most catastrophic war in modern European history.

States in Competition, 1648–1763

The Thirty Years' War brought France to the front rank of European power. As she attempted to pursue that advantage, she collided with England, which had emerged from relative insignificance in the late Middle Ages to become a major presence in Europe. As the duel between them proceeded, other rivalries were pursued by the new nations of eastern Europe (the term denoting the lands of modern Poland, the Czech Republic, Slovakia, Hungary, the eastern German region, and Austria), Prussia and Austria, the most successful remnants of the Holy Roman Empire, and a reinvigorated Russia.

By the 1660s, France possessed the largest army in Europe and nurtured vast ambitions. It sought to limit Habsburg power on its borders, and to annex nearby lands, especially Alsace-Lorraine and the southern, or Spanish, Netherlands. The French strategy was checked in 1688 by a coalition of alarmed nations. It was contained again in the War of the Spanish Succession (1701–1714), when again most of the other major European powers united to combat it.

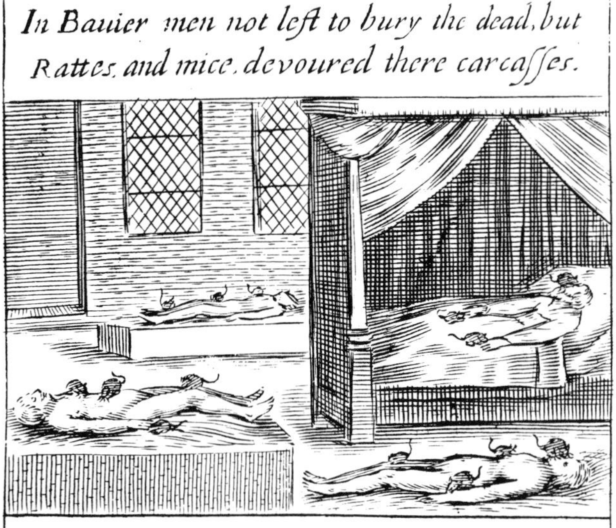

Carcasses devoured by rats and mice: *There were many tragic consequences of war. Casualties from the Thirty Years' War, 1618–48, where bodies, left unburied, were devoured by rats and mice, are shown in this woodcut from* The Lamentations of Germany, *1638.* (British Library, London)

This war was precipitated when the last Habsburg king of Spain, Charles II, died in 1700, having willed all of his possessions, to be kept intact, to the grandson of Louis XIV of France. Had the terms of the will been observed without protest, France would have dominated Europe (and much of the Western Hemisphere as well). An enormous alliance rose up against this possibility. The Peace of Utrecht of 1713 between England and France settled the conflict (although fighting continued between some parties for another year), and, together with the Peace of Rastatt (1714) drew new lines of authority in Europe. A French king of the Bourbon dynasty would rule in Spain and in Spanish America, but other Spanish dominions—principally the southern Netherlands and Spanish domains in Italy—were conveyed to Habsburg Austria. The rulers of the small states of Savoy and Prussia obtained territorial gains and the status of king, and the Dutch Republic received small concessions.

All contenders won something, but Great Britain (created by joining the crowns of England and Scotland in 1707) emerged the winner. She won the fortress of Gibraltar on the Spanish Mediterranean shore and parts of French Canada, which enabled her to pursue her maritime ambitions. Even more precious was the grant of the *asiento* ("contract") from Spain, giving Britain the right to carry African slaves to Spanish America (see Chapter 16). As a bonus, she also won a promise that France would not attempt to place a Catholic king on the British throne, which was now Protestant by law.

After some twenty-five years of relative peace, the European nations began fighting again in the 1740s, intent on gaining slips of territory and small advantages. An eight-year interlude between 1748 and 1756 was followed by the Seven Years' War (1756–1763), fought on three continents— not only in Europe but also in India and in North America, where it was known as the French and Indian War. Overarching all other issues was the continuing duel between Britain and France.

This time, the duel was fought largely overseas, as colonial possessions and foreign trade increasingly became the measure of national preeminence. By 1761, Britain had seized French possessions in India, and was poised for further ventures in the domination of that subcontinent. In 1759 a British force launched a surprise attack on the key French fortress at Quebec. After a ten-minute battle on the Plains of Abraham, outside the fortress, which the British won with disciplined musket volleys at close range, French prospects in North America were doomed. The Treaty of Paris of 1763 secured Britain's triumph over her main rival in India, in North America, and in Europe.

Eastern Europe By 1700, three states dominated eastern Europe: Austria, Prussia, and Russia. The homeland of the Habsburg family, Austria had a strong monarchy and an expansive agenda. It absorbed Hungary, Bohemia, Transylvania, and parts of the northern Balkans, knitting its empire together through the figure of the king, who ruled as monarch in each kingdom. It held the southeast frontier of Europe against the Ottoman Turks, whose vigor had waned since the siege of Vienna in 1529, though it resurged in 1683 to threaten that outpost once again.

The kingdom of Prussia developed from the ancestral lands of the Hohenzollern family: Brandenburg, some tiny states in the Empire, and the duchy of Prussia itself. These lands were patiently acquired over generations and combined to form an independent state; it was granted the status of kingdom by the Peace of Utrecht of 1713. Farther east, Tsar Peter I (r. 1682–1725), called "the Great," who had toured the successful nations of western Europe, learned what he could, and imported trained experts to Russia, now built a new capital city on the Baltic Sea and reoriented his political goals. For the first time, Russia looked westward, ready to engage as a great power in European struggles for sovereignty.

In 1713, Prussia, along with most other European nations, had agreed to the Pragmatic Sanction. Issued by the Holy Roman Emperor Charles VI (r. 1711–1740), this provided that his daughter and heir, Maria Theresa (r. 1740–1780), would inherit all the Habsburg lands intact (although, as a woman, she was ineligible to become Holy Roman Emperor). In 1740, on the basis of no other principle than *raison d'état*, the young king of Prussia, Frederick II (r. 1740–1786) broke this agreement. Frederick needed Silesia—a prosperous province under Austrian domination. And so he took it. Other nations entered into the fray, nibbling at the Habsburg lands. By the 1748 Peace of Aix-la-Chapelle, which settled the War of the Austrian Succession, Silesia was his. A few years later, in the Seven Years' War, Austria allied itself with France and Russia, to block Prussia's further expansion. Bankrolled by Britain but left to fight on its own, Prussia stayed firm and retained its position.

In 1772, Prussia was still hungry for territory to round out the boundaries of its domain. Along with Austria and Russia, it annexed small bits of Poland, an ailing republic dominated by a fractious nobility under an elected king, fatally resistant to centralization. In 1793 and 1795, Poland's neighbors completed her dismemberment. In the final "partition," it disappeared from the map, not to be reconstituted until after World War I. Prussia, Austria, and Russia, fat with new territory, now held unrivaled domination of eastern Europe. As recently as 1500, they had been overshadowed by the Holy Roman Empire, now in tatters; by the Ottoman Empire, in retreat through the Balkans; and by Poland, devoured whole.

During the early modern era, the violence that had characterized medieval Europe in an era of invasion became the official tool of the state. As a result, the map of Europe was radically altered as winners took their prizes and losers shrank behind their borders. Soon after 1500, the Italian cities yielded their primacy, as Machiavelli had feared, to more powerful nations beyond the Alps. By 1600, the most potent states in Europe were monarchies poised on the Atlantic coast: Spain, France, and England. Emerging as major players soon thereafter were the kingdom of Sweden, the newly constituted Dutch Republic, and the German electorate of Brandenburg, subsequently the kingdom of Prussia. Meanwhile, the Holy Roman Empire withered, while the Habsburg dynasty, which had long held the imperial title, raised its hereditary domain of Austria to international importance. Portugal, the rising star of the early 1500s, languished, and Poland was obliterated. Led by a series of tsars, who considered themselves the successors of Roman Caesars, Russia moved into the European arena.

AN AGE OF KINGS

As the nations of Europe competed, they also developed forms of government that endured into the modern era. This process usually involved the refinement of monarchy, as the ability to make laws and exercise force was concentrated in the figure of the king—or, in a few cases, the queen. Such kings were "absolute" monarchs, because they tried to rule "absolutely" (believing in complete, unrestricted powers due to their divine right), unchecked by representatives of the people. By the end of the eighteenth century, that newly evolved monarchy would be challenged and, in some places, limited. In diverse ways, monarchy developed in the direction of **absolutism** in several European countries: in Spain, France, and England in the western zone; and in Prussia, Austria, and Russia in the eastern one (see *Who's Who* on pp. 437 and 439).

Spain: Religious Zeal and Royal Absolutism

The autonomous kingdoms that formed on the Iberian peninsula in the Middle Ages were united by a common dedication to the centuries-long crusade called the *Reconquista* (see Chapter 9). After the fall of the last Moorish fortress at Granada in 1492, the Inquisition fostered the crusading spirit by pursuing lapsed converts to Christianity, as well as heretics. The same crusading spirit inspired Spanish missionaries to the Americas, to convert the native population. Before it became a nation, Spain was a culture united by its dedication to Roman Catholic orthodoxy. On this basis, kings from the fifteenth and sixteenth centuries built a strong, centralized state.

Crucial developments in this unifying process were achieved in the reigns of Ferdinand II of Aragon

(r. 1479–1516) and Isabella of Castile (r. 1474–1504), whose marriage in 1479 linked their two kingdoms. (Portugal had already taken a separate path to nationhood before the events about to be described.) Although the component states of Castile and Aragon retained their separate judicial, political, and administrative laws and institutions, a strong commonality of purpose marked the reigns of their two respective sovereigns—displayed most decidedly and dramatically by their conquest of Granada.

In 1516, on Ferdinand's death, a now-united Spain passed to his grandson, Charles I. The grandson also of the Holy Roman Emperor Maximilian I and Mary of Burgundy, Charles inherited the Habsburg lands on Maximilian's death in 1519 and, as Charles V (r. 1519–1556), became Holy Roman Emperor. A portrait of him by Titian is illustrated on p. 421. Ruler of several states, and required to manage the Italian Wars, the consequences of the Protestant Reformation, the rivalry of France, and the threat of Turkish invasion, Charles could not concentrate exclusively on Spain. When he abdicated in 1556, the Spanish inheritance (along with title to the Netherlands and parts of Italy) passed to his son Philip, and the Habsburg lands to his brother Ferdinand I.

Under Philip II (r. 1556–1598) the Spanish state rose to an apex of wealth and influence. Outside Madrid, Philip constructed the Escorial, a combined palace and monastery, vast and austere, which is depicted on p. 443. There he worshipped daily and ruled his far-flung possessions. Aided by diplomats and spies, he worked to extend Spanish rule and to reassert Catholic orthodoxy in Europe. Those goals were not implausibly grandiose, given that the great

WITNESSES

The Experience of War in Fiction and Fact

Early modern Europe pioneered the war against civilians that some historians see as distinctively modern. Armies besieged walled cities, battered their walls and gates, gained entry, and loosed their soldiers to loot, murder, and rape at will. That fate is depicted vividly in the words of William Shakespeare's character Henry V, ironically the late medieval English king perceived as most heroic. It is also the fate of the city of Magdeburg, as described by its mayor, an eyewitness.

King Henry V threatens the French city of Harfleur with battery, capture, rape, and sack:

How yet resolves the Governor of the town?
This is the latest parle we will admit:
Therefore to our best mercy give yourselves,
Or, like to men proud of destruction,
Defy us to our worst; for, as I am a soldier,
A name that in my thoughts becomes me best,
If I begin the batt'ry once again,
I will not leave the half-achieved Harfleur
Till in her ashes she lie buried.
The gates of mercy shall be all shut up,
And the fleshed soldier, rough and hard of heart,
In liberty of bloody hand shall range
With conscience wide as hell, mowing like grass
Your fresh fair virgins and your flow'ring infants. ...
... Therefore, you men of Harfleur,
Take pity of your town and of your people
Whiles yet my soldiers are in my command,
Whiles yet the cool and temperate wind of grace
O'erblows the filthy and contagious clouds
Of heady murder, spoil, and villainy.
If not—why, in a moment look to see
The blind and bloody soldier with foul hand
Defile the locks of your shrill-shrieking daughters;
Your fathers taken by the silver beards,
And their most reverend heads dashed to the walls;
Your naked infants spitted upon pikes,
While the mad mothers with their howls confused
Do break the clouds, as did the wives of Jewry
At Herod's bloody-hunting slaughtermen.
What say you? Will you yield, and this avoid?
Or, guilty in defense, be thus destroyed?

(Shakespeare, *Henry V*, 1600, III. iii. 1–14, 27–43; ed. J. R. Brown, 1998)

Eyewitness Otto von Guericke, mayor of Magdeburg, describes the destruction of his city by an imperial army during the Thirty Years' War (May, 1631): [The imperial troops and allies breached a gate and flooded into the city.] Thus it came about that the city and all its inhabitants fell into the hands of the enemy, whose violence and cruelty were due in part to their common hatred of the adherents of the Augsburg Confession, and in part to their being embittered by the chain shot which had been fired at them and by the derision and insults that the Magdeburgers had heaped upon them from the ramparts. Then was there naught but beating and burning, plundering, torture, and murder. ... Then, what with blows and threats of shooting, stabbing, and hanging, the poor people were so terrified that if they had had anything left they would have brought it forth if it had been buried in the earth or hidden away in a thousand castles. In this frenzied rage, the great and splendid city that had stood like a fair princess in the land was now, in its hour of direst need and unutterable distress and woe, given over to the flames, and thousands of innocent men, women, and children, in the midst of a horrible din of heart-rending shrieks and cries, were tortured and put to death in so cruel and shameful a manner that no words would suffice to describe, nor no tears to bewail it. . .

(Readings in European History, vol. 2, 1906; ed. J. H. Robinson)

wealth then pouring into Spain from its American possessions (see Chapter 16) could fund a formidable military organization. Philip succeeded in acquiring Portugal in 1580. With his marriage in 1554 to the queen of England, Mary Tudor (r. 1553–1558), came the opportunity, never realized, to add that kingdom to his other possessions and to restore it to the roster of Catholic nations.

The great success of sixteenth-century Spain faded during the seventeenth, as its silver imports from the Americas failed to enrich the nation. After 1665, the deterioration was rapid. Charles II, who ascended the throne in that year as a child, was sickly, stupid, and impotent. It was his death in 1700 that precipitated the War of the Spanish Succession, resulting in the importation to Spain of a French Bourbon dynasty. Spanish fortunes revived in the 1700s as Bourbon monarchs and ministers created administrative systems on the French model, but Spain no longer played its earlier role of foremost European monarchy.

HOW MANY?

Men in Arms 1600 and 1700, and Battlefield Deaths 1618–1763

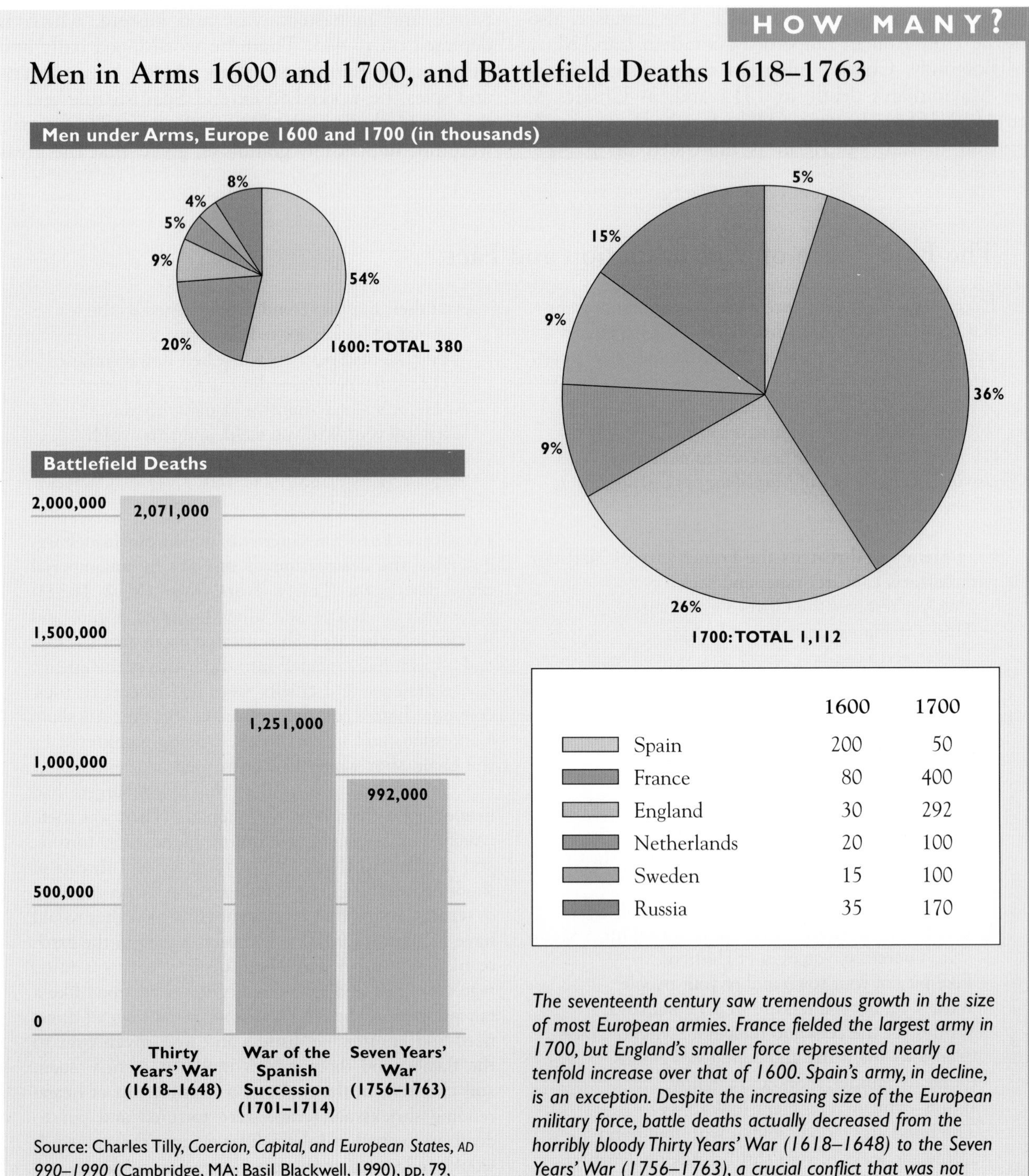

	1600	1700
Spain	200	50
France	80	400
England	30	292
Netherlands	20	100
Sweden	15	100
Russia	35	170

Source: Charles Tilly, *Coercion, Capital, and European States,* AD *990–1990* (Cambridge, MA: Basil Blackwell, 1990), pp. 79, 165–166.

The seventeenth century saw tremendous growth in the size of most European armies. France fielded the largest army in 1700, but England's smaller force represented nearly a tenfold increase over that of 1600. Spain's army, in decline, is an exception. Despite the increasing size of the European military force, battle deaths actually decreased from the horribly bloody Thirty Years' War (1618–1648) to the Seven Years' War (1756–1763), a crucial conflict that was not grossly wasteful of human life.

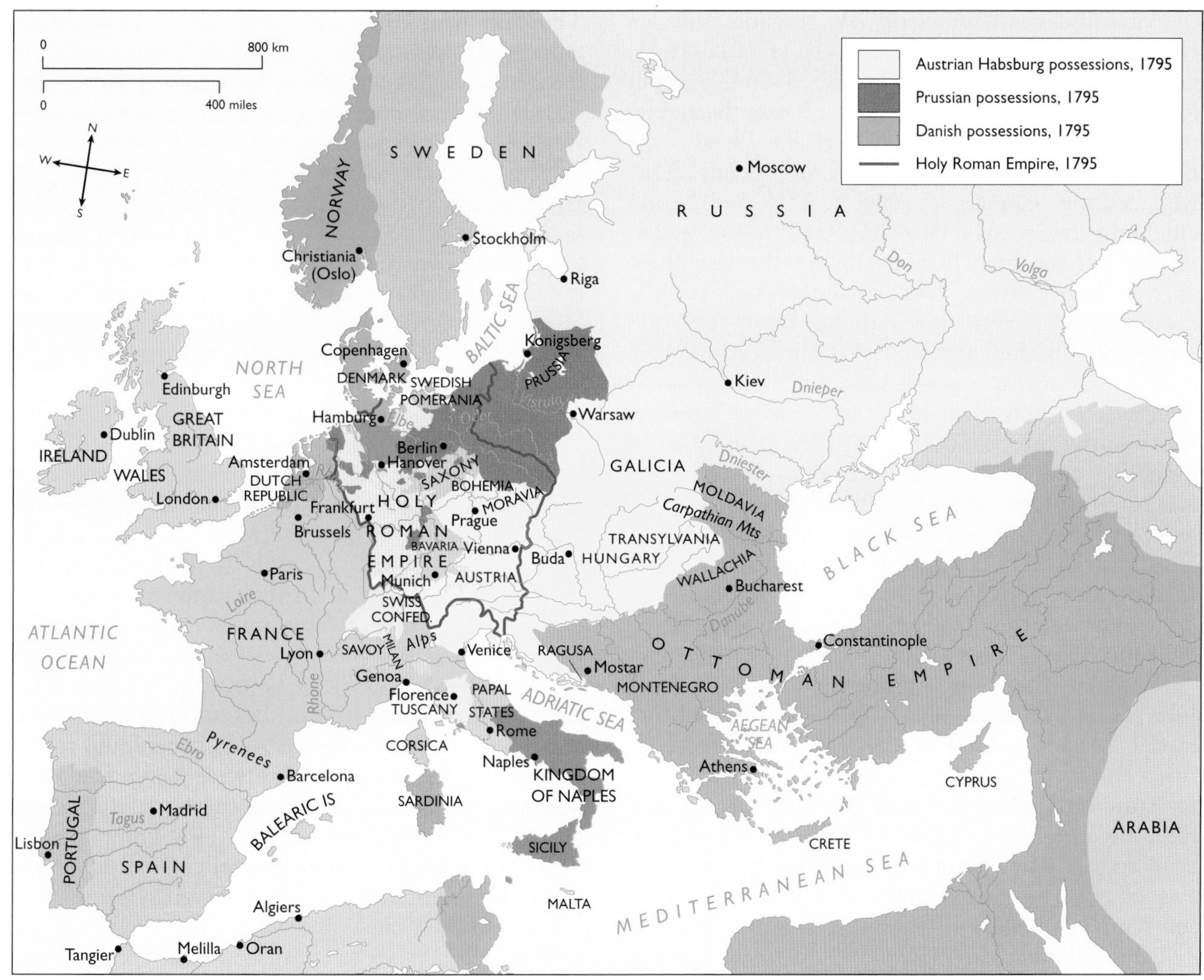

Map 15.2 The European States in 1795: *By 1795, France and England had fought their battles for supremacy, with France the loser in the global conflict that ended in 1763. Yet France remained a contender under its revolutionary leadership, and would soon strike out under Napoleon's leadership for hegemony in Europe. To the east the Ottoman Empire had weakened; Russia, Austria, and Prussia dominated the region, and by 1795 had partitioned and obliterated the once enormous Polish state.*

France: The Apogee of Absolutism

That role fell to France, which had lain in Spain's shadow in the sixteenth century, but towered above it in the next. Thanks to a larger and more productive population, the kings of France were able to build an impressive administrative machine, field an enormous army, and claim cultural leadership in Europe.

The French kings had already traveled far along the road toward sovereignty during the medieval centuries. They had gained recognition from the feudal nobility of their preeminence in the realm, and from the pope of their rights over the French clergy—the "Gallican liberties" won by the Pragmatic Sanction of Bourges in 1438 and the Concordat of Bologna in 1516. They had defended French territorial rights against other claimants, particularly the English, against whom they ultimately prevailed in the Hundred Years' War. The ascension to the throne of Henry IV (r. 1589–1610), the first of the Bourbon line, finally brought an end to the chaotic era of religious warfare. It also marked the opening of an especially fruitful era in the building of the French monarchy.

If Henry IV had done nothing else he would be remarkable for his promulgation in 1598 of the Edict of Nantes guaranteeing generous freedoms to his former coreligionists, the Huguenots. But Henry did much more. He saw to France's recovery from the civil wars, collected forgotten taxes and paid forgotten salaries, repaired roads and bridges and the mechanisms of government, administered justice, and promoted commerce. In the twenty-one years of his reign, he never summoned the Estates-General (an assembly of representatives of France's three **estates**, clergy, nobility, and commoners, comparable to the English Parliament). He thereby signaled the capacity of the monarch to rule without consulting a representative assembly. An unusually effective ruler, he laid the foundations for absolute monarchy in France.

After the death of Henry IV, the true ruler of France was neither his son Louis XIII (r. 1610–1643) nor his widow, Marie de' Medici (1573–1642), regent for Louis, then only nine years old. It was the nobleman and cardinal Armand Jean du Plessis, the Duke de Richelieu (1585–1642). This prudent cleric, who became secretary of state in 1616 and Louis's chief minister in 1624, devoted himself to the secular interests of the French monarchy. In the last phase of the Thirty Years' War he intervened on the Protestant side against the Catholic Habsburgs.

Cardinal Richelieu promoted commerce in France and in its overseas possessions, encouraging poor nobles to enrich themselves in business ventures and wealthy merchants to gain titles of nobility by funneling cash to the royal treasury. He reined in aristocratic pretensions, prohibited private dueling, and destroyed fortified castles not in royal service. He also stripped the Huguenot community of its right to bear arms and live in fortified towns, although he reaffirmed the freedom of worship guaranteed by Henry IV.

Cardinal Richelieu's protégé, the Italian-born Jules Mazarin (1602–1661), followed his mentor's model. Made Cardinal in 1641, Mazarin effectively ruled France from 1643 to 1661 as the chief adviser to Anne of Austria, widow of Louis XIII and regent for Louis XIV. Like Cardinal Richelieu, Mazarin managed domestic and international affairs in the interests of the French monarchy, deftly succeeding in surviving a rebellion of restive nobles and peasants called the Fronde.

The Bourbon dynasty benefited from the service of yet a third royal servant: Jean-Baptiste Colbert (1619–1683). The son of a merchant, Colbert began his career by monitoring Mazarin's investments. In 1665, recommended by his mentor, Colbert was employed by Louis XIV (r. 1643–1715) as France's chief financial minister, a position he held until his death in 1683. Colbert reduced France's debt, systematized its accounting methods, and attempted (unsuccessfully) to equalize tax burdens. Aiming at economic self-sufficiency, he encouraged commerce and discouraged misuse of natural resources, built roads and canals, set standards of quality for manufactured goods and agricultural products, increased foreign tariffs and reduced internal ones—all features of the strategy of **mercantilism**.

The French kings were brilliantly served by their ministers Richelieu, Mazarin, and Colbert. It was the genius of the third Bourbon ruler, Louis XIV, himself to raise the monarchy to a new zenith of power. Already under Henry IV, the Estates-General had ceased to function. After 1614, when a fruitless meeting of the Estates-General was dismissed, it was not summoned again until 1789. Those 175 years mark the span of royal absolutism in France—its achievement due principally to Louis XIV.

The Sun King Louis was four years old when his father died. His mother, assisted by Mazarin, ruled in his stead. He was ten when the Peace of Westphalia was signed, preparing the ground for France's assumption of European leadership. In 1661, Mazarin died and Louis, aged twenty-two, undertook personal rule. He guided France until 1715, when he was succeeded by his great-grandson. At that point he had reigned for seventy-two years and outlived two generations, his sheer endurance unmatched by other monarchs. Heir to the achievements of Richelieu and Mazarin, Louis labored for the supremacy of France in Europe, and of the king within France.

Louis may have said, as it is reported, "I am the state." If so, it would have been an accurate statement of the role of the absolute monarch, in whom were centered all the capacities of the political realm. Louis's central role in the French state and culture was expressed visually as well as politically: in the architecture, gardens, and rituals of the royal complex he built at Versailles, twelve miles outside the ancient capital of Paris.

Beginning in the 1660s, Louis converted the small royal hunting lodge at Versailles into the most splendid palace in Europe (see p. 443). According to the statesman Montesquieu, there were "more statues in [the king's] palace gardens than there are citizens in a large town." Palace and gardens, 1400 fountains (fed by a river diverted from its natural course), a panoply of nobles, administrators, and servants (more than 10,000 in all) and nearly as many well-stabled horses—all served to furnish an image of royal grandiloquence. Ranks of courtiers and servants attended the king's daily acts, from waking up to eating dinner to strolling through the gardens or meeting with important officials. Their attendance in itself, their rank and privilege indicated by their dress and proximity to the king, was the business of the court, where all of life was a ceremony underscoring the importance of the king—*le Roi Soleil*, as he was called, "the Sun King." As the prestige of the king rose, the status of the aristocracy sank and the patterns of French culture—costume, behavior, and diet, as well as music, literature, drama, and dance—became the standard in the West.

As Louis gathered the tamed nobles of France at Versailles to dance and play, he centralized in his court the administration of justice and the determination of law, eroding the authority of regional courts and assemblies (the ***parlements*** and "estates"). To supervise affairs in the provinces, he dispatched bureaucrats called ***intendants***, directly responsible to the crown. Royal appointees were often men from the middle classes who had purchased both their office and a title of nobility. These were members of the "nobility of the robe," to distinguish them from the ancient "nobility of the sword." In a further assertion of royal authority, Louis repealed the Edict of Nantes.

French Huguenots who wished to continue to worship as Protestants—among them many productive merchants and artisans—fled to the Dutch Republic, to England and to the Americas. An absolute monarch could not abide religious diversity.

In 1715, a child again ascended the throne of France—Louis XV (r. 1715–1774); again the country was governed by a regent. The aristocracy, which had been brought to heel by Louis XIV, now sought to recover their prestige and to curtail royal authority. The local *parlements* reasserted themselves, insisting on the right to register legislation and to assent to taxation. In this atmosphere of resurgent feudal claims, Louis XV and his grandson and successor, Louis XVI (r. 1774–1793), never enjoyed the absolute authority of their great ancestor. Louis XVI enlisted the aid of a series of capable and reform-minded finance ministers but never succeeded in winning the cooperation of the nobility. Indeed, he saw the principle of absolutism utterly defeated by the Revolution of 1789, which even cost him his life.

England: The Sharing of Power

The career of absolutism in England was different from the one it followed in Spain or France, for two principal reasons. First, England had a long tradition of the political rights of groups represented in its representative assembly, called Parliament. Second, England was, by the early 1600s, a Protestant nation; thus its kings could not bolster their authority, as did the Bourbon and Habsburg monarchs, by alignment with the Catholic Church. These realities tended against the accumulation of royal authority. Nevertheless, England achieved a strong, centralized monarchy; and, thereafter, a strong, centralized state, of which a limited monarch was titular head.

In 1485, the first king of the Tudor line, Henry VII (r. 1485–1509), acquired not only a throne, but the job of patching together a nation torn by the Wars of the Roses, fought between claimants from the York and Lancaster families. He succeeded in this task, organizing national finances, promoting trade and exploration, avoiding foreign entanglements, subduing rebellious nobles, and establishing the court of Star Chamber as a central judicial authority.

In 1509, his son Henry VIII (r. 1509–1547) succeeded him. Supported by shrewd ministers, Henry VIII pursued his father's centralizing strategies (but not his fiscal prudence). His concerns about the succession led him into a controversial series of marriages—six in all. Four of his unlucky wives were dismissed or beheaded; one died, and one survived him. The surviving progeny of these marriages were two daughters and, the youngest, a son—all of whom would accede to the throne, in 1547, 1553, and 1558 respectively: Edward (d. 1553), son of Henry's third wife, Jane Seymour; Mary (d. 1558), daughter of his first wife, Catherine of Aragon; and Elizabeth (d. 1603), daughter of his second wife, Anne Boleyn.

Great controversy surrounded the dissolution by annulment of Henry's first marriage. To effect it, Henry repudiated the pope and had himself declared the "supreme governor" of the Church in England, precipitating the Reformation in that country. His role as head of the Church enhanced Henry's authority. Later, religious controversy would flare up several times under his successors.

A child during most of his six-year reign (he died at fifteen), Edward VI was unable himself to act to shape the English monarchy. His advisers tended to the business of foreign affairs and the establishment of Protestant Christianity in England. On Edward's premature death, their labors on behalf of a Protestant Church were rendered futile. The young king's elder half sister Mary succeeded, having been passed over earlier in favor of the male heir. Granddaughter of Ferdinand and Isabella, raised by her mother an earnest Catholic, and married the year after her succession to the zealous Philip II of Spain, Mary sought to reestablish Catholicism in England. This attempt was thwarted by her death and the accession of Henry VIII's middle child, Elizabeth, whom Catholics considered illegitimate.

Elizabeth, portrayed on p. 434, overcame this liability and that of her sex in a forty-five year reign that is among the most remarkable in all of European history. A moderate Protestant, a classical scholar, and an extraordinarily intelligent leader, Elizabeth completed the task of forging an absolute monarchy begun by her Tudor forebears. Guided but not overshadowed by her very effective covey of ministers—notably Sir William Cecil (1520–1598), Sir Francis Walsingham (c. 1532–1590), and Robert Cecil (1563–1612)—she clarified the nature of English Protestantism, rallied popular support in foreign affairs, and guided financial and judicial institutions. Refusing to marry, she was able even as a woman to maintain authority in her own person and to command the respect of people and Parliament alike. Meanwhile, England's naval successes and deft diplomacy brought it recognition as a major nation.

In 1587, Elizabeth reluctantly authorized the execution—after eighteen years of imprisonment—of her cousin Mary Stuart (r. 1542–1567), the exiled queen of Scotland. (A Catholic with French ties, Mary was implicated in plots against Elizabeth just at the moment when Spain was planning to launch its Armada against England.) On her deathbed, in 1603, Elizabeth named as her successor the son of the woman she had executed, James VI, the reigning king of Scotland. As James I (r. 1603–1625), he assumed the thrones of England and Ireland as well, becoming the first of England's Stuart dynasty.

Twice a king, James was an advocate of absolutism in theory and reached for it in practice. As king in

Warriors and Peacemakers

Gentile Bellini, **Muhammad II,** *c. 1480*

Hans Holbein, **The Ambassadors,** *1533*

Gentile Bellini's portrait (above left) from the life of Muhammad II, the Ottoman Turkish ruler who conquered Constantinople and destroyed the Byzantine Empire, depicts its subject as poised and statesmanlike, in retirement from battle.

The two splendidly attired ambassadors painted by Holbein (above right), experts in the avoidance of war, are surrounded by astronomical and musical instruments, appropriately remote from the field of battle.

In contrast, the bronze statue by Verrocchio of the Italian mercenary captain Bartolommeo Colleoni (left) epitomizes the early modern warrior possessed of power and determination.

(top left: National Gallery, London; top right: National Gallery, London)

Andrea del Verrocchio, **Bartolommeo Colleoni,** *Venice, c. 1481–1496*

To continue your investigation of this topic, please go to www.prenhall.com/king for the related **WINDOWS** on the **WEB** activity

Scotland, he established royal authority over warring Protestant lords, his mother's Catholic friends and kin, and leaders of the Calvinist (called Presbyterian in Scotland) church. An author and scholar, he wrote in defense of royal absolutism: *The True Law of Free Monarchy*. In England, he chose to challenge or evade the authority of Parliament, acquiring the funds to manage the state and his lavish court from unpopular customs taxes or grants of monopoly.

The Parliament James antagonized included a growing number of Puritan representatives who were critical of the practices of the established Anglican Church. He also antagonized Catholics, who sought an amelioration of the civil disabilities under which they suffered. And the flagrant immorality of his court aroused general disapproval. Serious tensions persisted when James died in 1625 and his son Charles I (r. 1625–1649) succeeded.

Civil War and Commonwealth Married to a French Catholic Bourbon Charles soon revealed a tendency toward absolutism and was suspected of favoring his wife's religion. Whether or not that was so, he certainly did his best to impose the Anglican faith upon all of his subjects. His ministers took repressive measures against nonconforming Protestants, and angered the Presbyterian Scots to the point of armed rebellion. Charles followed his father's lead in relations with Parliament, ignoring it when it did not vote him funds and, not long after the French king's dissolution of the Estates-General, dismissing it altogether in 1629. Eleven years later, desperate for more funds, he recalled Parliament. In 1642, Parliament demanded to be granted greater powers, including approval of the king's ministers. Charles now raised his military standard against Parliament.

At least some of the members of the Parliament that assembled in 1640—called the Long Parliament —continued to meet until 1653 (after 1649, consisting of a remnant of some 100 members, it was called the "Rump" Parliament). They presided over a war between royalists and parliamentarians, and between Anglicans and other Protestants, which permanently changed the course of government in England. In 1649, the victorious parliamentarians created a High Court of Justice, which tried Charles for treason and condemned him to death. His execution followed. At the very moment of the triumph of royal absolutism on the Continent, the English had demonstrated the superiority of assemblies to kings. Although Charles I's sons would later reach for absolute power, the possibility of establishing such power in England had been gravely wounded.

In 1653, the leader of the parliamentary army, Oliver Cromwell (1599–1658), engineered his own elevation to "Lord Protector" of the new Commonwealth of England under a written constitution called the Instrument of Government. Cromwell enforced Puritan policies that suppressed, among other activities, theatrical performances and Sunday games on the village green. He repressed political dissent, such as that offered by the sectarian Ranters and Quakers, and harshly persecuted the Irish, whose religion and culture he attempted to crush. He did, however, favor religious tolerance within a Protestant community. Generally hated, Cromwell was a curious amalgam of religious zeal and military skill, a dictator who had destroyed a monarch. At his death in 1658, Englishmen from all sectors turned from his path and looked forward to the Restoration of the monarchy, which was accomplished in 1660.

Restoration and "Glorious Revolution" The Stuart line returned in the person of Charles II (r. 1660–1685), son of the executed Charles I. Mindful of the need to conciliate parliamentary opponents, Charles agreed to all the demands made by those groups—including a general amnesty to nearly all of those who had opposed and killed his father. He further conciliated both elites and people by setting a new cultural tone. During the Restoration, as the years of his reign are called, Puritan repression ended and the quest for pleasure was back in fashion.

Nevertheless, in the course of his reign Charles repeated the patterns that had led to friction before. He tended to Roman Catholicism, to a pro-French foreign policy, to noncooperation with Parliament, and to absolutism. Worse, as Charles had no legitimate children, his successor was his brother James, an avowed Catholic. One parliamentary faction, called "Whig," called for the exclusion of James from that inheritance, while another, called "Tory," supported the king. James in fact succeeded on Charles' death in 1685, with little opposition.

But Tories and Whigs joined in opposition to James II when, in 1688, his wife gave birth to a son, assuring the continuance of a Roman Catholic monarchy. Parliamentary leaders offered the throne jointly to Mary II (r. 1689–1694), James's elder and Protestant daughter, and her husband William III, the Prince of Orange (r. 1689–1702), zealous opponent of French expansionism in the Netherlands. William arrived with his army, the king's commanders disbanded, and James took refuge in France. These events constitute the "Glorious Revolution," a bloodless rechanneling of authority in perfect contrast to the Civil War which had resulted in the execution of a king and the elevation of a dictator.

By accepting Parliament's Declaration of Right of 1689, William and Mary accepted, as a condition of their joint rule, limits on monarchical power articulated in the Bill of Rights (also 1689). The Bill of Rights reaffirmed constitutional principles that had developed over the previous few stormy decades, providing that the king would not be able to suspend a law of Parliament nor raise taxes nor maintain an army without parliamentary consent; nor could any subject be arrested without full due legal process. Furthermore, the throne would pass to the descendants in turn of Mary and her younger sister Anne; but no Roman Catholic could ever succeed to the English monarchy. The Act of Settlement of 1701 reaffirmed these principles and extended the provisions for the succession. The Toleration Act in the same year protected the rights of non-Anglican Protestants to worship, though it continued to exclude them from political office—as Catholics had been so excluded since the Test Act of 1673. The guarantees in these key documents were added to the traditional rights of Englishmen inherited from medieval custom.

By the complicated events of the 1600s, the government of England achieved a delicate but fruitful balance between the king and Parliament, and of both with the established Anglican Church. The king could not hold absolute power, but would yield to decisions of Parliament. Kings and public officials could be neither Catholics nor non-Anglican Protestant dissenters, although private worship was tolerated (not, however, in Ireland, where Catholicism was illegal and vital). Even Jews, who had been expelled from England in 1290, had been permitted by Cromwell to return without conversion.

Over the next century, the struggle between kings and Parliament gave way to a government dominated by political parties, prominent ministers, and the policies of the Bank of England. Great Britain in the eighteenth century, under the last Stuart monarch, Anne, and the first three kings of the House of Hanover, all Georges, was a different world from that ruled by Stuart kings before 1688.

Kings and Queens

***Anonymous, Elizabeth I:** The kings and queens of Europe were the subjects of celebratory art. This sixteenth-century "Rainbow Portrait" of Elizabeth I shows her possessing the authority of a ruler, youthful despite increasing age.* (Hatfield House, Hertfordshire; Courtesy, Marquess of Salisbury)

Three New Empires: The Reshaping of Eastern Europe

The Thirty Years' War left central and eastern Europe in fragments. The Holy Roman Empire was a mere shell. Its more than 300 component cities and principalities, populated largely by German speakers, proceeded to develop independently. To the east of a line formed by the Elbe River and the mountains of Bohemia, largely Slavic and Hungarian peoples lived under Polish, Russian, or Ottoman overlordship. After 1648, three strong monarchies expanded to fill the vacuum of authority in central and eastern Europe—Austria, Prussia, and Russia. The main rulers are listed in *Who's Who* on p. 439.

Austria The Habsburgs had long ruled the principality of Austria and had held the title of Holy Roman Emperor since 1438. By 1714, these Austrian rulers had gained sovereignty over Bohemia, Hungary, and parts of the Balkans (wrested from the Ottoman Turks by 1699), as well as, in the west, the southern Netherlands, parts of Italy, and some Mediterranean possessions (taken from Spain). They were emperors over many different peoples who spoke different languages, practiced different religions, and possessed very different historical traditions.

Although Habsburg rulers managed this disparate empire with a fair amount of skill, it continually threatened to disintegrate. Ethnic rivalries among Magyars, Germans, Czechs, Poles, Croatians, and Italians were inevitable. Religious tensions were also severe. Austria had been re-Catholicized during the Thirty Years' War, and now imposed strict Catholic uniformity in all of its possessions. Yet the Polish and Czech nobility had strong Protestant leanings, and Eastern Orthodox (and later Muslim) subjects in the Balkans resisted Catholic preeminence. Partly to win over the landowning classes, Habsburg rulers permitted the enserfment or reenserfment of the peasantry, now an oppressed group perpetually liable to restlessness and revolt.

With the Pragmatic Sanction of 1713, Charles VI attempted to guarantee the inheritance of his daughter and only heir, Maria Theresa (r. 1740–1780). Yet on her succession in 1740, she faced the aggressions of other European states which little respected a female ruler when there was so much land to be had. Nevertheless, Maria Theresa managed to hold the bulk of her lands and even acquired additional territory by the first partition of Poland in 1772.

By that date Maria Theresa was ruling jointly with her son Joseph II (r. 1765–1790). After her death in 1780, Joseph ruled alone. He continued his mother's policy of centralizing authority, attempting agrarian reforms, and making the capital, Vienna, a center for the arts and learning. But he attempted more fundamental reforms than his mother would ever have countenanced. These included, notably, the abolition of serfdom in 1781; the creation of a civil service based on the principle of merit; and the reform of the justice system, including the abolition of torture and capital punishment. These and other of Joseph's projects aroused substantial opposition and were suspended after his death in 1790.

Prussia By the time of Joseph's death, Prussia was overtaking Austria as the major power of the fading Holy Roman Empire. Piecing together the small states of Brandenburg, Prussia, and Pomerania, lands scattered across the southern coast of the Baltic Sea, the "Great Elector" Frederick William (r. 1640–1688) had assembled a small nation. He had also built up a mighty army to defend it. His successor was granted the title "King in Prussia" in 1701 and reigned as Frederick I (r. 1688–1713). Frederick's son Frederick William I (r. 1713–1740) continued in his grandfather's path, hoarding his wealth, promoting the landowning class, from which he drew his officers, and modernizing and expanding the army.

These achievements were the inheritance of his son, the capable Frederick II, the Great (r. 1740–1786). The edifice of Prussian power rested on the army. Civil servants, the middle class, the serfs, were all subordinate to its needs and to the will of the aristocracy, who led an enormous military force consisting of 200,000 soldiers out of a population of only 6 million. The prince who ruled this successful state was also a flute-player and author of note, who corresponded easily with the finest minds of the age and shared their skeptical spirit. An absolute monarch himself, Frederick thought little of the theory of the divine right of kings (see below).

Russia By the time of Frederick the Great, Russia had developed from the medieval duchy of Muscovy to become a modern state, governed by an absolute ruler. Having won independence from their Mongol overlords after 1480, the grand princes of Muscovy continued a policy of annexing adjacent territories.

***Francisco de Goya,* Family of Charles IV:** *A more critical portrayal of a king and queen is seen in Goya's depiction of the Spanish royal family in 1800. The opulence of attire of Charles IV and his family does not disguise a weakness of intellect and will.* (Prado, Madrid)

Peter *Paul* Rubens, Marie de' Medici, Queen of France, Landing in Marseilles, 1622–25: *In 1622, Marie de' Medici, the widow of French king, Henri IV, called the Flemish artist Rubens to her court in Paris to paint a series of 21 canvases for her palace walls. Although her activities were only routine—like the one depicted in this painting—Rubens brilliantly employed mythological figures, sumptuous color and texture, and dramatic compositional strategies to elevate and glorify his patron.* (Louvre)

Under Ivan III, called "the Great" (r. 1462–1505), and Ivan IV, called "the Terrible" (r. 1533–1584), the new state of Russia became a powerful kingdom. The "Terrible" Ivan earned his designation by crushing the traditional landowner caste, the boyars, installing his own supporters as territorial lords, and supplying them with serfs. He further inspired fear when he established a corps of state spies, the *oprichniki*, the ancestor of the much-hated tsarist political police of the nineteenth century; and when, in 1581, he killed his own son in a fit of rage. Viewing himself as the heir to the Roman and Byzantine empires, Ivan had himself proclaimed "tsar" ("caesar") at his coronation in 1547. Anarchy followed his death in 1584, but in 1613, the establishment of the Romanov dynasty, destined to rule until 1917, restored stability.

Traditionally eastward-looking because of its history and because of its Orthodox Christianity, Russia turned westward under Peter I, "the Great" (r. 1682–1725). From 1689, when he ended the regency of his mother, Peter guided Russia to participation in the European cultural realm. He promoted the commercial and intellectual innovations of the West in order to develop the skills Russia needed to become a modern, sovereign state. The Church, too, was put under his control. He suppressed the old landed nobility and created a new aristocratic elite, subservient to the tsar but granted extraordinary powers over their serfs, who, since 1675, were reduced to the condition of slaves; that is, they could be bought and sold separately from the land. He required the sons of the nobles to gain a Western education, and directed the printing presses to publish newspapers and books like those read in such cities as Paris and London. He created a Baltic fleet, completely rebuilt the army, and encouraged industry (while punishing financial failure). Totally ruthless, he had his own son and heir condemned to death when that young man balked at the Tsar's cultural revolution.

By the time of Peter the Great, Russia had swollen far beyond the limits of old Muscovy. It extended eastward to the region of the Volga River, dominating the Asian descendants of the once-victorious Mongols, called Tatars. Passing the Ural Mountains, Russia reached still father across the arc of northern Asia into Siberia and to the Pacific shore. Pushing northward into the region of the Baltic Sea, it faced Sweden, which it stripped of vital territory in the Great Northern War (1700–1721). Here Peter constructed a new capital, facing west across the Gulf of Finland, named after himself: Saint Petersburg.

Pushing southward to the Black Sea, gateway to the Mediterranean, Russia faced Tatar chiefs who paid tribute to Ottoman Turkish rulers. To the west, it bordered the regions of Belarus and Ukraine, then under Polish domination. Much of this territory it acquired by the three eighteenth-century partitions of Poland accomplished under the most capable of Peter's successors, Catherine II, called "the Great" (r. 1762–1796).

A German princess by birth, Catherine came to the throne by the assassination of her husband, the grandson of Peter the Great. Although at first a committed reformer, seriously educated in political thought, she nevertheless worked to enhance the nobility's power over their serfs, at the same time insisting upon their obedience to herself. In foreign affairs she succeeded in expanding Russia's presence in the Middle East, and she acquired land from both Poland and the Ottoman Empire, including a precious outlet on the Black Sea. Considered an "enlightened" monarch, like her contemporaries in Austria and Prussia, Catherine, too, retained absolute power.

By the late eighteenth century, Europe was unique in being largely organized into nation-states (sovereign states containing a population linked by language, ethnicity, or history), and most Europeans were the subjects of monarchs who ruled, or wished to rule, absolutely. Of the continent's major political units, only Venice, the Swiss cantons, and the Dutch republic were not monarchies. Britain, though a monarchy, was a limited one, its king hedged around with constitutional restrictions. Yet although this was an age of

WHO'S WHO

Europe's Rulers in an Era of Concentrating Power, I

Charles V (r. 1519–1556, d. 1558) Habsburg emperor who briefly ruled much of Europe from the Iberian peninsula to the Ottoman border, including Italian possessions and Mediterranean islands, and much of the New World in addition.

Philip II (r. 1556–1598) Habsburg king of Spain, who from his monastic fortress (the Escorial) reigned over a Spanish Empire reaching to the New World and Italy, and defended Spanish naval supremacy and Atlantic monopoly.

Elizabeth I, "the Great" (r. 1558–1603) Queen of England who presided over the Anglican religious settlement, victory over the Spanish Armada, and the New World exploration.

Gustavus Adolphus (r. 1611–1632) King of Sweden who led reorganized Swedish army in Thirty Years' War.

Louis XIV (r. 1643–1715) King of France and patron of the court of Versailles, who best illustrates the concept of "absolute monarch," reportedly claiming: "I am the State."

Oliver Cromwell (r. 1653–1658) Parliamentary leader in English Civil War; subsequently, as Lord Protector, uncrowned ruler of England.

kings, the forces that would someday dethrone them were already gathering strength.

MIRRORS FOR PRINCES

In the thirteenth century, the saintly French King Louis IX (r. 1226–1270) had administered justice in a grove of trees, reclining against a great oak in order to hear the petitions of his subjects. In the seventeenth, his successor the "Sun King" Louis XIV was surrounded by circles of advisers and bureaucrats, laws and institutions, rituals and splendor. The four centuries that lie between saw the development of the notion of monarchy and the apparatus of the court—and, concurrently, the arguments for resistance to unjust power, and the theories of natural law and inborn rights that would in time dismantle both.

The Idea of the Prince

Almost as soon as kings appeared in Europe, writers began telling them how to rule. The same university-trained clerics who wrote on philosophy and theology wrote works on the ideal king. These "mirrors for princes," as they were called, urged moral values on the ruler: he should be kind, just, generous. The prince or king was to look into such books and see a perfected image of himself, which he was to emulate.

The idealized model of kingship projected by these works was remote from kingship in the flesh. Medieval monarchy had rested largely on force—military, judicial, personal. A theoretical understanding of the role of the sovereign, the figure in whom all authority resided, had not yet crystallized. Still less had the idea of the state as an abstract entity served by the king for the benefit of the people. From the fourteenth through seventeenth centuries, these concepts developed, culminating in the theoretical model of absolute monarchy.

The struggle between popes and emperors, originating in the eleventh century, stimulated in the fourteenth works challenging the notion of papal supremacy. Political theorists such as John of Jandun, Marsilius of Padua, and William of Ockham, as well as the poet Dante Alighieri aimed to free politics from papal ambitions and proposed the model of a universal monarchy. They observed that rulers operated in a realm of necessity separate from the realm of spirit, and made the decisions most beneficial to the state. These theories helped dismantle the secular authority of the papacy, which had peaked in the previous two centuries, and paved the way for the development of discrete secular monarchies in the two that followed.

Machiavelli's lawless prince, with whom this chapter opened, enters into consideration here. Italy, the arena where the struggle between pope and emperor took place, had no national monarchy until the nineteenth century. It was a patchwork of autonomous city republics and principalities. This region of fragmented authority and endemic violence was the context for Machiavelli's prince, a figure representing an abrupt departure from medieval tradition. He was to act unburdened by piety, compassion, or ideals of any sort. He was calculating, opportunistic, and ambitious for power. His aim was only to secure his state; the purpose of the state merely to exist, to avert conquest by another prince.

Machiavelli's contemporary Erasmus developed his own conception of the ideal monarch, in his *Education of the Christian Prince*, as well as in other treatises and letters. Like the subject of the medieval mirrors for princes, that figure was to be just, well-advised, and all-provident. But he had particularly Erasmian features, in addition: he would have a classical education, he would avoid war at all costs, and he would support with special diligence the productive middling and poorer citizens of his state. Erasmus's prince resembles not at all his Machiavellian counterpart.

Although Erasmus and Machiavelli differed in their view of the ideal monarch, they agreed that the modern world required a modern type of monarch. For Machiavelli, that new monarch, the "prince," would need to be ruthlessly focused on the problem of maintaining his power. For Erasmus, he would need to assume increased cultural, social, and economic responsibilities, and his ability to perform these primary duties would be jeopardized by the enormous costs of warfare.

Both were right. The ideal of the monarch developed by later sixteenth- and seventeenth-century theorists had both Machiavellian and Erasmian dimensions. The monarch would be truly sovereign, concentrating in himself all authority and pursuing all

HOW MANY?

European Wars, 1500–1763

The Italian Wars: 1494–1559 (Italian states, Papacy, Habsburg armies, France)

Dutch wars of independence: 1579–1648 (Provinces of Northern Netherlands, Spain)

Thirty Years' War: 1618–1648 (States of Holy Roman Empire [Bohemia, Palatinate], France, Austrian Habsburg Empire, Sweden)

English Civil War: 1642–1651 (England [Parliamentary and Royalist forces], Scotland)

War of the Spanish Succession: 1701–1714 (Spain, France, England, Netherlands)

Seven Years' War: 1756–1763 (Spain, France, England, Netherlands)

WHO'S WHO

Europe's Rulers in an Era of Concentrating Power, II

Peter I, "the Great" (r. 1682–1725) Tsar of Russia who labored on political, commercial, and cultural fronts to bring Russia into the world of western European nations.

Frederick II, "the Great" (r. 1740–1786) King of Prussia who continued to build his nation's military strength and who struck aggressively to annex further European territory.

Maria Theresa (r. 1740–1780) Habsburg Queen of the Austrian Empire, who struggled to secure and expand the multinational state left her by her father.

Catherine II, "the Great" (r. 1762–1796) German-born Tsar of Russia who extended her nation's boundaries, invited *philosophes* to St. Petersburg, and established a school for girls (see Chapter 17).

means necessary to further the interests of the state. At the same time, he would set standards in the cultural realm, promote the economic welfare of his subjects, secure peace and administer justice, and serve in his person as the symbol of national unity. He was an absolute monarch, who ruled by divine right.

The notion of the "divine right of kings" is implicit in the medieval worldview, with its hierarchies of perfection culminating in God. It was but a step more to declare that the king in his kingdom was comparable to God in the universe. Answering only to God, an absolute monarch might free himself of the laws passed by parliaments or urged by the Church or embodied in traditional customs. The king himself, deriving his powers from God, was the embodiment of law.

The French philosopher Jean Bodin (1530–1596) presented a classic statement of the theory of absolute monarchy in his *Six Books of the Commonwealth* of 1576 (see *Witnesses*, p. 440). Just as families fell under the authority of the father (a definition of patriarchy), so communities of families fell under the authority of the state and its prince. The sovereign power could maintain peace, make laws, ensure justice, promote well-being. He was not all-powerful, but was limited, like his subjects, by natural law. Those subjects, too, had rights, which the monarch was to respect. Bodin's theory implies an abstract state, a sovereign power embodied in the monarch but conceivable without him as an independent entity.

In his *Politics Drawn from the Very Words of Scripture* published posthumously in 1709 and quoted in *Witnesses* on p. 440, another Frenchman, Bishop Jacques-Bénigne Bossuet (1627– 1704), allowed kings more authority than did Bodin. As God's representatives, kings naturally produced judgments that were reasonable and just, like the will of God. While the king conformed to the divine law that reigned over all, what he willed, in the secular state, was the law itself. Bossuet verbalized the assumptions of power made by his own prince, Louis XIV.

Across the English Channel, too, the monarch's claims for absolute power were voiced—as in the *True Law of Free Monarchy* written in 1598 by James VI of Scotland, the future James I of England. James argued for the elevation of the king's will over Parliament, law, and custom. It was precisely such a claim that caused English absolutism to fail in the next generation, when Parliament dispatched monarchy for eleven years and absolute monarchy forever.

Yet in 1651, amid the throes of that revolution, the *Leviathan* (a reference to the Biblical monster appearing in the Book of Job, chapter 41) of Thomas Hobbes (1588–1679) promoted a different kind of absolutism: that of the state itself (see *Witnesses*, p. 442). Viewing human nature in an infamously negative light, Hobbes argued that people allowed their freedom would descend to anarchy, corruption, and violence—a "state of war." They must be reined in by a "Leviathan," a stern and vigilant government (not necessarily a king), to which they voluntarily conferred their obedience in an implicit contract. Thenceforth, the state would order the lives of those made desperate because their existence was, in Hobbes' memorably succinct and sad expression, "solitary, poor, nasty, brutish, and short."

The "Monstrous Regiment of Women" As theoreticians elevated the status of the king, the question of female monarchy was reexamined. What if the heir to the throne were a woman? A woman, it was believed, was unfit to rule. She would be fickle, deceitful, incapable of leading an army, obsessed with male relationships. In France, women were legally barred from ascending the throne.

Yet the early modern era boasts many female rulers. Isabella of Castile presided jointly with her husband, Ferdinand, over the *Reconquista* and the Spanish expansion into the New World. The British Isles saw three women rulers in the sixteenth century alone: Mary I, Elizabeth I, and their cousin Mary, Queen of Scots. In seventeenth-century Sweden, Christina (r. 1632–1654; d. 1689) succeeded her father Gustavus Adolphus. In the eighteenth century, Russia had four reigning empresses: Catherine I, Anna, Elizabeth, and Catherine II. The empress Maria Theresa (r. 1740–1780) ruled the disparate German, Hungarian, and Balkan areas of the Habsburg empire. In France, where a woman could not reign, Catherine de' Medici, Marie de' Medici, and Anne of Austria all ruled France as regents for their sons, its future kings.

Facing the ascension of Elizabeth I to the throne (in the wake of Queen Mary I) and with his native Scotland under the rule of Mary Stuart, the Protestant reformer John Knox (c. 1514–1572) wrote, in 1558, his *First Blast of the Trumpet against the Monstrous Regiment of Women* (see *Witnesses*, p. 441). For Knox, women were defects in nature, and rule by women was a hideous contradiction in terms. Assembling the various misogynist views of ancient philosophers, pagan poets, the Bible, and Church Fathers, he thundered that the English and Scottish nobility were worse than "brute beasts" for tolerating female sovereignty: "for that they do to women which no male amongst the common sort of beasts can be proved to do to their female, that is, they reverence them, and quake at their presence; they obey their commandments, and that against God."

In order to withstand such criticism, women who ruled often adopted the guise of androgyny. Queen Elizabeth I of England played with such male/female images—positive ones, of course—in representing herself to her subjects. She was a prince, and manly, she asserted, even though she was female, as recorded in *Witnesses* on p. 441. She was also (she claimed) a virgin, a condition essential to avoid the attacks of her opponents, for whom female nature always inclined to lust. In her last years, she defied the limits of female sexual identification. "My sex," she said, just before her death, "cannot diminish my prestige."

Catherine de' Medici skirted the boundaries of male and female identifications in the imagery she adopted to define her position. She chose as one symbol the figure of Artemisia, an androgynous ancient warrior-heroine, who combined a female persona with masculine powers. Thus clothed in androgynous imagery, these women rulers could, like their male counterparts, claim to be princes and absolute sovereigns.

Some later female rulers readily acknowledged and even exploited their gender. Maria Theresa, devoted to her wayward husband and to her thirteen children, was the embodiment of the motherly queen, while at the same time being an outstanding monarch. Catherine the Great indulged her own sexual appetites with the same freedom shown by male monarchs, taking numerous lovers—but never allowing them to distract her from affairs of state.

WITNESSES

A King's Right to Rule

During the sixteenth and seventeenth centuries, kings became more powerful and theorists rushed in to justify their claims to power. Here two French theorists, writing in that nation where "absolute monarchy" reached an apogee under Louis XIV, defend the king's right to make law (Bodin) and to rule as an agent of God himself (Bossuet).

Jean Bodin argues the king's right to impose laws without consent (1576): On the other hand it is the distinguishing mark of the sovereign that he cannot in any way be subject to the commands of another, for it is he who makes law for the subject, abrogates law already made, and amends obsolete law. No one who is subject either to the law or to some other person can do this. That is why it is laid down in the civil law [Roman law] that the prince is above the law, for the word *law* in Latin implies the command of him who is invested with sovereign power. ... From all of this it is clear that the principal mark of sovereign majesty and absolute power is the right to impose laws generally on all subjects regardless of their consent. ...

(Jean Bodin, *Six Books of the Commonwealth*, 1576, 1:8, 10; ed. R. Brown, 1990)

Jacques-Bénigne Bossuet claims that kings are God's ministers on earth (1678): It is God who establishes kings. ... Princes thus act as ministers of God and His lieutenants on earth. It is through them that he rules. ... This is why we have seen that the royal throne is not the throne of a man, but the throne of God himself. ... It appears from this that the person of kings is sacred, and to move against them is sacrilege. ... Since their power comes from on high, kings should not believe that they are its masters and may use it as they wish; they should exercise it with fear and restraint as a thing which has come to them from God, and for which God will demand an account. ...

Therefore let them respect their power, since is not theirs but the power of God, and must be used holily and religiously.

(Jacques-Bénigne Bossuet, *Politiques tirées des propres paroles de L'Ecriture sainte*, 1678; ed. W. F. Church, 1984)

Halls of Mirrors

Just as political philosophers developed the theory of absolute monarchy, architects designed spaces in which those monarchs might display their power. On grand staircases and in splendid reception rooms, such as the huge Hall of Mirrors built for Louis XIV at Versailles (and imitated in other royal courts) the king shone in glory; and those gathered around him, like glass, reflected his brilliant image. In addition to the crowds of courtiers pressing forward to catch a glimpse of majesty, the monarch was attended by poets and playwrights, composers and painters, all competing for the honor (and financial rewards) of royal patronage.

During the Middle Ages, as before, events of importance to the community had been celebrated with processions—solemn ritual marches, featuring a display of special objects. In the early modern era, kings adapted the ritual device of the procession to

WITNESSES

A Queen's Right to Rule

Although the sovereignty of the male monarch could be vigorously defended, the sovereignty of a woman monarch remained in question. In the first passage the Scottish reformer John Knox, whose own country and neighboring England were (to his fury) ruled by queens, denies that women can exercise authority as men do. In the second, Queen Elizabeth I presents herself to the English army, and declares her readiness and capacity to rule.

John Knox blasts his trumpet against rule by women (1558): The empire of a Woman is a thing repugnant to Nature. ... For who can deny but it is repugnant to nature, that the blind shall be appointed to lead and conduct such as do see? That the weak, the sick, and impotent persons shall nourish and keep the whole and strong? And finally, that the foolish, mad, and frenetic shall govern the discrete, and give counsel to such as be sober of mind? And such be all women, compared unto man in bearing of authority. For their sight in civil regiment [government} is but blindness; their strength, weakness; their counsel, foolishness; and judgment, frenzy, if it be rightly considered.
(John Knox, *The First Blast of the Trumpet against the Monstrous Regiment of Women*, 1558; ed. D. Laing, 1864, modernized)

Queen Elizabeth addresses the troops encamped at Tilbury (9 August 1588), asserting her sovereignty even in a military situation—the naval battle against the Spanish Armada had commenced–where her enemies might hope she would weaken: I know I have the body but of a weak and feeble woman; but I have the heart and stomach of a king, and of a king of England too, and think foul scorn that Parma or Spain or any prince of Europe should dare to invade the borders of my realm; to which, rather than any dishonor should grow by me, I myself will take up arms; I myself will be your general, judge, and rewarder of every one of your virtues in the field ... not doubting but by your obedience to my general, by your concord in the camp, and your valor in the field, we shall shortly have a famous victory over those enemies of my God, of my kingdoms, and of my people.
(Elizabeth I, "To the Troops at Tilbury, 1588"; ed. G. P. Rice, Jr., 1951)

their purposes. When a ruler was scheduled to enter a city, a team of artists, architects, and mechanics constructed props and scenery to make the arrival more imposing. Costume, music, and the careful choreography of the prince's retinue also enhanced the effect.

In the prince's private dwelling, too, sound, imagery, and movement were designed to reflect the sovereign's power. The paintings on the wall, the carving of the furniture, the patterns of the glass in the window, or the carpet on the floor—all could be designed to label the space inhabited by the prince. Throughout the Middle Ages, works of art and literature had been mainly religious, whether commissioned by the Church or by a private individual. In the early modern age, in the precincts of royal power, to communicate the authority and prestige of the prince was itself the business of the arts.

To convey their grandeur, kings built palaces increasingly distinct, in size and magnificence, from the homes of the subjects they ruled. Both the Escorial, near Madrid, and Versailles, near Paris, were not mere palaces, but immense complexes engineered to express the raw fact of royal power. The Austrian princes built palaces of commensurate grandeur and Peter the Great, of Russia, built a whole city, Saint Petersburg, in his image. Even the dukes and despots of Italy and the petty German princes of the Holy Roman Empire surrounded themselves with splendor.

The arrogance of royal power is nowhere expressed so eloquently as in these palaces, whose purpose was frankly not to live or to rule but to overawe. The claim to absolute power made by the kings of Europe and portrayed in stone, glass, and gilding would be challenged by other currents of early modern culture. In time these new ideas would variously reshape monarchy or abolish it, and would make of those palaces what most of them are today: museums, displaying the customs and values of a remote past.

Roman Law and Natural Right

As European monarchs accumulated power and as writers and artists celebrated it, traditions of law evolved that variously supported or undermined royal claims to authority. Concepts of natural right, based on both legal and philosophical traditions, also emerged to pose a challenge to political absolutism.

When Roman authority evaporated in the fifth century C.E., the peoples of Europe outside the old Empire—Celtic, Germanic, and Slavic—continued to follow the customs of their ancestors: tribal law. These customs satisfactorily regulated community life and disciplined criminal behavior so long as those communities remained simple. As tribes and villages became incorporated into nations, the increased complexity of life required the development of more complex systems of law. In many parts of western Europe, the sophisticated apparatus of Roman law, which had served the needs of the largest empire of the ancient Mediterranean world, was drawn upon to alter and even replace customary law.

While medieval philosophers fitted the concepts of Christian theology into the framework of Aristotelian metaphysics, medieval jurists studied the *Code* of Justinian. Centered at Bologna from the

WITNESSES

The Origins of Government in the Consent of the Citizens

While some political theorists labored to bolster the theory of monarchy, others thought about why and how citizens formed themselves into a political community. Foremost among these are Thomas Hobbes and John Locke, whose very different understandings of "civil society" are still important in political thought. Here Hobbes explains why subjects should and must obey a sovereign authority (who might or might not be a monarch), while Locke explains why individuals freely sacrifice some of their rights and join forces to form a civil body.

Thomas Hobbes shows how all citizens consent to the sovereign power (1651): II.17. The only way to erect such a common power, as may be able to defend [men] from the invasion of foreigners, and the injuries of one another, and thereby to secure them in such sort, as that by their own industry, and by the fruits of the earth, they may nourish themselves and live contentedly, is, to confer all their power and strength upon one man, or upon one assembly of men, that may reduce all their wills, by plurality of voices, unto one will. ... This is more than consent, or concord; it is a real unity of them all, in one and the same person, made by covenant of every man, in such manner, as if every man should say to every man, "I authorize and give up my right of governing myself, to this man, or to this assembly of men, on this condition, that thou give up thy right to him, and authorize all his actions in like manner." This done, the multitude so united in one person is called a "commonwealth," in Latin *civitas*. This is the generation of that great LEVIATHAN, or rather, to speak more reverently, of that "mortal god," to which we owe under the "immortal God," our peace and defence. For by this authority, given him by every particular man in the commonwealth, he has the use of so much power and strength conferred on him, that by terror thereof, he is enabled to perform the wills of them all, to peace at home, and mutual aid against their enemies abroad. And in him consists the essence of the commonwealth . ...

And he that carries this person is called "sovereign," and is said to have "sovereign power"; and every one besides, his "subject."
(Thomas Hobbes, *Leviathan*, 1651, 2:17; ed. E. Weber, 1990)

John Locke explains why people will surrender their freedom to form civil government (1690): Men, being, as has been said, by nature all free, equal, and independent, no one can be put out of this estate and subjected to the political power of another without his own consent. The only way whereby anyone divests himself of his own natural liberty and puts on the bonds of civil society, is by agreeing with other men, to join and unite into a community for their comfortable, safe and peaceable living one among another, in a secure enjoyment of their properties, and a greater security against any that are not of it. ... When any number of men have so consented to make one community or government, they are thereby presently incorporated, and make one body politic, wherein the majority have a right to act and conclude the rest. ...

If man in the state of nature be so free as has been said ... why will he part with his freedom? Why will he give up this empire, and subject himself to the dominion and control of any other power? To which it is obvious to answer, that though in the state of nature he has such a right, yet the enjoyment of it is very uncertain. ... This makes him willing to quit this condition which, however free, is full of fears and continual dangers; and it is not without reason that he seeks out and is willing to join in society with others who ... unite for the mutual preservation of their lives, liberties and estates, which I call by the general name—property.

The great and chief end, therefore, of men uniting into commonwealths, and putting themselves under government, is the preservation of their property. ...
(John Locke, *The Second Treatise on Government*, 1690; ed. E. Weber, 1990)

twelfth century, a series of jurists wrote commentaries showing how Roman law could be applied to the patterns of Christian society and medieval communities. Soon Roman legal concepts were employed by the advisers to the kings of Europe. Roman law had been developed for a state in which power was centered in a ruler, the emperor. Its concepts were now useful to kings seeking tools by which to discipline their nobility, administer their states, and become "emperors" in their own lands. Indeed, the very concept of a "state" was made available in the language of Roman law. It was the precondition of the further development of the nations of Europe.

In England, newly revived concepts of Roman law encountered an independent tradition of common law, developed during the Middle Ages and rooted in Anglo-Saxon and Norman practice. English common law was based on the principle that previous judicial decisions, rather than codes or statutes, established right. The jury system and the system of criminal procedure based on "grand" and "petty" inquests are components of English common law. The kings of England promoted common law, which was the law administered in the kings' courts, and shaped its procedures to the benefit of royal authority. In time, they also incorporated elements of Roman law into

The Royal Palace

***Pierre Patel the elder,* View of Versailles:** *In the sixteenth and seventeenth centuries, Europe's rulers built palaces to match their claims for glory. Greatest of these was Louis XIV's palace at Versailles, built between 1669 and 1686. This painting is an aerial view of the palace and its walks, fountains, and gardens.*

the tradition, especially those that tended to exalt the authority of the monarch. As elsewhere in Europe, the law of the Roman Church, or "canon law," which was modeled on Roman principles, also helped to shape common law.

If Roman law served to bolster the authority of the state and its ruler, it also conveyed another concept important in the development of modern politics: that of natural law. Roman jurists distinguished between the positive law by which Roman citizens were bound—the "law of nations" which regulated interactions between peoples—and natural law, which mirrored eternal principles of good and evil that were intrinsic in nature. Those concepts were transmitted in Christian Europe through the work of medieval jurists, and flourished anew in the early modern era. "The law of nature is a dictate of right reason," wrote the seventeenth-century Dutch theorist Hugo Grotius (1583–1645); an act is judged morally worthy if in accord with rational nature, or

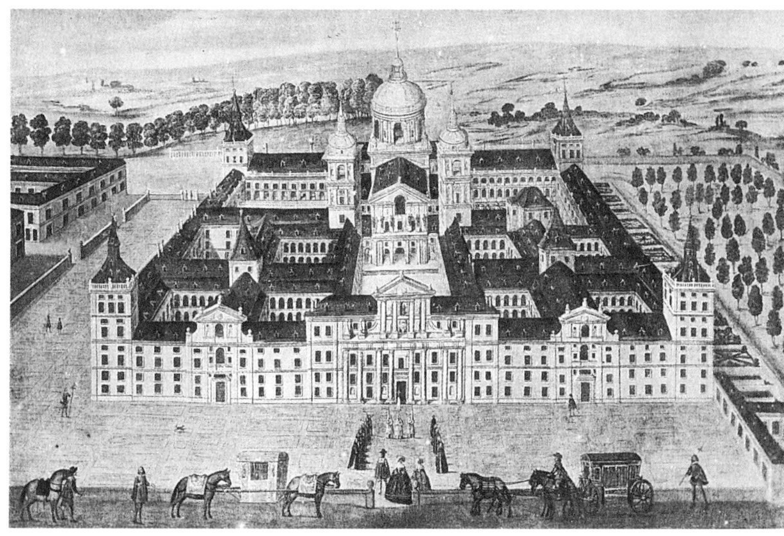

View of the Escorial: *The Spanish king Philip II's gloomier palace, the Escorial, was built outside Madrid between 1563 and 1584 more for labor and penitence than for the leisured elegance of Versailles.*

base if it is not. Human law, God's law, nature's law were all different, he maintained, but they could exist in congruence.

If medieval and Reformation thinkers wished to bring human activity into accord with divine mandates, some political thinkers of the early modern era wished to limit the state by the principles of natural law. Whereas Roman law favored state-building, the theory of natural law encouraged the building of states according to principles of right and justice which were unattached to any specific nation or people or system of belief.

Another school of political theory developed to justify resistance to states perceived as unjust. Some religious communities fostered an ethic of skepticism toward those in power, and even sanctioned disobedience to governments that violated independent standards of justice. These attitudes often prospered in radical Protestant groups, and in many cases they were extinguished as the adherents of such groups were suppressed. But similar attitudes also characterized the reformed churches radiating from Calvin's Geneva, born of a man who had himself fled a persecuting regime. "Obedience to man must not become disobedience to God," wrote that sober reformer. Next to God, Calvin acknowledged, we are subject to kings—but only so long as their command is godly. "If they command anything against Him, let it go unesteemed."

The right to resist unjust governors, cautiously but clearly stated here, is the proto-democratic germ of Calvinist political theory. The theme was not so prominent in Geneva (where Protestants were in power) as in the further reaches of the Calvinist network, where the reformers were opposed to the majority: in England, Scotland (until the late 1600s), Huguenot France, and Hungary, Poland and Bohemia before their re-conversion to Catholicism in the Thirty Years' War. Later Calvinist theorists went so far as to propose the notion that sovereignty lies in the people, who have the authority to make laws, appoint magistrates, and create kings.

It was but a step further to propose that government was based on a contract between the ruler and the ruled. Sovereignty resided in the people, who, by a kind of contract, agreed to surrender their independence in order to gain the benefits of a well-regulated state. These views form part of the famous analysis of civil government forged in the late seventeenth century by the English liberal John Locke.

A university-trained philosopher who witnessed in his youth the struggles of the English Civil War, John Locke (1632–1704) worked as secretary to a nobleman of the Whig party, which engineered the 1688 Revolution. By that time, Locke himself was living in the Dutch Republic, a center for the circulation of the latest and most daring ideas. From there in 1689–1690 he published four fundamental works: the *Letter on Toleration*, the *Essay Concerning Human Understanding*, and *Two Treatises on Civil Government*. Each was a groundbreaking work of momentous significance. The second of the two *Treatises* is specifically relevant here.

According to Locke, human beings were born absolutely free to pursue their own welfare as best they might amid the natural abundance that God provided at the Creation. All were born with fundamental rights: to life, to liberty, and to the pursuit of property. Some chose to labor diligently and acquire private property. When the others, propertyless, sought to seize what they had not labored to accumulate, the property-owners joined together to create civil government—which was, in effect, the result of a contract. That contract was reminiscent of that called for by Hobbes, but unlike his, it was reversible.

The participants chose representatives to a legislature, which reported to a king. If the government failed to perform the functions for which it was created, it could be dismantled and refounded on the original principles. If the king abused his position and interfered with the proper function of a just government, he could be removed. Locke's treatise is a roadmap at once for the creation of a society based on capitalist notions of the accumulation of property and for the founding of a government rooted in the consent and will of the people. These views passed directly to the authors of the American Declaration of Independence and inform its core principles.

Conclusion
POWER, RESISTANCE, AND THE MEANING OF THE WEST

Although Machiavelli's prince never appeared and Italy was lost, elsewhere the European monarchs of the early modern era adopted the objective that Machiavelli defined: the pursuit of power. By the mid-eighteenth century, the states of Europe were the most powerful in the world, and the rulers who governed them were, in most cases, absolute. Yet the possibility of resistance to unjust monarchy had also become apparent—in the example of the English Revolution on the one hand, and, on the other, in the philosophical vision of the proponents of natural law and social contracts. The tendencies to the concentration of power and, at the same time, to its limitation would both continue to characterize the civilization of the West, as Westerners set out to explore and to dominate the rest of the globe.

REVIEW QUESTIONS

1. Name major developments that changed the nature of power in the "early modern" era. How did gunpowder change warfare? Why did the foot soldier achieve dominance on the battlefield?

2. Explain how the following changed warfare: Italy, mercenary soldiers; Sweden, Gustavus Adolphus; England, Oliver Cromwell; France, Louis XIV; Prussia, Frederick the "Great Elector."

3. Explain the importance of the following wars: wars of Reformation; Dutch revolt in Spain; wars of Louis XIV; colonial conflicts in the New World; War of Austrian Succession; Seven Years' War.

4. What was the importance of Philip II's reign? Why did Spain decline as a great power? Why did France emerge as the strongest power in Europe? What were the contributions of Louis XIV?

5. How did England's development differ from Spain, France, and Austria? What were the issues that divided the English Parliament and the king? What was most significant about the Restoration and the Glorious Revolution?

6. How did the Thirty Years' War affect the development of emerging states in central and eastern Europe? Why did Prussia emerge as a major power? Explain the importance of Ivan the Terrible; Peter the Great; Catherine the Great.

SUGGESTED RESOURCES

Power and Gunpowder

Black, Jeremy, ed., *European Warfare, 1453–1815* (New York: St. Martin's Press, 1999). Nine historians look at major conflicts in Europe—in their social, cultural, and political contexts—painting a comprehensive picture of warfare from the Ottoman conquest of Constantinople to the fall of Napoleon.

Brewer, John, *The Sinews of Power: War, Money, and the English State, 1688–1783* (New York: Knopf, 1989). A methodical analysis of the fiscal-military complex that powered the English state through a period of nearly continuous warfare.

McNeill, William H., *The Pursuit of Power: Technology, Armed Force, and Society since A.D. 1000* (Chicago: University of Chicago Press, 1982). Argues that the emergence of free enterprise in Europe allowed wealth, technology, and political power to reinforce each other.

Parker, Geoffrey, *The Military Revolution: Military Innovation and the Rise of the West, 1500–1800*, 2nd ed. (Cambridge: Cambridge University Press, 1996). A classic description of a "military revolution" that was a major factor in Europe's achievement of global power during the early modern era.

Phillips, Carla Rahn, *Six Galleons for the King of Spain: Imperial Defense in the Early Seventeenth Century* (Baltimore: Johns Hopkins University Press, 1991). A study of shipbuilding, the logistics of naval defense, and the problems of the effort to defend the Spanish Atlantic Empire.

War Games

Anderson, Fred, *Crucible of War: The Seven Years' War and the Fate of Empire in North America, 1754–1766* (New York: Knopf, 2000). Traces the events that led to the Seven Years' War and its expansion over three of the continents, which shaped the development of Britain into a world empire.

DuPlessis, Robert S., *Lille and the Dutch Revolt: Urban Stability in an Era of Revolution, 1500–1582* (Cambridge–New York: Cambridge University Press, 1991). Shows that Lille remained loyal to Philip II during the Dutch revolt due to the political response of its ruling class.

Parker, Geoffrey, *The Thirty Years' War* (London–Boston: Routledge, Kegan Paul, 1984). A masterful account of this most devastating conflict of the early modern era.

An Age of Kings

Bonney, Richard, *The European Dynastic States, 1494–1660* (Oxford: Oxford University Press, 1991). An excellent overview of the political development of Europe's nation states in the early modern era.

Burns, J. H., *Lordship, Kingship and Empire: The Idea of Monarchy 1400–1525* (Oxford: Clarendon Press of Oxford University Press, 1988). An examination of lordship in late medieval and early modern France, England, Spain, the papacy, and the Holy Roman Empire.

Elliott, J. H. & L. W. B. Brockliss, eds., *The Age of the Favourite* (New Haven: Yale University Press, 1999). The absolute kings did not rule absolutely but shared power, tacitly, with their "favorites," men who gained importance because of their privileged access to and command over the monarch, and depicted in a variety of European settings in these essays.

Major, J. Russell, *From Renaissance Monarchy to Absolute Monarchy: French Kings, Nobles, and Estates* (Baltimore: Johns Hopkins University Press, 1994). Considers kings, aristocrats, and assemblies in the struggle for power, with the monarchy edging ahead in the end.

Mirrors for Princes

Brown, Jonathan and J. H. Elliott, *A Palace for the King: The Buen Retiro and the Court of Philip IV* (New Haven: Yale University Press, 1980). Analyzes the 1630s construction of the Buen Retiro palace, showing how the palace was a contrived presentation of kingship, intended to awe spectators and subjects.

Burke, Peter, *The Fabrication of Louis XIV* (New Haven–London: Yale University Press, 1992). An imaginative analysis of the staging of the French kingship during the high point of absolutism.

Frye, Susan, *Elizabeth I: The Competition for Representation* (Oxford: Oxford University Press, 1993). How Elizabeth appropriated the image-making machinery around her to advance her own construction of herself as both woman and monarch.

Life and Times of Queen Elizabeth I: http://www.elizabethi.org

Louise XIV, biography (Versailles):
http://www.chateauversailles.fr/en/210.asp

Constitutional goovernment, works of all periods, including Machiavelli, Grotius, Hobbes, Locke, Bodin, and Bossuet:
http://www.constitution.org/liberlib.htm

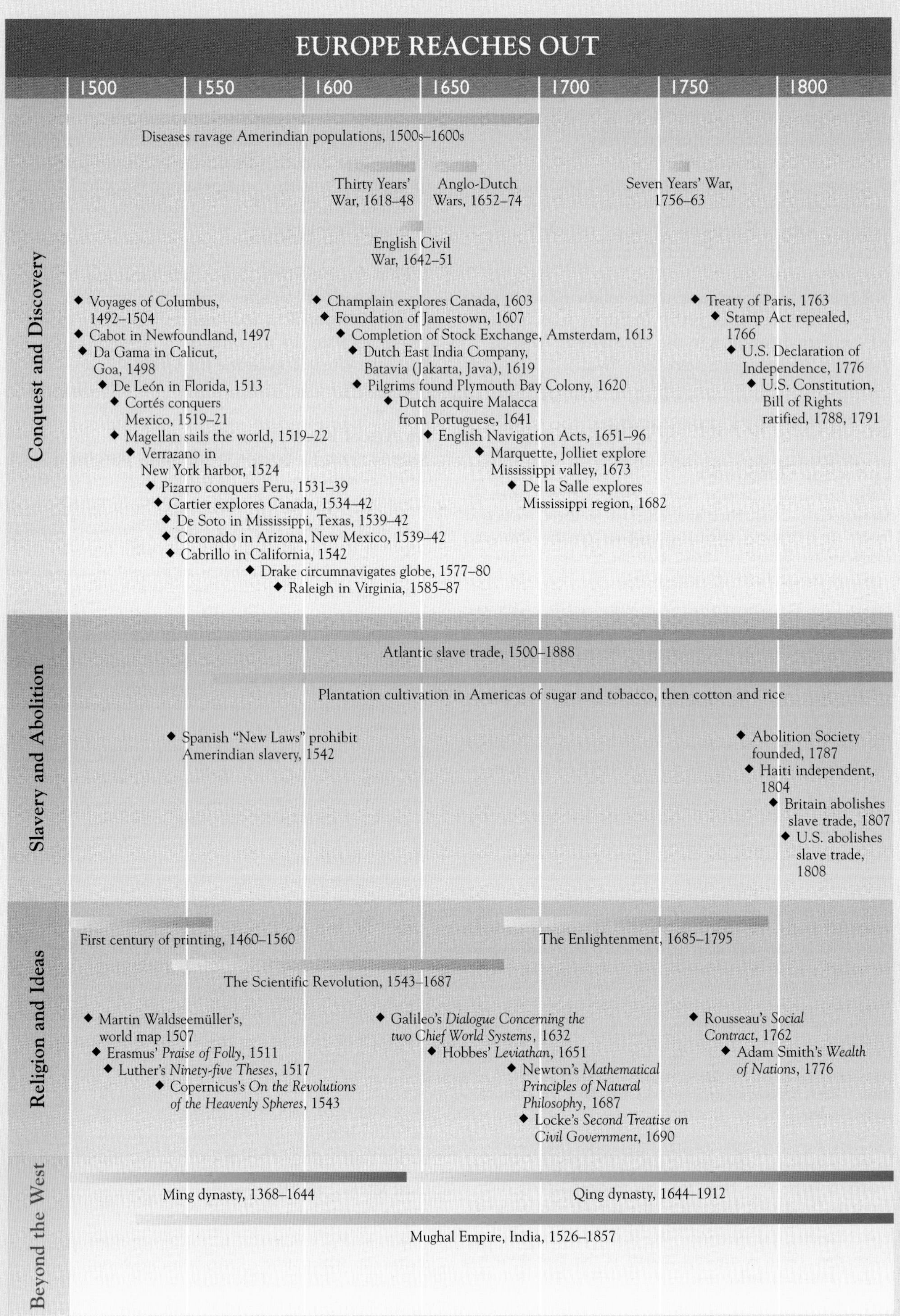
EUROPE REACHES OUT
1500
1550
1600
1650
1700
1750
1800
Conquest and Discovery
Diseases ravage Amerindian populations, 1500s–1600s
Thirty Years' War, 1618–48
Anglo-Dutch Wars, 1652–74
Seven Years' War, 1756–63
English Civil War, 1642–51
◆ Voyages of Columbus, 1492–1504
◆ Cabot in Newfoundland, 1497
◆ Da Gama in Calicut, Goa, 1498
◆ De León in Florida, 1513
◆ Cortés conquers Mexico, 1519–21
◆ Magellan sails the world, 1519–22
◆ Verrazano in New York harbor, 1524
◆ Pizarro conquers Peru, 1531–39
◆ Cartier explores Canada, 1534–42
◆ De Soto in Mississippi, Texas, 1539–42
◆ Coronado in Arizona, New Mexico, 1539–42
◆ Cabrillo in California, 1542
◆ Drake circumnavigates globe, 1577–80
◆ Raleigh in Virginia, 1585–87
◆ Champlain explores Canada, 1603
◆ Foundation of Jamestown, 1607
◆ Completion of Stock Exchange, Amsterdam, 1613
◆ Dutch East India Company, Batavia (Jakarta, Java), 1619
◆ Pilgrims found Plymouth Bay Colony, 1620
◆ Dutch acquire Malacca from Portuguese, 1641
◆ English Navigation Acts, 1651–96
◆ Marquette, Jolliet explore Mississippi valley, 1673
◆ De la Salle explores Mississippi region, 1682
◆ Treaty of Paris, 1763
◆ Stamp Act repealed, 1766
◆ U.S. Declaration of Independence, 1776
◆ U.S. Constitution, Bill of Rights ratified, 1788, 1791
Slavery and Abolition
Atlantic slave trade, 1500–1888
Plantation cultivation in Americas of sugar and tobacco, then cotton and rice
◆ Spanish "New Laws" prohibit Amerindian slavery, 1542
◆ Abolition Society founded, 1787
◆ Haiti independent, 1804
◆ Britain abolishes slave trade, 1807
◆ U.S. abolishes slave trade, 1808
Religion and Ideas
First century of printing, 1460–1560
The Enlightenment, 1685–1795
The Scientific Revolution, 1543–1687
◆ Martin Waldseemüller's, world map 1507
◆ Erasmus' *Praise of Folly*, 1511
◆ Luther's *Ninety-five Theses*, 1517
◆ Copernicus's *On the Revolutions of the Heavenly Spheres*, 1543
◆ Galileo's *Dialogue Concerning the two Chief World Systems*, 1632
◆ Hobbes' *Leviathan*, 1651
◆ Newton's *Mathematical Principles of Natural Philosophy*, 1687
◆ Locke's *Second Treatise on Civil Government*, 1690
◆ Rousseau's *Social Contract*, 1762
◆ Adam Smith's *Wealth of Nations*, 1776
Beyond the West
Ming dynasty, 1368–1644
Qing dynasty, 1644–1912
Mughal Empire, India, 1526–1857

CHAPTER

16 EUROPE REACHES OUT

Global Voyages and Cultural Encounters

1500–1750

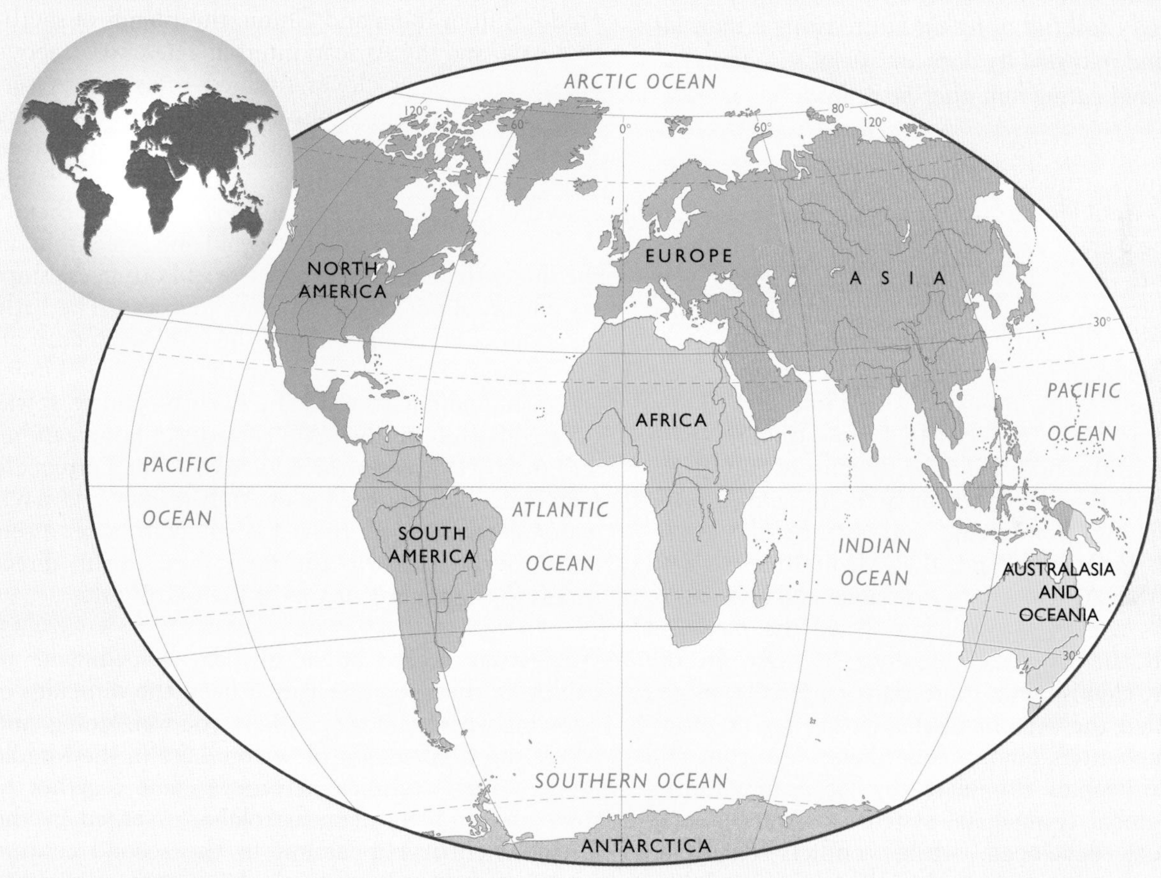

KEY TOPICS

- **The Open Seas:** Led by skilled Portuguese navigators, European merchants establish footholds in Africa, India, the East Indies, and East Asia.
- **Brave New World:** With Christopher Columbus in the vanguard, Spanish and Portuguese conquerors settle much of South and North America; the English, Dutch, and French follow them, as native Amerindians are increasingly displaced, and African slaves are imported to work the mines and the fields.
- **The Wealth of Nations:** New world commodities flood Europe, which exports its manufactures to the new colonies of the Western Hemisphere and the ancient markets of the east; "mercantilist" strategies are challenged by the proposition that free trade is an even better tool for building the wealth of nations.

*W**ho is the Cannibal?** The Tupinambá, wrote the sixteenth-century French essayist Michel de Montaigne (1533–1592) of the* **Amerindian** *inhabitants of Brazil, roasted and then ate their war captives. As the victims awaited their fate, they suffered without flinching the winners' abuse and mockery. A well-bred European of the ruling noble class, Montaigne did not quite admire this behavior, but neither did he condemn it. Did not Europeans perpetrate worse cruelties? "I think there is more barbarity in eating a man alive than in eating him dead," wrote Montaigne referring to then current judicial punishments, "and in tearing by torture and the rack a body still full of feeling, in roasting a man bit by bit, and mangled by dogs and swine ..., than in roasting and eating him after he is dead."*

Montaigne's attitude—at once curious, skeptical, and tolerant—could have crystallized only after Europeans began their great expansion into the other inhabited continents of the globe. During that 500-year venture, European peoples encountered the diverse peoples of Asia, Africa, Australia, and the Western Hemisphere. Non-Europeans and Europeans were transformed by the interactions that followed.

As Maps 16.1, 16.3, and 16.4 show, from the mid-fifteenth to the mid-seventeenth century, Europeans ranged over the globe, buying and selling, measuring and mapping, conquering and settling. First tiny Portugal ranged beyond the Mediterranean, and around the African coast to India and east Asia. Portugal's competitors quickly joined the race and extended the European presence in Asia. In the Western Hemisphere, European nations explored and settled the Americas, the setting for unanticipated encounters among Amerindian, African, and European peoples. Stimulated by European colonization, a global commercial system of unprecedented complexity developed, while conflicts flared up among competing nations which had committed their wealth and their people, and other peoples and their wealth too, in the quest for greater profits.

THE OPEN SEAS

In the late 1400s, European ships which had rarely ventured beyond the Mediterranean Sea launched out into the open ocean: the Indian, the Pacific, and the Atlantic, called the "Ocean Sea." These waters were the key to Europe's powerful leap forward in the early modern era. They were conquered by sturdy ships, refined navigational tools, cast-iron cannon, and better maps. The tiny Iberian state of Portugal took the lead, establishing footholds in Africa, India, China, Japan, and the famed "Spice Islands" or Moluccas (in modern Indonesia). Immense profits flowed into the port of Lisbon and the Portuguese royal treasury. Dutch, French, and English merchants followed their lure. By 1700, these nations had footholds of their own on the African coasts and in south and east Asia and the Pacific islands.

Portugal Takes the Lead

Since the earliest days of civilization, world trade had centered on the Mediterranean. In the Middle Ages, Byzantine, Arab, and Italian merchants carried across the Mediterranean goods hauled overland and over water from the three continents that surrounded it. Driving this commerce was the demand for luxury products from India and China, the islands of southeast Asia, and the African interior. These were, above all, spices—pepper, cloves, nutmeg—craved as preservatives and flavorings; also silks and cottons, exotic woods, ivory, and gems. Much as Europeans craved these luxury commodities, European merchants craved even more the gold with which to buy them.

It was in order to find both gold and spices that, in the fifteenth century, the captains of Portuguese ships set out on unprecedentedly long journeys. The little kingdom of Portugal bordered the Atlantic Ocean on the western edge of the Iberian peninsula. Under Moorish domination until the twelfth century, it was isolated both from the main currents of European life and from Mediterranean commerce. But Portuguese merchants had knowledge of Arab science and navigational tools, and enjoyed royal patronage, assets enabling them to win the prize they sought: direct access to the trading depots of the Old World.

Navigation Aids Previously, the impediment to exploring the open ocean had been the difficulty of knowing where you were, where you were going, and where the winds might blow you. Late in the Middle Ages, several technical advances came together to solve the problem. The **astrolabe**, invented by the Greek scientist Hipparchus in the second century B.C.E. and later refined by Arab scientists, permitted the navigator to measure the apparent height of a star and thus determine his latitude. Meanwhile, astronomers worked out detailed tables of the positions of the stars. These tables allowed the technician with an astrolabe to determine a ship's position.

The **quadrant** and, later, the more advanced **sextant**, also measured the altitude of heavenly bodies and thus determined position. Mechanical clocks could check the bearing of the sun—although longitude could not be measured until precision chronometers in the eighteenth century. The **compass**, used by Chinese navigators from around 1100, was adopted by Europeans, who designated as its four cardinal points the fixed directions North, South, East, and West. The device pointed to a magnetic, and therefore variable, north, rather than a true north, which limited its usefulness.

As nautical tools improved, so too did maps. **Portolan** charts gave sailing distances in clear quantities and bearings in straight lines. Lacking parallels and **meridians**, or any indication of the curvature of the earth, they could be used for enclosed seas, but not on the open oceans. Better charts became available as geographical knowledge improved.

Early in the fifteenth century, a copy of the *Geography* by the Greek scientist Ptolemy (c. 90–168 C.E.), began to circulate in western Europe, spurring the creation of a new generation of world maps. These first ventures of modern **cartography** (the science of mapmaking) sadly preserved Ptolemy's errors. He underestimated the circumference of the earth by one-sixth and imagined a huge "unknown land" covering much of the Southern Hemisphere. Portuguese expeditions enabled cartographers to partially correct the maps and charts and called for the drawing of at least one meridian and lines of latitude. By the mid-sixteenth century, map projections regularly described the earth as a sphere, as shown in *Windows On*, p. 453. Thereafter maps were more accurate than Ptolemy's, as science and experience improved on the knowledge inherited from antiquity.

As shipbuilding also improved, so too did ships (see Chapter 11). The ships of medieval Europe were square-masted and depended on oars for maneuverability and speed. Arab ships called **dhows**, designed for the deep waters of the Indian Ocean, were rigged with triangular, or **lateen**, sails. From these two types of vessel, Spanish and Portuguese shipbuilders developed the small, fast **caravel**. The key to the caravel's

Map 16.1 World Economies and Movements of Peoples around 1500: *On the eve of European expansion, advanced economies based on cultivation with the plow were found in Europe, Asia Minor and the Near East, South and East Asia and some of the Pacific islands, and a small fraction of mostly Mediterranean Africa—the areas of the original Eurasian civilizations and those regions that developed from contact with them. Here the production of food surplus had also made possible the intensive development of urban centers. Food gatherers, hand cultivators, and pastoralists occupied the rest of the inhabited globe, the major part of its surface. Beginning in the late fifteenth century, peoples from the more advanced areas and especially Europeans began the settlement, expansion, and transformation of those unvisited areas.*

speed was its enlarged sail area, achieved by increasing the number of masts and rigging the middle mast with a square sail or sails, the fore and aft with lateen sails. The stern rudder, a recent innovation, allowed for quick, precise steering. Navigators learned to overcome the westerly winds of the Atlantic and to make use of wind patterns on the Indian Ocean. Because oarsmen were unnecessary, their places could be taken by sailors, cargo, or soldiers.

These superior sailing ships also developed fighting capacity. In the 1400s, they carried cannon on deck, as well as soldiers armed with crossbows and arquebuses. By the early 1500s, guns were permanently mounted between the decks so as to fire broadside through special gunports. Hulls were strengthened, and the whole structure braced by multiple decks, so that the ship could withstand enemy bombardment and cannon recoil. Wherever they went, the new men-of-war (as these warships were called) out-powered other ships and even coastal defences. "At the rumor of our coming," a Portuguese general wrote his king in 1513, "the native ships all vanished, and even the birds ceased to skim over the water." This armed, oceangoing craft made possible the European domination of the seas.

Safe, fast, and formidable, well-steered and powered entirely by sails, manned by a smaller crew but equipped to sustain long journeys, these ships constituted an improvement over the Mediterranean carriers used by the Genoese and Venetians. They brought explorers to the New World, and escorted convoys of heavy merchant vessels across the oceans. (The "New World," designating the lands of the Western Hemisphere, was isolated from the Old World civilizations of Afro-Eurasia until Columbus' arrival in 1492.) By 1600, European ships, once inferior, were the best in the world.

The Lure of Faraway Places

Jan Vermeer, The Geographer: *In this painting of 1669 by the Dutch artist Vermeer can be seen different articles of navigation: a compass, maps, and a globe.* (Städelsches Kunstinstitut, Frankfurt)

The African Route The first nation to benefit from this improved technology was Portugal. Emerging from the wars of the *Reconquista*, Portugal entered upon its most glorious age around 1400, during the long reign of King John I (r. 1385–1433). John was not only a state-builder but the founder of Portugal's maritime success, even more brilliantly patronized by his brother Prince Henry the Navigator (1394–1460). In 1415, Henry participated in the Portuguese capture of Ceuta, a Moorish depot opposite Gibraltar. The next year he summoned cartographers and seamen to form an institute for navigation. Under Henry's patronage, dozens of vessels sailed straight from the shore into unknown waters, to Africa and beyond.

Plucking up the Atlantic archipelagoes of the Azores and Madeiras Islands on the way (while Spain took the Canaries), Portuguese sea captains turned south to plant garrisons along the west African shore. By the 1470s, they had founded permanent trading stations, where they loaded the gold, spices, ivory, and exotic woods of the interior on ships bound for home. Although their original objectives were gold and spices, they quickly developed an appetite for slaves. As early as 1433, Prince Henry approved the traffic in human cargoes. Soon the crown was taxing the revenues of this trade at 20 percent. The slave trade funded the Portuguese state.

Late in the fifteenth century, Portuguese exploration reached beyond the west coast of Africa. In 1488, Bartolomeu Dias (1430–1500) looped around Africa's southern tip (later named the Cape of Good Hope) and continued northeast along the further coast. Repelled by Arab merchants, and daunted by unfamiliar winds, Dias returned to Portugal.

Ten years later, and under Dias' tutelage, Vasco da Gama (c. 1460–1524) completed the mission his predecessor had launched. With four ships, he sailed past the Cape of Good Hope and into the Indian Ocean, previously the preserve of Arab merchants. In 1498, he anchored off Calicut, on the west (Malabar) coast of India, one of the main depots for the Asian spice trade, as described in *Witnesses* on p. 458. Although hostilities erupted between the Portuguese and the ruler of Calicut, Da Gama managed to return to Portugal with a quantity of pepper. That pepper signaled the accomplishment of a route to the east that started from the western coast of Europe.

Soon the Portuguese established a firm base at the city of Goa, farther north on the west coast of India. This would serve as the Asian capital of their commercial empire of "the Indies" (meaning at the time all of

***Alejo Fernandez,* Our Lady of the Navigators:** *This 1535 painting of the Virgin Mary as protectress of several known bold explorers (Columbus may be the figure at the left), and depicting some of the kinds of ships in which they would have sailed, was painted for the Casa de Contratación, or Trade House, in Seville, the center for New World shipping in Spain.*

Asia) which embraced merchant depots in the spice-rich Molucca islands, China, and Japan. Governor-general Afonso de Albuquerque (1453–1515) wrested the depot from Arab merchants and military forces who had long-established colonies there, committing terrible atrocities in the process. Portuguese merchants sent the precious commodities of the east directly back to Lisbon on an average of twelve ships per year. There they sold cheaply (the prices uninflated by the middlemen costs that Venice had had to pay), but at profits sufficient to make the tiny country rich. The kings of Portugal took 20 percent of the profit.

The Portuguese achievement was unprecedented. With a population of only 2 million, Portugal quickly acquired an empire vastly greater than itself. Its ships pierced the zone of Arab mercantile supremacy, crossed the Indian Ocean, and opened a European sea route to India, Indonesia, and China. The port at Lisbon now rivaled once-mighty Venice. After 1600, her mastery of the Mediterranean devalued by Portuguese competition, Venice was reduced to enjoying the small profits of Middle Eastern commerce. The future of merchant ventures lay on the open ocean.

Old World Ventures

In the early 1500s, the Dutch, English, and French followed the Portuguese into the commercial heart of the Old World, and had usurped their position by 1700. They did so by developing merchant empires, consisting of far-flung networks of garrisoned depots, often managed by **joint-stock** merchant companies which acted like nations in themselves.

Joint-stock companies were corporations more complex than the partnerships created by medieval Italian merchants. Now hundreds or thousands of individuals contributed funding for an ongoing commercial enterprise, and awaited, passively, a share of profits in return. The company itself had an identity independent of its participating partners, or shareholders. It sold its shares where merchants gathered—at the *bourse* (French for "purse"), or stock market, such as the one in Antwerp (Europe's first), founded in 1531, or the more important one in Amsterdam, completed in 1613. The company developed its own bureaucracy and hierarchy of officers and agents, and even its own security force, which looked much like a small army. A joint-stock company had the power not merely to buy and sell, but also to settle, manage, and defend a merchant **colony**.

The European agents of merchant companies pressed for trade privileges everywhere along the coasts of southern and eastern Asia. They succeeded especially well in establishing themselves in India, where most of the local rulers, possessing no naval capacity and at odds among themselves, were accustomed to commercial interaction with foreign merchants. Portuguese merchants maintained the base at Goa until it was reclaimed by an independent India in 1961. By 1700, English and Dutch competitors had taken over Indian trade with Europe. Their various enterprises in India were organized by the English East India Company, established in 1600, and the Dutch East India Company, established in 1602 (see *How Many?*, p. 454).

India As the Portuguese, English, and Dutch planted their commercial colonies on the coasts of India, great changes occurred in the interior. Since the Gupta kings died out on the Indian subcontinent in the mid-sixth century C.E., India had split into a multitude of states and kingdoms, but it still sustained a lively commercial life. By 1192, Islamic invaders from the frontier Sind region had conquered much of northern India and established a sultanate at Delhi which gained sovereignty in the northern part of the subcontinent. Meanwhile, Arab Muslim traders established commercial depots along the coasts. The Delhi sultanate fell in 1398 to the Mongol-Turkic conqueror Tamerlane (c. 1336–1405), to be succeeded by small Muslim kingdoms. After 1526, Tamerlane's descendant Babur (1483–1530) swept in, defeated the different petty states of the north, and established the Mughal Empire. The Great Mughals, as the emperors were called, gained dominion over much of the region, creating a united empire, and presided over a blossoming of culture.

By the early 1700s, the Hindu kingdoms of the center and south reasserted themselves, however, and by mid-century, the Mughal Empire had weakened, leaving India in a disarray the British then exploited. By 1757, the English East India Company, with bases at Bombay, Madras, and Calcutta, and employing its own army and diplomats, had become the principal power in the subcontinent (see Chapter 23). Over the next century it would defeat one regional power after another until it came to rule all of India—about two-thirds directly, and one-third indirectly.

China In China, European merchants never controlled local rulers as they did in India. Prosperous China was uninterested in the goods and services proffered by Europeans. Under the Ming dynasty (which replaced the Mongol Yuan dynasty in 1368), the Chinese people were better fed, clothed, and educated, and perhaps better ruled than peoples anywhere else. Even a poor boy from one of the remote farming villages could aspire to pass the difficult examinations that permitted entrance to the ruling bureaucracy. Steeped in the ancient Confucian tradition, these mandarins advocated self-sufficiency and disdained commercial enterprises and projects of territorial expansion.

Such attitudes had not always prevailed in China. Between 1405 and 1433 (two generations before Columbus' voyages), the emperor's Muslim eunuch Zheng He had made a quite remarkable series of

WINDOWS ON

Mapping the World

Grazioso Benincasa, Portolan chart of the east coast of Africa, 1468

Anonymous, Amerigo Vespucci, 1673

Perhaps the most important navigational device was the map. But advances in map creation had consequences beyond just practical considerations. Improved, realistic world maps based on data collected by acute explorers provided Europeans with an entirely new concept of the globe on which they lived. Shown here (above) is an example of a Portolan chart (showing the east coast of Africa), which guided navigators before the development of modern maps. The intersecting lines connect known locations, and the coastline is drawn freehand based on the careful observation of experienced sailors.

Amerigo Vespucci, Italian navigator, is shown (above right) complete with a compass, a map, and a globe.

Hondius' sophisticated map (below) shows the route followed during Sir Francis Drake's circumnavigation of the globe in 1580.

(top left: British Library, London)

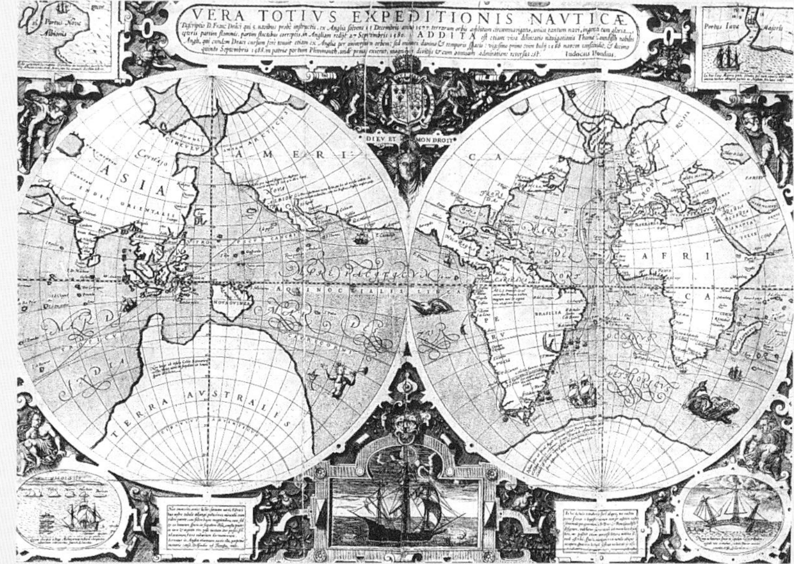

Hondius, World map showing Drake's voyage (1580), seventeenth century

To continue your investigation of this topic, please go to www.prenhall.com/king for the related **WINDOWS** on the **WEB** activity

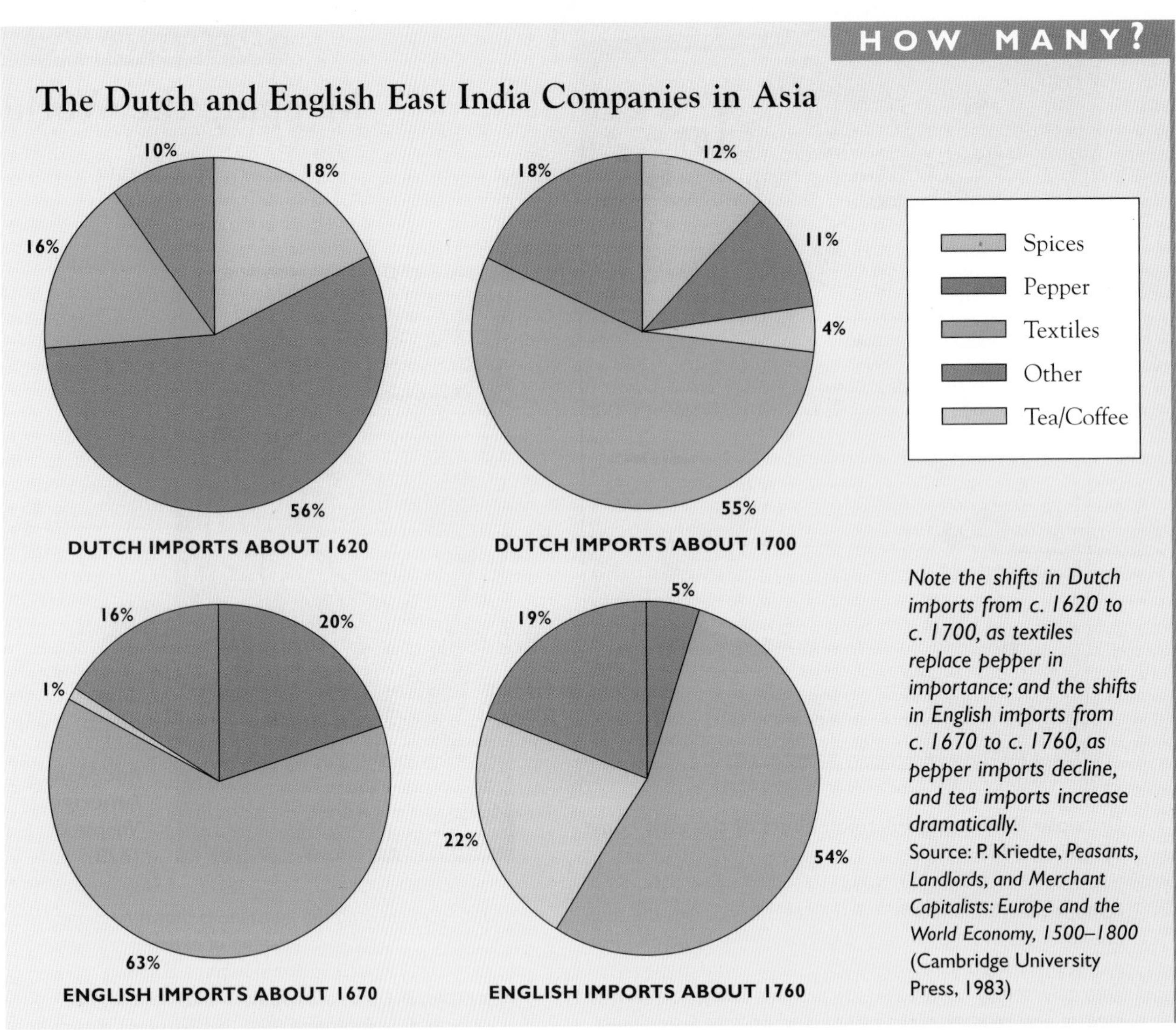

Note the shifts in Dutch imports from c. 1620 to c. 1700, as textiles replace pepper in importance; and the shifts in English imports from c. 1670 to c. 1760, as pepper imports decline, and tea imports increase dramatically.

Source: P. Kriedte, *Peasants, Landlords, and Merchant Capitalists: Europe and the World Economy, 1500–1800* (Cambridge University Press, 1983)

expeditions through the Indian Ocean to the east African coast. On the first occasion, Zheng had sailed with a fleet of sixty-two vessels, carrying 28,000 men. Advised by mandarin officials, Chinese rulers later halted these expeditions, and even banned the building of ships. Commerce had low priority for the ruling Chinese. But Europeans yearned to sell Chinese goods to the west—especially since the decline of the ancient caravan link between the Middle East and China, through which had flowed Chinese silks and luxury products. Chinese rulers stood firm, however. They might grant Europeans a trading base, such as that gained by the Portuguese at Macao in 1557, but they continued to insulate Chinese society from Europeans.

Japan Japanese rulers felt much the same way. From the twelfth century, Japan had been dominated by a class of warrior landowners—the **samurai**, roughly similar to the knights of medieval Europe—who owed obedience to an overlord, or shogun. Shoguns and samurai overshadowed the emperor, isolated in his court but protected from challenges by his divine descent. This Japanese elite opposed European influence. In 1636, the Japanese abandoned all seafaring activity and sealed themselves within their borders. In the 1630s, they expelled all Europeans except the Dutch, who were allowed to dock one ship each year and remain, segregated, on an island near Nagasaki. But the Dutch were to have no contact with Japanese, nor even learn that language; and the Japanese, similarly, were prohibited from learning Dutch, with the result that the two merchant communities were forced to converse in the language of the now-absent Portuguese. The Dutch merchant colony was the main link between Japan and the West until the nineteenth century.

The Dutch Initiative The Malay Peninsula (part of modern Malaysia), the islands of the South Pacific (including modern Indonesia and the Philippines), and other Pacific islands, including New Zealand and the continent of Australia, all became known to European merchant fleets between 1500 and 1800. The prime commercial target was the Moluccas, or Spice Islands, producers of cloves and nutmeg. In this vast Pacific region, as in India, the Portuguese were the first venturers, establishing a base at Malacca (in modern Malaysia) by 1511. But farther east the Dutch outpaced the Portuguese to win the prize. They gained title to the Moluccas by 1613, and in 1619 established an administrative center at Batavia (now Jakarta, in modern Indonesia). Dutch merchants became the main exploiters of the spice trade, and they were the first Europeans to sight New Zealand and Australia. The Dutch explorer Willem Schouten discovered the southern tip of South America in 1616 and named it Cape Hoorn (or Horn) after his birth place. In 1652 the Dutch settled the African Cape of Good Hope, indicating their leadership in world trade by their presence at these two southernmost outcroppings.

In the seventeenth century, the immense Pacific looked like a Dutch sea. How could such a tiny nation command so far-flung and efficient an empire, if only a merchant empire? The answer lay in its familiarity with the sea—a constant threat to the low-lying Dutch terrain but also a stimulus to shipbuilding. By 1600, the Dutch had 10,000 ships, which sailed the Baltic and Northern seas, as well as the Atlantic and Pacific oceans. The ***fluyt*** or "flyboat," a Dutch innovation, was an efficient vessel designed for inexpensive, utilitarian hauling. The Dutch became the common carriers of Europe, transporting both utilitarian and luxury goods and linking ports all over the globe. Of these entrepreneurs, the English writer Daniel Defoe (1660–1731) wrote with some awe: "They buy to sell again, take in to send out, and the greatest part of their vast commerce consists in being supplied from all parts of the world that they may supply all the world again."

From the coasts of Africa, across the Indian Ocean and on into the Pacific, merchant vessels probed the ports of the Old World. The next frontier lay on the far side of the Atlantic.

BRAVE NEW WORLD

As the human species evolved and developed communities in the Old World, the New World of the Western Hemisphere remained uninhabited. It acquired its first human immigrants around the time of the last Ice Age (which ended about 10,000 years ago). These peoples developed their own varied cultures and civilization in isolation from Old World influences. After 1492, explorers, conquerors, and settlers came in turn to the Western Hemisphere, overwhelming the New World's tens of millions of Amerindian natives, importing more than 10 million African strangers, and planting the seeds of new cultures descended from those of Europe. The New World became part of Western civilization; but its Amerindian and African inhabitants, whose labor enriched merchant and professional elites on both sides of the Atlantic, remained, to varying degrees, alienated from it.

Exploration and Conquest

The first explorers to visit the Western Hemisphere entered a world inhabited by defenseless peoples, rich in resources, and ripe for exploitation. They learned the extent and nature of the land and claimed it for the European nations that had sent them. Conquest followed exploration, resulting in the destruction of two advanced New World civilizations.

During the last Ice Age (from about 30,000 to 10,000 years before the present), Asian hunters wandered over the land bridge that stretched some 50 miles (80 km.) from Siberia (modern Russia) to Alaska—a region Europeans later called "Beringia," after the straits named for the Danish explorer Vitus Bering (1681–1741), (see Chapter 8). Others may have come from Asia by sea. These Asian migrants were the true discoverers of the lands of the Western Hemisphere. Material remains of their culture testify to their residence at various sites of North and South America from between 20,000 and 10,000 years ago.

Over thousands of years, the Amerindians migrated across the land mass to its southernmost tip, developing into numerous tribes and nations, speaking hundreds of languages. Most had not progressed beyond a Neolithic condition before the arrival of Europeans. Some remained hunters and gatherers, while others, beginning about 7000 years ago, learned to farm. More than half of them lived in Mexico and the Andes regions, where they developed, respectively, the Aztec and Inca civilizations. Perhaps 4 to 6 million lived in what is now the continental United States, and as many more in the Caribbean. In all, perhaps as many as 75 million Amerindians inhabited the Western Hemisphere before Europeans "discovered" that world and proclaimed it "new."

As early as the late tenth century, Viking sailors were exploring the waters of the north Atlantic near the coast of modern Canada. In 982 Erik the Red founded a settlement on the island of Greenland (so named by him to make it more attractive to

MUST READS

Tracing the Spanish Conquest of the Americas

Bernal Diaz del Castillo	*The Discovery and Conquest of Mexico* (c. 1527)
Bartolomé de las Casas	*Brief Relation of the Destruction of the Indies* (1552)
Christopher Columbus	*Diaries*
Hernán Cortés	*Letters*

colonists). A few years later some Viking sailors are believed to have accidentally discovered the Atlantic coast of North America; they reported their discovery to their compatriots in Greenland. Erik's son Leif Eriksson repeated the journey in 1003, naming the site of his landing as that of Vinland (possibly in Newfoundland). Two subsequent expeditions failed to establish a lasting settlement, and the Viking adventure was forgotten except in Greenland sagas. Nearly 500 years later, as Vasco da Gama and Dias were skirting Africa, a European expedition again arrived on the fringes of the Western Hemisphere. This time the newcomers stayed, and were followed by many others.

Columbus and the Spanish In 1492 the Genoese sea captain Christopher Columbus (1451–1506), funded by the Spanish monarchs Ferdinand and Isabella, set out with three ships on a daring expedition on the open ocean. His goal was to sail to the rich markets of the Indies, claiming for Spain any islands or mainlands he discovered en route. Assuming that Japan and China lay only 3000 miles (4380 km.) to the west, Columbus planned to reach Asia by traversing the Atlantic. This "Admiral of the Ocean Sea" died in 1506 still thinking he had reached Asia, called the "Indies", (see Map 16.2).

In fact, Japan lay more than 13,000 miles (20,900 km.) to the west—over half the circumference of the globe. Just under 4000 miles (6440 km.) away were the continents of the Western Hemisphere. Columbus first landed on the island he named San Salvador in the Bahamas, then visited other Caribbean islands. On a second journey, he established a base on the island he named Hispaniola (now shared by Haiti and the Dominican Republic). In two subsequent voyages he reached what is now Venezuela (1498) and the shores of Central America (1502)—and realized that his expedition had encountered not just some islands, but at least one huge land mass.

Columbus wanted to find gold, as he wrote in his notebook soon after the discovery: "I do not wish to delay but to discover and go to many islands to find gold." In Hispaniola, he established a trading depot. This was the first of a circuit of fortified mercantile settlements which, within a generation, ringed the Caribbean Sea along the coasts of Mexico, Central America, northern South America, and Florida, and on various islands including Cuba.

Within weeks of his arrival in the New World, Columbus had formed an opinion of its aboriginal residents, whom he named *Indios*, or Indians, thinking he had reached the Indies, or Asia. He concluded that the native Amerindians "would make good and industrious servants" and were "fit to be ruled" (see *Witnesses*, p. 464, and illustration on p. 461). Columbus's men put the Taino natives to work hauling the goods to be sent back to Spain. Appointed viceroy of the island, Columbus sparked a native revolt by his authoritarian rule. He was sent back to Spain in disgrace, but allowed to return again. In 1503, Queen Isabella granted his request for permission to enslave the Taino tribespeople. "Being as they are hardened in their bad habits of idolatry and cannibalism, I hereby give license and permission ... to capture them ... and to sell them and utilize their services. ..." Thus used, the Tainos were extinct within a century.

Meanwhile, Portugal laid claim to Spain's new possessions, announcing that they were an extension of the Atlantic islands of the Azores. Spain appealed to the reigning pope, Alexander VI (r. 1492–1503), who was Spanish by birth. In 1493, Alexander issued a series of papal bulls confirming Spanish possession of the new lands, and drawing an imaginary boundary between Spanish and Portuguese zones: a north-south line about 300 miles west of the Portuguese Azores. By the 1494 Treaty of Tordesillas between Spain and Portugal, the north-south line was redrawn farther west. The effect of the Treaty was that Portugal retained title to what is now Brazil, and Spain to the remaining lands of North and South America claimed by her explorers.

Papal intervention into the realm of geopolitics had a sound foundation. According to medieval theology, all property came from God. Who better to determine its allocation than the pope—according to Roman Catholic thought, God's representative on earth? Later Protestant participants in the race for New World properties were naturally unpersuaded by this line of reasoning.

Spurred by Columbus's example, a stream of explorers now journeyed across the Atlantic. Most were Italians or Portuguese in the employ of other nations. Soon after Columbus's first voyage, the Italian explorer Amerigo Vespucci (1454–1512), scion of an important commercial family of Florence and portrayed in *Windows On* on p. 453, set out in the employ of Spain and (later) Portugal. Probing the coast of South America, he found and explored some of the vast expanse of the Amazon River. He was the first to conclude that the new lands were not part of Asia but part of a previously unknown continent. He called it the "New World." The New World, ironically, was later named after him. In 1507, the German cartographer Martin Waldseemüller published an updated world map in which the New World lands were designated, in honor of the pioneering Florentine, "America."

Over the next fifty years, Spanish explorers crossed Panama to the Pacific Ocean (Vasco Nuñez de Balboa, 1475–1517), and claimed the lands of Florida (Juan Ponce de León, c. 1460–1521), Mississippi and Texas (Hernando de Soto, c. 1496–1542), Arizona and New Mexico (Francisco Vásquez de Coronado, c. 1510–1554), and California (Juan Rodríguez Cabrillo, d. 1543). Their expeditions in search of gold and of a miraculous "fountain of youth" were largely

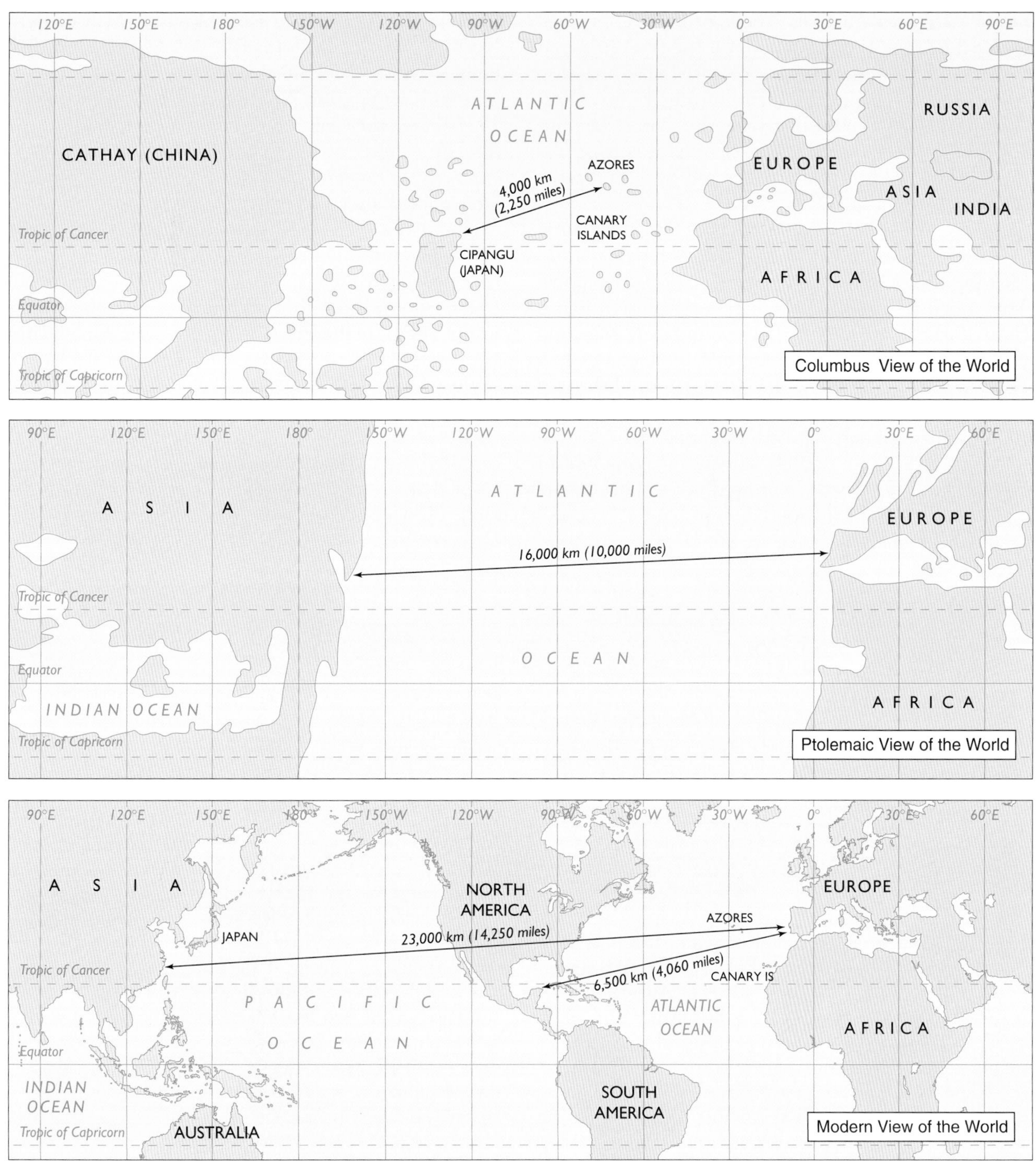

***Map 16.2 Columbus' World:** Columbus fully intended to reach Japan after a westward journey across some 3000 miles of the Atlantic—"correcting" the prevailing Ptolemaic (ancient Greek) model that placed Asia at a distance nearly three times that. Both theories were wrong, as the unknown continents of North and South America and the unknown Pacific Ocean lay between the coast of Spain and the coast of Asia.* (*Scientific Americans*, November 1992, p. 103)

fruitless, but they acquired for their Spanish overlords the lands of western North America stretching as far north as Utah.

The venture of the Portuguese navigator Ferdinand Magellan (c. 1480–1521) was of another sort. In Spain's employ, Magellan set out in 1519 to reach Asia. He sailed from Atlantic to Pacific through the strait near the tip of South America later named after him, the Strait of Magellan, and then across the Pacific, with a starving crew for sixty-eight days, described in *Witnesses* on p. 458, before reaching land (on the island of Guam). Touching on some islands which were later named the Philippines (after the future King Philip II of Spain), Magellan died in a battle with hostile natives. The expedition continued under the second in command. Of the five ships and 270 men who began the journey in 1519, one ship and a mere eighteen men returned in 1522. Accomplishing for the first time the feat of circumnavigating the globe, they had learned how vast was the Pacific, and how distant Asia was from Europe.

Opening up North America The other Atlantic nations now entered the race for American lands, focusing their efforts on the coast of North America. The English sent the Italian Giovanni Caboto (John Cabot, 1450–1499) with one small ship and eighteen sailors to explore in 1497. Cabot reached Newfoundland (in modern Canada), establishing a foothold on the basis of which England would later claim rights to much of North America.

Years later, the English adventurer Sir Walter Raleigh (c. 1552–1618) journeyed three times to the coast of what is now the southeastern United States—a land he named Virginia, in honor of the "Virgin Queen," Elizabeth I. On Roanoke Island (in modern North Carolina) he formed a colony, which failed. Francis Drake (c. 1540–1596), famed for his persistent raids on Spanish Atlantic commerce, repeated in 1577–1580 the feat of circumnavigation achieved first by Magellan's crew. Henry Hudson (d. 1611) explored for England Canada's immense northern bay, later named after him. For the Netherlands, Hudson explored the New York river also named after him, along which the Dutch established trading depots.

Hoping to find a "northwest passage"—an alternative northern route through the American land mass to the Pacific—the French sent the Italian navigator Giovanni da Verrazano (c. 1485–1528) in 1524 to explore the North American coast. Venturing south from Newfoundland, he entered what is now New York harbor. For over 200 years, French captains explored the Canadian coast and the Saint Lawrence, Great Lake, and Mississippi waterways as far as the Gulf of Mexico. Among the most notable were Jacques Cartier (1491–1557), Samuel de Champlain

WITNESSES

Exploration and Conquest

The expansion of European ventures into other regions of the world was accomplished with great brutality at times, yet also, at times, with great courage. The first passage reports the Portuguese plundering of an African town. The second presents the first, disappointing attempts byVasco da Gama to open trade at Calicut, in India. The third describes the enormous hardships suffered during a portion of the journey by a participant in Magellan's expedition to circumnavigate the globe.

João de Barros describes the sack of Mombasa, eastern Africa, by the forces of Portuguese grand-captain Dom Francisco d'Almeida (15–16 August 1505): The Portuguese attack and burn the town; the fire raged all night long, and many houses collapsed. ... [The next morning.] The Grand-Captain ordered that the town should be sacked. ... Then everyone started to plunder the town and to search the houses, forcing open the doors with axes and iron bars. ... A large quantity of rich silk and gold embroidered clothes was seized. ... [The next day] they also carried away provisions, rice, honey, butter, maize, countless camels and a large number of cattle, and even two elephants. ... There were many prisoners, and white women among them and children, and also some merchants. ...
(From G. S. P. Freeman-Grenville, *The East African Coast*, 1962)

Vasco da Gama arrives in Calicut, India (20–29 May 1498), according to an eyewitness: The king was in a small court, reclining upon a couch covered with a cloth of green velvet ... and upon this again a sheet of cotton stuff, very white and fine, more so than any linen. ... On the right side of the king stood a basin of gold, so large that a man might just encircle it with his arms. ... The canopy above the couch was all gilt. ...

On Tuesday the captain [da Gama] got ready the following things to be sent to the king, viz., twelve pieces of *lambel* [a striped cloth], four scarlet hoods, six hats, four strings of coral ... a case of sugar, two casks of oil, and two of honey. ... [The king's officials came] and when they saw the present they laughed at it, saying that it was not a thing to offer to a king, that the poorest merchant from Mecca, or any other part of India, gave more, and that if he wanted to make a present it should be in gold, as the king would not accept such things. When the captain heard this he grew sad, and said that he had brought no gold, that, moreover, he was no merchant, but an ambassador; that he gave of that which he had. ... Upon this they declared that they would not forward his presents, nor consent to his forwarding them himself.
(*A Journal of the First Voyage of Vasco da Gama, 1497–1499*; trs., ed. E. J. Ravenstein, 1848)

Eyewitness Antonio Pigafetta describes Magellan's Pacific crossing (1521): We were three months and twenty days without getting any kind of fresh food. We ate biscuit, which was no longer biscuit, but powder of biscuits swarming with worms, for they had eaten the good. It stank strongly of the urine of rats. We drank yellow water that had been putrid for many days. Rats were sold for one-half ducado apiece, and even then we could not get them. ... Had not God and His blessed mother given us so good weather we would all have died of hunger in that exceeding vast sea. ...
(From L. Wright, *Gold, Glory, and the Gospel*, 1970)

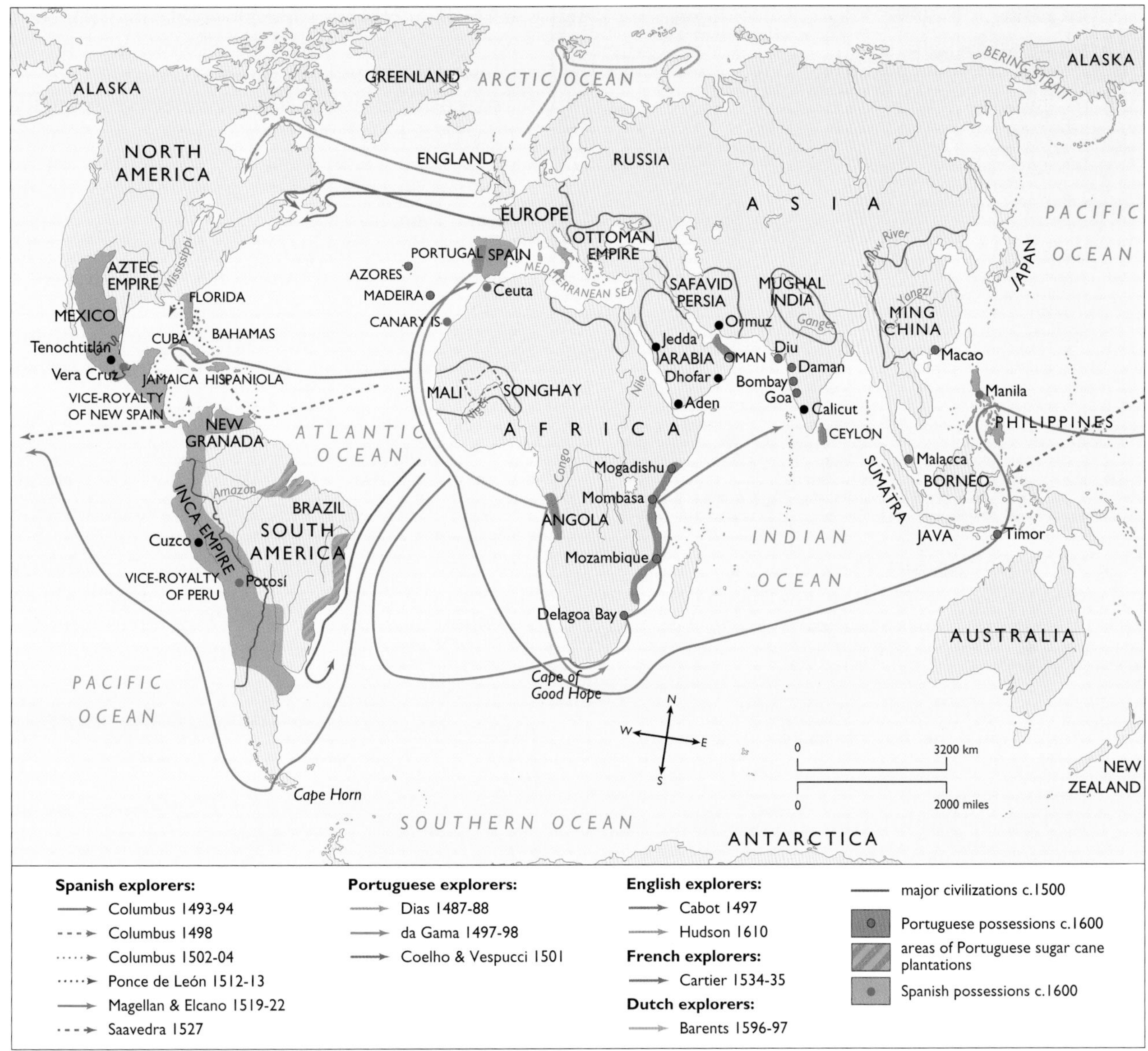

Map 16.3 European Exploration, 1450–1600: *By 1600, Spanish and Portuguese explorers and traders established settlements in South America and the Caribbean, and commercial depots on the coasts of Africa, India, the Pacific islands, China, and Japan—at a time when English, Dutch, and French explorations of North America had just begun.*

(1567–1635), Louis Jolliet (1645–1700), along with the priest Jacques Marquette (1637–1675), and Robert de la Salle (1643–1687).

The Aztecs Even before the English, French, and Dutch embarked on North American ventures, Spain had completed its conquest of much of the Americas. Most Amerindian communities succumbed quickly to European force. The Aztec and Inca empires, centered respectively in modern Mexico and Peru, promised serious resistance. In 1521 and 1533, two ***conquistadores***, conquerors from a nation with a long history of conquest, destroyed these civilizations within a brief time and with only a handful of men.

Spain had only just completed the reconquest of the Iberian peninsula from the Moors when it set out to conquer the lands of the New World. Behind it was a centuries-old military tradition, fueled by a religious zeal tinged deeply with intolerance. Ahead was a project that also invited the use of arms and the missionary muscle of the Roman Catholic Church. The goal of the medieval *Reconquista* was the recovery of Iberian land from foreign domination. That of the American conquest was gold. The extraction of gold from the earth—and later silver, in much greater abundance—was the major economic activity of the Spanish in the New World.

The Amerindian people who constructed the civilization that Europeans called "Aztec" (they called themselves the Mexicas) had moved into central Mexico in the middle of the thirteenth century, establishing a harsh dominion over existing tribal groups. There they claimed inheritance of the culture of the Olmecs and Maya, creators of successive Mesoamerican civilizations (see Chapter 8). On an

New World Encounters

Columbus' first voyage: *This woodcut by Giuliano Dati, 1493, depicts the imminent arrival of Columbus' ship in the Bahamas, with idealized representations of natives on the shore.*

island in the middle of Lake Texcoco, the Aztecs built their capital of Tenochtitlán (incorporated in modern Mexico City), the preeminent metropolis of pre-Conquest culture.

Tenochititlán bristled with temples, sculptures, and shrines, with palaces and schools, workshops and markets, interspersed with floating gardens and equipped with roads and movable bridges to the mainland. It had a population of about 100,000; few cities in contemporary Europe were larger or more splendid. A Spanish chronicler described the reaction of the soldiers—some of whom had seen Constantinople and the cities of Italy—who reported that "so large a market place and so full of people, and so well regulated and arranged, they had never beheld before."

The Aztecs worshiped many gods, especially a sun god having male and female attributes, the dual deity represented by an eagle on a cactus. Guided by Mayan traditions recorded in sacred picture books (for they had no written language), Aztec priests supervised religious life according to calendar cycles of worship, sacrifice, and feasting. Rite and sacrifice shaped the civilization—including human sacrifice, a celebration of the spilling of blood, in which the victim's still-beating heart was ripped from their chest and offered up to the divinity, as illustrated on this page. The need to secure sacrificial victims to appease the sun god stimulated wars of conquest. From childhood, young warriors were trained to capture rather than slay enemies, so that prisoners might be brought back for ceremonial deaths—"the flowered death by the obsidian knife"—on temple stones.

This was the civilization that fell to the conquistador Hernán Cortés (1485–1547). Arriving in 1519 with about 600 men and 11 vessels, in defiance of an order of recall from the Spanish governor of Cuba, Cortés and his troops made their way to Tenochtitlán. Having been received cordially, they proceeded to take prisoner the Aztec emperor, the oddly compliant Montezuma II (the familiar form of the name; more properly Moctezuma, r. 1502–1520). Cortés had burned his own ships, thereby closing off any escape for his men. He sallied from Tenochtitlán to meet a force of his own compatriots who had come to put an end to his mission. Defeating the leaders, he persuaded the men to return with him and pursue the conquest of Mexico.

In Cortés's absence, warfare broke out in Tenochtitlán, triggered by a Spanish massacre of a group of natives during a religious festival. Cortés returned; Montezuma died (possibly as a result of stoning by his angered people, possibly at the hands of the Spanish); and Cortés withdrew again during a "Sad Night" in which half his men were killed. Regrouping, the Spanish forces returned in 1521 to besiege the city, having constructed a fleet

Human sacrifice: *The Aztec practice of human sacrifice by excising the heart of a living victim, pictured in this sixteenth-century* Florentine Codex, *was condemned as barbaric by the conquerors.* (Biblioteca Medicea Laurenziana, Ms. Laur. Med. Palat. 218, c. 175v, Florence)

of twelve small oar- and sail-powered boats to do so. A few months later, after firing cannon from the decks of their ships, they seized and razed Tenochtitlán. A few Spanish soldiers armed with arquebuses and cannon achieved this military conquest (assisted by epidemic, caused by microbes for which the Aztecs had no immunity) over thousands of Mexicans armed merely with arrows and swords carved from obsidian, a volcanic glass. (An account of the Spanish forces is given in *Witnesses* on p. 464.) A cultural conquest followed. In an attempt to extinguish Aztec religion, the conquerors burned the sacred books and erected Christian churches, often on the sites of native temples.

The Incas The other great indigenous civilization was the Inca Empire at Cuzco (in modern Peru), in the Andes Mountains. The Inca domain, extending 2000 miles (3200 km.) along the Pacific coast of South America, included parts of modern Bolivia, Chile, Argentina, and Ecuador, as well as Peru. The empire had reached its greatest extent just prior to the arrival in 1531 of the Spaniard Francisco Pizarro (1475–1541), whose forces conquered and destroyed it.

The Inca emperor was an absolute monarch, whose legitimacy was marked by ceremonies of veneration for the mummies of his deceased ancestors. The emperor commanded the obedience of his subjects and was considered responsible for their welfare. The state owned virtually all property, which was sustained by the labor of the inhabitants. The agricultural wealth thus generated, and stored in an elaborate warehousing system, supported an elite of priests, government workers, and merchants, as well as the elderly, the ill, and widows. The priests managed the feasts, ceremonies, and sacrifices (including human ones) necessary to gain the favor of a roster of deities, among whom the sun god held sway.

The Incas used advanced engineering to terrace, drain, and irrigate the mountainous terrain and maximize productivity on plots as high as 9000 feet (2745 m.) above sea level. They were also expert builders, working from models rather than plans (as they had no system of writing) to create large cities. A network of roads and bridges extended more than 12,000 miles (19,000 km.), negotiating chasms, rivers, and solid rock. Metals buried in the earth, especially silver and gold, were reserved for the use of the emperor—until the arrival of Pizarro and his followers.

Pizarro arrived in Peru in 1531 with a mere 168 men, 67 horses, and 3 cannon, to assail an empire with a population of several millions and a military force of some 100,000. He captured, deceived, tortured, and executed the uncomprehending ruler Atahuallpa. Moving briskly to the capital at Cuzco, he began a conquest in which European guns and European steel swords overcame the force of wooden spears and clubs of the Incas. Pizarro's men accomplished the victory by unparalleled brutality, of which one participant has left this testimony: "I can bear witness that this is the most dreadful and cruel war in the world," in which both sides "give each other the cruelest deaths they can imagine." By 1539, the Spanish victors had quelled native resistance and established their colonial regime, subordinating almost as slaves a people who had administered one of the world's great empires. The Spanish soon opened the mines of Potosí (in modern Bolivia), an immense reservoir of silver, rich enough to supply the numerous Spanish **bullion** fleets for decades to come.

Silver mines: *Once conquered, Amerindians were pressed into service as laborers. At the "Silver Mountain" mines in Potosí (modern Bolivia), as in this engraving, c. 1584, 40,000 poorly paid laborers were employed to mine the silver which was then shipped back to Spain and made into coinage.* (Hispanic Society, New York)

Patterns of Settlement

After the first phase of New World exploration and conquest, settlers built European communities in what seemed like an endlessly fertile expanse. The pattern of settlement varied from region to region. Two main colonial zones emerged: the southern zone, or "Latin" America (including those regions of South America, the Caribbean, and Mexico where Spanish, Portuguese, or French—all derived from Latin—are spoken); and the northern zone, including much of North America, predominantly English- and French-speaking. The southern zone was settled earlier, and its main characteristics established by 1600. The northern zone was settled in the period after 1600. The administrative blocs in both areas were called colonies, each related to its own European "mother" country, or metropolis.

Latin America By the mid-1500s, Spanish settlers had organized the main population centers of Peru and Mexico. Spanish administrators and landowners, drawn primarily from the lesser nobility of the metropolis, recreated so far as they could the culture of their homeland. Their native Spanish language soon developed into a **creole**—a colloquial language containing elements of local Amerindian and African dialects. Their cities, modeled on European cities, boasted cathedrals, palaces, theaters, printing houses, and universities (five by 1636, when the first university of Anglo-America, Harvard, was founded). The new American culture was a mixture of imported Spanish and native Amerindian customs.

The Amerindian inhabitants worked for the proprietors of the *encomiendas* (royal land grants to the conquistadors), or as domestic and agricultural laborers on *haciendas*, the large ranches or plantations owned by the Spanish-speaking elite. The natives who lived on the land granted in *encomienda* owed labor services to the proprietor—who in turn owed the laborers protection, security, religious training, and even education. Haciendas drew on the labor services both of permanent residents—often **peons**, or debt slaves—and of seasonal workers from nearby Indian villages. These arrangements seemed to promise advantage to both laborer and contractor or landowner. In practice, the laborers were abused while the proprietors got richer.

The kingdom of Castile directly ruled the Spanish colonies and closely supervised their governance. Two governors—called viceroys ("vice-kings"), respectively, of "New Spain" (modern Mexico) and Peru—administered the whole of Spanish territory (the number of viceroys increased after 1700). Each viceroy presided over a regional advisory council established in the principal cities, and sent out inspectors to report on local administrations. The position of viceroy conferred high status and attracted ambitious noblemen from Spain. There, a Council of the Indies, based in Madrid, scrutinized the records of each viceroy's service upon completion, and intervened to direct the course of colonial events.

In contrast, Portuguese settlement in the New World followed the pattern of Portuguese expansion in Africa and Asia. Garrisoned merchant colonies were planted at key locations on the coast of Brazil, as fueling stations for fleets bound for the Caribbean. Later, Portuguese governors and landowners took over the settled areas of the interior, intending to control the native population more than to establish European communities.

By the late 1500s, settlers had brought to Brazil the **plantation system** (with lands worked by slave labor under supervision) for sugar cultivation developed in the Portuguese Atlantic islands, especially the island of São Tomé, just off the African coast. English, French, and Spanish landowners later adopted this system in the Caribbean (where tobacco, generally farmed on a smaller scale and yielding lower profits, had previously been the main cash crop). The Dutch, although possessing small colonial bases in the West Indies and on the north Brazilian coast, were more interested in trade than in settlement. Their Dutch West India Company, established in 1621, organized a profitable trade in Brazil and the Caribbean. From the West Indies ports of Havana (Cuba) and San Juan (Puerto Rico), the Spanish bullion fleets took off twice each year, an irresistible lure for Dutch, English, and French raiders.

North American Colonies After 1600, a northern zone of European settlement in the Americas established itself from Savannah (in modern Georgia) to Quebec (in modern Canada). Most of the settlers were English-speakers; some were French, German, or Dutch; there were even a few hundred Swedes. English settlement was at first organized by joint-stock companies. These obtained from the crown a charter enabling the creation of single agricultural communities, centered in Virginia and New England. Jamestown (in modern Virginia), settled by English emigrants, was founded on this pattern in 1607. The Virginia colony thrived, based as it was on the cultivation of tobacco as a cash crop.

In 1620, Plymouth (in modern Massachusetts) was the second English-speaking community to be established. The aim of the Plymouth **Separatists** (Puritans who had separated from the Church of England—later dubbed "Pilgrims") was not simply to gain farmland but also to secure the right to practice their own form of Protestant worship. Other Puritans settled the Massachusetts Bay Colony (1630), while other New England and mid-Atlantic settlements were also motivated by the quest for religious freedom.

By 1700, twelve colonies had been established (the thirteenth, Georgia, was founded in 1732), and about one-half million English-speakers dwelled in North America, equivalent to one-eighth to one-tenth of the population of England itself. Without initially planning to do so, the English had created a sizable empire abroad. Ruled theoretically by King and Parliament (although they had no representatives in Parliament), the colonies developed effective regional, representative governments.

The Dutch and French settlements more closely resembled the Portuguese pattern of coastal enclaves, and contained fewer colonists. These nationals established merchant colonies respectively in New Netherland (modern New York State) and New France (modern Canada, especially the province of Quebec). The Dutch merchants dealt in a variety of commodities, but the French (who competed with the Portuguese for fish in these northern waters) were particularly interested in the valuable furs that their hunters and traders obtained from the forested interior. French settlement was sparse. By the mid-1600s,

***Committed atrocities:** The conquerors treated the native population barbarically, as in this engraving by Théodore de Bry (from* Brevissima Relación, *1598, by Bartolomé de Las Casas) of Spaniards hanging and burning the inhabitants of a village.* (Bibliothèque Nationale, Paris)

there were only about 3000 Europeans in all of New France, many fewer than in the single English colony of Virginia. The French crown ruled its colony directly, sending military governors and financial supervisors responsible to officials in Paris.

In 1664 the Dutch lost their North American mainland possessions to their English challengers on the seas. The French would intermittently fight the British for theirs until an eventual British victory in 1763. By the time that the American War of Independence broke out in 1775 (see Chapter 19), the Atlantic region of North America was largely English both by language and tradition. Although the Spanish and the Portuguese had opened up the New World, the British eventually dominated in North America.

Religion played a major role in shaping the post-conquest civilizations of the New World. A main objective of many of the settlements, especially of the Spanish, was the conversion of Amerindian natives. In the English colonies of North America, as has been seen, a main motive for colonization was religious freedom—or freedom, in effect, from other Europeans. That impulse for liberation would express itself again, years later, when an ideology of political liberty took root in the same region. Meanwhile, the freedom sought by some colonists was steadily denied by all of them to the two "other" peoples with whom they interacted in the New World—the native Amerindians and the newcomer Africans.

Encountering Others

The "discovery" of the New World was more than the discovery by Europeans of lands previously unknown to them. It was a mutual discovery of different peoples, as European strangers, Amerindian natives, and, in time, African captives interacted. For the Amerindians, the encounter was deadly.

The Amerindians When Columbus and his sailors first landed on San Salvador, native Amerindian Tainos greeted them with an assortment of gifts. Impressed by the Europeans' unusual appearance, the Tainos concluded that they were gods. The European newcomers were equally startled by the appearance and customs of a people they had never seen before: largely naked, with painted bodies and long hair, smoking tobacco. The Tainos lived in stable communities, in well-constructed houses equipped with hammocks—an object the Europeans had never seen. Their enemies on nearby islands, the Caribs (after whom we name the Caribbean Sea), had a reputation for ferocity—specifically for cannibalism (although this is possibly undeserved). With such terrifying and amazing stories Columbus and later visitors impressed readers back in Europe.

The millions of natives inhabiting the Western Hemisphere before the European advent consisted of hundreds of nations and tribes and peoples too diverse to be considered as a single Amerindian culture. However, they did have some things in common. Their hundreds of languages ultimately descended from a common pool of Asian languages. None of these was a written language. Only the Mayan peoples acquired the ability to record spoken language in symbols. Although this skill vanished with their decline, the Maya transmitted to successor Mesoamerican peoples—who composed sacred texts using pictographs—a memory of writing and a respect for books.

Based on collectives of family, tribe, and clan, Amerindian societies could be highly stratified, with extended lineages generally traced in the male line. Some formed federations, while others developed representative assemblies. Respected priests, or shamans, were in charge of religious rites, medicine, and magic, all of which might overlap considerably. Some groups practiced human sacrifice, often of war captives. In many, women performed agricultural work.

Amerindians wielded as weapons spears, bows, and clubs of wood, stone, and, more rarely, copper or bronze; they had no iron and no sharp-edged swords, a key factor in their military defeat. They had no horses and no pack animals for hauling heavy loads long distances (the Andean llama could bear only a light burden) or for pulling plows—and perhaps for that reason never developed the wheeled vehicles

WITNESSES

New World Peoples and Customs

Exploration? Expansion? Conquest? Encounter? How should the European quest for land, wealth, knowledge, and power around the globe be titled? "Encounter" is certainly a term that could be used to describe one facet of that process, as Europeans encountered peoples previously unknown to them, and as remote peoples looked at Europeans for the first time. In these passages, Christopher Columbus observes the natives of the island he called Hispaniola; the king of the Mexican Aztecs, Montezuma, hears his agents' report of the Europeans arrived in his land; and the French Huguenot explorer Jean de Léry describes the customs of the Tupinamba natives of Brazil.

From Columbus' Diary: The arrival in the New World (1492): In order that they would be friendly to us ... to some of them I gave red caps, and glass beads which they put on their chests, and many other things of small value, in which they took so much pleasure and became so much our friends that it was a marvel. ...

But it seemed to me that they were a people very poor in everything. All of them go around as naked as their mothers bore them. ... They are very well formed, with handsome bodies and good faces. Their hair [is] coarse—almost like the tail of a horse—and short. ... And some of them paint their faces, and some of them the whole body, and some of them only the eyes, and some of them only the nose. ... They should be good and intelligent servants ... and I believe that they would become Christians easily, for it seemed to me that they had no religion.

(Christopher Columbus, *The Diario of Christopher Columbus' First Voyage to America, 1492–1493*; ed. trs. O. Dunn, J. E. Kelley Jr., 1969)

Aztec King Motecuhzoma (Montezuma) hears his messengers' report of Cortés' men (who they think are gods), according to an Aztec account (1521): Motecuhzoma was also terrified to learn how the cannon roared, how its noise resounded, how it caused one to faint and grow deaf. The messengers told him: "A thing like a ball of stone comes out of its entrails; it comes out shooting sparks and raining fire. The smoke that comes out with it has a pestilent odor, like that of rotten mud. ... If the cannon is aimed against a mountain, the mountain splits and cracks open. If it is aimed against a tree, it shatters the tree into splinters. ..."

The messengers also said: "Their trappings and arms are all made of iron. They dress in iron and wear iron casques [helmets] on their heads. Their swords are iron; their bows are iron; their shields are iron; their spears are iron. Their deer [horses] carry them on their backs wherever they wish to go. These deer, our lord, are as tall as the roof of a house. ... Their skin is white, as if it were made of lime. They have yellow hair, though some of them have black. ... Their dogs are enormous, with flat ears and long, dangling tongues. The color of their eyes is a burning yellow; their eyes flash fire and shoot off sparks. ... They bound here and there, panting, with their tongues hanging out. And they are spotted like an ocelot."

When Motecuhzoma heard this report, he was filled with terror. It was as if his heart had fainted, as if it had shriveled. It was as if he were conquered by despair.

(From M. L. Portilla, *The Broken Spears*, 1992)

Huguenot explorer Jean de Léry describes how the Tupinambá treat their war captives (1556): Now when the captive has hurled everything he could pick up near him on the ground—stones, even clods of earth—he who is to strike the blow ... approaches the prisoner with, for instance, "Are you not of the nation called Margaia, which is our enemy? And have you not yourself killed and eaten of our kinsmen and our friends?" The prisoner, more fearless than before, replies in his language ... "Yes, I am very strong, and have slain and eaten a great many." "... And for that reason," says he who is standing there ready to slaughter him, "since you are now in our power, you will presently be killed by men, and then roasted on the *boucan* and eaten by all the rest of us." "Very well," replies the prisoner ..., "my kinsmen will avenge me in turn." ... [He] who is there ready to perform this slaughter lifts his wooden club with both hands and brings down the rounded end of it with such force on the head of the poor prisoner that ... I have seen some who fell stonedead on the first blow. ...

(Jean de Léry, *History of a Voyage to the Land of Brazil, Otherwise called America*, 1556; trs., ed. J. Whatley, 1990)

such beasts might haul. They ate corn rather than wheat as a cereal staple. Where the climate permitted, they wore little or no clothing. They wore adornments crafted from stone and metal, shells, teeth, and feathers, and often painted their faces or bodies. Their skin was tawny.

The Amerindians worshiped many gods, among whom were gods of sun and sky like those the ancestors of the European newcomers had once worshiped. Their forests were alive with indwelling spirits—of the trees, of the eagles, of the jaguars. The land, like the air, was free for the use of all, and sacred in its generative power. To these communities, the European languages and their artifacts—treaties, contracts, documents, treatises of theology—must have seemed inexpressibly strange. The tools and weapons and clothing and armor and horses of the newcomers were awesome. Their guns were "iron which has a spirit." Their white skin seemed to be luminous. At Roanoke Island (modern North Carolina) in 1584, an eyewitness reported, the natives "wondered marvelously ... at the whiteness of our skins, ever coveting to touch our breasts, and to view the same." The religious rites, institutions, and personnel—the robed priests and friars with their crucifixes and sacred vessels—must have seemed odd and overwhelming.

The customs of Amerindian communities both shocked and surprised the European newcomers. They were impressed by the nakedness of the natives, and the brilliant hues of their adornments; their unfamiliar sexual customs, their generally meager technology and (in the European sense) their illiteracy; the ferocity and (from the European viewpoint) barbarous customs of a few—the cannibalism of the Caribs and the human sacrifices of the Aztecs and Incas. These permitted the invaders to label the inhabitants of the new land "primitive"; and because primitive, inherently suited to serve the new arrivals. Even if they

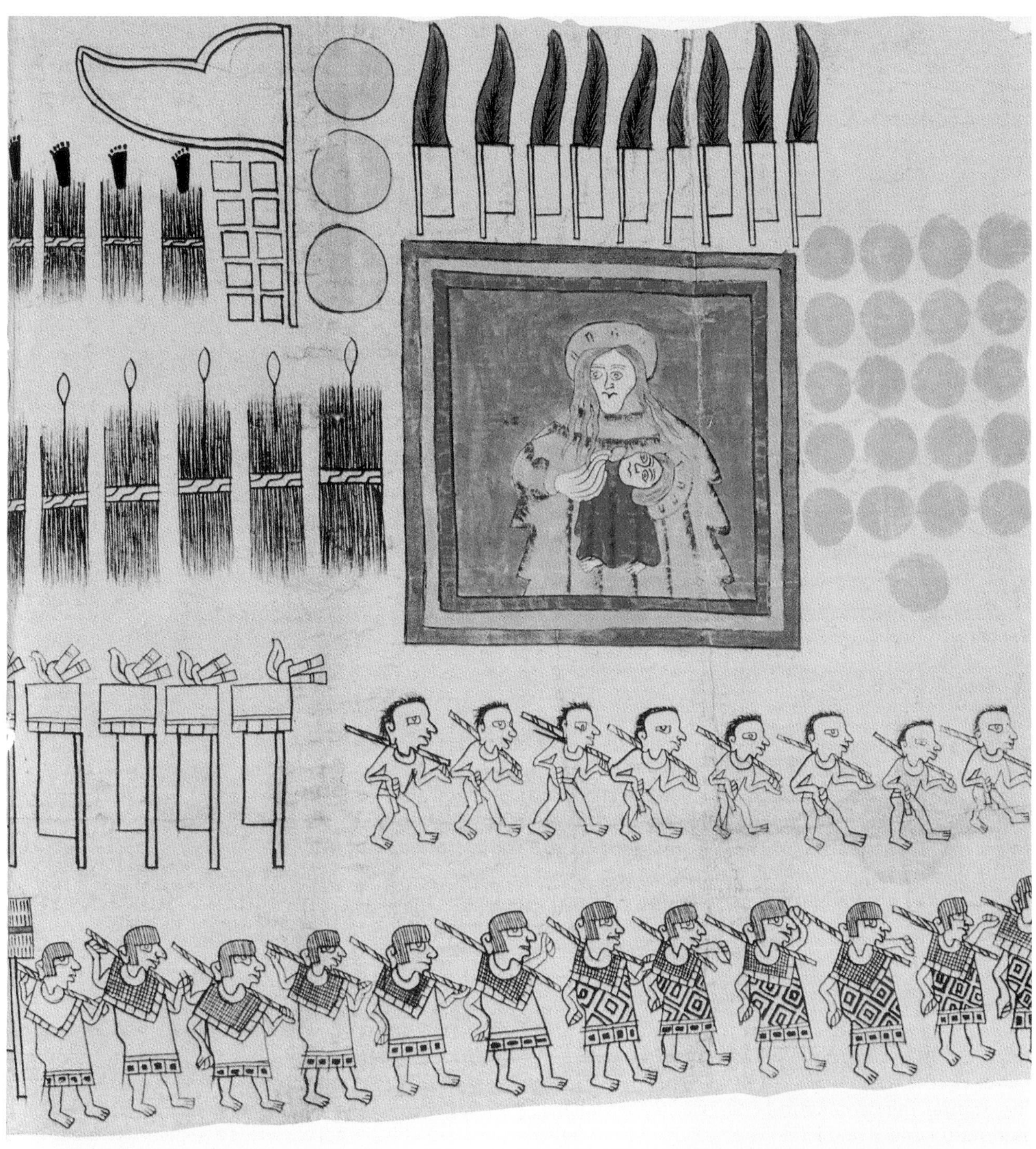

Huejotzingo Codex, 1531: *Constituting part of the testimony in a lawsuit brought by the Huejotzingo people in central Mexico to the Audiencia (high court) of New Spain, this detail shows a Christian image of the Virgin and child Jesus. Surrounding it are the objects representing the items brought in tribute by Amerindian workers to their masters.* (Library of Congress)

were not to serve, they were at least expected not to impede Europeans as they settled new lands that they considered to be empty wilderness.

Nevertheless, each group learned from the other. Europeans learned to eat corn and potatoes, to smoke or sniff tobacco, to equip their ships with hammocks (an improvement over the deck in terms of comfort and hygiene), and to employ some Amerindian methods of coping with the climate and cultivating crops. Amerindians learned to use horses and guns—to such an extent that some of them fundamentally changed their way of life. They craved European goods. One native hunter who delivered cherished beaver pelts to European fur traders observed contentedly that "the beaver does everything perfectly well"; and indeed, the beaver had netted him a fortune in "kettles, hatchets, swords, knives, bread."

Some Amerindians, often those who were kidnapped by settlers, learned to speak Spanish, Portuguese, English, or French, and served as translators and interpreters. The need to teach the natives the language of the conquerors encouraged the creation of language-teaching tools. The author of the first Castilian (Spanish) grammar, published in 1492, observed correctly that "language has always been the companion of empire."

So also was religion. Dominican, Franciscan, Augustinian, and, after 1540, Jesuit missionaries accompanied the Spanish expeditions. The Jesuits were especially active in Brazil. (Suspected of pursuing an agenda hostile to the monarchy, the Jesuits were expelled from several European nations in this period, and from the Portuguese colonies in 1759, the Spanish in 1767.) Missions constituted some of the first permanent European settlements in the Spanish American periphery, beyond the main regions of settlement in Mexico and the Andes. Missions were establishments modeled on European monastery communities; they offered medical assistance and skills training to Amerindian communities while urging conversion to Christianity. On a smaller scale, Protestant missionaries also attempted the conversion of native populations. Christian beliefs, institutions, and rituals were deeply alien to Amerindian belief systems. Conversions remained largely unsuccessful in the case of the Protestants, or incomplete in the case of the Roman Catholics, where native attitudes heavily colored alien doctrines. Each Amerindian group thought of itself as "the people," or "the true people," and were not disposed to adopt the spiritual habits of alien folk they considered inferior to themselves.

Over the same centuries, as Christian clergy attempted the conversion of the Amerindians, European farmers and landowners claimed their land. The original inhabitants were sometimes, initially, tolerated. More often, they were pushed away to more remote regions of the interior, or pressed into labor service. In the latter case, they worked as virtual serfs—dependent on a European owner and paid meager wages to work the land that had once been theirs. Others were labored under hideous conditions in the gold and silver mines that fed the Spanish Empire for nearly a century, as shown on p. 461.

Amerindian workers proved an unsatisfactory labor force—resistant to regimentation, prone to disease. The debased condition of the enslaved Amerindians prompted attempts at reform. The "Laws of Burgos" of 1512–1513 limited to 150 the number of forced laborers one person could maintain in Spanish America, but tacitly sanctioned the *encomienda* system. The "New Laws" of 1542 prohibited Amerindian slavery, even of war captives, and banned the *encomiendas*. The laws were not enforced.

During these years, the problem of Amerindian servitude aroused the attention of one of the West's most original and profound moralists: the priest Bartolomé de las Casas (1474–1566). As an owner of enslaved natives, de las Casas observed the harsh treatment of the Amerindians. In 1512 or 1513, he became a priest. In 1514, he gave up his slaves and committed himself to exposing the atrocities against American natives. His opposition was based on the view that natural laws and rights were common to all peoples, Christian and non-Christian. Moreover, the Amerindians were inherently a gentle, teachable, amenable people. He felt that if priests, and not armed conquerors, were sent to the New World, the Amerindians could be guided peacefully to live as Christians in a society based on European standards. Thus de las Casas did not propose to abandon plans to settle the New World and subordinate the Amerindians—but only to accomplish those projects without brutalizing them.

De las Casas described Spanish atrocities and his proposals for ideal Amerindian communities in works written over a long lifetime: in direct appeals to the Spanish monarchs, in a history of the new territories, in memoranda to the council that administered New World affairs, in a scathing *Brief Relation of the Destruction of the Indies* (see *Witnesses*, p. 470, and the illustration on p. 463). After the composition of this work, but before its publication in 1552, he held a public debate with the theologian Juan Ginés de Sepúlveda. Sepúlveda argued that slavery was natural, that the Amerindians were inherently suited to be slaves, and that the evils that accompanied the conquest were outweighed by the greater good achieved for civilization. In response, de las Casas swayed his audience by reporting vividly the tortures of innocent natives that he had witnessed.

In the end, he convinced King Philip II of Spain. In 1573, Philip approved new regulations decreeing that the occupation of the New World was not to be considered a "conquest," and that the natives were to be treated with love. "The Indians," read the ordinance, "[are] to be pacified and indoctrinated, but in no way are they to be harmed, for all we seek is their welfare and conversion." Such decrees ruled out the actual enslavement of the Amerindian population, but could not reverse (nor was that the intention) the destruction of its pre-conquest way of life.

The brutal conquest, the hideous conditions of labor, the disruption of Amerindian communities, the dispossession of the natives from their lands were terrible events. But these are responsible for only a small fraction of the Amerindian death toll that resulted from the European arrival in the New World. The rest were victims of "microbe shock."

Before the arrival of Columbus, the approximately 75 million Amerindian inhabitants of the Western Hemisphere constituted nearly one-fifth of the world population. A little more than 50 years later, only about 10 million remained. In Mexico, a pre-conquest native population of as many as 25 million inhabitants had, by 1600, sunk to about 1 million. The number of Caribs sank almost to zero. Most of the natives of the Western Hemisphere vanished in the first century after the arrival of the Europeans. They died from disease: smallpox, diphtheria, influenza, measles, mumps, and other illnesses. The inhabitants of the Old World had been exposed to the microbes causing these diseases, and had developed some immunity against them. New World populations, isolated from Eurasia for many millennia, had none. (Perhaps the New World retaliated; some scholars believe that syphilis, which infected Europe about the time of Columbus, originated in the Americas.) More than guns, more than abuse and dislocation, the common illnesses of Europe battered and nearly consumed the flourishing societies of the Americas. The continent became, it appeared, what the first European visitors proclaimed it to be: a wilderness.

HOW MANY?

Slave Imports to the Americas

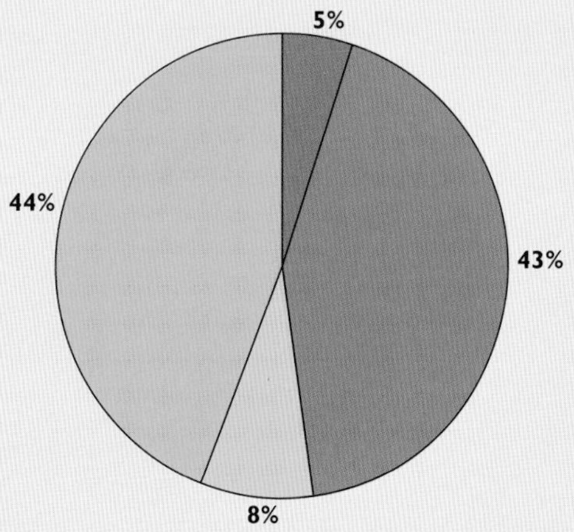

5%

44%

43%

8%

APPROX. TOTAL NUMBER IMPORTED 9,299,000

- North America excluding Mexico (400,000)
- Caribbean (4,000,000)
- Spanish South America including Central America and Mexico (769,000)
- Brazil and Guiana (4,130,000)

Of nearly ten million Africans imported to the Americas and enslaved, the greatest numbers remained in Brazil (and nearby Guiana) and the Caribbean (totalling 87% of the whole), with lesser numbers dispersed over the great areas of Spanish America and North or Anglo-America (totalling 13% of the whole).

Source: H. Spodek, *The World's History* (Upper Saddle River, NJ: Prentice Hall, 1998), p. 448

The African Solution

Amerindians became less available as a labor force because they were deemed not subject to enslavement, because they resisted the regimentation of the mines and plantations, and because they were ravaged by disease (imported from Europe) and declining in numbers. Europeans then turned to another labor source: that of African slaves. African slavery would have enormous consequences for the later development of American culture.

Two circumstances combined to trigger the exploitation of Africans in the New World by European landowners and entrepreneurs. The first was that the Portuguese had settled the west African coast at about the same time as the opening and exploitation of the Western Hemisphere. The second was that these same Portuguese had already experimented successfully, on their recently acquired Atlantic islands, with the plantation farming of sugar using African slave labor. Once the Portuguese inaugurated sugar planting in the Western Hemisphere, the importation there of the necessary slaves was inevitable. This happened in the 1530s, in Portuguese Brazil. Soon Dutch entrepreneurs had carried the system to the West Indies, where Spanish, French, and English landowners developed into a slakeless market for slaves.

Continuing a pattern begun in the first millennium C.E., the east African coastal cities, dominated by Arab traders, looked toward the mercantile zones of the Persian Gulf and Indian Ocean. Christian Ethiopia, facing the Red Sea, was also related to those trading centers. The states of North Africa were culturally Arab; their merchants traded south across the Sahara and on the Mediterranean, where they were trade rivals of Italian, Spanish, and Portuguese merchants. Egypt, in the northeast, previously part of the Arab network, and for nearly three centuries

(1250–1517) governed by the Mamluk sultans, became part of the Ottoman Empire in 1517.

In contrast to northern and eastern Africa, central and south Africa was characterized by village-based societies and small states. Though geographically more remote, these communities had been involved in local and even continental trade for centuries. West Africa was the zone of the great medieval kingdoms of Ghana, Mali, and Songhay, centers for commerce in gold and salt, and was still dominated by Songhay. Other, smaller states continued to form in west Africa. From these, and from the Kongo region to the south, flowed the stream of men and (in lesser numbers) women who were involuntarily removed to labor across the Atlantic Ocean.

Slaves were the major commodity that Portuguese merchants traded from their African depots. During the Middle Ages, most of the slaves exchanged in Mediterranean markets were Asian or Slavic—whence the word "slave" and its equivalents in European languages. The supply of these victims diminished in Europe after the conquest of Constantinople by the Ottoman Turks in 1453. Black African slaves took their place, and soon were exchanged in greater numbers than Eurasian captives had been earlier. Like the ancient Romans, Arab purchasers enslaved white and black workers indiscriminately.

North African Arab dealers supplied African slaves from the continent's interior to Mediterranean markets and to the courts and cities of Islamic Africa. After the Portuguese settlement on the west coast, mainly near modern Ghana, these dealers brought slaves also to the western coastal markets, where European traders waited to purchase them. European traders also recruited slaves directly from the nations and tribes of the interior, who willingly surrendered their war captives to the care of the new entrepreneurs. In exchange, African suppliers received textiles and hardware, especially guns. The guns permitted more war, and war produced more slaves.

From the 1440s, Portuguese ships brought African slaves to Europe. After 1503, slaves were transported across the Atlantic. Their numbers rose into the nineteenth century, to constitute the largest instance ever of the mass-transplantation of captive peoples. This trade enriched the Atlantic nations of Europe.

Different estimates are given for the numbers of slaves transported across the Atlantic, but recent research indicates the magnitude of that transshipment. Some 9 to 12 million African slaves arrived in the Western Hemisphere (in addition to one to 2 million others who died during the voyage) between the first shipment in 1503 and the last in the 1880s, as shown in *How Many?* on p. 467. The numbers were low at first (a few thousand per year in the 1500s), but mounted rapidly in the 1600s (20,000 per year) to peak in the late 1700s (nearly 100,000 per year). Before 1800, more Africans than Europeans crossed the Atlantic, carried first by the Portuguese, and then the Dutch and the British. Realizing annual profits of close to 10 percent, after 1730 the British became the chief traffickers in slaves.

Of the 9 to 12 million transported, men outnumbered women by two to one. Most were put to work in the Caribbean and South America, where the lives of laborers were short—slaves being, as one Portuguese official commented, "a commodity that died with such ease." They were swiftly replaced. The impact on African society of the steady removal of mostly young men can well be surmised. Only about 400,000 slaves came to North America, where they were able to reproduce themselves, so that plantation owners did not depend so heavily on new importation.

Captives awaiting transportation, 1890: *From around 1500, human slaves were the most important commodity that European traders exported from Africa. Often African chieftains acted as intermediaries. Depicted here is a group of captives, including a young child, who are bound, leashed, shackled, and immobilized in locked devices, awaiting whatever fate that the slavemaster may assign.* (Century Magazine, 1890)

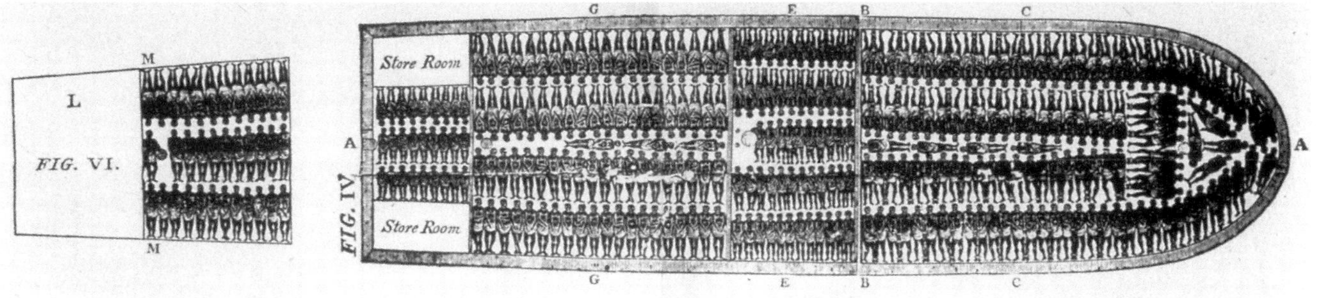

Commerce in Human Flesh

A slave ship: *In this drawing, 1789, of the slave ship* Brookes*, a slave cargo is arranged below decks for the horrific "Middle Journey" across the Atlantic. The slaves were squashed so tightly that they hardly had room to move. Contagious diseases spread quickly, leading to significant loss of life.* (Wilberforce House Museum, Hull, England)

The journey was punishing. Slavers brought the bands of new slaves to the ship, stripped them, and examined them—only the strong and healthy were valuable. For eight to twelve weeks, the slaves lived below deck, chained together and lying on shelves where they could neither sit up nor move about, as shown on this page. They were exercised on the deck, in which sessions females were vulnerable to rape. The food was scarce and shared from common buckets. Disease ran rampant. Vomit, mucus, excreta, and blood pooled in the slave quarters, breeding new waves of illness, described in *Witnesses* on p. 470. Despair drove many to suicide. The dead were thrown overboard. On the other side of the Atlantic, the survivors faced the degradation of the slave markets, depicted on this page and described in *Witnesses* on p. 470. Here, many were wrenched from family members and compatriots before being dispatched to a life of forced, unremunerated labor.

The system of African slavery developed to provide labor in places where Amerindians could not or would not work, and where Europeans were unavailable. Those circumstances differed in the northern and southern zones. In the south, especially in the Caribbean, African laborers were immediately impressed into labor on the sugar plantations—indeed, the numbers of slaves shipped rose directly in proportion to the increase of sugar farming. In the north, where sugar was not a key crop, slavery was slower to develop. In Brazil in later years, coffee plantations, displacing sugar as the main form of agriculture, eventually absorbed great numbers of slaves.

In the early years of North American settlement, European immigrants farmed the lands themselves. For additional labor services, they could employ convicted felons who had been transported to the colonies in lieu of punishment at home (a phenomenon also found in the West Indies). Or they could employ **indentured servants**, who worked without wages for a contractually defined period of years in exchange for the price of passage to the colonies and clothing, room, and board while in service. From the employment of these workers—tantamount to temporary slaves—it was not a long distance to the use of imported African slaves.

The first African laborers in the English colonies were brought to Virginia by Dutch traders in 1619, twelve years after the colony's founding. They worked as indentured servants, however. So long as tobacco—the first cash crop—was farmed on a small scale, there was little reason to resort to slaves. As late as 1660, there were only 1700 black workers in Virginia, when slaves in West Indian Barbados numbered 20,000. As tobacco plantations grew, slavery was established in Virginia. In the Carolinas, the cultivation of rice—requiring intense labor under unpleasant and dangerous conditions—also encouraged the adoption of slavery. The introduction of cotton in the warmer colonies in the early 1700s gave a further impetus to the use of slave labor. By 1700, there were 20,000 African slaves in the Chesapeake

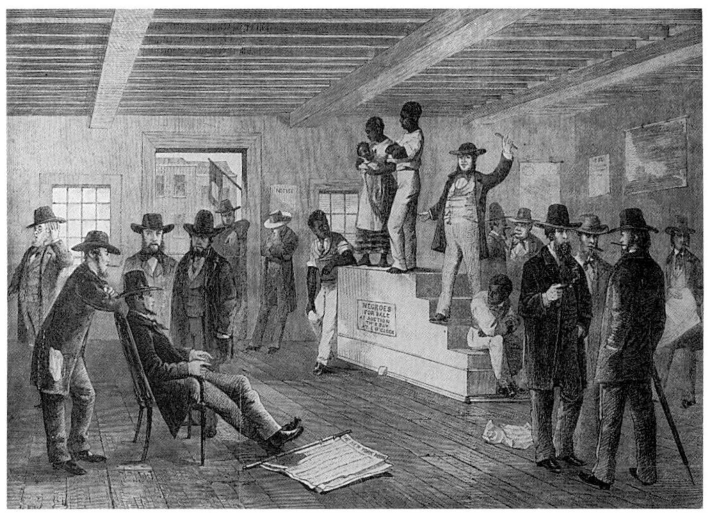

A slave auction: *A slave family is sold on the auction block in Virginia, 1861. The placard reads "Negroes for sale at Auction this day at 1 o'clock."*

WITNESSES

Voices of Protest

The slave trade, rampant within Africa for centuries before the European arrival, entered a new and horrible "Atlantic" phase for nearly four centuries thereafter, during which it supported a colonial economic system that enriched the planters and merchants who became the governors of new American states. Yet there were those who opposed it, and whose opposition, in time, led to its extinction. Here the priest Bartolomé de las Casas protests against the exploitation of the Amerindians; his intervention prefigures later protests against the evils of colonialism. More than two centuries later, the former slave Olaudah Equiano deplores the evils of slavery; and a British physician reveals the awful conditions on the ship that was to transport human cargo out of Africa and into slavery.

The Spanish Priest Bartolomé de las Casas describes the native Amerindians and condemns Spanish atrocities (1552): And of all the infinite universe of humanity, these people are the most guileless, the most devoid of wickedness and duplicity, the most obedient and faithful to their native masters and to the Spanish Christians whom they serve. ... And because they are so weak and complaisant, they are less able to endure heavy labor and soon die of no matter what malady. ... They are very clean in their persons, with alert, intelligent minds, docile and open to doctrine, very apt to receive our holy Catholic faith, to be endowed with virtuous customs, and to behave in a godly fashion. ...

[Towards these gentle people, for the last forty years, the Spaniards have been] ... acting like ravening beasts, killing, terrorizing, afflicting, torturing, and destroying the native peoples, doing all this with the strangest and most varied new methods of cruelty, never seen or heard of before, and to such a degree that this Island of Hispaniola, once so populous (having a population that I estimated to be more than three millions), has now a population of barely two hundred persons. ...
(Bartolomé de las Casas, *The Devastation of the Indies: A Brief Account*, 1552; ed. H. Briffault, 1974)

Former slave Olaudah Equiano describes the sale of his fellow slaves at auction (1789): We ... were sold after their usual manner, which is this: On a signal given ..., the buyers rush at once into the yard where the slaves are confined, and make choice of that parcel they like best. ... In this manner, without scruple, are relations and friends separated, most of them never to see each other again. ... O, ye nominal Christians! Might not an African ask you—Learned you this from your God, who says unto you, Do unto all men as you would men should do unto you? Is it not enough that we are torn from our country and friends, to toil for your luxury and lust of gain? Must every tender feeling be likewise sacrificed to your avarice? ... Why are parents to lose their children, brothers their sisters, or husbands their wives? Surely, this is a new refinement in cruelty, which ... adds fresh horrors even to the wretchedness of slavery.
("The Life of Olaudah Equiano, or Gustavus Vassa, the African," 1789; ed. A. Bontemps, 1969)

A British physician inspects slaves on a ship bound for Brazil (1843): After the first paroxysm of horror and disgust had subsided, I remarked on the poop another wretched group, composed entirely of females. Some were mothers with infants who vainly endeavoring to suck a few drops of moisture from the lank, withered, and skinny breasts of their wretched mothers ... most of them destitute even of the decency of a rag. ...

While employed in examining the negroes individually ... I obtained a closer insight into their actual condition. Many I found afflicted with a confluent smallpox, still more with purulent ophthalmia, and the majority of what remained, with dysentery, ulcers, emaciation, and exhaustion. ... Not the least distressing sight on that pest-laden deck was the negroes whom the ophthalmia had struck blind, and who cowered in seeming apathy to all that was going around. This was indeed the ultimatum of wretchedness. ... Deprived of liberty, and torn from their native country, there was nothing more of human misery but to make them the victims of a physical darkness as deep as they had already been made a moral one.
(Thomas Nelson, "Remarks on the Slavery and Slave Trade of the Brazils," 1843; from eds. P. Riley et al., 1998)

Bay region of Virginia and Maryland; by 1775, some 331,000 African slaves in the North American British colonies, outstripping the number of those on the islands of Barbados and Jamaica together. These slaves, generally better treated than in the West Indies, enjoyed a higher birth rate and lower mortality rate and were able to reproduce themselves.

New World Women Women of all races and peoples, such as Amerindian natives and African slaves, were another kind of "other" in the New World: they did not number among the explorers, conquerors, settlers, and governors, but instead were subordinate to them. They had the main responsibility for domestic labor, and they were sexually exploited by the men of the ruling elite. Although all women shared this subordinate position, European women were by far the most privileged. The wives and daughters of upper-class men lived comfortable and protected lives. Even those who began their lives in the Americas as servants or laborers might improve their status by marrying rich planters or professional men—for women were in high demand in the largely male communities of European settlers, and found unusual opportunity for social mobility through employment or marriage.

Quite the opposite was true of Amerindian and African women. In their own cultures, they were already subordinated, and very often assigned responsibility (in addition to domestic service) for agricultural work held in low esteem. Additionally, they were vulnerable to the sexual demands of European males. Often they were coerced into such sexual relationships, ranging from rape to concubinage or marriage, from fleeting to long-term. From these sexual relationships was born a whole new population of persons of mixed ancestry. In Spanish America, where intermixture of races was common, persons with mixed Amerindian and European ancestries were called ***mestizos***, meaning simply "mixed." Men and women with mixed African and European ancestries were called ***mulattoes***, an insulting term derived from the Spanish word for "mule." In the West Indies, light-skinned mulattoes, often slaves, in some circumstances obtained higher status than their fully black peers and kin.

In addition to sexual services, African slave women labored hard as field hands or domestics, often, in the latter case, bearing full responsibility for the functioning of the slave-owner's household. They served as nurses for the infants and the elderly members of the slave-owner's family, and their young children were the companions of the slave-owner's heirs, until separated in adolescence.

In time, slavery received the detestation it deserved. The French theoretician Montesquieu concluded as early as 1721 that the institution of slavery was opposed to natural law (see Chapter 17). In Britain, Quakers proclaimed an ardent anti-slavery message. Later in the century, the former slave Olaudah Equiano (c. 1750–1797) raised his voice for the abolition of slavery. Using the name Gustavus Vassa given him by his English purchaser, he published his compelling autobiography in 1789. In it he described his capture in Nigeria at age eleven and the cruelties of his passage across the Atlantic, the slave market where he was sold, and the different masters for whom he labored. Eventually he bought his freedom, taught himself to read and write, settled in England, and publicized his story. In this case, one man was instrumental in changing public opinion.

The system of African slavery gradually ceased over a period of nearly a hundred years. The London-based Abolition Society, founded in 1787, and the French Declaration of the Rights of Man of 1789 spelled out the principle of the fundamental evil of slavery—which was also implicit, but without immediate fruit, in the "all men are created equal" clause of the Declaration of Independence (1776) of the new United States. In 1794, the French decreed the abolition of slavery at home and in its colonies; but the system was later reinstated in the colonies by Napoleon and lasted until 1848. In 1804, nevertheless, the Caribbean nation of Haiti, populated almost entirely by slaves, won independence from France. In 1807 and 1808 respectively, Britain and the United States banned the slave trade. The former abolished slavery throughout the British Empire in 1838; the latter abolished it only in 1865.

In 1813, the independent government of Buenos Aires (Argentina) decreed that all children born of slaves would be deemed free, thus launching the process of emancipation in Latin America. New World slavery ended only in 1886 and 1888, when the Spanish colony of Cuba and the nation of Brazil, respectively, decreed abolition. The scar left by the institution of slavery on the societies of the new nations of the Americas was indelible. Like the metropolitan nations of Europe, the nations of the Americas are heirs of the civilization of the West—in all aspects, good and bad. We are all the descendants of societies that profited from slavery; and that fact has had persistent and inescapable consequences.

In the same way, these nations are the children of societies that dispossessed the Amerindian inhabitants of the Western Hemisphere. That heritage, too, conditions the civilization that American nations, north and south, have inherited.

THE WEALTH OF NATIONS

Just as the encounter among European, African, and Amerindian peoples shaped the cultural systems that developed in the New World, so did the economic dynamics that developed during the first hundred years of European presence in this vast region. The commercial energies of Europeans, which in previous centuries had built mercantile cities and trading empires, now produced modern capitalism. The origins of today's global economy lie in the Atlantic age that Columbus, it might be said, "discovered."

Bringing Home the Bacon

Before about 1500, Europe's foreign trade was fundamentally unbalanced. Wealthy nobles, prelates, and patricians craved the spices and gems, exquisite porcelains and finished silks found in the East. Having little of value to offer in exchange, Europe paid mostly in **specie,** with gold or silver coin. That pattern shifted after the opening of the New World. The Americas provided not only new sources of silver and gold, but also beneficial new commodities and raw materials for Europe's many manufacturing enterprises. By the 1700s the products of these enterprises had found markets in Asia. Eastern luxuries still satisfied the appetites of the rich, but other imports fed the European economy in more productive ways. By 1750, instead of draining Europe of coin, trade with other regions of the globe had, in fact, contributed to Europe's wealth.

The conquistadors, it was said, set out from Spain for "God, gold, and glory." They found gold and silver in abundance, as indicated in *How Many?* on p. 476, although not as much of the former as they would have liked. From the mid-1500s, annual shipments of bullion loaded on twenty to sixty ships escorted in convoy by two to six men-of-war left American ports for Spain (mostly) and Portugal. One-fifth of the wealth went directly to the royal treasury. From Columbus's first voyage until 1800, the New World supplied 85 percent of the world's silver and 70 percent of its gold; Spanish coins (the **reales**, each one-eighth of a **peso**, or "piece of eight") circulated worldwide.

Profitable New Crops Meanwhile, some people saw that a potentially greater treasure was present in a plant for which Europeans developed an enormous appetite—the sugar cane. In medieval Europe, honey was the principal sweetener, and sugar was rare. It was sold only in small pellets as a pharmaceutical, the ancestor of the modern candy bar. Sugar cane grew in Arab lands, including Sicily. From there, Portuguese entrepreneurs transplanted it to their newly settled Atlantic islands in the late fifteenth century, and to Brazil early in the sixteenth. From Brazil, sugar cultivation spread to the West Indies, where it grew on plantations owned by nationals of several different countries, with the labor of African slaves.

By itself, sugar constituted a whole economy, and its cultivation was a preeminent agricultural pursuit. It became doubly profitable when merchants learned to derive molasses and rum from it. In the eighteenth century, sugar and sugar products accounted for more imports to Britain (where their consumption reached huge proportions) than all the goods of the North American mainland, or all of those from Asia.

Of greater benefit to the European diet were some native American crops that proved to be cultivable in the Old World. None was more basic than the potato. Rich in vitamins, easily grown, capable of

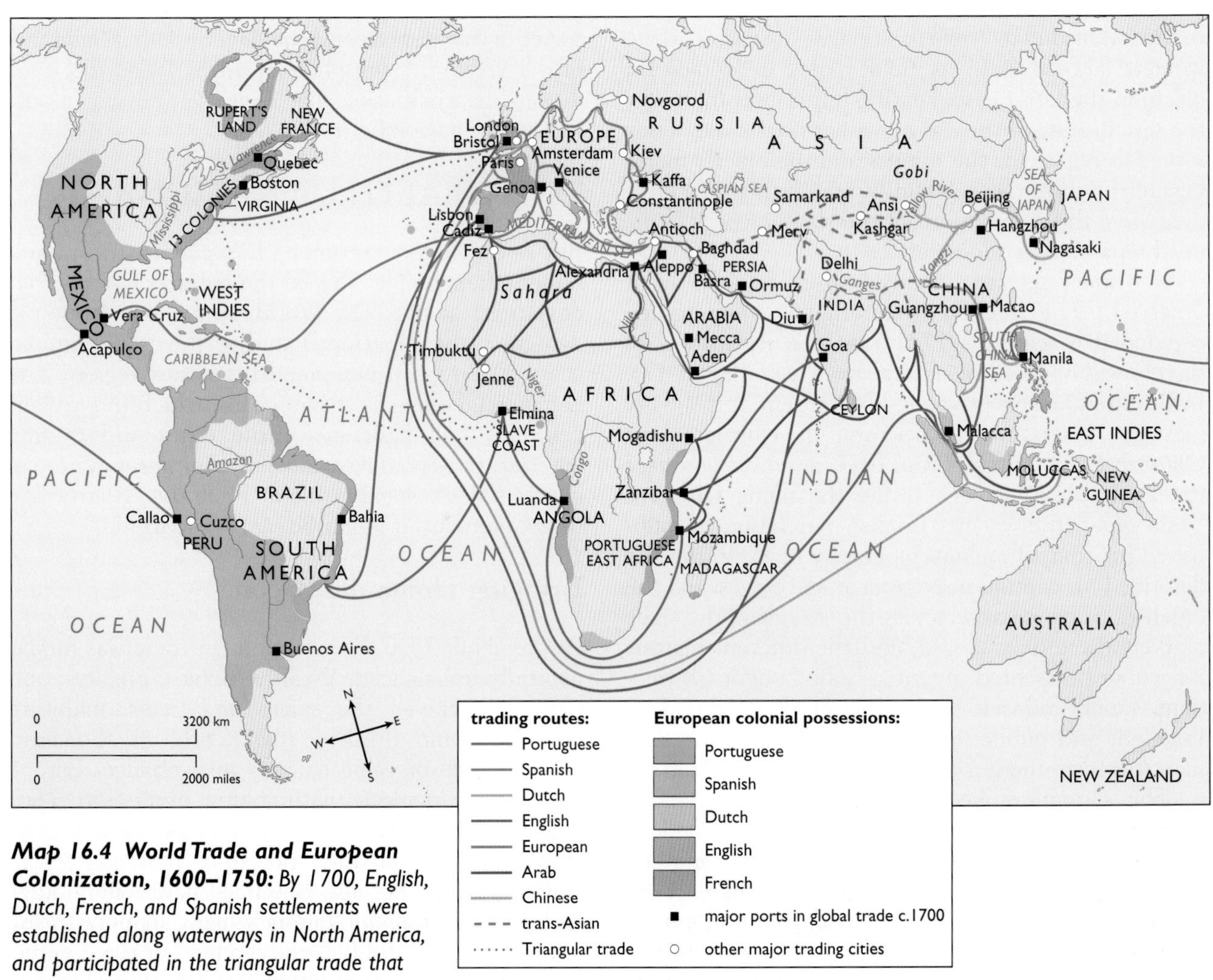

Map 16.4 World Trade and European Colonization, 1600–1750: *By 1700, English, Dutch, French, and Spanish settlements were established along waterways in North America, and participated in the triangular trade that circulated among European, African, and American ports. Meanwhile, French, Dutch, and English ships joined Portuguese and Spanish ones on the trade routes across the Indian and Pacific Oceans. Europeans had not yet fully explored the interiors of the Americas, Africa, and parts of Asia. They came to know of the existence of Australia and New Zealand only late in the eighteenth century.*

WITNESSES

The Profits of Trade

It was trade that enriched Europe so that Europeans might venture beyond their borders to other parts of the globe; and then trade again that enriched Europe and supported her political and cultural modernization. In these two passages, the French finance minister Jean-Baptiste Colbert and the Scottish economist Adam Smith think about the benefits of the circulation of goods in trade. For Colbert, trade will increase the nation's wealth, and thus its tax revenues, which can in turn support the nation in the event of war. For Smith, the effect of trade is the generation of wealth, and more is generated as each individual separately attempts to acquire as much of it as he can—through which selfish activity, as though by an "invisible hand," he is led to increase the wealth of the nation.

French Minister Jean-Baptiste Colbert instructs King Louis XIV about finances (1670): The palpable reward ... will be that by attracting a great quantity of wealth into the kingdom by trade, not only will you soon re-establish that due proportion between the money circulating in trade and the taxes paid by the people, but both will be increased proportionately, so that revenue will rise and the people will be in a condition to assist more effectively in the event of war or other emergency.

(Jean-Baptiste Colbert, "Mémoire au Roi sur les Finances," 1670; from ed. A. Lossky, trs. G. Symcox, 1967)

Scots economist Adam Smith criticizes mercantilist theories and argues for Free Trade and the regulation of an "Invisible Hand" (1776): The annual revenue of every society is always precisely equal to the exchangeable value of the whole annual produce of its industry. ... As every individual, therefore, endeavours as much as he can both to employ his capital in the support of domestic industry, and so to direct that industry that its produce may be of the greatest value; every individual necessarily labours to render the annual revenue of the society as great as he can. He generally, indeed, neither intends to promote the public interest, nor knows how much he is promoting it. ... [H]e intends only his own gain, and he is in this ... led by an invisible hand to promote an end which was no part of his intention. Nor is it always the worse for the society that it was not part of it. By pursuing his own interest he frequently promotes that of the society more effectually than when he really intends to promote it.

(Adam Smith, *The Wealth of Nations*, 1776; ed. E. Cannan, 1987)

being prepared in innumerable ways, this root vegetable which was already a prime source of nutrition (unlike sugar) for the Amerindian soon became a staple of the European (and African) diet. Its consumption in some places increasingly came to rival that of bread, which in Eurasia had held pride of place since antiquity.

Corn, tomatoes, yams, beans, squash, and cacao beans (for chocolate) and cashews also traveled to Europe, and even the ungainly turkey found some consumers on the eastern side of the Atlantic. Other North American animals were valuable not as food, but for the products they yielded. The beaver's fur (for warmth and fashion), the whale's blubber (for heat and light) were readily available in the huge forests and waters of the new continent. From a Mexican insect came the valuable dyestuff cochineal, which produced a rich red hue.

Some crops and beasts made the journey the other way. European pigs, sheep, horses, cattle, and chickens; honey bees; apple, peach, and pear trees; and, of course, wheat came with European farmers and thrived on new soil. Europeans also transplanted from Asia white rice (the Amerindian cereals were corn and wild rice), coffee and bananas, indigo (another dye), and cotton.

One other American crop added much to European culture, though nothing of benefit to its health: tobacco leaves, grown in southeastern North America. Europeans learned from Amerindian users to dry, age, and pulverize it into a powder called **snuff**, to be inhaled, or shred it into a coarse mix to be smoked in pipes, cigars, or in cigarettes, invented as early as the sixteenth century but refined in the later 1700s. This new luxury product complemented the spices, silks, porcelains, and other luxuries already imported from Asia.

European planters in warmer regions of North America experimented with crops native to tropical regions of the Old World. Rice, the staple grain of much of Asia, thrived in the marshy lands of the Carolinas, whose economy it boosted from the 1690s. Slaves first undertook its cultivation, using their experience of growing rice in Africa. The cotton plant, the source of the principal textile of the Indian subcontinent, could grow throughout the North American southeast. Cotton cultivation was already established in the 1600s, but really took off after 1800 to become the "king" of American agriculture (see Chapter 19). Both of these were plantation crops, grown by methods that were first developed for sugar cultivation in the West Indies, and absorbed the labor of African slaves. Coffee grown in Brazil also used forced labor. New World products greatly invigorated the European economy and made the Atlantic a theater of world trade as great as, and soon greater than, those of the Old World. But the old trade routes still functioned. At the height of Dutch sea trade in the 1600s, one-third of this trade was committed to the Baltic Sea, where Dutch ships had supplanted those of the medieval Hanseatic League after the late 1400s. The Baltic route, which extended from London in the west to Novgorod in the east, carried tar and timber, flax and hemp, honey, wax, and, most important, grain from the plains of eastern Europe. That ready supply of grain permitted some western European laborers to leave the soil and tend to manufacturing tasks—a precondition of subsequent industrialization.

European-made products and those transshipped from Asia—textiles above all, plus tools, furniture, nails, and tea—won ready markets on the western side of the Atlantic. The American colonists required these high-cost goods for survival and comfort and paid for them with low-cost raw materials in bulk. In the Atlantic trading system, trade was again unbalanced, but now in Europe's favor.

Trade Wars

With the creation of the Atlantic trade system, Europe's role in the global economy changed dramatically. Now she became the pivot of world trade (the nations of east Asia remaining aloof from the West for three more centuries). Her manufactures diversified, her appetite grew, her need for markets expanded, her merchant fleets swelled, and her treasuries fattened. The quest for profit, which had once driven Italian entrepreneurs to scour the Mediterranean, now drove the capitalists of Spain and Portugal, Britain and France, the Netherlands and Germany to expand their business empires to the farthest possible limits. By 1750, Europe was the wealthiest region on the globe. On the wave of this expansion, prices increased, populations soared, cities grew; and the ancient rivalries between European states increasingly gave way to a new generation of commercial competition and trade wars.

In the race for wealth, the European nation states took the lead in a departure from the medieval trade pattern, in which Italian merchants won the first fortunes of the modern West. But as navigation and commerce increasingly shifted to the Atlantic, these states developed under the aegis of newly powerful monarchies, whose rulers and chief ministers understood wealth to be the wealth of the nation.

This outlook was the outlook of mercantilism. Mercantilist strategies involved both economic and political measures, which sought to increase the nation's wealth in various ways: by encouraging domestic industries (often by grants of monopoly right), by limiting foreign imports, by assuring a favorable balance of trade, by securing ample quantities of gold and silver bullion, and by outpacing rival nations, whose increased wealth meant a relative decrease of their own. In mercantilist logic, these objectives were to be won, if necessary, by force. "Trade cannot be maintained without war, nor war without trade," pronounced an official of the Dutch East India Company, stating a commonplace of mercantilist thought.

Thus mercantilism pitted nation against nation in the race for wealth. The Portuguese were at first in the forefront, then were displaced by the Spaniards, who had meanwhile acquired the gold and silver resources of the Americas. Spanish ships laden with gold and silver attracted pirates and privateers, the semi-official raiding ships of the northern Atlantic nations which were ready to steal from Spain, but not yet to compete with her. The Spanish bullion hoards

Engines of Commerce

The great crane at Bruges: *Machines in early modern Europe speeded up enterprise but were powered by the energy of human beings or beasts, as shown in the operation by human beings of a treadmill in this sixteenth-century manuscript illumination.* (Bayerisches Staatsbibliothek, Munich)

***Jhiob Berckheyde*, A general scene at the Amsterdam Stock Exchange:** *At the Amsterdam stock exchange, completed in 1613, merchants might purchase shares in the commercial and industrial enterprises that fueled the prosperity of the age.* (Private Collection)

did not enrich the nation as planned (most of the money went to foreign bankers), and by the early seventeenth century Spain had fallen behind the Dutch.

For nearly a century, the Dutch were the masters of European trade, with England and France nipping at their heels. In those years, approximately three times as many Dutch ships as English ones set off for Asia. England's several Navigation Acts, passed between 1651 and 1696, aimed at undercutting Dutch competition. In the three Anglo-Dutch wars fought between 1652 and 1674, the English navy edged ahead of the Dutch. In the next century, with France as a primary rival, the British struggled to maintain economic supremacy, which it achieved at the close of the Seven Years' War in 1763.

From 1500 to 1800, foreign trade grew steadily, as more raw materials from the New World were used for European manufacture, and as more European products found markets in the west or in Asia. By 1700, almost half of England's merchant fleet was trading with America or India—the cargoes often guaranteed by Lloyd's, a new company which set the pattern for the modern insurance industry. In the following century, British exports to other parts of the world rose from a trickle to more than a third of the whole, while imports from those lands rose to over one-half of all imports. Meanwhile, France's foreign trade trailed Britain's and the Dutch share fell behind, while Spain and Portugal were no longer serious competitors.

The profits from this commerce went to merchant capitalists, but also to small investors, who sometimes greedily participated in unwise ventures: notoriously the "Louisiana bubble" (in France) and the "South Sea bubble" (in Britain). In these early-eighteenth-century episodes, private investors, sometimes pledging family estates and life savings, purchased stock in investment ventures that promised huge profits. Speculation proceeded unchecked, the stock values collapsed, and the investors were left with nothing from the exploded "bubble."

While western Europe's large nation-states seized the leadership of European trade, other areas were

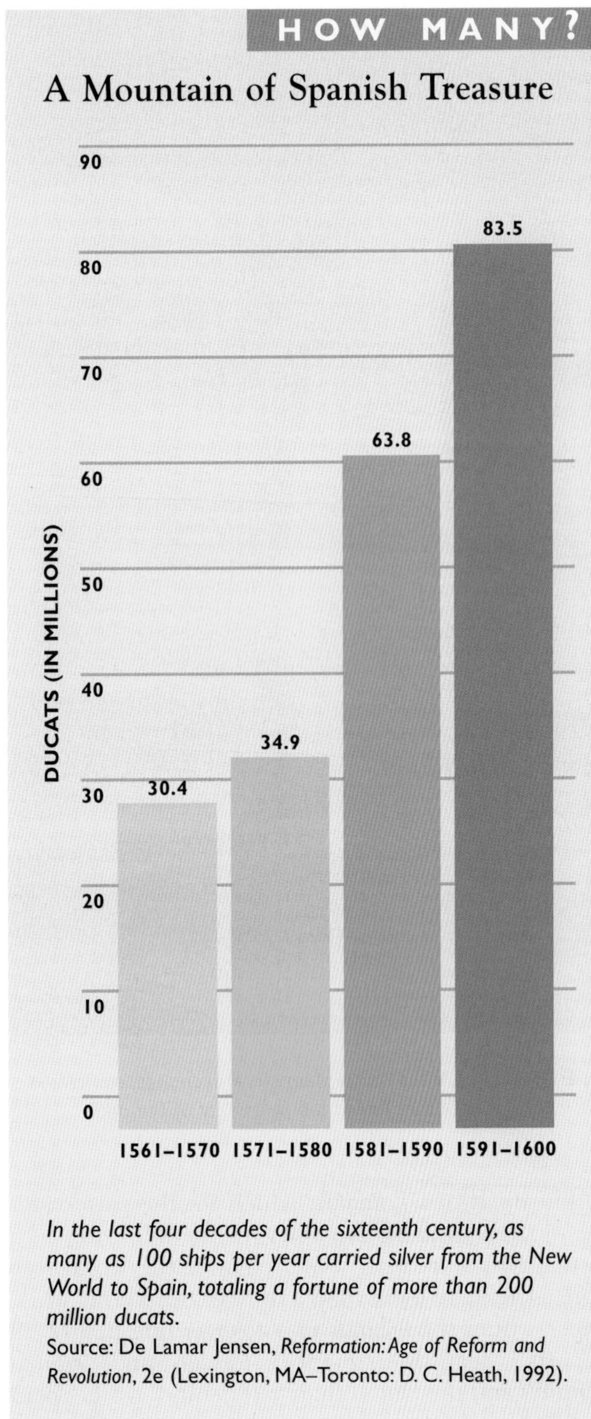

In the last four decades of the sixteenth century, as many as 100 ships per year carried silver from the New World to Spain, totaling a fortune of more than 200 million ducats.

Source: De Lamar Jensen, *Reformation: Age of Reform and Revolution*, 2e (Lexington, MA–Toronto: D. C. Heath, 1992).

quiescent, and still mainly agrarian in character. Eastern Europe turned deliberately to more intensive agricultural production. Italy lost its commercial preeminence in trade, although some Italian cities continued to produce profitable luxury goods, such as Venetian glass and lace.

Proto-industrialization Another way to enhance the wealth of the nation was to build up its manufacturing base. The old merchant and craft guilds that had generated economic growth during the Middle Ages had become restrictive, discouraging innovation or the circulation of personnel. Mercantilist projects tended to enliven the manufacturing sector, stimulating certain crafts or inviting joint-stock companies to undertake new endeavors. For example, Colbert (1619–1683), finance minister to Louis XIV, encouraged a variety of manufacturing enterprises (including the famous Gobelins tapestry workshop). To promote commerce, Colbert also oversaw the construction of new roads and canals, harbors and shipyards, and built up the French navy. The failure of Spain to support its industries, especially as silver imports dwindled, helps to explain its economic decline.

The devices that promoted the wealth of nations also enriched individuals, who accumulated enough wealth to fund extensive investments. Still, the wealthy merchants of the early modern era must be distinguished from later industrial capitalists, whose great factories won them previously extraordinary profits. These earlier merchants took commodities made by others and shipped them to distant markets. Or they supervised manufacturing enterprises, especially textiles, which worked on the domestic or "putting-out" system. In this system, the merchant acquired raw materials, distributed them to country workers who labored in their own cottages, and collected the finished goods for sale. Employing men, women, and children, this system flourished into the eighteenth century. It constituted a "proto-industrial" phase of European manufacturing, featuring rural production and city-directed exchange.

Technological innovations also contributed to the growth of the European economy. By 1500, Europe already had put machines to work in productive ways. Waterwheels and windmills helped grind grain, brew ale, pump water, make paper, saw wood, and treat textiles. The circulation of goods was facilitated by the building of canal networks which in turn was made possible by the invention of locks. Changes in ship design and gun manufacture have already been noted. Over the next centuries, other new machines and industrial processes improved textile and glass manufacturing, coal mining, and iron production.

All this growth, however, had a disadvantage: rapid inflation. The injection of new quantities of bullion into the European economy, the deliberate devaluation of existing currencies, and the steady climb of the European population caused an explosion of values and prices. Prices rose for goods, while wages and rents lagged, with regional variations: in Spain, prices more than tripled in the century before 1600; in England, the prices of basic goods rose nearly sixfold during the same period. The pattern of steep price increases affected different groups differently—it allowed merchants to accumulate capital for investment in more manufacture and trade, while it mercilessly pinched peasants and urban workers.

The forward wave of commercial economy favored population increase, which in turn undergirded the economic boom. European population generally increased until about 1600, when it surpassed for the first time the pre-Black Death level of 73 million. During the seventeenth century, population growth slowed again, owing in part to the disastrous effect of the Thirty Years' War, which reduced the population of central Europe by 30–40 percent. The marriage age increased in many regions, showing that people were adopting a familiar strategy to reduce the birth rate. Spain and Italy fell behind the north Atlantic nations, and France's rate of growth fell behind England's. In the eighteenth century, the population began again to increase as mortality rates declined. After a last outbreak of bubonic plague in Marseilles in 1720, the plague left Europe (perhaps because of unfavorable shifts in the ecology of the black rat, the critical carrier of the deadly infectious flea). The cycle of famine receded too, and the proto-industrial cottage industries, which allowed young persons to make a profit from their labor without delaying marriage, drove the numbers upward.

Despite economic growth, the steady upward pressure on prices and the increasing population brought hardship, especially to the rural poor. Grain prices rose by factors of three, four, even six, while the average price of manufactured goods merely doubled. Bread was expensive or scarce, while landowners strove to extract more labor from their workers. The real wages of agricultural workers fell catastrophically, and the force of hunger, briefly subdued in the aftermath of the Black Death, returned. The numbers of the landless increased, and beggars proliferated.

The high price of grain resulted not only from general inflationary trends but also from a shortage of good soil due to over-plowing and little fertilization. In England and the Netherlands, farmers opened up new land for cultivation of more grain. They drained low-lying lands, fenced off fields to raise stock, and systematized crop rotation to increase the yield of already-plowed soil. These practices were only slowly diffused to the rest of Europe.

Urbanization With economic growth came urbanization, as Map 16.5 below shows. Merchants concentrated in cities, where goods changed hands, where banks held funds, where artisans labored, and where consumers purchased. In the early modern centuries, towns became cities, cities expanded. For the first

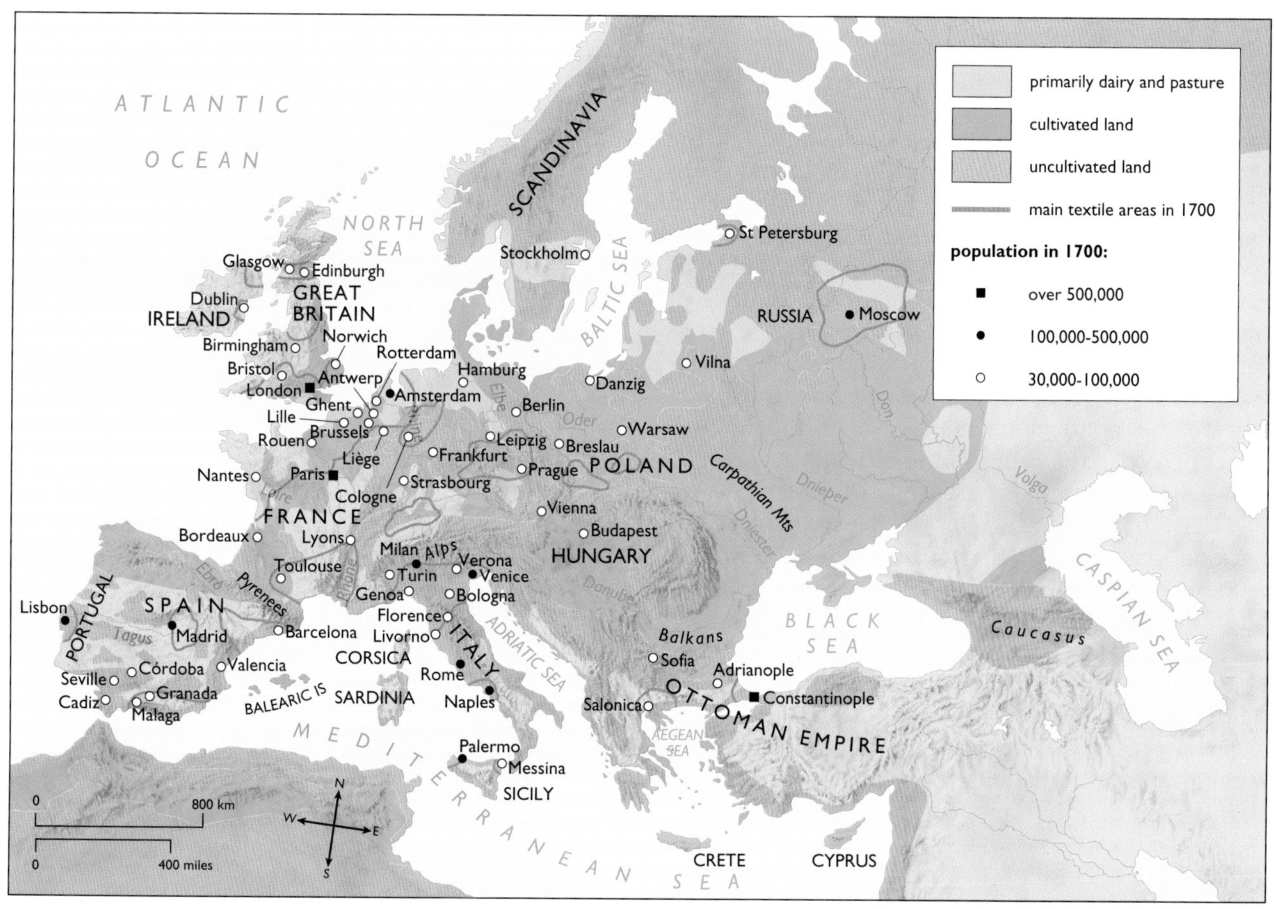

***Map 16.5 European Commerce, Industry, and Urbanization, 1550–1750:** The medieval centers of commerce in Italy and Flanders expanded from the fifteenth through the eighteenth centuries, while new areas of textile production and zones of intensive mining enriched the European economic scene. Population increased overall, and especially in towns, many of which grew to be cities, two approaching the million mark in population, while others, like Amsterdam and Madrid, surpassed 100,000.*

time, many European cities grew to exceed the largest cities previously known in the Western world (London, Paris, Naples, and Milan). Not only did large cities grow larger, but a greater proportion of Europeans lived in cities and towns; even country workers often migrated to the city for part of their lives before returning to their villages, their mental outlook forever changed. No longer islands in a world of fields, the cities were open to the countryside and linked to each other in large regional networks of economic activity.

Before 1500, few people lived in concentrations greater than 10,000. Between 1500 and 1800, the number of western European cities larger than 10,000 more than doubled (from 154 to 364). At the same time, the number of people living in those cities more than tripled (from 3,441,000 to 12,218,000). From 1500 to 1750, the percentage of Europeans living in cities of more than 10,000 inhabitants increased from 6.1 to 9.9 percent. The growth was heaviest in areas of new urbanization—western and northern Europe—rather than in Italy, whose cities had been the power centers of medieval commerce. Farther east—in Russia, for example—urbanization was minimal, and only a few towns held populations as large as 30,000.

Some individual cities mushroomed. By 1600 the populations of Seville (Spain), Lisbon (Portugal), and Antwerp (modern Belgium), all involved in transatlantic trade, had jumped to 100,000—the size previously reached only by the largest Italian cities. By the same year, the populations of London and Paris approached 200,000; by the end of the eighteenth century, they reached 800,000 and 670,000 respectively. Lyons, France's second commercial city, had nearly 100,000 inhabitants. Smaller cities, with populations hovering around 20,000, were nevertheless important centers of regional trade. The major German cities (Augsburg, Nuremberg, Cologne), subject to the political fragmentation of the Empire, never exceeded this range in the early modern period.

Medieval cities, concentrated in Italy and Flanders, had flourished in the absence of strong national governments. In contrast, the largest early modern cities were the centers of powerful nations, often the capitals. They looked the part. Their streets were straightened, for displays of military and state power and for the carriages of the wealthy. Their secular buildings—palaces, banks, **stock exchanges** and theaters—began to rival cathedrals in grandeur, both secular and sacred buildings being designed in styles that raised classical forms to new levels of opulence.

Amsterdam The city of Amsterdam is a noteworthy example of early modern urbanization. In the Middle Ages, Amsterdam had been a town of little importance, but the political developments of the sixteenth century boosted it to eminence. Nearby Antwerp, a port city with access to the Atlantic, had preceded

HOW MANY?

Population Growth: Region, Nations, Cities—1500 and 1750

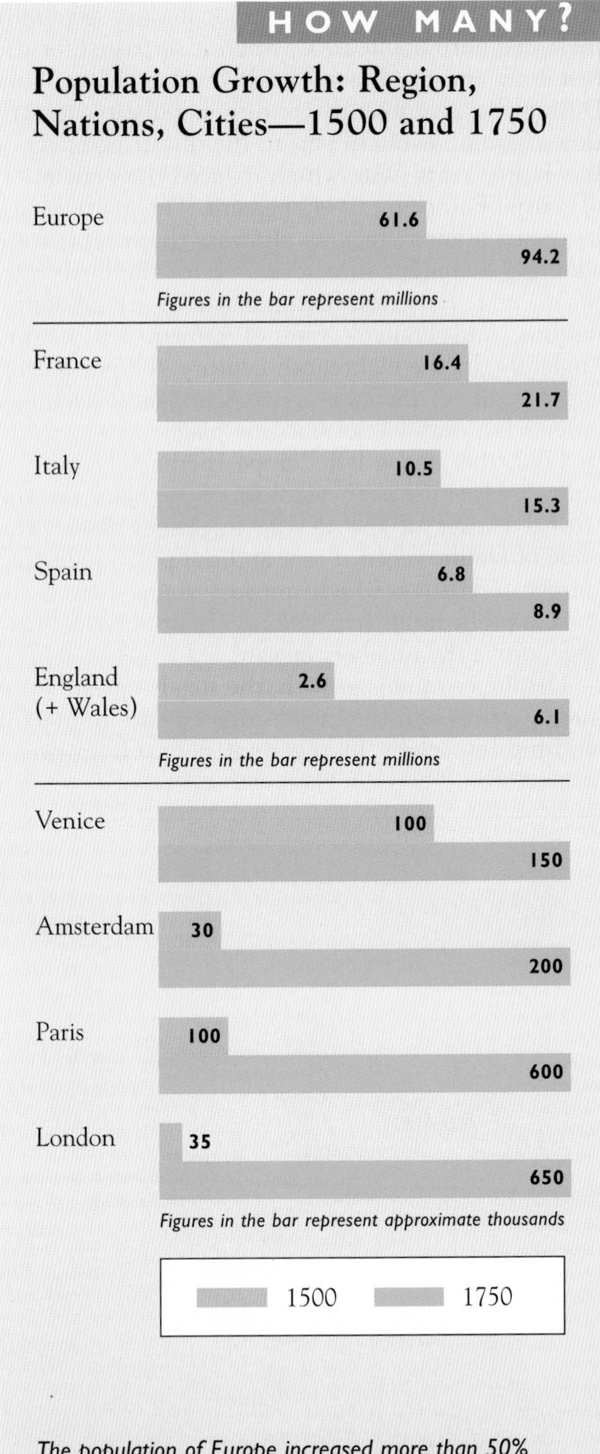

The population of Europe increased more than 50% (from a base of about 60 million) from 1500–1750. But nations and cities increased at different rates. While the population of France increased only about 32%, the population of England increased 135%, to reach by 1750 more than twice its 1500 figure. Meanwhile Venice, the front-ranking city of 1500, fell to a poor fourth place by 1750, when London, having increased more than twentyfold, reached preeminence with a population of 650,000.

Source: J. de Vries, *European Urbanization, 1500–1800* (Cambridge, MA: Harvard University Press, 1984)

Amsterdam as the major port (and thus the commercial and banking center) of northern Europe. It reigned supreme in the sixteenth century, when it handled much of Portuguese trade as well as the commerce of the textile manufactures of the region. But Antwerp's career suddenly declined around 1650, when the newly independent United Provinces were allowed (by the Treaty of Münster, 1648) to close the Scheldt River, the city's route to the sea. Located not far to the north of Antwerp and in closer proximity to the sea, Amsterdam took its place.

In the seventeenth and eighteenth centuries, Amsterdam was the banking center of Europe, the fulcrum of world trade. Its population grew from 30,000 in 1567 to over 200,000 by the early 1780s. Its bank, founded in 1609 on the model of the Venetian Rialto banks, issued its own gold florin. By 1700, the bank provided safety for more than 2000 depositors and the lowest interest rates in Europe (4 percent or less) on investment loans. At its stock exchange (completed 1613), illustrated on p. 475, merchants participated in ventures around the globe, trading in as many as 491 commodities by 1674 (when London, its rising competitor, dealt in 305). A weekly bulletin listed options and gave updated prices.

Even after the 1713 Peace of Utrecht, when the Netherlands fell behind the British and French as a European power, Amsterdam remained the center of European financial life. During the eighteenth century, the city lived on the capital it had accumulated over the previous 200 years, which now helped fund, at profitable rates of interest, nearly every major commercial venture in Europe.

The growing mercantilist commercial system of the sixteenth, seventeenth, and eighteenth centuries enriched European nations, swelled their towns and cities, and lavishly rewarded the merchant investors. It seemed a great success. And yet it also had many defects. The intervention of government into the business of business, while often protective, also retarded the pace of commerce. Tariffs set to shelter domestic manufactures and monopolies created by royal edict interfered with the free flow of trade and the mechanisms which, as later experts argued, allowed the market to regulate itself.

Such problems of mercantilist organization encouraged the Scottish professor Adam Smith (1723–1790) to argue for an alternative organization of manufacture and commerce. In his *Inquiry into the Nature and Causes of the Wealth of Nations* (published in 1776, the same year as the Declaration of Independence), part of which is quoted in *Witnesses* on p. 473, he argued that the absence of intervention would enhance production within the nation, as individuals pursuing their own self-interest would both yield high profits and benefit the public. Free trade policies would allow the entrepreneurs competing for foreign trade to realize the greatest possible wealth, and thus enrich the nation. Directed only by merchant interest and buyer need, "as though by an invisible hand," free trade would more greatly increase the "wealth of nations" than a trade system controlled by jealous states and governors. The nation states that had just matured in the political life of Europe were now instructed to limit themselves to defense and security. They did not easily retreat.

Conclusion

THE EXPANSION OF EUROPE AND THE MEANING OF THE WEST

From 1500 to 1750, Europe expanded beyond its earlier borders physically, economically, and psychologically. The expansion had begun even earlier, with the commercial revolution achieved by Italian merchants and the foreign adventures of the Crusades. The cultural and religious movements of the Renaissance and the Reformation, although contained within the geographical boundaries of Europe, entailed an enormous broadening of Europeans' mental horizons. Now, however, the expansion was fundamental and taking place on all fronts: it sent people of many nations around the world on new ships driven by new technology; it stimulated Europeans to reconsider their view of themselves upon contact with human communities previously unknown; it changed what ordinary people ate and wore, their work and their homes; it impacted on the lives of nearly every European, from the Dutch ship hand to the Polish peasant.

The same expansion made Europe the master of the globe. Europeans were involved in the rout of Amerindian culture, in the mass enslavement of Africans, and in the enlistment of Indian and Indonesian (if not yet east Asian) producers into the economy of the West. At the beginning of the episode of European expansion, Montaigne wrote about the Amerindian Caribs who ate their war captives. But he had already detected that, much as his fellow Europeans feared and deplored the cannibal, the cannibal had much to dread in the advent to his world of European civilization.

REVIEW QUESTIONS

1. Why was Portugal a leader in African and Asian explorations? Who were the shoguns and samurai of Japan? What advantages contributed to the rise of Dutch power?

2. What were the strengths and weaknesses of Columbus' accomplishments? How were other avenues to North America discovered? Who were the Aztecs and Incas and why were Cortés and Pizarro able to defeat them?

3. Describe the culture of Amerindians before European colonization. What role did missions play in colonial development?

4. What led to the emergence of the African slave trade? What was the final destination of most African slaves and why? What role did women of African and Amerindian descent play in colonial development?

5. How did the New World contribute to Europe's wealth? Explain the European colonial trade routes. Why did Spain and the Netherlands decline as colonial powers?

6. What was proto-industrialization? What were the positive and negative economic and social effects of colonial trade for Europe? Why was the burgeoning city of Amsterdam a good example of early modern urbanization?

SUGGESTED RESOURCES

The Open Seas

Chaudhuri, K. N., *Asia before Europe: Economy and Civilisation of the Indian Ocean from the Rise of Islam to 1750* (New York: Cambridge University Press, 1990). A study of cultural practices and beliefs: food and drink, architecture, clothing, symbolism, land, nomadism, urbanism.

Fernández-Armesto, Felipe, *Before Columbus: Exploration and Colonization from the Mediterranean to the Atlantic, 1229–1492* (Philadelphia: University of Pennsylvania Press, 1991). A collection of essays on the pre-Columbian European expansion in northwest Africa and the Atlantic islands.

Smith, Roger C., *Vanguard of Empire: Ships of Exploration in the Age of Columbus* (Oxford: Oxford University Press, 1993). Explores the advances in ship technology that allowed the Spanish and Portuguese to venture out on the deep seas for exploration and exploitation.

Voyages of discovery and exploration, biographies and links: **http://www.win.tue.nl/cs/fm/engels/discovery**

Columbus navigation homepage: **http://www1.minn.net/~keithp**

Sir Walter Raleigh, biography, resources, and links: **http://www.britishexplorers.com**

Brave New World

Axtell, James, *Beyond 1492: Encounters in Colonial North America* (Oxford: Oxford University Press, 1992). Essays on themes relating to interactions between Amerindians and Europeans.

Blackburn, Robin, *The Making of New World Slavery: From the Baroque to the Modern, 1492–1800* (New York: Verso, 1998). A discussion of New World slavery in a comparative and historical perspective.

Clendinnen, Inga, *The Aztecs: An Interpretation*. (Cambridge: Cambridge University Press, 1991). A provocative study of Aztec rituals and human sacrifice in terms of an all-consuming religious world-view.

Crosby, Alfred W., *Ecological Imperialism: The Biological Expansion of Europe 900–1900* (Cambridge: Cambridge University Press, 1993). A survey of the biological impact of European contact on the Americas, Africa, Asia, Australia, and the Pacific islands.

Curtin, Philip D., *The Rise and Fall of the Plantation Complex: Essays in Atlantic History* (Cambridge: Cambridge University Press, 1990). A study of plantation agriculture from the medieval Mediterranean to the Atlantic islands and the American tropics.

Josephy, Alvin M., Jr., ed., *America in 1492: The World of the Indian Peoples before the Arrival of Columbus*. 2nd ed. (New York: Knopf, 1993). A collection of essays surveying the Indian peoples by region and by theme—language, religion, trade, technology, etc.

Pagden, Anthony, *Lords of All the World: Ideologies of Empire in Spain, Britain and France, c. 1500–c. 1800* (New Haven: Yale University Press, 1995). A brilliant and fascinating reconstruction of the different ideological traditions that authorized European conquerors to dominate other peoples.

Stannard, David E., *American Holocaust: The Conquest of the New World* (Oxford: Oxford University Press, 1993). Describes the European conquest and wholesale destruction of the Indian populations of the Americas as a deliberate act of genocide, whose origins lie within the Christian traditions of the West.

Thomas, Hugh, *The Slave Trade: The Story of the Atlantic Slave Trade, 1440–1870* (New York: Simon and Schuster, 1998). Splended overview written for a general audience, that evokes the whole tragedy of the Atlantic slave trade, taking into its purview the slave traders, purchasers, collaborators, and the slaves themselves.

Indigenous peoples of the Americas, all regions, articles, and resources: **http://www.hartford-hwp.com**

The Wealth of Nations

De Vries, Jan & Ad Van der Woude, *The First Modern Economy: Success, Failure, and Perseverance of the Dutch Economy, 1500-1815* (Cambridge: Cambridge University Press, 1997). Presents the Dutch as the first to create a truly modern economy, with an integrated profitable agricultural sector, foreign trade, and capital market.

Mintz, Sidney, W., *Sweetness and Power* (New York: Penguin, 1985). A study of sugar in the rise of plantations and the world economy.

Price, Jacob M., *Perry of London: A Family and a Firm on the Seaborne Frontier, 1615–1753* (Cambridge MA: Harvard University Press, 1992). Traces the history of one family, and firm, which imported American tobacco into Britain in the 17th and 18th centuries; reveals the connectedness of social, economic, and political power.

Tracy, James D., ed., *The Rise of Merchant Empires: Long-Distance Trade in the Early Modern World, 1350–1750* (Cambridge: Cambridge University Press, 1990). Thirteen essays by leading scholars on merchant networks, the transatlantic slave trade, trans-Saharan trade, and Central Asian trade.

Picture Credits

All numbers refer to page numbers (t=top; b=bottom; l=left; r=right; c=center)

Chapter 1

3 Venus of Willendorf, c.25,000-21,000 B.C.E. Naturhistorisches Museum Vienna; 6 AKG London; 7l, 15, 22tr Hirmer Fotoarchiv, Munich; 7r Craig & Marie Mauzy, Athens; 12b Werner Forman Archive, London; 14 Spectrum Colour Library, London; 22tl India Office, London; 22b American School of Classical Studies

Chapter 2

31 detail of 45t; 37 Hirmer Fotoarchiv, Munich; 40, 45br Craig & Marie Mauzy, Athens; 41 Spectrum Colour Library, London

Chapter 3

57 detail of 79b; 61tl Louisa Eldridge McBurney Gift Fund, 1953, (53.11.6); 61br, 63t RMN-Hervè Lewandowski, Paris; 63b Bildarchiv Preussicher Kulturbesitz, Berlin; 75t Fletcher Fund, 1931, (31.11.10); 76 Hirmer Fotoarchiv, Munich

Chapter 4

83 detail of 99; 88l Fletcher Fund, 1932; 89 Fotografica Foglia, Naples; 92l Hirmer Fotoarchiv, Munich; 92c Alison Frantz; 97t Hulton Getty, London; 97c TAP © Archaeological Receipts Fund; 99 Bildarchiv Preussicher Kulturbesitz, Berlin

Chapter 5

111 The Battle of Issos (detail), Pompei, 2nd century B.C.E. Museo Archeologico Nazionale, Naples/Fotografica Foglia Naples; 115 Robert Harding, London; 116t Vincenzo Pirozzi, Rome; 116b Araldo Da Luca, Rome; 121, 127 Araldo De Luca, Rome; 123 AKG London

Chapter 6

139 detail of 161; 142, 143, 148tr, 148br Alinari; 152 Scala; 153, 161 Vincenzo Pirozzi, Rome; 154 Paul M.R. Maeyaert, Mont de l'Enclus (Orroir), Belgium; 155cl Fotografica Foglia, Naples

Chapter 7

167 Christ Pantocrator (detail) 6th century C.E./AKG London; 170 Vincenzo Pirozzi, Rome; 171 Christies Images; 172 RMN, Paris; 174 Werner Forman Archive, London; 175 Sonia Halliday, Weston Turville, UK; 179c Alinari; 184l Scala; 184r Araldo De Luca, Rome; 186 A.F. Kersting, London

Chapter 8

195 Ludovisi Sarcophagus (detail) c.250 C.E. Museo Nazionale Rome; 197t Alinari; 197b Hirmer Fotoarchiv, Munich; 198, 207b Spectrum Colour Library, London; 202 Bridgeman Art Library; 206 Sonia Halliday, Weston Turville, UK; 207t Cameraphoto Arte, Venice; 223t Aerofilms, Hertfordshire; 223bl Justin Kerr, New York; 223br Werner Forman Archive, London

Chapter 9

229 Les Très Riches Heures du Duc de Berry (detail), 1413-16, ms. 65, fol.6v, Museè Condè/Giraudon, Paris; 234 Alinari; 239t Frank Blackwell, Oxfordshire; 241 Spectrum Colour Library, London; 244r Giraudon, Paris

Chapter 10

257 detail of 262l; 259t Studio Fotografico Quattrone, Florence; 261 Wim Cox, Cologne; 264 Hirmer Fotoarchiv, Munich; 265, 286 Paul M.R. Maeyaert, Mont de l'Enclus (Orroir), Belgium; 272l Art Resource, New York; 272r Scala; 274 AKG London; 277r photo: C. Vignaud

Chapter 11

289 detail of 291; 291 RMN-Daniel Arnaudet, Paris; 292 Scala; 303t Alain Lonchampt/CNMHS, Paris; 305 Bridgeman Art Library

Chapter 12

323 Gentile Bellini, Procession of the Cross in Piazza San Marco (detail), 1496, Galleria dellíAccademia/Cameraphoto Arte Venice; 325 Higginson/Private Collection, London; 326-7 Studio Fotografico Quattrone, Florence; 328 CNMHS, Paris; 329t A.F. Kersting, London; 329b Bildarchiv Foto Marburg; 334, 336 AKG London; 344, 346 Scala

Chapter 13

353 Michelangelo, David, 1501-4 Galleria dellíAccademia, Florence/ Studio Fotografico Quattrone, Florence; 355, 359r, 367t, 371, 376, 377 Scala; 359bl RMN, Paris; 363, 397, 373 Studio Fotografico Quattrone, Florence; 367b Cameraphoto Arte, Venice; 370 Raffaello Bencini, Florence

Chapter 14

383 Hans Holbein the Younger, Erasmus of Rotterdam, c.1520, Louvre, Paris/RMN-Hervè Lewandowski; 386 Mary Evans Picture Library, London; 388 Bridgeman Art Library; 391tl, 403l, 410b, 413tr Higginson/Private Collection; 402 Scala; 405 Spectrum Colour Library, London; 410t RMN-Mich%ole Bellot, Paris; 411 photo: J.-C. Ducret; 413bl Araldo Da Luca, Rome; 413br Images/Charles Walker Collection, London

Chapter 15

417 The Battle of Pavia (detail), 1525, Museo di Capodimonte/Scala; 419t AKG London; 419b Mary Evans Picture Library, London; 420 English Heritage Photo Library; 432b Cameraphoto Arte, Venice; 436 RMN-Jean/Lewandowski, Paris; 443t RMN-Gèrard Blot, Paris; 443b Institut Amatller DíArt Hisp‡nic, Barcelona

Chapter 16

447 detail of 450; 450 Artothek, Peissenberg; 451 © Patrimonio Nacional, Madrid; 453tr, 468, 475 Mary Evans Picture Library, London; 453b, 469b Hulton Getty, London; 460t AKG London; 469t Bridgeman Art Library

Literary Credits

Augsburg Fortress: from *Luther's Works*, Volume 31, edited by Harold J. Grimm (Muhlenberg Press, 1957), © 1957 Fortress Press; **Beacon Press**: from *The Broken Spears* by Miguel Leon-Portilla (Beacon Press, 1992), © 1962, 1990 by Miguel Leon-Portilla; Expanded and Updated Edition © 1992 by Miguel Leon-Portilla; **Burns and Oates Ltd.**: from *Edict of Milan* by Constantine, with Licinius, in *Church and State Through the Centuries*, edited by S. Ehler and J. Morrall (Burns & Oates/Newman Press, 1954); **Center for Reformation and Renaissance Studies**, University of Toronto: from *On the Removal of Images* by Andreas Karlstadt in *A Reformation Debate: Three Treatises in Translation* by Bryan Mangrum and Giuseppe Scavizzi (CRRS, 1991); **Columbia University Press**: from *New Chronicle* by Giovanni Villani in *Medieval Trade in the Mediterranean World: Illustrative Documents*, edited by Robert S. Lopez and Irving W. Raymond (Columbia University Press, 1955), © 1955 Columbia University Press; from *Res gestae divi Augusti* by Augustus, *Letters* by Pliny the Younger, *History of Rome* by Livy, *The Elements of Oratory* by Quintilian, *Histories, 4* by Sallust, *Dialogue on Oratory* by Tacitus, and *Theodosian Code* by Emperor Theodosius, in *Roman Civilization: Selected Readings*, edited by Naphtali Lewis and Meyer Reinhold (Columbia University Press, 1990), © 1990 Columbia University Press; **Continuum Publishing Company**: from *The Devastation of the Indies: A Brief Account* by Bartolemé de las Casas, edited by Herma Briffault (The Seabury Press/Continuum, 1974), © 1974 by The Seabury Press; **DharmaNet International**: from *The Edicts of King Asoka*, translated by Ven. S. Dhammika (Dharma Net edition, 1993); **Dover Publications Inc**: from *Malleus maleficarum* by Heinrich Krämer and James Sprenger, translated by Montague Summers (1928; Dover Publications, 1971); Elizabeth Hadas: from *Edict on Prices* by Diocletian, preface to the *Institutes* by Justinian, *Moral Epistles* by Seneca, and *Histories* by Tactitus in *A History of Rome*, edited by Moses Hadas (Doubleday, 1956), © Estate of Moses Hadas; **Johns Hopkins University Press**: from Livy in *Women's Life in Greece and Rome: A Source Book in Translation*, edited by Mary R. Lefkowitz and Maureen B. Fant (Johns Hopkins University Press, 1982); **Kendall/Hunt Publishing Company**: from *Nemean VI* by Pindar in *Ancient Greece: Documentary Perspectives*, edited by Stylianos Spyridakis and Bradley Nystrom (Kendall/Hunt Publishing, 1985), © 1985 by Kendall/Hunt Publishing Company; **Manchester University Press**: from *Cronica de Don Manuel* by Damiao de Gois in *The Jews in Western Europe, 1440–1600*, translated by John Edwards (Manchester University Press, 1994); **Oxford University Press**: from *The Institutes of the Christian Church* by John Calvin in *Documents of the Christian Church*, edited by Henry Bettenson (Oxford University Press, 1952); from *The Goodman of Paris* in Le Menagier de Paris, edited by Georgine E. Brereton and Janet M. Ferrier (Clarendon Press, 1981); **Pegasus Press**: from *On the Equal or Unequal Sin of Adam and Eve* by Isotta Nogarola in *Her Immaculate Hand*, edited by Margaret King and Albert Rabil (SUNY, 1992); Penguin UK: from *The Prince* by Niccolo Machiavelli, translated by George Bull (Penguin Classics, 1961; third revised edition, 1981), © George Bull, 1961, 1975, 1981; from *Agricola* from *The Agricola and the Germania* by Tacitus, translated by H. Mattingly, revised by S.A. Handford (Penguin Classics, 1948; revised edition, 1971), © The Estate of H. Mattingly, 1948, 1970; S. A. Handford, 1970; from *The Life of Saint Teresa of Avilla by Herself*, translated by J. M. Cohen (Penguin Classics, 1957), © J. M. Cohen, 1957; from *The Peloponnesian War* by Thucydides, translated by Rex Warner (Penguin Classics, 1954), © Rex Warner, 1954; **Princeton University Press**: from *Ancient Near Eastern Texts Relating to the Old Testament*, edited by James B. Pritchard, 2nd edition, revised, © 1950, 1955, 1964, renewed 1978 by Princeton University Press; **Random House Archive and Library**: from *Epic of Gilgamesh*, translated by R. Temple, in *He Who Saw Everything: A Verse Translation of Gilgamesh* (Rider Books, 1991); from *The Medea* by Euripedes in *The Great Plays of Euripedes*, translated by Rex Warner (The Bodley Head/Signet), © 1958 and renewed © 1986 by Rex Warner; **Teachers College Press**: from *De ingenius moribus* by Pier Paolo Vergerio in *Vittorino da Feltre and Other Humanist Educators* by W. H. Woodward (Teachers College Press, 1964), © 1964 Teachers College, Columbia University; **Thames and Hudson Ltd**: from *The Origins of War: From the Stone Age to Alexander the Great* by Arthur Ferrill (Thames and Hudson, 1985); **University of California Press**: from *History of a Voyage to the Land of Brazil, Otherwise Called America* by Jean de Léry, edited/translated by Janet Whatley (University of California Press 1990), © 1990 The Regents of the University of California; **University of Chicago Press**: from *Ancient Records of Assyria and Babylon* by D. D. Luckenbill (1927; 1968); from *Works and Days* by Hesiod, from *On Law and Justice* by Solon in *Greek Lyrics*, edited by Richmond Lattimore (University of Chicago Press, 1960); from *Iliad* by Homer, edited by Richmond Lattimore (University of Chicago Press, 1951); from *Letter to Lucilia Vernacula* by Laura Cereta in *Collected Letters of a Renaissance Feminist*, translated by Diana Robin (University of Chicago Press, 1997); from *Oration on the Dignity of Man* by Giovanni Pico della Mirandola, translated by E. L. Forbes, in *Renaissance Philosophy of Man*, edited by Ernst Cassirer et.al. (University of Chicago Press, 1948); from *Persians* by Aeschylus, translated by S. G. Bernardette, in *The Complete Greek Tragedies*, edited by D. Grene and Richmond Lattimore (University of Chicago Press, 1992); University of Toronto Press: from *The Cruel Turks* by Erasmus in *The Erasmus Reader*, edited by Erika Rummel (University of Toronto Press, 1990); **Barbara Watterson**: *My god, my husband, I come to you...* in *Women in Ancient Egypt* by Barbara Watterson (St Martin's Press, 1991), © Barbara Watterson, 1991; **Renee Watkins**: from *On the Family* by Leon Battista Alberti in *Family in Renaissance Florence* (University of South Carolina Press, 1989); **Westminster/John Knox Press**: from *Letter of the Church of Smyrna to the Church of Philomelium* in *Early Christian Fathers*, edited by Cyril C. Richardson (Macmillan, 1970); **John Wiley and Sons Inc**: from *Lettere di una gentildonna fiorentina del secolo XV ai figliuoli esuli* by Alessandra Strozzi in *Social and Economic Foundations of the Italian Renaissance*, edited by Anthony Molho (John Wiley, 1969).

Every effort has been made to trace or contact all copyright holders. The publishers would be pleased to rectify any omissions brought to their attention at the earliest opportunity.

GLOSSARY

absolution: In some branches of Christianity, the act of pronouncing forgiveness and the remission of sins, performed by a priest in the sacrament of penance.

absolutism: A political system or project that concentrates power in the hands of the monarch. Absolutism came to prominence in Europe during the sixteenth through eighteenth centuries when monarchs sought to wrest power from the Church and the aristocracy, in order to create national states.

acropolis: The citadel of a Greek city, built at its highest point and containing the chief temples and public buildings.

agnate: A relative on the father's side, from a male line of descent. A cognate is a relative whose kinship is on the mother's side.

***agora*:** A central feature of the *polis*. Originally a marketplace, the *agora* also served as the main social and political meeting place. With the acropolis, the *agora* housed the most important buildings of the city-state.

alumnus, alumna, alumni: In ancient Rome, abandoned infants who were picked up and "adopted" into families, usually as servants. In present-day usage, an alumnus or alumna is a person who has been graduated from a particular school or university.

ambassador: The highest-ranking diplomatic representative of one country to another, usually accorded the privilege of guaranteed personal security, even when the countries represented are at war.

ambulatory: A curved aisle running around the east end of a church, originally used for processions.

Amerindians: Aboriginal peoples of the Western Hemisphere, American Indians. Preferred to "Indian" (used to refer to the peoples of the Indian subcontinent) and "Native American" (an anti-immigrant nineteenth-century American political party, called "the Know-Nothings").

animism: *See* **monotheism**.

anthropomorphism: The assigning of human characteristics to animals, natural phenomena or abstract ideas or, in the case of religion, to a deity or spirit.

anti-Semitism: The discrimination against, prejudice or hostility toward Jews.

anti-trinitarianism: *See* **unitarianism.**

apostle: An early follower of Jesus, including the original twelve disciples and the first missionaries.

apotheosis: *See* **deification**.

apprenticeship: Training in a craft or profession in which the master profits from the labor of the apprentice, and the apprentice receives training. *See also* **guild, master**.

apse: A domed or vaulted semicircular recess, especially at the east end of a church.

aristocracy: A government or social structure in which power and wealth is vested in a small minority, a hereditary nobility which claims to be best qualified to rule.

arquebus: A portable, long-barrelled gun, fired by a wheel-lock or match-lock, dating from the fifteenth century.

artisan: A skilled maker of things. Before mass manufacture, artisans produced earthenware, tools, jewelry, etc.

Aryan: Formerly a term that referred to the Indo-European language family, and an assumed racial category composed of people of Indo-European "blood." The notion of an Aryan race was created by nineteenth-century race theorists and adopted by Adolf Hitler. "Aryan" is now used to designate the Indo-Iranian language group, or, more narrowly, the Indo-Aryan (Indic) branch and the group of Indo-Aryan speakers who invaded the Indian subcontinent c. 1500 B.C.E.

astrolabe: The most important instrument used by astronomers and navigators from antiquity through the sixteenth century, used to measure the altitudes of celestial bodies. The altitude of the North Star yields the latitude, and the altitude of the sun and stars yields the time. In the eighteenth century, the astrolabe was superseded by the sextant.

atrium: The central rectangular, interior open-air hall of the Etruscan and Roman house, usually considered the most important room.

***auto-da-fé*:** An "act of faith," a penal sentence by the Spanish Inquisition; also, the execution of that sentence by burning at the stake.

barbarian: In ancient Greece, a word applied to non-Greek-speaking peoples, assumed to be inferior and uncivilized. Similarly used in Chinese civilization. Later and more generally, a person or group believed to lack cultural refinement.

basilica: An oblong building that ends in a semicircular protrusion (an apse), used in ancient Rome as a court of justice and place of public assembly; early Christians adapted this plan for their churches.

bastion: A projecting work in a castle wall or other fortification which allows the defenders to fire along the face of the wall.

bayonet: A short sword attached to the muzzle of a rifle. First used by European armies in the seventeenth century as an infantry weapon for close combat, eliminating the need for a corps of pikemen.

Bible: The sacred writings of Judaism and Christianity, known to Christians as the Bible, consist of two parts. The first, called the Old Testament by Christians, stands alone for Jews as the Hebrew Bible. The second, called the New Testament, includes accounts of Jesus's life attributed to four of Jesus's disciples—Matthew, Mark, Luke, and John—known as Gospels (meaning "good news") or collectively as the Gospel.

Black Death: A fourteenth-century epidemic that killed one-fourth to one-third of the population of Europe (about 75 million people), caused by the bacterium *yersinia pestis* and spread by fleas harbored by the black rat.

bourgeoisie: *See* **burgher**.

bourse: *See* **stock exchange**.

brahman: A priest or member of the priestly caste in Hinduism.

Bronze Age: An age in which bronze, an alloy of copper and tin, was used to manufacture tools, weapons, and other objects. The term originated as part of the nineteenth-century three-age system (Stone Age, Bronze Age, and Iron Age), but bronze technology actually appeared at different times in different parts of the world. Around 3000 B.C.E. in Mesopotamia and Egypt, bronze alloys were developed to make stronger tools, shields, and weapons.

bull: A letter issued by the pope stating a religious doctrine. In very early times, papal bulls (from Latin *bulla*, "leaden seal") were sealed with the pope's signet ring. Today only the most solemn bulls carry a leaden seal.

bullion: Uncoined gold and silver, molded into bars or ingots.

burgher: In medieval Europe, a citizen of a town (*burg, borough, bourg, borgo*). Burghers were members of the class of enterprising merchants, bankers, and long-distance traders ("the bourgeoisie").

caliph: The supreme leader of the Islamic world after Muhammad's death in 632 C.E. Secular and religious authority were combined in the office of the caliph, who claimed to be appointed by God.

canon law: A single ecclesiastical rule or law, or the body of ecclesiastical law. By extension, a set of rules or fundamental texts pertinent in any art or discipline.

canton: In Switzerland, an independent unit of local government; the Swiss Confederation is divided into twenty-three cantons.

capitalism: An economic system organized around the profit motive and competition, in which the means of production are privately owned by businessmen and organizations which produce goods for a market guided by the forces of supply and demand.

caravel: A type of sailing ship, first developed in Portugal and widely used by fifteenth- and sixteenth-century explorers, equipped with square and lateen sails or entirely lateen rigged.

cartography: The art and science of mapmaking.

caste: A system of rigid hereditary social stratification, characterized by disparities of wealth and poverty, inherited occupations, and strict rules governing social contact.

castle: In the Middle Ages, the fortified residence of a European noble or monarch. At first only a wood or stone tower built on a mound encircled by walls or moat, castles later became more complex, with thick walls topped by a parapet.

catacombs: A complex of underground rooms and tunnels, especially in Rome, used as a cemetery, with niches for tombs and graves.

chancery: A record office; the court of a chancellor.

chivalry: The qualities expected of a knight; the code of values associated with the medieval nobility, developed in response to church strictures and elaborated at court.

Christendom: The part of the world in which Christianity predominates; the collective body of Christian believers.

citizen: In ancient Greece, a free male inhabitant of a *polis*, with landowning and voting rights. In modern times, applied to any legal member of the state.

civic humanism: An engaged form of humanism that responded to the moral concerns of those who lived in cities. *See also* **humanism**.

civility: The set of manners and attitudes developed in European princely and royal courts from the later Middle Ages and into the early modern period.

civilization: A condition of society characterized by high cultural achievement and complex social development. A society is a civilization if it has (1) class stratification; (2) political and religious hierarchies; (3) a complex division of labor; (4) an economic system that creates agricultural surpluses; and (5) the skills to create architecture, tools, and weaponry.

civil law: *See* ***jus civile***

clan: A number of households that claim descent from a common ancestor.

classical: A term that refers to the ideals and styles of ancient Greek and Roman art, literature, and philosophy, and as reinterpreted by later generations. Classical ideals and styles have exemplified simplicity, harmony, restraint, proportion, and reason. Classicism also implies the finest period of artistic activity or the purest aesthetic. The era during which a society or art reaches its peak is often called classical, as in "Classical Greece" (fifth century B.C.E.).

clergy: A group ordained to perform religious functions. In Catholicism, the clergy is a hierarchical body headed by the pope.

cognate: *See* **agnate**.

cohort: A subdivision of the Roman legion, including infantry and cavalry.

***coloni*:** In imperial Rome, the class of poor tenant farmers, often the descendants of manumitted slaves. The *coloni* were the forerunners of the serfs of medieval Europe.

colonialism: The control by a country over an area outside its borders. The ancient Phoenicians, Greeks, and Romans were colonizers. In the Middle Ages, Venice and Genoa had colonies on the banks of the Black Sea and in the

Aegean. Modern European colonialism began after the discovery of America and of the sea route to the Far East.

comedy: A genre of humorous drama, typically with a happy or absurd ending, sometimes critical of social and political institutions, first developed in ancient Greece.

common: In medieval Europe, a centrally located area of land set aside for the free use of the community. Commons still exist in areas of England and the United States.

common law: A system of law developed after the Norman Conquest of England (1066), and still partly in use in most English-speaking countries. Unlike civil law (descended from the codified laws of the Roman Empire and from Napoleonic France), common law is not embodied in a text or code. Judges draw instead upon precedents that have been set by earlier court decisions.

commune: In the Middle Ages, a self-governing municipality with the right to regulate trade, collect taxes, and operate its own system of justice within the town walls. In northern Europe, communes were often granted charters by the royal government or local court. In Italy, communes were sworn associations of townspeople that arose in the eleventh century to overthrow local bishops or feudal magnates.

compass: A device that indicates direction on the earth's surface, and that is used as the principal instrument of navigation. A magnetic compass indicates movement relative to the earth's geomagnetic field.

condottiere: *See* **mercenary**.

confraternity: An association of laypeople linked by a common mission, which combined spiritual and charitable service.

conquistadors: Military adventurers who led the Spanish exploration and conquest of the New World during the sixteenth century.

consul: The two chief annual civil and military magistrates of Rome during the Republic.

contemplation: Quiet and solitary thought; the intellectual and religious ideal of medieval scholars who lived in monasteries and universities.

conversion: The act or experience associated with the decisive adoption of a particular religion and set of beliefs, often entailing the rejection of a previous religious identity.

cosmopolis: A culturally prestigious city whose population is composed of peoples from many parts of the world; an urban center where the most sophisticated customs, practices, and beliefs can be found.

coup d'état: The sudden, violent overthrow of a government by a small group.

courtier: A person in attendance at a court, and who seeks the ruler's favor.

creole: A fully-formed language that develops from a pidgin and becomes the primary language of a linguistic community. Most creoles have vocabularies derived from major European languages; some exist only or primarily in spoken form. The word also refers to combinations of European and non-European cultures, especially cooking and music, as well as to people of mixed racial heritage (*see also* **mestizo**).

culture: Learned behavior acquired by individuals as members of a particular group, in contrast to genetically endowed behavior. Each culture has different styles governing behavior and thought. "Culture" can include food preparation, politics, sculpture, architecture, painting, music, literature, philosophy, and a variety of other civilized pursuits.

cuneiform: A system of writing from Sumer and used for various Middle Eastern languages from c. 3000 B.C.E. until c. 100 C.E. It consisted of wedge-shaped characters inscribed on clay, stone, wax, or metal.

curtain wall: The plain wall of a castle or other fortified place, connecting two towers.

decurions: In cities of the Roman Empire, the elite hereditary class responsible for funding and administering municipal functions, and for collecting taxes.

deification: The process of attributing god-like attributes to a human being. In ancient Rome, a deceased emperor was often deified in a ritual known as apotheosis.

demesne: That part of a medieval landholding cultivated exclusively for the lord's use.

democracy: Term from the Greek words for "people" and "power." A form of government in which citizens monitor the state; as opposed to oligarchy or monarchy, where the state is controlled by a small minority or individual. In a direct democracy citizens vote in an assembly, as in ancient Athens. In an indirect democracy citizens elect representatives.

demotic: A simplified form of Egyptian hieroglyphic writing used for informal communication and by the masses; hieratic was a simplified form of writing used by the priesthood.

dhow: A type of sailing vessel with lateen sails, in common use from the Red Sea to the western coast of India.

dialectics: Logical argumentation, especially in the Western tradition according to the method of Aristotle and his followers. In modern times, the opposition or reconciliation of conflicting ideas or forces (as for Hegel and Marx).

dialogue: A literary genre favored by humanists, based on Classical models. Dialogue permitted an author to present two or more competing viewpoints and argue for each plausibly without committing himself.

diaspora: A Greek word meaning "dispersion," originally referring to the Jewish settlements of ancient Babylon and Egypt formed after the destruction of the Temple in 587 B.C.E. Later diasporas of Jews occurred, especially after Jewish revolts against Rome in the first and second centuries C.E. Today, "diaspora" is used of Jewry outside of the state of Israel and is also applied to other dispersions of peoples.

Diet: In the Holy Roman Empire, the assembly of the representatives of the estates.

diplomacy: Conducting negotiations in order to resolve differences, regulate commerce, make alliances, etc.

disputation: In medieval education, an exercise in logic that consists of arguments for and against a thesis, until a conclusion is reached. *See* **dialectics, sholasticism**.

distaff: A simple stick used in spinning. The distaff held raw fiber that was pulled and twisted into thread and wound on the spindle; later the spindle was the bobbin on the spinning machine that held spun thread.

dowry: The property a bride brings to her marriage. It correlates with the wealth or status of the bridegroom.

dualism: Any theory or system of philosophical or religious thought that recognizes two independent and mutually irreducible spiritual entities. The ancient Zoroastrian belief that the god of Good struggled against the god of Evil to determine human destiny was a form of dualism, influencing Judaism, Christianity, and Islam.

ducat: A gold coin with the portrait of the ruler (i.e. the duke, the doge) on it, first minted in 1284 by the city of Venice.

duchy: The territory of a duke or duchess.

dynasty: A succession of monarchs of the same line of descent; a group or family that maintains power for a long period of time.

elite: A small group of persons who control major institutions, exercise military and/or political power, possess superior wealth, or enjoy elevated status and prestige.

empiricism: The philosophy that knowledge derives from experience by the senses.

entrepreneur: A person who organizes and assumes the risks of a business.

epidemic: A contagious disease that periodically or episodically afflicts many people within a population, community, or region. Severe epidemics have killed large numbers of people, most notoriously the Black Death of fourteenth-century Europe.

estate: A social group, legally defined, invested with distinct powers, possessions, and property.

Eucharist: A central observance of the Christian churches, variously called the Lord's Supper, Holy Communion, and the Mass.

excommunication: The formal expulsion of a member from a religious group. In Roman Catholicism, the excommunicated are excluded from receiving the sacraments of the church.

façade: A French word meaning "face" or "front." In architecture, a façade is the side of a structure, normally the front, that is architecturally or visually most significant.

fallow: Cultivated land deliberately allowed to lie idle during a growing season in order to prevent soil exhaustion.

famine: A shortage of food sufficient to cause widespread privation and a rise in mortality. Famine may be caused by natural events; by war; or by certain agricultural practices that cause soil erosion.

feudal: *See* **fief.**

fief, feudal: Medieval relationships of lordship, landholding, and service are often called "feudal," and depended on the granting of a unit of land, the "fief," in usufruct.

florin: A coin first minted in 1252 by the city of Florence; later, any of several gold coins patterned after the Florentine florin.

fluyt: A "flyboat," in early modern Europe, a small, highly efficient vessel for inexpensive, utilitarian hauling, a Dutch innovation.

folk: The people as a whole; those who bear and transmit the cultural values of a people.

fresco: Italian for "fresh," a technique of durable wall painting used extensively for murals. In pure (*buon*) fresco paint is applied to a fresh wet layer of plaster; painting on a dry (*secco*) surface with adhesive binder is not permanent.

galley: A warship driven by oars in battle and with sails for cruising. It was the standard European battle vessel until the late sixteenth century, when the sail-powered, more heavily armed, galleon replaced it.

Gentile: A non-Jew, avoided by faithful Jews.

Geometric style: A style of Greek pottery produced in the ninth and eighth centuries B.C.E., marked by densely patterned lines, including zigzags and Greek key motifs.

ghetto: A segregated quarter where Jews were required to reside. In 1516, the first ghetto was established on the site of an iron foundry (the meaning of "ghetto") by the rulers of Venice. The term came to designate any urban area to which Jews were legally confined, or where Jews or any other socially marginalized group lived voluntarily.

Gospel: *See* **Bible**.

Gothic: An architectural style originating in twelfth-century France, which uses pointed arches and diagonal rib vaults.

grace: A central concept in Christian theology, referring to God's granting of salvation as a free and undeserved gift of love.

guild: An association of merchants or craftsmen. In medieval and early modern Europe, a guild normally comprised all self-employed members of an occupation in a town or district. Only guild members could practice that occupation.

gymnasium: In ancient Greece, a place where athletes exercised in the nude. Gymnasia served as meeting places for social events and intellectual exchange.

gynaeceum: The "women's quarters" of a Greek citizen's house; the workshop for women textile workers on an early medieval estate.

hegemony: The domination of one institution, sector, or state over others.

Hellas: The Greek name for Greece.
Hellenic: A term that designates the period of Greek culture and history from the Archaic Age (c. 700 to c. 500 B.C.E.) to the period of Alexander the Great (r. 336–323 B.C.E.).
Hellenistic: A term designating the period of Greek culture and history from the conquests of Alexander the Great until the eastern Mediterranean region fell under Roman domination (by 30 B.C.E.).
helot: In ancient Sparta, a serf who was forced to perform agricultural labor; originally, the Messenians, a group conquered by the Spartans and reduced to near slave status.
heresy: The rejection of the established doctrines of a group (e.g. a church) by a member or members of that group; from the Greek word meaning "to choose."
heterodoxy: Deviation from orthodoxy.
hierarchy: A series of persons, graded or ranked in order of authority.
hieratic: *See* **demotic**.
hieroglyph: Writing employing pictographic characters, developed in ancient Egypt.
hominid: The genus of human-like animals, comprising modern humans *(Homo sapiens)* and ancestral and related human and human-like species *(Homo sapiens neanderthalensis, Homo erectus, Homo habilis)*. *See* **species**.
***Homo erectus*:** *See* **hominid**.
***Homo habilis*:** *See* **hominid**.
***Homo sapiens*:** *See* **hominid** and **species**.
honor: A social value of growing importance in late medieval and early modern Europe, originally the reputation of a grand nobleman but also that of a patrician or bourgeois adult male; and dependent on the regulation of the sexuality of female kin.
hoplite: A heavily armored foot soldier of ancient Greece, who fought in close formation, each carrying a heavy bronze shield (a *hoplon*), a short iron sword, and a long spear.
hospice: A place of refuge for travelers and pilgrims. In the medieval context, very similar to the non-specialized hospital.
hospital: Generally church-related and increasingly funded by bequests, the hospital of the Middle Ages accommodated not only the sick but also abandoned children, "fallen" or deserted women, and the elderly. From the seventeenth century, it increasingly specialized in the treatment of the ill.
humanism: An intellectual movement that emerged in Italy in the late 1300s and spread throughout western and central Europe in the early modern period, centered around the revival of interest in ancient Greek and Roman literature, philosophy, and history.
icon: An image that represents a divine figure and is believed to possess some essential aspect of that divinity.
iconoclasm: A Christian religious movement opposed to the veneration of images (icons) of Christ and the saints. Controversy over the legitimacy of icons lasted for over a century (730–843 C.E.) in the Byzantine Empire. Iconoclasts (Greek for "image-breakers") often invaded churches, destroying the offending images, or icons.
illuminated manuscript: A handwritten book with pictures and ornamentation, "illuminating," or lighting up, the page.
immortality: Being exempt from death, also, human survival after physical death.
***imperator*:** Originally, in ancient Rome, a person who commanded an army. Augustus Caesar was the *imperator* of all the armies and institutions of government, and thus of Rome and its territories.
***imperium*:** The supreme command in war and in the execution of the law, granted at Rome to consuls and other magistrates; authority over a region or empire.
indentured servant: In the early years of North American settlement, a European immigrant who worked without wages for a contracted period in exchange for the price of passage to the colonies and clothing, board, and lodging while in service.
Indo-European: An extensive language family, originally derived from a common ancestor, Proto-Indo-European. The surviving languages include Hindi, Persian, Russian, Polish, Armenian, Albanian, Greek, Italian, French, Spanish, Portuguese, German, English, Dutch, and the Scandinavian languages.
indulgence: In medieval Catholicism, a document granting release from purgatorial punishment in recognition of extraordinary service.
infantry: Armed foot soldiers, as distinct from cavalry, air, or sea forces.
infidel: In Islam, a nonbeliever, someone outside the faith.
Inquisition: A church court to prosecute heretics. Inquisitory courts were harsh in their interrogation and punishment, obtaining confessions through torture.
***intendant*:** In seventeenth- and eighteenth-century France, the absolute monarchy's key regional administrator, regarded by French monarchs as more reliable than hereditary officials.
investiture: The ceremonial conferring of high office and rank. The question as to which authority should have power to invest church officials provoked the "Investiture Controversy" during the high Middle Ages between the papacy and secular rulers.
Iron Age: The period when iron replaced bronze as the material used for tools and weapons. Iron metallurgy began among the Hittites in eastern Anatolia, c. 1900–1400 B.C.E. and by 1000 B.C.E. had spread throughout the Middle East, Mediterranean region, and westward into Europe.
***isonomia*:** The principle in ancient Athenian society that citizens are entitled to equality before the law.
jihad: An Arabic word meaning "striving"; according to the Qu'ran, the religious duty of Muslims. Often translated as "holy war," it can be interpreted as a personal or collective spiritual battle against evil, or as a physical battle against unbelievers.
joint-stock company: A type of partnership similar to a corporation. A joint-stock company has transferable shares which are sold at a stock exchange. It is managed by a board of directors elected by the partners (shareholders) who, unlike modern corporations, are personally liable for the company's debts. The joint-stock company was instrumental in the expansion of mercantile capitalism and European colonialism.
jurisprudent: In ancient Rome, a citizen who was learned in law but who held no official position. Over time, jurisprudence came to mean a system or body of law, and jurisprudents became professionals in the imperial bureaucracy, whose documentation and analysis of past decisions constituted a system of law.
***jus civile*:** In the Roman Empire, the "civil law," based primarily on codified statute, most famously the *Corpus Juris Civilis* of the sixth-century C.E. emperor Justinian, rather than court rulings and precedents. Today, used in the legal systems of certain western European countries and their offshoots in Latin America, Asia, and Africa. In contrast, the *jus gentium* ("law of nations") was based on unwritten customary practice and *jus naturale* ("law of nature") on an unwritten (and superior) divine or philosophical law.
justification: In Christianity, the process through which an individual, alienated from God by sin, is reconciled to God and becomes righteous through faith in Christ.
knight: In medieval Europe, a mounted warrior. Most were nobles of low rank who gave a military service to their lords in exchange for a land grant or maintenance. Higher-status nobles also acquired knighthood, by which they were admitted to military rank. A knight was named by a noble superior, and often went through an elaborate ceremony of knighthood.
koine: The form of Greek commonly spoken and written in the eastern Mediterranean in the Hellenistic and Roman periods, allowing people of many different cultures to communicate.
***kore*, pl. *korai*:** A type of statue featuring a young, clothed female, developed in the Archaic Age (c. 700 B.C.E.).
***kouros*, pl. *kouroi*:** A statue featuring a young, male nude, first introduced in the Archaic Age (c. 700 B.C.E.) and common in the Classical era.
lateen sail: A triangular sail on a long yard, used by dhows and other light sailing vessels.
***latifundia*:** In Latin, literally "broad fields"; in Roman times a *latifundium* was a great landed estate, usually worked by slave labor.
layperson: A person who is not a member of the clergy; now commonly meaning a person who is not a member of a specific profession.
legitimacy: The claim of a right to power, which is based on hereditary succession, electoral rules, or natural law.
liturgy: The formal public rituals, prayers, and written texts of religious worship (from the Greek "people" and "work"), used of Christian services and the form of prayer in synagogues.
Lyceum: The philosophical school established by Aristotle; in the nineteenth century, the inspiration for secondary school education.
man of war: An armed, combatant naval vessel.
manor: In medieval Europe, a unit of social organization dominated by a lord, usually consisting of open fields, forest, and common grazing lands, a manor house and the lord's demesne, and one or more peasant villages. Peasants paid a portion of their produce and a number of days of labor each year to the lord. The lord was expected to provide military protection and to dispense justice.
manumission: The formal act of emancipating a slave, sometimes by written agreement or payment by the slave to his master.
martyr: A person who suffers the penalty of death (and/or painful torture) for adhering to a religion or cause.
Mass: The celebration of the Eucharist, the central religious service of the Roman Catholic Church and some other Christian churches.
master: An artisan who is self-employed or who employs journeymen, usually a member of a guild. A journeyman who could demonstrate truly superior skills might be admitted to the guild as a master. In the later Middle Ages, the guild membership was often limited to the sons of masters.
materialism: A philosophical theory, first developed in ancient Greece, that physical matter is the only reality. In modern usage, also a cultural style in which the goal is the satisfaction of physical desire and comfort.
mendicant: Someone dependent on alms for sustenance. In the Middle Ages, the mendicant orders lived by begging or on charitable gifts. The first mendicant order grew out of the efforts of St. Francis of Assisi (c. 1182–1226).
mercantilism: An economic system developed in the early modern era to unify and increase the power and monetary wealth of a nation by regulating the entire national economy. From the sixteenth through the eighteenth century, western European governments practiced mercantilism to build up their military and industrial strength.
mercenary: A professional soldier who fights for pay in the army of a foreign country.
Messiah: The prophesied king and redeemer of the Jews, who would restore the Jews to Israel and bring divine justice to the earth; derived from the Hebrew term for "anointed one." Translated into Greek as "Christos," the term became applied to Jesus.

***mestizo*:** A term of biological and cultural classification used in the Spanish-speaking world for persons of mixed Amerindian and white ancestry.
metaphysics: The branch of philosophy concerned with ultimate universal principles such as being and purpose.
metic: In ancient Greece, a merchant, usually a foreigner, who was a member of a class of resident non-citizens in the *polis*, with some, but not all, of the privileges of citizenship.
metropolis: A great city regarded as a center of business or politics. Applied to the ancient world, the term means the "mother" *polis* that established a colony. In that sense, it continues to be applied to nations that establish colonies.
Midrash: In Judaism, a method of interpreting biblical scriptures; later, compilations of stories and sermons commenting on, alluding to, or codifying biblical texts.
Milesian school: The first materialistic philosophers, Thales, Anaximander, and Anaximenes, who lived in the city of Miletus, in the sixth century B.C.E. They explained natural phenomena by reference to laws that governed growth and change, understood through observation and logic.
mintage, minting: The process by which metal money is coined by a government. A mint is the place where coins are manufactured from gold and silver bullion.
Mishnah: The oldest post-biblical codification of Jewish Oral Law, from the Hebrew "repetition" or "study." Together with the Gemara (later commentaries on the Mishnah), it forms the Talmud.
missionary: The missionary movement was the Christian effort to convert peoples. The first great missionary to the Gentiles, Paul, helped to spread Christianity until, by the end of the first century, it had reached most Mediterranean cities. The voyages of discovery in the fifteenth and sixteenth centuries and the expansion of European colonization began a surge of Roman Catholic missionary activity. Renewed missionary activity took place as part of nineteenth-century imperialism.
monarchy: Rule by a single individual, usually with life tenure and descended from a line of monarchs.
monasticism: The way of life of individuals who have chosen to pursue an ideal of perfection in a separate, dedicated religious setting. Monasticism is practiced in Buddhism, some forms of Christianity, and some other religions.
monotheism: Belief in a single God (as in Judaism, Christianity, and Islam). By contrast, polytheism is the belief that many gods exist; pantheism is the belief that God is suffused throughout, or is synonymous with, the universe; animism is the belief that spirits or divinities dwell inside objects and living things. Some religions are non-theistic (Confucianism, Buddhism), but permit belief in gods or spirits.
Moor: In medieval and early modern Europe, an inhabitant of Muslim North Africa, and, by extension, the Arab and Arabicized conquerors and inhabitants of Spain.
mosque: The Islamic place of public worship (from the Arabic *masjid*, "a place to prostrate one's self [in front of God]"), always oriented toward Mecca, the holy city of Islam. A mosque must have a place for ritual washing, a place from which a leader (*imam*) can start the prayer, and a minaret, a tower from which Muslims are called to prayer.
***mulatto*:** In former colonies of Spain, Portugal, and France, and in the United States, a term for a person of mixed Negro and European parentage.
museum: An institution where objects of aesthetic, educational, or historical value are preserved and displayed.
musket: A large-caliber, smooth-bore firearm aimed and fired from the shoulder, which first appeared in Spain in the mid-1500s and was used to fire a lead ball.
Mycenae: An ancient Greek city which rose to military power around 1500 B.C.E. Mycenaean civilization, influenced by Minoan Crete and the ancient Middle East, flourished until about 1300 B.C.E.
mystery cults: In the ancient world, religious cults whose members believed that the performance of secret rituals would give them special knowledge and a mystical union with the divine. Initiates ritually reenacted the death and rebirth of the divinity at the center of the cult.
mysticism: Religious experience in which the believer has or claims direct contact with the sacred. In Christianity this can take the form of a vision of, or sense of union with, God.
myths: Stories that narrate in an imaginative and symbolic way the basic practices and beliefs upon which a culture rests. Mythology means either a certain body of myths (e.g. Greek or Scandinavian) or the study of myths.
nave: The central space in a church, usually extending from the west door to the chancel, and often flanked by aisles.
Neolithic Period: The prehistoric development that followed the Paleolithic Period and preceded the Bronze Age. In the Neolithic ("New Stone Age," c. 9000–3000 B.C.E.), chipped stone tool manufacture became increasingly sophisticated; agriculture and the domestication of animals were introduced; and pottery and polished stone tools were developed.
Neoplatonism: An interpretation of Plato's philosophy that developed in the third century C.E., which influenced Christian and Islamic philosophy and theology. It holds that knowledge is possible only through the understanding of archetypes, essences that structure the objects and beings that make up the world of human experience. According to Neoplatonism, the human soul has within it a vision of these ideal forms, which are dependent on and created by the One (i.e. God).
nepotism: The practice of awarding jobs or privileges to a relative.
New Testament: *See* **Bible**.
nirvana: Release from bondage to physical desire and pain: a core belief of Buddhism, the ultimate state attained by the Buddha, and the goal of all Buddhists. In Hinduism, nirvana is achieved only through a complete cessation of the cycle of death and rebirth. In Buddhism a state of enlightenment can be achieved in this life, through spiritual or physical exercises.
notary: In medieval cities, a trained professional who drew up deeds, contracts, wills, and other documents essential for urban life.
***oecumene*:** A Greek word referring to "the inhabited world"; in antiquity designating a distinct cultural community. The ecumenical councils in the early church were so called because they represented the whole church. Today, the term "ecumenical" is applied to the collective effort of all Christians to repair differences and manifest unity.
***oikos*:** The household, the fundamental unit of private land and of domestic production in ancient Greece, consisting of a dominant man, his wife and children, and related and unrelated dependents, including slaves. The *oikos* was patrilineal and patriarchal.
Old Testament: *See* **Bible**.
oligarchy: A form of government in which a small minority holds ruling power in order to favor its own interests. Military dictatorships are often oligarchic, as are the political machines that sometimes run city governments in democracies.
Optimates: In late Republican Rome, die-hard defenders of patrician privilege (literally, the "best"). Opposing the Optimates were the Populares ("supporters of the people").
orthodoxy: The established (literally "correct") doctrine of a church or religious group.
ostracism: In ancient Athens, a method of banishment by popular vote, without trial. Each year the citizens would vote on whether anyone was so dangerous to the state that he should be ostracized, or exiled for ten years. Later, ostracism came to mean any form of political or social exclusion.
Paleolithic Period: Prehistoric cultural development that preceded the Neolithic Period. In the Paleolithic ("Old Stone Age"), which lasted from about 2.5 million to about 10,000 years ago, hominids and humans developed the manufacture of various chipped stone tools.
pantheism: *See* **monotheism**.
papacy: *See* **pope**.
papal bull: *See* **bull**.
papyrus: Writing paper made from the pith of a reed that grows wild in the Nile River, used from about 2400 B.C.E. by the people of Egypt, Palestine, Syria, and southern Europe. Connected together in strips and rolled up, it made scrolls, the books of antiquity.
parable: A brief moral tale (from the Greek *parabole*, "a setting beside"). In parables, a spiritual truth is articulated by telling a simple story. Well-known biblical examples include the Gospel stories of the Prodigal Son and of the Good Samaritan.
***parlement*:** In medieval and early modern France, a regional supreme court of criminal and civil law. At first the *parlements* were staffed by royal appointees who supported medieval monarchs, but in the seventeenth and eighteenth centuries, they often actually obstructed the absolutist agenda of Bourbon kings. The revolutionary National Assembly of 1789 abolished the *parlements*.
pastor: In Protestantism, a leader or minister (Greek *pastor*, "shepherd") of a congregation who presides at the weekly Sunday celebration and whose role is to teach scripture, rather than to confer grace (the role of the priest in Catholicism). Pastors, unlike celibate priests, are allowed to marry.
patriarchy: Social organization marked by the supremacy of the father, the legal dependence of wives and children, and the reckoning of and inheritance from the male line.
patricians: The hereditary aristocratic class of ancient Rome, initially entitled to privileges denied to commoners (the plebeians). In medieval and early modern cities, a hereditary elite of bourgeois office-holders, *rentiers*, and high-status merchants, to be distinguished from ordinary guild merchants.
patrilineal: The tracing of ancestry and kinship through the male line. Female offspring are valued insofar as they help preserve the male line, mainly through marriage. Patrilineal families may also be patriarchal.
patrimony: The accumulation of familial wealth which can be inherited; originally the wealth that flows through the male line of descent.
patronage: The conferring of jobs, favors, and commissions by a powerful patron to a client, in order to promote the patron's interests.
***pax romana*:** Literally, "the Roman peace." Under the empire consolidated by Augustus Caesar (27 B.C.E.), Rome's total domination of Europe, the Mediterranean, and the Middle East brought about 250 years of peace, albeit a peace secured by conquest and bloodshed.
pedagogue: In ancient Greece, originally a slave who accompanied children to school. Later, pedagogue came to mean a theorist of education or a teacher.
penance: A sacrament of the Roman Catholic, Eastern Orthodox, and some Protestant churches. The rite consists in the confession of sins to a priest, who then assigns the repentant sinner an act of penance in order to obtain forgiveness.

peon: A member of the landless agricultural laboring class of Spanish America; a person held in compulsory servitude to a master for the working out of a debt.

perspective: In art, the techniques used to represent three-dimensional spatial relationships on a two-dimensional surface; from the fifteenth century, one of the principal characteristics of western European art.

peso: In the early modern era, a widely circulated gold coin minted from gold mined in Spanish America (also known as a "piece of eight," because it was worth eight reales).

phalanx: In ancient Greece, a military formation in which heavily armed infantrymen lined up close together in deep ranks, defended by a wall of shields.

Pharisees: A major Jewish sect (flourished c. 100 B.C.E.–100 C.E.), noted for strict observance of rites and ceremonies and for their insistence on the validity of their own oral traditions concerning the written law. Pharisaism arose in opposition to the Sadducees; Pharisees argued that religious authority was not the sole prerogative of the priesthood. The Pharisees developed the idea of an afterlife and the resurrection of the body, and the concept of the Messiah. Pharisaism profoundly influenced the rabbinical Judaism of later centuries.

philosophy: The oldest form of systematic scholarly inquiry (Greek *philosophos*, "lover of wisdom"). Today "philosophy" has several related meanings: (1) the study of the principles underlying knowledge, being, and reality; (2) a particular system of philosophical doctrine; (3) the critical study of philosophical doctrines; (4) the study of the principles of a particular branch of knowledge; (5) a system of principles for guidance in everyday life.

phonogram: A character or symbol that represents a word, syllable, or language sound (phoneme) in writing.

pictograph: A simplified picture of an object that represents the object in writing.

***pietas*:** In Roman culture, the highest virtue, a selfless regard for the father and ancestors, with a determination to preserve the lineage. Our term "piety" is derived from *pietas*, but now means religious devotion.

pike: A weapon consisting of a long wooden shaft with a pointed steel head, used by foot soldiers until superseded by the bayonet.

pilgrimage: The practice, common to many religions, of journeying to a holy place or shrine to obtain blessings from God or as an act of devotion or penance.

plantation system: Cultivating crops on extensive lands worked by slave labor, developed in the sixteenth century by the Portuguese settlers for sugar cultivation on São Tomé and elsewhere, and later adopted by other European colonizers.

plebeians: Most of the free citizens of ancient Rome, originally denied most rights accorded the privileged, hereditary patrician class.

***plebs*:** The ordinary people of Rome; by the last century B.C.E., the increasingly dependent urban masses.

pluralism: In medieval and early modern Europe, the practice of holding several offices at the same time.

***polis*, pl. *poleis*:** In ancient Greece, a city-state.

politiques: A faction that emerged in the sixteenth-century civil war between Protestants and Catholics in France, who rejected religious considerations in favor of the secular goal of order and national unity.

polyglot: A term describing geographical areas or states in which many languages are spoken.

polytheism: *See* **monotheism**.

pope: The pope (literally, "father"), or bishop of Rome, is claimed by Roman Catholics as the successor to the apostle Peter, who is traditionally assigned preeminence over other apostles. The papacy comprises the pope and the system of ecclesiastical government of the Roman Catholic Church.

Populares: *See* **Optimates**.

portolan: From the thirteenth century onward, charts that gave sailing distances in miles and bearings in straight lines. Lacking parallels and meridians, or any indication of the curvature of the earth, these charts could not be used on the open oceans.

predestination: A Christian doctrine according to which a person's ultimate salvation or damnation is determined by God alone prior to, and apart from, any worth or merit on the person's part.

prelate: A clergyman of high rank.

Presocratic philosophy: Greek philosophy (c. 660–440 B.C.E.) prior to Socrates. The Presocratic philosophers challenged religious explanations of reality and sought to explain rationally the natural world and physical processes.

primogeniture: The preference given to the eldest son and his descendants in inheritance. Practiced in many regions of medieval Europe to maintain estates whole and intact.

***princeps*:** Literally, "first citizen," a title adopted by Augustus, the first Roman emperor. The system he created, based on the allegiance of the army and the people to the emperor (*imperator*) and on the collaboration between the emperor and the senatorial and equestrian classes, came to be known as the principate, the rule of the first citizen.

proletarian: In ancient Rome, the poorest citizens; the only class of citizens who were not required to serve in the army. The word means literally "bearer of children": the proletarian's only service to the state was to provide new generations of citizens.

proscription: In ancient Rome, the posting of names of the opponents of a faction in the Forum. Those whose names were posted were murdered and their wealth confiscated.

quadrant: An instrument used by astronomers and navigators from medieval times to measure the altitude of the sun or a star and for surveying. At its simplest, the quadrant is a flat plate in the shape of a quarter circle marked with a degree scale along the curved side; two sights are attached to one of the radial sides and a plumb bob hangs from the apex.

Qur'an: The sacred scripture of Islam. Muslims acknowledge the Qur'an, or Koran (Arabic, "reading" or "recital"), as the actual words of God given to the Prophet Muhammad between c. 610 and his death in 632.

rabbi: The title given to recognized Jewish religious teachers, sages, and leaders. Originally a term of respect (Hebrew, "my master"), around the first century C.E. it became a formal title for men authorized to interpret and expound Jewish law.

race: A population group, subspecies, or variety within the species *Homo sapiens*, set apart from other groups on the basis of arbitrarily selected, commonly visible criteria. The criteria most often selected are: skin color; "blood"; hair type; the shape and form of the body, head, and facial features; and alleged moral and/or behavioral attributes.

***raison d'état*:** French for "reason of state"; the justification given when the political interests of a nation-state override any moral principles governing the state's actions.

rationalism: The belief that the most fundamental knowledge is based on reason and that truth can be arrived at only by rational analysis of ideas, independent of empirical data, emotions, or prior authority.

real: In the early modern era, a small Spanish or Spanish-American silver coin, worth one-eighth of a peso.

regent: A person appointed to govern during the absence, childhood, or incapacity of a monarch.

relic: An object esteemed and venerated because of its association with a saint or martyr, often a body-part. Relics are often credited with curative or miraculous powers.

relief: A mode of sculpture in which forms project outward from a plane surface.

reliquary: A receptacle, usually richly decorated and made of precious materials, for the safekeeping or exhibition of a relic.

Renaissance: The period of European history from the early fourteenth to the mid-seventeenth century, derived from the French word for rebirth, originally referring to the revival of the values and artistic styles of Classical antiquity during that period, especially in Italy.

resurrection: The "rising again" to life of a dead person in the future or in heaven. The concept of resurrection from death is found in several religions, but is associated particularly with Christianity because of the central belief in the resurrection of Jesus.

rhetoric: The branch of written and oral discourse that concerns persuasion (Greek *rhetor*, "speaker in the assembly").

Romance languages: The family of languages that developed out of the provincial Latin spoken in various sections of the Roman Empire after its fall: Italian, French, Spanish, Portuguese, Romanian, and Romansch (spoken in some parts of Switzerland).

Romanesque: A style of art and architecture that flourished throughout western Europe from about 1050 to about 1200. The word originally meant "in the Roman manner"; Romanesque church architecture characteristically employs the Roman round arch and the major forms of antique Roman vaulting, and retains the basic plan of the early Christian basilica.

rosary: A circular string of beads used by Roman Catholics for counting recitations of such prayers as the Hail Mary (Ave Maria), the Our Father (Lord's Prayer), and the Glory Be to the Father (Gloria Patri).

sacrament: In Christianity, a sacred ritual conferring grace.

Sadducees: A powerful Jewish religious sect, identified with the priesthood and aristocracy, that flourished from about 200 B.C.E. until the fall of Jerusalem in 70 C.E. Unlike the Pharisees, the Sadducees did not believe in resurrection and the immortality of the soul, and opposed the use of Oral Law, holding only to the Pentateuch (the first five books of the Old Testament).

saint: A holy person (from the Latin *sanctus*, "holy") credited with the ability to work miracles of healing, or to pray effectively for others. In the New Testament "saint" refers to a baptized follower of Jesus Christ. Later the phrase "communion of saints" was used to refer to all members of the Church, living and dead. Still later, "saint" was defined as an individual who has died a heroic death for Christ (i.e. a martyr), or whose life has been marked by unusual signs of compassion. The Church came to regulate cults venerating such individuals by instituting a system of canonization in about 1000 C.E.

salvation: A religious concept that refers to the process through which a person is brought to ultimate, and eventually eternal, well-being. In Christianity, salvation (Latin *salus*, "health," "safety") refers to the process or state of being "saved" or "redeemed."

samurai: In medieval and early modern Japan, a class of warriors (from the Japanese *saburu*, "service"). The samurai were originally rural landowners who served as military retainers. Later they became military aristocrats and then military rulers.

Saracen: A term that Greek-speaking Byzantine chroniclers and other European peoples used for Muslim Arabs.

satrap: The governor of a province (satrapy) of the ancient Persian Empire.

schism: A formal division in a religious body. Two of the most important schisms in the history of Christianity were the division between the Eastern (Orthodox) and Western (Roman) Churches (traditionally dated 1054), and the period (1378–1417) during which the Western Church had two, and later three, competing lines of popes.

Scholasticism: A philosophical movement dominant in medieval European universities and writing from about the ninth century until the seventeenth century. Scholasticism combined Christian dogma, patristic philosophy (contained in the works of the Church Fathers), and Aristotelian philosophy.

sect: A dissenting religious body or political faction, often regarded as heretical or blasphemous by the larger body of believers.

secular: Of or relating to the worldly or temporal. Specifically in Catholicism, the term "secular" refers to a category of clergy that is not bound by monastic vows or rules.

Semitic: A branch of the Afroasiatic (or Hamito-Semitic) language group. Semites speak Semitic languages: Arabs, Aramaeans, Jews, and some Ethiopians, and in antiquity Babylonians, Assyrians, Phoenicians, Canaanites, and other groups. Speakers of a proto-Hamito-Semitic language may have migrated into Mesopotamia, the Middle East and the Arabian Peninsula from North Africa during the sixth millennium B.C.E.

Separatists: Seventeenth-century Puritans who separated from the Church of England and settled in North America to practice their form of worship.

serf: In medieval Europe, a peasant who was legally bound to the soil and obligated to give a portion of his produce to his lord. Up until about 1200, most peasants in western Europe were serfs.

sexagesimal: A numerical system based on the number 60, used by the Babylonians. Largely supplanted by the number 10 (decimal system), sexagesimal arithmetic presently survives in the use of 60 for the minute and hour cycle, the dozen, the foot (divided into 12 inches), and the 360° circle.

sextant: An optical instrument used in navigation since the mid-eighteenth century to measure the angles of celestial bodies above the horizon from the observer's position.

Shiite: One of the major branches of Islam, historically the dominant religious group in Persia (present-day Iran) and elsewhere a minority, in opposition to the dominant Sunnites. Following the death of Muhammad, disagreement arose as to who should succeed him as leader (imam) of the Muslim community. Shiites (from the Arabic *shiat Ali*, "the party of Ali") insisted that only descendants of Muhammad's son-in-law Ali could qualify.

Shintoism: The indigenous religious tradition of Japan, based on the worship of gods, nature spirits, and ancestors. After the eighth century C.E., Shintoism coexisted and blended with Buddhism and Confucianism.

shuttle: In weaving, a device or object used for passing the thread of the woof between the threads of the warp.

simony: In Christian canon law, the sale or purchase of a spiritual service or office.

slavery: A social practice in which a person is owned by and commanded to labor for the benefit of a master.

snuff: A preparation of dried, pulverized tobacco to be inhaled through the nostrils, chewed, or placed against the gums.

Sophists: A group of ancient Greek teachers of rhetoric, philosophy, and the art of living, fifth–fourth centuries B.C.E., known for their adroit and specious reasoning. "Sophistry" is now applied to any form of devious, but convincing, argument.

specie: Money in the form of coinage.

species: A biological classification designating a type of organism or population of animals potentially capable of interbreeding.

spindle: *See* **distaff**.

spinster: In medieval Europe, an unmarried woman who maintained herself by spinning thread. Later, the term came to designate an unmarried woman who is past the common age for marrying.

spiritualists: In sixteenth- and seventeenth-century Europe, inward-looking but radical Protestant sects, such as the Mennonites, Moravian Brethren, and English Society of Friends (Quakers). Spiritualist sects exalted the divine within the human and deliberately abstained from the demands of worldly existence.

stele, pl. **stelae:** An upright stone slab or column, decorated with inscriptions or figures, common in prehistoric and early historic cultures.

steppes: The Slavic term for the vast grasslands, flat, semi-arid, and subject to extremes of temperature, that stretch across central Eurasia.

stoa: A freestanding porchlike structure usually walled at the back with a front colonnade, designed to give pedestrians shelter and meeting places, often in the *agoras* of ancient Greek cities. The Stoic school of philosophy took its name from an Athenian stoa where its members first taught.

stock exchange, stock market: A place where brokers and dealers in stocks and bonds transact business together. Stock exchanges facilitated the financing of business and government activity by bringing together the buyers and sellers of the shares of joint-stock companies and, in later times, shares of corporations and bonds.

stratification: The division of society into separate groups, generally based on wealth, prestige, and/or ancestry.

suburb: A settlement immediately outside the walls of a city or fortification; in medieval Europe, sometimes the nucleus of a city.

sumptuary laws: Laws against luxury and extravagance (Latin *sumptus*, "expense"). Sumptuary laws prohibiting extravagance in dress or ceremony were designed to maintain moral standards and the distinctions between the social classes, and often particularly targeted women.

Sunnite: A follower of the Sunni branch of Islam to which most Muslims belong. Sunnites claim to strictly follow the *sunna* (practices) of the Prophet Muhammad, as defined and elaborated by the religious authorities (*'ulam*).

surrogate: A person who acts on behalf of another.

symposium: Originally, in ancient Greece, an all-male drinking party, where men composed drinking songs and engaged in lively conversation. The term is now usually applied to a meeting where speeches are given and discussions are held.

synagogue: A building where Jews gather for worship and religious instruction; the focus of Jewish communal life. In ancient Judaism, worship centered on the Temple in Jerusalem, where sacrificial rites were performed by a special caste of priests, with the masses excluded. In contrast, the synagogue is open to all Jews for prayer, ceremony, the reading of the Torah, religious instruction, and preaching. The synagogue provided the model for the Christian church and Islamic mosque.

syncretism: The fusion of cultural forms of different origin and character into a new formation.

Talmud: A compendium of law and lore that is regarded in Judaism as the sequel to the Hebrew Bible and the basis of Jewish religious life. There are two Talmuds: the Palestinian, composed in the third and fourth centuries C.E., and the Babylonian, completed about 500 C.E., with some later additions.

Tartars, Tatars: Descendants of the Mongols, who ruled part of eastern Europe and central Asia.

tax farmer: A free agent contracted by a ruler or state to collect taxes, from which he takes an agreed-upon commission or, more often, whatever percentage he can expropriate.

theocracy: Rule by a priesthood or religious elite, with rule of law based on religious doctrine or scripture.

***tholos*:** The bee-hive shaped tombs of the Mycenaean kings.

tithe: A "tenth part" of agricultural or other produce, exacted to support the Church.

Torah: The entire body of Jewish teaching incorporated in the Hebrew Bible, the Talmud, and later rabbinical commentaries. Applied sometimes to the written Mosaic law that is contained in the first five books of the Bible.

tragedy: A genre of drama, developed in ancient Greece, in which a hero meets death brought on by a flaw of character and circumstances beyond control.

transept: The part of the church that crosses the nave; also, either wing of the transept.

transubstantiation: In Roman Catholic or Eastern Orthodox church dogma, the miraculous change by which bread and wine at their consecration during the ritual of Mass become the body and blood of Christ.

Trinity: The Christian understanding of God as a unity of three persons (triune): Father, Son, and Holy Spirit. The idea of the Trinity is an attempt to reconcile the diverse statements about God contained in the Bible.

triumvirate: A ruling group of three persons; originally, in the last years of the Republic, Julius Caesar, Crassus, and Pompey.

tyranny: Rule by an illegitimate leader, the tyrant, who seizes power and holds it by violence. In ancient Greece, tyranny was seen as the opposite of monarchy. Both forms of rule concentrate power in a single figure.

unitarianism: A form of Protestant Christianity asserting that God is one person, rather than three persons in one (the Trinity).

urban: Relating to the city. Urbanization is the process of becoming more urban through the concentration of population, the performance of economic tasks, and the development of the mental outlook of a city.

usufruct: The legal right of using and enjoying the fruits or profits of something belonging to another. In medieval Europe, land held in usufruct and granted by another noble, or a king or an agent of the church, was often called a fief.

usury: Money-lending for profit.

utopia: An ideal society in which social, political, and economic evils have been entirely eradicated, and in which the state functions for the happiness of all.

vassal: A person under the protection of a feudal lord, to whom he vows homage and fealty. The vassals of powerful rulers might also in turn have vassals.

vernacular: In medieval and early modern Europe, the native spoken language of a region or country; not Latin, which was the language used for the writing of high literary, scientific, legal, and religious works. In time the main modern national vernaculars such as French, German, and Italian displaced Latin in most intellectual tasks.

warp, woof: The warp is a series of yarns extended lengthwise in a loom and crossed by the woof (or weft), together constituting, when complete, a woven textile.

wergeld: Among the Germanic tribes that lived outside the borders of the Roman Empire, a vengeance or compensation payment, which varied according to a person's status.

wet nurse: A lactating woman who is hired to breastfeed the baby of her employers.

INDEX

Figures in bold refer to picture captions and maps